Florida

The Panhandle
p451

Northeast
Florida
p351

Orlando &
Walt Disney
World®
p255

Tampa Bay &
Southwest Florida
p395

The Space
Coast
p333

Southeast
Florida
p211

The Everglades
& Biscayne
p154

Miami
p63

Florida Keys
& Key West
p175

D0950778

Anthony Ham,

Fionn Davenport, Adam Karlin, Vesna Maric, Trisha Ping, Regis St Louis

Contents

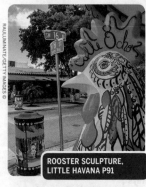

ROOSTER SCULPTURE,
LITTLE HAVANA P91

CRYSTAL RIVER P424

Contents

COVID-19

We have re-checked every business in this book before publication to ensure that it is still open after 2020's COVID-19 outbreak. However, the economic and social impacts of COVID-19 will continue to be felt long after the outbreak has been contained, and many businesses, services and events referenced in this guide may experience ongoing restrictions. Some businesses may be temporarily closed, have changed their opening hours and services, or require bookings; some unfortunately could have closed permanently. We suggest you check with venues before visiting for the latest information.

Right: Key West
(p191)

WELCOME TO
Florida

Even if I cared little for white-sand beaches, brilliantly imaginative theme parks or waterfront restaurants serving up some of the best seafood in the Americas, Florida would still top my travel list. Most of all I love how every trip here can be so different. Whether plotting a weekend getaway exploring street art and Latin rhythms in Miami, heading to the Everglades for a wilderness excursion, attending a renowned African American arts festival in Orlando or island-hopping in the Keys, Florida offers experiences you simply can't find anywhere else.

By Regis St Louis, Writer
🐦 @regisstlouis 📷 @regisstlouis
For more about our writers, see p544

STOCKDONKEY / SHUTTERSTOCK ©

Florida

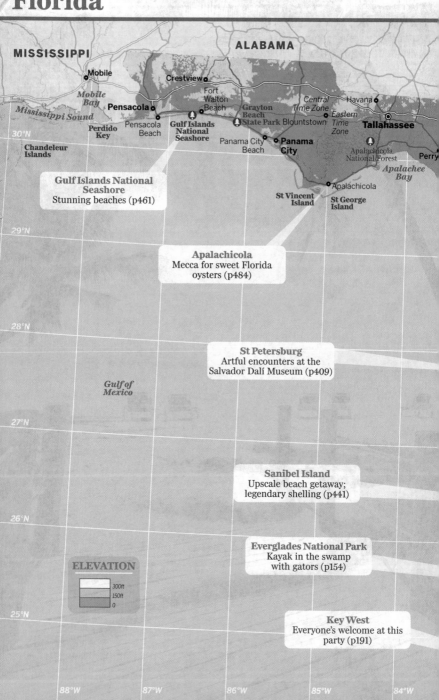

MISSISSIPPI

ALABAMA

Mobile

Crestview

Mobile Bay

Fort Walton Beach

Mississippi Sound

Pensacola

Central Time Zone

Havana

Perdido Key

Pensacola Beach

Gulf Islands National Seashore

Grayton Beach State Park

Blountstown

Eastern Time Zone

Tallahassee

30°N

Panama City Beach

Panama City

Chandeleur Islands

Apalachicola National Forest

Apalachee Bay

Perry

Apalachicola

Gulf Islands National Seashore
Stunning beaches (p461)

St Vincent Island

St George Island

29°N

Apalachicola
Mecca for sweet Florida oysters (p484)

28°N

St Petersburg
Artful encounters at the Salvador Dalí Museum (p409)

Gulf of Mexico

27°N

Sanibel Island
Upscale beach getaway; legendary shelling (p441)

26°N

Everglades National Park
Kayak in the swamp with gators (p154)

ELEVATION

	300ft
	150ft
	0

25°N

Key West
Everyone's welcome at this party (p191)

88°W   87°W   86°W   85°W   84°W

0 200 km
0 100 miles

GEORGIA

ATLANTIC OCEAN

31°N
30°N
29°N
27°N
25°N

Gainesville
An indie music scene that really rocks (p387)

St Augustine
Nation's oldest city is a time warp (p360)

Ocala National Forest
Outdoor paradise of hiking and crystal springs (p386)

Canaveral National Seashore
Kayak with dolphins (p337)

Kennedy Space Center
Fascinating legacy of space exploration (p335)

Universal Orlando Resort
Excellent rides and wonderful worlds (p292)

Walt Disney World®
Only the world's grandest theme park (p257)

Miami
Chic, sexy, Latin-spiced culture and nightlife (p63)

John Pennekamp State Park
Coral reef cities of uncommon abundance (p178)

THE BAHAMAS

Fernandina Beach, Amelia Island, Jacksonville, Lake City, Alachua, Gainesville, Palatka, St Augustine, Cross City, Suwannee, Cedar Key, Ocala, Ocala National Forest, Daytona Beach, Crystal River, Homosassa Springs, Orlando, Titusville, Cape Canaveral, Cocoa Beach, Kissimmee, Melbourne, Tampa, Lakeland, Clearwater, St Pete Beach, St Petersburg, Fort DeSoto Park, Sebring, Fort Pierce, Bradenton, Sarasota, Venice, Okeechobee, Charlotte Harbour, Lake Okeechobee, Palm Beach, Fort Myers, Captiva Island, Sanibel Island, Corkscrew Swamp Sanctuary, Delray Beach, Boca Raton, Naples, Alligator Alley, Fort Lauderdale, Cape Romano, Big Cypress National Preserve, Miami Beach, Miami, Everglades National Park, Shark Valley, Biscayne National Park, Shark Point, Florida City, John Pennekamp Coral Reef State Park, Flamingo, Key Largo, Dry Tortugas National Park, Islamorada, Marathon, Florida Keys, Florida Bay, Key West, FLORIDA, Florida's Turnpike (toll), Kissimmee River, St Johns River, Suwannee River, Straits of Florida

Florida's Top Experiences

LTTLENY/GETTY IMAGES ©

1 SEASIDE CULTURE

The wave-kissed coastline of Florida has much more going for it than just beaches and palm trees. Miami's booming arts scene, bohemian revelry in Key West and a burgeoning food and drink scene up and down the coast is just the beginning. There are also plenty of surprises, including the world-class Salvador Dalí museum in St Petersburg and little-known historical settlements such as oyster-loving Apalachicola on the Panhandle.

Above: Ocean Drive, South Beach (p68)

Key West

Boasting colorful Caribbean architecture, a vibrant arts scene and plenty of fabulous bars and eateries, Key West is a fine place to cut loose. Start with a sunset over Mallory Square, then embark on the infamous 'Duval Crawl' before catching live music at the Green Parrot. p191

Right: Cocktail at a Key West bar

Miami

For years Miami's loci of cool-kid activity have been Wynwood and the neighboring Design District. Many once industrial buildings have been transformed into galleries and studio spaces, and the nearby Wynwood Walls is a massive, ever-changing open-air art installation. p63

Above: Murals, Wynwood (p81)

St Augustine

Peel back the centuries in St Augustine, the oldest continuously occupied European settlement in the US. Tour magnificent Spanish cathedrals and forts, and Henry Flagler's ludicrously ornate resorts, take spooky ghost tours, join scurvy-dog pirate invasions then dine well when you're done. p360

Above: Castillo de San Marcos National Monument (p360)

2 WILDERNESS ENCOUNTERS

Some 10 million acres (4 million hectares) of Florida is protected, allowing nature to flourish in all its astonishing variety. Alligators prowl beside cypress-filled waterways, herons strut through inky black ponds and sea turtles nest along deserted beaches, while manatees glide through warm-water springs. Amid these animal kingdoms, there are myriad ways to connect with nature, whether canoeing through biologically diverse wetlands, bird-watching along the shores, or hiking and camping in hardwood forests.

The Everglades

Mottled by hammocks, cypress domes and mangroves, the alligator-filled wetlands of the Everglades are mesmerizing. Enticing boardwalks and a few elevated lookouts provide a glimpse of the scale and beauty of this place. p145

Below: Mahogany Hammock trail (p151)

Canaveral National Seashore

Virtually in the shadow of Kennedy's shuttle launch-pad, the dunes, lagoons and white-sand beaches of Canaveral National Seashore look much as they did 500 years ago when the Spaniards landed. Kayak with bottlenose dolphins and manatees, observe nesting sea turtles and swim on pristine beaches. p337

Above left: Roseate spoonbills

Ocala National Forest

Leave the well-trodden path behind and enter a world of subtropical forests, cypress stands, sinkholes and crystal springs in the Ocala National Forest. You can happily roam for days along hundreds of miles of forested trails and among countless lakes, with campgrounds en route. p386

Above right: A spring

3 BEACH BEAUTIES

There's no mystery to what makes Florida so appealing. Beaches as fine and sweet as powdered sugar, warm waters, rustling mangroves: all conspire to make our workaday selves dream of the Florida sunshine. Some desire a beachside getaway of swimming, seafood and sunsets. Others seek the seaside revelry of Miami's South Beach or classy beach towns such as Sarasota or Naples. No matter your vision of tropical paradise, Florida has you covered.

South Beach

Reason enough to make the trip to Florida, South Beach offers prime people-watching and memorable sunrise strolls past those iconic, colorfully painted lifeguard stations. p68

LEFT: OLGA YUDINA / SHUTTERSTOCK ©; TOP RIGHT: SIMON DANNHAUER / SHUTTERSTOCK ©; BOTTOM RIGHT: JOHN COLETTI / GETTY IMAGES ©

Fort DeSoto Park

Near St Petersburg, you'll find a jaw-dropping stretch of comely wave-kissed shoreline. Seven miles of white-sand beaches and a nature trail across five islands set the scene for a fine day's outing. p417

Bahia Honda State Park

The finest beach in the Keys invites long leisurely walks and frolicking in the aquamarine seas. Book early and you can camp or stay in a cabin here — pure heaven after the day-trippers depart. p188

4 FANTASY COME TO LIFE

Legoland (p330)

Florida's famous theme parks bring the fantastical to life, offering boundless amusement for visitors of all ages and creeds. Here you can curtsy with Cinderella, blast through outer space aboard the *Millennium Falcon*, and browse for wizarding wands in Diagon Alley. Greater Orlando is the epicenter for the magic, and no matter what you're after — adrenaline-fueled rides, storybook landscapes or animal safaris — you'll find it all right here.

Walt Disney World®

Want to set the bar of expectations high? Call yourself 'The Happiest Place on Earth.' Walt Disney World® does, then pulls out all the stops to deliver a place where a child is the most important character in the show. p257

Universal Orlando Resort

The theming, the creativity of the rides, the thrilling surprises, the silly fun – Universal is the smart and sassy class clown to Disney's teacher's pet. p292

Legoland

Pure fun without the stress of complicated planning, Legoland offers old-school amusement on its rides and waterpark. p330

Right: Legoland entrance

5 TROPICAL MOSAIC

America's third-largest state by population is a fascinating microcosm of the great American melting pot. From rural hunters and trappers in the north to retirees sitting side by side with arrivals from every Spanish-speaking nation in the world, Florida boasts astonishing diversity. Exploring the state's rich cultural history is one of the unsung rewards of travel here: whether catching Cuban bands on Miami's Calle Ocho or learning about Seminole and Miccosukee communities in the Everglades.

Zora! Festival

The historical African American settlement of Eatonville (today in present-day Orlando) throws a memorable arts festival in January celebrating the music, literature, art, filmmaking and fashion of the African diaspora. p316

Miccosukee Indian Village

In the Everglades, learn about the folkways of Florida's indigenous inhabitants on guided visits of traditional homes, boat rides, and music and dance performances. p156

Above right: Miccosukee carver

Cubaocho

For insight into Cuban culture, visit this long-standing icon in Little Havana. Best known for its concerts, Cubaocho also has changing art exhibitions, film screenings and other events. p137

Left top and bottom: Cubaocho

6 ISLAND ESCAPES

GNAGEL./GETTY IMAGES ©

Dry Tortugas National Park

Far off Key West and surrounded by azure seas, Dry Tortugas National Park makes a memorable outing for those making the journey by ferry or seaplane. You can snorkel coral reefs, tour a 19th-century fort and camp on Garden Key. p207

Left top: Fort Jefferson (p207)
Left bottom: Snorkeler explores a coral reef

IMAGE SOURCE / GETTY IMAGES ©

Gulf Islands National Seashore

The Panhandle's barrier islands boast almost-pure-white quartz-sand beaches, shimmering like freshly fallen snow. p461

Sanibel Island

This gorgeous island is famous for the bounty of colorful and exotic shells that wash up along its beaches; the 'Sanibel stoop' is the name for the distinctive profile of avid shellers. p441

The Florida peninsula is ringed with eye-catching barrier islands and verdant mangrove-fringed keys. Many are accessible by causeways and bridges, making it easy to make a quick escape from the mainland for a tropical-infused getaway. Other spots can be reached only by boat, adding to the sense of resplendent isolation. Wherever you roam, you won't be far from sparkling beaches, with palms rustling in the breeze, and night skies packed with stars.

7 THE MUSIC SCENE

With loud, fist-pumping rock, gator-swamp rockabilly and sweaty blues, Florida's northern cities flex their Southern roots. On the opposite end of the state, you have a mesmerizing mix of brassy Latin jazz, Cuban *trova* and cutting-edge indie rock spilling out of the drinking dens and ballrooms of Miami. Across the state, you'll find wide-ranging offerings from top-notch orchestras playing in state-of-the-art concert halls to barefoot cover bands jamming at open-air bars in the Keys.

Gainesville

If local boy Tom Petty is the patron saint of Gainesville's rock-music scene, the University of Florida – the nation's second-largest university – is the engine that keeps it going strong. p387

LEFT: JUSTIN FOULKES/LONELY PLANET ©; TOP RIGHT: MIA2YOU/SHUTTERSTOCK ©, ARCHITECT: CÉSAR PELLI; BOTTOM RIGHT: MSJBHADEEPM/SHUTTERSTOCK ©

Miami

The epicenter of the Latin music scene, Miami has plenty of joints for dance lovers. Downtown is also home to the Adrienne Arsht Center for the Performing Arts (top right; p136). p63

Bottom right: Street performer

The Keys

All along the Keys, you'll be well-placed for live music. At places such as Sundowners, you can admire the fiery sunsets while lingering over cocktails as Jimmy Buffet lookalikes work the crowd. p175

Above: Green Parrot (p204)

8 AQUATIC ADVENTURES

Christ of the Abyss statue, John Pennekamp Coral Reef State Park (p178)

Some of Florida's most breathtaking scenery is underwater. Almost everywhere, the peninsula is edged by more coral reefs than anywhere in North America, and their quality and diversity rival Hawaii and the Caribbean. There's fabulous snorkeling and diving, with countless wreck dives within easy access of the mainland. On the surface, there are wonderful destinations for kayakers and boaters – whether exploring islands of the Keys or taking dolphin-spotting trips off the Gulf.

John Pennekamp Coral Reef State Park

In the Upper Keys, this mostly underwater park has outstanding snorkeling and diving amid coral reefs, wrecks and even famous underwater Christ statue. You can also arrange glass-bottom boat tours. p178

10,000 Islands

The Everglades meet the ocean in this pristine aquatic wilderness. Arrange boat tours to spy on marine life, or head off on your own to kayak the isolated islands. p162

Cedar Key

Take nature tours by boat of the wildlife-rich Suwannee River, or go kayaking among the marshes and estuaries of this protected archipelago in the Panhandle. p489

Need to Know

For more information, see Survival Guide (p519)

Currency
US dollars ($)

Language
English, also Spanish in Tampa, Miami and South Florida, and Haitian Creole in South Florida.

Visas
Nationals qualifying for the Visa Waiver Program are allowed a 90-day stay without a visa; all others need a visa.

Money
ATMs widely available everywhere.

Cell Phones
Europe and Asia's GSM 900/1800 standard is incompatible with USA's cell-phone systems. Confirm your phone can be used before arriving.

Time
East of the Apalachicola River, Florida is in the US Eastern Time Zone (GMT/UTC minus five hours). West of the Apalachicola is US Central Time (GMT/UTC minus six hours).

When to Go

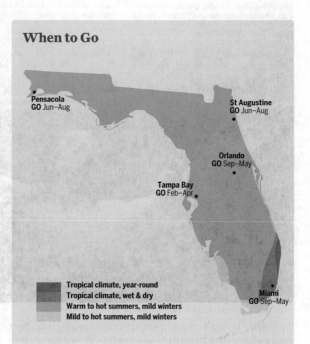

Pensacola
GO Jun–Aug

St Augustine
GO Jun–Aug

Orlando
GO Sep–May

Tampa Bay
GO Feb–Apr

Miami
GO Sep–May

Tropical climate, year-round
Tropical climate, wet & dry
Warm to hot summers, mild winters
Mild to hot summers, mild winters

High Season
(Mar–Aug)

➡ South Florida beaches (and Daytona) peak with spring break.

➡ Panhandle and northern beaches packed in summer.

➡ Orlando theme parks busiest in summer.

➡ Hot and humid (May to September).

Shoulder
(Feb & Sep)

➡ In South Florida, February has ideal dry weather, but no spring-break craziness.

➡ In september northern beaches/theme parks less crowded, still hot.

➡ Prices drop from peak by 20% to 30%.

Low Season
(Oct–Dec or Jan)

➡ Beach towns quiet until winter 'snowbirds' arrive.

➡ Hotel prices can drop from peak by 50%.

➡ November-to-April dry season is best time to hike/camp.

➡ Can be interrupted by public holidays when rates spike.

Useful Websites

Visit Florida (www.visitflorida.com) Official state tourism website.

Miami Herald (www.miamiherald.com) Main daily newspaper for metro Miami-Dade.

Tampa Bay Times (www.tampabay.com) News and views for the Gulf Coast.

Florida State Parks (www.floridastateparks.org) Primary resource for state parks.

Lonely Planet (www.lonelyplanet.com/florida) Destination information, hotel bookings, traveler forum and more.

Important Numbers

Country code	1
International access code	011
Emergency	911
Directory assistance	411

Exchange Rates

Australia	A$1	$0.78
Canada	C$1	$0.79
Euro zone	€1	$1.23
Japan	¥100	$0.97
New Zealand	NZ$1	$0.73
UK	UK£1	$1.36

For current exchange rates see www.xe.com.

Daily Costs

Budget:
Less than $140

➡ Dorm beds/camping: $25–50

➡ Supermarket self-catering per day: $25

➡ Beaches: free

➡ Bicycle hire per day: $25–35

Midrange:
$140–250

➡ Hotels: $100–200

➡ In-room meals and dining out: $50

➡ Theme park pass: $40–100

➡ Rental car per day: $40–50

Top End:
More than $250

➡ High-season beach hotel/resort: $250–400

➡ Miami gourmet dinner for two: $150–300

➡ All-inclusive, four- to seven-day theme-park blowout: $1500–4000

Opening Hours

Standard business hours:

Banks 8:30am to 4:30pm Monday to Thursday, to 5:30pm Friday; sometimes 9am to 12:30pm Saturday.

Bars Most bars 5pm to midnight; to 2am Friday and Saturday.

Businesses 9am to 5pm Monday to Friday.

Post offices 9am to 5pm Monday to Friday; sometimes 9am to noon Saturday.

Restaurants Breakfast 7am to 10:30am Monday to Friday; brunch 9am to 2pm Saturday and Sunday; lunch 11:30am to 2:30pm Monday to Friday; dinner 5pm to 9:30pm, later Friday and Saturday.

Shops 10am to 6pm Monday to Saturday, noon to 5pm Sunday.

Arriving in Florida

Miami International Airport (p526) Miami Beach Airport Express ($2.25) runs every 30 minutes, 6am to 11pm, to Miami Beach (35 minutes). Shuttle vans cost around $22 to South Beach. A taxi to South Beach is $35.

Orlando International Airport (p526) Lynx buses ($2) run from 6am to midnight. Public bus 11 services downtown Orlando (40 minutes), 42 services International Dr (one hour) and 111 services SeaWorld (45 minutes). Complimentary luggage handling and airport transport for guests staying at a Walt Disney World® Resort (Disney's Magical Express). Shuttle vans cost $20 to $37, depending where you're going. Taxi costs: Disney area, $52 to $68; International Dr and Universal Orlando Resort, $38 to $45; downtown Orlando, $38 to $45; Winter Park, $45 to $55.

Getting Around

Transportation in Florida revolves around the car.

Car Car-hire offices can be found in almost every town. Drive on the right.

Bus Greyhound and Megabus are cheap, if slow, and serve larger cities.

Train Amtrak's *Silver Service/Palmetto* runs between Miami and Tampa, and from there connects to a nationwide network. The *Auto Train* runs from the Washington, DC area to Sanford, near Orlando.

Cycling Flat Florida is good for cycling, although hot weather and a lack of highway bike lanes are hindrances.

For much more on **getting around**, see p528

What's New

Few states have the capacity to reinvent themselves quite like Florida, with new people, new ideas and new trends taking root here every year. At the same time, Florida is just as adept at absorbing everything that's new and making it its own.

New Disney Rides

Just when you think Disney (p257) can't get any better, they go and reinvent the whole meaning of fun. First it was *Avatar*- and *Harry Potter*-themed rides. Now they've introduced Star Wars: Galaxy's Edge – their Millennium Falcon: Smugglers Run and Rise of the Resistance are two world-class rides that together make up a high-tech, immersive universe. It also offers a town's worth of shops, restaurants and bars – all carefully themed to make you believe you're actually in the Black Spire Outpost.

Panhandle Biking

Tallahassee (p475) is garnering a quite a reputation as a center for mountain-biking. Given Florida's absence of mountains, *off-road* biking would probably be more accurate. Whatever you call it, Tallahassee is at the center of it, with around 700 miles of trails close to the city and a growing biking culture that takes in Panhandle beaches and inland forests.

Everglades Lodging

For far too long after the last hurricane, if you wanted to stay in the Everglades you had to go camping, either in a staffed campground or out on a mangrove island. Not any more. As of 2020, park concessioner Flamingo Adventures (www.flamingo everglades.com) has opened safari-style eco-tents with comfy beds and decks, plus fully equipped houseboats for off-the-beaten-path exploring. The southern location puts you close to so many canoeing and hiking trails — great spots to see wildlife.

Miami Arts

Miami (p63) has to be one of America's most restless and dynamic artistic scenes

---

LOCAL KNOWLEDGE

WHAT'S HAPPENING IN FLORIDA

Regis St Louis, Lonely Planet writer

Climate change remains the hot topic of the day in a state with one of America's most threatened coastlines. With sea levels expected to rise 10 to 20 inches by 2040, Floridians face a daunting future. Increasingly frequent flooding from everyday storms, more devastating hurricanes and a deeply eroded coastline are among the grave threats – not to mention damage to the state's fragile ecosystems (including die-offs in the vast reef system off the Keys and irreparable harm to the Everglades).

Some policy makers still believe it's not too late to prevent the most dire scenarios (such as one in eight Floridian homes being underwater by 2100). Preparing for the future, however, will require an estimated $76 billion to mitigate the effects of climate change in the form of sea walls and other infrastructure investments. The big challenge is getting everyone on board — no easy prospect in a state where 30% oppose government spending on climate change.

and the offerings just keep on improving. The world-class Rubell Museum (p96) has moved to a vast new exhibition space over in Allapattah. Down in South Beach, The Orb (www.thebetsyhotel.com/explore/arts-culture) is a cutting-edge artistic space for photography and video. Steps away from it, the Poetry Rail, an etched metal wall, takes poetry to a whole new audience.

Tampa Urban Renewal

For many years, Tampa (p396) was the poster child for unrestrained development and soulless urban sprawl, and for a downtown area that emptied of life as soon as workers left for the day. But things are changing. The beautiful Riverwalk promenade has become a magnet for outdoor relaxation, activities and festivals. Restaurants are starting to appear, while the free tram service connects the center with Ybor City's bright lights and busy streets.

Accessible Beaches

The beaches of the Sunshine State haven't always been easy to access for travelers with disabilities, but there are signs that this may be starting to change. In Pensacola Beach and other nearby beach towns, beach wheelchairs and mats have become widely available, with a number of places offering rentals. Here's hoping it catches on elsewhere.

Orlando Dining

Orlando's dining scene (p317) continues to expand and take on some serious culinary cred. Winter Park has long been considered the counterpoint to all of the fast-food and world's-biggest-McDonald's hype. But now the Mills 50 district, just north of downtown and with the largest Vietnamese population of any city outside of Vietnam, is abuzz with good eating options. They span the full range of international cuisines, from BBQ to sushi, with, as you'd expect, a strong tendency toward tasty Asian fusion.

Art in the Keys

While heading down the Keys (p175), it's worth trying to time your visit with Islamorada's monthly art walk (http://moradaway.org). On the third Thursday of the month, you can browse open studios, purchase art (and crafts) and sip local microbrews. Fur-

LISTEN, WATCH & FOLLOW

For inspiration and up-to-date stories, visit www.lonelyplanet.com/usa/florida/articles.

Visit Florida (https://twitter.com/visitflorida) Florida's official tourism Twitter account.

Miami New Times (www.miaminewtimes.com) News and happenings in Miami.

WDW Radio Show (www.wdwradio.com) All things Disney with a good podcast.

Florida Podcast Network (http://floridapodcastnetwork.com) Plenty of Florida-focused podcasts.

FAST FACTS

Food trend fried oysters; farm-to-table

Miles of beaches 825

Number of alligators 1.5 million

Pop 21.5 million

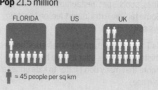

FLORIDA   US   UK

≈ 45 people per sq km

ther south, the iconic Studios of Key West (p195) has recently added a rooftop bar and expanded its lineup of cultural offerings.

A New Waterfront

In St Petersburg, the $93 million St Pete Pier (p410) has quickly became a new focal point for locals and tourists alike. The 26-acre space encompasses a promenade, greenery (native Florida species), picnic spots, playgrounds, waterfront dining and drinking spots, and a pretty beach. There are regular events (fitness classes, film screenings, outdoor music), and fine views across the bay.

Underwater Museum of Art

In 2018, North America's first permanent underwater sculpture gallery (p469) was unveiled off the coast of Grayton Beach State Park in the Florida Panhandle. Divers can swim amid striking works of art, which also serve as an artificial reef aimed at rejuvenating marine life in the area.

Accommodations

Find more accommodation reviews throughout the On the Road chapters (from p61)

Accommodation Types

Hotels Options range from cookie-cutter chain hotels to beautifully designed boutique and luxury hotels, with an equally varied price range.

Resorts Florida resorts aim to be so all-encompassing you'll never need, or want, to leave. Included are all manner of fitness and sports facilities, pools, spas, restaurants, bars and so on. Some tack an extra 'resort fee' on to rates; always ask.

B&Bs These often-charming small guesthouses and historical homes offer a more homey stay (but note that many don't cater to kids under a certain age).

Motels Cheaper and simpler than most hotels, these are clustered along interstates and sprinkled across rural Florida and along town outskirts.

Hostels Only a small number of these are found in Florida, and rarely beyond the larger cities. Most have communal dorm rooms and communal facilities where you can meet other travelers.

PRICE RANGES

The following price ranges refer to a standard double room at high-season rates, unless otherwise noted. Note that 'high season' can mean summer or winter depending on the region. Unless otherwise stated, rates do not include breakfast, bathrooms are private and all lodging is open year-round.

$ less than $120

$$ $120–200

$$$ more than $200

Camping Options range from primitive backcountry spots in the Everglades or serviced campgrounds in state parks to full-facility private campgrounds and RV sites.

Best Places to Stay

Best on a Budget

Florida can be tough going if you're on a tight budget, especially if you're traveling in high season – budget travel is not really the way Florida usually rolls. But if you know where to look, there are plenty of excellent places to put down your backpack and hang out with other like-minded travelers.

➡ Hoosville Hostel (p162), Florida City

➡ Floridian Hotel & Suites (p316), Orlando

➡ Universal's Endless Summer Resort (p296), Orlando

➡ SoBe Hostel (p104), South Beach

➡ Gram's Place Hostel (p401), Tampa

➡ Pirate Haus Inn (p365), St Augustine

Best for Families

Florida can seem custom-made for the perfect family holiday, from the theme parks of Orlando and seemingly endless miles of white sand and sheltered beaches to wildlife-filled wilderness areas with child-friendly activities. Orlando offers the richest pickings but anywhere with a beach will likely have a few places for the perfect family vacation.

➡ Legoland Florida Resort (p330), Winter Haven

➡ Cabana Bay Beach Resort (p296), Orlando

➡ Disney's Fort Wilderness Resort (p273), Orlando

➡ 'Tween Waters Inn (p443), Captiva Island

➡ Disney's Coronado Springs Resort (p281), Orlando

Best Resorts

Florida's coast is ringed with resorts, the kind of all-inclusive places that cater to your every need. Orlando and the surrounding area is another resort hotspot, where the focus is on keeping you close and preparing you for your immersion into theme-park heaven. Most, especially those in the Orlando cluster, are family-friendly, but some beach resorts aim for adults-only exclusivity.

➡ Four Seasons Resort Orlando at Walt Disney World® (p259), Orlando

➡ Lago Mar Resort (p218), Fort Lauderdale

➡ WaterColor Inn & Resort (p470), South Walton & 30A Beaches

➡ Hilton Orlando Bonnet Creek (p264), Orlando

➡ Breakers (p236), Palm Beach

Best B&Bs

Florida has some outstanding B&Bs, most of which promise an intimate stay, often in lovingly restored historical homes and watched over by owners who take hospitality seriously. They're found throughout Florida, and they're at their best in smaller towns or historical town centers, especially away from the glitz, glamor and bright lights of Southeast Florida.

➡ At Journey's End (p366), St Augustine

➡ Deer Run on the Atlantic (p190), Big Pine Key

➡ Addison (p378), Amelia Island

➡ Aunt Martha's Bed & Breakfast (p465), Fort Walton Beach

➡ Sundy House Inn (p227), Delray Beach

➡ Harrington House (p434), Sarasota Keys

HANDOUT / GETTY IMAGES ©

Cabana Bay Beach Resort (p296)

idea, nowhere more so than in Orlando and tourist beach towns.

Lonely Planet (lonelyplanet.com/hotels) Find independent reviews, as well as recommendations on the best places to stay – and then book them online.

Recreation.gov (www.recreation.gov) The best site for booking campsites in national parks, state parks and other public areas.

Reserve America (www.reserveamerica.com) An excellent resource for booking campsites and campgrounds across the state.

Visit Florida (www.visitflorida.com) Has a section on places to stay, including resorts, campgrounds, B&Bs and more.

Booking

High season runs from March to August – prices skyrocket, especially by the beach. Other peaks include spring break. February and September are cheaper and the weather can be excellent (unless a September hurricane looms on the horizon). November to April is best for camping. Booking ahead is almost always a good

Taxes

Taxes vary considerably between towns; in fact, hotels almost never include taxes and fees in their rate quotes, so always ask for the total rate with tax. Florida's sales tax is 6%, and some communities tack on more. States, cities and towns also usually levy taxes on hotel rooms, which can increase the final bill by 10% to 12%.

Month by Month

January

January falls in the middle of Florida's winter 'dry' season. In northern Florida, cool temps make this off-season. In southern Florida, after New Year's, January becomes shoulder season.

☆ College Football Bowl Games

On January 1, Floridians go nuts for college football. Major bowls are played in Orlando (Capital One Bowl), Tampa (Outback Bowl) and Jacksonville (Gator Bowl), while Miami's Orange Bowl (January 3) often crowns the collegiate champion (www.ncaa.com).

🎆 Gasparilla Pirate Festival

On the last Saturday of the month, the city of Tampa becomes a big pirate party. (p401)

February

Ideal month for less-crowded South Florida beaches; high season ramps up. Still too cool for tourists up north.

🎆 Edison Festival of Light

For two weeks, Fort Myers celebrates the great inventor Thomas Edison with a block party, concerts and a huge science fair. February 11, Edison's birthday, culminates in an incredible Parade of Light. (p438)

🎆 Florida State Fair

More tha a century old, Tampa's Florida State Fair is classic Americana: two mid-February weeks of livestock shows, greasy food, loud music and old-fashioned carnival rides. (p401)

☆ Daytona 500

One of the biggest annual events on the American sporting calendar, the Daytona 500 draws 200,000 to the Daytona International Speedway, with millions more watching on TV. (p353)

🎆 Mardi Gras

Whether it falls in late February or early March, Fat Tuesday inspires parties statewide. Pensacola Beach, closest to New Orleans, hosts Florida's best (www.pensacolamardigras.com).

March

Beach resort high season all over, due to spring break. Modest temps and dry weather make for an ideal time to hike and camp. Last hurrah for manatees.

🎆 Spring Break

Throughout March to mid-April, American colleges release students for one-week 'spring breaks.' Coeds pack Florida beaches for debaucherous drunken binges. The biggies? Panama City Beach, Pensacola, Daytona and Fort Lauderdale.

☆ Baseball Spring Training

Through March, Florida hosts Major League Baseball's spring training 'Grapefruit League' (www.floridagrapefruitleague.com): 15 pro teams train and play exhibition games around Orlando, Tampa Bay and the Southeast.

🎉 Carnaval Miami

Miami's premier Latin festival takes over for nine days in early March: there's a Latin drag-queen show, in-line-skate competition, domino tournament, the immense Calle Ocho street festival, Miss Carnaval Miami and more.

April

As spring-break madness fades, prices drop. It's the end of the winter dry season.

☆ Florida Film Festival

Held in Winter Park, near Orlando, this celebration of independent films is fast becoming one of the largest in the southeast. Sometimes held in late March. (p316)

🎉 Conch Republic Independence Celebration

Honor the (pseudo) independence of the (pseudo) republic of Key West with crazy parties and (pseudo) elections for (pseudo) office. (p197)

May

Summer 'wet' season begins: rain, humidity, bugs all increase with temps. Northern beach season ramps up; southern beaches enter off-season.

🏃 Sea Turtle Nesting

Beginning in May and extending through October, sea turtles nest on Florida

beaches; after two months (from midsummer through fall), hatchling runs see the kids totter back to sea.

☆ SunFest

Over five days in early May, West Palm Beach holds South Florida's largest waterfront music and arts festival. (p242)

🎉 Gay Memorial Day

For late May's Memorial Day weekend, Pensacola becomes one massive three-day gay party, with lots of DJs, dancing and drinking. (p458)

🎉 Florida Folk Festival

Held over the Memorial Day weekend, White Springs celebrates the huge Florida Folk Festival. It's been going since 1953 and draws everyone from gospel singers and banjo pluckers to Seminole storytellers. (p474)

🦀 Palatka Blue Crab Festival

For four late-May days, Palatka celebrates the blue crab and hosts the state championship for chowder and gumbo. (p380)

June

Oh my it's getting hot. It's also the start of hurricane season, which peaks in September/October. School's out for summer, so theme parks become insanely crowded.

🎉 Gay Days

Starting on the first Saturday of June and going for a week, around 170,000

people – especially members of the LGBT+ community – descend on the Magic Kingdom and other Orlando theme parks, hotels and clubs. Wear red. (p316)

🎉 Miami Fashion Week

Miami: so hot right now. Actually, it's hot all the time, in every sense of the word, but especially so during the city's Fashion Week (www.miamifashionweek. com).

🎉 Goombay Festival

In Miami's Coconut Grove, this massive street party draws well over 300,000 to celebrate the city's Bahamian culture with music, dancing and parades. It's one of America's largest black-culture festivals.

July

Northern-beach and theme-park high season continues. Swamp trails are unbearably muggy and buggy; stick to crystal springs and coastlines.

🎉 Fourth of July

America's Independence Day is cause for parades and fireworks, large and small, across the state. Miami draws the biggest crowd for the best fireworks and laser show.

August

Floridians do nothing but crank the A/C inside while foolish tourists swelter and burn on the beaches – and run from afternoon thundershowers.

September

Weather becomes just a little milder; look for shoulder-season deals in many resorts.

☆ Mickey's Not-So-Scary Halloween Party

At Disney World on select evenings over two months (starting in September), kids can trick or treat in the shadow of Cinderella Castle, with costumed Disney favorites and a Halloween-themed parade. (p273)

October

Temperatures drop, rains abate, school returns, crowds leave. Prices dip all over. The last hurricanes strike.

☆☆ MoonFest

West Palm Beach throws a rockin', riotous block party for Halloween on October 31. Guests are encouraged to come in costume and dozens of the best local bands play for free (www.moonfest.me).

☆☆ Fantasy Fest

Key West pulls out all the stops for this week-long costumed extravaganza culminating in Halloween. Everyone's even crazier than usual, and Key West's own Goombay Festival competes for attention the same week. (p198)

☆ Universal's Halloween Horror Nights

Magnificently spooky haunted houses, gory thrills and over-the-top Halloween shows. Watch for goblins, monsters and mummies roaming the streets and creeping up behind you. Parents should think carefully before bringing children 13 and under. (p293)

November

Florida's 'dry' winter season begins. Northern 'snowbirds' start flocking to their Florida condos. It's safe to hike again. Thanksgiving holidays spike tourism for a week.

☆☆ Fall Country Jamboree

Barberville in north-central Florida is the Cracker (rural Floridian) heartland, and on November's first weekend the Fall Country Jamboree hosts the state's best pioneer-heritage festival, with folk music and demonstrations of Cracker life. (p393)

December

High season begins for South Florida beaches. Manatees arrive in warm-water springs.

☆ Art Basel Miami Beach

Early December sees one of the biggest international art shows in the world (www.artbasel.com/miami-beach), with more than 150 art galleries represented and four days of parties.

☆☆ Ybor City Cigar Heritage Festival

Tampa's Ybor City has a long history as the cigar-making capital of the US. That heritage, and the cigars themselves, are celebrated in this fun festival. (p401)

Itineraries

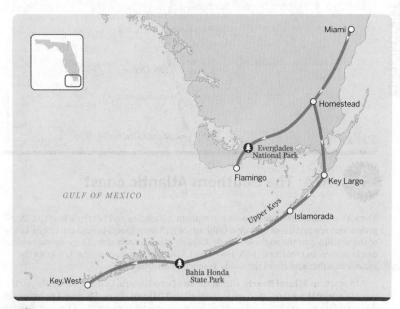

7 DAYS Iconic Florida

For sheer iconic box-ticking, you can't do better than spending a week taking in Miami, the Everglades and the Florida Keys.

First off, explore **Miami** for three solid days (more if you can). Florida's most exciting city offers everything from South Beach's pastel art deco hotels and hedonistic beach culture to Cuban sandwiches, Haitian *botanicas* and modern art to Latin hip-hop and *mojitos*. The list is endless.

Then take one day to visit the sunning alligators of **Everglades National Park**. On the way, **Homestead** has prime Florida roadside attractions (Coral Castle and Robert Is Here to name just two). The Everglades' **Flamingo Marina** offers opportunities to kayak among the mangroves, or simply spy crocs and manatees in the harbour.

Now spend three days (or more) in the Florida Keys. Stop first in **Key Largo**, for key lime pie, conch fritters and jaw-dropping coral reefs. Enjoy tarpon fishing in **Islamorada**, beach napping at **Bahia Honda State Park** and, finally, hit **Key West** to ogle the off-the-wall craziness of Mallory Sq and raise a libation as the tangerine sun drops into an endless ocean – *salut!*

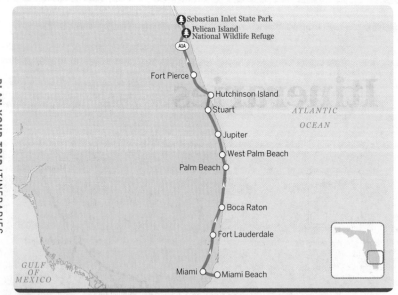

3 WEEKS A1A: The Southern Atlantic coast

Florida's southern Atlantic Coast is a symphony of beaches and barrier islands, of mangroves and sea turtles, of nostalgic Old Florida and nipped-and-tucked celebrity Florida, of the wealthy and the you've-got-to-be-kidding-me obscenely rich. Three driving routes can be mixed and matched (I-95, Hwy 1 and A1A), but scenic, two-lane A1A knits the islands together and edges the sands as much as any road can.

A1A starts in **Miami Beach**, within the Art Deco Historic District. Naturally you'll want to spend three days or so soaking up all that **Miami** offers. Then rent a convertible, don your Oakley sunglasses and nest a Dior scarf around your neck: it's time to road trip.

Whoops! There already? First stop is **Fort Lauderdale**. Preen along the promenade among the skating goddesses and be-thonged gay men, ride a romantic gondola through the canals, and enjoy fine art and gourmet cuisine: it's a suite of pleasures the Gold Coast specializes in.

After two or three days, pause for a quiet interlude on the gorgeous beaches of **Boca Raton**, then repeat your Lauderdale experience in **Palm Beach**. Ogle the uberwealthy as they glide between mansion and Bentley and beach, stop by the Flagler Museum to understand how this all got started, and each day decamp to **West Palm Beach**, the hipper, more happening sister city.

After several days, it's time to detox. Heading north, the Treasure Coast is known for unspoiled nature rather than condos and cosmopolitans. Stop first in **Jupiter**; among its pretty parks, don't miss the seaside geyser at Blowing Rocks Preserve.

Even better, spend several days in **Stuart**. From here you can kayak the Loxahatchee River, book a fishing charter, snorkel the reefs at St Lucie Inlet and escape the crowds while frolicking on nearby **Hutchinson Island** beaches.

In your last week, admire manatees (in winter) at **Fort Pierce** and snorkel its Spanish galleon. Surfers should pause at **Sebastian Inlet State Park**, and birders detour to the nation's first national wildlife refuge, **Pelican Island**.

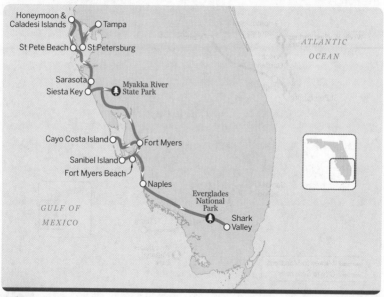

Gulf Coast Swing

3 WEEKS

Although it's less famous than Florida's eastern seaboard, Florida's Gulf Coast has its followers and here's why: the beaches aren't as built up, soporifically warm waters lap blindingly white sand, and the sun sets (rather than rises) over the sea. Plus, it's easy to mix urban sophistication with seaside getaways and swampy adventures – just like around Miami, only even more family- (and budget-) friendly.

On this trip, spend your first three to four days in **Tampa** and **St Petersburg**. Stroll the museums and parks along Tampa's sparkling Riverwalk, and spend a day enjoying historical Ybor City's Spanish cuisine, cigars and nightclubs. St Pete offers similar city fun, but above all, don't miss its Salvador Dalí Museum and the city's craft-brewing scene.

Now head west for the barrier islands. Take their full measure by spending one day on unspoiled **Honeymoon and Caladesi Islands**, then enjoy the hyper, activity-fueled atmosphere of **St Pete Beach**.

Next, drive down to **Sarasota** for three days. Take in the magnificent Ringling Museum Complex, the orchid-rich Marie Selby Botanical Gardens, perhaps catch the opera and still allow plenty of time to build sandcastles on the white-sand beaches of **Siesta Key**. With extra time, visit **Myakka River State Park** and kayak among the alligators.

Skip down to **Fort Myers** for two days of regional exploring. Take the ferry to **Cayo Costa Island** for a beach of unforgettable solitude, or go the party route and hit the crowded strands of **Fort Myers Beach**. Save at least two days for **Sanibel Island**. World famous for its shelling, it's also a bike-friendly island with great eats and wildlife-filled bays ripe for kayaking.

End with two to three days in **Naples**, the quintessential Gulf Coast beach town: upscale, artistic and welcoming of every age demographic, with perhaps Florida's most pristine city beach. It's easy to fit in a day trip to the **Everglades** – zip along the Tamiami Trail to **Shark Valley**, and take a tram tour or bike ride among the sawgrass plains and alligators.

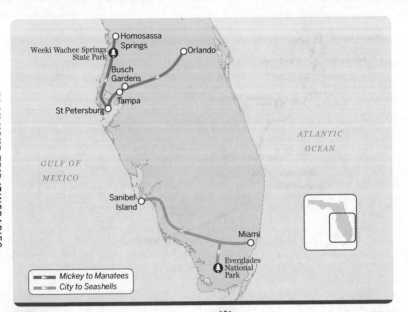

Mickey to Manatees
City to Seashells

10 DAYS Mickey to Manatees

The kids want Disney, but Mom and Dad want beach time, a good meal and some culture. Oh, and you've only got 10 days.

For the first three or four days, stay in **Orlando**. Rather than give in entirely to Walt Disney World®, spend two days there and another day at Universal Orlando Resort, particularly if you've read any of the Harry Potter books or seen the *Star Wars* movies.

For the next three or four days, hit Tampa Bay. Begin with the epic roller-coasters of **Busch Gardens**, a theme park that deserves its place among Florida's fun park elite. In **Tampa** choose between its tremendous zoo and aquarium and its fantastic museums, then end in historical Ybor City for Spanish cuisine with a side of flamenco. In **St Petersburg** even kids will find the Salvador Dalí Museum intriguing, and it's just the beginning for a fine portfolio of museums; you'll eat well here, too. Then squeeze in a day trip north for the mermaid shows at **Weeki Wachee** and the manatees of **Homosassa Springs**. Everybody's happy!

1 WEEK City to Seashells

You really don't want to miss high-energy Miami, but if you don't get some sandy, leave-me-alone-with-my-novel downtime you'll never make it when you return to work in [insert name of major metropolis here]. Oh, and you've only got a week.

Spend the first three days in **Miami** and have a party. Tour the art deco district hotels, enjoy the sophisticated art museums, shop for tailored shirts and racy designer dresses, and prance past the velvet ropes to celebrity-spot and dance all night to Latin hip-hop.

Next, spend one day peering at alligators through dark sunglasses in the **Everglades**, just so everyone back home won't be all 'What? You went to Florida and didn't even go?'

For the last three days, chill on **Sanibel Island**. Get a hotel on a private stretch of beach and do nothing but sun, sleep, read and collect handfuls of beautiful seashells as you kick along. Maybe take a bike ride and have a gourmet dinner. But each night, dig your toes in the sand and enjoy the setting sun in romantic solitude.

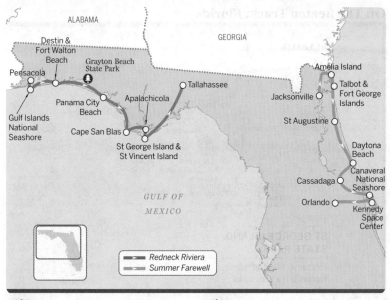

ALABAMA

GEORGIA

Destin &
Fort Walton
Beach   Grayton Beach
State Park
Pensacola

Amelia Island

Talbot &
Fort George
Islands

Jacksonville

Panama City
Beach   Apalachicola

Tallahassee

Gulf Islands
National
Seashore   Cape San Blas

St Augustine

St George Island &
St Vincent Island

Daytona
Beach

Canaveral
National
Cassadaga   Seashore

GULF OF

Orlando   Kennedy
MEXICO   Space
Center

Redneck Riviera
Summer Farewell

10 DAYS Redneck Riviera

Sure, Florida's Panhandle gets rowdy, yet there's family-friendly warmth and unexpected sophistication here alongside spectacular bone-white beaches.

Start your tour with a few days in **Pensacola**. Relax on the beaches of the **Gulf Islands National Seashore**, and enjoy Pensacola's historical village and its naval aviation history. The Blue Angels may even put on a show.

Spend another two days in the tourist towns of **Destin** and **Fort Walton Beach**, and don't miss the world-class sand of **Grayton Beach State Park**. If you have kids, a day among the hyperactive boardwalk amusements of **Panama City Beach** is a must.

Afterward shuffle along to the secluded wilderness of **Cape San Blas** and quaint **Apalachicola**, where the romantic historical center is charming on a hot Florida day.

St George and **St Vincent Islands** provide more secluded getaways, but if time is short spend your last day around **Tallahassee**. Unwind and get a little rowdy in some local live-music joints.

2 WEEKS Summer Farewell

This trip is good anytime, but Florida's north is particularly sweet as school starts and summer fades.

Fly into **Jacksonville**, but go straight to **Amelia Island** for several days of romantic B&Bs, luscious food and pretty sand. The good vibes continue as you kayak and explore the undeveloped beaches of **Talbot and Fort George Islands**, just south.

Then spend two to three days in **St Augustine**. The oldest city in the US preserves its heritage very well, with plenty of pirate tales enlivening the Spanish forts and basilicas. For a complete change of pace, worship at the shrine of all things NASCAR at **Daytona Beach** and the Daytona International Speedway.

Slow down again, this time for **Cassadaga**, a town of spiritualists and New Age wisdom in the middle of the backwoods, and have your fortune told.

A few more days means more kayaking in **Canaveral National Seashore**, and perhaps a day or two reaching for the stars at **Kennedy Space Center**. Spend whatever remaining time you have at the theme parks of **Orlando**.

Off The Beaten Track: Florida

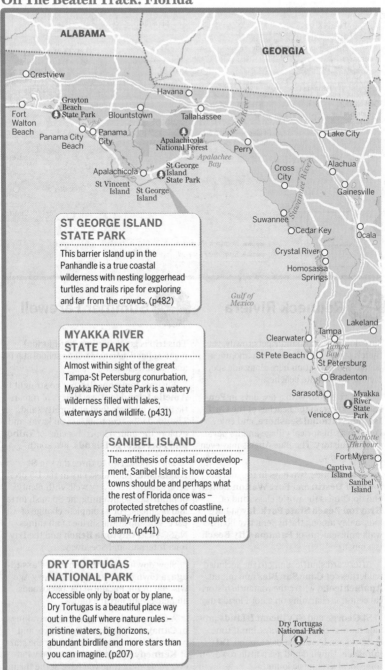

ST GEORGE ISLAND STATE PARK

This barrier island up in the Panhandle is a true coastal wilderness with nesting loggerhead turtles and trails ripe for exploring and far from the crowds. (p482)

MYAKKA RIVER STATE PARK

Almost within sight of the great Tampa-St Petersburg conurbation, Myakka River State Park is a watery wilderness filled with lakes, waterways and wildlife. (p431)

SANIBEL ISLAND

The antithesis of coastal overdevelopment, Sanibel Island is how coastal towns should be and perhaps what the rest of Florida once was – protected stretches of coastline, family-friendly beaches and quiet charm. (p441)

DRY TORTUGAS NATIONAL PARK

Accessible only by boat or by plane, Dry Tortugas is a beautiful place way out in the Gulf where nature rules – pristine waters, big horizons, abundant birdlife and more stars than you can imagine. (p207)

0 / 200 km
0 / 100 miles

PALATKA

Palatka is a world away from the busy Atlantic Coast, a one-time steamship terminus with a crab festival and small-town feel sliding gently towards obscurity. (p380)

ATLANTIC OCEAN

OCALA NATIONAL FOREST

One of the oldest forests in the eastern USA and the southernmost forest in the US, the 400,000-acre National Forest is a dense wilderness with so many quiet corners and deserted trails. (p386)

CANAVERAL NATIONAL SEASHORE

Wildlife and wilderness aren't something you usually associate with Florida's Atlantic Coast, but Canaveral is a wild and beautiful place, home to sea turtles and undeveloped beaches. (p337)

BIG CYPRESS NATIONAL PRESERVE

While everybody else heads to the Everglades, you can get much the same experience in Big Cypress National Preserve with swamps, mangroves and prairies. Watch for alligators, and even Florida panthers. (p154)

10,000 ISLANDS

An offshore echo of the Everglades, 10,000 Islands is a remote archipelago inhabited by dolphins and filled with secluded corners once used by pirates and smugglers. (p162)

Fernandina Beach
Amelia Island
Jacksonville
St Augustine
Palatka
Ocala National Forest
Daytona Beach
Canaveral National Seashore
Orlando
Titusville
Cape Canaveral
Kissimmee
Cocoa Beach
Melbourne
St Johns River
Florida's Turnpike (toll)
Kissimmee River
Sebring
Fort Pierce
Okeechobee
FLORIDA
Lake Okeechobee
Palm Beach
Corkscrew Swamp Sanctuary
Delray Beach
Boca Raton
Naples
Alligator Alley
Fort Lauderdale
Big Cypress National Preserve
Miami
Miami Beach
THE BAHAMAS
Cape Romano
Everglades National Park
Shark Point
Florida City
John Pennekamp Coral Reef State Park
Flamingo
Key Largo
Islamorada
Florida Bay
Marathon
Florida Keys
Straits of Florida
Key West

Plan Your Trip

Theme Park Trip Planner

Every year Walt Disney World®, Universal Orlando Resort and Legoland draw millions of visitors to Orlando, the theme-park capital of the world. There's also Busch Gardens near Tampa and a handful of other lesser-known parks. Here's the bottom line on what's what and how to tackle them.

When to Go

Peak Periods

Crowds and prices soar during US school vacations, including summer (June through August), spring break (March through mid-April), Thanksgiving weekend and, especially, the week between Christmas and New Year. If at all possible, do not visit during these high seasons.

Slow Times

The slowest times are mid-January through February, September through mid-October, the first half of May and the few weeks in between Thanksgiving weekend and mid-December.

Special Events

Some events worth planning for are the Epcot International Food & Wine Festival (late September through early November), Mickey's Very Merry Christmas Party (November to mid-December) and Universal Orlando's Halloween Horror Nights (October).

Florida's Theme Parks

Walt Disney World®

Walt Disney World® (p257) encompasses 42 sq miles and includes four completely separate and distinct theme parks, each with rides and shows: Magic Kingdom (p267), Hollywood Studios (p275), Epcot (p282), and Animal Kingdom (p279). There are also two water parks, Typhoon Lagoon (p289) and Blizzard Beach (p289); more than 20 hotels; almost 140 restaurants; and two shopping and nightlife districts, Disney Springs (p290) and Disney's Board-Walk (p289); as well as four golf courses, two miniature-golf courses, lagoons with water sports, and a spectator-sports complex, all connected by a system of free buses, boats and monorails.

For classic Disney at its best, head to the iconic Magic Kingdom, home to Cinderella Castle, fairy-tale rides and quintessential Disney parades, shows and fireworks. Garden-filled Epcot is another favorite, although it was undergoing a major refurbishment in 2020 and is expected to reach a whole new level when it reopens in 2021.

Africa-inspired Animal Kingdom has always been about rides and shows with zoo encounters, animal conservation and, oddly, a dash of dinosaur. To this, you can also add Pandora – The World of Avatar, easily Animal Kingdom's best feature, and that's saying something. Animal Kingdom is also home to *Finding Nemo: The Musical*, one of Disney's best live performances.

Hollywood Studios is now the home of the extraordinary Star Wars: Galaxy's Edge and its two fabulous rides – Millennium Falcon: Smugglers Run and Rise of the Resistance. They're so impressive that Hollywood Studios is now second in overall footfall to Magic Kingdom. And the word is out: expect waiting lines to be ridiculously long for the foreseeable future.

Universal Orlando Resort

In contrast to WDW, Universal Orlando Resort (p292) is a more intimate and walkable complex, with two excellent theme parks – Islands of Adventure (p301) and Universal Studios (p303) – and one water park – Volcano Bay (p306) – plus eight first-rate resorts and a carnival-like restaurant and nightlife district, CityWalk (p293), all connected by garden paths and a quiet wooden boat shuttle.

Universal's theme parks offer shamelessly silly, laugh-out-loud 'wow' for the whole family, with some of Orlando's best thrills, incredibly designed simulated experiences and water rides that leave you soaked.

At Islands of Adventure, each section has its own distinct tone and vibe. Seuss Landing surrounds visitors with the characters and landscapes of the Dr Seuss books and the Wizarding World of Harry Potter – Hogsmeade has proven a well-deserved runaway hit.

Universal Studios, just next door, has primarily movie- and TV-themed rides and scheduled shows, emphasizing comic-book superheroes and contemporary favorites such as *Despicable Me* and *The Simpsons*. Yet it also has a sweet Barney show, an excellent kids' play area, and Diagon Alley, an expansion of the park's enormously successful Potter-themed attractions. Guests with tickets for both theme parks can ride the Hogwarts Express through the 'British' countryside between Hogsmeade and Diagon Alley.

Volcano Bay is structured as an artificial Pacific island, centered on its own 200ft-high eponymous volcano. Some 18 attractions, ranging from family-friendly lazy rivers to adrenaline-pumping waterslides, beckon visitors to the park.

Legoland

Wonderful Legoland (p330) is as awesome and innovative as your favorite beloved Lego set, except this one is enormous and you can play on it for days. It may lack the polish of WDW, Universal Orlando Resort and Busch Gardens, but there's something appealing about the old-school theme-park vibe, the relative lack of hype and the much smaller crowds. There's a water park, Lego versions of famous US landmarks, botanical gardens, the Flight School roller-coaster and the play-learning-focused Imagination Zone.

Busch Gardens

A throwback to the days when theme parks meant roller coasters, Busch Gardens (p403) is for those who like their rides fast and scary. Divided into 10 different African-themed zones, Busch Gardens

Lego parrots, Legoland (p330)

also puts animal encounters front and center, and has various shows and musical entertainment.

The most exhilarating rides include Falcon's Fury (the highest freestanding drop tower in the US), Cheetah Hunt (which takes you forward at the speed of the fastest land animal on the planet), SheiKra (a 'dive coaster' that goes underground) and the Kumba (a 360-degree roller-coaster spiral). For something more sedate, head to Serengeti Plain, Nairobi, Morocco and the Sesame Street Safari of Fun & Bird Gardens.

Busch Gardens requires careful planning. Long queues form at the more popular rides (ie roller coasters) in the afternoons, so begin with these in the mornings and plan your route through the site carefully on their website.

Adventure Island

North of downtown Tampa, Adventure Island (p403) is a top-class water theme park with a wave pool, a lazy river and waterslides in all their adrenaline-rush glory. With plenty of picnic and recreation areas, it's a great day out for families.

Cheetah Hunt, Busch Gardens (p403)

Staying in the Resorts

Disney and Universal provide great perks for their hotel guests and both offer budget accommodations, so if you'll be spending several days exploring their parks, there's no compelling reason not to stay on-site.

If, however, you choose to stay off-site, resorts and national chains surround the parks, and many offer theme-park packages. Convenient locations for Disney parks are Lake Buena Vista, Kissimmee and the town of Celebration. International Drive is more convenient for Universal Orlando Resort and SeaWorld. Most hotels offer shuttles to some or all of the theme parks, but be warned that they can be a pain. They leave at prearranged times, make lots of stops, often require advance booking, and, for Disney in particular, you may need to take additional Disney transportation once the hotel shuttle drops you off. Always ask for *precise details* about shuttle logistics.

Disney and Universal hotel rates vary wildly by season and demand, as do hotel rates in Orlando in general, and prices can change dramatically (as in hundreds of dollars) within 24 hours. Stay flexible, be persistent and always ask about packages and specials. Most hotel rooms sleep at least four at no extra charge and several have bunk beds, suites and villas to accommodate larger parties.

Walt Disney World® Resort Hotels

With more than two dozen resort hotels, Disney has lodging for every budget, from camping to villas, motel-style complexes to full-service resorts. You're paying for convenience, location, recreational amenities and theming; quality-wise, except for the very best deluxe resorts, rooms are no better than good midrange chains elsewhere, and even the most expensive options pale in comparison to similarly priced luxury resorts elsewhere in Florida.

Guest Perks

Extra Magic Hours Each day, one theme park opens early and closes late for guests at Disney hotels only.

FastPass+ Advanced Reservations Reserve a one-hour window to FastPass+ lines at three attractions per person, per day up to 60 days in

Springfield: Home of the Simpsons (p304), Universal Studios.

advance, thus slashing wait times. Guests staying off-site can reserve attractions up to 30 days in advance. For the Avatar and Star Wars rides, you'll need to book 180 days in advance. This doesn't seem like much, but it makes a difference.

Disney transportation Despite the frustration of tackling Disney buses, boats and monorails, they can be more convenient than off-site hotel shuttles.

Free parking No fee at theme parks or hotels.

Disney's Magical Express Complimentary baggage handling and deluxe bus transportation from Orlando International Airport.

Baggage transfer If you change to a different Disney hotel during your stay, leave your bags in the morning and they'll be at your new hotel by evening.

Dining plans Only resort guests have access to the meal plans.

Universal Orlando Resort Hotels

Universal has eight resort hotels. They are top quality, extremely well situated within their more-intimate resort and highly recommended.

Guest Perks

Early admission to Wizarding World of Harry Potter Theme-park gates open one hour early for access to Harry Potter–themed attractions.

Unlimited Express Pass Up to five guests per room automatically receive unlimited access to Express Pass lines. This is a huge bonus, worth hundreds of dollars, but there are two major caveats. One: the major attractions at Wizarding World of Harry Potter do not have Express Pass lines. Two: this perk only applies to guests at some of the resorts – check which ones before booking.

Universal transportation Small boats run between the parks and deluxe resort hotels, and there's complimentary shuttle service to Cabana Bay (an on-site resort), Wet 'n Wild, Aquatica and SeaWorld.

Priority Seating Get first-available seating at select restaurants, but again, only for guests at some of Universal's resorts.

Dining & Character Meals

Eating at the theme parks falls into two general categories: quick service (a euphemism for 'fast food') and table service. Beyond this, your primary considerations are price, quality and theming fun. Sip on a Flaming Moe or Butterbeer at Universal Orlando Resort, eat under asteroid showers or in a mock drive-in theater at WDW, or watch giraffes and ostriches over African fare at Disney's Animal Kingdom Lodge. At Disney's Epcot, sample food and drink from around the world.

Beyond Disney and Universal, the creative twists to dining fade. There's certainly a nod to healthy and interesting, but generally it's the usual overpriced burgers and pizza served cafeteria-style. With the exception of Magic Kingdom, which serves alcohol at only one restaurant (wine and beer only), you'll find plenty of tantalizing cocktails and cold beer throughout the parks.

Disney allows table-service restaurant reservations 180 days in advance, and for a Disney character meal, dinner show or some of the more popular restaurants, you'll need to reserve the moment your 180-day window opens. Seriously. Some of the most coveted seats include Cinderella's Royal Table (p275) inside the castle, the *Beauty and the Beast*–themed Be Our

Top: Jurassic World
(p302), Islands of
Adventure

Bottom: Hogsmeade,
Islands of Adventure
(p294)

MIAZYOU/SHUTTERSTOCK ©

Guest (p274), dinner at California Grill (p261) with fireworks views, and the ultra-chic no-kids-allowed Victoria & Albert's (p261). Always ask about cancellation policies; generally, you can cancel with no penalty up to 24 hours in advance.

Snagging a table at Universal isn't nearly the trouble it is at Disney. Each park has two table-service restaurants that take advance reservations.

Note that restaurants inside theme parks require theme-park admission. But there are plenty of excellent eateries, including several that offer character meals, at entertainment districts and resort hotels outside the theme parks.

Essential Theme Park Strategies

In Advance

Purchase FastPass+ for the hottest Disney rides Avatar Flight of Passage and Millennium Falcon: Smugglers Run should be booked 180 days in advance, or else you won't get a spot.

Purchase advance tickets At many parks, tickets cost $10 to $20 less if purchased in advance. Online calendars allow you to peruse prices over several months.

Purchase multiple day-admission tickets and be flexible It's absolutely exhausting tackling the parks at 110% day after day. You'll enjoy the fun more if you allow room for downtime by the pool or beyond.

Reserve Disney dining up to 180 days in advance Select a few don't-miss eating experiences as the backbone of your Disney plans, and be sure to take location into consideration.

Stay at an on-site resort if going to Universal Orlando's Wizarding World of Harry Potter The quality of the accommodations, amenities and service, combined with the time- and stress-saving perks they offer, plus easy access to the parks, makes this a no-brainer if you can swing it.

Once There

Arrive early Come before park gates open, march straight to popular rides before lines get long, and consider leaving by lunch, when crowds are worst. This probably won't work every day, but a few efficient mornings make a real difference.

Pack snacks Something as simple as peanut-butter sandwiches and an apple stuffed in your bag will save time, money and stress.

Factor travel time When planning each day, carefully consider travel to and within the parks. At Disney especially, transportation logistics can waste hours and leave you drained.

Website, Apps & Podcasts

Google 'WDW' and you'll find pages upon pages of websites with detailed menus, crowd calendars, touring plans, photographs, discounts and more. There are dozens and dozens of apps to help you navigate the parks in real time. While it's easy to get buried in and stressed by infor-

---

ESSENTIALS

What to Wear

Floridians can be both laid-back and obsessive about fashion – this is the state where a guy in flip-flop sandals and no shirt can host a fancy dinner for guests recently arrived from an A-list party. In general, bring beachy clothes that can double as day outfits (eg a loose button-up). Men and women alike should pack one or two nice outfits if planning on a nice dinner or more expensive clubbing.

What to Take

➡ Sunscreen! That Florida sun will have you burned before you know it.

➡ Bug spray – to be fair, you can buy this in Florida, but buy it quickly.

➡ Proof of insurance.

➡ A driver's license issued from your home state or country.

Crowds approaching Universal Orlando Resort

mation overload, they can be helpful. Here are some of our favorites – most offer both apps and websites:

Walt Disney World® (www.disneyworld.disney.go.com) Official WDW website.

Universal Orlando Resort (www.universalorlando.com) Official Universal website.

My Disney Experience (www.disneyworld.disney.go.com/plan/my-disney-experience) Indispensable Disney app for creating WDW itineraries; reserve FastPass+ and meals.

Orlando Informer (www.orlandoinformer.com) Go-to for all things Universal Orlando, including crowd calendar.

Theme Park Insider (www.themeparkinsider.com) News from theme parks around the world, with painstaking details.

Undercover Tourist (www.undercovertourist.com) Disney, Universal and SeaWorld discounts, car rental, wait times etc.

All Ears (www.allears.net) Menus and advice.

WDW Info (www.wdwinfo.com) Go-to source.

MouseSavers (www.mousesavers.com) Money-saving tips.

> ### MYMAGIC
> MyMagic+ is Disney's system designed to help guests both plan and navigate their Disney vacation. It includes My Disney Experience, FastPass+ and MagicBands (p271).

Our Laughing Place (www.ourlaughingplace.com) WDW Transportation Wizard (TW) plots best routes. Several apps, including planning, TW and dining.

Mom's Panel (https://disneyparksmomspanel.disney.go.com) Perky Disney-sponsored discussion boards run by moms. Website only.

Touring Plans (https://touringplans.com) Tips on best use of FastPass+.

Disney Tourist Blog (www.disneytouristblog.com) Ride guides and more. Website only.

WDW Radio Show (www.wdwradio.com) Interviews, trivia, history and reviews.

The Disney Story Origins Podcast (www.disneystoryoriginspodcast.com) Goes in depth into classic Disney stories, movies etc.

Plan Your Trip

Outdoor Activities

Florida doesn't have mountains, valleys, cliffs or snow. What does it have? Water, and lots of it – fresh water, salt water, rainwater, spring water, swamp water. Florida's peninsula bends with more than 1200 miles of coastline, which includes more than 660 miles of the best beaches in the US. Plus coral reefs, prehistoric swamps, and forests, all teeming with Ice-Age flora and dinosaur-era fauna.

Getting Active in Florida

Hiking

From boardwalks across Everglades (p154) swamps to the Ocala National Forest (p386), Florida has some of the best hiking in the southern US. The Florida National Scenic Trail (www.fs.usda.gov/fnst) covers 1400 not-yet-contiguous miles.

Canoeing & Kayaking

There's no better way to explore Florida than by canoeing or kayaking its swamps and rivers, estuaries and inlets, and lagoons and barrier islands. The Everglades (p154) and 10,000 Islands are legendary but there are so many more fine waterways to explore.

Diving & Snorkeling

For diving and snorkeling, Florida has superlative coral reefs and wreck diving, while northern Florida is great for cave diving.

Cycling

Florida is too flat for mountain biking, but there are plenty of off-road opportunities, along with hundreds of miles of paved trails.

Hiking

Florida has some exceptional hiking, though the state's trails can be challenging, because of the weather and, in the Everglades, trail conditions when you stray from the boardwalk.

South Florida swamps tend to favor 1- to 2-mile boardwalk trails; these are excellent and almost always wheelchair accessible. But they can only take you so far. In the Everglades, you can also embark on 'wet walks,' which are wading trips deep into the blackwater heart of the swamps.

Just be warned: mosquitoes are an unavoidable reality, especially during the spring and summer months. Sunscreen is a must when hiking in Florida, and a good bug repellent (and insect-proof clothes) comes a close second.

Where to Hike

The Florida National Scenic Trail (www.fs.usda.gov/fnst) runs north from the swamps of Big Cypress National Preserve (p154), around Lake Okeechobee, through the Ocala National Forest (p386) and then west to the Gulf Islands National Seashore (p461) near Pensacola. The Everglades is not only boardwalks and swamp immersion – a number of hiking trails (p149) in the southern (Flamingo) reaches of the park are excellent half-day hikes.

Other prime areas for hiking include the remote pine wilderness, karst terrain and limestone sinkholes of Apalachicola National Forest (p487) and Paynes Prairie Preserve State Park (p393). Wekiwa Springs State Park (p321) also has excellent hiking.

Resources

For short hikes in national, state or regional parks, free park maps are perfectly adequate. Most outdoor stores and ranger stations sell good topographical (topo) maps.

Florida Greenways & Trails (www.visitflorida.com/en-us/things-to-do/outdoors-nature/trails-florida.html) The Florida Department of Environmental Protection has downloadable hiking, biking and kayaking trail descriptions.

Florida Hikes (www.floridahikes.com) A comprehensive, updated, easy-to-search online guide to hikes across the state.

Florida Office of Greenways & Trails (https://floridadep.gov/parks/ogt) The state's main database of current and future trails.

Florida State Parks (www.floridastateparks.org) Comprehensive state-park information and all cabin and camping reservations.

Florida Trail Association (www.floridatrail.org) Maintains the Florida National Scenic Trail (FNST); a wealth of online advice, descriptions and maps.

Leave No Trace (www.lnt.org) Advice on low-impact hiking and camping.

National Geographic (www.nationalgeographic.com) Custom and GPS maps.

Rails-to-Trails Conservancy (www.railstotrails.org) Converts abandoned railroad corridors into public biking and hiking trails; has a Florida chapter and reviews trails at www.traillink.com.

Recreation.gov (www.recreation.gov) Reserve camping at all national parks and forests, as well as many state parks.

Trails.com (www.trails.com) Create custom, downloadable topo maps.

US Geological Survey (www.usgs.gov/products/maps/overview) Online one-stop shop for maps and geological surveys of all US states.

Canoeing & Kayaking

Canoeing and kayaking are two brilliant ways to explore this watery state. The winter 'dry' season is best for paddling. That's because 'dry' in Florida is still pretty darn wet. So why come during the dry season? Because evaporation and receding waterlines force wildlife into highly visible concentrations amid the state's waterways and pools. In summer, canoe near cool, freshwater springs and swimming beaches.

Where to Canoe & Kayak

Choosing where to take to the water and paddle is a real joy in Florida. We have our own favourite spots to go kayaking, but the possibilities can seem endless.

In terms of rivers, the 207-mile Suwannee River (p474) is quintessential Florida. A meandering, muddy ribbon (ideal for multiday trips) decorated with 60 clear blue springs, it runs from Georgia's Okefenokee Swamp to the Gulf of Mexico. About 170 miles form an official wilderness trail (www.floridahikes.com/suwannee-river-wilderness-trail), and the section near Big Shoals State Park actually has some Class III rapids.

Other unforgettable rivers include: the Atlantic Coast's Loxahatchee River in the Jonathan Dickinson State Park (p246); Orlando's Wekiwa River in the Wekiwa Springs State Park (p321); and the Tampa region's placid Hillsborough River and alligator-packed Myakka River (p431).

You'll tell your grandchildren about Everglades National Park and its kayaking (p148); **Hell's Bay Canoe Trail** is a classic. The nearby 10,000 Islands (p42) are just as amazing, and nothing beats sleeping in the

AVOIDING HEATSTROKE

One thing Florida hikers never have to worry about is elevation gain. But the weather more than makes up for it. If your destination is South Florida, it's best to hike and camp from November through March. This is Florida's 'dry season,' when rain, temperatures, humidity and mosquitoes decrease to tolerable levels. In summer, hike before noon to avoid the midday heat and afternoon thundershowers.

Everglades in a 'chickee' (a raised wooden platform above the waterline). A truly great Florida adventure – indeed, one of the most unique wilderness experiences in North America – is paddling through the mangrove ecosystem that fringes the entirety of the southern Florida coast along the 99-mile **Wilderness Way**.

The remainder of the state's coasts are just as compelling. You'll kick yourself if you don't kayak Miami's **Bill Baggs Cape Florida State Park** (☑786-582-2673; www.floridastateparks.org/capeflorida; 1200 S Crandon Blvd; per car/person $8/2; ☺8am-sunset, lighthouse 9am-5pm; ℗) ℐ; Tampa Bay's Caladesi Island (p422); Sanibel Island's JN 'Ding' Darling National Wildlife Refuge (p441); and the Big Bend's Cedar Key (p489). There's even an entire 'blueway' – a collection of charted streams, coastline and rivers – within Lee County in southwest Florida.

On Florida's Atlantic Coast, more mangroves, waterbirds, dolphins and manatees await at Canaveral National Seashore (p337), particularly at Mosquito Lagoon. Also seek out Indian River Lagoon. Big Talbot Island (p381) and Little Talbot Island (p381) both provide more intercoastal magic.

Resources

Water-trail and kayaking information is also provided by Florida State Parks and Florida Greenways & Trails websites (p43) under Hiking. Here are more resources:

CAVE DIVING
· ·
Many diving spots line the Suwannee River. Try **Peacock Springs State Park** (www.floridastateparks.org/peacocksprings), one of the continent's largest underwater cave systems, **Troy Springs State Park** (www.floridastateparks.org/troyspring) and Manatee Springs State Park (p490). Another fun dive is Blue Spring State Park (p385), near Orlando. Note that you need to be cavern certified to dive a spring (an open-water certification won't do) and solo diving is usually not allowed. Local dive shops can usually arrange certification as well as trips.

American Canoe Association (www.americancanoe.org) ACA publishes a newsletter, has a water-trails database and organizes courses.

Florida Paddling Trails Association (www.floridapaddlingtrails.com) Divides the state into 15 sections and provides reports on paddle trails via an interactive map.

Florida Professional Paddlesports Association (www.paddleflausa.com) Provides a list of affiliated member kayak outfitters.

Kayak Online (www.kayakonline.com) A good resource for kayak gear, with links to Florida outfitters.

Paddle Florida (www.paddleflorida.net) Firsthand trip reports, maps, photos and detailed guides to dozens of paddling destinations in the state.

Swimming & Springs

Florida's beaches are the best in the continental United States and incredibly diverse. So let's start with two questions: do you prefer sunrise or sunset? Do you prefer surfing and boogie boarding or sunbathing and sand castles? For sunrise and surfing, hit the bigger, east-facing waves of the Atlantic Coast; for sand castles at sunset, choose the soporific, west-facing waters of the Gulf Coast and the Panhandle.

There are a few other elements of beachgoing we can certainly address: namely, the 'beach as casual escape' versus 'family destination' versus 'spring-break boozefest' versus 'spot to show off your fashion sense and spot celebrities.' If you're into the last of these, head for Palm Beach (p232), Fort Lauderdale (p215) and Miami Beach (p63). These are the spots where you'll see the stars and models decked out in swimwear. Those searching for a casual beach escape or a trip for the family may be better served by the tepid, calm waters of the Gulf; Sanibel Island (p441), off the coast of Fort Myers, may have the most family-friendly beaches in the state. You'll also feel less pressure to look stunning compared with in Southeast Florida and Miami. If you're into straight-up partying and a spring-break atmosphere, set your compass to towns such as Panama City (p471) and Daytona Beach (p353). Fair warning: while the Florida Keys seem like they would possess excellent swaths of sand, they are in fact mangrove islands with few natural beaches to speak of (though larger private resorts do tend to create their own artificial beaches).

Don't overlook Florida's lakes, rivers and springs. Taking a dip in one of the state's 700 freshwater springs – each 72°F (22°C) and, when healthy, clear as glass – is unforgettable. There are too many to list, but good swimming destinations include Crystal River (p424), the Suwannee River (p474), the Ichetucknee River (p392) and Ponce de León Springs State Park (p466).

Diving & Snorkeling

Florida has the continent's largest coral-reef system. The two best spots are John Pennekamp Coral Reef State Park (p178) in Key Largo (the uppermost of the Florida Keys) and Biscayne National Park (p164) south of Miami, at the tip of the Florida mainland. Biscayne is actually the only national park in the US park service system to exist primarily under the waves – 95% of the park is underwater. If you travel further along the Keys, you won't be disappointed at Bahia Honda State Park (p188) or Key West (p191).

Wreck diving in Florida is equally epic, and some are even accessible to snorkelers. So many Spanish galleons sank off the Emerald Coast, near Panama City Beach, that it's dubbed the 'Wreck Capital of the South.' But also check out wreck dives in Pensacola (p454), Sebastian Inlet State Park (p250), Troy Springs, Fort Lauderdale (p217), Biscayne National Park and Key West, a town that historically supported itself off the industry of wrecking (salvaging sunken ships and their cargo).

Named for its abundant sea turtles, the Dry Tortugas (p207) are well worth the effort to reach them.

As for Florida's freshwater action: every spring offers prime snorkeling. At times the clarity of the water is disconcerting, as if you were floating on air; every creature and school of fish all the way to the bottom feels just out of reach.

Resources

Ocean diving in Florida requires an Open Water I certificate. The state has plenty of certification programs (with good weather,

they take three days). To dive in freshwater springs, you need a separate cave-diving certification, and this is also offered throughout the state.

National Association for Underwater Instruction (www.naui.org) Information on dive certifications and a list of NAUI-certified Florida dive instructors.

Professional Diving Instructors Corporation (www.pdic-intl.com) Similar to NAUI, with its own list of PDIC-certified Florida dive instructors.

Cycling

Top off-roading spots include **Big Shoals State Park** (www.floridastateparks.org/bigshoals), with 25 miles of trails along the Suwannee River, and Paynes Prairie Preserve State Park (p393), with 20 miles of trails through its bizarre landscape. Also recommended is the Apalachicola National Forest (p487), particularly the sandy Munson Hills Loop.

To dip among the Panhandle's sugar-sand beaches, take the 19-mile **Timpoochee Trail**, which parallels Hwy 30A. In Tallahassee, the 16-mile Tallahassee-St Marks Historic Railroad State Trail (p477) shoots you right to the Gulf. Both paved and off-road trails encircle Lake Okeechobee, which is a great way to take in the surrounding countryside. One of the most unforgettable paved trails? Palm Beach's Lake Trail (p235), aka the 'Trail of Conspicuous Consumption' for all the mansions and yachts it passes.

For a more-involved overland adventure, the urban-and-coastal Pinellas Trail (p412) runs 47 miles from St Petersburg to Tarpon Springs.

In Florida's many beach towns, it's easy to find beach-cruiser-style bicycle rentals. These heavy-duty vehicles are made for lazy cycling along flat boardwalks – more a fun and casual trundle than serious ride. Sanibel Island (p441) is a calm little refuge, with a distinct lack of highway development, laced with dozens of bicycle paths.

Florida law requires that all cyclists under 16 wear a helmet (under 18 in national parks). As with hiking, avoid biking in summer, unless you like getting hot and sweaty.

TOP FIVE CYCLING TRAILS

We know this will start many an argument, but if we had to choose just five Florida cycling trails, they would be these:

Florida Keys Overseas Heritage Trail (p179) Ride alongside the shoulder of the road above the teal horizons of the ocean and Florida Bay for 70 non-contiguous miles.

Paisley Woods Bicycle Trail (p386) Think Florida has nothing for off-road bikers? You'll think again after pounding the scrub on this 22-mile ride through Ocala National Forest.

West Orange Trail (☑407-654-1108; www.orangecountyfl.net) This 24-mile trail passes through about 10 miles of lovely horse country just west of theme-park-studded Orlando.

Shark Valley Tram Road Trail (p155) This 15-mile paved track pierces the Everglades' gator-infested saw-grass river.

Legacy Trail (p429) Explore the countryside around Sarasota on this lovely 20-mile bike ride, which runs through forests, over bridges and behind backyards.

Resources

Bike Florida (www.bikeflorida.net) A good online resource for local cycling trails.

Florida Bicycle Association (https://florida bicycle.org) Advocacy organization providing tons of advice, a statewide list of cycling clubs, and links to off-road-cycling organizations, racing clubs, a touring calendar and more.

Fishing

Fishing in Florida is the best the US offers and, for variety and abundance, few places in the world can compete.

In Florida's abundant rivers and lakes, largemouth bass are the main prize. Prime spots, with good access and facilities, include **Lake Manatee State Park** (www.floridastateparks.org/parks-and-trails/ lake-manatee-state-park), south of St Petersburg; and Myakka River State Park (p431) for fly-fishing.

Near-shore saltwater fishing means redfish and mighty tarpon, snook, spotted sea trout and much more, up and down both coasts. Little Talbot Island (p381) is good for grand tidal fishing (mullet and sheepshead). The jetties at Sebastian Inlet (p250) are a mecca for shore anglers on the Atlantic Coast, while on the Gulf, Tampa's **Skyway Fishing Pier** is dubbed the world's longest fishing pier.

Other places to enjoy the quiet pleasures of pier fishing include Flagler Beach Fishing Pier (p359), Deerfield Beach International Fishing Pier, Anglin's Pier (p223) in Lauderdale-by-the-Sea, Venice Pier (p436), Fort DeSoto Park (p417) and Cocoa Beach Pier (p339).

In the Keys, Bahia Honda and Old Seven Mile Bridge on Pigeon Key are other shore-fishing highlights.

However, as 'Papa' Hemingway would tell you, the real fishing is offshore, where majestic sailfish leap and thrash. Bluefish and mahimahi are other popular deep-water fish. For offshore charters, head for Stuart, Fort Lauderdale, Lauderdale-by-the-Sea, Destin, Lake Worth and Miami. Steinhatchee is also good, as well as for scalloping, which you can also do at Crystal River. The best strategy is to walk the harborside, talking with captains, until you find one who speaks to your experience and interests.

Resources

All nonresidents 16 and over need a fishing license to fish and crab, and Florida offers several short-term options. There are lots of regulations about what and how much you can catch, and where. Locals can give you details, but do the right thing and review the official word on what's OK and what's not.

Florida Fish & Wildlife Conservation Commission (www.myfwc.com) The official source for all fishing regulations and licenses (purchase online or by phone). Also has boating and hunting information.

Florida Fishing Capital of the World (www.visitflorida.com/en-us/things-to-do/florida-fishing.html) State-run all-purpose fishing advice and information.

Top: Everglades National Park (p154)

Bottom: Manatees, Crystal River (p424)

Florida Sportsman (www.floridasportsman.com) Get the lowdown on sportfishing, tournaments, charters, gear and detailed regional advice.

Sailing

If you like the wind in your sails, Florida is your place. Miami is a sailing sweet spot, with plenty of marinas for renting or berthing your own boat – Key Biscayne is a particular gem. Fort Lauderdale is chock-full of boating options. In Key West, you can sail on a schooner with a real cannon, though tour operators are plentiful throughout the Keys. To learn how to sail, check out Pensacola's Lanier Sailing Academy (p462).

Golf

Fun fact: with more than 1250 courses (and counting), Florida has the most golf courses of any US state. We suspect it has something to do with Florida's high number of wealthy retirees. If you want to tee up, you won't have to look far.

Towns that are notable for golf include Palm Beach, Naples, Fort Myers, Orlando, Jacksonville, Miami and St Augustine. Near St Augustine is the World Golf Hall of Fame (p369); the US PGA (www.pgatour.com) has its headquarters at Palm Beach Gardens.

For a comprehensive list of Florida courses, see Florida Golf (www.floridagolf.com) and Florida Golfer Guide (www.floridagolferguide.com).

Surfing

Eleven-times world-champion surfer Kelly Slater is from Cocoa Beach, and four-times women's champion Lisa Anderson is from Ormond Beach. Both first learned how to carve in Space Coast waves, in the shadow of rockets, and Slater honed his aerials at Sebastian Inlet.

All of which is to say that while Florida's surf may be considered 'small' by Californian and Hawaiian standards, Florida's surfing community and history are not. Plus, Florida makes up in wave quantity what it may lack in wave size.

Nearly the entire Atlantic Coast has rideable waves, but the best spots are gathered along the Space Coast, which has surf lessons, rentals and popular competitions: shoot for Cocoa Beach (p338) – home of Ron Jon Surf Shop (p341) and the annual Easter Surf Festival (p339) – and nearby New Smyrna Beach. Also good are Indialantic (p347), Sebastian Inlet (p250) and Playalinda Beach (p338). However, you'll find tiny, longboard-friendly peelers from Fort Lauderdale down to Miami's South Beach, although the presence of the Bahamas' islands offshore prevents Miami from being a truly great surfing destination. In general, you'll find the big waves end at around Jupiter Beach.

Florida's northern Atlantic Coast is less attractive, partly due to chilly winter water, but consistent, 2ft to 3ft surf can be had at Daytona Beach (p353), from Flagler Beach (p359) up to St Augustine (p360), and around Amelia Island (p376).

The calm Gulf Coast isn't great for surfing, but you'll occasionally see folks hitting small waves in the area around Pensacola Beach or Destin, especially if the weather is rough.

Resources

Florida Surfing Association (www.floridasurfing.org) Manages Florida's surf competitions; also runs the surf school at Jacksonville Beach.

Surf Guru (www.surfguru.com) East Coast Florida surf reports.

Surfer (www.surfermag.com) *Surfer's* travel reports cover Florida and just about every break in the USA.

Plan Your Trip

Eat & Drink Like a Local

Florida's culinary scene is an enticing mix of ingredients: Gulf and Atlantic seafood, the best citrus fruits in the US, recipes from America's Deep South and Latin America, and some extremely talented chefs. Together, they give Florida serious culinary cred. Throw in quirky outliers, such as gator tail and fried snake, and there's so much to look forward to.

Food Experiences

Meals of a Lifetime

Būccan (p237) Small plates take diners on a gastronomic trip around the world down in Palm Beach.

Ulele (p404) This excellent Tampa restaurant serves up brilliant dishes influenced by Floridian Native American culinary traditions.

27 Restaurant (p98) Creative dishes, international influences from far and wide, and a lovely old Miami Beach home all come together here.

Cress (p384) Amazing, cutting-edge seasonal cuisine in...DeLand? Damn right. One of the state's culinary gems.

Ravenous Pig (p329) Locavore cooking at the forefront of Orlando's growing culinary sophistication.

Dare to Try

Boiled peanuts In rural North Florida, they take green or immature peanuts and boil them until they're nice and mushy, sometimes spicing them up with Cajun or other seasonings.

Alligator tail Alligator tastes like a cross between fish and pork. It's healthier than chicken, with as much protein but half the fat, fewer calories and

The Basics

Florida has a varied eating scene that jukes from white-tablecloth refinement to roadside fried seafood to themed restaurants in tourist towns and resorts. At higher-end places, especially in big cities such as Miami, you need to book seats in advance. At places with lower prices, or in smaller towns, you can usually show up and be seated.

Restaurants

You'll find restaurants in almost every town in Florida, serving any cuisine imaginable.

Bars

Pub grub and bar menus are increasingly popular in Florida nightspots.

Theme Parks

The food is often overpriced, but the atmosphere is generally delightful.

less cholesterol. Yearling Restaurant (p386) is a good place to try it.

Cracker cooking This being Florida, they don't stop at gators. Cracker (pioneer or rural Floridian) cooking also celebrates smoked eel and fried snake. Clark's Fish Camp (p372) is excellent.

Frogs legs Those who know say the 'best' legs come from the Everglades; imported ones are smaller and and have less flavor. Good frogs legs taste, honestly, like chicken, but with a more fishy texture. Try some at the Everglades Seafood Festival (p143) or Mill (p414).

Swamp Cabbage Heart of palm, or 'swamp cabbage,' has a delicate, sweet crunch. The heart of the sabal palm, Florida's state tree, it was a mainstay for Florida pioneers. Try it if you can find it served fresh (don't bother if it's canned; it won't be from Florida). There's even a **Swamp Cabbage Festival** (www.swampcabbagefestival.org) in February in LaBelle.

Where to Eat & Drink

Miami Florida's epicenter of all things gourmet, Miami has the greatest selection of ethnic cuisines. Miami is highly susceptible to buzzword-of-the-moment dining trends; at the time of writing, farm-to-table cuisine and an affected focus on rustic simplicity was all the rage.

PRICE RANGES

The following price ranges refer to a typical dinner main course. The Florida state sales and use tax is 6%, which will be added to the total of your bill. Some counties and municipalities may charge an additional percentage, but this is the exception not the rule. For good to excellent service, always tip 15% to 25% of the total bill.

For Miami and Orlando:

$	less than $15
$$	$15–30
$$$	more than $30

Elsewhere:

$	less than $12
$$	$12–25
$$$	more than $25

East Coast North of Miami and Miami Beach, Fort Lauderdale, Palm Beach and West Palm Beach offer the well-heeled foodie oodles of fun. Key West is, as in all things, more laid-back, but its dining scene is notably stocked with creative-fusion cool.

Southern Gulf Coast Tampa and St Petersburg are enjoying a culinary renaissance, with everything from Old World Iberian to locavore-inspired modern gastronomy. Skip south through Sarasota, Sanibel Island and Naples, and a memorable meal is just a reservation away.

Northern Florida As you go north, robust Southern cuisine comes to dominate. Great choices are sprinkled through Jacksonville, Amelia Island, St Augustine and Tallahassee; there's plenty of fresh, upscale seafood in Panhandle resort towns.

Local Specialties

Most Florida specialties incorporate distinctly local ingredients (such as oranges, seafood or alligator...) that have been given flavor by all manner of regional influences, from the north (America's Deep South) to the south (Latin America and the Caribbean). The result is a dynamic, exciting culinary scene filled with variety and flavor. Among the signature dishes to watch out for are grouper (try it blackened or in a sandwich), lobster (ever tried lobster mac-n-cheese?), smoked fish, and fried oysters. Other mainstays of the Florida table include:

Peel-and-eat shrimp A decidedly old-school Florida treat, peel-and-eat shrimp are served boiled and pink in their shells. There's an art to ripping off the legs and stripping down the shells to get to the sweet meat underneath; there's always cocktail sauce nearby.

Stone crabs The first recycled crustacean: only one claw is taken from a stone crab – the rest is tossed back into the sea (the claw regrows in 12 to 18 months, and crabs plucked again are called 'retreads'). The claws are so perishable that they're always cooked before selling. October through April is less a 'season' than a stone-crab frenzy.

Key lime pie Key limes are yellow and that's the color an authentic key lime pie should be. Pies are made from a custard of key lime juice, sweetened condensed milk and egg yolks in a cracker crust, topped with meringue. Avoid any slice that's green or stands ramrod straight.

Stone-crab claws

Tarpon Springs Greek salad We don't know why, but in Tarpon Springs, Greek restaurants started hiding a dollop of potato salad inside a regulation Greek salad – now you can find this odd combination throughout central Florida.

Homegrown Fruit & Vegetables

Today, most restaurants with upscale or gourmet pretensions promote the local sources of their produce. Florida has worked long and hard to become an agricultural powerhouse, and it's famous for its citrus fruits. The state is the nation's largest producer of oranges, grapefruits, tangerines and limes, not to mention mangoes and sugarcane. Bananas, strawberries, coconuts, avocados (once called 'alligator pears') and a gamut of tropical fruits and vegetables are also grown here. The major agricultural region is around Lake Okeechobee, with field upon field and grove upon grove as far as the eye can see.

Increasingly, there are appealing choices for vegetarians, especially in larger cities such as Miami, Orlando, Sanibel, Fort Lauderdale, St Petersburg and college towns. In many rural areas and in parts of North Florida, however, vegetarians can be forced to choose among iceberg-lettuce salads and pastas.

FLORIBBEAN CUISINE

'Floribbean' cooking refers to Florida's tantalizing gourmet mélange of just-caught seafood, tropical fruits and eye-watering peppers, all dressed up with some combination of Nicaraguan, Salvadoran, Caribbean, Haitian, Cajun, Cuban and even Southern influences. Some call it 'fusion,' 'Nuevo Latino,' 'New World,' 'nouvelle Floridian' or 'palm-tree cuisine,' and it could refer to anything from a ceviche of lime, conch, sweet peppers and scotch bonnets to grilled grouper with mango, adobo and fried plantains.

BEST FOR SOUTHERN COOKING

➡ Pig Floyd's Urban Barbakoa (p318), Orlando

➡ Bearded Pig (p371), Jacksonville

➡ Southern Charm (p372), Jacksonville

➡ Yardbird (p96), South Beach Miami

➡ Big Lee's (p385), Ocala

➡ Cypress (p479), Tallahassee

➡ Mr B's Real Grill BBQ (p479), Tallahassee

➡ Sand Dollar Cafe (p475), Port St Joe

Bounty of the Sea

Grouper is far and away the most popular fish. Grouper sandwiches are to Florida what the cheesesteak is to Philadelphia or pizza to Manhattan – a defining, iconic dish and the standard by which many places are measured. Hunting the perfect grilled or fried grouper sandwich is an obsessive Floridian quest – the issue of fried versus grilled has been known to provoke fights – as is finding the creamiest bowl of chowder.

Other popular fish include snapper (with dozens of varieties), mahimahi (which is sometimes labeled as dolphin, to the consternation of many a tourist) and catfish.

Florida really shines when it comes to crustaceans: try pink shrimp and rock shrimp, and don't miss soft-shell blue crab – Florida is well known for its blue-crab hatcheries, making them available fresh year-round. Locals boil their crabs, as is common across the American South, but plenty of Northeastern transplants means crabs are also steamed. Why not try both?

Winter (October to April) is the season for Florida spiny lobster and stone crab (out of season both will be frozen). Florida lobster is all tail, without the large claws of its Maine cousin, and stone crab is heavenly sweet, served steamed with butter or the ubiquitous mustard sauce. Usually, only the stone-crab claw is served.

Finally, the Keys popularized conch (a giant sea snail); now fished out, most conch is from the Bahamas. It has a slightly rubbery texture and a lovely, savory flavor. From July to September, Steinhatchee is the place for fresh scallops. In fall/winter, Apalachicola Bay produces 90% of Florida's small but flavorful oysters.

Southern Cooking

The further north you travel in Florida, the more Southern the cooking gets. This is the sort of cuisine that makes up in fat what it may lack in refinement. 'Meat and three' is Southern restaurant lingo for a main meat – such as fried chicken, catfish, barbecued ribs, chicken-fried steak or even chitlins (hog's intestines) – and three sides: perhaps some combination of hush puppies (small deep-fried maize cakes), cheese grits (a sort of cornmeal polenta), cornbread, coleslaw, mashed potatoes, black-eyed peas, fried green tomatoes, collard greens or buttery corn. End with pecan pie, and that's living. Po' boys are Southern hoagies (long rolls usually filled with fried nuggets of goodness).

Barbecue in the American South is all about the smoke. In fact, open flames are anathema to true American barbecue, which refers to a slow cooking process that involves smoke, smoke, more smoke, spices (sometimes), vinegar (maybe) and another dash of smoke.

Cracker cooking is Florida's rough-and-tumble variation on Southern cuisine, but with more reptiles and amphibians. And you'll find a good deal of Cajun and Creole as well, which mix in spicy gumbos and bisques from Louisiana's nearby swamps.

These days, Southern food isn't confined to North Florida. Fancy variations on the theme – haute Southern, if you will – are all the rage from Jacksonville to Key West.

Cuban & Latin American Cuisine

Cuban food is itself a mix of Caribbean, African and Latin American influences, and in Tampa and Miami it's a staple of everyday life. Sidle up to a Cuban

Top: Conch fritter stand, Mallory Square (p194)

Bottom: Key lime pie

KRS / SHUTTERSTOCK ©

loncheria (snack bar) and order a *pan cubano* or 'Cuban sandwich': a buttered, grilled baguette stuffed with ham, roast pork, cheese, mustard and pickles.

Integral to many Cuban dishes are *mojo* (a garlicky vinaigrette, sprinkled on sandwiches), adobo (a meat marinade of garlic, salt, cumin, oregano and sour orange juice) and *sofrito* (a stew-starter mix of garlic, onion and chili peppers); this is basically meat-and-starch cuisine, with an emphasis on huge portions. Main-course meats are typically accompanied by rice, beans and fried plantains.

With its large number of Central and Latin American immigrants, the Miami area is a culinary hotpot. Seek out Haitian *griot* (marinated fried pork), Jamaican jerk chicken, Brazilian barbecue, Central American *gallo pinto* (red beans and rice) and Nicaraguan *tres leches* ('three milks' cake).

In the morning, try a Cuban coffee, also known as *café Cubano* or *cortadito*. This hot shot of liquid gold is essentially sweetened espresso, while *café con leche* is just *café au lait* with a different accent: equal parts coffee and hot milk.

Another Cuban treat is *guarapo*, or fresh-squeezed sugarcane juice. Cuban snack bars serve the greenish liquid straight or poured over crushed ice, and it's essential to an authentic *mojito*. It also sometimes finds its way into *batidos*, a milky, refreshing Latin American fruit smoothie.

Florida Food Festivals

Food Fest! by Joan Steinbacher is the definitive guide to Florida's food festivals; her companion website (www.foodfestguide.com) lists festivals for the coming three months.

Everglades Seafood Festival (p159) In Everglades City; not just seafood, but gator, frogs legs and snakes.

Florida Strawberry Festival (www.flstrawberry festival.com; Plant City; ☺early Mar) More than half a million folks come annually to pluck, eat and honor strawberries at this 11-day event in Plant City, northeast of Tampa.

Carnaval Miami (p24) Negotiate drag queens and in-line skaters to reach the Cuban Calle Ocho food booths at this two-week Miami fest.

Isle of Eight Flags Shrimp Festival (p378) Pirates invade Amelia Island for shrimp at this three-day weekend event.

Palatka Blue Crab Festival (p380) Palatka hosts the state championship for chowder and gumbo.

Florida Seafood Festival (p485) Signature two-day oyster-shucking and -eating contests in Apalachicola.

Fort Myers Beach Shrimp Festival (p439) Dedicated to the Gulf pink shrimp with lots of cooking over two weekends.

BEST FOR CUBAN & LATIN AMERICAN

➡ El Nuevo Siglo (p124), Miami
➡ Versailles (p124), Miami
➡ Enriqueta's (p120), Miami
➡ Islas Canarias (p129), Miami
➡ Frontera Cocina (p291), Orlando
➡ Chucherias Hondureñas (p357), Daytona Beach

Plan Your Trip

Family Travel

The Sunshine State makes it so easy for families to have a good time that many return year after sandy, sunburned year. But with so many beaches, theme parks and kid-perfect destinations and activities, the challenge is deciding exactly where to go and what to do.

Children Will Love...

High-Octane Fun

Walt Disney World® (p257) Magic Kingdom, Hollywood Studios and mind-blowing rides such as Avatar and Star Wars.

Universal Orlando Resort (p292) First-rate attractions such as Universal Studios and the Wizarding World of Harry Potter.

Legoland (p330) Like walking into your own Lego movie, with old-school fun.

Kennedy Space Center (p335) Inspire your child's inner astronaut at this iconic complex dedicated to exploring space.

Daytona International Speedway (p353) Legendary NASCAR racetrack, with excellent tours and a brilliant Hall of Fame museum.

Beach Towns

St Augustine (p360) Pirates, forts, jails and re-enactors in a compact, walkable space.

Vero Beach (p251) Carefully zoned with grassy parks, a pedestrian-friendly downtown and wide, life-guarded beaches.

Stuart (p248) For outdoors-eager families, with getaway beaches and an aquarium-filled oceanographic center on Hutchinson Island.

Florida Keys (p175) The whole island chain brims with activities for all ages; check out the street performances at Key West's Mallory Sq.

Keeping Costs Down

Accommodations

Avoid high season (summer, spring break or school holidays). Most hotels do not charge extra for kids under 18.

Transportation

Bring your own car seat or, better still, your own car (if traveling from elsewhere in North America). Choose hotels with free airport and/or theme park shuttles.

Eating

Many Florida restaurants have kids' menus, and some that don't will happily prepare smaller portions for children.

Supplies

Although Florida supermarkets and pharmacies have plentiful supplies of most children's products, you can save money by bringing your own; this will also ensure you have your favorite brand.

Gasparilla Island (p443) Intimate, easy and blissfully free of high-rises, chain restaurants and hotels; ditch the car and tootle around in a golf cart.

Zoos

Zoo Tampa at Lowry Park (p400) Fantastic Tampa zoo with up-close encounters and Florida critters you may not see in the wild.

Zoo Miami (p96) Extensive and flagship city zoo, with all the big-ticket species.

Lion Country Safari (p241) An enormous drive-through safari park and rehabilitation center in West Palm Beach.

McCarthy's Wildlife Sanctuary (p239) West Palm Beach's first-rate animal rescue, featuring endangered animals and discarded exotic pets.

Naples Zoo at Caribbean Gardens (p445) Compact zoo with some local Florida specialties and inspiring conservation programs.

Wildlife Encounters

Everglades National Park (p154) Don't miss the Anhinga Trail, an easy stroll past alligators and beautiful birds; for family-friendly kayaking, head to Everglades City and Flamingo centers.

Ellie Schiller Homosassa Springs Wildlife State Park (p423) Old Florida don't-miss staple emphasizing Florida wildlife; underwater manatee observatory.

John D MacArthur Beach State Park (p246) Ranger-led sea-turtle watches, beautiful beaches and calm-water kayaking north of West Palm Beach.

Biscayne National Park (p164) Glass-bottom boat tours and snorkeling over an epic reef in Homestead, 30 miles south of Miami.

Ichetucknee Springs State Park (p392) Inner-tube along crystal-clear slow-moving water with manatees, otters and turtles at Fort White.

Region by Region

Miami

Miami has loads of attractions for young travelers. You'll find lovely beaches, grassy parks, nature trails, megamalls, zoos and other animal-centric attractions. Plus, there's plenty of great snacks, from Italian-style gelato to Venezuelan *arepas* (corn cakes). There are also loads of family-friendly hotels and restaurants.

The Everglades

Florida's best wildlife-watching destination has plenty to entertain kids. Manatees, river otters, weird-and-wonderful birds, and even the mere possibility of seeing bobcats and Florida panthers can all hold a child's attention, while alligators are everywhere and guaranteed to excite. Boardwalks and tours by tram or boat are easily accessible for families, while older kids will love kayaking through the swamps.

Florida Keys & Key West

Just the very idea of the Keys, with its lands reclaimed from the sea, is one that kids usually find pretty cool. And what's not to like when every aspect of life down here revolves around snorkeling, diving, fishing, boating and an all-around no-worries vibe.

Southeast Florida

Some of the best beaches anywhere in the state are the major calling card for families in the state's southeast. Upscale beachside towns mean excellent restaurants, while places such as Sebastian Inlet and Vero Beach provide a backdrop to hiking and kayaking.

Orlando & Walt Disney World®

If any place could be considered paradise for kids, it has to be Orlando and its theme parks. Many a family's Best Day Ever has been had here, and the rides are seriously world-class. The entire atmosphere and experience is geared toward families and putting a smile on every child's face.

The Space Coast

World-class beaches and sleepy coastal towns combine with vintage airplanes and all-things-space to make this 75-mile stretch of barrier islands a favorite. Kennedy Space Center (p335) is the perfect place for every child big and small who ever dreamed of being an astronaut, while Canaveral National Seashore (p337) means the chance to see nesting turtles and kayak or hike.

Northeast Florida

From the stories of pirates and conquistadores in St Augustine to the family-friendly beaches of Amelia Island or Jacksonville, the northeast has plenty to capture and hold a child's attention.

Tampa Bay & Southwest Florida

Great zoos, aquariums and museums, plus some of Florida's prettiest, most family-friendly beaches and alluring island getaways make the Southwest a fine family destination. Best of all, Busch Gardens (p403) has what many believe to be the best roller coasters on the planet.

The Panhandle

The Panhandle coastline has stunning white-sand beaches, crystal water and pockets of frenetic boardwalk amusements. It's also a terrific region for activities, excellent restaurants, and opportunities to explore nature in the numerous protected areas just inland from the Gulf shore.

Good to Know

Look out for the 🐾 for family-friendly suggestions throughout this guide.

Accommodations Most Florida hotels have cribs, roll-away beds and sleeper-sofas, suites and adjoining rooms, plus refrigerators and microwaves. Most full-service resorts offer children's programs.

High chairs Most restaurants have a few, but they can run out when things are busy – reserve ahead.

Baby change facilities Reasonably widespread.

Car seats Florida car-seat laws require that children must be in a rear-facing car-seat until they are 20lb and one year old; a separate or integrated child-safety seat until five; and a booster until seat belts fit properly (over 4ft 9in and 80lb). Rental-car companies are legally required to provide child seats, but reserve in advance.

Baby-gear rental Traveling Baby Company (www.travelingbabyco.com) offers cribs, strollers, car seats etc and infant supplies such as diapers and baby food etc. It gets delivered to your hotel.

Useful Resources

Lonely Planet Kids (www.lonelyplanetkids.com) Loads of activities and great family travel blog content.

Visit Florida (www.visitflorida.com/en-us/things-to-do/family-vacation.html) The local tourist board has plenty of suggestions for family travel.

Kids' Corner

Say What?

Slang for 'kid'	*Jit*
Slang for chillin' out	*Vibin*
Getting a clean in a pool rather than a shower	Florida bath
Flip flops	*chancleta* or *chanclas*

Did You Know? ℹ️

- More than 1.2 million alligators inhabit Florida, with 200,000 in the Everglades.

Have You Tried?

LENA GROTTLING / SHUTTERSTOCK ©

Alligator tail
An old Florida favorite.

Regions at a Glance

Miami

Museums
Nightlife
Food

Museums & the Arts

Miami is a real-time performance-art piece with major cultural institutions (the Bass, the Adrienne Arsht Center, the Lowe), vibrant gallery districts such as Wynwood, and architectural masterpieces such as South Beach's art deco district.

Miami's Vice

Indulgence, a love of beauty, youth and good times make up the Miami nightlife cocktail. It's part celebrity-spotting, drag shows and bottle service, part authentic Cuban dance halls and grotty dive bars, with bohemian lounges and bars thrown in.

Ethnic & Gourmet

Miami offers an ideal gastronomic mix of wealth, immigrants and agricultural abundance. Trendy, celebrity-chef-driven laboratories of gourmet perfection dot Miami Beach and Coral Gables, balanced out by hole-in-the-wall ethnic eateries.

p63

The Everglades & Biscayne

Wildlife-Watching
Activities
Quirky Florida

Find-the-Fauna

Alligators, manatees, bottlenose dolphions, river otters, bobcats, the Florida panther and more than 350 bird species all call these swamps home. The Everglades ranks among America's best wildlife destinations.

Outdoor Adventures

Ramble along raised wooden boardwalks, then kayak or canoe and let yourself be swallowed by the Everglades' watery wilderness for an unforgettable experience.

Roadside Attractions

Bizarre food, strange legends of mythical beasts, offbeat roadside stands, monuments to scorned love? Yep, all these and then some pepper this land.

p145

Florida Keys & Key West

Activities
Beaches
Nightlife

Islands & Outdoors

In addition to drinking and partying, people come to the Keys to do stuff: fish, snorkel North America's best coral reefs, dive, kayak, hike, bike, then fish some more and snorkel again.

Mangroves & Sand

Except for Bahia Honda, one of Florida's best beaches, Keys beaches aren't as uniformly perfect as elsewhere, yet they're still brilliant.

Crazy Key West

No nightlife scene in Florida matches Key West's peculiar mix of craziness, self-conscious performance, gay humor and drunken loutishness. Hemingway found his perfect bar here at the end of the world; he wasn't alone.

p175

Southeast Florida

Beaches
Activities
Entertainment

Buttery Beaches

The Gold Coast, the Treasure Coast: for once the hyperbole is true. Some of these towns – Palm Beach, Boca Raton, Fort Lauderdale – are über-wealthy and, wow, are these beaches gorgeous.

Sightseeing

Canal and gondola tours around Fort Lauderdale, river trips on the Loxahatchee, epic wreck diving, snorkeling Spanish galleons, surfing, sportfishing, turtle watches: there's plenty to see and do.

Waterfront Fun

Southeast beach towns are good fun, whether people-watching along Hollywood Broadwalk, partying in Fort Lauderdale bars, chilling in Jupiter or gaping at the mansions of Palm Beach.

p221

Orlando & Walt Disney World®

Theme Parks
Entertainment
Activities

Magic Kingdoms

If theme parks are worlds, then Orlando is its own galaxy. Walt Disney World® is itself a solar system of amusements; Universal Orlando Resort may be smaller but it's equally entertaining, with more attitude.

Family Parties

Start with Disney, which packs evenings with a magical light parade and Cirque du Soleil, or head to Universal, which dishes up a *luau* and the Blue Man Group.

Outdoor Exploring

In and around Orlando are plentiful opportunities to bike, golf, kayak, go river-tubing and even 'skydive' indoors, not to mention the water play at park resorts.

p255

The Space Coast

Activities
Beaches
History

Surfing & Kayaking

Surfing and kayaking are the Space Coast's unbeatable one-two punch; Cocoa Beach is the surfing scene's epicenter. Manatees and dolphins swim among protected, unspoiled lagoons and intercoastal waterways.

Cosmic Coast

Space Coast beaches are truly swell, with a relaxed and low-key vibe that you rarely find to the north or south. Seek out cute Vero Beach and escape on beautiful Apollo Beach.

Kennedy Space Center

The shuttle launches may have ended, but the space center is still a top-notch, immersive experience that throws you into the US space program and the life of an astronaut.

p333

Northeast Florida

Activities
Old Florida
Eccentric Experiences

Outdoor Adventures

Ocala National Forest beckons with forested hikes, crystal springs, rivers and fine camping. But the region's interior state parks are all special, and there's splendid kayaking.

Old & Oldest Florida

Old Florida survives in Cross Creek, where Cracker (backwoods Florida pioneer) life is lovingly preserved. Spanish-founded St Augustine is a splendid time warp back to the days of Spanish explorers, missionaries and real-life pirates.

Offbeat Fun

For a maritime getaway, choose Amelia Island, with its pirate parties and shrimp festivals. Or head to Cassadaga to have your fortune read in a town full of spiritualists.

p351

Tampa Bay & Southwest Florida

Beaches
Food
Museums

Gulf Breezes

The Gulf Coast from Tampa south enjoys some of Florida's best white-sand beaches. Siesta Key, Fort Myers Beach, Honeymoon Island, Naples, Fort DeSoto, St Pete Beach and Sanibel are all great.

Coastal Cuisine

Tampa has a big-city foodie scene, with several gourmet destinations, and St Petersburg is no slouch. Sophisticated Sarasota, Naples and Sanibel also offer excellent cuisine.

Arts & Culture

Two of Florida's best museums – the Salvador Dalí Museum and the Ringling Museum complex – are found here. Classy cultural institutions are highlights in Tampa, St Petersburg, Sarasota, Fort Myers and Naples.

p395

The Panhandle

Beaches
Activities
Entertainment

Country Coast

The 'Redneck Riviera,' is a place of glittering snow-white sands and gentle waters. The beaches are universally beautiful, whether bordered by coastal towns or pristine natural preserves.

Springs & Sinkholes

Kayaking Cedar Key is wonderful, and canoeing the Suwannee River is classic Florida. There's swimming, snorkeling and diving in crystal springs, and hiking and biking in Apalachicola National Forest.

Beaches & Blues

Enjoy blues clubs in Tallahassee, South Walton's chic boutique beach experience, glass-bottom boat tours in Wakulla Springs State Park, and Pensacola's Blue Angels and beach-bars.

p451

On the Road

AT A GLANCE

POPULATION
470,000

**NATIVE SPANISH
SPEAKERS**
60%

BEST FOOD MARKET
1 800 Lucky (p120)

**BEST RECORD
STORE**
Sweat Records (p139)

**BEST CUBAN
COCKTAILS**
Cafe La Trova (p137)

WHEN TO GO
Dec–Mar
Warm, dry weather
and festivals draw
in tourists; Miami's
liveliest season.

Apr–Jun
Not as muggy as
summer, but lusher
and greener than
winter.

Jul–Oct
Prices plummet.
When it's not as hot
as an oven, there
are storms: it's
hurricane season.

Wynwood Walls (p81)
DENNIZN/SHUTTERSTOCK ©

Miami

Miami is the ultimate synthesis of the United States, the Caribbean and Latin America, a place possessed of brash ambition, endless hustle and a ceaseless appreciation for beauty, good food, fun times and more beauty. This is a city of bewildering diversity, as measured by both citizens and neighborhoods. You can admire graffiti murals in Wynwood, sip a sugarcane and guava milkshake in Little Havana, rub shoulders with art mavens at a contemporary exhibition Downtown, then cross the bridge to the models and deco playgrounds of Miami Beach.

Nature lies just beyond the city fringes, encompassing verdant botanical gardens (Coral Gables), peaceful mangroves for kayaking (Virginia Key) and a vast estuarine park (Oleta River State Park). Miami will wear you out, but that's the price for exploring a city relentlessly dedicated to squeezing the juice out of life (and while we're at it, another sugarcane and guava smoothie, *por favor*).

INCLUDES

Miami Highlights

1 Art Deco Historic District (p68) Seeing South Beach's art-deco beauties at their most alluring.

2 Pérez Art Museum Miami (p74) Checking out the latest show and wandering the waterfront sculpture garden.

3 Wynwood Walls (p81) Being bowled over by the stunning murals at the epicenter of Wynwood.

4 South Beach (p68) Sitting on the sands with glamor-seekers from around the world.

5 Vizcaya Museum & Gardens (p92) Marveling at the eclectic collection of art and antiquities.

6 Bill Baggs Cape Florida State Park (p95) Walking the boardwalks and peaceful trails.

See South Beach (11th to 23rd Streets) Map (p76)

1 Art Deco Historic District

4 South Beach

Collins Ave

8 Wolfsonian–FIU

See South Beach (1st to 11th Streets) Map (p70)

ATLANTIC OCEAN

MacArthur Cswy

Miami Children's Museum

Jungle Island

Lummus Island

Virginia Key Beach North Point Park

Virginia Key

2 Pérez Art Museum Miami

Wynwood Walls **3**

Rubell Museum

See Downtown Miami Map (p100)

S Miami Ave

Hobie Island

Bear Cut

Rickenbacker Cswy

Crandon Park

Key Biscayne

6 Bill Baggs Cape Florida State Park

See Key Biscayne Map (p114)

See Little Havana Map (p140)

Cubaocho **9**

SW 22nd Ave

SW 27th Ave

Ermita de la Caridad

5 Vizcaya Museum & Gardens

See Coconut Grove Map (p126)

Biscayne Bay

Intracoastal Waterway

Miami International Airport

SW 37th Ave/Douglas Rd

SW 42nd Ave (Le Jeune Rd)

NW 7th St

W Flagler St

SW 8th St (Calle Ocho)

Dolphin Expwy

Granada Golf Course

SW 22nd St

10 Venetian Pool

See Coral Gables Map (p134)

COCONUT GROVE

Kampong

Maynada Blvd

Matheson Hammock Park

Fairchild Tropical Garden

Old Cutler Rd

Coral Way

Lowe Art Museum

SW 57th Ave/Red Rd

S Dixie Hwy

SW 72nd St (Sunset Dr)

Don Shula Expwy

KENDALL

Pinecrest Gardens

PINECREST

SW 112th St (Killian Dr)

Killian Dr

Dixie Hwy

Deering Estate at Cutler (1m)

N

5 km
3 miles

7 Little Haiti Cultural Complex (p91) Catching an exhibition at this colorful arts and music space.

8 Wolfsonian–FIU (p68) Browsing gorgeous 19th- and 20th-century works at this museum, dedicated to decorative arts and design.

9 Cubaocho (p137) Watching a live performance by top Latin musicians and artists.

10 Venetian Pool (p98) Splashing about the faux grottoes and coral cliffs.

DAY TRIPS FROM MIAMI

FORT LAUDERDALE

Miami's northerly neighbor is upscale and elegant, but it can also be as show off-y as the yachts that frequently dock at her canals. It's an attractive place inhabited by fairly attractive people, with a noticeable LGBTQ scene and a very Floridian commitment to enjoying the heck out of life.

☆ Best Things to See/Do/Eat

◉ Riverwalk The easiest way to soak up a good chunk of what Fort Lauderdale has to offer is a stroll along this pathway, which takes in much of the city's Latin-meets-Anglo opulence, Mediterranean-esque architecture, and some nice waterfront views besides. (p215)

Las Olas Gondola They call this city the American Venice, so let's just lean into the cliché, alright? There are more than 300 miles of canals here; get poled out among them on an actual Venetian gondola, complete with Italian music, and check out the homes of the rich and even more rich. (p217)

✖ Lester's Diner Fort Lauderdale can be overwhelmingly fancy. Offset the posh with a visit to this greasiest of spoon diners. Have some pancakes, hash browns, eggs, and wash it down with coffee and a good taste of pure Americana. (p219)

☆ How to Get There

Car I-95 and Florida's Turnpike can both get you to Fort Lauderdale, which is about 30 miles north of Downtown Miami.

Tri-Rail This commuter train runs between Miami Airport and Fort Lauderdale (one way $5, 45 minutes), among other locations. A feeder system of buses has connections at no charge. Free parking is provided at most stations. Provide ample cushion for delays. Amtrak also uses Tri-Rail tracks.

THE KEYS

It's a bit far to day-trip all the way out to Key West, which sits at the (imagine that) western end of this offshore archipelago. But a jaunt to the Upper Keys is quite doable, and will give you a good taste of the odd allure of Florida's own island chain.

☆ Best Things to See/Do/Eat

◉ Anne's Beach Contrary to popular perceptions, there aren't a ton of beaches in the Keys. But Anne's, on the island of Islamorada (Eye-luh-moe-raw-duh), is a very fine stretch of blue green water and squidgy tidal flats. (p182)

◉ John Pennekamp Coral Reef State Park Explore the first underwater park in the USA, which includes some 75 sq miles of watery environs. The snorkeling here (which can be arranged with the park) is some of the best in the Lower 48 states. (p178)

✖ Lazy Days Rock up and order some fresh bread, the catch of the day and a bowl of delicious conch chowder at this wonderful Islamorada restaurant, which captures the tropical laid-back elegance of fine Keys dining. (p183)

☆ How to Get There

Car The Keys are connected to the mainland by US Rte 1, known in these parts as the Overseas Hwy. It's a beautiful 90-mile drive from Miami to Islamorada over multiple causeways and bridges. Beware of weekend traffic, which can cause bumper-to-bumper gridlock.

THE EVERGLADES

One of the most unique ecosystems in North America sits mere miles from Miami: the 'River of Grass,' a flooded prairie and forest that contains within its green depths a collage of prehistoric wildlife and vistas of vast, gentle, tide-lapped beauty.

☆ **Best Things to See/Do/Eat**

◉ **Anhinga Trail** One of the most accessible trails in the Everglades is happily also one of the best, a series of walkways and boardwalks where you can almost always catch sight of a wild alligator, plus scores of wetland birds. (p150)

🕴 **Garl's Coastal Kayaking** Head to this outfitter in Homestead to get set up with paddling excursions and 'hikes' that are like wet-wading into the heart of the watery Glades (very fun and highly recommended!). (www.garlscoastalkayaking.com)

✖ **Robert Is Here** Part fruit stand, part farmers market, part petting zoo, all enjoyable, Robert's is an old Florida institution that happens to sell some of the best orange juice on the planet. (p163)

☆ **How to Get There**

Car It's a roughly 50- to 60-mile drive from Miami to the entrance to the eastern edge of Everglades National Park, but keep in mind the park spans 1.5 million acres. You need your own set of wheels to properly explore it.

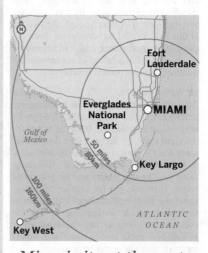

Miami sits at the center of South Florida's weird and wonderful buffet of attractions, which happens to include alligator swamps, mangrove-fringed offshore islands and the USA's own version of Venice.

◉ Sights

◉ South Beach

South Beach (SoBe) is everything Miami is known for – the sparkling beach, beautiful art-deco architecture, top-end boutiques, and buzzing bars and restaurants. Still, there's more to this district than velvet ropes and high-priced lodging (though there's a lot of this too). You'll find some great down-to-earth bars, good eating and cool museums, all set against a backdrop of relentlessly attractive pastel deco architecture.

★ Wolfsonian-FIU   MUSEUM
(Map p70; ☑ 305-531-1001; www.wolfsonian.org; 1001 Washington Ave; adult/child $12/8, 6-9pm Fri free; ⊙ 10am-6pm Mon, Tue, Thu & Sat, to 9pm Fri, noon-6pm Sun) Visit this excellent design museum early in your stay to put the aesthetics of Miami Beach into context. It's one thing to see how wealth, leisure and the pursuit of beauty manifest, but it's another to understand the roots and shadings of local artistic movements. By chronicling the interior evolution of everyday life, the Wolfsonian reveals how these trends manifested architecturally in SoBe's exterior deco.

Take a look at the Wolfsonian's own noteworthy architectural features with its Gothic-futurist angles and lion-head-studded grand elevator.

Art Deco Historic District   AREA
(Map p76; Ocean Dr) The world-famous art deco district of Miami Beach is pure exuberance: an architecture of bold lines, whimsical tropical motifs and a color palette that evokes all the beauty of the Miami landscape. Among the 800 deco buildings listed on the National Register of Historic Buildings, each design is different and strolling among these restored beauties from a bygone era is utterly enthralling. Classic art deco structures are positioned beautifully between 11th and 14th Sts – each bursting with individuality.

Close to 11th St, the Congress Hotel (p73) shows perfect symmetry in its three-story facade. About a block north, the Tides is one of the finest of the nautical-themed hotels, with porthole windows over the entryway, a reception desk of Key limestone (itself imprinted with fossilized sea creatures) and curious arrows on the floor, meant to denote the ebb and flow of the tide. Near 13th St, the Cavalier (Map p76; ☑ 305-673-1199; www.cavalier

southbeach.com; 1320 Ocean Dr; r $145-255, ste $285; P ✳ 🎧) plays with the seahorse theme, in stylized depictions of the sea creature, and also has palm-tree-like iconography.

Note that it's best to go early in the day when the crowds are thinnest and the light is best for picture-taking. For deeper insight into the architecture, take a guided walking tour of the area offered daily by the Miami Design Preservation League (p99).

SoundScape Park   PARK
(Map p76; www.nws.edu; 500 17th St) Outside of the New World Center, this park is one of the best places for open-air screenings in Miami Beach. During some New World Symphony performances, the outside wall of the Frank Gehry–designed concert hall features a 7000-sq-ft projection of the concert within. Bring a picnic and enjoy the free WALLCAST show. In addition, there are free once-monthly yoga sessions on the lawns. Check the website for dates.

Art Deco Museum   MUSEUM
(Map p70; ☑ 305-672-2014; www.mdpl.org; 1001 Ocean Dr; ⊙ 10am-5pm Tue-Sun) FREE This small museum is one of the best places in town for an enlightening overview of the art-deco district. Through videos, photography, models and other displays, you'll learn about the pioneering work of Barbara Baer Capitman, who helped save these buildings from certain destruction back in the 1970s, and her collaboration with Leonard Horowitz, the talented artist who designed the pastel color palette that became an integral part of the design visible today.

The museum also touches on other key architectural styles in Miami, including Mediterranean Revival – (typefied by the Villa Casa Casuarina (Map p76; ☑ 786-485-2200; www.vmmiamibeach.com; 1116 Ocean Dr; r $700-1400; P ✳ 🎧 ▣) – and the post-deco boom of MiMo (Miami Modern), which emerged after WWII, and is particularly prevalent in North Miami Beach. The guided art deco tour is $30 per person and takes around two hours (10:30am daily, plus 6:30pm Thursday) touching on art deco, MiMo and Mediterranean Revival movements.

South Beach   BEACH
(Map p76; Ocean Dr; ⊙ 5am-midnight) When most people think of Miami Beach, they envision South Beach, a label that applies to both the beach itself and the neighborhood that adjoins it. The latter includes clubs, bars, restaurants and a distinctive veneer

of art-deco architecture. The beach is a sweep of golden sands, dotted with colorful deco-style lifeguard stations and countless souls uploading panorama shots to their social media platforms. The shore gets crowded in high season (December to March) and most weekends.

You can escape the masses by avoiding the densest parts of the beach (5th to 15th Sts) – heading south of 5th street, to the area known as SoFi, is a good means of eluding the crowds. Keep in mind that there's no alcohol (or pets) allowed on the sand.

New World Center
NOTABLE BUILDING

(Map p76; ☑ 305-680-5866, tours 305-428-6776; www.nws.edu/new-world-center; 500 17th St; tours $5; ☺ tours 4pm Tue & Thu, 1pm Fri, 3pm Sat) Designed by Frank Gehry, this performance hall rises majestically out of a manicured lawn just above Lincoln Rd. Not unlike the ethereal power of the music within, the glass-and-steel facade encases characteristically Gehry-esque sail-like shapes that help create the magnificent acoustics and add to the futuristic quality of the concert hall. The grounds form a 2.5-acre public park aptly known as SoundScape Park.

Some performances inside the center are projected outside via a 7000-sq-ft projection wall (the so-called WALLCAST), which might make you feel like you're in the classiest (and free!) open-air theater on the planet. Reserve ahead for a 45-minute guided tour.

Holocaust Memorial
MEMORIAL

(Map p76; www.holocaustmmb.org; cnr Meridian Ave & Dade Blvd; ☺ 9:30am-10pm) Even for a Holocaust piece, this memorial is particularly powerful. With more than 100 sculptures, its centerpiece is the *Sculpture of Love and Anguish*, an enormous, oxidized bronze arm that bears an Auschwitz tattoo number – chosen because it was never issued at the camp. Terrified camp prisoners scale the sides of the arm, trying to pass their loved ones, including children, to safety only to see them later massacred, while below lie figures of all ages in various poses of suffering.

Around the perimeter of the memorial are dozens of panels, which detail the grim history that led to the greatest genocide of the 20th century. This is followed by names of many who perished. The memorial doesn't gloss over the past. The light from a Star of David is blotted by the racist label of *Jude* (the German word for 'Jew') representative of the

yellow star that Jews in ghettos were forced to wear. Two menorah sculptures, flanking the Dome of Contemplation descent to the center, show the transformation from life to death in a rather lurid fashion. It's impossible to spend time here and not be moved.

The memorial was completed in 1990 through the efforts of Miami Beach Holocaust survivors, local business leaders and sculptor Kenneth Treister. Download the excellent free app (Holocaust Memorial Miami Beach) for iPhone or Android to learn more about the sculpture as well as hear testimonials from survivors, peruse slideshows, and view interactive maps and additional audio and video.

The Bass
MUSEUM

(Map p76; ☑ 305-673-7530; www.thebass.org; 2100 Collins Ave; adult/child $15/8; ☺ 10am-5pm Wed-Sun) The best art museum in Miami Beach has a playfully futuristic facade, a crisp interplay of lines and a bright, white-walled space – like an Orthodox church on a space-age Greek isle. All designed, by the way, in 1930 by Russell Pancoast (grandson of John A Collins, who lent his name to Collins Ave). The collection isn't shabby either: there is a focus on cutting-edge contemporary art, although some temporary exhibitions showcase older work. The museum forms one point of the Collins Park Cultural Center triangle, which also includes the three-story Miami City Ballet (p136) and the lovingly inviting Miami Beach Regional Library, which is a great place for free wi-fi.

Jewish Museum of Florida-FIU
MUSEUM

(Map p70; ☑ 305-672-5044; www.jmof.fiu.edu; 301 Washington Ave; adult/student & senior $12/8, Sat free; ☺ 10am-5pm Tue-Sun, closed Mon & Jewish holidays) Housed in a 1936 Orthodox synagogue that served Miami's first congregation, this small museum chronicles the large contribution Jews have made to the state of Florida. After all, it could be said that while Cubans made Miami, Jews made Miami Beach, both physically and culturally. Yet there were times when Jews were barred from the American Riviera they carved out of the sand, and this museum tells that story, along with some amusing anecdotes (like seashell Purim dresses).

There are also walking tours of the area that take in famous local Jewish landmarks and businesses, as well as foodie tours of local Jewish restaurants (three-hour tour including food $48; two-hour tour without food $20).

MIAMI

South Beach (1st to 11th Streets)

See South Beach (11th to 23rd Streets) Map (p76)

500 m
0.25 miles

ART DECO HISTORIC DISTRICT

Wolfsonian-FIU 1

Promenade

Playground

South Beach

11th St

12
4
11
7
23
17

10th St

Ocean Dr

Ocean Ct

3
10

9th St
18

8th St

20
P

Collins Ave

Collins Ct

Washington Ave

7th St

6th St

5th St

4th St

Pennsylvania Ave

Euclid Ave

Meridian Ave

10th St

9th St

8th St

7th St

6th St

Jefferson Ave

Michigan Ave

Miami Beach Dr (5th St)

Euclid Ave

Meridian Ave

Jefferson Ave

Michigan Ave

Lenox Ave

8

Lenox Ave

4th St

Alton Rd

22

10th St

11th St

16

Alton Ct

West Ave

Pier B

Pier A

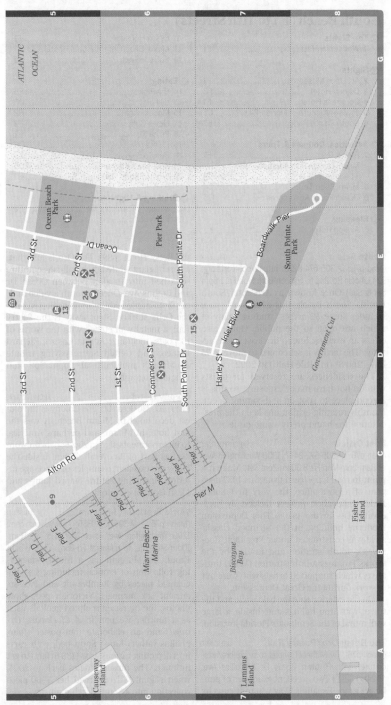

MIAMI

ATLANTIC OCEAN

Ocean Beach Park

3rd St
2nd St
Ocean Dr
Pier Park
South Pointe Dr

Boardwalk Pier
South Pointe Park

3rd St
2nd St
1st St
Commerce St
South Pointe Dr
Harley St
Inlet Blvd

Government Cut

Alton Rd

Pier C
Pier D
Pier E
Pier F
Pier G
Pier H
Pier J
Pier K
Pier L
Pier M

Miami Beach Marina

Biscayne Bay

Fisher Island

Causeway Island

Lummus Island

South Beach (1st to 11th Streets)

Oolite Arts   GALLERY
(Map p76; ☎ 305-674-8278; https://oolitearts.org;
924 Lincoln Rd, 2nd fl; ⊗ noon-6pm Mon-Fri, 1-6pm
Sat & Sun) Once known as ArtCenter/South
Florida South Beach, this exhibition space
includes some 52 artists' studios, many of
which are open to the public. Oolite also
offers an exciting lineup of classes and lectures. The facility is scheduled to move to 75
NW 72nd St (in Little Haiti) in 2022.

The residences are reserved for artists
who do not have major exposure, so this is
a good place to spot up-and-coming talent.
Monthly rotating exhibitions keep the pres-
entation fresh and pretty avant-garde.

Post Office   ARCHITECTURE
(Map p76; ☎ 305-672-2447; 1300 Washington Ave;
⊗ 8am-5pm Mon-Fri, 8:30am-2pm Sat) Make it a
point to mail a postcard from this 1937 deco
gem of a post office, the very first South
Beach renovation project tackled by pres-
ervationists in the 1970s. This Depression
moderne building in the 'stripped classic'
style was constructed under President Roosevelt's administration and funded by the
Works Progress Administration (WPA) initiative, which supported artists who were out
of work during the Great Depression.

On the exterior note the bald eagle and the
turret with iron railings and, inside, a large
wall mural of the Seminole's Florida invasion.

The Betsy Orb/Poetry Rail   PUBLIC ART
(Map p76; www.thebetsyhotel.com/explore/arts-
culture; 14th Pl btwn Ocean Dr & Collins Ave;
⊗ 24hr) FREE Two excellent examples of public art grace Española Way where it runs by
the Betsy Hotel (p89). The Orb is just that:
a sort of giant white beach ball-ish sculpture
squashed into an alley between Ocean Dr
and Collins Ave. Once a month a video and/
or photography exhibition is projected onto
the Orb's surface. Steps away is the Poetry
Rail, a metal wall etched with the words of
13 poets, including Adrian Castro, Richard
Blanco, and Gerald Stern, paying tribute
to Miami's multicultural population and
unique geography.

Colony Hotel   ARCHITECTURE
(Map p70; 736 Ocean Dr) The Colony is the oldest deco hotel in Miami Beach. It was the
first hotel in Miami, and perhaps America,
to incorporate its sign (a zigzaggy neon wonder) as part of its overall design. Inside the
lobby are excellent examples of space-age interiors, including Saturn-shaped lamps and
Flash Gordon elevators.

World Erotic Art Museum   MUSEUM
(Map p76; ☎ 305-532-9336; www.weam.com;
1205 Washington Ave; over 18yr $15; ⊗ 11am-
10pm Mon-Thu, to midnight Fri-Sun) The World
Erotic Art Museum has a frankly staggering collection of erotica, including sexually
charged pieces by Rembrandt and Picasso,
ancient sex manuals, Victorian peep-show
photos, the oversized sculpted genitals used
as a murder weapon in *A Clockwork Orange*, and an elaborate four-poster (four-
phallus rather) Kama Sutra bed, with carvings depicting various ways (138 in fact) to get
intimate. The museum dates back to 2005,
when Naomi Wilzig turned her 5000-piece
collection into a South Beach mainstay.

South Pointe Park
PARK

(Map p70; ☑305-673-7779; 1 Washington Ave; ☺sunrise-10pm; 🅿🏖) The very southern tip of Miami Beach has been converted into a lovely park, replete with manicured grass for lounging and warm, scrubbed-stone walkways, as well as a tiny water park for the kids. There's also a restaurant and refreshment stand for all the folks who want to enjoy the great weather and teal ocean views minus the South Beach strutting.

Promenade
WATERFRONT

(Map p76; Ocean Dr) This beach promenade, a wavy ribbon sandwiched between the beach and Ocean Dr, extends from 5th St to 15th St. A popular location for photo shoots, especially during crowd-free early mornings, it's also a breezy, palm-tree-lined conduit for inline skaters, cyclists, volleyball players (there's a net at 11th St), dog walkers, yahoos, locals and tourists.

The beach that it edges, called Lummus Park, sports six floridly colored lifeguard stands.

1111 Lincoln Rd
ARCHITECTURE

(Map p76; www.1111lincolnroad.com; 🅿) The west side of Lincoln Rd is anchored by a most impressive parking garage: a geometric pastiche of sharp angles, winding corridors and incongruous corners that looks like a lucid fantasy dreamed up by Pythagoras after a long night out.

In fact, the building was designed by Swiss architecture firm Herzog & de Meuron, who describe the structure as 'all muscle without cloth.' Besides parking, 1111 Lincoln Rd is filled with retail shops and residential units.

A1A
BRIDGE

The A1A causeway, coupled with the Rickenbacker Causeway in Key Biscayne, is one of the great bridges in America, linking Miami and Miami Beach via the glittering turquoise of Biscayne Bay.

To drive this road in a convertible or with the windows down, with a setting sun behind you, enormous cruise ships to the side, the palms swaying in the ocean breeze, and a synthwave playlist blasting, is like starring in your own music video.

Miami Beach Community Church
CHURCH

(Map p76; ☑305-538-4511; www.miamibeach communitychurch.com; 1620 Drexel Ave; ☺service 10:30am Sun) In rather sharp and refreshing contrast to all the uber-modern structures muscling their way into the art-deco design of South Beach, this community church puts one in mind of an old Spanish mission – humble, modest and elegantly understated in an area where overstatement is the general philosophy.

Fourteen stained-glass windows line the relatively simple interior, while the exterior is built to resemble coral stone in a Spanish Revival style. The congregation is LGBT-friendly and welcomes outside visitors.

Temple Emanu-El
SYNAGOGUE

(Map p76; www.tesobe.org; Washington Ave at 17th St) An art-deco temple? Not exactly, but the smooth, bubbly dome and sleek, almost aerodynamic profile of this Conservative synagogue, established in 1938, fits right in on SoBe's deco parade of moderne this and streamline that. Shabbat services are on Friday at 7pm and on Saturday at 10am.

Cardozo Hotel
ARCHITECTURE

(Map p76; 1300 Ocean Dr; 🅿) The Cardozo and its neighbor, the **Carlyle** (Map p76; 1250 Ocean Dr), were the first deco hotels saved by the Miami Design Preservation League (p99), and in the case of the Cardozo, we think it saved the best first. Its beautiful lines and curves evoke a classic automobile from the 1930s.

Congress Hotel
ARCHITECTURE

(Map p70; 1052 Ocean Dr) Close to 11th St, the Congress Hotel is an art-deco classic, with a perfectly symmetrical three-story facade. It has window-shading eyebrows and a long marquee down the middle that's reminiscent of the grand movie palaces of the 1930s.

Miami Beach Botanical Garden
GARDENS

(Map p76; ☑305-673-7256; www.mbgarden.org; 2000 Convention Center Dr; suggested donation $2; ☺9am-5pm Tue-Sun) FREE This lush but little-known 2.6 acres of plantings is operated by the Miami Beach Garden Conservancy, and is a veritable green haven in the midst of the urban jungle – an oasis of palm trees, flowering hibiscus trees and glassy ponds. It's a great spot for a picnic. While touring the garden, you can dial 305-423-1525 for a free self-guided tour.

⊙ North Beach

Aside from the beach, many of the sights in North Beach require some effort to access. You'll need a car for a day's exploring here.

Faena Forum
CULTURAL CENTER

(Map p108; ☎305-534-8800; www.faena.com; Collins Ave & 33rd St) This cultural center has been turning heads since its opening in late 2016. The circular Rem Koolhaas–designed building features rooms for performances, exhibitions, lectures and other events. Check the website to see what's coming up.

Oleta River State Park
STATE PARK

(☎305-919-1844; www.floridastateparks.org/oleta river; 3400 NE 163rd St; vehicle/pedestrian & bicycle $6/2; ⊙8am-sunset; P🚲) Tequesta people were boating the Oleta River estuary as early as 500 BCE, so you're following a long tradition if you canoe or kayak in this park. At almost 1000 acres, this is the largest urban park in the state and one of the best places in Miami to escape the madding crowd. Boat out to the local mangrove island, watch the eagles fly by, or just chill on the pretension-free beach.

On-site ROAM Oleta River Outdoor Center (p98) rents out kayaks, canoes, stand-up paddleboards and mountain bikes. It also offers paddling tours, yoga classes on stand-up paddleboards and other activities. The park is off 163rd St NE/FL 826 in Sunny Isles, about 8 miles north of North Miami Beach.

Fontainebleau
HISTORIC BUILDING

(Map p108; www.fontainebleau.com; 4441 Collins Ave) As you proceed north on Collins, the condos and apartment buildings grow in grandeur and embellishment until you enter an area nicknamed Millionaire's Row. The most fantastic jewel in this glittering crown is the Fontainebleau hotel (p109). The hotel – mainly the pool, which has since been renovated – features in Brian de Palma's classic *Scarface*.

This iconic 1954 leviathan is a brainchild of the great Miami Beach architect Morris Lapidus and has undergone many renovations; in some ways, it is utterly different from its original form, but it retains that early glamour.

Boardwalk
BEACH

(Map p108; www.miamibeachboardwalk.com; 21st -46th Sts) Posing is what many people do best in Miami, and there are plenty of skimpily dressed hotties on the Mid-Beach boardwalk, but there are also middle-class Latinos and Orthodox Jews, who walk their dogs and play with their kids here, giving the entire place a laid-back, real-world vibe that contrasts with the nonstop glamour of South Beach.

Haulover Beach Park
PARK

(☎305-947-3525; www.miamidade.gov/parks/haulover.asp; 10800 Collins Ave; per car Mon-Fri $5, Sat & Sun $7; ⊙sunrise-sunset; P🐕) Swimsuits are optional in at least part of this 40-acre beach park hidden behind vegetation from the sight of condos, highways and prying passersby. You don't have to get into your birthday suit if you don't fancy it – in fact, most of the beach is clothed and there's even a **dog park**. It is one of the nicer spots for sand in the area and is located about 4.5 miles north of 71st St on Collins Ave..

◉ Downtown Miami

Downtown Miami, the city's international financial and banking center, is split between tatty indoor shopping arcades, and new condos and high-rise luxury hotels in the area known as Brickell – said high-rises stretch all the way down Brickell Ave. At night, the towers are illuminated in hot pinks and cool blues, and the entire effect is unmistakably magical.

Even though construction is a near constant in this area, there are still pockets of small-scale, creative, authentic spaces, and the city's best museum.

★Pérez Art Museum Miami
MUSEUM

(PAMM; Map p100; ☎305-375-3000; www.pamm. org; 1103 Biscayne Blvd; adult/senior & student $16/12, 1st Thu & 2nd Sat of month free; ⊙10am-6pm Fri-Tue, to 9pm Thu; P) One of Miami's most impressive spaces, designed by Swiss architects Herzog & de Meuron, this museum integrates tropical foliage, glass, concrete and wood – a melding of tropical vitality and fresh modernism that fits perfectly in Miami. PAMM stages some of the best contemporary exhibitions in the city, with established artists and impressive newcomers.

The permanent collection rotates through unique pieces every few months – drawing from a treasure trove of work spanning the past 80 years. Don't miss it. The temporary shows and retrospectives bring major crowds. The outdoor space has hanging gardens that took an entire two months to install.

If you need a little breather amid all this contemporary culture, PAMM has a first-rate cafe, or you can simply hang out in the grassy park or lounge on a deck chair enjoying the views over the water.

This art institution inaugurated Museum Park, a patch of land that oversees the broad blue swath of Biscayne Bay.

🏃 City Walk
Art-Deco Miami Beach

START ART DECO MUSEUM
END 960 OCEAN DR
LENGTH 1.2 MILES; TWO TO THREE HOURS

Start at the ❶ **Art Deco Museum** (p68), at the corner of Ocean Dr and 10th St (named Barbara Capitman Way here, after the Miami Design Preservation League's founder). Step in for an exhibit on art-deco style, then head out and north along Ocean Dr. Between 12th and 14th Sts you'll see three examples of deco hotels: the ❷ **Leslie**, a boxy shape with eyebrows (cantilevered sunshades) wrapped around the side of the building; the ❸ **Carlyle** (p73), featured in the film *The Birdcage* and boasting modernistic styling; and the graceful ❹ **Cardozo Hotel** (p73), built by Henry Hohauser, owned by Gloria Estefan and featuring sleek, rounded edges.

At 14th St take a peek inside the sun-drenched ❺ **Winter Haven Hotel** (Map p76; ☑305-531-5571; www.winterhavenhotelsobe.com; 1400 Ocean Dr; r $140-390; P ❉ 🛜) to see its fabulous terrazzo floors, made of stone chips set in mortar that's polished when dry. Turn left and down 14th St to Washington Ave and the ❻ **US Post Office** (p72), at 13th St. It's a curvy block of white deco in the stripped classical style. Step inside to admire the wall mural, domed ceiling and marble stamp tables. Lunch at the ❼ **11th Street Diner** (p116), a gleaming aluminum Pullman car that was imported in 1992 from Wilkes-Barre, PA. Get a window seat and gaze across the avenue to the corner of 10th St and the stunningly restored ❽ **Hotel Astor**, designed in 1936 by T Hunter Henderson.

After your meal, walk half a block east from the Astor to the imposing ❾ **Wolfsonian-FIU** (p68), an excellent design museum, formerly the Washington Storage Company. Wealthy snowbirds of the '30s stashed their pricey belongings here before heading back up north. Continue walking on Washington Ave, turn left on 8th St and then continue north along Collins Ave to the ❿ **Hotel of South Beach**, featuring an interior and roof deck by Todd Oldham. L Murray Dixon designed the hotel as the Tiffany Hotel, with a deco spire, in 1939. Go two blocks to Ocean Dr, where you'll spy nonstop deco beauties; at ⓫ **960 Ocean Dr** you'll see an exterior designed in 1935 by deco legend Henry Hohauser.

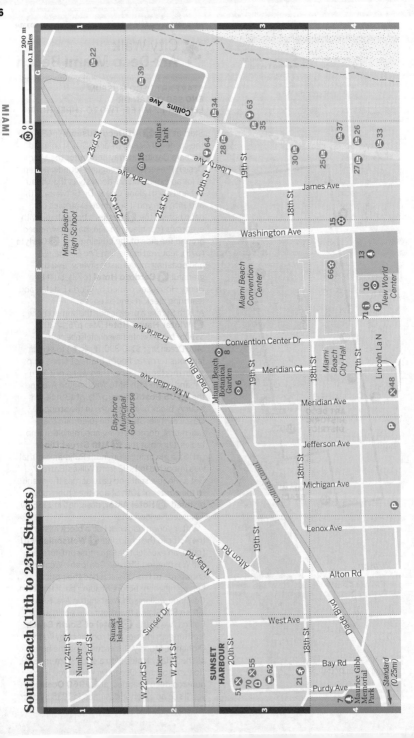

South Beach (11th to 23rd Streets)

South Beach (11th to 23rd Streets)

★ **Bayfront Park** PARK

(Map p100; ☎305-358-7550; www.bayfrontpark miami.com; 301 N Biscayne Blvd) Few American parks can claim to front such a lovely stretch of turquoise as Biscayne Bay, but Miamians are lucky like that. Notable park features are two performance venues: the Klipsch Amphitheater (p136), which boasts excellent views over the bay and is a good spot for live-music shows, and the smaller 200-seat (lawn seating can accommodate 800 more) **Tina Hills Pavilion**, which hosts free spring-time performances.

Look north for the **JFK Torch of Friend-ship**, and a fountain recognizing the accomplishments of longtime US congressman Claude Pepper. There are a huge variety of activities here, including flying trapeze classes and free yoga classes (p98), plus a great play-ground for the kids.

Noted artist and landscape architect Isamu Noguchi redesigned much of Bayfront Park in the 1980s and dotted the grounds with three sculptures. In the southwest corner is the **Challenger Memorial**, a monument designed for the astronauts killed in the 1986 space-shuttle explosion, built to resemble both the twisting helix of a human DNA chain and the shuttle itself. The Light Tower is a 40ft, somewhat abstract allusion to Japanese lanterns and moonlight over Miami. Our favorite is the Slide Mantra, a twisting spiral of marble that doubles as a playground piece for the kids.

HistoryMiami
MUSEUM

(Map p100; ☑305-375-1492; www.historymiami. org; 101 W Flagler St; adult/child 6-12yr $10/5; ☻10am-5pm Tue-Sat, from noon Sun; ⓜ) South Florida – a land of escaped slaves, guerrilla Native Americans, gangsters, land grabbers, pirates, tourists, drug dealers and alligators – has a special history, and it takes a special kind of museum to capture that narrative. This highly recommended place, located in the Miami-Dade Cultural Center, does just that, weaving together the stories of the region's successive waves of population, from Native Americans to Nicaraguans.

The collection is spread between two buildings. Start off in the permanent collection, which has interactive exhibits showing life among the Seminoles, early Florida industries such as sponge diving, and wealth made from 'wreckers' (those who salvaged treasure lost on the reefs). More recent-era exhibits touch on the history of Jewish and African American communities in South Beach, Cuban refugees and cultural expression in public spaces (highlighting traditions such as street art, parades, protests, vehicle customizing and religious practices). Get off the Metromover at the Govern-ment Center stop.

Patricia & Phillip Frost Museum of Science
MUSEUM

(Map p100; ☑305-434-9600; www.frostscience. org; 1101 Biscayne Blvd; adult/child $25/22; ☻9:30am-6pm; Ⓟⓜ) This sprawling new Downtown museum spreads across 250,000 sq ft that includes a three-level aquarium, a 250-seat state-of-the-art planetarium, and two distinct wings that delve into the wonders of science and nature. Exhibitions range from weather phenomena to creepy-crawlies, feathered dinosaurs and vital microbe displays, while Florida's fascinating Everglades and biologically rich coral reefs play starring roles.

Miami Riverwalk
WATERFRONT

(Map p100) This pedestrian walkway follows along the northern edge of the river as it bisects Downtown, and offers some peaceful vantage points of bridges and skyscrapers dotting the urban landscape. You can start the walk at the south end of Bayfront Park, and follow it under bridges and along the waterline till it ends just west of the SW 2nd Ave Bridge. The Riverwalk is one small section of the ambitious Miami River Greenway project, which aims to extend a green path along both banks of the river all the way to the river's intersection with the Dolphin Expwy.

Brickell City Centre
AREA

(Map p100; ☑786-475-5536; www.brickellcity centre.com; 701 S Miami Ave; ☻10am-9:30pm Mon-Sat, noon-7pm Sun) One of Miami's favorite shopping centers, this massive billion-dollar complex spreads across three city blocks, encompassing glittering residential towers, modernist office blocks and a soaring five-star hotel (the EAST, Miami; p110). There's much to entice both Miami residents and visitors to the center, with restaurants, bars, a cinema and loads of high-end retailers (Ted Baker, All Saints, Kendra Scott). You'll find shops scattered across both sides of S Miami Ave between 7th and 8th Sts, including a massive Saks Fifth Ave. There is a three-story Italian food emporium, with restaurants, cafes, a bakery, an enoteca and a culinary school.

MiamiCentral
NOTABLE BUILDING

(Virgin MiamiCentral; Map p100; https://virgin miamicentral.com; NW 1st Ave btwn NW 3rd St & NW 8th St; 🚇Government Center) FREE This train station has been converted into a 9-acre mixed-use complex that houses a food hall, shopping arcades, plus office and residential space. Architecturally, it's like the space age has landed in South Florida, an unmissable jumble of odd angles, enormous windows and twisted steel, designed by Skidmore, Owings & Merrill, the firm responsible for Dubai's Burj Khalifa. The station will be the Miami home of Brightline trains.

KEEPING IT KOSHER IN MIAMI BEACH

They are no shtetls, but Arthur Godfrey Rd (41st St) and Harding Ave between 91st and 96th Sts in Surfside are popular thoroughfares for the Jewish population of Miami Beach. Just as Jewish people have shaped Miami Beach, so has the beach shaped them: you can eat lox y arroz con moros (salmon with rice and beans) and while the Orthodox men don yarmulkes and the women wear headscarves, many have nice tans and drive flashy SUVs.

Freedom Tower
HISTORIC BUILDING

(Map p100; 600 Biscayne Blvd; ⊙10am-5pm) An iconic slice of Miami's old skyline, the richly ornamented Freedom Tower is one of two surviving towers modeled after the Giralda bell tower in Spain's Cathedral of Seville. As the 'Ellis Island of the South,' it served as an immigration processing center for almost half a million Cuban refugees in the 1960s. Placed on the National Register of Historic Places in 1979, it was also home to the *Miami Daily News* for 32 years.

In the beautifully restored lobby, above the elevators and stretching toward the coffered ceiling, you can see reliefs of men at work on the printing presses. The tower also houses the MDC Museum of Art & Design.

Black Archives
Historic Lyric Theater
HISTORIC BUILDING

(Map p100; ☑786-708-4610; www.bahlt.org; 819 NW 2nd Ave; ⊙archives 9:30am-4:30pm Tue-Fri) Duke Ellington and Ella Fitzgerald once walked across the stage of the Lyric, a major stop on the 'Chitlin' Circuit' – the black live-entertainment trail of pre-integration USA. As years passed both the theater and the neighborhood it served, Overtown, fell into disuse. Then the **Black Archives History & Research Foundation of South Florida** took over the building. Today the theater hosts occasional shows, while the Archives hosts exhibitions exploring African American heritage, both in Miami and beyond.

Brickell Avenue
Bridge & Brickell Key
ISLAND

(Map p100) Crossing the Miami River, the lovely Brickell Avenue Bridge, between SE 4th St and SE 5th St, was made wider and higher several years ago, which was convenient for the speedboat-driving drug runners being chased by Drug Enforcement Administration agents on the day of the bridge's grand reopening! Note the 17ft bronze statue by Cuban-born sculptor Manuel Car-bonell of a Tequesta warrior and his family, which sits atop the towering Pillar of History column. Walking here is the best way to get a sense of the sculptures and will allow you to avoid one of the most confusing traffic patterns in Miami. Brickell Key looks more like a floating porcupine, with glass towers for quills, than an island. To live the life of Miami glitterati, come here, pretend you belong, and head into a patrician hangout like the Mandarin Oriental Miami (p110) hotel, where the lobby and intimate lounges afford sweeping views of Biscayne Bay.

MDC Museum of Art & Design
MUSEUM

(Freedom Tower; Map p100; ☑305-237-7700; www.mdcmoad.org; 600 Biscayne Blvd; adult/student $12/5; ⊙1-6pm Wed & Fri-Sun, to 8pm Thu) Miami-Dade College operates a small but well-curated art museum in Downtown; the permanent collection includes works by Matisse, Picasso and Chagall, and focuses on minimalism, pop art and contemporary Latin American art. The museum's home building is art itself: it's set in the soaring 255ft (78m) Freedom Tower, a masterpiece of Mediterranean Revival, built in 1925.

Miami City Cemetery
CEMETERY

(Map p112; 1800 NE 2nd Ave; ⊙7am-3:30pm Mon-Fri, 8am-4:30pm Sat & Sun) This quiet graveyard, the final resting place of some of Miami-Dade's most important citizens, is a sort of narrative of the history of the city cast in bone, dirt and stone. The dichotomy of the past and modernity gets a nice visual representation in the form of looming condos shadowing the last abode of the Magic City's late, great ones. More than 9000 graves are divided into separate white, black and Jewish sections. Buried here are mayors, veterans (including about 90 Confederate soldiers) and the godmother of South Florida, Julia Tuttle, who purchased the first orange groves that attracted settlers to the area.

Miami Center for
Architecture & Design
MUSEUM

(Old US Post Office; Map p100; ☑305-448-7488; www.miamicad.org; 310 SE 1st St; ⊙10am-5pm Mon-Fri) FREE The Miami branch of the American Institute of Architects shares a building with the Downtown Miami Welcome Center. MCAD houses lectures and events related to architecture, design and urban planning, and hosts temporary exhibitions on all of the above subjects. Two-hour walking tours on alternate Saturdays depart from here (at 10am), and take in some of the historic buildings of Downtown. Visit the website for upcoming times and reservations.

Miami River
RIVER

(Map p100) For a taste of old Florida, take a stroll along the Miami River. A shoreline promenade (p79) leads past a mix of glittering high-rise condos and battered warehouses tinged with graffiti, with a few small tugboats pulling along the glassy surface. Fisherfolk float in with their daily catch – en route to places such as Casablanca (p119) – while fancy yachts make their way in and out of the bay.

There are some photogenic vantage points over the river from the bridges – particularly the Brickell Ave bridge at dusk, when the city lights glow against the darkening night sky.

Miami Children's Museum   MUSEUM

(☑305-373-5437; www.miamichildrensmuseum.org; 980 MacArthur Causeway; $22; ⊙10am-6pm; P♿) This museum, located between South Beach and Downtown Miami, is a bit like an uber-playhouse, with areas for kids to practice all sorts of adult activities – banking and food shopping, caring for pets, and acting as a local cop or firefighter. Adults must go accompanied by children, and vice versa.

Other imaginative areas let kids make music, go on undersea adventures, make wall sketches, explore little castles made of colored glass, or simply play on outdoor playgrounds.

Jungle Island   ZOO

(☑305-400-7000; www.jungleisland.com; 1111 Parrot Jungle Trail, off MacArthur Causeway; adult/child $40/25; ⊙10am-5pm; P♿) Jungle Island, packed with tropical birds, alligators, orangutans, chimps, lemurs and a Noah's Ark of other animals, is a ton of fun. It's one of those places kids (justifiably) beg to go, so just give up and prepare for some bright-feathered, bird-poop-scented fun in this artificial, self-contained jungle. Also on offer: rope bridges among the trees ($35), a flight-generating wind tunnel ($60), an escape room ($60) and Adventure Bay, an area with rock-climbing walls and kid-friendly bungee jumping ($60).

Miami-Dade Public Library   LIBRARY

(Map p100; ☑305-375-2665; www.mdpls.org; 101 W Flagler St; ⊙9:30am-6pm Mon-Sat) To learn more about Florida (especially South Florida), take a browse through the extensive Florida Collection, or ask about the Romer Photograph Collection, an archive of some 17,500 photos and prints that chronicles the history of the city from its early years to 1945.

⊙ Wynwood & the Design District

Wynwood is Miami's hippest neighborhood, and it knows it. This is an adult playground of graffiti, murals, restaurants, bars, shops and galleries. Whatever is cool and on trend in the world is emulated, if not started, on these streets, in the shadow of some excellent public art. The Design District is a high-end shopping area, where the line between neighborhood and mall is tough to draw.

★Wynwood Walls   PUBLIC ART

(Map p112; www.thewynwoodwalls.com; NW 2nd Ave btwn 25th & 26th Sts) FREE One of the most photographed locations in Miami (if social media hashtags are anything to go by), Wynwood Walls is a collection of murals and paintings laid out over an open courtyard that invariably bowls people over with its sheer exuberant colors and commanding presence. What's on offer tends to change with the coming and going of major arts events, such as Art Basel (p87), but it's always interesting stuff.

★Margulies Collection at the Warehouse   GALLERY

(Map p112; ☑305-576-1051; www.margulies warehouse.com; 591 NW 27th St; adult/student $10/5; ⊙11am-4pm Tue-Sat mid-Oct–Apr) Encompassing 45,000 sq ft, this vast not-for-profit exhibition space houses one of the best art collections in Wynwood – Martin Margulies' awe-inspiring 4000-piece collection includes sculptures by Isamu Noguchi, George Segal, Richard Serra and Olafur Eliasson, among many others, plus sound installations by Susan Philipsz and jaw-dropping room-sized works by Anselm Kiefer. Thought-provoking, large-format installations are the focus at the Warehouse, and you'll see works by some leading 21st-century artists here.

Bakehouse Art Complex   GALLERY

(BAC; Map p112; ☑305-576-2828; www.bacfl.org; 561 NW 32nd St; ⊙noon-5pm; P) FREE One of the pivotal art destinations in Wynwood, the Bakehouse has been an arts incubator since well before the creation of the Wynwood Walls. Today this former bakery houses galleries and some 60 studios, and the range of works is quite impressive. Check the schedule for upcoming artist talks and other events.

De La Cruz Collection   GALLERY

(Map p112; ☑305-576-6112; www.delacruz collection.org; 23 NE 41st St; ⊙10am-4pm Tue-Sat) FREE Housing one of Miami's finest private collections, this 30,000-sq-ft gallery has a treasure trove of contemporary works scattered across three floors, which you can roam freely. Rosa and Carlos de la Cruz, who originally hail from Cuba, have particularly strong holdings in postwar German paintings, as well as fascinating works by Jim Hodges, Ana Mendieta and Felix González-Torres. You have to ring the bell to gain admittance.

LOCAL KNOWLEDGE

WYNWOOD & THE DESIGN DISTRICT

Hangouts The Wynwood Marketplace embodies the spirit of this diverse 'hood, with food trucks, a bar (front and center), outdoor dining at picnic tables, and a changing lineup of music.

Beer lore Boxelder (p132) is the go-to spot for brew lovers, and showcases local beers in a friendly, unpretentious setting.

Art revelry On the second Saturday of the month, Wynwood and the Design District hold an Art Walk (p103), where galleries host special exhibitions, plus there's live music, a craft market and more.

Wynwood Marketplace   MARKET

(Map p112; 305-461-2700; www.wynwood-marketplace.com; 2250 NW 2nd Ave; ⊘1pm-2am Fri & Sat, noon-9pm Sun) An enormous open-air marketplace takes over several blocks of Wynwood real estate on weekend evenings, and plays hosts to artisan shops, food trucks, a performance stage, live music, art exhibitions, etc. The Marketplace is more or less a weekly carnival, and given Miami's consistently good weather, it's a pleasant one to stroll. While booze is sold, the vibe is family friendly.

Museum of Graffiti   MUSEUM

(Map p112; 786-580-4678; https://museumof graffiti.com; 299 NW 25th St; adult/child $16/free; ⊘11am-7pm Wed-Mon;) The Museum of Graffiti gives visitors a quick dive into the history of this particular art form, which is so obviously and brilliantly in evidence on the urban blocks of surrounding Wynwood. It's a bit small, but passionate: there are kids' art classes on Sundays (11am, free with parent admission), photos from graffiti's earliest days, temporary exhibitions from graffiti masters, and beginners' graffiti workshops ($100, 2pm Saturday). The gift shop alone is a must for anyone who likes graffiti or pop art.

Palm Court   COURTYARD

(Map p112; 140 NE 39th St) At the epicenter of the Design District is this lavish courtyard, which opened just before Art Basel back in 2014. It's set with tall palm trees, reflecting mirrors along the sides, two floors of high-end retailers and one eye-catching sculpture, namely the Fly's Eye Dome.

Fly's Eye Dome   SCULPTURE

(Map p112; 140 NE 39th St, Palm Court) Installed during Art Basel (p87) in 2014, Buckminster Fuller's striking geodesic dome looks otherworldly as it appears to float in a small reflecting pool surrounded by slender, gently swaying palm trees. The 24ft-tall sculpture was dubbed an 'autonomous dwelling machine' by Fuller when he conceived it back in 1965.

There are some fantastic vantage points for photographers both inside and outside the dome – which also serves as the covered entry/exit point connecting the below-ground parking lot with the plaza.

Locust Projects   GALLERY

(Map p112; 305-576-8570; www.locust projects.org; 3852 N Miami Ave; ⊘11am-5pm Tue-Sat) FREE Locust Projects has become a major name for emerging artists in the contemporary art scene. Run by artists as a nonprofit collective since 1998, LP has exhibited work by more than 250 local, national and international artists over the years. The gallery often hosts site-specific installations by artists willing to take a few more risks than those in more commercial venues.

Bacardi Building   ARCHITECTURE

(National YoungArts Foundation Headquarters; Map p112; 800-970-2787; www.youngarts. org/national-headquarters; 2100 Biscayne Blvd; ⊘tours 10am 2nd & 4th Tue of month, gallery 9am-5pm Mon-Fri) FREE The former Miami headquarters of Bacardi is a masterpiece of tropical architecture, and holds a spot on the National Register of Historic Places. The main event is a beautifully decorated jewel-box-like building built in 1973 that seems to hover over the ground from a central pillar supporting the entire structure. The building currently serves as the headquarters of the nonprofit YoungArts, which offers one-hour tours of the complex and also manages an on-site art gallery. Register for tours online.

One-inch-thick pieces of hammered glass cover the exterior in a wild Mesoamerican-style pattern modeled after a mosaic designed by German artist Johannes M Dietz. Also on-site is the older 1963 building, a tower covered with blue-and-white handmade tiles – some 28,000 in fact – in a striking ceramic pattern designed by Brazilian artist Francisco Brennand.

continued on p91

MICHAEL D EDWARDS/SHUTTERSTOCK ©

Art-Deco Miami

South Beach may be known for celebrity spotting, but the area's original cachet owes less to paparazzi and more to preservation. The art-deco design movement, the architectural and aesthetic backbone of SoBe, is powerfully distinctive and finds expression in soft lines, bright pastels and the integration of neon into structural facades.

Contents

Above Ocean Drive, South Beach (p68)

1. Post office (p72) 2. Cardozo Hotel (p73) 3. Lifeguard station 4. Essex House Hotel

SOLARISYS/SHUTTERSTOCK ©

Classical Deco South Beach Structures

In the past, South Beach architects distinguished themselves through decorative finials, parapets and neon signage. Miami Beach art deco relies on 'stepped-back' facades to disrupt the harsh, flat Florida light. Cantilevered 'eyebrows' jut out above windows to protect interiors from the sun.

Cardozo Hotel

This lovely building (p73) features unusual flourishes, including keystone trim, made of dyed porous limestone. Its two hubcap-like emblems on the upper facade and its sleek curves make it reminiscent of a 1937 Studebaker. Owned by Gloria Estefan, the hotel looks more impressive than ever following a four-year, $15 million renovation completed in 2019.

Essex House Hotel

Porthole windows lend this **hotel** (Map p70; ☎877-532-4006; www.clevelander.com; 1001 Collins Ave; r $160-500; ❇🛜🐾) the feel of a grand cruise ship, while its spire looks like a rocket ship, recalling art-deco's roots as an aesthetic complement to modernism and industrialism. Beautiful terrazzo floors also cool the lobby.

South Beach Lifeguard Stations

Besides being cubist-inspired exemplars of the classical art-deco movement, with their sharp, pleasing geometric lines, these stations (p73) are painted in dazzling colors. Found all along the beach from 1st to 17th Sts.

Post Office

This striking building (p72) has a round facade and a lighthouse-like cupola. Above the door is the characteristic art-deco stripe of glass blocks. Step inside for a glimpse of geometrically laid-out post boxes (painted gold) and a fantastical ceiling with an elaborate sunlike deco light fixture orbited by stars.

Deco Elements & Embellishments

As individualized as South Beach's buildings are, they share quirks and construction strategies. Canopy porches provide cool places to sit. To reflect heat, buildings were originally painted white (and later in pastels) with accent colors highlighting smaller elements. Some hotels resemble Mesoamerican temples; others evoke cruise liners.

Room Mate Waldorf Towers

Art deco pioneer L Murray Dixon designed the tower of this hotel at 860 Ocean Dr to resemble a lighthouse, surely meant to shine the way home for drunken Ocean Dr revelers.

Colony Hotel

The oldest deco hotel (p72) in Miami Beach, Colony was the first hotel in Miami, and perhaps America, to incorporate its sign (a zigzaggy neon wonder) as part of its overall design. Inside the lobby are excellent examples of space-age interiors, including Saturn-shaped lamps and Flash Gordon elevators.

Cavalier South Beach

This hotel (p68) makes clever allusions to nautical themes. The word 'cavalier,' a kind of horseman, is a play on 'seahorse,' stylized examples of which are depicted on the facade. The tropical theme continues with figurative palm trees, whose trunks run down both sides of the facade.

Wolfsonian-FIU

The lobby of this museum (p68) contains a phenomenally theatrical example of a 'frozen fountain.' The gold-leaf fountain, formerly gracing a movie-theater lobby, shoots vertically up and flows symmetrically downward.

Crescent Resort

Besides having one of Miami Beach's most recognizable neon facades, the signage of the **Crescent** (Map p76; 1420 Ocean Dr) attracts the eye down into its lobby, rather than up to its roof.

1. Colony Hotel (p72) 2. Cavalier South Beach (p68) 3. Crescent Resort 4. Room Mate Waldorf Towers

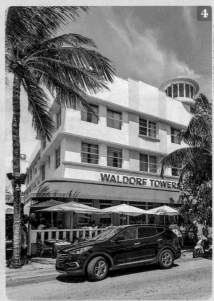

1. Delano (p106) 2. The Carlyle (p73) 3. The Betsy (p105)
4. Royal Palm (p106)

CHRISTIANTHIEL.NET/SHUTTERSTOCK ©

'New' Deco Hotels

Hoteliers such as Ian Schrager combine faith in technology with an air of fantastical glamour. Newer hotels such as the W and Gansevoort South have art-deco roots, but have expanded the architectural sense of scale, integrating deco style into Miami Modern's (enormous) proportions.

Delano

The top tower of Delano (p106) evokes old-school art-deco rocket ship fantasies, but the theater-set-on-acid interior is a flight of modern fancy. The huge backyard pool mixes jazz-era elegance with Miami muscular opulence.

The Carlyle

The 1941 Carlyle hotel (p73) was one of the last deco hotels built in Miami Beach. Here the eyebrow-like window coverings are semi-circular (rather than rectangular), and its name (borrowed from a hotel in NYC) was meant to evoke wealth and exclusivity. It also has cinematic cachet: *The Birdcage* was filmed here, as was the opening scene from *Miami Vice*.

The Betsy

One of the most unconventional landmarks of South Beach, the Betsy (p105) was designed by L Murray Dixon in 1942 and marries two wildly different styles: a deco wing facing Collins Ave, with a Florida-Georgian facade (the only one of its kind) overlooking Ocean Dr.

Royal Palm

This massive, beautifully restored hotel (p106) is an excellent place to feel a sense of seaborne movement. It has a *Titanic*-esque, ocean-liner back lobby. The mezzanine floor has modern dimensions in its enormity, mixed with classic deco styling.

Surfcomber

One of the best deco renovations on the beach, Surfcomber (p105) is offset by sleek, transit-lounge lines in the lobby and a lovely series of rounded eyebrows.

11th Street Diner (p116)

Quirky Deco Delights

Tropical deco is mainly concerned with stimulating the imagination. Painted accents lifted from archaeology sites might make a passer-by think of travel, maybe on a cruise ship. And hey, isn't it funny that the windows resemble portholes? Almost all of the preserved buildings here still inspire this childlike sense of wonder.

Avalon Hotel

The exterior of the **Avalon** (Map p70; ☎305-538-0133, 800-933-3306; www.avalonhotel.com; 700 Ocean Dr; r $185-240; ❄🐾) is a fantastic example of classic art-deco architecture – clean lines and old-school signage lit up by tropical-green deco, all fronted by a vintage 1950s Oldsmobile.

11th Street Diner

It doesn't get much more deco than dining in a classic Pullman train car (p116). Many buildings on Miami Beach evoke planes, trains and automobiles – this diner is actually located in one.

The Bass

One of the oldest art-deco buildings in Miami, The Bass (p69) has a facade made of fossilized Paleolithic coral. Adding to this wondrous element, bas-relief friezes by the sculptor Gustav Boland depict Spanish galleons, mangroves, pelicans and flying boats.

Winter Haven Hotel

Outside the Winter Haven Hotel (p75), you'll note shade-providing 'eyebrows,' and striking geometry, with an elegant zigzag of windows creating a vertical stripe down the center of the facade. Inside, check out the wild light fixtures that evoke futuristic elements (inspired perhaps by Fritz Lang's 1927 sci-fi film *Metropolis*).

continued from p82

◉ Little Haiti & the Upper East Side

These two neighborhoods are at the northern edge of mainland Miami gentrification with restaurants, hotels and galleries increasingly setting up shop every year. Little Haiti is the largest Haitian community in North America, and while it feels as Caribbean as the rest of Miami, it is also undeniably distinct: the Kreyol language dominates, as do Haitian businesses and community institutions. Further east, the Upper East Side is best known for its striking modernist buildings lining Biscayne Blvd.

Little Haiti Cultural Complex   GALLERY
(Map p122; ☑ 305-960-2969; www.littlehaiticultural center.com; 212 NE 59th Tce; ⊙10am-9pm Mon-Fri, 10am-4pm Sat) **FREE** This cultural center hosts an art gallery with often thought-provoking exhibitions from Haitian painters, sculptors and multimedia artists. You can also find dance classes, drama productions and a Caribbean-themed market during special events. The building itself is quite a confection of bold tropical colors, steep A-framed roofs and lacy decorative elements. Don't miss the mural in the palm-filled courtyard.

Miami Ironside   ARTS CENTER
(Map p122; ☑ 305-438-9002; www.miami ironside.com; 7610 NE 4th Ct; 🅿 👪) 🏊 Ironside is a pleasant hub of creativity in Miami in an otherwise industrial corner of the city. Here you'll find art and design studios, showrooms and galleries, as well as a few eating and drinking spaces. It's a lushly landscaped property, with some intriguing public art.

Opening hours vary between the on-site businesses; see the website for more details.

Morningside Park   PARK
(Map p122; 750 NE 55 Tce) On the waterfront, this aptly named park is a great spot to be in the morning, when the golden light is just right for getting a bit of fresh air. There's lots going on in the park, with walking paths, basketball courts, tennis courts, sports fields, a playground for kids and a swimming pool (admission $3). If you come on Saturday, you can rent kayaks (from $12 per hour) and stand-up paddleboards (from $20 per hour).

PanAmerican Art Projects   GALLERY
(PAAP; Map p122; ☑ 305-751-2550; www.pan americanart.com; 274 NE 67th St; ⊙10am-5pm Tue-Fri, from 11am Sat) Despite the name, Pan-American also showcases work from the occasional European artist. But much of what is on display comes from artists representing Latin America, the Caribbean and the USA.

Formerly located in Wynwood, PAAP made the move up to Little Haiti in 2016 – a growing trend as gallerists get priced out of the neighborhood they helped popularize.

◉ Little Havana

The Cuba-ness of Little Havana is slightly exaggerated for visitors, though it's still an atmospheric area to explore, with the crack of dominoes, the scent of wafting cigars and the sound of salsa spilling into the street. Keep an eye out for murals; older art often references the Cuban revolution, while newer pieces contain contemporary references to hip-hop and the Miami Heat.

Little Havana's main thoroughfare, Calle Ocho (SW 8th St), is the heart of the neighborhood. In many ways, this is every immigrant enclave in the USA – full of restaurants, mom-and-pop convenience shops and phone-card kiosks, except here you get intermittent tourists posing and taking selfies.

★ Máximo Gómez Park   PARK
(Map p140; cnr SW 8th St & SW 15th Ave; ⊙9am-6pm) Little Havana's most evocative reminder of Cuba is Máximo Gómez Park ('Domino Park'), where the sound of elderly men trash-talking over games of dominoes is harmonized with the quick clack-clack of slapping tiles – though the tourists taking photos all the while does take away from the experience. The heavy cigar smell and a sunrise-bright mural of the 1994 Summit of the Americas add to the atmosphere.

Cuban Memorial Boulevard Park   MONUMENT
(Map p140; SW 13th Ave btwn 8th & 11th Sts) Stretching along SW 13th Ave just south of Calle Ocho (SW 8th St), Cuban Memorial Boulevard Park contains a series of monuments to Cuban and Cuban American icons. The memorials include the **Eternal Torch in Honor of the 2506th Brigade**, for the exiles who died during the Bay of Pigs Invasion; a **José Martí memorial**; and a **Madonna statue**, supposedly illuminated by a shaft of holy light every afternoon.

There's also a map of Cuba, with a quote by José Martí. At its center is a massive ceiba tree, still revered by followers of Santería (a syncretic religion that evolved in Cuba among African slaves in the 18th century).

LITTLE HAVANA

Cuban style Pick up a new outfit at the Havana Collection (p140). *Guayaberas* are the unofficial dress shirts of the neighborhood and you'll fit right in.

Friday fun On the third Friday of the month, Little Havana lets her hair down in a spirited night of live music and special art exhibitions during Viernes Culturales (p104).

Supermarket dining Hidden in the grocery store of the same name, El Nuevo Siglo (p124) is a well-loved local haunt known for its delicious and reasonably priced cooking.

Bay of Pigs Museum & Library   LIBRARY

(Map p140; ☑ 305-649-4719; http://bayofpigs 2506.com; 1821 SW 9th St; ☺ 9am-4pm Mon-Fri) This small museum is more of a memorial to the 2506th Brigade, otherwise known as the crew of the ill-fated Bay of Pigs invasion. Whatever your thoughts on the late Fidel Castro and Cuban Americans, pay a visit here to flesh out one side of this contentious story. You may meet a few survivors of the Bay of Pigs, who like to hang out here surrounded by pictures of comrades who never made it back to the USA.

At the time of research, the museum's collection was slated to move to a new building way out in Hialeah Gardens, so call before visiting to check where things are at.

⦿ Coconut Grove

Coconut Grove was once a hippie colony, but these days its demographic is upper-middle-class, mall-going Miamians and college students. It's a pleasant place to explore, with intriguing shops and cafes, and a walkable village-like vibe. It's particularly appealing in the evenings, when residents fill the outdoor tables of its bars and restaurants. Coconut Grove backs onto the waterfront, with a pretty marina and some pleasant green spaces.

★ Vizcaya
Museum & Gardens   HISTORIC BUILDING

(☑ 305-250-9133; www.vizcaya.org; 3251 S Miami Ave; adult/child/6-12yr/student & senior $22/10/15; ☺ 9:30am-4:30pm Thu-Mon; ℗) If you want to see something that is 'very Miami,' this is it – lush, big and over the top, a patchwork of all that a rich US businessman might want to show off to his friends. Which is essentially what industrialist James Deering did in 1916, starting a Miami tradition of making a ton of money and building ridiculously grandiose digs. He employed 1000 people (then 10% of the local population) and stuffed his home with Renaissance furniture, tapestries, paintings and decorative arts.

The mansion is a classic of Miami's Mediterranean Revival stye. The largest room in the house is the informal living room, sometimes dubbed 'the Renaissance Hall' for its works dating from the 14th to the 17th centuries. The music room is intriguing for its beautiful wall canvases, which come from Northern Italy, while the banquet hall evokes all the grandeur of imperial dining rooms of Europe, with its regal furnishings.

On the south side of the house stretch a series of lovely gardens that are just as impressive as the interior of Vizcaya. Modeled on formal Italian gardens of the 17th and 18th centuries, these manicured spaces form a counterpoint to the wild mangroves beyond. Sculptures, fountains and vine-draped surfaces give an antiquarian look to the grounds, and an elevated terrace (the Garden Mound) provides a fine vantage point over the greenery. The on-site Vizcaya Cafe has light snacks and coffee to keep energy levels up while perusing the lavish collections.

Kampong   GARDENS

(☑ 305-442-7169; https://ntbg.org/gardens/kampong; 4013 Douglas Rd; adult/child/senior & student $20/5/15; ☺ tours by appointment only 9:30am-3pm Tue-Fri, from 10:15am Sat) David Fairchild, the Indiana Jones of the botanical world and founder of Fairchild Tropical Garden, would rest at the Kampong (Malay/Indonesian for 'village') in between journeys in search of beautiful and profitable plant life. Today this lush garden is listed on the National Register of Historic Places and the lovely grounds serve as a classroom for the National Tropical Botanical Garden. Self-guided tours (allow at least an hour) are available by appointment, as are $25 one-hour guided tours.

Peacock Park   PARK

(Map p126; 2820 McFarlane Rd) Extending down to the edge of the waterfront, Peacock Park serves as the great open backyard of Coconut Grove. Young families stop by the playground and join the action on the ball fields, while power-walkers take in the view on a scenic stroll along the bayfront.

Plymouth Congregational Church CHURCH
(Map p126; ☑305-444-6521; www.plymouth miami.org; 3400 Devon Rd; ⊙ services 10am Sun; P) This 1917 coral church is striking, from its solid masonry to a hand-carved door from a Pyrenees monastery, which looks like it should be kicked in by Antonio Banderas carrying a guitar case full of explosives and Salma Hayek on his arm. Architecturally this is one of the finest Spanish Mission– style churches in a city that does not lack for examples of the genre.

The church opens rarely, though all are welcome at the organ- and choir-led 10am Sunday service.

Ermita de la Caridad MONUMENT
(☑305-854-2404; https://ermita.org; 3609 S Miami Ave; ⊙ 7am-5:30pm, mass noon Mon-Sat, 11am & 3pm Sun) The Catholic diocese purchased some of the bayfront land from Deering's Villa Vizcaya estate and built a shrine here for its displaced Cuban parishioners. Symbolizing a beacon, it faces the homeland, exactly 290 miles due south. There is also a mural that depicts Cuban history. Just outside the church is a grassy stretch of waterfront that makes a fine spot for a picnic.

Barnacle Historic State Park STATE PARK
(Map p126; ☑305-442-6866; www.florida stateparks.org/thebarnacle; 3485 Main Hwy; admission $2, house tours adult/child $3/1; ⊙ 9am-5pm Wed-Mon; ❧) In the center of Coconut Grove village is the residence of pioneer Ralph Munroe, Miami's first honorable snowbird. The house, which was built in 1891, is open for guided tours (every 90 minutes between 10am and 2:30pm), and the 5-acre park it's located in is a shady oasis for strolling. Barnacle hosts frequent (and lovely) moonlight concerts, from jazz to classical.

Eva Munroe's Grave HISTORIC SITE
(Map p126; 2875 McFarlane Rd) Tucked into a small gated area near the Coconut Grove Library, you'll find the humble headstone of one Ms Eva Amelia Hewitt Munroe, Ralph Munroe's first wife. Eva, who was born in New Jersey in 1856 and died in Miami in 1882, lies in the oldest American grave in Miami-Dade County (a sad addendum: local African American settlers died before Eva, but their deaths were never officially recorded).

◉ Coral Gables

The lovely city of Coral Gables, filled with a pastel rainbow of Mediterranean-style buildings, feels a world removed from the rest of Miami. Here you'll find pretty banyan-lined streets and a walkable village-like center, dotted with shops, cafes and restaurants. The big draws are the striking Biltmore Hotel, a lush tropical garden and one of America's loveliest swimming pools.

★Fairchild Tropical Garden GARDENS
(☑305-667-1651; www.fairchildgarden.org; 10901 Old Cutler Rd; adult/child/senior $25/12/18; ⊙ 10am-4pm; P ❧) If you need to escape Miami's madness, consider a green day in one of the country's largest tropical botanical gardens. A butterfly grove, tropical plant conservatory and gentle vistas of marsh and keys habitats, plus frequent art installations from artists like Roy Lichtenstein, are all stunning. In addition to easy-to-follow, self-guided walking tours, a free 45-minute tram tour takes in the entire park, departing hourly on the hour from 10am to 3pm (till 4pm weekends).

A favorite among the garden's youngest visitors is the **Wings of the Tropics** exhibition. Inside an indoor gallery, hundreds of butterflies flutter freely through the air, the sheen of their wings glinting in the light. There are some 40 different species represented, including exotics from Central and South America, like blue morphos and owl butterflies. Visitors can also watch in real time as chrysalises emerge as butterflies at **Vollmer Metamorphosis Lab**.

CORAL GABLES

Theater Gables residents have a small but vibrant theater scene, with performances at GableStage (p138) in the Biltmore.

Markets In front of City Hall (p94), the Coral Gables Farmers Market is the spot to load up on seasonal fruits, fresh breads and other goodies. It happens Saturdays from 8am to 2pm mid-January through March.

Hangouts Threefold (p127) is a neighborhood institution, and a great place to start the day.

The lushly lined pathways of the Tropical Plant Conservatory and the Rare Plant House contain rare philodendrons, orchids, begonias, rare palms, rhododendrons, ferns and moss, while the Richard H Simons Rainforest, though small in size, provides a splendid taste of the tropics, with a little stream and waterfalls amid orchids, plus towering trees with lianas (long woody vines) and epiphytes up in the rainforest canopy. There are a couple of on-site cafes serving simple light fare or you can bring your own picnic and eat on the grounds.

Fairchild Tropical Garden lies about 6 miles south of Coral Gables downtown. It's easiest to get here by car or taxi. Another option is to take Metrorail to South Miami, then transfer to bus 57.

★ **Biltmore Hotel**   HISTORIC BUILDING
(Map p134; ☑855-311-6903; www.biltmore hotel.com; 1200 Anastasia Ave; P) In the most opulent neighborhood of one of the showiest cities in the world, the Biltmore still manages to stand out. This was the greatest of the grand hotels of the American Jazz Age and if it were a fictional character from a novel it would be, without question, Jay Gatsby. Al Capone had a speakeasy on-site and the Capone Suite is said to be haunted by the spirit of Fats Walsh, who was murdered here.

Back in the day, imported gondolas transported celebrity guests like Judy Garland and the Vanderbilts around because, of course, there was a private canal system out there back. It's gone now, but the largest hotel pool in the continental USA, which resembles a sultan's water garden from *One Thousand & One Nights*, is still here.

Lowe Art Museum   MUSEUM
(☑305-284-3535; www.lowe.miami.edu; 1301 Stanford Dr; adult/student/child $12.50/8/free; ☉10am-4pm Tue-Sat, from noon Sun) The Lowe, located on the campus of the University of Miami, has a solid collection of modern art, a lovely permanent collection of Renaissance and baroque paintings, Western sculpture from the 18th to 20th centuries, and archaeological artifacts, art, and crafts from Asia, Africa, the South Pacific and pre-Columbian America.

Coral Gables City Hall   HISTORIC BUILDING
(Map p134; 405 Biltmore Way; ☉8am-5pm Mon-Fri) It's a little funny to think of the often tedious grind of city council business being conducted in this grand building, which opened in 1928 and, architecturally, suggests romance and power, as opposed to parking ordinances. Check out Denman Fink's *Four Seasons* ceiling painting in the tower, as well as his framed, untitled painting of the underwater world on the 2nd-floor landing.

There's a small farmers market on site from 8am to 2pm on Saturdays from mid-January to March.

Granada Entrance   LANDMARK
(Map p134; cnr Alhambra Circle & Granada Blvd) Coral Gables–designer George Merrick planned a series of elaborate entry gates to the city. The Granada Entrance is among the completed gates worth seeing.

Coral Gables Congregational Church   CHURCH
(Map p134; ☑305-448-7421; www.gablesucc.org; 3010 De Soto Blvd; ☉hours vary) Developer George Merrick's father was a New England Congregational minister, so perhaps that accounts for him donating the land for the city's first church. Built in 1924 as a replica of a church in Costa Rica, the yellow-walled, red-roofed exterior is as far removed from New England as...well, Miami. The interior is graced with a beautiful sanctuary and the grounds are landscaped with stately palms.

It isn't open much, though you can stop in for a look during Sunday services at 9am and 11am.

Matheson Hammock Park   PARK
(☑305-665-5475; www.miamidade.gov/parks/matheson-hammock.asp; 9610 Old Cutler Rd; per car weekday/weekend $5/7; ☉sunrise-sunset; P🚻) This 630-acre county park is the city's oldest, and one of its most scenic. It offers good swimming for children in an enclosed tidal pool, lots of hungry raccoons, dense mangrove swamps and (pretty rare) alligator-spotting. It's just south of Coral Gables.

◉ **Key Biscayne**

Key Biscayne and neighboring Virginia Key are a quick and easy getaway from Downtown Miami. Once you pass those scenic causeways you'll feel like you've left Miami for a floating suburb with magnificent beaches, lush nature trails in state parks and aquatic adventures aplenty. The stunning skyline views of Miami alone are worth the trip out.

★ **Bill Baggs Cape Florida State Park** STATE PARK
(Map p114; ☑786-582-2673; www.floridastate
parks.org/capeflorida; 1200 S Crandon Blvd; per
car/person $8/2; ☺8am-sunset, lighthouse 9am-
5pm; P🚹🐾) ⌀ If you don't make it to the
Florida Keys, come to this park for a taste
of their unique island ecosystems. The 494-
acre space is a tangled clot of tropical fauna
and dark mangroves – look for the 'snorkel'
roots that provide air for half-submerged
mangrove trees – all interconnected by
sandy trails and wooden boardwalks, and
surrounded by miles of pale ocean. A concession shack rents out kayaks, bikes, in-line
skates, beach chairs and umbrellas.

At the state recreation area's southernmost tip, the 1845 brick **Cape Florida Lighthouse** is the oldest structure in Florida (it
replaced another lighthouse that was severely damaged in 1836 during the Second Seminole War). Free tours run at 10am and 1pm
Thursday to Monday. If you're not packing a
picnic, there are several good places to dine
in the park, including Boater's Grill (p128)
and **Lighthouse Cafe** (Map p114; ☑305-361-
8487; www.lighthousecafekb.com; mains $12-36;
☺9am-7pm).

**Virginia Key Beach
North Point Park** STATE PARK
(off 3861 Rickenbacker Causeway, Virginia Key;
per car weekday/weekend $6/8; ☺8:15am-5pm
Nov-Mar, 9:15am-6pm Apr-Oct) This lovely
green space has several small but pleasing
beaches, and some short nature trails. Pretty waterfront views aside, there are two big
reasons to come here. The first is to get out
on the water by hiring kayaks or stand-
up paddleboards at Virginia Key Outdoor
Center (p99). The second is to go mountain
biking in a gated-off section known as the
Virginia Key North Point Trails (p99), with
a series of trails ranging from beginner to
advanced.

The mountain bike trails, which are
tucked away at the northern tip of the park,
are free to use, but you'll need your own
bike (and helmet), which you can rent from
the nearby Virginia Key Outdoor Center.
Coming from Miami, this is the first park
entrance (the second leads to the smaller
Historic Virginia Key Beach Park).

Historic Virginia Key Park STATE PARK
(Map p114; www.virginiakeybeachpark.net; 4020
Virginia Beach Dr, Virginia Key; per car weekday/
weekend $5/8, bike & pedestrian free; ☺9am-5pm

Mon-Thu, 7am-5pm Fri-Sun; 🚹) A short drive
(or bike ride) from Downtown Miami, the
Historic Virginia Key Park is a fine place
for a dose of nature, with a small but pretty
beachfront and playgrounds for the kids (as
well as a carousel). From time to time there
are concerts, ecology-minded family picnics
and other events. Coming from Downtown
Miami, this is the second park entrance on
the left (just past the entrance to the Virginia Key Beach North Point Park).

In the dark days of segregation, this
beachfront, initially accessible only by
boat, was an official 'colored only' recreation site (African Americans were not
allowed on other beaches). Opened in
1945, it remained a major destination for
African American communities (as well as
Cubans, Haitians and many others from
Latin America) seeking to enjoy a bit of the
Miami coastline. It was popular until the
early 1960s when the city's beaches were
finally desegregated.

**Marjory Stoneman Douglas
Biscayne Nature Center** MUSEUM
(Map p114; ☑305-361-6767; www.biscayne
naturecenter.org; 6767 Crandon Blvd, Crandon
Park; ☺10am-4pm; P🚹) ⌀FREE Marjory
Stoneman Douglas was a beloved environmental crusader and worthy namesake
of this child-friendly nature center. It's
a great introduction to South Florida's
unique ecosystems, with hands-on exhibits as well as aquariums in the back full
of parrot fish, conch, urchins, tulip snails
and a fearsome-looking green moray eel.
You can also stroll a nature trail through
coastal hammock (hardwood forest) or enjoy the pretty beach in front.

Once a month, the center hosts naturalist-
led walks ($14 per person) through sea-
grass in search of marine life. It's always a
big hit with families. Reserve ahead.

Crandon Park PARK
(Map p114; ☑305-365-2320; www.miamidade.
gov/parks/crandon.asp; 6747 Crandon Blvd; per
car weekday/weekend $5/7; ☺sunrise-sunset;
P🚹🐾) This 1200-acre park boasts **Crandon
Park Beach**, a glorious stretch of sand that
spreads for 2 miles. Much of the park consists
of a dense coastal hammock and mangrove
swamps. The beach here is clean and unclut-
tered by tourists, faces a lovely sweep of teal
goodness, and is regularly named one of the
best beaches in the USA. Pretty cabanas at
the south end of the park can be rented by
the day ($40).

◉ Greater Miami

★ Rubell Museum
GALLERY

(☑ 305-573-6090; www.rubellmuseum.org; 1100 NW 23rd St; ⊙ 10:30am-5:30pm Wed-Sun; ℗) The Rubell family's private art collection made Miami synonymous with the contemporary art scene, and their Wynwood museum helped set the stage for that neighborhood's gentrification. The family museum has relocated to Allapattah, where an enormous campus has been converted into one of the largest private contemporary art institutions in North America. The sleek museum consists of some 100,000 sq ft of soaring exhibition space divided into 40 galleries. Artists on display include Kehinde Wiley, Jeff Koons, Cindy Sherman and Cady Noland.

Zoo Miami
ZOO

(Metrozoo; ☑ 305-251-0400; www.zoomiami.org; 12400 SW 152nd St; adult/child $23/19; ⊙ 10am-5pm; ℗ ⓓ) Miami's tropical weather makes strolling around the Metrozoo almost feel like a day in the wild. Look for Asian and African elephants, rare and regal Bengal tigers prowling an evocative Hindu temple, pygmy hippos, Andean condors, a pack of hyenas, cute koalas, colobus monkeys, black rhinoceroses and a pair of Komodo dragons from Indonesia. For a quick overview (and because the zoo is so big), hop on the Safari Monorail; it departs every 20 minutes.

Deering Estate at Cutler
LANDMARK

(☑ 305-235-1668; www.deeringestate.org; 16701 SW 72nd Ave; adult/child under 14yr $15/7; ⊙ 10am-5pm; ℗ ⓓ) The Deering estate is sort of 'Vizcaya lite,' which makes sense as it was built by Charles, brother of James Deering (of Vizcaya mansion fame; p72). The 150-acre grounds are awash with tropical growth, an animal-fossil pit of bones dating back 50,000 years and the remains of Native Americans who lived here 2000 years ago. There's a free tour of the grounds at 3pm included in admission, and the estate often hosts jazz evenings under the stars.

Arch Creek Park
PARK

(☑ 305-944-6111; www.miamidade.gov/parks/arch-creek.asp; 1855 NE 135th St; ⊙ 9am-5pm Wed-Sun; ℗ ⓓ) This compact and cute park, located near Oleta River, encompasses a cozy habitat of tropical hardwood species that surrounds a pretty, natural limestone bridge. Naturalists can lead you on kid-friendly ecotours of the area, which include a lovely butterfly garden, or visitors can peruse a small but well-stocked museum of Native American and pioneer artifacts. The excellent Miami EcoAdventures (p91) is based here. The park is just off North Biscayne Blvd, 7 miles north of the Design District.

Ancient Spanish Monastery
CHURCH

(☑ 305-945-1461; www.spanishmonastery.com; 16711 W Dixie Hwy; adult/child $10/5; ⊙ 10am-4:30pm Mon-Sat, from 11am Sun; ℗) Finding a fully intact medieval monastery in North Miami Beach is yet another reason why the moniker 'Magic City' seems so fitting. Constructed in 1141 in Segovia, Spain, the Monastery of St Bernard de Clairvaux is a striking early-Gothic and Romanesque building that rather improbably found its way to South Florida. The property – today a church that's part of the Episcopal diocese – gets busy for weddings, so call before making the long trip out here. It's roughly 15 miles north of Downtown Miami.

Pinecrest Gardens
PARK

(☑ 305-669-6990; www.pinecrest-fl.gov/gardens; 11000 SW 57th Ave; adult/child/senior $5/5/3; ⊙ 9am-6pm; ℗ ⓓ) When Parrot Jungle – now Jungle Island (p81) – flew the coop for the big city, the village of Pinecrest purchased the property in order to keep it as a municipal park. It's now a quiet oasis with some of the best tropical gardens this side of the Gulf of Mexico, topped off by a gorgeous centerpiece banyan tree. Outdoor movies and jazz concerts are held here, and all in all this is a total gem that is utterly off the tourism trail.

Monkey Jungle
ZOO

(☑ 305-235-1611; www.monkeyjungle.com; 14805 SW 216th St; adult/child/senior $30/24/28; ⊙ 9:30am-5pm, last entry 4pm; ℗ ⓓ) Step into the cage while monkeys run around, wild and free! Indeed, you'll be walking through screened-in trails, with primates swinging, screeching and chattering all around you. It's incredibly fun, and just a bit odorous. The big show of the day takes place at feeding time, when crab-eating monkeys and Southeast Asian macaques dive into the pool for fruit and other treats.

Museum of Contemporary Art North Miami
MUSEUM

(MOCA; ☑ 305-893-6211; www.mocanomi.org; 770 NE 125th St; adult/student/child under 12yr $10/3/free; ⊙ 11am-5pm Tue-Fri & Sun, 1-9pm Sat; ℗) The Museum of Contemporary Art has long been a reason to hike up to North Miami – its galleries feature excellent rotating exhibitions of contemporary art by local, national and international artists, usually themed along socially engaged lines of interest. There is a 'pay what you wish' gallery policy during Jazz@MOCA from 7pm to 10pm on the last Friday of every month, when live outdoor jazz concerts are held.

Activities

Miami doesn't lack for ways to keep yourself busy. From sailing the teal waters to hiking through tropical undergrowth, yoga in the parks and (why not?) trapeze artistry above the city's head, the Magic City rewards those who want an active holiday.

South Beach

Fritz's Skate, Bike & Surf   SKATING
(Map p76; ☑305-532-1954; www.fritzsmiami beach.com; 1620 Washington Ave; bike & skate rental per hour/day/5 days/7 days $10/24/69/89; ⊙11am-9pm) Rent your wheels from Fritz's, which offers skateboards, longboards, in-line skates, roller skates, scooters and bicycles (cruisers, mountain bikes, kids' bikes). Protective gear is included with skate rentals, and bikes come with locks. Be mindful that there's a deposit for each rental – skates $100, longboards $150 and bicycles $200.

Spa at the Setai   SPA
(Map p76; ☑855-923-7908; www.thesetaihotels. com; 101 20th St, Setai Hotel; treatments $190-750; ⊙9am-9pm) Pamper yourself with a day in this silky Balinese haven, itself located in one of South Beach's most beautiful hotels (p105). Services include Balinese massages, rose petal and Himalayan salt baths, and full-body kneading.

Green Monkey Yoga   YOGA
(Map p76; ☑305-397-8566; www.greenmonkey.net; 1800 Bay Rd; drop-in class/1-week pass $25/89) This yoga studio has a beautiful setting with

huge windows on the top floor of a building in Sunset Harbour. There's a wide range of classes throughout the day, including Vinyasa, power yoga, hip-hop flow and meditation. If you're around for a while ask about the new student special ($69 for one month of unlimited classes).

SoBe Surf   SURFING
(☑321-926-6571; www.sobesurf.com; group/private lessons from $70/120) This outfit offers surf lessons both in Miami Beach and in Cocoa Beach, where there tends to be better waves. Instruction on Miami Beach usually happens around South Point. All bookings are done by phone or email.

Glow Hot Yoga   YOGA
(Map p76; ☑305-534-2727; www.glowhotyoga miami.com; 1560 Lenox Ave; drop-in class/weekly unlimited rate $27/59) This company offers excellent hot yoga classes in a big, inviting studio that's kept sparkling clean. There's also an outdoor patio where you can unwind after an intense Bikram class. Located just south of Lincoln Rd.

North Beach

Russian & Turkish Baths   MASSAGE
(Map p108; ☑305-867-8315; www.russianand turkishbaths.com; 5445 Collins Ave; treatments from $40; ⊙noon-midnight) This is an excellent spot for getting reasonably priced wellness treatments in a local – very local – environment. Go for a *platza*: a treatment where you're beaten by oak-leaf brooms called *venik* in a lava-hot spa (for $40). The Russians swear by it. There's Dead Sea salt and mud exfoliation ($55), plus the on-site cafe serves delicious borscht, blintzes and dark bread with smoked fish. The crowd is interesting too: hipsters, older Jews, model types, Europeans and tons of Russian expats.

CYCLING IN MIAMI

The Miami-Dade County Parks and Recreation Department maintain a list of traffic-free cycling paths as well as downloadable maps on its website (www.miamidade.gov/parksmasterplan/bike-trails-map.asp). For less strenuous rides, try the side roads of South Beach or the shady streets of Coral Gables and Coconut Grove. Some good trails include the Old Cutler Trail, which starts at the traffic circle at Ingraham Terrace Park and continues south for 4 miles on to Pinecrest Gardens, passing Fairchild Tropical Garden and Matheson Hammock Park on the way. The Rickenbacker Causeway takes you up and over the bridge to Key Biscayne for an excellent workout combined with gorgeous water views (from the mainland to Bill Baggs State Park is about 7 miles). A bit further out, the Oleta River State Park has a challenging dirt trail with hills for off-road adventures. Need to rent a trail bike? Try Bike & Roll (p103).

Carillon Miami Wellness Resort SPA
(Map p108; ☑866-800-3858; www.carillonhotel.
com; 6801 Collins Ave, Carillon Hotel; treatments
$179-345; ☺8am-9pm) For pure pampering
the Carillon's 70,000-sq-ft spa and wellness
center is hard to knock. It has an excellent
range of treatments and fitness classes (spinning, power yoga, meditation, core work-
outs) plus pretty views of the crashing waves.

**ROAM Oleta River
Outdoor Center** WATER SPORTS
(☑786-274-7945; https://oletariveroutdoors.
com; 3400 NE 163rd St; kayak/canoe rental per
90min $30/45; ☺9am-6pm Mon-Fri, 8am-7pm Sat
& Sun; ⊛) Located in the Oleta River State
Park, this outfitter rents loads of watersports
gear; two-hour rental options include single/
tandem kayaks ($35/45), canoes ($50), stand-
up paddleboards ($40) and bikes (from $30).

It also organizes group tours: sunset paddles (on Fridays, from $35), once-a-month
full-moon paddles ($50), stand-up paddle-
board classes ($40), and stand-up paddle-
board yoga classes (Sundays at 10:30am, $30).

Normandy Isle Park & Pool SWIMMING
(Map p108; ☑305-673-7750; 7030 Trouville Esplanade; adult/child $10/6; ☺6:30am-8:30pm; ⊛)
For a fun day out, head to this family-friendly
four-lane pool. It's lap swimming only at various times of day (before 9am and after 7pm),
but otherwise it's open to all. There's also an
outdoor splash-play area for the kids, with
cascades to keep things interesting.

**YOGA WITH A SIDE
OF SALT BREEZE**

The beach is definitely not the only place
to salute the sun in Miami. There are
Yoga by the Sea (Map p126; ☑305-
442-6866; www.thebarnacle.org; 3485 Main
Hwy, Coconut Grove; class $15; ☺6:30-
7:45pm Mon & Wed) lessons offered at
the Barnacle Historic State Park (p93)
in Coconut Grove. If you don't feel like
breaking out your wallet, try the free
yoga classes at Bayfront Park (p78),
held outdoors at Tina Hills Pavilion, at
the south end of the park.

Studios offer a large range of classes;
bring your own mat (though some
places rent out mats as well for around
$2 a class).

⬆ Downtown Miami

Yoga at Tina Hills Pavilion YOGA
(Map p100; www.bayfrontparkmiami.com/Yoga
Classes.html; Biscayne Blvd, Bayfront Park; ☺6pm
Mon-Thu, 9am Sat) FREE Tina Hills is a small
open-air pavilion in Bayfront Park (p78)
that frequently hosts free events, including
free 75-minute yoga sessions, suitable for all
levels.

Spa at Mandarin Oriental Miami SPA
(Map p100; ☑305-913-8332; www.mandarin
oriental.com/miami/brickell-key/luxury-spa; 500
Brickell Key Dr, Mandarin Oriental Miami; manicures
$55-95, spa treatments $165-555; ☺9:30am-
8:30pm Mon-Thu, 8:30am-9:30pm Fri-Sun)
Calling this spa over the top is an under-
statement. Treatments utilize materials like
bamboo and rice paper, and services include
Ayurvedic herbal baths, aromatherapy, oiled
massages and lots more self-care.

⬆ Little Haiti &
the Upper East Side

★**Venetian Pool** SWIMMING
(Map p134; ☑305-460-5306; www.coralgables.
com/venetian-pool; 2701 De Soto Blvd; adult/child
Sep-May $15/10, Jun-Aug $20/15; ☺11am-6:30pm
Mon-Fri, 10am-4:30pm Sat & Sun Jun-Aug, closed
Dec-Feb, reduced hours Mar-Apr & Oct-Nov; ⊛)
One of the few pools listed on the National Register of Historic Places, this is a wonderland of rock caves, cascading waterfalls,
a palm-fringed island and Venetian-style
moorings. Back in 1923 rock was quarried
for one of the most beautiful Miami neighborhoods, leaving an ugly gash – cleverly, it
was laden with mosaic and tiles, and filled
up with water.

It looks like a Roman emperor's aquatic
playground, an absolute delight. Take a swim
and follow in the footsteps of stars like Esther
Williams and Johnny 'Tarzan' Weissmuller.

KOTR Konpa Dance Studio DANCING
(Map p122; www.wikotr.com; 5706 NE 2nd Ave) We
can't imagine a more appropriate activity
in Little Haiti than learning *konpa* dancing. *Konpa* (also called *compas*) is a sort
of merengue, and widely considered Haiti's
national genre of music. KOTR offers several
different *konpa* classes that are open to the
public; check the website for times, but classes usually run for an hour in the evening and
cost $10. Some courses are for women only.

LOCAL KNOWLEDGE

MIAMI CRITICAL MASS

If you're in Miami at the beginning of the weekend late in any given month, you may spot hordes of cyclists and, less frequently, some skateboarders, roller-skaters and other self-propelled individuals. So what's it all about?

It's Miami Critical Mass. The event is meant to raise awareness of cycling and indirectly advocate for increased bicycle infrastructure in the city. Anyone is welcome to join; the mass ride gathers at Government Center by HistoryMiami (p79) on the last Friday of each month.

The event is loosely organized, but you can usually find information on it at www.themiamibikescene.com. Generally, the riders gather around 6:30pm, before departing on the 12-to-18-mile trek at 7:15pm. The average speed of the ride is a not-too-taxing 12mph, and you will be expected to keep up (at the same time, you're not to go faster than the pacesetters). All in all it's a fun experience, and a good way to meet members of the local cycling community.

🕊 Key Biscayne

★ **Virginia Key Outdoor Center** OUTDOORS
(VKOC; ☑ 786-224-4777; www.vkoc.net; 3801 Rickenbacker Causeway, Virginia Key; 2hr kayak or 4hr bike rental from $35, 2hr paddleboard $40; ⊗ 9am-6pm Mon-Fri, 8am-7pm Sat & Sun Mar-Aug, reduced hour Sep-Feb) This highly recommended outfitter will get you out on the water in a hurry with kayaks and stand-up paddleboards, which you can put in the water just across from its office. The small mangrove-lined bay (known as Lamar Lake) has manatees, and makes for a great start to the paddle before you venture further out.

One of the highlights is partaking in one of VKOC's guided sunset and full moon paddles, which happen several times a month. You can also rent mountain bikes for the nearby Virginia Key North Point Trails.

**Virginia Key
North Point Trails** MOUNTAIN BIKING
(☑ 786-224-4777; 3801 Rickenbacker Causeway, Virginia Key Beach North Point Park; ⊗ 10am-5pm Mon-Fri, 8am-6pm Sat & Sun) FREE In a wooded section at the north end of the Virginia Key Beach North Point Park, you'll find a series of short mountain-bike trails, color coded for beginner, intermediate and advanced. It's free to use the trails, though you'll have to pay for parking at the Virginia Key Beach North Point Park to get here. If you are not traveling with a bike, rent one from the nearby Virginia Key Outdoor Center.

Crandon Golf Course GOLF
(Map p114; ☑ 305-361-9129; www.golfcrandon.com; 6700 Crandon Blvd; 18 holes $176; ⊗ 6:30am-7:45 pm) On Key Biscayne, this course has great views over the water. Avid golfers consider it to be one of the loveliest and most challenging par-72 courses in Florida.

Miami Kiteboarding WATER SPORTS
(Map p114; ☑ 305-345-9974; www.miamikiteboarding.com; 6747 Crandon Blvd, Crandon Park; private/semiprivate classes from $360/240; ⊗ 10am-6pm Apr-Sep, 9am-5pm Oct-Mar) This outfit offers a range of private lessons on how to kiteboard – basically sail over the water while attached to a parachute. Semiprivate classes never have more than two students per instructor.

🛶 Courses & Tours

☞ South Beach

**Miami Design
Preservation League** WALKING
(MDPL; Map p70; ☑ 305-672-2014; www.mdpl.org; 1001 Ocean Dr; guided tours adult/student $30/25) The Miami Design Preservation League tells the stories and history behind the art-deco buildings in South Beach. The lively regular guided tours last 90 minutes. It also offers tours of Jewish Miami Beach, Gay & Lesbian Miami Beach, and tours of Mediterranean architecture and the MiMo district by request. Check the website for details and for tour days and times.

Miami Food Tours FOOD & DRINK
(Map p70; ☑ 786-361-0991; www.miamifoodtours.com; 429 Lenox Ave; South Beach tour adult/child $58/35, Wynwood tour $75/55, Swooped with Forks $129/109; ⊗ tours South Beach 11am & 4:30pm daily, Wynwood 10:30am Mon-Sat) This highly rated tour explores various facets of the city – culture, history, art and, of course,

MIAMI

Downtown Miami

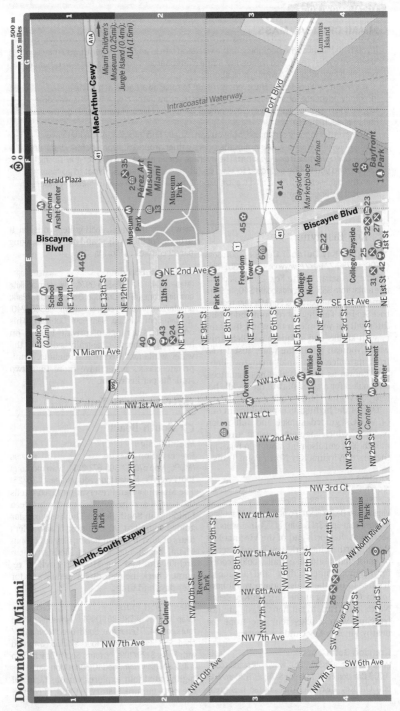

Miami Children's Museum (0.25mi); Jungle Island (0.4mi); A1A (1.6mi)

MacArthur Cswy

Intracoastal Waterway

Port Blvd

Lummus Island

Herald Plaza

Adrienne Arsht Center

Biscayne Blvd

Pérez Art Museum Miami

Museum Park

Museum Park

Bayside Marketplace

Marina

Bayfront Park

Biscayne Blvd

College/Bayside

School Board

NE 14th St

NE 13th St

NE 12th St

Freedom Tower

College North

NE 2nd Ave

11th St

Park West

SE 1st Ave

NE 1st St

Esotico (0.1mi)

N Miami Ave

NE 10th St

NE 9th St

NE 8th St

NE 7th St

NE 6th St

NE 5th St

NE 4th St

NE 3rd St

NE 2nd St

NE 1st St

Overtown

Wilkie D Ferguson Jr

Government Center

NW 1st Ave

NW 1st Ct

NW 1st Ave

NW 2nd Ave

NW 3rd St

NW 2nd St

Government Center

NW 3rd Ct

NW 12th St

Gibson Park

North-South Expwy

NW 9th St

NW 8th St

NW 5th Ave

NW 6th St

NW 5th St

NW 4th Ave

NW 4th St

Lummus Park

NW North River Dr

NW 10th St

Reeves Park

NW 9th Ave

NW 8th St

NW 7th St

NW 6th St

NW 6th St

NW 7th St

NW 3rd St

SW S River Dr

NW 2nd St

Culmer

NW 7th Ave

NW 10th Ave

NW 7th Ave

SW 7th St

SW 6th Ave

500 m

0.25 miles

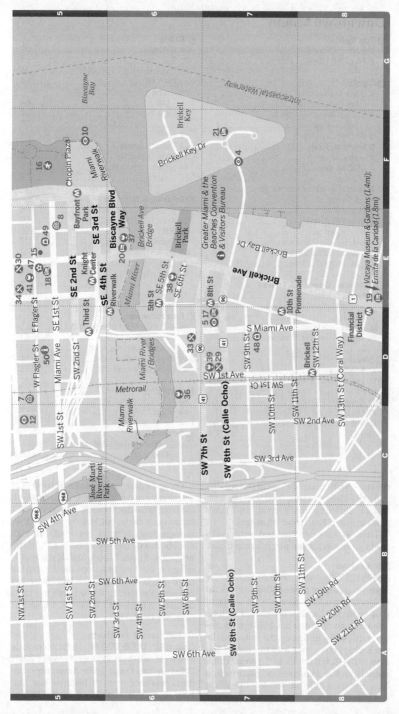

Biscayne Bay

Intracoastal Waterway

Brickell Key

Brickell Key Dr

21

4

Chopin Plaza

Miami Riverwalk

10

16

Bayfront Park

8

Miami Center

Knight

SE 2nd St

SE 3rd St

SE 4th St

Biscayne Blvd Way

20

37

Brickell Ave Bridge

Brickell Park

Greater Miami & the Beaches Convention & Visitors Bureau

Brickell Bay Dr

30

47

15

18

49

34

41

E Flagler St

SE 1st St

Third St

Miami River

5th St

SE 5th St

38

SE 6th St

Brickell Ave

5 17

8th St

96

10th St Promenade

Vizcaya Museum & Gardens (1.4mi); Ermita de la Caridad (1.8mi)

19

1

Financial District

W Flagler St

50

7

12

Miami Ave

SW 2nd St

SW 1st St

Metrorail

Miami River / Bridges

33

96

39

29

41

36

41

SW 1st Ave

S Miami Ave

SW 9th Ave

48

Brickell

SW 12th St

SW 13th St (Coral Way)

SW 1st Ct

SW 1st St

SW 10th St

SW 11th St

SW 2nd Ave

José Martí Riverfront Park

Miami Riverwalk

968

SW 4th Ave

SW 5th Ave

SW 6th Ave

SW 7th St

SW 8th St (Calle Ocho)

SW 3rd Ave

NW 1st St

SW 1st St

SW 2nd St

SW 3rd St

SW 4th St

SW 5th St

SW 6th St

SW 6th Ave

SW 8th St (Calle Ocho)

SW 9th St

SW 10th St

SW 11th St

SW 19th Rd

SW 20th Rd

SW 21st Rd

Downtown Miami

cuisine – while making stops at restaurants and cafes along the way. It's a walking tour, though distances aren't great, and takes place in South Beach and Wynwood.

There is also the Swooped with Forks food tour that takes you places in a golf cart.

Rumbachiva BUS
(☎ 305-925-7571; www.rumbachiva.com; single/group pass per person $50/35; ⊙ Fri & Sat 8:30am-11:30pm) How do you want to spend your nights in Miami? If the answer is, 'Ride around in an open-top bus blasting reggaeton music while hitting up the clubs,' maybe you should book a tour with this outfit? You have to BYOB, but there's a DJ, you get drink specials and/or free cover at participating bars, and for a little bit, you feel like you're in a Pitbull video.

Group rates are available for a crowd of 15 or more. You work out pickup locations with the company after booking. The bus doesn't follow a set route, but instead sort of slowly meanders (15 miles per hour) through neighborhoods like Wynwood, South Beach, Brickell and Coral Gables. Mainly you're partying on the bus; bar stops are for buying more drinks or going to the bathroom. You can book the bus Sunday through to Thursday, but you have to book the whole bus ($525 for two hours).

Ocean Force Adventures BOATING
(Map p70; ☎ 305-372-3388; https://oceanforce adventures.com; tours $150; ⊙ 2hr tours 9:30am, 11:45am & 3pm) Ocean Force Adventures conducts two-hour tours of Biscayne Bay that take in seaside mosaics, celebrity homes,

inter-coastal islands, and Stiltsville, the remains of a village built on the water once inhabited by smugglers, gamblers and those who just couldn't fit in on dry land.

Island Queen, also offers infrequent trips to Stiltsville (approximately once a month), on three-hour tours narrated by Dr Paul George. Check www.historymiami.org/citytour for the latest schedule.

Bike & Roll CYCLING

(Map p70; ☑ 305-604-0001; www.bikemiami.com; 210 10th St; rental per 2/4hr from $15/20, per day from $25, tours $49; ☉ 9am-7pm) This well-run outfit offers a good selection of bikes, including single-speed cruisers, geared hybrids and speedy road bikes; all rentals include helmets, lights, locks and maps. Staff move things along quickly, so you won't have to waste time waiting to get out and riding. Bike tours are also available (daily at 10am).

☞ Downtown Miami

History Miami Tours TOURS

(☑ 305-375-1492; www.historymiami.org/citytour; tours $30-60) Historian extraordinaire Dr Paul George leads fascinating walking tours, including culturally rich strolls through Little Haiti, Little Havana, Downtown and Coral Gables at twilight, plus the occasional boat trip to Stiltsville and Key Biscayne. Tours happen once a week or so. Get the full menu and sign up online.

Urban Tour Host WALKING

(Map p100; ☑ 305-416-6868; www.miamicultural tours.com; 25 SE 2nd Ave, Suite 1048; tours from $20) Urban Tour Host runs a program of custom tours that provide face-to-face interaction in all of Miami's neighborhoods. For something different, sign up for a Miami cultural community tour that includes Little Haiti and Little Havana, with opportunities to visit Overtown, Liberty City and Allapattah. Other tours take in South Beach, Downtown and Coral Gables; Wynwood and the Design District; and the Everglades, among other places.

Island Queen BOATING

(Map p100; ☑ 844-292-2610; www.islandqueen cruises.com; 401 Biscayne Blvd; adult/child from $28/20; ☉ 11am-6pm, boats leave hourly) This outfit, based out of the Bayside Marketplace, runs 90-minute boat tours that take in Millionaire's Row, the Miami River and Fisher Island.

MIAMI ECOADVENTURES

The Dade County parks system leads a variety of **Miami EcoAdventures** (☑ 305-666-5885; www.miamidade.gov/ ecoadventures; bike tours $5, kayaking & canoeing $30-45) tours, including excellent bike tours on Key Biscayne and out in the Everglades. You can also go on one of six different canoe trips, out on the Oleta River, on the Matheson Mangrove trek or paddling to Indian Key down in the Keys. There's also kayaking, snorkeling trips, walking tours and birdwatching. Trips depart from different locations; call or go online for details.

☞ Wynwood & the Design District

Art Classes in Wynwood ARTS & CRAFTS

(Map p112; https://artclasseswynwood.com; 151 NW 36 St; 2/3hr classes $35/45) If you're going to explore the ostensibly artsiest neighborhood in Florida, you might as well take an art class while you're here, right? Check the website or call for a full schedule; classes run for two or three hours, and cover topics such as clay sculpture, painting and drawing.

Wynwood Art Walk WALKING

(☑ 305-814-9290; www.wynwoodartwalk.com; tours from $29) Not to be confused with the monthly art celebration of the same name, this Wynwood Art Walk is actually a 90-minute guided tour taking you to some of the best gallery shows of the day, plus a look at some of the top street art around the 'hood. It also offers other tours like a golf cart trip around the area's best graffiti ($39).

☞ Coral Gables

Coral Gables Tours OUTDOORS

(Map p134; ☑ 305-603-8067; www.coralgables museum.org/tours; 285 Aragon Ave; tours $10) The Coral Gables Museum runs various tours throughout the month, including downtown walking tours (Saturdays at 11am, $10), exhibition tours at the museum (Sundays at 1pm, free with admission) and bike tours (third Sunday of the month at 10am, $10).

Best of all are the two-hour paddling tours on the Coral Gables Waterway (last Sunday of the month at 9:30am, $40)

Call ahead to reserve a spot on a tour.

MIAMI'S TOP EVENTS

➡ Art Basel Miami Beach (p26), December

➡ Art Deco Weekend (www.artdecoweekend.com), January

➡ Coconut Grove Arts Festival (www.coconutgroveartsfest.com), February

➡ Carnaval Miami (p25), March

➡ Ultra Music Festival (www.ultramusicfestival.com), March

✦✦ Festivals & Events

Viernes Culturales   CULTURAL
(Cultural Fridays; www.viernesculturales.org; ⊙7-11pm 3rd Fri of month) No wine-sipping art walk this; Cultural Fridays in Little Havana are like little carnival seasons, with music, old men in *guayaberas* (Cuban dress shirts) crooning to the stars, and Little Havana galleries throwing open their doors for special exhibitions.

The Little Havana Arts District has an energetic strip of galleries and studios (concentrated on 8th St between SW 15th and SW 17th Aves), and there's no better time to visit it all than on the third Friday of each month for Viernes Culturales.

Wynwood Art Walk Block Party   ART
(☎305-461-2700; www.wynwoodartwalkblockparty.com; ⊙1pm-midnight 2nd Sat of month) The Wynwood Art Walk Block Party has become an incredibly popular (free) nightlife option where a big party of people wander around murals and galleries with food trucks, ever-flowing drinks (not always free), live music and special markets. The party is centered on the Wynwood Marketplace (p82), which is a good spot to get things started.

Sounds of Little Haiti   CULTURAL
(https://littlehaiticulturalcenter.com/sounds-of-little-haiti; 212 NE 59 Terrace, Little Haiti Cultural Center; ⊙6-10pm 3rd Fri of month; ☷) FREE This family-friendly fest, held on the third Friday of every month, is an easy introduction to Haitian culture. The celebration is rife with music, Caribbean food and kids' activities.

🛏 Sleeping

Miami has some of the finest hotels in the world, bar none, boasting lodging options that balance cutting-edge design with amenity breakthroughs. Indeed, both Miami Beach's initial heyday in the 1920s, and its revitalization in the 1980s, was fueled by a blossoming of art-deco hotel architecture.

You are spoiled for choice, from boutique beauties in South Beach to Downtown high-rises with sweeping views and endless amenities to historic charmers in Coral Gables to mid-century modern – MiMo – 'motels' along Biscayne Blvd.

🛏 South Beach

Note that rates in South Beach can swing wildly week by week depending on events, festivals and concerts.

SoBe Hostel   HOSTEL $
(Map p70; ☎305-534-6669; www.sobe-hostel.com; 235 Washington Ave; dm $15-22, r $100; ❄@☎) On a quiet end of SoFi (the area south of 5th St, South Beach), this massive multilingual hostel has a happening common area and spartan rooms. The staff are friendly and the on-site bar (open 24/7) is a good spot to meet other travelers. Free breakfasts are included in the rates. There are loads of activities on offer – from volleyball games to mojito-making nights, screenings of big games and bar crawls.

Aqua Hotel   BOUTIQUE HOTEL $
(Map p76; ☎305-538-4361; www.dot-hotels.com/aqua-hotel-miami-beach; 1530 Collins Ave; r $100-200; P❄☎) On the outside this hotel stays true to name and embraces marine-like hues, while the rooms within have a crisp white paint job, with wood floors and a few touches of artwork. Although there's no pool, you can escape the noise of Collins Ave in the small backyard. Rates include breakfast.

Standard   BOUTIQUE HOTEL $$
(☎305-673-1717; www.standardhotels.com/miami; 40 Island Ave; r $160-285; P❄☎≋❄) Look for the upside-down 'Standard' sign on the old Lido building on Belle Island (between South Beach and Downtown Miami) and you'll find the Standard – which is anything but. This boutique hotel blends a bevy of spa services, hipster funk and South Beach sexiness, and the result is a '50s motel gone glam.

There are raised white beds, spa rain showers and gossamer curtains that open onto a courtyard of earthly delights, including a heated *hammam* (Turkish bath).

Miami Beach
International Hostel   HOSTEL $$
(Map p70; ☎305-534-0268; www.hostelmiamibeach.com; 1051 Collins Ave; dm $22-34, r $130-150; ❄@☎) An extensive makeover has turned this reliable old hostel into something like a boutique club with dorm rooms. Bright plas-

ter, marble accents, deco-and-neon decor and hip, clean rooms all make for a good base in South Beach. Wallflowers need not apply: there's a party-friendly social vibe throughout.

Greystone Miami Beach HOTEL $$

(Map p76; ☎ 305-847-4000, reservations 833-895-1918; www.greystonemiamibeach.com; 1920 Collins Ave; r $140-280; ❄ 🛜 ⛱) With rounded walls, half-circle 'eyebrows' providing shade, and porthole windows, the Greystone is a deco gem. It's also a 21 and over hotel with bright white rooms offset by little Aegean swatches of blue. Cocktail bar and restaurants are onsite, and if you want some sand, the beach is just mere steps away.

Catalina Hotel BOUTIQUE HOTEL $$

(Map p76; ☎ 305-674-1160; www.catalinahotel.com; 1732 Collins Ave; r $128-248; P ❄ 🛜 ⛱) The Catalina is a lovely example of midrange deco style. Most appealing, besides the playfully minimalist rooms, is the vibe – the Catalina doesn't take itself too seriously, and staff and guests all seem to be having fun as a result. The back pool, concealed behind the main building's crisp white facade, is particularly attractive and fringed by a whispery grove of bamboo trees. It was renovated to incorporate the Dorset, next door, which means that it now has two pools, a roof terrace and a reasonable Mexican restaurant.

★ 1 Hotel HOTEL $$$

(Map p76; ☎ hotel 305-604-1000, reservations 833-625-3111; www.1hotels.com/south-beach; 2341 Collins Ave; r $430-1155, ste $909-2829; ❄ 🛜 ⛱) 🏄 One of the top hotels in the USA, the 1 Hotel has 400-plus gorgeous rooms that embrace both luxurious and ecofriendly features – including tree-trunk coffee tables/desks, custom hemp-blend mattresses and salvaged driftwood feature walls, plus in-room water filtration (no need for plastic bottles). The common areas are impressive, with four pools, including an adults-only rooftop infinity pool.

The list of amenities is long, with a lavish spa, a 14,000-sq-ft gym (with many classes), water-sports activities, a kids' club and, of course, direct access to the fine sands of South Beach. The Seedlings program provides daily 'adventures' and low-key excursions for kids.

★ Betsy Hotel BOUTIQUE HOTEL $$$

(Map p76; ☎ hotel 305-531-6100, reservations 844-539-2840; www.thebetsyhotel.com; 1440 Ocean Dr; r $340-670, ste $1300-1800; P ❄ 🛜 ⛱ 🐕) One of South Beach's finest hotels, the Betsy is a historic gem with two wings

and rooms set in either a tropical Colonial style or an art-deco aesthetic. The owners are committed to the local literary scene; the Betsy frequently hosts writers and public readings, and has heavily curated photography exhibitions on-site. Thoughtful touches include orchids in the rooms, a 24-hour fitness center, two swimming pools and rather curious bathroom mirrors with inbuilt LCD TVs. The property is pet friendly, to the point that you can get a couples massage with your dog.

★ Washington Park Hotel BOUTIQUE HOTEL $$$

(Map p76; ☎ 305-421-6265; www.wphsouthbeach.com; 1050 Washington Ave; r $200-500; ❄ 🛜 ⛱) In a great location two blocks from the beach, the Washington Park is spread among five beautifully restored art-deco buildings fronted by a pool and a palm-fringed courtyard. The rooms are all class, with muted color schemes, distressed laminate wood flooring and elegant design touches like bedside globe lamps and wood and cast-iron work desks. The vibe is welcoming and fun, with bocce in the courtyard, complimentary yoga classes, and stylish green Martone bikes for zipping about town.

★ Surfcomber HOTEL $$$

(Map p76; ☎ 305-532-7715; www.surfcomber.com; 1717 Collins Ave; r $200-480; P ❄ 🛜 ⛱ 🐕) The Surfcomber has a classic art-deco exterior with strong lines and shade-providing 'eyebrows' that zigzag across the facade. But the interior is the really impressive part – rooms have undeniable appeal, with elegant lines in-keeping with the art-deco aesthetic, while bursts of color keep things contemporary.

The lobby and adjoining restaurant are awash with bold colors, decorative wood elements, playful tropical themes and skylights, while a terrace overlooking Collins Ave connects indoor and outdoor spaces. Head around the back for a dazzling view: a massive sun-drenched pool, fringed by palm trees and backed by lovely oceanfront, with the beach just steps away.

★ Setai BOUTIQUE HOTEL $$$

(Map p76; ☎ 305-600-3099; www.thesetaihotel.com; 2001 Collins Ave; ste $725-2650; P ❄ 🛜 ⛱) Inside a deco building, the Setai has a stunning interior that mixes elements of Southeast Asian temple architecture and contemporary luxury. The spacious rooms are decked out in chocolate teak wood, with clean lines and Chinese and Khmer embellishments. The amenities are exquisite, with a heavenly spa, three palm-fringed swimming pools, a top restaurant and a great beach location.

Gale South Beach
HOTEL **$$$**

(Map p76; ☑ 305-673-0199; www.galehotel.com; 1690 Collins Ave; r $185-410; P✳🛜🏊) The Gale's exterior is an admirable re-creation of classic boxy deco aesthetic expanded to the grand dimensions of a modern SoBe super-resort. This blend of classic and haute South Beach carries on indoors, where you'll find bright rooms with a handsome color scheme, sharp lines and a retro chic vibe inspired by the mid-century modern movement. The elegant rooftop pool is rather narrow but gets sun all day, plus a crowd of pretty people.

Royal Palm
HOTEL **$$$**

(Map p76; ☑ 305-604-5700; www.royalpalm southbeach.com; 1545 Collins Ave; r from $120, ste $529-1310; P✳🛜🏊) Even the tropical fish tank with its elegant curves and chrome accents has a touch of deco flair, to say nothing of the streamlined bar with mint-green accents – all of which adds up to South Beach's most striking example of building-as-cruise-liner deco theme. The shipboard style carries into the plush rooms, which are also offset by bright whites and minty subtle marine-like hues.

As with other big properties anchored between the beach and Collins Ave, the Royal Palm has extensive amenities, including two pools and good drinking and dining spaces, including Byblos, a recommended Greek restaurant.

Stiles Hotel
BOUTIQUE HOTEL **$$$**

(Map p76; ☑ 305-674-7800; www.thestileshotel. com; 1120 Collins Ave; r $209-409; P✳🛜🏊) Bring the beach to your room at the Stiles; guest chambers balance pale sandy hues and crisp, sunny whites with natural fiber carpeting, modular bedside lamps and blackout curtains. The courtyard, with three small spa pools, is a fine spot to unwind.

Shore Club
BOUTIQUE HOTEL **$$$**

(Map p76; ☑ 305-695-3100; www.shoreclub.com; 1901 Collins Ave; r $250-1000; P✳@🏊) In a highly coveted location in South Beach (backing onto lovely beachfront), the Shore Club has airy but rather simply furnished rooms with a few color splashes amid the otherwise white design scheme. There are some appealing areas for amusement, including the **Skybar** (h4pm-2am Mon-Wed, to

3am Thu-Sat), which is a fine garden-like spot for a drink (though located rather surprisingly at ground level).

Redbury South Beach
BOUTIQUE HOTEL **$$$**

(Map p76; ☑ 305-604-1776; www.theredbury.com/ southbeach; 1776 Collins Ave; r $180-370; ✳🛜🏊) What sets the Redbury apart is its refusal to toe the line of identikit South Beach minimalist rooms. Rather, the interior here references art across the 20th century, with fun but easygoing comfort in mind (striped carpets, Italian linens, and in-room record players – and albums! – available upon request). A rooftop pool makes for some chilled-out lounging, while the lobby channels East Asian exoticism, plus there's a giant ornamental cage just outside the entrance.

W Hotel
RESORT **$$$**

(Map p76; ☑ 305-938-3000; www.wsouthbeach. com; 2201 Collins Ave; r $440-720, ste $1160-2800; P✳🛜🏊) There's an astounding variety of rooms available at the South Beach outpost of the W chain, which touts the whole W-brand mix of luxury and style in a big way. The 'spectacular studios' balance long panels of reflective glass with cool tablets of Cipollino marble, while the Oasis suite lets in so much light you'd think the sun had risen in your room. The attendant bars, restaurants, clubs and pool built into this complex are some of the best-regarded on the beach.

Sagamore
BOUTIQUE HOTEL **$$$**

(Map p76; ☑ 305-535-8088; www.sagamore hotel.com; 1671 Collins Ave; r $220-455, ste $770-830; P✳🛜🏊) This hotel-cum-exhibition-hall likes to blur the boundaries between interior decor, art and conventional hotel aesthetics. Almost every space here, from the lobbies to the rooms, doubles as an art gallery thanks to a talented curator and an impressive roster of contributing artists. Rooms? Soft whites and rich tones, accented by artsy photography and sleek designer touches.

Delano
BOUTIQUE HOTEL **$$$**

(Map p76; ☑ 305-672-2000; www.delano-hotel. com; 1685 Collins Ave; r $314-389; P✳🛜🏊) The Delano opened in the 1990s and immediately started ruling the South Beach roost. If there's a quintessential 'I'm-too-sexy-for-this...' South Beach moment, it's when you walk into the Delano's lobby, which has all the excess of an overbudgeted theater set. Rooms are almost painfully white and bright: all long, smooth lines, reflective surfaces and modern, luxurious amenities. The pool area resembles the courtyard of a Disney princess's palace.

MIAMI SLEEPING

Mondrian South Beach RESORT $$$
(Map p76; ☎ 305-514-1500; www.mondrian-miami.com; 1100 West Ave; r $235-505; P ❋ 🛜 ☲) Morgan Hotel Group hired Dutch designer Marcel Wanders to crank it up to 11 at the Mondrian. The theme's inspired by Sleeping Beauty's castle – columns carved like giant table legs, a 'floating' staircase and spectacular bay views from the floor-to-ceiling windows. Upstairs the design whimsy continues with plush rooms sporting Delft tiles with beach scenes instead of windmills, and chandelier-like rainfall showers.

🛏 North Beach

★**Freehand Miami** BOUTIQUE HOTEL $$
(Map p108; ☎ 305-531-2727; www.thefreehand.com; 2727 Indian Creek Dr; dm $28-55, r $120-340; ❋ 🛜 ☲) The Freehand is the brilliant reimagining of the old Indian Creek Hotel, a classic of the Miami Beach scene. Rooms are sunny and attractively designed, with local artwork and wooden details. The vintage-filled common areas are the reason to stay here though – especially the lovely pool area and backyard that transforms into one of the best bars in town. Dorms serve the hostel crowd, while private rooms are airy and decorated with pop art. There are also bungalows for self-catering groups.

Palihouse Miami Beach BOUTIQUE HOTEL $$
(Map p108; ☎ 305-763-8006; www.palisociety.com/hotels/miami-beach; 3101 Indian Creek Dr; r $185-215, ste $255-295; 🛜 ☲ ❋) From the sunset-toned rooms with bohemian vintage decor accented by Mediterranean tiles, to an airy, deco-inspired lobby, the Palihouse evokes Miami Beach's early-20th-century heyday, while providing guests with a 21st-century hotel experience. The property gets bonus points for maximum utilization of natural light, and for allowing four-legged friends (up to 30 pounds, and charges a $150 registration fee).

Croydon Hotel BOUTIQUE HOTEL $$
(Map p108; ☎ 305-938-1145; www.hotelcroydonmiamibeach.com; 3720 Collins Ave; r $128-435; ❋ 🛜 ☲) The Croydon earns high marks for its bright, classically appointed rooms with dark-wood floors, luxurious beds and modern bathrooms with CO Bigelow products. Head to the ground-floor restaurant with its elaborately patterned ceramic floors for good meals. Fringed by palms, the terrace around the pool has a crisp modern design.

There's also beach service – though the hotel is a block away from the sands.

HOTEL POOLS

Miami has some of the most beautiful hotel pools around, and they're more about seeing and being seen than swimming. Most of these pools double as bars, lounges or even clubs. Some hotels have a guests-only policy when it comes to hanging out at the pool, but if you buy a drink at the poolside bar you should be fine.

➡ Delano (p106)

➡ Shore Club (p106)

➡ Kimpton EPIC Hotel (p110)

➡ Biltmore Hotel (p112)

➡ Fontainebleau (p109)

Landon Hotel BOUTIQUE HOTEL $$
(☎ 305-868-4141; www.thelandon.com; 9660 E Bay Harbor Dr; r $129-289; P ❋ 🛜) The Landon is a cheerful, hip option about 3 miles north of Miami Beach. It looks, from the outside, like a large B&B that's been fashioned for MTV and Apple employees. This vibe continues in the lobby and the rooms: cool, clean lines offset by bright, bouncy colors, plus a nice list of amenities such as flat-screen TVs, in-room Keurig coffeemakers, gym access and the rest.

Circa 39 BOUTIQUE HOTEL $$
(Map p108; ☎ 305-538-4900; www.circa39.com; 3900 Collins Ave; r $120-300; P ❋ 🛜 ☲) If you love South Beach style but loathe South Beach attitude, Circa has got your back. The lobby has molded furniture and wacky embellishments, and staff go out of their way to make guests feel welcome. Chic (if small) rooms, bursting with lime green and subtle earth tones, are attractive enough for the most design-minded visitors.

Red South Beach BOUTIQUE HOTEL $$
(Map p108; ☎ 305-531-7742; www.redsouthbeach.com; 3010 Collins Ave; r $165-400; ❋ 🛜 ☲) Red is indeed the name of the game, from the cushions on the sleek chairs in the lobby to the flashes dancing around the marble pool to deep, blood-crimson headboards and walls wrapping you in warm sexiness in the small but beautiful guest rooms. Come evening, the pool-bar complex is a great place to unwind and meet fellow guests. If you score an online deal, Red can be good value for money. Friendly, down-to-earth staff add to the appeal.

North Beach

0 _____ 1 km
0 _____ 0.5 miles

A **B** **C** **D**

Normandy Isle

N Shore Dr

77th St
Josh's Deli (1.6mi);
Mendel's Backyard BBQ (1.6 mi);
Landon Hotel (2.3mi);
Chayhana Oasis (5 mi);
Jelly & Burger (7.5 mi);

Collins Ave

Normandy Shores Golf Course

S Shore Dr

Normandy Dr

Harding Ave

☆24

⊗23

⊗18 ⊗19

22 71st St
71st St Bridge

4 ✪

Trouville Esplanade

5

JFK/79th St Cswy 21

NORTH BAY VILLAGE

W 63rd St

La Gorce Country Club

6 ✪

A1A

Biscayne Bay

Alton Rd

La Gorce Dr
Pine Tree Dr

Collins Ave

Enlargement

8

9 Indian Creek Dr
Collins Ave

Miami Beach Boardwalk

7

2

14 16
11

MID-BEACH

15

13 1

South Beach

12
17

0 _____ 200 m
0 _____ 0.1 miles

907

Alton Rd

Dade Blvd

10

3

A1A

195 **Julia Tuttle Cswy**

41st St/Arthur Godfrey Rd
20

Sheridan Ave
Pine Tree Dr

See Enlargement

Sunset Islands

N Bay Rd
Alton Rd
N Chase Ave

Bayshore Municipal Golf Course

N Chase Ave

W 28th St

Indian Creek Dr
Collins Ave

South Beach

A **B** **C** **D**

North Beach

MIAMI SLEEPING

★ **Faena Hotel Miami Beach**   HOTEL $$$
(Map p108; ☎844-798-9712; www.faena.com/miami-beach; 3201 Collins Ave; r $780-970, ste $1065-2425; ❋☞❅) The Faena has lavish, artfully designed spaces inside and out. The rooms, set with a royal red and teal color scheme, are full of beauty and whimsy: animal-print fabrics, coral and seashell decorative touches, and window seats (or terraces) for taking in the views. Each room also has butler service, because this is Miami, damn it.

Gilded columns and exquisite tropical murals line the lobby, with a pretty pool in back – a few paces away from a fully intact gold-covered woolly mammoth skeleton created by British artist Damien Hirst. The hotel boasts a massive spa that takes up one whole floor of the hotel, plus lavish drinking dens and a 150-seat theater inspired by Europe's grand old auditoriums.

Miami Beach Edition   HOTEL $$$
(Map p108; ☎786-257-4500; www.editionhotels.com/miami-beach; 2901 Collins Ave; r $489-1400, ste $1499-6859; ❋☞❅) Design guru Ian Schrager spearheaded the gorgeous retooling of this 1950s Mid-Beach classic. Luxurious rooms are kitted out in warm-ish neutral tones meant to evoke the presence of the beach in your bedchambers, while the artfully designed lobby and common spaces stay true to mid-century style, showcasing minimalist geometric design and flashes of tropical color.

The best features are the pool with its hanging gardens, the plush spa, a top restaurant (Matador by Jean-Georges), a Studio 54–esque nightclub (called Basement Miami) and an indoor skating rink.

Fontainebleau   RESORT $$$
(Map p108; ☎800-548-8886; www.fontainebleau.com; 4441 Collins Ave; r $409-569, ste $619-2070; ℙ❋☞❅❀) The grand Fontainebleau opened in 1954, when it became a celeb-sunning spot. Numerous renovations have added beachside cabanas, a shopping mall, a fabulous swimming pool and a nightclub. The rooms are bright and cheerful, with an unpretentious elegance.

Eden Roc Miami Beach   RESORT $$$
(Map p108; ☎786-801-6886; www.nobueden roc.com; 4525 Collins Ave; r $330-579, ste $619-799; ℙ❋☞❅❀) The Roc's immense inner lobby draws inspiration from the Rat Pack glory days of Miami Beach cool, and rooms in the Ocean Tower boast lovely views over the Intracoastal Waterway. All the digs here have smooth, modern embellishments and a beautiful ethereal design – we prefer the lofts, two-level rooms that efficiently maximize your space.

The amenities are staggering: three swimming pools, two Jacuzzis, an extensive spa, 24-hour fitness center and on-site restaurants, cafes and bars

Casa Faena   HOTEL $$$
(Map p108; ☎305-604-8485; www.faena.com/casa-faena; 3500 Collins Ave; r $325-400; ❋) Part of the growing Faena empire in Mid-Beach, this 1928 Mediterranean-style palace feels like an (Americanized) Tuscan villa, with a honey-stone courtyard, frescoed walls and gleaming stone floors. The sunny rooms have abundant old-world charm, and some have private terraces.

Palms Hotel   HOTEL **$$$**

(Map p108; ☑ 305-534-0505; www.thepalmshotel. com; 3025 Collins Ave; r $200-470; P ❋ @ 🛜 🏊) The Palms' lobby manages to be imposing and comfortable all at once; the soaring ceiling, cooled by giant, slow-spinning rattan fans, makes for a Colonial-villa-on-convention-center-steroids vibe. Upstairs the rooms are perfectly fine, though a touch on the masculine side. Thoughtful touches include comfy high-end mattresses, iPod docking stations, in-room coffeemakers and Aveda bath products.

🛏 Downtown Miami

Eurostars Langford   HERITAGE HOTEL **$$**

(Map p100; ☑ 305-420-2200; www.eurostars hotels.co.uk/eurostars-langford.html; 121 SE 1st St; r $180, ste $240-530; ❋ 🛜) Set in a beautifully restored 1925 beaux-arts high-rise, the Langford's 126 rooms blend comfort and nostalgia, with elegant fixtures and vintage details, including oak flooring and lush furniture. Thoughtful design touches abound, and there's a rooftop bar and an excellent ground-floor restaurant on-site.

YVE   HOTEL **$$**

(Map p100; ☑ 305-358-4555; www.yvehotelmiami. com; 146 Biscayne Blvd; r $120-200; ❋ 🛜 🏊) The YVE is a simple but trendy choice for those who want to be close to the pulsing neon heart of the Downtown experience at a competitive rate. Rooms mix dark carpets with minimalist white bedding. A fitness center is on-site, and pets can stay for $50 extra.

EAST, Miami   HOTEL **$$$**

(Map p100; ☑ 305-712-7000; www.east-miami. com; 788 Brickell Plaza; r $279-549; ❋ 🛜 🏊) Part of the burgeoning Brickell City Centre development, this cosmopolitan hotel has loads of style in its 352 spacious, attractively furnished rooms and suites. Apart from the beach (a 20-minute drive away), you've got everything at your fingertips, with swimming pools, a state-of-the-art fitness center, an excellent Uruguayan-style grillhouse, and a tropically inspired rooftop bar.

Kimpton EPIC Hotel   HOTEL **$$$**

(Map p100; ☑ 305-424-5226; www.epichotel.com; 270 Biscayne Blvd Way; r $265-550, ste from $605; P ❋ 🛜 🏊) Epic indeed! This massive Kimpton hotel is one of the more attractive Downtown options and it possesses a coolness

cred and youthful energy that could match any spot on Miami Beach. Of particular note is the outdoor pool and sun deck, which overlook a gorgeous sweep of Brickell and the surrounding condo canyons. The rooms are outfitted in designer-chic furnishings and some have similarly beautiful views of greater Miami-Dade.

Mandarin Oriental Miami   HOTEL **$$$**

(Map p100; ☑ 305-913-8288; www.mandarin oriental.com/miami; 500 Brickell Key Dr; r $299-419, ste $799-1589; P ❋ 🛜 🏊) The Mandarin shimmers on Brickell Key, which is actually annoying – you're a little isolated from the city out here. Not that it matters; there's a luxurious world within a world inside this exclusive compound, from swanky restaurants to a private beach and skyline views that look back at Miami from the far side of Biscayne Bay.

The Guild Downtown Miami   APARTMENT **$$$**

(Map p100; ☑ 512-623-7480; https://theguild. co; 230 NE 4th St; apt $200-550; P ❋ 🛜 🏊) If you're staying downtown and want some privacy to complement the Miami skyline, consider these one-, two- and three-bedroom apartments, which feature furniture that has a contemporary, design-forward vibe, and cool, light-filled common spaces. Guests will have access to a patio, pool, parking and gym, and kids are more than welcome.

Four Seasons Miami   HOTEL **$$$**

(Map p100; ☑ 305-358-3535; www.fourseasons. com/miami; 1435 Brickell Ave; r/ste from $435/640; P ❋ 🛜 🏊) The marble common areas double as art galleries, a massive spa caters to corporate types, and there are sweeping, could-have-been-a-panning-shot-from-*Miami-Vice* views over Biscayne Bay in some rooms. The 7th-floor terrace bar, Edge, is pure mojito-laced swankiness.

🛏 Wynwood & the Design District

Krymwood Flats   APARTMENT **$**

(Map p112; ☑ 954-763-2000; www.krymwood flats.com; 145 NW 29th St; apt $67-108; ❋ 🛜) These fully furnished apartments, ranging from studios to one-bedroom flats, make an attempt at Wynwood-y bohemian funkiness with mixed results – some rentals have graffiti and contemporary art aplenty, others look pretty plain. Still, they're clean and comfortable, and the cheaper ones are really a steal given their proximity to the heart of the action.

Fortuna House APARTMENT **$**
(Map p112; ☑954-232-4705; www.fortunahouse. com; 432 NE 26th St; apt $90-190; ❊ ☎) The Fortuna House is an affordable base for exploring the neighborhood's galleries and bars – though it's still a good 20-minute (1-mile) walk to Wynwood's epicenter. It's set in an attractive but aging three-story building on a quiet street. The accommodations are small and minimally furnished, but not a bad option for short stays.

Real Living Residence APARTMENT **$$**
(Map p112; ☑877-707-0461; www.rlmiami.com; 2700 N Miami Ave, entrance on N 28th St; apt $150-350; P ❊ ☎ ☒) A short stroll to the galleries and restaurants of Wynwood, this modern place has studio apartments with a minimal design of polished-concrete floors, tall ceilings and high-end furnishings. The best (and priciest) studios are rather spacious with a living room and dining area (though still within the one-room space). All have small kitchen units, washer-dryer, satellite TV and free parking.

🛏 Little Haiti & the Upper East Side

New Yorker HOTEL **$**
(Map p122; ☑305-759-5823; wwww.hotelnewyorker miami.com; 6500 Biscayne Blvd; r $100-180; P ❊ ☎ ☒) Dating back to the 1950s, the New Yorker has an eye-catching design that's right at home in the architecturally rich MiMo district. The New Yorker has comfortable rooms done up with pop art, geometric designs and solid colors. Catch a drink at the excellent outside **Patio Bar** (☑305-759-0357; 589 Northeast 65th St; ☺5pm-1am Tue-Thu, to 3am Fri & Sat, to 11pm Sun).

★**Vagabond Hotel** BOUTIQUE HOTEL **$$**
(Map p122; ☑305-400-8420; www.thevagabond hotelmiami.com; 7301 Biscayne Blvd; r $170-340; P ❊ ☎ ☒) An icon in the MiMo district, the Vagabond is a 1953 motel and restaurant where Frank Sinatra and other Rat Packers used to hang out. Today it's a boutique hotel, though it's lost none of its allure, with plush retro-inspired rooms that stepped out of a mid-century modern design catalogue, and a lushly landscaped pool complete with gurgling fountain. There's also a great bar (p133) fronting the pool – well worth visiting even if you're not lodging here.

🛏 Coconut Grove

Mutiny Hotel HOTEL **$$**
(Map p126; ☑305-441-2100; www.providentresorts. com/mutiny-hotel; 2951 S Bayshore Dr; 1-bedroom ste $170-320, 2-bedroom ste $400-600; P ❊ ☎ ☒) This small, luxury bayfront hotel, with one- and two-bedroom suites featuring balconies, boasts indulgent staff, high-end bedding, gracious appointments, fine amenities and a small heated pool and Jacuzzi. Although it's on a busy street, you won't hear the traffic once inside. The property has fine views over the water.

Mr C BOUTIQUE HOTEL **$$$**
(Map p126; ☑305-800-6672; www.mrchotels.com/ mrccoconutgrove; 2988 McFarlane Rd; r/ste from $167/434; P ❊ ☎ ☒) It was only a matter of time before the hip Mr C boutique hotel brand came to Miami. Many thought the Magic City's outpost would be in South Beach, but instead it occupies this gorgeous, unique, art-deco-meets-the-space-age structure. A stylized wall of futuristic portholes adjoins a five-story building filled with rooms decked out in neutral colors and cool pastels.

A lush back courtyard adjoins an elegant lobby that is far more vintage chic than the ultramodern exterior.

Life House Little Havana BOUTIQUE HOTEL **$$$**
(Map p140; ☑866-466-7534; www.lifehousehotels. com/hotels/miami/little-havana; 528 SW 9th Ave; r $215-290; ☎) Life House is a design-conscious hotel brand, and its Little Havana outpost is a fabulous blend of minimalist decor and old Havana vibe: elegant dark wooden touches and vintage photos enliven crisp minimalist rooms. The roof terrace is a jungly escape from the street, and offers wonderful views of the Downtown skyline. If you're in a group, consider a bunk bed quad room ($270).

🛏 Coral Gables

Extended Stay HOTEL **$$**
(Map p134; ☑305-443-7444; www.extendedstay america.com; 3640 22nd St; r $120-180; P ❊ ☎ ☒) Sure it's a chain hotel, but this place has spacious, modern rooms that are decent value for the price, and the good location puts you within walking distance of Coral Gables' attractions and eateries.

Rooms get plenty of light and are well equipped with small kitchens.

Wynwood & the Design District

Hotel St Michel   HOTEL **$$**
(Map p134; ☏ 305-444-1666; www.hotelstmichel.
com; 162 Alcazar Ave; r $180-282; P❋☎) Built
in 1926, this building exudes class, with an
elegant sense of style that feels more Old Eu-
rope than South Florida. Renovations have
added more light and a refined look to the
rooms, while still maintaining the histori-
cal charm beneath. You won't have to go far
for a meal. An excellent Italian restaurant
opened on the property in 2017 – though the
hotel's location puts you within walking dis-
tance of other appealing spots in downtown
Coral Gables.

★Biltmore Hotel   HISTORIC HOTEL **$$$**
(Map p134; ☏ 855-311-6903, 305-445-1926; www.
biltmorehotel.com; 1200 Anastasia Ave; r $329-
699, ste from $730; P❋☎⛱) A stay here is a
chance to sleep in one of the great laps of US
luxury. The grounds are so palatial it would
take a week to explore everything the Biltmore has to offer – sunbathe underneath
enormous columns and take a dip in the
largest hotel pool in continental USA. Rooms
themselves are surprisingly business-like,
with some baroque furniture flashes.

Wynwood & the Design District

MIAMI EATING

🛏 Key Biscayne

Silver Sands Beach Resort   RESORT $$
(Map p114; ☎305-361-5441; www.silversandskey
biscayne.net; 301 Ocean Dr; r $169-189, cottages
$329-349; 🅿❋🛜🏊) Silver Sands: aren't you
cute, with your one-story, stucco tropical
tweeness? How this little, Old Florida–style
independent resort has survived amid the
corporate competition is beyond us, but
it's definitely a warm, homey spot for those
seeking some intimate, individual attention
– to say nothing of the sunny courtyard, garden area and outdoor pool.

Ritz-Carlton Key Biscayne   RESORT $$$
(Map p114; ☎305-365-4500; www.ritzcarlton.com;
455 Grand Bay Dr; r $424-770, ste $820-1400;
🅿❋🛜🏊) Many Ritz-Carlton outposts feel
a little cookie-cutter, but the Key Biscayne
outpost of the empire is pretty impressive.
There's the magnificent lobby, vaulted by
four giant columns lifted from a Cecil B

DeMille set. Tinkling fountains, the view of
the bay and the marble grandeur speak less
of a chain hotel and more of early-20th-cen-
tury glamour. Rooms and amenities are pre-
dictably excellent.

🍴 Eating

Miami has tons of immigrants from every inhabited continent, and it's a sucker for food
trends. Thus you get a good mix of cheap
ethnic places to eat and high-quality top-end
cuisine, alongside some poor-value dross in
touristy zones. You can eat well anywhere
here, from cutting-edge trendsetters Downtown to tiny Cuban cafes in Little Havana.

🍴 South Beach

Panther Coffee   CAFE $
(Map p76; ☎305-677-3952; www.panthercoffee.
com; 1875 Purdy Ave, Sunset Harbour; coffees $3-
6; ☉7am-7pm) Panther has the best coffee
in Miami Beach, though the location is not

Key Biscayne

Virginia Key
Outdoor Center (1mi);
Virginia Key
North Point Trails (1.5mi)

Arthur Lamb Jr Rd

Rickenbacker Cswy

Bear Cut

Northwest Point

VIRGINIA KEY

Crandon Park Marina

Biscayne Bay

Crandon Park

West Point

Crandon Blvd

Crandon Park Beach

KEY BISCAYNE

ATLANTIC OCEAN

Harbor Dr

East Dr

Village Green Park

E Heather Dr

Key Biscayne

Galen Dr

Harbor Point

W Wood Dr

Southwest Point

W Mashta Dr

S Mashta Dr

Crandon Blvd

Bill Baggs Cape Florida State Park

Cape Florida Channel

Crandon Blvd

Biscayne Bay

Cape Florida

Cape Florida Lighthouse

Key Biscayne

all that convenient if you're on the beach. It has the same elegant vintage-chic vibe as its Wynwood branch, plenty of pastries, and outdoor seating to boot.

Taquiza   MEXICAN $
(Map p76; ☑305-203-2197; www.taquizatacos. com; 1351 Collins Ave; tacos $3.50-5; ☺noon-midnight) Taquiza has acquired a stellar reputation among Miami's street-food lovers. The takeout stand with a few outdoor tables serves delicious perfection in its steak, pork, shrimp or veggie tacos (but no fish options) served on handmade blue-corn tortillas. They're small, so order a few. It also serves craft beers.

True Loaf   BAKERY $
(Map p76; ☑786-216-7207; 1894 Bay Rd, Sunset Harbour; pastries $3-5; ☺7am-5pm Mon-Sat, from 8am Sun) The best bakery in South Beach is True Loaf, a small space where you can pick up heavenly croissants and berry tarts. With nowhere to eat these goodies, you'll have to take them around the corner to the waterfront **Maurice Gibb Memorial Park** (Map p76; 18th St & Purdy Ave, Sunset Harbour; �§) – stopping for Panther Coffee (p113) on the way of course. Fair warning: True Loaf may run out of its best baked goods by lunchtime.

Lincoln Eatery   FOOD HALL $
(Map p76; ☑305-695-8700; www.thelincoln eatery.com; 723 N Lincoln Ln; mains $8-17; ☺8am-10pm Mon-Thu, to 11pm Fri-Sun) It's easy to feel overwhelmed with food choice in South Beach, which is why we love the Lincoln Eatery. OK, to be fair, this is a food hall, so there are still a lot of choices: taco spots, sushi counters, even a kosher barbecue stand. But at least all of these options are concentrated in one easy-to-navigate arcade.

Moshi Moshi   JAPANESE $
(Map p76; ☑305-531-4674; www.moshimoshi.us; 1448 Washington Ave; mains $10-15; ☺noon-5am; ✆) The best-known name in South Beach when it comes to sushi, Moshi Moshi serves up mouthwatering perfection in its tender rolls, daikon salads and steaming noodle soups. Prices are fair and it's open late, meaning you can join the party crowd when sushi cravings strike at 3am.

Puerto Sagua   CUBAN $
(Map p70; ☑305-673-1115; 700 Collins Ave; mains $8-18; ☺7:30am-2am) Puerto Sagua challenges the US diner with this reminder: Cubans can greasy-spoon with the best of them. If you're never leaving South Beach, at least get a taste of authentic Cuban cuisine at this beloved institution, which has been slinging hash since 1962. Portions of favorites such as *picadillo* (spiced ground beef) are enormous.

La Sandwicherie   SANDWICHES $
(Map p76; ☑305-532-8934; www.lasandwicherie. com; 229 14th St; mains $6-11; ☺7am-5am; ✆) Closed for just a few hours each day, this boxcar-long eatery does a roaring trade in filling baguette sandwiches sold at rock-bottom prices. Ingredients are fairly classic: roast beef, smoked salmon, avocado or combos like prosciutto with mozzarella, though you can load up with toppings for a deliciously satisfying meal. Seating is limited to stools lining the restaurant's outside counter, but you can always get it to go and head to the beach.

Segafredo L'Originale   CAFE $
(Map p76; ☑305-673-0047; www.sze-originale. com; 1040 Lincoln Rd; mains $8-16; ☺10am-1am Sun-Thu, to 2am Fri & Sat; ✆) Immensely popular with Europeans and South Americans, this chic cafe serves up tasty snacks – pizzas, sandwiches, antipasti plates – and, of course, excellent Segafredo coffee. Credited with being the first Lincoln Rd business to open its trade to the outside street.

MIAMI EATING

11th Street Diner
DINER **$**

(Map p76; ☑305-534-6373; www.eleventhstreet diner.com; 1065 Washington Ave; mains $10-20; ☺7am-midnight Mon & Tue, 24hr Wed-Sun) A gorgeous slice of Americana, this Pullman-car diner trucked down from Wilkes-Barre, PA, is where you can replicate Edward Hopper's *Nighthawks* – if that's something you've always wanted to do. The food is as classic as the architecture, with oven-roasted turkey, baby back ribs and mac 'n' cheese among the hits, plus breakfast at all hours.

A La Folie
FRENCH **$**

(Map p76; ☑305-538-4484; www.alafoliecafe. com; 516 Española Way; mains $10-20; ☺9am-midnight; ✍) It's easy to fall for this charming French cafe on the edge of picturesque Española Way. You can enjoy duck confit salad, a decadent onion soup and savory galettes (buckwheat crepes) before satisfying your sweet tooth with dessert crepes – try the Normande (with caramelized apples and Calvados cream sauce). Vine-trimmed outdoor seating makes for a peaceful setting – and a fine break from the mayhem of Ocean Dr.

Pizza Rustica
PIZZA **$**

(Map p70; ☑305-674-8244; www.pizza-rustica. com; 863 Washington Ave; slices $5-7, pizzas $9-27; ☺11am-6am) One of South Beach's favorite pizzerias has several locations to satisfy the demand for crusty Roman-style slices topped with an array of exotic offerings. A slice is a meal unto itself and sure hits the spot after a night of drinking (hence the late hours).

★Yardbird
SOUTHERN US **$$**

(Map p76; ☑305-538-5220; www.runchicken run.com; 1600 Lenox Ave; mains $18-38; ☺11am-midnight Mon-Fri, from 9am Sat & Sun; ✍) Yardbird has earned a die-hard following for its haute Southern comfort food. The kitchen churns out some nice shrimp and grits, St Louis–style pork ribs, and biscuits with smoked brisket, but it's most famous for its supremely good plate of fried chicken, spiced watermelon and waffles with bourbon maple syrup. The setting is a shabby-chic interior of distressed wood, painted white brick columns, wicker basket-type lamps and big windows for taking in the passing street scene.

★Pubbelly
FUSION **$$**

(Map p76; ☑305-532-7555; http://pubbelly global.com; 1424 20th St; plates $9-24; ☺noon-11pm Sun-Thu, to midnight Fri & Sat; ✍) A mix of Asian and Latin flavors, Pubbelly serves hip fusion takes on small plates, and sushi such as grilled miso black cod with spring onions, beef tartare rolls with mustard and truffle poached egg, and Japanese fried chicken with kimchi. Super-popular and decently priced, it's a South Beach foodie spot that delivers.

Macchialina
ITALIAN **$$**

(Map p70; ☑305-534-2124; www.macchialina.com; 820 Alton Rd; mains $21-40) This buzzing Italian trattoria has all the right ingredients for a terrific night out; namely great service and beautifully turned-out cooking, served in a warm rustic-chic interior of exposed brick and chunky wood tables (plus outdoor tables in front).

Lilikoi
CAFE **$$**

(Map p70; ☑305-763-8692; www.lilikoiorganic living.com; 500 S Pointe Dr; mains $12-21; ☺8am-7pm Mon-Wed, to 8:30pm Thu-Sun; ✍) Head to the quieter, southern end of South Beach for healthy, mostly organic and veg-friendly dishes at this laid-back, indoor-outdoor spot. Start the morning off with big bowls of açai and granola or bagels with lox (and eggs Benedict on weekends); or linger over kale Caesar salads, mushroom risotto and falafel wraps at lunch.

Rossella's Kitchen
ITALIAN **$$**

(Map p70; ☑305-397-8852; www.rossellas sobe.com; 110 Washington Ave; mains lunch $12-18, dinner $16-29; ☺8:30am-11pm; ✍) Rossella's well-executed Italian fare served in SoFi ('south of Fifth St') makes this a favorite haunt morning, noon and night. The outdoor tables on the sidewalk feel like the perfect spot for good Italian cooking made with care.

Big Pink
DINER **$$**

(Map p70; ☑305-532-4700; https://myles restaurantgroup.com/big-pink; 157 Collins Ave; mains $13-26; ☺8am-midnight Mon-Wed, to 2am Thu, to 5am Fri & Sat) Big Pink does American comfort food with joie de vivre and a dash of whimsy. The Americana menu is consistently good throughout the day; pulled Carolina pork holds the table next to a nicely done Reuben. The interior is somewhere between a '50s sock hop and a South Beach club; expect to be seated at a long communal table.

Spiga
ITALIAN **$$**

(Map p76; ☑305-534-0079; www.spigarestaurant. com; 1228 Collins Ave; mains $16-32; ☺6pm-midnight) This romantic nook is a perfect place to bring your partner and gaze longingly at one another over candlelight, before you both snap out of it and start digging into excellent traditional Italian such as baby clams

SELF-CATERING

If you can tear yourself away from the Cuban sandwiches, celebrity hot spots and farm-to-table gems, Miami has a decent selection of options for self-caterers offering fresh produce and obscure ingredients aplenty.

Many of the more than two dozen **Publix** supermarkets throughout Miami are quite upscale, and the **Whole Foods Market** (Map p70; ☎305-938-2800; www.wholefoods market.com; 1020 Alton Rd; ☺8am-9pm) is the biggest high-end grocery store around, with an excellent produce department, a pretty good deli and a so-so salad bar; its biggest draw is for vegetarians or health nuts who are seeking a particular brand of soy milk or wheat-free pasta.

There are six **Milam's** markets around town that offer high-end ingredients, from stone-crab claws to filet mignon. Out on Key Biscayne, Golden Hog (p128) is a brilliant spot for fine meats and cheeses, while the iconic Marky's (p124) offers excellent ingredients beloved by any number of South Florida ethnic communities: Spanish deli meats and tinned fish, Italian truffles, kosher smoked salmon, and, most famously, genuine Russian caviar.

over linguine or red snapper with kalamata olives, tomatoes and capers.

Planta
VEGETARIAN $$

(Map p70; ☎305-397-8513; www.plantarestaurants.com/location/planta-miami; 850 Commerce St; mains $18-25; ☺noon-3pm Mon-Fri, from 11am Sat & Sun, 5:30-10pm Sun-Thu, to 11pm Fri & Sat; ☝) Planta brings South Beach diners a garden-to-table vegetarian and vegan experience. Mushroom and squash pizza is made with almond parmesan, udon noodles come with truffle cream, and a long list of small plates includes cauliflower tots and split-pea fritters. The setting is open and airy, located in the quieter corner of SoFi.

Front Porch Cafe
AMERICAN $$

(Map p76; ☎305-531-8300; www.frontporchocean drive.com; 1458 Ocean Dr; mains $12-29; ☺7am-11pm; ☝) An open-sided perch just above the madness of the cruising scene, the Porch has been serving salads, sandwiches and the like since 1990 (eons by South Beach standards). Breakfast is justifiably popular; the challah French toast is delicious, as are fluffy omelets, eggs Benedict and strong coffees.

Osteria del Teatro
ITALIAN $$

(Map p76; ☎305-538-7850; www.osteriadel teatro.miami; 1200 Collins Ave; mains $18-40; ☺6-11pm Sun-Thu, to midnight Fri & Sat) A main-stay of the fine Italian dining scene in these parts, Osteria remains a gem. When you get here, let the gracious Italian waiters seat you, coddle you, and guide you along the first-rate menu, with temptations such as polenta with wild mushrooms, black squid-ink linguine and locally caught red snapper.

News Cafe
AMERICAN $$

(Map p70; ☎305-538-6397; www.newscafe.com; 800 Ocean Dr; mains $11-32; ☺7am-11am Sun-Thu, 24hr Fri & Sat; ☝) News Cafe is an Ocean Dr landmark that attracts thousands of travelers. We find the food to be pretty uninspiring, but the people-watching is good, so take a perch, eat some over-the-average but not-too-special food and enjoy the anthropological study that is South Beach as it skates, salsas and otherwise shambles by.

Chotto Matte
PERUVIAN $$$

(Map p76; ☎305-690-0743; https://chotto-matte.com; 1664 Lenox Ave; small plates $13-29, mains $18-55; ☺4pm-midnight Mon-Fri, noon-1am Sat & Sun; ☝) Chotto Matte is a strong contender for most physically beautiful restaurant in Miami, and that's saying something in this city of impressive design. Peruvian-Japanese cuisine – such as avocado doused with a truffle ponzu or beef in a spicy teriyaki sauce – is served in a roofless space that encloses a tropical garden. Even if you're not hungry, pop by for a drink and to gawk at the layout.

Juvia
FUSION $$$

(Map p76; ☎305-763-8272; www.juviamiami.com; 1111 Lincoln Rd, access via Lenox Ave elevator; mains $27-46; ☺6-11pm daily, noon-3pm Sat & Sun) Juvia blends the trendsetters that have staying power in Miami's culinary world: France, Latin America and Japan. Chilean sea bass comes with maple-glazed eggplant, while sea scallops are dressed with okra and oyster mushrooms. The big, bold, beautiful dining room and open-air terrace, which sit on the high floors of 1111 Lincoln Rd (p73), are quintessential South Beach glam.

On top of the regular menu are dishes cooked on a Binchotan charcoal grill (ie fancy Japanese charcoal); shrimps, steaks and the like cooked on the grill will run you $40 to $160.

✗ North Beach

Josh's Deli
DELI $

(☑ 305-397-8494; 9517 Harding Ave; sandwiches $14-18; ⊙ 8:30am-3:30pm) Josh's is simplicity itself. Here in the heart of Jewish Miami, you can nosh on thick cuts of house-cured pastrami sandwiches and matzo-ball soup for lunch or challah French toast, eggs and house-cured salmon for breakfast. It's a deliciously authentic slice of Mid-Beach culture.

Roasters 'n Toasters
DELI $

(Map p108; ☑ 305-531-7691; www.roastersn toasters.com; 525 Arthur Godfrey Rd; mains $10-18; ⊙ 6am-3:30pm) Given the crowds and the satisfied smiles of customers, Roasters 'n Toasters meets the demanding standards of Miami Beach's large Jewish demographic, thanks to juicy deli meat, fresh bread, crispy bagels and warm latkes. Sliders (mini-sandwiches) are served on challah bread, an innovation that's as charming as it is tasty.

★ 27 Restaurant
FUSION $$

(Map p108; ☑ 786-476-7020; www.freehandhotels. com; 2727 Indian Creek Dr, Freehand Miami Hotel; mains $17-30; ⊙ 6-11:30pm Mon-Sat, 11am-3pm Sat & Sun; ✐) Part of Freehand Miami and the very popular bar Broken Shaker (p130), 27 has a lovely setting – akin to dining in an old tropical cottage, with worn floorboards, candlelit tables, and various rooms slung with artwork and curious knickknacks, plus a lovely terrace. Try the braised octopus, crispy pork shoulder, kimchi fried rice and yogurt-tahini-massaged kale. Book ahead. Brunch is also quite popular.

Cafe Prima Pasta
ITALIAN $$

(Map p108; ☑ 305-867-0106; www.cafeprimapasta. com; 414 71st St; mains $17-29; ⊙ 5-11pm Mon-Thu, to 11:30pm Fri & Sat, 4-10:30pm Sun) We're not sure what's better at this Argentine-Italian place: the much-touted pasta, which deserves every one of the accolades heaped on it, or the atmosphere, which captures the dignified sultriness of Buenos Aires. You can't go wrong with the small, well-curated menu, with standouts including gnocchi formaggi, baked branzino, and squid-ink linguine with seafood in a lobster sauce.

Chayhana Oasis
UZBEK $$

(☑ 305-917-1133; http://chayhanaoasis.com; 250 Sunny Isles Blvd; mains $13-34; ⊙ noon-11pm) Chayhana claims to be an oasis, but with its elaborate tile work and light fixtures, it feels more like a Samarkand palace. A flush and flash Central Asian, Russian and American crowd dine here on steamed dumplings filled with spiced lamb meat, pea soup served with yogurt, *samsa* (traditional savory baked Uzbek pastries) and other Silk Road delights.

Shuckers
AMERICAN $$

(Map p108; ☑ 305-866-1570; www.shuckers barandgrill.com; 1819 79th St Causeway; mains $12-26; ⊙ 11am-1am; ☎) With excellent views overlooking the waters from the 79th St Causeway, Shuckers has to be one of the best-positioned restaurants around. The food is pub grub: burgers, fried fish and the like. The chicken wings, basted in several mouthwatering sauces, deep-fried and grilled again, are famous.

Mendel's Backyard BBQ & Brew
BARBECUE $$

(☑ 305-763-8818; www.backyardbbqmiami.com; 9472 Harding Ave; mains $13-42; ⊙ noon-11pm Sun-Thu, to 3pm Fri, 8-11pm Sat; ☝) If you didn't think 'kosher barbecue' was a restaurant genre, come to Mendel's Backyard. Chicken, fish, and beef (but not pork, obviously) are slow-smoked to perfection, yielding a tasty if oddly hybridized menu of Southern American and Ashkenazi Jewish gastronomy: schnitzel on the one hand, burgers and ribs on the other. Speaking of ribs, give the lamb ribs a go. Popular with families, not least because of its kids' menu.

✗ Downtown Miami

★ All Day
CAFE $

(Map p100; ☑ 305-699-3447; www.alldaymia.com; 1035 N Miami Ave; coffee from $3.50, breakfast $10-19; ⊙ 7am-5pm Mon-Fri, from 9am Sat & Sun; ☎) ✐ All Day is positively Miami's best cafe – with locally sourced ingredients forming the basis of its simple menu, as well as excellent coffees, teas, beer and wine, and an airy, light Scandinavian-style decor, this is a winner all-around. Stylish chairs, wood-and-marble tables, friendly staff and an always enticing soundtrack lend it an easygoing vibe. Featuring ingredients sourced from small Florida farms, the cooking is first rate.

Manna Life Food
VEGAN **$**

(Map p100; ☎786-717-5060; www.mannalifefood. com; 80 NE 2nd Ave; mains $8-12; ☺10am-6pm Mon-Fri, 11am-4pm Sat; ☑) This airy, stylish eatery has wowed diners with its plant-based menu loaded with superfoods. Filling 'life bowls,' *arepas* (corn cakes) and *noritos* (like a burrito but wrapped with seaweed rather than a tortilla) are packed with flavorful ingredients. There's also healthy smoothies, delicious soups and a decadent guacamole. It's all plant based and entirely vegan save for a few dishes with raw honey.

Bali Cafe
INDONESIAN **$**

(Map p100; ☎305-358-5751; 109 NE 2nd Ave; mains $10-15; ☺11am-4pm daily, 6-10pm Mon-Fri; ☑) It's odd to think of the clean flavors of sushi and the bright richness of Indonesian cuisine coming together in harmony, but they're happily married in this tropical hole-in-the-wall. Have some spicy tuna rolls followed by *soto betawi* – beef soup cooked with coconut milk, ginger and shallots.

La Moon
COLOMBIAN **$**

(Map p100; ☎305-860-6209; www.lamoon restaurant.com; 97 SW 8th St; mains $7-17; ☺11am-midnight Sun & Tue-Thu, to 6am Fri & Sat) Nothing hits the spot after a late night of partying quite like red beans, rice, sausage, pork belly and plantains, or sweetcorn cakes stuffed with steak. These street-food delicacies are available well into the wee hours on weekend nights, plus La Moon is conveniently located within stumbling distance of bars including Blackbird Ordinary (p131).

★NIU Kitchen
SPANISH **$$**

(Map p100; ☎786-542-5070; www.niukitchen. com; 134 NE 2nd Ave; sharing plates $14-26; ☺noon-3:30pm & 6-10pm Mon-Thu, to 11pm Fri, 1-4pm & 6-11pm Sat, 6-10pm Sun; ☑) NIU is a stylish living-room-sized restaurant serving delectable contemporary Catalan cuisine. It's a showcase of culinary pyrotechnics, featuring imaginative sharing plates like Ous (poached eggs, truffled potato foam, *jamón ibérico* and black truffle) or Toninya (smoked tuna, green *guindillas* and pine nuts). The wine list is excellent.

Verde
AMERICAN **$$**

(Map p100; ☎786-345-5697; www.pamm.org/ dining; 1103 Biscayne Blvd; mains $15-25; ☺11am-4pm Mon, Tue & Fri, to 9pm Thu, to 5pm Sat & Sun; ☑) Inside the Pérez Art Museum Miami (p74), Verde is a local favorite for its tasty market-fresh dishes and great setting – with outdoor seating on a terrace overlooking the bay. Crispy mahimahi (dorado fish) tacos, pizza with squash blossoms and goat cheese, and grilled endive salads are among the temptations.

River Oyster Bar
SEAFOOD **$$**

(Map p100; ☎305-530-1915; www.therivermiami. com; 650 S Miami Ave; mains $12-40; ☺noon-10:30pm Sun-Thu, to midnight Fri & Sat) A few paces from the Miami River, this buzzing little spot with a classy vibe whips up excellent plates of seafood. Start off with their fresh showcase oysters and ceviche before moving on to grilled red snapper or yellowfin tuna. For a decadent meal, go for a grand seafood platter ($125), piled high with Neptune's culinary treasures.

Garcia's Seafood Grille & Fish Market
SEAFOOD **$$**

(Map p100; ☎305-375-0765; www.garciasmiami. com; 398 NW N River Dr; mains $10-28; ☺11am-10pm Mon-Fri, to 11pm Sat & Sun) Crowds of office workers lunch at Garcia's, which feels more like you're in a smugglers' seafood shack than the financial district. Expect freshly caught and cooked fish and pleasant views of the Miami River.

Casablanca
SEAFOOD **$$**

(Map p100; ☎305-371-4107; www.casablanca seafood.com; 400 N River Dr; mains $14-40; ☺11am-10pm Mon-Thu, to 11pm Fri, 7am-10pm Sat & Sun) Perched over the Miami River, Casablanca serves excellent seafood. The setting is a big draw – with tables on a long wooden deck just above the water, and the odd seagull winging past. But the fresh fish is the real star here.

CVI.CHE 105
PERUVIAN **$$**

(Map p100; ☎305-577-3454; www.ceviche105. com; 105 NE 3rd Ave; mains $12-30; ☺noon-10pm Sun-Thu, to 11pm Fri & Sat) White is the design element of choice in Juan Chipoco's ever-popular Peruvian Downtown eatery. Beautifully presented ceviches, *lomo saltado* (marinated steak) and *arroz con mariscos* (seafood rice) are ideal for sharing and go down nicely with a round of Pisco Fuegos (made with jalapeño-infused pisco) and other specialty Peruvian cocktails.

Soya e Pomodoro
ITALIAN **$$**

(Map p100; ☎305-381-9511; www.soyae pomodoro.com; 120 NE 1st St; lunch $10-19, dinner $13-29; ☺11:30am-4:30pm Mon-Fri, 7-11:30pm Wed-Sat) Soya e Pomodoro feels like a bohemian retreat for Italian artists and filmmakers, who can dine on bowls of fresh pasta under vintage posters, rainbow paintings and curious wall hangings. Adding to the vibe is live Latin jazz (on Thursday nights from 9pm to midnight), plus readings and other arts events that take place here on select evenings.

Pollos & Jarras PERUVIAN $$
(Map p100; ☑786-567-4940; www.pollosy jarras.com; 115 NE 3rd Ave; $9-26; ⊙11:30am-10pm Mon-Thu, to 11pm Fri & Sat, noon-10pm Sun) The same celebrated team behind CVI.CHE 105 (p119) next door also operate this festive spot with an outdoor patio. The focus is less on seafood and more on meat: namely outstanding barbecued chicken (and chicken crackling – ie deep-fried skin – oh yes!), though of course signature dishes (including ceviche) are also available.

✖ Wynwood & the Design District

★ **Enriqueta's** LATIN AMERICAN $
(Map p112; ☑305-573-4681; 186 NE 29th St; mains $6-14; ⊙6am-4pm Mon-Fri, to 2pm Sat) Enriqueta's is an outpost of pre-gentrification Miami in the heart of that city's most gentrified neighborhood, a roadhouse diner where local Spanish speakers, as opposed to international installation artists, rule the roost. Notable for its excellent coffee, *pan con bistec* (steak sandwiches), *croquetas* (croquettes), Cuban sandwiches, and daily specials such as *picadillo* and *lechón asado* (roast pork).

1 800 Lucky FOOD HALL $
(Map p112; ☑305-768-9826; wwww.1800lucky.com; 143 NW 23rd St; mains $7-16; ⊙noon-2am Mon-Thu, to 3am Fri-Sun) Another example of Wynwood becoming a sort of adult playground for cosmopolitan world wanderers, 1 800 Lucky tries to recreate an Asian food hall in the midst of South Florida. The atmosphere is excellent: red lanterns, booming lounge and hip-hop, a slick bar, beautiful people. The food is pretty good too, ranging from sashimi bowls to Thai-style chicken wings to Chinese pork belly buns. The food hall becomes an outdoor bar as the night wears on, as popular as any packed Miami club.

Coyo Taco MEXICAN $
(Map p112; ☑305-573-8228; www.coyo-taco.com; 2300 NW 2nd Ave; mains $7.50-13; ⊙11am-3am Mon-Sat, to 11pm Sun; ☑) If you're in Wynwood and craving tacos, this is the place to be. You'll have to contend with lines day or night, but those beautifully turned-out tacos

are well worth the wait – and come in creative varieties such as chargrilled octopus, marinated mushrooms or crispy duck, along with the usual array of steak, grilled fish and roasted pork.

Kush AMERICAN $
(Map p112; ☑305-576-4500; www.kushwynwood. com; 2003 N Miami Ave; mains $12-16; ⊙noon-11pm Sun-Tue, to midnight Wed & Thu, to 1am Fri & Sat; ☑) Gourmet burgers plus craft brews is the simple but winning formula at this lively eatery and drinking den on the southern fringe of Wynwood. Juicy burgers topped with hot pastrami, Florida avocados and other decadent options go down nicely with drafts from Sixpoint and Funky Buddha. There are great vegetarian options too, including a house-made black-bean burger and vegan jambalaya.

Panther Coffee CAFE $
(Map p112; ☑305-677-3952; www.panthercoffee. com; 2390 NW 2nd Ave; coffees $3-6; ⊙7am-9pm Sun-Thu, to 11pm Fri & Sat; ☑) Miami's best independent coffee shop specializes in single-origin, small-batch roasts, fired up to perfection. Aside from sipping on a zesty brewed-to-order Chemex-made coffee (or a creamy latte), you can enjoy microbrews, wines and sweet treats. The front patio is a great spot for people-watching.

SuViche FUSION $
(Map p112; ☑305-501-5010; www.suviche. com; 2751 N Miami Ave; sushi $7-12, ceviche $8-15; ⊙11:30am-11pm Mon-Thu, to midnight Fri, noon-midnight Sat, noon-11pm Sun) SuViche is just fun: an open-sided setting of garrulous couples chatting over swinging chairs, graffiti-esque murals and good beats. The menu – and you may have guessed this based off the name – is a blend of Peruvian dishes and sushi, which goes down nicely with the creative *macerados* (pisco-infused cocktails). Visit the website for other locations, including South Beach and Brickell.

Zak the Baker DELI $
(Map p112; ☑786-294-0876; www.zakthebaker.com; 295 NW 26th St; sandwiches $8-17; ⊙7am-7pm Sun-Fri) This kosher bakery is admired by all for its delicious breads, bagels and sandwiches. Lines will often stretch around the block for all of the above, but the wait is worth it.

Salty Donut DONUTS $
(Map p112; ☑305-639-8501; www.saltydonut.com; 50 NW 23rd St; doughnuts $3-6; ⊙7:30am-6pm

Tue-Fri, from 8am Sat & Sun; 🖥) Although 'artisanal doughnuts' sounds pretentious, no one can deny the merits of these artfully designed creations featuring seasonal ingredients. Maple and bacon, guava and cheese, and brown butter and salt are a few classics, joined by changing hits such as pistachio and white chocolate or strawberry and lemon cream.

Buena Vista Deli   CAFE $
(Map p112; 📞305-576-3945; www.buenavista deli.com; 4590 NE 2nd Ave; mains $8-15; 🕐7am-11pm) Never mind the uninspiring name: French-owned Buena Vista Deli is a charming Parisian-style cafe that warrants a visit no matter the time of day. Come in the morning for fresh croissants and other bakery temptations, and later in the day for thick slices of quiche, big salads and hearty sandwiches – plus there's wine, beer and good coffees.

Lemoni Café   CAFE $
(Map p112; 📞305-571-5080; www.mylemoni cafe.com; 4600 NE 2nd Ave; mains $10-18; 🕐11am-10:30pm Mon-Sat, to 6pm Sun; 🖥) Lemoni is a small, dimly lit cafe with a creative Mediterranean-inspired menu in its panini, salads and appetizers (including hummus, bruschetta and spicy Moroccan eggplant). Weekend brunch (till 2pm Saturday, till 5pm Sunday) features beautifully turned-out French toast and blueberry pancakes. Located in the pretty Buena Vista neighborhood, this is a fine place to grab a sidewalk alfresco lunch or dinner.

Dasher & Crank   ICE CREAM $
(Map p112; 📞305-213-1569; www.dasherand crank.com; 2211 NW 2nd Ave; ice cream $5-10; 🕐11am-11pm Sun-Thu, to noon Fri & Sat; 🖥) Escape the heat of the concrete jungle at Dasher & Crank, which (literally) churns out ice cream in delectable flavors, ranging from Salty Beach (coconut, salt and graham cracker) to lemon and speculoos cookie cream. Many varieties are vegan friendly.

⭐ Kyu   FUSION $$
(Map p112; 📞786-577-0150; www.kyumiami.com; 251 NW 25th St; sharing plates $17-44; 🕐noon-11:30pm Mon-Sat, 11am-10:30pm Sun, bar till 1am Fri & Sat; 🖥) 🍴 Kyu has been dazzling locals and food critics alike with its creative Asian-inspired dishes, most of which are cooked over the open flames of a wood-fired grill. Try the Florida red snapper, beef tenderloin and a magnificent head of cauliflower. There's also grilled octopus, soft-shell-crab steamed buns and smoked beef brisket. Book well ahead, or turn up and wait (usually around an hour).

Michael's Genuine   MODERN AMERICAN $$
(Map p112; 📞305-573-5550; www.michaelsgenuine. com; 130 NE 40th St; mains lunch $16-29, dinner $17-48; 🕐11:30am-11pm Mon-Sat, to 10pm Sun) This upscale tavern combines excellent service with a well-executed menu of wood-fired dishes, bountiful salads and raw bar temptations (including oysters and stone crabs). Michael's tends to draw a well-dressed crowd, and the place gets packed most days. There's also outdoor dining on the plant-lined pedestrian strip out front.

Butcher Shop   AMERICAN $$
(Map p112; 📞305-846-9120; www.butchershop miami.com/tbs; 165 NW 23rd St; mains $12-39; 🕐11am-midnight Sun-Thu, to 2am Fri & Sat) It's called the Butcher Shop for a reason, and that reason is it is unashamedly aimed at carnivores. From bone-in rib eyes to smoked sausages to full charcuterie, meat lovers have reason to rejoice. Beer lovers too: this butcher doubles as a beer garden, which gets lively as the sun goes down.

Mandolin   GREEK $$
(Map p112; 📞305-749-9140; www.mandolinmiami. com; 4312 NE 2nd Ave; mains $16-44; 🕐noon-11pm; 🖥) It's all Mediterranean whites and blues at this Greek restaurant in the midst of the Buena Vista neighborhood. The back courtyard is beautifully lit in the evenings and the Greek cooking is good – try grilled sea bass marinated in lemon and olive oil, lamb kabobs with spicy yogurt or satisfying mezes, such as smoked eggplant and grilled octopus.

Palmar   CHINESE $$
(Map p112; 📞305-573-5682; www.palmar miami.com; 180 NW 29 St; mains $15-27; 🕐6-11pm Tue-Fri, from noon Sat & Sun) Palmar is putting the hipster Wynwood spin on Chinese classics in a sweet space bedecked with rattan lamps. Discerning diners pack in for Mongolian chicken with fermented chili, kimchi fried rice, *char siu* (pork) ribs, and a whole slew of dim sum, ranging from duck confit dumplings to crispy prawns with passion-fruit chili sauce.

Harry's Pizzeria   PIZZA $$
(Map p112; 📞786-275-4963; www.harryspizzeria. com; 3918 N Miami Ave; pizzas $13-17, mains $12-24; 🕐11:30am-10pm Sun-Thu, to midnight Fri & Sat; 🖥) A stripped-down yet sumptuous dining

MIAMI EATING

Little Haiti & the Upper East Side

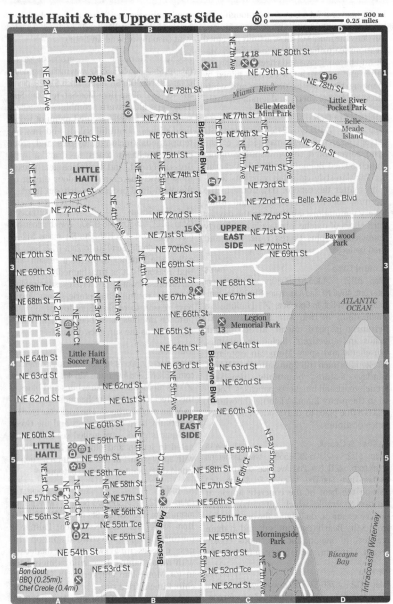

experience awaits pizza lovers in the Design District. Harry's tiny kitchen and dining room dishes out deceptively simple wood-fired pizzas topped with creative ingredients (shrimp, lemon and manchego, or spicy pepperoni). Add in some not-to-be missed appetizers like polenta fries and you have a

great, haute-cuisine meal served for a very reasonable rate.

Maska   INDIAN **$$**
(Map p112; ☑786-971-9100; www.maskamiami.
com; 3252 NE 1st Ave; mains $16-32, lunch thali
$22-28; ⊙noon-3pm & 6-11pm Tue-Thu, to mid-

Little Haiti & the Upper East Side

night Fri & Sat, noon-3:30pm & 6-10pm Sun) Maska is at the forefront of high-end Indian dining in Miami. The dining room, awash in subcontinental art and contemporary-design flourishes, accommodates diners feasting on crunchy soft-shell buns, tandoori lamb chops, and Kashmiri short ribs. Come at lunch for solid *thalis* (an all-you-can-eat plate of curries, chutneys, vegetables and starches).

★ **Alter** MODERN AMERICAN $$$
(Map p112; ☑305-573-5996; www.altermiami.com; 223 NW 23rd St; set menu 5/7 courses $90/110; ☉7-11pm Tue-Sun) Alter's changing menu showcases high-quality Florida ingredients from sea and land in seasonally inspired dishes with Asian- and European-flavored haute cuisine. Expect dishes such as eggs with sea-scallop foam, truffle pearls and Siberian caviar, or 'Pelin' duck with dashi, turnip, and Jamaican ginger beer. Reserve soon, preferably yesterday.

Amara at Paraiso AMERICAN $$$
(Map p112; ☑305-702-5528; https://amaraatparaiso.com; 3101 NE 7th Ave; mains $24-150; ☉11:30am-3pm & 5:30-11pm Mon-Thu, to midnight Fri & Sat, to 10pm Sun) You pay for the privilege at this gorgeous waterfront restaurant, but the rewards are delicious: new American/Latin American hybrid cuisine like a bone-in rib eye the size of a small child, a banana-wrapped mixed seafood grill, vegetarian cilantro rice, and grilled sweetbreads with chimichurri.

✖ Little Haiti & the Upper East Side

Chef Creole HAITIAN $
(☑305-754-2223; www.chefcreole.com; 200 NW 54th St; mains $10-22; ☉11am-10pm Mon-Wed, to 11pm Thu-Sat) When you need Caribbean food on the cheap, head to the edge of Little Haiti and this excellent takeout shack. Order up fried conch, oxtail or fish, ladle rice and beans on the side, and you'll be full for a week. Enjoy the food on nearby picnic benches while Haitian music blasts out of tiny speakers – as island an experience as the food.

Jimmy's East Side Diner DINER $
(Map p122; ☑305-754-3692; 7201 Biscayne Blvd; mains $7-13; ☉6:30am-4pm) Come to Jimmy's, a classic greasy spoon (that happens to be very LGBTQI+-friendly; note the rainbow flag out front), for big cheap breakfasts of omelets, French toast or pancakes, and turkey clubs and burgers later in the day. As an aside, the diner played a starring role in the final scene of Barry Jenkins' powerful film *Moonlight*, which won the Oscar for Best Picture in 2017.

Legion Park Farmers Market MARKET $
(Map p122; cnr Biscayne Blvd & 66th St, Legion Park; ☉9am-2pm Sat) For a taste of local culture, stop by this small farmers market held each Saturday in the Upper East Side's Legion Park. It's got all the produce (especially tropical fruits), cheese and breads you'd need for a good picnic, and as with most markets of this ilk, it's a nice place to wander and soak up the community vibe. It's open year-round.

★ Blue Collar
AMERICAN $$

(Map p122; ☑ 305-756-0366; www.bluecollar
miami.com; 6730 Biscayne Blvd; mains $17-27;
⊙ 11:30am-3:30pm daily, 6-10pm Sun-Thu, to
11pm Fri & Sat; 🅿 🖉 🏠) 🍴 True to name, Blue
Collar tosses pretension aside and fires up
American comfort food done to perfection
in a classic 1960s coffee-shop-style interior.
Start off with shrimp and grits or the four-
cheese Mac(aroni) before moving on to
seared rainbow trout, a smoky plate of ribs
or lip-smacking jambalaya.

A well-curated veg board keeps non-
carnivores happy.

Phuc Yea
VIETNAMESE $$

(Map p122; ☑ 305-602-3710; www.phucyea.com;
7100 Biscayne Blvd; mains $16-27; ⊙ 6-10pm Mon-
Thu, to 11pm Fri & Sat, 11:30am-3:30pm & 6-9pm
Sun) Phuc Yea started as a pop-up and went
wildly popular with its delicious Cajun-
Vietnamese cooking (the name got about
as much attention). Get yourself some
lobster summer rolls, the excellent fish
curry, spicy chicken wings, and other great
sharing plates.

The venue is industrial with graffiti, soft
lighting and loud hip-hop. The raw bar in
front doles out sushi, fresh oysters and creative cocktails (happy hour from 5pm to
7pm). There's also outdoor dining in a paper-
lantern-filled garden.

Bon Gout BBQ
BARBECUE $$

(☑ 305-381-5464; www.bongoutbbq.com; 99 NW
54th st; mains $10-25; ⊙ noon-10pm Tue-Sat, to
6pm Sun) A small dining room conceals a
kitchen turning out enormous platters of
meat that should get any proper carnivore
salivating. Yes, you are in Little Haiti, and
there is a tropical edge to the flavors, but
the primary palette here is fantastically
executed smokiness, which infuses all of
the barbecue, from ribs to brisket to chick-
en wings.

Fried fish and *griot* (fried pork) add
more Haitian color to the menu.

Andiamo
PIZZA $$

(Map p122; ☑ 305-762-5751; www.facebook.com/
andiamopizzamiami; 5600 Biscayne Blvd; pizzas
$12-21; ⊙ 11am-11pm Sun-Thu, to midnight Fri &
Sat; 🍴) Miami's best thin-crust pizzas come
from the brick oven at this converted industrial space (once a tire shop). With more than
30 varieties, it's a lively setting to start off the
night, with flickering tiki torches scattered
around the outdoor tables and large screens
showing sports on big-game nights.

Cake Thai
THAI $$

(Map p122; ☑ 786-534-7906; www.cakethaikitchen.
com; 7919 Biscayne Blvd; mains $12-24; ⊙ noon-
9:30pm Mon-Thu, to 11pm Fri & Sat, to 10:30pm Sun;
🍴) Chef Phuket Thongsodchaveondee (who
goes by the name 'Cake') is a Godfather of
Thai cuisine in Miami, whipping up roast-
ed duck salad, Panang pork belly, baby back
ribs with garlic and black pepper, and pad
thai with prawns – plus several variations of
fried rice for good measure.

★ Boia De
ITALIAN $$$

(Map p122; ☑ 305-967-8866; www.boiade
restaurant.com; 5205 NE 2nd Ave; small plates $8-
24; ⊙ 5:30-10:30pm Sun-Thu, to 11:30pm Fri & Sat)
Tucked into a faceless strip mall, Boia De is
not your average Miami Italian eatery. The
kitchen crew of punk rock-y chefs have an
uncompromising commitment to their food,
and no see-and-be-seen vibe has crept in (yet).
The menu has a small plates approach, and
you'll likely need more than one dish to fill
up. Reservations are recommended.

Marky's Gourmet
RUSSIAN $$$

(Map p122; ☑ 305-758-9288; www.markys.com; 687
NE 79th St; ⊙ 9am-7pm Mon-Wed, to 9pm Thu-Sat,
10am-5pm Sun) A Miami institution among
Russians, Russophiles and those that simply
love to explore global cuisine, Marky's has
been going strong since 1983. In-the-know
foodies from afar flock here to load up on
gourmet cheeses, olives, European-style sau-
sages, wines, teas, jams, caviar and much
more. As in the good old days of the Soviet
Union, service does not come with a smile.

✕ Little Havana

★ Versailles
CUBAN $

(☑ 305-444-0240; www.versaillesrestaurant.com;
3555 SW 8th St; mains $6-21; ⊙ 8am-1am Mon-
Thu, to 2:30am Fri & Sat, 9am-1am Sun) Versailles
is an institution – one of the mainstays of
Miami's Cuban gastronomic scene, and per-
haps the most iconic Cuban restaurant in
the nation. Try the excellent black bean soup
or the fried yucca before moving onto heart-
ier meat and seafood plates. Generations of
Cuban Americans, along with Miami's Latin
political elite, all rub elbows here.

★ El Nuevo Siglo
LATIN AMERICAN $

(Map p140; ☑ 305-854-1916; 1305 SW 8th St; mains
$7-13; ⊙ 7am-9pm) Clouds of locals come to El
Nuevo Siglo supermarket and rock up at the
shiny black countertop counter for delicious
cooking at excellent prices, plus unfussy am-

bience. Everything is good: nibble on roast meats, fried yucca, tangy Cuban sandwiches, grilled snapper with rice, beans and plantains, and other daily specials.

Lung Yai Thai Tapas THAI $

(Map p140; ☑786-334-6262; www.lung-yai-thai-tapas.com; 1731 SW 8th St; mains $10-15; ⊙noon-3pm & 5pm-midnight Tue-Thu, to 1am Fri & Sat, 5pm-midnight Sun) This tiny gem in Little Havana has some excellent Thai cooking – and provides a nice change of palate in the area. Chef and owner Bas Trisransi produces a menu ideal for sharing, hence the 'tapas' in the name. Try the perfectly spiced fried chicken wings, tender duck salad or a much-revered *kaho soi gai* (a rich noodle curry).

Taqueria Viva Mexico MEXICAN $

(Map p140; ☑786-350-6360; 502 SW 12th Ave; tacos $2.50-3; ⊙11am-9pm Tue-Thu, to 11pm Fri & Sat, to 6pm Sun) Head up busy 12th Ave for some of the best tacos in Little Havana. From a takeout window, smiling Latin ladies dole out heavenly tacos topped with steak, tripe, sausage and other meats. You can also grab a quesadilla ($6 to $12), if that's your thing. There are a few outdoor tables – or get it to go.

Yambo LATIN AMERICAN $

(1643 SW 1st St; mains $5-12; ⊙24hr) If you're a bit drunk in the middle of the night and can find a cab or a friend willing to drive to Little Havana, direct them to Yambo. At night Yambo does a roaring trade selling trays and takeout boxes about to burst with juicy slices of *carne asada* (grilled beef), piles of rice and beans, and sweet fried plantains.

San Pocho COLOMBIAN $

(Map p140; ☑305-854-5954; www.sanpocho.com; 901 SW 8th St; mains $6.50-17; ⊙7am-8pm Mon-Thu, to 9pm Fri-Sun) For a quick journey to Colombia, head to friendly, always hopping San Pocho. The meat-centric menu features hearty platters such as *bandeja paisa* (with grilled steak, rice, beans, an egg, an *arepa* and fried pork skin). There's also *mondongo* (tripe soup) as well as Colombian-style tamales and requisite sides such as *arepas*.

Azucar ICE CREAM $

(Map p140; ☑305-381-0369; www.azucaricecream.com; 1503 SW 8th St; ice cream $4-6; ⊙11am-9pm Mon-Wed, to 11pm Thu-Sat, to 10pm Sun) One of Little Havana's oldest ice-cream parlors serves delicious ice cream just like *abuela* (grandmother) used to make. Deciding isn't easy with dozens of tempting flavors,

including rum raisin, dulce de leche, guava, mango, cinnamon, jackfruit and lemon basil.

El Exquisito Restaurant CUBAN $

(Map p140; ☑305-643-0227; www.elexquisitomiami.com; 1510 SW 8th St; mains $9-13; ⊙7am-11pm) Great Cuban cuisine in the heart of Little Havana – the roast pork has a tangy citrus kick and the *ropa vieja* (spiced shredded beef and rice) is wonderfully rich. Even standard sides such as beans and rice and roasted plantains are executed with a little more care and are extra tasty. Prices are a steal, too.

★El Carajo SPANISH $$

(☑305-856-2424; www.el-carajo.com; 2465 SW 17th Ave; tapas $5-15; ⊙noon-10pm Sun-Wed, to 11pm Thu-Sat; ☑) Walk past the motor oil inside the Citgo gas station on SW 17th Ave (yes, really!) into this Granadan wine cellar and get yourself a seat at the bar. Order the divine bacon-wrapped stuffed dates, fluffy *tortilla de patata* (thick Spanish omelets) and don't miss the sardines – cooked with a bit of salt and olive oil till they're dizzyingly delicious.

★Doce Provisions MODERN AMERICAN $$

(Map p140; ☑786-452-0161; www.doceprovisions.com; 541 SW 12th Ave; mains $12-25; ⊙noon-3:30pm & 5-10pm Mon-Thu, noon-3:30pm & 5-11pm Fri, noon-11pm Sat, noon-9pm Sun) For a break from old-school Latin eateries, stop in at Doce Provisions. The industrial interior is stylish and sets the stage for dining on creative American fare – rock shrimp mac 'n' cheese, fried chicken with sweet plantain waffle, short-rib burgers and truffle fries – plus local microbrews. Brunch is justifiably popular on Sunday (11am to 3pm). There's a nice leafy terrace out back.

✖ Coconut Grove

Coral Bagels DELI $

(☑305-854-0336; www.coralbagels.com; 2750 SW 26th Ave; mains $7-11; ⊙6:30am-8pm Tue-Fri, 7am-8pm Sat, to 4pm Sun, 6:30am-3pm Mon; ☑☑) Miami has a large 'Juban' (Jewish-Cuban) population, and this spot is sort of like a Juban given brick-and-mortar restaurant form. The buzzing little deli serves proper bagels, rich omelets and decadent potato pancakes with apple sauce and sour cream. You'll be hard-pressed to spend double digits, and you'll leave satisfied.

Bianco Gelato ICE CREAM $

(Map p126; ☑786-717-5315; www.biancogelato.com; 3137 Commodore Plaza; ice cream $3.50-7;

Coconut Grove

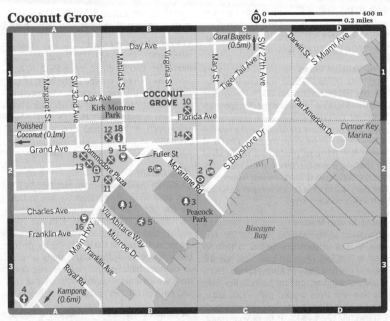

Coconut Grove

⊙ noon-11pm Mon-Thu, to 11:30pm Fri, 11am-11:30pm Sat, 11am-11pm Sun) A much-loved spot in the neighborhood, Bianco whips up amazing gelato that's all made from organic milk and natural ingredients. Flavors change regularly, but a few hits have included guava and cheese, avocado with caramelized nuts, hazelnut and vegan chocolate.

Last Carrot VEGETARIAN **$**
(Map p126; ☎ 305-445-0805; 3133 Grand Ave; mains $5-9; ⊙ 10:30am-6pm Mon-Sat, 11am-4:30pm Sun; 🖋 🖶) Going strong since the 1970s, and set in a decidedly unglamorous corner of Coconut Grove, the Last Carrot serves fresh juices, delicious pita sandwiches, avocado melts, veggie burgers and rather-famous spinach pies. The Carrot's endurance is testament to the quality of its good-for-your-body food.

Spillover MODERN AMERICAN **$$**
(Map p126; ☎ 305-456-5723; www.spillovermiami.com; 2911 Grand Ave; mains $17-32; ⊙ noon-10pm Sun-Thu, to 11pm Fri, 11am-11pm Sat, 11am-10pm Sun; 🖥 🖋) Tucked down a pedestrian strip

near the CocoWalk, the Spillover serves locally sourced seafood and creative bistro fare in an affected vintage setting (cast-iron stools and recycled doors around the bar, suspenders-wearing staff, brassy jazz playing overhead). Come for crab cakes, buffalo shrimp tacos, spear-caught fish and chips, or a melt-in-your-mouth lobster Reuben.

LoKal AMERICAN $$
(Map p126; ☑ 305-442-3377; www.lokalmiami.com; 3190 Commodore Plaza; burgers $15-16; ☉ noon-10pm Mon & Tue, to 11pm Wed-Fri, 11:30am-11pm Sat, 11:30am-10pm Sun; ✱☑☻) ✐ This little Coconut Grove joint does two things very well: burgers and craft beer. The former come in several variations, all utilizing excellent beef (bar the oat and brown-rice version). When in doubt, go for the *frita*, which adds in guava sauce, melted Gruyère and crispy bacon.

Atchana's Homegrown Thai THAI $$
(Map p126; ☑ 305-774-0404; https://atchanas.com; 3194 Commodore Plaza; mains $16-21; ☉ noon-10pm Sun-Thu, to 11pm Fri & Sat; ☻) Woodsy, airy environs are the setting at this standout Thai restaurant, which takes diners on a culinary tour of many of the regional cuisines from that nation. Yes, you can get massaman curry, but there's also *khao soi* from northern Thailand (coconut curry chicken soup) and rarer treats like a crispy fried whole red snapper. It also has a kids' menu.

Bombay Darbar INDIAN $$
(Map p126; ☑ 305-444-7272; www.bombaydarbar. com; 2901 Florida Ave; mains $17-22; ☉ noon-3pm Mon-Sat, 6-10pm Mon-Thu, to 11pm Fri & Sat, noon-10pm Sun; ☻) Indian food can be tough to find in Miami and all the more so in Coconut Grove, which makes Bombay Darbar even more of a culinary gem. Run by a couple from Mumbai, this upscale but friendly place hits all the right notes, with its beautifully executed tandooris and tikkas, best accompanied by piping-hot naan.

GreenStreet Cafe AMERICAN $$
(Map p126; ☑ 305-444-0244; www.greenstreet cafe.net; 3468 Main Hwy; mains $15-31; ☉ 7:30am-12:30am Sun-Tue, to 2am Wed-Sat) Sidewalk spots don't get more popular than Green-Street, where the Grove's pretty and gregarious congregate at sunset. The menu of high-end pub fare ranges from roast vegetable and goat cheese lasagna to blackened *mahimahi*.

✗ Coral Gables

Threefold CAFE $
(Map p134; ☑ 305-704-8007; www.threefoldcafe. com; 141 Giralda Ave; mains $10-16; ☉ 7:30am-3pm Mon, to 4pm Tue-Fri, 7am-4pm Sat & Sun; ☎☑) One of Coral Gables' most talked-about cafes is a buzzing, Aussie-run charmer that serves perfectly pulled espressos (and a good flat white), along with creative breakfasts and lunch fare. Start the morning with waffles and berry compote, smashed avocado toast or a slow-roasted leg of lamb with fried eggs.

Frenchie's Diner FRENCH $$
(Map p134; ☑ 305-442-4554; www.frenchiesdiner. com; 2618 Galiano St; mains lunch $12-36, dinner $21-36; ☉ 11am-3pm & 6-10pm Tue-Fri, 6-10pm Sat) Located on a side street, Frenchie's has a tucked-away appeal that is quite, well, French. But if the location is 'French-y,' the restaurant itself is the eating out equivalent of blasting 'La Marseillaise'. There are black-and-white checkered floors, a chalkboard menu, old prints on the walls, and lots of bistro classics.

Matsuri JAPANESE $$
(Map p134; ☑ 305-663-1615; 5759 Bird Rd; mains $7-22; ☉ 11:30am-2:30pm Tue-Fri, 5:30-10pm Sun & Tue-Thu, 5:30-11pm Fri & Sat) There are many trendy sushi spots in Miami, but while this strip mall restaurant lacks scene, it is often packed with customers seeking real deal, delicious Japanese cuisine (including quite a few South American Japanese). Spicy *toro* (fatty tuna) and scallions, and grilled mackerel with natural salt are all *oishii* (delicious).

Bulla Gastrobar SPANISH $$
(Map p134; ☑ 786-810-6215; www.bullagastrobar. com; 2500 Ponce de Leon Blvd; small plates $7-19; ☉ noon-10pm Mon & Tue, to 11pm Wed & Thu, to midnight Fri & Sat, 11am-10pm Sun; ☻) With a festive crowd chattering away, this stylish spot has great ambience that evokes the lively eating and drinking dens of Madrid. *Patatas bravas* (spicy potatoes), and *huevos* 'bulla' (eggs, *serrano* ham and truffle oil) keep the crowds coming throughout the night.

Ortanique On the Mile CARIBBEAN $$$
(Map p134; ☑ 305-446-7710; https://ortanique restaurants.com; 278 Miracle Mile; mains lunch $17-26, dinner $25-58; ☉ 11:30am-10pm Mon-Thu, to 11pm Fri, 6-11pm Sat, 5:30-9:30pm Sun; ☻) Eating at Caribbean-derived Ortanique is like a white tablecloth version of having a Red Stripe on the beach, which totally scans,

MIAMI EATING

LOCAL KNOWLEDGE

A LITTLE WINDOW ON VENTANITA CULTURE

What's the most common kind of restaurant in Miami? Chain fast-food joints? Hotel bars? Yet *another* Peruvian-Japanese fusion place?

Escucha, dear readers, and learn about the *ventanita*. The word means 'little window,' and these places are just that: small windows attached to storefronts, gas stations, some auntie's house etc, that typically serve small cups of rocket fuel Cuban coffee, also known as a *cafe Cubano* or *cafecito* (espresso with foam made from beating sugar and coffee).

Also on the menu – usually – is *cafe con leche* (a cup of steamed milk served alongside a shot of espresso), loaves of buttered Cuban bread, *pastelitos* (flaky, filled pastries; the most common fillings are guava, cheese, guava and cheese, and meat), sandwiches, etc – the options are fairly limitless.

Many *ventanitas* are attached to larger restaurants (there's a very good one at Versailles; p124), but they can be found almost anywhere in the city that hasn't become overly gentrified. Even if you order a *cafecito* at a *ventanita* (and you should), we recommend just watching the bustle at these coffee stands on any given morning. Customers get together, talk trash, flirt, make predictions about the Heat, etc. You might say they're a fascinating *little window* into Miami's day to day.

seeing as one of the best appetizers is Red Stripe steamed clams and mussels. Other standouts are jerked Cornish hen, seared ahi tuna with mango salsa, and an ever-changing slate of vegetarian specials.

Eating House Miami AMERICAN $$$
(☑305-448-6524; www.eatinghousemiami.com; 804 Ponce de Leon Blvd; small plates $7-16, large plates $18-34; ⊙11:30am-10pm Tue-Thu, to 11pm Fri, 11am-11pm Sat, to 3pm Sun) Eating House is one of the stars of the Gables fine dining scene, but the vibe is consciously counterculture: graffiti on the walls, and a playful menu of souped-up Miami comfort food, from chicken and waffles to pork-belly-and-arborio-rice *croquetas*. We recommend ordering lots of small plates, then going wild.

Pascal's on Ponce FRENCH $$$
(Map p134; ☑305-444-2024; 2611 Ponce de Leon Blvd; mains lunch $22-31, dinner $31-45; ⊙11:30am-2:30pm Mon-Fri, 6-10pm Mon-Thu, to 11pm Fri & Sat) They're fighting the good fight here: sea scallops with beef short rib, crispy duck confit with wild mushroom fricasée and other French fine-dining classics set the stage for a night of high-end feasting. Pascal's is a favorite among Coral Gables foodies who appreciate time-tested standards.

The menu and the atmosphere rarely change, and frankly that's not a bad thing. After all, if it ain't broke...

Caffe Abbracci ITALIAN $$$
(Map p134; ☑305-441-0700; www.caffeabbracci.com; 318 Aragon Ave; mains $26-47; ⊙11:30am-3:30pm Mon-Fri, 6-11pm Sun-Fri, to midnight Sat)

Perfect moments in Coral Gables come easy. Here's a simple formula: you, a loved one, a muggy Miami evening, some delicious pasta and a glass of red at a sidewalk table at Abbracci – one of the finest Italian restaurants in the Gables.

✖ Key Biscayne

La Boulangerie Boul'Mich CAFE $
(Map p114; ☑305-365-5260; www.laboulangerieusa.com; 328 Crandon Blvd; mains $12-15, pastries $3-6; ⊙7:30am-8pm Mon-Sat, 8am-4pm Sun; ☎⏎) This delightful French-style bakery whips up delicious quiches, satisfying veggie- or meat-filled empanadas, heavenly pastries and, of course, perfectly buttery croissants. It's also a fine place for breakfast (fruit platters, eggs Benedict) or lunch (prosciutto and mozzarella sandwiches, four-cheese gnocchi, quinoa salads). The shop may close earlier if it runs out of stuff.

Golden Hog Gourmet SUPERMARKET $
(Map p114; ☑305-361-1300; https://thegoldenhogmarket.com; 91 Harbor Dr; mains $8-15; ⊙8am-9pm Mon-Sat, to 7pm Sun) Tucked into a small shopping complex, this is the best place in Key Biscayne to grab picnic fare before hitting the beach or state parks. Aside from good cheeses, bakery items, tasty spreads and fresh fruits, there are various counters where you can order takeout sandwiches, soups and ready-made dishes.

Boater's Grill SEAFOOD $$
(Map p114; ☑305-361-0080; www.boatersgrill.com; 1200 S Crandon Blvd, Bill Baggs Cape Florida

State Park; mains $14-41; ⊘9am-8:30pm Sun-Wed, to 10pm Thu-Sat) Located in Bill Baggs Cape Florida State Park, this waterfront restaurant (actually there's water below and all around) has a menu that is packed with South Florida maritime goodness: stone crabs, mahimahi, and seafood paella.

Kebo
SPANISH $$

(Map p114; ☑305-365-1244; www.facebook.com/keborestaurant; 200 Crandon Blvd; mains $16-39; ⊘noon-10pm Sun-Thu, to 11pm Fri & Sat) This fantastic Spanish restaurant would be packed on the mainland; as it is, Kebo is very popular, but its Key Biscayne location gives it an out-of-the-way romantic atmosphere. This is all underlined by a pleasantly austere interior, and courses such as wild mushroom risotto, grilled prawns, and Galician octopus – the attention to detail, and resulting flavors, are outstanding.

Novecento
ARGENTINE $$$

(Map p114; ☑305-362-0900; www.novecento. com; 620 Crandon Blvd; mains $15-39; ⊘11:30am-11pm Mon-Thu, to midnight Fri & Sat, to 10pm Sun) Need a nice night out on this little urban island? Tough to do better than this Argentine mainstay, especially if you're a fan of a nicely marbled steak. Other delights include tagliatelle with meat sauce, octopus salad, and a nice gnocchi in a four-cheese sauce.

✕ Greater Miami

★Islas Canarias
CUBAN $

(☑305-559-6666; http://islascanariasrestaurant. com; 13695 SW 26th St; mains $6-18; ⊘7am-10pm Sun-Thu, to 11pm Fri & Sat; ℗) If you ask Miami natives where the city's best Cuban food is served, an argument will probably break out. But Islas Canarias will likely as not be mentioned multiple times. Located a fair drive from the main tourism districts, this spot is particularly famous for its *ropa vieja*, Cuban coffee, and *croquetas*, but really, everything is outstanding. Don't pass up on the signature homemade chips, especially the ones cut from plantains.

★Stephen's Deli
JEWISH $

(☑https://www.stephensdeli.com; www.stephens deli.com; 1000 E 16th St, Hialeah; sandwiches $11-15; ⊘11am-5pm) Stephen's is a Jewish deli for the 21st century. Yes, it has a '50s malt-shop vibe, and there is a literal shrine to the show *Seinfeld*. But all of the above is done with a 21st-century self-referential sense of playfulness. Also, the food is *good*. All deli

meats, especially the pastrami, corned beef, and turkey, are mouthwateringly juicy, while the bread is fresh and fragrant. Don't miss this one.

Jelly & Burger
VENEZUELAN $

(☑305-760-2149; 17010 W Dixie Hwy; mains $6-13; ⊘8am-3:30pm; ℗) Odd name? A bit, but the food makes up for it at this takeout spot where you can get, yes, excellent burgers (including the *lechón* – marinated pulled pork), but also savor Venezuelan favorites like *cachapas*, a thick, soft, delicious corn cake, similar but distinct from an *arepa*.

☂ Drinking & Nightlife

Miami has an intense variety of bars, ranging from grotty jazz and punk dives (with excellent music) to beautiful lounges, cocktail bars blended with tropical gardens, and Cuban dance halls. Miami's nightlife reputation for being all about wealth, good looks and phoniness is thankfully mostly isolated to the South Beach scene.

☂ South Beach

★Sweet Liberty
BAR

(Map p76; ☑305-763-8217; www.mysweet liberty.com; 237 20th St; ⊘4pm-5am Mon-Sat, from noon Sun) A much-loved local haunt near Collins Park, Sweet Liberty has all the right ingredients for a fun night out: friendly, easygoing bartenders who whip up excellent cocktails (try a mint julep), great happy-hour specials (including 75¢ oysters) and a relaxed crowd. The space is huge, with flickering candles, a long wooden bar and the odd band adding to the cheer.

★Mac's Club Deuce Bar
BAR

(Map p76; ☑305-531-6200; www.macsclub deuce.com; 222 14th St; ⊘8am-5am) The oldest bar in Miami Beach (established in 1926), the Deuce is a real neighborhood bar and hype-free zone. It's just straight-up seediness, which depending on your outlook can be quite refreshing. Plan to see everyone from tourists to drag queens to off-shift bar staff – some hooking up, some talking rough, all having a good time.

Bodega
COCKTAIL BAR

(Map p76; ☑305-704-2145; www.bodega taqueria.com; 1220 16th St; ⊘noon-5am) Bodega looks like your average cool-kid Mexican joint – serving delicious tacos ($3 to $5) from a converted Airstream trailer to

MIAMI DRINKING & NIGHTLIFE

SOUTH BEACH SIPPIN'

Greater Miami's coffee scene has improved in leaps and bounds in recent years, though Miami Beach still has limited options (we don't count stand-up Cuban coffee counters, as you can't sit there and read a book or work on your laptop, although if you speak Spanish, they're a good place for hearing local gossip). That said, there are a handful of decent options in Miami Beach.

➡ Panther Coffee (p113) The Wynwood chain has opened a great spot in Sunset Harbour.

➡ A La Folie (p116) A *très* French cafe with some excellent pastries.

➡ Segafredo L'Originale (p115) Pulls an excellent espresso on Lincoln Rd.

➡ Lilikoi (p116) The best spot in SoFi for a pick-me-up.

a party-minded crowd. But there's actually a bar hidden behind that blue porta-potty door on the right. Head inside (or join the long line on weekends) to take in a bit of old-school glam in a sprawling drinking den.

Mango's Tropical Café
BAR

(Map p70; ☑ 305-673-4422; www.mangos.com; 900 Ocean Dr; $10, dinner & show ticket $26; ⊙ 11:45am-5am) Visitors from across the globe mix things up at this famous bar on Ocean Dr. Every night feels like a celebration, with a riotously fun vibe, and plenty of entertainment: namely minimally dressed staff dancing on the bar, doing Michael Jackson impersonations, shimmying in feather headdresses or showing off some amazing salsa moves. It's a kitschy good time, which doesn't even take into consideration the small dance floor and stage in the back, where brassy Latin bands get everyone moving.

Kill Your Idol
BAR

(Map p76; ☑ 305-672-1852; www.facebook.com/killyouridolmiami; 222 Española Way; ⊙ 8pm-5am) Kill Your Idol is a lovable hipster dive, with graffiti and shelves full of retro bric-a-brac covering the walls, plus drag shows on Monday and DJs spinning danceable old-school grooves. The crowd is a mix of cool-kid locals and fashionable out-of-towners.

Story
CLUB

(Map p70; ☑ 305-479-4426; www.storymiami.com; 136 Collins Ave; ⊙ 11pm-5am Thu-Sat) For the big megaclub experience, Story is a top destination. Some of the best DJs (mostly EDM) from around the globe spin at this club, with parties lasting late into the night. It has a fairly roomy dance floor, but gets packed on weekend nights. Be good-looking and dress to impress, as getting in can be a pain.

Lost Weekend
BAR

(Map p76; ☑ 305-672-1707; www.sub-culture.org/lost-weekend-miami; 218 Española Way; ⊙ 4pm-5am) The Weekend is a grimy, sweaty dive, filled with pool tables, cheap domestics and – hell yeah – *Golden Tee* and *Big Buck Hunter* arcade games. God bless it. It is popular with local waiters, kitchen staff and bartenders.

Abbey Brewery
MICROBREWERY

(Map p76; ☑ 305-538-8110; www.abbeybrewinginc.com; 1115 16th St; ⊙ 1pm-5am) The oldest brewpub in South Beach is on the untouristed end of South Beach (near Alton Rd). It's friendly and packed with folks listening to throwback hits (grunge, '80s new wave) and slinging back some excellent homebrew: give Father Theo's stout or the Immaculate IPA a try.

🍸 North Beach

★ Broken Shaker
BAR

(Map p108; ☑ 305-531-2727; www.freehandhotels.com; 2727 Indian Creek Dr, Freehand Miami Hotel; ⊙ 5:30pm-2am Mon-Thu, 4:30pm-3am Fri, 1pm-3am Sat, to 2am Sun) A single small room with a well-equipped bar produces expert cocktails, which are mostly consumed in the beautiful, softly lit garden – all of it part of the Freehand Miami hotel (p107). There's a great soundtrack at all times, and the drinks are excellent.

The clientele is a mix of hotel guests (young and into partying) and cool locals.

Bob's Your Uncle
BAR

(Map p108; ☑ 786-542-5366; www.bobsyouruncle miami.com; 928 71st St; ⊙ 3pm-3am) Bob's Your Uncle's name doesn't just derive from the saying. 'Bob' is simple, and so is this bar:

classic cocktails, good beer, spacious seating, old games, friendly service, and the chillest vibe in Miami Beach. It's just a decently priced spot where you can grab a drink and catch up with friends, and that's something beautiful.

On The Rocks SPORTS BAR
(Map p108; 305-864-2444; https://ontherocks miamibeach.com; 217 71st St; 8am-5am) This convivial neighborhood dive feels pulled from another era, a feeling underlined by the multiple racks of old liquor bottles behind the bar and the nicely faded feel of the whole establishment. Grab a cold beer, watch the game with locals on either side of you, and relax.

Downtown Miami

★ **Lost Boy** BAR
(Map p100; 305-372-7303; www.lostboydry goods.com; 157 E Flagler St; noon-2am Mon-Sat, to midnight Sun) Miami is a city full of impressive-looking bars, but few pull off vintage aesthetics like Lost Boy, which makes sense, as it is housed in one of the oldest-standing buildings in Downtown. Vintage Cuban furniture, brass knobs, exposed brick and lots of old wood come together into an enormous pub with straightforward cocktails and beers served in imperial pint glasses.

★ **The Corner** BAR
(Map p100; 305-961-7887; www.thecorner miami.com; 1035 N Miami Ave; 4pm-5am Sun-Thu, to 8am Fri & Sat) This excellent bar sits near Eleven Miami, which is ironic as the Corner couldn't have a more different vibe. The interior, all dark wood and dim lighting, looks like it could double as a fancy old British library. Many folks still choose to drink outdoors – this is Miami – sipping classic cocktails and cold beers. It attracts a non-fussy, creative professional crowd.

★ **Baby Jane** BAR
(Map p100; 786-623-3555; www.babyjane miami.com; 500 Brickell Ave; noon-3am Sun-Thu, to 5am Fri & Sat) Small but sexy, Baby Jane is a Brickell outpost filled with tropical accents, neon, and Pacific Rim meets the Caribbean cocktails like the Big Trouble in Little Havana, which features *flor de caña* rum infused with wontons, a sentence we could only write in Miami. The crowd seems to mainly be Downtown cool kids, but the vibe is laid back.

Blackbird Ordinary BAR
(Map p100; 305-671-3307; www.blackbird ordinary.com; 729 SW 1st Ave; 3pm-5am Mon-Fri, from 5pm Sat & Sun) This is an excellent bar, with great cocktails and a vibe that manages to strike a good balance between laid-back and Miami hedonism. The only thing 'ordinary' about the place is the sense that all are welcome for a fun and pretension-free night out. You can often catch great live music, and on quiet nights there's always a pool table.

Mama Tried BAR
(Map p100; http://mamatriedmia.com; 207 NE 1st St; 3pm-5am Mon-Fri, from 5pm Sat & Sun) She really did. And she pulled off a very fine bar here in the heart of Downtown. Look for an orange neon sign, then walk into a dark bar with a speakeasy feel, giant metallic light fixtures, and a big square bar. It's got a laid-back, even neighborhood vibe on weekdays, but turns into an absolute Miami dance party on weekend nights.

Esotico COCKTAIL BAR
(305-800-8454; www.esoticomiami.com; 1600 NE 1st Ave; 5pm-1am Mon-Thu, to 2am Fri & Sat) Who knew there was a jungle in the middle of Downtown Miami? That's the sense one gets after walking into Esotico, all leafy plants, green murals and hot neon. Tiki drinks are as sultry as the setting, ranging from Zombies to new spins on the Colada. A breakfast cocktail of rum, ginger syrup, lime juice and bananas is flat-out stunning.

Eleven Miami CLUB
(E11EVEN; Map p100; 786-460-4803; www.11 miami.com; 29 NE 11th St; 24hr) Since its opening in 2014, Eleven Miami has remained one of the top Downtown clubs. There's much eye candy here (and not just the attractive club-goers): go-go dancers, aerialists and

LOCAL KNOWLEDGE

DOWNTOWN MIAMI

Bar-hopping Have a stumbling pub crawl from Mama Tried to Lost Boy.

Yoga in the park The open-air views of the bay are the perfect backdrop to sun salutations at free classes by the Tina Hills Pavilion (p98).

Hangouts Linger over excellent coffee and breakfast served at all hours at All Day (p118).

DON'T MISS

ROOFTOP BARS

Miami's high-rises are put to fine use by the many rooftop bars you'll find scattered around the city. These are usually located in high-end hotels found in Miami Beach and in Downtown. The view is of course the big reason to come – and it can be sublime, with the sweep of Biscayne Bay or a sparkling beachfront in the background. Despite being in hotels, some spots are a draw for locals and it can be quite a scene, with DJs, a dressy crowd and a discriminating door policy at prime time on weekend nights. If you're here for the view and not the party, come early. Happy hour is fabulous – you can catch a fine sunset and getting in is usually not a problem.

racy (striptease-esque) performances, amid a state-of-the-art sound system, with top DJs working the crowd into a frenzy.

Sugar
LOUNGE

(Map p100; ☑786-805-4655; www.east-miami. com/en/restaurants-and-bars/sugar; 788 Brickell Plaza, EAST, Miami Hotel, 40th fl; ⊘noon-1am Sun-Wed, to 3am Thu-Sat) One of Miami's hottest bars sits on the 40th floor of the EAST, Miami hotel (p110). Calling it a rooftop bar doesn't quite do the place justice. Verdant oasis is more like it, with a spacious open-air deck full of plants and trees – and sweeping views over the city and Key Biscayne.

Area 31
ROOFTOP BAR

(Map p100; ☑305-424-5234; www.area31restaurant. com; 270 Biscayne Blvd Way, Klimpton Epic Hotel; ⊘6-10pm Sun-Thu, to 11pm Fri & Sat) On the rooftop of the Kimpton Epic Hotel (p110), this open-air bar draws in the after-work happy-hour crowd, which morphs into a more party-minded gathering as the evening progresses. The view – overlooking the river and the high-rises of Downtown – is stunning.

American Social Club
SPORTS BAR

(Map p100; ☑305-570-4468; https://american socialbar.com/brickell; 690 SW 1st Ct; ⊘11:30am-1am Mon-Wed, to 2am Thu, to 3am Fri & Sat, to midnight Sun) There's a surprising lack of waterfront bars in Downtown Miami, but American Social Club fills the gap nicely. This is a big bar with a frat-y vibe that attracts a mix of conference attendees, pro athletes and locals who want a riverside drink.

🍷 Wynwood & the Design District

Wood Tavern
BAR

(Map p112; ☑305-748-2828; www.facebook.com/ woodtavern; 2531 NW 2nd Ave; ⊘5pm-3am Tue-Sat, 3pm-midnight Sun, 5pm-2am Mon) The crowd here is local kids who want something stylish, but don't want South Beach. Food specials are cheap, the beer selection is excellent and the crowd is friendly. The outdoor space has picnic benches, a wooden stage complete with bleachers, a giant Jenga game, and an attached art gallery with rotating exhibits.

Boxelder
BAR

(Map p112; ☑305-942-7769; www.bxldr.com; 2817 NW 2nd Ave; ⊘4pm-midnight Mon, 1pm-midnight Tue-Thu, to 2am Fri & Sat, to 10pm Sun) This long, narrow space is a beer-lover's Valhalla, with a menu of brews from near and far, though its 20 rotating beer taps give pride of place to South Florida beers. There's also more than 100 different varieties by the bottle. The down-to-earth vibe keeps the place humming.

Gramps
BAR

(Map p112; ☑305-699-2669; www.gramps.com; 176 NW 24th St; ⊘11am-1am Sun-Wed, to 3am Thu-Sat) Friendly and unpretentious (just like some grandpas), Gramps always has something afoot whether it's live music and DJs, dueling synthesizers (awesome) or bingo. The big draw though is really just the sizable backyard that's perfect for alfresco drinking and socializing.

R House
BAR

(Map p112; ☑305-576-0201; www.rhouse wynwood.com; 2727 NW 2nd Ave; ⊘3-10pm Wed & Thu, to 3am Fri, 11:30am-3am Sat, to 9pm Sun, brunch 11:30am & 2:30pm Sat & Sun) R House specializes in a lot: cocktails, happy hours, and shareable happy-hour bites ($3 to $7).But it's best known for its immensely popular drag brunch. You need to reserve seats ($45 to $65, food included) *way* in advance for this raucous affair that has a deserved reputation as one of the best midday parties in Miami.

Coyo Taco
BAR

(Map p112; ☑305-573-8228; www.coyo-taco.com; 2300 NW 2nd Ave; ⊘11am-3am Mon-Sat, to 11pm Sun) Secret bars hidden behind taco stands are all the rage in Miami. To find this one, head inside Coyo Taco, down the corridor past the bathrooms and enter the unmarked door. Inside you'll find a classy low-lit spot with a DJ booth, with brassy Latin rhythms and Afro Cuban funk filling the space.

Lagniappe   BAR
(Map p112; ☑305-576-0108; www.lagniappe house.com; 3425 NE 2nd Ave; ☺6pm-2am Sun-Thu, to 3am Fri & Sat) Lagniappe copycats a New Orleans model of outdoors drinking spaces fronted by an old-fashioned bar packed with art, faded vintage furnishings and weathered walls. There's live music (9pm to midnight, 10pm to 1am Friday and Saturday), in a sprawling back garden filled with palm trees and fairy lights. It gets *very* crowded here on weekends.

⬤ Little Haiti & the Upper East Side

★The Anderson   BAR
(Map p122; ☑786-401-6330; www.theanderson miami.com; 709 NE 79th St; ☺5pm-2am Sun-Thu, to 4am Fri & Sat) The Anderson is a great neighborhood bar with a dimly lit interior sprinkled with red couches, animal-print fabrics, and neon wallpaper that will put you in mind of an '80s dance-music video. Head to the large outdoor back area for more of a tropical-themed setting where you can dip your toes in the sand (never mind the absent oceanfront).

Vagabond Pool Bar   BAR
(Map p122; ☑305-400-8420; www.thevagabond hotelmiami.com; 7301 Biscayne Blvd; ☺5pm-midnight Mon-Fri, from noon Sat & Sun) Tucked behind the Vagabond Hotel, this is a great spot with perfectly mixed cocktails courtesy of pro bartenders (the kind who will shake your hand and introduce themselves). The outdoor setting overlooking the palm-fringed pool and eclectic crowd pairs nicely with elixirs such as the Lost in Smoke (mezcal, amaro, amaretto and orange bitters).

Churchill's   BAR
(Map p122; ☑305-757-1807; www.churchillspub. com; 5501 NE 2nd Ave; ☺3pm-3am Sun-Thu, to 5am Fri & Sat) A Miami icon that's been around since 1979, Churchill's is a Brit-owned pub in the midst of what could be Port-au-Prince. There's a lot of live music here, mainly punk, indie, hip-hop, and more punk.

Boteco   BAR
(Map p122; ☑305-345-7615; www.botecomiami.com; 916 NE 79th St; ☺noon-11pm Sun-Thu, to midnight Fri & Sat) If you're missing the *cidade maravilhosa* (aka Rio de Janeiro), come to Boteco on Friday evening to see the biggest Brazilian expat reunion in Miami. *Cariocas* (Rio natives) and their compatriots flock here to listen to samba and bossa nova, and chat each other up over the best caipirinhas in town.

⬤ Little Havana

★Los Pinareños Frutería   JUICE BAR
(Map p140; ☑305-285-1135; 1334 SW 8th St; snacks & drinks $3-6; ☺7am-6pm Mon-Sat, to 3pm Sun) Nothing says refreshment on a sultry Miami afternoon like a cool glass of fresh juice (or *batidos* – milkshakes) at this fruit and veggie stand, beloved by generations of Miamians. Sip a *guarapa* (sugarcane extract) *batido* while roosters cluck and folks gossip and argue in Cuban-accented Spanish; this is as Miami as it gets, short of being in a Pitbull song.

Ball & Chain   BAR
(Map p140; ☑305-643-7820; www.ballandchain miami.com; 1513 SW 8th St; ☺11am-midnight Mon-Wed, to 2am Thu, to 3am Fri & Sat, to 1am Sun) The Ball & Chain has survived several incarnations over the years. Back in 1935, when 8th St was more Jewish than Latino, it was the sort of jazz joint Billie Holiday would croon in. That iteration closed in 1957, but today's Ball & Chain is still dedicated to music and good times – specifically, Latin music and tropical cocktails.

ART WALKS: NIGHTLIFE MEETS ART

Ever-flowing (not always free) wine and beer, great art, a fun crowd and no cover charge (or velvet rope): welcome to the wondrous world where art and nightlife collide. The Wynwood and Design District Art Walks are among the best ways to experience an alternative slice of Miami culture. Just be careful, as a lot of galleries in Wynwood are separated by short drives (the Design District is more walkable). Art Walks (p104) take place on the second Saturday of each month, from 7pm to 10pm (some galleries stretch to 11pm); when it's all over, lots of folks repair to Wood Tavern or the **Sylvester** (Map p112; ☑305-814-4548; www.thesylvesterbar.com; 3456 N Miami Ave; ☺5pm-2am Tue-Thu & Sun, to 3am Fri & Sat). Visit www.artofmiami. com/maps/art-walks for information on participating galleries.

Coral Gables

Coral Gables

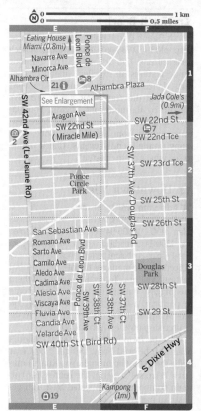

Coral Gables

Seven Seas BAR

(Map p134; ☑ 305-266-6071; www.facebook.com/sevenseasbar; 2200 SW 57th Ave; ☉ noon-1am Sun-Wed, to 2am Thu-Sat) Seven Seas is a genuine Miami neighborhood dive, decorated on the inside like a nautical theme park and filled with University of Miami students, Cuban workers, gays, straights, lesbians and folks from around the way.

Come for the best karaoke in Miami on Tuesday, Thursday and Saturday, and for trivia on Monday.

Copper 29 BAR

(Map p134; ☑ 786-580-4689; http://copper29bar.com; 206 Miracle Mile; ☉ 5pm-1am Mon & Tue, to 2am Wed & Thu, 4pm-2am Fri, noon-2am Sat, to 1am Sun) Portraits of celebrities like Brad Pitt in a Napoleonic military uniform or the Mona Lisa in hipster glasses gaze at a crowd of Coral Gables pretty people throwing back serious cocktails like the La Vie en Rose (tequila, mezcal, blood orange and vanilla foam). There's a dark and sexy speakeasy vibe, although come the weekend the spot becomes more of a dance-y lounge.

Titanic Brewing Company MICROBREWERY

(☑ 305-668-1742; www.titanicbrewery.com; 5813 Ponce de Leon Blvd; ☉ 11:30am-1am Sun-Thu, to 2am Fri & Sat) By day Titanic is an all-American-type brewpub, but at night it turns into a popular University of Miami watering hole. Titanic's signature brews are refreshing and there's good pub grub on hand, including sriracha wings and peel-and-eat shrimp.

☆ Entertainment

Miami's arts scene draws from an enviable creative demographic base. Immigrants from around the world come here to create a better life, and in the process they've also created world-class art, live music and theater – all of it given a unique, sexy twist thanks to the sultry weather and sheer compressed diversity of South Florida.

☆ South Beach

New World Symphony CLASSICAL MUSIC

(NWS; Map p76; ☑ 305-680-5866; www.nws.edu; 500 17th St) Housed in the New World Center (p69) – a funky explosion of cubist lines and geometric curves, fresh white

⚑ Coconut Grove

Taurus BAR

(Map p126; ☑ 305-529-6523; https://taurusbeerandwhiskey.com; 3540 Main Hwy; ☉ 4pm-3am Mon-Fri, from noon Sat & Sun) The oldest bar in Coconut Grove is a cool mix of wood paneling, smoky-leather chairs, about 100 beers to choose from and a convivial vibe – as Miami neighborhood bars go, this is one of the best.

Barracuda BAR

(Map p126; ☑ 305-918-9013; https://barracuda-taphouse-grill.business.site; 3035 Fuller St; ☉ noon-3am Tue-Sun, from 6pm Mon) Coconut Grove has its share of divey, pretension-free bars, and Barracuda is one of the better ones, with a fine jukebox, pool table, darts, and sports playing on the various TV screens. It's a fine retreat from the Grove's shiny shopping vibe – the inside is decorated with wood salvaged from an old Florida shrimp boat.

against the blue Miami sky – the acclaimed New World Symphony (NWS) holds performances from October to May. The deservedly heralded NWS serves as a three- to four-year preparatory program for talented musicians from prestigious music schools.

Colony Theatre PERFORMING ARTS
(Map p76; ☑305-674-1040, box office 800-211-1414; www.colonymb.org; 1040 Lincoln Rd) The Colony was built in 1935 and was the main cinema in upper South Beach before it fell into disrepair in the mid-20th century. It was renovated and revived in 1976 and now boasts 465 seats and great acoustics. It's an absolute art deco gem, with a classic marquee and Inca-style crenelations, and now serves as a major venue for performing arts.

O Cinema South Beach CINEMA
(Map p76; ☑786-471-3269; www.o-cinema.org/venue/o-cinema-south-beach; 1130 Washington Ave) This much-loved nonprofit cinema screens indie films, foreign films and documentaries. You'll find thought-provoking works you won't see elsewhere. The venue itself is a hybrid theater/bookstore/library that occupies the old Miami Beach city hall, built in 1927 by real-estate mogul Carl Fischer.

Miami City Ballet DANCE
(Map p76; ☑305-929-7010; www.miamicityballet.org; 2200 Liberty Ave) Formed in 1985, this troupe is based out of a lovely three-story headquarters designed by famed local architectural firm Arquitectonica. The facade allows passersby to watch the dancers rehearsing through big picture windows, which makes you feel like you're in a scene from *Fame*, except the weather is better and people don't spontaneously break into song.

Fillmore Miami Beach PERFORMING ARTS
(Map p76; ☑305-673-7300; www.fillmoremb.com; 1700 Washington Ave) Built in 1951, South Beach's premier showcase for touring Broadway shows, orchestras and other big musical productions has 2700 seats and excellent acoustics.

Jackie Gleason chose to make the theater his home for the long-running 1960s TV show, but now you'll find an eclectic lineup: Catalan pop or indie rock one night, the comedian Bill Maher or an over-the-top vaudeville group the next.

☆ North Beach

North Beach Bandshell LIVE MUSIC
(Map p108; ☑786-453-2897; www.northbeachbandshell.com; 7275 Collins Ave) This outdoor venue features an excellent lineup of concerts, dance, theater, opera and spoken word throughout the year. Some events are free. It's run by the nonprofit Rhythm Foundation, and the wide-ranging repertoire features sounds from around the globe, with many family-friendly events. Check online to see what's on the roster.

☆ Downtown Miami

★ Adrienne Arsht Center for the Performing Arts PERFORMING ARTS
(Map p100; ☑305-949-6722; www.arshtcenter.org; 1300 Biscayne Blvd; ⊘box office noon-5pm Mon-Fri, plus 2hr before performances) This magnificent venue manages to both humble and enthrall visitors. Today the Arsht is where the biggest cultural acts in Miami come to perform; a show here is a must-see on any Miami trip. There's an Adrienne Arsht Center stop on the Metromover.

This performing-arts center is Miami's beautiful, beloved baby. Designed by César Pelli (the man who brought you Kuala Lumpur's Petronas Towers), the center has two main components, connected by a thin pedestrian bridge.

Inside the theaters there's a sense of ocean and land sculpted by wind; the rounded balconies rise up in spirals that resemble a sliced-open seashell. Hidden behind these impressive structures are highly engineered, state-of-the-art acoustics ensuring that no outside sounds can penetrate, creating the perfect conditions to enjoy one of the 300 performances staged at the center each year.

Klipsch Amphitheater LIVE MUSIC
(Map p100; www.klipsch.com/klipsch-amphitheater-at-bayfront-park; 301 N Biscayne Blvd, Bayfront Park) In Bayfront Park in Downtown Miami, the Klipsch Amphitheater stages a wide range of concerts throughout the year. The open-air setting beside Biscayne Bay is hard to top.

American Airlines Arena STADIUM
(Map p100; ☑786-777-1000; www.aaarena.com; 601 N Biscayne Blvd) Resembling a massive spaceship that perpetually hovers

at the edge of Biscayne Bay, this arena has been the home of the city's NBA franchise, the **Miami Heat**, since 2000. The **Waterfront Theater**, Florida's largest, is housed inside; throughout the year it hosts concerts, Broadway performances and the like.

Olympia Theater   PERFORMING ARTS
(Map p100; ☎ 305-374-2444; www.olympiatheater. org; 174 E Flagler St) This elegantly renovated 1920s movie palace services a huge variety of performing arts including film festivals, symphonies, ballets and touring shows. The acoustics are excellent.

Miami loves modern, but the Olympia Theater at the Gusman Center for the Performing Arts is vintage-classic beautiful. The ceiling, which features 246 twinkling stars and clouds cast over an indigo-deep night, frosted with classical Greek sculpture and Vienna Opera House–style embellishment, will melt your heart. The theater first opened in 1925.

☆ Wynwood & the Design District

Light Box at Goldman Warehouse   PERFORMING ARTS
(Map p112; ☎ 305-576-4350; www.miamilight project.com; 404 NW 26th St) The Miami Light Project, a nonprofit cultural foundation, stages a wide range of innovative theater, dance, music and film performances at this intimate theater. It's in Wynwood, and a great place to discover cutting-edge works by artists you might not have heard of. It is particularly supportive of troupes from South Florida.

Punch Bowl Social   KARAOKE
(Map p112; ☎ 786-796-5242; https://punchbowl social.com; 2660 NW 3rd Ave; bowling $16-18, karaoke rooms $35-45; ☉ 11am-11pm Mon-Fri, from 10:30am Sat & Sun) It's hard to pin down just what Punch Bowl Social is, other than fun. Let's tick off the constituent parts: a big, industrial facility with hip lighting; a large bar that serves cocktails, both in glasses and shareable via punch bowls; a bowling alley; a place to rock out with karaoke; or play pool, or Ping-Pong...yeah. Hard to define. Fun to be at.

Note the bowling is duckpin bowling, a variation on the game with a smaller ball.

☆ Little Haiti & the Upper East Side

Villain Theater   COMEDY
(Map p122; ☎ 786-391-2241; www.villaintheater. com; 5865 NE 2nd Ave; tickets $5-15) This laid-back theater showcases local stand-up artists, improv and sketch comedy, which makes this villain kind of a hero in our book (see what we did there?). The performance calendar is packed, and there's free improv classes on the first Saturday of the month from 4pm to 6pm – bonus.

☆ Little Havana

★ Cafe La Trova   LIVE MUSIC
(Map p140; ☎ 786-615-4379; www.cafelatrova.com; 971 SW 8th St; ☉ noon-midnight Mon-Thu, to 2am Fri & Sat, 11am-midnight Sun) A lot of Miami places try to (re)create a romanticized old Cuba. La Trova, with its wood accents, immaculately dressed bartenders, and faded Havana-esque walls, really executes the concept. Regular live shows featuring classic Cuban dance music accompanied by a crowd decked out in their best dresses and *guayaberas* is insanely fun; if the scene here doesn't get you dancing, we're not sure what will.

You've got the Cuban trifecta of food, drink and music going here, including a menu serving Cuban sandwiches and braised pork (mains $14 to $34). The house-made cocktails have an old-school tropical theme, and a good sense of humor – we had to chuckle at a strong drink named *La Chancleta* (the term for a cheap plastic sandal Cuban and Puerto Rican moms use to enforce discipline in the house).

★ Cubaocho   LIVE PERFORMANCE
(Map p140; ☎ 305-285-5880; www.cubaocho.com; 1465 SW 8th St; ☉ 11am-3am) Jewel of the Little Havana Art District, Cubaocho is renowned for its concerts, with excellent bands from across the Spanish-speaking world. It's also a community center, art gallery and research outpost for all things Cuban. The interior resembles an old Havana cigar bar, yet the walls are decked out in artwork that references both the classical past of Cuban art and its avant-garde future.

Aside from the busy concert schedule, Cubaocho also has film screenings, drama performances, readings and other events.

Tower Theater   CINEMA
(Map p140; ☑ 305-237-2463; www.towertheater miami.com; 1508 SW 8th St; tickets $11.75) This renovated 1926 landmark theater has a proud deco facade and a handsomely renovated interior, thanks to support from the Miami-Dade Community College. In its heyday it was the center of Little Havana social life and, via the films it showed, served as a bridge between immigrant society and American pop culture. Today it frequently shows independent and Spanish-language films (sometimes both).

☆ Coral Gables

Coral Gables Art Cinema   CINEMA
(Map p134; ☑ 786-385-9689; www.gablescinema. com; 260 Aragon Ave) In the epicenter of Coral Gables' downtown, you'll find one of Miami's best art-house cinemas. It shows indie and foreign films in a modern 144-seat screening room. Check out cult favorites shown in the original 35mm format at Saturday midnight screenings (part of the After Hours series).

GableStage   THEATER
(Map p134; ☑ 305-445-1119; www.gablestage.org; 1200 Anastasia Ave) Founded as the Florida Shakespeare Theatre in 1979 and now housed on the property of the Biltmore Hotel in Coral Gables, this company still performs an occasional Shakespeare play, but mostly presents contemporary and classical pieces.

☆ Greater Miami

Miami Symphony Orchestra   CLASSICAL MUSIC
(☑ 305-275-5666; www.themiso.org; tickets $20-50) Miami's well-loved hometown symphony has many fans. Its yearly series (from November to May) features world-renowned soloists performing at either the Adrienne Arsht Center for the Performing Arts (p136) or the Fillmore Miami Beach (p136).

Hard Rock Stadium   FOOTBALL
(☑ 305-943-8000; www.hardrockstadium.com; 347 Don Shula Dr, Miami Gardens; tickets from $35) The renovated (and renamed) Hard Rock Stadium (formerly known as Sun Life Stadium) is the home turf of the Miami Dolphins. 'Dol-fans' are respectably crazy about their team, even if a Super Bowl showing has evaded them since 1985. Games are wildly popular and the team is painfully successful, in that they always raise fans' hopes but never quite fulfill them.

🛍 Shopping

Miami boasts plenty of high-end fashion, designer sunglasses, vintage clothing, books, records, Latin American crafts, artwork, gourmet goodies and more. While there are plenty of malls in Miami, new shopping centers are often built in the style of outdoor arcades or bazaars, allowing shoppers to enjoy the sunny weather.

🔒 South Beach

Taschen   BOOKS
(Map p76; ☑ 305-538-6185; www.taschen.com; 1111 Lincoln Rd; ⊙ 11am-9pm Mon-Thu, to 10pm Fri & Sat, noon-9pm Sun) An incredibly well-stocked collection of art, photography, design and coffee-table books from this high-quality illustrated-books publisher. Check out David Hockney's color-rich art books, the *New Erotic Photography* (always a great conversation starter) and Annie Liebovitz's witty society portraits.

Books & Books   BOOKS
(Map p76; ☑ 305-532-3222; www.booksand books.com; 927 Lincoln Rd; ⊙ 11am-9pm) Stop in this fantastic indie bookstore for an excellent selection of new fiction, beautiful art and photography books, award-winning children's titles and more. The layout – a series of elegantly furnished rooms – invites endless browsing, and there's a good restaurant and cafe in front of the store.

Sunset Clothing Co   FASHION & ACCESSORIES
(Map p76; www.facebook.com/SunsetClothingCo; 1895 Purdy Ave; ⊙ 10am-7pm Mon-Fri, to 6pm Sat, 11am-4pm Sun) A great little men's and women's fashion boutique in Sunset Harbour for stylish gear that won't cost a fortune (though the merchandise isn't cheap either). You'll find well-made long-sleeved shirts, soft cotton T-shirts, lace-up canvas shoes, nicely fitting denim (including vintage Levi's), warm pullover sweaters and other casual gear. Helpful, friendly service too.

Alchemist   FASHION & ACCESSORIES
(Map p76; ☑ 305-531-4815; 1111 Lincoln Rd; ⊙ 11am-8pm) Inside one of Lincoln Rd's most striking buildings, this high-end boutique has a wild collection of artful objects, including Warhol-style soup-can candles, heavy gilded corkscrews, Beats headphones by Dr Dre, and mirrored circular sunglasses that are essential for the beach. The clothing here tends to be fairly avant-garde (straight from the runway, it seems).

🔒 Downtown Miami

Mary Brickell Village   SHOPPING CENTER
(Map p100; ☑305-381-6130; www.marybrickell
village.com; 901 S Miami Ave; ☺10am-9pm Mon-
Sat, noon-6pm Sun) This outdoor shopping
and dining complex has helped revitalize
the Brickell neighborhood, with a range of
boutiques, restaurants, cafes and bars. It's a
magnet for new condo residents in the area,
with a central location in the heart of the
financial district.

Supply & Advise   CLOTHING
(Map p100; ☑305-960-2043; www.supplyand
advise.com; 223 SE 1st St; ☺11am-7pm Mon-Sat)
Supply & Advise brings a heavy dose of
men's fashion to Downtown Miami, with
rugged, well-made and handsomely tailored
clothing, plus shoes and accessories, set in
a historic 1920s building. Most merchandise
here is made in the USA. There's also a bar-
bershop, complete with vintage chairs and
that impeccable look of bygone days.

🔒 Wynwood & the Design District

Nomad Tribe   CLOTHING
(Map p112; ☑305-364-5193; www.nomadtribe
shop.com; 2301 NW 2nd Ave; ☺noon-8pm) 🌿
This boutique earns high marks for carrying only ethically and sustainably produced merchandise. You'll find cleverly
designed jewelry from Miami-based Kathe
Cuervo, Osom Brand socks (made of up-
cycled thread), ecologically produced graphic T-shirts from Thinking MU, and THX
coffee and candles (which donates 100% of
profits to nonprofit organizations), among
much else.

Art by God   GIFTS & SOUVENIRS
(Map p112; ☑305-573-3011; www.artbygod.com;
60 NE 27th St; ☺10am-5pm Mon-Fri, 11am-4pm
Sat) Purses? Jackets? *Pssht.* When we go
shopping, we like to buy fossilized dinosaur
poop, and clumps of amethysts, and stuffed
full-sized zebras. It's all on offer at Art by
God, as well as rhino heads, dinosaur bones,
and more portable things like home furnishings from all of earth's continents.

Rupees   GIFTS & SOUVENIRS
(Map p112; ☑305-576-4368; www.facebook.com/
rupeessareesmiami; 415 NW 27th St; ☺11am-
6:30pm Mon-Sat) Rupees feels like the sort
of old-school international goods store that
wouldn't hack it in ultramodern Wynwood,

but it is going strong, selling South Asian
crafts and gifts, along with a huge range of
fabrics, alongside books about the local con-
temporary-art scene.

Out of the Closet   THRIFT STORE
(Map p112; ☑305-764-3773; www.outofthe
closet.org; 2900 Biscayne Blvd; ☺10am-7pm
Mon-Sat, to 6pm Sun) You'll find all manner
of treasure-trash at this sizable thrift store
on busy Biscayne Blvd: men's and women's
clothing, accessories, books, CDs, records,
housewares and more. Friendly staff can
help guide you on the search. The store benefits the AIDS Healthcare Foundation.

Harold Golen Gallery   ART
(Map p112; ☑305-989-3359; https://harold
golen.gallery; 2294 NW 2nd Ave; ☺noon-7pm)
Original artwork is exhibited at this small
gallery, mainly of a very animation/anime/
tiki-influenced pop art variety, often painted in rainbow palettes set to neon levels of
bright. There is also a ton of art-adjacent
gifts – posters, books, stickers, patches and
prints – influenced by this playful aesthetic.
One of the few Wynwood galleries younger
kids will get a kick out of.

Malaquita   ARTS & CRAFTS
(Map p112; www.malaquitadesign.com; 2613 NW
2nd Ave; ☺11am-8pm) This artfully designed
store has merchandise you won't find elsewhere, including lovely handblown vases,
embroidered clothing, Mesoamerican tapestries, vibrantly painted bowls, handwoven
palm baskets and other fair-trade objects –
some of which are made by indigenous artisans in Mexico.

🔒 Little Haiti & the Upper East Side

Sweat Records   MUSIC
(Map p122; ☑786-693-9309; www.sweatrecords
miami.com; 5505 NE 2nd Ave; ☺noon-10pm Mon-
Sat, to 5pm Sun) Sweat's almost a stereotypical
indie record store – there's funky art and
graffiti on the walls, it sells weird Japanese
toys, there are tattooed staff with thick glasses arguing over LPs and EPs you've never
heard of and, of course, there's coffee and
vegan snacks.

Libreri Mapou   BOOKS
(Map p122; ☑305-757-9922; http://mapoubooks.
com; 5919 NE 2nd Ave; ☺11am-7pm Mon-Fri, 10am-
8pm Sat, 11am-5pm Sun) The center of literary
life in Little Haiti, this bookstore specializes

Little Havana

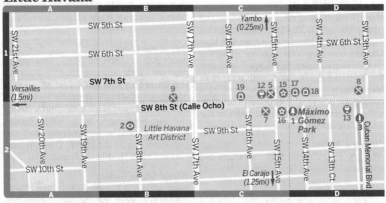

Little Havana

in English, French and Creole titles and periodicals, with thousands of great titles and live events. The owner, Jan Mapou, is a writer and political thinker, of some distinction.

🛍 Little Havana

Havana Collection   CLOTHING
(Map p140; ☑786-717-7474; www.facebook.com/TheHavanaCollection; 1421 SW 8th St; ◷10am-6pm) One of the best and most striking collections of the classic traditional *guayaberas* in Miami can be found in this shop. Prices are high (plan on spending about $85 for a shirt), but so is the quality, so you can be assured of a long-lasting product.

La Isla   ART
(Map p140; ☑786-317-3051; https://laislausa.com; 1561 SW 8th St; ◷9am-5pm) This hip outpost of the new(er) Little Havana showcases

Cuban-inspired pop art, graphic design and clever gifts (a poster of a certain *Star Wars* droid smoking a cigar titled 'Arturito' had us cracking up). La Isla promotes a Cuba more rooted in contemporary cool than black-and-white photos of cigar rollers, and is a great spot for a unique souvenir.

Guantanamera   CIGARS
(Map p140; ☑786-618-5142; www.guantanameracigars.com; 1465 SW 8th St; ◷10:30am-8pm Sun-Wed, to 10pm Thu, to 3am Fri & Sat) In a central location in Little Havana, Guantanamera sells high-quality hand-rolled cigars, plus strong Cuban coffee. It's an atmospheric shop, where you can stop for a smoke, a drink (there's a bar here) and some friendly banter. There's also some great live music most nights of the week. The rocking chairs in front are a fine perch for people-watching.

Books & Books

BOOKS

(Map p134; ✆305-442-4408; https://booksand books.com; 265 Aragon Ave; ⊗9am-11pm Sun-Thu, to midnight Fri & Sat) The best indie bookstore in South Florida – with branches across town – is a wonderful place to stock up on your beach reading material and see authors in action at one of the frequent in-store events. There's a nice cafe and restaurant, with dining on a Mediterranean-like patio fronting the shop.

Boy Meets Girl

CHILDREN'S CLOTHING

(Map p134; ✆305-445-9668; www.bmgkids. com; 358 San Lorenzo Ave, Village of Merrick Park; ⊗10am-8pm Mon-Sat, 11am-7pm Sun) Fantastically upscale and frankly expensive clothing for wee ones – if the kids are getting past puberty, look elsewhere, but otherwise they'll be fashionable far before they realize it.

Coconut Grove

Polished Coconut

FASHION & ACCESSORIES

(✆305-443-3220; www.facebook.com/Polished Coconut; 3600 Grand Ave Village West; ⊗11am-6pm Mon-Sat, noon-5pm Sun) 🍽 Colorful textiles from Central and South America are transformed into lovely accessories and home decor at this eye-catching store in the heart of Coconut Grove. You'll find handbags, satchels, belts, sun hats, pillows, bedspreads and table runners made by artisans inspired by traditional indigenous designs.

Midori Gallery

ANTIQUES

(Map p126; ✆305-443-3399; www.midorigallery. com; 3168 Commodore Plaza; ⊗11am-6pm Tue-Sat) Filled with antiques and oddities from across Asia, the Midori Gallery also surprises with a lacquer Japanese sake flash here and a standing Burmese Buddha there. It feels like the sort of shop Indiana Jones uses to decorate his study.

Coral Gables

★ Retro City Collectibles

MUSIC

(Gables Records n Comics; Map p134; ✆786-879-4407; 277 Miracle Mile, 2nd fl; ⊗3-6pm Wed-Fri, 1-7pm Sat, to 4pm Sun) This cluttered little upstairs den of geekery is a fun place to browse, with all manner of eye-catching and collectible genre artifacts. You'll find comic books, records, baseball cards, Pez dispensers, old film posters and action figures (*Star Wars, Star Trek, Doctor Who* etc).

Key Biscayne

Boheme Boutique

CLOTHING

(Map p114; ✆305-361-7474; www.modaboheme. com; 650 Crandon Blvd; ⊗11am-8pm Mon-Sat) Simple-but-chic dresses, flow-y wraps, wispy tunics: there's an aesthetic to the clothes here, one that is is light and linen-y, and perfect for Miami's more relaxed offshore island. Bonus points for the friendly, enthusiastic staff.

❶ Information

MEDICAL SERVICES

Mount Sinai Medical Center (✆305-676-6496, emergency room 305-563-8026; www. msmc.com; 4300 Alton Rd; ⊗24hr) The area's best emergency room.

TOURIST INFORMATION

Art Deco Welcome Center (Map p70; ✆305-672-2014; www.mdpl.org; 1001 Ocean Dr, South Beach; ⊗9:30am-5pm Fri-Wed, to 7pm Thu) Run by the Miami Design Preservation League (MDPL), it has tons of art-deco-district information and organizes excellent walking tours. There's a museum (p68) attached to the center that provides a great overview of the art deco district.

Greater Miami & the Beaches Convention & Visitors Bureau (Map p100; ✆305-539-3000; www.miamiandbeaches.com; 701 Brickell Ave, 27th fl; ⊗8:30am-6pm Mon-Fri) This visitors bureau offers loads of info on Miami and keeps up-to-date with the latest events and cultural offerings. It is located in an oddly intimidating high-rise building.

LGBT Visitor Center (Map p76; ✆305-397-8914; www.gogaymiami.com; 1130 Washington

Ave; ⊙ 9am-6pm Mon-Fri, 11am-4pm Sat & Sun) An excellent source for all LGBT info on Miami, this friendly welcome center has loads of recommendations on sights, restaurants, nightlife and cultural goings-on. It also hosts meetings and other events.

Check the website for Pink Flamingo–certified hotels, ie hotels that are most welcoming to the LGBT crowd.

❶ Getting There & Away

The majority of travelers come to Miami by air, although it's feasible to arrive by car, bus or even train. Miami is a major international airline hub, with flights to many cities across the USA, Latin America and Europe. Most flights come into Miami International Airport (MIA), although many are also directed to Fort Lauderdale-Hollywood International Airport (FLL). Figure 3½ hours from New York City, five hours from Los Angeles, and 10 hours from London or Madrid.

Flights, tours and rail tickets can be booked online at www.lonelyplanet.com/bookings.

AIR
Miami International Airport

Located 6 miles west of Downtown, the busy **Miami International Airport** (MIA; ☑ 305-876-7000; www.miami-airport.com; 2100 NW 42nd Ave) has three terminals and serves more than 45 million passengers each year. Around 60 airlines fly into Miami. The airport is open 24 hours and is laid out in a horseshoe design. There are left-luggage facilities at Concourse E in the Central Terminal (call 305-869-1163 for more information).

Fort Lauderdale-Hollywood International Airport

Fort Lauderdale-Hollywood International Airport (FLL; www.fll.net), around 26 miles north of Downtown Miami, largely serves domestic passengers and is well connected to major hubs like New York and Atlanta.

BOAT

Though it's doubtful you'll be catching a steamer to make a trans-Atlantic journey, it is quite possible that you'll arrive in Miami via a cruise ship, as the **Port of Miami** (☑ 305-347-4800; www.miamidade.gov/portmiami), which receives around five million passengers each year, is known as the cruise capital of the world. Arriving in the port will put you on the edge of Downtown Miami; taxis and public buses to other local points are available from nearby Biscayne Blvd.

BUS

For bus trips, **Greyhound** (www.greyhound.com) is the main long-distance operator. Megabus offers a service to Tampa and Orlando.

Greyhound's main bus terminal is near the airport.

If you are traveling very long distances (say, across several states), bargain airfares can sometimes undercut buses. On shorter routes, renting a car can sometimes be cheaper. Nonetheless, discounted (even half-price) long-distance bus trips are often available by purchasing tickets online seven to 14 days in advance.

TRAIN

The main Miami terminal of **Amtrak** (☑ 305-835-1222; www.amtrak.com; 8303 NW 37th Ave, West Little River), about 9 miles northwest of Downtown, connects the city with several other points in Florida (including Orlando and Jacksonville) on the Silver Service line that runs up to New York City. Travel time between New York and Miami is 27 to 31 hours. The Miami Amtrak station is connected by Tri-Rail to Downtown Miami and has a left-luggage facility.

MiamiCentral (p79) station, located Downtown, will be the home of Brightline trains, which will connect to West Palm Beach and Orlando.

❶ Getting Around

TO/FROM THE AIRPORT
Miami International Airport

Buses Metro buses leave from Miami Airport Station (connected by electric rail to the airport) and run throughout the city; fares are $2.25. The Miami Beach Airport Express (bus 150) also costs $2.25 and makes stops all along Miami Beach, from 41st to the southern tip; it runs from 6am to 11:40pm.

Shuttles Some hotels offer free shuttles.

Taxi From Miami International Airport, taxis charge a flat rate, which varies depending on where you're heading. It's $22 to Downtown, Coconut Grove or Coral Gables; $35 to South Beach; and $44 to Key Biscayne. Count on 40 minutes to South Beach in average traffic, and about 25 minutes to Downtown. Note that 'average traffic' is more of a happy exception than the rule in this town. Rush hours and/or accidents could mean you're spending an hour in the cab.

Fort Lauderdale-Hollywood International Airport

Shuttles Shared van service is available from the airport with **GO Airport Shuttle** (☑ 773-363-0001; https://goairportshuttle.com). Prices are around $25 to South Beach.

Taxi Count on at least 45 minutes from the airport to Downtown by taxi, and at least an hour for the ride to South Beach. Prices are metered. Expect to pay about $75 to South Beach and $65 to Downtown.

Train Take the free shuttle (with stops at the west end of terminal 1, between terminals 2 and 3, and between terminals 3 and 4) to the airport's Tri-Rail station (www.tri-rail.com). There you can hop aboard this commuter train into Miami ($3.75 to $5), which connects with Miami-Dade's Metrorail Orange Line. The schedule is infrequent though (trains run every 30 to 60 minutes), so be mindful of departure times to avoid long waits.

BICYCLE

Citi Bike (☑ 305-532-9494; https://www.citibikemiami.com; rental per 30min $4.50, 1/2/4hr $6.50/10/18, day $24) is a bike-share program where you can borrow a bike from scores of kiosks spread around Miami and Miami Beach. Miami is flat, but traffic can be horrendous (abundant and fast-moving), and there isn't much of a biking culture (or respect for bikers) just yet. Free paper maps of the bike network are available at some kiosks, or you can find one online. There's also a handy app that shows you where the nearest stations are.

For longer rides, clunky Citi Bikes are not ideal (no helmet, no lock and only three gears).

Note that a variety of scooters are also available to rent via third party apps throughout Miami Beach, Downtown and Wynwood.

BUS

Miami's local bus system is called **Metrobus** (☑ 305-891-3131; www.miamidade.gov/transit/routes.asp; tickets $2.25). It can get you most places you're trying to go, but it won't get you there very quickly. Each bus route has a different schedule and routes generally run from about 5:30am to 11pm, though some are 24 hours. Rides cost $2.25 and must be paid in exact change (coins or a combination of bills and coins) or with an Easy Card (available for purchase from Metrorail stations and some shops and pharmacies). An easy-to-read route map is available online. Note that if you have to transfer buses, you'll have to pay the fare each time if paying in cash. With an Easy Card, transfers are free.

Megabus (https://us.megabus.com; Miami International Center, 3801 NW 21st St) Megabus offers a bus service to Orlando and Tampa. Buses depart from a stop near the airport.

MIAMI TROLLEYS

A free bus service serves Miami, Miami Beach, Coconut Grove, Little Havana and Coral Gables, among other locations. Called the Trolley (www.miamigov.com/trolley) it's actually a hybrid-electric bus disguised as an orange-and-green trolley. There are numerous routes, though they're made for getting around neighborhoods and not *between* them.

The most useful for travelers are the following:

Biscayne Travels along Biscayne Blvd; handy for transportation from Brickell to Downtown and up to the edge of Wynwood.

Brickell Connects Brickell area (south of the Miami River in the Downtown area) with the Vizcaya Museum & Gardens.

Coral Way Goes from Downtown (near the Freedom Tower) to downtown Coral Gables.

Wynwood Zigzags through town, from the Adrienne Arsht Center for the Performing Arts up through Wynwood along NW 2nd Ave to 29th St.

MIAMI BEACH TROLLEYS

Miami Beach has four free trolleys (www.miamibeachfl.gov/transportation) running along different routes, with arrivals every 10 to 15 minutes from 6am to midnight (from 8am on Sundays).

Alton-West Loop Runs up (north) Alton Rd and down (south) West Ave between 6th St and Lincoln Rd.

Collins Link Runs along Collins Ave from 37th St to 73rd St. Catch it southbound from Abbott Ave and Indian Creek Dr.

Middle Beach Loop Runs up Collins Ave and down Indian Creek Dr between 20th and 44th Sts (southbound it also zigzags over to Lincoln Rd).

North Beach Loop Runs 65th to 88th St.

TRAIN

The **Metromover** (☑ 305-891-3131; www.miamidade.gov/transit/metromover.asp; ☺ 5am-midnight), which is equal parts bus, monorail and train, is helpful for getting around Downtown Miami. It offers visitors a great perspective on the city and a free orientation tour of the area.

Metrorail (www.miamidade.gov/transit/metrorail.asp; one-way ticket $2.25) is a 21-mile-long heavy-rail system that has one elevated line running from Hialeah through Downtown Miami and south to Kendall/Dadeland. Trains run every five to 15 minutes from 6am to midnight. Pay with either the reloadable Easy Card or single-use Easy Ticket, which are sold from vending machines at Metrorail stations.

The regional **Tri-Rail** (☑ 800-874-7245; www.tri-rail.com) double-decker commuter trains run the 71 miles between Dade, Broward and Palm Beach counties. Fares are calculated on a zone basis; the shortest distance traveled costs $4.40 round-trip; the most you'll ever pay is for the ride between MIA and West Palm Beach ($11.55 round trip). No tickets are sold on the train, so allow time to make your purchase before boarding. All trains and stations are accessible to riders with disabilities. For a list of stations, log on to the Tri-Rail website.

AT A GLANCE

★

POPULATION
95,000

BIRD SPECIES
350

BEST FRUIT STAND
Robert Is Here (p163)

BEST GUIDED WALK
Slough slog (p151)

BEST RESTAURANT
Havana Cafe (p160)

WHEN TO GO
Dec–Mar
Dry season: top wildlife viewing along watercourses, but some kayaking will be difficult.

Apr–Jun
Although the weather gets pretty hot, there's a good mix of water and wildlife.

Jul–Nov
Lots of heat, lots of bugs and chances of hurricanes.

Anhinga Trail (p150)
CHRISTIAN OUELLET/SHUTTERSTOCK ©

The Everglades & Biscayne

There is no wilderness in America quite like the Everglades. Called the 'River of Grass' by Native American inhabitants, this is not just a wetland, or a swamp, or a lake, or a river, or a prairie, or a grassland – it is all of those, twisted together into a series of soft horizons, long vistas, and sunsets that stretch across your entire field of vision, all animated by an extraordinary cast of wild creatures.

The park's quiet majesty is evident when you see anhinga flexing their wings before breaking into a corkscrew dive, or the slow, rhythmic flap of a great blue heron gliding over its domain while being watched by alligators below, or the shimmer of light on miles of untrammeled saw grass as the sun sets behind hunkering cypress domes. In a nation where natural beauty is measured by its capacity for drama, the Everglades subtly, contentedly flows on.

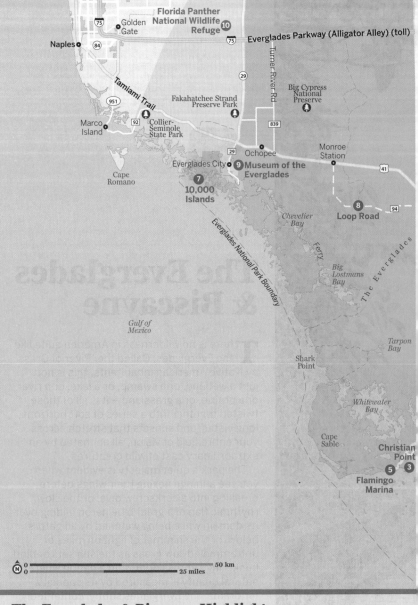

Florida Panther
National Wildlife
Refuge **10**

75 Golden
Gate

Naples ●

84

Everglades Parkway (Alligator Alley) (toll)

75

Tamiami Trail

951

Fakahatchee Strand
Preserve Park

29

Turner River Rd

Big Cypress
National
Preserve

839

Marco
Island

92

Collier-
Seminole
State Park

29 Ochopee

Monroe
Station

41

Cape
Romano

Everglades City ● **9** Museum of the
Everglades

7
10,000
Islands

8
Loop Road

94

Chevelier
Bay

Everglades National Park Boundary

Ferry

The Everglades

Big
Lostmans
Bay

Gulf of
Mexico

Tarpon
Bay

Shark
Point

Whitewater
Bay

Cape
Sable

Christian
Point

5 **3**

Flamingo
Marina

N 0 ——————————— 50 km
0 ——————————— 25 miles

The Everglades & Biscayne Highlights

1 **Anhinga Trail** (p150)
Spotting alligators by day or
night, and watching nesting
waterbirds.

2 **Shark Valley** (p155)
Spying gators, turtles and birds
on a walk, bike ride or tram tour.

3 **Christian Point** (p150)
Hiking one of the best walks in
the southern Everglades.

4 **Hell's Bay Canoe Trail**
(p149) Paddling through
scenic swamps and mangrove
creeks.

5 **Flamingo Marina** (p156)
Looking for manatees and
crocodiles in the far south.

6 **Pa-hay-okee Overlook**
(p157) Watching the sun set
over the ingress road from the
roof of your car.

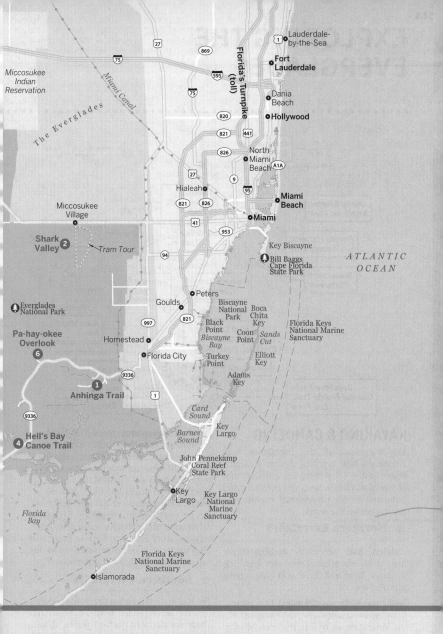

EXPLORING THE EVERGLADES

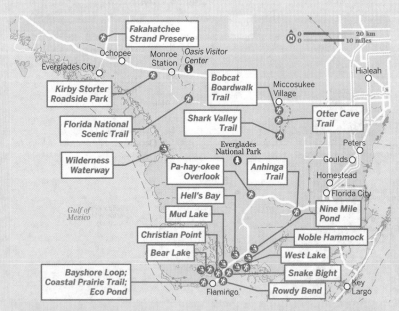

Fakahatchee Strand Preserve
Ochopee Monroe Oasis Visitor
Station Center
Everglades City
Hialeah
Kirby Storter Roadside Park
Bobcat Boardwalk Trail
Miccosukee Village
Florida National Scenic Trail
Shark Valley Trail
Otter Cave Trail
Everglades National Park
Peters
Wilderness Waterway
Pa-hay-okee Overlook
Anhinga Trail
Goulds
Homestead
Hell's Bay
Florida City
Gulf of Mexico
Mud Lake
Nine Mile Pond
Christian Point
Noble Hammock
Bear Lake
West Lake
Bayshore Loop; Coastal Prairie Trail; Eco Pond
Snake Bight
Flamingo
Rowdy Bend
Key Largo

KAYAKING & CANOEING

The waterways of the Everglades rank among the best kayaking destinations anywhere in the US – there are infinite trails, plenty of wildlife to keep you company, and numerous highly professional operators to get you out on the water.

☆ Northern Everglades

Paddlers have seemingly endless choice here, with countless Everglades channels to choose from and the 10,000 Islands lying just offshore.

Wilderness Waterway (99 miles) This route between Everglades City and Flamingo is the longest canoe trail in the area. Most islands are fringed by narrow beaches with sugar-white sand, but note that the water is brackish, and very shallow most of the time. It's not Tahiti, but it's fascinating. You can camp on your own island for up to a week.

Everglades Adventures (p160) This highly recommended outfitter offers a range of half-day kayak tours, from sunrise paddles to twilight trips through mangroves that return under a sky full of stars. Tours shuttle you to places like Chokoloskee Island, Collier-Seminole State Park, Rabbit Key or Tiger Key for excursions. Everglades Adventures also provides one-way shuttle services (from Flamingo back to Everglades City) for those making the seven- to 10-day trip along the Wilderness Waterway.

☆ Southern Everglades

The real joy in this part of the park is paddling into the bracken-filled heart of the swamp. There are plenty of push-off points, all with names that sound like they come from Frodo's map to Mordor, including Hell's Bay, Snake Bight and Graveyard Creek. If you plan to camp along any of the following trails, you need to pick up a backcountry permit (p158) from any park visitor center. Rent canoes and kayaks at Flamingo Everglades (p151).

A little local knowledge can take you a very long way in the Everglades. Hike along trails and boardwalks, kayak the waterways or take a tour to get the expert low-down on this spectacular wilderness.

Nine Mile Pond (3- or 5.2-mile loop) Paddle through grassy marshes and mangrove islands, following the numbered white poles; for the shorter version, take the cut-through from marker #44. Allow four hours for the full loop. It's good for spotting alligators, wading birds and turtles.

Noble Hammock (2 miles return) Short loop with some challenging tight corners; check water levels in the dry season before setting out.

Hell's Bay (5.5 miles one way) Despite the frightening name (and terrible mosquitoes), this can be a magnificent place to kayak. 'Hell to get into and hell to get out of' was how this sheltered launch was described by old Glades aficionados, but once inside you'll find a capillary network of mangrove creeks, saw-grass islands and shifting mudflats, where the brambles form a green tunnel and all you can smell is sea salt and the dark organic breath of the swamp. Three *chickee* (wooden platform above the waterline) sites are spaced along the trail. Allow six to eight hours for the return trip.

West Lake (7.7 miles one way) Cross open lakes linked by narrow creeks to Alligator Creek; good for alligators and crocodiles.

Mud Lake (7 miles return) Paddle through mangroves between Coot Bay Pond and Mud Lake.

Bear Lake (11.5 miles one way) Classic Everglades trail, but closed since 2017 due to hurricane damage; check at the Flamingo Visitor Center to see if it has reopened.

On the property of the Robert Is Here (p163) fruit stand, **Garls Coastal Kayak-ing Everglades** (☑ 305-393-3223; www.garlscoastal kayaking.com; 19200 SW 344th St, Homestead; single/double kayak per day $40/55, half-/full-day tour $125/160) leads highly recommended excursions into the Everglades. A full-day 'Day in the Glades' outing includes hiking (more of a wet walk or slog into the lush landscape of cypress domes), followed by kayaking in both the mangroves and in Florida Bay, and, time

permitting, a night walk. For a DIY adventure, you can also hire kayaks as well as other equipment – including tents, sleeping bags and fishing gear.

The most isolated portion of the park is a squat marina where you can go on a back-country boat tour or rent boats. Due to its isolation, this area is subject to closure during bad weather. You can rent kayaks and canoes from Flamingo Everglades (p151); if you do, you're largely left to explore the channels and islands of Florida Bay on your own. During rough weather be cautious, even when on land, as storm surges can turn an attractive spread of beach into a watery stretch of danger fairly quickly.

HIKING

Getting out on the water may allow you to go deeper into the Everglades wilderness, but the numerous hiking trails are more accessible, even to those with very basic levels of fitness. Most trails are no longer than 1 mile return, although there are a couple of longer trails to really leave the world behind you.

☆ Northern Everglades

All along the Tamiami Trail, short and well-signposted boardwalk tracks take you just beyond the road. The Fakahatchee Strand Preserve (p155) is another possibility.

Kirby Storter Roadside Park (1 mile return) Probably the pick of the short walks close to the main road. Though short in terms of length, this elevated **boardwalk** (☑ 239-695-2000; www.nps.gov/bicy/planyourvisit/kirby-storter-roadside-park.htm; ☉ 24hr) FREE leads to a lovely overlook where you can often see a variety of birdlife (such as ibis and red-shouldered hawks) amid tall cypresses and strangler figs, plus of course alligators.

Bobcat Boardwalk Trail (0.5-mile loop) At the park entrance going into Shark Valley, this easy trail makes a loop through a thick copse of tropical hardwoods before emptying you out right back into the Shark Valley parking lot.

Otter Cave Trail (0.25 miles one-way)
In a similar area, this trail heads over a limestone shelf that has been Swiss-cheesed into a porous sponge by rainwater. Animals now live in the eroded holes (although it's not likely you'll spot any) and Native Americans used to live on top of the shelf.

Shark Valley Trail (15 miles return) This excellent trail takes you past small creeks, tropical forest and 'borrow pits' (human-made holes that are now basking spots for gators, turtles and birdlife). The pancake-flat trail is perfect for bicycles, which can be rented at the entrance for $10 per hour. Bring water.

Florida National Scenic Trail There are some 31 miles of the Florida National Scenic Trail within Big Cypress National Preserve. From the southern terminus, which can be accessed via Loop Rd, the trail runs 8.3 miles north to US 41. The way is flat, but it's hard going: you'll almost certainly be wading through water, and you'll have to pick through a series of solution holes (small sinkholes) and thick hardwood hammocks (forests). There is often no shelter from the sun, and the bugs are...plentiful. There are three primitive campsites with water wells along the trail; pick up a map and a free hiking permit (required) at the Oasis Visitor Center (p158).

☆ Southern Everglades

Anhinga Trail (0.8 mile one way) You'll get a close-up view of gators and birds on this short trail that begins at the Royal Palm Visitor Center (p157). The park also offers periodic ranger-led walks along the boardwalk at night, though you can always do this by yourself.

West Lake Trail (1.8 miles one way) This trail runs through the largest protected mangrove forest in the Northern Hemisphere.

Snake Bight (1.8 miles one way) Signposted off the main park road a few miles northeast of the Flamingo Visitor Center (p158), this walk skirts a bay and passes through tropical hardwood hammock, a real Everglades specialty; high tide brings good birdlife.

Rowdy Bend (2.6 miles one way) Follow an overgrown access road through buttonwoods and coastal prairie; the trail has an option to connect with the Snake Bight Trail.

Christian Point (2 miles one way) This dramatic walk takes you under tropical forest, past columns of white cypress and over a series of mudflats, and ends with a dramatic view of the windswept shores of Florida Bay.

Bear Lake (1.6 miles one way) Hardwood hammock and mangroves line the Homestead Canal along a trail rich in woodland birds and Caribbean tree species. You can drive to the trailhead from the main State Rd 9336; otherwise, add 2 miles to the walk one way.

Anhinga Trail

BLUEBARRONPHOTO/SHUTTERSTOCK ©

BEST FREE PARK ACTIVITIES

The $30 entrance fee for the Everglades National Park ends up being great value if you take advantage of the park's many free ranger-led activities. Reserve popular activities (canoeing, biking) up to one week in advance. Among the highlights:

Slough slog Escape the crowds and immerse yourself in the wilderness on a 1–2 mile guided walk/wade through muddy and watery terrain into a cypress dome. Wear long pants, socks and lace-up shoes that can get wet. Meets at Royal Palm Visitor Center (p157).

Starlight walk Evening walk along the Anhinga Trail looking for gators and other creatures by nightfall. Bring a flashlight.

Bike hike A 2½-hour bike ride exploring the Everglades on two wheels. Bikes and helmets provided. Departs from Ernest Coe Visitor Center (p156).

Canoe the wilderness A three-hour morning paddle through some of the Everglades' best scenery. Meets at Flamingo Visitor Center (p158) and at Gulf Coast Visitor Center (p158).

Early bird walk Join a morning hike looking for, and learning about, some of the Everglades' feathered species. Meets at Flamingo Visitor Center (p158).

Glades glimpse Learn about some of the wonders of the Everglades at a daily talk given by rangers at the Royal Palm Visitor Center (p157) and at the Shark Valley Visitor Center (p158), typically from 1:30pm to 2pm.

Coastal Prairie Trail (7.5 miles one way) Follow the traditional path of fishers across open prairies and stands of buttonwoods. It begins at the Flamingo Campground (p158); a shorter version off the main trail called **Bayshore Loop (2-mile loop)** is an alternative for those with limited time.

Eco Pond (0.5 mile return) Across the main road from the Flamingo Visitor Center, this short loop around Eco Pond is good for seeing birds and gators.

Other Short Walks All of the following are half a mile long. **Mahogany Hammock** leads into an 'island' of hardwood forest floating on the waterlogged prairie, while the **Pinelands** takes you through a copse of rare spindly swamp pine and palmetto forest. Further on, **Pa-hay-okee Overlook** (p157) is a raised platform that has some of the best views in the Everglades.

BOAT TOURS

The best selection of boat tours operate in the northern Everglades, from along the Tamiami Trail, Everglades City, and out into the 10,000 Islands. In addition to the other operators, the Gulf Coast Visitor Center (p158) rents out kayaks and canoes in Everglades City. Be sure to take a map with you (they're available in the visitor center). Boaters will want to reference NOAA Charts 11430 and 11432. Keep an eye out for manatees in the marina. In the southern Everglades, **Flamingo Everglades** (☏855-798-2207; www.flamingoeverglades.com; tours per adult/child $40/20, canoe rental 2/4/8hr

$20/28/38, kayak rental half-/full-day $35/45; ⏱marina 7am-7pm Mon-Fri, from 6am Sat & Sun) also runs guided boat tours. Listed below are outfits operating boat tours:

Everglades National Park Boat Tours (☏239-695-2591; www.nps.gov/ever/planyourvisit/guidedtours.htm; 905 Copeland Ave) Tours, lasting just under two hours, go either into the mangrove wilderness (adult/child $50/25) or out among the 10,000 Islands (adult/child $40/20), where it's lucky you may see dolphins.

Everglades Florida Adventures (☏855-793-5542; https://evergladesfloridaadventures.com; 815 Oyster Bar Lane; adult/child $40/20) Departing from the marina next to the Gulf Coast Visitor Center, this is a 90-minute boat trip into the 10,000 Islands. Houseboat and kayak rentals are also available.

Everglades Adventure Tours (EAT; ☏800-504-6554; www.evergladesadventuretours.com; 40904 Tamiami Trail E; 2hr kayak/pole-boat tour per person from $99/108) The EAT guys are based out of the same headquarters as the Skunk Ape people and offersome of the best private Everglades tours. Whether you go on a swamp hike, a 'safari' or a night tour, being poled around in a canoe or skiff by some genuinely funny guys with deep local knowledge of the Grassy Waters is an absolute treat.

Smallwood Store Boat Tour (p162) Departing from a dock below the Smallwood Store (p159), this small family-run outfit offers excellent private tours taking you out among the 10,000 Islands. You'll see loads of birds, and more than likely a few bottlenose dolphins.

History

Following the European settlement of Florida, some pioneers saw the potential for economic development of the Grassy Waters.

Cattle ranchers and sugar growers, attracted by mucky waters and Florida's subtropical climate (paradise for sugarcane), successfully pressured the government to make land available to them. In 1905 Florida governor Napoleon Bonaparte Broward personally dug the first shovelful of earth for a diversion that connected the Caloosahatchee River to Lake Okeechobee. Hundreds of canals were cut through the Everglades to the coastline to 'reclaim' the land, and the flow of lake water was restricted by a series of dikes. Farmland began to claim areas previously uninhabited by humans.

In her famous book, *The Everglades: River of Grass*, Marjory Stoneman Douglas (1890–1998) revealed that Gerard de Brahm, a colonial cartographer, named the region the River Glades, which became Ever Glades on later English maps.

Native American Everglades

The Everglades were an utter wilderness for thousands of years. Even Native Americans avoided the Glades; the 'native' Seminole and Miccosukee actually settled here as exiles escaping war and displacement from other parts of the country.

When a changing climate helped to form the Everglades as we now know it around 5000 years ago, two Native American peoples, the Calusa and Tequesta, inhabited the area; the former's territory centred on Fort Myers and as far north as Tampa, while the latter lived in Florida's southeast. Both were hunter-gatherer peoples and while they fished and hunted in the Everglades, they never lived within them, save for temporary campsites. As was the case for so many indigenous groups, the arrival of Spanish explorers and settlers from the 17th century onward wrought devastation upon indigenous society, and very few survived.

The Muscogee (Creek) Nation, originally from Alabama and Georgia, incorporated the remnants of other, smaller tribes, as well as, according to some reports, a number of escaped former slaves. In the process of migrating south through Florida, some of these bands became known as the Seminoles – the name is believed to come from a Spanish word that may mean 'those who have broken away.' By the mid-19th century, the Seminole and Miccosukee, another band of descendants from the Muscogee (Creek) nation, were living in the Everglades region, as well as further north. The three Seminole Wars pitted the US army against Native Americans, and more than 4000 Native Americans were killed or displaced; many Native Americans were removed from the area and resettled in Oklahoma. Rather than surrender, more than 100 Seminole and Miccosukees sought refuge in the Everglades. There they lived in what became known as 'hammock camps,' and they survived relatively undisturbed for almost a century.

BOOKS ABOUT THE EVERGLADES

➡ *The Everglades: River of Grass* (Marjory Stoneman Douglas, 1947) This landmark book introduced the Everglades to the outside world and was a call to action to protect the Everglades ecosystem.

➡ *Death in the Everglades: The Murder of Guy Bradley, America's First Martyr to Environmentalism* (Stuart B McIver, 2003) True crime story that takes you into the murky world of the resistance faced by conservationists who would save the Everglades.

➡ *The Swamp: The Everglades, Florida, and the Politics of Paradise* (Michael Grunwald, 2007) Fascinating and highly readable journey through Everglades history, with detailed studies of the threats to the Everglades and some of the conservation efforts to save it.

➡ *Shadow Country* (Peter Matthiessen, 2008) National Book Award–winning novel set in the 10,000 Islands and surroundings during the pioneer days. There is no more beautiful evocation of the Everglades and its history.

➡ *Swamplandia* (Karen Russell, 2011) Fast-paced fictional family drama set in the Everglades and a gator-wrestling theme park.

ℹ️ EVERGLADES PRACTICALITIES

Gateway Towns

Although you could visit from Naples or Miami, the main gateway towns for Everglades National Park are Everglades City (p159), northwest of the park, and Homestead and Florida City (p161), for the east and southeast.

Park Entrances

There are three main entrances and three main areas of the park:

Gulf Coast section The park's northwest region, past Everglades City.

Shark Valley section At the central-north side on the Tamiami Trail.

Ernest Coe section Along the southeast edge near Homestead and Florida City.

Admission Fee

The admission fee – $30 per vehicle, $15 per hiker and cyclist – covers the whole park, and is good for seven consecutive days. Because the Tamiami Trail is a public road, there's no admission to access national park sights along this highway, aside from Shark Valley.

Throughout the 20th century, the growing settler population in south Florida, the building of roads like the Tamiami Trail, the development of towns such as Everglades City, and increasing tourism infrastructure and visitors all contributed to the decline of traditional ways of life. Most Seminole and Miccosukee people now depend upon indigenous-owned casinos and tourism for their livelihoods. Most of those who remain in the region are descendants of those who hid out in the Everglades during and after the Seminole Wars.

For a glimpse of traditional life, visit the Miccosukee Indian Village (p156) along the Tamiami Trail or the Ah-Tah-Thi-Ki Seminole Indian Museum (p156) in the Big Cypress Preserve.

Natural History

It's tempting to think of the Everglades as a swamp, but 'flooded prairie' may be a more apt description. The Glades, at the end of the day, are grasslands that happen to be flooded for most of the year: visit during the dry season (winter) and you'd be forgiven for thinking the Everglades was the Everfields.

So where's the water coming from? Look north on a map of Florida, all the way to Lake Okeechobee and the small lakes and rivers that band together around Kissimmee. Florida dips into the Gulf of Mexico at its below-sea-level tip, which happens to be the lowest part of the state geographically

and topographically. Run-off water from central Florida flows down the peninsula via streams and rivers, over and through the Glades, and into Florida Bay. The glacial pace of the flood means this seemingly stillest of landscapes is actually in constant motion. Small wonder the Native Americans called the area Pa-hay-okee (grassy water).

So what happens when nutrient-rich water creeps over a limestone shelf? The ecological equivalent of a sweaty orgy. Beginning at the cellular level, organic material blooms in surprising ways, clumping and forming into algal beds, nutrient blooms and the ubiquitous periphyton, which are basically clusters of algae, bacteria and detritus (ie stuff).

Periphyton ain't pretty: in the water it resembles streaks of vomit, and the dried version looks like hippo turds. But you should kiss this biological soup when you see it (well, maybe not) because in the great chain of the Everglades, this slop forms the base of a very tall organic totem pole. The smallest tilt in elevation alters the flow of water and hence the content of this nutrient soup, and thus the landscape itself: all those patches of cypress and hardwood hammock (not a bed for backpackers; in this case, hammock is a fancy Floridian way of saying a forest of broadleaf trees, mainly tropical or subtropical) are areas where a few inches of altitude create a world of difference between ecosystems.

EVERGLADES NATIONAL PARK

This vast **wilderness** (☑305-242-7700; www.nps.gov/ever; 40001 State Rd 9336, Homestead; vehicle pass $30, pedestrian & cyclist $15; ☺visitor center 9am-5pm; 🅿), encompassing 1.5 million acres, is one of America's great natural treasures and certainly the best place to see wildlife in Florida. Utterly unlike anywhere else in the state, this is a place where the natural world takes over, with a vast network of islands and watery channels sheltering plenty of alligators, abundant birdlife and a real sense of being far from the world and its noise. There's much to see and do – from hiking past basking alligators as herons stalk patiently through nearby waters in search of prey, to kayaking through mangrove canals and on peaceful lakes. You can also wade into murky knee-high waters among cypress domes on a rough-and-ready 'slough slog.'

There are sunrise strolls on boardwalks amid the awakening of birdsong, and moonlit glimpses of gators swimming gracefully along narrow channels in search of dinner. Backcountry camping, bicycle tours and ranger-led activities help bring the magic of this place to life. The biggest challenge is really just deciding where to begin.

WILDLIFE: THE BEST PLACES TO SEE...

Alligator Shark Valley, Anhinga Trail (p150), Fakahatchee Strand Preserve

Crocodile Flamingo Marina (p156), 10,000 Islands (p162)

Manatee Flamingo Marina (p156), Gulf Coast Visitor Center (p158), Big Cypress Swamp Welcome Center (p158)

Bottlenose Dolphin 10,000 Islands (p162)

Birdlife Anhinga Trail (p150), Shark Valley

Florida Panther Everywhere and nowhere... Big Cypress National Preserve, Florida Panther National Wildlife Refuge (p160)

☉ Sights & Activities

☉ Northern Everglades

As you fly over the northern Everglades on your approach into Miami International Airport, the incongruity of this extraordinary wilderness is impossible to miss. One minute, there are watery grasslands and barely a sign of human life as far as the eye can see. The next, you're in Miami, that poster child for Florida's all-consuming coastal development. Once on the ground, the Tamiami Trail/Hwy 41 cuts through the Everglades, from Calle Ocho in Miami's Little Havana to the Gulf of Mexico. All along this road, in whichever direction you're traveling, this trip traverses long landscapes of flooded forest, pine woods, gambling halls, swamp-buggy tours and roadside food shacks.

Ochopee   VILLAGE
(38000 Tamiami Trail E; ☺8-10am & noon-4pm Mon-Fri, 10-11:30am Sat) Drive to the hamlet of Ochopee (population about four), then pull over and break out the cameras: Ochopee's claim to fame is the country's smallest **post office**. It's housed in a former toolshed and set against big park skies; a friendly postal worker patiently poses for snapshots.

Big Cypress National Preserve   PARK
(☑239-695-4758; www.nps.gov/bicy; 33000 Tamiami Trail E; ☺24hr; 🅿🅵) 🅵 FREE The 1139-sq-mile Big Cypress National Preserve (named for the size of the park, not its trees) is the result of a compromise between environmentalists, cattle ranchers and oil-and-gas explorers. The area is integral to the Everglades' ecosystem: rains that flood the preserve's prairies and wetlands slowly filter down through the Glades. About 45% of the cypress swamp (actually mangrove islands, hardwood hammocks, orchid flowers, slash pine, prairies and marshes) is protected.

Skunk Ape Research Headquarters   PARK
(☑239-695-2275; www.skunkape.info; 40904 Tamiami Trail E; adult/child $15/8; ☺9am-5pm; 🅿) This only-in-Florida roadside attraction is dedicated to tracking down southeastern USA's version of Bigfoot, the eponymous Skunk Ape (a large gorilla-man who supposedly stinks to high heaven). We never saw a Skunk Ape, but you can see a corny gift shop and, in the back, a reptile-and-bird zoo run by a true Florida eccentric, the sort of guy who wraps albino pythons around his neck for fun.

EVERGLADES IN...

One Day

If you only have a day in the Everglades, choose between a day in the north or a day in the south – where you start the day will most likely determine which works best. If you're in the north, consider driving the Loop Rd (p156), go for a short walk at the Kirby Storter Roadside Park (p149), or hike part of the Shark Valley Trail (p150) in the morning and then go kayaking with Everglades Adventures (p160) in the afternoon. If you're in the south, drive all the way to the Flamingo area, then hike the Anhinga Trail (p150), walk to the Pa-hay-okee Overlook (p157), and rent a kayak for an afternoon paddle.

Two Days

If you have two full days to dedicate to the park, spend one of the days exploring the northern reaches of the park, the other in the south – the order doesn't matter, but doing both will give you a good overview of the park and its possibilities.

Three Days

If you've done the main activities on days one and two, consider a deeper immersion for day three. If you're in the south, you could spend a whole day and into the evening getting out onto the water, hiking through the swamp, and taking a night walk with Garls Coastal Kayaking Everglades (p149). In the north, do the whole Shark Valley Trail, either on foot or by bike, and/or take a boat tour out toward the 10,000 Islands (p162), through the Gulf Coast Visitor Center (p158) or Smallwood Store Boat Tour (p162).

Shark Valley PARK
(☑305-221-8776; www.nps.gov/ever/planyourvisit/svdirections.htm; 36000 SW 8th St; car/cyclist & pedestrian $30/15; ☉9am-5pm; P ⊞) ✔ Shark Valley sounds like it should be the headquarters for the villain in a James Bond movie, but it is in fact a slice of National Park Service grounds heavy with informative signs and knowledgeable rangers. Shark Valley is located in the cypress, hardwood and riverine section of the Everglades, a more traditionally jungly section of the park than the grassy fields and forest domes surrounding the Ernest Coe visitor center.

If you don't feel like exerting yourself, the most popular and painless way to immerse yourself in the Everglades is via the two-hour **tram tour** (☑305-221-8455; www.sharkvalleytramtours.com; adult/child under 12yr/senior $25/19/12.75; ☉departures 9:30am, 11am, 2pm, 4pm May-Dec, 9am-4pm Jan-Apr hourly on the hour) that runs along Shark Valley's entire 15-mile trail. If you only have time for one Everglades activity, this should be it, as guides are informative and witty, and you may see gators sunning themselves on the road. Halfway along the trail is the 50ft-high **Shark Valley Observation Tower**, an ugly concrete tower that offers dramatically beautiful views of the park.

Big Cypress Gallery GALLERY
(☑239-695-2428; https://clydebutcher.com; 52388 Tamiami Trail; ☉10am-5pm; P) ✔ This gallery showcases the work of Clyde Butcher, an American photographer who follows in the great tradition of Ansel Adams. His large-format black-and-white images elevate the swamps to a higher level. Butcher has found a quiet spirituality in the brackish waters. You'll find many gorgeous prints, which make fine mementos of the Everglades experience (though prices aren't cheap).

★**Fakahatchee Strand Preserve** PARK
(☑239-695-4593; www.floridastateparks.org/parks-and-trails/fakahatchee-strand-preserve-state-park; 137 Coastline Dr, Copeland; vehicle/pedestrian/bicycle $3/2/2; ☉8am-sunset; P ⊞) ✔ The Fakahatchee Strand, besides having a fantastic name, also houses a 20-mile by 5-mile estuarine wetland that looks like something from the beginning of time. A 2000ft boardwalk traverses this wet and wild wonderland, where panthers still stalk their prey amid the black waters. While it's unlikely you'll spot any panthers, there's a great chance you'll see a large variety of blooming orchids, birdlife and reptiles ranging in size from tiny skinks to grinning alligators.

DETOUR: LOOP ROAD

The 24-mile-long Loop Rd, off Tamiami Trail (Hwy 41), offers some unique sites.

➡ The homes of the Miccosukee, some of which have been considerably expanded by gambling revenue. You'll see some traditional *chickee*-style huts (wooden platforms above the waterline) and some trailer homes with massive add-on wings that are bigger than the original trailer – all seem to have shiny new pickup trucks parked out front.

➡ Great pull-offs for viewing flooded forests, where egrets that look like pterodactyls perch in the trees, and alligators lurk in the depths below.

➡ Houses with large 'Stay off my property' signs; these homes are as much a part of the landscape as the swamp.

➡ The short, pleasantly jungly **Tree Snail Hammock Nature Trail**. Though unpaved, the graded road is in good shape and fine for 2WD vehicles.

True to its name, the road loops right back onto the Tamiami; expect a leisurely jaunt on the Loop to add an hour or two to your trip.

Ah-Tah-Thi-Ki
Seminole Indian Museum   MUSEUM

(☑ 877-902-1113; www.ahtahthiki.com; Big Cypress Seminole Indian Reservation, 34725 West Boundary Rd, Clewiston; adult/child/senior $10/7.50/7.50; ☉ 9am-5pm) If you want to learn about Florida's Native Americans, come to the Ah-Tah-Thi-Ki Seminole Indian Museum, 17 miles north of I-75. All of the excellent educational exhibits on Seminole life, history and the tribe today were funded by gaming proceeds, which provide most of the tribe's multimillion-dollar operating budget.

The museum is located within a cypress dome cut through with an interpretive boardwalk, so from the start it strikes a balance between environmentalism and education. The permanent exhibit has several dioramas with life-sized figures depicting various scenes out of traditional Seminole life, while temporary exhibits have a bit more academic polish (past examples have included lengthy forays into the economic structure of the Everglades). There's an old-school 'living village' and re-created ceremonial grounds as well. The museum is making an effort to not be a cheesy Native American theme park, and the Seminole tribe has gone to impressive lengths to achieve this.

Miccosukee Indian Village   MUSEUM

(☑ 305-552-8365; www.miccosukee.com; Mile 70, Hwy 41; adult/child/child 5yr & under $15/8/free; ☉ 9am-5pm; 🅿 ♿) Just west of the turnoff to Shark Valley, this 'Indian Village' is an informative open-air museum that showcases the culture of the Miccosukee via guided tours of traditional homes, a crafts gift store, dance and music performances, and an airboat ride (additional $20) into a hammock-cum-village of raised *chickee* (wooden platforms above the waterline) huts. The art and handmade crafts from the on-site art gallery make good souvenirs. There's a somewhat desultory restaurant as well, if you get hungry.

◉ Southern Everglades

Head south of Miami to drive into the heart of the park and the biggest horizons of the Everglades. Plus there are plenty of side paths and canoe creeks for memorable detours. You'll also see some of the most quietly exhilarating scenery the park has to offer on this route.

Flamingo Marina   MARINA

(State Rd 9336) The chief draw here is taking either a boat tour or hiring a kayak or canoe – all arranged through Flamingo Everglades (p151), a short stroll from the visitor center (p158). Do spend some time hanging out near the water's edge. This is a great place for seeing manatees, alligators and even the rare American crocodile.

Ernest Coe Visitor Center   VISITOR CENTER

(☑ 305-242-7700; www.nps.gov/ever; 40001 State Rd 9336; ☉ 9am-5pm mid-Apr–mid-Dec, 8am-5pm mid-Dec–mid-Apr) Near the entrance to the Everglades National Park, this friendly visitor center has some excellent exhibits, including a diorama of 'typical' Floridians (the fisherman looks like he should join ZZ Top).

★ **Pa-hay-okee Overlook**   VIEWPOINT

State Rd 9336 cuts through the soft heart of the park, past long fields of marsh prairie, white, skeletal forests of bald cypress and dark clumps of mahogany hammock. Further on, the Pa-hay-okee Overlook is a raised platform that peeks over one of the prettiest bends in the River of Grass.

Royal Palm Visitor Center   PARK

(☎ 305-242-7237; www.nps.gov/ever/planyour visit/royal-palm.htm; State Rd 9336; ☺ 9am-4:15pm) Four miles past Ernest Coe Visitor Center, Royal Palm offers the easiest access to the Glades in these parts. Two trails, the Anhinga (p150) and **Gumbo Limbo** (the latter named for the gumbo-limbo tree, also known as the 'tourist tree' because its bark peels like a sunburned tourist), take all of an hour to walk and put you face to face with a panoply of Everglades wildlife. There's a small information station and bookstore.

🛏 Sleeping & Eating

Options within the park, as opposed to the gateway towns, are largely restricted to camping, although 24 new and extremely comfortable cabins are slated to open in the southern Flamingo area of the park. Built from recycled shipping containers but repurposed to a hotel standard, they will be bookable through the national park website.

If you plan to camp in the park, make reservations months in advance. Otherwise, base yourself in Homestead or Florida City (both of which have dozens of hotels across all budgets) and visit the park during the day.

🛏 Northern Everglades

Monument Lake   CAMPGROUND $

(☎ 239-695-1205; www.recreation.gov; 50215 Tamiami Trail E; tent/RV sites $24/28) Reserve months ahead to book one of 10 tent sites (or 26 RV sites) at this appealing campground in the Big Cypress National Preserve. The lake looks quite enticing, but there's no swimming (alligators live here after all). There's plenty of greenery, but not a whole lot of shade.

Swamp Cottage   COTTAGE $$$

(☎ 239-695-2428; https://clydebutcher.com/big-cypress/vacation-rentals; 52388 Tamiami Trail; cottage $250-350; P 🛜) 🍴 Want to get as close to the swamp as possible, without giving up on amenities? Book a bungalow or a two-bedroom cottage, tucked amid lush greenery behind the Big Cypress Gallery (p155). The

lodging is comfortably appointed, if not luxurious, and is certainly cozy, though the best feature is having one of America's great wetlands right outside your door.

Joanie's Blue Crab Cafe   AMERICAN $$

(☎ 239-695-2682; www.joaniesbluecrabcafe.com; 39395 Tamiami Trail E; mains $8-17; ☺ 11am-5pm Thu-Tue, closed seasonally, call to confirm; 🍴) This long-standing Everglades shack, east of Ochopee, with open rafters, shellacked picnic tables and alligator kitsch, serves filling food of the 'fried everything' variety on paper plates. Crab cakes are the thing to order. There's live music on some Saturdays and Sundays from 12:30pm and a rockabilly-loving jukebox at other times.

Glades Eats   AMERICAN $$

(☎ 305-894-2374; www.facebook.com/GladesEats; Tamiami Trail, Hwy 41; mains $12-16; ☺ 8am-4pm) Part of the Miccosukee complex of attractions along the Tamiami Trail close to the Shark Valley turnoff, Glades Eats does everything from Cuban sandwiches and quesadillas to BBQ spare ribs and a decent Wagyu beef burger.

🛏 Southern Everglades

Quality dining options are fairly sparse here, though there are some good, inexpensive Mexican restaurants in Florida City and Homestead.

> **NATIONAL PARK SERVICE CAMPING**
>
> There are campgrounds run by the National Park Service (NPS) located throughout the park. Sites are fairly basic, though there are showers and toilets. Depending on the time of year, the cold water can be either bracing or a welcome relief. The NPS information offices provide a map of all campsites, as does the park website. Visit www.nps. gov/ever/planyourvisit/camping.htm for more information.
>
> There are also many backcountry tent sites ($2 per night). For these you'll also need a permit ($15) and to reserve ahead at one of the visitor centers. Sites are free during the off season (May to October). Note that these sites are accessible only by canoe or kayak (excepting one site that can be reached on foot from Flamingo).

WILDERNESS CAMPING

Three types of **backcountry campsites** (☑239-695-3311, 239-695-2945; www.nps.gov/ever/planyourvisit/backcamp.htm; permit Nov-Apr/May-Oct $15/free, plus per person per night $2; ⊙Flamingo & Gulf Coast Visitor Centers 8am-4:30pm) are available: beach sites on coastal shell beaches and in the 10,000 Islands; ground sites, which are basically mounds of dirt built up above the mangroves; and *chickees*, wooden platforms built above the waterline where you can pitch a freestanding (no spikes) tent. *Chickees*, which have toilets, are the most civilized – there's a serenity found in sleeping on what feels like a raft levitating above the water. Ground sites tend to be the most bug infested.

Warning: if you're paddling around and see an island that looks pleasant for camping but isn't a designated campsite, beware – you may end up submerged when the tides change.

From November to April, backcountry camping permits cost $15, plus $2 per person per night; from May to October sites are free, but you must still self-register at either Flamingo or Gulf Coast Visitor Centers or call 239-695-2945. And pick up the *Wilderness Trip Planner* brochure from Flamingo Visitor Center; it has maps and information on campsites.

Some backcountry tips:

➡ Store food in a hand-sized, raccoon-proof container (available at gear stores).

➡ Bury your waste at least 10in below ground, but keep in mind some ground sites have hard turf.

➡ Use a backcountry stove to cook. Ground fires are only permitted at beach sites, and you can only burn dead or downed wood.

Flamingo Campground CAMPGROUND $
(☑877-444-6777; www.nps.gov/ever/planyourvisit/flamdirections.htm; Flamingo Lodge Hwy; tent sites with/without hookups $20/30) There are over 200 campsites at the Flamingo Visitor Center, some of which have electrical hookups. Escape the RVs by booking a walk-in site. Reserve well ahead (via www.reserveamerica.com) for one of the nine waterfront sites.

Long Pine Key Campground CAMPGROUND $
(☑305-242-7700; www.nps.gov/ever/planyourvisit/camping.htm; Off State Rd 9336; tent & RV sites $20; ⊙closed Jun–mid-Nov) This is a good bet for car campers, just west of Royal Palm Visitor Center. It has 108 sites, available on a first-come basis (no reservations).

ℹ Information

Big Cypress Swamp Welcome Center
(☑239-695-4758; www.nps.gov/bicy/planyourvisit/big-cypress-swamp-welcome-center.htm; 33000 Tamiami Trail E; ⊙9am-4:30pm) About 2.5 miles east of the turnoff to Everglades City, this big visitor center is a good one for kids, with a small nature center where you can listen to recordings of different swamp critters. There's also a viewing platform overlooking a canal where you can sometimes spot manatees. Good spot for information on the reserve.

Flamingo Visitor Center (☑239-695-2945; www.nps.gov/ever; State Rd 9336; ⊙8am-4:30pm mid-Nov–mid-Apr) The visitor center is at the end of State Rd 9336. It's being rebuilt after sustaining hurricane damage, so they're operating out of a trailer until repairs are done.

Gulf Coast Visitor Center (☑239-695-3311; www.nps.gov/ever; 815 Oyster Bar Lane, off Hwy 29, Everglades City; ⊙9am-4:30pm mid-Apr–mid-Nov, 8am-5pm mid-Nov–mid-Apr; ♿) This is the northwestern-most ranger station for Everglades National Park, and provides access to and information on the 10,000 Islands area.

Oasis Visitor Center (☑239-695-1201; www.nps.gov/bicy; 52105 Tamiami Trail E; ⊙9am-4:30pm; ♿) This visitor center, about 20 miles west of Shark Valley, has hands-on exhibits and info on nearby walks in the Big Cypress National Preserve. A platform overlooking a small water-filled ditch is a great spot to see alligators, particularly in the dry season (December to May).

Shark Valley Visitor Center (☑305-221-8776; www.nps.gov/ever/planyourvisit/svdirections.htm; national park entry per vehicle/bicycle/pedestrian $25/8/8; ⊙9am-5pm) A good place to pick up information about the Everglades, including trails, wildlife watching and free ranger-led activities.

ℹ Getting There & Away

The largest subtropical wilderness in the continental USA is easily accessible from Miami. The Glades, which comprise the 80 southernmost miles of Florida, are bound by the Atlantic Ocean to the east and the Gulf of Mexico to the west. The Tamiami Trail (Hwy 41) goes east–west, parallel to the more northern (and less interesting) Alligator Alley (I-75).

❶ Getting Around

You need a car to properly enter and explore the Everglades, or at least to get as far as the hiking trailheads or kayak jumping-off points. Once you're in, wearing a good pair of walking boots is essential to penetrate the interior. Having a canoe or a kayak helps as well; these can be rented from outfits inside and outside the park, or you can seek out guided canoe and kayak tours. Bicycles are well suited to the flat roads of Everglades National Park, particularly in the area between Ernest Coe and Flamingo Point. Road shoulders in the park tend to be dangerously small.

EVERGLADES CITY & CHOKOLOSKEE ISLAND

🎵 239 / POP 426

On the edge of Chokoloskee Bay, you'll find this Old Florida fishing village of raised houses, turquoise water and scattershot emerald-green mangrove islands. 'City' is stretching it for Everglades City – this is really a friendly fishing town where you can easily disappear from the modern world for a day or three. You'll find some intriguing vestiges of the past here, including an excellent regional museum, as well as delicious seafood.

◉ Sights

★ **Museum of the Everglades**　MUSEUM
(🎵 239-252-5026; www.evergladesmuseum.org; 105 W Broadway, Everglades City; ◷ 9am-4pm Mon-Fri, to 5pm Sat; 🅿️) FREE For a break from the outdoors, don't miss this small museum run by volunteers who have a wealth of knowledge on the region's history. Located in the town's former laundry house, the collection delves into human settlement in the area from the early pioneers of the 1800s to the boom days of the 1920s and its tragic moments (Hurricane Donna devastated the town in 1960), and subsequent transformation into the quiet backwater of today.

The most important player here is Barron Collier, Florida's largest landowner of the early 20th century, who essentially created the town from scratch to serve as the base for building the ambitious Tamiami Trail through the Everglades (completed in 1929). Photographs, models and films tell the story of this engineering marvel, as well as what life was like for the early settlers, the workers and the wealthy developers.

Smallwood Store　MUSEUM
(🎵 239-695-2989; www.smallwoodstore.com; 360 Mamie St, Chokoloskee; adult/child $5/free; ◷ 10am-5pm Dec-Apr, 11am-5pm May-Nov) Perched on piers overlooking Chokoloskee Bay, this wooden building dates back to 1906, when a pioneer by the name of Ted Smallwood opened his rustic trading post, post office and general store. The wooden shelves are lined with antiques and old artifacts, along with descriptions of events and characters from those rough and tumble days of life on a remote island frontier.

Don't miss the peaceful views (particularly around sunset) over the waterfront from the pier just below the store. You can also arrange boat tours here.

✹ Festivals & Events

Everglades Seafood Festival　FOOD & DRINK
(www.evergladesseafoodfestival.org; 102 Copeland Ave; ◷ Feb) In Everglades City, this three-day festival features plenty of feasting, as well as kids rides and live music. The star of the show is of course glorious seafood – stone crab, conch fritters, crab cakes, coconut shrimp, mussels, and calamari – though there's also fried gator, frog's legs, pulled-pork barbecue and key-lime pie on a stick!

⏾ Sleeping

Reserve ahead, especially from December to March.

Outdoor Resorts of Chokoloskee　MOTEL $$
(🎵 239-695-2881; www.outdoorresortsofchokolskee.com; 150 Smallwood Dr, Chokoloskee; r $125; ✲ ⊠) At the northern end of Chokoloskee Island, this good-value place is a big draw due to its extensive facilities, including several swimming pools, hot tubs, tennis and shuffleboard courts, a fitness center and boat rentals. The fairly basic motel-style rooms have kitchenettes and a back deck overlooking the marina. It's popular with the RV crowd (there are 283 sites versus only eight motel units).

Parkway Motel & Marina　MOTEL $$
(🎵 239-695-3261; www.parkwaymotelandmarina.net; 1180 Chokoloskee Dr, Chokoloskee; r $108-155; 🅿️✲) A friendly couple runs this veritable testament to the old-school Floridian lodge: cute small rooms and one cozy apartment in a one-story motel building. It's in a peaceful spot on the island of Chokoloskee, and owners Bill and Geri have a wealth of knowledge on the region.

FLORIDA PANTHER NATIONAL WILDLIFE REFUGE

The critically endangered Florida panther is one of the Everglades' most charismatic characters and its most secretive – very few visitors see one here, although the chance of doing so animates any visit. The **Florida Panther National Wildlife Refuge** (239-657-8001; www.fws.gov/refuge/florida_panther; State Rd 29; sunrise-sunset) **FREE**, north of Everglades National Park, covers 26,400 acres and is home to an estimated 12 to 16 of the 200 or so Florida panthers that remain in the wild. Also living on the refuge are bobcats, black bears and alligators.

Most of the refuge is off-limits to visitors, but there are two hiking trails where you can get a glimpse of the panther's habitat of hardwood hammocks, pine flatwoods, and flooded prairies. The trails run for 0.3 miles and 1.3 miles; watch for panther footprints along the longer trail in particular. Call ahead to check on trail conditions, as they can be impassable after heavy rains. Both trails are well signposted with brown signs on the west side of the road between a quarter- and a half-mile north of where State Road 29 intersects with I-75. Early morning and late afternoon are the best times to visit.

The refuge lies 20 miles east of Naples. Take I-75 South, then turn off at Exit 80.

Ivey House Bed & Breakfast   B&B **$$**
(877-567-0679; www.iveyhouse.com; 605 Buckner Ave N, Everglades City; inn $100-200, lodge $90-100, cottage $180-250; P ❄ 🎧 ≋) This friendly, family-run tropical inn offers a variety of well-appointed accommodations: bright spacious inn rooms overlooking a pretty courtyard, cheaper lodge rooms (with shared bathrooms) and a freestanding two-bedroom cottage with a kitchen and screened-in porch. The pool (covered in winter) is a great year-round option for a swim.

This is a top place to book nature trips with **Everglades Adventures** (www.iveyhouse.com/everglades-adventures; 107 Camellia St, Everglades City; 3-4hr tours adult/child from $99/59, canoe/kayak rental per day from $45/55) 🍃, from daytime paddles to six-day packages that include lodging, tours and some meals.

Everglades City Motel   MOTEL **$$**
(239-695-4224; www.evergladescitymotel.com; 309 Collier Ave, Everglades City; r from $149; P ❄ 🎧) With large rooms that have all the mod cons (flat-screen TV, fridge, coffeemaker) and friendly staff who can hook you up with boat tours, this motel provides good value for those looking to spend some time near the 10,000 Islands.

🍴 Eating

Triad Seafood Cafe   SEAFOOD **$**
(239-695-0722; www.triadseafoodmarketcafe.com; 401 School Dr, Everglades City; mains $10-23, stone-crab meals $26-46; 10:30am-6pm Sun-Thu, to 7pm Fri & Sat) Triad is famous for its stone-crab claws, but it serves up all kinds of coastal seafood that you can enjoy on picnic tables perched over the waterfront. Should you impress the friendly owners with your ability to devour crustaceans (or their claws, anyway), you get the dubious honor of having your picture hung on the Glutton Board.

⭐ **Havana Cafe**   LATIN AMERICAN **$$**
(239-695-2214; www.havanacafeoftheeverglades.com; 191 Smallwood Dr, Chokoloskee; breakfast $9-12, lunch mains $7-19; 7am-4pm Sun-Thu, 5-8pm Fri & Sat mid-Oct–mid-Apr, closed mid-Apr–mid-Oct) The Havana Cafe is famed far and wide for its deliciously prepared seafood served with Latin accents. Lunch favorites include stone-crab enchiladas, blackened grouper with rice and beans, and a decadent Cuban sandwich. The outdoor dining amid palm trees and vibrant bougainvillea – not to mention the incredibly friendly service – adds to the appeal.

Reservations are essential on Friday and Saturday nights, when foodies from out of town arrive for stone-crab feasts. Order in advance the astonishingly good seafood paella or seafood pasta – both $50 but serving at least two people.

⭐ **Camellia Street Grill**   SEAFOOD **$$**
(239-695-2003; www.facebook.com/camelliastreetgrill; 202 Camellia St, Everglades City; mains $12-26; 11am-9pm; 🅿) In a barnlike setting with fairy lights strung from the rafters and nautical doodads lining the walls, Camellia is an easygoing spot for a down-home seafood feast. Come before sunset to enjoy the pretty views from the waterfront deck. Don't miss the tender stone-crab claws in season.

❶ Information

Everglades Area Chamber of Commerce
(☏239-695-3941; cnr Hwys 41 & 29 Everglades City; ⏱9am-4pm) General information about the region.

❶ Getting There & Away

There is no public transportation out this way. If you're driving, it's a fairly straight 85-mile drive west from Miami. The trip takes about 1¾ hours in good traffic.

HOMESTEAD & FLORIDA CITY

☏305 / POP 70,477 (HOMESTEAD), 12,077 (FLORIDA CITY)

Homestead and neighboring Florida City, 2 miles to the south, have little obvious appeal upon arrival – they're closer in spirit to Miami than the wild Everglades. Part of the ever-expanding subdivisions of South Miami, this bustling corridor can feel like an endless strip of big-box shopping centers, fast-food joints, car dealerships and gas stations. However, look beneath the veneer and you'll find much more than meets the eye: strange curiosities like a 'castle' built single-handedly by one lovestruck immigrant, an animal rescue center for exotic species, a winery showcasing Florida's produce (hint: it's not grapes), an up-and-coming microbrewery, and one of the best farm stands in America.

This area makes a great base for forays into the southern reaches of Everglades National Park.

◉ Sights

★Coral Castle   CASTLE
(☏305-248-6345; www.coralcastle.com; 28655 S Dixie Hwy, Homestead; adult/senior/child $18/16/8; ⏱9am-6pm Sun-Thu, to 7pm Fri & Sat) 'You will be seeing unusual accomplishment,' reads the inscription on the rough-hewn quarried wall. That's an understatement. There is no greater temple to all that is weird and wacky about South Florida. The legend goes that a Latvian man got snubbed at the altar, came to the US and settled in Florida, and hand-carved, unseen, in the dead of night, a monument to unrequited love.

Everglades Outpost   WILDLIFE RESERVE
(☏305-247-8000; www.evergladesoutpost.org; 35601 SW 192nd Ave, Homestead; adult/child $15/10;

⏱10am-5:30pm Mon, Tue & Fri, 10am-6pm Sat & Sun) The Everglades Outpost houses, feeds and cares for wild animals that have been seized from illegal traders, abused, neglected or donated by people who could not care for them. Residents of the outpost include a lemur, wolves, a black bear, a zebra, cobras, alligators and a majestic tiger (who was bought by an exotic dancer who thought she could incorporate it into her act). Your money goes toward helping the outpost's mission.

Downtown Homestead   AREA
(☏305-323-6564; www.homesteadmainst.org; Krome Ave) You could pass a mildly entertaining afternoon walking around Homestead's almost quaint main street, which essentially comprises a couple of blocks of Krome Ave extending north and south of the **Historic Town Hall** (☏305-242-4463; www.townhall museum.org; 41 N Krome Ave; ⏱1-5pm Wed-Sat). The town hosts one big monthly event from September to April, including concerts, food fests, holiday parades and other events at **Losner Park** (across the street from the Historic Town Hall).

Fruit & Spice Park   PARK
(☏305-247-5727; www.redlandfruitandspice.com; 24801 SW 187th Ave, Homestead; adult/child/child under 6yr $10/3/free; ⏱9am-5pm; ⓟ) Set on the edge of the Everglades, this 35-acre public park grows all those great tropical fruits you usually have to contract dysentery to enjoy. The park is divided into 'continents' (Africa, Asia etc) and it makes for a peaceful wander past various species bearing in total around 500 different types of fruits, spices and nuts. Unfortunately, you can't pick the fruit, but you can eat anything that falls to the ground (go early for the best gathering!).

Schnebly Redland's Winery   WINERY
(☏305-242-1224; www.schneblywinery.com; 30205 SW 217th Ave, Homestead; wine tastings/tours $13/8; ⏱noon-5pm Mon-Thu, noon-10pm Fri & Sat, 11am-5pm Sun) Given the climate, you won't find malbec, pinot noir or zinfandel – wines here are made of mango, passion fruit, lychee, avocado, coconut and other flavors from the tropics, and are surprisingly good. Tucked along a quiet farm road west of Homestead, Schnebly has the distinction of being the southernmost winery in America. You can stop in for tastings, available any time, or for a tour (weekends only, hourly 1pm to 5pm). There's also a good restaurant here, and a pretty back garden next to a small gurgling waterfall.

10,000 ISLANDS

One of the best ways to experience the serenity of the Everglades is by paddling the network of waterways that skirt the northwest portion of the park. Out here, apart from a few pleasure craft, other tourists are a rarity and they're easy to avoid in the labyrinth of islands and channels. The 10,000 Islands consist of tiny islands and a mangrove swamp that hugs the southwestern-most border of Florida. And there aren't really 10,000 of them, just a few hundred, but once you're among them it can feel like many more.

The 10,000 Islands run from Cape Romano, the southernmost tip of Marco Island, to the mouth of what's known as Lostman's River, close to Everglades City. In places it can be difficult to tell which are genuine islands (ie the tips of landscapes submerged in the shallow waters) and which are mangroves (plant life that grows between the point of high and low tide) that have grown atop oyster mounds; the mangroves occupy an estimated 230 sq miles, making it one of the most extensive areas of mangrove forest in the US. The southern islands fall within Everglades National Park.

Archaeologists have found evidence of Native American habitation from around 3500 years ago, although some of these sites have since disappeared beneath rising sea waters. You may also come across the remains of huts, occupied by pioneers who inhabited the islands in the 19th century. Chokoloskee Island, next to Everglades City, is the largest of the islands, and one of very few inhabited today. The absence of any nighttime light pollution makes the islands ideal for stargazing.

Exploring the Islands

Most travelers who explore the 10,000 Islands do so as part of a tour. Everglades Adventures (p160), operating out of Everglades City, is a recommended operator for kayak tours, while **Smallwood Store Boat Tour** (☑ 239-695-0016; www.smallwood storeboattour.com; 360 Mamie St, Chokoloskee; 1hr tour $40; ⊞) runs guided boat trips out into the islands from Chokoloskee Island; the latter operates one tour that follows the story of pioneers such as Edgar J Watson, the main (and real-life) protagonist in Peter Matthiessen's epic novel, *Shadow Country*, which was set in the region.

Getting around the 10,000 Islands is pretty straightforward if you're a competent navigator and you religiously adhere to National Oceanic & Atmospheric Administration (NOAA) tide and nautical charts. Going against the tides is the fastest way to make a miserable trip. The Gulf Coast Visitor Center (p158) sells nautical charts and gives out free tidal charts. You can also purchase charts prior to your visit – call 305-247-1216 and ask for charts 11430, 11432 and 11433.

👉 Tours

Hoosville Hostel offers fantastic tours of the eastern Everglades. You can either paddle into the bush, or if you don't mind getting a little damp, embark on a 'wet walk' into a flowered and fecund cypress dome, stepping through black water and around the edges of an alligator wallow. Half-day/full-day kayaking tours start from $135/160.

🛏️ Sleeping

Aside from an excellent hostel in Florida City, unique lodging options are rare here. You will find plenty of chain hotels scattered along Rte 1 Krome Ave. Higher-end options tend to be close to the busy Ronald Reagan Turnpike.

⭐ **Hoosville Hostel**   HOSTEL $

(☑ 305-248-1122; www.hoosvillehostel.com; 20 SW 2nd Ave, Florida City; tent sites per person $18, dm $35, r $60-240; P ❄ 🛜 🐾) Formerly the Everglades International Hostel, the Hoosville has kept the good-value dorms, private rooms and 'semi-privates' (you have an enclosed room within the dorms and share a bathroom with dorm residents). The creatively configured backyard is the best feature. There's a small rock-cut pool with a waterfall and a gazebo.

We should add the crowd is made up of free-spirited international types, and the hostel leads excellent tours into the Everglades.

Hotel Redland

HOTEL $

(☑305-246-1904; 5 S Flagler Ave, Homestead; r $110-150; ❄❅) On the edge of Homestead's quaint downtown, the Hotel Redland is set in a 1904 building that has a warm, cozy feel thanks to its gracious hosts. The 12 rooms are comfortable, but dated in a charming, grandmotherly way (quilted bedspreads, floral curtains, old photos or framed paintings on the walls). There's a good restaurant here – which is just as well as the area feels deserted at night, so you'll need to get around by car.

✖ Eating & Drinking

★ Robert Is Here

MARKET $

(☑305-246-1592; www.robertishere.com; 19200 SW 344th St, Homestead; juices $7-10; ☺8am-7pm) More than a farmers stand, Robert's is an institution. This is Old Florida at its kitschy best, in love with the Glades and the agriculture that surrounds it. You'll find loads of exotic, Florida-grown fruits you won't get elsewhere – including black sapote, carambola (star fruit), dragon fruit, sapodilla, guanabana (soursop), tamarind, sugar apples, longans and passion fruit. The juices are fantastic.

There's also a petting zoo and a waterplay area for kids (bring your own towels), live music on weekends, and plenty of homemade preserves and sauces.

Rosita's

MEXICAN $

(☑305-246-3114; www.rositasmexicanrestaurant fl.com; 199 W Palm Dr, Florida City; mains $8-13; ☺8am-9pm) There's a working-class Mexican crowd here, testament to the sheer awesomeness of the tacos and burritos. Everyone is friendly, and the mariachi music adds to the authenticity.

Gator Grill

AMERICAN $

(☑786-243-0620; www.facebook.com/everglades gatorgrill; 36650 SW 192nd Ave, Homestead; mains $9-17; ☺11am-6:30pm) A handy pit stop before or after visiting the Everglades National Park, the Gator Grill is a white shack with picnic tables, where you can munch on all manner of alligator dishes. There are gator tacos, gator stir-fry, gator kabobs and straight-up fried alligator served in a basket.

Non-reptile eaters will find veggie burgers, pulled-pork sandwiches and grouper tacos, plus egg sandwiches (with or without gator) for breakfast.

White Lion Cafe

AMERICAN $$

(☑305-248-1076; www.whitelioncafe.com; 146 NW 7th St, Homestead; mains $12-26; ☺11am-3pm & 5-10pm Tue-Sat) There's a comfy cabin vibe to this place near downtown Homestead, with indoor and outdoor seating. The menu features American fare along the lines of meatloaf, crab cakes, fried chicken and fresh fruit cobbler.

Miami Brewing Company

BREWERY

(☑305-242-1224; www.miamibrewing.com; 30205 SW 217th Ave, Homestead; ☺noon-6pm Sun-Wed, to 10pm Thu, to midnight Fri & Sat) You'll find first-rate craft brews in this enormous warehouse-style tasting room. The brewers here bring more than a hint of Floridian accents to beers like Shark Bait mango wheat ale, Big Rod coconut blond ale and Vice IPA with citrus notes.

There are big screens for game days, a pool table, outdoor picnic tables and live music (or DJs) on weekends.

THE EVERGLADES & BISCAYNE HOMESTEAD & FLORIDA CITY

AIRBOATS & SWAMP BUGGIES

Airboats are flat-bottomed skiffs that use powerful fans to propel themselves through the water. Their environmental impact has not been determined, but one thing is clear: airboats can't be doing much good, which is why they're not allowed in the park. Swamp buggies are large balloon-tired vehicles that can go through wetlands, creating ruts and damaging wildlife.

Airboat and swamp-buggy rides are offered all along US Hwy 41 (Tamiami Trail). Think twice before going on a 'nature' tour. Loud whirring fanboats and marsh jeeps are the antithesis of the Everglades' quiet serenity. If you do decide to take such a tour, Coopertown (☑305-226-6048; www.coopertownairboats.com; 22700 SW 8th St; adult/child $23/11; ☺9am-5pm; ⊞) is one of the longest-running airboat operators (since 1945) and is still one of the best. Friendly, knowledgeable guides have a knack for spotting wildlife and giving a good overview of this unique environment.

LOCAL KNOWLEDGE

GUARDIAN OF THE EVERGLADES

In a state known for iconoclasts, no one can hold a candle to **Marjory Stoneman Douglas** – not just for her quirks, but for her drive. A persistent, unbreakable force, she fueled one of the longest conservation battles in US history.

Born in 1890, Douglas moved to Florida after her failed first marriage. She worked for the *Miami Herald* and eventually as a freelance writer, producing short stories that are notable for both the quality of the writing and their progressive themes: *Plumes* (1930) and *Wings* (1931), published in the *Saturday Evening Post*, addressed the issue of Glades bird-poaching when the business was still immensely popular (the feathers were used to decorate ladies' hats).

In the 1940s Douglas was asked to write about the Miami River for the Rivers of America Series and promptly chucked the idea in favor of capturing the Everglades in her classic, *The Everglades: River of Grass*. Like all of Douglas' work, the book is remarkable for both its exhaustive research and lyrical, rich language.

River of Grass immediately sold out of its first print run, and public perception of the Everglades shifted from 'nasty swamp' to 'national treasure.' Douglas went on to be an advocate for environmental causes, women's rights and racial equality, fighting, for example, for basic infrastructure in Miami's Overtown.

Today she is remembered as Florida's favorite environmentalist. Always immaculately turned out in gloves, dress, pearls and floppy straw hat, she would bring down engineers, developers, politicians and her most hated opponents, sugar farmers; by force of her oratory alone. She kept up the fight, speaking and lecturing without fail, until she died in 1998 at the age of 108.

Today it seems every environmental institution in Florida is named for Douglas, but were she around, we doubt she'd care for those honors. She'd be too busy planting herself in the CERP office, making sure everything was moving along on schedule.

❶ Information

There are several info centers where you can get tips on attractions, lodging and dining.

Chamber of Commerce (☑ 305-247-2332; www.southdadechamber.org; 455 N Flagler Ave, Homestead; ⊙9am-5pm Mon-Fri)

Tropical Everglades Visitor Association (☑ 305-245-9180; www.tropicaleverglades. com/homestead.php; 160 N 1st St, Florida City; ⊙8am-5pm Mon-Sat, 10am-2pm Sun)

❶ Getting There & Away

From December or January until April, Homestead runs a free weekend **trolley bus service** (☑ 305-224-4457; www.cityofhomestead.com; ⊙Sat & Sun Dec or Jan-Apr), which takes visitors from Losner Park (downtown Homestead) out to the Royal Palm Visitor Center (p157) in Everglades National Park. It also runs between Losner Park and Biscayne National Park. Call for the latest departure times.

BISCAYNE NATIONAL PARK

Just to the east of the Everglades and right on Miami's southern doorstep is Biscayne National Park (☑ 305-230-1144, boat tours 786-335-3644; www.nps.gov/bisc; 9700 SW 328th St, Homestead; ⊙7am-5:30pm) **FREE**, 95% of which is made up of the waters of Biscayne Bay and the Atlantic. A portion of the world's third-largest reef sits here off the coast of Florida, along with mangrove forests and the northernmost Florida Keys. This is some of the best reef viewing and snorkeling you'll find in the USA, outside Hawaii and nearby Key Largo.

This unique 300-sq-mile park is easy to explore independently with a canoe, or via a boat tour. Generally summer and fall are the best times to visit the park. The offshore Keys, accessible only by boat, offer pristine opportunities for camping. There is no park fee for day admission to the park.

⚑ Activities

Long Elliott Key has picnicking, campsites and hiking among mangrove forests; tiny Adams Key has only picnicking; and equally tiny Boca Chita Key has an ornamental lighthouse, picnicking and campsites. These little islands were settled under the Homestead Act of 1862, which gave land freely to anyone willing to spend five years turning a scratch of the tropics into a working pineapple and key-lime farm.

Boating & Kayaking

Boating is naturally very popular, but you'll need to get some paperwork in order. Boaters will need to get tide charts from the park (ask at Dante Fascell Visitor Center or download them from www.nps.gov/bisc/planyourvisit/tide-predictions.htm). Make sure you comply with local slow-speed zones, designed to protect the endangered manatee. If you'd rather be taking in the scenery than be at the helm, take one of the park-led tours run by the Biscayne National Park Institute.

If you end up on Boca Chita Key, allow time to walk part of the 6-mile trail and look for the 65-foot-high lighthouse. Other highlights include Jones Lagoon, with its rich marine life and bird rookeries, and Sands Key, another rarely visited lagoon.

Diving & Snorkeling

The Maritime Heritage Trail (www.nps.gov/bisc/learn/historyculture/maritime-heritage-trail.htm) takes visitors through one of the only trails of its kind in the US. If you've ever wanted to explore a sunken ship, this may well be the best opportunity in the country. Six are located within the park grounds; the trail experience involves taking visitors out, by boat, to the site of the wrecks where they can swim and explore among derelict vessels and clouds of fish.

There are even waterproof information site cards placed among the ships. Three of the vessels are suited for scuba divers, but the others – particularly the *Mandalay*, a lovely two-masted schooner that sank in 1966 – can be accessed by snorkelers.

Biscayne National Park Institute also offers snorkeling opportunities.

Wherever you go, there's plenty to see – Biscayne National Park has shipwrecks, more than 500 different kinds of fish (including parrotfish, angelfish, wrasses and butterfly fish) as well as sea cucumbers and the gloriously named Christmas tree worm.

☞ Tours

The Biscayne National Park Institute (☑ 786-335-3644; www.biscaynenationalparkinstitute.org; Convoy Point; tours per person $44-159) is the hub for activities and tours within the park. Options include a three-/four-hour boat cruise ($44/70), 3¼-hour snorkeling trip ($64) and six-hour boat trips ($159). Most adventures begin at Convoy Point.

🛏 Sleeping & Eating

Primitive campsites are available on Elliott and Boca Chita Keys, though you'll need a boat to get there. No-see-ums (tiny flies) are invasive, and their bites are nasty. Make sure your tent is devoid of minuscule entry points.

Tent sites cost $25 per night from October to April, but are free the rest of the year. Visit www.nps.gov/bisc/planyourvisit/camping.htm for more information.

ⓘ Information

Dante Fascell Visitor Center (☑ 305-230-7275; www.nps.gov/bisc; 9700 SW 328th St, Homestead; ⊘ 9am-5pm) Located at Convoy Point, this center shows a great introductory film for an overview of the park, and has maps, information and excellent ranger activities. The grounds around the center are a popular picnic spot on weekends and holidays, especially among families from Homestead. Also showcases local artwork.

ⓘ Getting There & Away

To get here, you'll have to drive about 9 miles east of Homestead (the way is pretty well signposted) on SW 328th St (North Canal Dr) into a long series of green-and-gold flat fields and marsh.

The Everglades Environment

The Everglades is one of the most important wilderness areas in the Lower Forty Eight, a fragile ecosystem rich in astonishing wildlife that is also under existential threat from human-led and natural causes. Charismatic wildlife is an Everglades specialty, from alligators and manatees to bobcats, river otters and, if you're *really* lucky, the Florida panther. Whether the Everglades can be protected from the many things that threaten it will be a bellwether for the future of the US environment.

Everglades Wildlife

The Everglades provides rich habitat for a wide range of animals. These include more than 40 species of mammals, 50 different reptiles, 300 fish species, 700 different plants and more than 360 bird species. Of these, one species of snake, four turtles, and one bat species, as well as the Florida panther and West Indian manatee, are among those species considered to be endangered.

Alligators

Alligators are the most commonly seen large animal in the park, although not so much in the 10,000 Islands, as they tend to avoid salt water. They are a keystone species in the Everglades, where they play an important role in the ecosystem – alligator dens, for example, are often used later by other species. More than 200,000 are thought to inhabit the Everglades (the Florida-wide gator population is around 1.5 million).

American alligators (*Alligator mississippiensis*) love freshwater swamps, lakes and rivers, although they can inhabit salt water for short periods; unlike crocodiles, they don't possess a gland that gets rid of the salt.

Female alligators in the Everglades rarely exceed 10ft. They dig dens, where they then give birth, but due to the dangers of flooding, these dens are usually above the waterline and can be up to 3.5ft high. They also use them for shelter when temperatures fall. Eggs usually take around two months to hatch. If the eggs incubate at temperatures between 90°F and 93°F (around 32°C to 34°C), baby male alligators emerge. Female babies are produced when incubation temperatures range between 82°F and 86°F (27.7°C and 30°C). Mixed litters are born when temperatures are between these two ranges during incubation. Once the eggs hatch, the mother carries up to 10 babies at a time on her tongue and then releases them into the water. Young alligators remain close to their mother for between one and three years.

Males in the Everglades generally grow to around 13ft to 15ft. Younger alligators have bright yellow bands across their backs which, when combined with their black base color, provides a form of camouflage during the early years when they are at their most vulnerable.

Young alligators feed on insects, small fish and frogs, but they graduate to larger fish, turtles, mammals, birds and other

1. Alligator 2. Airboat tour (p151)

reptiles when they become adults. When temperatures drop below 68°F (20°C), alligators stop feeding and cease most activities. Even their color – from olive to brown to nearly black – depends on their surroundings: in waters with a high algae content they tend toward green, while skin colors are darker where there are lots of overhanging trees.

If you do see an alligator, it probably won't bother you unless you do something overtly threatening or angle your boat between it and its young. If you hear an alligator making a loud hissing sound, get the hell out of Dodge. That's a call to other alligators when a young gator is in danger. Finally, never feed an alligator – it's dangerous and illegal.

Crocodiles

The American crocodile (*Crocodylus acutus*) was once found across the southern US. Although they have been sighted further north in Florida and as far north as the South Carolina coast, only a few hundred remain in the US, and only in any numbers in Florida's far south. There are also populations across Central and northern South America. Crocodiles are less commonly seen in the Everglades,

as they prefer coastal and predominantly saltwater habitats, including islands; they're commonly seen in the 10,000 Islands and around Flamingo Marina.

Males can grow up to 20ft in length and weigh up to 880lb. They are more aggressive than alligators.

Marine Mammals

If you're traveling along the coastal sections of the Everglades, including the 10,000 Islands, look out for **bottlenose dolphins**. Beautiful, streamlined creatures, they are usually between 10ft and 14ft in length and have smooth gray skin. They live in highly complex social groups and are considered among the smartest of all mammals.

The **West Indian manatee** is a common sight in the warm waters along the coast of Florida. Manatees are shy, utterly peaceful mammals that look like obese seals with vaguely elephantine noses. Despite weighing between 1500lb and 1800lbs, they're surprisingly graceful, able to swim at around 15mph for short periods. But typically, they drift around, feeding on vegetation just below the water's surface (hence their none-too-flattering nickname of 'sea cow'). After grabbing a bite, manatees come up for air and often float just beneath the surface.

Another charismatic Everglades presence is the playful **river otter**, sometimes known as the 'playboy of the Everglades.' River otters are rarely out of the water during daylight hours – their webbed feet, sleek design and powerful jaws combine to make them swift swimmers and excellent hunters of turtles, fish and even baby alligators; the latter are relatively easy prey if caught alone. Your best chance of seeing a river otter is along the Anhinga Trail (p150) and in the waterways of Shark Valley (p155).

Florida Panthers

The critically endangered Florida panther is the state's official animal. As recently as the early 1990s, the Florida panther was in deep trouble, with as few as 10 (and no more than 30) left in the wild. There were, and remain, no other known populations of mountain lions (also known as cougars, pumas and, here in

ALLIGATOR OR CROCODILE?

Alligators and crocodiles are closely related, but how can you tell the difference between them?

For a start, if you're in the Everglades' freshwater channels, swamps and lakes (which make up most of the subcoastal areas of the national park), it's more than likely that you're looking at an alligator. Crocodiles are more likely to be seen in coastal, saltwater areas.

Secondly, the alligator's long snout has more of a 'U' shape, while crocodile snouts have a long, pointier 'V' shape.

When an alligator's mouth is closed, the upper jaw is wider than the lower jaw and no teeth are visible. In contrast, the fourth tooth from the front on each side of a crocodile's mouth sticks out when it's closed.

River otter

Florida, the Florida panther) east of the Mississippi. Those that did inhabit southwestern Florida had already developed a number of genetic problems (including heart defects) that came from close inbreeding. In the mid-1990s, scientists brought in eight female mountain lions from Texas. The population in Florida began to grow, the genetic flaws began to disappear, and estimates of the number of Florida panthers now range between 130 and 200. In November 2016, a female panther became the first of her kind to cross the Caloosahatchee River; although males had crossed the river before, the female, who soon had cubs, represented an important milestone for the species.

Many challenges remain, however. As usual, humans have been the culprits behind this predator's demise. Widespread habitat reduction (ie the arrival of big subdivisions) is the major cause of concern. Breeding units (one male and two to five females) require about 200 sq miles, and that often puts panthers in the way of one of Florida's most danger-

ous beasts: drivers. Some 31 panthers were killed by cars in 2016, with 26, 24 and 23 killed in the following three years. Underpasses have been critical in reducing road fatalities. Planned major new roads, including one between Orlando and Naples, will cut through habitat considered essential if the Florida panther population is to grow.

Florida panthers are rather magnificent golden-brown hunting cats. They are extremely elusive and only inhabit 5% of their historic range. They're found in the northern Everglades region, with denser concentrations in Big Cypress National Preserve (p154) and Florida Panther National Wildlife Refuge (p160). Sightings are also possible in **Corkscrew Swamp Sanctuary** (📞239-348-9151; www.corkscrew. audubon.org; 375 Sanctuary Rd W; adult/child 6-18yr $14/4; ⏰7am-5:30pm, last entry 4:30pm).

To learn more about the battle to save the panther, track down *Cat Tale* (Craig Pittman; 2020).

Raccoon

Other Mammals

One of the Everglades' most commonly seen mammals is the **white-tailed deer**. Deer in the Everglades have no need for the extra layer of fat that protects deer from winter cold elsewhere. Here, they're often seen grazing on saw grass in open prairie. During spring, watch for recently born fawns (with white spots for camouflage).

If you're *really* lucky, you might just see a **bobcat** lurking in the mangroves. Found throughout the continental United States, the bobcat is a member of the lynx family, and has beautiful markings, with black spots and streaks against a gray to brown undercoat, as well as affecting tufts on the ears. One of the most adaptable of all wild cat species, it is found anywhere from the desert regions of the American West to the Everglades subtropical swamps, and is an opportunistic hunter, killing fish, small mammals and birds; in 2015 one enterprising bobcat was even photographed pulling a shark from the ocean shallows...

Other mammals include **raccoon**, dwindling numbers of **marsh rabbit**, and the Everglades' only pouched marsupial, the **opossum**. The **gray fox** of the Everglades is the only fox species known to climb trees.

PROTECTING MANATEES

The manatee has become the poster child of Floridian environmentalism. Pollution is a big problem, but their biggest killers are pleasure boaters.

Manatees seek warm, shallow water and feed on vegetation. South Florida is surrounded by just such an environment, but it also has one of the highest concentrations of pleasure boats in the world. Despite pleas from environmental groups, wildlife advocates and the local, state and federal governments, which have declared many areas 'Manatee Zones,' some pleasure boaters routinely exceed speed limits and ignore simple practices that would help protect the species.

Manatees spend a lot of their time grazing gently just below the water's surface. When speedboats zoom through the area, manatees are hit by the hulls and either knocked away or pushed under the boat, whose propeller then gashes the mammal as the boat passes overhead. Few manatees get through life without propeller scars, and many are killed.

Save the Manatee (www.savethemanatee.org) works with teams from the Dolphin Research Center to respond to reports of injured manatees, dolphins and whales, but they're fighting a losing battle. The Florida Fish & Wildlife Commission reported that 136 manatees were killed by watercraft in 2019 – an all-time high. The commission also reported a five-year average of nearly 100 manatees killed by watercraft every year.

Threats to the Everglades

Unfortunately, the whole 'River of Grass' needs the river to survive and the Everglades acts as a hurricane barrier and kidney. Kidney? All those wetlands leached out pollutants from the Florida Aquifer (the state's freshwater supply). But when farmland wasn't diverting the sheet flow, it was adding fertilizer-rich wastewater to it. Result? Bacteria, and eventually plant life, bloomed at a ridiculous rate (they call it fertilizer for a reason), upsetting the fragile balance of resources vital to the Glades' survival.

Despite the tireless efforts of environmentalists, today the Florida Aquifer is in serious danger of being contaminated and drying up. The number of wading birds nesting has declined by 90% to 95% since the 1930s. Currently there are more than 60 threatened and endangered plant and animal species in the park.

The diversion of water away from the Glades and runoff pollution are the main culprits. This delicate ecosystem is the neighbor of one of the fastest-growing urban areas in the US. The current water-drainage system in South Florida was built to handle the needs of two million people; the local population is now closer to 10 million. Scientists estimate the wetlands have been reduced to as little as a quarter of their original size.

Nature has done some damage as well. During 2005's Hurricane Wilma, for example, six storm water treatment areas (artificial wetlands that cleanse excess nutrients out of the water cycle) were heavily damaged by powerful winds. Without these natural filtration systems, the Glades are far more susceptible to nutrient blooms and external pollution. In 2016 nearly 4000 acres went up in flames in wildfires near Long Pine Key. And, of course, rising sea levels associated with climate change could also have a devastating impact on the Everglades.

Restoration of the Everglades

Efforts to save the Everglades began in the late 1920s, but were sidelined by the Great Depression. In 1926 and 1928 two major hurricanes caused Lake Okeechobee to overflow; the resulting floods killed hundreds. The Army Corps of Engineers did a really good job of damming the lake. A bit too good: the Glades were essentially cut off from their source, the Kissimmee watershed.

BURMESE PYTHONS

As the name would suggest, the Burmese python (*Python bivittatus*) belongs in tropical Asia, not subtropical Florida. How they came to be in Florida is simple: Burmese pythons make popular pets – their beautiful, traditional python markings make them one of the prettier snakes in the pet-snake market. However, the small young pythons sold by pet stores and importers of exotic pets have a tendency to just keep growing – the longest Burmese python recorded in Florida reached 17.5ft in length. Burmese pythons are one of the five largest snake species in the world and can grow up to 23ft in length. And so many pet owners who couldn't take care of such a massive creature with a ravenous appetite dumped the animals into the swamp.

Burmese pythons first began turning up in the Everglades in the 1980s. The latest estimates suggest that at least 30,000, but possibly as many as 300,000, may now live in the wild in southern Florida. It has been illegal to import Burmese pythons into the US since 2012, although at this point it is of course too late to turn back the clock.

As an invasive species, the Burmese python has had a devastating impact on the Everglades environment. A female python can lay up to 50 eggs and live for 20 years. The pythons have also preyed on a whole range of species – marsh rabbits have been nearly wiped out from the Everglades, while populations of everything from raccoon and fox to bobcat have been devastated. In 2017 one *Palm Beach Post* reporter even stumbled upon a large python devouring an alligator just off Loop Rd.

Programs to reduce the number of Burmese pythons in the Everglades have ranged from hunting using dogs right through to offering bounties and biological methods, but have had very limited effect.

In the meantime, conservationists began donating land for protection, starting with 1 sq mile of land donated by a garden club. The Everglades was declared a national park in 1947, the same year Marjory Stoneman Douglas' *The Everglades: River of Grass* was published.

By draining the wetlands through the damming of the lake, the Army Corps made huge swaths of inland Florida inhabitable. But the environmental problems created by shifting water's natural flow, plus the area's ever-increasing population, now threaten to make the whole region uninhabitable. The canal system sends, on average, more than 1 billion gallons of water into the ocean every day. At the same time, untreated runoff flows unfiltered into natural water supplies. Clean water is disappearing from the water cycle while South Florida's population gets bigger by the day.

The Comprehensive Everglades Restoration Plan (CERP; www.evergladesrestoration.gov) is designed to address the Everglades' water

problems. The plan is to unblock the Kissimmee, restoring Everglades lands to predevelopment conditions, while maintaining flood protection, providing fresh water for South Florida's populace and protecting regions against urban sprawl. Political battles, cost overruns and bureaucratic red tape have significantly slowed the implementation of CERP.

A major portion of CERP is the Central Everglades Planning Project (CEPP), the rare public works project that is supported by environmentalists and industry alike. The CEPP's aim is to clean polluted water from Florida's agricultural central heartland and redirect it toward the Everglades. The River of Grass would be rewatered, and toxic runoff would no longer flow to the sea. In 2016 the US Congress approved $976 million of funding for CEPP as part of its Water Infrastructure Improvements for the Nation Act. Congress authorized a further $111 million for restoration projects in 2018 and 2019, with $200 million allocated in the 2020 budget.

Black vulture flying over wetlands

AT A GLANCE

POPULATION
79,000

**NUMBER OF
ISLANDS**
1700

**BEST WILDLIFE
ENCOUNTERS**
National Key Deer
Refuge (p188)

**BEST FISH
SANDWICHES**
Key Largo Fisheries
(p180)

BEST CRAFT BEER
Florida Keys Brewing
Company (p184)

WHEN TO GO
Dec–Mar The dry,
sunny days are
perfect, though
lodging is at its most
expensive.

Apr–Jun Sea breezes
help keep the sum-
mer heat down, and
hotel rates drop
precipitously.

Jul–Nov There's
some rain (and
maybe hurricanes),
but also unbeatable
low-season prices.

Florida Keys & Key West

Curving beneath Southern Florida, this 113-mile-long archipelago is a land of mangrove and sandbar islands, teal waters and magnificent sunsets. A memorable journey down the Overseas Highway takes you from the bustle of Key Largo to Key West, passing arts-loving villages, old-fashioned roadside eateries and stretches of verdant hardwood forest, crossing some 42 bridges along the way.

Paddling across mirror-like coves and joining the free-spirited party people in Key West is just a sample of the great Florida Keys experience. You can also take in the unusual plant and animal life and explore the fascinating history still visible on these shores – from abandoned railroad trestles built in the early 20th century to grand homes and museums filled with treasures.

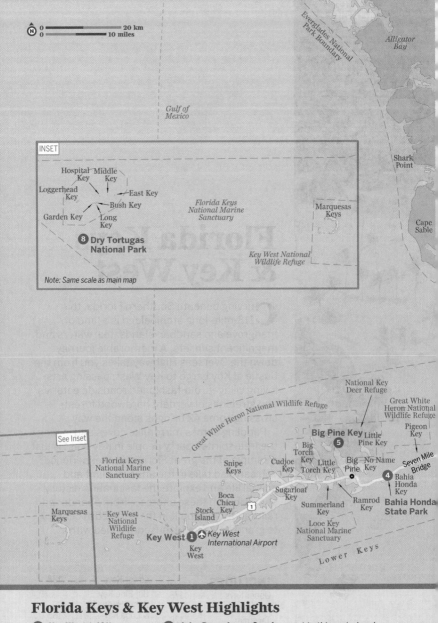

Florida Keys & Key West Highlights

① **Key West** (p191)
Shopping and dining amid the pastel-hued cottages of the Bahamian Village, followed by drinks on Duval St.

② **John Pennekamp Coral Reef State Park** (p178) Diving around the rainbow reefs.

③ **Indian Key Historic State Park** (p182) Paddling

out to this eerie, lonely, beautiful park.

④ **Bahia Honda State Park** (p188) Basking on the sands of one of South Florida's prettiest beaches.

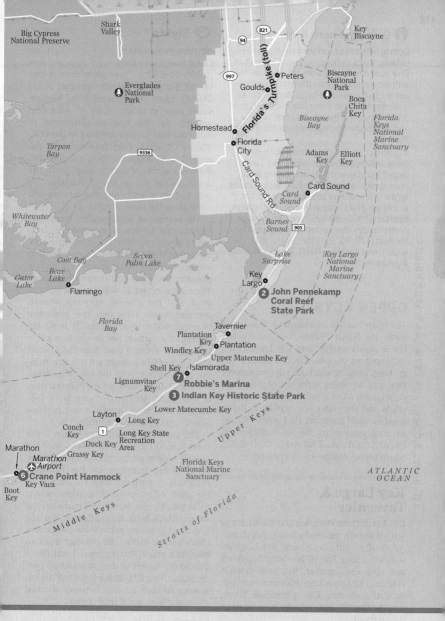

5 Big Pine Key (p188)
Looking for tiny Key deer and other wildlife on nature trails near the Blue Hole.

6 Crane Point Hammock (p185) Strolling through the palm hammock, mangroves and gorgeous shoreline near Marathon.

7 Robbie's Marina (p182) Feeding the giant tarpon, then hiring a kayak for a paddle to forest-covered Lignumvitae Key.

8 Dry Tortugas National Park (p207) Taking an island-hopping day trip or detour.

❶ Getting There & Away

Getting here can be half the fun – or, if you're unlucky, inject a whopping dose of frustration. On a good day, driving along the Overseas Hwy with the windows down – the wind in your face and the twin sisters of Florida Bay and the Atlantic stretching on either side – is the US road trip in tropical perfection. On a bad day, you end up sitting in gridlock behind a midlife-crisis Harley.

Greyhound (www.greyhound.com) buses serve all Keys destinations along Hwy 1 and depart from Downtown Miami and Key West; you can pick up a bus along the way by standing on the Overseas Hwy and flagging one down. If you fly into Fort Lauderdale or Miami, the **Keys Shuttle** (☑ 305-289-9997; www.keysshuttle. com) provides door-to-door service to most of the Keys ($70/80/90 to the Upper and Middle Keys/Lower Keys/Key West). Reserve 48 hours in advance.

UPPER KEYS

The huge blanket of mangrove forest that forms the South Florida coastline spreads like a woody morass into Key Largo; little differentiates the island from Florida proper. Keep heading south and the mangroves give way to wider stretches of road and ocean, until all of a sudden you're in Islamorada and the water is everywhere. If you want to avoid traffic on US 1 south of Florida City, you can try the less trafficked FL 997 and Card Sound Rd to FL 905 (toll $1), which passes Alabama Jack's (p181).

Key Largo & Tavernier

Key Largo (both the town and the island itself) is slightly underwhelming at a glance. As you drive onto the islands, Key Largo resembles a long line of low-lying hammock and strip development. But head down a side road and duck into this warm little bar, or that converted Keys plantation house, and the island's idiosyncrasies become more pronounced.

The 33-mile-long Largo, which starts at Mile Marker 106, is the longest island in the Keys, and those 33 miles have attracted a lot of marine life, all accessible from the biggest concentration of dive sites in the islands. The town of Tavernier (Mile Marker 93) is just south of the town of Key Largo.

◎ Sights

★ **John Pennekamp
Coral Reef State Park**   STATE PARK
(☑ 305-451-6300;   www.pennekamppark.com; Mile 102.6 oceanside; car with 1 person/2 people $4.50/9, cyclist or pedestrian $2.50; ⊙ 8am-sunset, aquarium to 5pm; 🅿 📵) ✒ John Pennekamp has the singular distinction of being the first underwater park in the USA. There's 170 acres of dry parkland here and more than 48,000 acres (75 sq miles) of wet: the vast majority of the protected area is the ocean. Before you get out in that water, be sure to take in some pleasant beaches and stroll along the nature trails.

The **Mangrove Trail** is a good boardwalk introduction to this oft-maligned, ecologically awesome species (the trees, often submerged in water, breathe via long roots that act as snorkels). Stick around for nightly campfire programs and ranger discussions. The visitor center is well run and informative, and has a small saltwater **aquarium** and nature films that give a glimpse of what's under those waters. To really get beneath the surface, you should take a 2½-hour **glass-bottom boat tour** (adult/child $24/17). You'll be brought out in a safe, modern 38ft catamaran to the splendid Molasses Reef, where you'll see see filigreed flaps of soft coral, technicolor schools of fish, dangerous-looking barracuda and perhaps massive, yet graceful, sea turtles.

The park's most famous attraction is the coral-fringed *Christ of the Abyss*, an 8.5ft, 4000lb bronze sculpture of Jesus – a copy of a similar sculpture off the Portofino Peninsula in northern Italy. On calm days, the park offers **snorkeling trips** (adult/child $30/25, plus equipment rental) to the statue, which is six miles offshore. You can also arrange **diving excursions** (six-person charter from $500). DIY-ers may want to take out a canoe ($20 per hour), kayak (from $12/30 per hour/half day) or stand-up paddleboard (from $25/50 per hour/half day) to journey through a 3-mile network of trails. Phone for boat-rental information.

**Laura Quinn Wild
Bird Sanctuary**   WILDLIFE RESERVE
(☑ 305-852-4446;   www.keepthemflying.org; 93600 Overseas Hwy, Mile 93.6; donations accepted; ⊙ sunrise-sunset; 🅿 📵) ✒ This 7-acre sanctuary serves as a protected refuge for a wide variety of injured birds. A boardwalk leads through various enclosures where you

FLORIDA KEYS OVERSEAS HERITAGE TRAIL

One of the most rewarding ways to see the Keys is by bicycle. The flat elevation and ocean breezes are perfect for cycling, and the **Florida Keys Overseas Heritage Trail** (☎305-853-3571; www.floridastateparks.org/trail/Florida-Keys) gives gorgeous vantage points along the way. Around 90 miles (out of 106 miles) of this multiuse trail are complete. A complete, safe bike trail covering the entire length of the Keys is still a distant dream (damage from Hurricane Irma in 2017 brought expansion to a close, though work may resume in the years ahead).

If you are keen to ride, it's currently possible to bike through the Keys along portions of this trail, though it's not always easy to follow (sometimes crossing from bayside to oceanside and back). On the incomplete parts of the trail, you can ride along the shoulder of the highway if you don't mind traffic whizzing by at 50mph (crossing the Seven-Mile Bridge is particularly harrowing; taxis in Marathon have bike racks, saving you the stress). Bring plenty of spares (road debris makes quick work of non-Kevlar-lined tires). You can download a map on www.floridastateparks.org.

Among the most peaceful stretches are the Old Road from Mile Marker 90 to 80 in Islamorada, the historical 2.2-mile Long Key Bridge (near Mile Marker 66), and the fine coastal scenery from Mile Markers 15 to 5 near Key West.

For two-day biking trips between Key Largo and Key West, book a tour with Key Largo Bike and Adventure Tours. It also rents out bikes for those who want to go it alone.

can learn a bit about some of the permanent residents – those unable to be released back in the wild. The species here include masked boobies, great horned owls, green herons, brown pelicans, double-crested cormorants and others.

Keys Meads
DISTILLERY

(☎305-204-4596; www.keysmeads.com; 99353 Overseas Hwy; mead tasting $8; ⊙noon-7pm Tue-Sat, to 6pm Sun) For something completely different, stop in for a tasting at this artisanal, family-run mead producer which opened back in 2017. Owner Jeff Kesling has an encyclopedic knowledge of all things mead related, and has created many unique varieties of his award-winning libation (one of the world's oldest alcoholic drinks), all made from locally sourced honey.

During a tasting, you can try up to 12 different meads (small pours since the alcohol content ranges from 7% to 14%), with a regularly changing lineup including a spicy habanero, Jamaican cherry and star fruit. Bottles (from $16) make fine gifts.

Harry Harris Park
PARK

(50 East Beach Rd, Mile 92.6, Tavernier; admission free Mon-Fri, $5 Sat, Sun & holidays; ⊙7:30am-sunset; 🐾🎣) This small park is a good place to take the kids – there's a small playground, picnic tables, grills for barbecuing, basketball courts and ball fields. Unusual for the Keys, there's also a good patch of white sand fronting a warm lagoon that's excellent for swimming.

Activities

Key Largo Bike and Adventure Tours
CYCLING

(☎305-395-1551; www.keylargobike.com; 90775 Old Hwy, Tavernier; 3hr tour $75) This outfit offers various tours, including three-hour jaunts around Islamorada and two-day tours from Key Largo to Key West ($575). It also hires out bikes for those who want to go it alone – the $375 package includes one-way bike rental to Key West (the staff will transfer your bags for you and pick up the bike when you finish).

Key Largo Princess
BOATING

(☎305-451-4655; Key Largo Holiday Inn, 99701 Overseas Hwy; adult/child from $37/21; ⊙cruises 10am, 1pm & 4pm; 🐾) Get a glimpse of the Key's undersea beauty on a glass-bottom boat tour. Popular with families, these 75ft, 129-passenger vessels give you the opportunity to see lots of colorful coral, plus sea fans, sharks, tropical fish and the odd sea turtle winging along.

African Queen
BOATING

(☎305-451-8080; www.africanqueenflkeys.com; Key Largo Holiday Inn, 99701 Overseas Hwy; cruises from $59) The steamboat used in the 1951 movie starring Humphrey Bogart and Katharine Hepburn has been restored to its former splendor, and offers cinematic tours through the Port Largo canals and out to the ocean. It was built in England in 1912 and used in

FLORIDA KEYS & KEY WEST KEY LARGO &TAVERNIER

Africa to transport goods, missionaries and hunters, before becoming a movie star.

Jacob's Aquatics Center WATER PARK

(☑305-453-7946; http://jacobsaquaticcenter. org; 320 Laguna Ave, Mile 99.6; adult/child/ student/family weekday $10/6/8/25, weekend $12/8/10/30; ☻10am-6pm; ☝) Jacob's has an eight-lane pool for lap and open swimming, an accessible therapy pool and water aerobic courses. For the kids there's a small waterpark with waterslides, a playground and, of course, kiddie-sized pools.

🛏 Sleeping

John Pennekamp
Coral Reef State Park CAMPGROUND $

(☑information 305-676-3777, reservations 800-326-3521; www.reserveamerica.com; 102601 Overseas Hwy; tent & RV sites $38.50; ℗) You don't even have to leave Pennekamp at closing time if you opt for tent or RV camping, but you'll need to make a reservation well in advance (up to 11 months ahead), as the 47 sites fill up fast. Leashed, well-behaved pets are welcome.

Bay Harbor Lodge MOTEL $$

(☑305-852-5695; www.bayharborkeylargo.com; 97702 Overseas Hwy bayside; r $150-350; ❄☎🏊) This lush 2.5-acre property has its own private beach (and free kayaks), a temperature-controlled pool and tropical gardens alive with birdsong. The spacious and comfortable cottage-style rooms are painted in cheery colors and come with small kitchen units and outdoor seating areas. The homemade scones (available in the morning along with freshly brewed coffee) are all the rage. Excellent value.

MB at Key Largo HOTEL $$

(☑305-852-6200; www.mbatkeylargo.com; 147 Seaside Ave; r $175-400; ℗❄☎🏊) This midsized hotel fronting the Atlantic Ocean offers bright rooms that have an old-school tropical vibe with lemon-hued walls, wood and rattan furniture and earth-colored carpeting. Some rooms have small balconies that catch a fine breeze. It's a family-friendly spot and you can borrow bikes and kayaks or just lounge away by the seaside pool.

Kona Kai Resort
& Gallery RESORT $$$

(☑305-852-7200; www.konakairesort.com; Mile 97.8 bayside; r $320-530; ℗☎🏊) This hideaway is one of the only botanical gardens we can think of that integrates a hotel onto its grounds – or is that the other way around?

Either way, this spot, backing onto peaceful waterfront, is lush. The 13 airy rooms and suites (some with full kitchens) are all bright and comfortable, with good natural light and an attractive modern design.

Jules' Undersea Lodge HOTEL $$$

(☑305-451-2353; www.jul.com; 51 Shoreland Dr, Mile 103.2 oceanside; s/d/tr $675/800/1050) If you fancy diving to your hotel, this place is for you. Once a research station, this module has been converted into a delightfully cheesy Keys motel, but wetter. In addition to two private guest rooms, there are common rooms, a kitchen-dining room and a wet room with hot showers and gear storage. Telephones and an intercom connect guests with the surface.

🍴 Eating

Harriette's AMERICAN $

(☑305-852-8689; www.facebook.com/harriettes restaurant; 95710 Overseas Hwy bayside; mains $8-15; ☻6am-3pm) This sweet, breadbox-sized eatery is famed far and wide for its utterly addictive key lime muffins (so big you'll need a knife and fork to eat them). There's also classic American fare – pancakes, bacon and eggs, and not-to-be-missed fluffy biscuits for breakfast, which is the best time to come.

★**Key Largo Fisheries** SEAFOOD $$

(☑305-451-3782; www.keylargofisheries.com; 1313 Ocean Bay Dr; mains $12-24; ☻10am-5:30pm Tue-Sat) At this laid-back dockside spot, you can sit at picnic tables and watch the boats bobbing in the marina while tucking into scrumptious seafood caught the same day. Famous fish sandwiches (such as the blackened mahimahi) are massive and pair nicely with local microbrews. The on-site market has a good selection of fresh catch if you're self-catering.

Fish House SEAFOOD $$

(☑305-451-4665; www.fishhouse.com; Mile 102.4 oceanside; mains lunch $13-21, dinner $23-30; ☻11:30am-10pm; ℗☝) The Fish House delivers on the promise of its title – very good fish, bought from local fishers and prepared fried, broiled, jerked, blackened or chargrilled. Because the Fish House only uses fresh fish, the menu changes daily based on what is available.

Key Largo Conch House FUSION $$

(☑305-453-4844; www.keylargoconchhouse.com; Mile 100.2 oceanside; mains lunch $11-18, dinner $18-30; ☻8am-10pm; ℗❄☝) This innovative kitchen likes to freshen up local classics (grilled mahimahi stuffed with blue crab and mango, or yellowfin tuna with coconut and sesame served with sriracha rice cake and seaweed).

Mrs Mac's Kitchen AMERICAN $$
(☏305-451-3722; www.mrsmacskitchen.com; Mile 99.4 bayside; mains breakfast & lunch $9-21, dinner $16-30; ☺7am-9:30pm Mon-Sat; P🛈) When Applebee's stuffs its wall full of license plates, it's tacky. When Mrs Mac's does it, it's homey. Probably because the service is warm and personable, and the meals are delicious.

Sal's Ballyhoo's SEAFOOD $$$
(☏305-852-0822; www.ballyhoosrestaurant.com; 97860 Overseas Hwy; mains $23-37; ☺11am-10pm; 🅿) A rather ho-hum-looking building along the highway serves up outstanding seafood dishes. Try the decadent yellowtail Hemingway (parmesan-crusted snapper topped with crab meat and key-lime butter) or pasta loaded with scallops, mussels, mahimahi and shrimp. There's also stone crabs in season (mid-October to mid-May) and vegetarian options (sweet-potato burgers, black-bean tacos, vegan grilled cheese).

On clear nights, grab an outdoor table on the front patio.

Drinking & Nightlife

Sundowners BAR
(☏305-451-4502; www.sundownerskeylargo.com; 103900 Overseas Hwy; ☺11am-10pm; 🅿) The best place in town to watch the sunset is this buzzing bar and restaurant sitting pretty on the Florida Bay. There's ample outdoor seating, good happy hour drink specials (from 4pm to 7pm), live music most nights and a first-rate pub grub and seafood menu (mains $14 to $38). There's also a glass-walled dining room if you need to escape the elements.

Alabama Jack's BAR
(☏305-248-8741; 58000 Card Sound Rd; ☺11am-7pm) Welcome to your first taste of the Keys: zonked-out fishermen, exiles from the mainland and Harley-heads swilling beers on a mangrove bay. This is the line where Miami-esque South Florida gives way to the country-fried American South. The laid-back vibe is the perfect setting for conch fritters, crab cakes and mahimahi tacos, among other favorites (mains $11 to $20).

Just watch out for dive-bombing gulls along the deck (though the oversized red buoys seem to keep them away), and the

evening onslaught of mosquitoes – which is why Alabama Jack's closes at 7pm every night. Country bands take the stage on Saturday (2pm to 5pm) and Sunday (2pm to 7pm). It's located just before the tollbooth over the Card Sound Bridge.

ℹ Information

Mariners Hospital (☏305-434-3000; www.baptisthealth.net; Mile 91.5 bayside, Tavernier; ☺24hr) The best hospital in the area with a 24-hour emergency room. If you're diving, this is the only place in the Keys that has a hyperbaric chamber.

ℹ Getting There & Away

The Greyhound bus stops at Mile Marker 99.6 oceanside. It stops twice a day traveling between Miami and Key West.

Islamorada

☏305 / POP 6400

Islamorada (is-luh-murr-*ah*-da) is also known as 'The Village of Islands.' A beautiful string of pearls, or rather, six keys – Plantation, Upper and Lower Matecumbe, Shell and Lignumvitae (lignum-*vite*-ee) – shimmers as one of the prettiest stretches of the islands. The scrubby mangrove is replaced by unbroken horizons of ocean and sky, one perfect shade of blue mirroring the other. Islamorada stretches across some 20 miles, from Mile Marker 90 to Mile Marker 74.

◎ Sights

★ **Keys History & Discovery Museum** MUSEUM
(☏305-922-2237; www.keysdiscovery.com; 82100 Overseas Hwy, Islander Resort; adult/child $15/6; ☺10am-5pm Wed-Sun) It's easy to spend a few hours at this fascinating interactive museum that delves into the people and major events that have shaped the Keys' past. The first floor takes in coral reefs (with several aquariums boasting live coral as well as elegant angelfish, butterfly fish and otherworldly lionfish), aboriginal peoples and Spanish treasure fleets (and the salvagers and pirates who thrived off of them).

There's also a handsome scale model of Indian Key (which was a small flourishing village in the 1830s), and stories of the homesteaders, fisherfolk, botanists and hermit artists who settled here over the years. Upstairs, a comfy theater screens a number of worthwhile films that capture the incredible challenges of building Henry Flagler's Overseas Railway (completed in 1912) and survivors' accounts of the horrific 1935 Labor Day Hurricane.

The museum also hosts a lecture series (admission $10) on topics including reef restoration, pirate stories and underwater exploration. It happens twice monthly from October to April.

★ **Anne's Beach**   BEACH
(Mile 73.5 oceanside; 🅿) FREE Named after local environmentalist Anne Eaton, this tiny beach is one of the finest seascapes in these parts. The small ribbon of sand opens onto a sky-bright stretch of tidal flats and a green tunnel of hammock and wetland. A short (quarter-mile) boardwalk leads through the mangroves with lookouts and picnic tables along the way.

**Florida Keys History of
Diving Museum**   MUSEUM
(🖉305-664-9737; www.divingmuseum.org; Mile 83; adult/child $15/7; ◷10am-5pm, 10am-6:45pm 3rd Wed of month; 🅿🖫) You can't miss the diving museum – it's the building with the enormous mural of whale sharks on the side. This journey 'under the sea' covers 4000 years, with fascinating pieces including the 1797 Klingert's copper kettle diving machine, a whimsical room devoted to Jules Verne's Captain Nemo, massive deep-diving suits and an exquisite display of diving helmets from around the world.

**Windley Key Fossil Reef
Geological State Site**   STATE PARK
(🖉305-664-2540; www.floridastateparks.org; Mile 85.5 oceanside; admission $2.50, tour $2; ◷8am-5pm Thu-Mon) To get his railroad built across the islands, Henry Flagler had to quarry out some sizable chunks of the Keys. The best evidence of those efforts can be found at this former quarry turned state park. Windley has leftover machinery scattered along an 8ft former quarry wall, with fossilized evidence of brain, star and finger coral embedded right in the rock. The wall offers a cool (and rare) public peek into the stratum of coral that forms the substrate of the Keys.

There are also various short trails through tropical hardwood hammock that make for a pleasant glimpse into the Keys' wilder side. Borrow a free trail guide from the visitor center. From December to April, ranger-led tours are offered at 10am and 2pm Friday to Sunday for $2 per person.

Rain Barrel Village   ARTS CENTER
(🖉305-521-2043; www.rainbarrelvillage.com; 86700 Overseas Hwy; ◷9am-5pm) Once you see the giant spiny lobster, you know you've arrived. Welcome to the Rain Barrel, a craft emporium that is packed with souvenir-y tourist tat, beach wear, island-themed artwork, pottery, glasswork and plenty of other eye candy – though not everything is made locally.

Indian Key Historic State Park   ISLAND
(🖉305-664-2540; www.floridastateparks.org/indiankey; Mile 78.5 oceanside; $2.50; ◷8am-sunset) This quiet island was once a thriving city, complete with a warehouse, docks, streets, a hotel and about 40 to 50 permanent residents. There's not much left at the historical site – just the foundation, some cisterns and jungly tangle. Arriving by boat or kayak is the only way to visit. Robbie's Marina hires out kayaks for the paddle out here – around 30 minutes one way in calm conditions.

**Lignumvitae Key
Botanical State Park**   ISLAND
(🖉305-664-2540; www.floridastateparks.org/lignumvitaekey; admission/tour $2.50/2; ◷8am-5pm Thu-Mon, tours 10am & 2pm Fri-Sun Dec-Apr) This key, only accessible by boat, encompasses a 280-acre island of virgin tropical forest ringed by alluring waters. The official attraction is the 1919 Matheson House, with its windmill and cistern; the real draw is a nice sense of shipwrecked isolation. From December to April, guided walking tours (1¼ hours) are given at 10am and 2pm Friday to Sunday. Get out here by hiring a kayak (about an hour's paddle) from Robbie's Marina.

Strangler figs, mastic, gumbo-limbo, poisonwood and lignum vitae trees form a dark canopy that feels more South Pacific than South Florida. Prepare for fierce mosquitoes outside of winter.

🏃 Activities

★ **Robbie's Marina**   BOATING
(🖉305-664-8070; https://robbies.com; Mile 77.5 bayside; kayak & stand-up paddleboard rentals $50-80; ◷7am-8pm; 🖫) Robbie's covers all the bases – it's a local flea market, tacky tourist shop, sea pen for tarpons (massive fish), waterfront restaurant and jumping-off point for fishing expeditions, all wrapped into one driftwood-laced compound. Boat rental and tours available. You can quickly escape the mayhem by hiring a kayak for a peaceful

paddle through nearby mangroves, hammocks and lagoons.

You can also book a snorkeling trip ($36), which takes you out on a very smooth-riding Happy Cat vessel for a chance to bob amid coral reefs. If you don't want to get on the water, you can feed the freakishly large tarpons from the dock ($4 per bucket, $2.25 to watch).

🛏 Sleeping

Ragged Edge Resort
RESORT $$
(☎305-852-5389; www.ragged-edge.com; 243 Treasure Harbor Dr; apt $160-330; P✳🛜🌊) This low-key and popular apartment complex, far from the maddening traffic jams, has 10 quiet units (all renovated in 2018) and friendly hosts. The larger studios have screened-in porches, and the entire vibe is happily comatose. There's no beach, but you can swim off the dock and in the heated pool.

There are kayaks, bikes and hammocks for guest use.

Sunset Inn
MOTEL $$
(☎305-664-3454; www.sunsetinnkeys.com; 82200 Overseas Hwy; r $150-300; P✳🛜🌊) After a stylish makeover, this once boxy motel along the highway has earned a new following for its bright, spacious rooms and appealing amenities. Oversized TVs, Keurig coffee makers, refrigerators and attractive bathrooms (brass fixtures, subway tiles) come standard in the rooms, and old photos of bygone days channel Keys nostalgia.

You can borrow bikes, use the outdoor games (table tennis, giant Jenga and chess) or fire up the barbecue.

Lime Tree Bay Resort Motel
MOTEL $$$
(☎305-664-4740; www.limetreebayresort.com; Mile 68.5 bayside; r $250-480; ✳🛜🌊) Hammocks and lawn chairs provide front-row seats for the spectacular sunsets at this 2.5-acre waterfront hideaway. The rooms are comfortable, airy and elegant, with wood floors and decorative rope details – the best have balconies overlooking the water. The extensive facilities include tennis courts, bikes, kayaks and stand-up paddleboards, plus a pool and Jacuzzi.

Casa Morada
HOTEL $$$
(☎305-664-0044; www.casamorada.com; 136 Madeira Rd, off Mile 82.2; ste incl breakfast $440-710; P✳🛜🌊) Contemporary chic comes to Islamorada, but it's not gentrifying away the village vibe. Rather, Casa Morada adds a welcome dash of sophistication to Conch chill: a keystone standing circle, freshwater pool, artificial lagoon – plus a *Wallpaper*-magazine-worthy bar that overlooks Florida Bay – all make this 16-suite boutique hotel worth a reservation. Go to the bar to catch a drink and a sunset.

Ask about yoga on the pier, private sunset sails on a 30ft Skipjack, and free use of kayaks and/or stand-up paddleboards.

🍴 Eating

Bad Boy Burrito
MEXICAN $
(☎305-509-7782; www.badboyburritoislamorada.com; 103 Mastic St, Mile 81.8 bayside; mains $8-24; ⏰10am-9pm Mon-Sat; 🎗) Tucked away in a small shopping plaza complete with gurgling fountain, orchids and swaying palms, Bad Boy Burrito whips up superb fish tacos and its namesake burritos – with quality ingredients (skirt steak, duck confit, zucchini and squash) and all the fixings (shaved cabbage, chipotle mayo, housemade salsa). Top it off with a hibiscus tea or a fruit smoothie and some chips and guacamole.

Midway Cafe
CAFE $
(☎305-664-2622; www.midwaycafecoffeebar.com; 80499 Overseas Hwy; mains $6-11; ⏰7am-3pm Mon-Sat, to 2pm Sun; P🛜🎗) A homey cafe that is a favorite stopover on the journey to the Keys for its excellent coffee and good sandwiches, wraps, salads and omelets. The lovely folks who run this cafe roast their own beans and make delectable baked goods. Everything is best enjoyed on the tiny patio beside the cafe.

⭐Lazy Days
SEAFOOD $$
(☎305-664-5256; www.lazydaysislamorada.com; 79867 Overseas Hwy oceanside; mains lunch $12-24, dinner $20-35; ⏰11am-9:30pm Sun-Thu, to 11pm Fri & Sat; 🎗) One of Islamorada's culinary icons, Lazy Days has a stellar reputation for its fresh seafood plates. Start off with a conch chowder topped with a little sherry, before moving on to a decadent grouper Lorenzo (fish topped with crab cake, key-lime butter and béarnaise sauce) or the creative Key West salad (spinach, coconut shrimp, sliced peaches, oranges and toasted almonds).

⭐Square Grouper Islamorada
SEAFOOD $$
(☎786-901-5678; www.squaregrouperislamorada.com; 80460 Overseas Hwy; mains lunch $12-31, dinner $18-39; ⏰11am-2:30pm & 5-10pm Wed-Mon; P🎗) In a peaceful spot overlooking a small marina, Square Grouper serves up beautifully

executed appetizers (such as seared tuna with ponzu sauce) and mouthwatering seafood platters, as well as creative salads and jasmine rice bowls topped with lobster tails, portobello mushrooms, scallops or other delicacies.

Bayside Gourmet   AMERICAN **$$**
(305-735-4471; www.baysidegourmet.com; Mile 82.7 bayside; mains breakfast $8-10, lunch & dinner $10-22; ⊗6am-9:30pm Mon-Sat, 11am-9pm Sun) This friendly deli and restaurant is a family-run affair and adds a dash of style to the average Keys seafood shack. The diverse menu serves up something for all palates: from pancakes and breakfast burritos to grouper sandwiches, lasagna and delicious thin-crust pizzas. There's outdoor dining in the palm-fringed back courtyard and old-school arcade games up front.

Beach Café & Bar
at Morada Bay   AMERICAN **$$$**
(☑305-664-0604; https://moradabaykeys.com/dining/beach-cafe; Mile 81.6 bayside; mains lunch $17-42, mains dinner $20-38; ⊗11:30am-10pm Sun-Thu, to 11pm Fri & Sat; P) The Beach Café & Bar has a lot going for it, namely a lovely, laid-back Caribbean vibe, a powder-white sandy beach, nighttime torches, tapas and outstanding seafood. It's also a good place to bring the kids, with room to run around, and the adults can come back for a monthly full-moon party, with live music, special cocktails and a beach barbecue.

🍸 Drinking & Nightlife

★**Florida Keys**
Brewing Company   MICROBREWERY
(☑305-916-5206; www.floridakeysbrewingco.com; 81611 Old Hwy; ⊗11am-10pm) Locally owned and operated, Florida Keys brews innovative,

well-balanced beers with a hint of the tropics (including flavor notes such as hibiscus, star fruit and key lime). Come in to the friendly tap room, order a flight and have a chat with one of the knowledgeable bartenders.

You can relax in the back garden, catch live music several nights a week, or join in another of the brewery's regular events such as movie nights and trivia quizzes.

🛍 Shopping

Old Road Gallery   ARTS & CRAFTS
(☑305-852-8935; www.oldroadgallery.com; Mile 88.8 oceanside; ⊗10am-5pm Thu-Tue) Specializing in pottery and sculpture, the Old Road Gallery embodies the Key's most creative side. After browsing the ceramics, jewelry and bronze works in the shop, take a stroll along the winding forested path to the cottage – a house built by the Red Cross in the aftermath of the 1935 Labor Day Hurricane, and home to yet more works of art.

ℹ Getting There & Away

The Greyhound bus stops at the Burger King at Mile Marker 82.5 oceanside. It goes twice daily to both Key West and Miami.

MIDDLE KEYS

On this stretch of the Keys, the bodies of water get wider, and the bridges get more impressive. This is where you'll find the famous Seven Mile Bridge, one of the world's longest causeways and a natural divider between the Middle and Lower Keys. In this collections of islands you'll cross specks such as Conch Key and Duck Key; green, quiet Grassy Key; and Key Vaca, where Mar-

---

DOLPHINS IN CAPTIVITY

Aquariums and marine life centers are popular destinations in Florida, particularly those with shows featuring dolphins and other marine mammals. Some even offer one-on-one interaction with dolphins. While swimming across a pool being towed by Flipper may sound like a memorable photo op, such practices raise deep ethical concerns.

The harsh reality of life for dolphins in captivity is hidden from visitors. Dolphins are highly intelligent and complex animals, and an artificial environment prevents them from communicating, hunting, playing and mating as they would in the wild. The stress of living in captivity often leads to a greater incidence of illness, disease and behavioral abnormalities. As a result, dolphins in captivity often live much shorter lives than those in the wild. Those dolphins that remain 'voluntarily' in captivity often do so simply to remain close to food.

You can read more about captive marine life at World Animal Protection (www.world animalprotection.us), Whale and Dolphin Conservation (www.whales.org/issues/swimming-with-dolphins) and the World Cetacean Alliance (www.worldcetaceanalliance.org).

athon, the second-largest town and most Key-sy community in the islands, is located.

Grassy Key

◉ Sights

Curry Hammock State Park STATE PARK
(☑305-289-2690; www.floridastateparks.org; Mile 56.2 bayside; car/cyclist $5.50/2.50; ☺8am-sunset; P♿) ✎ Curry Hammock is a popular spot for paddling through some lovely coastal scenery: you can rent a kayak (single/double for two hours $18/22) or stand-up paddleboard ($22 for two hours). You can also hike a 1.5-mile trail amid preserved tropical hardwood and mangrove habitats. The trailhead is one mile past the park's main entrance on the bayside (heading towards Marathon); look for the parking area on the right.

🛏 Sleeping & Eating

Rainbow Bend HOTEL $$$
(☑305-289-1505; www.rainbowbend.com; Mile 58 oceanside; r $260-480; P🐾♨) Experience intensely charming Keys-kitsch in these big pink cabanas, which have all been renovated following a big hit from Hurricane Irma in 2017. Inside, the 23 rooms are modern and attractively furnished, with cheerful color schemes and extras including small kitchen units in the bigger suites. The beachfront location and fine-dining restaurant add to the appeal.

SS Wreck Galley & Galley Grill AMERICAN $$
(☑305-517-6484; www.wreckgalleygrill.com; Mile 59 bayside; mains $12-28; ☺11am-9pm Sun & Tue-Thu, to 10pm Fri & Sat; P) The SS Wreck is a Keys classic, where fisherfolk types knock back brews and feast on wings. It's definitely a local haunt, where island politicos like to prattle on about the issues (fishing). The food is excellent: it grills one of the best burgers in the Keys, and fires up satisfying daily specials.

Marathon

☑ 305, 786 / POP 8700

Marathon sits right on the halfway point between Key Largo and Key West, and it's a good place to stop on a road trip across the islands. Outside Key West, it is perhaps the most 'developed' key (though that might be pushing the definition of the word 'devel-oped') – it has large shopping centers and a population of more than 8000. It's still a place where exiles from the mainland fish, booze it up and have a good time; while Marathon is more family-friendly than Key West, it has maintained its wild side.

◉ Sights

★Crane Point Hammock NATURE RESERVE
(☑305-743-9100; www.cranepoint.net; Mile 50.5 bayside; adult/child $15/10; ☺9am-5pm Mon-Sat, from noon Sun; P♿🐾) ✎ For a look at a Keys ecosystem in a near pristine state, don't miss this 63-acre reserve encompassing dense tropical hammock, solution holes, mangroves, a butterfly meadow and a lovely stretch of coastline. A looping 1.5-mile trail with various boardwalk detours transports you quickly into the wild side.

Highlights along the way include the restored Adderley House (built by Bahamian immigrants in 1903), the jungle-like palm hammock (which only grows between Mile Markers 47 and 60), and a wild bird center (where injured birds are nursed back to health). Start off with a short film that gives an overview of the park, and have a look at the natural history museum (dugout canoes, pirate exhibitions, a simulated coral reef). It's a great spot for kids.

Pigeon Key National Historic District ISLAND
(☑305-743-5999; www.pigeonkey.net; Mile 47 oceanside; adult/child $12/9; ☺tours 10am, noon & 2pm) For years tiny Pigeon Key, located 2 miles west of Marathon (basically below the Old Seven Mile Bridge), housed the rail workers and maintenance men who built the infrastructure that connected the Keys. Today you can tour the structures of this National Historic District or relax on the beach and get in some snorkeling. Buy tickets from the **visitor center** (2010 Overseas Hwy; ☺9:30am-4pm) at Mile 47.5 on the main highway; boats leave from the pier in back – parking is available at the Hyatt Place next door.

Restoration is underway on the 2-mile stretch of the Old Seven Mile Bridge that connects Marathon to Pigeon Key. Once complete (perhaps by 2021), visitors will be able to walk or bike to the island along this historical former rail line.

Florida Keys Aquarium Encounters AQUARIUM
(☑305-407-3262; www.floridakeysaquarium encounters.com; 11710 Overseas Hwy, Mile 53.1

bayside; adult/child $25/18, animal encounters from $30; ⊙9am-5pm; 🐾) A visit to this small, interactive aquarium starts with a free guided tour of some fascinating marine ecosystems. There are also more immersive experiences, where you snorkel in the coral reef aquarium or the tropical fish–filled lagoon.

Some of the ecosystems you will encounter include a mangrove-lined basin full of tarpon, a tidal pool tank with queen conch and horseshoe crabs, and a 200,000-gallon coral reef tank with moray eels, grouper and several different shark species.

You can also observe mesmerizing lionfish, a pig-nosed turtle, juvenile alligators and various fish species from the Everglades, plus snowy egrets and little blue herons that come by for a visit.

Sightly more controversial are the 'touch tanks' and 'stingray encounters' where you can handle shallow-water marine species and touch stingrays (the barbs have been trimmed). Please note that the stress of human interaction can be detrimental to the well-being of aquatic creatures.

Sombrero Beach   BEACH
(Sombrero Beach Rd, off Mile 50 oceanside; ⊙7:30am-dusk; P🐾🎽) One of the few white-sand, mangrove-free beaches in the Keys. It's a good spot to lounge on the sand or swim, and there's also a small playground.

Turtle Hospital   WILDLIFE RESERVE
(☑305-743-2552; www.theturtlehospital.org; 2396 Overseas Hwy; adult/child $27/13; ⊙9am-6pm; P🐾) 🐢 Injured sea turtles in the Keys hopefully end up in this motel-cum-sanctuary. It's sad to see the injured and sick ones, but heartening to see them so well looked after. Ninety-minute tours are educational, fun and offered on the hour from 9am to 4pm.

🏃 Activities

Keys Kayak   KAYAKING
(☑305-743-8880; www.keyskayakllc.com; 10499 Overseas Hwy; tour $50-70; ⊙8:30am-5:30pm) This professional outfit runs highly rated two- to three-hour kayaking tours, including paddles through the mangroves off Sombrero Beach and sunset trips off Grassy Key. If you prefer DIY adventures, you can rent kayaks (single/double $30/55 per day) and stand-up paddleboards ($50 per day).

Tilden's Scuba Center   DIVING
(☑305-743-7255; www.tildensscubacenter.com; 4650 Overseas Hwy; snorkel/dive trip $60/85, full scuba gear hire $120-150, snuba trip $165; ⊙8am-6pm) This knowledgeable and respected outfit offers snorkeling and diving expeditions through nearby sections of the coral reef. Reef trips typically depart twice daily at 8am and 1pm. Inexperienced divers can try snuba, allowing you to dive to depths of 20ft, while breathing through an air hose tethered to the surface.

🛏 Sleeping

Ranch House Motel   MOTEL $$
(☑305-743-2217; www.theranchhousemotel.com; 7251 Overseas Hwy; r $130-230; P❄🐾) For the money, this friendly, family-run place right off the highway is one of the best-value lodging options in the Keys. The owners go the extra mile to make guests feel at home. The rooms are clean and well maintained, with wood-paneled walls, comfy beds, fluffy towels (and modern bathrooms), wall-mounted TVs, and a fridge and microwave in each.

Sea Dell Motel   MOTEL $$
(☑305-743-5161; www.seadellmotel.com; 5000 Overseas Hwy; r $180-250; P❄🐾🏊) The Sea Dell is a Keys classic: bright, low-slung rooms with a pastel color scheme and floral bedspreads. The rooms are well equipped (coffeemaker, fridge and microwave), and can comfortably accommodate small families. The small pool entices after a day of exploring.

Seascape Motel & Marina   MOTEL $$$
(☑305-743-6212; www.seascapemotelandmarina. com; 1075 75th St Ocean E, btwn Mile 51 & 52; r $290-550; P❄🐾🏊) The understated luxury of this B&B manifests in its 12 rooms, with their minimalist sleek decor. There is a waterfront pool, kayaks, stand-up paddleboards and bikes for guests to use, and its secluded setting will make you feel like you've gotten away from it all. Seascape also offers guests complimentary wine and beer at 5pm.

Tranquility Bay   RESORT $$$
(☑305-289-0667; www.tranquilitybay.com; Mile 48.5 bayside; r $320-970; P❄🐾🏊) If you're serious about going upscale, you should book in here. Tranquility Bay is a massive condo-hotel resort with plush townhouses, a lagoon-style pool (as well as two others), a waterfront tiki bar, fitness room, and a top-notch restaurant – while the inviting, palm-studded beach is just steps away from your bed. The grounds are enormous and activity-filled; they really don't want you to leave.

✕ Eating

Wooden Spoon
AMERICAN $

(7007 Overseas Hwy; mains $6-12; ⊘5:30am-1pm; 🅿️) Never mind the sometimes surly service; the Wooden Spoon whips up the best breakfast for miles around, and always warrants a visit. The fluffy pancakes (ideally with blueberries) are outstanding, and you can also opt for perfectly baked biscuits covered in thick sausage gravy or a spicy Mexican omelet and other favorites. The down-at-the-heels diner ambience is a Keys classic.

★ Keys Fisheries
SEAFOOD $$

(☑866-743-4353; www.keysfisheries.com; 3502 Louisa St; mains $14-33; ⊘11am-9pm; 🅿️♿) The lobster Reuben is the stuff of legend. Sweet, chunky, creamy – so good you'll be daydreaming about it afterward. But you can't go wrong with any of the excellent seafood here, all served with sass. Expect some seagull harassment as you dine on a working waterfront.

The rambling waterfront property also includes an upstairs bar with cold beer, oysters and sweeping views over the marina.

Sunset Grille
AMERICAN $$

(☑305-396-7235; www.sunsetgrille7milebridge. com; 7 Knights Key Blvd, Mile 47 oceanside; mains lunch $12-17, dinner $20-35; ⊘8am-10pm; ♿) Overlooking the Seven Mile Bridge, this huge, festive spot has an unbeatable location (it's not called Sunset for nothing) and wide-ranging appeal: namely a huge menu of seafood and grilled meat dishes, plus a raw bar, sushi and plenty of kid-friendly options. There's also an appealing swimming pool (heated in winter) that's free and open to all.

Burdines Waterfront
AMERICAN $$

(☑305-743-9204; www.burdineswaterfront.com; 1200 Oceanview Ave, end of 15th St, Mile 48 oceanside; mains $10-19; ⊘11am-9pm; ♿) For a taste of old-school Marathon, head to this barnlike upper-story shack on the waterfront. It's a much-loved local haunt where you can take a seat around the thatch-roof bar or at a picnic table and take in the breezy views while munching on mahimahi Reuben sandwiches, fresh tuna melts and the best burgers (and hand-cut fries) in the Keys.

🍺 Drinking & Nightlife

Sparky's Landing
BAR

(☑305-363-2959; www.sparkyslanding.com; 13205 Overseas Hwy; ⊘11am-10pm) Newly reborn after being wiped off the face of the earth by Hurricane Irma in 2017, Sparky's is the go-to spot for easygoing waterfront drinking. There's live music most nights, a buzzing happy hour (4pm to 6pm) and a first-rate food menu (fish tacos, pizza, seafood platters).

It's hidden behind a Holiday Inn Express. Look for the steep thatched roof.

Hurricane
BAR

(☑305-743-2200; www.facebook.com/hurricane gillemarathon; Mile 49.5 bayside; ⊘11am-midnight) Locals, tourists, mad fisherfolk and rednecks saddle up here for endless Jägerbombs before dancing the night away to any number of consistently good live acts. With sassy staff and heartwarming (strong) drinks, this is one of Marathon's best dive bars.

Island Fish Company
BAR

(☑305-743-4191; https://islandfishco.com; Mile 54 bayside; ⊘8am-10pm) The Island has friendly staff pouring strong cocktails on a seabreeze-kissed tiki island overlooking Florida Bay. Chat with your friendly bartender – tip well, and they may top up your drinks without you realizing it. The laid-back, by-the-water atmosphere is quintessentially Keys. Pretty sunsets, great seafood plates and a raw bar add to the allure.

☆ Entertainment

Marathon Cinema & Community Theater
CINEMA

(☑cinema 305-743-0288, theater 305-743-0994; www.marathontheater.org; 5101 Overseas Hwy) An iconic single-stage theater that shows plays and movies in big reclining seats (with even bigger cup holders); the snack bar serves wine and beer.

ℹ️ Information

Fishermen's Hospital (☑305-743-5533; 3301 Overseas Hwy; ⊘24hr) Has a major emergency room, as well as a walk-in clinic for less severe health issues.

ℹ️ Getting There & Away

Only chartered planes currently fly into **Marathon Airport** (☑305-289-6060; Mile 50.5 bayside), which is in the center of the island – and serves as the Greyhound bus stop. There's also regular bus service to Key West on **Key West Transit** (☑305-600-1455; www.kwtransit.com; day pass $4-8).

LOWER KEYS

The people of the Lower Keys vary between winter escapees and native Conchs. Some local families have been Keys castaways for generations, and there is somewhat of a more insular feel than other parts of the Overseas Hwy. The islands get at their most isolated and rural before opening onto (relatively) cosmopolitan, heterogeneous and free-spirited Key West.

People aside, the big draw in the Lower Keys is nature. You'll find the loveliest state park in the Keys here, and one of its rarest species. For paddlers, there is a great mangrove wilderness to explore in a photogenic and pristine environment.

Big Pine Key, Bahia Honda Key & Looe Key

Big Pine is home to endless stretches of quiet roads, Key West employees who found a way around astronomical real-estate rates, and packs of wandering Key deer. Bahia Honda has everyone's favorite sandy beach, while the coral-reef system of Looe offers amazing reef-diving opportunities.

◉ Sights

★ **Bahia Honda State Park**   STATE PARK
(☑ 305-872-3210; www.bahiahondapark.com; Mile 37; car $4.50-8.50, cyclist & pedestrian $2.50; ⊙ 8am-sunset; 🏊) 🏖 This park, with its long, white-sand (and at times seaweed-strewn) beach, named Sandspur Beach by locals, is the big attraction in these parts. As Keys beaches go, this one is probably the best natural stretch of sand in the island chain. There's also the novel experience of walking on the old Bahia Honda Rail Bridge, which offers nice views of the surrounding islands. Heading out on kayaking adventures (from $12/36 per hour/half day) is another great way to spend a sun-drenched afternoon.

You can also check out the nature trails and science center, where helpful park employees can assist you to identify stone crabs, fireworms, horseshoe crabs and comb jellies. The park concession offers daily 1½-hour snorkeling trips at 9:30am and 1:30pm (adult/child $30/25). Reserve ahead in high season. Many parts of the park were badly damaged by Hurricane Irma, but the park should be fully operational again by 2021.

No Name Key   ISLAND
Perhaps the best-named island in the Keys, No Name gets few visitors, as it's basically a residential island. It's one of the most reliable spots for Key deer watching. From Overseas Hwy, go onto Watson Blvd, turn right, then left onto Wilder Blvd. Cross Bogie Bridge and you'll be on No Name.

There are several barely signed trails here, including one off to the right about 0.8 miles after crossing Bogie Bridge. It leads through mangrove forest (badly damaged by Hurricane Irma) and out to the waterfront, passing an old rock quarry with abandoned machinery along the way.

National Key Deer Refuge Headquarters   WILDLIFE RESERVE
(☑ 305-872-0774; www.fws.gov/refuge/National_Key_Deer_Refuge; 30587 Overseas Hwy; ⊙ 10am-3pm Mon-Sat; 🏊) What would make Bambi cuter? Mini Bambi. Introducing the Key deer, an endangered subspecies of white-tailed deer that prance about primarily on Big Pine and No Name Keys. The folks here are an incredibly helpful source of information on the deer and all things Keys related. The refuge sprawls over several islands, but the sections open to the public are on Big Pine and No Name.

The headquarters also administers the **Great White Heron National Wildlife Refuge** – 200,000 acres of open water and mangrove islands north of the main Keys that is only accessible by boat. There's no tourism infrastructure in place to get out here, but you can inquire about nautical charts and the herons themselves at the office.

Blue Hole   LAKE
(Key Deer Blvd, off Mile 30.5) This little pond (and former quarry) is now the largest freshwater body in the Keys. That's not saying much, but the hole is a pretty little dollop of blue (well, algal green) surrounded by a small path and information signs. The water is home to turtles, fish, wading birds and the odd alligator. A quarter-mile further along the same road is **Watson's Nature Trail** (less than 1 mile long) and **Watson's Hammock**, a small Keys forest habitat.

Looe Key National Marine Sanctuary   PARK
(☑ 305-809-4700; www.floridakeys.noaa.gov) Looe (pronounced 'loo') Key, located 5 nautical miles off Big Pine, isn't a key at all but a reef, and is part of the Florida Keys National Marine Sanctuary. This is an area of some 2800 sq nautical miles of 'land' managed

NATURAL WONDERS OF THE KEYS

It's easy to think of the Keys, environmentally speaking, as a little boring. The landscape isn't particularly dramatic (with the exception of those sweet sweeps of ocean visible from the Overseas Hwy); it tends toward low brush and...well, more low brush.

Hey, don't judge a book by its cover. The Keys have one of the most remarkable, sensitive environments in the USA. The difference between ecosystems here is measured in inches, but once you learn to recognize the contrast between a hammock and a wetland, you'll see the islands in a whole new tropical light. Some of the best introductions to the natural Keys can be found at Crane Point Hammock (p185) and the Florida Keys Eco-Discovery Center (p195).

But we want to focus on the mangroves – the coolest, if not most visually arresting, habitat in the islands. They rise from the shallow shelf that surrounds the Keys (which also provides that lovely shade of Florida teal), looking like masses of spidery fingers constantly stroking the waters. Each mangrove traps the sediment that has accrued into the land your tiki barstool is perched on. That's right, no mangroves = no Jimmy Buffett.

The three different types of mangrove trees are all little miracles of adaptation. Red mangroves, which reside on the water's edge, have aerial roots, called propagules, allowing them to 'breathe' even as they grow into the ocean. Black mangroves, which grow further inland, survive via 'snorkel' roots called pneumatophores. Resembling spongy sticks, these roots grow out from the muddy ground and consume fresh air. White mangroves grow furthest inland and actually sweat out the salt they absorb through air and water to keep healthy.

The other tree worth a mention here isn't a mangrove. The lignum vitae, which is limited to the Keys in the USA, is also intriguing. Its sap has long been used to treat syphilis, hence the tree's Latin name, which translates to 'tree of life.'

by the National Oceanic & Atmospheric Administration. The reef here can only be visited through a specially arranged charter-boat trip, best arranged through any Keys diving outfit, the most natural one being Looe Key Dive Center.

Big Pine Flea Market MARKET
(www.bigpinefleamarket.com; Mile 30.5 oceanside; ⊗8am-2pm Sat & Sun late Nov-May; P) FREE This market is an extravaganza of locally made crafts, antiques, vintage clothes, handbags, sunglasses, souvenir T-shirts and beach towels, wood carvings, wind chimes and hand tools – plus all the secondhand gear you might need for a fishing trip.

🏃 Activities

★ **Big Pine Kayak Adventures** KAYAKING
(☑305-872-7474; www.keyskayaktours.com; tours depart from 1791 Bogie Dr; half-day backcountry tour per person from $150) For backcountry paddling tours in the Keys, there's no better operator than the highly regarded Big Pine Kayak Adventures. It's run by Bill Keogh, a highly experienced naturalist guide who has written the book on South Florida aquatic tours (literally – check out his extensively

researched *Florida Keys Paddling Guide*, published in 2004).

Whether you go with Bill or another of Big Pine's guides, you're in for a treat. You'll paddle across pristine coves with mirror-like waters, through mangrove forests, and sponge and grass flats while looking for wildlife (Key deer, starfish, jellyfish, sponges, herons and loads of other bird life). Tours depart from the Old Wooden Bridge Resort & Marina. Book ahead.

Old Wooden Bridge Resort & Marina BOATING
(☑305-872-2241; www.oldwoodenbridge.com; 1791 Bogie Dr; 2hr single/double kayak ride $25/35, motorboat half-/full-day rental from$150/200; ⊗8:30am-5pm) At the foot of the bridge that takes you over to No Name Key, you can hire kayaks and small motor boats for the day (multiday discounts available). This is a lovely area to explore.

Looe Key Dive Center DIVING
(☑305-872-2215; www.diveflakeys.com; 27340 Overseas Hwy, Ramrod Key; snorkel/dive from $40/70; ⊗8am-7pm) Located in a resort of the same name, the Looe Key Dive Center on Ramrod Key runs recommended day trips out to Looe Key departing in the morning

(8am) and afternoon (12:45pm). This two-tank/two-location dive is $70 plus gear for scuba divers, $40 plus gear for snorkelers, and $25 for 'bubblewatchers' who want to come along for the ride.

🛏 Sleeping

Bahia Honda State Park
Campground   CAMPGROUND $
(☎ 800-326-3521; www.reserveamerica.com; Mile 37, Bahia Honda Key; campsites/cabins $50/175; P 🛜) 🐾 Bahia Honda has the best camping in the Keys. There's nothing quite like waking up to the sky as your ceiling and the ocean as your shower (and: Ow! Sand flies. OK, it's not paradise...). The park has six cabins, each sleeping four to six people, and 80 campsites a short distance from the beach. Reserve months in advance.

⭐ Deer Run on the Atlantic   B&B $$$
(☎ 305-872-2015; www.deerrunontheatlantic. com; 1997 Long Beach Dr, Big Pine Key, off Mile 33 oceanside; r from $355; P 🛜 @ 🛜 🐾) 🐾 This state-certified green lodge and pet-friendly B&B is isolated on a lovely stretch of Long Beach Dr. One of the hardest hit places by Hurricane Irma, Deer Run has gone through an extensive restoration inside and out since 2017. The four bright, ecofriendly rooms have sparkling views over the water, and guests have free use of bikes and kayaks.

🍴 Eating

Good Food
Conspiracy   VEGETARIAN $
(☎ 305-872-3945; www.goodfoodconspiracy.com; 30150 Overseas Highway, Big Pine Key, Mile 30 oceanside; sandwiches $9-15; ⊗ 10am-6pm Mon-Sat; P 🐾) 🐾 Rejoice, health-food lovers: all the greens, sprouts, herbs and tofu you've been dreaming about during that long, fried-food-studded drive down the Overseas Hwy are available at this friendly little macrobiotic organic shop. There is a good sandwich and fresh-juice bar on-site, where you can get avocado melts, fresh salads, veggie burgers, homemade soup and fruit smoothies.

No Name Pub   PIZZA $$
(☎ 305-872-9115; www.nonamepub.com; N Watson Blvd, Big Pine Key, off Mile 30.5 bayside; mains $13-27; ⊗ 11am-10pm; P) The No Name's one of those off-the-track places that everyone seems to know about. Despite the isolated location, folks come from all over to this divey spot to add their dollar bills to the walls, drink locally brewed beer, enjoy some classic rock playing overhead, and feast on pizzas, burgers and pub grub.

Take in the kooky ambience from a barstool or head out back to a shaded yard full of picnic tables. Note: the name of this place implies that it is located on No Name Key, but it is on Big Pine Key, just over the causeway.

🍷 Drinking & Nightlife

Kiki's Sandbar   BAR
(☎ 305-872-4500; www.kikissandbar.com; 183 Barry Ave, Mile 28.3 bayside; ⊗ 11am-midnight) For drinks with a view, Kiki's is hard to beat. You can have a chat around the bar or retreat for a bit of sunset watching or stargazing from one of the picnic tables on the waterfront lawn – or better yet stroll to the pier, which can be a magical setting when the moon is on the rise.

❶ Getting There & Away

Greyhound (www.greyhound.com) has two buses daily that stop in Big Pine Key on the run between Miami and Key West (one way from $12).

Key West Transit (p187) runs nine buses daily between Key West and Marathon, stopping in Big Pine Key. The one-way fare is $4.

Sugarloaf Key & Boca Chica Key

This is the final stretch before the holy grail of Key West. There's not much going on – just bridges over lovely swaths of teal and turquoise, and a few good dining options, including longtime Key classics and a newer hot spot serving cutting-edge fare.

This lowest section of the Keys goes from about Mile Marker 20 to the start of Key West.

🛏 Sleeping & Eating

Sugarloaf Lodge   MOTEL $$
(☎ 305-745-3211; www.sugarloaflodge.net; Sugarloaf Key, Mile 17; r $180-280; P 🛜 🐾) The 55 motel-like rooms with wood paneling are nothing special, though every single one has an excellent bay view from the balcony or patio (1st floor), and the service is friendly. There's plenty of extras on hand including an excellent restaurant, an appealing tiki bar and a neighboring marina, where you can hire kayaks and arrange fishing charters.

FLORIDA KEYS & KEY WEST SUGARLOAF KEY & BOCA CHICA KEY

Baby's Coffee
CAFE $

(📞 305-744-9866; www.babyscoffee.com; Mile 15 oceanside; ⏰ 6:30am-6pm) This very cool coffee counter has an on-site bean-roasting plant and sells bags of the aromatic stuff along with excellent hot and cold java brews. Other essentials are sold, from yummy baked goods to fruit smoothies.

Mangrove Mama's
CARIBBEAN $$

(📞 305-745-3030; www.mangrovemamas20.com; Mile 20 bayside; ⏰ 11am-10pm; P 🅿 🍴) This groovy roadside eatery serves globally inspired seafood – scallops with linguine, plantain-crusted hogfish, blackened mahimahi tacos – best enjoyed on the backyard patio and accompanied by a little live music (daily 6pm to 9pm).

Square Grouper
MODERN AMERICAN $$$

(📞 305-745-8880; www.squaregrouperbarandgrill. com; Mile 22.5 oceanside, Cudjoe Key; mains lunch $13-31, dinner $18-39; ⏰ 11am-2:30pm & 5-10pm Tue-Sat; 🍴) Reason enough to venture out of Key West, the Square Grouper hits all the right notes with fresh, locally sourced ingredients, innovative recipes and great service, all dished up in one elegant but unpretentious dining room. Local fish-of-the-day tacos, seared sesame-encrusted tuna loin and a rich seafood stew are among the highlights, though it's worth investigating daily specials.

Reserve ahead. And don't forget to have a pre- or post-dinner drink in the upstairs lounge My New Joint.

🍷 Drinking & Nightlife

★ My New Joint
COCKTAIL BAR

(📞 305-745-8880; www.mynewjoint420lounge. com; Mile 22.5, Cudjoe Key; ⏰ 4:20pm-11pm Tue-Sat) My New Joint brings a serious dash of style to the Lower Keys. This spacious, warmly lit lounge has artfully made cocktails, excellent brews on tap (including local varieties), great tapas plates and platters of oysters, and live music most nights (from 7pm).

❶ Getting There & Away

Key West Transit (p187) runs nine buses a day between Key West and Marathon, stopping in both Boca Chica and Sugarloaf Key. The one-way fare is $4.

KEY WEST
📞 305. 786 / POP 24,600

Key West is the far frontier: edgier and more eccentric than the other Keys, and far more captivating. At its heart, this 7-sq-mile island feels like a beautiful tropical oasis, where the moonflowers bloom at night and the classical Caribbean homes are so sad and romantic it's hard not to sigh at them.

While Key West has obvious allure, it's not without its contradictions. On one side of the road, there are literary festivals, Caribbean villas, tropical dining rooms and expensive art galleries. On the other, you may see an S&M fetishist parade, frat boys passing out on the sidewalk and grizzly bars filled with bearded burnouts. With all that in mind, it's easy to find your groove in this setting, no matter where your interests lie.

As in other parts of the Keys, nature plays a starring role here, with some breathtaking sunsets – cause for nightly celebration down on Mallory Sq.

◉ Sights

★ Museum of Art & History at the Custom House
MUSEUM

(📞 305-295-6616; www.kwahs.com; 281 Front St; adult/child $12/5; ⏰ 9:30am-4:30pm) This excellent museum, set in a grand 1891 red-brick building that once served as the Custom House, covers Key West's history. Highlights are the archival footage from the building of the ambitious Overseas Hwy (and the hurricane that killed 400 people), a model of the ill-fated USS *Maine* (sunk during the Spanish–American War), exhibitions on the role of the navy (once the largest employer in Key West) and the 'wreckers' of Key West, who scavenged sunken treasure ships.

★ Key West Butterfly & Nature Conservatory
WILDLIFE RESERVE

(📞 305-296-2988; www.keywestbutterfly.com; 1316 Duval St; adult/child $15/11; ⏰ 9am-5pm; 🚼) This huge domed conservatory lets you stroll through a lush, enchanting garden of flowering plants, tiny waterfalls, colorful birds (including flamingos) and up to 1800 fluttering butterflies comprising some 50 different species – all live imports from around the globe. The shimmery blue morpho butterflies winging past are particularly captivating. Don't miss the small viewing area, where butterflies emerge from their chrysalises (most frequently in the morning).

Key West

Latitudes
(0.25mi)

Key West Bight

Land's
End Marina

Sunset
Key

Historic
Seaport

Schooner
Wharf

58

54

19

39

Front St

8

Greene St

68

11

18

65

Key West
Chamber of
Commerce

Dey St

William St

**Museum of Art
& History at the
Custom House**

Ann St

Caroline St

Elizabeth St

2

12

53

23

56

42

62

30

16

67

Eaton St

21

Duval St

52

31

13

Front St

Whitehead St

63

27

49

Bahama St

28

Pier B

10

14

48

Fleming St

64

55

3

57

50

25

BAHAMA
VILLAGE

Whitehead St

51

Emma St

35

59

Submarine
Basin

Truman
Waterfront
Park

Angela St

66

32

38

Gay Key West
Business
Guild

6

47

60

Petronia St

Thomas St

9

4

Angela St

Fort St

Emma St

Olivia St

Julia St

Howe St

P

Naval Air
Station –
Truman Annex

5

Fort Zachary
Taylor
State Park

20

Whitehead
Spit

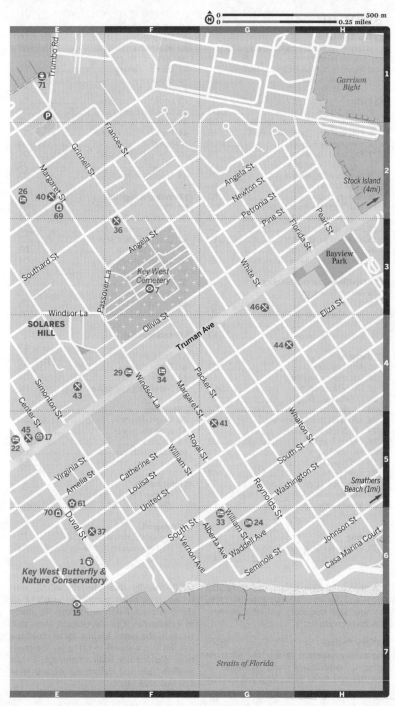

0 500 m
0 0.25 miles

E

Trumbo Rd
71
P
Grinnell St
Frances St
Margaret St
26 40
69
36
Southard St
Passover La
Angela St
Key West Cemetery
7
Windsor La
SOLARES HILL
Olivia St
Simonton St
43
Center St
45
22 17
Virginia St
Amelia St
61
70
Duval St 37
1
Key West Butterfly & Nature Conservatory
15

F

Angela St
Newton St
Petronia St
Pine St
White St
Olivia St
Truman Ave
29 34
Margaret St
Packer St
Windsor La
41
Royal St
William St
Catherine St
Louisa St
United St
South St
Vernon Ave
Alberta Ave
33
Waddell Ave
William St
24
Seminole St

G

Garrison Bight

Stock Island (4mi)

Florida St
Pearl St
Bayview Park
Eliza St
46
44
Whalton St
South St
Washington St
Reynolds St
Smathers Beach (1mi)
Johnson St
Casa Marina Court

H

Straits of Florida

1
2
3
4
5
6
7

Key West

A tiny exhibition center has intriguing videos and displays describing the life cycle, anatomy and migratory patterns of these wondrous creatures.

Mallory Square SQUARE
(www.mallorysquare.com; P ⛵) Take all those energies, subcultures and oddities of Keys life and focus them into one torchlit, family-friendly (but playfully edgy), sunset-enriched street party. The result of all these raucous forces is Mallory Sq, home to a cinematic, if tourist-clogged, show that starts in the hours leading up to dusk, the sinking sun a signal to bring on the madness. Watch a dog walk a tightrope, a man swallow fire, and British acrobats tumble and sass each other.

Hemingway House HOUSE

(☑ 305-294-1136; www.hemingwayhome.com; 907 Whitehead St; adult/child $15/6; ☺ 9am-5pm) Key West's biggest darling, Ernest Hemingway, lived in this gorgeous Spanish Colonial house from 1931 to 1940. Papa moved here with his second wife, a *Vogue* fashion editor and (former) friend of his first wife; Hemingway left the house when he ran off with his third wife. *The Short Happy Life of Francis Macomber* and *The Green Hills of Africa* were produced here, as were many cats, whose descendants basically run the grounds.

Nancy Forrester's Secret Garden GARDENS

(www.nancyforrester.com; 518 Elizabeth St; adult/child $10/5; ☺ 10am-3pm; ⊞) Nancy, an environmental artist and fixture of the Keys community, invites you into her backyard oasis where chatty rescued parrots and macaws await visitors. She gives an overview of these marvelously intelligent and rare birds ('Parrot 101' as she calls it) between 10am and 11am daily. It's a great place for kids, who often leave inspired by the hands-on interactions. Musicians are welcome to bring their instruments to play in the yard. The birds love it – particularly flutes!

Duval Street AREA

Key West locals have a love-hate relationship with the most famous road in Key West (if not the Keys). Duval, Old Town Key West's main strip, is a miracle mile of booze, tacky everything and awful behavior – but it's a lot of fun. The 'Duval Crawl' is one of the wildest pub crawls in the country. The mix of neon drink signs, drag shows, T-shirt kitsch, local theaters, art studios and boutiques is more charming and entertaining than jarring.

Florida Keys Eco-Discovery Center MUSEUM

(☑ 305-809-4750; https://floridakeys.noaa.gov/eco_discovery.html; 35 East Quay Rd; ☺ 9am-4pm Tue-Sat; ℗ ⊞) 🏄 FREE This 6000-sq-ft center is one of the best places in the Keys to learn about the extraordinary marine environments of South Florida. Start off with the 20-minute film which has some beautiful footage of life among the reefs, hardwood hammocks, seagrass beds and mangroves. Continue to the exhibits of life above the waterline, then look at sea creatures in the small aquarium tanks that make up the 'Living Reef' section.

Studios of Key West GALLERY

(TSKW; ☑ 305-296-0458; www.tskw.org; 533 Eaton St; ☺ 10am-4pm Tue-Sat) FREE This nonprofit showcases about a dozen artists' studios in a three-story space, and hosts some of the best art openings in Key West on the first Thursday of the month. Besides its public visual-arts displays, it also hosts readings, literary and visual workshops, concerts, lectures and community discussion groups. Don't miss Hugh's Views, a new rooftop deck that opened in 2020 and offers a fine perspective over town.

Key West Cemetery CEMETERY

(www.friendsofthekeywestcemetery.com; cnr Margaret & Angela Sts; ☺ 7am-6pm; ⊞) A darkly alluring Gothic labyrinth beckons at the center of this pastel town. Built in 1847, the cemetery crowns Solares Hill, the highest point on the island (with a vertigo-inducing elevation of 16ft). Some of the oldest families in the Keys rest in peace – and close proximity – here. With body space at a premium, mausoleums stand practically shoulder to shoulder. Island quirkiness penetrates the gloom: seashells and macramé adorn headstones with inscriptions such as, 'I told you I was sick.'

Get chaperoned by a guide from the **Historic Florida Keys Foundation** (☑ 305-292-6718), with guided tours ($20 per person) offered periodically. Call to reserve a spot.

Fort Zachary Taylor State Park STATE PARK

(☑ 305-292-6713; www.fortzacharytaylor.com; 601 Howard England Way; vehicle/pedestrian/bicycle $7/2.50/2.50; ☺ park 8am-sunset, fort 8am-5pm) 'America's Southernmost State Park' is home to an impressive fort, built in the mid-1800s, that played roles in the American Civil War and in the Spanish–American War. The **beach** here is the best one Key West has to offer – it has white sand to lounge on (but is rocky in parts), water deep enough to swim in and tropical fish under the waves. It's also a fine spot for sunset viewing. Learn more about the fort on free guided tours offered at 11am.

There's a fine cafe on-site, and you can hire lounge chairs and umbrellas, as well as snorkeling gear. If coming by foot, it's about a half-mile walk (12 minutes) from the entrance to the beach.

Mel Fisher Maritime Museum MUSEUM

(www.melfisher.org; 200 Greene St; adult/student/child $16/14/7; ☺ 8:30am-5pm Mon-Fri, from 9:30am Sat & Sun) For a fascinating glimpse into Key West's complicated history, pay a visit to this popular museum near the waterfront. It's best known for its collection of gold coins, rare jewels and other treasures scavenged from Spanish galleons by Mel Fisher and crew. More thought-provoking is the exhibition devoted to the slave trade, with artifacts from the wreck of the *Henrietta Marie,* a merchant slave ship that sank in 1700.

Key West First Legal Rum   DISTILLERY

(☑ 305-294-1441; www.keywestlegalrum.com; 105 Simonton St; ☺ 10am-8pm Mon-Fri, 11am-7pm Sat, 10am-6pm Sun, tours 1pm, 3pm & 4pm Mon-Sat, 1pm & 3pm Sun) Opened back in 2013 by a kitesurfing pioneer, this distillery makes some mighty fine rums, which are made with Florida sugarcane and infused with coconut, vanilla and key lime. Try up to eight rums in the shop by buying a shot glass ($10 to $18). The entertaining chef-guided tours in the production room include a tasting.

Fort East Martello
Museum & Gardens   MUSEUM

(☑ 305-296-3913; www.kwahs.org/museums/fort-east-martello/history; 3501 S Roosevelt Blvd; adult/child $12/5; ☺ 9:30am-4:30pm) This old fortress was built to resemble an old Italian Martello-style coastal watchtower, a design that quickly became obsolete with the advent of the explosive shell. Now the fort serves a new purpose: preserving the past. There's historical memorabilia exploring Key West's role in the Civil War, its heyday in the wrecking and cigar industries, plus the folk art of Mario Sanchez and 'junk' sculptor Stanley Papio, who worked with scrap metal.

Perhaps the most haunted thing in Key West, infamous museum resident 'Robert the Doll' is a terrifying child's toy from the early 1900s who reportedly causes much misfortune to those who question his powers (get the backstory on www.robertthedoll.org). Creepy music playing overhead adds to the sense of unease.

Little White House   HISTORIC BUILDING

(☑ 305-294-9911; www.trumanlittlewhitehouse.com; 111 Front St; adult/child $23/11; ☺ 9am-5pm) This sprawling 1890s mansion (a former naval officer's residence) is where President Harry S Truman used to vacation when he wasn't molding post-WWII geopolitics. It's beautifully preserved and open only for guided tours, although you are welcome to visit one small gallery with photographs and historical displays (and a short video) on the ground floor.

Tennessee Williams Museum   MUSEUM

(☑ 305-204-4527; www.kwahs.org; 513 Truman Ave; $7; ☺ 9:30am-4:30pm) Tennessee Williams, who lived in Key West for more than three decades, was one of the great playwrights of the 20th century. Although he actually lived a mile away (at 1431 Duncan St), this small museum is a great place to learn about his contributions to the literary and theatrical world. On display are photos, manuscripts, one of Williams' typewriters, newspaper articles and a dollhouse-sized model of his one-story home.

Key West Lighthouse   LIGHTHOUSE

(☑ 305-294-0012; www.kwahs.org; 938 Whitehead St; adult/child/senior $12/5/9; ☺ 9:30am-4:30pm) Climb up 88 spiraling steps to the top of this snowy-white lighthouse, opened in 1848, for a decent view (perhaps not as striking as it was in the days when a men's clothing-optional resort was next door). You can also visit the lighthouse keeper's cottage, which has photographs and artifacts with historical tidbits on the lives of the keepers of the light.

Southernmost Point   LANDMARK

(cnr South & Whitehead Sts) Though it's the most-photographed spot on the island, this red-and-black buoy isn't even the southernmost point in the USA (that's in the off-limits naval base around the corner). Worth a quick snapshot if you happen to be walking or cycling past.

 Activities

Yoga on the Beach   YOGA

(☑ 508-737-3211; www.yogaonbeach.com; Fort Zachary Taylor State Park; class $18; ☺ 8:15am-9:45am) If you're a yoga fan, you won't want to miss a session on the beach at Fort Zachary Taylor State Park (p195). The daily 90-minute class, held on the sands overlooking gently lapping waves, is simply exhilarating. The class fee includes park admission for the day, and mats are available.

Sunset Watersports   OUTDOORS

(☑ 855-378-6386; Smathers Beach, S Roosevelt Blvd; kayak/paddleboard/windsurfer/hobie cat per hr from $25/25/35/50; ☺ 9am-5pm) For a down day on Smathers Beach, this outfit rents out all the essentials: chairs and umbrellas, kayaks, paddleboards, windsurfing gear and Hobie Cats for a sailing adventure. The same company also runs snorkeling trips, sunset cruises and other outings from the dock at 201 William St.

Jolly Rover CRUISE
(☑305-304-2235; www.schoonerjollyrover.com; Schooner Wharf, cnr Greene & Elizabeth Sts; day cruise adult/child $45/25, sunset cruise $65/34) This outfit has a gorgeous, tanbark (red-dish-brown) 80ft schooner that embarks on daily two-hour cruises under sail. It looks like a pirate ship and has the cannons to re-inforce the image. You can bring your own food and drink (including alcohol) – small coolers only.

☞ Tours

Key West Food Tours FOOD & DRINK
(☑305-570-2010; www.keywestfoodtours.com; food tour adult/child $75/50) Created by a born-and-raised Conch with a passion for Key West, these three-hour walking tours celebrate the island's food and culture. You'll learn about Key West's Cuban and Caribbean connections, while stopping for fish tacos, conch fritters, key-lime pie and other delights. The same outfit also runs an evening pub crawl, taking you to alternative spots well off the Duval St strip.

Conch Tour Train TOURS
(☑888-916-8687; www.conchtourtrain.com; cnr Front & Duval Sts; adult/child $35/20; ⊘tours 9am-4:30pm; 🖮) This tour outfit seats you in breezy linked train cars on a 70-minute narrated tour; there are three stops (includ-ing one near the Hemingway House), where

you can hop off and take a later train. Offers discounted admission to the Hemingway House as well as Ghosts and Graveyards night tours. The best place to board is at the Front St depot.

Key West Ghost & Mysteries Tour TOURS
(☑305-292-2040; www.keywestghostandmyster-iestour.com; adult/child $23/15; ⊘tours 9pm; 🖮) A playfully creepy ghost tour that's as fami-ly-friendly as this sort of thing gets – in oth-er words, no big chills or pop-out screaming. Tours depart near the corner of Duval and Caroline Streets.

🎆 Festivals & Events

Key West Literary Seminar LITERATURE
(www.kwls.org; ⊘Jan) A feast for the literary minded, this annual four-day event draws top novelists, poets and historians from around the country (although it costs more than $700 to attend). Most book signings and presentations take place in the San Carlos Institute (☑305-294-3887; www.in-stitutosancarlos.org; 516 Duval St; ⊘noon-5pm Fri-Sun).

Year-round, you can catch one of its lit-erary-themed walking tours ($30), held on Friday at 5pm and Saturday at 10am.

Conch Republic Independence Celebration CULTURAL
(www.conchrepublic.com; ⊘Apr) A 10-day trib-ute to Conch Independence; vie for (made-up) public offices and watch a drag queen footrace.

THE CONCH REPUBLIC: ONE HUMAN FAMILY

A Conch (pronounced 'conk' as in 'bonk') is someone born and raised in the Keys. It's a rare title to achieve. Even transplants can only rise to the rank of 'freshwater Conch.' You will hear reference to, and see the flag of, the Conch Republic everywhere in the islands, which brings us to an interesting tale.

In 1982 US border patrol and customs agents erected a roadblock at Key Largo to catch drug smugglers and illegal aliens. As traffic jams and anger mounted, many tourists disappeared. They decided they'd rather take the Shark Valley Tram in the Ever-glades, thank you very much. To voice their outrage, a bunch of fiery Conchs decided to secede from the USA. After forming the Conch Republic, they made three declarations (in this order): secede from the USA; declare war on the USA and surrender; and request $1 million in foreign aid. The roadblock was eventually lifted, and every April, Conchs celebrate the anniversary of those heady days with nonstop parties, and the slogan 'We Seceded Where Others Failed.'

Today the whole Conch Republic thing is largely a marketing gimmick, but that doesn't detract from its official motto: 'One Human Family.' This emphasis on tolerance and mutual respect has kept the Keys' head and heart in the right place, accepting peo-ples of all backgrounds, sexual orientations and religions.

Hemingway Days Festival   CULTURAL

(www.fla-keys.com/hemingwaymedia; ⊙late Jul) Held on days surrounding the author's birthday (July 21), this long-running fest brings parties, a 5km run, a fishing tournament, arm-wrestling contests, a 'Papa' look-alike contest and the running of the bulls (with mock animals pulled on wheels).

Womenfest   LGBT

(http://gaykeywestfl.com/womenfest; ⊙Sep) One of North America's biggest lesbian celebrations, Womenfest is four days of merrymaking, with pool parties, art shows, roller derby, drag brunches, sunset sails, flag football, and a tattoo-and-moustache bicycle ride. It's great fun, with thousands descending on Key West from all corners of the USA and beyond.

★Fantasy Fest   CULTURAL

(www.fantasyfest.com; ⊙late Oct) Akin to New Orleans' riotous Mardi Gras revelry, Fantasy Fest is 10 days of burlesque parties, parades, street fairs, concerts and loads of costumed events. Bars and inns get competitive about decorating their properties, and everyone gets decked out in the most outrageous costumes they can cobble together (or get mostly naked with daring body paint).

Goombay Festival   CULTURAL

(⊙late Oct; 🏠) Held during the same out-of-control week as Fantasy Fest, this is a Bahamian celebration of food, crafts and culture. The family-friendly event runs over two days (typically a Friday and Saturday).

🛏 Sleeping

There's a glut of boutique hotels, cozy B&Bs and four-star resorts here at the end of the USA. Unfortunately, the one thing lacking is inexpensive lodging. Aside from sleeping in the town's only hostel, it's not easy to find a bed for less than $300 a night during the high season. During low season (June to November, excluding big festivals), prices listed here can drop by up to 50%.

Seashell Motel & Key West Hostel   HOSTEL $

(☎305-296-5719; www.keywesthostel.com; 718 South St; dm $74; ᴘ✳🛰) This place isn't winning any design awards, but the staff is kind, and the dorms are some of the only lower-priced choices on the island. The Seashell also offers much pricier double rooms (starting at $265 in high season). Wherever you stay, you'll find white tile floors, a cheery

paint job, and a back patio where you can meet other travelers.

There's also a kitchen for guests, laundry service and bikes for hire.

El Patio   MOTEL $$

(☎305-296-6531; www.elpatiomotel.com; 800 Washington St; r $200-330; ✳🛰🏊) One of Key West's more affordable options, El Patio has spacious rooms set in a two-story art deco building on a quiet residential street. Rooms are simple with a rather old-fashioned Floridian design, but the beds are comfy and the mini-fridges are a nice touch (some rooms have kitchens). There's also ample (free) parking, a rooftop deck, pool and bike rental.

★Mermaid & the Alligator   GUESTHOUSE $$$

(☎305-294-1894; www.kwmermaid.com; 729 Truman Ave; r winter $370-430, summer $270-330; ᴘ✳🛰🏊) It takes a real gem to stand out amid Key West's grand guesthouses, but this converted 1904 mansion never fails to impress. Lush tropical gardens designed by a landscape architect are set with a trickling fountain, plunge pool and enticing hammocks (there's also a cabana for massages). Each of the nine individually designed rooms boasts a mix of modern comfort and artful details.

Guests can enjoy cookies and lemonade at 3pm and wine and cheese at 5pm. The breakfasts (included) are outstanding – not surprising since the owner is a trained chef (and a great resource on Key West's dining scene).

Tropical Inn   BOUTIQUE HOTEL $$$

(☎888-611-6510; www.tropicalinn.com; 812 Duval St; r $300-500; ✳🛰🏊) The Tropical Inn has excellent service and a host of individualized rooms spread out over a historical home property. Each room comes decked out in bright pastels and shades of mango, lime and seafoam. A delicious breakfast is included and can be enjoyed in the jungly courtyard next to a lovely sunken pool.

Gardens Hotel   HOTEL $$$

(☎305-294-2661; www.gardenshotel.com; 526 Angela St; r $440-780; ᴘ✳🛰🏊) This boutique, environmentally friendly property lives up to its name with extravagant greenery surrounding lavish rooms and cottages. Shaded walkways meander past palms, orchids, a koi pond, an aviary and fountains with peaceful seating areas to relax. Inside, Caribbean accents mesh with antique furniture, polished wood floors, designer linens and marble bathrooms to create some of Key West's most enticing rooms.

Artist House
B&B **$$$**

(✑ 305-296-3977; www.artisthousekeywest.com; 534 Eaton St; r $330-420; ❄️ 🛜) A picture-perfect Queen Anne Victorian a short hop from Duval Street, this 1890s mansion has attractive rooms with tall ceilings, polished wood floors and a dash of originality (large paintings in some, vintage wallpaper in others). Breakfast is served on the palm-shaded back terrace, and there's also a complimentary happy hour.

The historical property was once the residence of the painter Robert Eugene Otto and his creepy sidekick, Robert the Doll (the artist named it after himself), which today casts its curses inside the Fort East Martello Museum (p196).

Casablanca Key West
GUESTHOUSE **$$$**

(✑ 305-296-0815; www.keywestcasablanca.com; 900 Duval St; r $275-725; ❄️ 🛜🏊) On the quieter end of Duval St, the Casablanca is a friendly guesthouse with eight bright rooms, all with polished wood floors and comfy beds; some have small balconies. This lush, tropical and elegant inn, once a private house, was built in 1898.

Old Town Manor
BOUTIQUE HOTEL **$$$**

(✑ 305-292-2170; www.oldtownmanor.com; 511 Eaton St; $330-485; ❄️ 🛜🏊) While it bills itself as a B&B (and breakfast is included), the Old Town feels more like a boutique operation that offers a variety of rooms spread throughout lush gardens. The digs come in a subdued, tropically inspired palette, with quality furnishings (four-poster beds in some) and thoughtful extras including coffeemakers and mini-fridges. The best rooms open onto verandas.

L'Habitation
GUESTHOUSE **$$$**

(✑ 305-293-9203; www.lhabitation.com; 408 Eaton St; r $292-410; ❄️ 🛜) A beautiful, classical Keys cottage, L'Habitation has fine rooms kitted out in light tropical shades, with cozy quilts and lamps that look like contemporary art pieces. The friendly bilingual owner welcomes guests in English or French. The front porch, shaded by palms, is a perfect place to stop and engage in Keys people-watching.

Key West Bed & Breakfast
B&B **$$$**

(✑ 305-296-7274; www.keywestbandb.com; 415 William St; r $350, with shared bathroom $125-230; ❄️ 🛜) Sunny, airy and full of artistic touches, this adults-only B&B has 10 unique rooms, each bursting with personality. Some rooms are lined with Dade County pine, others have mahogany four-poster beds, antique furniture, or access to a private deck. If you're on a budget, book early to score one of four rooms with shared bathrooms. The kindhearted host has loads of great travel tips.

There's also a tiny single (the so-called Nun's Room) that's a steal at $125.

Seascape Tropical Inn
B&B **$$$**

(✑ 305-296-7776; www.seascapetropicalinn.com; 420 Olivia St; r $250-460; ❄️🛜🏊) Had this B&B existed back in the day, Hemingway could have stumbled into it after one of his epic drinking binges – it's within hollering distance of his old house. Crash in one of seven rooms, each uniquely designed with floral comforters and artwork on the walls. The best rooms have French doors opening onto private terraces.

Silver Palms Inn
BOUTIQUE HOTEL **$$$**

(✑ 305-294-8700; www.silverpalmsinn.com; 830 Truman Ave; r $475-610; 🅿️❄️🛜🏊) 🏄 Royal blues, sweet teals, bright limes and lemon-yellow color schemes pervade the interior of this boutique property, which also boasts bicycle rentals, a saltwater swimming pool and a green certification from the Florida Department of Environmental Protection.

Mango Tree Inn
B&B **$$$**

(✑ 305-293-1177; www.mangotree-inn.com; 603 Southard St; r $250-420; ❄️🛜🏊) This down-to-earth B&B offers a courtyard pool and attractive accommodation in a number of airy rooms, each decorated with swaths of tropical-chic accoutrements, from rattan furniture to flowering hibiscus. Rates dip as low as $160 in the low season.

Curry Mansion Inn
HOTEL **$$$**

(✑ 305-294-5349; www.currymansion.com; 511 Caroline St; r $290-400; 🅿️❄️🛜🏊) In a city full of stately 19th-century homes, the Curry Mansion is especially handsome. All the elements of an aristocratic American home come together here, from plantation-era Southern colonnades to a New England-style widow's walk and, of course, bright Floridian rooms with canopied beds.

LAZY DAYS IN KEY WEST

With its walkable town center, easygoing bars and friendly locals happy to share a story or two, Key West seems like it was made for lazy days. After you've seen the sights, take a day for seaside relaxing and enjoying the Keys' lesser-known charms.

BEACH LOUNGING

Although not known as a beach destination, Key West has some pretty spots for a day by the ocean. Fort Zachary Taylor State Park (p195) has a palm-backed stretch of white sand and clear water, plus snorkel gear for hire and a peaceful cafe.

BRUNCH & COCKTAILS

The classic way to start the day in Key West is over a long, leisurely brunch. You can join the roosters for a bit of backyard nibbling at Blue Heaven (p204), or linger over America's finest Bloody Mary at Burgundy Bar (p204).

BACKYARD OASIS

At Nancy Forrester's Secret Garden (p195), Nancy happily introduces visitors to her remarkable parrots and macaws, all with unique personalities. If you play an instrument, these birds always enjoy a concert!

NO NAME KEY

An easy 45-minute drive from Key West is No Name Key (p188), where endangered Key deer feed in the forests near the road. You can take some short walks in the National Key Deer Refuge (p188) and stop for a meal at the famous No Name Pub (p190).

MIAZVOU/SHUTTERSTOCK ©

1. Key deer, National Key Deer Refuge (p188)
2. Fort Zachary Taylor State Park (p195)
3. Blue Heaven (p204)

STOCK ISLAND

Just east of Key West, Stock Island is home to boatyards, fishing marinas and grid-like housing strips favored by Key West's largely immigrant workforce. While most visitors pass quickly over the island, it's well worth making a detour here to discover a bit of vintage South Florida coupled with some recent revitalization.

Sheriff's Animal Farm (Monroe County Sheriff's Office Animal Farm; ☎ 305-293-7300; www.facebook.com/keysanimalfarm; 5501 College Rd, Stock Island; ⏱ 1-3pm 2nd & 4th Sun of the month or by appointment; P) is a longtime favorite with Key West families. This Monroe County shelter houses miniature horses, pot-bellied pigs, sloths, birds, snakes, alpacas, an ostrich, lemurs and some massive tortoises.

Drawn to the (slightly) cheaper rents and bigger spaces, artists continue to colonize abandoned spaces on the island. There is a growing number of creative spaces, including **Art Shack** (www.facebook.com/TheArtShackKeyWest; 6404 Front St; ⏱ 11am-7pm Tue-Sun), a collective of galleries and studios, and also a venue for live music, painting classes and other periodic events. A great time to take in Stock Island's cultural scene is during the Art Stroll, held on the second Saturday of every month, from 11am to 4pm (find other upcoming events at www.ilovestockisland.org).

There are several good restaurants on the island. The long-running **Hogfish Bar & Grill** (☎ 305-293-4041; www.hogfishbar.com; 6810 Front St; mains $15-30; ⏱ 11am-midnight Mon-Sat, from 9am Sun) is a charmingly ramshackle eatery perched over Safe Harbor Marina that serves excellent seafood. It's also the favored watering hole for Stock Island's shrimpers, fisherfolk, artists and other assorted characters. For a more cutting-edge culinary experience, reserve a spot for the **Lost Kitchen Supper Club** (www.lostkitchenkeywest.com), held monthly at Hogfish.

Though it opened the same year Hurricane Irma hit, the architecturally striking **Perry Hotel** (☎ 305-296-1717; www.perrykeywest.com; 7001 Shrimp Road, Stock Island Marina; r $395-600; ⏱ restaurant 8am-2pm & 6-10pm; P ❄ 🛜 🐾) was spared from destruction. Bright, stylishly furnished rooms afford fine views over the waterfront, and the amenities are top notch. Even if you don't stay here, it's worth booking a table at its award-winning **Matt's Stock Island Kitchen & Bar** (mains $24 to $38) for an outstanding meal.

✗ Eating

BO's Fish Wagon SEAFOOD $
(☎ 305-294-9272; www.bosfishwagon.com; 801 Caroline St; mains $12-20, lunch specials $12-18; ⏱ 11am-9:30pm) Looking like a battered old fishing boat that smashed onto the shore, BO's is awash with faded buoys, lifesavers and rusting license plates strung from its wooden rafters (in some spots you needn't step outside to peer up at the moon). Regardless, the seafood is fantastic – with rich conch fritters, soft-shell crab sandwiches and tender fish tacos.

Date & Thyme HEALTH FOOD $
(☎ 305-296-7766; www.dateandthyme.com; 829 Fleming St; mains $6-15; ⏱ cafe 8am-4pm, market to 6pm;) 🌿 Equal parts market and cafe, Date & Thyme whips up deliciously guilt-free breakfast and lunch plates, plus energizing smoothies and juices. Try the açai bowl with blueberry, granola and coconut milk for breakfast, or lunch favorites such as Thai coconut curry with mixed vegetables and quinoa. There's a shaded patio in front, where roaming chickens nibble underfoot (don't feed them).

5 Brothers Grocery & Sandwich Shop DELI $
(☎ 305-296-5205; http://5brotherskw.com; 930 Southard St; sandwiches $6-10; ⏱ grocery 6:30am-3pm, kitchen 7am-3pm Mon-Sat) A Key West icon, this tiny grocery store has a loyal local following who come for first-rate Cuban-style espresso. Stop in for early-morning *café con leche* (coffee with steamed milk), guava pastries and bacon and egg rolls, or come later for delectable roast pork sandwiches.

Garbo's Grill FUSION $
(☎ 305-304-3004; www.garbosgrillkw.com; 409 Caroline St; mains $10-15; ⏱ 11am-10pm Mon-Sat, noon-6pm Sun) Just off the beaten path, Garbo's whips up delicious tacos with creative toppings including mango ginger habanero-glazed shrimp, Korean barbecue, and

fresh mahimahi with all the fixings, as well as gourmet burgers and hot dogs. It's served out of a sleek Airstream trailer, which faces onto a shaded brick patio dotted with outdoor tables.

Pierogi Polish Market EASTERN EUROPEAN **$**
(☑305-292-0464; www.facebook.com/PierogiPolishMarket; 1008 White St; mains $6-12; ⊙10am-7pm Mon-Sat; P ♪) The Keys has an enormous seasonal population of temporary workers largely drawn from Central and Eastern Europe. This is where those workers can revisit their homeland, via pierogies, dumplings, blinis and a great sandwich selection. The market is a great place to assemble a picnic with smoked fish, sausages, rye bread and quality Czech beer.

★Santiago's Bodega SPANISH **$$**
(☑305-296-7691; www.santiagosbodega.com; 207 Petronia St; tapas $8-16, meals for two $48-90; ⊙11am-10pm; ♪) A much-loved local icon, Santiago's has easygoing front porch tables, an elegant dining room filled with whimsical artwork, and a zigzagging wooden bar in back that you won't want to miss during happy hour. Small plates are ideal for sharing, with standouts including prosciutto-wrapped dates stuffed with goat cheese, yellowfin tuna ceviche, and blue-cheese-topped beef tenderloin. There is a good selection of wines by the glass.

Stop in from 3pm to 6pm for wine and sangria specials, and a $5 tapa that changes daily.

Thirsty Mermaid SEAFOOD **$$**
(☑305-204-4828; www.thirstymermaidkeywest.com; 521 Fleming St; mains $17-33; ⊙11am-10pm; ♪) The lovely Thirsty Mermaid serves outstanding seafood in an elegant, easygoing space. The menu is a collection of sea-life culinary treasures such as an oyster bar, ceviche, middleneck clams and caviar. Among the main courses, seared diver scallops or spiced tuna with jasmine rice and lemon aioli are outstanding. There are also luxurious sandwiches with lobster, fried oysters or local snapper fillings.

The Café FUSION **$$**
(☑305-296-5515; www.thecafekw.com; 509 Southard St; mains $13-24; ⊙9am-10pm; ♪) The oldest (mostly) vegetarian spot in Key West is a sunny luncheonette by day that morphs into a buzzing, low-lit eating and drinking spot by night. The cooking is outstanding, with an eclectic range of dishes: spicy Szechuan stir-fries, grilled portobello salads, udon noodle bowls, pizza with shaved Brussels sprouts, and a famous veggie burger.

Banana Cafe FRENCH **$$**
(☑305-294-7227; www.bananacafekw.com; 1215 Duval St; mains breakfast & lunch $10-21, dinner $17-29; ⊙7:30am-10pm; 🛜♪) One of the best places in town to start off the day, the sun-drenched two-story Banana Cafe serves creatively topped eggs Benedict (try it with blackened shrimp or Florida lobster), fluffy omelets and delicious savory or sweet crepes.

For lunch and dinner, the antique- and vintage-poster-filled eatery leans heavily toward French cooking, with mussels and *frites*, tuna Niçoise (with blackened yellowfin), baked *escargots* as well as satisfying comfort fare such as fish and chips and baguette sandwiches.

El Siboney CUBAN **$$**
(☑305-296-4184; www.elsiboneyrestaurant.com; 900 Catherine St; mains $12-20; ⊙11am-9:30pm) This is a rough-and-ready Cuban joint where the portions are big and there's no messing around with high-end embellishment or bells and whistles. Classic ingredients – rice, beans, grilled grouper, roasted pork, barbecue chicken, sweet plantains – are all cooked with pride for belly-filling satisfaction.

Point5 FUSION **$$**
(☑305-296-0669; www.915duval.com/point5; 915 Duval St; mains $14-22, small plates $8-16; ⊙6pm-midnight; ♪) This sophisticated upstairs hideaway with well-placed balcony tables trades in fusion-style tapas with a global influence: think Greek flatbread with lamb and feta, walnut pistachio tacos, shishito peppers and marinated octopus salad. All go nicely with wines by the glass and creative cocktail selections.

Heartier plates include seafood risotto, lobster ravioli and fall-off-the-bone Mongolian ribs.

Mo's Restaurant CARIBBEAN **$$**
(☑305-296-8955; 1116 White St; mains $12-24; ⊙11am-10pm Mon-Sat) The words 'Caribbean' and 'home cooking,' when used in conjunction, are generally always enough to impress. But it's not just the genre of cuisine that wins us over at Mo's – it's the execution.

The dishes are mainly Haitian, and they're delicious – the spicy pickles will inflame your mouth, which you can then cool down with a rich vegetable 'mush' over rice, or try the incredible signature snapper.

★ **Little Pearl** SEAFOOD $$$

(☏305-204-4762; www.littlepearlkeywest.com; 632 Olivia St; mains $24-42; ⊙5-10pm) The same team behind the Thirsty Mermaid opened this vaguely nautical-themed restaurant (and four-seat bar) to much acclaim back in 2018.

Sink into a cerulean blue banquette and let the evening unfold while indulging in Asian-accented dishes such as king crab and papaya salad, Bangkok octopus (with mint and basil), seared diver scallops with baby bok choy slaw, or (for the nonpescatarians) duck breast with cognac shallot butter.

★ **Blue Heaven** AMERICAN $$$

(☏305-296-8666; www.blueheavenkw.com; 729 Thomas St; mains breakfast & lunch $13-25, mains dinner $24-42; ⊙8am-10:30pm; ✐) This is one of the quirkiest venues on an island of oddities – customers, together with free-ranging fowl, flock to dine in the ramshackle, tropical-plant-filled garden where Hemingway once officiated boxing matches. This place gets packed with customers who come for the delectable breakfasts and Keys cuisine with French touches. Entrance on Petronia St.

Nine One Five FUSION $$$

(☏305-296-0669; www.915duval.com; 915 Duval St; mains lunch $14-26, dinner $26-45; ⊙5-11pm Mon & Tue, 11:30am-11pm Wed-Sun; ✐) Classy Nine One Five certainly stands out from the Duval dens of drunkenness and '80s cover bands. Ignore all that and enter this modern and elegant space, which serves a creative, changing New American menu with global accents. It's all quite rich – imagine yellowtail snapper with Thai chili sauce and basmati rice, mojito-cured salmon tartare or duck confit with parsley pesto.

Latitudes SEAFOOD $$$

(☏305-292-5300; www.sunsetkeycottages.com; Sunset Key; mains lunch $18-28, dinner $32-56; ⊙7am-2:15pm & 5-10pm) For a memorable meal on your own private island (well, plus the other diners and resort guests), Latitudes is hard to top. The palm-studded 27-acre key sits around 500m off Key West, and offers gorgeous views over the water and breathtaking sunsets (time your visits well). The seafood is excellent, but pricey (it's the unrivaled location you're paying for).

The ferry dock to the island is tucked behind a parking garage on Front St (just south of the Mel Fisher Maritime Museum). For a long, leisurely lunch without the rush, book a 1:15pm or 1:45pm reservation.

 Drinking & Nightlife

Duval St is Key West's famed nightlife strip, which is lined with all manner of drinking dens – from frat-boy party hubs to raucous drag-loving cabarets.

★ **Green Parrot** BAR

(☏305-294-6133; www.greenparrot.com; 601 Whitehead St; ⊙10am-4am) The oldest bar on an island of bars – 'A sunny place for shady people' being one of its mottos – this rogues' cantina opened in the late 19th century and keeps going. Its ramshackle interior, with local artwork on the walls and a parachute stretched across the ceiling, only adds to the atmosphere, as does the fun-loving, colorful crowd.

The Green Parrot books some of the best bands – playing funk-laden rock, brassy jazz, juke-joint blues and Latin grooves – that hail from Miami, New Orleans, Atlanta and other places. There's never a cover charge.

Cuban Coffee Queen CAFE

(☏305-294-7787; www.cubancoffeequeen.com; 5 Key Lime Square; ⊙7am-7pm) Key West's best coffee is served at this open-sided cafe (one of several branches in town), tucked down a tiny lane behind Duval St. The *café con leche* is simply perfection, though there are plenty of other options including iced coffee (the ice cubes are also made of coffee) and the delicious, caffeine-free, Ayurvedi turmeric *con leche.*

Lagerheads BAR

(☏305-509-7444; www.lagerheadsbeachbar.com; 0 Simonton St; ⊙9am-sunset) Walk to the end of Simonton St to find this peaceful beach bar, with umbrella-shaded lounge chairs for hire in the sand, and a small swimming area where you can cool off. It's a great spot for cold drinks, conch salad and a legendary smoked fish dip – particularly around sunset, for fine views without the Mallory Square mob.

Burgundy Bar BAR

(☏305-294-3200; www.sainthotels.com/bite-sip; 417 Eaton St; ⊙1-11pm) Inside the Saint Hotel, this small, convivial bar deserves special mention for its outstanding Bloody Marys – among the best you'll find in this country. It's also a fine setting for a cocktail and high-end pub grub – and feels secreted away from the chaos of nearby Duval St.

Vinos on Duval WINE BAR

(☏305-294-7568; www.vinosonduval.com; 810 Duval St; ⊙2pm-12:30am Mon-Wed, from noon

Thu-Sun) On the less rowdy end of Duval St, Vinos pours a good selection of wines from around the globe – Spanish tempranillos, Argentine malbecs, Californian cabs – in a cozy setting with a touch of Key West eccentricity. Grab a seat at the bar and have a chat with the knowledgeable staff, or retreat to one of the tables on the porch.

Captain Tony's Saloon   BAR
(📞305-294-1838; www.capttonyssaloon.com; 428 Greene St; ⊙10am-2am) Propagandists would have you believe the nearby megabar complex of Sloppy Joe's was Hemingway's original bar, but the spot where the old man famously drank was right here, in the original Sloppy Joe's location (before it was moved onto Duval St and into frat-boy hell). According to legend, Martha Gellhorn, Hemingway's third wife, seduced him in this very bar.

Conch Republic   BAR
(📞305-294-4403; www.conchrepublicseafood.com; 631 Greene St; ⊙11:30am-midnight) Overlooking the waterfront, this sprawling, open-sided eatery and drinking space is a fun place to get you in the Key West spirit. The allure: a festive happy hour, a chatty laid-back crowd, island breezes and live music (nightly from 5:30pm to 9pm, plus noon to 4pm on Saturday and Sunday). The seafood is also quite good (mains $16 to $32).

Viv   WINE BAR
(📞305-517-6799; www.vivez-joyeux.com; 300 Petronia St; ⊙noon-11pm) This French-run wine bar is tiny but utterly charming, with velvety red wines by the glass or bottle from an impressive rotation of French and American wine growers. You can pair those wines with first-rate cheese, charcuterie and other snacks. The owners also run the very charming crêperie next door.

Bourbon St Pub   GAY & LESBIAN
(📞305-293-9800; www.bourbonstpub.com; 724 Duval St; ⊙10am-4am) A celebratory crowd, great DJs and striking male dancers (who shimmy on top of the bar from 10pm onward) keep the party going at this iconic spot on Duval St. The garden bar in back, with pool and Jacuzzi, is open to men only, and occasionally hosts clothing-optional afternoon parties. Tuesday nights are for women.

Garden of Eden   BAR
(224 Duval St; ⊙noon-4am) Take the stairs to the rooftop to discover Key West's own clothing-optional drinking patio. Lest you get too excited, cameras aren't allowed and most people forego the striptease. Regardless, the views over town are great, the mixed crowd is up for a fun time, and it's an obligatory stop when bar-hopping along Duval.

Aqua   GAY & LESBIAN
(📞305-294-0555; www.aquakeywest.com; 711 Duval St; ⊙3pm-2am) Aqua hosts some of the best drag shows on the island and attracts people of all ages and sexual orientations – including couples and groups – all wanting to see what the excitement is about. Shows happen nightly at 9pm, plus 7pm on Thursday, and 7pm and 11pm on Friday and Saturday.

☆ Entertainment

La Te Da   CABARET
(📞305-296-6706; www.lateda.com; 1125 Duval St; tickets $33; ⊙piano bar shows 8:30pm daily, cabaret 9pm Mon-Sat) While the outside bar is where locals gather for mellow chats over beer, you can catch high-quality drag acts – big names come here from around the country – upstairs at the fabulous Crystal Room on weekends. More low-key cabaret acts grace the downstairs piano bar (admission free). The Sunday tea dance – an afternoon dance party (4pm to 6:30pm) by the pool – is great fun.

Virgilio's   LIVE MUSIC
(📞305-296-8118; http://latrattoria.us/index.php/virgilios; 524 Duval St; ⊙6pm-3am) This barstage is as 'un-Keys' as they come, and frankly, thank God for a little variety. It's a dark, candlelit martini lounge where you can chill to blues or jazz and get down with some salsa. Enter on Applerouth Lane.

Tropic Cinema   CINEMA
(📞305-396-4944; www.tropiccinema.com; 416 Eaton St) Great art-house movie theater with deco frontage.

Waterfront Playhouse   THEATER
(📞305-294-5015; www.waterfrontplayhouse.org; 407 Wall St, Mallory Sq) Catch high-quality musicals and dramas from the oldest-running theater troupe in Florida. The season generally runs from October through early June.

Red Barn Theatre   THEATER
(📞305-296-9911; www.redbarntheatre.com; 319 Duval St; ⊙box office 1-8pm Tue-Fri, 4-8pm Sat & Sun) An occasionally edgy and always fun local playhouse, the quaint Red Barn Theatre stages indie productions such as *Tiny*

FLORIDA KEYS & KEY WEST KEY WEST

Beautiful Things by Cheryl Strayed or Steve Martin's *Meteor Shower*. The season runs from December through April.

Shopping

Salt Island Provisions — GIFTS & SOUVENIRS
(☑ 305-517-6088; www.saltislandprovisions.com; 830 Fleming St; ☺10am-5pm) You'll find delicate jewelry made by local artisans, beeswax candles, honey and, of course, salt in its many incarnations: namely salt scrubs and gourmet cooking salts in infusions of merlot, sriracha, curry and white truffle.

The Green Pineapple — FASHION & ACCESSORIES
(☑ 305-509-7378; www.facebook.com/thegreen pineapple; 1130 Duval St; ☺9am-8pm Mon-Sat, to 6pm Sun) 🍍 An inviting and sustainably minded boutique with handmade jewelry, skincare products and beautifully made apparel, as well as sunglasses, wide-brimmed hats, sandals and other South Florida essentials. The Green Pineapple also offers yoga classes and has a cafe on-site for smoothies, light organic meals and glasses of wine, with happy hour specials (you're still in Key West, after all).

Books & Books — BOOKS
(☑ 305-320-0208; www.booksandbookskw.com; 533 Eaton St; ☺10am-6pm) Miami's best indie bookshop has a branch in Key West, and it's a magnet for the literary minded. You'll find plenty of titles of local interest (particularly on Key West and Cuba), great staff picks and thought-provoking new releases. Regular book signings and author readings take place throughout the year.

The Key West branch was founded by children's book author Judy Blume and her writer husband George Cooper, who often work in the store.

Bésame Mucho — GIFTS & SOUVENIRS
(☑ 305-294-1928; www.besamemucho.net; 315 Petronia St; ☺10am-6pm Mon-Sat, to 4pm Sun) It's hard not to be lured inside this handsomely designed boutique with its old-world charm (gilt-framed mirrors, exposed brick, antique display counters) in the Bahama Village. There's a wide range of temptations, including high-end bath, fragrance and skincare products, antique-inspired jewelry, sustainably sourced clothing and eye-catching ceramics and other housewares.

Kermit's — FOOD
(www.keylimeshop.com; 200 Elizabeth St; ☺9am-9:30pm) Satisfy your innermost cravings for all things key-lime-related at this long-running institution near the waterfront. You'll find salsa, barbecue sauce, candies, ice cream, dog biscuits and even wine bearing that distinctive key-lime flavor. Purists may prefer to settle for a pie (mini pies available) or perhaps a chocolate-dipped key-lime Popsicle.

❶ Information

Key West Chamber of Commerce (☑ 305-294-2587; www.keywestchamber.org; 510 Greene St; ☺9am-5:30pm) An excellent source of information.

Lower Keys Medical Center (☑ 305-294-5531; www.lkmc.com; 5900 College Rd, Mile 5, Stock Island) Has a 24-hour emergency room.

Gay Key West Business Guild (☑ 305-294-4603; www.gaykeywestfl.com; 808 Duval St; ☺9am-5pm Mon-Sat) Serves as a welcome center for LGBTIQ+ travelers. Loads of great tips on restaurants, bars, lodging and outdoor activities in Key West.

❶ Getting There & Away

Key West International Airport (EYW; ☑ 305-809-5200; www.eyw.com; 3491 S Roosevelt Blvd) is off S Roosevelt Blvd on the east side of the island. You can fly into Key West from some main US cities, such as Miami, Chicago, Atlanta, Charlotte and Newark. From Key West airport, a quick and easy taxi ride into Old Town costs a fixed $9 per person (solo travelers pay the meter, usually less than $20).

Greyhound (☑ 305-296-9072; www.grey hound.com; 3439 S Roosevelt Blvd; ☺7:30-9am & 4:30-6pm) has two buses daily between Key West and Downtown Miami. Buses leave Miami for the 4½-hour journey at 12:25pm and 6:25pm and Key West at 8:30am and 5:45pm going the other way (from $20 to $44 each way).

You can take a boat ride from Fort Myers to the Keys on the **Key West Express** (☑ 239-463-5733; www.seakeywestexpress.com; 100 Grinnell St, Key West; adult/senior/junior/child round-trip $155/145/92/62, one way $95/95/68/31), which departs from Fort Myers beach daily at 8am and does a 3½-hour cruise to Key West. Returning boats depart the seaport at 6pm.

❶ Getting Around

Once you're in Key West, the best way to get around is by bicycle (rentals from the Duval St area, hotels and hostels cost from $10 a day). For transportation within the Duval St area, the free Duval Loop shuttle (www.carfreekeywest.com/duval-loop) runs from 6am to midnight.

Other options include Key West Transit (p187), with color-coded buses running about every 15 minutes; mopeds, which generally cost from $35 per day ($60 for a two-seater); or the open-sided electric tourist cars, aka 'Conch cruisers,' which travel at 35mph and cost about $140/200 for a four-/six-seater per day.

A&M Scooter Rentals (📞305-896-1921; www.amscooterskeywest.com; 523 Truman Ave; bicycle/scooter/electric car per day from $10/35/140; ⊙9am-7pm) rents these, plus scooters and bicycles, and offers free delivery.

Parking can be tricky in town. There's a free **parking lot** on Fort St off Truman Ave.

DRY TORTUGAS NATIONAL PARK

After all those keys, connected by that convenient road, the nicest islands in the archipelago require a little extra effort – the **Dry Tortugas** (📞305-242-7700; www.nps.gov/drto) are accessible only by boat or plane.

The park is open for day trips and overnight camping, which provides a rare phenomenon: a quiet Florida beach. Reserve months in advance through the **Yankee Freedom III** (📞800-634-0939; www.drytortugas.com; Key West Ferry Terminal, 100 Grinell St; adult/child/senior $180/125/170), which provides ferry service to the island. The sparkling waters offer excellent snorkeling and diving opportunities. A **visitor center** is located within fascinating Fort Jefferson.

In March and April, there is stupendous bird-watching, including aerial fighting. Stargazing is mind-blowing any time of the year.

⊙ Sights

Dry Tortugas National Park is America's most inaccessible national park. It rewards you for your effort in getting there with amazing snorkeling amid coral reefs full of marine life. You'll also get to tour a beautifully preserved 19th-century brick fort, one of the largest such fortifications in the USA despite its location 70 miles off the coast of Key West.

On paper, the Dry Tortugas covers an extensive area – more than 70 sq miles. In reality, only 1% of the park (about 143 acres) consists of dry land; much of the park's allure lies under the water with the opportunity to see tarpon, sizable groupers and lots of colorful coral and smaller tropical fish, plus the odd sea turtle.

Explorer Ponce de León named this seven-island chain Las Tortugas (The Turtles) for the sea turtles spotted in its waters. Thirsty mariners who passed through and found no water later affixed 'dry' to the name. In subsequent years, the US Navy set an outpost here as a strategic position into the Gulf of Mexico. But by the Civil War, **Fort Jefferson**, the main structure on the islands, had become a prison for Union deserters and at least four other people, among them Dr Samuel Mudd, who had been arrested for complicity in the assassination of Abraham Lincoln. Hence a new nickname: Devil's Island. The name was prophetic; in 1867 a yellow-fever outbreak killed 38 people, and after an 1873 hurricane the fort was abandoned. It reopened in 1886 as a quarantine station for smallpox and cholera victims, was declared a national monument in 1935 by President Franklin D Roosevelt, and was upped to national park status in 1992 by George Bush Sr.

🛏 Sleeping

There's no lodging on the island, but you can camp here if you plan well in advance. Garden Key has 10 campsites ($15 per person, per night), which are given out on a first-come, first-served basis. You'll need to reserve eight to 12 months ahead on the ferry *Yankee Freedom III*, which takes only 10 campers per day to and from the island. There are toilets, but no freshwater showers or drinking water; bring everything you'll need. You can stay up to three nights.

ℹ Getting There & Away

If you have your own boat, the Dry Tortugas are covered under National Ocean Survey chart No 11438. Otherwise, the Yankee Freedom III operates a fast ferry between Garden Key and the Historic Seaport (at the northern end of Margaret St). The round-trip fare (2¼ hours each way) costs per adult/child $180/125. Reservations are essential. Continental breakfast, a lunch buffet, snorkeling gear, a 45-minute tour of the fort and park admission fee are all included.

Key West Seaplanes (📞305-293-9300; www.keywestseaplanecharters.com; half-day trip adult/child $361/288, full-day trip $634/508) can take up to 10 passengers (flight time 40 minutes each way). The half-day tour is four hours, allowing 2½ hours on the island. The eight-hour full-day excursion gives you six hours on the island. Again, reserve at least a week in advance. Passengers over age 16 arriving by plane also need to pay an added $10 park admission fee (cash only). Flights depart from Key West International Airport.

ON THE WATER IN THE KEYS

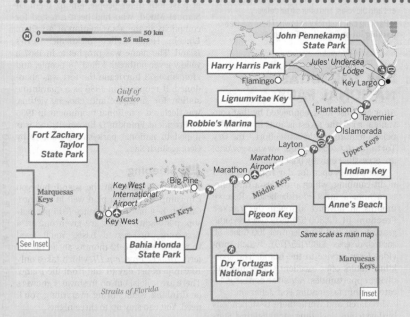

KAYAKING

There are paddling hot spots up and down the keys. Many hotels include kayak rental with accommodation, making it easy to head off on some DIY exploring when the water is calm. Keep an eye out for manatees, stingrays and sharks, plus winged residents including cormorants, frigate birds, herons and ospreys. With its protected mangroves, **John Pennekamp Coral Reef State Park** (p178) is a superb place for kayaking.

For something more immersive, consider booking a guided backcountry tour. On a memorable outing, you'll make your way across grass flats and through mangrove-filled inlets, spotting wildlife along the way. One of the best operators in the business is **Big Pine Kayak Adventures** (p189) in the Lower Keys. You can arrange customized tours with experienced paddler Bill Keogh, who wrote the iconic guide to paddling in the Florida Keys.

SNORKELING & DIVING

Colorful coral reefs are within a short boat trip from the Keys. Key Largo makes a great base for exploring offshore wonders. True to its name, **John Pennekamp Coral Reef State Park** (p178) draws visitors more for its underwater attractions than its shoreline trails. For snorkeling enthusiasts, this should figure high on an itinerary. Trips depart regularly, and on calm days, you might have the opportunity to snorkel above the open-armed *Christ of the Abyss* – a massive statue sunk in 25ft of water and surrounded by reefs. Divers can also plan trips in the area, though you'll have to charter your own vessel. It's easier to join trips (or take classes) offered by the well-run **Looe Key Dive Center** (p189) in the Lower Keys. Avid divers can even overnight in the **Jules' Undersea Lodge** (p180), located in 30ft of water in a protected lagoon.

Paddling through sun-dappled mangroves, walking the shorelines of forest-covered islands and setting off on a sunset cruise: there are many ways to experience the life aquatic in the Florida Keys.

Near Islamorada, **Robbie's Marina** (p182) offers snorkeling trips as well as myriad other activities.

BOATING & SAILING

Key West is one of the great boating capitals of South Florida. You can head off for a kitschy pirate-themed tour on the **Jolly Rover** (p197), or hire a Hobie Cat for sailing adventures off **Smathers Beach** (p196). There are loads of options – dinner cruises, sunset trips and dolphin-watching tours. The waterfront along Key West Bight is where many agencies dock.

Elsewhere, you'll find some gems: step back in time by booking passage on the **African Queen** (p179), the small steamboat depicted in the 1951 Humphrey Bogart and Katharine Hepburn film. Docked in Key Largo, it makes regular forays through the Port Largo canals, with guides (slightly less wisecracking than Bogart) sharing historical details along the way. For something completely different, sign up for a glass-bottom boat tour in the **John Pennekamp Coral Reef State Park** (p178).

BEACHES

The Keys aren't known for their sandy shores, but there are still a handful of small but captivating stretches of coastline where you can enjoy a waterside afternoon in between island-hopping. Chief among them, **Bahia Honda State Park** (p188) has one of the most alluring stretches of beachfront anywhere in Florida.

Harry Harris Park (p179) is a local favorite in Tavernier for its small but photogenic lagoon. **Anne's Beach** (p182), near Islamorada, has a sandy beach and a boardwalk stretching through mangroves. In Marathon, **Sombrero** (p186) is another obligatory stop for beach lovers.

Key West has its share of sandy seduction: at **Fort Zachary Taylor State Park** (p195) you can swim, snorkel, stretch out under palm trees, join an outdoor yoga class or watch a (usually) spectacular sunset.

ISLAND ADVENTURES

You'll get a far different perspective of the keys when you leave behind the busy main highway and head out to explore one of many islands reachable only by boat.

Near Islamorada, you can visit two very different islands – both state parks – that make for fascinating exploring. The larger of the two, **Lignumvitae Key** (p182), is home to old-growth tropical hardwood hammock and a solution hole (good for spying bird life), with rangers leading guided tours several times a week. At **Indian Key** (p182), you can slip into the past while looking for ruins on a walk across the 11-acre island. In the 1830s, this was once a bustling community based on salvaging cargo from shipwrecks. Reach either island by kayak, which you can hire from **Robbie's Marina** (p182) in Islamorada.

Pigeon Key (p185) gives a first-hand glimpse of what life was like for the workers who built the Overseas Railway (completed in 1912). Tours take in the restored structures that once made up the work camp (later used by railway maintenance), with downtime on the small beach afterwards.

Far beyond Key West, the **Dry Tortugas National Park** (p207) isn't easy to reach. But those who make the effort can snorkel coral reefs, lounge on the beach and explore a historical 19th-century fortress. You'll have to book well in advance for a spot on a boat or a seaplane that makes the journey out. You can also camp on the island.

AT A GLANCE

★

POPULATION
3.9 million

OLDEST LIGHTHOUSE
Jupiter Inlet
Lighthouse (p247)

BEST BEACH
Hutchinson Island
(p248)

BEST GLOBAL FARE
Little Moir's Food
Shack (p247)

BEST MERMAID SHOW
Wreck Bar (p221)

📅

WHEN TO GO
Mar–Apr Spring
break hits, packing
beaches with the
partying college
crowd.

Jun–Jul Sweltering
temperatures bring
low-season prices;
it's also turtle-
nesting season.

Dec–Feb Perfect
beach weather with
dry, sun-drenched
days and ample
events (such as
Lake Worth's Street
Painting Festival).

Fort Lauderdale Beach & Promenade (p215)
MARIAKRAY/SHUTTERSTOCK ©

Southeast Florida

Florida's southeast coast has luscious beaches and excellent surfing, as well as some beautiful nature enclaves with secluded islands, moss-draped mangrove swamps, wild rivers and empty dunes. Sebastian Inlet, a protected area, has miles of beach, hiking and bird-spotting opportunities. The beach towns – a world away from Miami's vibrant multiculturalism and glitz – are a somewhat bizarre mixture of extreme wealth (think Trump's Mar-a-Lago resort in Palm Beach), evangelical zealots and staggering death statistics due to the opioid crisis.

Nightlife lovers will enjoy the activity-packed, gay- and family-friendly Fort Lauderdale, and surf-loving Vero Beach, while those looking for something more quiet can explore laid-back Lauderdale-by-the-Sea and the rugged coast of Jupiter.

Southeast Florida Highlights

1 **Dr Von D Mizell-Eula Johnson State Park** (p214) Gliding through mangroves past undisturbed beaches.

2 **Morikami Museum & Japanese Gardens** (p227) Sipping matcha at Delray Beach's serene gardens.

3 **Loggerhead Marinelife Center** (p251) Getting up close and personal with loggerhead and leatherback turtles as they recuperate.

4 **Jupiter** (p246) Kayaking the wild, scenic Loxahatchee River for close-up views of cypress knees, mangrove forests and sunning alligators.

5 **Sebastian Inlet** (p250) Hiking, biking and birding along the Atlantic and the Indian River, and long and beautiful beaches.

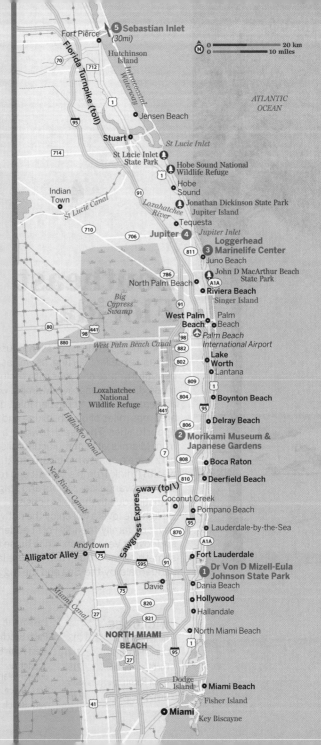

GOLD COAST

Though the 70-or-so miles of sparkling Atlantic shoreline from Hollywood to Jupiter earned its nickname from the gold salvaged from area shipwrecks, it could easily have come from the mix of sapphire skies, glowing sands and ritzy residents.

Here the coastline has a split personality. There's slow-going Rte 1 along the ocean front, a pleasant drive revealing vistas of unspoiled beaches and endless condos. Then there's the older Dixie Hwy, running parallel to Rte 1 but further inland, past dive bars and working-class communities. Drive both stretches; each is rich with divergent offerings.

Hollywood

📞 754, 954 / POP 148,770

Hollywood positions itself as a gateway to Fort Lauderdale. It's divided into two sections: the bustling waterfront, and the small, pleasant historical downtown, a couple of miles west. Most visitors come for the waterfront, which has earned a sizable wedge of the spring break market since Lauderdale gave revelers the boot. The resulting influx each March brings concerts in the sand, beach-volleyball tournaments and assorted debauchery. In recent times the city has tried to glam up its image with several new South Beach–style developments.

◉ Sights

Anne Kolb Nature Center   PARK
(www.broward.org/parks; 751 Sheridan St; admission $1.50; ◉9am-7:30pm) This lovely 1500 acres of coastal mangroves is on one side of West Lake, while opposite is the recreation area (referred to as West Lake Park. The entirely 'wild' section, Anne Kolb Nature Center, is criss-crossed by hiking trails and offers views over West Lake. Such a natural park is a rarity in Broward County. Fortunately environmentalists in the 1970s managed to save it from development, forever preserving its mangroves, wetlands and wildlife.

These days it's one of the most accessible natural places for kayaking, biking and hiking within a largely built-up area. A variable schedule of environmental boat tours departs from the West Lake Marina (adult/under 18 $5/3) - the tours are on a first come, first served basis

West Lake Park   PARK
(📞954-357-5161; www.broward.org/parks; 1200 Sheridan St; kayak rental per 1/2/4hr $14/24/33; ◉9am-7:30pm) Connected to the Anne Kolb Nature Center, this is more of a recreation section, with a marina, tennis courts and picnic ground. You can paddle across West Lake and through the mangroves via various locales marked as red, white and green trails.

Hollywood Broadwalk   WATERFRONT
Reminiscent of California's famed Venice Beach, this beach and adjacent promenade teem with scantily clad rollerbladers and fanny-pack-wearing tourists. The Broadwalk itself is a 2.5-mile, six-person-wide path, extending from pretty North Beach Park, where the route is lined with sea grape trees, all the way to South Surf Rd. It's regularly clogged with skaters, strollers and entire families pedaling enormous group bikes.

If you feel like joining the rollers along the Broadwalk, a dozen or so vendors rent out bikes ($12/30 per hour/day), in-line skates and other beach gear.

North Beach Park   PARK
(3601 N Ocean Dr; ◉8am-7:30pm) FREE This is the formal name for the beach, though there is a suburban-style green space behind the boardwalk with picnic tables and barbecue grills.

🛏 Sleeping

Hollywood Beach Suites   HOTEL $
(📞954-391-9441; www.hollywoodbeachsuitehotel. com; 320 Arizona St; r from $93; P ❀ @ 🛜) This slick complex comprises a warren of whitewashed, vaguely Moroccan-looking motel units that are branded as 'boutique.' This is generally a quiet place (versus a party palace), which appeals to families. Surfboards are available for use. The reception desk is at the street number cited above.

★**Walkabout Beach Resort**   BOUTIQUE HOTEL $$
(📞954-272-6000; www.walkaboutbeachresort. com; 2500 North Surf Rd; d $180-280; ❀🛜) This classic, baby-pink art-deco hotel, built in 1947, sits on the Broadwalk. There are just eight rooms, all of which are equipped with kitchenette and dining table. Wooden and terrazzo floors, vintage black-and-white photographs and furnishings, and an on-site tiki bar all combine to create a retro beachside getaway.

On the July 4 you'll have front-row seats for the fireworks. The suite located in the gorgeous rounded 'tower' costs a bit more because of its larger size.

Sea Downs APARTMENT **$$**
(☑954-923-4968; www.seadowns.com; 2900 North Surf Rd; apt $115-230; P✸✿⌬) This cozy, unpretentious little spot has faded charm, featuring tidy studios and one-bedroom apartments equipped with everything you need to roll out of bed in the morning and stroll along the beach and promenade. It's right on the beach, so you can forgive the dated decor.

Seminole Hard Rock Hotel & Casino HOTEL **$$$**
(☑866-502-7529; www.seminolehardrockholly wood.com; 1 Seminole Way; r $249-600; ✸⌬✿) If you're wondering what that enormous guitar-shaped building is on the horizon, you'll be delighted to know that it's none other than the Seminole Hard Rock Hotel, which includes casinos, restaurants, theaters, a day spa, swanky guestrooms and some of the most alluring concert bills in the state. The 4.5-acre lagoon-style pool surrounding a bar is out of this world.

✗ Eating

Taco Beach Shack MEXICAN **$**
(www.tacobeachshack.com; 334 Arizona St; tacos $4-10; ⊙11am-10pm) Hipsters and hangers-on lounge around on wicker chaises at this open-air taqueria. The menu has a very of-the-moment mix of ethnic flavors – try the Korean short rib and kimchi tacos. Margarita Mondays have these classic cocktails at $2 a pop. DJs play thumping techno all day on weekends.

ArtsPark STREET FOOD **$**
(Young Circle, off US 1; ⊙5:30pm-10pm Mon) If you're in town on a Monday head downtown to the ArtsPark, where you'll find a gathering of food trucks.

Le Comptoir FRENCH **$$**
(☑786-718-9441; 1902 Harrison St; mains $14-26; ⊙5-10pm) It's worth making the trip downtown for this classic, excellent-value bistro. You'll dine on bowls heaped high with mussels stewed in white wine and Provençal sauces, and garnished with vibrant green parsley. Other signature French dishes include duck with an orange glaze, and succulent peppered steak.

Le Tub AMERICAN **$$**
(☑954-921-9425; www.theletub.com; 1100 N Ocean Dr; mains $9-20; ⊙11am-1am Mon-Fri, noon-2am Sat & Sun) Decorated exclusively with flotsam collected along Hollywood Beach, this quirky burger joint is routinely named 'Best in America.' Everything is prepared from scratch and in a small kitchen so expect a wait, both for seating and cooking time. It's worth it.

❶ Getting There & Away

An old-fashioned trolley known as the Sun Trolley travels between downtown Hollywood and the beach. Fares are $1. Bright-colored signs mark the stops but don't hold your breath; you could be waiting a long time. (The Sun Trolley's cell phone app might help with timing a trolley.)

Broward County Transit (BCT; www.broward. org/bct; single fare/day pass $2/5) buses serve Hollywood, connecting to Fort Lauderdale. Fares are $2.

To go north to West Palm Beach or south to Miami, head to the Fort Lauderdale–Hollywood International Airport (p526) on BCT bus 1 and jump on **Tri-Rail** (☑954-783-6030; www.tri-rail. com). Route 4 heads along Hollywood Blvd into the historical downtown.

Parking at the beach in Hollywood is hellacious – if you can't find on-street parking (around $2 per hour), try the parking deck at Margaritaville.

Dania Beach

☑754 / POP 30,183

Dania (dane-ya) feels like an extension of the 'burbs of Hollywood; the vestiges of a mellow little town, with a fledgling antiques district and a breezy fishing pier, are largely disappearing. The main appeal is the Dr Von D Mizell-Eula Johnson State Park on Dania Beach's outskirts.

◎ Sights

Dr Von D Mizell-Eula Johnson State Park STATE PARK
(☑954-923-2833; www.floridastateparks.org/ mizell; 6503 N Ocean Dr; vehicle/cyclist $6/2; ⊙8am-sunset) Named after the Civil Rights Movement leaders at the front of the 'wade-in' protests to desegregate South Florida beaches in the 1950s and '60s, this is now a popular kayaking spot. The dense mangrove-lined route meanders 1.5 miles through the park, and is shallow and calm. There's also 2.5 miles of undisturbed beach to enjoy. The northern end has the Port Everglades inlet, past which cruise ships and

yachts sail, and the southern end houses the Dania Beach fishing pier.

The park also offers good offshore snorkeling and diving, and is an important turtle nesting area. The **Whiskey Creek Hideout** (https://whiskeycreekhideout.com) at the north end of the park provides kayak and canoe rentals ($20 per hour).

✕ Eating

★**Tarks of Dania Beach**   SEAFOOD $
(☏954-925-8275; 1317 S Federal Hwy; mains $6-15; ⊙11am-10pm) This jaunty clam stand has been going strong since 1966 and is now a local landmark. Most of the tiny, very fuggy interior is taken up with the cooking counter, where they broil, fry and steam daily specials. These usually include a combination of steamed, fried and raw clams alongside shrimp, oysters, snow crab and spicy chicken wings.

It can get crazy busy, but the food usually vanishes so fast you won't be waiting long.

Jaxson's Ice Cream Parlor   ICE CREAM $
(www.jaxsonsicecream.com; 128 S Federal Hwy; ice cream from $5; ⊙11:30am-11pm Sun-Thu, 11:30am-midnight Fri & Sat; ⊕) Established in 1956, this place has 80-plus flavors of homemade ice cream that come in very large portions.

❶ Getting There & Away

Broward County Transit (☏954-357-8400; www.broward.org/bct) buses serve Dania, connecting to Fort Lauderdale. Fares are $2.

To go north to West Palm Beach or south to Miami, head to the Fort Lauderdale–Hollywood International Airport (p526) on BCT bus 1 and jump on Tri-Rail.

Fort Lauderdale

☏754 / POP 180,072
After years of building a reputation as *the* destination for beer-swilling college students on raucous spring breaks, Fort Lauderdale now angles for a slightly more mature crowd. Think martinis rather than tequila shots; jazz concerts instead of wet T-shirt contests – though there's still plenty of carrying-on within the confines of bars and nightclubs.

Few visitors venture far inland except to dine and shop along Las Olas Blvd; most

spend the bulk of their time on the beach, which is long and sandy (though crowded).

Fort Lauderdale has an international yachting scene, spiffy hotels and fancy restaurants. The city's Port Everglades is one of the busiest cruise-ship ports in the world, with megaships departing daily for the Caribbean, Mexico and beyond.

◉ Sights

★**Bonnet House**   HISTORIC BUILDING
(Map p216; ☏954-563-5393; www.bonnethouse.org; 900 N Birch Rd; adult/child $20/16, grounds only $10; ⊙9am-4pm Tue-Sun) This pretty plantation-style property was once the home of artists and collectors Frederic and Evelyn Bartlett. It is now open to guided tours that swing through its art-filled rooms and studios. Beyond the house 35 acres of lush, subtropical gardens protect a pristine barrier-island ecosystem, including one of the finest orchid collections in the country.

Fort Lauderdale Beach & Promenade   BEACH
(Map p216; N Atlantic Blvd; ⓟ⚕🐾) Fort Lauderdale's promenade – a wide, brick, palm-tree-dotted pathway swooping along the beach and the A1A – is a magnet for runners, in-line skaters, walkers and cyclists. The white-sand beach, meanwhile, is one of the nation's cleanest and best. Stretching 7 miles to Lauderdale-by-the-Sea, it has dedicated family-, gay- and dog-friendly sections. Boating, diving, snorkeling and fishing are all extremely popular.

Riverwalk   LANDMARK
(Map p220; www.goriverwalk.com) Curving along the New River, the meandering Riverwalk runs from Stranahan House to the Broward Center for the Performing Arts. Host to culinary tastings and other events, the walk connects a number of sights, restaurants and shops.

Las Olas Riverfront   WATERFRONT
(Map p220; cnr SW 1st Ave & Las Olas Blvd) A giant alfresco boardwalk area with stores, restaurants and live entertainment nightly; it's also the place to catch many river cruises.

Hugh Taylor Birch State Recreation Area   PARK
(Map p216; ☏954-564-4521; www.floridastateparks.org/park/Hugh-Taylor-Birch; 3109 E Sunrise Blvd; vehicle/bike $6/2; ⊙8am-sunset) This lusciously tropical park contains one of the last significant maritime hammocks

Fort Lauderdale Beach

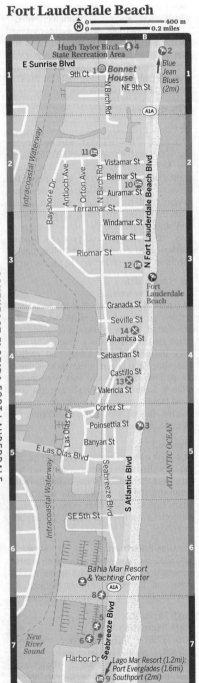

Fort Lauderdale Beach

in Broward County. There are mangroves, a freshwater lagoon system (great for birding) and several endangered plants and animals (including the golden leather fern and gopher tortoise). You can fish, picnic, stroll the short Coastal Hammock Trail or cycle the 1.9-mile park drive.

Stranahan House   HISTORIC BUILDING
(Map p220; ☏954-524-4736; www.stranahan-house.org; 335 SE 6th Ave; adult/student $12/7; ⊙tours 1pm, 2pm & 3pm) Constructed from Dade County pine, grand Stranahan House is a fine example of Florida vernacular design, and one of the state's oldest homes. It served as both home and store for Ohio transplant Frank Stranahan, who built a small empire trading with the Seminoles. He then committed suicide by jumping into the New River after real-estate and stock-market losses in the late 1920s. The house has many of the original furnishings, and is open daily for three hour-long tours.

Docents from the house also guide a fun hour-long River Ghost Tour ($25 per person) in conjunction with the water taxi. Tours depart from the house (and include a tour inside) at 7:30pm every Sunday.

NSU Art Museum
Fort Lauderdale
MUSEUM

(Map p220; ☎954-525-5500; www.nsuart
museum.org; 1 E Las Olas Blvd; adult/student/chil-
dren under 12 $12/5/free; ☉11am-5pm Tue-Sat,
from noon Sun) A Florida standout with an interesting spilled rainbow design outside, the
museum is known for its William Glackens
collection and its exhibitions on wide-ranging themes from northern European art
and contemporary Cuban art to American
pop art and contemporary photography. On
first Thursdays of the month, the museum
stays open to 8pm and hosts lectures, films
and performances, as well as a happy hour
in the museum cafe. Day courses and workshops are also available. Check the website
for details.

Museum of
Discovery & Science
MUSEUM

(Map p220; ☎954-467-6637; www.mods.org; 401
SW 2nd St; adult/child Mon-Fri $24/19, Sat and Sun
$19/16; ☉10am-5pm Mon-Sat, noon-6pm Sun; ⊞)
A 52ft kinetic-energy sculpture greets you
here, and fun exhibits include Gizmo City
and Runways to Rockets – where it actually
is rocket science. Plus there's an Everglades
exhibit and IMAX theater. You can even
have an 'Otter Encounter' for $50 per per-
son (Wednesdays, Saturdays and Sundays,
by reservation only), where you can feed
otters, participate in a training, and learn
about their habits and diet.

Canine Beach
BEACH

(Map p216; cnr Sunrise Blvd & N Atlantic Blvd;
weekend permits $7; ☉3-7pm winter, 5-9pm sum-
mer) This dog-friendly beach is the 100-yard
swath running from E Sunrise Blvd to lifeguard station 5.

🏃 Activities

★ Sea Experience
SNORKELING

(Map p216; ☎954-770-3483; www.seaxp.com; 801
Seabreeze Blvd; snorkeling adult/child $40/25,
2-tank dive $65 (not incl gear); ☉10:15am &
2:15pm; ⊞) Sea Experience takes guests in a
glass-bottom boat along the Intracoastal and
into the ocean to snorkel on a natural reef,
thriving with marine life, in 10ft to 20ft of
water. Tours last 2½ hours. Also offers scuba
trips to multiple wreck sites.

Broward BCycle
CYCLING

(☎754-200-5672; https://broward.bcycle.com;
first 30min/additional 30min $5/5, maximum per
day $25) Flat Fort Lauderdale is an easy town

to traverse by bicycle. Broward Count
erated bicycle sharing stations can be fo
throughout town, and provide easy access ,
two-wheeled exploration.

Water Taxi
BOATING

(☎954-467-6677; www.watertaxi.com; day pass
adult/child $28/14) For the best unofficial tour
of the city hop on the water taxi; the drivers
offer a lively narration as they ply Fort Lauderdale's canals and waterways from Oakland
Park Boulevard to the Riverwalk Arts District. Other routes head down the coast to
Hollywood. Check online for locations. After
5pm prices are a flat $18 for all passengers.

Bahamas Paradise
CRUISE

(☎800-995-3201; www.bahamasparadisecruise.
com; trips from $119) Leaves Palm Beach in the
afternoon, heads out overnight, then spends
two full days in Grand Bahama, before returning overnight on the third night. The
boat is furnished with several bars, a casino,
four restaurants, a spa and a kids club, and
cabins range from bare-bones to luxe.

Fort Lauderdale
Parasail
WATER SPORTS

(Map p216; ☎954-361-9965; www.ftlauderdale
parasail.com; 1005 Seabreeze Blvd; per person $95)
If you're curious how the mansions along
Millionaires' Row look from above, sign up
for a parasailing trip. You'll soar on a 600ft
and 1000ft line (around 300ft to 500ft sailing height) above the waves while strapped
securely to an enormous smiley-face
parachute.

Fish Lauderdale
FISHING

(Map p216; ☎954-839-0083; www.fishlauder
dale.com; 1005 Seabreeze Blvd; up to 6 people
per hour from $125; ☉8am-sunset) The waters
off Fort Lauderdale are rich with marlin,
sailfish, snapper, tarpon, wahoo and more.
Naturally there are plenty of fishing charters
available – this outfit has four boats to take
you trolling for dinner.

👉 Tours

Las Olas Gondola
BOATING

(Map p220; ☎954-727-8870; www.lasolas
gondola.com; SE 1st Ave; tours from $100 per per-
son) Explore the 'Venice of America' with a
romantic ride in an original Venetian gondola, accompanied by Italian music. The
tour lasts roughly 75 minutes and takes you
through the canals and past the homes of
the rich and famous.

954-642-1601; www.carriebcruis-
... New River Dr E; tours adult/child
... 11am, 1pm & 3pm, closed Tue
...) Hop aboard this replica
...tury riverboat for a 90-minute 'life-
...tyles of the rich and famous' narrated tour
of the ginormous mansions along the Intracoastal and New River. Tours leave from Las
Olas at SE 5th Ave.

Jungle Queen Riverboat BOATING
(Map p216; 954-462-5596; www.junglequeen.
com; 801 Seabreeze Blvd; adult/child $24/14;
tour hours vary) Runs three-hour tours
along the waterfront, Millionaires' Row and
part of the Everglades on a Mississippi-style
paddle-wheeler. In addition to taking daily
sightseeing cruises, you can hop aboard the
four-hour evening barbecue cruise at 6pm.
It has all-you-can-eat shrimp or ribs, and entertainment (adult/child $43/23).

🛏 Sleeping

⭐ **Island Sands Inn** B&B $$
(954-990-6499; www.islandsandsinn.com; 2409
NE 7th Ave, Wilton Manors; r $185-245; P ❋ 🛜 🐾)
It's hard to say whether it's the beach towels,
the luxurious bed and bedding, the thought-
ful attention to detail (tissues, bath prod-
ucts, mini-bar, microwave) or the utterly
unpretentious ease of this four-room place
that makes Island Sands Inn so comfortable.
The charming hosts, Mike and Jim, unob-
trusively ensure that you get the best from
your stay.

Tranquilo MOTEL $$
(Map p216; 954-565-5790; www.tranquilo
fortlauderdale.com; 2909 Vistamar St; r $154-205;
P ➹ ❋ 🛜 🐾) This white-on-white retro
1950s motel offers fantastic value for families. Rooms range over five buildings, each
with its own pool, and some include newly
refurbished kitchens along with access to
outdoor grills and laundry services. No shuttle, but the beach is three blocks away. The
main pool has an accessible entry for those
with mobility needs.

B Ocean Resort HOTEL $$
(Map p216; 954-524-5551; www.bhotelsand
resorts.com; 1140 Seabreeze Blvd; r from $145;
P ➹ ❋ 🛜 🐾) Defining the southern end
of Seabreeze Blvd, this hotel straddles the
uberpopular South Beach and offers breezy
ocean views from the majority of its airy
rooms. Built by M Tony Sherman in 1956, it

looks like a giant cruise ship tethered to the
sidewalk.

Its 'hull', the Wreck Bar (p221), is a his-
torical landmark, and offers porthole views
on the underwater world of the swimming
pool. Come at the weekend and you'll be
able to catch the mermaid show at 7pm.
There's adult-only burlesque at 10pm.

Premiere Hotel HOTEL $$
(Map p216; 954-566-7676; www.premiere
hotel.com; 625 N Fort Lauderdale Beach Blvd; r from
$165, ste from $255; P ❋ 🛜 🐾) This recently re-
modeled, family-run spot is large enough to
have good infrastructure – a small bar/cafe
and food menu – but small enough to not
feel like you're gobbled up by a resort. It's
quiet despite being opposite the beach, and
has simple, white rooms and studio apart-
ments with kitchenette. It's a good-value,
reliable bet, especially in low season.

Riverside Hotel HOTEL $$
(Map p220; 954-467-0671; www.riversidehotel.
com; 620 E Las Olas Blvd; r/ste from $189/399;
P ❋ 🛜 🐾) This Fort Lauderdale landmark
(c 1936) – fabulously located downtown on
Las Olas, and with plush floral carpet and an
air of grandeur – has two room types: large,
executive rooms in the newer 12-story tow-
er, and those in the historical 1936 building.
The classic rooms overlooking Las Olas are
the pick of the bunch. Valet parking costs a
hefty $27 per night.

⭐ **Lago Mar Resort** RESORT $$$
(954-523-6511; www.lagomar.com; 1700 S
Ocean Lane; r $300-700; P ➹ ❋ @ 🛜 🐾) On
the south end of South Beach, this wonderfully noncorporate resort has it all: private
beach, grand lobby, massive island-style
rooms, full-service spa, on-site restaurants,
lagoon-style pool set amid tropical plantings
and the personal touch of family ownership.
A lovely fish mosaic graces the lobby floor.
(Not to be confused with Donald Trump's
Mar-a-Lago!)

This is unpretentious, but with old-fashioned manners and the feeling of a well-
cared-for guesthouse.

⭐ **W Fort Lauderdale** HOTEL $$$
(Map p216; 954-414-8200; www.wfortlauder
dalehotel.com; 401 N Fort Lauderdale Beach Blvd; r
$289-699; P ❋ @ 🛜 🐾) With an exterior re-
sembling two giant sails and an interior that
looks like the backdrop for a J Lo video, this
is where the glitterati stay – bust out your
glad rags and join them. The massive lobby

is built for leisure, with a silver-and-aqua lounge area, a moodily lit bar and a deck lined with wicker chaises.

Pineapple Point
GUESTHOUSE $$$

(☑888-844-7295; www.pineapplepoint.com; 315 NE 16th Tce; r from $329; P❋@🐾🏊) Tucked away in a quiet residential neighborhood, this guesthouse caters exclusively to a loyal gay male clientele. Suites and apartments are bright, all clustered around a handful of pools, hot tubs and tree-shaded sitting areas. Daily happy hours ensure mingling, and the super-friendly staff know all the best restaurants and gay bars in town.

✗ Eating

Lester's Diner
DINER $

(☑954-525-5641; www.lestersdiner.com; 250 W State Rd 84; mains $6-19; ⊙24hr) Hailed endearingly as a greasy spoon, retro-since-it-was-new Lester's Diner has been keeping folks happy since the late 1960s. Everyone makes their way here at some point, from business types on cell phones to clubbers to travel writers needing pancakes at 4am.

A must-visit for non-Americans.

Tacocraft
MEXICAN $

(Map p220; www.tacocraft.com; 204 SW 2nd St; mains $5-15; ⊙11:30am-midnight Mon, Wed & Thurs, to 1am Tues, Fri & Sat, to 11pm Sun) One of a stable of funky eateries and bars along this strip, this taqueria and tequila bar serves up a great atmosphere, even better drinks and very good tacos. It attracts both a younger crew and mature hipster crowd who head here for pork belly and ahi tuna fillings.

Tuesday serves up $3 tacos.

Gran Forno Bakery
ITALIAN $

(Map p220; ☑954-467-2244; http://granforno. com; 1235 E Las Olas Blvd; mains $6-12; ⊙7am-6pm) This old-school Milanese-style bakery and cafe is a good takeout lunch spot downtown: warm crusty pastries, bubbling pizzas and fat golden loaves of ciabatta, sliced and stuffed with ham, roast peppers, pesto and other delicacies.

Pizza Craft
PIZZA $

(Map p220; ☑954-616-8028; https://pizzacraft pizzeria.com; 330 Himmarshee St; pizza $15-18; ⊙Tue-Fri 4:30pm-11pm, Sat 11am-11pm, Sun 4-9:45pm) Excellent pizzas from a wood-fired oven; choices such as the 'forager', fragrant with truffles and wild mushrooms, are a treat. Try the fennel and orange salad,

Vegan Fine Foods
VEGAN $

(Map p220; ☑954-533-6412; www.veganfine foods.com; 330 SW 2nd Street; mains $8-15; ⊙Tue-Sun noon-8pm;🐾) A cafe with plant-based everything from quinoa burgers to mac and nut-cheese, decent breakfasts and wraps, and a variety of smoothies. This is a good place for a light and affordable lunch or snack. The adjoining market has vegan wines, ice cream and skincare, and many of their products are made by local vegan entrepreneurs.

Louie Bossi's
ITALIAN $$

(www.louiebossi.com; 1032 E Las Olas Blvd; mains $16-30; ⊙11am-11pm Mon-Thu, to 1am Fri & Sat, 10am-late Sun) Sit back and enjoy the bossiness (managers), the business (servers) and the bolshiness (waiting clients)...this is as Roman an experience as you can ever hope to have in the US. Servers race, crack pepper, sprinkle parmesan cheese. Chatter volume is on boom-box blasting levels. Pizzas are churned out of the 900-degree oven every 90 seconds.

Casablanca Cafe
MEDITERRANEAN $$

(Map p216; ☑954-764-3500; www.casablanca cafeonline.com; 3049 Alhambra St; mains $10-34; ⊙11:30am-2am) Try to score a seat on the front terrace of this Moroccan-style home where Mediterranean-inspired food and Florida-style ocean views are served. It won't knock your socks off, but it's a classic and an excellent location. Live music Tuesday to Saturday. Drinkers enjoy its piano bar.

★ Burlock Coast
INTERNATIONAL $$$

(Map p216; ☑954-302-6460; www.burlockcoast. com; Ritz Carlton, 1 N Fort Lauderdale Beach Blvd; mains $19-46; ⊙7am-10pm) Situated in the Ritz Carlton Hotel, this chic, casual spot somehow manages to be all things to all people: a cafe, bar, market and upmarket restaurant. The menu has been crafted to the ethos of local farmers and vendors. The menu changes seasonally but leans toward modern international, such as pulled pork or simple fish-and-chips. The deck outside is prime for people-watching.

15th Street Fisheries
SEAFOOD $$$

(☑954-763-2777; www.15streetfisheries.com; 1900 SE 15th St; bar mains $7-16, restaurant mains $38-55; P) Tucked away in Lauderdale Marina

Fort Lauderdale

with an open-fronted deck offering a front-row view of yachts, this place is hard to beat for waterfront dining. The wooden interior is kitted out like an Old Florida boathouse. The fine-dining restaurant is upstairs and a more informal dockside bar serves shrimp, crab and grilled mahimahi. You can feed the tarpon, too, which is popular with kids.

At the weekend there's live music from 6pm to 10pm. You can also reach the Fisheries via the water taxi.

Casa D'Angelo   ITALIAN $$$
(☑954-564-1234; http://casa-d-angelo.com; 1201 N Federal Hwy; mains $26-50; ◷5:30-10:30pm) Chef Angelo Elia presides over an impressive kitchen specializing in Tuscan and southern Italian dishes, many handed down by his mother. Seasonality and quality translate into intense flavors and delightful textures: the sunburst taste of just-ripe tomatoes, peppery arugula, silken sea bass and surprisingly spicy cinnamon gelato. The restaurant has one of the finest wine lists in the state.

🍷 Drinking & Nightlife

Fort Lauderdale bars can stay open until 4am on weekends and 2am during the week. A handful of great bars and pubs are found in the Himmarshee Village area on SW 2nd

St, while the beach offers plenty of open-air seating.

⭐**BREW Urban Cafe**   CAFE
(☑954-357-3934; https://brewurbancafe.com; 537 NW 1st Ave; ◷7am-7pm; 🛜) Brew is the coolest thing going in Fort Lauderdale: a kick-ass cafe located in a weird, semi-abandoned studio space filled with floor-to-ceiling bookshelves. It looks like a British lord's library that got lost in an '80s warehouse party. It feels like you're heading to nowhere, but it's worth it. Look out for a big NEXTDOOR sign above the door.

⭐**Stache**   COCKTAIL BAR
(Map p220; ☑954-449-1044; www.stacheftl.com; 109 SW 2nd Ave; ◷7am-5pm Mon & Thu, to 4am Fri, 8pm-4am Sat) The town's favorite speakeasy serves a wide range of whiskeys and both classic and crafted cocktails. It rocks a blend of rock/funk/soul and R&B. At weekends there's live music, dancing and burlesque – dress up and have fun. It serves Panther Coffee coffee during the day. It's open late on weekends only. 'Non-binary night' is one of its themed evenings.

Warsaw Coffee Company   CAFE
(815 NE 13th St; ◷7am-10pm Mon-Sat, to 6pm Sun) The coffee spot to come to if you're serious about your brew. It's inside the Milk Money

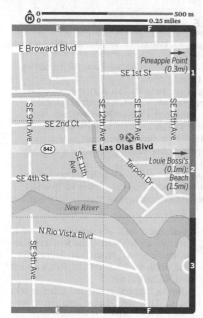

Bar & Kitchen space. The main features of this industrial space are concrete, Tolix-style designer chairs and floor-to-ceiling windows. Fabulous, if pricey, coffee.

Unfortunately the outlook is nothing much – the usual suburban car park – but the rest of the ambience is spot on. Fabulous baked items, too.

The Living Room Lounge BAR
(Map p216; ☑954-414-8200; www.wfortlauderdalehotel.com/living-room; The W Hotel, 401 N Fort Lauderdale Beach Blvd; ⊙5-10pm Mon-Thu, to 2am Fri & Sat, to midnight Sun) W Fort Lauderdale, the city's poshest digs, is proud of its 'living room' lounge. Created to be accessible and casual, it has the air of a relaxed and spacious bar rather than a nightclub. You can sit at sofas or barstools and the ambience is a cut above the rest in terms of style and clientele.

Patrons who aren't looking at their cell phones over a classic cocktail are ogling the crowd (and pretending they're not).

Laser Wolf BAR
(☑954-667-9373; 901 Progresso Dr, Suite 101; ⊙6pm-2am Mon-Thu, to 3am Fri, 8pm-3am Sat) An arty dive bar that serves a wide variety of craft beer in a tiny space. The atmosphere is friendly; if you're looking for an authentic local place to have a drink and perhaps chat

to some locals, this is it. There's a nice outdoor area too.

Wreck Bar BAR
(B Ocean Resort Fort Lauderdale; Map p216; ☑954-524-5551; www.bhotelsandresorts.com/b-ocean-resort/eat-drink/wreck-bar; 1140 Seabreeze Blvd; ⊙6pm-2am Mon-Sat, 11am-3pm Sun) After one too many cocktails you might wonder whether you're seeing things as you look through the Wreck Bar's 'portholes' to see three or four mermaids swimming seductively past. It's a piece of priceless Florida kitsch. The show begins at 7pm, but get there early for a spot.

There are nightly 21-and-over 10pm burlesque shows with the mermaids too (reservations required), as well as a weekly ladies-themed mermen show.

Rosie's GAY
(☑954-563-0123; www.rosiesbng.com; 2449 Wilton Dr; ⊙11am-10pm) A low-key, 'anyone's welcome' neighborhood gay bar with a solid American menu, a wonderful outdoor patio and a popular Sunday brunch menu (from 10am).

Ramrod GAY
(☑954-763-8219; www.ramrodbar.com; 1508 NE 4th Ave; ⊙noon-2am Sun-Thurs, to 3pm Fri & Sat)

GAY & LESBIAN FORT LAUDERDALE

Sure, South Beach is a hot location for gay travelers, but Fort Lauderdale nips at the heels of its southern neighbor. Compared to South Beach, Lauderdale is a little more rainbow-flag-oriented and a little less exclusive. And therein lies the charm for the hordes of gay men who flock here, either to party or to settle down.

Fort Lauderdale is home to several dozen gay bars and clubs, as many gay guesthouses, and a couple of way-gay residential areas. **Victoria Park** is an established gay hub just northeast of downtown Fort Lauderdale. A bit further north, **Wilton Manors** is a more recently gay-gentrified area boasting endless nightlife options. Look for Rosie's (p221), a low-key neighborhood watering hole; The Manor, for nationally recognized performers and an epic dance floor; and Georgie's Alibi. Spots such as Stache (p220) offer non-binary nights. Or check out the leather/bear/cowboy club, Ramrod (p221).

Gay guesthouses are plentiful; visit www.gayftlauderdale.com. Consult the glossy weekly *Hot Spots* (www.hotspotsmagazine.com) to keep updated on gay nightlife. For the most comprehensive list of everything gay, log on to www.jumponmarkslist.com.

A leather/bear/cowboy club with plenty to experience (both on the dance floor and at the regular themed events). Uniforms, leather and shirtless guys in jeans are in order. It will surely be a memorable night.

Georgie's Alibi GAY
(☑954-565-2526; www.alibiwiltonmanors.com; 2266 Wilton Dr; ⊙11am-2am) Georgie's is Wilton Manors' gay landmark, a nightclub featuring a playlist of Top 40s and country blockbusters along with cheap drinks after 9pm and ever-popular performers (see the website).

The Manor CLUB
(☑954-626-0082; www.themanorcomplex.com; 2345 Wilton Dr; cover $10-20; ⊙varies) This epic nightclub features nationally recognized singers, fashion and runway shows, burlesque, drag and stand-up comedians, plus a young crowd (18 to 30) and a hot and sweaty dance floor.

☆ Entertainment

★**Savor Cinema** CINEMA
(Cinema Paradiso; Map p220; ☑954-525-3456; 503 SE 6th St) This funky church-turned-cinema offers plush velvet seats, film festival entries, independent and European films, and plenty of kid-friendly programs. It's a great rainy-day standby. Events and films are posted on its Facebook page.

Blue Jean Blues JAZZ
(☑954-306-6330; www.bjblive.com; 3320 NE 33rd St; ⊙11am-2am Sun-Thu, to 3am Fri & Sat) Get away from the beach for a low-key evening of jazz and blues at this cool little neighborhood bar, often packed. There's live music

seven nights and four afternoons a week, featuring a who's who of the southern Florida music scene. From East Sunrise Blvd head north for 2.3 miles and then turn left onto NE 33rd Street.

Serves burgers, pizzas and other snacks ($9 to $17), too. Happy hour, with half-priced mixed drinks, domestic beers and house wine, goes from 11am all the way to 7pm daily.

🛍 Shopping

Swap Shop MARKET
(www.floridaswapshop.com; 3291 W Sunrise Blvd; ⊙9am-5pm Mon-Fri, 8am-6pm Sat & Sun) Perhaps the most fun shopping in town, the state's biggest flea market has acres of stalls selling everything from underwear to antique cookie jars to pink lawn flamingos, and a carnival atmosphere of mariachi music, hot-dog trucks and a 14-screen drive-in movie theater. You'll find it slightly northwest of downtown.

❶ Getting There & Away

Fort Lauderdale is served by its own international airport (p526).

If you're driving here, I-95 and Florida's Turnpike run north–south and provide good access to Fort Lauderdale. I-595, the major east–west artery, intersects I-95, Florida's Turnpike and the Sawgrass Expwy. It also feeds into I-75, which runs to Florida's west coast.

AIR

Fort Lauderdale–Hollywood International Airport (p526) is off I-95 between Lauderdale and Hollywood. The airport has four terminals (following a recent expansion and massive investment) and is served by more than 35 airlines, including many low-cost carriers and nonstop flights from Europe.

From the airport, it's a short 20-minute drive to downtown, or a $25 cab ride.

BOAT

Port Everglades (www.porteverglades.net; 1850 Eller Drive) cruise port is considered one of the busiest ports in the world, accommodating both cruise ships and containers. From the port, walk to SE 17th St and take bus 40 to the beach or to Broward Central Terminal.

If you're heading to Fort Lauderdale in your own boat (not that unlikely here), head for the **Bahia Mar Resort & Yachting Center** (Map p216; ☑ 954-627-6309; www.bahiamaryachtingcenter.com; 801 Seabreeze Blvd; ☺7am-6pm).

BUS

The **Greyhound Station** (☑ 954-764-6551; www.greyhound.com; 515 NE 3rd St) is about four blocks from Broward Central Terminal, the central transfer point for buses in the area.

TRAIN

Tri-Rail (☑ 800-874-7245; www.tri-rail.com; 6151 N Andrews Ave) runs between Miami Airport and Fort Lauderdale (one way $5, 45 minutes). A feeder system of buses has connections at no charge. Free parking is provided at most stations. Provide ample cushion for delays. **Amtrak** (☑ 800-872-7245; www.amtrak.com; 200 SW 21st Tce) also uses Tri-Rail tracks.

❶ Getting Around

Sun Trolley (☑ 954-876-5539; www.suntrolley.com; free; ☺10:30am-5pm) runs between Las Olas and the beaches between 9:30am and 6:30pm Friday to Monday. Broward County Transit (p214) operates between downtown, the beach and Port Everglades. From **Broward Central Terminal** (Map p220; 101 NW 1st Ave), take bus 11 to upper Fort Lauderdale Beach and Lauderdale-by-the-Sea; bus 4 to Port Everglades; and bus 40 to 17th St and the beaches.

The fun, yellow water taxi (p217) travels the canals and waterways between 17th St to the south, Atlantic Blvd/Pompano Beach to the north, the Riverwalk to the west and the Atlantic Ocean to the east. There are also services to Hollywood ($15 per person).

Lauderdale-by-the-Sea

☑ 754 / POP 6544

In the late 1800s southern Florida was a wild frontier, home to a few dozen Seminole families and some hardy settlers. Remnants of this early history can be found in the flow of beachside communities north of Fort Lauderdale along the Intracoastal Waterway. This includes Lauderdale-by-the-Sea, the closest community to Fort Lauderdale. If you enter from the busy highway you'll find it hard to distinguish from Fort Lauderdale's city sprawl. Turn coastward for a mile, however, and you'll find yourself in a pretty town with a laid-back, beach resort feel.

◉ Sights & Activities

Anglin's Pier   LANDMARK
(admission $2; ☺24hr) This popular fishing pier has a 24-hour tackle shop, night fishing lights and rod rental for $18. The pier itself was built in 1963 after storms destroyed the original, which was constructed in 1942 and had cannons perched on its end in anticipation of attack during WWII.

South Florida Diving Headquarters   DIVING
(☑954-783-2299; www.southfloridadiving.com; 101 N Riverside Dr, Pompano Beach; 2-tank dive/snorkeling $65/35; ☺trips 8:30am & 1:30pm) Dive natural and artificial reefs, or float along one of the area's famous drift dives with this PADI-certified company. Snorkeling trips will keep nondivers happy.

🛏 Sleeping

⭐**Blue Seas Courtyard**   HOTEL **$$**
(☑954-772-3336; http://blueseascourtyard.com; 4525 El Mar Dr; r from $155; ▣✿🛜🏊) Standing out from the crowd with a hacienda-style roof of clay barrel tiles, Mexican-themed yellow exterior and hand-stenciled decoration, Blue Seas seems to embody the sunny, laid-back disposition of Lauderdale-by-the-Sea. Owners Marc and Cristie have been at the helm since the 1970s, and provide a truly attentive and personalized service that keeps rooms booked up weeks in advance.

⭐**High Noon Beach Resort**   MOTEL **$$**
(☑954-776-1121; www.highnoonresort.com; 4424 El Mar Dr; r/ste/apt from $188/222/239; ✿@🛜🏊) Smack bang in the middle of the action and spilling onto the beach, this ultraclean resort includes a number of properties in a row. You have a choice of rooms, efficiencies and apartments; these are modern and spotless. The friendly owner's parents bought one of the properties in 1961 and it's been family-run ever since.

Seacrest Hotel HOTEL **$$**

(☑ 954-530-8854; www.hotelseacrest.com; 4562 Bougainvillea Dr; r $179-265; P❄🅿🛜🏊) One of the best-kept secrets in Lauderdale-by-the-Sea, the Seacrest is set back from the beach and offers the polished standards of a hotel within the intimate confines of a converted home. Pad across cool travertine marble floors to enormous beds with plump pillowtops before flicking on your favorite HBO show. There's a generous private pool, and the beach is just five minutes' walk away.

✖️ Eating

Pan'e Dolci CAFE **$**

(Italian Bakery; ☑ 954-635-2385; 207 Commercial Blvd; snacks $5-10; ⊗ 8am-11:30pm Mon-Thu, to midnight Fri-Sun) This smart Italian *dolceria* (cake shop) serves the most expensive cappuccino around ($5), but it's worth it for the authentic and oh-so-delicious Italian cakes. The panini ($10) make a great takeout for the beach. It's handily located on the main drag.

Frenchy's Table FRENCH **$$**

(☑ 954-533-2580; https://frenchystable.com; 235 Commercial Blvd; 2-/3-course meal from $29/36; ⊗ 5pm-late Tues-Sat) The owner, Edith, does the lot here: serves, cooks and chats. This means that the experience is neither harried nor hurried, so don't come if you want to eat and run. It's as French as Limoges (where Edith is from) and the interior is white and chic. It's got a touch of French elegance with zero snootiness.

Vinnie's ITALIAN **$$**

(☑ 954-772-8111; http://vincents.kitchen; 106 E Commercial Blvd; mains $16-41; ⊗ noon-midnight) This Italian American raw bar and pizzeria is popular for locals who like to be seen, and the modern, industrial-chic space that opens onto the pavement has a sociable, if very loud, ambience.

🍷 Drinking & Nightlife

The Village Pump BAR

(www.villagegrille.com; 4404 El Mar Dr; ⊗ 9am-2am) Serving sturdy drinks in a nautical wood-paneled room since 1949, the Village Pump simply hums at the daily happy hour where middle-aged regulars spill out onto the streets.

ℹ️ Getting There & Away

Tri-Rail (p214) heads north from Fort Lauderdale. If you're driving, try to take A1A (sometimes called Ocean Blvd): the drive is glorious.

Broward County Transit (p214) buses connect to beaches north of Fort Lauderdale and south to Las Olas in Fort Lauderdale itself. Fares are $2.

Deerfield Beach

☑ 754 / POP 80,571

Wherever you go along this coastline you are spoiled for choice for beaches, but Deerfield Beach is the best of the bunch. Deerfield Beach has a small core backed (unfortunately, like most of the southeastern coastline) by the US 1 highway. It's friendly, lacks pretension or snobbery, has a lovely stretch of beach and some good restaurants.

⦿ Sights

Deerfield Beach Historical Society MUSEUM

(☑ 954-429-0378; www.deerfieldhistory.org; 380 E Hillsboro Rd; ⊗ 10am-2pm) **FREE** This volunteer-run organization oversees several sites from Deerfield Beach's early days in the 1920s. Back then the community was 1300 people strong and the town consisted of four or five stores, a lodge, a post office and two hotels. The Old Deerfield School, Kester Cottage and the Butler House museum are all open for tours on the first and third Saturday of the month.

Deerfield Beach BEACH

(www.deerfield-beach.com) Deerfield Beach is an award-winning 'Blue Wave' beach with pristine water, nine lifeguard towers and a designated surfing area north of the pier and south of Tower 7.

Butterfly World NATURE RESERVE

(www.butterflyworld.com; 3600 W Sample Rd, Coconut Creek; adult/child $33/23; ⊗ 9am-5pm Mon-Sat, from 11am Sun; 🅿) The first indoor butterfly park in the US is also one of the largest butterfly exhibits anywhere. It features thousands of live, exotic species, such as the bright blue morphos or camouflaged owl butterfly. Various exhibits highlight different creatures, from butterflies to hummingbirds. Butterfly World is an excellent place to spend the better part of a day, especially with wide-eyed children or shutterbugs.

🏃 Activities

Ski Rixen
WATER SPORTS

(www.skirixenusa.com; cable pass per hr/half-day $25/40; ⊙noon-8pm Tue-Sun) Deerfield's Quiet Waters Park is home to South Florida's only cable waterski system. Using an innovative cabling system suspended from towers surrounding a half-mile course, water-skiers (and wakeboarders) are pulled over a wake-free watercourse. Obstacles are available for advanced tricksters; otherwise riders can perfect their waterskiing techniques without the hassle of a boat.

Skiers under 18 must have a waiver form notarized and signed by their parents.

Island Water Sports
SURFING

(☑954-427-4929; www.islandwatersports.com; 1985 NE 2nd St; surfboard rental per hr from $10) This central spot is the kingdom of all things 'hang ten,' from surfboard, bodyboard and stand-up paddleboard rental to surf lessons. To tantalize you, they offer free lessons every Saturday (7am to 9am).

Splash Adventure
Water Park
WATER PARK

(☑955-357-5100; www.broward.org/parks/things todo/pages/splashadventure.aspx; 401 S Powerline Rd, Quiet Waters Park; admission per person/car $1.50/6; ⊙10am-5:20pm; 🏊) The 430-acre Splash Adventure Water Park rings with the squeals of kids and grown-ups enjoying all kinds of wet'n'wild fun. This water playground has a shallow pool and fountains spraying every which way. Hours may change seasonally.

🍴 Eating

⭐Tucker Duke's Lunchbox
BURGERS $

(☑954-708-2035; http://tuckerdukes.com; 1101 S Powerline Rd; mains $6-18; ⊙10am-10pm) Superior burgers and Southern comfort food made from local, seasonal ingredients. The brain behind the brand (yes, it's a chain) is Florida native and *Cutthroat Kitchen* winner chef Brian Cartenuto, who is passionate about getting back to basics in the kitchen.

The Whale's Rib
and Raw Bar
SEAFOOD $$

(☑954-421-8880; www.whalesrib.com; 2301 NE 2nd St; mains $11-21; ⊙11am-11pm Sun-Thurs, 11am-midnight Fri & Sat) If you ask a local where to eat, the Whale's Rib is a frequent suggestion. This seafood joint is renowned for its dolphin fingers and dolphin wrap. And before you report us to animal welfare authorities, they're 'talking mahimahi, not Flipper here,' as we were told. They also serve up tasty and generous helpings of chicken sandwiches and clams over linguine.

❶ Getting There & Away

Broward County Transit (☑954-357-8400; www.broward.org/bct) buses serve Deerfield Beach, connecting to Fort Lauderdale. Fares are $2.

Boca Raton

☑561 / POP 98,150

Boca Raton, or simply 'Boca,' is the quintessential glitzy retiree town. What began as a sleepy residential community was plumped up in the mid-1920s by architect Addison Mizner, who relied on his love of Spanish architecture to give this town its particular look. Although his fingerprints remain on numerous structures throughout the area, his name is most often invoked when talking about the popular alfresco mall, Mizner Park. The rest of Boca is a mostly mainstream collection of chain stores and restaurants and, as you near the ocean, some peaceful beaches and parks. Most people don't come to Boca on vacation unless they have family here, as there are almost no beachfront hotels.

◉ Sights

⭐Gumbo Limbo
Nature Center
PARK

(☑561-544-8605; www.gumbolimbo.org; 1801 N Ocean Blvd; suggested donation $5; ⊙9am-4pm Mon-Sat, noon-4pm Sun; 🏊) Boca's best asset is this stretch of waterfront parkland. It's a preserve of tropical hammock and dunes ecosystems, and a haven for all manner of sea creatures and birds. Dedicated to educating the public about sea turtles and other local fauna, the natural-history displays include saltwater tanks full of critters. The highlight is the sea-turtle rehabilitation center.

Boca Raton
Museum of Art
MUSEUM

(☑561-392-2500; www.bocamuseum.org; 501 Plaza Real; adult/student $12/free; ⊙11am-7pm Wed-Sun) In Mizner Park, this elegant museum showcases the minor works of modern masters such as Picasso, Chagall and Modigliani (note: these may rotate). It also has a genuinely worthwhile collection of pieces by 20th- and 21st-century American and European painters, sculptors and photographers. Regular exhibitions to boot.

Mizner Park
PLAZA

(www.miznerpark.com) Since Boca lacks a cohesive downtown, Mizner Park generally serves as the city's center. At the north end the Count de Hoernle Amphitheater accommodates more than 4000 people for symphonies, ballet, rock concerts and other cultural events. This Spanish-style outdoor shopping mall, bookended on one side by the Boca Raton Museum of Art, has valet parking and a slew of chichi restaurants and upscale chain stores.

Red Reef Beach
BEACH

(1 N Ocean Blvd; per vehicle Mon-Fri $16, Sat & Sun $18; ⊘8am-sunset; 🅿) Sadly Hurricane Sandy buried most of the artificial reef in 2012, but this beach – one of three in the area – is still tops for water-lovers. There are lifeguards and great shallow pools for beginner snorkelers. Together with neighboring South Beach Park, the beaches encompass some 60 acres of wild shores.

 ## Tours

Loxahatchee Everglades Tours
ECOTOUR

(📞800-683-5873; www.evergladesairboattours. com; 15490 Loxahatchee Rd, Parkland; 50min tour adult/child under 12yr $65/35; ⊘9:30am-2:30pm Mon-Sat) Ten miles west of downtown, Wild Lyle's Loxahatchee Everglades Tours offers 50-minute ecoexplorations of the Everglades on one of eight custom airboats (a boat using a fan instead of a propeller to push it over the water). Guests enjoy an adventure ride through swampy marsh, around papyrus and hurricane grass and past longwinged birds. turtles and gators sunning themselves.

🍽 Sleeping & Eating

La Boca Casa
APARTMENT $$

(📞561-392-0885; 356 N Ocean Blvd; apt from $195) One of the couple of options in Boca Raton, this surprising find is opposite the beach. The modern self-contained units (19 in total) are housed in a long, white, contemporary building and surrounded by lush, green lawns. It makes a good base for exploring the coast. Minimum two-night stay.

Ben's Kosher Deli
DELI $

(www.bensdeli.net; 9942 Clint Moore Rd; mains $7-15; ⊘9am-7:30pm Mon-Thurs, 9am-8pm Fri-Sun) The Florida outpost of a well-loved New York–based deli, Ben's sprawling menu covers all the Jewish classics: corned-beef sandwiches, knishes (potato-stuffed pastries), sweet-and-sour beef tongue and eggs with smoked salmon. The deli is 8 miles northwest of the Mizner Plaza in downtown Boca Raton.

Casimir French Bistro
FRENCH $$

(📞561-955-6001; www.casimirbistro.com; 416 Via De Palmas Ste 81; mains $13-22; ⊘Mon- Sat 11:30am-10pm) A great option for a casual lunch at the Mizner Plaza – go for half a sandwich and a bowl of delicious French onion soup, or a steak and fries.

STaR
AMERICAN $$$

(Six Tables, A Restaurant; 📞561-347-6260; www. sixtablesrestaurant.com; Mizner Plaza, 112 NE 2nd St; menu $99; ⊘7-10pm Thu-Sat) Chef Jonathan Fyhrie offers an elegant and romantic dining experience for just six lucky tables. The evening starts with the chef drawing the curtains and locking the door, then a shared glass of bubbles, some cheese puffs and a presentation. Settle in for a flavorful five-course fixed-price menu, which often includes a peerless lobster bisque and chateaubriand.

🛈 Getting There & Away

Boca Raton is 30 miles from both Fort Lauderdale–Hollywood International Airport (p526) (FLL) and Palm Beach International Airport (p245) (PBI), and sprawls several miles east and west of I-95.

The **Tri-Rail Station** (www.tri-rail.com; 680 Yamato Rd) has shuttle services to both airports. Palm Tran bus 94 connects downtown Boca with the Tri-Rail station.

Palm Tran (http://discover.pbcgov.org/ palmtran; per ride $2, day pass $5) serves southeast Florida between Jupiter and Boca Raton. From the Tri-Rail station, bus 2 takes you to PBI and bus 94 to Florida Atlantic University, where you can transfer to bus 91 to Mizner Park. From Mizner Park, take bus 92 to South Beach Park.

Delray Beach

📞 561 / POP 68,749

Founded by Seminoles, and later settled in the 18th and 19th centuries by African Americans and Japanese agriculturists who farmed pineapples just east of I-95, this melting pot retooled itself for the tourist trade when the railroads chugged through Delray Beach in 1896. Local hotels and clubs turned a blind eye to Prohibition laws and accommodated everyone. Perhaps this eclectic mix of early residents – from the industrious to the lawless – is the reason Delray so effortlessly juggles a casual yet sophisticated vibe.

⦿ Sights

★ Morikami Museum & Japanese Gardens
MUSEUM

(☑561-495-0233; www.morikami.org; 4000 Morikami Park Rd; adult/child $15/9; ⊙10am-5pm Tue-Sun) Japanese immigrant and pineapple farmer Sukeji 'George' Morikami, a member of the original Yamato settlement, donated his spectacularly landscaped 200-acre property for the establishment of a museum showcasing Japanese culture. Today you can wander more than a mile of pine-lined nature trails around koi-filled ponds, experiencing different Japanese gardens from bonsai to a 12th-century *shinden* (pleasure) garden modeled on a noble estate. The outstanding museum showcases more than 5000 Japanese antiques, objects and works of fine art.

On the third Saturday of the month you can take part in a tea ceremony in the **Seishin-An Teahouse** ($5 with admission to the museum). Cultural and educational events and classes are also offered. Check out the website for details.

The museum's Cornell Cafe (p228) serves neo-Japanese cuisine such as sweet-potato tempura, ginger-roasted duck and sushi rolls. It is considered one of the best museum restaurants in the country.

The museum is located 7.5 miles southwest of Old School Square.

Old School Square
ARTS CENTER

(☑561-243-7922; http://oldschoolsquare.org; 51 N Swinton Ave) This highly successful preservation project encompasses Delray's 1913 elementary school, 1925 high school and 1926 gymnasium. The buildings house the Cornell Art Museum, showcasing rotating exhibitions of local, national and international arts and crafts; the **Crest Theatre**; and a vibrant **School of Creative Arts**, sponsoring a program of classes, events, theater and exhibitions.

Cornell Art Museum
MUSEUM

(http://oldschoolsquare.org/about/cornell-museum; Old School Square; adult/child $8/free; ⊙10am-4:30pm Tue-Sat, from 1pm Sun) Housed in the restored 1913 Delray Elementary building within Old School Square, this charming museum hosts rotating exhibits featuring an eclectic mix of local, national and international fine art, crafts and pop culture.

Public Beach
BEACH

(Ocean Blvd) A hip gathering spot for young locals and visitors, with lifeguards and excellent surf for swimming.

Atlantic Dunes Park
PARK

(www.downtowndelraybeach.com; 1600 Ocean Blvd) Has 7 acres of shorefront, clean restroom facilities, volleyball courts and picnic areas.

🛏 Sleeping

★ Parliament Inn
GUESTHOUSE $$

(☑561-276-6245; www.florida-info.com; 1236 George Bush Blvd; 2-person ste $99-220, 4-person ste $107-260; P❋❀🛜❄) This lushly planted hideaway is tucked just off Delray's spectacular 2-mile beach. It's easy to miss given the eight lemon-yellow, single-story units are situated in a gorgeous tropical garden shaded by towering palms. The trees are strung with hammocks from where you can idly contemplate the turquoise pool. Each unit has a kitchen, living space and a private porch.

★ Sundy House Inn
B&B $$$

(☑561-272-5678; www.sundyhouse.com; 106 S Swinton Ave; r Sun-Thu from $300, Fri & Sat from $350; P❋❀🛜❄) The best place to stay along the entire stretch of this coast, stepping into this sumptuous B&B feels like being transported to Bali. Pathways twine through a dense garden of trumpet flowers, hibiscus and coconut palms, the vegetation occasionally parting to reveal vintage bird cages or Chinese lion statues. Guestrooms are stylish, with heavy wood furniture and dark shutters.

Crane's Beach House
GUESTHOUSE $$$

(☑561-278-1700; www.cranesbeachhouse.com; 82 Gleason St; studio/apt from $346/from $475; P❋@🛜❄) This hidden garden guesthouse has 28 spacious rooms and apartments (with kitchenette), brightly appointed in colorful Key West style with loads of funky local art. Palm-shaded grotto swimming pools and a tiki bar (Thursday to Saturday) and weekend live music add a fun, sociable spirit. The ultrafriendly staff love to chat and help out with tips and restaurant recommendations.

Eating

★ El Camino
MEXICAN $

(☑ 561-865-5350; www.elcaminodelray.com; 15 NE 2nd Ave, Pineapple Grove; mains $10-19; ⊙ 11am-11pm) It's hard to know what's better: the industrial-chic in this former car garage (complete with original hoists), the new-age interpretation and ambience of a traditional Mexican cantina, or the fabulous array of tacos, burritos and margaritas. The tacos are a bite of Mexican *paradiso*, and we love the smoked brisket served in an enchilada or quesadilla.

Ramen Lab
RAMEN $

(☑ 561-750-4448; https://ramenlabeatery.com; 25 NE 2nd Ave; ramen $13-16; ⊙ 11:30am-10:30pm Mon-Thu, 11:30am-1am Fri-Sun) A lovely place for a bowl of hearty ramen, with a choice of six types of broth - from pork tonkotsu ramen to veggie broth vegan ramen. If it's too hot for soup, go for the cooling poke bowl ($15) or a Korean bulgogi ($11). All are delicious.

The New Vegan
VEGAN $

(☑ 561-404-5301; www.thenewvegan.com; 528 NE 2nd St; mains $8-17; ⊙ 10am-3:30pm & 5:30-9:30pm Wed-Sun; 🖋) This light, simple, cafe-style place makes vegans swoon with plant-based burgers, salads, wraps and melts.

Cornell Cafe
ASIAN $$

(mains $9-20; ⊙ 11am-3pm Tue-Sun) On the grounds of the Morikami Museum & Japanese Gardens (p227), Cornell Cafe serves neo-Japanese cuisine such as sweet-potato tempura, ginger-roasted duck and sushi rolls. It is definitely 'up there' when it comes to museum restaurants. It's 7.5 miles southwest of Old School Square.

Joseph's Wine Bar
MEDITERRANEAN $$$

(☑ 561-272-6100; www.josephswinebar.com; 200 NE 2nd Ave 107; lunch mains $10-15, dinner mains $22-39; ⊙ 11am-10pm) Hosted by the gregarious Joseph, lunch or dinner at this friendly eatery is an elegant and convivial affair. Everything is made fresh to order so relax, take a wine recommendation from Joseph and await a vibrant selection of dips (including a deliciously smokey baba ghanoush), salads and wraps at lunchtime, and a sophisticated selection of mains in the evening. The baked rack of lamb in an unctuous Chianti sauce is a particular highlight.

★ Sundy House Restaurant
AMERICAN $$$

(☑ 561-272-5678; www.sundyhouse.com; 106 S Swinton Ave; mains $28-42, Sunday brunch $58; ⊙ 6-9pm Tue-Sun, brunch 10:30am-2pm Sat & Sun) Nibble on a charcuterie selection and the likes of braised pork shank or seared scallops at Delray's most romantic restaurant, overlooking the primeval Taru Gardens at the Sundy House Inn. The Sunday brunch, complete with made-to-order crepes and a prime-rib-carving station, is an extravaganza. (Saturday brunch is à la carte.) You must definitely reserve ahead.

🍷 Drinking & Nightlife

★ Dada
BAR

(☑ 561-330-3232; http://sub-culture.org/dada; 52 N Swinton Ave; ⊙ 5-11pm) Join the cool cats lounging in this two-story bungalow to sip cocktails, hear poetry readings or live bands, and nibble on ravioli, salads and hummus. The front porch with its outdoor lanterns adds to the romantic charm.

Subculture Coffee
CAFE

(☑ 561-808-8482; http://subculturecoffee.com; 20 W Atlantic Ave; ⊙ 7am-6pm Sun-Thu, 7am-8pm Fri & Sat) Join the locals for a break at long shared tables or comfy armchairs. There is even a small porch at the front for alfresco coffee. They roast their own beans. This is one of two cafes: the other is in West Palm Beach (p244). Great coffee and breakfast/brunch options.

☆ Entertainment

★ Arts Garage
ARTS CENTER

(☑ 561-450-6357; https://artsgarage.org; 94 Northeast 2nd Ave) Delray's community arts center hosts anything from bands and musical performances to radio shows and theater. Patrons can bring their own wine and snacks and, given the intimate size, there isn't a bad seat in the house.

🔒 Shopping

Murder on the Beach Mystery Bookstore
BOOKS

(☑ 561-279-7790; www.murderonthebeach.com; 104 W Atlantic Ave; ⊙ 10am-6pm Mon-Sat, noon-5pm Sun) For those looking for a good beach read, the rather particular Murder on the Beach bookstore specializes in Floridian mystery authors. You can also pick up general interest books on Florida here. There are literary events for mystery genre fans.

ℹ️ Getting There & Away

Delray Beach is about 20 miles south of West Palm Beach and 45 miles north of Miami on I-95, US Hwy 1 or Hwy A1A.

The **Greyhound Station** (📞561-272-6447; www.greyhound.com; 1587 SW 4th Ave) is served by Palm Tran (p226). Bus 2 takes you to Palm Beach International Airport or Boca Raton; bus 81 services the Tri-Rail station, Amtrak and downtown Delray. Amtrak, half a mile south of Atlantic Ave, shares a station with **Tri-Rail** (📞800-874-7245; www.tri-rail.com; 345 S Congress Ave).

Lake Worth

📞561 / POP 38,107

Billing itself as 'Where the tropics begin,' this bohemian community sits further east than any place in South Florida and it's where the Gulf Stream flows further west than anywhere along the coast. Such geographical good fortune gives Lake Worth warm weather year-round. The town has a famous casino, a decent collection of restaurants, and a spectacular sliver of public-access beachfront. Most visitors come for either the casino or the surf.

👁️ Sights & Activities

Lake Worth Beach   BEACH
This stretch of sand is universally considered to be the finest between Fort Lauderdale and Daytona. Surfers come from miles around to tame the waves; everyone else comes to enjoy the fine white sand.

Snook Islands Natural Area   PARK
(www.lakeworth.org/visitors/parks; Lake Avenue Bridge) The 20-mile long Lake Worth Lagoon is Palm Beach County's largest estuary and an important warm-water refuge for manatees. Stretching 1.2 miles north from Lake Avenue into the lagoon, this $18 million natural area was created to reverse some of the damage from years of development. Restoring miles of mangroves and laying down new oyster beds to encourage the growth of sea grasses, a favorite manatee snack, has enabled a startling number of birds and marine life to return.

Kayak Lake Worth   KAYAKING
(📞561-225-8250; http://kayaklakeworth.com; kayaks 2/4hr $40/50, tours per person $40-60) This mobile kayak and paddleboard operator can kit you up with all the necessary equipment for kayaking, paddleboarding and fishing, mainly Snook Islands Natural Area and Bingham Islands. Two- to three-hour eco, sunset and moonlight tours are also available with knowledgeable local guides Bryce and Emily.

🎊 Festivals & Events

Street Painting Festival   CULTURAL
(www.streetpaintingfestivalinc.org; ⊙Feb) If you're visiting in February, don't miss the fantastic Street Painting Festival, when artists come from far and wide to cover Lake Worth's pedestrianized main streets with more than 200 surreal images of superheroes and Old Masters. Wander the open-air gallery while snacking on barbecue, tacos or cheese sandwiches, then settle down for live music in the park.

🛏️ Sleeping & Eating

⭐**Sabal Palm B&B**   B&B $$
(📞561-582-1090; www.sabalpalmhouse.com; 109 N Golfview Rd; r winter $179-249, summer $109-199; ❄️🛜) A classic knickknack-filled B&B, this smart and spotless 1936 house has eight rooms named after artists. It's frilly, but neatly so; if that's not your thing, opt for the Dali Room that has an art deco, modern vibe. Owners Colleen and John are most helpful. Discount for longer stays.

It's opposite the golf course and the beach is a 10-minute walk over the bridge that spans the Intracoastal Waterway.

Pelican   DINER $
(610 Lake Ave; mains $3-10; ⊙7am-1pm Mon-Fri, to 2pm Sat & Sun; 🅿️) This early-risers' place offers hearty portions of perfectly prepared breakfast, plus a carnival of vegetarian-friendly specials with Pakistani flavors (the owners are Pakistani). It's an old-style diner with dated decor and you can sit at the bar or at inside or outside tables. Don't miss the Nihari beef shank ($17.95).

Hachi   ASIAN $
(📞561-582-5800; www.hachiasiancuisinegrill.com; 809 Lake Avenue; mains $12-18; ⊙Mon-Fri 11:30am-10pm, Sat noon-11pm, Sun noon-10pm) With its gorgeous, crimson diner decor, friendly service and a range of Asian dishes from Thailand to Korea via Japan, Hachi makes a great escape to a different set of flavors than you might otherwise find in Lake Worth. Try a spicy kimchi stew or rolls of

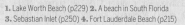

1. Lake Worth Beach (p229) 2. A beach in South Florida
3. Sebastian Inlet (p250) 4. Fort Lauderdale Beach (p215)

JUSTIN MICHAEL PHOTO /SHUTTERSTOCK ©

Top Beaches in Southeast Florida

Deerfield Beach

Deerfield Beach (p224) is an award-winning 'Blue Wave' beach with pristine water, nine lifeguard towers and a designated surfing area north of the pier and south of Tower 7.

Hutchinson Island

A stunning array of unspoiled beaches (p248), all with free access. Excellent for walking, swimming and some snorkeling. The beaches get less touristy the further north you go.

Sebastian Inlet

Stretching along a narrow strip of the barrier island (p250), this busy park, popular with fishers, surfers, boaters and families, is divided into two sections by the inlet bridge. On the north side swimming is safe for children in the calm-water lagoon. Surfers enjoy the waves.

Red Reef Beach

Hurricane Sandy buried most of the artificial reef (p226) in 2012, but this beach – one of three in the area – is still tops for water-lovers. There are lifeguards and great shallow pools for beginner snorkelers. Together with neighboring South Beach Park, the beaches encompass some 60 acres of wild shores.

Fort Lauderdale Beach

Fort Lauderdale's white-sand beach (p215) is one of the nation's cleanest and best. Stretching 7 miles to Lauderdale-by-the-Sea, it has dedicated family-, gay- and dog-friendly sections. Boating, diving, snorkeling and fishing are all extremely popular.

Lake Worth Beach

The finest stretch of sand (p229) between Fort Lauderdale and Daytona. Surfers come from miles around to tame the waves; everyone else comes to enjoy the fine white sand.

crisp sushi, or choose a hot tom yum noodle soup.

Downtown Pizza
PIZZA **$$**

(☑ 561-586-6448; 608 Lake Ave; pizza $11-22; ⊙ 11am-11pm) In business for more than 20 years, this sliver of a restaurant serves up delicious pizza with generous toppings (up to 18-inch bases). Meat-lovers should try the Philly cheesesteak pizza with shredded steak tips, peppers and onions.

★ Paradiso Ristorante
ITALIAN **$$$**

(☑ 561-547-2500; www.paradisolakeworth.com; 625 Lucerne Ave; mains $38-56; ⊙ 11:30am-3pm & 5:30-10pm) From the elegant interior to exquisitely presented dishes of homemade pasta, sheep-ricotta gnocchi and succulent veal fillet, this is a dining experience to savor. Seasonal delights such as truffles, chestnuts and huckleberries call from the specialty menu. Scheduled wine dinners and theater packages are arranged in conjunction with the Lake Worth Playhouse.

Reservations are recommended.

🍷 Drinking & Nightlife

CWS
BAR

(☑ 561-318-5637; www.cwslw.com; 522 Lucerne Ave; ⊙ 4pm-midnight Mon, 8am-midnight Tue, 8am-1am Wed & Thu, 8am-2am Fri, noon-2am Sat, 11am-midnight Sun) This trendy gastropub has a fabulous speakeasy vibe and whiskey den feel (apt, as there are more than 400 types on offer here). A beer garden attracts the younger crowd for live music but clients of all ages find their own niche and tuck into beers, classic cocktails and a dram or three of whiskey.

There are fabulous meals (menu changes regularly). The handmade pasta is our fave but go with the specials.

Igot's Martiki Bar
BAR

(☑ 561-582-4468; www.facebook.com/igotsmartikibar; 702 Lake Ave; ⊙ noon-2am) Get acquainted with Lake Worth's most eccentric locals at this surf-themed watering hole. It's open-sided so you can either sit at the high tops at the bar and watch the ball game or take a pew streetside and watch the sidewalk scene. Drinks are poured strong, and there's live music Thursday through Sunday.

☆ Entertainment

★ Lake Worth Playhouse
THEATER

(☑ 561-586-6410; www.lakeworthplayhouse.org; 713 Lake Ave; tickets $23-35) Housed in a restored 1924 vaudeville venue, this intimate spot stages classic community theater. The attached Stonzek Studio Theatre screens independent films (tickets $7 to $9). The Dinner + Theater package with Paradiso Ristorante is an absolute bargain; prices start from $60.

Bamboo Room
LIVE MUSIC

(☑ 561-585-2583; http://bambooroommusic.com; 25 S J St; ⊙ 7pm-2am Mon-Sat) This is where to go for club nights, salsa nights, and all sorts of DJ music. Check their calendar for what's on.

Lake Worth Drive-In
CINEMA

(☑ 561-965-4518; 3438 Lake Worth Rd; tickets adult/child $7/2) When was the last time you went to the drive-in? Screening first-run movies under the stars seven nights a week – drive in, tune in and sit back. Coolers are welcome; dogs are not.

ℹ Getting There & Away

The **Tri-Rail station** (www.tri-rail.com; 1703 Lake Worth Rd) is at the intersection of A St. Palm Tran (p226) bus 61 connects the station to downtown.

Palm Beach

☑ 561 / POP 8,751

The third-wealthiest city in America, Palm Beach, a barrier island connected by bridges to the mainland, is home to dozens of billionaires and looks every inch the playground for the rich and famous. Palatial Greco-Roman mansions line the shore; Bentleys and Porsches cruise the wide avenues of downtown; you may even see an entirely chrome Rolls Royce or two. Life here revolves around charity balls, designer shopping and cocktail-soaked lunches. Though all the bling may make you intimidated, fear not: much of Palm Beach is within the reach of all travelers. Stroll along the truly golden Gold Coast beach, ogle the massive gated compounds on A1A or window-shop along uber-ritzy Worth Ave – all for free.

Palm Beach is frequently in the news as Donald Trump's mansion-cum-private-club Mar-a-Lago is here.

Despite all the glitz, Palm Beach's architecture and history is nothing but fascinating, and offers some insight into how it might have been to live during the Gilded Age of late-19th-century USA.

⊙ Sights

★ Flagler Museum   MUSEUM
(📱561-655-2833; www.flaglermuseum.us; 1 White-hall Way; adult/child $18/10; ☉10am-5pm Tue-Sat, from noon Sun) This museum is housed in the spectacular 1902 mansion built by Henry Flagler as a gift for his bride, Mary Lily Kenan. The beaux-arts-styled Whitehall was one of the most modern houses of its era and quickly became the focus of the winter season. It was designed by John Carrère and Thomas Hastings, both students of the Ecole des Beaux-Arts in Paris and collaborators on other Gilded Age landmarks such as the New York Public Library.

Its modish, pink aluminum-leaf wallpaper was more expensive, at the time, than gold. Downstairs, public rooms such as the 4750-sq-ft Grand Hall, the Library with its painted cast plaster ceiling, and the silk-and wood-lined Drawing Room wow visitors with their detailed craftmanship and opulence. Upstairs, intimate bedrooms give an insight into family life. Of particular interest is the Flagler/Kenan History Room, which chronicles, through letters, newspaper clippings and photographs, Flagler's personal and professional life and Mary Lily's family history.

If you'd like more than to simply wander around the house, take a look at the website for a whole host of lectures, talks and exhibits, as well as the critically acclaimed Music Series that features intimate chamber concerts in the West Room, followed by a champagne reception ($70 per person).

Time your visit right and you can segue into a 'Gilded Age Style' lunch in the Café des Beaux-Arts (p237), which is housed in the Pavilion.

The second level portico, originating from 1902, has been renovated, and is quite delightful.

Free, one-hour docent-led tours depart at 11am, 12:30pm and 2pm Tuesday to Saturday, and hourly on Sundays from 12:30pm to 2:30pm; alternatively, you can pick up a free audioguide. This is a fabulous, not-to-be-missed experience and if there's one place to visit to immerse yourself in the Gilded Age, this is it.

★ Society of the Four
Arts Botanical Garden   GARDENS
(www.fourarts.org; 100 Four Arts Plaza, via Royal Palm Way; ☉10am-5pm) FREE These stunning gardens were originally designed and cultivated by the Garden Club in 1938 as 'demonstration gardens' to showcase tropical plants that suited the South Florida climate. This included a garden suitable for a Spanish-style house, a moonlight garden of white plants, plus Chinese, rose and jungle gardens, and others with fountains and tropical fruit trees. A landscape architect was employed in the 1950s to bring the elements together, although the 2004 hurricanes destroyed much of the area.

The painstakingly reconstructed gardens provide a lovely respite for locals and visitors.

Worth Avenue   AREA
(www.worth-avenue.com) This quarter-mile, palm-tree-lined strip of more than 200 high-end brand shops is like the Rodeo Dr of the East. You can trace its history back to the 1920s when the now-gone Everglades Club staged weekly fashion shows and launched the careers of designers such as Elizabeth Arden. Even if you don't have the slightest urge to sling a swag of glossy bags over your arm, the people-watching is priceless, as is the Spanish Revival architecture.

To learn more, don't miss the historical walking tour (p236).

Sea Gull Cottage   NOTABLE BUILDING
(60 Cocoanut Row) Sea Gull Cottage was constructed in 1886 overlooking what was a freshwater lake (now the Intracoastal Waterway) by RR McCormick, the Denver railroad and land developer. This was Henry Flagler's first Palm Beach residence, purchased in 1893. It is the oldest house on the island, although it used to be located next to the Royal Poinciana Hotel, Flagler's first resort hotel in Palm Beach. It was moved to its current site for preservation in 1984.

Built in the Florida vernacular style, the shingle cottage was famous as the 'showplace along the shores,' so pretty were its stained glass windows, Georgian marble floors and commanding viewing turret. You can't enter the building, but it's worth viewing its exterior.

Bethesda-by-the-Sea   CHURCH
(📱561-655-4554; www.bbts.org; 141 S County Rd; ☉9am-5pm Mon-Sat, 7am-4pm Sun) After visiting Tiffany's windows on Worth Ave, head to Bethesda-by-the Sea to admire *its* glorious Tiffany window and grand Gothic architecture. Built in 1926 to replace the first Protestant church of Palm Beach, it has a long

Palm Beach

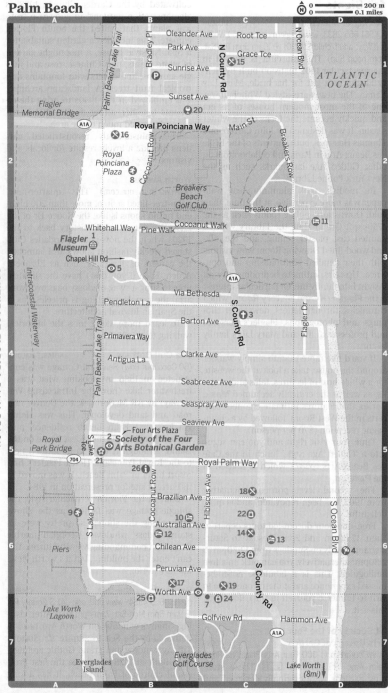

Palm Beach

SOUTHEAST FLORIDA PALM BEACH

community history and has hosted many a celebrity wedding, including those of Donald Trump to Melania Trump, and Michael Jordan.

To the side is a tranquil English-style cloister and the lovely Cluett Memorial Garden.

Palm Beach
Municipal Beach BEACH
(Ocean Blvd, btwn Royal Palm Way & Hammon Ave; ⊙sunrise-sunset) This is one of Palm Beach's two beautiful public beaches, both of which are kept seaweed-free by the town. This beach can get crowded.

For privacy, head north along S Ocean Blvd and turn left onto Barton Ave. There's free two-hour parking near the church before S County Rd and public access to the beach across from Clarke Ave.

Phipps Ocean Park BEACH
South of Southern Blvd on Ocean Blvd, before the Lake Worth Bridge, this is another place to catch rays.

🏃 Activities

★ **Palm Beach**
Lake Trail CYCLING
(Royal Palm Way, at the Intracoastal Waterway) Running along the Intracoastal Waterway, this 5-mile paved path stretches from Worth Ave (in the south) to Indian Rd (in

the north). Nicknamed 'The Trail of Conspicuous Consumption,' it is sandwiched between two amazing views: Lake Worth lagoon to the west, and an unending series of mansions to the east, and it originally allowed Flagler hotel guests to check out the social scene.

To get here from Worth Ave walk west to S Lake Dr and follow the path north to the Sailfish Club. For an abbreviated version, park in the metered lot off Royal Palm Way (or in the supermarket's lot on Sunset Ave) and head west to pick up the trail. Another nice stretch runs along N County Rd. Park on Sunset Ave and head north on the path running to Palm Beach Country Club. At just under 2 miles, the route is lined with houses and magnificent trees and there are plenty of exotic side streets to explore.

If bike rentals are not available at your hotel head to Palm Beach Bicycle Trail Shop. There's a 10mph speed limit on the trail.

Palm Beach
Bicycle Trail Shop CYCLING
(☑561-659-4583; http://palmbeachbicycle.com; 50 Cocoanut Row, Suite 117, In the Slat House; bikes/electric bikes per day $49/89; ⊙9am-5:30pm Mon-Sat, 10am-5pm Sun) This shop rents out bikes and electric bikes at a convenient spot for cycling. Helmets cost $5 extra.

⛳ Tours

★ Island Living Tours
CULTURAL

(📞561-309-5790; www.islandlivingpb.com; tours $35-150; ⏱appt only) Intriguing driving and cycling tours led by local resident Leslie Diver hint at some of the personal stories and history behind all the glitz. Her spiel covers the history, architecture and details about famous and infamous residents. Tours vary and can be tailored accordingly, and last between 90 minutes and 2½ hours or more, depending on the content.

Historical Walking Tour
CULTURAL

(📞561-659-6909; www.worth-avenue.com; 256 Worth Ave; $10; ⏱10:30am Wed) If you are here on a Wednesday be sure to head off on a walking tour with local historian and character, Rick Rose. The 1¼-hour tour covers the history of Worth Avenue, giving fabulous context to the Spanish Revival era, the social scene and the fashion behind the town since the Gilded Age.

Tours are popular among middle-aged (mainly) women and groups can get a bit large, but if you are happy with the odd elbow, this is not to be missed. The ticket price is donated to an animal rescue outfit. Meet opposite Tiffany & Co.

🛏 Sleeping

Palm Beach Historic Inn
B&B $$

(📞561-832-4009; www.palmbeachhistoricinn.com; 365 S County Rd; r/suite from $309/409; ❄🛜🛁) Housed on the 2nd floor of a landmark building brimming with character, this intimate European-style hotel has 13 small, light-filled rooms with hardwood floors and period Palm Beach furnishings. It was renovated in 2018 and the rooms and suites are fresh and airy. Stroll a block to the beach, or two to Worth Ave.

★ Brazilian Court
HOTEL $$$

(📞561-655-7740; www.thebraziliancourt.com; 301 Australian Ave; r $599-699, ste $799-1200;) Built in 1926, this elegant resort is an excellent choice for those who want pampering but not obsequiousness. Trendy but timeless, it's got a lovely Mediterranean style, a romantic courtyard and fashionable suites that effortlessly blend sleek lines and soft comfort. The on-site Frédéric Fekkai salon and renowned (and ultraromantic) French Café Boulud are major draws, too.

Heading to the beach? Hitch a ride in the hotel's house car – your driver will supply you with chairs, umbrellas, towels, bottled water and magazines. Bliss. Low season rates are significantly lower. Valet parking costs $27 per night.

★ Breakers
RESORT $$$

(📞833-200-7279; www.thebreakers.com; 1 S County Rd; r/ste from $700/2000; 🅿🐕❄@🛜🛁) 🏊 Originally built by Henry Flagler (in 1904 rooms cost $4 per night, including meals), today this 538-room resort sprawls across 140 acres and boasts a staff of 2000 plus, fluent in 56 languages. Just feet from the county's best snorkeling, this palace has two 18-hole golf courses, a mile of semiprivate beach, four pools and the best brunch around.

For opulence, elegance and old-world charm, there's no other choice; it's one of those once-in-a-lifetime experiences. Green Lodging certified.

Also worth noting is that prices fluctuate enormously and are drastically reduced in low season.

Chesterfield
HOTEL $$$

(📞561-659-5800; www.chesterfieldpb.com; 363 Cocoanut Row; r/ste from $310/from $535; 🅿❄🛜🛁🐕) From its old-fashioned room keys to the cookie jar in the lobby, this hotel aims for a British-inspired, old-world elegance that's much appreciated by its loyal guests, many of whom have been returning for decades. Room decor varies (each room is unique) from a 'Great White Hunter' feel with plaid wallpaper and murals of monkeys gamboling around the jungle, to padded-fabric walls.

The hotel's Leopard Lounge (p238), with its painted ceilings and tiger-print banquettes, is a perennial favorite for long lunches and evening piano music. You can even have high tea in the small library ($38 per person).

🍴 Eating

Green's Pharmacy
DINER $

(📞561-832-0304; www.greenspb.com/restaurant; 151 N County Rd; mains $4-11; ⏱7am-4pm Mon-Fri, to 3pm Sat, to 1pm Sun) Housed inside a working pharmacy, this place hasn't changed since John F Kennedy, looking to slip away from the Secret Service, would stroll across the mint-green linoleum to grab a bite. Choose between a table or a stool at the Formica counter and order from the paper menu just like everyone else, from trust-fund babies to beach-bound college women.

You'll be largely ignored if you're not a regular, but it's all part of the fun.

Surfside Diner
DINER $

(☑561-659-7495; https://surfsidediner.com; 314 S County Rd; mains $8-13; ☺8am-3pm) This classy remake of a classic diner serves decent breakfasts and brunch. Pancakes, chicken breakfast burritos and French toast are all tasty. For lunch there's grilled cheese and tomato soup, BLTs, PB&Js and sliders.

★HMF
INTERNATIONAL $$

(The Breakers Resort, 1 S County Rd; mains $16-27; ☺5pm-1am) HMF stands for the man himself: Henry Morrison Flagler. This stunning bar-cum-lounge is within the building's North Loggia where you'll definitely feel the ghosts of glitterati past. While the dress codes might differ these days (although most arrive elegantly attired), the party atmosphere – and whispers about the 'who's who, what and where' – is still going strong.

It's chic, sophisticated and a delightful spot for a cocktail and a selection of wines, plus delicious small plates with a very global influence.

Pizza al Fresco
PIZZA $$

(☑561-832-0032; www.pizzaalfresco.com; 14 Via Mizner; pizzas $16-25, salads $11-22; ☺11am-10pm; 🐾) If Worth Ave shopping is making you feel fatigued, duck into quaint Via Mizner and take the strain off your feet at this alfresco pizza place. Light-spangled palm trees provide evening romance, while efficient waitstaff whisk out orders of whole wheat and traditional flat crusts lathered with generous and inventive toppings. A local fave.

It also serves a good selection of salads and sandwiches.

Palm Beach Grill
MODERN AMERICAN $$

(☑561-209-2799; www.hillstone.com; 340 Royal Poinciana Way; mains $19-49; ☺11:30am-9pm) This restaurant is a great compromise between Palm Beach chic and casual. During the season it's perpetually packed thanks to good food and a buzzing bar. Securing one of the dining room's leather booths can be nearly impossible at the weekend, so book well ahead.

★Būccan
AMERICAN $$$

(☑561-833-3450; www.buccanpalmbeach.com; 350 S County Rd; mains $18-40; ☺5pm-10pm Sun-Thu, to 11pm Fri & Sat) With its modern American menu and James Beard-nominated chef, Clay Conley, at the helm, Būccan is the 'it' place to eat in Palm Beach. Flavor-hop with a selection of small plates, including smoked chicken sliders, and move on to snapper ceviche. Reservations recommended.

The bar will stay open later if it's busy, to midnight Sunday to Thursday and to 1am on Friday and Saturday.

★Café Boulud
FRENCH $$$

(☑561-655-6060; www.cafeboulud.com/palm beach; 301 Australian Ave; mains $16-58, fixed-price menu $38/$42; ☺cafe 7am-11pm, bar to midnight) Created by renowned New York chef Daniel Boulud, the restaurant at the Brazilian Court hotel is one of the few places in Palm Beach that truly justifies the sky-high prices. The warm dining room, terrace and beautiful lit-marble bar complement a rich menu of classic French and fusion dishes, all displaying Boulud's signature sophistication and subtlety.

Kinder on the purse, the Boulud brunch is a delicious feast. Happy hour is from 4pm to 6pm in the lounge and there's live jazz post-brunch on Sundays, with a fixed-price menu from 5:30pm to 6:30pm Sunday to Thursday,

Circle
INTERNATIONAL $$$

(☑877-724-3188; www.thebreakers.com; 1 S County Rd, The Breakers Resort; adult/child $110/50; ☺7am-11am Mon-Sat, to 2:30pm Sun) Sure, it's steep, but brunch at the Breakers' storied restaurant will certainly rank among the most amazing you'll ever enjoy. Beneath soaring 30ft frescoed ceilings, surrounded by ocean views and entertained by a roving harpsichordist, guests begin their feast at the breakfast bar, which features homemade doughnuts, tropical fruits and on-demand omelets.

In high season you'll need to reserve weeks in advance.

Café des Beaux-Arts
CAFE $$$

(☑561-655-2833; www.flaglermuseum.us; 1 Whitehall Way, Flagler Museum; tea $40 (includes museum admission); ☺11:30am-2:30pm Tue-Sat, noon-3pm Sun) Housed in the Pavilion alongside Flagler's private railroad car is this period cafe, built in the style of a 19th-century iron-and-glass railway palace. Here you can daintily dine on finger sandwiches, scones and custom-blended teas while looking out over Lake Worth.

SOUTHEAST FLORIDA PALM BEACH

Ta-Boo

MODERN AMERICAN $$$

(☎ 561-835-3500; www.taboorestaurant.com; 221 Worth Ave; mains $22-49; ☺11am-10pm) If you believe the legend, the Bloody Mary was invented here, mixed to soothe the hangover of Woolworth heiress Barbara Hutton. Today the restaurant boasts the most coveted window seats on Worth Ave. Competition to get in is as stiff as the heiress' drinks. Get past the intricate woodwork and jungle murals, and you'll enjoy a well-executed American bistro meal.

 Drinking & Nightlife

Leopard Lounge

LOUNGE

(www.chesterfieldpb.com; 363 Cocoanut Row; ☺7am-2:30pm & 5:30-11pm Mon-Fri, to midnight or later Sat & Sun) This gold, black and red lounge attracts a mature crowd and the occasional celeb (neither photos nor autograph hounds are allowed). The piano player and the waitstaff give off a there's-a-place-they'd-rather-be vibe, but if you want to relax with a drink or strike up a chat with someone next to you, this is the spot.

Cucina Palm Beach

CLUB

(www.cucinapalmbeach.com; 257 Royal Poinciana Way; ☺7am-3am) Reminiscent of a Florentine cafe, this high-end eatery overflows with warm colors, art and some of the finest glitterati in Palm Beach. Around 10pm they shove the tables out of the way and blast the music. There's a women's night called Kiss Me Thursdays, with food and DJs.

 Entertainment

Society of the Four Arts

PERFORMING ARTS

(☎ 561-655-7227; www.fourarts.org; 2 Four Arts Plaza) The concert series here includes cabaret, the Palm Beach Symphony, chamber orchestras, string quartets and piano performances.

 Shopping

Church Mouse

VINTAGE

(☎ 561-659-2154; www.bbts.org/about-us/churchmouse; 141 S County Rd; ☺10am-5pm Mon-Sat) Sponsored by Bethesda-by-the-Sea, this little donation-based resale shop has raised more than $4.5 million for Palm Beach charities in the last 20 years. It stocks 'gently' used castaways, and if you browse carefully you can find Palm Beach classics from Lilly Pulitzer or Chanel.

Il Sandalo

Fabio Tesorone

SHOES

(☎ 561-805-8645; https://ilsandaloinc.business.site; via Gucci Courtyard, 240 Worth Ave; ☺10am-6pm Mon-Sat) Handcrafted leather sandals from Neapolitan brothers Fabio and Pier Paolo Tesorone. Classic styles are embellished with glittering laminates, coral and, in some cases, semi-precious stones. If you can't find anything you like, have a pair made on-site to your exact specifications.

C. Orrico

FASHION & ACCESSORIES

(☎ 561-659-1284; www.corrico.com; 336 S County Rd; ☺10am-6pm Mon-Sat, from 11am Sun) Lilly Pulitzer, the Palm Beach princess of prints who created a fashion uniform for wealthy socialites, passed away in February 2013 aged 81. Pay homage to this enduring Palm Beach style icon by purchasing one of her lurid print dresses from C. Orrico, and pair it with similarly psychedelic sandals and jewelry.

Stubbs & Wootton

SHOES

(☎ 561-655-6857; www.stubbsandwootton.com; 340 Worth Ave; ☺10am-6pm Tue-Sat) If you want to fit in with the no-socks Palm Beach set, head straight to this high-end slippers and sandals shop. Wedges made from woven raffia handcrafted in Spain, hand-embroidered velvet slippers with custom-designed monograms and cool chambray cotton espadrilles are all *very* Palm Beach.

 Getting There & Away

Palm Tran (p226) bus 41 covers the bulk of the island, from Lantana Rd to Sunrise Ave; transfer to bus 1 at Publix to go north or south along Hwy 1. To get to Palm Beach International Airport (p245) in West Palm Beach, take bus 41 to the downtown transfer and hop on bus 44.

West Palm Beach

☎ 561 / POP 110,222

When Henry Flagler decided to develop what is now West Palm Beach, he knew precisely what it would become: a working-class community for the labor force that would support his glittering resort town across the causeway. And so the fraternal twins were born – Palm Beach, considered the fairer of the two, and West Palm Beach, a cooler work-hard-play-hard community. West Palm has a surprisingly diverse collection of restaurants, friendly inhabitants (including a strong gay community) and a gorgeous waterway that always seems to reflect the perfect amount of starlight.

◉ Sights

★**Norton Museum of Art**   MUSEUM
(☑ 561-832-5196; www.norton.org; 1451 S Olive Ave; adult/child $18/free, free on Fri & Sat; ⊙ 10am-5pm Mon, Tue, Thu & Sat, to 10pm Fri, from 11am Sun) This is the largest art museum in Florida and arguably the most impressive. It opened in 1941 to display the enormous art collection of industrialist Ralph Hubbard Norton and his wife Elizabeth. The Nortons' permanent collection of more than 5000 pieces (including works by Matisse, Warhol and O'Keeffe) is displayed alongside important Chinese, pre-Columbian Mexican and Southwestern USA artifacts, plus some wonderful contemporary photography and regular traveling exhibitions.

To enhance your visit, you can join one of the free docent-led tours through the galleries (2pm and 3pm Monday to Friday, 2pm Saturday). Alternatively, drop by on Friday from 5pm to 10pm for the fun 'Art After Dark' series, which includes anything from lectures and live music to conversations with curators and wine tastings.

★**Ann Norton**
Sculpture Garden   GARDENS
(☑ 561-832-5328; www.ansg.org; 253 Barcelona Rd; adult/child $15/7; ⊙ 10am-4pm Wed-Sun) This serene collection of sculptures is a real West Palm gem. The historical house, verdant grounds and monumental sculptures are all the work of Ralph Norton's second wife, Ann. After establishing herself as an artist in New York in the mid-1930s, she became the first sculpture teacher at the Norton School of Art, and created this luxurious garden as a place of repose.

After poking through Norton's home (the 1st floor has temporary exhibitions), you can wander the grounds and uncover her soaring feats of granite, brick, marble and bronze. Perhaps most awe-inspiring is the 1965 *Cluster,* a collection of seven burka-clad women in pink granite. Before leaving, be sure to peek into Norton's light-filled studio, where dusty tools lie just as she left them.

McCarthy's
Wildlife Sanctuary   WILDLIFE RESERVE
(☑ 561-790-2116; www.mccarthyswildlife.com; 12943 61st St N, Loxahatchee; adult/child $35/25; ⊙ tours 11am, noon, 1pm Tue-Sat) With entry by reservation only, this wildlife sanctuary takes unwanted exotics and treats dozens of native animals that are sick or injured and then releases them back to the wild. On the two-hour guided tour you'll get to see white tigers, panthers and barred owls all from 3ft away. Children under five are not permitted.

The sanctuary is 16 miles northwest of Clematis St, downtown West Palm Beach.

Peanut Island   ISLAND
(http://discover.pbcgov.org; $12 round-trip; ⊙ 11am-4pm Thu-Sun) Plopped right off the northeastern corner of West Palm, Peanut Island was created in 1918 by dredging projects. Originally named Inlet Island, the spit was renamed for a peanut-oil-shipping operation that failed in 1946. There is even a disused nuclear fallout bunker that was constructed for John F Kennedy during the days of the Cuban Missile Crisis (closed at the time of research).

The island has long been a popular spot for boaters to moor and party by day, and in 2005 the county invested $13 million into island rehabilitation, resulting in **Peanut Island Park**, which includes a pier, an artificial reef and some pretty sweet campsites (p242). There are no roads to the island. Visitors can get there via the shuttle boat that departs every 15 minutes from the Riviera Beach Marina.

Palm Beach County
History Museum   MUSEUM
(☑ 561-832-4164; www.hspbc.org; 300 N Dixie Hwy; ⊙ 10am-2pm Mon, to 5pm Tue-Fri, to 4pm Sat Sep-May) FREE For all the region's activities and museums, it can be hard for outsiders to get an insight into the history and people of the Sunshine State. This small museum, housed in the restored 1916 courthouse and staffed by volunteers, aims to change that. Quirky exhibits – featuring models, photographs and period artifacts – highlight individuals who have contributed to the growth and prosperity of Palm Beach County.

Informative plaques on everyone from Flagler and Mizner to Alligator Joe and the first settlers make the tour a fascinating one. Also has temporary exhibitions that change annually.

Palm Beach Zoo &
Conservation Society   ZOO
(☑ 561-547-9453; www.palmbeachzoo.com; 1301 Summit Blvd; adult/child $25/19; ⊙ 9am-5pm; 🐾) The highlight of this compact zoo is the

West Palm Beach

0 — 500 m
0 — 0.25 miles

Northwood Village (1.2mi);
Rapids Water Park (6.4mi)

Quadrille St

A1A

Flagler Memorial
Bridge

Piers

6th St
5th St
4th St
3rd St
2nd St

5th St
14

N Tamarind Ave
N Sapodilla Ave
N Rosemary Ave
N Quadrille St
N Dixie Hwy
Federal Hwy

Clear
Lake

Banyan St

3

N Narcissus
Ave

19

22

Centennial
Square

Clematis St
25   23
Datura St

9
Evernia St

Trolley line

S Quadrille Blvd
S Dixie Hwy
Federal Hwy
Flagler Rd

15

17

Fern St   21
Gardenia
St
20
Amtrak
Station
Iris St

12

Hibiscus St

Iris St

Trinity
Park

Trinity Ave

Lakeview Ave

704

Okeechobee Blvd

Royal Park
Bridge

S Tamarind Ave

Pembroke Pl
Chicago St
Kings Ct
Gruber Pl

L St
M St
N St

Acacia Rd

Waterside Path

Howard
Park
New Jersey
St

Newark St

6

Woodlawn
Cemetery

Norton Museum
of Art
2

Lake Ave

Cranes
Nest Way

Palm St
7 Penn St

Lake Worth
Lagoon

5
Park Pl

Queens Ct
16

Kanuga Dr

Flamingo Dr

Biscayne Dr

Claremore Dr

Charles St

Dock St

Parker Ave

Georgia Ave

Vallette Way
Orange Ct

S Dixie Hwy

11

Flamingo Dr
10
Barcelona Rd

Flagler Dr

1
Ann Norton
Sculpture
Garden

Ardmore Rd

Upland Rd

Florida Ave

4   EL CID
DISTRICT

Cordova Rd

Granada Rd

Intracoastal Waterway

Palm Beach
International (1mi);
International Polo Club (15mi);
McCarthy's Wildlife Sanctuary (16mi);
Lion Country Safari (18.5mi)

Westwood Dr

Valencia Rd

Olive Ave

Sunset Rd

18

Sunset Rd

Belvedere Rd

13

Lake Blvd

Gotham Ct

24

8

South Florida Science Center &
Aquarium, Palm Beach Zoo (2mi);
National Croquet Center (2.8mi);
Rhythm Cafe (3mi)

West Palm Beach

Tropics of the Americas exhibit, a 3-acre recreation of a rainforest, stocked with jaguars, monkeys, snakes, macaws and other tropical creatures. The zoo's also home to a few of the last remaining Florida panthers, North America's rarest mammal. Other unusual residents include Komodo dragons (the largest lizard in the world), capybaras (the largest rodent in the world) and one lone red kangaroo.

Like any zoo the animals are caged, which may be distressing for animal lovers, but many around these parts generously fund the museum to ensure good conditions. The zoo is a brief drive south of downtown.

Lion Country Safari WILDLIFE RESERVE
(☏561-793-1084; www.lioncountrysafari.com; 2003 Lion Country Safari Rd; adult/child $39/30; ⊙9:30am-5:30pm; 🚸) The first cageless drive-through safari in the country, this incredible animal park has 900 creatures roaming freely. Equal parts conservation area and safari, the park's 500 acres are home to bison, zebra, white rhinos, chimpanzees and, of course, lions. You tour in your car (unless it's a convertible, in which case short-term rentals are available), driving slowly, hoping the animals approach the vehicle.

The best time to go is when it rains, because the animals are more active when it's cool. The park is 20 miles west of downtown West Palm.

South Florida Science Center & Aquarium MUSEUM
(☏561-832-1988; www.sfsciencecenter.org; 4801 Dreher Trail North; adult/child $18/14; ⊙9am-5pm Mon-Fri, 10am-6pm Sat & Sun) A great little hands-on science center, aquarium and planetarium with weekend programs, traveling exhibits, a science trail, mini-golf and butterfly garden. On the last Friday of the month the museum stays open from 6pm to 9pm so you can view the night sky from the county's only public observatory (weather permitting). Prices change according to the exhibition.

Ragtops Motorcars Museum MUSEUM
(www.ragtopsmotorcars.com; 420 Claremore Dr; donations appreciated; ⊙10am-5pm Wed-Sat) This spot was originally a classic-car dealership with three convertible Mercedes, but Ty Houck's incredible automobile collection quickly grew, compelling area automotive enthusiasts to stop by for a look-see. Today you can test-drive many of the vehicles on display, though it helps to have serious intent to buy. Otherwise you're free to browse the rarities displayed, including an amphibious 1967 Triumph, a regal 1935 Bentley and a 1959 Edsel station wagon.

🏃 Activities

Rapids Water Park WATER PARK
(☏561-848-6272; www.rapidswaterpark.com; 6566 North Military Trail, Riviera Beach; weekday/weekend $46/52; ⊙10am-5pm mid-Mar-Dec, to

SOUTHEAST FLORIDA WEST PALM BEACH

7pm or 9pm Jun-Aug) South Florida's largest water park features 30 action-packed acres of wet and wild rides. Don't let the squeals of fear and delight from the Big Thunder funnel put you off. Awesome fun. Parking costs an extra $15.

Tours

Palm Beach Water Taxi
BOATING

(☑561-844-1724; www.sailfishmarina.com; 98 Lake Dr, Singer Island) Water taxis run between downtown West Palm and Singer Island ($16), as well as to Peanut Island (round-trip $13), leaving from Singer Island. Additionally, this outfit offers guided tours along the Intracoastal, including 90-minute narrated tours of Palm Beach mansions (adult/child $32/16.50).

Diva Duck
BOATING

(☑561-844-4188; www.divaduck.com; adult/child $31/5; ⊞) This hybrid bus-boat gives quacky 75-minute narrated tours of downtown's historical district, CityPlace (p245), the surrounding waterways and the shores of Peanut Island (p239). Yes, the bus really does float in the water. Tours start at CityPlace.

Courses

National Croquet Center
SPORTS

(☑561-478-2300; www.nationalcroquetclub.com; 700 Florida Mango Rd; ⊙9am-5pm) FREE Get a real taste of the upper-crust Palm Beach lifestyle at the largest croquet facility in the world. Here genteel sportspeople dressed in crisp whites hit balls through wickets on 12 of the world's biggest, greenest, most manicured lawns. It's members-only, but the public is invited to free lessons on Saturday mornings at 10am.

The pro shop, inside the plantation-style clubhouse, has all the latest in mallets and croquet wear. The center is about a 10-minute drive southwest of downtown West Palm.

Armory Art Center
ART

(☑561-832-1776; www.armoryart.org; 811 Park Place) FREE With more than a dozen state-of-the-art studios, the center hosts numerous adult and youth courses in ceramics, jewelry, painting, drawing, printmaking, photography and sculpture. Special events, lectures and rotating gallery exhibits also aim to educate and enrich. From June to early August, the Armory hosts a Summer Art Camp for kids between the ages of five and 17.

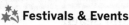 Festivals & Events

Clematis by Night
MUSIC

(☑561-822-1515; http://wpb.org/clematis-by-night; ⊙6-9:30pm Thu) Every Thursday night the city shuts down the eastern terminus of Clematis St, brings in food carts and crafts vendors, and stages a free outdoor music festival under the stars.

Free Outdoor Concerts
MUSIC

(www.cityplace.com; ⊙6-10pm Fri & Sat) On Friday and Saturday evenings, CityPlace hosts free outdoor concerts in front of the gorgeous CityPlace Fountain. Bands stick to familiar rock, R&B and occasionally country sounds.

SunFest
CULTURAL

(www.sunfest.com; ⊙May) Florida's largest waterfront music and art festival, SunFest attracts more than 175,000 visitors for five days in early May.

Sleeping

Peanut Island Camping
CAMPGROUND $

(☑561-845-4445; http://discover.pbcgov.org; tent sites $35) This tiny island has 20 developed campsites by reservation only. There are some restrictions, so call or visit the website.

Hotel Biba
MOTEL $

(☑561-832-0094; www.hotelbiba.com; 320 Belvedere Rd; r $99-179; P❋🛜❆) With plain, white, slightly missing-a-small-something rooms, this place isn't the liveliest, but is one of the better (if only) budget options around. It's well located – only a block from the Intracoastal, and perched on the edge of the El Cid district. Suffice to say it's clean and fine if you just want a bed. Includes a simple continental breakfast.

★ Grandview Gardens
B&B $$

(☑561-833-9023; www.grandview-gardens.com; 1608 Lake Ave; r $139-255; P❋🛜❆) Book a room at this intimate resort and you'll feel like a local in no time. Hidden in a tropical garden on Howard Park, the enormous suites with their wrought-iron and four-poster beds access the pool patio through French doors. They're decorated to reflect the Spanish Mediterranean style that is so popular in these parts.

The house is a period 1925 structure typical of the historical neighborhood and sits opposite the Armory Art Center, so is perfect for longer stays for the arts-inclined. The Norton is a few blocks away, and the

Grandview Public Market is visible across a ball field.

Fabulous breakfasts are included. Incredibly, prices are significantly lower outside of high season.

Palm Beach Hibiscus
B&B $$

(☑ 561-833-8171; www.palmbeachhibiscus.com; 213 S Rosemary Ave; r $199-315; ❋ ☎) Fabulously located just a block from CityPlace (p245), this pair of 1917 homes has four-poster beds, floral prints, abundant light and a front porch with wooden rockers. Watch the world – including the city trolley, which stops out front – roll by. On the property is a tiki bar lounge that's popular among some locals: sociable, though it dampens the sense of privacy.

Casa Grandview
B&B $$$

(☑ 561-655-8932; www.casagrandview.com; 1410 Georgia Ave; r $199-449; ℙ ❋ ☎ ☀) Hidden behind hedgerows in the historical Grandview Heights neighborhood, this intimate little compound has five B&B rooms, seven cottages and five apartments. B&B rooms are in the main house, which has a charming-if-odd medieval-Spanish feel, with a narrow stone staircase and elf-sized wooden doors in the walls. We love the cozy Library Suite – small but plush.

Luxurious cottages have a stylized 1940s beach chic, with vintage signs and bright tiled kitchens. They're great for families.

✖ Eating

★ Mediterranean Market & Deli
MIDDLE EASTERN $

(☑ 561-659-7322; www.mediterraneanmarketand deli.com; 327 5th St; ☺ 8am-6pm Mon-Fri, 8am-5pm Sat; mains $3-12) Don't be put off by the nondescript warehouse exterior – this Middle Eastern deli serves up some of the most flavorful lunches in town. Fresh-baked pita is stuffed with homemade hummus, feta and kefta accompanied by zingy lima bean salad and tabbouleh. You can then order honey-drenched baklava or lady fingers to go.

Johan's Jöe
CAFE $

(Swedish Coffee House & Cafe; www.johansjoe. com; 401 S Dixie Hwy; mains $9-13; ☺ 7am-5pm) A delightful array of pastries and cakes for the Scandinavian expats in town. Since this is Sweden in Palm Beach, the interiors are white, minimalist and stylish. The sweets are not the only winners; it's hard to go past the likes of pickled herrings, meatballs, and authentic Swedish salads and sandwiches.

Paris Bakery & Cafe
FRENCH $

(www.parisbakerycafe.com; 212 S Olive Ave; mains $9-13; ☺ 8am-2:30pm Mon & Tue, 8am-2:30pm & 5-9pm Wed-Fri, 9am-2pm & 5-9pm Sat) French owned and operated, this '70s style and very authentic patisserie serves continental breakfasts of crepes any style, well-priced lunches of smoked salmon and béchamel sauce, and sandwiches stuffed with *paysanne* chicken. On Saturday lines form down the block for 'Le Frunche.'

Curbside Gourmet
FOOD TRUCK $

(☑ 561-371-6565; http://curbsidegourmet.com; 2000 S Dixie Hwy) This bright, peppermint truck is Palm Beach's first mobile food truck dedicated to bringing good, seasonal staples to resident gourmets. The short, sweet menu includes a breakfast burrito, BLTs, crab-cake sliders, fresh fish and pork tacos, and a daily panini or frittata. Fries are hand cut; add-ons include heritage tomatoes and

SOUTHEAST FLORIDA WEST PALM BEACH

THE WILDLIFE CORRIDOR

Florida's human population is increasing at a staggering rate – around 1000 people move to the state every day. Suburban building is predicted to take up 5 million acres of wildlife habitat in fifty years – or by 2070 – which would spell out disaster not only for the animals living in the wild, but for the humans who aim to live in these suburban sprawls.

The **Florida Wildlife Corridor** (http://floridawildlifecorridor.org) is an organisation that aims to 'connect, protect and restore a statewide network of lands and waters that supports wildlife and people.' The Corridor provides habitat for 42 federally listed endangered, 24 threatened and 15 candidate species.

The project aims to speed up conservation efforts against the mass suburban sprawls and increase conservation in Florida by 10% annually. Their immediate aim is to protect 300,000 acres within the Corridor, connecting the rivers, streams and protected land that provide the necessary drinking water and roaming space that wild animals so desperately need.

Applewood smoked bacon; and dessert is caramelized grapefruit. Yum.

Belle & Maxwell's
INTERNATIONAL $$

(☑561-832-4449; www.belleandmaxwells.com; 3700 S Dixie Hwy; mains $18-32; ⊙11am-4pm Mon, to 9pm Tue-Sat) Situated in the middle of Antique Row, this tearoom/cafe is the place to come after some browsing; it's a favorite among the ladies-who-lunch crowd. It looks like the interior of a swap shop, with stained-glass pieces, eclectic furniture and lamp-shades. Wonderful crabmeat salad ($18) and roast beef and brie sandwich ($14).

Darbster
VEGAN $$

(☑561-586-2622; www.darbster.com; 8020 S Dixie Hwy; mains $12-18; ⊙5-10pm Tue-Fri, 10:30am-3pm & 5-10pm Sat, to 9pm Sun; ☑) This place is out on a limb in many respects: it's 5 miles south of town in an incongruous location by the S Dixie Hwy on the Palm Beach canal; the menu is 100% vegan; all profits go to a foundation for animal care; and it attracts everyone from Birkenstock-wearing hippies to diamond-dripping Palm Beachers.

Howley's
AMERICAN $$

(4700 S Dixie Hwy; mains $14-25; ⊙11am-2pm Mon-Thu, to 5am Fri & Sat) Open almost all night, this mint-green 1950s diner's tagline is 'cooked in sight, must be right.' The food (shake 'n' bake pork chops, crab hash, tiki-style tuna burgers and banana pancakes) might be described as 'upscale retro' and certainly tastes right – especially at 2am.

Grato
ITALIAN $$

(☑561-404-1334; http://gratowpb.com; 1901 S Dixie Hwy; mains $18-25; ⊙11:30am-10pm; ☑) Service can be a bit hit and miss as it gets so busy at this smart Italian brasserie-cum-pizzeria, but it's popular for good reason. It spins out great pizzas (including a vegan option), and pasta that is truly *squisito* (delicious!). Throw in two bars for cocktails, a choice of sitting areas, and you've got yourself a relaxing night with the locals.

Sailfish Marina
SEAFOOD $$

(☑561-842-8449; www.sailfishmarina.com; 98 Lake Dr, Singer Island; mains $26-41; ⊙7am-10pm) On Singer Island, Sailfish Marina is a good place for a seafood meal, but it's especially fine for Sunday brunch between 8am and 1pm (adults/kids $24/16). Grab a seat close to the water, slowly chew your smoked salmon, tropical fruit or Belgian waffles and watch the resident pelicans paddle around the yachts, searching for their own breakfast.

★ Table 26 Degrees
AMERICAN $$$

(☑561-855-2660; www.table26palmbeach.com; 1700 S Dixie Hwy; mains $20-49; ⊙11:30am-2pm Mon-Sat, from 10:30am Sun, plus 4:30-10pm Sun-Thu, to 11pm Fri & Sat) Don't be put off by the prices at this sophisticated restaurant. It is filled with locals, conversation and the clinking of glasses for good reason. They flock here for the bar (great happy hour 4:30pm to 6:30pm daily) plus the share plates and mains that are divided by water, land, field, and hands (the latter covers fried chicken and burgers).

★ Rhythm Cafe
FUSION $$$

(☑561-833-3406; www.rhythmcafe.cc; 3800 S Dixie Hwy; mains $21-30; ⊙5:30-10pm Wed-Sat, to 9pm Sun) There's no lack of flair at this colorful, upbeat bistro set in a converted drugstore in West Palm's antiques district. It's strung with Christmas lights and hung with bright, bobbing paper lanterns. The menu is equally vibrant, bopping happily from goat's cheese pie to 'the best tuna tartare ever' to the pomegranate-infused catch of the day.

Kitchen
MODERN AMERICAN $$$

(☑561-249-2281; http://kitchenpb.com; 319 Belvedere Road #2; mains $20-40; ⊙6-10pm) Book well ahead if you want to snag a seat at one of the 10 tables in chef Matthew Byrne's contemporary American brasserie. The concept is simple: the freshest ingredients, presented in the simplest, most flavorful manner. Highlights include organic chicken schnitzel dressed in Panko breadcrumbs and topped with charred lemon and a sunny fried egg.

🍷 Drinking & Nightlife

★ Subculture Coffee
CAFE

(☑561-318-5142; http://subculturecoffee.com; 509 Clematis St; ⊙7am-midnight Sun-Thu, to 2am Fri & Sat) Head here for the best coffee at West Palm, located right on Clematis St. Apart from the excellent, single-origin beans and well-made brews, it has a wonderful space with bookshelves and a large bar, furniture à la 1950s, and vintage photos.

★ Blind Monk
WINE BAR

(☑561-833-3605; http://theblindmonk.com; 410 Evernia St #107; ⊙9am-1pm Sat & Sun, 4pm-midnight (or later) daily) With a team of knowledgeable sommeliers behind it, the Blind

Monk is arguably the best wine bar in West Palm. It offers an extensive list of wines by the glass, including international labels and local craft beers. Small plates of cheese, salami, grapes, pickles and nuts soak up the vino, while silent old movies play on the wall. It offers daytime bites as well, including a great brunch.

Roosters GAY
(📞561-832-9119; www.roosterswpb.com; 823 Belvedere Rd; ⊙3pm-3am Sun-Thu, to 4am Fri & Sat) A mainstay of West Palm's thriving gay community, this bar has been offering popcorn, hot dogs, bingo and male dancers since 1984.

⭐ Entertainment

Harriet Himmel Theater THEATER
(📞561-318-7136; www.cityplace.com; 600 S Rosemary Ave) The centerpiece of CityPlace is this theater situated in an attractive Mediterranean plaza. The 11,000-sq-ft historical venue hosts a program of live concerts, art exhibitions, fashion shows and high-school proms. Named after its major benefactor, Harriet Himmel, the 1926 building was previously the Methodist Church. It's regarded as one of the largest Colonial Revival structures of its time.

**Palm Beach
Dramaworks** THEATER
(📞561-514-4042; www.palmbeachdramaworks. org; 201 Clematis St) 'Theater to Think About' is the tagline of this award-winning resident theater, which is committed to presenting underrated classic and contemporary plays from the likes of Lorca, Steinbeck, Pinter, Hansberry and Stoppard.

CityPlace CONCERT VENUE
(📞561-366-1000; www.cityplace.com; 700 S Rosemary Ave; ⊙10am-10pm Mon-Sat, noon-6pm Sun) This massive entertainment and shopping complex is the crown jewel of West Palm Beach's urban-renewal initiative. At its center is the Harriet Himmel Theater.

There's also a bowling alley, a 20-screen cinema theater, dozens of restaurants and a slew of stores.

Respectable Street LIVE MUSIC
(📞561-832-9999; www.respectablestreet.com; 518 Clematis St; ⊙9pm-3am Wed-Thu, to 4am Fri & Sat) Respectables has kept South Florida jamming to great bands for two decades; it also organizes October's MoonFest, the city's best block party. Great DJs, strong drinks and a breezy chill-out patio are added bonuses.

See if you can find the hole that the Red Hot Chili Peppers' Anthony Kiedis punched in the wall when they played here.

International Polo Club SPECTATOR SPORT
(📞561-204-5687; www.internationalpoloclub.com; 3667 120th Ave S, Wellington; general admission $10, lawn seating from $30; ⊙Sun Jan-Apr) Between January and April the International Polo Club hosts 16 weeks of polo and glamour. As one of the finest polo facilities in the world, it not only attracts the most elite players but also the local and international glitterati who whoop it up in head-turning fashion over champagne brunches ($125; $325 with bottle of Veuve Clicquot). Why not?

🛍 Shopping

⭐Kismet VINTAGE
(📞561-865-7895; www.kismetvintage.com; 540 Clematis St; ⊙Thu-Mon 3pm-8pm) A fantastic vintage shop that has an impeccably curated and reasonably priced selection of both designer names and odd finds, always perfectly pitched. Choose from YSL jumpsuits, 1970s kaftans, hand-dyed silk blouses or embroidered Palm Beach slippers. There's always a great playlist on, and the staff is friendly.

Antique Row ANTIQUES
(📞561-822-2222; www.westpalmbeachantiques. com; S Dixie Hwy) Just south of town along S Dixie Hwy, between Belvedere Rd and Southern Blvd, this strip of shops over several blocks has more than 30 antique vendors. You might unearth an incredible find from a Palm Beach estate.

Opening hours vary by shop.

ℹ Getting There & Away

Palm Beach International Airport (PBI; 📞561-471-7420; www.pbia.org; 1000 James L Turnage Blvd) is served by most major airlines and car-rental companies. It's about a mile west of I-95 on Belvedere Rd. Palm Tran (p226) bus 44 runs between the airport, the train station and downtown ($2).

Greyhound (📞561-833-8534; www. greyhound.com; 205 S Tamarind Ave; ⊙6am-10:45pm), **Tri-Rail** (📞800-875-7245; www. tri-rail.com; 203 S Tamarind Ave) and **Amtrak** (📞800-872-7245; www.amtrak.com; 209 S Tamarind Ave) share the same building: the historical Seaboard Train Station. Palm Tran serves the station with bus 44 (from the airport).

A cute and convenient (and free!) trolley runs between Clematis St and CityPlace starting at 11am.

SOUTHEAST FLORIDA WEST PALM BEACH

DON'T MISS

JOHN D MACARTHUR BEACH STATE PARK

While this **state park** (☎561-624-6950; www.macarthurbeach.org; 10900 Jack Nicklaus Dr; per vehicle/bicycle $5/2; ⊙8am-sunset) is one of the smallest in the region (438 acres), it has some of the best turtle-watching programs around. Loggerhead, green and leatherback turtles nest along the beach between May and August. It's home to aquariums and a spectacular 1600ft boardwalk spanning the mangroves of Lake Worth Cove. The on-site nature center offers kayak rental (unguided; single kayak $12 per hour).

In June and July, lucky visitors might catch a glimpse of hatching baby sea turtles during the ranger-led turtle walks, led nightly at 8:30pm.

TREASURE COAST

The Treasure Coast gets its name for being the site of numerous treasure-laden shipwrecks over the years. Today the Treasure Coast is where you'll find Florida's true jewel: unspoiled beach paradise.

Industrialist billionaire John D MacArthur (1897–1978) once owned almost everything from Palm Beach Gardens to Stuart, and he kept it mostly pristine during his life. Over time he grew concerned that Florida's real-estate bonanza would compromise – or destroy – what he considered paradise. In his will he stated that thousands of acres would be kept wild, and the rest would be deeded out incrementally in order to save the oceanfront property from Miami's fate. And you know what? His plan worked. Well, almost... In true American style, swaths of highway run north–south along the coast.

Jupiter & Jupiter Island

☑561 / POP 64,976

Jupiter is a largely ritzy residential area with one of the wealthiest communities in America. There is no central core to speak of, and for visitors Jupiter is best seen as a jumping-off point for exploring the area's parks, nature preserves and beaches. Unlike those of its southerly neighbors Palm Beach and Boca Raton, the beaches around here are largely untouched by condo development.

◎ Sights

Hobe Sound National Wildlife Refuge   WILDLIFE RESERVE

(☎772-546-6141; www.fws.gov/hobesound; 13640 SE Federal Hwy; parking $5; ⊙sunrise-sunset) A 1091-acre federally protected nature sanctuary, Hobe Sound has two sections: a small slice on the mainland, opposite the Jonathan Dickinson State Park; and the refuge grounds at the northern end of Jupiter Island. The Jupiter Island section has 3.5 miles of beach (it's a favorite sea-turtle nesting ground), while the mainland section is a pine scrub forest. In June and July, nighttime turtle-watching walks take place twice a week (changing days; reservations necessary).

Blowing Rocks Preserve   NATURE RESERVE

(www.nature.org; 574 S Beach Rd; $2; ⊙9am-4:30pm) This preserve encompasses a mile-long limestone outcrop riddled with holes, cracks and fissures. When the tide is high and there's a strong easterly wind, water spews up as if from a geyser. (At low tide, nothing happens.) When seas are calm you can hike through four coastal biomes: shifting dune, coastal strand, interior mangrove wetlands and tropical coastal hammock.

Jonathan Dickinson State Park   STATE PARK

(☎772-546-2771, activities 561-746-1466; www.floridastateparks.org/parks-and-trails/jonathan-dickinson-state-park; 16450 SE Federal Hwy; vehicle/bicycle $6/2; ⊙8am-sunset) With almost 11,500 acres to explore, this is an excellent state park between US Hwy 1 and the Loxahatchee River. There's no ocean access in the park, but its attraction lies in its several habitats: pine flatwoods, cypress stands, swamp and increasingly endangered coastal sand-pine scrub. Ranger-led nature walks leave at 2pm on Fridays and Sundays from the Cypress Creek Pavilion, and campfire programs are offered Saturday at dusk next to the Pine Grove campground.

You can rent canoes and kayaks from the concession stand. Guided-tour boat rides of the Loxahatchee River are available throughout the day (adult/child $24/14).

Several short-loop hiking and bicycle trails can be explored. Most popular is the Kitching Creek Trail just north of the boat landing, a short 1.5 miles, but other trails extend from this. Visit www.clubscrub.org for details on cycling options.

Jupiter Inlet Lighthouse　　LIGHTHOUSE
(www.jupiterlighthouse.org; 500 Capt Armour's Way; adult/child $12/6; ⊙10am-5pm Tue-Sun) Built in 1860, this historical lighthouse hasn't missed a night of work in more than 100 years and is among the oldest lighthouses on the Atlantic coast. Visitors can climb the 105 steps to view the surrounding area and ocean. To visit the lighthouse, you must take a tour; these depart regularly between 10am and 4pm depending on visitor numbers.

There's some interesting Seminole and pioneer Florida memorabilia in the small but smart museum.

🏃 Activities

Jupiter Outdoor Center　　KAYAKING
(☑561-270-4920; www.jupiteroutdoorcenter.com; 9060 W Indiantown Rd, Jupiter; double/single kayaks per day $85/60) For a great day exploring the various aquatic preserves, Jupiter Outdoor Center provides access to these lush waterways. From the launch, paddle to the right for thick, verdant waterways overhung with fallen branches and a small but thumping rapid; paddle to the left for open vistas and plentiful picnic areas.

Jonathan Dickinson State Park Concession Stand　　BOATING
(☑561-746-1466; www.floridaparktours.com; 2 hr canoes & kayaks single/double $20/30; ⊙9am-5pm) Rents canoes and kayaks. Guided-tour boat rides of the Loxahatchee River are available throughout the day (adult/child $20/12).

🛏 Sleeping & Eating

Jupiter Waterfront Inn　　HOTEL $$
(☑561-747-9085; www.jupiterwaterfrontinn.com; 18903 SE Federal Hwy; r $145-185; P❄🐾🛜🏊) As sunny and friendly as can be, this unpretentious, highway-side inn has huge rooms with flat-screen TVs, Intracoastal views and a marina for boaters. Decor is beachy, with Spanish tile floors and cheerful yellow walls. For romance, ask for a room with an in-suite Jacuzzi tub. The inn's own 240ft fishing pier is a big hit with anglers.

It backs onto the major highway, but it's excellent value. Prices include a continental breakfast.

⭐ Jupiter Donut Factory　　BAKERY $
(☑561-741-5290; http://jupiterdonuts.com; 141 Center St; doughnuts from $0.80, dozen $9; ⊙6am-1pm) These fresh-baked doughnuts are what doughnuts dream of being, so get here early or you'll miss out; the doughnuts are usually polished off by mid-morning. If you can't decide between raspberry jelly, banana coconut, s'mores or red velvet, just stick with the most popular order: the bacon maple syrup.

Dune Dog Cafe　　AMERICAN $
(☑561-744-6667; http://dunedog.com; 775 A1A Alternate; mains $10-19; ⊙11am-9pm) This indoor-outdoor, ultra-casual fried food joint on the highway has mini palm trees, pink and blue barstools, tables made from surf boards and plastic fast food baskets. Regulars come for combo platters of snow crabs and steak or lobster bisque.

⭐ Little Moir's Food Shack　　SEAFOOD $$
(www.littlemoirsfoodshack.com; 103 S US 1; mains $9-24; ⊙11am-9:30pm Mon-Wed, to 10pm Thu-Sat) If you didn't know to look, you'd walk right past this strip-mall hole-in-the-wall. But then you'd miss out on one of Florida's genuine food finds, a neo-Caribbean cafe serving a mouthwatering blend of global flavors: sweet-potato crusted fish, Jamaican pepper-pot soup, lobster egg rolls. The seafood is as fresh as you'd expect (but so rarely find) in a seaside town.

Leftovers Cafe　　CAFE $$
(☑561-627-6030; www.littlemoirsjupiter.com/ leftovers-cafe; 451 University Blvd; mains $8-24; ⊙11am-9:30pm Mon-Wed, to 10pm Thu-Sat) Food guru Mike Moir, who runs Little Moir's Food Shack, also operates the first-class Leftovers Cafe, which serves a lighter menu of sandwiches, salads and sweets.

🍸 Drinking & Nightlife

Square Grouper　　BAR
(www.squaregrouper.net; 1111 Love St; ⊙11am-midnight Sun-Thu, to 1am Fri & Sat) If this Old Florida dive looks familiar, it's because the video for the Alan Jackson and Jimmy Buffett tune *It's Five O'Clock Somewhere* was shot here. Perched on the water, with an ample (sandy) dance floor, this place is an ultra-casual gem in an otherwise well-heeled town. Snacks available from $5 to $17.

☆ Entertainment

Roger Dean Stadium   STADIUM
(📞561-775-1818; www.rogerdeanstadium.com; 4751 Main St; tickets spring training $29-42) It may not be a 'nature' activity, but an afternoon here will get you outdoors. This small but immaculate stadium is home to spring-training action for the Miami Marlins, the St Louis Cardinals and various minor-league baseball teams. Ticket prices vary; call for details.

❶ Getting There & Away

Though I-95 is the quickest way through this area, do yourself a favor and get off the freeway. US Hwy 1 (US 1) runs up the coastline, and Hwy A1A jumps back and forth between the mainland (where it's the same as US 1) and various barrier islands.

Stuart

📞772 / POP 16,543

Often overlooked in favor of its more famous southern neighbors, Stuart has long been a hush-hush destination for sporty millionaires and their gleaming yachts. Fishing is tops here, which explains Stuart's nickname: 'Sailfish Capital of the World.' It wasn't until the late 1980s that Stuart got its first exit off I-95, which is when the wave of rich people, leaving places like Boca, started coming in earnest.

Though Stuart's retro, sherbet-colored downtown has some reasonable restaurants and boutiques, the real draws of the region are the adjacent beach areas of Jensen Beach and Hutchinson Island. Jensen Beach, on the mainland facing the Indian River Lagoon, caters to fishers and arty types, with a tiny downtown lined with craft shops and tackle stores. Just across the water by the bridge, narrow Hutchinson Island is where visitors go for sun and fun.

◉ Sights & Activities

Elliott Museum   MUSEUM
(📞407-225-1961; https://hsmc-fl.com/elliott-museum; 825 NE Ocean Blvd, Hutchinson Island; adult/child $14/6; ⊘10am-5pm) The eccentric Elliott collection has a focus on early 20th-century technology, and for good reason – the museum was founded by Harmon Elliott, the son of Sterling Elliott, who invented the kingpin and steering knuckle (which led to steerability for four-wheeled vehicles). Hence the spectacular collection

of vintage vehicles, displayed in a $20 million gallery complete with robotic racking system, which ferries cars to the foreground and rotates them for viewing.

Florida Oceanographic Coastal Science Center   AQUARIUM
(📞772-225-0505; www.floridaoceanographic.org; 890 NE Ocean Blvd, Hutchinson Island; adult/child $12/6; ⊘10am-5pm Mon-Sat, noon-4pm Sun; ⊕) This center is great for kids, who'll be mesmerized by the four 300-gallon tropical-fish aquariums, a worm reef and touch tanks with crabs, sea cucumbers and starfish. There's an excellent menu of guided tours and nature programs, from guided nature walks at 10:15am (except Sundays) and daily stingray feedings to summer sea-turtle-spotting expeditions.

Hutchinson Island   BEACH
This long, skinny barrier island, which begins in Stuart and stretches north to Fort Pierce, features a stunning array of unspoiled beaches. All beaches have free access, and are excellent for walking, swimming and even a bit of snorkeling. The beaches get less touristed the further north you go.

Lady Stuart   FISHING
(📞772-286-1860; www.ladystuart.com; 555 NE Ocean Blvd, Stuart; adult/child Sat-Thu $50/40 Fri $60/50) The crew will take you out, bait your hook, and clean and fillet any fish you catch. They make no guarantees of hooking dinner, but know where to sink their lines. Trips depart 8am to 1pm Saturday through Thursday, and 8am to 3pm Friday.

🛏 Sleeping & Eating

★**Old Colorado Inn**   HOTEL $$
(📞772-215-3437; www.oldcoloradoinn.com; 211 Colorado Ave, Stuart; r & ste $169-399; 🅿❄🛜) With its pastel-colored Key West vibe and easy charm, the excellent-value 1914 Colorado Inn is a lovely spot. Spacious studio rooms and suites come with gleaming wooden floors and ceilings, tasteful modern furnishings, grand beds and kitchenettes. Hosts Steven and Ashley brim with insightful tips on Stuart and the surrounding beaches.

River Palm Cottages & Fish Camp   COTTAGE $$
(📞772-334-0401; www.riverpalmcottages.com; 2325 NE Indian River Dr, Jensen Beach; apt from $99-259; 🅿❄🛜🐾🛶) Perched on Indian River, this complex has adorable, if simple,

cottages with kitchens. Some have waterfront views and all sport cool tiled floors and a breezy, Caribbean style. The peaceful grounds are lush with palm trees, guava and the exotic praying-hands banana tree. There's a private beach, a ping-pong table and a pier for watching sunrises.

Conchy Joe's CARIBBEAN $$
(www.conchyjoes.com; 3945 NE Indian River Dr, Jensen Beach; mains $10-22; ⊙11:30am-10pm) Overlooking St Lucie River, Conchy Joe's offers the flavor of old Florida with exotic drinks and pub grub at a palm-tree-filled bar. It gets very lively when the band's jamming.

★**11 Maple St** AMERICAN $$$
(☑772-334-7714; www.elevenmaple.com; 3224 NE Maple St, Jensen Beach; mains $25-59; ⊙5:30-10pm Tue-Sat) This romantic spot, a series of rooms inside a historical cottage, has a daily changing menu of eclectic large and small plates, from roasted pompano with saffron essence to grilled elk tenderloin. This is your best bet for special-occasion dinners short of driving south to Palm Beach.

The Gafford INTERNATIONAL $$$
(☑772-221-9517; www.thegafford.com; 47 SW Flagler, Stuart; mains $13-38) The closest thing around here to a gastropub, this blandly decorated but popular and loud eatery has good food. Try the Seminole beef filet mignon, Scottish salmon or a burger (with brisket – heaven). Bar seats are available but usually taken; happy hour (4pm to 7pm) is popular.

❶ Getting There & Away

I-95 is the quickest way to and from this area. South of Stuart, US 1 runs up the coastline and then jogs west, into and through town. If you're headed between Stuart and Fort Pierce, the best route is the slow-but-scenic NE Indian River Dr.

Fort Pierce

☑772 / POP 45,581
Fort Pierce – also locally known as Port Fierce – has a sleepy feel to it, but offers top sportfishing and some great beaches. Downtown often feels like a ghost town, with lots of vacancies and few people. Orange Ave is the main drag and is far more vibrant than adjoining blocks.

◉ Sights

Manatee Observation Center MUSEUM
(☑772-429-6266; www.manateecenter.com; 480 N Indian River Dr; $1; ⊙10am-5pm Tue-Sat, noon-4pm Sun Oct-Jun, 10am-5pm Thu-Sat Jul-Sep; ♿) A small center educating the public on the plight of the manatee. Videos and exhibits teach boaters how to avoid hurting the creatures, and enlightens the rest of us on how our lifestyle has indirectly eradicated most of the manatee population. Manatee sightings are common-ish in winter in waters along the museum's observation deck.

Fort Pierce Inlet State Park STATE PARK
(www.floridastateparks.org/parks-and-trails/fort-pierce-inlet-state-park; 905 Shorewinds Dr; vehicle/bicycle $6/2; ⊙8am-sunset) This 700-acre park has everything you'd want in a waterfront recreation spot: sandy shores, decent surf, verdant trails, mangrove swamps with a beautiful bird population, and a family-friendly picnic area.

UDT-SEAL Museum MUSEUM
(☑772-595-5845; www.navysealmuseum.com; 3300 North Highway A1A; adult/child $15/7; ⊙10am-4pm Tue-Sat, noon-4pm Sun) The world's only museum dedicated to the warriors of Naval Special Warfare, this Hutchinson Island exhibit features once-top-secret tools and weapons used by the most elite combat forces of the US.

Urca de Lima SHIPWRECK
(☑850-245-6444) FREE In 1715 a Spanish flotilla was decimated in a hurricane off the Florida coast. One of the ships, the *Urca de Lima,* went down (relatively) intact. Today the wooden-hulled ship is partly exposed within snorkeling distance from the beach at Fort Pierce. To get here, exit Ocean Blvd (Hwy A1A) at Pepper Beach Park and walk north along the beach about half a mile from the park boundary.

☞ Tours

Dolphin Watch Boat Tours BOATING
(☑772-464-6673; http://dolphinwatchboattours. com; adult/under 12yr $45/35) Wild dolphins are spotted routinely in the Indian River Lagoon, occasionally from the riverbank. To increase your chances of seeing them you need to get on the water. Capt Adam Pozniak

seems to know instinctively where to find them on these two-hour dolphin-spotting tours on his 25ft pontoon. He's also extremely knowledgeable about the lagoon and its flora and fauna.

🛌 Sleeping

Savannas Recreation Area CAMPGROUND $
(☑ 772-464-7855; www.stlucieco.gov/parks/savannas.htm; 1400 Midway Rd; tent sites $25; ⊙ Nov-May) Covering 550 acres and five distinct biological communities – pine flatwoods, wet prairie, marsh, lake and scrub – the Savannas features both primitive and developed campsites.

ℹ Getting There & Away

Fort Pierce is reachable via the I-95 or US 1 (a gorgeous drive that's highly recommended as a trip in itself). To get downtown from I-95, take the Orange Ave exit east, crossing US 1 (here called N 4th St).

Sebastian Inlet

☑ 772 / POP 21,929

Heading south from Melbourne Beach along Hwy A1A toward Sebastian Inlet, development trickles nearly to a halt. You'll find plenty of access to beaches, and hiking and birding along both the Atlantic Coast and the Indian River here, as well as mile after mile of tidy hedges and bike paths lining the highway.

◎ Sights

★ Pelican Island National Wildlife Refuge WILDLIFE RESERVE
(☑ 772-581-5557; www.fws.gov/pelicanisland; Hwy A1A; ⊙ 7:30am-sunset) **FREE** Established in 1903 as a refuge for the endangered brown pelican, Pelican Island was America's first federal bird reservation, the forerunner of today's national wildlife-refuge system. The preserve now encompasses 500 acres along the Indian River Lagoon as well as the 2.2-acre Pelican Island, which can be seen from the observation tower at the end of the **Centennial Trail**. Two trails loop 2.5 miles along the shore and are perfect for bike rides and long hikes.

Pelican Island itself can also be viewed by boat and there are several public boat ramps to access the refuge waters.

Sebastian Inlet State Park STATE PARK
(☑ 321-984-4852; www.floridastateparks.org/parks-and-trails/sebastian-inlet-state-park; 9700 South State Rd; cyclist/vehicle $2/8; ⊙ 24hr) Stretching along a narrow strip of the barrier island, this busy park, popular with fishers, surfers, boaters and families, is divided into two sections by the inlet bridge. On the north side swimming is safe for children in the calm-water lagoon. In June and July you can join ranger-led sea-turtle-nesting walks (reservations necessary).

On the southern side you'll find the Sebastian Inlet Marina.

McLarty Treasure Museum MUSEUM
(☑ 772-589-2147; Hwy A1A; adult/child under 6yr $2/free; ⊙ 10am-4pm) In 1715 a Spanish colonial ship carrying pillaged gold and treasure went down in a hurricane, and survivors built a makeshift camp. This small museum, featuring a 45-minute movie, dioramas and artifacts from the shipwreck, sits on the site of that camp. Even today, folks looking for a pretty shell sometimes stumble upon treasures washed ashore. The museum is 1 mile south of Sebastian Inlet State Park.

🏃 Activities

★ Honest John's Fish Camp KAYAKING
(☑ 321-727-2923; www.honestjohnsfishcamp.com; 750 Mullet Creek Rd; kayaks per hr $15, boats per half/full day $70/105; ⊙ 6am-6pm Wed-Mon) Rent kayaks and motorboats from this 1890s Florida Cracker homestead on the edge of Indian River Lagoon. Set in an old citrus grove on Mullet Creek, it's a prime spot for fishing and spotting manatees. The camp is 10 miles south of Melbourne Beach.

Sebastian Inlet Marina BOATING
(☑ 321-724-5424; 9502 South Hwy A1A; ⊙ 8am-5pm Mon-Fri, to 6pm Sat & Sun) On the south side of Sebastian Inlet you'll find a well-equipped marina offering boat ($175 per half day) and kayak ($20 per half day) rental, a small fishing museum and an uninspiring campground (from $31 per site).

🛌 Sleeping

★ Seashell Suites RESORT $$
(☑ 321-409-0500; www.seashellsuites.com; 8795 S Hwy A1A; r $225-250; 🅿) 🍃 This low-key eco-resort has been designed to blend in with its pristine natural setting. With only eight two-bedroom suites, the atmosphere is intimate and environmental standards are high: there's a saltwater pool and cleaning

LOGGERHEAD MARINELIFE

Juno Beach lies six miles north of John D MacArthur Beach State Park (p251) on the scenic A1A. If you're traveling with a four-legged companion you can jump out here to enjoy one of the county's only dog-friendly beaches (from Xanadu Lane to Marcinski Rd). It's also a popular place for families with short-term rentals. But the main reason to visit is the fascinating **Loggerhead Marinelife Center** (☑561-627-8280; www.marinelife.org; 14200 US 1, Juno Beach; suggested donation $5; ⊘10am-5pm), which gives you an up-close-and-personal experience with these beautiful creatures.

View recovering sea turtle patients in specially designed outdoor tanks and watch through the window while surgeons treat the animals. Volunteers stand by turtle tanks with information on their charges: how they sustained their injuries, how they're healing and whether they're good or grumpy patients. It's a privilege to see and learn at such close quarters. All four species – greens, hawksbills, Kemp's ridleys and loggerheads – frequent the local waters.

Around 100 turtles are treated here and returned to the wild annually. The center runs a host of educational programs, leads ecotours ($25) and a nature tour (free) through the dune system, tells 'hatchling tales' to younger kids (10:30am Wednesdays) and offers guided turtle walks (by reservation; $18) from Tuesday to Saturday evenings in June and July.

agents are toxin free. Beach chairs, bikes, umbrellas and bodyboards are all complimentary, and the digital library has a good stock of movies. Rates are reduced for weekly stays.

⊕ Getting There & Away

Sebastian Inlet lies 35 miles south of Cocoa Beach on Hwy A1A, and 15 miles north of Vero Beach. Transport via car makes the most sense, but the **GoLine Bus System** (☑772-569-0903; www.golineirt.com; ⊘6am-7pm Mon-Fri, 9am-3pm Sat) travels between Vero Beach and Sebastian.

Vero Beach

☑772 / POP 16,919

This coastal town has lovely grassy parks, wide ivory beaches and a pedestrian-friendly downtown. Vero's lack of high-rise buildings gives the place a less developed feel, with consistently better sea views than neighboring beach communities.

And while many visitors are happy to lose themselves in the lull of beach life, Vero Beach residents (many with sky-high net worth) are committed to supporting both the arts and the environment.

⊙ Sights

★**Vero Beach Museum of Art** MUSEUM
(☑772-231-0707; www.vbmuseum.org; 3001 Riverside Park Dr; adult/under 17yr $12/free; ⊘10am-4:30pm Mon-Sat, 1-4:30pm Sun) With changing fine-art exhibitions and regular outdoor jazz concerts, this sleek, white museum in Riverside Park could easily hold its own against any big-city heavy hitter. Look for signs on Hwy A1A.

★**McKee Botanical Gardens** GARDENS
(☑772-794-0601; www.mckeegarden.org; 350 US 1; adult/child 3-12yr $15/8; ⊘10am-5pm Mon-Sat, noon-5pm Sun; last entry 4pm; ⋈) In Vero's early-1920s tourist heyday, Waldo Sexton and Arthur McKee joined forces to open the 80-acre McKee Jungle Gardens, which delighted visitors for decades until Disney stole the show in the 1970s. Much of the land was sold off for development, but passionate locals managed to save 18 acres of tropical garden, which now grows thick with native plants, palms and lily ponds.

Admission prices are subject to seasonal fluctuations.

There is a lovely garden cafe that serves simple dishes such as quiche and salad, where you can have lunch amid the greenery (mains from $6).

Environmental Learning Center NATURE RESERVE
(☑772-589-5050; www.discoverelc.org; 255 Live Oak Dr; adult/child under 12yr $7/5; ⊘8am-4pm Mon-Sat, 9am-4pm Sun; ⋈) This 64-acre reserve, dedicated to educating visitors about the fragile environment of the Indian River estuary, offers hands-on displays and a boardwalk through the mangroves. Check the website for details on **EcoVentures:**

guided nature trips including canoe and pontoon boat trips and nature walks.

Activities

Adventure Kayaking KAYAKING
(☑ 772-567-0522; https://adventurekayakingtours.com; adult/child under 12yr $60/25) Daily Indian River Lagoon kayak tours run to Round and Pelican Islands, Sebastian River and Blue Cypress Lake. Multiday camp-and-kayak tours ($275 to $350 per person per day) are also offered on the lagoon and further afield to the Everglades.

Orchid Island
Bikes & Kayaks CYCLING
(☑ 772-299-1286; www.orchidislandbikesandkayaks.com; 1175 Commerce Ave; bikes per day/week $24/59, kayaks single/tandem per half-day $79/129, SUP half-day/day/week $45/75/235) Vero Beach is the perfect place to ditch the car for a bike, as even kids can easily pedal to restaurants, hotels and the beach. Alternatively, rent kayaks or paddleboards and tootle around Indian River Lagoon.

Tours

★**Sail Moonraker** BOATING
(☑ 772-696-2941; www.sailmoonraker.com; Vero Beach Marina, 3611 Rio Vista Blvd; 2-8hr cruises for up to 6 guests $475-1000; ⚐) Captain Bruce offers customized dolphin-watching, swimming and sunset cruises in Indian River Lagoon, excellent for children, grandparents and everyone in between, aboard his 40ft catamaran. Cash only.

🛏 Sleeping

Caribbean Court
Boutique Hotel BOUTIQUE HOTEL $$
(☑ 772-231-7211; www.thecaribbeancourt.com; 1601 S Ocean Dr; r & ste $149-359; P ❀ 🛜 ❄ 🐾) In a quiet residential area a block off South Beach, this lovely spot expertly blends understated elegance with a casual beach vibe. Bougainvillea and palm trees hide a small garden pool, and handsome whitewashed rooms with earthy accents have rattan furnishings, decorative tiled sinks, thick towels and a refrigerator stocked with goodies. Ask about weekday discounts.

★**Costa d'Este**
Beach Resort & Spa RESORT $$$
(☑ 772-562-9919; www.costadeste.com; 3244 Ocean Dr; r $200-300; P ❀ ❄ 🐾) Owned by Gloria Estefan and her husband, this chic Miami Beachesque resort drips with style. From the ostentatious entryway fountain to the dazzling sundeck and oceanfront pool (where frozen grapes are always available), every detail reflects the unique and sophisticated taste of the Estefans. A cruise-ship theme dominates throughout shared spaces and the 94 rooms, with porthole-shaped art abounding.

Eating

Barefoot Cafe CAFE $
(☑ 772-770-1733; www.thebarefootcafe.com; 2036 14th Ave; wraps $8-12; ⌚ 10am-3pm Mon-Fri) Although it doesn't have a beachside location, this laid-back deli is a surf shack in its soul. Salads, soups and wraps (the most popular of which is the Tuscan wrap) are homemade daily. There's seating inside and out, and the service is super friendly.

★**Riverside Café** SEAFOOD $$
(☑ 772-234-5550; www.riversidecafe.com; 3341 Bridge Plaza Dr; mains $12-26; ⌚ 11am-late Mon-Sat, 10am-late Sun) This casual waterfront eatery and dock sits right on the Indian River Lagoon, with incredible sunset views and excellent tuna nachos. There's a huge wood-floored terrace where you can enjoy your food over the water. In the evenings things get a bit rowdy, as sports fans and salty folks pack the bar.

Waldo's SEAFOOD $$
(☑ 772-231-7091; www.historicwaldos.com; 3150 Ocean Dr, Driftwood Resort; mains $10-22; ⌚ 11am-1am Mon-Sat, 10am-9pm Sun; P 🐾) Built out of driftwood by pioneering Vero settler Waldo Sexton in 1935, this is a Vero Beach institution for dinner and music (from 9pm). Eat blackened mahimahi wraps on the deck overlooking the ocean or prop up the rustic bar with the locals.

Tides MODERN AMERICAN $$$
(☑ 772-234-3966; www.tidesofvero.com; 3103 Cardinal Dr; mains $20-38; ⌚ 5pm-late) This is the hottest fine dining around, with New American and Floridian cuisine spiced up with French, Caribbean, Southern and Latin flair, plus an award-winning wine list with a perfect pair for any dish. The seafood is fresh and local, with top choices including the crab cake appetizer (very meaty) and a tender, flavorful hogfish that's often on special.

If you don't make a reservation far in advance, the hostess will laugh at you.

Maison Martinique FRENCH **$$$**
([☎]772-231-7299; Caribbean Court Boutique Hotel,
1603 S Ocean Dr; mains $24-42; [⊙]5-10pm Tue-Sat)
Maison Martinique offers American cuisine
with a first-rate service and intimate atmos-
phere. Go for the excellent crab cakes ($15),
the juicy rack of lamb ($45) or tangy and
delicious lemon chicken ($30). On warm
evenings eat by the little pool; for something
more casual, head to the romantic Havana
piano bar upstairs.

Drinking & Nightlife

★ **Kilted Mermaid** PUB
([☎]772-569-5533; https://kiltedmermaid.com;
1937 Old Dixie Hwy; [⊙]5pm-late Tue-Sun) Do as
they say and 'drink outside the box' at this
excellent local pub that serves more than 80
craft and imported beers. Then order char-
cuterie or fondue (cheese or chocolate!) to
keep the party going. There's an open mike
on Wednesday, trivia on Thursday and live
music every Friday and Saturday.

Grind + Grape WINE BAR
([☎]772-231-5536; www.facebook.com/grindand
grape; 925 Bougainvillea Lane; [⊙]8am-2am Mon-
Sat, to 1am Sun) Coffee shop by day, wine
bar by night, this place has decent coffee, a
vast tequila selection, delicious pastries and
handcrafted cocktails. There's live music
every evening at 7:30pm on the patio.

❶ Getting There & Away

Vero Beach lies 53 miles south of Cocoa Beach
on Hwy A1A. The closest international airports
are in Orlando, 90 minutes to the northwest;
West Palm Beach, 90 minutes to the south;
and Melbourne, 30 minutes up the coast. **Vero
Beach Airport Shuttle** ([☎]772-794-8300; www.
verobeachairportshuttle.com; Melbourne/Palm
Beach/Orlando airport $95/175/175) provides
an airport-shuttle service.

Vero Beach Regional Airport ([☎]772-978-
4930; 3400 Cherokee Dr) now offers Elite Air-
ways flights to and from Newark direct.

AT A GLANCE

⭐

POPULATION
2.5 million (Greater Orlando)

ANNUAL VISITORS
75 million

BEST ROLLER COASTER
Mako (p309)

BEST WATER PARK
Typhoon Lagoon (p289)

BEST FOOD MARKET
East End Market (p319)

📅

WHEN TO GO
Sep–Oct Theme-park crowds thin, accommodations rates drop and summer's sizzle fades.

Mid-Mar–May Warm weather generally dry skies and lower prices (excluding Easter and spring break).

Thanksgiving–mid-Dec Enjoy seasonal festivities (though be aware of soaring prices and bigger crowds).

Orlando skyline
SEAN PAVONE / SHUTTERSTOCK ©

Orlando & Walt Disney World®

Once upon a time, Orlando was a sleepy citrus town in the heart of central Florida. Then, in the mid-1960s, Walt Disney began buying up acres of cheap land and suddenly Orlando's fortunes were on the turn.

When Walt Disney World® opened in 1971 it soon cemented the theme park experience in the American imagination and made it synonymous with fantasy, fun and perpetual childhood. It's since been joined by Universal Orlando Resort, SeaWorld and Legoland, and together they draw in 75 million visitors a year, making Orlando not just the theme park capital of the world but its most visited city bar none.

Away from the hubbub of the parks is a wonderful city in its own right, home to world-class museums, oodles of parks and lakes, and a sparkling dining scene.

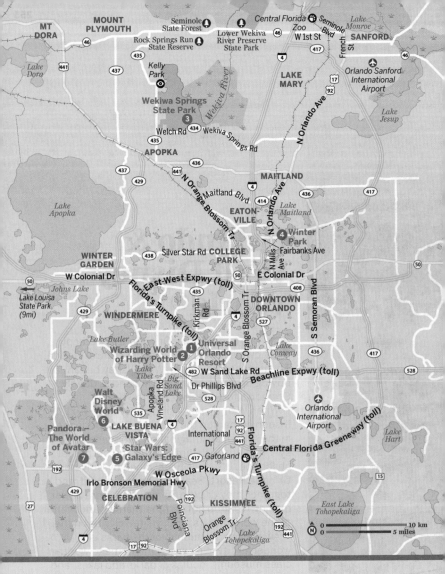

Orlando & Walt Disney World® Highlights

① **Universal Orlando Resort** (p292) Getting your adrenaline to sky-high levels on the hair-raising rides.

② **Wizarding World of Harry Potter** (p294) Wandering Hogsmeade's cobblestone streets and flying through Hogwarts at Universal Orlando Resort.

③ **Wekiwa Springs State Park** (p321) Paddling quietly past alligators and blue herons on the Wekiva River.

④ **Winter Park** (p326) Poking through art museums, window-shopping and some of the region's best dining.

⑤ **Star Wars: Galaxy's Edge** (p276) Travelling to a galaxy far,

far away at Disney's Hollywood Studios.

⑥ **Walt Disney World®** (p257) Stimulating all your senses at four theme parks, two water parks and more.

⑦ **Pandora – The World of Avatar** (p280) Exploring this simply gorgeous land at Disney's Animal Kingdom.

WALT DISNEY WORLD®

Cinderella Castle in Magic Kingdom. Epcot's Spaceship Earth. The Tree of Life in Animal Kingdom. The Tower of Terror in Hollywood Studios. These aren't just the easily recognizable symbols of the world's most famous theme park, but deeply embedded cultural icons that evoke memories of childhood and the promise of a magically fun time – just as Walt Disney intended when he designed the park that opened in 1971 to be the 'Happiest Place on Earth.'

Most of the headlines today are made by the high-tech rides in the likes of Pandora – The World of Avatar and Star Wars: Galaxy's Edge, but what makes **Walt Disney World®** (☑ 407-939-5277; www.disneyworld.com; Lake Buena Vista, outside Orlando; daily rates vary, from around $109, see website for discount packages & tickets up to 10 days; 🚇) truly special are the perennials. The castle and the fireworks. A photo op with Mickey and Minnie. A ride on 'It's a Small World.' This is the magic of Disney, sprinkled like pixie dust over all those who enter the parks. It's powerful stuff too, able to turn a child's tantrum into pure happiness and make adults forget those long lines and sore feet. All you have to do is surrender to it.

History

When Disneyland opened in southern California, it took off in a huge way, fundamentally transforming the concept of theme parks. Walt Disney, however, was irritated at the hotels and concessions that were springing up in a manner that he felt was entirely parasitic. In 1965, after a secret four-year search, he bought 27,000 acres of swamp, field and woodland in central Florida. His vision was to create a family vacation destination and he wanted to control every aspect – hotels, restaurants, parking and transportation.

Alas, Walt died of lung cancer the following year at the age of 65; his brother Roy took over responsibility for development. Walt Disney World's Magic Kingdom – with 'Walt' added in tribute – opened on October 1, 1971, but 10 weeks later Roy died of a brain hemorrhage. Epcot opened in 1982, Hollywood Studios in 1989 and Animal Kingdom in 1998.

⊙ Sights

Walt Disney World® is indeed a network: the area covers 42 sq miles and includes

ⓘ ADVANCE PLANNING

Three months before Snag a table at Disney character, themed and high-end restaurants.

Two months before Book your hotel, purchase theme-park tickets and reserve Disney FastPass+ attractions (if not staying on site, reserve 30 days in advance).

Three weeks before Check hotel prices and make changes if necessary – cancellation policies are generous and prices fluctuate dramatically. Buy theater tickets.

four separate (walled) theme parks and two water parks (plus some leisure attractions including golf courses), all connected by a complicated system of monorail, boat and bus, and intersected by highways and roads. Attractions, primarily in the form of rides, character interactions, movies and shows, are spread out among the six parks, resort hotels and, to a far lesser extent, two entertainment districts.

The six parks are: Magic Kingdom (p267), Epcot (p282), Disney's Animal Kingdom (p279), Disney's Hollywood Studios (p275), Blizzard Beach (p289) and Typhoon Lagoon (p289).

🏃 Activities

Disney offers a dizzying array of recreational activities, most based at Disney hotels and none requiring theme-park admission. Call Walt Disney World® Recreation (407-939-7529) for reservations and details on everything from water-skiing lessons to bike rental, tennis to cycling, horseback riding to carriage rides. For general information on activities at Walt Disney World®, check www.disneyworld.com.

Walt Disney World®
Bicycle Rental   CYCLING
(☑ 407-939-7529; www.disneyworld.com; select Walt Disney World® resorts; per day $20, surrey bikes per 30min from $25) There are eight bike-rental places throughout Walt Disney World® that rent on a first-come, first-served basis. A few places, including Disney's BoardWalk, rent two-, four- and six-person surrey bikes, with four wheels, candy-striped tops and bench seats.

Winter Summerland
Miniature Golf
GOLF

(☑ 407-560-3000; www.disneyworld.com; 1548 W Buena Vista Dr, Walt Disney World®; adult/child $14/12; ⊙10am-11pm) Two holiday-inspired, season-themed (as in both summer and winter) miniature golf courses located next to Blizzard Beach.

Fantasia Gardens &
Fairways Miniature Golf
GOLF

(☑ 407-560-4870; www.disneyworld.com; 1205 Epcot Resorts Blvd, Walt Disney World®; adult/child $14/12; ⊙10am-11pm; ⊞) Two sweet fairy-land-themed courses based on the classic animation *Fantasia*.

Disney's Lake Buena
Vista Golf Course
GOLF

(☑ 407-939-4653; www.golfwdw.com; 1960 Broadway, Walt Disney World®; per round from $49) A championship golf course, designed in classic country-club style, with lakes and pine forests. Test out your approach shot – a major feature is its elevated bunkered greens.

Disney's Magnolia
Golf Course
GOLF

(☑ 407-939-4653; www.golfwdw.com; 1950 W Magnolia Palm Dr, Disney's Grand Floridian Resort & Spa; per round from $49) The longest of Disney's five golf courses, this one-time regular on the PGA Tour (Tiger Woods and Jack Nicklaus have both won the contest here) is notable for its testing length and handsome magnolia trees.

Disney's Oak
Trail Golf Course
GOLF

(☑ 407-939-4653; www.golfwdw.com; 1950 W Magnolia Palm Dr, Disney's Grand Floridian Resort & Spa; per round from $45) Family-friendly, nine-hole walking course.

Disney's Palm Golf Course
GOLF

(☑ 407-939-4653; www.golfwdw.com; 1950 W Magnolia Palm Dr, Disney's Grand Floridian Resort & Spa; per round from $40) This Arnold Palmer–designed, 18-hole championship course is one of Disney's most picturesque, with palm trees, lakes and sloping greens.

Fort Wilderness
Tri-Circle-D Ranch
HORSEBACK RIDING

(☑ 407-824-2832; www.disneyworld.com; 4510 Fort Wilderness Trail, Disney's Fort Wilderness Resort & Campground; rides from $8; ☐ Disney, ☑ Disney) Guided trail, pony, wagon, hay and carriage rides.

Disney Boat Rental
BOATING

(☑ 403-939-7529; www.disneyworld.com; select Disney resort hotels; rental per boat per hour from $15) Disney rents canoes, kayaks, Sunfish and catamaran sailboats, pedal boats and motorized boats at several resort hotels, including Disney's Port Orleans (p259), Disney's Caribbean Beach Resort (p285) and Disney's Fort Wilderness Resort (p273). Consider reserving a pontoon to watch the fireworks over the Magic Kingdom castle.

Sammy Duvall's
Watersports Centre
WATER SPORTS

(☑ 407-939-0754; www.sammyduvall.com; 4600 World Dr, Disney's Contemporary Resort; personal watercraft per hour $135, water skiing, wakeboarding & tubing up to 5 people per hour $165; ⊙10am-5pm; ☐ Disney, ☑ Disney, ☐ Disney) Lessons, rentals and parasailing.

☞ Tours

Disney Tours
TOURS

(☑ 407-939-8687, VIP tours 407-560-4033; www.disneyworld.com; Walt Disney World®; prices vary) Disney offers all kinds of guided tours and specialty experiences, including the **Wild Africa Trek** private safari and backstage Disney tours. For the ultimate in hassle-free touring, with front-of-the-line access to attractions and insider information on the park and its history, consider a **VIP tour** ($400 to $600 per hour per group of up to 10 people).

Note that tours inside theme parks require theme-park admission in addition to the cost of the tour.

☆ Festivals & Events

In November and December, millions of lights and hundreds of Christmas trees, specialty parades and holiday shows celebrate the season throughout Walt Disney World®.

See the individual park coverage later in this chapter for park-specific festivals and events.

🛏 Sleeping

Disney resort hotels are divided according to location (Magic Kingdom, Epcot, Animal Kingdom and Disney's BoardWalk) and category (value, moderate, deluxe and deluxe villa). Prices vary drastically according to the season, week and day.

While deluxe resorts are the best Disney has to offer (deluxe villas are just that), note that you're paying for Disney theming and location convenience, not necessarily luxury. Most hotels offer multiroom suites and villas, upscale restaurants, children's programs and, crucially, free transport to the theme parks.

See the individual parks for accommodations options within them.

Disney's Port Orleans French Quarter & Riverside Resorts RESORT $$
(☑ French Quarter 407-934-5000, Riverside 407-934-6000; www.disneyworld.com; 1251 Riverside; r from $175; P ❋ @ 🛜 ☲; 🚌 Disney, 🚢 Disney) Lush gardens and a jubilant Mardi Gras motif blend in an effort to create a Louisiana feel to these sister resorts. Though the result sometimes falls flat and the simple rooms feel dated, the resort is a mecca for activities and includes a sea-serpent water slide, boat rental, horse-drawn-carriage rides and evening s'mores.

This is one of the biggest resorts at Disney; a boat connects the two properties, or it's a 15-minute walk.

★ Four Seasons Resort Orlando at Walt Disney World® RESORT $$$
(☑ 800-267-3046; www.fourseasons.com; 10100 Dream Tree Blvd; r from $600; P ❋ @ 🛜 ☲) Greater Orlando's only five-star hotel has all of the luxury, quality and attention to detail you'd expect from a Four Seasons resort. It's one of the few non-Disney properties within the resort and is marvelously removed from the Disney vortex. A superb experience. Rates fluctuate tremendously; check online.

✖ Eating

With the exception of Epcot, expect mediocre fast food, bad coffee and cafeteria cuisine at premium prices. Table-service restaurants accept 'priority seating' reservations up to 180 days in advance. Reserve through Disney Dining (☑ 407-939-3463), at www.disneyworld.com or through the My Disney Experience app. Remember: while restaurants in the theme parks require theme-park admission, resort hotel restaurants do not.

Disney also offers character meals, dinner shows and specialty dining.

Many of the best sit-down dining options at Walt Disney World® are located in the park's resort hotels, as opposed to within the pedestrian areas within the park itself. See later in this chapter for food options within each individual park.

Sanaa SOUTH INDIAN $$
(☑ 407-939-3463; www.disneyworld.com; 3701 Osceola Pkwy, Kidani Village, Disney's Animal Kingdom Lodge; mains $15-25; ⊙ 11:30am-3pm & 5-9:30pm; ✍ 🖐; 🚌 Disney) Lovely cafe with savanna views – giraffes, ostriches and zebras graze outside the window. You almost forget you're in Florida, but, hey, that's Disney. The food is South Indian – try the slow-cooked tandoori chicken, ribs, lamb or shrimp; the delicious salad sampler with tasty watermelon, cucumber and fennel salad; and a mango margarita.

PICK YOUR PARK

Magic Kingdom (p267) Low on thrills and high on nostalgia, with Cinderella Castle and nightly fireworks. The most popular park of them all.

Epcot (p282) A handful of rides on one side; country-based food, shopping and attractions on the other. Undergoing a major transformation from 2020.

Disney's Animal Kingdom (p279) Part zoo and part county fair, with a heavy dusting of Disney-styled Africa. Home to Pandora – The World of Avatar.

Disney's Hollywood Studios (p275) Movie-based attractions including the new Star Wars: Galaxy's Edge area.

Typhoon Lagoon (p289) Water park particularly excellent for families.

Blizzard Beach (p289) Ski-resort-themed water park with high-speed twists and turns.

Disney's BoardWalk (p289) Intimate waterfront boardwalk with a handful of shops, restaurants and entertainment; no admission fee.

Disney Springs (p290) Mostly retail area (including the world's largest Disney store) but also restaurants, live music and attractions; no admission fee.

Walt Disney World®

Space
Mountain
8

Splash 9
Mountain

Floridian Pkwy

5
Magic
Kingdom
27

Bay
Lake

South
Lake

Seven Seas
Lagoon

Timberline Dr
35

W Wilderness Way

Fort Wilderness Tr

21

22

30

31

23

Seven Seas Dr

Transportation &
Ticket Center (TTC)

Disney's Fort
Wilderness Resort
& Campground

37

29

Vista Blvd

World Dr

Bonnet Creek Pkwy

Epcot Center Dr

33

Soarin' Around
the World

45
19
Epcot

4

Frozen Ever Afte

Epcot Resort Blvd

36

12

43

World Showcase

44

41

15

International Gateway:
Epcot Back Entrance

34

Crescent
Lake

24

Disney's
BoardWalk

26

28

17

Rock 'n' Roller Coaster
Starring Aerosmith

7

3

Disney's Hollywood
Studios

Avatar: Flight
of Passage

1

Disney's Animal
Kingdom

2

13

16

10

Star Wars: Rise of
the Resistance

25

32

Pandora –
6
The World
of Avatar

42

Blizzard
Beach

Osceola Pkwy

World Dr

Hourglass
Lake

Century Dr

192
530

W Irlo Bronson
Memorial Hwy

W Buena Vista Dr

Victory Way

Exit 65

4

ESPN
Wide World
of Sports

46

192
530

Irlo Bronson Memorial Hwy
Exit 64B

0 ——— 1 km
0 ——— 0.5 miles

Lake Sheen

Winter Garden Vineland Rd

Grand
Cypress
Golf Club

S Apopka Vineland Rd

**LAKE
BUENA VISTA**

Disney Vacation Club Way

E Buena Vista Dr

Grand Cypress Blvd

39

Hotel Plaza
Blvd

20

Buena Vista
Watersports
(0.7mi)

Village
Lake

11 The Void

P

Orlando
Premium
Outlets –
Vineland Ave
(1mi)

E Buena Vista Dr

P

14

18 Typhoon
Lagoon

Epcot Center Dr

Exit 67

38

40

S International Dr

W Osceola Pkwy

Central Florida Greeneway (toll)

Celebration
Ave

530 192

Florida Plaza
Blvd

Celebration
(0.8mi)

★**Boma** BUFFET $$$

(☎407-938-4744, 407-939-3463; www.disney-world.com; 2901 Osceola Pkwy, Disney's Animal Kingdom Lodge; adult/child breakfast $38/20, dinner $49/27; ☻7:30-11am & 5-9:30pm; 🛜🚻; 🚍Disney) Several steps above Disney's usual buffet options, this African-inspired eatery offers wood-roasted meats, interesting soups such as coconut curried chicken and plenty of salads. Handsomely furnished with dark woods, decorated with African art and tapestries, and flanked by garden-view windows on one side, Boma offers not only good food but unusually calm and pleasant surrounds.

★**Victoria & Albert's** AMERICAN $$$

(☎407-939-3862; www.victoria-alberts.com; 4401 Floridian Way, Disney's Grand Floridian Resort; prix-fixe from $235, wine pairing $150; ☻5-9:20pm; 🛜; 🚍Disney, 🚍Disney, 🚍Disney) With one sitting per evening and a prix-fixe menu as the only choice (vegetarian option available), this opulent Victorian-themed dining room provides one of the poshest meals in all of Florida. Everything is beautifully prepared, and desserts by pastry chef Kristine Farmer are divine. You must reserve directly (not through the Disney Dining number) and well in advance.

Everything here is elegant, from the linen to the crystal glasses and the live cello music. Dinner at the intimate Chef's Table or Queen Victoria's room includes 13 courses; there's also the option of a caviar-tasting course ($295), where you get a half-ounce each of Siberian Osetra, Snake River sturgeon and Royal Belgian Platinum. Children must be aged 10 and over.

California Grill AMERICAN $$$

(☎407-939-3463; www.disneyworld.com; 4600 World Dr, Disney's Contemporary Resort; mains $37-52; ☻5-10pm; 🚻; 🚍Disney, 🚍Disney, 🚍Disney) Disney's signature gourmet restaurant has commanding rooftop views of the Magic Kingdom fireworks, which for many is reason enough to bag a table. But the clincher is the superb menu, with everything from quirky sushi to triple-cheesed flatbreads. Reservations should be made well in advance (up to 180 days for peak season).

Jiko – The Cooking Place AFRICAN $$$

(☎407-938-4733; www.disneyworld.com; 2901 Osceola Pkwy, Disney's Animal Kingdom Lodge; mains $35-60; ☻5:30-10pm; 🚗🚻; 🚍Disney) Excellent food, with plenty of grains, vegetables

Walt Disney World®

and creative twists, a tiny bar, and rich African surrounds make this a Disney favorite for both quality and theming. You can relax with a glass of wine on the hotel's back deck, alongside the giraffes and other African beasts.

For a less-expensive option, enjoy an appetizer (the Taste of Africa features various dips and crackers) at the bar. Swing by for dinner, or at least a cocktail, after a day at Animal Kingdom.

Chef Mickey's   AMERICAN $$$
(☑ 407-939-3463; www.disneyworld.com; 4600 World Dr, Disney's Contemporary Resort; adult/child from $50/33; ⊙ 7-11:15am, 11:30am-2:30pm & 5-9:30pm) Nothing says Walt Disney World® Resort more than Mickey Mouse and the monorail, so what better way to start your classic Disney day than a buffet breakfast with Mickey Mouse, Minnie Mouse, Pluto, Donald Duck and Goofy under the roar of the monorail. Head to Chef Mickey's for an early breakfast.

(Reservations required well in advance; prices differ for the various meals.) After this, hop on the monorail and get to Magic Kingdom when the gates open.

Storybook Dining with
Snow White at Artist Point   AMERICAN $$$
(📞407-939-3463; www.disneyworld.com; 901 Timberline Dr, Disney's Wilderness Lodge; mains $30-50; ⏱4-9pm; 🅿🚼; 🚌Disney, 🚢Disney) Modeled on the arts-and-crafts Old Faithful Inn at Yellowstone National Park, this lodge-style restaurant serves up delicious Pacific Northwest fare (roast venison, wild salmon,

grilled buffalo) themed after the story of Snow White and accompanied by the bulk of its characters. The good news is that the 'Poison' Apple dessert only works on the Evil Queen.

🍷 **Drinking & Nightlife**

Disney Springs and the much smaller Disney's BoardWalk are the designated drinking (and entertainment and shopping) districts at Walt Disney World®, but you'll find bars and sometimes live music at most Disney resorts and within the theme parks. Magic

Kingdom sells beer and wine only, available at the more formal, sit-down restaurants. At Epcot, you'll find a broad choice of spirits and cocktails from around the world.

Tambu Lounge BAR
(www.disneyworld.com; Disney's Polynesian Resort; 🖳 Disney, ⬤ Disney) Escape to the islands, Disney-style, with umbrella-topped tropical drinks and Blue Glow-tinis. There's also an excellent selection of bar food, including pulled pork nachos and kebabs, and it's an easy boat or monorail from here to Magic Kingdom.

☆ Entertainment

Go to www.buildabettermousetrip.com/wdw-outdoor-movie-schedule for a schedule of free outdoor screenings of Disney movies at Disney hotels and other locales at Disney's Fort Wilderness. You'll find fabulous performances in each of the parks, as well as singalongs specifically aimed at kids and three dinner shows.

★ Chip 'n' Dale Campfire Singalong CINEMA
(☑ 407-939-7529; www.disneyworld.com; 4510 N Fort Wilderness Trail, Disney's Fort Wilderness Resort; ⏰ 8pm; 🖳 Disney, ⬤ Disney) This intimate and low-key character experience offers

singing and dancing with Chip and Dale, campfires for roasting marshmallows, and a free outdoor screening of a Disney film. Every night is a different movie, and Disney doesn't post a schedule on its website – call or search online.

You can buy generously portioned s'mores supplies, and though there are split-log benches, it's better to bring a blanket and pillows to snuggle down on. Cars are not allowed in Fort Wilderness; park at the parking area after the entry gate, or take a Disney bus or boat to the resort, and catch a shuttle the few minutes to the Meadow Recreation Area.

ESPN Wide World of Sports SPECTATOR SPORT
(☑ 407-939-4263, visitor center 407-541-5600; www.espnwwos.com; 700 S Victory Way, Walt Disney World®) This 230-acre sports facility at Walt Disney World® hosts Atlanta Braves spring training and hundreds of amateur and professional sporting events.

Shopping

There are endless stores throughout Walt Disney World®, most of which are thematically oriented. So near the Winnie-the-Pooh ride you'll find lots of bear stuff; and, in Star Wars: Galaxy's Edge, well, light sabres and everything else to turn you into your favour-

---

NON-DISNEY HOTELS

There are a bunch of non-Disney hotels within the Walt Disney World® limits, including the following:

Hilton Orlando Bonnet Creek (☑ 407-597-3600; www.hiltonbonnetcreek.com; 14100 Bonnet Creek Resort Lane, Greater Orlando; r from $200, resort fee per day $45, self/valet parking $29/37; P @ 🛜 ⬤) Surrounded by Walt Disney World®, this quintessential full-service resort (it also has a big pool with a lazy river and a slide) has a slight corporate feel but makes an excellent alternative to comparable resorts on Disney property. No, you won't enjoy the benefits of staying at a Disney hotel, but the quality more accurately mirrors the price.

The on-site Harvest Bistro serves rather pricey fresh and tasty fare, though children pay half-price for breakfast and are free for dinner. A better bet is treating yourself to **La Luce** (☑ 407-597-3675; www.laluceorlando.com; 14100 Bonnet Creek Resort Lane; mains $18-46; ⏰ 6-11pm; P) for dinner.

Waldorf Astoria (☑ 407-597-5500; www.waldorfastoriaorlando.com; 14200 Bonnet Creek Resort Lane, Greater Orlando; r $200-400, ste $450-600, resort fee per day $45, valet-only parking $37; P @ 🛜 ⬤) Though this elegant classic doesn't offer the benefits of on-site Disney hotels, it's located within the gates of Walt Disney World® and the quality of its rooms, amenities and service is impeccable. There's an excellent buffet breakfast, two grandly styled pools bordering the golf course, and a spa. Hilton Orlando Bonnet Creek shares amenities with the Waldorf.

Bus shuttle to Disney is complimentary but unreliable if there's traffic – it makes several stops on the way to/from your destination, stretching what should be a 15-minute ride closer to an hour, and so rendering null the benefit of close proximity to Disney.

DISNEY DINNER SHOWS

Disney's three dinner shows sell out early, so make your reservation for these up to 180 days in advance; you can cancel up to 48 hours in advance with no penalty. They are each held at a Disney resort, include beer and wine, and do not require theme park admission.

Hoop-Dee-Doo Musical Revue (☑407-939-3463; www.disneyworld.com; 4510 N Fort Wilderness Trail, Disney's Fort Wilderness Resort; adult $64-72, child 3-9yr $38-43; ☺4pm, 6:15pm & 8:30pm daily; ♠; ☐Disney, ☀Disney) Nineteenth-century vaudeville show at Disney's Fort Wilderness Resort, with ribs delivered to your table in metal buckets, corny jokes and the audience singing along to 'Hokey Pokey' and 'My Darling Clementine.' This is one of Disney's longest-running shows and is great fun, once you grab your washboard and get into the spirit of it all.

Mickey's Backyard Barbecue (☑407-939-3463; www.disneyworld.com; 4510 N Fort Wilderness Trail, Disney's Fort Wilderness Resort; adult $62-72, child 3-9yr $37-47; ☺hours vary; ♠; ☐Disney, ☀Disney) The only dinner theater with Disney characters. Join in on country-and-western singin', ho-down-style stompin' and goofy Mickey antics at this Disney favorite.

Spirit of Aloha (☑407-939-3463; www.disneyworld.com; 1600 Seven Seas Dr, Disney's Polynesian Resort; adult $66-78, child 3-9yr $39-46; ☺5:15pm & 8:15pm; ☐Disney, ☀Disney, ☐Disney) Hula-clad men and women leap around the stage, dance and play with fire in this South Pacific–style luau at Disney's Polynesian Resort. Pulled pork, barbecue ribs and island-themed specialties like pineapple-coconut bread are served family-style.

ite character. For a one-stop shop, Disney Springs (p290) has the largest Disney character store in the country, with 12 massive rooms chock-a-block with everything you can imagine.

ⓘ Information

INTERNET ACCESS

Strong, complimentary wi-fi (presumably to encourage constant social media use) is available throughout Walt Disney World® parks, entertainment districts, theme parks, water parks and resort hotels. Select Walt Disney World® Resort network, and call ☑ 407-827-2732 if you have technical problems.

MAPS

Park maps with listings of the day's scheduled events and activities (including character meets) are available at the park entrances, Guest Services and all retail locations throughout the parks. Otherwise, the My Disney Experience app has geo-locator maps of every inch of Disney property to help you orient yourself.

MEDICAL SERVICES

Medical facilities are located within each theme park and at both Disney water parks. The closest hospital is Florida Hospital Celebration Health (p326). If you need care at your hotel room, Doctors on Call Service (p326) provides medical service 24/7.

Lake Buena Vista Centra Care (☑407-934-2273, for pickup 407-938-0650; www.centracare.org; 12500 S Apopka Vineland Rd;

☺8am-midnight Mon-Fri, to 8pm Sat & Sun) Nonemergency-care medical facility, offering adult and pediatric care, x-rays, and free transportation to and from area hotels and attractions.

MONEY

You will find ATMs throughout Walt Disney World®. Guest Services at each park offer limited currency exchange.

OPENING HOURS

Walt Disney World theme-park hours change not only by season, but day to day within any given month. Generally, parks open at 8am or 9am and close sometime between 6pm and 10pm. Every day one of the four theme parks opens one hour early or closes late for guests of Walt Disney World® hotels only – these 'Magic Hours' are a major perk of staying at a Disney resort hotel.

TOURIST INFORMATION

For on-site questions and reservations, head to Guest Services, just inside each theme park, or the concierge at any Disney resort hotel.

Important Telephone Numbers

Walt Disney World® (☑ 407-939-5277) Central number for all things Disney, including packages, tickets, room and dining reservations, and general questions about hours and scheduled events. They'll connect you to anything you need.

Walt Disney World® 'Disney Dining' (☑407-939-3463) Book priority dining reservations up to 180 days in advance, including character meals, dinner shows and specialty dining. You can also book online, by phone or through your

ORLANDO & WALT DISNEY WORLD® WALT DISNEY WORLD®

ⓘ STROLLER RENTAL

Strollers (single/double per day $15/31, multiday $13/27) are available on a first-come, first-served basis at Disney's four theme parks and Disney Springs, and you can also purchase umbrella strollers.

My Disney Experience app (www.disney world.com).

Walt Disney World® 'Enchanting Extras Collection' (Recreation) (☎ 407-939-7529) Horseback riding, boating and more.

Walt Disney World® 'Enchanting Extras Collection' (Tours) (☎ 407-939-8687) Tours at all of Disney's four theme parks. One of these gives a 'behind the scenes' look; excellent for return visitors.

Walt Disney World® 'Theme Parks Lost & Found' (☎ 407-824-4245) Items are sent to this central location at the end of each day; also see Guest Services at individual parks.

ⓘ Getting There & Away

TO & FROM AIRPORT

If you're staying at a Walt Disney World® hotel and are arriving at Orlando International Airport (as opposed to Sanford), arrange in advance for complimentary luggage handling and deluxe bus transportation with **Disney's Magical Express** (☎ 866-599-0951; www.disneyworld.com). They will send you baggage labels in advance, collect your luggage at the airport and, if during your stay you transfer from one Disney hotel to another, the resort will transfer your luggage while you're off for the day.

BUS

Orlando's Lynx (p331) bus 50 connects the downtown central station to Disney's Transportation & Ticket Center and Disney Springs, but it's an hour ride. Bus 56 runs along Hwy 192, between Kissimmee and Disney's Transportation & Ticket Center. From there, you can connect to any theme park or hotel.

CAR & MOTORCYCLE

Disney lies 25 minutes' drive south of downtown Orlando. Take I-4 to well-signed exits 64, 65 or 67.

Alamos and National car rental is available inside the Walt Disney World® Dolphin Resort.

Parking

If you're staying at a Disney resort, parking at all the theme parks and hotels is free; otherwise, it costs $25 per day. Note: it's not made clear, but parking tickets bought at one park are good all day for all Disney parks.

TICKETS

One-day tickets Valid for admission to Magic Kingdom. Separate one-day tickets at slightly lower prices are valid for admission to Epcot, Disney's Hollywood Studios or Animal Kingdom.

Multiday tickets Valid for one theme park per day for each day of the ticket (you can leave/re-enter the park but cannot enter another park).

Park Hopper Gives same-day admission to any/all of the four Walt Disney World® parks. Fair warning: hopping between four parks requires a lot of stamina. Two parks a day is more feasible.

Park Hopper Plus The same as Park Hopper, but you can toss in Blizzard Beach, Typhoon Lagoon and Oak Trail Golf Course. The number of places you can visit increases the more days you buy (eg a four-day ticket allows four extra visits; a five-day ticket allows five).

DAYS	MULTIDAY PRICES (AGE 10+/AGE 3-9)	PARK HOPPER (AGE 10+/AGE 3-9)	PARK HOPPER PLUS (AGE 10+/AGE 3-9)
2	$202/192	$267/257	$287/277
3	$294/279	$369/354	$389/374
4	$372/356	$447/431	$467/451
5	$390/370	$475/455	$495/475
6	$402/384	$487/469	$507/489
7	$406/392	$491/477	$511/497
8	$424/400	$509/485	$529/505
9	$432/414	$517/499	$537/519
10	$440/420	$525/505	$545/525

Disney Dining Offers Complex Disney Dining Plans are available to guests of Disney resort hotels; see www.disneyworld.com for prices, and remember – you can add in a dining plan on any day leading up to the time of your reservation.

Buying tickets at the gate This is $20 more expensive than buying online.

Parking lots sit directly outside the gates of all the parks, except for Magic Kingdom; if you're driving to Magic Kingdom, you have to park at the Transportation & Ticket Center and take a monorail or ferry to the park. Parking at Disney Springs, the water parks, ESPN Wide World of Sports and all the golf courses is free, but there is no transportation from these attractions to any of the four theme parks. Valet parking at deluxe hotels costs around $30 per day.

The **Transportation & Ticket Center** (www. disneyworld.com; Walt Disney World®; Magic Kingdom parking $20) is Disney's transportation epicenter. From here, one monorail goes to Magic Kingdom, Disney's Polynesian Resort, Disney's Contemporary Resort and Disney's Grand Floridian Resort; a second monorail connects directly to Epcot; a third monorail connects directly to Magic Kingdom; ferries go to Magic Kingdom; and buses service attractions and hotels throughout Walt Disney World®.

TAXI

Taxis can be found at hotels, theme parks, the Transportation & Ticket Center and Disney Springs.

ⓘ Getting Around

The Disney transportation system utilizes boats, buses and even a monorail to shuttle visitors to hotels, theme parks and other attractions within Walt Disney World®. The Transportation & Ticket Center operates as the main hub of this system. Note that it can take an hour to get from point A to point B using the Disney transportation system, and there is not always a direct route.

BOAT

Disney World Water Transportation (www. disneyworld.com/guest-services/water-transportation; Walt Disney World®) runs complimentary Disney boats that connect Magic Kingdom to Magic Kingdom resorts and the Transportation & Ticket Center; and Epcot resorts to Disney's Hollywood Studios, Disney's BoardWalk and Epcot.

Water launches (water taxis) circulate directly between Magic Kingdom and Disney's Grand Floridian Resort and Disney's Polynesian Resort; a second route connects Magic Kingdom to Disney's Contemporary Resort, Disney's Fort Wilderness Resort & Campground and Disney's Wilderness Lodge; and a third route, utilizing 600-passenger ferries, connects Magic Kingdom to the Transportation & Ticket Center.

Boats also loop between Epcot, Disney's Hollywood Studios, Disney's BoardWalk, Disney's Yacht & Beach Club Resorts, and Walt Disney World® Swan & Dolphin Resorts.

Finally, boats connect Disney Springs to Disney Springs resort hotels.

BUS

Everything at Disney World is accessible by a free bus, but not all destinations are directly connected. Buses from Disney Springs, for example, do not connect directly to any theme parks. To this end, some routes may involve a combination of bus, monorail or boat. So-called 'cast members' (that is, staff) are willing to assist.

CABLE CAR

The relatively new **Disney Skyliner** (www.disney world.com/guest-services/disney-skyliner) is a nifty gondola system that connects Disney's Hollywood Studios and International Gateway at Epcot with four resort hotels: Disney's Caribbean Beach Resort, Disney's Art of Animation Resort, Disney's Pop Century Resort and Disney's Riviera Resort.

MONORAIL

Three separate monorail routes service select locations within Walt Disney World®. The Resort Monorail loops between the Transportation & Ticket Center, Disney's Polynesian Resort, Disney's Grand Floridian Resort, Magic Kingdom and Disney's Contemporary Resort. A second monorail route connects the Transportation & Ticket Center directly to Magic Kingdom; and a third route connects the Transportation & Ticket Center directly to Epcot.

Magic Kingdom

When most people think of Walt Disney World®, they're thinking of just one of the four theme parks – the **Magic Kingdom** (☑407-939-5277; www.disneyworld.com; 1180 Seven Seas Dr, Walt Disney World®; $109-129, prices vary daily; ◷9am-11pm, hours vary; ▢Disney, ▣Disney, ▢Disney). The home of Cinderella Castle, Splash Mountain and many a dream come true isn't just quintessential Disney but the template for all theme park development – even now, nearly a half century after it first opened. Hardly surprising that of Disney's 65-odd-million annual visitors, nearly 50 million of them will come here, to the smallest of the four parks.

For most of them, this isn't just a visit but a pilgrimage to the origin of a million childhood fantasies, made real by the iconic castle and its grand approach, Main Street, USA.

A horse-drawn carriage and an old-fashioned car run for the first hour from the park entrance to the castle (most people walk), and from there paths lead to the four 'lands' – Fantasyland, Tomorrowland, Adventureland and Frontierland, as well as

TOP TIPS FOR A SUCCESSFUL FAMILY VACATION TO DISNEY

Disney expectations run high, and the reality of things can be disappointing. Long waits, and getting jostled and tugged through crowds and lines, can leave the kids, and you, exhausted. There are two ways to do this. The first is to plan ahead with scrupulous attention to detail. Make dinner reservations, plan when to go where based on parade and show schedules, decide in advance what attractions to tackle once you're there and reserve FastPass+ selections. The final tip might come as a shock to some (but it worked for us).

Here are some simple tips:

Buy tickets that cover more days than you think you'll need It's less expensive per day, and it gives the freedom to break up time at the theme parks with downtime in the pool or at low-key attractions beyond theme-park gates.

Stay at a Walt Disney World® resort hotel While it's tempting to save money by staying elsewhere, the value of staying at a Walt Disney World® resort lies in the convenience offered. They do vary in standards, however, and are divided into value, midrange and deluxe categories.

Download the Disney app 'My Disney Experience' You can make reservations, reserve FastPass+ attractions, view listings and programs as well as your own schedule.

Take advantage of 'My Disney Experience' Reserve your three FastPass+ attractions per day (www.disneyworld.com) up to 60 days in advance (30 days for nonresort guests) – this will give you three guaranteed short lines each day. You can redeem additional FastPasses after you use the first three.

Stock up on snacks Even if it's nothing more than some snack packets and some bananas, you'll save the irritation of waiting in line for bad, overpriced food. Or, to avoid the lines, buy a sandwich early on the way in and have a picnic at your leisure.

Pimp your stroller Can you recognize your stroller in a sea of them? The sprawling stroller parking zones are just that, so make sure to adorn yours with something recognizable, like a flag.

Arrive at the park at least 30 minutes before gates open Don't window shop or dawdle – just march quickly to the rides and then kick back for the afternoon. If you can only manage this on one day of your trip, make it the day you're going to Magic Kingdom. Factor in the time to get here from the Transportation & Ticket Center (this can take up to an hour).

Speed up, slow down Yes, there's a time to hurry, as 10 minutes of pushing the pedal to the metal could save two hours waiting in line, but allow days to unfold according to the ebbs and flows of your children's moods.

Program 'Disney Dining' into your cell phone While you'll want to make some plans well in advance, once you have a sense of where you'll be at mealtime, call 407-939-3463 to make reservations at table-service restaurants at all four theme parks, Disney resort hotels and at Disney's two shopping districts, Disney Springs and Disney's BoardWalk (or go online). Also, check for last-minute cancellations to dinner shows or character meals.

Transportation and accommodations When booking accommodations it's worth considering your transportation options. All Disney resorts offer bus transportation, but those offering boat and monorail transportation are far more convenient (and, except for camping at Fort Wilderness, more expensive).

Go with the flow This is about managing expectations. If you build up the idea that your child will definitely hug Belle in a so-called 'character meet,' only to see the line is ridiculous, then recalibrate. Suggest initially that you're going to spot, rather than visit, a character. Believe us, you'll end up spotting them in parades or by chance. In addition to your three FastPass+ experiences, you can head to any of the activities listed in the daily schedule/map.

two other areas: Liberty Square and Main Street, USA.

Sights

Main Street, USA

All visits to the Magic Kingdom begin and end on Main Street, which was fashioned after Walt Disney's hometown of Marceline, MO, but given the full Disney treatment. Built to four-fifths scale, the Victorian-style, pastel-colored buildings are power-hosed every night and repainted regularly, all to cast that spell that is at the heart of Disney's own brand of magic.

At the top of the street is **Central Plaza**, which is the main gathering point for the crowds who congregate for the nightly fireworks-and-light shows. There are no big-ticket attractions, but you can meet Mickey Mouse, and Tinker Bell and her friends from Pixie Hollow at the **Town Square Theater Meet and Greets** (FastPass+); peruse the miniature dioramas of Peter Pan and Snow White in the street windows; pop in to catch the black-and-white movie reels of old Disney cartoons; and browse the hundreds of thousands of must-have Disney souvenirs.

The only ride – Walt Disney World Railroad – is closed pending the construction of a new *Tron*-themed ride in nearby Tomorrowland, which should be completed by 2021.

Fantasyland

Spread out like a miniature Alpine village under the towers of Cinderella Castle, Fantasyland is the spellbinding heart of the Magic Kingdom, especially for the eight-and-under crowd and grown-ups looking for a nostalgic taste of classic Disney. Littlies, especially, love the character-focused experiences and attractions.

Fantasyland offers all kinds of excellent character-interaction opportunities. Watch a princess tale at the little stone grotto of **Fairytale Garden**; listen to Belle tell a story at **Enchanted Tales with Belle**; meet Ariel at **Ariel's Grotto** and Gaston by **Gaston's Tavern**; or hop in line and catch a handful of princesses in **Fairytale Hall**. And, of course, always keep an eye out for Cinderella, Alice in Wonderland and other favorites hanging out throughout.

Note: Mary Poppins is, er, a 'floater'; she appears at different lands at different times. Ask a staff member (known as 'cast characters') where she might be appearing.

Peter Pan's Flight RIDE
(www.disneyworld.com; Magic Kingdom, Fantasyland; theme-park admission required; ⊙9am-9pm, hours vary; 🖥 Disney, 🚌 Disney, 🚈 Lynx 50, 56) A Fantasyland classic, this indoor ride starts in the Darling family's house before taking you on an easygoing flight aboard a pirate ship that makes its way through the fog and stars over London before arriving in Never Land. All things end well as Peter saves Wendy and Captain Hook dances on the snout of a crocodile. It's very popular so use a FastPass+ or get here early to avoid long lines.

Mickey's PhilharMagic CINEMA
(www.disneyworld.com; Magic Kingdom, Fantasyland; theme-park admission required; ⊙9am-9pm, hours vary; 🖥 Disney, 🚈 Lynx 50, 56) Undoubtedly the best 3D show in Disney, Mickey's PhilharMagic takes Donald Duck on a whimsical adventure through classic Disney movies. Ride with him through the streets of Morocco on Aladdin's carpet and feel the champagne on your face when it pops open during *Beauty and the Beast's* 'Be Our Guest.' Fun, silly and lighthearted, this is Disney at its best.

it's a small world RIDE
(www.disneyworld.com; Magic Kingdom, Fantasyland; theme-park admission required; ⊙9am-9pm, hours vary; 🖥 Disney, 🚌 Disney, 🚈 Lynx 50, 56) Fantasyland's most enduring ride is this sweet boat trip around the globe, which has captivated children since it debuted at the 1964 New York World's Fair. Small boats gently glide through country after country, each decked out from floor to ceiling with elaborate and charmingly dated sets inhabited by hundreds of automated animals and children. Yes, it's so well known how the song sticks irritatingly in your head for weeks, that it's become a Disney cliché.

Seven Dwarves Mine Train RIDE
(www.disneyworld.com; Magic Kingdom, Fantasyland; theme-park admission required; ⊙9am-9pm, hours vary; 🖥 Disney, 🚌 Disney, 🚈 Lynx 50, 56) Race and 'heigh-ho' your way through a diamond mine in this family roller coaster that is a Fantasyland favorite. The audio-animatronics are great, but it's the singing that's really infectious.

Many Adventures of Winnie-the-Pooh
RIDE

(www.disneyworld.com; Magic Kingdom, Fantasyland; theme-park admission required; ⊙9am-9pm, hours vary; 🚌Disney, 🚇Disney, 🚌Lynx 50, 56) Take a sweet journey through the Hundred Acre Wood aboard a 'Hunny Pot' as Winnie and the gang wish you a 'Happy Windsday.' A nice dream sequence with Heffalumps and Woozles ends in a satisfying cloudburst. One of Fantasyland's better-done rides.

◉ Adventureland

Adventure Disney-style means pirates and jungles, magic carpets and tree houses, and whimsical and silly representations of the exotic locales from storybooks and imagination.

Kids love flying around on **Magic Carpets of Aladdin**, but skip the slow train of folks climbing 116 steps at **Swiss Family Treehouse**, a replica tree house of the shipwrecked family from the book and movie *The Swiss Family Robinson*. Animatronic birds sing and dance Hawaiian-style at **Walt Disney's Enchanted Tiki Room**, a silly and rather bizarre two-bit attraction that opened in 1963 and continues to enjoy a curious cult following. You won't find lines, and it makes for a perfect spot to relax out of the heat for a bit.

Pirates of the Caribbean
RIDE

(www.disneyworld.com; Magic Kingdom, Adventureland; theme-park admission required; ⊙9am-9pm, hours vary; 🚌Disney, 🚇Disney, 🚌Lynx 50, 56) The ride that spawned the hugely successful movie series remains one of Disney's most popular attractions. Drunken pirates sing pirate songs, sleep among the pigs and sneer

ALSO IN FANTASYLAND

Ride through the *Little Mermaid* on **Under the Sea: Journey of the Little Mermaid**. At **Dumbo the Flying Elephant** toddlers love jumping on a Dumbo and riding slowly around and around, up and down, and thrill at the chance to control how high they go. Lines here can be unbelievably long and slow, and the ride is incredibly short – hit this when the park gates open. The **Mad Tea Party** is a basic spinning ride, and you and others in the teacup decide just how much you'll be twirling.

over their empty whiskey bottles, but unless you're scared of the dark or growling pirates, it's a giggle not a scream. It's busy, but the lines generally move pretty quickly. Ride in the late afternoon for minimum waiting times.

Jungle Cruise
RIDE

(www.disneyworld.com; Magic Kingdom, Adventureland; theme-park admission required; ⊙9am-9pm, hours vary; 🚌Disney, 🚇Disney, 🚌Lynx 50, 56) This boat ride through a bunch of simulated jungle waterways populated by animatronic animals and people is quite fun, if you can stomach the skipper's cheeseball humor. Bad word play, silly jokes...they're all part of the experience.

◉ Frontierland

The theme at this land is 19th-century America, and as you walk through it you may notice a historical timeline, beginning with the establishment of the frontier in the early 1800s to the period just before the Civil War.

★ Splash Mountain
RIDE

(www.disneyworld.com; Magic Kingdom, Frontierland; theme-park admission required; ⊙9am-9pm, hours vary; 🚌Disney, 🚇Disney, 🚌Lynx 50, 56) Wild West Disney-style Splash Mountain (FastPass+) depicts the misadventures of Br'er Rabbit, Br'er Bear and Br'er Fox, complete with chatty frogs, singing ducks and other critters. The ride is half a mile long and the 40mph drop into the river makes for one of the biggest thrills in the park – and you will get very wet! The best ride in Frontierland and a highlight of any visit to Walt Disney World®.

◉ Tomorrowland

Although the Jetsons-inspired peek into the future falls flat, Tomorrowland holds a couple of wildly popular Disney highlights.

At the interactive comedy show **Monsters, Inc Laugh Floor**, monsters from the film must harness human laughter rather than screams. A screen projects characters from the movie, each doing a stand-up comedy routine that surprises audience members by unexpectedly incorporating them. It's pretty funny, and every show is different.

Kids can put the pedal to the metal on grand-prix-style cars at **Indy Speedway**, but the cars are fixed to the track and you don't control the steering. Note that kids must be

MY DISNEY EXPERIENCE: FASTPASS & MAGICBAND

FastPass+ is Disney's free ride reservation system, designed to help you plan your visit in advance and reduce waiting times in lines. Visitors can reserve a specific time for up to three attractions per day through My Disney Experience (www.disneyworld.com), accessible online or by downloading the free mobile app. There are also kiosks in each park where you can make reservations.

Resort guests receive a **MagicBand** – a plastic wristband that serves as a room key, park entrance ticket, FastPass+ access and room charge. As soon as you make your room reservation, you can set up your My Disney Experience account and begin planning your day-by-day Disney itinerary. A MagicBand will be sent to you in advance or it will be waiting for you when you check into your hotel. Your itinerary, including any changes you make online or through the mobile app, will automatically be stored in your wristband.

Once at the park, head to your reserved FastPass+ ride or attraction anytime within the preselected one-hour timeframe. Go to the FastPass+ entrance, scan your MagicBand and zip right onto the attraction with no more than a 15-minute wait. Though it's a simple system, there are some kinks, so a few tips can help you navigate it smoothly with optimal benefit.

➡ If you're staying at a Disney Resort, you can access My Disney Experience and start reserving FastPass+ attractions up to 60 days in advance; nonresort guests with purchased theme-park tickets can reserve FastPass+ attractions 30 days in advance.

➡ You can use FastPass+ selections for rides, character greeting spots (where lines can rival the most popular rides), fireworks, parades and shows.

➡ Some parks use a tiered FastPass+ system – you must choose one attraction from group one and two from group two.

➡ Make reservations for meals and character dining through My Disney Experience.

➡ Change your selections anytime through the website or mobile app. Once you've used the three prebooked FastPass+ attractions, you can add additional FastPass+ at on-site kiosks for free. But note you must use *all three* reserved selections before adding new ones.

➡ Do not waste your limited FastPass+ options on attractions that do not have long lines; carefully consider your day's plan to maximize the benefits of this system. Disney planning websites offer all kinds of tips. At the Magic Kingdom, lines for the most popular rides can be very long; same with Avatar: Flight of Passage at Animal Kingdom and Millennium Falcon: Smuggler's Run at Hollywood Studios.

➡ FastPass+ won't be available for Star Wars: Rise of the Resistance at Hollywood Studios until late 2020 or early 2021.

➡ Use your FastPass+ for sequential afternoon times for the super headliners and big-ticket attractions and use the morning, when your patience and energy are stronger and the lines are shorter, for other attractions.

➡ Check the website or call for updated information, as the system is always in flux.

52in tall to 'drive' on their own, which pretty much eliminates this ride's target audience.

A new *Tron*-themed ride will open here in 2021.

★**Space Mountain**　RIDE
(www.disneyworld.com; Magic Kingdom, Tomorrowland; theme-park admission required; ⊘9am-9pm, hours vary; ☒Disney, ☒Disney, ☒Lynx 50, 56) The Magic Kingdom's most popular ride is this indoor coaster that rockets its way through the star-studded galaxies of outer space. It's fast (in Disney terms at least) and while there are no long drops, the sudden turns and near darkness are what give this classic coaster its thrills. It's in Tomorrowland's most futuristic-looking structure. Come first thing or use FastPass+.

**Buzz Lightyear's
Space Ranger Spin**　RIDE
(www.disneyworld.com; Magic Kingdom, Tomorrowland; theme-park admission required; ⊘9am-9pm, hours vary; ☒Disney, ☒Lynx 50, 56) Join Buzz

TOP TIPS:
MAGIC KINGDOM

➡ Best attractions to use as your three FastPass+ selections are Peter Pan's Flight, Big Thunder Mountain Railroad, Splash Mountain, Space Mountain, Seven Dwarf's Mine Train, Princess Fairytale Hall and Enchanted Tales with Belle; alternatively, hit them when the park gates open.

➡ it's a small world, Mickey's PhilharMagic and Monsters, Inc Laugh Floor are air-conditioned attractions with short waits.

in his efforts to save the world from the evil Emperor Zurg. A cross between a ride and a video game, the aim is to shoot a laser at targets projected onto the screens. It's a tad clunky but brilliant fun.

◉ Liberty Square

Disney does the American Revolution and the birth of the USA with suitably elegant Federal and Colonial architecture surrounding the **Liberty Tree**. This live Southern Oak is a 130-plus-year-old homage to the famous Liberty Tree that stood on Boston Common but was cut down by loyalists in 1775.

All sorts of presidential memorabilia decorates the waiting area of the **Hall of Presidents**, where people are herded into a theater to watch a superpatriotic flick on US history, ending with every US president standing before you on stage. More fun is the regular **The Muppets Present...Great Moments in American History** show, a zany 8-minute trip through US history that takes place throughout the day on the square.

You can take to the water aboard the **Liberty Belle Riverboat**, which departs every half hour and goes for a 15-minute cruise around Tom Sawyer Island.

Haunted Mansion RIDE
(www.disneyworld.cm; Magic Kingdom, Liberty Square; theme-park admission required; ◷9am-9pm, hours vary; 🚌Disney, 🚶Disney, 🚌Lynx 50, 56) Liberty Square's best attraction is this classic favorite, which is a low-on-thrill, high-on-silly bit of fun. Cruise slowly past the haunted dining room, where apparitions dance across the stony floor, but beware of those hitchhiking ghosts – don't be surprised if they jump into your car unin-

vited. While it's mostly lighthearted ghosty goofiness, kids may be frightened by spooky preride dramatics.

🧭 Tours

Keys to the Kingdom WALKING
(📞407-939-8687; www.disneyworld.com; Magic Kingdom; tours $99, theme-park admission required; ◷8am, 8:30am, 9am & 9:30am) Quintessential Disney, this popular five-hour tour peeks into the Magic Kingdom's underground tunnels and backstage secrets – it's strictly for over-16s, so as not to destroy the magic! Lunch is included.

🎆 Festivals & Events

⭐**Happily Ever After** FIREWORKS
(www.disneyworld.com; Magic Kingdom; theme-park admission required; ◷8pm, hours vary; 🚌Disney, 🚶Disney, 🚌Lynx 50, 56) The grand finale to many a visitor's day in Magic Kingdom is the simply spectacular fireworks-and-light show that lights up the sky above Cinderella Castle. Images from Disney staples – *Frozen*, *Cinderella*, *The Hunchback of Notre Dame*, *Monsters, Inc* and others – are projected onto the castle walls, all to tell the story of determination and realizing your dreams.

Fun fact: the show costs $45,000 *a night* to put together and Disney is the second-biggest user of explosives in the United States after the Department of Defence. All this magic clearly takes a huge effort. Look out for Tinker Bell's flight toward the end of the show.

⭐**Festival of Fantasy** PARADE
(www.disneyworld.com; Magic Kingdom; theme-park admission required; ◷morning & afternoon daily, hours vary; 🚌Disney, 🚶Disney, 🚌Lynx 50, 56) The vivid pageantry of Fantasyland and its colorful cast of characters are part of this parade that makes its way down Main Street, USA. Characters from *Frozen*, *The Little Mermaid* and *Brave* feature, as do Rapunzel, Peter Pan and Sleeping Beauty. Plus Maleficent, the fire-breathing dragon.

Once Upon a Time LIGHT SHOW
(www.disneyworld.com; Magic Kingdom; theme-park admission required; ◷nightly, hours vary; 🚌Disney, 🚶Disney, 🚌Lynx 50, 56) Seasonally changing light-and-music show that's projected onto Cinderella Castle. It highlights Disney movies and characters, and takes place before or after Happily Ever After (aka the 'Nighttime Spectacular').

Mickey's Not-So-Scary Halloween Party

CARNIVAL

(☑407-939-5277; www.disneyworld.com; Magic Kingdom; adult/child $65/60, theme-park admission required; ☻select nights Sep & Oct; ▣Disney, ▣Disney, ▣Lynx 50, 56) Characters decked out in costumes, trick-or-treating and Halloween-inspired fireworks, parade and events. Discounted tickets available if purchased in advance online.

Mickey's Very Merry Christmas Party

CHRISTMAS

(☑407-939-5277; www.disneyworld.com; Magic Kingdom; prices vary; ☻select nights 7pm-midnight Nov-Dec; ▣Disney, ▣Disney, ▣Lynx 50 & 56, ▣Disney) Christmas songs, decorations and festivities Disney-style saturate Disney's Magic Kingdom park, including a Christmas parade, snowfall on Main Street and seasonal shows. Prices change annually and are posted nearer the event.

🛏 Sleeping

The fancier resorts near the Magic Kingdom are all on the monorail line; those further away (including Wilderness Lodge and the campsite) are a bit further away but easily reached by boat or bus.

★Disney's Fort Wilderness Resort

CAMPGROUND, CABIN $

(☑407-939-5277, 407-824-2900; www.disneyworld.com; 4510 N Fort Wilderness Trail; tent sites from $82, RV sites $108-158, 6-person cabins $387; ✳@🛜🛜🛜; ▣Disney, ▣Disney) Located in a huge shaded natural preserve, Fort Wilderness caters to kids and families with its hay rides, fishing and nightly campfire sing-alongs. Cabins sleep up to six and are hardly rustic, with cable TV and full kitchens, and while cars aren't allowed within the gates, you can rent a golf cart to toodle around in.

Staff keep a strict eye on after-hours noise, the grounds are meticulously maintained and there's a wonderfully casual and friendly state-park-like tone to the entire resort.

★Disney's Grand Floridian Resort & Spa

RESORT $$$

(☑407-939-5277; www.disneyworld.com; 4401 Floridian Way; r from $646; 🅿✳@🛜🛜; ▣Disney, ▣Disney, ▣Disney) One easy monorail stop from Magic Kingdom (and with good views of Cinderella Castle), the Grand Floridian rides on its reputation as the grandest, most elegant property in Disney World, and

it does indeed exude a welcome calm and charm – as well as a pianist in the five-story lobby playing jazz standards and Disney classics.

At its heart, though, this is Disney. Sparkling princesses ballroom dance across the Oriental rugs; exhausted children sit entranced by classic Disney cartoons; and babies cry. In contrast to the massive ferries from the Transportation & Ticket Center, small wooden boats shuttle folks back and forth to the Magic Kingdom.

Disney's Contemporary Resort

RESORT $$$

(☑407-824-1000, 407-939-5277; www.disneyworld.com; 4600 N World Dr; r from $654; 🅿✳@🛜🛜; ▣Disney, ▣Disney, ▣Disney) The granddaddy of Disney resorts, the Contemporary's futuristic A-frame opened in Walt Disney World® in 1971, but a series of upgrades means the name still applies. Rooms are among the nicest in Disney, with dark wood and warm tones offset by splashes of green and yellow. And yes, it's still cool to see the monorail zip silently through the lobby.

Balcony rooms front Magic Kingdom and an excellent top-floor restaurant lures folks with its drop-dead views of Disney's fireworks.

Disney's Wilderness Lodge

RESORT $$$

(☑407-824-3200, 407-939-5277; www.disneyworld.com; 901 Timberline Dr, Magic Kingdom; r from $370; 🅿✳🛜🛜; ▣Disney, ▣Disney) The handsome lobby's low-lit tepee chandeliers, hand-carved totem pole and dramatic 80ft fireplace echo national-park lodges of

---

ℹ STAYING ON BAY LAKE

The number-one advantage of staying at one of the resorts on Bay Lake is that they are one easy monorail or boat ride from Magic Kingdom – they're the only hotels at Walt Disney World® where you can get to classic Disney with no need for transfers. This may not sound like much, but when you're slogging home with three exhausted children or are desperate for a quick afternoon dip in the pool, it makes a world of difference. You can also take the monorail to Epcot, though you have to transfer at the Transportation & Ticket Center, and there are nonstop buses to Animal Kingdom and Disney's Hollywood Studios.

America's old West. But this is Disney, not John Muir country, so there's a fake geyser, singing waiters and – for those rooms overlooking the lobby – too much noise from the (not quite) Whispering Canyon cafe.

Disney's Polynesian Resort
RESORT $$$

(☑407-939-5277, 407-824-2000; www.disney world.com; 1600 Seven Seas Dr; r from $508; P❋@🖅🖅; 🖵Disney, 🖳Disney, 🖵Disney) A South Pacific theme runs through this resort, so think lots of (faux) bamboo, a jungle motif in the lobby and an abundance of co-conut-shell cups and shell necklaces in the store. The rounded lagoonside pool features a slide, a zero entrance perfect for little ones and an excellent view of Cinderella Castle, directly across the lagoon.

✗ Eating

Eating at Magic Kingdom is less about great food than theming, festive environs and character dining opportunities. There are snacks, fast-food options and table-service restaurants at every turn, but there's little here worth seeking out. For sit-down meals, make a reservation at one of Disney's Magic Kingdom Resorts (Disney's Polynesian, Disney's Contemporary, Disney's Grand Floridian) – they're an easy monorail or boat hop from Magic Kingdom.

Gaston's Tavern
AMERICAN $

(www.disneyworld.com; Magic Kingdom; mains $8-10, theme-park admission required; ◷9am-park closing; 🖅🖪; 🖵Disney, 🖳Disney, 🖵Lynx 50, 56) The manliest of manly Disney characters gets a themed snack bar, where you can get fresh sandwiches and cinnamon rolls. Try Le Fou's Brew, Disney's counter to Universal's runaway hit Butterbeer.

Columbia Harbour House
AMERICAN $

(www.disneyworld.com; Magic Kingdom; mains $9-16, theme-park admission required; ◷11am-park closing; 🖅🖪; 🖵Disney, 🖳Disney, 🖵Lynx 50, 56) One of the better counter-service restaurants in the Magic Kingdom is this nautical-themed spot with an interior styled like an old boat. Seafood and fish make up the bulk of the menu (the grilled salmon is lovely), but there's also chicken, mac 'n' cheese and a decent hummus-and-tomato sandwich.

Sleepy Hollow
AMERICAN $

(www.disneyworld.com; Magic Kingdom; snacks $6-9, theme-park admission required; ◷9am-park closing; 🖵Disney, 🖳Disney, 🖵Lynx 50, 56) This small walk-up 'window' produces a yummy ice-cream sandwich with oozing vanilla ice cream squished between warm, fresh-baked chocolate-chip cookies. Look for the brick house in Liberty Square, just across the bridge from Cinderella Castle. Ideal snacks for the fireworks.

★ Jungle Navigation Co Ltd Skipper Canteen
INTERNATIONAL $$

(☑407-939-5277; www.disneyworld.com; Magic Kingdom; mains 19-36; ◷11:30am-9pm) This adventure-themed spot has three delightful areas based around boat skippers' tropical headquarters in the days of boat exploration. Enjoy a meal in the Secret Society of Adventurers Room, the Jungle Room or the Mess. It's the most atmospheric of options in the park and the meals are large, but by far the healthiest.

The menu features 'sustainable fish' and Skip's Beefy Bakes pasta.

Liberty Tree Tavern
AMERICAN $$

(☑407-939-3463; www.disneyworld.com; Magic Kingdom; mains $20-39, theme-park admission required; ◷11am-park closing; 🖵Disney, 🖳Disney, 🖵Lynx 50, 56) One of the better options in the Magic Kingdom is this Colonial-themed restaurant with six dining rooms that commemorate an important figure from US history. The food – classic American fare from Revolutionary Meatloaf to the Pilgrim's Feast (basically a Thanksgiving Day dinner of carved turkey breast) – is very tasty. Plus beer and wine are served.

★ Be Our Guest
AMERICAN $$$

(☑407-939-3463; www.disneyworld.com; Magic Kingdom; mains breakfast $29, lunch $6-19, prix-fixe dinner adult/child $62/37; ◷8am-10:30am, 11am-2:30pm & 4-10pm, hours vary; 🖅🖪; 🖵Disney, 🖳Disney, 🖵Lynx 50, 56) Set inside the Beast's marvelously detailed castle, this experience is a must for *Beauty and the Beast* fans. Breakfast and lunch are a counter-service affair, but the table-service dinner is a treat. Specialties in the three-course prix-fixe plan include the French onion soup, the pork tenderloin and the dark chocolate truffle.

Come for quick-service lunch when the door opens or expect upwards of two hours' wait; reservations are accepted for dinner only, but you'll need to make them as close to six months in advance as you can. The Beast makes regular appearances and after your meal you can explore his castle and have your picture taken with him in his study.

Cinderella's Royal Table
AMERICAN $$$

(📞407-934-2927; www.disneyworld.com; Cinderella Castle, Magic Kingdom; adult/child from $75/45; ⏰8-10:15am, 11:30am-2:50pm & 4-10:20pm, hours vary; 📶♿; 🚃Disney, ⛴Disney, 🚌Lynx 50, 56) Cinderella greets guests and sits for a portrait (included in the price), and a sit-down meal with princesses (Aurora, Ariel and Snow White) is served upstairs. The food's good, but it's the sight of those deliriously happy kids in princess costumes that makes it special. This is the only restaurant in the castle – make reservations six months in advance.

Crystal Palace
AMERICAN $$$

(📞407-939-3463; www.disneyworld.com; Magic Kingdom; buffet adult/child $55/36, theme-park admission required; ⏰8-10:45am, 11:30am-2:45pm & 3:15-9:15pm, hours vary; 🚃Disney, ⛴Disney, 🚌Lynx 50, 56) The buffet at this character meal inside Magic Kingdom is surprisingly tasty. At lunch, there's a wide selection of salads, glazed carrots, mashed potatoes and green beans, as well as a carving station with ham and steak. The real draw, though, is the glass-enclosed garden atmosphere and Winnie-the-Pooh and friends mingling around the tables.

🔒 Shopping

Bibbidi Bobbidi Boutique
COSMETICS

(📞407-939-7895; www.disneyworld.com; Magic Kingdom; hair & makeup from $79; ⏰10am-8pm, hours vary) Inside Cinderella Castle, fairy godmothers finalize your kid's transformation from shorts and T-shirt to bedazzling princess with fanciful hairstyling and makeup.

Girls aged from three to 12 can choose from the Crown (hair and makeup from $79), the Carriage (add a store-branded t-shirt, from $99), the Courtyard (add tutu, from $149) or the Castle (hair, makeup, nails, full costume and photograph, from $199). For boys, there's the Knight Package (hair, a sword and a shield, $19), whose deluxe version ($79) includes a knight outfit. It's a more expensive and elaborate version of the spiky green hair or a pink updo and Disney sequins ($10 to $20) at the Harmony Barber Shop on Magic Kingdom's Main Street. There's a second Bibbidi Bobbidi Boutique in Disney Springs.

ℹ Getting There & Away

The only direct way to get to Magic Kingdom is by water taxi or monorail from Disney's Contemporary Resort, Disney's Grand Floridian or Disney's Polynesian Resort; by water taxi from Disney's Fort Wilderness Resort and Disney's Wilderness Lodge; by passenger ferry or monorail from the Transportation & Ticket Center; or by bus from any Disney resort hotel or the Transportation & Ticket Center.

If you drive, you *must* park at the Transportation & Ticket Center and then take the monorail, bus or the ferry to the park. With its massive parking lot and endless lines for bus shuttles, the Transportation & Ticket Center, however, can be unbearable, with tempers on edge and impatient people – and you'll pay $22 a day for the privilege.

Consider hopping on the monorail or water launch to a Magic Kingdom resort and then taking a cab to your hotel. If you coordinate reserved breakfast or dinner at one of these resorts, and many offer character meals, this works particularly nicely, and you can park at resort hotels free of charge if you have restaurant reservations. Note that you can get to Magic Kingdom via monorail from Epcot, but you must switch trains at the Transportation & Ticket Center.

For the first hour after opening, a horse-drawn carriage or old-fashioned car carries folk back and forth down Main Street, USA, from the entrance gate to Cinderella Castle. The open-air Walt Disney World® Railroad follows the perimeter of the park and stops at Main Street, USA, Fantasyland and Frontierland.

Disney's Hollywood Studios

Hollywood's Golden Age is the thematic inspiration for Disney's Hollywood Studios (📞407-939-5277; www.disneyworld.com; 351 S Studio Dr, Walt Disney World®; $109-129, prices vary daily; ⏰9am-8pm, hours vary; 🚃Disney, ⛴Disney), which was Disney's response to the announcement that Universal would build an Orlando version of its successful theme park in Hollywood. Disney-MGM Studios opened in 1989 (Universal Studios in 1990) and through the art-deco entrance we were transported into an ersatz Hollywood of the 1930s: there's Sunset Boulevard, Grauman's Chinese Theater and the Brown Derby.

Hollywood's heyday may provide the ambience, but this park is all about contemporary attractions. In 2008 the name was changed following the acquisition of Pixar, which brought *Toy Story, Monsters, Inc,*

Finding Nemo and *The Incredibles* into the fold, but they've all since been overshadowed by the opening in August 2019 of Star Wars: Galaxy's Edge.

◎ Sights & Activities

◎ Sunset Boulevard

The heart of the original park evokes the glamour of 1940s Hollywood. There are lots of eating options, as well as some of the park's better rides.

★ Rock 'n' Roller

Coaster Starring Aerosmith   RIDE
(www.disneyworld.com; Disney's Hollywood Studios; theme-park admission required; ◎ 9am-9pm, hours vary; 🚌 Disney, 🚇 Disney) One of the best indoor coasters in Orlando, where you take off up a ramp, going from 0mph to 57mph in three seconds before twisting into an inversion at a g-force of 5. A bunch of loops and twists later and you've arrived – all to a raucous Aerosmith soundtrack. Not for the fainthearted: the speed and twists are one thing, but doing them in semi-darkness will put others off. Not us, though. Can we go again? It's at the top of Sunset Boulevard.

Twilight Zone
Tower of Terror   RIDE
(www.disneyworld.com; theme-park admission required; ◎ 9am-9pm, hours vary; 🚌 Disney, 🚇 Disney) On your tour of this now decrepit Hollywood hotel, the elevator taking you to the 13th floor experiences a series of strange events, including sudden drops and lifts and then… OK, we don't want to give anything away, but this is a brilliantly executed ride, full of minutely observed detail. From the top, you can get a (quick) glimpse of the whole park.

◎ Star Wars: Galaxy's Edge

The transformation of this 14-acre backlot into the **Black Spire Outpost**, a spaceport on remote Batuu, is Disney's most ambitious technological accomplishment to date. Every detail is remarkable, from the 200,000 sq ft of rock work to the live actor performances. There's a full-scale *Millennium Falcon*, lots of themed retail outlets and two superb rides – Millennium Falcon: Smuggler's Run and Star Wars: Rise of the Resistance. It's a new standard in immersive theme park design.

Although the Black Spire Outpost is an entirely new creation, there are strong echoes of the infamous Mos Eisley spaceport about it, which will no doubt satisfy even the most ardent *Star Wars* fans. In this 'wretched hive of scum and villainy', the First Order is on the lookout for any hint of rebellion, and visitors are automatically immersed in the storyline as soon as they enter the land. Get in the way of the fierce-looking

---

DISNEY PARADES, FIREWORKS & LIGHT SHOWS

It takes a little bit of planning to coordinate your schedule to hit Disney's parades and nighttime spectaculars. Note that times vary according to day and season. In addition to the following cornerstones, check www.disneyworld.com for holiday celebrations and specialty parties.

Festival of Fantasy (p272) Elaborate floats and dancing characters, including Dumbo, Peter Pan and Sleeping Beauty.

Happily Ever After (p272) This fireworks and light-show extravaganza (often promoted as the 'Nighttime Spectacular') is the last word in Disney displays and the grand finale to many a visit.

Fantasmic (p278) A water, music and light show featuring Mickey Mouse as the Sorcerer's Apprentice from *Fantasia* using all kinds of wizardry to defeat a cast of Disney villains.

Star Wars: A Galactic Spectacular (https://disneyworld.disney.go.com/entertainment/hollywood-studios/star-wars-galactic-spectacular/; Disney's Hollywood Studios; ◎ nightly, hours vary) A firework and light show topped off with projected clips of the *Star Wars* movies on the Chinese Theater.

Rivers of Light: We Are One (p282) Animal Kingdom's light show features its beautiful baobab tree, the 'tree of life.'

stormtroopers or an angry-looking Kylo Ren and they will bark at you to move.

You can declare your loyalty for either side at the **Resistance Supply** or the **First Order Cargo**, design your own lightsaber at **Savi's Workshop** or get that droid you've always wanted at the **Droid Depot**. For everything else there's the **Black Spire Outfitters**.

The idea is that you can still be part of the experience without getting on either of the rides, which, at the time of writing, were the most popular by far across all four parks.

★**Star Wars:**
Rise of the Resistance   RIDE
(www.disneyworld.com; Disney's Hollywood Studios, Star Wars: Galaxy's Edge; theme-park admission required; ⊘ 9am-9pm, hours vary; 🔲 Disney, 🔲 Disney) Rise of the Resistance isn't so much a ride as a 20-minute-long, multi-part piece of high-tech theater that seamlessly blends four ride systems and a stunning walk-through experience that drew gasps of delighted wonder when we visited. The plot is straightforward: you're a crew member on a transport that is captured by the First Order and, after being tractor-beamed into the belly of an Imperial Star Destroyer, your task is to escape.

Disney's imagineers flexed their considerable creative muscles to create the experience, which combines cutting-edge audio-animatronics, live actor performances and a trackless vehicle that interacts convincingly with the surrounding environment, so when you come face to face with a pair of menacing AT-ATs, the vehicle jerks back and turns to find a better escape route.

The detail of the actual physical structures you move around in is extraordinary, and equally matched by the quality of the graphics and imagery. We don't want to give too much away, but there are a couple of moments of pure wish fulfilment for *Star Wars* fans that make this one of the very best experiences Disney has ever created.

In order to deal with the massive numbers looking to get on the ride, Disney instituted a virtual line system, which is available through the My Disney Experience app but only works once you're in the park. You join a boarding group and then receive a time slot for joining the ride. At the time of writing, the boarding groups were usually filled pretty quickly after the park opened, so you'll have to be there early to have a

chance. Until the hype dies down, you won't be able to use FastPass+ to gain entry.

Millennium Falcon:
Smuggler's Run   RIDE
(www.disneyworld.com; Disney's Hollywood Studios, Star Wars: Galaxy's Edge; them-park admission required; ⊘ 9am-9pm, hours vary; 🔲 Disney, 🔲 Disney) Climb aboard the mythical *Millennium Falcon* and your crew of six – two pilots, two gunners and two engineers – try to fly the 'fastest hunk of junk in the galaxy' on a less-than-legit mission. The special effects (including jumping to light speed) are very good, but this is effectively an immersive video game where you just press a lot of buttons, which may disappoint some. However, the thrill of being aboard a full-scale version of Han and Chewy's ship might suffice.

On board, everything is instantly recognizable to fans, not least the table in the main hold, which has the chess-type Dejarik laid out just as it does in the films (you can buy the game in one of the retail outlets).

⊙ Hollywood Boulevard & Echo Lake

This is where you'll find the Star Wars-themed **Star Tours** (FastPass+), one of Disney's best 3D-simulated experiences, the over-the-top stunt show **Indiana Jones Epic Stunt Spectacular** (FastPass+), held in a huge outdoor theater, and Frozen's **For the First Time in Forever Sing-Along**.

Star Tours:
The Adventure Continues   RIDE
(www.disneyworld.com; Disney's Hollywood Studios; theme-park admission required; ⊘ Disney's Hollywood Studios hours; ✚; 🔲 Disney, 🔲 Disney) Board a *StarSpeeder 1000* and blast into the galaxy at this 3D *Star Wars*-themed simulation ride.

Jedi Training:
Trials of the Temple   MARTIAL ARTS
(www.disneyworld.com; Disney's Hollywood Studios; theme-park admission required; ⊘ from 9am, up to 15 times daily) Children, aged four to 12, don brown robes, pledge the sacred Jedi oath and grab a lightsaber for on-stage training by a Jedi Master. It's first-come, first-served, so get to Disney's Hollywood Studios when gates open and line up at the Indiana Adventure Outpost, near the 50's Prime Time Café, to sign up for one of the many daily classes.

◉ Toy Story Land

Everything is oversized in this 11-acre land – but that's because you've been shrunk to the size of a toy and are now in Andy's backyard, where you can play with all the other toys from the *Toy Story* universe.

Alien Swirling Saucers is a pleasant tea-cup ride, while **Slinky Dog Dash** is a family-friendly roller coaster. This is a lovely part of the park, especially for younger kids.

Toy Story Midway Mania! RIDE
(www.disneyworld.com; Disney's Hollywood Studios; theme-park admission required; ⊙9am-9pm, hours vary; 🚍Disney, 🚤Disney) Don your 3D glasses and you'll be transported inside Andy's toy box, where from inside your car you shoot at all kinds of carnival targets to rack up points.

✯ Festivals & Events

Fantasmic LIGHT SHOW
(☑407-939-5277; www.disneyworld.com; Disney's Hollywood Studios; theme-park admission required; ⊙nightly; 🚻; 🚍Disney, 🚤Disney) This water, music and light show features Mickey Mouse as the Sorcerer's Apprentice from *Fantasia*, and involves him using all kinds of wizardry to defeat a cast of Disney villains. The plot's a bit weak but no matter: the effects are spectacular, and get a lot of oohs and aahs from the huge crowd.

Seating for the 25-minute show begins 90 minutes in advance, and even though the outdoor amphitheater seats more than 6000 people, it's always crowded.

✖ Eating

Disney's Hollywood Studios offers some of the most novel eating experiences. From a meal at a drive-in in your very own car, to enjoying hospitality in a 1950s kitchen, there's much themed fun to be had as you chomp down everything from a burger to upscale tapas.

★ Sci-Fi Dine-In Theater AMERICAN $$
(☑407-939-3463; www.disneyworld.com; Disney's Hollywood Studios; mains $17-33, theme-park admission required; ⊙11am-8:30pm; 🚻; 🚍Disney, 🚤Disney) Burgers, ribs and glow-in-the-dark drinks served drive-in style. Climb into your convertible Cadillac, order from the car hop, sip on a Lunar Landing and sit back for animations, a silly horror movie or sci-fi flick (on loop for 47 minutes). This is Disney theming at its best.

There's a handful of normal tables on the side, but if you want your table in a car, request one up to six months in advance.

★ 50's Prime Time Café AMERICAN $$
(☑407-939-3463; www.disneyworld.com; Disney's Hollywood Studios; mains $17-28, theme-park admission required; ⊙11am-park closing; 🚻; 🚍Disney, 🚤Disney) Step into a quintessential 1950s home with TVs, linoleum floors, some of the funkiest of funky retro furniture around and, of course, home-cooked meals, including Grandma's Chicken-Pot-Pie, Aunt Liz's Golden Fried Chicken and Mom's Old-Fashioned Pot Roast, served up on a Formica tabletop.

Waiters in pink plaid and white aprons banter playfully and admonish those diners who don't finish their meals, putting their elbows on the table with a sassy 'shame, shame, shame.' Such, such fun.

Hollywood Brown Derby Lounge TAPAS $$
(☑407-939-3463; www.disneyworld.com; Disney's Hollywood Studios; tapas $11-20; ⊙11am-park closing; 🚻; 🚍Disney, 🚤Disney) Upscale, small-bite menu with lump-crab cocktail, mussels and beef sliders, and an excellent selection of cocktails. It's generally pretty easy to snag a table at the bistro-style sidewalk patio, a great place to relax and people-watch over a flight of scotch, champagne, martinis or margaritas, or order a drink to go. Not exactly fast food, but reservations are not accepted.

Hollywood Brown Derby AMERICAN $$$
(☑407-939-3463; www.disneyworld.com; Disney's Hollywood Studios; mains $19-49, theme-park admission required; ⊙11:30am-park closing; 🚻; 🚍Disney, 🚤Disney) Semi-upscale surroundings modeled after the LA original, with an odd selection of gourmet eats ranging from a vegetarian pho (noodle soup) to charred fillet of beef and, of course, that Derby classic, the Cobb salad. This is heavy fare, not the place for a quick light lunch.

🍺 Drinking

Oga's Cantina BAR
(www.disneyworld.com; Disney's Hollywood Studios, Star Wars: Galaxy's Edge; alcoholic drinks $17-18, nonalcoholic drinks $7-13, theme-park admission required; ⊙9am-9pm, hours vary; 🚍Disney, 🚤Disney) The Black Spire Outpost's main watering hole is Oga's, a popular gathering spot for bounty hunters, smugglers and other rogues. For regular visitors, this bar in the

MEETING DISNEY CHARACTERS

Folks of all ages pay a lot of money and spend hours in line to get their photo taken with Winnie-the-Pooh, Donald Duck, Elsa and other Disney favorites – Mickey and Minnie are still top of most wish lists. If this is what makes you swoon (versus just spotting them from a short distance, which can also be fun), see www.disneyworld.com. There is a plethora of opportunities to sidle up next to a princess, villain or furry friend.

Note that character experiences in the resort hotels do not require theme-park tickets.

Disney Character Dining (☑ 407-939-3463; www.disneyworld.com; Walt Disney World® theme parks & resort hotels; prices vary widely) Make reservations up to six months (yes, six!) for any of the 20 or so character-dining meals at Walt Disney World®. They're hardly relaxing and are rather loud and chaotic. Characters stop at each table to pose for a photograph and interact briefly. Disney's Grand Floridian Resort (p273) has a buffet breakfast featuring Winnie-the-Pooh, Mary Poppins and Alice in Wonderland, plus it holds the **Perfectly Princess Tea Party**. There's a jam-packed breakfast and dinner with Goofy, Donald Duck and pals at **Chef Mickey's** in Disney's Contemporary Resort (p273); princesses mingle in Epcot's Norway at the Akershus Royal Banquet (p287); and the 100 Acre Wood folk come to Magic Kingdom's **Crystal Palace** for three meals a day.

Character Spots Each Walt Disney World® theme park has specific spots where Disney characters hang out, and you can simply hop in line (and wait and wait) to meet them and have your photo taken. A few character spots, such as **Enchanted Tales with Belle**, include a short performance. In addition, check your map and Times Guide for times and locations of scheduled character greetings, and always keep your eyes open – you never know who you'll see!

Cinderella's Royal Table (p275) Cinderella greets guests and sits for a formal portrait (included in the price), and a sit-down meal with princesses is served upstairs. This is the only opportunity to eat inside the iconic castle – make reservations six months in advance. Hours vary.

Chip 'n' Dale Campfire Singalong (p264) A campfire sing-along at Disney's Fort Wilderness Resort.

---

heart of Star Wars: Galaxy's Edge serves a mix of alcoholic and nonalcoholic drinks to a musical soundtrack provided by droid DJ R-3X. Keep your head down: there may be trouble.

❶ Getting There & Away

A paved waterfront walkway and a boat shuttle connect Disney's Hollywood Studios, Disney's BoardWalk, Disney Epcot resorts (BoardWalk Inn, Yacht & Beach Clubs, Swan & Dolphin) and Epcot. It is about a 25-minute walk from Epcot to Disney's Hollywood Studios along a pleasant path. Look for the sign near Jellyrolls and the Atlantic Dance Hall.

Disney buses provide transportation to other parks, hotels and the Transportation & Ticket Center, sometimes requiring a transfer.

You cannot take the monorail to Epcot and then walk or take a boat to Hollywood Studios unless you have a Park Hopper ticket. The monorail is at Epcot's front entrance, and access to Hollywood Studios is from Epcot's back entrance.

Disney's Animal Kingdom

Set apart from the rest of Disney both in miles and in tone, **Animal Kingdom** (☑ 407-939-5277; www.disneyworld.com; 2901 Osceola Pkwy, Walt Disney World®; $109-129, prices vary daily; ☺ 9am-7pm, hours vary; ☐ Disney) blends theme park and zoo, carnival and African safari, with a healthy dose of Disney characters, storytelling and transformative magic.

Animal Kingdom is made up of six 'lands': the Oasis, Discovery Island, DinoLand USA, Africa, Asia and Pandora – The World of Avatar. The 500-acre park has relatively few attractions, and the layout can be frustrating: to get to the themed areas, you are forced to double back through Discovery Island.

Due to the enormous popularity of the Pandora rides, guests are usually allowed in up to an hour before official opening, when most of Pandora is already up and running.

◎ Sights

★ Pandora – The World of Avatar AREA
(www.disneyworld.com; Animal Kingdom; theme-park admission required; ⊙9am-6pm, hours vary; 🖾Disney) Welcome to the Valley of Mo'ara, where floating islands and the beautifully lush vegetation leave you in no doubt that this is a land far away from earth – 4.3 light years away, to be exact. Drift slowly through the stunningly detailed bioluminescent forest on the Na'vi River Journey (p280) or soar through Pandora atop a banshee on Avatar: Flight of Passage (p280). This is James Cameron and Disney imagineers at their absolute best.

Avatar buffs will note that the setting is not connected to *Avatar* the movie or any of its characters, but to Pandora long after the events of the film: the Na'vi and the humans have sorted out their differences and are now collaborating to protect Pandora's fragile ecosystem, which is so exquisitely rendered around a giant floating mountain as to draw gasps from first-time visitors.

Inevitably, the two rides are *incredibly* popular and you'll want to use your Fast-Pass+ (booked as long in advance as possible) – but as they're both Tier A options, you can only pick one on any given day. Flight of Passage is by far the most memorable, but it has a height restriction of 44in, so if you're with little kids stick to Na'vi River Journey.

Pandora is beautiful during the day, but its otherworldly qualities really come out after sunset, when the bioluminescence makes you feel like you're on an alien planet. Which you are, of course.

★ Avatar: Flight of Passage RIDE
(www.disneyworld.com; Animal Kingdom; theme-park admission required; ⊙9am-6pm, hours vary; 🖾Disney) After a pre-flight briefing explaining the concept of pairing with a banshee, you and 15 other cadets enter a chamber where you each strap into a vehicle (that looks vaguely like a motorcycle), put on your 3D goggles and then soar above Pandora atop your own banshee. This is one of the best and most immersive rides of any theme park, anywhere.

Although now a few years old, the 3D visuals are still breathtaking. The jungle landscapes and seascapes feel completely real, and for added authenticity you can smell

the faint must of the undergrowth and, as you skim the surface of the water, you feel a light splash on your face. The seat pulsating beneath you gives the sensation of the banshee 'breathing' – just another layer of magic that helps you immerse completely into the experience.

This is one of the most popular rides in all of Walt Disney World®, so you'll want to use your FastPass+ as far in advance as possible. Another alternative for avoiding long lines is to get in line 30 minutes before closing time, when lines aren't as long and the park will let you ride even if you get on after the park has closed.

Na'vi River Journey RIDE
(www.disneyworld.com; Animal Kingdom; theme-park admission required; ⊙9am-6pm, hours vary; 🖾Disney) This slow meander through the bioluminescent world of Pandora is short on thrills but very high on beauty: over 4½ minutes in a four-seater boat you drift past glowing flora and mysterious fauna. The ride climaxes in an encounter with the Na'vi Shaman of Songs, Pandora's life force, wonderfully rendered in audio-animatronics.

Africa AREA
(www.disneyworld.com; Animal Kingdom; theme-park admission required; ⊙9am-6pm, hours vary; 🖾Disney) Board a jeep and ride through the African savanna on Kilimanjaro Safaris, pausing to look at zebras, lions, giraffes and more, all seemingly roaming free. This is one of the Animal Kingdom's most popular attractions, so come early or use your FastPass+.

Most of the park's live entertainment options are in Africa, including the long-running Festival of the Lion King, a song-and-dance performance based on the popular Disney animation set in its own theater.

The Gorilla Falls Exploration Trail passes gorillas, hippos, a great bat display and a hive of naked mole rats – nothing more than you'd find in any zoo, but those mole rats sure are cute.

Asia AREA
(www.disneyworld.com; Animal Kingdom; theme-park admission required; ⊙9am-6pm, hours vary; 🖾Disney) Home to two of Animal Kingdom's three most popular rides: Expedition Everest, a great roller coaster with a yeti twist, and Kali River Rapids, a water ride. Owls, peregrine falcons and many other birds dazzle audiences at Flights of Wonder. It's got

some cheesy dialogue, but the animals are spectacular as they zoom around over your head on cue.

Maharajah Jungle Trek is a self-guided path past Bengal tigers, huge fruit bats and Komodo dragons.

Discovery Island   AREA
(www.disneyworld.com; Animal Kingdom; theme-park admission required; ⏱9am-6pm, hours vary; 🖥Disney) The centrepiece of this land (and of the whole park) is the **Tree of Life**, a carefully constructed baobab tree that's 14 stories high and carved with over 325 animals. Paths at the base lead to the *Bugs' Life*–themed **It's Tough to Be a Bug!**, a 4D movie that includes periods of darkness, dry ice and flashing lights. It's a lot of fun, but little 'uns may find it all a bit too scary.

DinoLand USA   AREA
(www.disneyworld.com; Animal Kingdom; theme-park admission required; ⏱9am-6pm, hours vary; 🖥Disney) This bizarre dinosaur-themed section seems more like a tired carnival than Disney Magic, with garish plastic dinosaurs, midway games and 'Trilo-Bite' snacks, but **DINOSAUR** is a really fun jeep ride with a *Jurassic Park* twist.

Rafiki's Planet Watch   ZOO
(www.disneyworld.com; Animal Kingdom; theme-park admission required; ⏱9am-6pm, hours vary; 🚼; 🖥Disney) Veterinarians care for sick and injured animals at the **Conservation Station**. You can check out pet sheep and goats at **Affection Section**. On the **Habitat Habit!** trail check out the adorable, fist-sized tamarin monkeys. But ultimately, the **Wildlife Express Train** you take to get here might just be the best part of this Disney enigma.

Oasis   ZOO
(www.disneyworld.com; Animal Kingdom; theme-park admission required; ⏱9am-6pm, hours vary; 🚼; 🖥Disney) Oasis is the first themed section of Animal Kingdom. It has cool critters, including a giant anteater, but it's best to move along to other attractions and pause to enjoy the animals on your way out.

🛏 Sleeping

Along with Disney's value resorts, the hotels here are the most inconveniently located of all Disney hotels. They are the furthest from all the parks except Animal Kingdom and the only Disney transportation is by bus.

Disney's Coronado Springs Resort   RESORT $$
(☎407-939-1000, 407-939-5277; www.disney world.com; 1000 W Buena Vista Dr; r from $200; P❋@🛜🏊; 🖥Disney) Disney's only mid-range convention hotel is so big that it's served by three shuttle bus stops. Rooms are divided between the stylishly contemporary Gran Destino tower and the casita-style two- and three-story buildings spread throughout, some with private pools. The overall vibe is the traditional American Southwest, but the feel is much more contemporary. An excellent family option.

There's plenty of grass, and little beaches with hammocks. At the central pool, an open-air slide zooms down a Maya pyramid. Suites and casitas sleep up to five.

Disney's Animal Kingdom Lodge   RESORT $$$
(☎407-938-3000, 407-939-5277; www.disney world.com; 2901 Osceola Parkway Blvd; r from $400; P❋@🛜🏊; 🖥Disney) With an abutting 33-acre savanna parading a who's who of Noah's Ark past hotel windows and balconies, park rangers standing ready to answer questions about the wildlife, and African-inspired food being served at the recommended restaurants, this resort offers particularly fun and quirky theming.

Ask about storytelling and singing around the fire. If you want to see giraffes and ostriches out your room window, you'll have to reserve the more expensive savanna-view rooms, but anyone can enjoy the animals from the observation decks. Even if you're not staying here, swing by for a drink after an afternoon at Animal Kingdom.

🍴 Eating

Plenty of quick counter-service joints disguised behind African names and offering nods to a somewhat tribal feel define eating options at Animal Kingdom.

Yak & Yeti   ASIAN $$
(☎407-939-3463, 407-824-9384; www.disney world.com; Animal Kingdom; mains $14-18, theme-park admission required; ⏱11am-park closing; 🛜📷🚼; 🖥Disney) Sharing the name of Kathmandu's exclusive digs in the real Nepal, decorated with a vaguely Nepalese-infused decor, and serving a mix of Asian dishes like dim sum and Korean chicken, this recommended getaway at Mt Everest's base transports you from Disney to the Himalayas. The

food is surprisingly good and is one of the best bets for eating inside the park.

Satu'li Canteen INTERNATIONAL $$

(www.disneyworld.com; Animal Kingdom; mains $13-17; ⏲ 11am-closing; 🚍 Disney) In this Pandora-themed restaurant, the signature is to create your own bowl, where you pick a protein, base and sauce, and end up with, say, a super-healthy chicken, quinoa and chimichurri sauce bowl. Other options include things like cheeseburger *bao*, quesadillas or hot dogs. It's all a cut above typical theme park food.

Flame Tree Barbecue BARBECUE $$

(www.disneyworld.com; Animal Kingdom; mains $12-22, theme-park admission required; ⏲ 11am-6pm; 🛜 👶; 🚍 Disney) Counter-service barbecue ribs and chicken; a favorite with in-the-know Disney fans.

🍷 Drinking & Nightlife

Dawa Bar BAR

(www.disneyworld.com; Animal Kingdom; theme-park admission required; ⏲ 11am-park closing; 🛜 👶; 🚍 Disney) The best place in Animal Kingdom for a cocktail. Sidle up to the flat-roofed bar, kind of like an African 'shebeen,' order a sugarcane mojito and rest those Disney-weary bones.

☆ Entertainment

★ Finding Nemo: the Musical PERFORMING ARTS

(www.disneyworld.com; Animal Kingdom; theme-park admission required; ⏲ several shows daily; 👶; 🚍 Disney) Arguably the best show at Walt Disney World® and a favorite of both kids and adults, this sophisticated musical theater performance features massive and elaborate puppets on stage and down the aisles, incredible set design and fantastic acting.

The music was composed by Robert Lopez and Kristen Anderson-Lopez, who also wrote *Frozen's* Academy Award–winning 'Let It Go,' and the spectacular puppets were created by Michael Curry, the creative and artistic force behind the puppets in Broadway's *The Lion King*.

Rivers of Light: We Are One SHOW

(www.disneyworld.com; Animal Kingdom; ⏲ 7:15pm, 8:30pm, times vary) This sound-and-light show over water focuses on the theme of nature. It presents stunning effects, from fireflies flitting across the lake to 'spirit forms' of the world's animals, and is a fitting end to this little, tropical, ever-so-controlled and very animal-sanitized 'paradise.' Reserve ahead with your FastPass+.

❶ Getting There & Away

Disney buses stop at Animal Kingdom, but be warned that the ride here can be up to 45 minutes, maybe longer. There is parking just outside the park gates.

Epcot

If the Magic Kingdom is the most iconic of Disney's theme parks, **Epcot** (✆ 407-939-5277; www.disneyworld.com; 200 Epcot Center Dr, Walt Disney World®; $109-129, prices vary daily; ⏲ 9am-9pm, hours vary; 🚍 Disney, 🚝 Disney) – an acronym of Experimental Prototype Community of Tomorrow – is perhaps the closest to Walt Disney's own personal interests and vision.

There are no roller coasters screeching overhead, no parades or water rides. Instead this is a version of Walt's vision of the American city of the future, where self-driving cars and prefab solar-powered homes would be found inside a huge geodesic dome. This vision was pretty radical for the 1960s, but in the 2020s it's all a bit tired.

The good news is that Walt Disney World® knows it too, and is in the midst of a huge refurb of the park. The year 2020 saw the opening of Remy's Ratatouille Adventure, and 2021 will welcome a Guardians of the Galaxy indoor roller coaster and a new play-themed pavilion to replace the Wonders of Life showcase. The work is scheduled to be completed in time for the 50th anniversary celebrations in 2021, but until then you should be prepared for a much-diminished theme park.

Epcot is divided into two themed areas: **Future World**, divided into east and west and where most of the refurb is taking place; and **World Showcase**, a 40-acre spread where pavilions recreate 11 individual countries, complete with country-specific food, shopping and entertainment. For added authenticity, pavilion staff come from the countries they represent – it's all part of an international college program. It's like a permanent version of a World's Fair, another of Walt Disney's great interests.

There are two entrances (though only one is shown on the official map). The main entrance, next to the bus and monorail stations, sits at the landmark geodesic dome of Spaceship Earth in Future World (it, too, is getting a major overhaul). The back entrance ('International Gateway') is for those catching a boat from Disney's BoardWalk, Hollywood Studios and Disney Epcot resort hotels.

◉ Sights & Activities

★**World Showcase** AREA
(www.disneyworld.com; Epcot; theme-park admission required; ◷9am-6pm, hours vary; ⬚Disney, ⬚Disney, ⬚Disney) Who needs the hassle of a passport and jet lag when you can travel the world right here at Walt Disney World®? World Showcase, one of two themed sections of Epcot, comprises 11 countries arranged around a lagoon. Watch belly dancing in Morocco, eat pizza in Italy and buy personally engraved bottles of perfume in France, before settling down to watch fireworks about world peace and harmony. Disney was right: it truly is a small world after all.

Seasoned travelers may scoff at the ersatz quality of it all, but so what? The idea here is to prompt you to hop on a plane and explore the real thing; in the meantime, this is a fun way to show kids a little something about the world.

The best way to experience the World Showcase is to simply wander as the mood moves you, poking through stores and restaurants, and catching what amounts to Bureau of Tourism promotional films and gentle rides through some of the countries. Highlights include the **American Adventure** in the USA pavilion, a 30-minute dash through US history complete with stirring music, a huge screen and 35 audio-animatronic figures; travelling through Mexico with Donald Duck and his pals in **Gran Fiesta Tour Starring the Three Caballeros**; and the immensely popular **Frozen Ever After** boat ride in Norway.

The featured countries from left to right around the water are Mexico, Norway, China, Germany, Italy, USA ('The American Adventure'), Japan, Morocco, France, the UK and Canada.

★**Frozen Ever After** RIDE
(www.disneyworld.com; Norway, Epcot; ◷9am-6pm, hours vary) The hottest ride in the World Showcase is this *Frozen*-themed slow boat journey aboard a dragon-headed longboat through the film's familiar settings. There's all of your favorite tunes and some of the film's best-loved characters, brilliantly ren-

ⓘ WORLD SHOWCASE PASSPORT
....
If your kids' attention risks waning at World Showcase, you might consider investing $12 in the World Showcase Passport (available from vendors), which the kids can get stamped at every pavilion.

dered in animatronic form. The journey ends, inevitably, at Elsa's ice palace. The cold definitely won't bother you.

★**Soarin' Around the World** RIDE
(www.disneyworld.com; Future World, Epcot; theme-park admission required; ◷9am-6pm, hours vary; ⬚Disney, ⬚Disney, ⬚Disney) Soar up and down, hover and accelerate as the giant screen in front of you takes you over and around the globe. Sounds straightforward, but this is an extraordinarily visceral experience as aroma effects blast the smells of the earth at you as you ride (such as the elephants and grasses of Africa). Ask for a front-row seat; feet dangling in front of you can ruin the effect.

While not at all scary in terms of speed or special effects, people with agoraphobia or motion sickness may feel a bit uneasy. Reserve a FastPass+ or hit this first thing in the morning, as it's one of the best rides at Disney.

Mission: Space RIDE
(www.disneyworld.com; Future World, Epcot; theme-park admission required; ◷9am-6pm, hours vary; ⬚Disney, ⬚Disney) The year is 2036 and you're a test pilot at the International Space Training Center. You're assigned a seat in the four-person launch capsule and then it's liftoff. This is an intense simulator ride designed to replicate the g-force of takeoff and a moment of zero-gravity weightlessness. The ride's intensity may cause motion sickness, so choose orange to be on the spinning version of the ride or green on the non-spinning team.

Seas with Nemo & Friends Pavilion RIDE
(www.disneyworld.com; Future World, Epcot; theme-park admission required; ◷9am-6pm, hours vary; ⬚Disney, ⬚Disney, ⬚Disney) Kids under 10 won't want to miss the two *Nemo*-themed attractions at Epcot's Future World. Ride a clamshell through the ocean with Nemo on

TRAVEL WITH CHILDREN

The challenge for families vacationing in the Theme Park Capital of the World is digging through the overwhelming options and inflated rhetoric to find what best suits your time, budget and family. If time is limited, stick to Disney's iconic Magic Kingdom (p267) and the edgier, less-stressful Universal Orlando Resort, home to the marvelously themed Wizarding World of Harry Potter (p295).

Though part of the Disney magic is how it magically makes your money disappear, there are plenty of inexpensive highlights in and around Orlando. Tubing at **Kelly Park** (☑407-254-1902; www.ocfl.net/cultureparks; 400 E Kelly Park Rd, Apopka; per vehicle $3-5; ☉8am-8pm Mar-Oct, to 6pm Nov-Feb; 🚗), canoeing at Wekiwa Springs State Park (p321) and a visit to the lovely Bok Tower Gardens (p321) make perfect day trips. The free outdoor movie at Disney's Chip 'n' Dale Campfire Singalong (p264) is one of the best things at Disney. The science-is-fun experiences and exhibits at WonderWorks (p309) are also a good bet, especially for older kids.

Everything in Orlando is an opportunity to attract tourists, and eating is no exception. There are **character meals** both inside the parks and at resort hotels; **dinner shows** at Walt Disney World®, Universal Orlando Resort and venues around town; and **themed restaurants** offering everything from dining under asteroid showers to burgers and milkshakes in a mock drive-in theater.

You may be ready for bed once the sun sets, obsessively checking your watch to see if it's time yet to collapse, but there's more fun to be had. With the exception of Animal Kingdom, all of Disney's theme parks offer **light shows** or **fireworks**. Orlando's performing-arts scene includes excellent **children's theater**, Disney's Drawn to Life (p292) performs nightly, and Universal's Blue Man Group (p308) is full of silly shenanigans. Disney's BoardWalk, Disney Springs and Universal Orlando Resort's CityWalk all make for a festive evening, with street performers and plenty of eye candy, but if you've had enough adrena-

Seas with Nemo & Friends and talk face-to-face with Crush in the interactive **Turtle Talk with Crush**, a Disney highlight.

A small blue room with a large movie screen holds about 10 rows of benches with sitting room for kids in front. Crush talks to the children staring up at him, taking questions from the 'dude in the dark-blue shell' and cracking jokes about how sea grass gives him the bubbles. Dory shows up and gets squished against the screen by the whale, and there's plenty of silliness and giggling.

Test Track   RIDE
(www.disneyworld.com; Future World, Epcot; theme-park admission required; ☉9am-6pm, hours vary; 🚇 Disney, 🚌 Disney) Board a car and ride through heat, cold, speed, braking and crash tests. At one point a huge semi with blinding lights heads right for you, its horn blaring. When testing the acceleration, the car speeds up to 60mph within a very short distance, but there are few turns and no ups and downs like a roller coaster.

At the ride's entrance you can virtually design your own car, and at the exit you'll find all kinds of car-themed games and simulators.

Spaceship Earth   RIDE
(www.disneyworld.com; Future World, Epcot; theme-park admission required; ☉9am-6pm, hours vary; 🚇 Disney, 🚌 Disney) Epcot's iconic dome is home to this cult favorite ride that explores human progress and the development of communications. From cave paintings to computers, the history of human progress is tracked in slow-moving, kitschy, out-of-date animatronic detail. It's Western-centric, completely devoid of excitement and yet... there's always a line to get on.

At the time of writing there were vague plans to update this ride completely.

🎇 Festivals & Events

The perennially popular IllumiNations fireworks and laser show came to an end in late 2019. For the time being, it's been replaced by **Epcot Forever**, a tribute to the park's ideas and rides, but a more permanent replacement, A Celebration of Disney Music, will start soon.

Epcot International Food & Wine Festival   FOOD & DRINK
(☑407-939-5277; www.disneyworld.com; Epcot; theme-park admission required; ☉Aug-early Nov,

line for one day, kick back in small-town **Celebration** or **Winter Park**. Children appreciate the slow pace, and on a summer evening, after a day slogging through parks, sitting with a glass of wine while the children play in Celebration's lakefront fountain may just be heaven.

Sprinkle in the big-bang, high-energy fun judiciously. Yes, you might ride the Winnie-the-Pooh seven times in a row, and yes, you may never make it to the Finding Nemo musical in Animal Kingdom. If only we had gotten up earlier, if only we hadn't waited in line for that Mickey ice cream, if only we had scurried out of the park after the fireworks: if only, if only, if only we'd seen this, that and the other thing.

Forget it. There's too much, and you'll never win that game. In the end it's what you do that kids remember, not what you missed.

Baby Basics at the Parks

Hitting Orlando's theme parks with a baby in tow? Children three years and younger do not pay admission. Once in the gates, a few things help navigate your day.

Child Swap (Walt Disney World® and Universal Orlando Resort) Allows caregivers to wait in line together, and then take turns staying behind with a baby or child while the other rides. Perfect for families traveling with multiple-age children or for kids who want a parent to check out the scare-factor before riding. Other parks offer similar options, but can be a bit complicated, so ask the ride attendant.

Disney's Baby Care Centers (Disney theme parks) Toys and Disney cartoons. You can purchase diapers, over-the-counter children's medication and more, and there's a full kitchen.

SeaWorld's Baby Center (SeaWorld) The cute house with rocking chairs on the porch in Shamu's Happy Harbor, with similar facilities to Disney. Women only.

changing dates; 💻 Disney) Disney-fied food and drink from around the world. You need to pay park admission, and then pay anywhere from $3 to $10 for food samples of varying quality by chefs from 25 different countries. There are wine tastings, demonstrations and seminars. This is a very popular event – come early, expect crowds, and allow at least half a day.

Epcot International
Flower & Garden Festival   FAIR
(📞 407-939-5277; www.disneyworld.com; Epcot; theme-park admission required; ⊙ Mar-May; 💻 Disney) Spectacular Disney-themed topiary and garden displays, with 1200 species and 30m flowers and plants. All the countries in the World Pavilion celebrate spring with seasonal delicacies.

🛌 Sleeping

One of the best parts about this cluster of hotels on the shore of Crescent Lake is their easy access to restaurants and entertainment in Epcot, Hollywood Studios and Disney's BoardWalk. The area is pedestrian-friendly and it's a pleasant walk or an easy boat ride to Epcot and to Hollywood Studios.

Disney's Caribbean
Beach Resort   RESORT $$
(📞 407-939-5277, 407-934-7639; www.disneyworld.com; 900 Cayman Way, Walt Disney World®; r from $172; ❄🐾 🛌 Disney) A Disney taste of the islands means painted beds, pastel rooms, a food court that looks like a street festival during Carnival and a pool with a vague resemblance to ancient temple ruins. This hotel sits along 45-acre Barefoot Bay, and does not have convenient boat transportation to Epcot and Hollywood Studios.

Rooms, some pirate-themed, spread out among two-story, motel-like buildings.

⭐ Walt Disney World®
Swan & Dolphin Resort   RESORT $$$
(📞 407-934-4000; www.swandolphin.com; 1500 Epcot Resorts Blvd; r $200-650; 🅿❄@🛌; 💻 Disney, 🚤 Disney) These two Michael Graves–designed, high-rise luxury hotels, which face each other on Disney property and share facilities, offer a distinctly toned-down Disney feel but have many of the the Disney perks, including Magic Hours (where

a theme park opens early and closes late for guests at Disney hotels only). Large swan and dolphin statues grace the grounds.

Perched along the bay between Epcot and Hollywood Studios, these are the only non-Disney hotels next to a theme park; thus, the 'Magic Band' payment system is no good here – they need real dollars, not mouse money. They are also differently owned: Dolphin is a Sheraton property, Swan a Westin. Online and last-minute deals can save literally hundreds of dollars.

Disney's Riviera Resort
HOTEL $$$

(☑407-939-5277; www.disneyworld.com; 1080 Esplanade Ave, Walt Disney World®; r from $600) Disney's first resort hotel in seven years opened in late 2019 with a mature, European theme: think elegant tiles and soothing tones rather than primary colors and Disney characters. Beautiful furnishings and bedrooms burnished with Italian and French flavors make this one of the most adult of all Disney properties. It connects to the parks via the Disney Skyliner (p267).

Disney's Yacht Club Resort
& Disney's Beach Club Resort
RESORT $$$

(☑Beach Club 407-934-8000, Walt Disney World® 407-939-5277, Yacht Club 407-934-7000; www.disneyworld.com; 1700 & 1800 Epcot Resorts Blvd, Walt Disney World®; r from $457; ❈🛜🏊; 🚡Disney, 🚢Disney) These handsome sister resorts, on the water just a five-minute walk from Epcot, strive for that old New England beachside charm. The Victorian cottage-like Beach Club's rooms go for a summery tan-and-blue vibe, the nautically themed Yacht Club blue-and-white with laminate 'hardwood' floors. Both have been refurbished. Great pools – there's a sandy shore and slide off a ship's mast.

✖ Eating

Eating at Epcot is as much about the experience as the food, and many of the restaurants go overboard to create an atmosphere characteristic of their country. Cuisine here is a cut above that at other theme parks.

La Cantina de San Angel
MEXICAN $

(www.disneyworld.com; Mexico, Epcot; mains $12-14, theme-park admission required; ⊘11am-park closing; 🛜🔧; 🚡Disney, 🚢Disney) One of the best fast-food places in the park. Try the tacos, served with surprisingly tasty *pico de gallo* (fresh salsa of tomatoes, onion and

jalapeños) and fresh avocado. Great guacamole, too.

Les Halles
Boulangerie Patisserie
FRENCH $

(www.disneyworld.com; France, Epcot; snacks $6-14, theme-park admission required; ⊘9am-park closing; 🚡Disney, 🚢Disney) Most folks come for cakes, éclairs and cookies, but it also sells French-bread pizza, quiche and those baguette sandwiches that are ubiquitous in France, as well as wine and champagne.

Yorkshire County
Fish Shop
BRITISH $

(www.disneyworld.com; UK, Epcot; fish & chips $11.50, theme-park admission required; ⊘11:30am-park closing; 🛜🔧; 🚡Disney, 🚢Disney) Crispy fish with vinegar and Bass Ale at the walk-up window outside the pub in the UK pavilion of World Showcase.

★Tutto Gusto
ITALIAN $$

(☑407-939-3463; www.disneyworld.com; Italy, Epcot; mains $22-36; ⊘11:30am-9pm; ❈🛜) Full marks for this authentic Italian brasserie and wine bar. It oozes style and serves delicious small plates, including meats and cheeses. Definitely the place to come for an excellent glass of Italian wine and homemade pasta served at the bar, high bar tables or while you're nestled in a sofa. Recommended for dinner before the night spectaculars at Epcot.

Restaurant Marrakesh
MEDITERRANEAN $$

(☑407-939-3463; www.disneyworld.com; Morocco, Epcot; mains $21-33, theme-park admission required; ⊘11:30am-park closing; 🛜✎🔧; 🚡Disney, 🚢Disney, 🚢Disney) Belly dancers shimmy and shake past the massive pillars and around the tables of the Sultan's Palace, magnificently decorated with mosaic tiles, rich velvets and sparkling gold. While the beef kebabs, vegetable couscous and other basics are OK, the windowless elegance is a fun escape from the searing sun and kids love to join in the dancing.

La Hacienda de San Angel
MEXICAN $$

(☑407-939-3463; www.disneyworld.com; Mexico, Epcot; mains $25-33, theme-park admission required; ⊘4pm-park closing; 🔧; 🚡Disney, 🚢Disney, 🚢Disney) Authentic Mexican rather than Tex Mex, this lagoonside eatery is tops for location and features excellent specials from chicken to seared-meat specialties. Why not make a day of it with on-the-rocks margari-

DISNEY'S VALUE RESORTS

Five value resorts, the least-expensive Disney properties available (not including camping), have thousands of motel-style rooms and suites; are garishly decorated according to their theme; connect to all the parks by bus only; and cater to families and traveling school groups – expect cheerleader teams practicing in the courtyard or a lobby of teenagers wearing matching jerseys. You will definitely feel the difference because of the lower price: instead of proper restaurants, there are food courts and snack bars, and things are particularly bright, hectic and loud. Some value resorts offer family suites with two bathrooms and a kitchenette.

Disney's Art of Animation Resort (407-938-7000, 407-939-5277; www.disneyworld.com; 1850 Animation Way; r from $130; P ❄ @ 🎐 ❄; Disney) Inspired by four animated Disney classics (*Finding Nemo, Lion King, Cars* and *Little Mermaid*) and the newest of Disney's Value Resorts (finished in 2012), this dazzlingly bright hotel is the best bet for budget-conscious Disney travel.

Disney's All-Star Resorts Three self-contained hotels (three of Disney's five 'value' accommodations options); take your pick between movie, music and sports themes.

Disney's Pop Century Resort (407-939-5277, 407-938-4000; www.disneyworld.com; 1050 Century Dr; r from $120; P ❄ @ 🎐 ❄; Disney) Each section pays homage to a different decade of the late 20th century, with massive bowling pins that extend beyond the roof and giant Play Doh.

---

tas, ranging from avocado-infused to a classic with cactus lemongrass salt on the rim?

Tokyo Dining
SUSHI **$$**

(407-939-3463; www.disneyworld.com; Japan, Epcot; mains $21-34, theme-park admission required; 11am-park closing; Disney, Disney, Disney) The delicate business of good sushi is the mainstay at this coolly elegant restaurant, but you can also get teriyaki, tempura and other Japanese classics. Try for a seat by the windows overlooking the pavilion – much better than by the screens that display a rotating mix of iconic Japanese sites.

★ Monsieur Paul
FRENCH **$$$**

(407-939-3463; www.disneyworld.com; France, Epcot; mains $41-47, prix fixe $89; theme-park admission required; 5:30-9pm; Disney, Disney, Disney) This exemplary French restaurant atop the France Pavilion bears the imprint of French culinary royalty. Jérôme Bocuse, son of legendary chef Paul, serves up exquisite dishes that would pass muster even in the most discerning Parisian restaurant. The only reminder that you're in Disney is if you sit by the window looking down on World Showcase.

Teppan Edo
JAPANESE **$$$**

(407-939-3463; www.disneyworld.com; Japan, Epcot; mains $30-38, theme-park admission required; 11am-park closing; 🛗; Disney, Disney, Disney) Chefs toss the chicken, fling the

chopsticks and frenetically slice and dice the veggies in this standard cook-in-front-of-you eatery next to Japan's gardens. It's housed in a stunning Japanese building, decked out in a black-and-red color theme and with contemporary flair. Its sister restaurant, Tokyo Dining (p287), is next door.

Akershus Royal Banquet Hall
NORWEGIAN **$$$**

(407-939-3463; www.disneyworld.com; Norway, Epcot; buffet adult/child $63/41, theme-park admission required; 8-11am, noon-3:30pm & 5-8:30pm; Disney, Disney) Join Disney princesses (a selection of Snow White, Cinderella, Belle, Aurora or Ariel) for a Norwegian-inspired feast in a medieval castle setting – Disney-style, of course, so you'll find pizza and Minute Maid lemonade with a glowing Ariel alongside Norwegian meatballs with lingonberries. It's one of the better character meals, both in terms of ambience and food.

Le Cellier Steakhouse
STEAK **$$$**

(407-939-3463; www.disneyworld.com; Canada, Epcot; mains $34-57, theme-park admission required; 12:30pm-park closing; 🎐🛗; Disney, Disney, Disney) If you love meat, this place is for you. Juicy filet mignons, rib-eyes and a tasty New York strip loin...you get the picture. Dark and cavernous, with stone walls and lanterns, it makes a good spot to escape the heat, but the dense sauces and decadent desserts might not be the best fuel to get you through the day.

Biergarten GERMAN $$$

(📞407-939-3463; www.disneyworld.com; Germany, Epcot; buffet adult/child $46/29; theme-park admission required; ⏲noon-9pm; 🚌🚴; 🚊Disney, 🚤Disney, 🚝Disney) Satisfy a hearty appetite with a buffet of classic German dishes, including sausage, sauerkraut, *spaetzle* (egg-noodle dumplings) and a particularly good pretzel bread, all washed down with a massive stein of brew. The restaurant interior is made to look like an old German village, with cobblestones, trees and a Bavarian oompah band in the evening. *Guten appetit!*

Drinking & Nightlife

★ **La Cava del Tequila** BAR

(📞407-939-3463; www.disneyworld.com; Mexico, Epcot; theme-park admission required; ⏲11am-park closing; 🚊Disney, 🚤Disney, 🚝Disney) Pop in for a cucumber, passion fruit or blood-orange margarita. Can't decide? Try a flight of margaritas or shots. The menu features more than 220 types of tequila, and it's a cozy, dark spot, with tiled floors, Mexican-styled murals and a beamed ceiling.

La Cava is connected to San Angel Inn, a full-service, sit-down restaurant, but it does not take reservations.

Entertainment

Awesome Planet CINEMA

(www.disneyworld.com; Epcot, Future World; theme-park admission required; ⏲9am-6pm, hours vary; 🚊Disney) A 10-minute tribute to the wonder of planet earth delivered as a realtor's sales pitch, Awesome Planet does exactly what it says on the can, with humor. Ty Burrell, aka Phil Dunphy from *Modern Family,* tells the earth's four-billion-year-old story in Disney-like wonder and with stunning camerawork made even better by the huge screen.

The film climaxes with an appeal to do what we can to reverse the threat of climate change and protect this pretty awesome place.

❶ Getting There & Away

A pleasant, well-lit, paved waterfront path or water taxi connects Epcot to Hollywood Studios, Disney's BoardWalk and Epcot resorts. The monorail runs a direct line between Epcot and the Transportation & Ticket Center; from there, catch a monorail, ferry or bus (slower) to Magic Kingdom. Disney buses depart from Epcot's main gate to Disney resorts, Hollywood Studios and Animal Kingdom.

❶ Getting Around

Within the park, a ferry shuttles folks to and from International Gateway from two boat docks just outside Future World.

Typhoon Lagoon & Blizzard Beach

In addition to the four theme parks, Disney boasts two distinctly themed water parks. Of the two, Blizzard Beach boasts the better

---

INTERACTIVE DISNEY

Disney parks offer self-paced, treasure-hunt-styled experiences that attract fans of all ages.

Sorcerers of the Magic Kingdom (Magic Kingdom) Join Merlin in his efforts to find and defeat Disney villains. Key cards activate hidden game portals throughout Magic Kingdom and the spell cards work magic. Stop by the firehouse by the main gate on Main Street to sign up.

Pirates Adventure – Treasure of the Seven Seas (Magic Kingdom) Pick up a talisman at the Crow's Nest (Adventureland) and help Captain Jack collect the pirate gold.

Agent P's World Showcase Adventure (Epcot) *Phineas and Ferb*–themed game. Make the beer steins in Germany sing, see the soldiers dance and activate surprises from China to the UK.

Wilderness Explorers (Animal Kingdom) Pick up a Wilderness Explorers Handbook and follow the adventures of Russell and Dug the dog (from the movie *Up!*) through jungles, forests and woods while completing self-guided activities. Collect a badge as a reward. Grab the guide from Wilderness Explorer stops or from 'headquarters,' on the bridge between Discovery Island and the Oasis.

thrills and speed, but Typhoon Lagoon has the far superior wave pool, a fantastic lazy river and tots' play area, and plenty of room to splash on the beach.

Be prepared to spend upwards of 30 minutes in line for a ride that's over in less than a minute, and take those wait times seriously – if it says the wait is 60 minutes, it's 60 minutes. Yes, 60 minutes for one slide. Both parks have fast-food restaurants and an outdoor pool bar.

Disney's water-park hours vary seasonally and by the day, but are generally open from 10am to 5pm and from 9am to 10pm in the summer. From late October through March one water park is closed for refurbishment.

◉ Sights

Typhoon Lagoon   AMUSEMENT PARK
(☑ 407-560-4120, 407-939-5277; www.disney world.com; 1145 Buena Vista Dr, Walt Disney World®; adult/child $73/63, prices vary daily; ◷ hours vary; ▣ Disney) An abundance of palm trees, a zero-entry pool with a white sandy beach, high-speed slides and the best wave pool in Orlando make this one of the most beautiful water parks in Florida. The most thrilling slide of them all is the **Crush 'n' Gusher water coaster**, but little ones will love floating along **Castaway Creek** and splashing at **Ketchakiddee Creek**.

Blizzard Beach   AMUSEMENT PARK
(☑ 407-560-3400, 407-939-5277; www.disney world.com; 1534 Blizzard Beach Dr, Walt Disney World®; adult/child $73/63, incl in Water Park Fun & More with Magic Your Way theme park ticket; ◷ hours vary; ▣ Disney) The newer of Disney's two water parks, themed as a melted Swiss ski resort complete with a ski lift, Blizzard Beach is the 1980s Vegas Strip hotel to Typhoon Lagoon's Bellagio. At its center sits **Mt Gushmore**, home to **Summit Plummet**, a 12-story free-fall slide with speeds up to 55mph.

ⓘ Information

Swimsuits with buckles or metal parts aren't allowed on most of the rides. Hours vary by day and by season; call the individual parks for current hours. From October through March, only one Disney water park is open at a time.

You can buy individual park tickets; Park Hopper Plus tickets include entrance to both the water parks.

ⓘ Getting There & Away

Disney buses stop at both Typhoon Lagoon and Blizzard Beach, and there is complimentary self-parking at both parks.

Disney's BoardWalk

The quarter-mile-long **Disney's BoardWalk** (☑ 407-939-5277; www.disneyworld.com; 2101 Epcot Resorts Blvd, Walt Disney World®; ▣ Disney, ▣ Disney) area is located across from Epcot and along Crescent Lake. It's designed to echo a waterfront promenade of turn-of-the-century New England seaside resorts. On Thursday to Saturday evenings magicians, jugglers and musicians give a festive vibe, and there are a handful of good restaurants and bars. Pick up a doughnut or cute li'l Mickey Mouse cakes at the bakery, and toot around on a surrey-with-the-fringe-on-top bike.

Far less harried and crowded than Disney Springs, Disney World's entertainment district is free to the public, and the bridge connecting the boardwalk to the Yacht and Beach club is a good spot to watch the Epcot fireworks.

⌕ Sleeping & Eating

★**Disney's BoardWalk Inn**   RESORT $$$
(☑ 407-939-5277; www.disneyworld.com; 2101 Epcot Resorts Blvd; r from $550; ⓟ ⊛ ✳ @ ⓢ ✳; ▣ Disney, ▣ Disney) This resort embodies the seaside charm of the 1930s Atlantic City Boardwalk in its heyday, with a waterfront the color of saltwater taffy, tandem bicycles with candy-striped awnings, and even a splintery boardwalk. The lovely lobby features sea-green walls, hardwood floors and vintage seating areas. Elegant rooms have a terrace or balcony.

The resort is divided into two sections, the Inn and the Villas; the Inn, with cute picket-fenced suites, quiet pools and plenty of grass, is far nicer and subdued. Accommodations range from rooms sleeping up to five to two-bedroom cottages.

Flying Fish   SEAFOOD $$$
(☑ 407-939-3463, 407-939-2359; www.disney-world.com; Disney's BoardWalk; mains $33-59; ◷ 5-9:30pm; ⚆ ♿; ▣ Disney) Specializing in complicated and innovative seafood dishes, Flying Fish is one of the best upscale dining spots at Disney. It's a contemporary, slick spot with a modern ocean theme (note the bubble chandeliers). Be sure to reserve

ahead. Kids' meals are significantly cheaper (from $14 to $23).

The oak-grilled salmon and plancha-seared Hokkaido scallops are two of the most popular dishes.

Drinking & Nightlife

★ Belle Vue Room BAR
(☑407-939-6200; www.disneyworld.com; 2101 Epcot Resorts Blvd, Disney's BoardWalk Inn; ⊘6:30-11am & 5pm-midnight; ▣Disney, ▣Disney) On the 2nd floor of Disney's BoardWalk Inn (p289), this is an excellent place for a quiet drink. It's more like a sitting room: you can relax and play a board game, listen to classic radio shows such as *Lone Ranger,* or simply take your drink to a rocking chair on the balcony and watch the comings and goings along Disney's BoardWalk.

Atlantic Dance Hall CLUB
(www.disneyworld.com; Disney's BoardWalk; ⊘9pm-2am) DJs spin '80s, top 40 and EDM tunes while a massive screen plays videos by request. As Disney nightclubs go, this is your only option, but it is often booked out by corporate clients. You need to be over 21 to enter.

Big River Grille & Brewing Works BREWERY
(☑407-560-0253; www.disneyworld.com; Disney's BoardWalk; ⊘11am-11pm) Open-air microbrewery with unique brews sold only on location, plus soups and pastas. Lovely outdoor seating along the water.

Jellyrolls BAR
(☑407-560-8770; www.disneyworld.com; Disney's BoardWalk; cover $12; ⊘7pm-2am) Comedians on dueling pianos encourage the audience to partake in all kinds of musical silliness and sing-alongs.

ESPN Club SPORTS BAR
(☑407-939-5100; www.disneyworld.com; Disney's BoardWalk; ⊘11am-midnight) So many TVs screening the hottest games that even in the bathroom you won't miss a single play.

❶ Information

Public areas at Disney's BoardWalk are open from 6:30am to 2am.

❶ Getting There & Away

A well-lit paved walking path (unsigned) and small boats connect Disney's BoardWalk to Epcot and Hollywood Studios, as well as to Disney Epcot resorts (BoardWalk Inn, Yacht & Beach Clubs and Swan & Dolphin). Disney buses stop at the BoardWalk Resort (at the entrance to the BoardWalk) and there's also parking here – be sure to say you're visiting the BoardWalk and you won't be charged.

Disney Springs

Stretching along the shore of Lake Buena Vista, the **Disney Springs** (☑407-939-6244; www.disneyworld.com; 1490 E Buena Vista Dr, Walt Disney World®; ⊘8:30am-2am; ▣Disney, ▣Disney, ▣Lynx 50)' smart outdoor pedestrian mall lures tourists with a huge number of restaurants, bars, music venues and shops.

This is also where you'll find the stage show Drawn to Life (p292) and the largest Disney store in the world. There's a Disney-styled party atmosphere, particularly on the weekends, with street performers dancing on stilts, parents pushing strollers loaded with Disney shopping bags, and hundreds upon hundreds of people enjoying the waterside drinking and excellent cuisine.

◉ Sights

★ The Void AMUSEMENT PARK
(www.thevoid.com; 1732 E Buena Vista Dr, Disney Springs; $39.95; ⊘10am-11pm Sun-Thu, to 11:30pm Fri & Sat; ▣Disney, ▣Disney, ▣Lynx 50) Don a pack and VR goggles and lose yourself in your choice of two adventures. In **Star Wars: Secrets of the Empire** you're disguised as a stormtrooper and have to solve and blast your way to survival. In **Ralph Breaks VR**, you join Wreck-it-Ralph and Vanellope von Schweetz to sneak into the internet's coolest video games – and get involved in a food fight. As good a VR experience as you'll find anywhere.

NBA Experience AMUSEMENT PARK
(☑407-828-3800; www.disneyworld.com; 1620 East Buena Vista Dr, Disney Springs; adult/child from $34/29; ⊘noon-11pm; ♿; ▣Disney, ▣Disney, ▣Lynx 50) As close as most of us will ever get to stepping into the (very big) shoes of a professional basketball player. There are 13 basketball-themed activities in a high-tech, interactive setting that will see you playing in front of virtual fans. Personalize your experience by entering your age, favorite team, skill level and nickname.

Aerophile RIDE
(☑407-939-7529; www.disneyworld.com; 1620 East Buena Vista Dr, Disney Springs; adult/child $20/15; ⊘8:30am-midnight; ▣Disney, ▣Disney,

Lynx 50) Guests climb onboard the basket of this massive tethered gas balloon and ascend 400ft into the air for 360-degree views. Between 8:30am and 10am there's a special for $10 per person.

🛏 Sleeping & Eating

There are no hotels at Disney Springs, though several are within a few miles.

Disney Springs is becoming a magnet for some well-known chefs-about-town, so the quality of nosh is high and refreshingly unthemed. There are also plenty of casual and takeout options.

Earl of Sandwich
SANDWICHES $
(www.disneyworld.com; 1620 East Buena Vista Dr, Disney Springs; sandwiches $6-9; ⏱8:30am-11pm; P 🛜 🖓; 🚌 Disney, 🚢 Disney, 🚌 Lynx 50) Surprisingly good toasted sandwiches ranging from basic to exotic. One of the most satisfying lunches at Disney, with plenty of bang for your buck, but in the end, it's a fast-food sandwich chain.

★ Frontera Cocina
MEXICAN $$
(📞407-560-9197; www.fronteracocina.com; 1620 East Buena Vista Dr, Disney Springs; mains $24-38; ⏱11am-10pm Sun-Wed, 11am-10:45pm Thu-Sat; 🚌 Disney, 🚢 Disney, 🚌 Lynx 50) A smart, trendy version of modern Mexico where, thanks to Chef Rick Bayless, corn, chili and salsa are whipped up into contemporary tastes in a delightfully light, bright and bustling environment. A pleasant change from some Southern flavors. Fun margarita-filled happy hours, too.

Chef Art Smith's Homecomin'
AMERICAN $$
(📞407-560-0100; www.disneyworld.com; Disney Springs; mains $22-31; ⏱11am-11pm; 🚌 Disney, 🚢 Disney, 🚌 Lynx 50) Chef Art Smith is a local celebrity chef, so local fans love his Floridian farm-to-fork, old-style-meets-modern flavors. We're talkin' fried chicken, shrimp and grits, and pork barbecue.

Boathouse
SEAFOOD $$
(📞407-939-2628; www.theboathouseorlando.com; 1620 East Buena Vista Dr, Disney Springs; mains $21-34; ⏱11am-1:30am) All kinds of seafood fills the menu at this upscale waterfront spot, as well as classic craft cocktails and a good wine list (that showcases American wines). Nightly music entertains you well into the morning. After dinner and drinks, head off for a spin and a float in a genuine amphic-

ar (📞407-939-2628; www.theboathouseorlando.com; 1620 East Buena Vista Dr, Disney Springs; up to 3 people 25min $125; ⏱10am-10pm; 🚌 Disney, 🚢 Disney, 🚌 Lynx 50).

T-Rex Cafe
AMERICAN $$
(📞407-828-8739; www.disneyworld.com; 1620 East Buena Vista Dr, Disney Springs; mains $18-22; ⏱11am-11pm Sun-Thu, to midnight Fri & Sat; P 🛜 🖓; 🚌 Disney, 🚢 Disney, 🚌 Lynx 50) Over-the-top multisensory overload, with massive autotronic dinosaurs, volcanoes erupting, light shows and meteor showers every 15 minutes. The menu features Woolly Mammoth Chicken, Caveman Punch and Chocolate Extinction – you get the idea. Kids will love it and the food is better than you might expect.

Paradiso 37
SOUTH AMERICAN $$$
(📞407-934-3700; www.paradiso37.com; 1620 East Buena Vista Dr, Disney Springs; mains $31-43; ⏱11am-11pm Sun-Thu, 11am-midnight Fri & Sat; P 🛜 🖓; 🚌 Disney, 🚢 Disney, 🚌 Lynx 50) With a menu representing 37 countries of the Americas, this contemporary waterfront spot is one of Disney Spring's best bets. It's very family-friendly, but nighttime has live music, a fiesta atmosphere – and 75 types of tequila. Plan accordingly. Call directly for reservations – it often has more flexibility and openings than Disney Dining.

🍷 Drinking & Nightlife

★ Jock Lindsay's
BAR
(www.disneyworld.com; 1620 East Buena Vista Dr, Disney Springs; ⏱11:30am-midnight; 🚌 Disney, 🚢 Disney, 🚌 Lynx 50) According to, er...'old' Disney folklore, Jock (the pilot in Raiders of the Lost Ark) 'arrived here in 1938 while chasing down a mythology-based tip in central Florida.' He liked the natural springs and lush terrain, and so bought some land. His hangar (his home base) became popular for world travelers and locals...and here you now are.

Yes, it's heavily themed and that's the idea. But the alcohol and fun are very real.

Raglan Road
PUB
(📞407-938-0300; www.raglanroad.com; 1620 East Buena Vista Dr, Disney Springs; ⏱10am-2am; 🛜 🖓; 🚌 Disney, 🚢 Disney) Traditional Irish ditties. Irish dancing, solid tasty fare, cozy pub decor and beer flights with Guinness, Harp, Smithwick's and Kilkenny complete the leprechaun mood.

☆ Entertainment

★ Drawn to Life
PERFORMING ARTS

(☑407-939-7600, 407-939-7328; www.cirquedu-soleil.com; 1478 Buena Vista Dr, Disney Springs; adult $67-179, child $65-145; ☺6pm & 9pm Tue-Sat; ⬛Disney, ⬛Disney, ⬛Lynx 50) A Disney animator's desk is the stage and the characters are both lithe and alive in this new show that debuted in 2020. It combines the visual genius of Walt Disney Imagineering with the mind-boggling acrobatic feats of Cirque du Soleil. This is a small horseshoe theater, with roughly 20 rows from the stage to the top, and no balcony.

Disney built the theater specifically to house the show's predecessor, La Nouba – there are no bad seats. See the website for black-out dates.

AMC Downtown Disney 24 – Dine-In Theatres
CINEMA

(☑888-262-4386; www.amctheatres.com/dinein; 1500 E Buena Vista Dr, Disney Springs; tickets $9-16; ⬛) Several screens offer Fork and Screen Theater, where you can order meals and have them delivered to your seat, and the bar sells beer, wine and cocktails to take into the movie.

House of Blues
LIVE MUSIC

(☑407-934-2583; www.houseofblues.com; 1490 Buena Vista Dr, Disney Springs; ☺10am-11pm Mon-Thu, to midnight Fri & Sat, 10:30am-11pm Sun; ⬛⬛; ⬛Disney, ⬛Disney, ⬛Lynx 50) Top acts visit this national chain serving Southern cooking and blues. It's particularly popular for the Sunday Gospel Brunch buffet.

🛍 Shopping

Lego Imagination Center
TOYS

(☑407-828-0065; www.disneyworld.com; 1672 Buena Vista Dr, Disney Springs; ☺9am-11pm; ⬛Disney, ⬛Disney, ⬛Lynx 50) Life-size Lego creations, tables to create your own masterpieces and a wall of individually priced Lego pieces.

Once Upon a Toy
TOYS

(☑407-824-4321; www.disneyworld.com; 1375 Buena Vista Dr, Disney Springs; ☺10am-11:30pm; ⬛Disney, ⬛Disney, ⬛Lynx 50) Design a personalized My Little Pony, build your own lightsaber and create your own tiara at one of the best toy stores anywhere. You'll find old-school classics such as Mr Potato Head and Lincoln Logs, board games, action figures, stuffed animals and more.

World of Disney
GIFTS & SOUVENIRS

(☑407-939-6224; www.disneyworld.com; Disney Springs; ☺9am-11pm; ⬛Disney, ⬛Disney, ⬛Lynx 50) Room after room of Disney everything at this Disney mega-super-duper store (the country's largest).

ℹ Information

Public areas at Disney Springs are open from 10am to midnight.

ℹ Getting There & Away

Disney Springs is accessible by water taxi from Disney Springs resorts and by bus from everywhere else. There is complimentary self parking, but no direct Disney transportation to any of the theme parks. Lynx bus 50 services Disney Springs from downtown Orlando and SeaWorld.

ℹ Getting Around

You can walk the 1.8 miles from one end of Disney Springs to the other or catch a boat shuttle.

UNIVERSAL ORLANDO RESORT

If Walt Disney World® is about finding the child in all of us, Universal Orlando Resort (Map p311; ☑407-363-8000; www.universalorlando.com; 1000 Universal Studios Plaza; single park adult/child from $80/74, two parks adult/child from $174/169, two-day three parks ticket from $350/340; ☺daily, hours vary; ⬛Lynx 21, 37 & 40, ⬛Universal) is all about our inner teenager. The rides are faster and the shows are sassier, and while this is still strictly a family-friendly resort with lots for tots to enjoy, the overall experience is unabashedly PG-13 compared to Disney's more G-rated fun.

With three parks and a dining and entertainment district, Universal Orlando Resort is also smaller and much easier to navigate. Universal Studios has mostly movie-based attractions and shows, including the Wizarding World of Harry Potter; Islands of Adventure has the bulk of the thrill rides; and Volcano Bay is a Polynesian-themed water park of thrills, splashes and state-of-the-art rides centred around a 200ft volcano.

By the time you read this, construction on a fourth park, Universal's Epic Universe, will be well underway. Scheduled to open in 2023, rumors abound about what you will find here: Super Nintendo World; some DreamWorks franchises like *How to Train*

BEST OF UNIVERSAL ORLANDO RESORT

Universal and its top-notch ride engineers have designed some of the most incredible simulated rides you'll see anywhere. They are constantly updating and rethinking its attractions, pushing the limits of ride engineering and incorporating new movies and shows into its repertoire.

On top of that, Universal's Express Pass system almost eliminates line anxiety on all but a few rides, and, if you're OK riding without your friends and family, many rides offer single-rider lines that are usually much shorter than the standard line – always ask.

Universal Studios

The Simpsons Ride (p304)

Hollywood Rip Ride Rockit (p303)

Revenge of the Mummy (p303)

Race Through New York Starring Jimmy Fallon (p304)

Harry Potter and the Escape from Gringotts (p295)

Despicable Me: Minion Mayhem (p304)

Skull Island: Reign of Kong (p302)

Islands of Adventure

Harry Potter and the Forbidden Journey (p294)

Incredible Hulk Coaster (p301)

Hagrid's Magical Creatures Motorbike Adventure (p294)

Amazing Adventures of Spider-Man (p301)

Dudley Do-Right's Ripsaw Falls (p302)

Your Dragon, Kung-Fu Panda and *Madagascar;* and perhaps even a third *Harry Potter* land.

In between Universal Studios and Islands of Adventure is CityWalk (Map p311; ☑407-363-8000; www.citywalk.com; 6000 Universal Studios Blvd, Universal Orlando Resort; ⊘7am-2am, hours vary; ☐ Lynx 21, 37 or 40, ⊠ Universal), which has restaurants and bars as well as a small selection of retail outlets. Universal also has eight resort hotels, and connections between them to the parks and CityWalk is a mix of buses, water taxis and pleasant walking paths.

Multiday and multipark tickets are available, so check online for the latest combinations and offers.

🎊 Festivals & Events

★ **Halloween Horror Nights** CARNIVAL
(www.halloweenhorrornights.com/orlando; Universal Orlando Resort, Universal Studios; $99-147, plus theme-park admission; ⊘select nights Sep & Oct; ☐ Lynx 21, 37 or 40) The best Halloween event in the US sees 10 warehouses converted into scary mazes themed according to either a well-known horror franchise or Universal's

own dastardly creations. The effects are exceptional and the frights very real – watch for bloodied zombies with chainsaws creeping up behind you on the streets. Parents should think carefully before bringing children 13 and under.

There are also a couple of excellent live shows. This is a very popular event and tickets are limited; advanced purchase recommended.

★ **Mardi Gras** CARNIVAL
(www.universalorlando.com; Universal Orlando Resort, Universal Studios; theme-park admission required; ⊘nightly Feb & Mar; ☐ Lynx 21, 37 or 40) Parades, live music and Cajun food mimic the iconic New Orleans street festival, Universal-style. The crowds really get into the whole spirit of catching beads and the dozen or so floats are beautifully decorated.

Grinchmas CARNIVAL
(www.universalorlando.com; Universal Orlando Resort, Islands of Adventure; theme-park admission required; ⊘Dec; ♿; ☐ Lynx 21, 37 or 40) A whimsical holiday spectacular at Seuss Landing pays homage to that classic Christmas story.

ORLANDO & WALT DISNEY WORLD® UNIVERSAL ORLANDO RESORT

WIZARDING WORLD OF HARRY POTTER

You don't have to be a huge Harry Potter fan to appreciate the genius of the magnificently whimsical **Wizarding World of Harry Potter**, which invites muggles to lose themselves in JK Rowling's imagination. First opened in 2010 and expanded in 2014, this is theme park development at its absolute best. Not since Cinderella Castle has there been such a fantastically realized experience, and today its only rival for imaginative scale and attention to detail is the recently opened Star Wars: Galaxy's Edge at Disney's Hollywood Studios.

The Wizarding World of Harry Potter tickles the fancy at every turn, from the screeches of the mandrakes in the shop windows to the groans of Moaning Myrtle in the bathroom; keep your eyes peeled for magical happenings. Don't forget to down some (oh-so-addictive!) Butterbeer.

The land is divided into two sections, each with rides, attractions and over-the-top detailed theming: **Hogsmeade** sits in Islands of Adventure and **Diagon Alley** is in Universal Studios. If you have a park-to-park ticket, you can ride the **Hogwarts Express** from one section to the other.

Hogsmeade (Islands of Adventure)

Wizarding World of Harry Potter – Hogsmeade (Map p311; ☏407-363-8000; www.universalorlando.com; Islands of Adventure; theme-park admission required; ⊙9am-6pm, hours vary; ☐Lynx 21, 37 or 40) Poke around among the cobbled streets and impossibly crooked buildings of Hogsmeade, munch on Cauldron Cakes and mail a card via Owl Post – all in the shadow of Hogwarts Castle. Two of Orlando's best rides are here – Harry Potter and the Forbidden Journey and the new Hagrid's Magical Creatures Motorbike Adventure. Come first thing when the park gates open, before the lines get too long and the crowds become unbearable. Guests staying at Universal Orlando Resort hotels get one hour early admission.

Harry Potter and the Forbidden Journey Wind through the corridors of Hogwarts, past talking portraits to one of the best rides in Orlando. You'll feel the cold chill of Dementors, escape a dragon attack, join a Quidditch match and soar over the castle with Harry, Hermione and Ron. Though it's not a fast-moving thrill ride, this is scary stuff. Little ones can enjoy the castle but sit out the ride with a parent in the Child Swap waiting room. There's a single rider line as well, but it's tricky to find – ask at the Hogwarts entrance.

Hagrid's Magical Creatures Motorbike Adventure There are no big hills or stomach-churning loops, but this coaster where you sit on either Hagrid's motorcycle or sidecar is one of the best in the park for its newfangled trickery, including a vertical tunnel that leads to a backward helix and an unexpected free-fall drop.

Ollivander's Wand Shop Floor-to-ceiling shelves crammed with dusty wand boxes and a winding staircase set the scene for a 10-minute show that brings to life the iconic scene in which the wand chooses the wizard. Come first thing, as the line quickly extends upwards of an hour.

Flight of the Hippogriff (Express Pass) This family-friendly coaster passes over Hagrid's Hut; listen for Fang's barks and don't forget to bow to Buckbeak!

Honeydukes Sweet Shop Bertie Botts Every Flavor Beans, Chocolate Frogs, Rock Cakes and other Harry Potter–inspired goodies.

Owl Post & Owlery Buy Wizarding World stamps and send a card officially postmarked Hogsmeade.

Filch's Emporium of Confiscated Goods Souvenir shop featuring the Marauders Map on display.

Three Broomsticks & Hog's Head Tavern Surprisingly good shepherd's pie, pumpkin juice and Hog's Head Brew.

Dervish & Banges Magical supplies and Hogwarts robes for sale.

Diagon Alley (Universal Studios)

Wizarding World of Harry Potter – Diagon Alley (Map p311; www.universalorlando.com; Universal Studios; theme-park admission required; ⊘ from 9am; 🚌 Lynx 21, 37 or 40) Lined with magical shops selling robes, Quidditch supplies, wands, brooms and more, Diagon Alley leads to the massive Gringotts Bank, home to one of Universal Studio's multisensory thrill rides, **Harry Potter and the Escape from Gringotts** (⊘ 9am-6pm, hours vary; 🚌 Lynx 21, 37 or 40). To get here, you must walk through Muggles' London at Universal Studios or, if you have a park-to-park ticket, ride the **Hogwarts Express** from Islands of Adventure's Hogsmeade to King's Cross Station. Keep an eye on the **fire-breathing dragon** above the bank.

Grab some bangers and mash at the **Leaky Cauldron**, a scoop of quirky wizarding-themed ice cream at **Florean Fortescue's Ice-Cream Parlor** and wander down Knock-turn Alley to pick up tools of the Dark Arts at **Borgin and Burkes**. There's a bigger branch of **Ollivander's** (in its rightful location as per the books), where you can also take part in the wand-choosing ceremony.

Given the creative spirit and success of Islands of Adventure's Hogsmeade, Diagon Alley is theme-park magic at its best.

Interactive Wands

Wands at Universal Orlando's Wizarding World of Harry Potter come in two varieties: interactive ($55) and noninteractive ($49). Interactive wands, including Hermione's and Harry's, can be used in both Diagon Alley and Hogsmeade to activate magical windows and displays. Make it rain down on an umbrella, illuminate lanterns, watch the marionettes dance. They can be a bit touchy to get used to – use small, gentle movements, and if you have trouble, ask a nearby wizard for help.

Gold medallions on the ground indicate spots where you can cast your spells, and how to move your wand to cast the spell, and each wand comes with a map. Some secret spell locations, however, aren't marked at all, either on the map or by a gold medallion, but we're not telling where they are. Hint: secret spells respond to a triangle swoop.

Top Tips for Visiting Harry Potter's Hogsmeade & Diagon Alley

Universal's Wizarding World of Harry Potter is no place for the faint-hearted during high season. The lines for almost everything can risk breaking even the most indomitable spirit, but don't be deterred: with a little bit of smart planning, a visit to Hogsmeade and Diagon Alley can be magnificently joyful, easy and stress-free.

Stay at a Universal Orlando Resort Hotel Harry Potter attractions open one hour early for guests at four on-site hotels. Arrive at least 30 minutes before the gates open to the general public, and do not dawdle.

Strategize Head to Islands of Adventure's Hogsmeade on one morning. Hit Harry Potter and the Forbidden Journey, Hagrid's Magical Creatures Motorbike Adventure, Flight of the Hippogriff, and finally shops and restaurants (in that order). The other morning, zip straight to Universal Studio's Diagon Alley, hop on Escape from Gringotts, and then explore at leisure. There is an Ollivander's Wand Shop in both parks – on one of the two days, make this your first stop.

Buy a park-to-park ticket This allows you to ride the Hogwarts Express between Diagon Alley and Hogsmeade.

Visit during low season Do not go Christmas through early January, March and summer.

Take advantage of Universal's 'return time' tickets If the Wizarding World of Harry Potter *does* reach capacity during your visit (usually after 10:30am), it only allows new guests to enter once others have left. This electronic ticket allows you to enjoy other attractions and return for entry into the Wizarding World within a specific window of time. Look for the blue banner directing you to the easy-to-use kiosks.

At the center is a musical production of *How the Grinch Stole Christmas*.

Macy's Holiday Parade PARADE
(www.universalorlando.com; Universal Orlando Resort, Universal Studios; theme-park admission required; ⊘ select nights Dec; 🚌 Lynx 21, 37 or 40) Echoes the real thing in New York City, with giant balloons, Santa Claus, Christmas music and a tree-lighting ceremony. Dates can change slightly.

🛏 Sleeping

Universal Orlando Resort has eight excellent resort hotels divided into four pricing categories: value, prime value, preferred and premier. The bulk of its hotels are themed to evoke a summery vibe of yesteryear, and for the most part they work. Staying at a resort eliminates many logistical hassles: it's a pleasant gardened walk or a quiet boat ride to the parks; most offer Unlimited Express Pass access to park attractions and priority dining; several popular rides, such as the Wizarding World of Harry Potter, open one hour early for all guests; and the Loews Loves Pets program welcomes Fido as a VIP.

Universal's Endless Summer Resort HOTEL $
(Map p311; ☑ 407-503-7000; www.universal orlando.com; 7000 Universal Blvd, Universal Orlando Resort; r/ste from $79/120; 🚌 Universal) The theme of Universal's newest hotel is California surf culture in the 1960s, and you can choose between the 750-room Surfside or the 1100-room Dockside, which opened in 2020. Brightly colored standard rooms sleep up to four; the family suites sleep six. As both are value properties, guests can avail of early admission to the parks but not free Universal Express.

★ Cabana Bay Beach Resort RESORT $$
(Map p311; ☑ 407-503-4000; www.universalorlando.com; 6550 Adventure Way, Universal Orlando Resort; r from $116, parking $15; 🅿 ✴ 🐾 🏊 ; 🚌 Universal) Evoking the spirit of road trips c 1957, Cabana Bay Beach Resort has a beautifully themed, hip, retro-Florida vintage vibe. It offers moderate and good-value accommodations. Family suites have kitchenettes and sleep six, and there are two pools, a bowling alley, a food court and a lazy river.

While guests can enjoy early admission to the Wizarding World of Harry Potter (a huge plus), they do not benefit from perks afforded to guests at the other Universal Resorts, including Unlimited Express Pass, priority dining status and boat transportation to the parks. A Universal bus goes every 15 minutes to CityWalk and the theme parks.

Universal's Aventura Hotel HOTEL $$
(Map p311; ☑ 407-503-6000; www.universalorlando.com; 6725 Adventure Way, Universal Orlando Resort; r/ste from $116/210, parking $45; 🚌 Universal) Universal's nod to the streamlined, curvilinear mid-century modern style is this glass tower block with all the usual amenities, including a pool, a kids' splash zone, a gym and a virtual-reality games room. Standard rooms are smaller than those at the similarly priced Cabana Bay, but the views from the rooftop restaurant are exceptional.

Loews Sapphire Falls Resort HOTEL $$
(Map p311; ☑ 407-503-5000; www.universalorlando.com; 6601 Adventure Way; r from $165, self-/valet parking per day $38/45; 🅿 ✴ 🐾 🏊) A Caribbean-inspired hotel with a tropical vibe and a mélange of eras, from Colonial to the 1950s. The property's water features include lovely rivers and waterfalls. Rooms have a weird mix of Caribbean colors and patterned decor, but as with everything park-Orlandesque, it's all about the theming. It's got some great restaurant and bars, including the Strong Water Tavern (p299).

Loews Royal Pacific Resort RESORT $$$
(Map p311; ☑ 407-503-3000; www.loewshotels.com/royal-pacific-resort; 6300 Hollywood Way, Universal Orlando Resort; r/ste from $225/326, self-/valet parking per day $42/45; 🅿 ✴ @ 🐾 🏊 ; 🚌 Universal) The glass-enclosed Orchid Court, with its reflecting pool, Balinese fountains and carved stone elephants, sits at the center of the airy lobby at this friendly South Pacific–inspired resort. The grounds are gorgeous with lush tropical plantings, flowers and palm trees. Excellent on-site restaurants. Rates include one-hour early entrance to the Wizarding World of Harry Potter and an Unlimited Express Pass.

Kids will love the family-friendly pool, with real sand, and the 6pm 'dive-in movie' where they can swim while watching a poolside screen showing the likes of Harry Potter and Universal favorites. Note that the rooms here tend to be smaller than those at other Universal hotels. Rates are significantly lower outside peak season.

Loews Portofino Bay Hotel RESORT $$$
(Map p311; ☑ 407-503-1000; www.loewshotels.com/portofino-bay-hotel; 5601 Universal Blvd,

Universal Orlando Resort; r/ste from $270/517, self/valet parking per day $30/42; P❋@🌐❄❄; 💻Universal) Universal's most exclusive hotel is sumptuously designed to evoke the relaxing charm of seaside Italy. And while everything here is undoubtedly elegant, including the excellent Mama Della's Ristorante, the hotel could do with a little spruce up. Rates include one-hour early entrance to the Wizarding World of Harry Potter and an Unlimited Express Pass.

Hard Rock Hotel
RESORT $$$

(Map p311; 📞407-503-2000; www.hardrockhotels.com/orlando; 5800 Universal Blvd, Universal Orlando Resort; r/ste from $258/405, self-/valet parking per day $30/42; P❋@🌐❄❄; 💻Universal) From the grand lawn with the massive guitar fountain at its entrance to the pumped-in, underwater music at the pool, the modern and stylized Hard Rock embodies the pure essence and energy of rock 'n' roll cool. Rates include one-hour early entrance to the Wizarding World of Harry Potter and an Unlimited Express Pass.

There's a huge zero-entry pool with a waterslide, and families mingle harmoniously alongside a young party crowd, but the loud live band that sometimes plays in the lobby and the rockin' vibe may be overkill for folk looking for a peaceful getaway.

✗ Eating

The only restaurants in the theme parks that take advance reservations are Finnegan's Bar & Grill (p305) and Lombard's Seafood Grille (p305) in Universal Studios, and Mythos Restaurant (p303) and Confisco Grille (p303) in Islands of Adventure.

Each Universal resort has high-quality bars and restaurants that you can enjoy even if you're not a guest. For kids, some even offer 'character dining' options where Universal characters visit one of the resort hotel restaurants.

✗ Resort Hotels

Emack & Bolio's Marketplace
ICE CREAM $

(Map p311; 📞407-503-2432; www.emackandbolios.com; 5800 Universal Blvd, Hard Rock Hotel; ice cream $4-9; ⏰6am-10pm; 🌐📶; 💻Universal) Originally from Boston, Emack and Bolio's ice cream beats other national chains hands down. And of course, only at this bastion of rock 'n' roll will you find a flavor called Deep Purple.

★ Mama Della's Ristorante
ITALIAN $$

(Map p311; 📞407-503-3463; www.universalorlando.com; 5601 Universal Blvd, Loews Portofino Bay Hotel; mains $20-38; ⏰5:30-11pm; 🅿📶; 💻Universal) Charming, cozy and friendly, with vintage wallpaper, dark wood and several rooms with romantic nooks. You really do feel like you're a welcomed guest at a private home nestled in Italy. Strolling musicians entertain tableside and the simple Italian fare is both fresh and excellent; the service is efficient but relaxed.

Good wine, old-fashioned soda in a bottle and a bowl of pasta at Mama Della's makes a very nice ending to a day at the parks, for both kids and adults.

Amatista Cookhouse
CARIBBEAN $$

(Map p311; 📞407-503-5200; www.universalorlando.com; 6601 Adventure Way, Loews Sapphire Falls Resort; mains $18-39; ⏰7-11am, 11:30am-2:30pm & 5-10pm) A wide range of Caribbean-influenced dishes, from mojo-marinated rotisserie chicken to a spicy linguine, served in a large, airy dining room with big windows and an open kitchen. Comfortable, friendly and, most importantly, delicious.

Kitchen
AMERICAN $$

(Map p311; 📞407-503-2430; www.loewshotels.com/hard-rock-hotel/dining/restaurant; 5800 Universal Blvd, Hard Rock Hotel; mains $22-38; ⏰7am-10pm Sun-Thu, to 11pm Fri & Sat; 📶; 💻Universal) Music paraphernalia and patio poolside dining. Come for flatbreads, steak and comfort food such as chicken potpie and roast chicken. Children can head to the Kids' Crib, which has bean-bag chairs, cartoons and toys, while parents dine in the big-people restaurant. Every night two characters visit tables.

Orchid Court Sushi Bar
JAPANESE $$$

(Map p311; 📞407-503-3000; www.universalorlando.com; 6300 Hollywood Way, Loews Royal Pacific Resort; rolls $8-17, sushi platters $40-125; ⏰6-11am & 5-11pm; 📶; 💻Universal) This small, informal sushi bar oozes calm inside the light-and-airy, glass-enclosed lobby of the Royal Pacific Resort, and is decked out with cushioned couches and chairs. Try the Yokohama Selfie (Roku gin, sweet-potato *shōchū*, mint, cucumber and absinthe; $15). It's also open for breakfast.

Palm Restaurant
STEAK $$$

(Map p311; 📞407-503-7256; www.thepalm.com; 5800 Universal Studios Blvd, Hard Rock Hotel; mains $35-60; ⏰5-10pm; 💻Universal) The

UNIVERSAL FOR CHILDREN

Universal Orlando Resort's primary target may be tweens and older kids, but it is a master at blending attractions for all ages into one easily digestible and navigable package of fun. Dr Seuss' Grinch, superheroes and all kinds of Universal favorites make appearances at theme parks, and characters from *Despicable Me* and other kid-friendly shows swing by hotel restaurants. CityWalk is very family-friendly, despite its many bars and live music, with a sci-fi-themed miniature golf course and a splash fountain.

Most of the kid-friendly attractions cluster at Universal Studios' Woody Woodpecker's KidZone (p305), and Islands of Adventure's Seuss Landing (p302) and Toon Lagoon (p301), and the Wizarding World of Harry Potter (p294). Bring a change of clothes, as both parks have attractions designed to get kids wet!

Best for Kids: Islands of Adventure

One Fish, Two Fish, Red Fish, Blue Fish Ride a Seussian fish around, slowly up and down, with just enough spin to thrill.

Caro-Seuss-al Hop on a fanciful Seuss character.

The Cat in the Hat Classic ride through a storybook.

The High in the Sky Seuss Trolley Train Ride Soar gently over the park.

If I Ran the Zoo Colorful interactive play area with water-spurting triggers.

Me Ship, the Olive Kids crawl, climb and squirt on Popeye's playground ship and zoom down tunnel waterslides.

Popeye & Bluto's Bilge-Rat Barges (p302) Float, twist, bump and giggle along on a circular raft – you will get drenched!

Hogwarts Little (and big) ones too young for the scary Harry Potter and the Forbidden Journey ride can walk through the magical charms of the famous wizardry school. The separate line for this isn't marked, so ask the accommodating Universal folks. Other kid-friendly highlights in the Wizarding World of Harry Potter are Ollivander's Wand Shop (10-minute show) and family coaster the Flight of the Hippogriff.

Best for Kids: Universal Studios

A Day in the Park with Barney Delightfully gentle theater-in-the-round live performance and sing-along.

Animal Actors on Location! Big stage show that highlights the exploits of animal actors like Marley, from *Marley & Me*.

Curious George Goes to Town Best tiny-tot water-play area in any of the theme parks, and a giant room of nerf balls to throw and shoot from cannons.

E.T. Adventure (p304) Board a bike and ride through the woods, the police in hot pursuit, before rising safely into the sky through outer space to E.T.'s fanciful home planet. Prepare kids for darkness, loud noises and steam – but there are no spins, speeds or plummets.

Fievel's Playground Imagine you've been shrunk to the size of a mouse...and let loose. Kids have a ball.

Woody Woodpecker's Nuthouse Coaster Gentle coaster for kids three and up.

Best for Kids: Volcano Bay

Tot Tiki Reef A mini volcano, small wave pool and fountains perfect for toddlers.

Puka Uli Lagoon Small leisure pool for families.

original Palm opened in New York City in 1926 and, though there are now more than 30 locations, it remains a family-owned bedrock American steakhouse, albeit up there in the price stakes, too. Classic cocktails, a steady din and big plates of steak, lobster and Italian fare.

Drinking & Nightlife

★ Strong Water Tavern   BAR

(Map p311; www.universalorlando.com; Loews Sapphire Falls Resort, Universal Orlando Resort; ⊙4pm-2am; ☎) This sophisticated rum and tapas bar will transport you to the Caribbean. Rum barrel lids are suspended overhead, and other wood accents transform this hotel bar into an atmospheric, stylish place. You can take a journey through different types of rum (there are more than 60 to try) and a rum counsel is on hand to advise.

Jake's American Bar   BAR

(Map p311; www.universalorlando.com; Loews Royal Pacific Resort, Universal Orlando Resort; ⊙11am-1:30am; ☺Universal) Glide into this pleasant South Seas island experience run by 'Jake,' imaginary pilot of an island-hopper aircraft (his seaplane is floating in the lagoon). The 'pilot log book' menu (mains $15 to $20) complements the drinks, including beer flights. It is a stylish locale, worthy of the Royal Pacific.

☆ Entertainment

CityWalk (p306), Universal Orlando's entertainment district (free access to the public) is a popular destination for Orlandoans who come to enjoy the restaurants, bars and clubs.

Wantilan Luau   LUAU

(Map p311; ☎407-503-3463; www.universalorlando.com; 6300 Hollywood Way, Loews Royal Pacific Resort; adult $71-91, child 3-9yr $36-51; ⊙6pm Sat; ☺Universal) Pacific Island fire dancers shimmy and shake on stage while guests enjoy a tasty buffet of roast suckling pig, guava-barbecued short ribs and other Polynesian-influenced fare. The atmosphere is wonderfully casual and, like everything at Universal Orlando, this is simple unabashed silliness and fun. Unlimited mai tais, beer and wine are included in the price.

The Maori warriors' roar can be rather scary and the fire a bit close for comfort in the eyes of little ones, but there's a pleasant grassy area next to the open-air dining theater where kids can muck about. Reservations accepted up to 60 days in advance.

ℹ Information

INTERNET ACCESS

Strong, complimentary wi-fi is available throughout all three parks and CityWalk – they don't want you to miss those Instagram moments. Universal Orlando Resort hotels all have their own wi-fi but it's for guests only; however, nonguests can log on to a free service in the hotel lobbies.

LOCKERS

Available inside both Islands of Adventure and Universal Studios parks from $10 per day. Several rides require that all loose items, including backpacks and small purses, be secured in complimentary short-term lockers. If you are carrying something too big for the locker, you can take advantage of the Bag Swap option – wait in line together, one person rides while the other holds the bag, and then swap.

MAPS

Pick up a free map at each park entrance (and dotted around at stands within the park). They also list the attractions, with a schedule outlining events, shows and locations of free character interactions. The monthly *Times & Info Guide* lists larger parades and events, too.

MEDICAL SERVICES

Each theme park has medical facilities. A handy hospital for all parks is Dr P Phillips Hospital (p326), 5.5 miles south on Turkey Lake Rd.

OPENING HOURS

Universal Orlando Resort theme-park hours change seasonally and daily. Generally, parks open at 8am or 9am and close sometime between 6pm and 10pm. Guests at any of the on-site hotels can enter the parks one hour before official opening times.

TOURIST INFORMATION

Guest Services inside each Universal Orlando Resort park and at CityWalk can help with anything you need, and there are concierge desks at the on-site hotels. Furthermore, the front desk of just about any Orlando area hotel provides Universal Orlando Resort tourist information.

Important Telephone Numbers

Dining CityWalk & Theme Parks (☎407-224-9255) Advanced priority seating for CityWalk, Islands of Adventure and Universal Studios.

Dining Resort Hotels (☎407-503-3463) Advanced priority seating for Loews Portofino Bay, Hard Rock and Loews Royal Pacific Resorts.

Guest Services (☎407-224-6350, 407-244-4233)

Resort Hotel Reservations (888-273-1311, for vacation packages 888-343-3636) Accommodations at Universal's on-site resort hotels.

Universal Orlando Resort (407-363-8000, toll-free 800-232-7827) Central number for all things Universal (although infuriatingly automated).

Universal Orlando Resort Lost & Found (407-224-4233) Located inside Guest Services.

Websites

Orlando Informer (www.orlandoinformer.com) Excellent and detailed information on all things Universal, including park changes, money-saving tips, menus and a crowd calendar.

Universal Orlando Resort (www.universal orlando.com) Official site for information, accommodations and tickets.

TRAVELERS WITH DISABILITIES

➧ The *Universal Orlando Rider's Guide,* available online at www.universalorlando.com and at Guest Services, includes ride requirements and attraction accessibility details for travelers with disabilities. There are also sign-language-interpreting, closed-captioning and assistive-listening devices available at some attractions, and large-print and braille maps. TDD-equipped (Telecommunications Device for the Deaf) telephones are located throughout the park.

❶ Getting There & Away

BOAT

Universal Orlando Water Taxis (Map p311; www.universalorlando.com; Universal Orlando Resort; 7am-2am) Water taxis, which leave each point roughly every 15 minutes, shuttle regularly and directly between four of the five deluxe Universal hotels (Cabana Bar excepted) and CityWalk. From here, it's a five-minute walk across the canal to the theme parks.

BUS

Lynx buses 21, 37 and 40 service the Universal Orlando Resort parking garage (40 runs directly from the downtown Orlando Amtrak station). International Dr's I-Ride Trolley (p331) stops at Universal Blvd, a 0.6-mile walk away.

CAR

From I-4, take exit 74B or 75A and follow the signs. From International Dr, follow the signs west onto Universal Blvd.

Parking

Parking for Universal Studios, Islands of Adventure and CityWalk is available inside a giant garage structure (self-/valet parking $25/40). Hotels charge per day for self-parking (from $25) or valet (from $30). For Volcano Bay, you have to park at CityWalk and get the shuttle.

TICKETS

Tickets for the three Universal Orlando Resort Parks (Islands of Adventure, Universal Studios and Volcano Bay) cost the following:

NO OF DAYS	ONE PARK ($) ADULT/CHILD	TWO PARKS ($) ADULT/CHILD	THREE PARKS ($) ADULT/CHILD
1	119/114 (Volcano Bay 80/75)	174/169	n/a
2	190/185	235/225	310/300
3	n/a	255/245	330/320
4	n/a	265/255	350/340

➧ Tickets are good anytime within 14 consecutive days, and multiple-day tickets include admission to paid venues in CityWalk. Universal Orlando Resort participates in the Orlando Flex Ticket available online or in person at the Orlando Official Visitor Center (p325).

➧ Avoid lines at designated Islands of Adventure and Universal Studios rides by flashing your Express Pass at the separate Express Pass line. The standard one-day pass (for Islands of Adventure and Universal Studios from $70; for Volcano Bay from $20) allows one-time Express Pass access to each attraction; the unlimited version allows you unlimited access to rides (from $90; Volcano Bay from $40). If you are staying at one of Universal Orlando's deluxe resort hotels – Universal Orlando's Loews Portofino Bay, Hard Rock or Loews Royal Pacific Resort – up to five guests in each room automatically receive an Unlimited Express Pass. A limited number of passes per day are available online or at the park gates. Check www.universalorlando.com for a calendar of prices and black-out dates. Note that Unlimited Express Passes are sold bundled to park admission online, but, if they're available, you can add them to an existing ticket at the park.

➧ Florida residents pay roughly 30% less than out-of-state visitors.

❶ Getting Around

Universal Orlando Resort – that is, Universal Orlando's resort hotels, Islands of Adventure and Universal Studios theme parks and City-Walk – are linked by pedestrian walkways. It's a 10- to 15-minute walk from the theme parks and CityWalk to the deluxe resort hotels. Cabana Bay Beach Resort is about a 25-minute walk. Several hotels outside the park are within a 20-minute walk, but it's not a very pleasant journey.

Rent strollers, wheelchairs and electric convenience vehicles (ECVs) at the entrance to each park and manual wheelchairs at the Rotunda section of the parking lot. To reserve an ECV in advance, call ☑407-224-4233.

Islands of Adventure

Built to offer a competitive alternative to Disney's Magic Kingdom, Islands of Adventure (Map p311; ☑407-363-8000; www.universalorlando.com; 6000 Universal Blvd, Universal Orlando Resort; 1 day adult $119, child $114; ☺from 9am, closing hours vary; ☐Lynx 21, 37 or 40, ☒Universal) is a more adrenalized version of the world's most popular theme park. Right from the entrance everything is designed for no-holds-barred, laugh-out-loud kind of fun. Marvel Super Hero Island is packed with thrill rides and hair-raising coasters; Toon Lagoon is like stepping into a cartoon; while next door, Skull Island is all about the brilliantly executed menace of the world's biggest – and most misunderstood – ape, King Kong. The Lost Continent covers the ancient world, and Seuss Landing is all about Dr Seuss' rhyming and colorful fun.

And then there's Harry Potter. Here you'll find the theme-park game-changing Wizarding World of Harry Potter – Hogsmeade (p294), which is connected to Universal Studios' Wizarding World of Harry Potter – Diagon Alley (p295) via the Hogwarts Express train, but you'll need a park-to-park ticket to ride it.

◉ Sights

◉ Marvel Super Hero Island

Bright, loud and fast moving, Marvel Super Hero Island (Map p311; www.universalorlando.com; Islands of Adventure; theme-park admission required; ☺9am-6pm, hours vary; ⛟; ☐Lynx 21, 37 or 40) is sensory overload and a thrill-lover's paradise. Comic-book characters patrol this area, so keep an eye out for your favorites and check your map for scheduled meet-and-greet times.

★Incredible Hulk Coaster   RIDE
(Map p311; www.universalorlando.com; Universal Orlando Resort, Islands of Adventure; theme-park admission required; ☺9am-6pm, hours vary; ☐Lynx 21, 37 or 40) Our favorite coaster across all three of Universal's parks starts with a takeoff that takes you from 0mph to 40mph in *two seconds,* followed by a quick twist and a 100ft drop.The rest of the ride is a mix of twists, turns and dives that replicate the g-force of a jet fighter. Fabulous stuff.

★Amazing Adventures of Spider-Man   RIDE
(Map p311; www.universalorlando.com; Universal Orlando Resort, Islands of Adventure; theme-park admission required; ☺9am-6pm, hours vary; ☐Lynx 21, 37 or 40) One of the best simulator 4D rides in the park, this high-def, high-tech adventure pits you against some of Spider-Man's deadliest enemies while coursing through the streets of New York. You'll feel every bump, every blast of heat and a splash of water from Hydro-Man – but there's always Spidey to make sure you're OK.

Doctor Doom's Fearfall   RIDE
(Map p311; www.universalorlando.com; Univeral Resort Orlando, Islands of Adventure; theme-park admission required; ☺9am-6pm, hours vary; ☐Lynx 21, 37 or 40) Doctor Doom has a plan for you, but first you have to strap into his dastardly contraption. As you blast 200ft upwards with your feet dangling below you, his plan becomes clear. The ride itself isn't nearly as scary as the apprehension that precedes it, but that's all part of the fun.

◉ Toon Lagoon

Island of Adventure's sparkly, lighthearted cartoon-themed Toon Lagoon (Map p311; www.universalorlando.com; Islands of Adventure; theme-park admission required; ☺9am-6pm, hours vary; ⛟; ☐Lynx 21, 37 or 40) transports visitors to the days when lazy weekends included nothing more than mornings watching *Popeye* and afternoons playing in the sprinkler. Most of the attractions here include water: be warned that you will get drenched, so protect phones and cameras, wear water-friendly shoes and bring a change of clothes. If you forget, there are, of course, plenty of shops that sell towels, flip-flops and clothes.

Dudley Do-Right's Ripsaw Falls   RIDE

(Map p311; www.universalorlando.com; Universal Orlando Resort, Islands of Adventure; theme-park admission required; ⊙9am-6pm, hours vary; 🖵Lynx 21, 37 or 40) A flume ride through the Canadian Rockies that ends in a big drop. Does Dudley Do-Right rescue his girlfriend Nell Fenwick from the clutches of Snidely Whiplash? Sure, why not? All we know is this is a great ride that *will* leave you wet.

Popeye & Bluto's Bilge-Rat Barges   RIDE

(Map p311; www.universalorlando.com; Universal Orlando Resort, Islands of Adventure; theme-park admission required; ⊙9am-6pm, hours vary; 🖵Lynx 21, 37 or 40) This whitewater rafting ride is brilliant fun for the whole family, but be prepared to get very, very wet – the ride is designed so that you do.

⊙ Skull Island

Although it gets its own island, Skull Island is just the setting for one of Universal's most talked about rides.

Skull Island: Reign of Kong   RIDE

(Map p311; www.universalorlando.com; Islands of Adventure; theme-park admission required; ⊙9am-6pm, hours vary; 🖵Lynx 21, 37 or 40) Board a trackless 72-seat, open-sided vehicle 'driven' by a wise-cracking animatronic tour guide and head deep into Skull Island, where high-tech 3D screens bring its collection of over-sized beasts to life. The biggest threat comes from a ferocious V-rex dinosaur...or is it Kong himself? Suffice to say, not for littlies.

⊙ Lost Continent

Magic and myth from across the seas and the pages of fantasy books inspire this mystical corner of the park. In **Lost Continent** (Map p311; www.universalorlando.com; Universal Orlando Resort, Islands of Adventure; theme-park admission required; ⊙9am-6pm, hours vary; 🚹; 🖵Lynx 21, 37 or 40) you'll find dragons and unicorns, psychic readings and fortune-tellers. And don't be startled if that fountain talks to you as you walk past. The **Mystic Fountain** banters sassily, soaking children with its waterspouts when they least expect it and engaging them in silly conversation.

At the swashbuckling **Eighth Voyage of Sinbad Stunt Show** (Express Pass), Sinbad and his sidekick Kabob must rescue Princess Amoura from the terrible Miseria and, of course, Sinbad has to tumble and jump around to do it. Or head into the ancient Temple of Poseidon in **Poseidon's Fury** with an archaeologist who leads you deep into the temple...until you're 'trapped' in a massive battle with lasers, water and fireballs.

⊙ Seuss Landing

Anyone who has ever fallen asleep being read *Green Eggs and Ham* or learned to read with *Sam I Am* knows the world of Dr Seuss: the fanciful creatures, the lyrical names, the rhyming stories. **Seuss Landing** (Map p311; www.universalorlando.com; Islands of Adventure; theme-park admission required; ⊙9am-6pm, hours vary; 🚹; 🖵Lynx 21, 37 or 40), realized in magnificently designed 3D form, is Dr Seuss' imagination. The Lorax guards his truffula trees; Thing One and Thing Two make trouble; and creatures from all kinds of Seuss favorites adorn the shops and the rides.

Drink moose juice or goose juice, eat green eggs and ham, and peruse shelves of Dr Seuss books before riding through **The Cat in the Hat** or around and around on an elephant-bird from *Horton Hears a Who!* Seuss Landing is one of the best places for little ones in all of Orlando's theme parks, bringing the spirit and energy of Dr Seuss' vision to life. So come on in, walk into his world and take a spin on a fish.

⊙ Jurassic World

At the time of writing, Jurassic World was in the midst of a substantial overhaul centred on the construction of the **Jurassic World VelociCoaster**, which is slated to open in summer 2021. Expected thrills along the 4700ft track include a 360-degree barrel roll, a zero-gravity inverted stall and a 155ft skyward launch before plunging into an 80-degree drop.

In the meantime, **Jurassic Park River Adventure** (Map p311; www.universalorlando.com; Universal Resort Orlando, Islands of Adventure; theme-park admission required; ⊙9am-6pm, hours vary; 🚹; 🖵Lynx 21, 37 or 40) remains a favorite, a gentle boat tour of Jurassic Park that... Oh no! Why did the boat turn suddenly and head for the maintenance facilities? At **Pterandoon Flyers** (Map p311; www.universalorlando.com; Universal Resort Orlando, Islands of Adventure; theme-park admission required; ⊙9am-6pm, hours vary; 🖵Lynx 21, 37 or 40), kids fly over the lush landscape and robotic dinosaurs of Jurassic Park. Note that you must be between 36in and 56in tall to fly, and adults can't fly without a kid (also note: it sways quite severely; you don't just 'float' along). Waits can be upwards of an hour for the 80-second ride and there's no Express Pass.

🍴 Eating

All the usual fast-food suspects are sold throughout the park, but with a commitment to theme that you don't see elsewhere. Sip a Predator Rocks in the lush foliage of the Cretaceous period in Jurassic Park or grab a Hog's Head Brew in Hogsmeade.

★Three Broomsticks　　　BRITISH $

(Map p311; www.universalorlando.com; Islands of Adventure; mains $15-17, theme-park admission required; ⊘9am-park closing; 🐾; 🚇 Lynx 21, 37 or 40) Fast-food-styled British fare inspired by Harry Potter, with cottage (shepherd's) pie and Cornish pasties, and rustic wooden bench seating. There's plenty of outdoor seating out back, too, by the river.

**Confisco Grille
& Backwater Bar**　　　AMERICAN $$

(Map p311; ☎407-224-4406; www.universalorlando.com; Islands of Adventure; mains $17-24, theme-park admission required; ⊘11am-4pm Mon-Thu, to 6pm Fri-Sun; 🐾🐾; 🚇 Lynx 21, 37 or 40) Under-the-radar and often overlooked, the recommended Confisco Grille has outdoor seating, freshly made hummus, wood-oven pizzas and a full bar. Plant-based veggie or vegan options are available.

Mythos Restaurant　　　MEDITERRANEAN $$

(Map p311; ☎407-224-4534; www.universalorlando.com; Islands of Adventure; mains $19-36, theme-park admission required; ⊘11am-1hr before park closes; 🐾🐾; 🚇 Lynx 21, 37 or 40) Housed in an ornate underwater grotto with giant windows and running water and overlooking a lake, this successfully combines Mediterranean flavors with tastes of Asian cuisine and a healthy dollop of American cooking. The menu changes seasonally but you can chomp on anything from pad Thai noodles to risotto. New plant-based options have been added to the menu.

🍺 Drinking & Nightlife

Hog's Head Pub　　　PUB

(Map p311; www.universalorlando.com; Islands of Adventure, Universal Studios; drinks $4-8, theme-park admission required; ⊘park opening-park closing; 🚇 Lynx 21, 37 or 40) Butterbeer, frozen or frothy, real beer on tap, pumpkin cider and

more. Keep an eye on that hog over the bar – he's more real than you think! If the lines at the Butterbeer carts outside are too long, head inside. Same thing, same price.

Universal Studios

Divided geographically by film-inspired and region-specific architecture and ambience, and themed as a Hollywood backlot, **Universal Studios** (Map p311; ☎407-363-8000; www.universalorlando.com; 1000 Universal Studios Plaza, Universal Orlando Resort; 1 day adult $119, child $114; ⊘from 9am, closing hours vary; 🚇 Lynx 21, 37 or 40, 🚤 Universal) has shows and magnificently designed, simulation-heavy rides dedicated to silver-screen and TV icons. Drink Duff beer, a Homer favorite, in Springfield; ride the Hogwarts Express into Diagon Alley; and challenge the host of *The Tonight Show* to a scavenger hunt. And if you're looking for thrills, Hollywood Rip Ride Rockit and Revenge of the Mummy are two of Orlando's best coasters.

The park is divided into eight areas – Hollywood, New York, Production Central, San Francisco, Springfield: Home of the Simpsons, Woody Woodpecker's KidZone, World Expo and The Wizarding World of Harry Potter (Diagon Alley) – but as most of the rides aren't necessarily connected to their area's theme, we've listed them here in order of preference.

👁 Sights

★Hollywood Rip Ride Rockit　　　RIDE

(Map p311; www.universalorlando.com; Universal Orlando Resort, Universal Studios; theme-park admission required; ⊘9am-6pm, hours vary; 🚇 Lynx 21, 37 or 40) This high-thrill coaster is not for the faint-hearted. You *Rip* up to 65mph, *Ride* 17 stories above the theme park and down a crazy-steep drop, and *Rockit* to your choice of song from a menu in your seat. You can get a video of the whole ride to see how calm you were throughout!

There's a 'hidden' menu of songs you can access via a quick internet search and keeping one of the buttons pressed down until the list appears. The only disadvantage is you won't be able to get a video.

★Revenge of the Mummy　　　RIDE

(Map p311; www.universalorlando.com; Universal Orlando Resort, Universal Studios; theme-park admission required; ⊘9am-6pm, hours vary; 🚇 Lynx 21, 37 or 40) One of the best rides in the park combines roller-coaster speed and twists with in-your-face special effects. Head deep into ancient Egyptian catacombs in near pitch black, but don't anger Imhotep the mummy – in his wrath he flings you past fire, water and more.

Springfield: Home of the Simpsons AREA

(Map p311; www.universalorlando.com; Universal Studios; theme-park admission required; ☺9am-6pm, hours vary; 🚹; 🚍Lynx 21, 37 or 40) In 2013 Universal opened *Simpsons*-themed Springfield, home to that iconic American TV family. Hang at Moe's Tavern, grab doughnuts at Lard Lad, and meet Krusty the Clown, Sideshow Bob and the Simpson family themselves. The child-friendly **Kang & Kodos' Twirl & Hurl** offers an interactive twist to whirling, and don't miss **The Simpsons Ride** (Express Pass).

It's one of the best simulated experiences at Universal, a highlight even if you're not a *Simpsons* fan. Kids will want to try Springfield's signature drink, a bubbling and steaming **Flaming Moe** that rivals the theming fun of Harry Potter's Butterbeer and tastes surprisingly good! Sure, it's just an orange soda, but it's a pretty cool orange soda, the cup makes a good souvenir, and in the eyes of an eight-year-old, it's worth every penny of that nine bucks.

Despicable Me:
Minion Mayhem RIDE

(Map p311; www.universalorlando.com; Universal Orlando Resort, Universal Studios; theme-park admission required; ☺9am-6pm, hours vary; 🚍Lynx 21, 37 or 40) Fans of *Despicable Me* won't want to miss the chance to become one of Gru's minions in this 3D simulated ride, one of Universal's best 3D experiences. There's lots of silliness, in the best of Minion traditions, and there's nothing particularly scary. Note that even ExpressPass+ lines can soar upwards from 30 minutes, so come first thing.

Race Through New York
Starring Jimmy Fallon RIDE

(Map p311; www.universalorlando.com; Universal Orlando Resort, Universal Studios; ☺9am-6pm, hours vary; 🚍Lynx 21, 37 or 40) You don't have to be a fan of *The Tonight Show* to get a kick out of this 3D simulator ride that sees you race host Jimmy Fallon through the streets of New York and then up to the moon. The pre-ride experience, where you're serenaded by the Ragtime Gals and have a meet-and-greet with Hashtag the Panda, is as good as the ride itself.

A nice touch – very much in keeping with the cool tenor of the show itself – is the safety instruction, delivered in a freestyle rap by show bandleader Tariq of the Roots.

Transformers: The Ride 3D RIDE

(Map p311; www.universalorlando.com; Universal Studios; theme-park admission required; ☺9am-6pm, hours vary; 🚍Lynx 21, 37 or 40) Get into the transport, don your 3D glasses and almost immediately you're catapulted into the middle of an epic battle to save the planet. Autobots including Optimus Prime and Bumblebee go head-to-head with nasty Decepticons as you whirl, bash, rise and fall. The effects are excellent and you'll be relieved the Autobots win.

E.T. Adventure RIDE

(Map p311; www.universalorlando.com; Universal Studios; theme-park admission required; ☺from 9am; 🚍Lynx 21, 37 or 40) This is one of Universal's classic rides and one for the nostalgia seekers. For some people, *E.T.* is Universal. Jump aboard the flying bicycle and assist E.T. to save the planet. Dodge the baddies while soaring into the stars and into E.T.'s magical world. Sure it might be dated compared to some hi-tech 'competitors,' but it's sweet. And after all, who can resist a little, shriveled alien.

Fast & Furious:
Supercharged RIDE

(Map p311; www.universalorlando.com; Universal Orlando Resort, Universal Studios; theme-park admission required; ☺9am-6pm, hours vary; 🚍Lynx 21, 37 or 40) After checking out a couple of the cars that featured in the $5-billion franchise and a quick recap of the films' basic premise, you board the 'party bus' and soon find yourself in a chase that gets pretty fast, if not all that furious. The 4K projections are pretty good, but they pale in comparison to the immersive 3D of Skull Island: Reign of Kong in Islands of Adventure.

✕ Eating

There are both the usual suspects and some fun themed eateries at Universal, including lots of burgers and ice-cream offerings. But for something different, head to Duff Brewery in Springfield for a Flaming Moe, a nonalcoholic orange-flavored concoction that gurgles like a volcano, or an icy mug of Homer Simpson's favorite brew.

Florean Fortescue's
Ice-Cream Parlour   ICE CREAM $

(Map p311; www.universalorlandoresort.com; Diagon Alley, Universal Studios; ice cream $5-10, theme-park admission required; ☺ park opening-1hr before park closing; ☐ Lynx 21, 37 or 40) In *Harry Potter and the Prisoner of Azkaban,* young Harry spends several weeks living at the Leaky Cauldron and Florean Fortescue gives him free ice cream whenever he pops into the store. His bright and charming shop, just across from the fire-spewing dragon on top of Gringotts Bank, is now open to muggles.

Bizarre and delectable flavors include Butterbeer, sticky toffee pudding and clotted cream, as well as pumpkin juice.

Mel's Drive-In   BURGERS $

(Map p311; www.universalorlando.com; Universal Studios; mains $11-16, theme-park admission required; ☺ 11am-park closing; ⊕; ☐ Lynx 21, 37 or 40, ☑ Universal) Based on the movie *American Graffiti,* this rockin' rollin' joint features classic cars and performing bands outside, '50s-diner style inside. This is a fast-food eatery, not very different really from your standard well-known burger joint, but it's a lot more fun!

Leaky Cauldron   BRITISH $$

(Map p311; www.universalorlando.com; Universal Studios; mains $12-22, theme-park admission required; ☺ 8am-park closing; ☐ Lynx 21, 37 or 40) Wizard servers in marvelous Harry Potter surrounds with classic English breakfasts, shepherd's pie, Guinness beef stew and sticky toffee pudding. You order fast-food style and the food is brought to your table – refectory of course, à la Potteresque boarding-school experience. No surprise, but this is one of the most popular restaurants in the whole park. Be prepared to wait.

The only drinks are Potter-themed delights, including nonalcoholic Peachtree Fizzing Tea and Fishy Green Ale, as well as dark ale Wizard's Brew and the malty Dragon Scale.

Lombard's Seafood Grille   SEAFOOD $$

(Map p311; ☎ 407-224-6401; www.universalorlando.com; Universal Studios; mains $17-28, theme-park admission required; ☺ 11am-1hr before park closes; ☎⊕; ☐ Lynx 21, 37 or 40) A more upmarket experience (and good for older folk). Features carpet and tile floors, a huge fish tank and a solid seafood menu. It's a calming respite from Universal Orlando's energy and the prices are, well, at least not astronomical.

Finnegan's Bar & Grill   PUB FOOD $$

(Map p311; ☎ 407-224-3613; www.universalorlando.com; Universal Studios; mains $15-26, theme-park admission required; ☺ 11am-1hr before park closes; ☎⊕; ☐ Lynx 21, 37 or 40) An Irish pub with live acoustic music plopped into the streets of New York. Serves Cornish beef pasties and Scotch eggs, as well as Harp, Bass and Guinness on tap. Annoyingly (as with many establishments, it seems), the prices are not shown on the outside menu.

🍸 Drinking & Entertainment

★ Moe's Tavern   BAR

(Map p311; www.universalorlando.com; Springfield, Universal Studios; drinks $3-9, theme-park admission required; ☺ 11am-park closing; ☎; ☐ Lynx 21, 37 or 40) Brilliantly themed *Simpsons* bar with Isotopes memorabilia, the Love Tester and Bart Simpson crank-calling the red rotary phone; it's as if you walked straight into your TV to find yourself at Homer's favorite neighborhood joint. Buy a Krusty Burger from the neighboring food court and sidle up for a Duff Beer, Duff Lite or Duff Dry.

Duff Brewery   BAR

(Map p311; www.universalorlando.com; Springfield, Universal Studios; snacks $6-15, theme-park admission required; ☺ 11am-park closing; ☎; ☐ Lynx 21, 37 or 40) Outdoor lagoonside bar serving Homer Simpson's beer of choice, on tap or by the bottle, and Springfield's signature

GETTING TO VOLCANO BAY

If you're staying at a Universal property, shuttle buses will bring you directly to the park (guests at Cabana Bay or Aventura can access the park on foot via a special entrance). If you're staying off-site, you'll have to go to CityWalk by bus or taxi and get a shuttle from there, as there's no drop-off zone at Volcano Bay.

Flaming Moe. Look for the topiary Seven Duffs out front – Tipsy, Queasy, Surly, Sleazy, Edgy, Dizzy and Remorseful.

★**Universal Orlando's
Cinematic Celebration** CINEMA
(Map p311; ☑ dining reservations 407-224-7554; www.universalorlando.com; Universal Studios; theme-park admission required; ☉ evenings, times vary; ☐ Lynx 21, 37 or 40) The 40ft-wide water curtains pull back on this nighttime spectacular that uses 120 water fountains, fireworks and crystal clear projections of some of Universal's most popular attractions, including *Jurassic World*, *Despicable Me*, *Fast & Furious*, *E.T.* and *Harry Potter*. The show takes place over the lagoon in Universal Studios as 6500 people gather on the grass at Central Park.

**Universal Orlando's
Horror Make-Up Show** LIVE PERFORMANCE
(Map p311; www.universalorlando.com; Universal Orlando Resort, Universal Studios; theme-park admission required; ☉ 9am-6pm, hours vary; ☐ Lynx 21, 37 or 40) A lively and very funny insight into how make-up artists create film monsters, this terrific 25-minute show pulls the bandages back and reveals how fake wounds, severed limbs and all that movie gore are created. The light-touch comedy means that even pre-teens can handle it, although you might want to make it clear that it's not real.

Volcano Bay

Volcano Bay (Map p311; www.universal orlando.com; 6000 Universal Blvd, Universal Orlando Resort; 1 day adult $80, child $75; ☉ from 10am, closing hours vary; ☐ Universal) is not a water park. It's a water *theme* park. Universal Orlando's biggest expansion since the opening of Islands of Adventure and CityWalk in 1999, the park is a Polynesian-themed, 28-acre pleasure paradise of flumes, slides and rides designed around a 200ft volcano. Although it's divided into four separate lands, its 28 acres are pretty compact and its 18 attractions are all close to each other.

There are winding rivers with family raft rides, wave pools, tube slides, a sandy beach and a handful of retail outlets and restaurants. It's located alongside Islands of Adventure and Universal. Hold your spot in line with a waterproof **TapuTapu** wristband, which you can link to your credit card and use to pay for food and retail goods.

★**Kala & Tai Nui
Serpentine Body Slides** RIDE
(Map p311; www.universalorlando.com; Universal Orlando Resort, Volcano Bay; theme-park admission required; ☉ 10am-6pm, hours vary; ☐ Universal) The beating of the drums gets louder and more frenetic, and then the trapdoor is released – and you're sliding down a snaking tube that delivers you to the bottom of the volcano. You have a choice between a green and blue slide; the green one is slightly quicker.

★**Krakatau Aqua Coaster** RIDE
(Map p311; www.universalorlando.com; Universal Orlando Resort, Volcano Bay; theme-park admission required; ☉ 10am-6pm, hours vary; ☐ Universal) Volcano Bay's signature ride is this coaster where you board a four-person canoe and then take off on a 60-second toboggan-style run that sees you rounding corners and shooting down straights at speed, all the while climbing and dropping for extra thrills. The launch effect is all thanks to linear induction motor technology, which makes this one of the best coasters in Orlando.

Ko'okiri Body Plunge RIDE
(Map p311; www.universalorlando.com; Universal Orlando Resort, Volcano Bay; theme-park admission required; ☉ 10am-6pm, hours vary; ☐ Universal) The tallest trapdoor plunge ride in North America is 208 steps up the towering volcano. It delivers you 125ft down to earth (well, to a splash pool) much more quickly than it took you to get up those steps.

CityWalk

Across the canal from the three theme parks is CityWalk, Universal's entertainment district comprising a pedestrian mall with restaurants, clubs, bars, the best multiplex movie theater in town, miniature golf and shops. Live music and *mucho* alcohol sums up the entertainment options here. Although nights can be packed with partying 20-somethings, bachelorette parties and general drunken mayhem, there's a distinct family-friendly vibe and several bars have reasonable food. Oh, and although it feels like a partying theme park in its own right, you can come here even if you're not visiting the Universal theme parks.

✖ Eating

The entrance hub to the theme parks, CityWalk is lined with some great restaurants and bars. Many of these shift to become live-music venues at night that charge covers after 9pm. To avoid the individual cover charges, you can purchase a CityWalk Party Pass ($12; free with multiday theme-park admission) for unlimited all-night club and bar access; add dinner and a movie for an extra $16. If you're driving, parking is free after 6pm; otherwise it's a flat rate of $25.

★ Voodoo Doughnut   DESSERTS $
(Map p311; ☑ 407-224-3663; www.universal orlando.com; 6000 Universal Blvd, CityWalk; doughnuts $2-5; ⊙ 7am-midnight Sun-Thu, to 1am Fri & Sat; ◈; ▣ Lynx 21, 37 or 40, ▣ Universal) Born in Portland, America's most original doughnut shop has brought its brand of raised yeast magic to CityWalk. How about an Old Dirty Bastard, made with Oreo cookies and peanut butter and covered in chocolate frosting, or a Bacon Maple Bar, a rectangular-shaped doughnut with maple frosting and crispy bacon on top? Vegan options available.

Toothsome Chocolate Emporium
& Savory Feast Kitchen   INTERNATIONAL $
(Map p311; www.universalorlando.com; CityWalk; ⊙ 11am-11pm Sun-Thu, to 11:30pm Fri & Sat; ◈; ▣ Universal) A delightfully quirky steampunk-meets-Willy-Wonka experience. Oh, and did we mention chocolate? If this description doesn't make sense, it isn't meant to, for that would spoil the surprise. Follow your nose here – head behind the smokestacks and into a world of chocolatey wonder with gadgets, gizmos and the 'creator,' Prof Dr Penelope Tibeaux-Tinker Toothsome.

Bob Marley –
A Tribute to Freedom   JAMAICAN $
(Map p311; ☑ 407-224-3663; www.universal orlando.com; CityWalk; mains $12-18; ⊙ 4pm-2am; ▨; ▣ Lynx 21, 37 or 40, ▣ Universal) Jerk-spiced chicken, monk stew and veggie patties with yucca fries served in a replica of the reggae

master's Jamaican home. There's live reggae in the courtyard every evening, and after 9pm you must be 21 to enter.

★ Bigfire   AMERICAN $$
(Map p311; ☑ 407-224-2074; www.universal orlando.com; 6000 Universal Blvd, CityWalk; mains $16-27; ⊙ 4-11pm Sun-Thu, to midnight Fri & Sat; ▣ Lynx 21, 37 or 40, ▣ Universal) The grill is central to everything at CityWalk's newest restaurant, with a menu designed to evoke memories of cooking over a campfire. Don't know about you, but we've never managed to cook anything as well as they do here: perfect steaks, succulent chicken and a really tasty cauliflower steak. Don't miss out on the s'mores, which you cook yourself.

Cowfish   AMERICAN $$
(Map p311; ☑ 407-224-3663; www.universal orlando.com; CityWalk, Universal Orlando Resort; mains $16-26; ⊙ 10:30am-11pm Sun-Thu, to midnight Fri & Sat; ▣ Lynx 21, 37 or 40, ▣ Universal) 'Burgushi'...this is something you'd only find in the US. Surely. Yes, a fusion between a burger and sushi. In reality, it's more sushi with a burger component rather than fusion cuisine. But it's good. Cowfish (getting the idea, here?) is a mighty popular spot with a fabulous bar.

Throw in a sake or three or a craft beer and you've got yourself a fun CityWalk experience.

Hard Rock Café   AMERICAN $$
(Map p311; ☑ 407-351-7625; www.hardrock. com/cafes/orlando; CityWalk; mains $14-28; ⊙ 8:30am-midnight; ◈; ▣ Lynx 21, 37 or 40, ▣ Universal) Excellent burgers and a rock 'n' roll theme make this a fan favorite. Plus it's open for breakfast – handy for a prepark carbo-fill. Reservations not accepted, but you can ring ahead for 'priority seating,' meaning that if there's a wait, you can queue-jump (but are not guaranteed a seat).

NBC Sports Grill & Brew   AMERICAN $$
(Map p311; www.universalorlando.com; CityWalk, Universal Orlando Resort; mains $14-30; ⊙ 11am-1:30am; ▣ Lynx 21, 37 or 40, ▣ Universal) This massive sports grill and brew has a 120ft-wide screen (playing the greatest moments in NBC sports history), but another 100 smaller screens showing live coverage of all types of games. Oh, and there's food too – the expansive menu has everything from chicken wings to a seven-layer Big Banana Cake – and more than 100 beers, from craft to regional brews.

MEETING CHARACTERS AT UNIVERSAL ORLANDO RESORT

Characters roaming Universal Studios and Islands of Adventure may include anyone/anything from the likes of Curious George and SpongeBob Square Pants to Marilyn Monroe, as well as the cast of characters from *The Simpsons*, *Shrek* and Dr Seuss books. Some favorites have scheduled meet-and-greets, so be sure to check your park map for times and places. In addition, Universal offers several character dining options.

Drinking

★ Pat O'Brien's
BAR

(Map p311; ☑ 407-224-2106; www.universal orlando.com; CityWalk; after 10pm $7; ⊙ 4pm-2am, piano bar from 5pm; 🚌 Lynx 21, 37 or 40, 🚤 Universal) A replica of the New Orleans classic, this lively bar serves Cajun food (like crawfish étouffée, Louisiana blackened redfish and po'boys; mains $15 to $21), and has a pleasant outdoor patio and duelling pianos. Order a Hurricane and settle in for a night of raucous fun.

Red Coconut Club
CLUB

(Map p311; ☑ 407-224-4233; www.universal orlando.com; CityWalk; after 10pm $7; ⊙ 8pm-2am Sun-Thu, from 6pm Fri & Sat; 🚌 Lynx 21, 37 or 40, 🚤 Universal) Modeled on a Vegas ultralounge, with a '50s Havana club and Polynesian tiki bar thrown in for good measure, this is where 'tropical meets trendy,' but the kitschiness works. There's a martini bar, a rooftop balcony and a VIP bottle service. Live music on weekends.

Groove
CLUB

(Map p311; ☑ 407-224-2165; www.universal orlando.com; CityWalk; after 10pm $7; ⊙ 9pm-2am; 🚌 Lynx 21, 37 or 40, 🚤 Universal) Dance club with sleek blue neon walls, multiple bars, three themed lounges and a mix of R&B, chart stuff, EDM and live bands.

☆ Entertainment

7Hard Rock Live
LIVE MUSIC

(Map p311; ☑ 407-351-5483; www.hardrock.com; CityWalk; tickets $25-55; ⊙ box office 10am-9pm; 🚌 Lynx 21, 37 or 40, 🚤 Universal) This 3000-person-capacity landmark draws some fairly big rock 'n' roll names and comedy acts. Full bar.

CityWalk's Rising Star
KARAOKE

(Map p311; ☑ 407-224-4233; www.universal orlando.com; CityWalk; cover $7; ⊙ 8pm-2am; 🚌 Lynx 21, 37 or 40, 🚤 Universal) A live band karaoke bar that invites you to test your chops in front of a (mostly) supportive audience split across two floors. There's backing singers to help if you slip, and heaps of cocktails for courage; just hope you don't get called *after* some of the professionals that make regular appearances. Still, it's a great night out.

Blue Man Group
PERFORMING ARTS

(Map p311; ☑ 407-258-3626; www.universal orlando.com; CityWalk; adult/child from $64/30; ⊙ times vary; 🚌 Lynx 21, 37 or 40, 🚤 Universal) Originally an off-Broadway phenomenon in 1991, this high-energy, comedy theatrical troupe at Universal Orlando Resort features all kinds of multisensory craziness – percussion 'instruments,' paintballs, marshmallows, modern dancing and general mayhem.

Universal Cinemark
CINEMA

(Map p311; ☑ 407-354-3374; www.amctheatres. com; adult/child from $12/9; 🚌 Lynx 21, 37 or 40, 🚤 Universal) The most comfortable movie theater in Orlando, where every seat in all 20 screening rooms is a luxury recliner and all movies are projected in 4K. There's even a liquor bar selling beer and wine. There's free parking for all matinee performances before 6pm, but there's a minimum two-ticket purchase.

ORLANDO

It's so easy to get caught up in Greater Orlando – in the isolated, fabricated worlds of Disney or Universal Orlando (for which, let's face it, you're probably here) – that you forget all about Orlando itself. Which is a shame, as 'The City Beautiful' isn't an ironic nickname but a fair representation of a downtown with lovely, tree-lined neighborhoods, a fabulous dining and nightlife scene, a wealth of museums and performing arts venues, several gorgeous gardens and nature preserves, and a delightfully slower pace free of manic crowds.

International Drive – aka I-Drive – is Orlando's tourist hub, packed with restaurants (including the world's biggest McDonald's), bars, stores, accommodations and Orlando attractions both tired and new. It parallels I-4 to its east, stretching 17 miles from Orlando Premium Outlets south to World Dr, just east of Walt Disney World®. The section between the convention center and Sand Lake Rd is lined with palm trees and museums, and is a relatively pleasant walking district (you'll find the visitor center here). From Sand Lake Rd north to the dead end at the outlet mall, it is Orlando tourism at full throttle.

◉ Sights

◉ International Drive

★**WonderWorks**   MUSEUM
(Map p311; ☏407-351-8800; www.wonderworks online.com; 9067 International Dr; adult/child 4-12yr $34/25; ⊙9am-midnight; ⛸; ⛟Lynx 8, 38, 42, ⛟I-Ride Trolley Red Line Stop 18 or Green Line Stop 10) Housed in a hard-to-miss, upside-down building, this is a bright, loud, frenetic landmark, and is a cross between a children's museum, a video arcade and an amusement park. Several stories of interactive exhibits offer high-speed, multisensory education. Lie on a bed of nails, sit inside a hurricane simulator and so on.

Younger children may find the pulse disorienting and frightening, but older ones will probably enjoy the cool stuff there is to do. There's also a 36ft indoor ropes course, a 4D theater with changing shows, laser tag and the nightly (and very funny) **Outta Control Magic Show**.

SeaWorld   AMUSEMENT PARK
(Map p311; ☏407-545-5550; www.seaworld parks.com; 7007 Sea World Dr; $99, discounts online, prices vary daily; ⊙9am-8pm; ⛸⛟; ⛟Lynx 8, 38, 50, 111, ⛟I-Ride Trolley Red Line Stop 28) One of Orlando's largest theme parks, SeaWorld's aquatic theme mixes marine animal shows with up-close sea-life encounters and three of the best roller coasters around. Its traditional drawcard were the live shows featuring trained dolphins, sea lions and killer whales, but the company is slowly pivoting away from these shows in reaction to the negative PR and falling visitor numbers that resulted from the 2013 documentary *Blackfish*, which alleged serious mistreatment of its captive orcas.

The film is a damning portrayal of the effects of keeping killer whales in captivity and charts the life of Tilikum, an orca at

SeaWorld Orlando that was involved in the deaths of three people, including one of its trainers during a live show. Since its release, many animal welfare groups have come out in support of the film. Research by conservationists shows it is harmful and stressful to keep such sensitive, complex creatures inside an enclosed tank.

While SeaWorld initially countered that the filmmakers were guilty of giving false and misleading information, the fallout from the controversy was severe enough to cost one CEO's job and a thorough re-evaluation of the park's focus, which is now geared firmly toward its roller coasters and its animal encounters, with a strong emphasis on education and conservation. The much criticised 'One World' killer whale show has been replaced by the twice daily 'Orca Encounter,' where you learn about these animals rather than watch them do tricks. Of every penny you spend in the park, 5% goes to various marine life conservation programs.

SeaWorld's marine-themed, adrenaline-pumping roller coasters, however, brook no argument. **Kraken** is a whiplash zip of twists and turns in carriages with no floor so your feet dangle free. On **Manta** you lie horizontally, face down, several to a row, so that the coaster vaguely resembles a manta ray, and dive and fly through the air in this position, reaching speeds of almost 60mph. The newest ride, **Mako**, is the best of the three: replicating the high-speed twists and turns of a mako shark in full flow, the glass-smooth hyper coaster has a top speed of 73mph and features serious airtime as you 'float' over some of the bumps. There are also many attractions for the under-10s.

Wheel at Icon Park   AMUSEMENT PARK
(Map p311; www.iconorlando.com; I-Drive 360, 8401 International Dr, International Drive; from $28; ⊙10am-10pm Sun-Thu, to midnight Fri & Sat) Orlando's massive Ferris wheel gives you bird's-eye views of the theme parks and the surrounding area. Greater Orlando is pretty flat, so visibility on clear days extends up to 50 miles as far as Cape Canaveral. iPads in the high-tech capsules help you locate all of the major landmarks. Check ahead as it sometimes closes for private events.

Combination tickets are available with **Madame Tussauds** (Map p311; ☏866-630-8315; www.madametussauds.com/orlando; 8387 International Dr, International Dr; from $20; ⛟I-Ride Trolley Red Line 14, Green Line 8) and Sea Life (p310).

ORLANDO & WALT DISNEY WORLD® ORLANDO

WORTH A TRIP

LOCH HAVEN PARK

Just a couple of miles north of downtown is picturesque Loch Haven Park, with 45 acres of parks, including the exquisite **Harry P Leu Gardens** (Map p318; ☑ 407-246-2620; www.leugardens. org; 1920 N Forest Ave, Loch Haven Park; adult/child 6-17yr $10/1; ☉ 9am-5pm, last admission 4:30pm; ☐ Lynx 38, 8, 50), and a handful of the city's best art museums: the **Orlando Museum of Art** (Map p318; ☑ 407-896-4231; www.omart. org; 2416 N Mills Ave, Loch Haven Park, Downtown; adult/child $15/5; ☉ 10am-4pm Tue-Fri, from noon Sat & Sun; ☖; ☐ Lynx 125, ☒ Florida Hospital Health Village) and, especially, the **Mennello Museum of American Art** (Map p318; ☑ 407-246-4278; www.mennellomuseum.org; 900 E Princeton St, Loch Haven Park; adult/child 6-18yr $5/1; ☉ 10:30am-4:30pm Tue-Sat, from noon Sun; ☐ Lynx 125, ☒ Florida Hospital Health Village). The nearby **Orlando Science Center** (Map p318; ☑ 407-514-2000; www.osc.org; 777 E Princeton St, Loch Haven Park; adult/child $21/15; ☉ 10am-5pm Thu-Tue; ☖; ☐ Lynx 125, ☒ Florida Hospital Health Village) is a great pitstop for young kids.

Fun Spot America – Orlando AMUSEMENT PARK
(Map p311; ☑ 407-363-3867; http://fun-spot.com; 5700 Fun Spot Way, International Dr; admission free, unlimited all-day rides adult/child under 54in $46/40, per ride $3-9; ☉ 10am-midnight; ☐ I-Ride Trolley Red Line Stop 1, 2) County-fair-like amusement park, with go-carts, kiddy rides, a wooden roller coaster and more. There's a small section called 'Gator Spot,' an overflow area owned by Gatorland (p322), with around 100 young 'gators.

Sea Life AQUARIUM
(Map p311; ☑ 866-622-0607; www.visitsealife. com/orlando; 8449 International Dr, International Dr; adult/child $30/25; ☉ 10am-9pm) Orlando's version of this global franchise dedicated to underwater marine life is divided into many themes, and has an educational, sustainable line to its exhibits, including talks and feeding sessions. The 360-degree glass tunnel is the highly promoted centerpiece. Online prices are $5 less per person. Combination tickets are available with the Wheel at Icon Park and Madame Tussauds.

Aquatica AMUSEMENT PARK
(Map p311; ☑ 407-351-3600; www.aquaticaby seaworld.com; 5800 Water Play Way; online advance $55, daily pass $65, with SeaWorld Orlando per day $151; ☉ 9am-6pm; ☖; ☐ Lynx 8, 38, 50, 111, ☐ SeaWorld shuttle, ☐ I-Ride Trolley Red Line Stop 30) Water slides, lazy rivers, splash zones and wave pools are the main attractions at this Pacific-themed waterpark. The newest slide is **Riptide Race**, where you can race friends down two 650ft tubes sliding from a 68ft tower. Of its 40-odd slides and rides though, still the most thrilling of all is the free-fall experience of **Ihu's Breakaway Falls**, where a slide door drops you into a tube that eventually makes its way to a pool at the bottom.

The park is owned by SeaWorld, and while there are no controversial dolphin or whale shows, the twice-daily feeding exhibitions of its four black-and-white Commerson's dolphins have been pared back in response to scrutiny by animal welfare organizations.

Discovery Cove AMUSEMENT PARK
(Map p311; ☑ 877-434-7268; www.discovery cove.com; 6000 Discovery Cove Way, International Dr; day entry from $144, incl SeaWorld & Aquatica from $171, SeaVenture extra $59-79, prices vary daily; ☉ 8am-5:30pm; ☖; ☐ Lynx 8, 38, 50, 111) Discovery Cove's big draw is the chance to snorkel in a fish- and ray-filled reef, float on a lazy river and relax in an intimate tropical sanctuary of white-sand beaches. For an extra charge you can also swim with dolphins, which is strongly opposed by animal-welfare groups and marine scientists, who say it's debilitating and stressful for these sensitive and complex creatures. Advance reservations are required for the all-day experience.

◉ Downtown

Lake Eola Park PARK
(Map p314; 195 N Rosalind Ave; ☉ 6am-midnight; ☖) Pretty and shaded, this little city park sits between downtown and Thornton Park. A paved sidewalk circles the water, there's a waterfront playground and you can rent swan paddleboats ($15 for 30 minutes). On Sunday mornings, the park is home to the Orlando Farmers Market (p325).

Wells' Built Museum MUSEUM
(Map p314; ☑ 407-245-7535; www.wellsbuilt.org; 511 W South St; adult/child $5/3; ☉ 9am-5pm Mon-Fri) This small museum is dedicated to Orlando's African American history and culture. It's housed in the former Wells' Hotel, built in 1921 by Dr William Monroe

International Drive

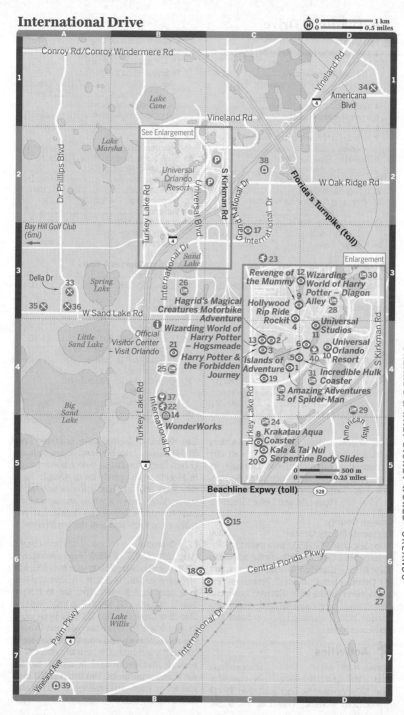

International Drive

Wells to host African American performers forbidden from staying in the city's strictly segregated accommodations. Through its doors passed many an influential performer, including Count Basie, Cab Calloway, Billie Holiday, Ella Fitzgerald and Duke Ellington.

Orange County
Regional History Center   MUSEUM
(Map p314; ☑ 407-836-8500; www.thehistory center.org; 65 E Central Blvd, Downtown; adult/child 5-12yr $8/6; ☺ 10am-5pm Mon-Sat, from noon Sun; ♿) Orlando before Disney? Permanent exhibits cover prehistoric Florida, European exploration, race relations and citrus production, with a recreated pioneer home and 1927 courtroom.

🏃 Activities

I-Drive NASCAR   AMUSEMENT PARK
(Map p311; ☑ 407-581-9644; www.idrivenascar. com; 5228 Vanguard St; race adult/child $19/17; ☺ noon-10pm Mon-Thu, 11am-11pm Fri & Sat,

11am-10pm Sun; ☐ I-Ride Trolley Red/Green Lines Stop 4) Inside a huge blue-and-yellow container building is the fastest indoor go-kart track in Florida, with speeds up to 45mph. Each race lasts around eight minutes and when you're done, there's a whole amusement arcade to explore before you decide that you really want to try and beat the track record.

I Fly Orlando   ADVENTURE SPORTS
(Map p311; ☑ 407-337-4359; www.iflyworld.com; 8969 International Dr; 2-flight adult from $50, with VR experience $110; ☺ 11:30am–8:30pm Mon-Thu, to 9:30pm Fri, 9:30am–9:30pm Sat, to 8:30pm Sun; ♿; ☐ Lynx 8, 38, 42, ☐ I-Ride Trolley Red Line Stop 18 or Green Line Stop 10) This is as close as you'll get to skydiving without leaving the room. Suit up and take to the 12ft-high, 1000HP wind tunnel, where the effect is so realistic that skydiving clubs use the facility for training purposes. You can add VR goggles for an extra-real experience. It's fun and safe, even for kids as young as 4.

Grand Cypress Golf Club GOLF
(📞407-239-1909; www.grandcypress.com; 1 N Jacaranda St; from $70) A beautiful 18-hole Scottish-links-style course (including deep pot bunkers) designed by Jack Nicklaus, just outside Walt Disney World®. Rates vary according to time and season.

Dubsdread Golf Course GOLF
(Map p318; 📞407-246-2551; www.historical dubsdread.com; 549 W Par St, College Park; green fee from $44) Old-school Orlando course opened in 1924 and renovated in 2008; it was the host of the Orlando Open between 1945–47. Sits in the College Park neighborhood, just west of I-4 and south of Winter Park.

West Orange Trail Bikes & Blades CYCLING
(📞407-877-0600; www.orlandobikerental.com; 17914 State Rd 438, Winter Garden; bikes per hour $8-12, per day $30-50, per week $99-149, delivery/pickup $40; ⏰9am-5pm Mon-Fri, from 7:30am

Sat & Sun) This bike shop lies 20 miles west of Orlando and sits at the beginning of the West Orange Trail. It offers bike rental and comprehensive information, both online and on site, on biking in and around Orlando.

Orange Cycle CYCLING
(Map p318; 📞407-422-5552; www.orangecycle orlando.com; 2204 Edgewater Dr; ⏰10am-7pm Mon-Fri, 10am-5pm Sat) Provides printable maps to Orlando bike trails and is an excellent source of information for all things biking in and around Orlando. Sells and repairs bikes, but does not rent.

Buena Vista Watersports WATER SPORTS
(📞407-239-6939; www.bvwatersports.com; 13245 Lake Bryan Dr; per hour kayak, canoe or paddleboard $25, jet ski $105; ⏰9am-6:30pm; 🅿) Just outside the Disney gates, with a low-key vibe. Water skiing and tube riding include driver/instructor (per hour per boat $165).

ORLANDO & WALT DISNEY WORLD® ORLANDO

Downtown Orlando

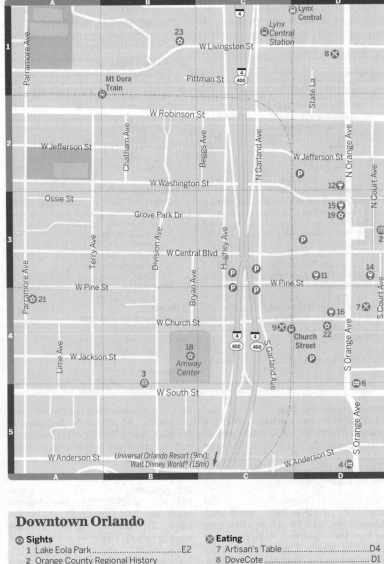

Downtown Orlando

◉ Sights
1 Lake Eola Park	E2
2 Orange County Regional History Center	D3
3 Wells' Built Museum	B4

🛏 Sleeping
4 Aloft Orlando Downtown	D5
5 EO Inn & Spa	G2
6 Grand Bohemian Hotel	D5

✗ Eating
7 Artisan's Table	D4
8 DoveCote	D1
9 Hamburger Mary's	C4
10 Stubborn Mule	G4

🍷 Drinking & Nightlife
Bösendorfer Lounge	(see 6)
11 Cocktails & Screams	D3
12 Courtesy Bar	D2

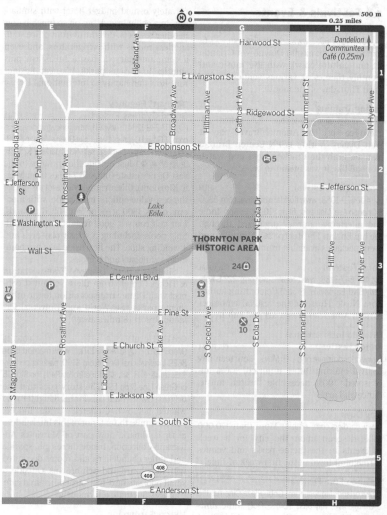

13 Eola Wine Company		G3
14 Hanson's Shoe Repair		D3
15 Independent Bar		D3
16 Latitudes		D4
17 Mathers Social Gathering		E3

☺ Entertainment

18 Amway Center		B4
19 Beacham & the Social		D3

20 Dr Phillips Center for the		
Performing Arts		E5
21 Exploria Stadium		A4
22 Mad Cow Theatre		D4
23 Orlando Ballet		B1

🛍 Shopping

24 Orlando Farmers Market		G3

✨ Festivals & Events

Thursday Gallery Hop　CULTURAL
(☎407-648-7060; www.orlandoslice.com; ⏲6-9pm 3rd Thu of the month) Downtown Orlando art and culture crawl, with live music and monthly themes at various venues on the third Thursday of the month.

Spring Training　SPORTS
(www.springtrainingonline.com; tickets from $4; ⏲mid-Feb–Apr) The Atlanta Braves play at Walt Disney World's ESPN Center. Bring a blanket, grab the Cracker Jacks and watch baseball like it was meant to be.

Florida Film Festival　FILM
(☎407-629-1088; www.floridafilmfestival.com; 1300 S Orlando Ave, Maitland; films $10-13; ⏲Apr) Indie and alternative movies organized through the hip Enzian Theater (p324). Multifilm and event packages available from $55.

Zora! Festival　CULTURAL
(☎407-647-3188; www.zorafestival.org; 227 E Kennedy Blvd, Eatonville; ⏲Jan) Celebrating author Zora Neale Hurston, the festival embraces African American music, art and culture.

Orlando International Fringe Festival　CULTURAL
(www.orlandofringe.org; ⏲May) Fourteen-day festival offering '100% unjuried, 100% uncensored, 100% accessible theater, music, dance and art.'

Gay Days　LGBT
(www.gaydays.com; ⏲Jun) More than 170,000 folks descend upon the city for a week of events in the theme parks and venues throughout town in the first week of June.

Orlando Film Festival　FILM
(www.orlandofilmfest.com; Cobb Plaza Cinema, 155 S Orange Ave; day pass $24; ⏲Oct) Indie films screen in downtown Orlando at Cobb Plaza Cinema Cafe. Various packages available.

🛏 Sleeping

I-Drive is close to the parks and in the heart of the tourist action, while Downtown has some lovely privately owned options, which can be a blessed relief from the resorts.

🛏 International Drive

⭐ Floridian Hotel & Suites　HOTEL $
(Map p311; ☎407-212-3021; www.floridianhotelorlando.com; 7531 Canada Ave, International Drive; r from $80; P🐕❄🏠🛆) A wonderful, privately owned budget hotel with similarities to a chain brand, but oh so much better in other respects: delightful front office staff, spotless rooms with refrigerators, and even a complimentary (if basic) breakfast, plus shuttles to various parks. It's near Restaurant Row and handy to International Dr.

⭐ Hyatt Regency Grand Cypress Resort　RESORT $$
(☎407-239-1234; www.hyattregencygrandcypress.com; 1 Grand Cypress Blvd, Lake Buena Vista; r $150-350, resort fee per day $38, self-/valet parking $25/35; P@❄🏠🛆🐕) Just outside the entrance to the vast Disney estate (but still 7 miles from Magic Kingdom), this atrium-style resort is one of the best-value options in Orlando, with modern rooms, 1500 acres of palm-filled grounds, four golf courses, good restaurants and multiple pools, including a splash play area and a winding slide. The beachside lake has hammocks, sailboats and bicycles.

Shuttles go to Disney's Transportation & Ticket Center (from there you must connect with Disney transportation to the other theme parks), SeaWorld and Universal Orlando Resort (8 miles away).

Castle Hotel　HOTEL $$
(Map p311; ☎407-345-1511; www.marriott.com; 8629 International Dr; r from $160, parking per day $15; P@❄🏠🛆; 🚋I-Ride Trolley Red Line Stop 15 or Green Line Stop 69) The story goes that the original owner built this for his daughter who wanted her own Cinderella castle. Indeed, you can't miss the exterior of this International Dr landmark, now part of Marriott's Autograph Collection. Inside there's gilt, sparkle and antler chandeliers, and rooms decorated with faux lizard and rich browns. Outside, a small pool sits next to a garden-inspired cafe.

Prices fluctuate enormously.

Hilton Garden Inn International Drive North　MOTEL $$
(Map p311; ☎407-363-9332; www.hiltongardenorlando.com; 5877 American Way, International Dr; r $120-270; P@❄🛆; 🚋I-Trolley Red Line Stop 5) With an airy garden-style lobby, a poolside tiki bar and an on-site restaurant, this is an excellent midrange option for visiting Universal Orlando. It's less than a mile to the parks and, although it sits on I-4, it's quiet and set apart from I-Drive's overdrive.

Hilton Homewood Suites　MOTEL $$
(Map p311; ☎407-226-0669; http://homewoodsuites1.hilton.com; 5893 American Way, International Dr; ste $140-280; @❄🛆; 🚋I-Ride Trolley Red

Line Stop 5) Comfy one- and two-bedroom suites, each with a fully equipped kitchen and a low-key feel that is lacking at comparable chain hotels in Orlando. There's a complimentary hot breakfast, a dinner buffet (Monday to Thursday) and a 24-hour snack shop. Great choice, particularly if you're going to Universal Orlando Resort; there's a free shuttle from the hotel.

★ **Grande Lakes Orlando –**
JW Marriott & Ritz-Carlton   HOTEL $$$
(Map p311; ☑ JW Marriott 407-206-2300, Ritz-Carlton 407-206-2400; www.grandelakes.com; 4012 Central Florida Pkwy – Ritz Carlton, 4040 Central Park Pkwy – JW Marriott; r from $330, resort fee per day $39, self/valet parking $29/37; P@🐾🏊) Two properties, one a Ritz and the other a Marriott, share facilities. The grounds, peaceful and elegant, with plenty of greenery and the best lazy river pool in Orlando, sit in a sheltered oasis of quiet and luxury. The spa is divine, the service impeccable, the food outstanding and most rooms have balconies overlooking the pool and golf course.

Excellent for honeymooners and families alike, this hotel is the rare Orlando find that seamlessly combines child- and adult-friendly facilities. Rates fluctuate enormously.

🛏 **Downtown**

EO Inn & Spa   BOUTIQUE HOTEL $$
(Map p314; ☑ 407-481-8485; www.eoinn.com; 227 N Eola Dr, Thornton Park; r $150-500; P✳@🛜) Small and understated hotel, and one of the only options on the northeastern shore of Lake Eola, with an easy walk to Thornton Park and downtown Orlando bars and restaurants. The rooms vary dramatically in size. It's got a not-quite-there ambience, but is good value at the lower end of the scale (note: prices fluctuate enormously).

Grand Bohemian Hotel   HOTEL $$$
(Map p314; ☑ 407-313-9000; www.grandbohemianhotel.com; 325 S Orange Ave, Downtown; r from $350, ste from $470, valet-only parking per day $29; P@🛜🏊) Downtown Orlando's most luxurious and elegant option has marble floors, a stunning art-deco bar with massive black pillars, weekend jazz and rich urban rooms. The small rooftop pool echoes 1950s Miami Beach. With no shuttle transport to the parks and no kid-friendly amenities, the hotel appeals to an atypical Orlando visitor.

Aloft Orlando Downtown   BUSINESS HOTEL $$$
(Map p314; ☑ 407-380-3500; www.aloftorlandodowntown.com; 500 S Orange Ave, Downtown; r from $220, parking $25; P🐾@🛜🏊) Open, streamlined and decidedly modern, this one-time utilities building has been successfully converted into a sleek hotel with carefully constructed minimalist decor. It's a 45-minute drive from the theme parks, but downtown's bars and restaurants are on your doorstep.

🍴 Eating

Whatever you're craving, you'll find a version of it on International Dr. Just off the main drag is Sand Lake Rd, aka Restaurant Row, which has about two dozen casual and upscale spots for a good meal. Just northeast of Downtown, Mills 50 is fast becoming a foodie hub to rival Winter Park, which has a long-established restaurant scene. I-Drive is the heartland of the midrange chain restaurant, including the world's biggest McDonald's (at the north end of International Dr, at the intersection with Destination Pkwy).

🍴 International Drive

Slate   AMERICAN $$
(Map p311; ☑ 407-500-7528; www.slateorlando.com; 8323 W Sand Lake Rd, Restaurant Row; mains $21-42; ⏱11am-12:30pm & 5-10pm Mon-Fri, 10:30am-3pm & 5-11pm Sat, 10:30am-3pm & 5-9pm Sun) One of Restaurant Row's brightest spots is this place that serves wood-fired meats and pizzas as well as seafood and light bites. The brain-child of Atlanta-based Concentrics, seating is divided between private and communal tables, as well as the wood room, a veranda-style space with a fireplace. It's Orlando, so cocktails are right on point.

Pharmacy   AMERICAN $$
(Map p311; ☑ 407-985-2972; https://thepharmacyorlando.com; 8060 Via Dellagio Way, Sand Lake Rd; mains $19-34; ⏱5-9pm Tue-Sat) This speakeasy-style joint in a high-end mall is renowned for the quality of its craft cocktails and exceptional farm-to-fork cuisine. Burgers, pizzas, steaks and a particularly good mac 'n' cheese are served in huge portions, and are all the better for it. Finding the place is part of the fun: look for an unmarked elevator door.

🍴 Downtown

★ **Kabooki Sushi**   SUSHI $
(Map p318; ☑ 407-328-3839; www.kabookisushi.com; 3122 E Colonial Dr; mains $8-18; ⏱5-10pm

Greater Orlando

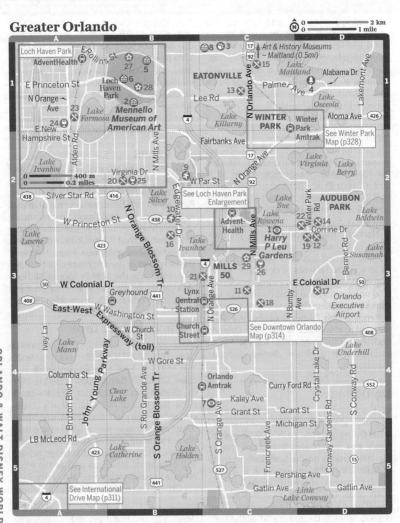

Sun-Thu, to 11pm Fri & Sat) In an unassuming strip mall just east of Downtown is the best budget sushi spot in Orlando. Chef Henry Moso crafts nigiri, sashimi and *makimono* (sushi rolls) of such exquisite delicacy and flavor that the James Beard people saw fit to nominate him for a 2020 Rising Star Chef of the Year award. Best budget? Maybe just the best, period.

P is for Pie
BAKERY $

(Map p318; ☑ 407-745-4743; www.crazyforpies.com; 2806 Corrine Dr, Audubon Park; pies from $2.50; ☺ 7:30am-4:30pm Mon-Sat) Clean-lined with an artisan twist to classic pies (as in sweet tarts with a biscuit base), offering mini and specialty options based on seasonal availability – try caramel maple pumpkin in winter and triple berry in summer. Sublime.

Pig Floyd's Urban Barbakoa
BARBECUE $

(Map p318; ☑ 407-203-0866; https://pigfloyds.com; 1326 Mills Ave; mains $9-18; ☺ 11am-10pm Mon-Thu & Sun, 11am-11pm Fri & Sat) A spin-off of the popular Treehouse food truck, this shack-style spot serves up sizzling Southern barbecue – brisket, ribs, pork belly and slaw. Throw in some Caribbean, Latin and Asian flavours (how about a Korean kimcheeze taco, or a crisp pork belly *bánh mì*?) and you've got the best BBQ joint in town. The lines are worth it.

Greater Orlando

East End Market MARKET $
(Map p318; ☑231-236-3316; www.eastendmkt.com; 3201 Corrine Dr, Audubon Park; ☺8am-7pm Mon-Thu, to 9pm Fri & Sat, 11am-6pm Sun; ☑🚼) Look for the raised vegetable beds and picnic tables outside this hip, earthy little organic collection of locally sourced places to eat and markets.

Inside there's Lineage, a fabulous coffee stand; a bar offering Florida beer and wine; Gideon's Bakehouse, with fabulous cakes and cookies; the excellent raw-vegan bar Skybird Juicebar & Experimental Kitchen; Olde Hearth Bread Company; and more.

Stardust Video & Coffee CAFE $
(Map p318; ☑407-623-3393; www.stardustvideoandcoffee.wordpress.com; 1842 E Winter Park Rd, Audubon Park; mains $8-15; ☺7am-midnight Mon-Fri, from 8am Sat & Sun; ℗🛜☑) A 'weirdo eclectic' hangout (to quote Tess, the server) with folks hiding behind laptops munching on veggie treats or sipping on freshly squeezed juices by day. It's an atmospheric craft cocktail and artisan-beer hot spot by night. There's even a snapshot machine. Call for information on weekly live music and the Monday evening farmers market.

Paper lanterns and twinkly lights dangle from the ceiling, snapshot-style photographs hang haphazardly from the concrete walls, and there are private booths that have a church confessional feel.

Anh Hong VIETNAMESE $
(Map p318; ☑407-999-2656; https://anhhongorlando.com; 1124 E Colonial Dr; mains $9-15; ☺9am-10pm) This award-winning Vietnamese restaurant looks plain enough, but the massive menu – there are over 200 dishes – is anything but. Fresh, healthy ingredients are combined to create classic dishes. Its specialties are *pho*-noodle and rice-noodle soups and Vietnamese sandwiches.

Bikes, Beans & Bordeaux CAFE $
(Map p318; ☑407-427-1440; www.b3cafe.com; 3022 Corrine Dr, Audubon Park; mains $7-14; ☺7am-9pm Mon-Fri, from 8am Sat, 8am-5pm Sun; ℗🛜☑) Started by keen cyclists for their fellow enthusiasts, the word soon spread. This casual little spot serves up good sandwiches and salads that are much healthier than you'll find elsewhere. The menu is themed along cycling events: sandwiches are named Tour de France and Tour Mediterranean etc. Kids can have 'training wheels' bites, aka smaller meals such as peloton pizzas.

There's weekend live music, couches for lounging and local art.

Eden Bar AMERICAN $
(Map p318; ☑407-629-1088; www.enzian.org; 1300 S Orlando Ave, Maitland; mains $9-12; ☺11am-10pm Sun-Thu, to 11pm Fri & Sat; ☑) Island-vibe outdoor dining under the giant cypress of the ultracool Enzian Theater (p324). The delightfully eclectic menu ranges from pear prosciutto pizza and

ORLANDO & WALT DISNEY WORLD® ORLANDO

quinoa-stuffed peppers to fried chicken and country fried steak. Try the Mexican mojito.

Keke's Breakfast Cafe   CAFE $

(Map p311; ☑407-226-1400; www.kekes.com; 4192 Conroy Rd, Suite 100; mains $10-16; ◷7am-2:30pm; 🖐) Orlando go-to spot for great breakfasts, including stuffed French toast, eggs Benedict and banana-nut pancakes. It's a Florida-wide chain; other Orlando locations include one in Winter Park (☑407-629-1400; www.kekes.com; 345 W Fairbanks Ave; mains $10-16; ◷7am-2:30pm; 🖐) and one in Restaurant Row (Map p311; ☑407-354-1440; www.kekes.com; 7512 Dr Phillips Blvd; mains $10-16; ◷7am-2:30pm; 🖐).

★Maxine's on Shine   AMERICAN $$

(Map p318; ☑407-674-6841; https://maxines onshine.com; 337 N Shine Ave; dinner mains $14-27, brunch mains $12-17; ◷5-10pm Tue-Fri, 10am-10pm Sat, 10am-4pm Sun) This friendly bistro and retro bar is a firm neighborhood favorite. The mixed menu of European-infused dishes is tasty at any time, but the big draw is brunch. Chicken and waffles is the signature dish, while the Bloody Mary with a beer floater, bacon stir stick and shrimp cocktail garnish is almost a meal in itself.

★DoveCote   FRENCH $$

(Map p314; ☑407-930-1700; www.dovecote orlando.com; 390 N Orange Ave, Suite 110; lunch mains $11-29, dinner mains $18-32; ◷11:30am-2:30pm & 5-10pm Mon-Sat, 10:30am-2:30pm Sun) The decor – vivid blue, gold and other colors – is straight out of a Klimt painting, but this restaurant in the Bank of America building serves some mighty fine cuisine, best described as 'comfort French.' Sit in the brasserie and tuck into a delicious croque monsieur or a piping hot bowl of onion soup. There's also a coffee stop.

Reyes Mezcaleria   MEXICAN $$

(Map p318; ☑407-868-9007; www.reyesmex.com; 821 N Orange Ave; mains $15-24; ◷11am-10pm Sun-Thu, to 11pm Fri & Sat) This stylish, airy cantina-style Mexican joint in the heart of Downtown serves delicious tacos, empanadas and other Mexican classics. There's a fine selection of wines, but ignore the margaritas and you're missing out on half the fun.

Stubborn Mule   MODERN AMERICAN $$

(Map p314; www.thestubbornmuleorlando.com; 100 S Eola Dr, Suite 103, Downtown; mains $19-32; ◷11am-11pm Tue-Sat, 11am-9pm Sun) A trendy and very popular gastropub that serves handcrafted cocktails with flair (yes, plenty of mules) and good ol' locally sourced, delicious food that's nothing but contemporary – the likes of polenta cakes, smoked Gouda grits and roasted winter vegetables. Live music on weekends can make the outdoor seating a rather noisy affair.

Hamburger Mary's   BURGERS $$

(Map p314; ☑321-319-0600; www.hamburger marys.com; 110 W Church St, Downtown; mains $12-18; ◷11am-10pm Sun & Mon, 11am-10:30pm Tue-Thu, 11am-11:30pm Fri & Sat) Downtown high-energy diner specializing in over-the-top burgers with sweet-potato fries and serious cocktails. There's a Broadway Brunch with show tunes, Tuesday night drag shows and all kinds of interactive entertainment.

BAY HILL

Quiet and genteel Bay Hill Club & Lodge (☑407-876-2429; www.bayhill.com; 9000 Bay Hill Blvd; r $250-700; 🅿️➗❄️@🛜🏊) feels like a time warp, as though you're walking into a TV set or your grandmother's photo album. Though the lodge seems to attract an older, golfing clientele, and there is nothing trendy or fancy about its pool or amenities, families will find Bay Hill's comforting cocoonlike atmosphere a welcoming oasis after a day tackling Orlando. It's reassuringly calm and simple.

Theme parks and restaurants are an easy drive. Handsome rooms are spread among a series of two-story buildings bordering the Arnold Palmer–designed golf course (☑407-876-2429; www.bayhill.com; 9000 Bay Hill Blvd; rates connected to room rates at Bay Hill Club & Lodge), which hosts a prestigious invitational on the PGA Tour in March. You'll find some terrific deals online, with room rates occasionally slashed by 50%.

Set in a residential golf community and sporting only a small sign, Bay Hill is difficult to find. Head west from Apopka Vineland Rd on Bay Hill Blvd and look for it after 1 mile, on the right. There is no daily parking fee or resort fee.

WILD ORLANDO

After a few days (or hours, depending on who you ask) in a theme park, the sheer mass of Orlando's artificial environments can get a little overwhelming. If that last sentence made you long for some real fresh air and the smell of dirt, never fear – there are actually a fair few parks and nature preserves in the Greater Orlando area.

Located 30 minutes west of Walt Disney World®, **Lake Louisa State Park** (☑ general 850-245-2157, park 352-394-3969; www.floridastateparks.org/park/Lake-Louisa; 7305 US 27, Clermont; car $5, campsites per person from $5, hookups $24, 6-person cabins $120; ☺ 8am-sundown) is an easy getaway. There are several peaceful lakes, lovely beaches and 25 miles of hiking trails through fields, woods and orange groves. For boating on Dixie Lake, you can rent three-person canoes and single-rider kayaks (from $20 to $30) at the ranger station. Twenty cabins, each with two bedrooms (linen included), a fully equipped kitchen and front porch, offer lake views. Camping and cabin reservations can be made up to 11 months in advance.

Fancy a swim? Head to **Wekiwa Springs State Park** (☑ 407-884-2009; www.floridastateparks.org/parks-and-trails/wekiwa-springs-state-park; 1800 Wekiwa Circle, Apopka; admission $6, campsites per person $5, hookups $24; ☺ 7am-dusk), located about 20 miles northwest of downtown Orlando, and cool off in the icy spring-fed swimming hole. You can also hike miles of trails and paddle the tranquil, still waters of the Wekiva River. Central Florida Nature Adventures, inside the park, offers 2½-hour guided tours, rents kayaks and canoes (two hours $17, per additional hour $3) and provides overnight camping supplies. Reserve primitive riverside campsites in advance.

At **Orlando Wetlands Park** (☑ 407-568-1706; www.orlandowetlands.org; 25115 Wheeler Rd, Fort Christmas; ☺ sunrise-sunset; ⊞) you'll find woodlands, lakes and marshes flush with migrating birds, alligators, deer and all kinds of other critters. There are 20 miles of hiking trails and dirt roads, as well as restrooms, picnic tables and charcoal grills at the main entrance. Biking is limited to unpaved berm roads. The park, 30 miles east of downtown Orlando, sits about halfway between Orlando and Titusville, home to Canaveral National Seashore and the Kennedy Space Center.

While it's not a nature park per se, **Bok Tower Gardens** (☑ 863-676-1408; www.boktowergardens.org; 1151 Tower Blvd, Lake Wales; adult/child $15/5, house tour $7; ☺ 8am-6pm, last admission 5pm; ⊞) is still a breath of clean air from a lovingly designed green lung. Designed by Frederick Law Olmsted Jr and showcasing the meticulously carved, 205ft stone bell tower, this 250-acre National Historic Landmark features beautiful gardens, twice-daily carillon concerts, the Mediterranean-style Pinewood Estates (c 1930s) and a garden cafe. Kids can pick up special paper at the entry and make a treasure hunt out of looking for the iron rubbing posts, each with a different animal to rub. The gardens host outdoor classical-music concerts, and sit an hour south of Orlando, close to Legoland.

Artisan's Table AMERICAN $$
(Map p314; ☑ 407-730-7499; www.artisanstable-orlando.com; 55 W Church St, Suite 128; mains $12-29; ☺ 7am-10pm Mon-Thu, 7am-midnight Fri, 9am-midnight Sat, 9am-10pm Sun) Chow down on the likes of a breakfast bowl of eggs and grits, or opt for steel-cut oats with agave and an organic smoothie at this under-the-radar locavore favorite offering an ever-changing and eclectic menu. It's extremely accommodating to dietary requirements, too. There's even coffee and cocktails to start and end the day.

If you want both, don't miss the cafe tequila, all fed through a fandangled gravity infusion tower ($7 per shot).

White Wolf Café & Bar DINER $$
(Map p318; ☑ 407-895-9911; www.whitewolfcafe.com; 1829 N Orange Ave, Ivanhoe Village; mains $16-24; ☺ 8am-3pm Sun-Tue, 8am-9pm Wed & Thu, 8am-10pm Fri & Sat; ☐ Lynx 102) Old-style, neighborhood diner cafe, with Tiffany-styled chandeliers, a massive wooden bar and a mishmash of antiques. Come for the stick-to-your-bones breakfasts and a Bloody Mary.

★ **K Restaurant** AMERICAN $$$
(Map p318; ☑ 407-872-2332; www.krestaurantorlando.com; 1710 Edgewater Dr, College Park; mains $25-39; ☺ 5-9pm Mon-Thu, 5:30-10pm Fri & Sat, 5:30-8pm Sun; ☑) ☙ Chef and owner Kevin Fonzo, one of Orlando's most celebrated

WORTH A TRIP

GATORLAND

With no fancy roller coasters or drenching water rides, this mom-and-pop **park** (📞 407-855-5496; www.gatorland.com; 14501 S Orange Blossom Trail/Hwy 17, Kissimmee; adult/child $30/20; ⏱ 10am-5pm; 🅿; 🚌 Lynx 108) hearkens back to Old Florida – and is all the better for it. The 'alligator capital of the world' is home to thousands of alligators big and small, as well as crocodiles, snakes and brightly colored macaws. The whole place is a lot of fun: there's a zipline, a swamp buggy ride and, if you have the nerve, the chance to feed the gators up close.

Of the 2000-odd alligators, look out for Chester, the biggest one in the park, and brothers Ferris Zombi and Trezo Je, two of only 12 leucistic alligators in the world. Their partial albinism earns them the nickname 'swamp ghost' and, according to Cajun folklore, looking into their bright blue eyes is meant to bring good luck.

The rather tongue-in-cheek shows are charmingly free of special effects, dramatic music and spectacular light design. At the **Jumparoo Show**, 10ft-long alligators leap almost entirely out of the water to grab whole chickens from the trainer. **Up-Close Encounters** involves mysterious boxes holding animals the public has sent to the park. The trainers are too scared to open them, so they drag audience members down to help.

The **Screamin' Gator Zipline** (per two hours $70, including park admission) features various ziplines over the park. The newest attraction is the **Stompin' Gator Off-Road Adventure** ($10), a 10-minute swamp buggy ride of big bumps and lots of funny wordplay by the guide. There's also the chance to be a Trainer for a Day ($129), a three-hour backstage experience where you meet some of the gators and learn about taking care of them.

Note: Lonely Planet does not condone the practice of having your photo taken sitting on a gator and some of the shows feature animal interaction some might find disturbing.

Gatorland is in Kissimmee, 18 miles south of Orlando via Florida's Turnpike; turn off at E Osceola Pkwy. Parking is free.

and established field-to-fork foodie stars, earns local and national accolades year after year, but this neighborhood favorite remains wonderfully unassuming. There's a wraparound porch, and a lovely little terrace, and herbs and vegetables come from the on-site garden.

Hemingways SEAFOOD $$$
(📞 407-239-1234; www.hemingwaysorlando.com; 1 Grand Cypress Blvd, Hyatt Regency Grand Cypress Resort, Buena Vista; mains $29-55; ⏱ 5-10pm) The atmosphere is Key West in the 1940s, but the cuisine is all kinds of contemporary sophistication. Try the particularly tasty crab cakes, with big chunks of lump crab and very little filler, or the Maine Lobster – deconstructed whole lobster with saffron butter. Ask for a table on the screened-in porch.

 Drinking & Nightlife

With so many vacationers around, it's hardly surprising that Orlando likes to enjoy itself. For the majority of visitors, I-Drive is where most of the action takes place, but the best bars and clubs are spread throughout Downtown.

 International Drive

Icebar BAR
(Map p311; 📞 407-426-7555; www.icebarorlando.com; 8967 International Dr; entry at door/advance online $20/15; ⏱ 5pm-midnight Sun-Wed, to 1am Thu, to 2am Fri & Sat; 🚋 I-Trolley Red Line Stop 18 or Green Line Stop 10) More classic Orlando gimmicky fun. Step into the 22ºF (-5ºC) ice house, sit on the ice seat, admire the ice carvings and sip the icy drinks. Coat and gloves are provided at the door (or upgrade to the photogenic faux fur for $10), and the fire room, bathrooms and other areas of the bar are kept at normal temperature.

Adults over 21 welcome anytime; folks aged between eight and 20 are allowed between 5pm and 9pm only.

 Downtown

⭐ **Mathers Social Gathering** COCKTAIL BAR
(Map p314; www.mathersorlando.com; 30 S Magnolia Ave; ⏱ 4pm-2am Tue-Sat) Our favorite bar in Orlando is on the 3rd floor of the 19th-century Mather Building, with a carefully designed speakeasy vibe and a killer

menu of vintage, craft cocktails that are the best you'll have anywhere in town. Highly recommended.

★ **Cocktails & Screams** COCKTAIL BAR
(Map p314; ☑ 407-885-3558; https://cocktails andscreams.com; 39 W Pine St; ⊙ 7pm-2am Tue-Sat, to midnight Sun) It's Halloween year-round at this bar that opened in 2019 and quickly became an Orlando favorite – and not just with fans of all things horror and Gothic. It's part bar, part attraction in its own right and almost every night has themed events – Wednesday is Addams Family Night, so dress up! You'll scream, but mostly in delight.

Around the walls of the bar are clues that will eventually lead you to the **Craft**, a 'secret coven bar' that serves even more potent cocktails.

Hanson's Shoe Repair COCKTAIL BAR
(Map p314; ☑ 407-476-9446; www.facebook.com/hansonsshoerepair; 3rd fl, 27 E Pine St, Downtown; cocktails $16; ⊙ 8pm-2am Tue-Thu & Sat, from 5pm Fri, from 3pm Sun) Orlando *loves* the Prohibition-era speakeasy theme, and this spot does it better than most, down to the historically accurate cocktails and a secret daily password for entry. Once inside, it's a cozy nest of folks having a quiet good time. Call or check its Twitter account (@hansonsshoeshop) for the password. There's a dress code – no sloppy gear.

Wally's Mills Ave Liquors BAR
(Map p318; ☑ 407-896-6975; www.wallysonmills.com; 1001 N Mills Ave, Thornton Park; ⊙ 11:30-2am Mon-Sat, to midnight Sun) It's been around since the early '50s, before Orlando became Disney, and while its peeling, naked-women wallpaper could use some updating, it wouldn't be Wally's without it. Nothing flashy, nothing loud, just a tiny, windowless, smoky bar with a jukebox and cheap, strong drinks – as much a dark dive as you'll find anywhere.

Wednesday night is $3 microbrews, Monday is $2 PBR beer, and the attached package store sells beer, wine and liquor.

Tin Roof BAR
(Map p311; ☑ 407-270-7926; www.tinrooforlando.com; 8371 International Dr, I-Drive 360, International Dr; ⊙ 11am-2am) The famous live-music joint that encourages performances of all standards. It's part of the I-Drive 360 complex (think the Wheel and more). Serves up reasonable (bordering on very nice) junk food – burgers, mac 'n' cheese – and things that will fuel you until the wee hours.

Bösendorfer Lounge LOUNGE
(Map p314; ☑ 407-313-9000; www.grand bohemianhotel.com; 325 S Orange Ave, Westin Grand Bohemian; ⊙ 11am-2am) Zebra-fabric chairs, gilded mirrors, massive black pillars and marble floors ooze pomp and elegance. This hotel bar is popular for after-work drinks and the lounge picks up with live jazz at 7pm. The name comes from the lounge's rare Imperial Grand Bösendorfer piano, with its sculpted tree legs and music stand in the shape of a peacock with unfurled feathers.

Courtesy Bar COCKTAIL BAR
(Map p314; ☑ 407-450-2041; www.thecourtesybar.com; 114 N Orange Ave, Downtown; drinks from $5; ⊙ 7pm-2am Mon & Sat, 5pm-2am Tue-Fri, 3pm-2am Sun) Housed in a historic Orlando space, with brick walls and Jefferson filament bulbs, this old-school cocktail bar serves up high-quality spirits with fresh and quirky artisan twists such as Himalayan pink salt, fresh honeydew juice and dandelion-eucalyptus tincture. We don't even know what all of it means, but what delights! There's also an excellent selection of beer and wine.

Keeps odd hours.

PULSE MEMORIAL

In 2019 plans were finalized for a permanent memorial to commemorate the victims of the attack on the Pulse nightclub of June 12, 2016, when 49 people were killed and 53 injured – all members of the LGBTIQ community and mostly Latinx, as the club was hosting a Latin night.

The winning design incorporates the nightclub building – bought by the city in the aftermath of the shootings – and will include a reflecting pool decorated with 49 stripes of different colors and an outdoor garden with 49 trees. The central building will also serve as an open-air museum and will include an educational center focused on the power of positive activism.

The memorial won't be completed until 2022, but until then a **temporary wall** (Map p318; www.onepulsefoundation.org; 1912 S Orange Ave; ⊙ 24hr) filled with photos and messages of solidarity, sorrow and love is a moving tribute to the victims and a powerful reminder that Orlando remains united against any kind of hatred or prejudice.

ORLANDO & WALT DISNEY WORLD® ORLANDO

Imperial Wine Bar & Beer Garden
BAR

(Map p318; 407-228-4992; www.imperial winebar.com; 1800 N Orange Ave, Loch Haven Park; snacks $9-16; 5pm-midnight Mon-Thu, to 2am Fri & Sat; Lynx 102) With its exposed ceiling pipes, glass mosaic light fixtures and antique furniture, this is a furniture store by day (hence the price tags everywhere) and a neighborhood boho bar by night. Sip on a Cigar City in the quiet nook of a beer garden out back and choose a bite from the limited menu of local fare.

Matador
COCKTAIL BAR

(Map p318; 407-872-0844; www.thematador orlando.com; 724 Virginia Dr, Mills 50; 7pm-2am) Deep-red walls, a pool table and furniture you'd expect in your grandmother's parlor. Low-key vibe perfect for sipping that Bulleit Rye.

Eola Wine Company
WINE BAR

(Map p314; 407-481-9100; www.eolawine company.com; 430 E Central Blvd, Thornton Park; 4:30-11:30pm Mon-Thu, to 12:30am Fri & Sat, 11:30am-9pm Sun) A California-style menu of light foods designed to be paired with wine or quirky independent-label beers. You can also get a flight of beer or wine, and a charcuterie and cheese plate.

Latitudes
BAR

(Map p314; 407-649-4270; www.churchstreet bars.com; 33 W Church St, Downtown; 4:30pm-2am) An Orlando classic, the island-inspired Latitudes, a rooftop bar with tiki lanterns and city views, is always hopping. You have to walk up past thumping bars on the first two floors to get here, but once up it's a pleasant place to enjoy the Florida night skies.

Independent Bar
CLUB

(Map p314; 407-839-0457; http://independent bar.net; 70 N Orange Ave, Downtown; varies, often $10; 10pm-2:30am Sat-Thu, from 9:30pm Fri) Half dive bar, half dance club, the 'I-Bar' squarely appeals to the non-EDM crowd with a menu of Top 40, old-school rock, '80s new wave and other popular retro genres. Hardly surprising that it promotes itself as the 'club for people who don't like clubs.'

☆ Entertainment

★ Mad Cow Theatre
THEATER

(Map p314; 407-297-8788; www.madcowtheatre. com; 54 W Church St, Downtown; tickets from $30) A model of inspiring regional theater, with classic and modern performances in a Downtown Orlando space (located on the 2nd floor).

★ Enzian Theater
CINEMA

(Map p318; 407-629-0054; www.enzian.org; 1300 S Orlando Ave, Maitland; adult/child $12/10; 5pm-midnight Tue-Fri, noon-midnight Sat & Sun) 'Film is Art' is the slogan of this clapboard-sided theater that could be the envy of any college town. Independent and classic films are the mainstay, while the excellent Eden Bar (p319) restaurant has primarily local and organic fare. Have a veggie burger and a beer on the patio underneath the cypress tree or opt for table service in the theater.

John & Rita Lowndes Shakespeare Center
THEATER

(Map p318; 407-447-1700; www.orlandoshakes. org; 812 E Rollins St, Loch Haven Park; tickets $15-65) Set on the shores of Lake Estelle in grassy Loch Haven Park, this lovely theater includes three intimate stages hosting professional classics such as *Pride and Prejudice* and *Beowulf,* excellent children's theater and up-and-coming playwrights' work.

Beacham & the Social
LIVE MUSIC

(Map p314; 407-246-1419; www.thebeacham. com; 46 N Orange Ave, Downtown; 9pm-3am) Both the Beacham and the more intimate and recommended Social next door are cornerstones of Orlando's nightclub and live-music scene. They host bands from punk to reggae on the weekends and hop all week long with music and dancing. Shows are designated 'all ages,' '18 plus' or '21 plus.'

Orlando Repertory Theater
THEATER

(Map p318; 407-896-7365; www.orlandorep.com; 1001 E Princeton St, Loch Haven Park; tickets $12-30) Performances for families and children run primarily in the afternoons or early evenings. Shows run the gamut of styles and content, including *Nancy Drew* and *Curious George.*

Will's Pub
LIVE MUSIC

(Map p318; 407-898-5070; www.willspub.org; 1042 N Mills Ave, Thornton Park; tickets $10-20; 4pm-2am Mon-Sat, from 6pm Sun) With $3 Pabst on tap, pinball and vintage pin-ups on the walls, this is Orlando's less-polished music scene, but it enjoys a solid reputation as one of the best spots in town to catch local and nationally touring indie music. Smoke-free; beer and wine only.

Dr Phillips Center
for the Performing Arts   ARTS CENTER
(Map p314; ☑844-513-2014; www.drphillipscenter.org; 445 S Magnolia Ave, Downtown; ☻box office 10am-4pm Mon-Fri, noon-4pm Sat) Covers the full gamut of top-quality entertainment from ballet and opera to jazz and classical music performances.

Orlando Philharmonic
Orchestra   PERFORMING ARTS
(☑407-770-0071; https://orlandophil.org) Classics, pop, opera and more, including family-friendly events, performed at venues in and around Orlando, including outdoor performances at Loch Haven Park.

Orlando Ballet   BALLET
(Map p314; ☑407-426-1739; http://orlando ballet.org; from $30) Performs primarily at downtown Orlando's Bob Carr Performing Arts Center (401 W Livingston St).

Amway Center   SPECTATOR SPORT
(Map p314; ☑407-440-7000; www.amwaycenter.com; 400 W Church St, Downtown) The Orlando Magic (National Basketball Association), the Orlando Predators (Arena Football League) and the Orlando Solar Bears (East Coast Hockey League) play here.

Exploria Stadium   SPECTATOR SPORT
(Map p314; www.orlandocitysc.com; 655 W Church St; tickets from $31; ☻mid-Feb–Oct) This 25,000-seat stadium in the heart of Downtown is the home of Major League Soccer team Orlando City FC and Orlando Pride of the National Women's Soccer League.

🔒 Shopping

Orlando's best shopping is in the handful of outlet malls found around International Dr. Otherwise, it's all about souvenirs and kitschy must-haves. With the exception of Winter Park and its collection of individual boutiques, the rest of the city isn't especially known for its retail opportunities.

Orlando Farmers Market   MARKET
(Map p314; www.orlandofarmersmarket.com; Lake Eola; ☻10am-4pm Sun) Local produce and a beer and wine garden on the shores of downtown Orlando's Lake Eola.

Orlando Premium Outlets –
Vineland Ave   MALL
(Map p311; ☑407-238-7787; www.premium outlets.com/outlet/orlando-vineland; 8200 Vineland Ave; ☻10am-11pm Mon-Sat, to 9pm Sun; ☒I-Ride Trolley Red Line 38) Popular outlet

mall just outside Walt Disney World® – you'll know you're close when you're stuck in stand-still traffic for upwards of half an hour for no apparent reason. There's another branch (Map p311; ☑407-352-9600; www.premiumoutlets.com/outlet/orlando-international; 4951 International Dr; ☻10am-11pm Mon-Sat, to 9pm Sun; ☒Lynx 8 or 42, ☒I-Ride Trolley Red Line 1) just off International Dr.

ℹ️ Information

DANGERS & ANNOYANCES
Crime Tangelo Park (behind International Dr and Kirkman Rd, not far from Universal Orlando Resort) and the Orange Blossom Trail (OBT), especially between North Rosemont and Turnpike South, have issues with drugs and crime. The north end of International Dr isn't particularly dangerous, but be on the lookout for petty thievery – where there are tourists there are often pickpockets looking for an easy score.

Heat Summer temperatures soar and bring with them a killer humidity. Stay well hydrated and use a high-SPF sunscreen.

Wildlife Central Florida is home to alligators and snakes, which may be found in some waterways and marshes in residential areas and on golf courses and the like.

Hurricanes Hurricane season is between June and November.

OPENING HOURS
Bars 4pm to 1am or 2am weekdays, 3am on weekends.

Museums 10am to 5:30pm.

Nightclubs 9pm to 1am or 2am weekdays, 3am on weekends.

Restaurants Breakfast 7am or 8am to 11am; lunch 11am or 11:30am to 2:30pm or 3pm; dinner 5pm or 6pm to 10pm Sunday to Thursday, to 11pm or midnight Friday and Saturday.

Shops 10am to 7pm Monday to Saturday, noon to 6pm Sunday.

Theme Parks 9am to 6pm, often later and sometimes as late as 1am; check websites for daily hours.

TOURIST INFORMATION
Official Visitor Center (Map p311; ☑407-363-5872; www.visitorlando.com; 8102 International Dr; ☻8am-8pm; ☒I-Ride Trolley Red Line 11)

TRAVELERS WITH DISABILITIES
➜ Accommodations in Florida are required by law to offer wheelchair-accessible rooms. For questions about specialty rooms at Walt Disney World® Resort call ☑407-939-7807.

➜ Parks allow guests with special needs to avoid waiting in line, but do not offer front-of-the-line access. Disney issues a Disability

NORTH OF ORLANDO

About 8 miles north of Orlando, the quiet town of Maitland is home to the wonderful **Audubon Center for Birds of Prey** (Map p318; ☑ 407-644-0190; http://fl.audubon.org/audubon-center-birds-prey; 1101 Audubon Way, Maitland; adult/child 3-12yr $8/5; ⊙10am-4pm Tue-Sun; ⓓ) and the one-time art colony that is now an **art and history museum** (☑ 407-539-2181; http://artandhistory.org; 231 W Packwood Ave, Maitland; adult/child $3/2; ⊙11am-4pm Tue-Sun). Six miles northeast of here, in Eatonville, is the **Zora Neale Hurston National Museum of Fine Arts** (Map p318; ☑ 407-647-3307; 227 E Kennedy Blvd, Eatonville; ⊙9am-4pm Mon-Fri, 11am-1pm Sat) **FREE**.

Access Service card and Universal Orlando Resort issues the Attraction Assistance Pass (AAP). Guests take the card to the attraction they want to experience and they are given a return time based on current wait times. Both are available at Guest Services inside the park.

➡ Wheelchair and electric convenience vehicle (ECV) rental is available at Guest Services at Walt Disney World® Resort, Universal Orlando Resort and SeaWorld.

➡ Go to individual park websites or Guest Services for details on accessibility, services for guests with cognitive disabilities, services for guests who are deaf or have hearing impairments, and services for guests who are visually impaired. Sign-language interpreting services require advance reservations.

Resources
➡ **Autism at the Parks** (www.autismatthe parks.com) provides comprehensive information on visiting Orlando theme parks with someone on the autism spectrum.

➡ Download Lonely Planet's free Accessible Travel guide from https://shop.lonelyplanet.com/products/accessible-travel-online-resources-2019.

MEDICAL SERVICES
Arnold Palmer Hospital for Children (☑ 407-649-9111; www.arnoldpalmerhospital.com; 1414 Kuhl Ave; ⊙24hr) Orlando's primary children's hospital. Located just east of I-4 at exit 81.

Centra Care Walk-In Medical (☑ 407-934-2273; www.centracare.org; ⊙8am-midnight Mon-Fri, to 8pm Sat & Sun) Walk-in medical center with more than 20 locations.

Doctors on Call Service (DOCS; ☑ 407-399-3627; www.doctorsoncallservice.com; ⊙24hr) Twenty-four-hour doctors on-call to your hotel, including to Walt Disney World® and Universal Orlando Resort.

Dr P Phillips Hospital (☑ 407-351-8500; www.orlandohealth.com/facilities/dr-p-phillips-hospital; 9400 Turkey Lake Rd; ⊙24hr) Closest hospital to Universal Orlando Resort, SeaWorld and International Drive.

Florida Hospital Celebration Health (☑ 407-303-4000; www.floridahospital.com/celebration-health; 400 Celebration Pl, Kissimmee; ⊙24hr) Closest hospital to Walt Disney World®.

❶ Getting There & Away

Amtrak (www.amtrak.com; 1400 Sligh Blvd) Offers daily trains south to Miami (from $46) and north to New York City (from $150).

Greyhound (Map p318; ☑ 407-292-3424; www.greyhound.com; 555 N John Young Pkwy) Serves numerous cities from Orlando.

❶ Getting Around

BUS
LYMMO (www.golynx.com; free; ⊙6am-10:45pm Mon-Fri, from 10am Sat, 10am-10pm Sun) circles downtown Orlando for free with stops near Lynx Central Station, near SunRail's Church St Station, at Central and Magnolia, Jefferson and Magnolia and outside the Westin Grand Bohemian.

SHUTTLE
Call **Mears Transportation** (☑ 855-463-2776; www.mearstransportation.com) one day in advance to arrange personalized transport between a long list of hotels and many attractions, including Universal Orlando Resort and SeaWorld. It costs between $25 and $35 per round-trip per person.

Casablanca Transportation (☑ 407-927-2773; www.casablancatransportation.com) provides good service to the airport and in and around Orlando.

TRAIN
SunRail (www.sunrail.com), Orlando's commuter rail train, runs north–south. It doesn't stop at or near any theme parks.

In addition to the Downtown station, Amtrak serves Winter Park, Kissimmee and Winter Haven (home to Legoland).

WINTER PARK

☑ 407 / POP 26,243

When Orlandoans want to wax lyrical about how beautiful their city is, a lot of them will point you to Winter Park, a bucolic town (well, city) north of Downtown founded in the mid-19th century as a winter getaway for wealthy northerners. The town grew up around liberal-arts school Rollins College, Florida's oldest institute of higher learning. Here are some of Orlando's best-kept secrets, including the city's best art museum and some of the most talked about restaurants in town, all within a few shaded, pedestrian-friendly streets. Shops, wine bars and sidewalk cafes line Park Ave.

◉ Sights

★ Charles Hosmer Morse Museum of American Art   MUSEUM
(📞 407-645-5311; www.morsemuseum.org; 445 N Park Ave; adult/child $6/free; ⏲ 9:30am-4pm Tue-Sat, from 1pm Sun, to 8pm Fri Nov-Apr; 🚻) Internationally famous, this stunning and delightful museum houses the world's most comprehensive collection of Louis Comfort Tiffany art. Highlights include the chapel interior designed by the artist for the 1893 World's Columbian Exhibition in Chicago; 10 galleries filled with architectural and art objects from Tiffany's Long Island home, Laurelton Hall; and an installation of the Laurelton's Daffodil Terrace.

Albin Polasek Museum & Sculpture Gardens   MUSEUM
(www.polasek.org; 633 Osceola Ave; adult/child $10/free; ⏲ 10am-4pm Tue-Sat, from 1pm Sun) Listed on the National Register of Historic Places and perched on the shore of Lake Osceola, this small yellow villa was home to Czech sculptor Albin Polasek. The house serves as a small museum of his life and work, and the gardens house some of his sculptures. Also hosts rotating exhibitions.

Cornell Fine Arts Museum   MUSEUM
(www.rollins.edu/cfam; Rollins College, 1000 Holt Ave; ⏲ 10am-7pm Tue, to 4pm Wed-Fri, noon-5pm Sat & Sun) FREE This tiny lakeside museum (accredited by the American Alliance of Museums) sits on the campus of Rollins College and houses US, European and Latin American art. Among the highlights are some exquisite old European Master works, as well as a good-sized contemporary collection. The collection is on display both here at the museum and at the nearby Alfond Inn (p327), a college-owned boutique hotel. Both have guided tours for visitors, and the museum hosts many other events throughout the year.

Hannibal Square Heritage Center   MUSEUM
(📞 407-539-2680; www.hannibalsquareheritage center.org; 642 W New England Ave; ⏲ noon-4pm Tue-Fri, 10am-2pm Sat) FREE As far back as 1881, Winter Park's Hannibal Square was home to African Americans employed as carpenters, farmers and household help. The *Heritage Collection: Photographs and Oral Histories of West Winter Park 1900–1980*, on permanent display at this little museum, celebrates and preserves this community's culture and history.

Kraft Azalea Gardens   PARK
(Map p318; https://cityofwinterpark.org/depart ments/parks-recreation/parks-playgrounds/parks/ kraft-azalea-garden; 1365 Alabama Dr; ⏲ 8am-dusk) Quiet lakeside park with enormous cypress trees. Particularly stunning January through March, when the azaleas burst into bloom. There's a dock, but no barbecues or picnic tables.

🎎 Festivals & Events

Winter Park Sidewalk Art Festival   CULTURAL
(📞 407-644-7207; www.wpsaf.org; Winter Park; ⏲ Mar) One of the oldest art festivals in the country where more than 220 artists display work along the sidewalks of small-town Winter Park.

🛏 Sleeping

Park Plaza Hotel   BOUTIQUE HOTEL $$
(📞 407-647-1072; www.parkplazahotel.com; 307 S Park Ave; r from $160; 🛜) Brick walls, spartan wood furniture, antiques and luscious white cotton bedding create a distinct arts-and-crafts sensibility at this historic two-story hotel. Rooms lining Park Ave share a narrow balcony, each with a private entrance and a few wicker chairs hidden from the street by hanging ferns.

It was built to house the workmen who were building the railway; note: some rooms still receive the blast of the passing warning hoots. It's a wonderful atmosphere, though there are more modern and sparklier options.

★ Alfond Inn   BOUTIQUE HOTEL $$$
(📞 407-998-8090; www.thealfondinn.com; 300 E New England Ave; r from $300; 🅿️@🛜♨️🐾) Contemporary white-walled elegance, a low-key welcoming vibe and colorful interiors in well-appointed rooms give this Winter Park gem a distinct style. The hotel has a strong

Winter Park

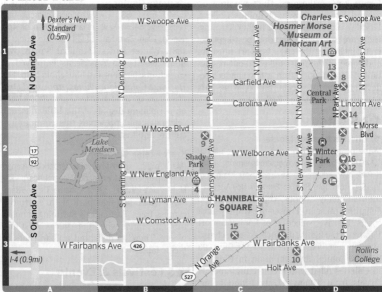

commitment to the arts: not only does it house the Alfond Collection of Contemporary Art, part of the permanent collection at Cornell Fine Arts Museum (p327), but all profits fund liberal-arts scholarships at Rollins College.

There's a lovely rooftop pool and an excellent restaurant that serves locally sourced food on courtyard tables.

✗ Eating

★ Ethos Vegan Kitchen   VEGAN $

(☑407-228-3898; www.ethosvegankitchen.com; 601b S New York Ave; mains $9-14; ⊙11am-11pm Mon-Fri; ☑) ✿ The welcome sign at this meat-free stop says 'get off at Platform One' for a vegan arrival. Ethos Vegan Kitchen offers a range of delights such as pizza with broccoli, banana peppers, zucchini and seitan; meat-free shepherd's pie; pecan-encrusted eggplant; homemade soups; and various sandwiches with names such as A Fungus Among Us and Hippie Wrap.

It's a casual spot with a good student vibe, a wide range of craft brews and a selection of New World wines.

Coop   SOUTHERN US $

(☑407-843-2667; www.asouthernaffair.com; 610 W Morse Blvd; mains $12-16; ⊙7am-8pm Mon-Thu, to 9pm Fri & Sat) Line up for massive plates of smothered pork chops, fried chicken or chicken pot pie, with sides of fried okra, creamed corn, maple-glazed carrots and other Southern classics. Cafeteria-style, with 'make-a-friend' tables or call ahead for sidewalk pickup.

Croissant Gourmet   CAFE $

(☑407-622-7753; www.facebook.com/thecroissant gourmet; 120 E Morse Blvd; mains $9-14; ⊙7am-6pm Sun-Thu, to 8pm Fri & Sat, kitchen closes 6pm daily) Befitting Winter Park's European vibe, start the day with coffee and a pastry at the tiny Paris-perfect Croissant Gourmet. There are classic éclairs, delicious blueberry tarts and massive cinnamon twists, as well as sweet and savory crepes, traditional French breakfasts and lunches, and wine by the glass.

Orchid Thai Cuisine   THAI $

(☑407-331-1400; www.orchidthaiwinterpark.com; 305 N Park Ave; mains $9-17; ⊙11am-9pm Mon-Wed, 11am-10pm Thu-Sat, noon-9pm Sun; ☑) Contemporary and tasty with pleasant pavement seating. Don't miss the delectable 'Thai Doughnuts': dough balls fried with a sweet condensed-milk dressing and sprinkled with crushed peanuts.

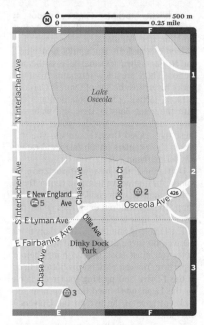

Briarpatch   CAFE **$**

(☎ 407-628-8651; www.thebriarpatchrestaurant. com; 252 N Park Ave; mains $8-16; ⏰ 7am-5pm Mon-Sat, from 8am Sun; 🖑) Massive multilayer cakes and hearty breakfasts in whitewashed, shabby-chic tearoom environs. A locals' fave for brunches, judging by the lines forming outside!

★Prato   ITALIAN **$$**

(☎ 407-262-0050; www.prato-wp.com; 124 N Park Ave; mains $15-17; ⏰ 11:30am-4:30pm Mon & Tue, to 11pm Wed-Sat, to 10pm Sun) A hopping go-to spot with high ceilings, exposed beams and a bar extending the length of the room. Offers inspired interpretations of classic Italian dishes, house-cured meats and excellent wood-oven pizza.

Dexter's New Standard   AMERICAN **$$**

(Map p318; ☎ 407-316-2278; www.newstandard wp.com; 1035 Orlando Ave, Suite 101; mains $15-26; ⏰ 11am-2am) Creative American fare built on locally sourced ingredients is the menu's mainstay at this upscale bistro, which doubles as a terrific live-music venue, with something on almost every night. There's also a raw bar with stone crab claws and ceviche, and an eye-catching glass oyster bar that's filled daily.

Bosphorous Turkish Cuisine   TURKISH **$$**

(☎ 407-644-8609; www.bosphorousrestaurant. com; 108 S Park Ave; mains $12-22; ⏰ 11am-10pm Sun-Thu, to 11pm Fri & Sat; 🖈) An interesting menu and huge helpings of good food make this place stand out along this strip. Try the *lavas* (hollow bread) or the lamb shank ($28).

Luma on Park   AMERICAN **$$**

(☎ 407-599-4111; www.lumaonpark.com; 290 S Park Ave; mains $25-32; ⏰ 5:30-10pm Mon-Thu, to 11pm Fri & Sat, to 9pm Sun) 🍽 A must for upscale foodie delights, not to mention people-watching. The menu features rather complicated pairings such as 'red snapper with black and white quinoa, braised watermelon radish, English pea, delta asparagus and citrus olive tapenade.' The recommended $35 prix-fixe menu is offered Sunday, Monday and Tuesday only.

★Ravenous Pig   AMERICAN **$$$**

(☎ 407-628-2333; www.theravenouspig.com; 565 W Fairbanks Ave; mains $21-48; ⏰ 11:30am-3pm & 5-10pm Mon-Sat, 10:30am-3pm & 5-9pm Sun) 🍽 The cornerstone of Orlando's restaurant trend for locally sourced food, this chef-owned hipster spot is all about letting the food do the talking: locavore, omnivore, carnivore – take your pick. Really ravenous pigs can get their teeth into the pork porterhouse or the local seafood (the shrimp and grits is a must; $15). Don't miss.

The menu changes seasonally. Happy Hour (from 3pm to 6pm) in the attached bar, its on-site brewery, offers $3 draft beers, $6 cocktails and cheap pub-fare plates.

Drinking & Nightlife

Wine Room   WINE BAR
(☑ 407-696-9463; www.thewineroomonline.com; 270 S Park Ave; tastings from $4; ☺ 2pm-midnight Mon-Wed, from noon Thu, 11:30am-1:30am Fri & Sat, noon-11pm Sun) It's a bit of a gimmick, but you purchase a wine card and put as much money on it as you'd like. Then simply slide your card into the automated servers for whichever wine looks good, press the button for a taste or a full glass, and enjoy. More than 150 wines, arranged by region and type.

❶ Getting There & Away

From downtown Orlando, take I-4 to Fairbanks Ave and head east for about 2 miles to Park Ave.

Orlando's SunRail (www.sunrail.com) stops at downtown Winter Park.

Lynx 102 bus services Orange Ave from downtown Orlando to Winter Park.

WINTER HAVEN

Legoland is sleepy Winter Haven's main draw (and a lovely one at that), but you'll also find a handful of reasonable restaurants in the small historic downtown. Lovely Bok Tower Gardens (p321) sits just 15 miles to the southwest.

◉ Sights

★Legoland   AMUSEMENT PARK
(☑ 863-318-5346; www.legoland.com/florida; 1 Legoland Way; 1-/2-day tickets adult $100/120, child 3-12yr $89/109; ☺ 10am-5pm, sometimes later; 🖼; ▣ Legoland Shuttle) Legoland is a joy. With manageable crowds and lines, and no bells and whistles, this lakeside theme park maintains an old-school vibe – you don't have to plan like a general to enjoy a day here, and it's strikingly stress-free and relaxed. This is about fun (and yes, education) in a colorful and interactive environment. Rides and attractions, including the attached water park, are geared towards children aged two to 12. Opening hours vary seasonally, and new things are regularly being added.

Highlights include **Flight School**, a coaster that zips you around with your feet dangling free, **Miniland**, a Lego recreation of iconic American landmarks and cities, and **Ninjago**, the park's martial-arts-themed section. There are a few remnants from the park's history as the site of Cypress Gardens (c 1936), including lovely botanical gardens with the giant Banyan Tree, and water-ski shows and a classic wooden roller coaster, these days called **Coastersaurus**. The water-ski show centers on a bizarre and rather silly pirate theme.

Don't miss the **Imagination Zone**, a wonderful interactive learning center that's heavily staffed with skilled Lego makers happy to help children of all ages create delights with their blocks.

The Legoland Shuttle ($5) runs daily from I-Drive 360 (near the Wheel at Icon Park). Note: you must book this 24 hours before departure. You can park on the bottom floor of the I-Drive 360 parking lot (free). Look for the Legoland-themed bus stop near the back entrance of the Eye on the Universal Blvd side.

You can rent strollers/wheelchairs/ECVs with shade ($16/14/56) and lockers ($9 to $15). Parking costs $23.

🛏 Sleeping

★Legoland Florida Resort   HOTEL $$$
(☑ 863-318-5346; 1 Legoland Way, Winter Haven; r from $400, resort fee $25; 🅿🐕❄🛜🏊) The exterior of this remarkable spot was designed to look like a child built it with Lego bricks. And it succeeds. Bright primary colors and its block-like facade give way to a fun factory. Each floor is based on a different Lego theme and the 152 rooms and suites have peepholes at the level of a child's, not adult's, eyes.

There's a treasure hunt in each room, Lego figures and blocks galore in the lobby, and young guests can even sign up for free master model builder workshops. Nighttime brings on a PJ dance party. In short, it's a little person's paradise. (Info for the adult: it doesn't come cheap.) Even the key drop is made of Lego.

🍴 Eating

Donut Man   BREAKFAST $
(☑ 863-293-4031, 863-514-7727; 1290 6th St; doughnuts from $1.50; ☺ 5:30am-10pm; 🖼) Classic roadside retro dive, with a 1967 exterior, Formica-counter dining, and delicious dough-

nuts made daily. Flavors vary, but bacon is a tasty option, as are the croissant doughnuts. The drive-up window is actually a real window that the server leans out of to give you your order. Locals know everyone else by name. Old school. It's 5 miles from Legoland.

❶ Getting There & Away

Winter Haven is a 33-mile drive southwest of Walt Disney World®.

❶ Getting There & Away

AIR

Orlando International Airport (p526) One of the busiest airports in the US, Orlando International is 30 minutes from downtown and I-Drive, and around 40 minutes from Walt Disney World® and Universal Studios Orlando. Also serves the Space Coast.

Orlando Sanford International Airport (✆ 407-585-4000; www.flysfb.com; 1200 Red Cleveland Blvd) Small airport 30 minutes north of downtown Orlando and 45 minutes north of Walt Disney World®.

BUS

A Greyhound bus originating in NYC, with stops including Washington, DC, and Daytona Beach, FL, terminates in Orlando (one way from $80 to $200, 24 hours).

CAR

Orlando is 285 miles northwest of Miami; the most direct route is a 4½-hour road trip via Florida's Turnpike. From Tampa it is an easy 60 miles along I-4. Both the Beachline Expressway and Hwy 50 will take you east to beaches on the Space Coast in just under an hour.

TRAIN

Amtrak's 97 Silver Meteor and 91 Silver Star from New York to Miami stop at Winter Park, downtown Orlando and Kissimmee. It's a 21½-hour ride from NYC (from $125). The daily Auto Train from Lorton, VA, terminates at Sanford, 30 miles north of downtown Orlando.

GETTING AROUND

Shuttle

Many hotels provide shuttles to Walt Disney World®, Universal Orlando Resort and SeaWorld, to varying timetables. Most hotels just outside Universal Studios and along International Dr provide free shuttle service to Universal Orlando Resort, but many are first-come, first-served. Always ask for details including how often they run and whether or not they take reservations. Contact Mears Transportation (p326) one day in advance to arrange personalized shuttle service; it's also got an app so you can track your ride.

Car & Motorcycle

➔ Hwy I-4 is the main north–south thoroughfare, though it's labeled east–west: to go north, take the I-4 east (toward Daytona Beach), and to go south, hop on the I-4 west (toward Tampa). Just about every place you'd want to go can be located through an I-4 exit number. From south to north, exits 62 through 87, you will find Walt Disney World®, SeaWorld, Aquatica and Discovery Cove, Universal Orlando Resort, downtown Orlando and Thornton Park, Loch Haven Park and Winter Park.

➔ Both Orlando International and Orlando Sanford International Airports, Walt Disney World® and many hotels have car-rental agencies.

Public Transportation

I-Ride Trolley (✆ 407-354-5656; www.iride trolley.com; rides adult/child 3-9yr $2/1, passes 1/3/5/7/14 days $5/7/9/12/18; ⊗ 8am-10:30pm) Services International Dr, from south of SeaWorld north to the Universal Orlando Resort area. Buses run at 20- to 30-minute intervals and exact change is required.

Lynx (Map p314; ✆ 407-841-2279, route info 407-841-8240; www.golynx.com; 455 Garland Ave, Downtown; per ride/day/week $2/4.50/16, transfers free; ⊗ call center 8am-8pm Mon-Fri, 8am-6pm Sat & Sun) Orlando's public bus covers greater Orlando, but service is limited after 8pm.

Scooter, Stroller & Wheelchair Rental

Tackling Orlando's theme parks requires a huge amount of walking and standing, and can be exhausting for all ages. You can rent at the parks, but they don't all take reservations and you can't use the equipment outside the park. Several companies offer stroller, wheelchair or scooter rentals for the duration of your visit (and will deliver to your hotel).

Walker Mobility	https://walker mobility.com	✆ 888-726-6837
Kingdom Strollers	www.kingdom strollers.com	✆ 407-271-5301
Orlando Stroller Rentals	www.orlando strollerrentals. com	✆ 800-281-0884

Taxi

Cabs sit outside the theme parks, Disney Springs, resorts and other tourist centers, but otherwise you'll need to call to arrange a pickup. A ride from the Disney area to downtown Orlando takes 30 minutes and costs about $65; from Universal Orlando Resort to Disney takes 15 minutes and costs $40. Just getting around *within* Walt Disney World® can easily cost $30 in fares.

Casablanca Transportation (✆ 407-927-2773; www.casablancatransportation.com)

Mears Transportation (p326)

AT A GLANCE

★

POPULATION
188,000

**NUMBER OF BIRD
SPECIES**
300

**BEST ANIMAL
ENCOUNTERS**
Black Point Wildlife
Drive (p337)

BEST SEAFOOD
Dixie Crossroads
(p349)

**BEST OCEANFRONT
BAR**
Sand on the Beach
(p347)

📅

WHEN TO GO
Jul Crowds diminish
as temperatures soar
(with tropical storms
a possibility); prices
drop; loggerhead sea
turtles nest.

Apr More sunny
days than any other
month, and most
spring-breakers
have gone.

Sep–Nov Peak
migratory-bird sea-
son and drier weather
make for prime
wildlife-spotting.

Rocket Garden, Kennedy Space Center (p335)
NAUGHTYNUT / SHUTTERSTOCK ©

The Space Coast

More than 40 miles of barrier-island Atlantic Coast stretch from Canaveral National Seashore south to Melbourne Beach, encompassing undeveloped stretches of endless white sand, an entrenched surf culture and pockets of Old Florida.

The Kennedy Space Center and several small museums dedicated to the history and science of the United States' space program give the Space Coast its name, and the region's tourist hub of Cocoa Beach is just south of Cape Canaveral's launching point for massive cruise ships. But beyond the 3D space movies, tiki-hut bars and surf shops, the Space Coast offers quintessential Florida wildlife for everyone from toddlers to seniors. Kayak with manatees, camp on a private island or simply stroll along miles and miles of sandy white beaches – it's easy to find a quiet spot.

The Space Coast Highlights

1 Kennedy Space Center (p335) Experiencing the awe and wonder of America's space program and the passion of its astronauts.

2 Merritt Island National Wildlife Refuge (p336) Kayaking with manatees and dolphins.

3 Titusville (p348) Watching a rocket launch from Space View Park or grabbing a craft beer in the historic downtown.

4 Canaveral National Seashore (p337) Spotting nesting turtles and diving pelicans.

5 Cocoa Beach Pier (p339) Surfing Florida's hottest waves or simply soaking up the scene.

❶ Getting Around

Space Coast Area Transit (www.321transit.com) operates a local bus service including routes from Titusville down the coast, from Cape Canaveral to Cocoa Beach and from Cocoa Beach to Cocoa Village. There are also buses circling through Titusville, Merritt Island, Cocoa Village and Melbourne. Surfboards and bikes are allowed on the bus, space permitting. Greyhound (www.greyhound.com) buses stop along the mainland.

Merritt Island

📧 321 / POP 34,743

In 1958, in the aftermath of WWII, the US government selected the east coast of Florida as the base of its newly formed National Aeronautics and Space Administration (NASA). From here new-age captains would launch rockets, telescopes and shuttles into the orbiting circle of the Earth to discover new worlds and galaxies. Thousands of acres of scrubland were commandeered at the northern end of Merritt Island; a third of it was cleared to form the new NASA base, while the remainder was given over to the US Fish and Wildlife Service to operate as the Merritt Island National Wildlife Refuge and the Canaveral National Seashore. The refuge and seashore provide the military with a secure and impenetrable buffer zone while also offering some 500 species of wildlife a pristine coastal habitat of saltwater marshes, hardwood hammocks, pine flatwoods and scrub.

◉ Sights

Merritt Island is home to a triumvirate of the Space Coast's main attractions: Kennedy Space Center, Merritt Island National Wildlife Refuge (p336) and Canaveral National Seashore (p337). The 43-mile strip of coast from the southern end of Cape Canaveral Air Force Station to the tip of Canaveral National Seashore is the longest stretch of undeveloped beach on Florida's Atlantic Coast, and one of the most important turtle-nesting beaches in the US with 7470 recorded nestings in 2015.

★ **Kennedy Space Center**   MUSEUM
(📞 855-433-4210; www.kennedyspacecenter.com; NASA Pkwy, State Rd 405; adult/child 3-11yr $57/47; ⏱ 10am-4pm, special events to 8pm) Whether you're mildly interested in space or a die-hard sci-fi fan, a visit to the Kennedy Space Center is awe-inspiring. To get a good overview start at the Early Space Exploration exhibit, progress to the 90-minute bus tour to the Apollo/Saturn V Center (where you'll find the best on-site cafe) and finish at the awesome *Atlantis* exhibit, where you can walk beneath the heat-scorched fuselage of a shuttle that traveled more than 126,000,000 miles through space on 33 missions.

➔ **Visitor Complex**
The Visitor Complex, with several exhibits showcasing the history and future of US space travel and research, is the heart of the Kennedy Space Center. Here you'll find the **Rocket Garden**, featuring replicas of classic rockets towering over the complex; **Heroes & Legends** and the **U.S. Astronaut Hall of Fame**, with films and multimedia exhibits honoring astronauts; and the hour-long **Astronaut Encounter**, where a real, live astronaut fields questions from the audience. A NASA Now exhibit includes **Journey to Mars**, a collection of related shows and interactive exhibits, and two delightful **IMAX films**: *A Beautiful Planet* offers footage of Earth from space and an optimistic look at the future of the planet (narrated by Jennifer Lawrence), and *Journey to Space 3-D* features interviews with astronauts and an overview of NASA's past, present and future endeavors.

The stunningly beautiful **Space Mirror Memorial**, a shiny granite wall standing four stories high, reflects both literally and figuratively on the personal and tragic stories behind the theme-park energy that permeates the center. Several stone panels display the photos and names of those who died in shuttle disasters.

➔ **Kennedy Space Center Bus Tour**
This 90-minute bus tour is the only way to see beyond the Visitor Complex without paying for an add-on tour. The bus winds through the launch facilities to the **Apollo/Saturn V Center**, where you don't want to miss the multimedia show in the Firing Room. Video footage on three screens depicts America's first lunar mission, the 1968 launch of *Apollo VIII*, before you're ushered through to an enormous hangar displaying the real *Apollo 14* Command Module and the 363ft *Saturn V* moon rocket. This 6.5 million pound marvel of engineering boosted men into space on November 9, 1967.

Tours depart every 15 minutes from 10am to 3:30pm. Look for the coach buses and long lines to the right when you enter the Visitor Complex.

➡ Space Shuttle Atlantis

Blasted by rocket fuel and streaked with space dust, space shuttle *Atlantis*, the final orbiter among NASA's fleet, is the most impressive exhibit in the complex. Suspended in a specially designed, $100-million space, it hangs just a few feet out of reach, nose down, payload doors open, as if it's still orbiting the earth. It's a creative and dramatic display, preceded by a chest-swelling film that tells the story of the shuttle program from its inception in the 1960s to *Atlantis'* final mission in 2011. Around the shuttle, interactive consoles invite visitors to try to land it or dock it at the International Space Station, touchscreens offer details of missions and crews, and there's a full-size replica of the Hubble Space Telescope and a not-very-scary 'shuttle launch experience.' Docents, many of whom worked on the shuttle program, are stationed around the exhibits to answer questions and tell tall space tales.

➡ Heroes & Legends and the U.S. Astronaut Hall of Fame

Next to the Rocket Garden, the newest exhibit at the center celebrates pioneers of NASA's early space programs, inspiring a new generation to keep their intergalactic dreams alive. It starts with a 360-degree film on the lives of astronauts, then guides visitors through displays of a Redstone rocket, space shuttles and astronauts' personal belongings, along with stations organized under character traits of astronauts, such as 'passionate,' 'tenacious' and 'disciplined.' The exhibit also features the *Mercury* Mission Control room and the 4D movie *Through the Eyes of a Hero*, about the lives of the 93 Hall of Fame inductees. Finally, inside the relocated and revamped U.S. Astronaut Hall

of Fame, visitors are welcomed by a statue of Alan Shepard, along with interactive video displays of the astronauts and their missions.

➡ Add-on Experiences

Extended tours offer the opportunity to visit the **Cape Canaveral Air Force Station** and *Mercury* and *Gemini* launch sites. Great for kids, **Dine with an Astronaut** offers a chance to hang out with a real astronaut, while the **Cosmic Quest** is an action-oriented game-play experience featuring real NASA missions involving a rocket launch, redirection of an asteroid and building a martian habitat. You can also **Fly with an Astronaut** and take part in the **Astronaut Training Experience (ATX)** to encounter some of the rigors involved in preparing for a journey to Mars.

ℹ Getting There & Away

Bus Gray Line offers round-trip transportation from Orlando locations ($59).

Car The Space Center is east across the NASA Pkwy on SR 405. Parking costs $10.

Merritt Island National Wildlife Refuge

Sharing a boundary with the Kennedy Space Center, the Merritt Island National Wildlife Refuge (☎321-861-5601; www.fws.gov/merritt island; Black Point Wildlife Dr, off FL 406; vehicle $10; ☉dawn-dusk) is one of the most diverse natural habitats in America. The 140,000-acre wilderness ranges from saltwater marshes and estuaries to hardwood hammocks, pine flatwoods, scrub and coastal dunes that support more than 1500 species of plants and animals, 15 of which are listed as threatened or endangered. Between October and May the refuge is also filled with migrating and wintering birds; the best viewing is on Black Point Wildlife Dr during the early morning and after 4pm.

🏃 Activities & Tours

Hiking along one of the refuge's seven trails is best during fall, winter and early spring. The shortest hike is 0.25 miles along a raised boardwalk behind the visitor center, while the longest is the 5-mile **Cruickshank Trail**, which forms a loop around Black Point Marsh, making it an excellent place to view wading birds.

MEET AN ASTRONAUT

You can meet an astronaut at the **Astronaut Encounter**, held daily inside the Astronaut Encounter Theater and included in park admission. Don't confuse this with the Mission Status Briefing, which is held in the same theater. Check your park map for times. Alternatively, **Dine with an Astronaut** (adult/child $30/16) is a lunch lecture followed by a Q&A. Register in advance online or check same-day availability at the Ticket Plaza upon entering the park.

A Day Away Kayak Tours   KAYAKING
(☑321-268-2655; www.adayawaykayaktours.com; day tours $40-75, night tours $45-75) Launching from Haulover Canal, these kayak tours offer the opportunity to glide alongside manatees and dolphins. On night tours the dark waters sparkle as comb jellyfish and bioluminescence illuminate cleaving paddle blades.

Mosquito Lagoon   KAYAKING
Hugging the western side of the barrier-island strip, Mosquito Lagoon is an incredibly peaceful waterway connected to the ocean by the Ponce de León Inlet. Barely 4ft deep, it's a great place to paddle between island hammocks and dense mangroves while observing the birds, manatees and dolphins. The lagoon is aptly named, so bring bug repellent.

A manatee observation deck can be found on the northeastern side of the Haulover Canal, which connects the lagoon to the Indian River Lagoon. This also makes a great launch point for kayaks. Boat launches (requiring a Refuge Day Pass, $5) are available at Bairs Cove, Beacon 42 and the Bio Lab.

Black Point Wildlife Drive   BIRDWATCHING
(off FL-406; day pass per vehicle $10; ☺sunrise-sunset) One of the best places to see wildlife is on this self-guided, 7-mile drive through salt- and freshwater marshes. A trail brochure detailing 12 stops and the habitats and wildlife found there is available at the entry point. On view are some of Florida's finest bucket-list birds: roseate spoonbills, tricolored herons, snowy egrets, bald eagles, ibis and more.

Birds aren't the only cool thing here. There's also the possibility of seeing alligators, bobcats, otters and reptiles, especially in the early morning and late afternoon. The drive takes approximately 40 minutes.

Sleeping & Eating
There are no accommodations or restaurants in the refuge. Titusville, Cape Canaveral and Cocoa Beach offer a variety of nearby options.

Information
The helpful Visitor Information Center (☑321-861-0669; www.fws.gov/merrittisland; off FL 402; ☺8am-4pm) offers displays on the refuge's habitats and wildlife, information on conservation programs and hiking trail maps. You can also check out the schedule of bird tours (usually at 9am and 1pm) and sign up for seasonal turtle-nesting tours (p338) along the Canaveral National Seashore in June and July.

Getting There & Away
You'll need a car, and can access the refuge via the A. Max Brewer Memorial Pkwy from Titusville.

Canaveral National Seashore
☑321, 689
Part of America's national-park system, spectacular Canaveral National Seashore (☑321-267-1110; www.nps.gov/cana; car/bike/pedestrian $20/15/10; ☺6am-8pm Mar-Nov, to 6pm Dec-Feb) is 24 miles of pristine, windswept beaches comprising the longest stretch of undeveloped beach on Florida's east coast. Two roads squeeze along a skinny bridge of barrier island, one heading 6 miles south from the small beach town of New Smyrna Beach and another 6 miles north from Merritt Island National Wildlife Refuge. Each road dead-ends, leaving about 16 miles of wilderness beach between them.

The best time to visit the park is between October and April, when migrating birds flock to the beaches. During the drier months wildlife-viewing opportunities are also better and there are fewer mosquitoes.

The beaches include family-friendly Apollo Beach on the north end with its gentle surf, untrammeled Klondike Beach in the middle – a favorite of nature lovers – and Playalinda Beach to the south, which is surfer central and includes a nudist section near lot 13.

Mosquito Lagoon, with islands and mangroves teeming with wildlife, hugs the west side of the barrier island. Rangers offer two-hour pontoon boat tours ($20 per person) from the visitor information center on Friday, Saturday and Sunday. In June and July rangers lead groups on nightly turtle-nesting tours (adult/child eight to 16 years $14/free; 8pm to midnight); reservations required.

Sights
★Klondike Beach   BEACH
The stretch between Apollo and Playalinda is as pristine as it gets: there are no roads and it's accessible only on foot or by bike (if you are skilled enough to ride your bike over sand). You need to obtain a back-country permit ($10 per person per day) from the entrance station before setting off.

Turtle Mound   ARCHAEOLOGICAL SITE
Located at the northern end of Mosquito Lagoon, Turtle Mound is the largest shell

midden in the mainland United States. It stands around 50ft high and consists of 1.5 million bushels (53 million liters) of oyster shells, the remains of the Timucuan culture, an ancient civilization that hunted rodents, reptiles and birds on these shores for five centuries prior to European contact. It can be reached via hiking trails from Apollo Beach and offers panoramic views.

Apollo Beach
BEACH

This 6-mile beach at the northern end of the park and immediately south of New Smyrna attracts families. It has boardwalk access (wheelchair accessible), and a longer stretch of road along the dunes with fewer parking lots than at Playalinda. There are several hiking trails nearby, including the **Eldora Trail**. It feels more isolated and is perfect for cycling or turtle-watching in June and July.

Playalinda Beach
BEACH

At the southern end of Mosquito Lagoon, Playalinda is popular with surfers. Boardwalks provide beach access, but only 2 miles of park road parallel the dunes and there are more parking lots than at Apollo, with fewer opportunities to access the lagoon. Note that the remote areas north of parking lot 13 are often populated by nudists.

Eldora State House Museum
HISTORIC BUILDING

(⊙noon-4pm Tue-Sun) Eldora was a small waterfront community of around 100 citrus farmers and fishers, many of them veterans of the Civil War, who settled here between 1877 and 1900. The town depended on the waterway for supplies, tourists and transport. It was fairly prosperous – at least prosperous enough for the construction of the colonial-revival Eldora House, which has now been renovated as a small house museum detailing the life of the settler community via photos, videos and artifacts.

To reach the house take the Eldora Trail at parking area 8 in the North District. The trail winds through a coastal hammock to the shoreline of Mosquito Lagoon, where you'll find the house.

☞ Tours

★ Sea-Turtle Nesting Tours
ECOTOUR

(☑386-428-3384; adult/child 8-16yr $15/free; ⊙8pm-midnight Jun & Jul) In the summer rangers lead groups of up to 30 people on these nightly tours, with about a 75% chance of spotting the little guys. Reservations are required (beginning May 15 for June trips, June 15 for July trips); children under eight years are not allowed.

Pontoon Boat Tours
BOATING

(☑386-428-3384; per person $20) Two-hour ranger-led tours leave from the Visitor Information Center on Friday, Saturday and Sunday.

🍽 Sleeping & Eating

Permits for tent camping are required as the only option for staying here. They're available up to seven days in advance. Be sure to bring plenty of water.

At the gate there's a vending machine that sells water and other beverages. But once inside there are no designated picnic areas, food, phones or drinking water. Come prepared.

Island Camping
CAMPGROUND $

(www.recreation.gov; tent sites $20) Fourteen primitive campsites scattered throughout the islands in Mosquito Lagoon are available year-round.

ℹ Information

Canaveral National Seashore Visitor Information Center (☑386-428-3384; www.nps. gov/cana; 7611 S Atlantic Ave, New Smyrna; ⊙8am-6pm Oct-Mar, to 8pm Apr-Sep) is located just south of the North District entrance gate. Alternatively the visitor center at Merritt Island National Wildlife Refuge (p336) can also provide information.

There is a fee station at both the North and South District entrances. There is a toilet at most beach parking areas.

Note that the park can experience temporary closures around launch time. For information on launch closures call ☑321-867-4077.

ℹ Getting There & Away

To get to the North District take I-95 to SR 44 (exit 249), head east to New Smyrna Beach and then south on A1A, 7 miles to the entrance gate.

Access to the South District is 12 miles east of Titusville, through Merritt Island National Wildlife Refuge (I-95 exit 220 to SR 406).

There is no public transportation to or within the park and no road access to Klondike Beach.

Cocoa Beach

☑ 321 / POP 11,325

As America raced to the moon in the wake of WWII, Cocoa Beach hustled to keep up with growth, building dozens of motels and gaining a reputation as a party town. That vibe has remained largely intact, and the area seems perenially populated with beer-wielding, scantily clad youth.

Cocoa Beach's other claim to fame: surfing. Eleven-time surfing world champion Kelly Slater, born and raised here, learned his moves in Cocoa Beach and thus established it as one of Florida's best surf towns.

Sights

Cocoa Beach Pier PIER
(fishing info 321-783-7549; www.cocoabeachpier.com; 401 Meade Ave; parking $15) Souvenir shops, restaurants and bars stretch along this 800ft pier built as a family attraction in 1962. It remains the focus of annual events such as the Easter Surf Festival. Fishing rods are available to rent for $20, and there's a $7 fee to fish on the pier with your own equipment.

Lori Wilson Park PARK
(1500 N Atlantic Ave) A 32-acre coastal park with a mellow vibe and facilities including wheelchair access, a playground, picnic tables, grills and a small dog-play area. Parking is free and plentiful. The sand is soft and the water is shallow, with small, consistent waves that are great for anyone learning to surf.

Sidney Fischer Park BEACH
(Hwy A1A; parking $5) The closest beach to downtown Cocoa Beach, Fischer Park is crowded with surfers.

Activities

Cocoa Beach Aerial Adventures OUTDOORS
(321-613-0047; http://cocoabeachadventurepark.com; 6419 N Atlantic Ave; adult/child 7-15yr/child 5-6yr $45/35/25; 10am-5pm Sun-Thu, to 6pm Fri & Sat) Constructed among century-old oaks, this aerial adventure park is like a playground in the air, complete with ziplines and seven rope courses featuring more than 50 obstacles. The most challenging tasks take place at 40ft in the air, and once each is complete a zipline back to the main tower is the ultimate reward.

Ron Jon Surf School SURFING
(321-868-1980; www.ronjonsurfschool.com; 150 E Columbia Ln; 1/2hr private surf lesson $65/95, group surf lesson $50; 9am-5pm) The long-running Ron Jon Surf School offers lessons for everyone from groms (that's surf talk for beginners) to experts.

Courses & Tours

Surf Art Camps SURFING
(321-799-3432; www.marymoonarts.com; per child $295; 9am-3pm Jun-Aug) Beach Place Guesthouses hosts weeklong Surf Art Camps for children aged five to 17.

Fin Expeditions KAYAKING
(321-698-7233; www.finexpeditions.com; 599 Ramp Rd; per person $44-69;) The calm waters, stable kayaks and attentive and enthusiastic guides make this an excellent tour company for families. You'll likely see a few mangrove species, cormorants, horseshoe crabs and even a dolphin or a manatee at the right time of year. Reservations required; cash only.

Festivals & Events

Easter Surf Festival SURFING
(321-799-0493; Cocoa Beach Pier) Hosted by Ron Jon Surf School, this Easter weekend surfing festival has been a tradition since 1964 and now draws crowds of more than 100,000 fans to watch some of the best surfers in the world.

Sleeping

★**Beach Place Guesthouses** APARTMENT **$$**
(321-783-4045; www.beachplaceguesthouses.com; 1445 S Atlantic Ave; ste $199-399;) A slice of heavenly relaxation in Cocoa Beach's partying beach scene, this laid-back two-story guesthouse has roomy suites with hammocks and a lovely deck, all just steps from the dunes and beach. Colorful art and greenery abound on the property. No pets.

Sea Aire Motel MOTEL **$$**
(321-783-2461; www.seaairemotelcocoa.com; 181 N Atlantic Ave; r $110-145;) This retro mom-and-pop motel has been around since the 1950s. The place is affordable and right on the beach, with comfortable units containing kitchenettes and homey wood paneling.

Surf Studio MOTEL **$$**
(321-783-7100; http://surf-studio.com; 1801 S Atlantic Ave; r & ste $155-195;) This old-school, single-story, family-owned motel sits on the ocean and offers basic doubles and apartments surrounded by grass and palms. One-bedroom apartments sleeping six cost from $215; there's no charge for children under 10.

Cocoa Beach

Fawlty Towers　　　　　　　　MOTEL **$$**
(📞 321-784-3870; 100 E Cocoa Beach Causeway; r $105-265; P⊖❄🛜🏊) It's all about location, location, location. This motel is gloriously garish and extremely pink: unmissable. It has clean, nonfancy rooms with an unbeatable beachside location, a quiet pool and a BYOB tiki hut. Sometimes a decent room is what you need.

✗ Eating

Pita Paradise　　　　　　　　LEBANESE **$**
(📞 321 784 4874; www.facebook.com/pitaparadise cocoabeach/; 225 W Cocoa Beach Causeway; mains $8-16; ⊙ Mon-Sat 11am-8.30pm) The best restaurant name around, Pita Paradise is a welcome international eatery in the sea of Americana options. The decor is like a faded 1970s dream of an oasis, with a wooden interior and an entire wall depicting a beach scene. The menu offers Lebanese/Middle Eastern staples, from falafel to tabbouleh, kibbe and *kofte*. Finish with an aromatic Lebanese coffee.

Green Room Cafe VEGETARIAN $
(✐ 321-868-0203; www.greenroomcafecocoabeach.
com; 222 N 1st St; mains $7-13; ☺10:30am-9pm
Mon-Sat; ✐) Focusing its energies on the
'goodness within,' this cafe delights with
fruit-combo acai bowls, wheat- and gluten-
free sandwiches, real fruit smoothies, and
homemade soups and wraps. If the 'Tower
of Power' smoothie (acai, peach, strawberry,
honey and apple juice) fails to lift you, the
vibrant decor and friendly company will.

Those who don't surf might wonder at
the name, which comes from the chamber of
green water one finds when inside the barrel of a wave. Ecominded folk will appreciate
the no straws policy.

Simply Delicious CAFE $
(✐ 321-783-2012; 125 N Orlando Ave; mains $8-16;
☺8am-3pm Tue-Sat, to 2pm Sun) In a darling little yellow house on the southbound stretch
of A1A, this homey establishment packs in
locals for a scrumptious menu with unusu-
ally delicious delights including fresh strawberry crepes and malted waffles.

Umami JAPANESE $$
(✐321 676 5159; www.myumamisushi.com;
3042 W New Haven Ave; mains $15-22; ☺Mon-
Fri 11.30am-2pm & 5pm-9pm, Sat 5pm-9pm, Sun
4.30pm-8.30pm) This excellent little Japanese
place in a bland strip mall will awaken your
taste buds and your umami sense. The noo-
dles and soups (try the Miso Seafood Nabe,
rich with seafood, fish, tofu and scallions)
are excellent, and the sushi is crisp, fresh
and full of flavour. The decor is tasteful and
elegant, and the service good.

Slow and Low Barbecue BARBECUE $$
(✐321-783-6199; www.slowandlowbarbeque.com;
306 N Orlando Ave; mains $7-20; ☺11am-10pm)
After a day on the beach nothing satisfies
better than a plate overflowing with barbecue ribs, fried okra, turnip greens and sweet
fried potatoes. There's a daily happy hour
and live music Thursday through Sunday. A
second location opened recently on Stadium
Pkwy in Rockledge, south of Cocoa Village.

Squid Lips
Overwater Bar & Grill SEAFOOD $$
(✐321-783-1350; www.squidlipsgrill.com; 2200 S
Orlando Av; mains $15-26; ☺11am-10pm Wed-Sun)
With its outdoor seating, this newest mem-
ber of the three-restaurant franchise pretty
much rules. You cross a moat filled with

koi to enter, and the views out over the Ba-
nana River are stunning. The Cajun bacon-
wrapped scallops and stuffed flounder are
excellent.

⭐**Pompano Grill** AMERICAN $$$
(✐321-784-9005; www.pompanogrill.com; 110 N
Brevard Ave; mains $17-30; ☺5.30-9pm Tue-Sat)
A small, family-run restaurant with mother
and daughter (Jackie and Erika) at the helm,
this place specializes in fresh, daily and locally caught fish, carefully picked ingredients and exquisite flavor. Erika is the wine
expert here, and as well as explaining the
chef's ingredient combo she will guide you
through the wine and dish pairing.

⭐**Fat Snook** SEAFOOD $$$
(✐321-784-1190; www.thefatsnook.com; 2464 S
Atlantic Ave; mains $27-42; ☺4-9pm) Hidden
inside an uninspired building, tiny Fat
Snook stands out as an oasis of fine cooking.
Under the direction of Mona and John Foy,
gourmet seafood is expertly prepared with
unexpected herbs and spices influenced by
Caribbean flavors. Reservations strongly
recommended.

🍷 **Drinking & Nightlife**

Rikki Tiki Tavern BAR
(www.cocoabeachpier.com; Cocoa Beach Pier;
☺11am-8pm) Kick back at this bar at the
very tip of Cocoa Beach Pier and soak up the
surfing-town mood.

Coconuts on the Beach BAR
(✐321-784-1422; www.coconutsonthebeach.com;
2 Minutemen Causeway; mains $8-21; ☺11am-mid-
night Mon-Thu, to 1am Fri & Sat, 9am-midnight Sun)
Coconut isn't just a name here, it's a favored
ingredient. The oceanfront 'party deck' hosts
regular live music and gets packed with rev-
elers, especially during the high season and
on spring break.

☆ **Entertainment**

Beach Shack LIVE MUSIC
(✐321-783-2250; www.facebook.com/beachshack
cocoabeach; 1 Minutemen Causeway; ☺10am-
1am Mon-Thu, to 2am Fri-Sun) A classic Tiki-
decorated locals' bar with two pool tables, a
beachfront patio and blues Thursday to Sat-
urday. A larger bar is across the street if the
beachside option fills.

🛍 Shopping

Sunseed
Food Co-op   FOOD & DRINKS
(☎321-784-0930;   www.sunseedfoodcoop.com;
6615 N Atlantic Ave; ◉9am-7pm Mon-Sat, 10am-
6pm Sun) Swing by this healthy oasis for locally grown fruit, veggies, microbrew beers,
wines and aftersun lotions.

Ron Jon Surf Shop   CLOTHING
(☎321-799-8888; www.ronjonsurfshop.com; 4151
N Atlantic Ave; ◉24hr) With live music, classic cars and a warehouse jammed with
everything you could possibly need for a day
at the beach, the massive 52,000-sq-ft Ron
Jon is more than a store. And should you
find yourself needing surf wax at 4am, no
worries – it's open 24 hours a day.

ℹ Getting There & Away

Three causeways – Hwy 528, Hwy 520 and Hwy
404 – cross Indian River Lagoon, Merritt Island
and Banana River to connect Cocoa Beach to the
mainland. At Ron Jon's, Hwy 528 (also known as
Minutemen Causeway) cuts south and becomes
Hwy AIA (also Atlantic Ave), a north–south strip
with chain hotels and restaurants, tourist shops
and condos. Hwy A1A divides into two one-way
roads (southbound Orlando Ave and northbound
Atlantic Ave) for a couple of miles, reconnects
and continues south along the barrier-island
coast 53 miles to Vero Beach and beyond.

Cocoa Beach is also served by **SCAT** (☎321-
633-1878; www.321transit.com; per ride $2,
10-ride/30-day pass $14/44; ◉schedule varies)
buses. Rte 9 connects it with Cape Canaveral,
and Rte 26 connects it with beaches to the south
all the way to Indialantic.

Cape Canaveral

☎321 / POP 10,450

In 1951 the US Army Corps of Engineers
carved out an inlet to facilitate the shipping
of goods to the Space Center. In the process
it laid the foundations for Port Canaveral,
the second-busiest cruise port in the United
States.

To the north of the port Cape Canaveral Air Force Station remains the primary
launch head of the nation's Eastern Range.
To the south Cape Canaveral has evolved
into a quiet, residential community for
space workers and their families, though
several chain hotels and restaurants here
cater to cruise-ship passengers and space
tourists.

◉ Sights

Jetty Park   PARK
(☎321-783-7111; www.portcanaveral.com/jpc; 9035
Campground Circle; nonresident/resident per car
$15/5; ◉5am-11pm) Facing the distant Cape
Canaveral Lighthouse, this 35-acre coastal
park is a prime spot for sunbathing, fishing
and watching cruise ships set sail. Chairs,
umbrellas, kayaks and paddleboards can all
be rented at the beach, which is patrolled
by lifeguards. There are also grills, a playground and a couple of food concessions.

Ongoing port construction has increased
noise levels temporarily, though not between 7pm and 7am.

🛏 Sleeping & Eating

There are quite a few chain hotels here,
largely catering to families visiting Kennedy Space Center and cruise-ship passengers
coming and going. Jetty Park is a good option for camping.

Jetty Park   CAMPGROUND $
(☎321-783-7111;   www.portcanaveral.com/jpc;
9035 Campground Circle; campsites $27-49, cab-
ins $84; P🅿🛜🐾) Jetty Park offers cabins, fire
pits for RV sites, a playground, two pavilions, 93 barbecue grills, beach access and a
fishing pier.

Construction of a new cruise ship dock
has increased noise, but 7pm to 7am is
quiet time.

Residence Inn
Cape Canaveral   HOTEL $$$
(☎321-323-1100; www.marriott.com; 8959 Astro-
naut Blvd; r $240-300; P❄🛜🐾) If you want
to get away from the Cocoa Beach party
scene, book into this comfortable Marriott
hotel. Rooms may be corporate, but they
offer acres of space, comfortable beds and
kitchenettes. Staff are also extremely ac-
commodating and there's a pretty pool area.
Park-n-cruise packages are popular. The big
astronaut in the lobby is amusing for kids.

★ Seafood Atlantic   SEAFOOD $$
(☎321-784-1963; www.seafoodatlantic.org; 520
Glen Cheek Dr, Port Canaveral; mains $8-19;
◉11am-7pm Wed-Sun, seafood market from 10am)
With deep roots in Canaveral's fishing industry, this restaurant (with outdoor deck) is
one of the few places to serve locally sourced
shrimp, crabs, mussels, clams, oysters and
fish. If they're in, order a bucket of Florida's
deep-sea golden crab, which has a delicious-

SPACE MISSIONS THEN & NOW

Early Space Exploration

In 1949 President Harry S Truman established the Joint Long Range Proving Grounds at Cape Canaveral for missile testing. The first rocket was launched on July 24, 1950, and in 1958 the National Aeronautics and Space Administration (NASA) was born to 'carry out the peaceful exploration and use of space.'

Though Soviet cosmonaut Yuri Gagarin took the honor of the first man in space on April 12, 1961, Alan Shepard became the first American one month later. In February 1962 John Glenn launched from Cape Canaveral, circled the Earth three times in the world's first orbital flight, and landed four hours later in the Atlantic Ocean off Bermuda.

Project Apollo & Space Shuttle Program

John Glenn's seminal voyage fueled support for the space program, and President John F Kennedy vowed to land a man on the moon by the end of the decade. On July 16, 1969, a *Saturn V* rocket shot out from Kennedy Space Center. Four days later Neil Armstrong spoke the immortal phrase: 'That's one small step for man, one giant leap for mankind.' Between 1969 and 1972 six more Apollo missions were launched to explore the moon.

In 1976 NASA introduced the space shuttle, a reusable occupied space vehicle designed to rocket into space with a booster (which is later shed), orbit the earth and glide back safely to solid ground. Five years later, in 1981, NASA's successful launch of the *STS-1*, piloted by John Young and Robert Crippen, opened a new era of American space exploration. Tragedy struck, however, with the January 28, 1986 *Challenger* explosion. Seven astronauts were killed, as was schoolteacher Christa McAuliffe, who was to be the first ordinary citizen to go into space. NASA stopped all launches until that of shuttle *Discovery* in 1988. Throughout the 1990s shuttles allowed American astronauts to maintain the Hubble Space Telescope and help construct the International Space Station.

On February 1, 2003, *Columbia* exploded upon re-entry, again killing all seven astronauts on board, and NASA again stopped the shuttle program. Missions resumed in 2005, but closed indefinitely in 2011.

Future Space Exploration

NASA is currently developing the most advanced rocket ever created, the *Orion* spacecraft, and has plans to send astronauts beyond the moon, eventually reaching destinations including Mars sometime in the 2030s. Meanwhile Elon Musk plans to run regular commercial trips into space as part of his SpaceX venture starting in 2021 – for a minimum cost of $55m per passenger.

---

ly moist and creamy texture. Bring a bag and stock up at the market next door.

If you've been missing the swampy taste of Florida gator, they have that too. Plus, you can take home recipe cards for popular items.

Drinking & Nightlife

Preacher Bar   BAR

(☑321-613-4629; www.preacherbar.com; 8699 Astronaut Blvd; ⊙11am-1am) This bizarre and colorful watering hole is decked out in Day of the Dead portraits, animal skulls and stained-glass windows. Seating is communal and the bartenders are clad in plaid skirts. Try a homemade Moscow mule with ginger-infused vodka.

Getting There & Away

There are two ways to arrive in Cape Canaveral: traveling north on A1A from Cocoa Beach, or west on A1A across the Banana River via Merritt Island.

Cape Canaveral is served by SCAT buses. Rte 9 connects it with Cocoa Beach and Rte 4 connects it with Cocoa Village.

Cocoa Village

📞 321 / POP 5937

Originally a trading post along the Indian River Lagoon, Cocoa Village started serving tourists in the late 19th century when steamboat travelers disembarked along Riverfront Park to stretch their legs. Now the historic downtown offers a pleasant

WHAT'S AILING THE INDIAN RIVER LAGOON?

The Indian River Lagoon is the largest marine nursery in the US and the most biologically diverse estuary in North America. Straddling temperate and subtropical zones, the lagoon (actually an ecosystem of three separate estuaries) stretches 156 miles from New Smyrna to Jupiter Inlet and is washed by tidal waters through six inlet channels. The resulting warm, shallow, soupy water is a dynamic environment for 4300 species of animal, plant and bird and exploring it is one of the true highlights of this coastline.

But all is not well in this natural paradise. In March 2016 the lagoon experienced its worst fish kill in history after an algal bloom, seemingly caused by pollution from septic tanks, fertilizers and/or storm-water runoff, stripped the lagoon of oxygen. Thousands of fish carcasses washed up onshore from Melbourne to Titusville, appalling residents and visitors and raising health concerns.

The poor state of the lagoon is nothing new. For years unprecedented runoff from Lake Okeechobee has lowered the salinity of the lagoon, flushed it with silt and created high levels of nitrogen and phosphorus from industrial agriculture and domestic fertilizer. The result has been a 60% decline in seagrass beds along with poisonous algal blooms. In 2013 scientists reported that these issues caused the deaths of 84 dolphins and more than 120 manatees.

In early 2017 Governor Rick Scott finally included the Indian River Lagoon in the state budget proposal. He asked for $60 million to help residents switch from septic tanks to sewer systems in affected areas, and to improve water quality by adding storage areas for polluted water to the north, east and west of Lake Okeechobee. With an annual economic impact of $4 billion and thousands of livelihoods at stake, figuring out exactly what's ailing the lagoon (and fixing it) remains the biggest environmental and economic challenge facing the Sunshine State.

alternative to Cocoa Beach. Its main drag, Delannoy Ave, is lined with historic structures such as the SF Travis Building, which houses a hardware store (the village's oldest existing business).

⊙ Sights & Activities

Indian River Queen   BOATING
(☏321-454-7414; www.indianriverqueen.com; Cocoa Village Marina, 90 Delannoy Ave; cruises $35-65) Take a trip back in time on this romantic paddleboat. The history-themed tour includes a narrated presentation on 19th-century Cocoa Village, when paddleboats were the norm and homesteaders hung a white cloth at the end of their pier to flag them down. Dinner and sunset booze cruises are also available. Check the website for the schedule.

Grasshopper Airboat Eco Tours   ECOTOUR
(☏321-631-2990; www.airboatecotours.com; 8190 West King St (State Road 520); tours $70) Often referred to as the Central Florida Everglades, the marshy shallows of the St Johns River are packed with alligators and migrating birds. Hop on board with US Coast Guard Master Captain Rick for thrilling ecotours through the marshy shallows. Afternoon tours see the best alligator sunbathing.

✖ Eating

★**Crydermans Barbecue**   BARBECUE $
(☏321-877-0796; 401 Florida Ave; sandwiches $10; ⊗11am-6.30pm Tue-Sat) Incredibly aromatic oak wood, Texas-style barbecue meat classics are dished out at this former gas station. It's very straightforward, with pork or beef brisket stuffed in a bun, plus sides (pickles, coleslaw) and rather loud rock on the speakers on the terrace (the only seating area). The taste is incomparable.

Meat is sold by weight – best are beef brisket ($22 per pound) and pulled pork ($18 per pound).

Ossorio   CAFE $
(☏321-639-2423; https://ossorio.com/; 316 Brevard Ave; mains $7-9; ⊗8am-7pm Tue-Sat, 9am-6pm Sun) Fuel up pre- or post-beach at this sunny cafe serving sandwiches, flatbread pizza, ice cream and coffee.

Cocoa Village Farmers Market   MARKET $
(Myrt Tharpe Sq; ⊗10am-3pm Thu) Weekly farmers market with fresh, organic produce, local honey and more.

Lone Cabbage Fish Camp   SEAFOOD $$
(☏321-632-4199; www.twisterairboatrides.com; 8199 Hwy 520; mains $8-17; ⊗10am-9pm Sun-Thu,

to 10pm Fri & Sat) Come to this fish camp for cold beers, fried gator tail and sunset views over the Indian River. You can even scoot around the lagoon on its airboats (adult/child $29/17). You'll find it west of Cocoa Village on Hwy 520.

★**Crush Eleven**   MODERN AMERICAN $$$
(☑321-634-1100; www.crusheleven.com; 923 E New Haven Ave; mains $18-49; ⊙5-9pm daily, 11am-2pm lunch Wed-Sun) Sister restaurant to the Fat Snook (p341), Crush Eleven gets top marks for its modern American menu and crafted cocktails. Don't miss the bacon-infused Old Fashioned cocktail.

Café Margaux   MEDITERRANEAN $$$
(☑321-639-8343; http://margaux.com; 220 Brevard Ave; mains $15-45; ⊙11:30am-2pm & 5-9pm Mon-Sat) A longtime favorite of Cocoa Village regulars is this creative Mediterranean restaurant. Dine on the patio or in one of the themed dining rooms on chili-seared red snapper or syrah-braised short ribs. To accompany your meal choose from a wine list that runs to 4000 labels.

☆ **Entertainment**

There are a couple of decent pubs in the area, and the best spot for craft cocktails is Crush Eleven.

Cocoa Village Playhouse   PERFORMING ARTS
(☑321-636-5050; www.cocoavillageplayhouse.com; 300 Brevard Ave) Stages locally produced plays on the site of the ornate Historic Cocoa Village Playhouse, built in 1924.

🛍 **Shopping**

★**Mrs Mango & Co**   MEDICINAL HERBS
(☑321-631-1194; www.mrsmangoandcompany.com; 3500 South US Hwy 1, Rockledge; ⊙10am-4pm, Tue-Sat) One of those total gems that you'd never know were there if you did not have the good fortune to get a recommendation, Mrs Mango's has been selling medicinal herbs, powders, teas and potions for the last 40 years in this creaky little house by the highway. There's also raw local honey, teas, essential oils and good advice on nature's remedies.

Any ailments, aches or pains you might have, bring 'em here. It's in Rockledge, just south of Cocoa.

Village Outfitters   SPORTS & OUTDOORS
(☑321-633-7245; www.villageoutfitters.com; 229 Forrest Ave; ⊙10am-5pm Mon-Fri, 8:30am-4pm Sat) Outdoor and camping gear as well as kayak rental.

ℹ **Information**

Space Coast Office of Tourism (☑321-433-4470; www.visitspacecoast.com; 430 Brevard Ave; ⊙9am-5pm Mon-Fri) Inside the Bank of America, one block south of the Village Playhouse.

ℹ **Getting There & Away**

Cocoa Village stretches west from S Cocoa Blvd to the Indian River Lagoon and south from King St about five blocks. Having a car is the most convenient, but Rte 1 SCAT (p342) buses pass through Cocoa Village on a north–south route, as does the Rte 4 SCAT bus which connects to Merritt Island and Cocoa Beach.

ℹ **Getting Around**

Cocoa Village is best explored on foot as it's only about five city blocks long and wide.

Melbourne

☑321 / POP 82,011
Historic Melbourne was established in the 1870s by freed slaves and pineapple farmers who built homesteads on a small peninsula between the Indian River Lagoon and Crane Creek. A fire destroyed the burgeoning town in 1919, but the newly reconstructed downtown along New Haven Ave remains much as it was in the 1920s, offering a small-town feel with several good restaurants, coffee shops and bars.

Across the lagoon, Melbourne Beach has a more chill vibe and a variety of beachfront accommodations.

◉ **Sights**

★**Brevard Zoo**   ZOO
(☑321-254-9453; www.brevardzoo.org; 8225 N Wickham Rd; adult/child 2-12yr $25/15, Tree Top Trek adult/small child $45/15; ⊙9.30am-5pm) For more than two decades this community-built zoo has set standards for imaginative design, immersive wildlife experiences, education and conservation. Since hammer-holding locals came out in force in March 1994 to start construction, the zoo's landscape has evolved via winding boardwalks through hardwood hammocks into distinct geographical zones featuring wildlife from Florida, South America, Africa and Australia. Specially designed enclosures merging with the undergrowth and

free-flight aviaries give a real sense of wandering through a wilderness.

The zoo's best experiences are the **kayak tours** past gangling giraffes down the Nyami Nyami river and the **Tree Top Trek**, an aerial adventure course incorporating ziplines over wetland ponds and alligator pools.

Once you've got over the enjoyment of wandering around the zoo's unique environment, you'll begin to notice its dedication to the serious work of conservation and wildlife education. The **Paws On** children's area invites kids to build, explore and splash around on a real sand beach, engage in hookless fishing and pet the resident pygmy goats and alpacas. Volunteers work tirelessly to create oyster mats for the oyster-reef-regeneration project in Indian River, and the **Wildlife Detective Training Academy** encourages curiosity and inquiry in older kids through self-guided mystery tours designed around the zoo.

In addition there are night hikes, a Junior Zoo Keeper's Club, summer camps, animal-adoption programs and well-attended community events, including the popular **Boo at the Zoo** Halloween celebration. For kids and animal lovers this may well outshine the Space Center.

Melbourne Beach   BEACH

(Ocean Park, Atlantic St) Backed by **Ocean Park** with its boardwalk, gazebo and showers, Melbourne Beach, along with its neighbor Indialantic Beach (to the north), offers miles and miles of white, sandy shoreline unspoiled by high-rise condos and commercialism. Pick up picnic essentials at the Melbourne Beach Market.

Ryckman Park   PARK

(cnr Ocean Ave & Riverside Dr, Melbourne Beach) Located in Melbourne's historic district, this family-friendly park features a large playground, bocce and basketball courts, and the nationally registered **Melbourne Beach Pier** (1889). The latter extends into the fish-rich Indian River Lagoon, making it a fantastic fishing spot.

🛏 Sleeping

There aren't many good options in the downtown area, with the exception of Crane Creek Inn. Head over to Melbourne Beach for oceanfront stays with lots of local character.

Crane Creek Inn Waterfront Bed & Breakfast   B&B $$

(📞 321-768-6416; www.cranecreekinn.com; 907 E Melbourne Ave; r $185; P❄🖥🛏) Two blocks from downtown Melbourne, this attractive 1925 home sits directly on Crane Creek, where manatees, dolphins and waterbirds can be seen. The five rooms are furnished in period style with lazy ceiling fans, and there is a two-person hammock beside the river.

Sea View Motel   MOTEL $$

(📞321-723-0566; www.seaviewmelbourne.com; 4215 S Hwy A1A, Melbourne Beach; r & ste from $185; ❄🖥🛏) Directly on the beach, this renovated 1950s motel has eight simple rooms with quilts, wood floors and fully equipped kitchens.

⭐ **Port d'Hiver**   BOUTIQUE HOTEL $$$

(📞321-722-2727; www.portdhiver.com; 201 Ocean Ave, Melbourne Beach; r $279-339, ste $479-529; P❄🖥🛏) Constructed in 1916, this cypress-built, colonial-style beach house sits amid tall palms, hidden behind flowering bougainvillea and bright pink allamanda. Brick-paved courtyards connect the main house with seven cabana rooms and the carriage-house suite, and views of the Atlantic are complemented by artful interior decor incorporating French printed fabrics, candelabra chandeliers, antique dressers and four-poster beds.

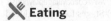 Eating

Seafood is top-notch both downtown and out at the beach.

Ichabods Dockside   AMERICAN $

(📞321-952-9532;www.ichabodsbarandgrille-florida. com; 2210 Front St; mains $8-14; ⊙11am-10pm Sun-Thur, to midnight Fri & Sat) Eddy Fisher's laid-back bar is a local favorite for its easygoing barside banter and top-quality burgers, jerked grouper wraps and mind-blowingly good buffalo wings.

El Ambia Cubano   CUBAN $

(www.elambiacubano.com; 950 E Melbourne Ave; mains $8-15; ⊙11am-2:30pm & 5-9pm Mon-Sat) Conga stools, weekend salsa, jazz and acoustic guitar, and tasty family cooking in a tiny spot across from Crane Creek.

Melbourne Beach Market   MARKET $

(📞321-676-5225; 302 Ocean Ave; ⊙8am-8pm Mon-Sat, to 7pm Sun) Pick up picnic essentials here, including ready-to-eat Greek and Italian meals.

Matt's Casbah SUSHI $$
(☑321-574-1099; www.mattscasbah.com; 801 E New Haven Ave; mains $10-15; ☺11am-midnight Mon-Thu, to 2am Fri & Sat, to 10pm Sun) This popular eatery in the heart of downtown features a delicious sushi bar, exotic options such as fried whole fish and desserts that arrive flaming in 151 rum. Check the website for nightly specials, live music and other event announcements.

★**Ocean 302** SEAFOOD $$$
(☑321-802-5728; www.ocean302.com; 302 Ocean Ave; charcuterie $20, mains $21-36; ☺4-10pm Mon-Sat, to 9pm Sun, brunch 11am-3pm Sat & Sun) Melbourne Beach's favourite dock- and farm-to-table establishment is situated in an otherwise unimpressive shopping plaza. With an adventurous and ever-changing menu, this place is luring foodies from up and down the Space Coast. The incredible 'Goddess' salad is king sized. Reservations recommended.

🍷 Drinking & Nightlife

On Friday and Saturday nights East New Haven Ave in downtown Melbourne is transformed into an urban block party.

Meg O'Malley's IRISH PUB
(☑321-952-5510; www.megomalleys.com; 812 E New Haven Ave; ☺10:30am-10pm Mon & Tue, to 11pm Wed, to 1am Thu, to 1:30am Fri & Sat, 10am-11pm Sun) This authentic, ever-hoppin' Irish pub serves up Guinness and 18¢ bowls of Parliament soup, with live music.

Foo Bar & Lotus Gallery LOUNGE
(☑321-728-7179; 816 E New Haven Ave; ☺5pm-2am Mon-Fri, 3pm-2am Sat & Sun) Draws an older crowd with an Asian-themed menu, craft cocktails and an exquisite interior gallery. Cabaret shows and '80s nights are frequently scheduled.

Sand on the Beach BAR
(☑321-327-8951; www.sandonthebeach.com; 1005 Atlantic St; ☺8am-10pm Mon-Fri, 7am-11pm Sat, to 10pm Sun) The only place where you have a private beach in front of you and a margarita in your hand. With bars on two levels, you've got sea views for miles in either direction.

Main Street Pub PUB
(☑321-723-7811; http://mainstreetpub.cc; 705 E New Haven Ave; ☺11:30am-late Tue-Sat) Offers a good selection of beers and a nice deck.

☆ Entertainment

While Cocoa Beach pays homage to the gods of commercialism, Melbourne prefers to pay its dues to those of culture with a thriving community arts, music and theater scene.

★**Melbourne Civic Theatre** THEATER
(☑321-723-6935; www.mymct.org; 817 E Strawbridge Ave; tickets $31; ☺box office 11am-3pm Tue-Fri, 2pm-6pm Sat) The Space Coast's oldest community theater stages early Broadway productions and popular contemporary pieces in a tiny spot in the shopping plaza La Galerie. They're a talented bunch and with only 90 seats in the auditorium it's an exciting space to experience live performances.

Brevard Symphony Orchestra CLASSICAL MUSIC
(☑321-345-5052; https://brevardsymphony.com; King Center, 3865 N Wickham Rd) This 65-strong, not-for-profit orchestra has been bringing music to Melbourne residents for more than 60 years and is one of the finest in the country. For the July 4 celebrations the symphony plays at the Cocoa Riverfront Park beneath a spectacular fireworks display.

Henegar Center ARTS CENTER
(☑321-723-8698; www.henegar.org; 625 E New Haven Ave) Melbourne's one-time high school now houses a community arts center and a 500-seat proscenium-style theater that stages musicals and comedies.

ⓘ Getting There & Away

Driving to and from Melbourne is the most sensible option, although several SCAT (p342) routes do connect Melbourne to most neighboring destinations and loop through several areas of the city.

The **Orlando Melbourne International Airport** (☑321-723-6227; www.mlbair.com; 1 Air Terminal Pkwy) is located to the northeast of the city and works with a limited number of commercial airlines.

Indialantic

☑321 / POP 2894

Indialantic, a small and cute town that hooks onto Melbourne, is homey. It has some lovely cafes and the usual gorgeous surf and white sand. If you don't have your own surfboard you can rent one and hop on the waves.

🏃 Activities

Longboard House   SURFING
(✆321-951-8001; www.longboardhouse.com; 101
5th Av; per day surfboard/bodyboard $29/10;
☉8:30am-9pm Mon-Sat, to 6pm Sun) Long-
standing surf shop with an impressive selection of surfboards for rent and purchase.

Paddleboard House   WATER SPORTS
(✆321-676-9773; www.paddleboardhouse.com;
110 S Miramar Av; 3hr/day $30/50; ☉noon-6pm
Tue-Thur, 9am-6pm Fri-Sun) This place rents
paddleboards at reasonable rates.

Bob's Bicycle Shop   CYCLING
(✆321-725-2500; http://bobsbicycles.com; 113
5th Ave; road bike per day/week $65/180, cruisers
per day/week $30/80; ☉10am-6pm Mon-Sat)
Rents road bikes and cruisers and sells fat
bikes, which are especially fun to ride in
the sand.

🛏 Sleeping & Eating

There are a few scattered cottages along the
coastline in Indialantic, but head north to
Cocoa Beach or south to Melbourne Beach
for a wider variety of options.

★ Beachside Cafe   CAFE $
(✆321-953-8444; www.thebeachsidecafe.com;
109 5th Ave; mains $6-12; ☉7am-2pm; 🖼) Grab
a booth at this wonderfully vintage, friendly, family-owned and fantastic-value downtown breakfast cafe, where servers regularly
top up coffee. Get a plate of stuffed French
toast, skillet eggs or griddled Belgian
waffles.

**Bizarro Famous
NY Pizza**   PIZZA $$
(✆321-724-4799; www.theoriginalbizzarro.com;
4 Wave Crest Ave; pizza $11-36; ☉11am-10pm
Mon-Sat, noon-10pm Sun) This NY-style pizza
joint sits in a majestic spot beside the
beach in Indialantic. Service is brusque,
but the spinach slice is divine with extra
marinara sauce.

Scott's on Fifth   MEDITERRANEAN $$$
(✆321-729-9779; www.scottsonfifth.com; 141 5th
Ave; mains $26-39; ☉5:30-9pm Tue-Sun) This
elegant restaurant on 5th Ave serves up
European classics as part of a seasonally
appropriate menu that changes daily, with
highlights often including grouper specials, escargot and stuffed shrimp. It's easy
to miss as it's tucked behind a tiny store-
front. There are only 12 tables, so reserve in
advance.

🍷 Drinking & Nightlife

Copperhead Tavern   CRAFT BEER
(✆321-802-4700; www.copperheadtavern.com;
205 5th Av; ☉2-10pm Sun-Thur, to midnight Fri &
Sat) The best (and only) bar in town, Copperhead Tavern offers craft beer, juicy burgers and a fire pit in the outdoor beer garden.

Titusville

📍 321 / POP 46,263

Essentially NASA's bedroom community, the
small but quaint town of Titusville is just
across the Indian River Lagoon from the
Kennedy Space Center, and its prosperity
is inextricably tied to that of the space program. When humans go to Mars, Titusville
will boom.

In the meantime the historic downtown
has shown signs of life, with the addition of a
hip craft brewery and plans for a bicycle trail
segment that will eventually extend across
Florida all the way to St Petersburg. There's
a quirky B&B, a couple of good restaurants
and a park for watching spacecraft launches.

👁 Sights

**Valiant Air Command
Warbird Museum**   MUSEUM
(✆321-268-1941; www.valiantaircommand.com;
6600 Tico Rd; adult/military/child $20/18/5;
☉9am-5pm; 🖼) What started off as a hob-
by for 12 combat veterans has grown into
a 1500-member-strong club and fascinating museum, which celebrates the region's
aviation heritage with an impressive stock
of more than 45 classic planes. A memorabilia hall kicks off the tour, then you're free
to roam through three hangars, one a restoration workshop and the other two housing
vintage aircraft from WWII, the Vietnam
War and the Korean War.

The VAC's flagship, the *Tico Belle,* a 1942
C-47A that dropped paratroopers at the
D-Day landings, sits combat-ready next to a
restored *Top Gun*–style Grumman Wildcat
that took more than 30,000 hours to restore.

In March or April the museum hosts a
family-friendly air show where combat veterans put on a three-hour aerial display and
offer the chance to fly in a unique piece of
history. Alternatively drop by on the second Saturday of the month to enjoy a fly-in
breakfast ($12; available 8am to 10:30am)
and ask about 'champagne flights,' which
fly the coast in a WWII C-47 about once a
month ($250 per person).

Space View Park PARK

(17 Orange St) Directly across the Indian River Lagoon from Kennedy Space Center, this park is one of the best spots on the coast from which to observe launches. Its 2-plus acres also contain the U.S. Space Walk of Fame, a collection of monuments, exhibits and plaques commemorating space missions.

🛏 Sleeping & Eating

★**Casa Coquina del Mar** B&B $$

(☑ 321-268-4653; www.casacoquina.com; 4010 Coquina Av; r $105-174; P❋☀) This quirky, family-owned B&B is set in a 1927 mansion with eight rooms, each uniquely furnished and named for gemstones (most impressive is the Black Pearl, spacious and beautifully adorned with Asian antiques). There's a huge replica of a knight riding a horse in the downstairs living room, and a hot tub in the gazebo out the back.

In the mornings the owners serve up an impressive buffet breakfast including freshly baked bread, an egg dish, baked ham, fresh fruit, coffee, tea and juice.

Wild Ocean Seafood MARKET $

(www.wildoceanmarket.com; 688 S Park Ave; mains $9-12; ◷11am-6pm Mon-Tue & Thur, from 10am Fri & Sat, 11am-4pm Sun) With more than 80 species of harvestable Florida seafood, Wild Ocean Seafood market believes in diversifying consumers' palates and therefore carries low trophic level fish as well as predatory species. They serve prepared seafood right in the store, including a mouthwatering Asian tuna burger and a 'not-from-a-can' tuna melt, and hold tastings and attend food festivals to educate the public.

There's a second location in Cape Canaveral.

★**Dixie Crossroads** SEAFOOD $$

(☑ 321-268-5000; www.dixiecrossroads.com; 1475 Garden St; mains $8-46; ◷11am-8pm Sun-Thu, to 9pm Fri & Sat; ⊞) Rodney Thompson developed the rock-shrimp fishery off Canaveral's coast in the early 1970s, and in 1983 his daughter Laurilee opened the Dixie Crossroads Seafood Restaurant. The aim: to put local shrimp back on the Canaveral's tables. Today this local landmark continues to serve up seasonal shrimp, including sweet, blush-colored royal reds, succulent white shrimp and melt-in-your-mouth broiled rock shrimp.

Rock shrimp are ordered by the dozen ($16), and arrive sliced open by a wondrous machine invented by the Thompsons and are accompanied by two side dishes. Other menu highlights include fresh Indian River Lagoon red mullet, oysters and juicy prime rib. Despite the generous seating in the funky wooden chalet, there's often a queue at peak times, so order a drink in the gazebo bar. Look for the tuxedo-wearing shrimp 'valets' outside and you'll know you've arrived.

★**Chef Larry's** MODERN AMERICAN $$

(☑ 321-368-9123; www.cheflarrysspice.com; 1111 S Washington Ave; lunch mains $7-10, dinner mains $12-15; ◷11am-1:30pm Tue-Fri, 5-7pm Fri & Sat) The best meal in Titusville is procured in a historic pink home filled with old Americana and run by a Hollywood chef who 'retired' to Titusville. He runs a tight, somewhat odd ship, opening for just a couple of hours on particular days (definitely reserve ahead) and serving just a few dishes, most notably teriyaki bourbon barbecue baby back ribs. Cash only.

🍷 Drinking & Nightlife

Playalinda Brewing Company MICROBREWERY

(☑ 321-225-8978; www.playalindabrewingcompany.com; 305 S Washington Ave; ◷4-9pm Mon-Wed, to 10pm Thur, 11:30am-10pm Fri, noon-10pm Sat, to 7pm Sun) In historic downtown Titusville, this microbrewery is set in a 100-year-old former hardware store and features a great selection of local and national craft beer, including a few very tasty stouts and porters. The brewery also serves delicious food, including the Ploughman's Platter (charcuterie with cheese, fruits and veggies) and a pretzel-bowl, beer-cheese soup.

Brix Project BAR

(☑ 321-567-5974; www.playalindabrewingcompany.com; 5220 S Washington Ave; ◷4-9pm Mon-Wed, 11.30am-10pm Thur-Sat, 10am-8pm Sun) Playalinda's second location, the Brix Project is housed in an aesthetically pleasing reformed lumberyard. With excellent beer, good food and a lovely back garden, it's a real treat.

ℹ Getting There & Away

A car is the best way to go in Titusville, which is accessible via Hwy 1 from the north and south. On the northern end of town, the A Max Brewer Memorial Pkwy extends east over the Indian River Lagoon to Merritt Island National Wildlife Refuge. To the south, NASA Pkwy stretches east over the lagoon to the Kennedy Space Center Visitor Complex.

SCAT (p342) bus Rte 1 connects Titusville with the cities to the south (including Cocoa Village) and Rte 2 loops around Titusville.

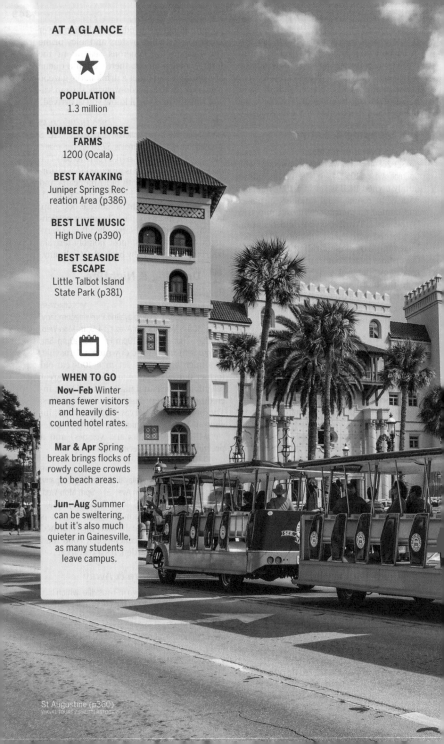

AT A GLANCE

⭐

POPULATION
1.3 million

NUMBER OF HORSE FARMS
1200 (Ocala)

BEST KAYAKING
Juniper Springs Recreation Area (p386)

BEST LIVE MUSIC
High Dive (p390)

BEST SEASIDE ESCAPE
Little Talbot Island State Park (p381)

📅

WHEN TO GO
Nov–Feb Winter means fewer visitors and heavily discounted hotel rates.

Mar & Apr Spring break brings flocks of rowdy college crowds to beach areas.

Jun–Aug Summer can be sweltering, but it's also much quieter in Gainesville, as many students leave campus.

St Augustine (p360)
VIAVAL TOURS / SHUTTERSTOCK ©

Northeast Florida

F lorida's northeastern corner is a reminder that there's more to the state than seemingly endless miles of soft, sandy beaches (although the northeast has those too). For a start, there's St Augustine, the oldest continuously occupied city in the US, and its historic core is a real charmer. History also looms large in the historic quarter of pretty Amelia Island, with its great restaurants and fun activities. Then there's Gainesville, a university town peppered with fair-trade coffee shops, craft cocktail bars and live-music bars.

Natural attractions abound in Ocala National Forest, Cumberland Island and De Leon Springs State Park. Jacksonville sprawls across the northeast and has a buzzing culinary and craft brewery scene, not to mention gorgeous beaches in abundance.

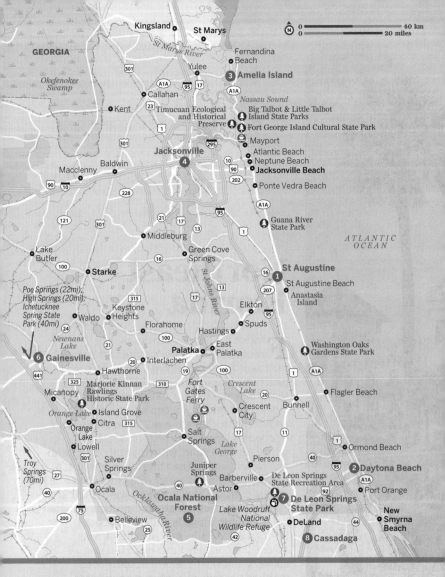

Northeast Florida Highlights

1 St Augustine (p360)
Exploring Spanish-colonial architecture, fascinating museums and centuries of history in America's oldest city.

2 Daytona Beach (p353)
Indulging your inner NASCAR fan then heading for the beach.

3 Amelia Island (p376)
Kayaking into the waterways

that surround this pretty barrier island.

4 Jacksonville (p369)
Discovering craft breweries and creative cooking in Florida's biggest city.

5 Ocala National Forest (p386)
Hiking, canoeing and camping your way through this pristine, wildlife-dense forest.

6 Gainesville (p387)
Rocking out in the home of Florida's largest university.

7 De Leon Springs State Park (p383) Marveling at the cool azure waters.

8 Cassadaga (p382) Having your fortune read in this spiritualist camp-cum-small town.

ATLANTIC COAST

Florida's northern Atlantic Coast – known as the 'First Coast' because this is where the European settlement of Florida (and the US) began – is a land of long beaches shadowed by tall condo complexes and seaside mansions, serving as an exurb riviera for the Southern USA. Heading from south to north, you'll pass the speedway and biker bars of Daytona Beach, go down through the gears in mellow Flagler Beach, and on to historic St Augustine, one of Florida's loveliest towns and certainly its oldest.

Sprawling but buzzy, Jacksonville combines an urban break with fine beaches and affluent coastal living. Continue north from here to charming Amelia Island near the Florida–Georgia border. Along the way you'll discover a jumbled necklace of grassy barrier islands, interlaced with tidal inlets, salt marsh flats and dark clumps of maritime forest.

Daytona Beach

📍 386 / POP 68,866

Daytona Beach is an icon of American life. While it goes by the self-appointed moniker of 'the World's Most Famous Beach,' for once in Florida the beach is overshadowed by something far bigger. This is the birthplace and spiritual home of NASCAR, the motor-racing phenomenon that's one of America's most popular (and most passionately followed) forms of entertainment. It all revolves around the awesome Daytona International Speedway, peaking in February for the Daytona 500, but with events throughout the year.

Beyond the race track, if you can see past the dated beachside barricade of '70s high-rise blocks, nightclubs and tourist traps, you might witness the phenomena of nesting sea turtles (in season) or explore a handful of interesting and worthwhile cultural attractions.

◎ Sights

★ **Daytona International Speedway** STADIUM
(📞 800-748-7467; www.daytonainternationalspeedway.com; 1801 W International Speedway Blvd; tours from $19; ⏰ tours 9:30am-3:30pm) Race fans never forget the first time they visit Daytona. The combination of sheer scale, the weight of history and the passion of NASCAR fans makes this one of America's most significant

sporting temples. Unless you're here for one of the race events, in which case you should start planning months in advance, take a tour of the track in all its glory and visit the Motorsports Hall of Fame afterwards.

The biggest race of the year is the **Daytona 500** (www.daytonainternationalspeedway.com; tickets from $99; ⏰ Feb), and it's this event that provides much of the Daytona lore and many of its legends. If you can't watch the race live in February, you'll get a taste of all the excitement on one of the tours that run most days. Highlights include getting up close with the maximum (and rather frightening) 31-degree gradient in some sections of the track – cars travel over 160mph through these turns, and they'll start to slide down the hill if they go less than 70mph! The main stand has 101,500 seats and the whole speedway can cater to 150,000 people; the seats are painted in such a way that the stand looks full on TV even when there's not a soul there.

All tours end with a visit to the Motorsports Hall of Fame, and you can pay $4 person more to get downloadable photos. Tours begin and end at the northern end of the complex, near the corner of W International Speedway Blvd and Bill France Blvd.

The 30-minute **Speedway Tour** (adult/child $19/13; 11:30am, 1pm, 2pm and 3:30pm) covers the basics, including a 'tram' ride around part of the track and a visit to Gatorade Victory Lane. For the full experience, take the 90-minute **All Access Tour** (adult/child $26/20; hourly 9:30am to 2:30pm), which visits the media center, fan zone and gives you a bird's-eye view from the stands. The three-hour **VIP Tour** ($55; 1pm Tuesday, Thursday and Saturday) covers everything NASCAR from the comfort of an air-conditioned coach.

If that's all a bit sedate, treat yourself to the NASCAR Racing Experience (p356), which allows you to either ride shotgun around the track or take a day to become a driver.

Southeast Museum of Photography MUSEUM
(📞 386-506-3894; www.smponline.org; 1200 W International Speedway Blvd, Mori Husseini Center; ⏰ 11am-5pm Tue, Thu & Fri, to 6pm Wed, 1-5pm Sat) FREE We love this hidden treasure in Daytona. This vibrant modern gallery with excellent lighting and facilities doesn't shy away from provocative subjects in its rotating exhibitions. Best of all, it's free (though donations are welcome)!

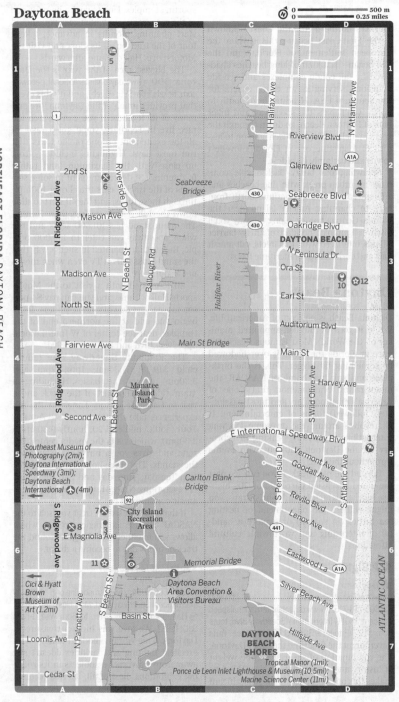

0   500 m
0   0.25 miles

Daytona Beach

◎ Sights
1 Daytona Beach..................................D5
2 Jackie Robinson Ballpark &
   Museum..B6

◐ Activities, Courses & Tours
3 Angell & Phelps Chocolate
   Factory...A6

◒ Sleeping
4 Plaza Resort & Spa...........................D2
5 River Lily Inn B1

◉ Eating
6 Chucherias Hondureñas A2
7 Dancing Avocado Kitchen.................A6
8 The Cellar A6

◐ Drinking & Nightlife
9 Daytona Taproom C2
10 Mai Tai Bar......................................D3

◉ Entertainment
11 Cinematique of Daytona A6
12 Daytona Beach Bandshell.................D3

Marine Science Center   AQUARIUM
(📞 386-304-5545; www.marinesciencecenter.
com; 100 Lighthouse Dr, Ponce Inlet; adult/child
$5/2; ⊙10am-4pm Tue-Sat, noon-4pm Sun Labor
Day-Memorial Day, 10am-5pm Tue-Sat & noon-5pm
Sun rest of year; ⊕) ✦ We were impressed by
this center's rescue, rehab and release programs for sea turtles and seabirds that nest
on Daytona's beaches. It's a fun and environmentally conscious place where adults and
kids can enjoy learning about our underwater friends. Exhibits include a 5000-gallon
reef aquarium, a stingray touch pool and a
bird-observation tower.

Daytona Beach Drive-In Church   CHURCH
(📞 386-767-8761; www.driveinchurch.net; 3140 S
Atlantic Ave; ⊙ services 8:30am & 10am Sun; 🅿)
Only in Daytona. At Daytona Beach Drive-In
Church you can get your dose of (Protestant)
religion from the comfort of your car. Pull in
to the former drive-in movie theater, hook
up a speaker or tune your radio to 680AM
or 88.5FM and behold the word of the Reverend. He and the choir hold services on a
balcony overlooking the sea of cars. There's
free coffee and doughnuts between services.
That's right...free doughnuts.

The church dates back to 1954. When the
old Neptune Drive-In Theater closed, this
car-obsessed town devised a novel solution

for increasing church attendance: getting
the good news while sitting in your vehicle.

Cici & Hyatt Brown
Museum of Art   MUSEUM
(📞 386-255-0285; www.moas.org; 352 S Nova Rd;
adult/child $13/7, free 1st Tue of month; ⊙10am-
5pm Mon-Sat, 11am-5pm Sun) This striking
must-see museum, designed to look like a
rural Floridian house, tells the story of the
Sunshine State via the largest collection of
Florida-themed oil and watercolor paintings
in the world.

Tomoka State Park   STATE PARK
(📞 386-676-4050; www.floridastateparks.org/
Tomoka; 2099 N Beach St, Ormond Beach; per
vehicle/pedestrian from $4/2; ⊙8am-sunset;
🅿 ♿) ✦ The 20-minute drive here from
downtown Daytona Beach is almost as
pleasant as the park itself, a bird-watchers'
heaven of former-indigo-fields-turned-
hardwood-forests. A canopy of trees overhangs the two-lane road like a green tunnel,
letting in only the stray dapple of sunlight.
It's a beautiful place with echoes of the
Deep South.

Jackie Robinson
Ballpark & Museum   STADIUM
(📞 386-257-3172; www.daytonacubs.com; 105 E
Orange Ave; ⊙9am-5pm; ♿) **FREE** 'The Jack'
made history when, in 1946, the Montreal
Royals, Jackie Robinson's team, were in
Florida to play an exhibition against their
parent club, the Brooklyn Dodgers: other
Florida cities refused to let the game proceed due to segregation laws, but Daytona
Beach cried, 'Play ball!' Robinson went on
to be the first African American baseball
player in the majors. The ballpark here was
renamed in his honor in 1990. A small open-
air museum tells the story.

Gamble Place   MUSEUM
(📞 386-304-0778; www.moas.org/explore/gamble-
place/index; 1819 Taylor Rd, Port Orange; adult/
child $3/free, with guided tour $6/3; ⊙8am-5pm
Wed-Sun; 🅿) Twenty minutes south of Daytona but a million miles away, the winter
estate of the Gamble family (of Procter &
Gamble fortune) lies in a sun-dappled glade.
The Cracker-style house and several whimsically-named cottages (including a replica
Snow White and the Seven Dwarfs house)
are closed to the public unless you're on a
guided tour (10-person minimum), but you
can walk the grounds of the estate.

Daytona Beach

BEACH

(per car $20; ⊙beach driving 8am-7pm May-Oct, sunrise-sunset Nov-Apr) This long stretch of sand was once the city's raceway. Sections of the beach still welcome drivers to the sands at a strictly enforced top speed of 10mph. Beachside rentals for ATVs, fat-tired cruisers, recumbent trikes and all manner of water sports are ubiquitous. Of course you're free to frolic anywhere on the beach, off the roadway.

☞ Tours

NASCAR Racing Experience

DRIVING

(☎740-886-2400; www.nascarracingexperience. com; 1801 W International Speedway Blvd; from $99; ⊙dates vary) If merely watching NASCAR drivers streak around the track isn't adrenaline-pumping enough for you, get in the car yourself via the NASCAR Racing Experience. Choose from several levels of death-defying action, from the three-lap passenger-seat Race Ride (from $99) to the intensive Advanced Experience ($4000), with multiple laps, celeb meetings and even a certificate on completion. Dates vary; check online.

Angell & Phelps Chocolate Factory

TOURS

(☎386-252-6531; www.angellandphelps.com; 154 S Beach St; ⊙tours 10am, 11am, 1pm, 2pm 3pm, 4pm Mon-Sat, open but no tours noon-5pm Sun) **FREE** Get your cacao fix at Angell & Phelps Chocolate Factory, a downtown Daytona tradition since 1925. Free 20-minute tours of the production area include a sweet taste of the goods. While you're here, snag a bag of chocolate-covered potato chips, chocolate gators or the factory's signature creation: a caramel, cashew and chocolate confection known as the Honeybee.

⊨ Sleeping

River Lily Inn

B&B $$

(☎386-253-5002; www.riverlilyinnbedandbreak fast.com; 558 Riverside Dr; r $149-249; P🐾🛜🏊) There's a grand piano in the living room, Belgian waffles for breakfast and, oh yes, a heart-shaped pool in the backyard. What more could you want in a B&B? Add to that a quiet location on an oak-shaded property overlooking the river, elegant rooms with high ceilings (some with private balconies) and friendly-as-can-be owners, and you've got the recipe for a perfect getaway.

Plaza Resort & Spa

RESORT $$

(☎844-284-2685, 855-327-5292; www.plaza resortandspa.com; 600 N Atlantic Ave; r $109-149;

P🐾❄🛜🏊) Built in 1888, Daytona's most historic resort has undergone extensive renovations in its time, but still maintains its old-world charm. If only the walls, painted an unfortunate shade of yellow, could talk... From the miles of honey-colored marble lining the lobby to the 42in plasma TVs and cloud-soft beds in the rooms, to the 15,000-sq-ft spa, this resort coos luxury.

A variety of room types are available – not all face the ocean.

Hyatt Place Daytona Beach Oceanfront

HOTEL $$

(☎386-944-2010; www.hyatt.com/en-US/hotel/ florida/hyatt-place-daytona-beach-oceanfront/dab-zd; 3161 S Atlantic Ave, Daytona Beach Shores; r from $125; P@🛜🏊) Some of Daytona's freshest, funkiest and most functional rooms can be found here. All rooms feature balconies, plush bedding, separate living and sleeping areas and a nifty panel to easily connect your laptop or phone to the 42in panel TV.

Home2 Suites

HOTEL $$

(☎386-400-2300; www.hilton.com; 200 Fentress Blvd; r $99-200; P❄@🛜🏊) If you're here to soak up the NASCAR atmosphere, this place is a fine choice. Large, contemporary-styled rooms with kitchenettes, comfier-than-average beds and pillows, sofas, and, wait for it, views towards Daytona International Speedway from half of the rooms – ask for a southeast-facing room on the 4th floor.

✖ Eating

Cracked Egg Diner

BREAKFAST $

(☎386-788-6772; www.thecrackedeggdiner.com; 3280D S Atlantic Ave, Daytona Beach Shores; breakfast mains $5-12; ⊙7am-3pm; P♿) Brainchild of brothers Chris and Kevin, one of whom will usually greet you at the door with a smile, this place is the finest in Daytona Beach for breakfast. There's everything from eggs Benedict to the Chunky Monkey Pancakes.

Dancing Avocado Kitchen

CAFE $

(☎386-947-2022; www.dancingavocadokitchen. com; 110 S Beach St; mains $7.50-13; ⊙10am-3pm Mon-Sat; 🌱♿) Not the sort of place you expect to find in red-meat-loving Daytona Beach. Gluten-free and predominantly vegetarian-friendly items feature at this colorful kitchen serving breakfasts, lunches and light meals, although you'll still find the occasional chicken or ham among the tofu, hummus and liberal servings of fresh avocado. Healthy and delicious!

Aunt Catfish's on the River
SOUTHERN US $$
(☎386-767-4768; www.auntcatfishontheriver.
com; 4009 Halifax Dr, Port Orange; mains $10-29,
brunch adult/child $23/10; ⊙11:30am-9pm Mon-
Sat, 9am-9pm Sun; P🚼) Fresh-from-the-boat
grouper and mahimahi lolling in butter
or deeply and deliciously fried, as well as
Southern-style Cajun-spiced catfish, make
this riverside seafood establishment insane-
ly popular with tourists: table waits can be
expected. It's just outside Daytona Beach in
Port Orange. A kids play area gives the little
ones something to do while you wait.

★ Rose Villa Southern
Table and Bar
AMERICAN $$$
(☎386-615-7673; www.rosevillarestaurant.com; 43 W
Granada Blvd, Ormond Beach; mains $12-44; ⊙11am-
9pm Sun-Thu, to 10pm Fri & Sat; P) Intimate and
delightful, this under-the-radar fine-dining
bistro occupies a charming historic Victorian
house and garden a few miles north of Daytona. The eclectic menu skews toward haute
Southern, and does it well – among other
choices, try the lobster mac 'n' cheese or crab
cakes while you decide on your main.

Chucherias Hondureñas
LATIN AMERICAN $$$
(☎386-239-0548; https://chucheriasrestaurant.
com; 101 2nd St; mains $21-56; ⊙11am-9pm Wed-
Sun; P) One of the brightest stars in the
local culinary firmament, Chucherias' cui-
sine is a blend of bold, rich Latin American

and Caribbean flavors – shellfish are dressed
with *chimol* (a Central American salsa),
while pork is roasted with citrus and garlic.
An interior of white-linen tablecloths and
paintings on the walls plus friendly manage-
ment make this one a don't-miss.

The Cellar
ITALIAN $$$
(☎386-258-0011; www.thecellarrestaurant.com;
220 Magnolia Ave; mains $23-46; ⊙5-10pm Tue-
Sat, to 9pm Sun; P) Now you can tell your
friends that you've dined in the summer
mansion of 29th US President Warren G
Harding. The classic, upscale Italian fare
and elegant ambience have made it Daytona's go-to spot for special-occasion dinners.

🍷 Drinking & Nightlife

Daytona Taproom
CRAFT BEER
(☎386-872-3298; 310 Seabreeze Blvd; ⊙noon-
3am Thu-Sat, to 12:30am Sun-Wed; 🐾) A bright
spot among the biker and beach bum status
quo, this 'burger joint with a drinking problem' has 50 taps of regional and national
microbrews and pretty damn fine burgers to
boot. May close earlier in slow season.

Mai Tai Bar
BAR
(☎386-947-2493; www.maitaibar.com; 250 N
Atlantic Ave; ⊙4pm-2am Mon-Fri, 11am-2am Sat
& Sun) A party-happy crowd downs crayon-
colored rum drinks at this Hawaiian-
themed bar overlooking the Atlantic Ocean.

NORTHEAST FLORIDA DAYTONA BEACH

DAYTONA CALENDAR

Daytona International Speedway hosts a busy calendar of racing events. For most of
them, expect Confederate flags, loud motorcycles, jacked-up pickup trucks and plenty of
folks who love all of the above. To help with planning, these are the biggest.

Rolex 24 at Daytona (www.daytonainternationalspeedway.com; ⊙late Jan) This 24-hour
epic takes place in late January. It utilises the main race track as well as part of the race-
way's internal field; teams use two-driver teams.

Daytona 500 (p353) Over a week in February a bunch of races lead up to the big event,
the Daytona 500, the grand highlight among many on the Daytona racing calendar. At
the same time, 200,000 rowdy folks do a lot of partying.

Daytona Supercross (www.daytonainternationalspeedway.com; ⊙Mar) In early March,
the lawns in front of the main stand are transformed into a supercross course that draws
local and international stars.

Bike Week (www.officialbikeweek.com; ⊙Mar) For 10 days in March, 500,000 bikers drool
over each other's hogs and party around the clock.

Spring Break (www.dbspringbreak.com) For spring break, which usually happens in early
March, more than 100,000 exuberant, hormone-fueled youths from all corners of the US
party at the beach, in bars, clubs and on the streets. Keg-stands galore.

Biketoberfest (www.officialbikeweek.com; ⊙mid-Oct) Lots of drinking, loud bikes, burly
men, tattoos and all the rest. It generally begins the weekend following Columbus Day.

NASCAR & THE DAYTONA 500

National Association for Stock Car Auto Racing (NASCAR) has its origins in the years of Prohibition (1920 to 1933), a period when the production and transportation of alcoholic drinks was prohibited in the USA. Illegal operations to circumvent the ban, particularly in the Appalachian Mountains of Kentucky, Virginia and West Virginia, relied on small, extremely fast cars to escape the law. The ban may have been lifted in 1933, but the love affair with these cars in the American heartland continues to this day, no doubt helped by the fact that the sport's origins involved a rebellious, anti-government story.

NASCAR fast outgrew its Southern redneck roots to become popular across the US, but Daytona was at the heart of this very American passion since the earliest days. Daytona Beach was where drivers and manufacturers broke numerous land speed records in the 1920s and 1930s, and it was the natural home for the official NASCAR launch in 1948, when a road circuit was used. William 'Bill' France was the father of NASCAR, and it was he who oversaw the construction of the Daytona International Speedway, which opened in 1959.

There are numerous aspects of the NASCAR year, although the NASCAR Cup Series (NCS) is the most popular with 36 races held over ten months each year. Of these, the 500-mile Daytona 500 is considered the most prestigious, and it holds pride of place as the opening race of the NCS calendar.

Often called 'The Great American Race,' the Daytona 500 is the stuff of legend for motorsports enthusiasts. If given the chance over a beer or bourbon or three, any serious NASCAR fan can recount in intimate detail Denny Hamlin's 0.010-second victory in 2016, or the three days it took the authorities to declare Lee Petty the winner in the 1959 inaugural race, so close was the finish. Similarly, those who win a Daytona 500 are assured of NASCAR immortality. Richard Petty, son of first winner Lee Petty, won seven titles between 1964 and 1981, while more recently, Denny Hamlin was victorious in his third Daytona 500 in 2020.

Late-night happy hours (9pm to 1am Monday to Saturday, 4pm to midnight Sunday) are hard to argue with, as is the sand for a late-night stumble.

☆ Entertainment

★ Cinematique of Daytona
CINEMA

(☑ 386-252-3778; www.cinematique.org; 242 S Beach St; tickets from $8) Daytona's only arthouse cinema screens independent and foreign films and serves booze and snacks to your table/highboy/sofa in its intimate screening room.

Daytona Beach Bandshell
LIVE MUSIC

(☑ 386-671-3462; www.daytonabandshell.com; 70 Boardwalk) Constructed in 1937 from coquina shell, this landmark venue with a killer beachfront location stages a free summer concert series and summer outdoor movies.

🛍 Shopping

J&P Cycles Destination Daytona Superstore
SPORTS & OUTDOORS

(☑ 386-615-0950; www.jpcycles.com/daytona; 253 Destination Daytona Ln, Ormond Beach; ⊙ 9am-6pm Mon-Sat, 10am-5pm Sun) Just north of Daytona Beach at the Junction of I-95 and US 1, this is the place to go to gear up for Bike Week: you're bound to find something to make you look and feel the part among the 15,000 sq ft of aftermarket motorcycle accessories and clothing.

Daytona Flea & Farmers Market
MARKET

(☑ 386-253-3330; www.daytonafleamarket.com; 1425 Tomoka Farms Rd; ⊙ 9am-5pm Fri-Sun) With more than 1000 booths and 600 vendors, this gargantuan market is one of the world's largest. Fans of garage and car-boot sales will not want to miss this: allocate plenty of time. It's at the corner of US 92 at I-95, a mile southwest of the Speedway.

ℹ Information

Daytona Beach Area Convention & Visitors Bureau (☑ 386-255-0415; www.daytonabeach. com; 126 E Orange Ave; ⊙ 8:30am-5pm Mon-Fri) In person or online, these guys are *the* authority on all things Daytona Beach.

ℹ Getting There & Away

Daytona Beach is close to the intersection of two major interstates, I-95 and I-4. The I-95 is the quickest way to Jacksonville (about 90 miles) and Miami (260 miles). The I-4 is the fastest route to Orlando (55 miles).

Daytona Beach International Airport (p527) Just east of the Speedway; is served by Delta and US Airways, and all major car-rental companies.

Greyhound (✆386-255-7076; www.greyhound. com; 138 S Ridgewood Ave) Services to Orlando (from $17, 1¼ hours, two daily) and Jacksonville (from $19, two hours, three daily), with plenty of onward connections.

Flagler Beach

✆386 / POP 5081

Isolated Flagler Beach is the sort of place that Floridians and sunbirds from elsewhere come when they want Florida's sun without the glitz. Around 21 miles – and a real shift in culture and tempo – north of rowdy Daytona, Flagler has a 6-mile stretch of beach backed by modest residences, a smattering of shops and not a tower block in sight: there's a three-story cap on buildings here. The results? A quiet seaside community where the spectacular sunrises don't hide behind the buildings.

◉ Sights

Washington Oaks Gardens State Park STATE PARK
(✆386-446-6780; www.floridastateparks.org/index.php/parks-and-trails/washington-oaks-gardens-state-park; 6400 N Oceanshore Blvd; per vehicle/bicycle $5/2; ◎8am-sunset; P) ◢ On the fishing and hunting grounds of the Timucuan Native Americans, the landscaped grounds here were once owned by Owen and Louise Young and have been converted into a small, gorgeous park that's a lovely spot for a picnic; you can also cycle or hike along the 1.7-mile trail loop. The experience is more manicured gardens than wilderness, but watch for sea turtles and manatees in the water. Otherwise, explore the camellia- and bird-of-paradise-filled gardens.

Flagler Beach Fishing Pier LANDMARK
(✆386-517-2436; www.cityofflaglerbeach.com/thepier; 105 S 2nd St; entry $1.50, fishing pole & permit $6; ◎6am-midnight) Rent a pole and some bait to try your luck against the deep blue sea by fishing off this historic landmark, or just walk the pier at a leisurely pace: it's breathtaking at sunrise.

⊨ Sleeping

Sleepy Flagler Beach has a small but good range of accommodations, and makes an alternative to garish Daytona – you'll have miles of sandy shores largely to yourself.

Gamble Rogers Memorial State Recreation Area CAMPGROUND $
(✆386-517-2086; https://floridastateparks.reserve america.com; 3100 S Ocean Shore Blvd; per vehicle $5, tent & RV sites $28; ◎8am-sunset; P) ◢ Nature lovers can camp beachside at Gamble Rogers Memorial State Recreation Area, which straddles the A1A. Kayaks, canoes and bicycles are available for rent at the ranger station.

Flagler Beach Motel MOTEL $
(✆386-517-6700; www.flaglerbeachmotelandvacationrentals.com; 1820 S Oceanshore Blvd; studio from $100, 2-bed unit from $150; ❀❀) Of several inexpensive motels, the standout is the Flagler Beach Motel. Its spotless studio and one- and two-bedroom motel-style units – many with full kitchen facilities and views of the Atlantic – feature artwork by local artists. Located across the road from the beach, this is a wonderful place to disappear for a while.

Island Cottage Oceanfront Inn & Spa INN $$$
(✆386-439-0092; www.islandcottagevillas.com; 2316 S Oceanshore Blvd; r $229-369; P❀) If romance is on the agenda, head to the Island Cottage Oceanfront Inn & Spa for a little pampering and indulgence. The floral and frilly decor won't be to everyone's taste, but the level of attentive service offered is otherwise hard to come by and the plush four-poster beds and double Jacuzzis aren't difficult to enjoy!

✖ Eating

Vessel Sandwich Company SANDWICHES $
(✆386-693-5085; www.vesselsandwichco.com; 213 S 2nd St; sandwiches $7-10; ◎11am-4pm Mon-Thu & Sat, to 9pm Fri; P◢⊛) After a swim in the ocean, a shrimp sandwich is kind of perfect, right? It's even more perfect if it's served at this excellent joint, which also slings a good *banh mi*, a brisket Sloppy Joe, aged cheddar and apple grilled cheese, and chicken sandwiches slathered in Alabama white barbecue sauce.

High Tides at Snack Jack SEAFOOD $$
(✆386-439-3344; www.snackjacks.com; 2805 Hwy A1A; mains $9-23; ◎11am-9pm; P❀⊛) The valet parking adds to the fun of this wonderfully laid-back, open-to-the-elements beachfront bar and diner, loved by locals and visitors alike for its location, vibe and

flavor. Food runs along the line of cheeseburgers, coconut shrimp and decadent fried seafood platters.

ⓘ Getting There & Away

Flagler Beach is 21 miles north of Daytona Beach, and 35 miles south of St Augustine. You'll find beachside rentals stretching along the A1A in each direction.

St Augustine

◪ 904 / POP 14,576

The oldest continuously occupied European settlement in the US, charming St Augustine was founded in 1565 and is one of Florida's standout attractions. What makes St Augustine's 144-block National Historic Landmark District so genuinely endearing is the accessibility of its rich history via countless top-notch museums and its well-preserved, centuries-old architecture, monuments and narrow cobbled lanes. Yes, there are moments when the line between authenticity and tacky tourist-trap elements becomes blurred – there are miniature theme parks, tour operators at almost every turn and horse-drawn carriages clip-clopping past townsfolk dressed in period costume – but they distract only momentarily from the palpable sense of history, wonderful B&Bs, cozy cafes, lamp-lit pubs and excellent restaurants.

History

In 1513 Spanish explorer Juan Ponce de León sighted land, came ashore and claimed La Florida (Land of Flowers) for Spain. In 1565 his compatriot Don Pedro Menéndez de Avilés arrived on the feast day of Augustine of Hippo, and accordingly christened the town San Augustín: 42 years prior to the founding of Jamestown, Virginia, and 55 years before that of Plymouth, Massachusetts.

Menéndez quickly established a military base against the French, who had established Fort Caroline near present-day Jacksonville. The French fleet did him the favor of getting stuck in a hurricane; Menéndez' men butchered the survivors. By the time Spain ceded Florida to the US in 1821, St Augustine had been sacked, looted, burned and occupied by pirates and Spanish, British, Georgian and South Carolinian forces.

Today the city's buildings, made of coquina – a DIY concrete made of sedimentary rock mixed with crushed shells – lend an enchanting quality to the slender streets. The city's long and colorful history is palpable, narrated vividly by what seems like innumerable museums, monuments and galleries.

◉ Sights

◉ Downtown St Augustine

Long, pedestrian-only **St George St** is the main thoroughfare through the old town, lined with historic buildings, galleries, cafes, and museums. Narrow little **Aviles St** is the oldest European-settled street in the country.

★Castillo de San Marcos National Monument   FORT
(◪ 904-829-6506; www.nps.gov/casa; 1 S Castillo Dr; adult/child under 15yr $15/free; ⊙ 9am-5pm; 🅿 ♿) ✎ This photogenic fort is an atmospheric monument to longevity: it's the country's oldest masonry fort, completed by the Spanish in 1695. In its time, the fort has been besieged twice and changed hands between nations six times – from Spain to Britain to Spain Part II to the USA to the Confederate States of America to the USA again. Park rangers lead programs hourly and shoot off cannons most weekends.

There is a parking lot on site, but blink your eye and it will be filled up.

★Lightner Museum   MUSEUM
(◪ 904-824-2874; www.lightnermuseum.org; 75 King St; adult/child $15/8; ⊙ 9am-5pm, last entry 4pm) Henry Flagler's former Hotel Alcazar is home to this wonderful museum with a little bit of everything, from ornate Gilded Age furnishings to collections of marbles and cigar-box labels. The dramatic and imposing building itself is a must-see, dating back to 1887 and designed in the Spanish Renaissance Revival style by New York City architects Carrère & Hastings.

Villa Zorayda Museum   MUSEUM
(◪ 904-829-9887; www.villazorayda.com; 83 King St; adult/child $12/5; ⊙ 10am-5pm Mon-Sat, 11am-4pm Sun; 🅿) Looking like a faux Spanish castle from a medieval theme park, this gray edifice was built out of a mix of concrete and local coquina shells in 1883. The structure was the fantasy (and maybe fever dream) of an eccentric millionaire who was obsessed with Spain's 12th-century Alhambra Palace. Today it's an odd but engaging museum. The Moorish-style atrium and rooms contain quirky antiques, archaeological pieces and other artifacts: highlights being a

NATIVE AMERICAN ST AUGUSTINE

St Augustine makes a big deal about being the oldest European settlement on US soil, but save for a few passing references in the historical displays at the Visitor Information Center (p369), the Native American people who lived here when the Spanish settlers arrived have been largely erased from the town's story.

The Timucuan people are believed to have settled what is now St Augustine in about 1000 BCE. They were largely a coastal people, hunting alligators and fishing, as well as cultivating corn, beans, squash and tobacco in the coastal hinterland. Timucuan culture was organized through matrilineal descent and political power rested in a series of chiefdoms. They lived in circular huts made of palm thatching, and their artisans used shell, stone and wood to fashion a range of household and ceremonial objects. At their height, the Timucuans ruled over a territory that stretched from Florida's northeastern coast to the Gulf of Mexico and into southeastern Georgia, with a population of 200,000 people living under 35 different chiefs; perhaps 50,000 remained in 1565.

The largest Timucuan settlement, Seloy, was at the site where the Fountain of Youth (p363) now stands, and where the first Spanish settlement began in 1565. Relations between the two nations were at first uneasy but civil, but within a year, Timucuan hostility drove the Spaniards to move their settlement across the channel to Anastasia Island. They returned seven years later, and Timucuan culture went into a decline from which it never really recovered. By 1595, disease had wiped out 75% of the Timucuan population, and barely 1000 remained by 1700; by 1763, fewer than 100 remained, and most of these were taken to Cuba by retreating Spanish forces.

2400-year-old mummy's foot and an Egyptian 'Sacred Cat Rug.'

Ximenez-Fatio House   MUSEUM
([☎]904-342-8887; www.ximenezfatiohouse.org; 20 Aviles St; adult/student/family $10/8/25; ⊙10am-4pm Mon-Sat) Dating to 1798, this fascinating museum complex includes the main house building, the area's only detached kitchen building and a reconstructed washhouse. All are set on immaculately manicured grounds, dating back to St Augustine's original town plan of 1572. Magnificently restored and chock-a-block full of artifacts and relics, the museum focuses primarily on the property's role as a boarding house/inn during the period from 1826 to 1875. Tours run every half hour.

Hotel Ponce de León   HISTORIC BUILDING
(Flagler College; [☎]904-810-6400; http://legacy.flagler.edu/pages/tours; 74 King St; tours adult/child $14/free; ⊙tours hourly 10am-3pm mid-May–mid-Aug, 10am & 2pm during school year) This striking former luxury hotel, built in the 1880s, is now the world's most gorgeous dormitory, belonging to Flagler College, which purchased and saved it in 1967. Guided tours are recommended to get a sense of the detail and history of this magnificent Spanish Renaissance building. At the very least, take a peek inside the lobby for free.

Oldest Wooden
School House   HISTORIC BUILDING
([☑]888-653-7245; www.oldestwoodenschoolhouse.com; 14 St George St; adult/child $5/4; ⊙9am-6pm Sun-Thu, to 8pm Fri & Sat) Built from red cedar and cypress, the 200-year-old building contains animatronic teachers and students, and provides a glimpse into 18th-century life and education. Naughty kids may be frightened into civility when they see the dungeon. It claims to be the oldest surviving wooden schoolhouse in the US.

Colonial Quarter   MUSEUM
([☑]888-991-0933; www.colonialquarter.com; 33 St George St; adult/child $14/8; ⊙10am-5pm, tours 10:30am, noon, 1:30pm & 3pm) See how they did things back in the 18th century at this re-creation of Spanish Colonial St Augustine, complete with craftspeople demonstrating blacksmithing, leather working, musket shooting and all sorts of historical stuff. A replica Spanish *caravel* (ship) is among the items.

Pirate & Treasure Museum   MUSEUM
([☑]877-467-5863; www.thepiratemuseum.com; 12 S Castillo Dr; adult/child $15/8; ⊙10am-7pm; [♠]) Historical accuracy may not always be the priority here, but this celebration of all things pirate is *fun*. Little kids and big kids alike will enjoy this mash-up of theme park and museum with genuine historical treasures (including

St Augustine

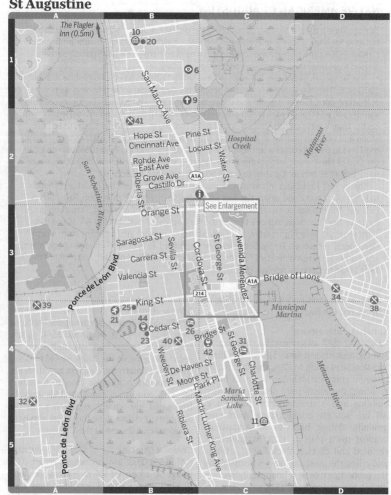

real gold), animatronic pirates, blasting cannons and a kid-friendly treasure hunt.

Plaza de la Constitution
SQUARE

In the heart of downtown, this grassy square, the oldest public park in the US and a former marketplace for food (and slaves), has an attractive gazebo, some cannons, the remains of the town well and a monument to Confederate veterans.

Cathedral Basilica of St Augustine
CHURCH

(☏ 904-829-0620; www.thefirstparish.org; 38 Cathedral Pl; tour adult/child $12/10; ⊘ mass 7am, tours 11am & 3pm Mon, 3pm Tue-Thu, 1pm 1st Sun of mth) FREE With its magnificent bell tower lording it over the Plaza de la Constitution, this Spanish-mission-style cathedral is the country's oldest parish – the first mass was celebrated here on September 8, 1565. After an earlier church was destroyed by the British, the current church was finished in 1797. The sanctuary is a pretty, airy mix of wood and murals. Masses are held daily; check the website for other times.

Governor's House
HISTORIC BUILDING

(☏ 904-825-5034; www.staugustine.ufl.edu/gov house.html; 48 King St; ⊘10am-5pm) FREE A

tions, leeching, the whole shebang. Housed in a reconstruction of the original hospital, the museum will make you glad you're not a patient in 1791. Discounted tickets can be reserved online.

Oldest House   MUSEUM
(✐904-824-2872; www.saintaugustinehistorical society.org; 14 St Francis St; adult/student/family $10/4/23; ⊙10am-5pm; Ⓟ) ✎ Also known as the González-Alvarez House, this is the oldest surviving Spanish-era home in Florida, dating to the early 1700s and sitting on a site occupied since the 1600s. The house is part of a complex that also contains two small historical museums and a lovely ornamental garden.

Mission of Nombre de Dios   CHURCH
(✐904-824-2809; www.missionandshrine.org; 27 Ocean Ave; ⊙museum 9am-5pm Mon-Sat, noon-4pm Sun; Ⓟ) **FREE** Just north of downtown on the A1A, the mission dates back to the earliest days of Spanish settlement. Today the peaceful memorial gardens feature a replica of the original altar, a tiny, ivy-shrouded chapel and a small museum.

Old Jail   HISTORIC BUILDING
(✐904-829-3800; 167 San Marco Ave; adult/child $10/6; ⊙tours every 20min 9am-4:30pm) Built in 1891, this is the former prison and residence of the town's first sheriff, Charles Joseph 'the terror' Perry (towering menacingly at 6ft 6in tall and weighing 300lb). Today costumed 'deputies' escort visitors through cellblocks and detail the site's arresting history.

Fountain of Youth   HISTORIC SITE
(✐904-829-3168; www.fountainofyouthflorida. com; 11 Magnolia Ave; adult/child $18/10; ⊙9am-6pm; 🐾) Insert tongue firmly in cheek and step right up for a cup of eternal youth at this kitschy 'archaeological park.' As the story goes, Spanish explorer Juan Ponce de León came ashore here in 1513, considered this freshwater stream the possible legendary Fountain of Youth, and promptly charged folks 18 bucks to take a gander. We may be kidding about that last part. Expect some child-friendly reenactments.

◉ St Augustine Beach Area

Cross the Bridge of Lions and take Anastasia Blvd right out to the beach. The 7-mile stretch of St Augustine Beach is a great place to soak up rays, and the road fronting it has a small handful of hotels, family restaurants and bars.

government building has stood on this site since 1598 and served as a residence, courthouse, administrative headquarters and post office. Today it is maintained by the University of Florida as a public museum and exhibition space showcasing temporary exhibitions on Florida history.

Spanish Military
Hospital Museum   MUSEUM
(✐904-342-7730; www.spanishmilitaryhospital. com; 3 Aviles St; adult/child $10.50/5.50; ⊙9am-5pm) Not for the faint of heart, guided tours of this museum discuss Colonial-era medical techniques in all their gory glory: amputa-

NORTHEAST FLORIDA ST AUGUSTINE

St Augustine

St Augustine Beach BEACH
(350 A1A Beach Blvd) This white-sand beach almost gets lost in the historical mix, but, this being Florida, a visit wouldn't be complete without a little bit of sun and surf. There's a visitor information booth at the foot of St Johns Pier, where you can rent a rod and reel (two hours for $15). About three blocks south of the pier, the end of A St has – as Florida goes – some fine waves.

Anastasia State Recreation Area BEACH
(☎904-461-2033; www.floridastateparks.org/anastasia; 300 Anastasia Park Rd; car/bicycle $8/2; ☺8am-sunset) Locals come to escape the tourist hordes at this terrific park, which is a beautiful quilt of estuarine marsh, maritime forest, boardwalk paths and sandy beach. There's also a campground (campsites $28) and rentals for all kinds of water sports.

St Augustine Lighthouse LIGHTHOUSE
(☎904-829-0745; www.staugustinelighthouse.com; 81 Lighthouse Ave; adult/child $13/11;

☺9am-6pm) The light produced by this 1870s striped lighthouse beams all the way downtown. A great place to bring kids six and older than 44in tall (since all climbers must be able to ascend and descend the tower under their own power). Check the website for special themed tours, such as the spooky 'Dark of the Moon' paranormal tour and the 'Lost Ships' archaeology tour.

Alligator Farm Zoological Park ZOO
(☎904-824-3337; www.alligatorfarm.com; 999 Anastasia Blvd; adult/child $28/17; ☺9am-5pm Sep-May, to 6pm Jun-Aug; ⊕) Welcome to the only zoo on the planet with every species of crocodilian in residence. Look for albino alligators, gorgeous gharials and seven species of endangered monkey, including the world's smallest, the pygmy marmoset. There are talks and shows throughout the day; catch hungry alligators snapping their jaws at feeding times (noon and 3pm).

The park is a five-minute drive from downtown St Augustine along Anastasia Blvd.

☞ Tours

See p366 for culinary tours.

★ St Augustine Eco Tours   KAYAKING

(☎904-377-7245; www.staugustineecotours.com; 111 Avenida Menendez; boat tour adult/child $40/35, kayak tour adult/child $45/35) ✍ This eco-outfitter has certified naturalists who take kayakers on 3-mile ecology trips. It also runs 1½-hour boat tours that explore the estuary and use hydrophones to search for bottlenose dolphins, as well as two-hour guided kayak nature tours. A portion of profits goes to environmental organizations.

Ripple Effect Ecotours   KAYAKING

(☎904-347-1565; www.rippleeffectecotours.com; 101 Tolstoy Lane; tours adult/child from $55/45) ✍ Explore the hundreds of channels and backwaters that lace through northeast Florida with this outfit, which works with the University of Florida's Whitney Laboratory for Marine Bioscience. It also offers a tour on a boat powered by vegetable oil culled from nearby restaurants. Can also arrange kayak rentals (half day from $40).

St Augustine City Walks   WALKING

(☎904-825-0087; www.staugcitywalks.com; 4 Granada St; tours per person $25-89; ⊙9am-8:30pm) Fun walking tours of all kinds, from silly to serious, including history and haunted pub walks.

Old Town Trolley Tours   TROLLEY TOURS

(☎844-388-6452; www.trolleytours.com; 167 San Marco Ave; adult/child $25/10; ⊞) These 22-stop hop-on, hop-off narrated trolley tours are family-friendly and underwhelming, but if you want a historical introduction to the town and prefer not to walk, this is an option.

🛏 Sleeping

For convenience and atmosphere, stay in the historic downtown area where there are numerous classic B&Bs; check out the selection on www.staugustineinns.com. Otherwise, head to the beach. St Augustine is a popular weekend escape for Floridians – prices go up by about 30% on weekends and a minimum two-night stay is often required.

Pirate Haus Inn   HOSTEL $

(☎904-808-1999; www.piratehaus.com; 32 Treasury St; r from $75-109; ℗🖳🛜) Although far from St Augustine's fanciest digs, this family-friendly, European-style guesthouse/hostel may well be the cheapest and most cheerful. Kids love it – themed private rooms are squeaky clean, the location is hard to beat and who doesn't love fresh 'pirate pancakes' for breakfast and pirate maps on some walls? Staff speak a variety of languages.

Bachelor/bachelorette parties are banned, which is a pro move as far as we're concerned.

The Flagler Inn   MOTEL $$

(☎877-342-7938; www.flaglerinn.com; 2700 N Ponce de León Blvd; r from $139; 🛜🖳) This motel has fresh and funky decor in an aquamarine color scheme that works. Beds are big and comfy, continental breakfast is included and free bikes will get you whizzing around in no time. There's an on-site restaurant as well.

THERE BE PIRATES

Pirates routinely ransacked St Augustine, given its vulnerable seaside location. Lying in wait along the coast, pirates would pounce on silver- and gold-laden fleets returning to Europe from Mexico and South America. When ships weren't around, they'd simply raid the town (which was home to the Spanish Royal Treasurer for Florida, no less).

Among the many brutal attacks on St Augustine was Sir Francis Drake's raid in June 1586, when he and his cohort pillaged the township before burning it down. Perhaps even more violent was Jamaican pirate Robert Searle's attack in 1668. After capturing a Spanish ship, Searle and his crew went on a plundering and killing spree. No one was safe: one of Searle's victims was a five-year-old girl, whose ghost, it is said, haunted him to madness and ultimately suicide.

Both events are meticulously reenacted every year in St Augustine. If you're interested in participating, get thee to St Augustine in March (to reenact Searle's raid) or June (for Drake's). For more information, log on to www.searlesbucs.com. Other local pirate activities include September's Talk Like a Pirate Day (www.talklikeapirate.com) and late-January's Old City Pirate Fest (www.visitstaugustine.com/event/old-city-pirate-fest).

★ **At Journey's End** B&B $$
(☑ 904-829-0076; www.atjourneysend.com; 89 Cedar St; r $179-349; P ଵ ♠) Free from the grannyish decor that defines many St Augustine B&Bs, this pet-friendly, kids-welcome and gay-friendly spot is outfitted in a chic mix of antiques and modern furniture and is run by kind, knowledgeable hosts. Mouthwatering breakfasts, concierge services and other thoughtful touches set At Journey's End apart. It's walking distance from the old town on a quiet street.

Casa de Solana B&B $$
(☑ 904-824-3555; www.casadesolana.com; 21 Aviles St; r $149-300; P ଵ) Just off pedestrian-only Aviles St in the oldest part of town, this utterly charming little inn remains faithful to its early-1800s period decor. Rooms aren't the largest in town, but the location and atmosphere more than compensate. Rumors of a resident ghost might sway some potential guests in (or drive them off).

Beachfront B&B B&B $$
(☑ 904-461-8727; www.beachfrontbandb.com; 1 F St, St Augustine Beach; r from $185; ଵ ♠) This sun-drenched, oceanfront beach house features canopy beds, rich pine floors and has a private heated pool. Most rooms feature private entrances, and fireplaces for romantic wintry nights.

★ **Casa Monica** HISTORIC HOTEL $$$
(☑ 904-827-1888; www.casamonica.com; 95 Cordova St; r $200-310, ste from $435; P ଵ ♠) ✿
Built in 1888, this is *the* luxe hotel in town, with turrets and fountains adding to the Spanish-Moorish castle atmosphere. Rooms are appropriately richly appointed, with wrought-iron, triple-sheeted beds and Bose sound systems in every room. Some suites have decadent Jacuzzis, and the location can't be beaten.

Carriage Way Inn Bed & Breakfast B&B $$$
(☑ 904-829-2467; www.carriageway.com; 70 Cuna St; r $189-279; ❄ ଵ) Stunning rooms with period charm, supremely comfortable beds and bold colors in a fine old-town location

---

CULINARY TOURS & TASTINGS

St Augustine has one of the best eating scenes in the state, provided you know where to go and which overcrowded, overpriced tourist traps to avoid. Many Floridians visit for the weekend just for the food. If you're only here for a short time, a tour can be a fine entry point into the gastronomic charms of the town.

St Augustine City Walks (p365) The 2½-hour food- and wine-tasting tour is our favorite. It visits half a dozen restaurants and food shops, and tells St Augustine's culinary story.

Ancient City Pour Tour (☑ 904-515-7050; www.ancientcitypourtour.com; 119 Avenida Menendez; per person from $55) Sample around 12 microbrews at four St Augustine craft breweries on this three- to four-hour tour. Hotel pickups can be arranged. Check the website for upcoming tour dates and times.

San Sebastian Winery (☑ 904-826-1594; www.sansebastianwinery.com; 157 King St; ⊙ 10am-6pm Mon-Sat, 11am-6pm Sun) FREE The 45-minute tours at this winery are capped with wine tastings and a video about Florida wine-making since the 1600s; if you're around in August, join the squishy fun during the annual grape-stomping competitions. There's an upstairs **bar** (⊙ 11:30am-6pm Thu & Sun, to 11pm Fri & Sat) with live jazz in the afternoons.

St Augustine Distillery (☑ 904-825-4962; www.staugustinedistillery.com; 112 Ribera St; ⊙ 10am-6pm) FREE Take a 45-minute tour to see how the distillery makes its own vodka, gin, rum and bourbon using all-Florida ingredients. Tasting is an obligatory part of the experience, of course.

Whetstone Chocolates (☑ 904-217-0275; www.whetstonechocolates.com; 139 King St; adult/child $8/5.50; ⊙ 10am-3.30pm) St Augustine's chocolatier of longest standing, Whetstone Chocolates runs factory tours five times daily from Monday to Thursday, and nine times daily from Friday to Sunday. You'll learn the history of chocolate-making, see how it's done and learn how to distinguish between different types of chocolate the only way possible – by tasting the end product.

make adults-only Carriage Way a favorite. Local wines and a warm welcome round out one of the best packages within walking distance of everything that matters.

St Francis Inn INN $$$
(☑ 904-824-6068, 800-824-6062; www.stfrancis inn.com; 79 St George St; r $179-340; ❄ ☎) St Augustine's oldest inn has been in continuous operation since 1791. Crushed-coquina-shell and ancient wood-beam architecture create a period ambience, abetted by open fireplaces, a maze of antique-filled nooks and crannies, beds with handmade quilts and a lush walled courtyard. Sumptuous buffet breakfasts, free local wine and complimentary evening desserts round out the picture.

✖ Eating

Maple Street Biscuit Company AMERICAN $
(☑ 904-217-7814; www.maplestreetbiscuits.com; 39 Cordova St; mains $6-9; ☉ 7am-2pm Mon-Thu, to 3pm Fri & Sat; ☷) The name of this place delivers on its promise: they do biscuits (the Southern flaky kind, not British cookies), and they do them *right*. There's plenty of variations; we love the Sticky Maple, which comes with fried chicken, maple syrup and bacon. Order it with fried green tomatoes and turn your back on that diet forever.

Present Moment Cafe VEGAN $
(☑ 904-827-4499; www.presentmomentcafe.com; 224 W King St; mains $10-16; ☉ 11am-8pm Sun, Mon, Wed & Thu, 11am-9:30pm Fri & Sat; ☷) Dishing up 'Kind Cuisine,' this folksy restaurant serves only vegan cooked, dehydrated or raw food, all bursting with flavor. If you need something a little bit naughty with your nice, try the chocolate ganache pie – one to turn even the most die-hard nonvegans.

Back 40 Urban Cafe CAFE $
(☑ 904-824-0227; www.back40cafe.com; 40 S Dixie Hwy; items $9-13; ☉ 11am-9pm) Flavored with the spices of Mexico and the Southwest, this cozy, unpretentious joint is favored by locals for its cheap and tasty tacos, burgers and comfort foods. We couldn't overlook the chili mac bowl. There's a good selection of cold beer too.

Hyppo DESSERTS $
(☑ 904-217-7853; www.thehyppo.com; 48 Charlotte St; popsicles $5; ☉ 11am-10pm Sun-Thu, to 11pm Fri & Sat; ☷) On steamy St Augustine afternoons, seek out the Hyppo, a slip of a popsicle shop with an ever-changing whiteboard menu of outrageous flavors – pineapple-cilantro,

mango mojito and blackberry cheesecake. Keep your eyes open for anything containing datil pepper, a high-octane local chili beloved by Spanish settlers – it goes great with strawberry.

★ Uptown Scratch Kitchen STREET FOOD $$
(☑ 904-377-6050; www.facebook.com/uptown scratchkitchen; 1280 N Ponce de León Blvd; mains $13-16; ☉ 7am-9pm Mon-Sat, 8am-8pm Sun) St Augustine's favorite food truck ranges far and wide in its influences, from Italy to the Caribbean via New Orleans and Philadelphia. The New Orleans Po Boy sandwich (shrimp or fish, with salad, BBQ sauce and onion rings) is an outstanding example of what they do.

Gas Full Service MODERN AMERICAN $$
(☑ 904-217-0326; www.gasrestaurant.com; 9 Anastasia Blvd; mains $10-28; ☉ 11am-9pm Tue-Thu, to 10pm Fri & Sat) You'll likely be vying for a table at this fantastic retro gas-station-esque cafe. The buzz is about the burgers: freshly baked buns, local beef, fried green tomatoes and crispy bacon all feature. How about the 'bunless burger Benedict,' smothered in hollandaise? And did we mention Reuben egg rolls?

O'Steen's SEAFOOD $$
(☑ 904-829-6974; www.osteensrestaurant.com; 205 Anastasia Blvd; mains $12-23; ☉ 11am-8:30pm Tue-Sat) Locals claim this seafood shack has the best shrimp on the East Coast and they're close to the mark; the tilapia and catfish (broiled or fried) are pretty good too. O'Steen's ain't no secret, so prepare to wait for a table or plan to take out and picnic. No credit cards accepted but there's an on-site ATM.

★ Collage INTERNATIONAL $$$
(☑ 904-829-0055; www.collagestaug.com; 60 Hypolita St; mains $30-48; ☉ 5-9pm) ✍ This upscale restaurant is renowned for its impeccable service, intimate atmosphere and the consistency of its cuisine: the menu makes the most of St Augustine's seaside locale and nearby local farms. It's all here: artisan salads, chicken, lamb, veal and pork, lobster, scallops and grouper. A subtle mélange of global flavors enhances the natural goodness of the freshest farm-to-table produce.

Preserved AMERICAN $$$
(☑ 904-679-4940; www.preservedrestaurant.com; 102 Bridge St; mains $22-31; ☉ 4-9pm Wed-Sat, 10am-2pm & 4-9pm Sun; ☷) If you're looking to do a date night in St Augustine, it's hard to

WORTH A TRIP

FORT MATANZAS NATIONAL MONUMENT

The tiny, 1742-built **Fort Matanzas National Monument** (☎904-471-0116; www.nps. gov/foma; 8635 Hwy A1A, Rattlesnake Island; ⊙9am-5:30pm; ℗) is located on Rattlesnake Island, near where Menéndez de Avilés executed hundreds of shipwrecked French soldiers and colonists when rations at St Augustine ran low. Today it makes a terrific excursion via a free 10-minute ferry that launches every hour (at half-past) from 9:30am to 4:30pm, weather permitting. Once there, the ranger provides an overview and lets you wander.

'Rattlesnake Island is located about 15 miles south of downtown St Augustine, and can be reached via Florida A1A.

To catch the 35-person ferry to the monument – the last free thing in Florida – go through the visitor center, pick up a free boarding pass and head out to the pier.

beat Preserved. It takes the locally sourced Southern genre to new culinary heights in its airy, historic-chic dining room; shrimp and grits come with creamed corn and bacon lardons, while roasted chicken comes with glistening black-eyed peas and cornflour dumplings. Make reservations.

The Gourmet Hut CAFE $$$
(☎904-824-7477; 17 Cuna St; mains $18-29, brunch $11-21; ⊙10am-9pm Sun & Tue-Thu, to 10pm Fri & Sat) ✔ A pretty garden setting and fresh tastes like shrimp and Brie grits, Creole crab cakes or glazed duck with Grand Marnier make this a fine choice. There's a commitment to local produce, a terrific drinks list, and there are few places we'd rather be on a balmy summer's evening.

🍷 Drinking & Nightlife

★**Odd Birds Bar** COCKTAIL BAR
(☎904-679-4933; www.oddbirdsbar.com; 33 Charlotte St; ⊙5pm-2am Mon-Fri, 1pm-2am Sat & Sun) Odd Birds embodies just about everything one could want in a quirky, totally unique craft cocktail bar: innovative, imaginative, often playful drinks; bartenders that are serious about their art (they even invite bartender 'diplomats' from other bars to spend an evening sharing their tricks of the trade); and a casual setting that's unpretentious (even though it could be).

Forgotten Tonic COCKTAIL BAR
(☎904-827-9055; https://forgottentonic.com/; 6 Aviles St; ⊙noon-11pm Sun-Thu, to midnight Fri & Sat) Cocktail bar meets wine bar meets craft beer taproom at this classy little place on St Augustine's oldest street. The food is excellent, but it's the drinks menu that excels: numerous local wines by the glass, a good mix of classic and contemporary cocktails

and all manner of craft beers. The 3pm-to-6:30pm Happy Hour, when cocktails cost $6, is St Aug's best deal.

Kookaburra CAFE
(☎904-209-9391; www.kookaburrashop.com; 24 Cathedral Pl; ⊙6:30am-9pm Sun-Thu, to 10pm Fri & Sat; 🛜) ✔ Ethically sourced Australian-American coffeehouse serving real Aussie meat pies for breakfast and lunch, and easily the best barista coffee in the historic quarter.

Dog Rose Brewing CRAFT BEER
(☎904-217-3355; www.dogrosebrewing.com; 77 Bridge St; ⊙noon-11pm Sun-Thu, to 1am Fri & Sat) This relative newcomer (it opened in October 2017) has pale ales, amber ales and an IPA among its home-brewed beers on tap. We like the combination of taking seriously the art of brewing (these are seriously good beers) with a playful atmosphere (there is live music, cookie-and-beer pairings and bar games). The outfit also makes boutique wines. Cool place.

Ice Plant BAR
(☎904-829-6553; www.iceplantbar.com; 110 Riberia St; ⊙11:30am-2am Tue-Fri, 10am-2am Sat, 10am-midnight Sun, 11:30am-midnight Mon; 🛜) The hottest spot in St Augustine flaunts exposed concrete, raw brickwork and soaring windows surrounding a vintage, dual-facing centerpiece bar all carved out of a former ice factory. Here visitors imbibe some of Florida's finest cocktails, mixed by overall-clad bartenders, and snack on farm-to-table bites.

TradeWinds Lounge LOUNGE
(☎904-826-1590; www.tradewindslounge.com; 124 Charlotte St; ⊙11am-2am) Great live music and big hairdos rule this nautical-themed dive. Smelling sweetly of stale beer, the classic dive bar has survived two locations and

six decades. Crowds tumble out the door during happy hour, and there's live music – mostly Southern rock or '80s – nightly. It's all fun and very old school.

Shopping

★ **The Ancient Olive Gourmet** FOOD
(844-336-5483; www.theancientolive.com; 47 King St; ⊙10am-7pm Mon-Thu, to 8pm Fri & Sat, to 6pm Sun) One of the best gourmet food shops in Florida, this fabulous place specializes in olive oils in all their glory – you can try most of them – as well as all manner of delectables, including carefully chosen cured meats, mustards, cookies-and-cream malted milk sweets, bottled sauces, alcoholic gourmet sweets…

Second Read Books BOOKS
(904-829-0334; 51 Cordova St; ⊙10am-7pm Sun-Thu, to 8pm Fri & Sat) This small, old-town, secondhand bookstore is a lovely place to browse, with books across a range of genres and friendly, knowledgeable staff.

❶ Information

Visitor Information Center (904-825-1000; www.visitstaugustine.com; 10 W Castillo Dr; ⊙8:30am-5:30pm) Helpful, period-dressed staff sell tour tickets and can advise you on everything St Augustinian. The nearby parking garage is your best bet if you can't find parking elsewhere.

❶ Getting There & Away

Driving from the north, take I-95 exit 318 and head east past Hwy 1 to San Marcos Ave; turn right and you'll end up at the Old City Gate, just past the fort. Alternatively, you can take Hwy A1A along the beach, which intersects with San Marco Ave, or Hwy 1 south from Jacksonville. From the south, take exit 298, merge onto Hwy 1 and follow it into town.

From the **Greyhound bus station** (904-829-6401; www.greyhound.com; 3 Cordova St), just a few blocks north of the visitor center, there are services to/from Daytona Beach (from $17, one hour, one daily), Jacksonville (from $12, 50 minutes, two daily) and Orlando (from $14, 2¼ hours, one daily).

❶ Getting Around

Cars are a nightmare downtown, with one-way and pedestrian-only streets and severely limited parking (from $2.50 per hour or $10 to $15 per day); outside the city center, you'll need wheels.

Solano Cycle (904-825-6766; www.solanocycle.com; 32 San Marco Ave; 2hr/5hr/24hr $8/11/18; ⊙10am-6pm) rents bicycles – great for exploring flat St Augustine.

Jacksonville

904 / POP 903,889

Jacksonville has a lot going for it, but it requires careful planning. That's because it's *big*. At a whopping 840 sq miles, Jacksonville is the largest city by area in the contiguous United States and the most populous in Florida. The city sprawls along three meandering rivers, with sweeping bridges and twinkling city lights reflected in the water. Its charms too often lie hidden: the glut of high-rises, corporate HQs and chain hotels can make 'Jax' feel a little soulless. But the city's museums are excellent, and the Five Points and San Marco neighborhoods are charming, walkable areas lined with bistros, boutiques and bars. And beyond the downtown, the Jacksonville area beaches – a 30- to

---

WORLD GOLF VILLAGE

They don't do anything by halves here in Florida, and golf is no exception. The **World Golf Village** (888-948-4653; www.worldgolfvillage.com; 1 World Golf Pl) is a massive resort, golf-course complex, golf museum and all-around golf-themed attraction.

Fans of the sport flock here to the **World Golf Hall of Fame** (904-940-4000; www.worldgolfhalloffame.org; 1 World Golf Pl; adult/child $21/5; ⊙10am-6pm Mon-Sat, noon-6pm Sun), a museum with, of course, 18 exhibits: the front nine cover the history of the sport and the back nine examine modern professional golf. Separating them is the Hall of Fame itself, with multimedia exhibits on inductees. Admission includes nine holes on a putting green designed to PGA specifications, and an IMAX film.

Two legendary on-site courses, **King & Bear** and **Slammer & Squire**, are open for public tee times. Budding Hall of Famers can try the two- to five-day PGA Tour Golf Academy (www.worldgolfvillage.com/pga-tour-academy). Private lessons start at $100 per hour.

World Golf Village is just off I-95 via exit 323, about halfway between St Augustine and Jacksonville.

50-minute drive from the city – are a completely different world.

◉ Sights

★ Cummer Museum of Art & Gardens
MUSEUM

(☏ 904-356-6857; www.cummermuseum.org; 829 Riverside Ave; adult/student $10/6; ⏱ 11am-9pm Tue & Fri, to 4pm Wed, Thu & Sat, noon-4pm Sun) This handsome museum, Jacksonville's premier cultural space, has an excellent collection of American and European paintings, Asian decorative art and antiquities. Among the highlights of the permanent collection are paintings by, among others, Peter Paul Rubens and Norman Rockwell, and there are usually high-class temporary exhibitions to enjoy. An outdoor area showcases classical English and Italian gardens and is one of the loveliest outdoor spaces in the city.

★ Museum of Contemporary Art Jacksonville
MUSEUM

(MOCA; ☏ 904-366-6911; https://mocajacksonville. unf.edu; 333 N Laura St; adult/child $8/5; ⏱ 11am-5pm Tue, Wed, Fri & Sat, to 9pm Thu & 1st Wed of month, noon-5pm Sun) The focus of this ultra-modern space extends beyond painting: get lost among contemporary sculpture, prints, photography and film for a wonderfully diverse creative experience. Check out www. jacksonvilleartwalk.com for details of the free MOCA-run Art Walk, held on the first Wednesday of every month from 5pm to 9pm: it has more than 56 stops and is a great way to see the city.

Jacksonville Zoological Gardens
ZOO

(☏ 904-757-4463; www.jacksonvillezoo.org; 370 Zoo Pkwy; adult/child $25/20; ⏱ 9am-5pm; P 🐾) Northeast Florida's only major zoo opened in 1914 with one deer; today it's home to over 1800 exotic animals and hectares of beautiful gardens. Favored fauna from around the world include elephants, jaguars, lions and okapis, and American highlights including bobcats, manatees, gators, coyotes and the Burmese python, an introduced species causing havoc in Florida's Everglades. There's an elevated viewing platform that brings you face to nose with giraffes. The zoo is 15 minutes north of downtown off I-95.

Treaty Oak
LANDMARK

(1123 Prudential Dr, Jessie Ball duPont Park) At first glance, it looks like a small forest is growing in the middle of the concrete on Jacksonville's south side, but upon closer inspection you'll see that the 'forest' is really one single enormous tree, with a trunk circumference of 25ft and a shade diameter of nearly 200ft. According to local lore, the live oak tree is the oldest thing in Jacksonville – it's estimated to be at least 250 years.

Southbank Riverwalk
WATERFRONT

This 1.2-mile boardwalk, on the south side of the St Johns River, opposite downtown, has excellent views of the city's expansive skyline; the firework displays, best seen from here on July 4 and New Year's Eve, are a real blast. The Southbank Riverwalk connects the museums flanking Museum Circle and makes a pleasant promenade.

Museum of Science & History
MUSEUM

(MOSH; ☏ 904-396-6674; www.themosh.org; 1025 Museum Circle; adult/child $15/12; ⏱ 10am-5pm Mon-Thu, to 8pm Fri, to 6pm Sat, noon-5pm Sun; 🐾) Traveling with kids? This awesomely named museum (MOSH) offers dinosaurs, all things science and exhibits on Jacksonville's cultural and natural history. Be sure to check out the Bryan Gooding Planetarium, one of the largest single-lens planetariums in the country. Shows and their times vary: check the website for details.

🛏 Sleeping

★ Riverdale Inn
B&B $$

(☏ 904-354-5080; www.riverdaleinn.com; 1521 Riverside Ave; r $150-198, ste $220-315; P 🛜) In the early 1900s this was one of 50 or so mansions lining Riverside. Now there are only two left, and you're invited to enjoy the Riverdale's tastefully decorated rooms, within walking distance of the Five Points, with full breakfast. Expect Persian carpets, four-poster beds and old-world elegance.

Hotel Indigo Jacksonville
HOTEL $$

(☏ 904-996-7199; www.hoteldeerwoodpark.com; 9840 Tapestry Park Circle; r from $169; P ⊖ ❄ 🛜 🐾 🐾) Lush blue accents and airy, design-conscious rooms with hardwood floors, fluffy king beds, flat-screen TVs and a general sense of stylish yet accessible luxury define the experience at this excellent branch of the Indigo chain. The pool makes for a relaxing spot to get some sun. Located about 11 miles south of downtown Jacksonville.

Homewood Suites by Hilton Downtown
HOTEL $$

(☏ 904-396-6888; www.homewoodsuites.com; 1201 Kings Ave; r from $123; P @ 🛜) These tasteful, modern suites in the central San Marco neighborhood feature full kitchens and business traveler–style rooms that are efficient and comfy, if not terribly exciting.

Omni Jacksonville Hotel · HOTEL $$

(☎904-355-6664; www.omnihotels.com; 245 Water St; r from $110; P🐾🖥️🏊) This stylish, 354-room downtown hotel has lavish, amenity-laden rooms, acres of marble, a heated rooftop pool and free wi-fi. The classy rooms have splashes of color and some have expansive views.

✗ Eating

The Five Points neighborhood, southwest of downtown, and the San Marco neighborhood, across the river from downtown, are where you'll find the most trendy cafes and bars with outdoor seating. The city's suit-and-tie financial industry means lots of steakhouses and upscale bistros.

Hawkers Asian Street Fare · ASIAN $

(www.eathawkers.com; 1001 Park St; mains $5-12; ⊙11am-9pm Sun-Thu, to 10pm Fri & Sat; 🥢) This small local chain tries to recreate an Asian food hawker court à la Singapore. There are no plastic stools to squat on, but the food is varied and good: curry duck noodles, *laksa* (noodle soup), *roti canai* (flaky flat bread with dipping sauce), grilled skewers and summer rolls are just a sampling of an intimidatingly large menu.

This is the sort of place you'll want to order a bunch of dishes and share.

Beach Road Fish House & Chicken Dinners · SOUTHERN US $

(☎904-398-7980; www.beachroadrestuarant. com; 4132 Atlantic Blvd; items $7-17; ⊙11am-8:30pm Tue-Sat, to 6pm Sun) You know a place does it right if its signature meal predates the Cold War, and this deliciously retro joint has been frying chicken since 1939. Tear off a chunk of tender thigh meat and wrap it up in a fluffy biscuit, and you'll understand why people line up every day at this much-loved shack.

★ Bearded Pig · BARBECUE $$

(☎904-619-2247; www.thebeardedpigbbq.com; 1224 Kings Ave; mains $9-32; ⊙11am-10pm Mon-Sat, 11:30am-9pm Sun; P🍽️) At this San Marco spot, barbecue and a beer garden meet in perfect marriage. It's got flawlessly smoked sausage, brisket and pork ribs, and cold draft beer on tap. Why are you still reading?

❶ FINDING YOUR WAY AROUND JACKSONVILLE

Jacksonville is *big* and can be tricky to navigate. A few things to know:

➡ Jacksonville is trisected by a very rough T formed by the St Johns River. Downtown Jacksonville is on the west side of the St Johns.

➡ I-95 comes in straight from the north to a junction just south of downtown with I-10. Follow I-10 east into downtown, where a maze of state highways offers access to surrounding areas.

➡ Three bridges cross the river and will take you to San Marco: Fuller Warren (I-10), Acosta (Hwy 13) and Main St Bridge.

➡ I-295 breaks off from I-95, forming a circle around the city.

➡ Though the city is enormous, most sites of interest are concentrated along the St Johns River's narrowest point: downtown; Five Points, just south of downtown along the river; and the elegant San Marco Historical District along the southern shore.

★ Black Sheep Restaurant · AMERICAN $$

(☎904-380-3091; www.blacksheep5points.com; 1534 Oak St; lunch mains $12-21, dinner mains from $15-34; ⊙5-9pm Wed & Thu, 11am-10pm Fri & Sat, to 9pm Sun; 🍴) 🌿 A commitment to good, local ingredients, delicious food, plus a bar with a retractable rooftop and a craft cocktail menu? Sign us up! Try wild Georgia shrimp and grits, pastrami sandwiches made from in-house deli meat, or blackened pork rinds with maple-smoked mayo; it's all good. The cardamom pancakes and salmon on bagels served for weekend brunch are pretty fine too.

bb's · FUSION $$

(☎904-306-0100; www.facebook.com/bbsrestaurant; 1019 Hendricks Ave; lunch/dinner mains from $11/24; ⊙11am-10:30pm Mon-Thu, 11:30am-midnight Fri & Sat) This groovy establishment, with its molded-concrete bar, clean, modern lines and daily cheese selection champions fresh local produce that is crafted into arty, flavorful dishes from scratch: a gourmand's delight. Suggested wine pairings keep things simple. Connoisseurs of dessert needn't look elsewhere – the chocolate ganache cake alone is worth the trip.

Downtown Jacksonville

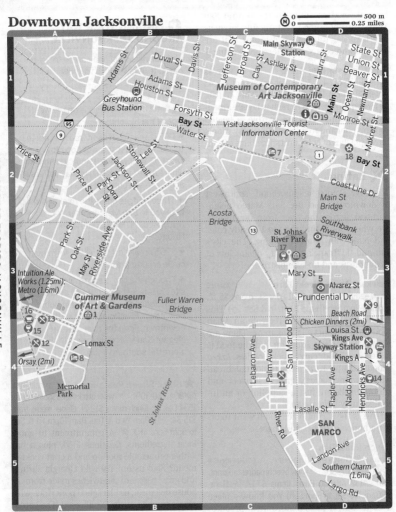

Southern Charm   AMERICAN **$$**

(☑ 904-517-3637; www.facebook.com/artscracker
cooking; 3566 St Augustine Rd; mains $8-19;
⊙ 11:30am-2:30pm & 5-8:30pm Tue-Fri, 6:30-9pm
Sat, 11:30am-3pm Sun) Yes, this is Southern
Charm: the place that looks like an automo-
tive garage on a torn-up stretch of sidewalk.
The restaurant, run by beloved Jacksonville
chef and all-round character Art Jennette,
serves enormous, cardiac-straining portions
of Southern and soul food: pork chops, fried
fish, collard greens and fried green toma-
toes. Atmosphere of the moon, but food of
the gods, people.

Note that hours may be dependent on
how busy the place is – and when food runs
out, it's out.

Clark's Fish Camp   SOUTHERN US **$$**

(☑ 904-268-3474; www.clarksfishcamp.net; 12903
Hood Landing Rd; mains $10-23; ⊙ 4:30-9:30pm
Mon-Thu, to 10pm Fri, 11:30am-10pm Sat, to 9pm
Sun; ℗) Sample Florida's Southern Cracker
(rural Floridian) cuisine surrounded by the
surreal animal menagerie of one of America's
largest private taxidermy collections, which
resembles the freakish love child of Tim Bur-
ton and Mr Kurtz from *Heart of Darkness*.
This swamp shack is unforgettable: gator

Downtown Jacksonville

tail, smoked eel, fried snake and frogs legs all make menu appearances amid more prosaic offerings such as catfish and steak.

If the grotesque taxidermy menagerie – monkeys prowl the ceiling, while leopards glare glassily from the corners – puts you off, you can always sit outside by the murky water. But a word to the wise: don't feed the gators. It's far south of downtown Jacksonville.

Orsay FRENCH, SOUTHERN $$$
(☑904-381-0909; www.restaurantorsay.com; 3630 Park St; mains $20-52; ⊗4-10pm Mon-Fri, 11:30am-3:30pm & 5-10pm Sat & Sun; 🛜) This minimalist bistro in Riverside merges traditional French fare with Southern intuition, leading to a menu chock-full of rich and vibrant dishes, most of which are locally sourced. We may or may not have delighted ourselves silly sopping up our incredible bouillabaisse gravy with black truffle mac 'n' cheese, chased with a few of the creative cocktails.

Bistro Aix FRENCH, MEDITERRANEAN $$$
(☑904-398-1949; www.bistrox.com; 1440 San Marco Blvd; lunch mains $13-22, dinner mains $14-42; ⊗11am-10pm Mon-Thu, to 11pm Fri, 5-11pm Sat, to 9pm Sun) Dine with the fashionable food mavens on fusion-y Mediterranean dishes at Aix, which offers a menu bursting with global flavors, from wine-braised chicken to duck cassoulet. There are over 250 wines by the bottle, and 50 by the glass. Reservations recommended.

🍷 **Drinking & Nightlife**

Downtown, Five Points and San Marco are peppered with interesting bars.

★**Birdies** BAR
(☑904-356-4444; www.birdiesfivepoints.com; 1044 Park St; ⊗4pm-2am Mon-Fri, 1pm-2am Sat & Sun) There's a lot to see at this funky spot. Local art graces the walls, there's a photo booth, and old-timers and twenty-somethings will be sharing the pool tables while indie rock fills the place. It has DJs on the weekends, making for even more good vibes.

Wall Street Deli BAR
(☑904-355-6969; 1050 Park St; ⊗2pm-2am Mon-Fri, noon-2am Sat & Sun) We guess they serve sandwiches here, but not to suited-up brokers coming off the trading floor. This place is a dive, straight up, and it's full of a cross-section of Jacksonville, and they're all getting tipsy (or more) on strong drinks served with little embellishment, besides maybe an extra finger of booze.

BREW Five Points CAFE
(☑904-374-5789; www.brewfivepoints.com; 1024 Park St; ⊗7:30am-2pm Mon, to 10pm Tue & Wed, 8am-midnight Thu & Fri, 9am-midnight Sat, to 9pm Sun) BREW sits at an odd juncture: it's a hybrid craft beer bar and espresso cafe, for those days when you need a pick-me-up *and* a sedative, we guess. The coffee is excellent, the beer list is extensive and the vibe is modern and friendly, so we're all on board.

Metro GAY
(☑904-388-8719; www.metrojax.com; 849 Willow Branch Ave; ⊗2pm-2am Sun-Thu, to 2:30am Fri & Sat) Jacksonville's top gay entertainment complex has a disco, a cruise bar, a piano bar, a games room with pinball machines,

a smoke-free chill-out loft, a leathery boiler room and a show bar.

☆ Entertainment

★ Florida Theatre
THEATER

(☑ administrative office 904-355-5661, box office 904-355-2787; www.floridatheatre.com; 128 E Forsyth St) Home to Elvis' first indoor concert in 1956, during which a local judge ensured Presley was not overly suggestive, this opulent 1927 venue is an intimate place to catch big-name musicians, musicals and movies.

🛍 Shopping

Chamblin's Uptown
BOOKS

(☑ 904-674-0868; www.chamblinbookmine.com; 215 N Laura St; ⊙ 8am-5pm Mon, Tue, Thu & Fri, to 9pm Wed, 9am-4pm Sat, noon-5pm Sun) We could spend (and have spent) hours in this wonderful secondhand bookstore with a brilliant collection across most genres. There is an even larger store on the city outskirts.

❶ Information

Florida Times-Union (www.jacksonville.com) Conservative daily paper, in print and online; Friday's *Weekend* magazine features family-oriented events listings.

Visit Jacksonville Tourist Information Center (☑ 800-733-2668; www.visitjacksonville.com; 208 N Laura St, Suite 102; ⊙ 9am-5:30pm Mon-Fri, 11am-4pm Sat & Sun) Has all there is to know about Jax and surrounds.

❶ Getting There & Away

Jacksonville International Airport (p527), about 18 miles north of downtown on I-95, is served by major and regional airlines and car-rental companies. A cab downtown costs around $40. Otherwise, follow the signs for shuttle services: there are numerous licensed providers and reservations aren't necessary.

The **Greyhound bus station** (☑ 904-356-9976; www.greyhound.com; 1111 W Forsyth St) is at the west end of downtown, with twice-daily services to Savannah, GA (from $24, 2¾ to 3½ hours, two daily) and Orlando (from $18, 2½ to 3¾ hours). The **Amtrak station** (☑ 904-766-5110, reservations 800-872-7245; www.amtrak.com; 3570 Clifford Lane) is less convenient, 5 miles northwest of downtown.

❶ Getting Around

The Jacksonville Transportation Authority (www.jtafla.com) runs buses and trolleys around town and the beaches (fare $1.75), as well as a free, scenic (and underused) river-crossing Skyway (monorail).

JACKSONVILLE CRAFT BREWERIES

Jacksonville has a buzzing (and growing) craft brewery scene. Visit www.visitjacksonville.com/jax-ale-trail/breweries for the long list, but we've included some of our favorites here:

Intuition Ale Works (☑ 904-683-7720; www.intuitionaleworks.com; 720 King St; ⊙ 3-10pm Tue-Thu, to 11pm Fri, 11am-11pm Sat, to 8pm Sun) Stop by for a glass or three in the taproom of this funky local brewery serving, you guessed it – beer only! With more than a dozen homemade brews on tap, this is a must for beer fans.

Aardwolf Brewing Company (☑ 904-301-0755; www.aardwolfbrewing.com; 1461 Hendricks Ave; ⊙ 3-11pm Wed & Thu, to midnight Fri, noon-midnight Sat, to 9pm Sun) Fine ales and lagers – try the German pilsner or any of the IPAs – and some surprising combinations in beers like Foreseen Consequences (a stout with chocolate and peanut butter) and Abomination of Desolation (with cherry and pomegranate).

River City Brewing Company (☑ 904-398-2299; www.rivercitybrew.com; 835 Museum Circle; ⊙ 2-10pm Mon-Thu, to midnight Fri, 11:30am-midnight Sat, 10:30am-4pm Sun; 🛜) Having a fine riverfront restaurant is only half the story here – the home-brewed ales (including the Nutty Floridian Pecan Brown Ale) and bourbon are our favorite reasons for coming.

Wicked Barley Brewing (☑ 904-379-7077; www.wickedbarley.com; 4100 Baymeadows Rd; ⊙ noon-8pm) It's worth the taxi ride south of downtown for Wicked Barley's award-winning ales and lagers; the pumpkin spice beer is wickedly good.

Green Room Brewing (☑ 904-201-9283; www.greenroombrewing.com; 228 3rd St N, Jacksonville Beach; ⊙ 4pm-midnight Tue-Thu, to 2am Fri, noon-2am Sat, to 10pm Sun) Over in Jacksonville Beach, nine of the 16 taps at Green Room rotate through the brewery's considerable portfolio of pale ales, stouts and IPAs. It's a fab place to drink just a few blocks back from the beach.

Jacksonville Area Beaches

Jacksonville's beaches are its prime tourism draw, and with good reason: besides the usual appeal of sun, sand and salt water, there's a nicely chilled atmosphere here. Local beachgoers are mellow compared with the folks in south Florida, or even the rest of north Florida, for that matter – it's difficult not to be here.

Moving from south to north, **Ponte Vedra Beach** is the posh home of the ATP and PGA golf tours: you'll find golf courses, resorts and mansions here. Urban **Jacksonville Beach** is where to eat, drink and party, while cozy **Neptune Beach** is more subdued, as is **Atlantic Beach**.

◎ Sights & Activities

Kathryn Abbey Hanna Park   PARK
(☑904-249-4700; www.coj.net; 500 Wonderwood Dr, Atlantic Beach; vehicle/bicycle entry $5/3; ⊗8am-8pm Apr-Oct, to 6pm Nov-Mar; 🅿🚻) 🏊 If you want a beach that's away from any crowds – and is a slice of Atlantic Coast natural beauty – come to this 450-acre park, which boasts 2.5 miles of undeveloped shoreline, dune ecosystems and maritime forest dripping with Spanish moss.

Rent Beach Stuff   CYCLING
(☑904-305-6472; www.rentbeachstuff.com; 11 1st St N, Jacksonville Beach; ⊗9:30am-5pm) The roads are flat and the towns are small: why not rent a bike? In addition to a bunch of other beach and water-sports equipment, these guys will deliver a 26in beach cruiser bike to your hotel for $30 per day.

🛏 Sleeping

Kathryn Abbey Hanna Park   CAMPGROUND $
(☑904-249-4700; www.coj.net; 500 Wonderwood Dr, Atlantic Beach; tent/RV sites $22/34, cabins $36; 🅿) This pleasant park and shaded campground is a stone's throw from Atlantic Beach and has its own freshwater lake. Basic cabins require two-night minimum stays.

★Hotel Palms   HOTEL $$
(☑904-241-7776; www.thehotelpalms.com; 28 Sherry Dr, Atlantic Beach; r $125-195, ste from $200; 🛜) An old-school courtyard motel turned into a chic little property with reclaimed headboards, concrete floors and open, airy design. Treat yourself to an outdoor shower, free beach-cruiser bicycles, an outdoor fireplace and some gorgeous rooms looking like they've been pulled straight off some fancy interior decorator's Instagram.

Courtyard by Marriott
Jacksonville Beach Oceanfront   HOTEL $$
(☑904-435-0300; www.marriott.com; 1617 1st St N, Jacksonville Beach; r from $179; 🅿🛜) Of the smattering of chain hotels in Jax Beach we love this waterfront property for its practical, pleasant rooms and friendly, attentive staff. It's right on the beach and has everything you need to drop in and chill out.

One Ocean   HOTEL $$
(☑904-249-7402; www.oneoceanresort.com; 1 Ocean Blvd, Atlantic Beach; r from $127; 🛜⊠) This stylish resort hotel has been favored by A-list celebs for its low-key oceanfront locale. The grand lobby is modern and elegant: white marble, rippling iridescent walls and suited staff. Rooms follow suit with clean, contemporary lines, touches of silver, pewter and sea green – most have views. Complete your indulgence with a treatment in the day spa.

Lodge at Ponte Vedra   RESORT $$$
(☑888-774-1477; www.pontevedra.com; 100 Ponte Vedra Blvd, Ponte Vedra Beach; r from $275; 🅿🛜⊠) Well-heeled families love this opulent Mediterranean-style resort – a historic landmark – where kids play by the pool while the grown-ups enjoy a beachfront massage. Rooms and suites are plush and airy, with tasteful sage-and-sand decor and super-luxe granite-and-marble bathrooms.

✖ Eating

European Street   CAFE $
(☑904-249-3001; www.europeanstreet.com; 992 Beach Blvd, Jacksonville Beach; items $7-13; ⊗10am-9pm; 🅿) Assemble the perfect picnic (or just get a great sandwich) at this excellent combination chocolatier, deli, bar (boasting 150 imported beers) and gourmet market, with a huge menu of salads, sandwiches and German fare.

Beach Hut Café   SOUTHERN US $
(☑904-249-3516; 1281 3rd St S, Jacksonsville Beach; mains $4.50-12; ⊗6am-2:30pm) Don't let its strip-mall location deceive you: the food here is finger-lickin' good. Famous for its big, all-day Southern breakfasts, it draws *huge* lines – especially on weekends.

Metro Diner   DINER $$
(☑904-853-6817; www.metrodiner.com; 1534 N 3rd St, Jacksonville Beach; mains $9-17; ⊗6:30am-2:30pm; 🅿🚻) An excellent breakfast/brunch

spot in Jacksonville Beach, this tried-and-true diner has been in business since 1938. These days it's usually packed, especially on weekends. Benedicts for brunch, meatloaf, big fish sandwiches and chicken pot pie all feature.

Eleven South   MODERN AMERICAN $$$

(☑ 904-241-1112; www.elevensouth.com; 216 11th Avenue S, Jacksonville Beach; mains $13-30; ⊙ 11am-11pm Tue-Fri, 5-11pm Sat-Mon) Eleven South, where the date-night atmosphere is thick and the rack of lamb is as memorable as the lobster paella, is Jacksonville Beach's classiest restaurant. Reservations are recommended, especially on weekends. Try for a seat on the patio.

🍺 Drinking & Nightlife

Surfer the Bar   BAR

(☑ 904-372-9756; www.surferthebar.com; 200 1st St N, Jacksonville Beach; ⊙ 11am-2am) This enormous spot is what happens when you blend a beach bar with a contemporary interiors magazine; if you're wondering about the design sense (and name), this is a brick-and-mortar bar operated by *Surfer* magazine. There are two levels, an indoor Airstream trailer selling food, live music on some nights, and, generally, big crowds looking to get a little crazy by the water.

Casa Marina   BAR

(☑ 904-270-0025; www.casamarinahotel.com; 691 N 1st St, Jacksonville Beach; ⊙ 3pm-midnight Mon-Thu, to 2am Fri, 1pm-2am Sat, noon-midnight Sun; 🛜) Atop the restored 1925 Casa Marina hotel you'll find a compact yet happening beachfront bar with killer views and ambient tunes from its ample rooftop deck. There's a live DJ Thursday to Saturday nights.

❶ Getting There & Away

Traveling by car from Jacksonville, follow I-10 to Atlantic Beach, and Hwy 90 (Beach Blvd) directly to Jacksonville Beach. Coming from St Augustine, you follow Hwy A1A due north.

Jacksonville Transportation Authority (www.jtafla.com) operates buses from Jacksonville to the beaches ($1.75).

Amelia Island

Just 13 miles from the Georgia border, Amelia Island is a moss-draped, sun- and sand-soaked blend of the Deep South and Florida coast. It is believed the island's original inhabitants, the Timucuan tribes-

people, arrived as early as 4000 years ago. Since that time, eight flags have flown here, starting with the French in 1562, followed by the Spanish, the English, the Spanish again, the Patriots, the Green Cross of Florida, the Mexican Rebels, the US, the Confederates, then the US again. Amelia is sometimes called Eight Flags Island.

Vacationers have flocked to Amelia since the 1890s, when Henry Flagler converted a coast of salt marsh and unspoiled beaches into a vacation spot for the wealthy. The legacy of that era is evident in the central town of Fernandina Beach, 50 blocks of historic buildings, Victorian B&Bs and restaurants housed in converted fishing cottages. Dotting the rest of the island are lush parks, green fairways and miles of shoreline.

◉ Sights

Fort Clinch State Park   STATE PARK

(☑ 904-277-7274; www.floridastateparks.org/fort-clinch; 2601 Atlantic Ave, Fernandina Beach; car/pedestrian $6/2; ⊙ park 8am-sunset, fort 9am-5pm; 🅿) 🌿 Although construction commenced in 1847, rapid technological advancements rendered Fort Clinch's masonry walls obsolete by as early as 1861, when the fort was taken easily by Confederate militia in the Civil War and later evacuated. Federal troops again occupied the fort during WWII. Today, the park offers a variety of activities, serene beaches for shelling (of the nonmilitary kind) and 6 miles of peaceful, unpaved trails for hiking and cycling.

Twice a year, spring and fall, authentically outfitted troops perform a reenactment of the Confederate evacuation that extends to cooking in the old kitchen's massive iron cauldron and sleeping on straw mats in the soldiers' barracks. They also do a living history reenactment of the Union Garrison every first full weekend of the month, with 20 to 40 people in period dress acting as if they were in Civil War times. Candlelight tours ($3.50; May to September) are a treat.

Amelia Island Museum of History   MUSEUM

(☑ 904-261-7378; www.ameliamuseum.org; 233 S 3rd St, Fernandina Beach; adult/student $8/5, Fri 4-6pm free; ⊙ 10am-4pm Mon-Thu & Sat, to 6pm Fri, 1-4pm Sun) Housed in the former county jail (1879–1975), this oral-history museum is tiny but has informative exhibits exploring Native American history, the Spanish Mission period, the Civil War and historic preservation. A variety of tours are availa-

WORTH A TRIP

CUMBERLAND ISLAND NATIONAL SEASHORE

The largest wilderness island in the US, **Cumberland Island** (☑912-882-4336; www.nps.gov/cuis; $10) lies just over the Georgia state line. At 17.5 miles long and 3 miles wide, almost half of its 36,415 acres is marshland, mudflats and tidal creeks. Only 300 visitors at any given time are allowed on the island, which is accessible by a 45-minute ferry ride.

Ashore, rangers lead free one-hour tours concluding at the ruins of Thomas and Lucy Carnegie's 1884 mansion, Dungeness. Along the way rangers interpret the rich bird and animal life – including sandpipers, ospreys, painted buntings, nesting loggerhead turtles, armadillos and deer – and detail 4000 years of human history that spans Timucuans, British colonists and Spanish missionaries.

After the Civil War, freed slaves purchased parcels of land at the island's northern end and founded the First African Baptist Church in 1893. The tiny, 11-pew, white-painted wooden church was rebuilt in the 1930s, and the late John Kennedy Jr and the late Carolyn Bessette were married in it in 1996. It's open to the public, but it's a hefty 15-mile hike from the ferry drop through moss-draped thickets.

The historic village of **St Marys** (www.stmaryswelcome.com) is the island's charming gateway: there are no shops on the island. Bring food, insect repellent and your camera! Accommodation options on the island range from an opulent mansion to rugged camping. Check the St Marys website for details.

For some interesting backstory to the fight to save Cumberland, track down John McPhee's classic *Encounters with an Archdruid* (1971) – Part 2 is all about the island.

Ferries (☑877-860-6787; www.cumberlandislandferry.com; E Saint Marys St & Ready St, St Marys; round-trip adult/senior/child $30/28/20) depart at 9am and 11:45am, returning at 10:15am and 4:45pm (an additional ferry runs at 2:45pm Wednesday to Saturday from March to November; no ferries run on Tuesday or Wednesday from December to February). Reservations are recommended.

From northern Florida, take I-95 north to St Marys Rd exit 1. Turn right onto GA-40/St Marys Rd E and follow it to the end.

---

ble, including the eight-flags tour (11am and 2pm Monday to Saturday and 2pm Sunday), providing lively interpretations of the island's fascinating history, as well as architecture tours and pub crawls.

American Beach Museum MUSEUM
(☑904-510-7036; www.americanbeachmuseum.org; 1600 Julia St, American Beach; adult/student $4/2; ⊙10am-2pm Fri & Sat, 1-5pm Sun; Ⓟ) This small museum offers a vibrant overview of life in American Beach, one of the few seaside resort communities built for African Americans in the segregated South. Call ahead for potential tours by appointment.

Activities

Egan's Creek Greenway WALKING
(☑904-310-3363; 2500 Atlantic Ave, Fernandina Beach) **FREE** A network of grassy trails covering over 300 acres, the Egan's Creek Greenway is the perfect place to spot alligators, snakes, bobcats and countless species of birds. Interpretive displays line

the trails. Well-soled, covered footwear is recommended.

Tours

★ **Kayak Amelia** KAYAKING
(☑904-261-5702, 904-251-0016; www.kayakamelia.com; 4 N 2nd St, Fernandina Beach; tours adult/child from $65/55, kayak rental half-day single/double from $40/55) The charms of Amelia Island are best appreciated through a quiet day on the water, with the sun glinting off the estuaries and cordgrass. That's the experience offered by Kayak Amelia, which leads paddling excursions into the watery ecosystem that ensconces the Atlantic barrier island. It also offers stand-up paddleboarding (SUP) classes and SUP yoga (both $30).

You can also book SUP ecotours (from $55) or rent kayaks and stand-up paddleboards. For four weeks in spring, Kayak Amelia offers a dusk firefly tour into local maritime forests that is especially magical. Bikes are $7 an hour or $20 a day.

Amelia River Cruises
BOATING

(☑904-261-9972; www.ameliarivercruises.com; 1 N Front St, Fernandina Beach; adult/child from $23/17; ♿) Explore Amelia and nearby Cumberland Island, GA, stopping to marvel at plantation ruins and dense tracts of Spanish-moss-covered forest. In summers (June to August), this outfit runs a cool **shrimping ecotour** (adult/child $27/17) where guests learn to operate an Otter Trawl shrimp net. The boat then traverses backwaters and creeks, before the caught shrimp are released back into the water.

✦ Festivals & Events

Isle of Eight Flags
Shrimp Festival
FOOD & DRINK

(www.shrimpfestival.com) Pirates (the fake, fun kind, not the real, scary version) invade Amelia Island for shrimp and a juried art show in late April or early May.

🛌 Sleeping

Fort Clinch State Park
CAMPGROUND $

(☑904-277-7274; www.floridastateparks.org/fortclinch; 2601 Atlantic Ave; tent & RV sites $26; P) 🐾 Take your pick (if you're lucky) of riverside or oceanfront sites in this lovely and extremely popular park. The oak-and-moss-protected Amelia River sites are more private than the exposed beach sites. Be sure to make reservations well in advance.

★ Amelia Hotel at the Beach
HOTEL $

(☑904-206-5600; https://ameliahotel.com; 1997 S Fletcher Ave, Fernandina Beach; r with/without partial ocean view $119/79; P❀🏱🏊) Away from the historic center but just across the road from the beach, this family-run hotel has modern, light-filled rooms and friendly service. It's nothing special – just a good honest hotel that represents outstanding value.

Florida House Inn
HISTORIC HOTEL $$

(☑904-491-3322; www.floridahouseinn.com; 22 S 3rd St, Fernandina Beach; r $142-201; P🏱) Florida's oldest hotel features an atmospheric structure dating to 1857 that is battling real estate with an ever-expanding 400-year-old oak tree. Past that, you've got your choice of 17 rooms, most of which are heavy on the lace-curtain-and-quilt vibe, and polished dark-wood floors.

★ Addison
B&B $$$

(☑904-277-1604; www.addisononamelia.com; 614 Ash St, Fernandina Beach; r $225-340; P🏱) 🐾 Built in 1876, the Addison has modern upgrades (Jacuzzi tubs, deluge showers,

Turkish-cotton towels and wi-fi) that'll trick you into thinking it was finished last week. Its white, aqua and sage color scheme is bright and totally unstuffy. Enjoy daily happy hours overlooking a delightful courtyard.

Ecoconscious guests take note: the inn's water- and energy-saving efforts have earned it a Green Lodging certification from the state. It also offers free tennis equipment, bikes and beach gear.

Fairbanks House
B&B $$$

(☑904-277-0500; www.fairbankshouse.com; 227 S 7th St, Fernandina Beach; r/ste/cottage from $200/250/250; P🏱🏊) You could imagine Indiana Jones retiring to a place like this grand Gothic Victorian property; it's stuffed to the gills with silk carpets, heavy leather-bound books and global knickknacks. Over-sized guestrooms are individually styled to suit the period of the house. If you're not sleeping, make use of the small pool and butterfly garden in the backyard.

Elizabeth Pointe Lodge
B&B $$$

(☑800-772-3359; https://elizabethpointeamelia island.com; 98 S Fletcher Ave, Fernandina Beach; r/ste from $280/360; P🏱) Atmosphere oozes from this eccentric yet stylish 1890s Nantucket-shingle-style maritime inn, perched on the ocean, 2 miles from downtown. Rocking-chair-laden porches offer the best seats on the island for beholding a sunrise. Classic, elegant rooms have plush, chunky beds and oversized tubs (some are jetted).

Ritz Carlton
HOTEL $$$

(☑904-277-1100; www.ritzcarlton.com; 4750 Amelia Island Pkwy, Fernandina Beach; r from $325; P🔄❀@🏱🏊) The height of luxury, decadence and impeccable service awaits at this unexpectedly located Ritz Carlton. Set on 13 miles of pristine beaches, with its own private 18-hole golf course, and lavish rooms and suites furnished with casual elegance, this is a property for those with fat wallets, accustomed to the best in life, or for that very special vacation experience.

Hoyt House
B&B $$$

(☑904-277-4300; www.hoythouse.com; 804 Atlantic Ave, Fernandina Beach; r from $215; P🏱🏊) This stately, award-winning Victorian B&B perched on the edge of downtown boasts an enchanting gazebo that begs idle time with a cool drink. Each of the 10 rooms has its own stylish mix of antiques and found treasures. Room service is available.

AFRICAN AMERICAN HERITAGE ON AMERICAN BEACH

Insurance magnate AL Lewis, Florida's first black millionaire, founded American Beach in 1935, creating the first black beach community on Florida's segregated shores. In its heyday American Beach catered to throngs of African Americans who arrived by the busload to enjoy the beaches and African American–owned motels, restaurants and nightclubs, where shows with Ray Charles, Louis Armstrong and others made for some of the biggest bills in Florida. In 1964, however, Hurricane Dora destroyed many homes and businesses; shortly thereafter desegregation allowed African Americans to stroll the beaches closer to their homes. Golf courses and gated communities have encroached upon what's left of American Beach, though beach access is possible via Lewis St, off Hwy A1A, on the south end of Amelia Island.

Once here, you'll find a quiet, pleasant stretch of shoreline dotted with some information boards that give insight into the area's history. Although it's only open during limited hours, you can also check out the American Beach Museum (p377).

✖ Eating

T-Ray's Burger Station
BURGERS $
(☑904-261-6310; www.traysburgerstation.com; 202 S 8th St, Fernandina Beach; mains $7-14; ☺7am-2:15pm Mon-Fri, 8am-1pm Sat) Inside a decommissioned gas station, this high-carb, high-fat, low-pretense diner and takeout joint is worth the cholesterol spike. Revered by locals, the big breakfasts are just that, and daily specials sell out fast. Juicy burgers, chunky fries, fried shrimp and tender crab cakes all make the mouth water. Believe the hype.

Hola Cuban Cafe
CUBAN $
(☑904-206-1985; www.holacubancafe.com; 117 Centre St, Fernandina Beach; mains from $7.50; ☺9am-4pm Mon & Thu-Sat, 10:30am-4pm Sun; P⛄) This may be as far north as you can get good Cuban food in Florida (yes, yes, we realize there's still Cuban food in the rest of the country). Have a hot Café Cubano, then down a classic Cuban sandwich hot off the *plancha* (sandwich press). Or just snack on some sweet *maduros* (fried plantains). It's all good.

29 South
SOUTHERN US $$
(☑904-277-7919; www.29southrestaurant.com; 29 S 3rd St, Fernandina Beach; lunch mains $8-14, dinner mains $13-28; ☺5:30-9:30pm Mon-Thu, to 10pm Fri, 10am-2:30pm & 5:30-10pm Sat, 10am-2:30pm & 5:30-9:30pm Sun; P) Lobster corn dogs, sweet-tea-brined pork chops, homemade doughnut-bread pudding and mocha ice cream – we're in business. Tucked into a pale-purple cottage, this neo-Southern bistro takes culinary risks and executes them well. It's casual yet classy and full of flavor.

Crab Trap
SEAFOOD $$
(☑904-261-4749; www.ameliacrabtrap.com; 31 N 2nd St, Fernandina Beach; lunch mains $8-13, dinner mains $16-30; ☺4:30-9pm Mon-Fri, noon-9pm Sat & Sun) Around for over four decades, this brick-lined family-run restaurant does lobster mac 'n' cheese, snow crab, shrimp and grits and fine steaks and burgers. It gets packed on weekends, and deservedly so.

Café Karibo & Karibrew
FUSION $$
(☑904-277-5269; www.cafekaribo.com; 27 N 3rd St, Fernandina Beach; mains $9-29; ☺11am-3pm Mon, to 9pm Tue-Sat, 10:30am-3pm Sun; 🛜) This funky side-street favorite serves a large and eclectic menu of sandwiches, soups, salads and healthy treats in a sprawling two-story space with a shady patio hung with twinkling Christmas lights. Have a blackened mahimahi sandwich or down a Sloppy Skip's Stout at the adjacent Karibrew brewpub, which has its own menu of global pub grub.

Burlingame Restaurant
MODERN AMERICAN $$$
(☑904-432-7671; www.burlingamerestaurant.com; 20 S 5th St, Fernandina Beach; mains $22-41; ☺5-10:30pm Mon-Sat; P✎) ✒ Amelia – a marsh and forest island in a brackish estuary that feeds into the Atlantic – has an incredible wealth of fish, game and produce, and this bounty is treated with love at Burlingame, which serves up seasonally inspired regional cuisine of the highest order. Shrimp and grits and rabbit cassoulet are two of our favorites. Reservations recommended.

☕ Drinking & Nightlife

★ Palace Saloon
BAR
(☑844-441-2444; www.thepalacesaloon.com; 113-117 Centre St, Fernandina Beach; ☺noon-2am) Push through the swinging doors at the oldest continuously operated bar in Florida (since 1903) and the first thing you'll notice is the 40ft gas-lamp-lit bar.

Knock back the saloon's rum-laced Pirate's Punch in dark, velvet-draped surroundings, curiously appealing to both bikers and Shakespeare buffs.

Shopping

Eight Flags Antique Market ANTIQUES
(☑ 904-277-8550; 602 Centre St, Fernandina Beach; ⊙ 10am-6pm Mon-Sat, noon-6pm Sun) Three dozen antique dealers sprawl across one large indoor space. Bargains from the 'treasures' of a hundred Southern attics await to be discovered.

ℹ Information

Amelia Island Visitor Center (☑ 904-277-0717; www.ameliaisland.com; 102 Centre St, Fernandina Beach; ⊙ 10am-4pm) Useful information and maps in the old railroad depot.

Shrimping Museum & Welcome Center
(☑ 904-261-7378; 17 S Front St, Fernandina Beach; ⊙ 10am-4pm Mon-Sat, from 1pm Sun) This small museum on the harborfront has local maps and pamphlets.

ℹ Getting There & Away

Hwy A1A splits in two directions on Amelia Island, one heading west toward I-95 and the other following the coast; both are well marked.

To get to Amelia, the fastest route from the mainland is to take I-95 north to exit 373 and head east about 15 miles straight to the island.

Want a prettier route? Heading from Jacksonville Beach to the town of Mayport, catch the **St Johns River Ferry** (☑ 904-241-9969;

JUST ACROSS THE BORDER

If you've made it to Amelia Island, Georgia is just on your doorstep, and its attractions close by are worth the detour.

Cumberland Island (p377) Island wilderness, acts as an antidote to some of the tourist-overwhelmed islands along Florida's east coast.

Savannah (www.visitsavannah.com) One of the loveliest cities of the American South, with antebellum mansions and plenty of historical architecture, a vibrant waterfront and great restaurants.

Okefenokee National Wildlife Refuge (www.fws.gov/refuge/okefenokee) Part of the vast Okefenokee Swamp, which is rich in wildlife (alligators, birdlife and the Florida black bear).

---

http://stjohnsriverferry.com; per pedestrian/motorcycle/car from $1/6/7; ⊙ from Maryport every 30min 6am-7pm Mon-Fri, 7am-8:30pm Sat & Sun; from George Island every 30min 6:15am-7:15pm Mon-Fri, 7:15am-8:45pm Sat & Sun), which runs around every 30 minutes.

Palatka

☑ 386 / POP 10,465

Welcome to small-town Florida, a place where the past overshadows the present. In its heyday, Palatka (pronounced puhl-*at*-kuh), almost midway between St Augustine and Gainesville, was the furthest south you could travel by steamship, and boasted more than 7000 hotel rooms for wealthy snowbirds using it as a gateway to Florida and its sun. Today, visitors are trickling back to this sweet, sleepy-verging-on-comatose town for fishing, Memorial weekend's Blue Crab Festival, and simply to escape the coastal crowds.

◉ Sights

Ravine Gardens State Park GARDENS
(☑ 386-329-3721; www.floridastateparks.org/parks-and-trails/ravine-gardens-state-park; 1600 Twigg St; per car/cyclist/pedestrian $5/2/2; ⊙ 8am-sunset; P) ✔ A two-mile walkable road loops the inner boundary of this 182-acre state park. A shallow ravine slices through the center of this pristine picnic spot, with the gorge views best enjoyed from the swinging suspension footbridge. Come between late February and early March when pink and red azaleas weave through the otherwise deep-green foliage.

🎆 Festivals & Events

Palatka Blue Crab Festival FOOD & DRINK
(https://bluecrabfestivalpalatka.com; ⊙ Memorial Day weekend) A terrific time to be in town, the Blue Crab Festival hosts the state championship for chowder and gumbo. There's also music, food stalls and lots of outdoor entertainment.

✖ Eating

Angel's Dining Car AMERICAN $
(☑ 386-325-3927; www.facebook.com/angels palatkafl; 209 Reid St; mains $4-10; ⊙ 6am-9pm Sun-Thu, to 10pm Fri & Sat; P) Looking like the offspring of a soda can and a subway car, Angel's offers curbside service and sit-in dining. Honk your horn or slide into a vinyl booth for iconic menu items like Monnie (mini) burgers, black-bottom eggs

(scrambled with hamburger meat) and Pusalow (pronounced 'puss-uh-loh'): chocolate milk with vanilla syrup and crushed ice.

Opened in 1932, this is Florida's oldest diner and a real slice of local life.

ⓘ Getting There & Away

Palatka is located about 60 miles south of Jacksonville (via US 17 or I-95), and 30 miles west of St Augustine (via SR 207).

Talbot Island & Fort George Island

Between Amelia Island and Jacksonville, this pair of fantastic green diversions hold high appeal for history and nature lovers. Along the shorelines and amid the breezy woods of Fort George and Talbot Islands, there's exceptional kayaking, distinctive state parks, and riverbank and beachside camping galore. It's a wonderful day trip, and an invigorating breath of fresh air after escaping the developments that clog the Atlantic Coast.

⊙ Sights

★ **Little Talbot Island State Park**   STATE PARK
(☏904-251-2320; www.floridastateparks.org/parks-and-trails/little-talbot-island-state-park; 12157 Heckscher Dr; per vehicle/cyclist $5/2; ⊗8am-sunset; ℗) ✈ This pristine island (which despite the name is almost the same size as Big Talbot Island) has 5 miles of unspoiled beaches, river otters, marsh rabbits, bobcats and grand tidal fishing for mullet and sheepshead. Camping available.

Big Talbot Island State Park   STATE PARK
(☏904-251-2320; www.floridastateparks.org/parks-and-trails/big-talbot-island-state-park; State Rd A1A N; per vehicle $3; ⊗8am-sunset; ℗) ✈ Deposit your fee in the blue envelope and pull into the lone parking lot at this stark but lovely park. Take your camera on the short trail to Boneyard Beach, where salt-washed skeletons of live oak and cedar trees litter the white sand, framed by a 20ft bluff of eroded coastline. Magical and wild, and makes you wonder what the rest of Florida must have looked like before the developers arrived.

Fort George Island Cultural State Park   STATE PARK
(☏904-251-2320; www.floridastateparks.org/parks-and-trails/fort-george-island-cultural-state-park; 11241 Fort George Rd; ⊗8am-sunset; ℗) FREE Although the exact location of the fort erected by the British in 1736 remains uncertain, the island still bears its name. In its pre-WWII glory days, flappers flocked here to the ritzy Ribault Club, built in 1928, for lavish Gatsby-esque bashes. Now housing the visitor center, the meticulously restored mansion flaunts grand archways and three dozen French doors. It's the starting point of the 4.4-mile Saturiwa loop trail, which you can walk, bike or drive.

🛏 Sleeping & Eating

Little Talbot Island Camping   CAMPGROUND $
(☏800-326-3521; http://floridastateparks.reserveamerica.com; tent & RV sites $24; ℗) There are few more beautiful ways of waking up in Florida than doing so on one of her last undeveloped barrier islands. Campsites have electricity, and are nestled amid rolling dunes and shady spreads of marine hammock forest.

Sandollar   SEAFOOD $$
(☏904-251-2449; www.sandollarrestaurantjax.com; 9716 Heckscher Dr, Fort George Island; mains $11-24; ⊗11am-9pm Sun-Thu, to 10pm Fri & Sat; ℗ 🍴) This classic waterfront spot does tasty seafood with a view out to the breeze-kissed water. Enjoy a drink and some blackened mahimahi or a basket of shrimp and wash it down with a craft beer. Located about 5 miles south of Little Talbot Island. There's live music on the deck Friday through Sunday.

ⓘ Information

Ribault Club (☏904-251-2802; www.nps.gov/timu/learn/historyculture/ricl_visiting.htm; 11241 Fort George Rd, Fort George Island; ⊗9am-5pm Wed-Sun) The Fort George Island Visitor Center is located within the Ribault Club, built in 1928 as a venue for millionaires who needed a warmer spot to perfect their *Great Gatsby* parties.

ⓘ Getting There & Away

Talbot Island is about 11 miles south of Amelia Island; you can arrive here via State Road A1A. If you're coming from Jacksonville, you can either take FI 105 to the A1A, or head north from the beaches along A1A and jump on the St Johns River Ferry in Mayport, which heads to Fort George (connected by road to Talbot Island).

THE TIMUCUAN PRESERVE

Tour portions of the oldest standing plantation house in Florida as well as the remains of 23 tabby-construction slave cabins at **Kingsley Plantation** (☑904-251-3537; www.nps.gov/timu; 11676 Palmetto Ave, Fort George Island; ☉9am-5pm; 🅿), a former cotton and citrus plantation. The main house is under near-constant restoration due to termites and humidity, but the sprawling shaded grounds and mangroves make a unique spot for a picnic. Weekend tours leave on a limited basis from 11am to 3pm; call ahead to determine availability.

Purchased by Zephaniah Kingsley in 1814, the plantation was managed with his wife, Anna Jai, whom he had purchased as a slave and later married in a traditional African ceremony, subsequently freeing both her and their children.

NORTH CENTRAL FLORIDA

In one of the least visited parts of the state, you'll discover crystal-clear springs, meandering back roads and small Victorian gingerbread towns reminiscent of a time before Florida became a byword for tourism overdevelopment. North Central Florida is more 'Southern' than almost anywhere else in Florida; Confederate flags are not unusual here.

The many-horse town of Ocala is as bucolic as Florida gets, while Gainesville, home of the University of Florida, is a charming college town worth a day's diversion. And don't forget to have your fortune read in spiritualist Cassadaga. Otherwise, soak up the region's beauty; you'll find more rolling countryside here than you might expect in a state like Florida.

Cassadaga

☑386 / POP 105

Cassadaga is a tiny, quirky place, the sort of place where the spiritual weighs heavily upon every aspect of the town's story. It's Florida's New Age poster-child and a curious place to visit if you're in the area.

Tiny Cassadaga doesn't have an ATM or gas station.

🛏 Sleeping & Eating

Cassadaga Hotel HOTEL **$**
(☑386-228-2323; https://hotelcassadaga.com; 355 Cassadaga Rd; r from $75; ❄ 🛜) The original Cassadaga Hotel burned down in 1926. Today ghosts reportedly lurk in the shadows of the rebuilt hotel (sniff for Jack's cigar smoke and listen for two girls terrorizing the upstairs halls). Past all that, the hotel has a charming Old Florida vibe, and there are psychics on hand to provide readings (starting at $20); that's concierge service.

Sinatra's Ristorante ITALIAN **$$**
(☑386-218-3806; www.sinatras.us; 355 Cassadaga Rd; mains $8-28; ☉11am-8pm Mon & Tue, to 9pm Wed & Thu, to 10pm Fri & Sat, 8am-4pm Sun) Look, we like old-school, red-sauce Italian cuisine as much as the next traveler, and the chicken stewed in tomato sauce and Tuscan seafood stew here are great. But it's even better because you can have a glass of wine and a tarot reading at the same time, seeing as Sinatra's is located in the Cassadaga Hotel.

This place also hosts dueling piano nights, because nothing adds to the surreal vibe of an Italian meal in a psychic colony like competing takes on Gaga's 'Bad Romance.'

❶ Getting There & Away

You wouldn't find Cassadaga if you weren't looking for it. The easiest way here is via I-4; take exit 116 onto Orange Camp Rd to get here. If you're using a GPS, enter the address of the Cassadaga Camp Bookstore: 1112 Stevens St, Lake Helen, FL.

DeLand

☑386 / POP 33,532

While much of Florida seems frantic to cover itself in neon and high-rises, stoic, small-town DeLand shrugs that off as nonsense. The quaint, walkable Woodland Blvd, bisecting the east side of town from the west, is home to independent shops and restaurants. Ancient oaks lean in to hug each other over city streets, Spanish moss dribbles from their branches, and picture-perfect Stetson University forms the town's heart. The whole scene whispers Old Florida.

These days DeLand is most famous for skydiving – the tandem jump was invented here.

◉ Sights & Activities

Several historic buildings are open for tours. Check out the West Volusia Historical Society for info (www.delandhouse.com).

De Leon Springs State Park STATE PARK
(☑ 386-985-4212; www.floridastateparks.org/parks-and-trails/de-leon-springs-state-park; 601 Ponce de León Blvd, De Leon Springs; car/bike $6/2; ⊗ 8am-sunset; P ⏃) ✎ Fifteen minutes north of town, these natural springs flow into the 18,000-acre Lake Woodruff National Wildlife Refuge and were used by Native Americans 6000 years ago. Today they're a popular developed swimming area that's great for kids. Water-equipment rentals and boat tours are available: inquire at the park office. Experienced hikers can attack the robust, blue-blaze 4.2-mile Wild Persimmon Trail, meandering through oak hammocks, floodplains and open fields.

Museum of Art – DeLand MUSEUM
(☑ 386-734-4371; www.moartdeland.org; 600 N Woodland Blvd; adult/child $5/free; ⊗ 10am-4pm Tue-Sat, 1-4pm Sun; P ⏃) A slate of innovative temporary exhibitions comes to the gallery space and attractive atrium of this energetic local museum, which has been bringing art to the region for six decades. There is a satellite modern gallery space and museum store located at 100 N Woodland Blvd.

DeLand House Museum MUSEUM
(☑ 386-740-6813; www.delandhouse.com; 137 W Michigan Ave; adult/child $5/3; ⊗ noon-4pm Tue-Sat; P) FREE This historical home, built in 1886, now serves as the headquarters of the West Volusia Historical Society and a museum for the county. You'll find lots of memorabilia and artifacts and earnest tour guides – it's like peeking into grandma's attic, if grandma were a Central Florida county.

Skydive DeLand SKYDIVING
(☑ 386-738-3539; www.skydivedeland.com; 1600 Flightline Blvd; tandem jumps $199) A short briefing and a seasoned professional strapped to your back is all it takes to experience the least-boring two minutes of your life above some glorious countryside with Skydive DeLand. Experienced skydivers can jump solo or advance their skills at this first-rate facility.

SPIRITUAL CASSADAGA

In 1894, 27-year-old New Yorker George Colby was suffering from tuberculosis. Seneca, Colby's Native American spirit guide, told him to head south to a lake and establish a spiritualist community, where he'd be healed. Colby did it, and Cassadaga (pronounced kassuh-*day*-guh) was born.

Today, Colby's camp – a collection of mainly 1920s Cracker (rural Floridian) cottages – is a registered historic district, the oldest active religious community in the US, and home to the Southern Cassadaga Spiritualist Camp Meeting Association, who believe in infinite intelligence, prophecy, healing and communicating with the dead. Some say the area is part of an energy vortex where the spirit and earthly planes are exceptionally close, creating a portal between the two.

There are 30-some spiritual practitioners in 'town' who offer a variety of psychic readings, starting at around $20 for a quick question-and-answer session and increasing to $50 for a good half-hour deep-dive into your consciousness. Many psychics practice out of the 2nd floor of the Cassadaga Hotel.

The hub of so much happening here is the **Cassadaga Camp Bookstore** (☑ 386-228-2880; www.cassadaga.org; 1112 Stevens St, Lake Helen; ⊗ 10am-6pm Mon-Sat, 11.30am-5pm Sun; P) FREE, which sells New Age books, crystals and incense, and serves as the visitor center for the town. Attached is an old spiritualist camp meeting hall, adorned with signs and photos from the camp's early days circa the late 19th and early 20th centuries.

The whiteboard in the back room of the bookstore connects you with which psychics are working that day. The store also organizes **historical tours of the village** (☑ 386-228-2880; www.cassadaga.org; adult/child/under 6 $15/7.50/free; ⊗ 2pm Thu-Sat) that are as enjoyably eccentric as Cassadaga itself. The tours provide a fairly on-brand message about local history, the importance of spirituality and expanded consciousness. Nighttime tours that seek out spirit-energy hot spots and where photographers shoot glowing balls of light – reportedly spirits from another world – are held at 7:30pm on Saturdays (adult $25, child $15). A $1 donation gets you a camp directory, allowing you to take a pretty good self-guided tour. Mandatory stop: Spirit Lake, where residents scatter the ashes of the departed.

🛏 Sleeping & Eating

Artisan Downtown   HOTEL $$
(☑386-873-4675; www.delandartisaninn.com; 215
S Woodland Blvd; r $178-225; 🛜) This centrally
located boutique hotel features the trendi-
est rooms in DeLand, with whirlpool baths
and cozy sitting areas. The on-site bar and
restaurant is a nice bonus, and noise doesn't
appear to be an issue.

Buttercup Bakery   BAKERY $
(☑386-736-4043; www.facebook.com/buttercup-
bakerydeland; 197 E Church St; snacks $3.50-8;
⊗8am-5pm Mon-Thu, from 9am Fri, 10am-3pm
Sat; 🅿) Inside this sunny yellow cottage the
pastry cases are stacked high with luscious
sweets: lemon-curd bars, white chocolate
and apricot bars, chocolate-chip bread pudding and more. It also serves organic coffee,
tea and salad.

★Cress   AMERICAN $$$
(☑386-734-3740; www.cressrestaurant.com; 103
W Indiana Ave; lunch mains $14-18, dinner mains
$21-35; ⊗11:30am-2pm & 5-9pm Tue-Sat) This
is a can't-miss restaurant if you're in the
area and citified foodies have been known
to trek to sleepy DeLand just to eat at this
cutting-edge bistro, whose menu might offer
such delights as local seafood *mofongo* (a
classic Caribbean dish), Indonesian shrimp
curry, and a salad of delicate pea tendrils
with passion-fruit emulsion. Advance reservations are highly recommended.

🍷 Drinking & Nightlife

Abbey Bar   BAR
(☑386-734-4545; www.oddelixir.com/abbey-bar-
deland; 117 N Woodland Blvd; ⊗11:30am-1am Mon-
Thu, to 2am Fri, 12:30pm-2am Sat, 1pm-midnight
Sun) This is a genuinely funky, fun drinking
option in the heart of town. The bar has
some great craft brews on tap, board games
in the corner, a house selection of mead
(why not?) and a quirky, neighborhood-
pub feel that is immediately warm and
enjoyable.

☆ Entertainment

Athens Theatre   THEATER
(☑386-736-1500; www.athensdeland.com; 124 N
Florida Ave) Dating back to 1922, this historic
theater, designed in a gorgeous Italian Renaissance style, is a good spot for live music
and drama performances courtesy of an in-
house theater company.

❶ Information

West Volusia Tourism (☑386-734-0162;
https://visitwestvolusia.com; 116 W New York
Ave; ⊗8:30am-5pm Mon-Fri) Everything you
ever wanted to know about DeLand but never
thought to ask.

❶ Getting There & Away

DeLand sits off I-4 and is bisected by Hwy 17. It's
located roughly 50 miles north of Orlando, 25
miles west of Daytona Beach and 60 miles east
of Ocala. There is no Greyhound out here: you
really need a car to explore the area.

Ocala

☑352 / POP 60,429

Ocala's surroundings are much more beautiful than the town itself. Blanketed by velvety paddocks where sleek-limbed horses
neigh in the misty morning air, the outskirts
of Greater Ocala look like the US Dept of
Agriculture–certified 'Horse Capital of the
World' *should* look. There are about 1200
horse farms in Marion County, with more
than 45 breeds represented.

Downtown Ocala, however, ain't so
grand – there's a reason locals call it 'Slocala.'
('Strip-Mall-Cala' would also be accurate, if
not as clever with the wordplay.) But it's not
the downtown you're here for – this rural
city is surrounded by beautiful clear springs
and the best backyard in Florida: Ocala National Forest.

◉ Sights & Activities

Silver Springs State Park   STATE PARK
(☑352-236-7148; www.floridastateparks.org/silver
springs; 1425 NE 58th Ave; car/pedestrian $8/2;
⊗8am-sunset; 🅿) �êThis state park was
once an amusement park – glass-bottomed
boats were invented here in 1878. to show
visitors the natural springs and stunningly
clear waters of the Silver River. Although
the amusement side of things closed in
2013, the natural beauty and the boat tours
(adult/child $12/11) over Mammoth Spring
remain. The spring is the world's largest
artesian limestone spring, gushing 550
million gallons of 99.8%-pure spring water
per day.

Don Garlits Museums   MUSEUM
(☑352-245-8661; www.garlits.com; 13700 SW 16th
Ave; adult/child $20/10; ⊗9am-5pm; 🅿) Local
drag racer Don 'Big Daddy' Garlits won 144
national events and 17 World Championship

WORTH A TRIP

BLUE SPRING STATE PARK

The largest spring on the St Johns River, **Blue Spring State Park** (☏386-775-3663; www.floridastateparks.org/parks-and-trails/blue-spring-state-park; 2100 W French Ave, Orange City; car/bike $6/2; ☺8am-sunset; P) maintains a constant 72°F (22°C). Between November and March it becomes the winter refuge for up to 200 West Indian manatees. The best time to see them is before 11am; there's a wheelchair-accessible path to the viewing platform. This tranquil state park, about 8 miles from DeLand, is a revitalizing spot to swim (prohibited when manatees are present), snorkel or canoe.

You can also spend two hours cruising the peaceful waters with **St Johns River Cruises** (☏386-917-0724; 2100 West French Ave, Orange City; adult/child $28/18; ☺tours 10am & 1pm), whose nature tours offer a thoughtful insight into this fragile ecosystem.

titles, shattering numerous records in hand-built breakneck speedsters along the way. In his **Museum of Drag Racing**, you'll find engine collections and an impressive line-up of dragsters, including Garlits' custom-designed 'swamp rats.' The adjacent Antique Building, also known as the **Museum of Classic Cars** (10am to 4pm daily), houses Don's impressive attic of automobiles, including the two-toned 1950 Mercury driven by the Fonz in *Happy Days*.

Cactus Jack's Trail Rides HORSEBACK RIDING
(☏352-266-9326; https://floridahorseriding.com; 11008 S Hwy 475A; 1hr from $50) You're in the horse capital of America, so saddle up and let Cactus Jack's take you trotting through shady forests and clover-green fields on the backs of handsome quarter horses and thoroughbreds.

☞ Tours

Farm Tours Ocala OUTDOORS
(☏352-895-9302; www.farmtoursofocala.com; 801 SW 60th Ave; $50) Ocala is one of the most important agricultural towns in Florida. On this tour, you'll get an unvarnished, informative peek into life on a working horse farm, and learn some of the ins and outs of raising, breeding and training thoroughbred horses. Tours start at 8:30am and conclude at noon. The outfit also runs food tours to local restaurants.

🛏 Sleeping & Eating

Silver River State Park CAMPGROUND $
(☏352-236-7148; www.floridastateparks.org/silversprings; 1425 NE 58th Ave; tent & RV sites $24, cabins $110; 🐾) Pets are welcome at any of the 59 campsites nestled among the woods at this 5000-acre park. If you want something more sumptuous (but canine-free), try

the park's fully equipped cabins, which sleep up to six – they have a two-night minimum stay policy on weekends and holidays.

Hilton Ocala HOTEL $$
(☏352-854-1400; www.hiltonocala.com; 3600 SW 36th Ave; r $120-185; 🅿🏊) Ocala's paddockside Hilton has its own Clydesdale horse, Buddy (and free horse cookies for you to feed him), who waits patiently to take guests on free carriage rides. There's a jogging trail, too. Cookie-cutter rooms, but the surroundings make this a better option than downtown.

★**Big Lee's** BARBECUE $$
(☏352-304-9105; www.mybigleesbbq.com; 3925 SE 45th Ct; mains $10.50-28; ☺11:30am-3:30pm Wed-Sat; P) It's a little ways out of town, and there's not even a restaurant to sit in, just a food truck and some picnic tables. So why come? Because this is some damn fine barbecue. The char on the skin is crunchy, the brisket glistens like a jewel and the enormous beef ribs taste like smoky heaven.

If they run out of food, they'll close. *Don't miss it.*

ℹ Information

Ocala & Marion County Visitors Center
(☏352-438-2800; www.ocalamarion.com; 109 W Silver Springs Blvd; ☺9am-5pm Mon-Fri) has all the information that you could ever need on Ocala.

ℹ Getting There & Away

Greyhound (☏352-732-2677; www.greyhound.com; 4032 Hwy 326 W) is in the Central Transfer Station, at the corner of NE 5th St, just a few blocks from downtown. Services include Gainesville (from $9, 40 minutes, four daily), Tampa (from $29, 4½ hours, three daily) and Orlando (from $16, 1½ hours, five daily).

WORTH A TRIP

MARJORIE KINNAN RAWLINGS HISTORIC STATE PARK

Marjorie Kinnan Rawlings (1896–1953) was the author of the Pulitzer Prize–winning novel *The Yearling*, a coming-of-age story set in what's now Ocala National Forest. Her former **Cracker-style home** (☑ 352-466-3672; www.floridastateparks.org/parks-and-trails/marjorie-kinnan-rawlings-historic-state-park; 18700 S CR 325, Cross Creek; per vehicle $3; ⊙ 9am-5pm, tours 10am, 11am, 1pm, 2pm, 3pm & 4pm Thu-Sun Oct-Jul; P) is open for tours. You can stroll the orange groves, farmhouse and barn on your own – pick up a self-guided walking brochure from the car park. The estate is 23 miles north of Ocala in the small town of Cross Creek, off Hwy 325 between Island Grove and Micanopy.

Hungry? Cross Creek's cedar-shingled **Yearling Restaurant** (☑ 352-466-3999; www.yearlingrestaurant.net; 14531 Hwy 325, Hawthorne; mains $11-26; ⊙ noon-8pm Thu & Sun, to 9pm Fri & Sat; P 🛋) serves 'Cracker cuisine' like gator tail, frog legs, hush puppies and catfish in an atmospheric wood-paneled dining room decorated with historical photos and paintings. It's worth a stop just to try its famous sour orange pie. Live music performances kick off on a pretty regular basis.

Rawlings' career flourished only after Max Perkins, Rawlings' (and also Ernest Hemingway's and F Scott Fitzgerald's) editor, told her that her letters about her friends and neighbors were more interesting than her Gothic fiction, inspiring her to write *Cross Creek*, a book about her life in old Cracker Florida.

Amtrak (☑ 352-629-9863; www.amtrak.com; 531 NE 1st Ave) has bus services from here that will drop you off at the Jacksonville Amtrak train station.

Ocala National Forest

The oldest national forest east of the Mississippi River and the southernmost national forest in the continental US, the 400,000-acre **Ocala National Forest** (☑ 352-669-7495; www.fs.usda.gov/main/ocala; off FL 40; P 🐾) 🌿 **FREE** is one of Florida's most important natural treasures. An incredible ecological web, the park is a tangle of springs, biomes (sand-pine scrub, palmetto wilderness, subtropical forest) and endangered flora and fauna.

With 18 developed campgrounds and 24 primitive ones, 219 miles of trails and 600 lakes (30 for boating), there are enormous opportunities for swimming, hiking, cycling, horseback riding, canoeing, bird- and wildlife-watching – or just meditating on how great it is that the government got here before the theme parks did.

Two highways cross the region: Hwy 19 runs north–south and Hwy 40 runs east–west.

🏃 Activities

Paisley Woods Bicycle Trail   CYCLING
(www.pwbt.weebly.com) 🌿 Passing through prairies and live-oak domes, the popular backwoods Paisley Woods Bicycle Trail rolls 22 miles from Alexander Springs to the north and Clearwater Lake to the south (it's shaped like a figure eight so you can do either half as a loop). Bring a bike that can handle off-road conditions, and plenty of water (there is none available along the trail).

**Juniper Springs
Recreation Area**   OUTDOORS
(☑ 352-625-3147; www.fs.usda.gov/ocala; 26701 Hwy 40, Silver Springs; $6; ⊙ 8am-8pm) 🌿 Ocala National Forest's flagship recreation area was developed in the mid-1930s as part of the work of the Civilian Conservation Corps. Swimming is sublime at Juniper Springs: the water is a crisp 72°F (22°C) year-round. Concessions sell groceries and firewood, and rent kayaks and canoes ($35 per day) for making the 7-mile, palmetto- and cypress-lined run down Juniper Creek. Also has campsites ($21).

There's a pickup and return shuttle at the end of the creek ($6 per person and $6 per boat).

**Alexander Springs
Wilderness Area**   OUTDOORS
(☑ 352-625-2520; www.fs.usda.gov/ocala; 49525 County Rd 445, Altoona; $6; ⊙ 8am-8pm) 🌿 This picturesque recreation area has one of the last untouched subtropical forests left in Florida. The stunning sapphire-blue freshwater spring attracts wildlife,

swimmers, scuba divers (an extra $7 fee) and sunbathers. Canoe rental (two hours/daily $17/40) includes a welcome re-haul at the end of the 7-mile paddle. Has campsites ($23), too.

Salt Springs
Recreation Area OUTDOORS
(📞352-685-2048; www.fs.usda.gov/recarea/ocala; 13851 N Hwy 19, Salt Springs; $6.50; ⏱8am-8pm) 🚣 Enriched by mineral deposits that include potassium, magnesium and sodium salts (hence the name), and rumored to have curative powers, Salt Springs is a favorite with RV owners for its lovely shady areas (sites with/without hookups $35/23). There's lovely swimming available, and local canoeing is supremely relaxing.

🛏 Sleeping & Eating

There are dozens of different camping options in the national forest. Campsites are available from $22 and there are cabins available that sleep up to 10 people (weekend/week $430/820). Visit the National Forest website (www.fs.usda.gov/recarea/ocala) for a full breakdown of all campsites; book through www.recreation.gov.

Stock up on food in Ocala or DeLand before arriving. Be careful how you store food – the forest boasts Florida's largest population of wild black bears.

❶ Information

Rangers serve most of the area and all campgrounds have resident volunteers who are good sources of information. There's no single admission fee and no one number to call; day-use areas are generally open 8am to 8pm. Pick up free literature and maps or buy a topographical version at any of the visitor centers, all open 8am to 5pm.

Lake George Ranger District (📞352-625-2520; 17147 E SR 40, Silver Springs; ⏱7:30am-4pm Mon-Fri) can answer questions about the region.

❶ Getting There & Away

Several entrances can be used to access Ocala National Forest. From Orlando take Hwy 441 north to the Eustis turnoff and continue north on Hwy 19 (about 40 miles); from Daytona take Hwy 92 west to DeLand, then head north on Hwy 17 to Barberville and west on SR 40 (about 30 miles); from Ocala take Silver Springs Blvd due west about 6 miles to the forest's main entry.

Gainesville

📞 352 / POP 133,857

The state's premier college town is an energetic change of pace from rural, conservative north Florida. While Gainesville is hardly hippie or hipster central, its attractive and compact downtown has graffiti murals, fair-trade coffee, funky music and similar amenities that all add a little diversity to the state's inner north.

Originally a whistle-stop along the Florida Railroad Company's line, today this town is home to the nation's second-largest university, the sprawling University of Florida (UF). The campus itself is 2 miles from downtown, but the student vibe infuses the entire city, which is why Gainesville has such a thriving music scene: Tom Petty and the Heartbreakers hail from here, and there's an old-school, vibrant punk rock scene.

◉ Sights

★ **Florida Museum**
of Natural History MUSEUM
(📞352-846-2000; www.floridamuseum.ufl.edu; 3215 Hull Rd; museum free, Butterfly Rainforest adult/child $14/7; ⏱10am-5pm Mon-Sat, to 1pm Sun; 🅿♿) **FREE** The highlight of this excellent natural-history museum is the expansive Butterfly Rainforest. Hundreds of butterflies from 55 to 65 species flutter freely in the soaring, screened vivarium. As you stroll among waterfalls and tropical foliage,

---

OCALA FOREST TRAILS

Also referred to as the Ocala Trail, roughly 61 miles of the Florida National Scenic Trail spears the center of the forest north–south. Marked with orange blazes, pickup points include Juniper Springs, Alexander Springs and Clearwater Lake recreation areas. Outside hunting season, hikers can camp anywhere 200ft from the trail, but if you prefer to commune with others you'll find spur trails to developed campgrounds every 10 to 12 miles.

The 8.5-mile St Francis Trail (blue blazes) winds through riverine and bayhead swamp to the abandoned 1880s pioneer town of St Francis on the St Johns River. No buildings remain, but you'll see the old logging railroad bed and levee built for rice growing.

peek at scientists preparing specimens in the rearing lab of this, the world's largest butterfly research facility. Other exhibits include displays on fossils and Floridian ecosystems.

Bat House & Bat Barn LANDMARK
(www.floridamuseum.ufl.edu/bats; Museum Rd; P) FREE Across from Gainesville's little Lake Alice, adjacent to a student garden, stands what appears to be two oversized birdhouses. However, these stilted gray-roofed structures are actually home to a family of Brazilian free-tailed bats. Built in 1991 after the flying mammals' poop began stinking up the campus, the population has since exploded to more than 300,000. Each night just after sundown, the bats drop from their roost – at the amazing rate of 100 bats per second – and fly off to feed.

Samuel P Harn Museum of Art GALLERY
(☑352-392-9826; www.harn.ufl.edu; 3259 Hull Rd; ⊙11am-5pm Tue-Fri, 10am-5pm Sat, 1-5pm Sun; P) FREE Peer in at ancient Native American sculptures and contemporary paintings at this excellent art gallery on the University of Florida campus. Also open on the second Thursday of the month (6pm to 9pm).

Kanapaha Botanical Gardens GARDENS
(☑352-372-4981; www.kanapaha.org; 4700 SW 58th Dr; adult/child $10/5; ⊙9am-5pm Mon-Wed & Fri, to dusk Sat & Sun; P 🐾) 🌿 Central Florida's lush native plants – azaleas, rare double-crowned cabbage palms, southern magnolias – are on proud display at this highly rated 62-acre garden, a domesticated version of wild Florida with hiking paths, a labyrinth, a children's koi pond and special herb and ginger gardens. Especially cool is the dense bamboo garden, whose dark groves look like fairy homes. Dogs are welcome!

Devil's Millhopper State Geological Site PARK
(☑352-955-2008; www.floridastateparks.org/parks-and-trails/devils-millhopper-geological-state-park; 4732 Millhopper Rd; car/pedestrian $4/2; ⊙9am-5pm Wed-Sun; P) 🌿 As the name indicates, this is not your average park and it's a vaguely surreal experience. The site centers on a 120ft-deep, 500ft-wide funnel-shaped rainforest which you enter by descending a 232-step wooden staircase. Water trickles down the slopes from the surrounding springs; some of it flows into a natural drain and ultimately to the Gulf of Mexico.

The park is about 20 minutes northwest of downtown by car.

University of Florida UNIVERSITY
(UF; ☑352-392-3261; www.ufl.edu; Welcome Center, cnr Museum Rd & Reitz Union Dr) The city is dominated by the UF campus, the second largest in the country. Pop in to the Welcome Center for tips on where best to wander around to check out the student vibe.

🎉 Festivals & Events

Gainesville Native American Festival CULTURAL
(www.gainesvillenativeamericanfest.com; 3100 NE 39th Ave, Alachua County Fairgrounds; ⊙Mar) In much of Florida you could be forgiven for thinking that the state's Native American past has been airbrushed from the public mind. Not in Gainesville. This fine little festival over a weekend in mid-March features Native American music, crafts, food, and even re-enactments of traditional rituals and live bands.

👉 Tours

Gainesville has a unique citywide cell-phone audio tour – when you spot a placard, dial the number listed for information about historical and cultural sites.

🛏 Sleeping

Prices soar during football games and graduations, when a minimum stay may be required and rooms fill rapidly. Many inexpensive motels are just east of UF, along SW 13th St or on approach roads. Just east of downtown, the historic district has a handful of elegant B&Bs in restored Victorian homes.

★ Hampton Inn & Suites – Gainesville Downtown HOTEL $$
(☑352-240-9300; www.hamptoninnandsuites-gainesville.com; 101 SE 1st Ave; d from $150; P 🐾) In the heart of downtown Gainesville, you couldn't ask for a better location from which to explore this quaint district. The attractive facade of this new hotel is echoed in the stylish interior, with contrasting colors offset by pale green accents and rooms have plenty of space. Free wi-fi and a light hot breakfast is provided, and there's plenty to eat, drink and enjoy nearby.

Magnolia Plantation B&B $$
(☑352-375-6653; www.magnoliabnb.com; 309 SE 7th St; r/cottages from $150/215; P 🐾) Lovingly

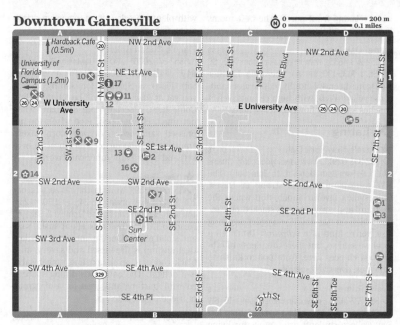

Downtown Gainesville

restored, this French Second Empire–style mansion was unique to Gainesville when constructed by a woodworker in 1885. It's still unique today. The main house boasts five rooms, 10 fireplaces (check the detailing in those mantels) and snacks around the clock. Outside, a tangled hidden garden has a pond and chairs for relaxing.

Sweetwater Branch Inn　　　　B&B **$$**
(☎800-595-7760, 352-373-6760; www.sweetwater inn.com; 625 E University Ave; r $145-185; @☒) In this wedding cake mansion that evokes America's Deep South, you'll find 20 rooms – no two exactly alike – decorated in an Old Florida aesthetic, with hardwoods, classic furniture and artwork that recalls the state's natural beauty and history. An on-site pool and mod-cons like cable TV and noise diffusers add the right touch of contemporary comfort.

Camellia Rose　　　　B&B **$$**
(☎352-395-7673; www.camelliaroseinn.com; 205 SE 7th St; r $165-225; P☯☜) Modern upgrades (like Jacuzzi tubs) integrate seamlessly with antique furniture in this fabulously restored 1903 Victorian building featuring a

wide, relaxing front porch. The best rooms have hardwood floors.

Laurel Oak Inn

B&B $$

(☑352-373-4535; www.laureloakinn.com; 221 SE 7th St; r $135-190; P 🛜) The 1885 Lassiter House has been splendidly redone as a handsome yellow B&B, with high ceilings, velvet couches and fresh flowers everywhere.

✕ Eating

★ Dave's New York Deli

DELI $

(☑352-333-0291; www.davesnydeli.com; mains $7-13; ⊙9am-8pm Mon-Sat, to 3pm Sun) The NYC-transplant force is strong at Dave's, Gainesville's favorite lunch stop where the pastrami and corned beef is stacked precariously high on rye, and if you order anything else, you're kind of a *schmuck*. Don't tell a local we said so, but there are plenty of other good choices here, from potato knish to delicious, oversized salads.

Crane Ramen

JAPANESE $

(☑352-727-7422; www.craneramen.com; 16 SW 1st St; mains $12-14; ⊙11am-4pm & 5-11pm Tue-Sun) College students are famous for living on ramen, but those packaged noodles are roughly a thousand steps below the quality of the soup served at this elegant, playful eatery. Seven variations on ramen broth can be accessorized into whatever seriously good soup your heart desires, and chased

with plenty of sake off an extensive drinks menu to boot.

Flaco's Cuban Bakery

CUBAN $

(☑352-371-2000; 200 W University Ave; mains $4-7; ⊙11:30am-2:30am Tue-Fri, noon-2:30am Sat) 'Flaco' is Spanish for 'skinny', and if you eat at Flaco's, you will be anything but. Come here, especially late at night (when not much else is open, food-wise), for hot pressed sandwiches, *arepas* (corn cakes), empanadas, *ropa vieja* (pulled braised brisket) and other Latin American favorites.

★ Dragonfly

JAPANESE $$

(☑352-371-3359; www.dragonflyrestaurants.com; 201 SE 2nd Ave; mains $8-24; ⊙11:30am-2pm Thu & Fri, 5-10pm Sun-Thu, to 11pm Fri & Sat; 🅿) Head to Dragonfly for excellent sushi, sake and small plates done Japanese style. Grilled tiger shrimp is fire-kissed and savory, miso black cod is a revelation and ginger salad is a delight. The enormous dining space is colorful, bustling and great for a big group of friends. Cool place.

Satchel's Pizza

PIZZA $$

(☑352-335-7272; www.satchelspizza.com; 1800 NE 23rd Ave; pizzas from $14; ⊙11am-10pm Tue-Sat; 🅿) Satchel's makes a strong claim to the best pizza within range of Florida's east coast, a reputation buttressed by enormous crowds of happy patrons. Grab a seat

---

LIVE MUSIC IN GAINESVILLE

Live music is to Gainesville what mouse ears are to Orlando, and many bars double as music venues. For an up-to-the-minute overview of local music, visit www.gainesville shows.com.

High Dive (☑352-872-5949; https://highdivegainesville.com; 210 SW 2nd Ave; ⊙8pm-2am Wed-Sat) Around since forever, and ranked in the Top 100 American live music venues by the respected Consequences of Sound blog in 2016, this stalwart of the Gainesville night is best-known for down-home rock-n-roll; if a good rock band comes to Florida, they'll play here. There are no frills; a beer garden and food truck go with the great music.

Hardback Cafe (☑352-317-1997; www.facebook.com/hardbackgainesville; 920 NW 2nd St; ⊙6pm-2am Wed-Fri, 7pm-2am Sat) Bar upstairs, live music downstairs, and a cool sound system that means you hear the music wherever you are. Gigs range from rock to acoustic, but check the Facebook page to see what's coming up.

Bull (☑352-672-6266; www.thebull-gnv.com; 18 SW 1st Ave; ⊙4pm-2am Mon-Sat) There's never a cover and almost always some music happening at The Bull, and if music isn't going down, there's art on the walls, craft beer on tap, strong coffee brewing and a mellow atmosphere that attracts a lot of local artists and musicians.

Lillian's Music Store (☑352-372-1010; 112 SE 1st St; ⊙2pm-2am Mon-Sat, to midnight Sun) The crowd's a little older than in the clubs along University Ave, so they appreciate that elegant stained-glass partition and the 3ft-tall gorilla at the entrance. Monday night jam sessions really pack 'em in.

at a mosaic courtyard table or in the back of a gutted 1965 Ford Falcon. Most nights there's live music in the Back 40 Bar, with its head-scratchingly eccentric collection of trash and treasure.

There's always a wait, so just kick back, down a beer and enjoy the ride.

The Top FUSION $$
(📋 352-376-1188; www.thetopgainesville.com; 30 N Main St; mains $10-29; ⏱ 5pm-2am Tue-Sun, 10am-2pm & 5pm-2am Sun) Combining 1950s kitsch, hunter-lodge decor and the well-known genre of giant owl art, this place is both hip and comfortable. The burgers are particularly awesome. Just as popular for the nightlife as it is for food.

Paramount Grill MODERN AMERICAN $$$
(📋 352-378-3398; www.paramountgrill.com; 12 SW 1st Ave; lunch mains $12-16, dinner mains $16-41; ⏱ 5-9:30pm Mon, 11am-2pm & 5-9:30pm Tue-Fri, 5-9:30pm Sat, 10am-3pm & 5-9:30pm Sun) Very Scandinavian chic, with minimalist wood tables and apple-green walls decorated with vintage sailor photos, this is the top spot for innovative upscale-casual eats in Gainesville. A globally influenced menu spans crab cakes, duck dishes and homemade ravioli.

Embers Wood Grill STEAK, SEAFOOD $$$
(📋 352-380-0901; https://embersofflorida.com; 3545 SW 34th St; mains $20-59; ⏱ 5-9:30pm Mon-Sat) Consistently ranked by locals as their favorite spot for steak and seafood, Embers is a bit of a hike from the center, but dishes like Alaskan king crab and perfectly seared steaks make it worth the drive.

 Drinking & Nightlife

⭐ **Dime** COCKTAIL BAR
(📋 352-692-0068; www.facebook.com/thedime bargvl; 4 E University Ave; ⏱ 4pm-2am Mon-Sat, 2pm-2am Sun) A small bar, some dim lighting, talented bartenders and strong, delicious cocktails – that's what you get at The Dime, a joint that feels like it made a wrong turn in 1930s Manhattan and ended up in central Florida.

⭐ **oak** BAR
(original american kitchen; 📋 352-283-8646; www.oakgainesville.com; 15 SE 1st Ave; ⏱ 11:30am-10pm Mon-Thu, to 2am Fri, 11am-2am Sat, to 10pm Sun) It's not every day you can sidle into a bar and pour yourself your own craft beer of choice. But oak does just that: buy a prepaid 'Brews & Barrels' card and use it to fill your mug with over a dozen craft brews on tap.

It has tasty cocktails too, if you're not in the mood for malt and hops.

Arcade Bar BAR
(www.arcadebargainesville.com; 6 E University Ave; ⏱ 5pm-2am) Three floors of old-school arcade goodness are the order of the day at Arcade Bar, which is filled with coin-operated games, pinball machines and plenty of other diversions that – we know, we know – you're *really* good at, unless you've had a bunch of beers, which is inevitably what ends up happening if you stick around for a while.

Curia On the Drag CAFE
(📋 352-792-6444; www.curiaonthedrag.com; 2029 NW 6th St; ⏱ 7am-11pm Mon-Fri, 9am-11pm Sat & Sun; 📶) There's plenty of good coffee in this college town, but we love Curia, both for its good coffee and its young, smart, accommodating staff. Food is funky but good, and there's a food truck: try the ever-popular Bagel Bomb or the Jackfruit quesadilla. Yes, it's a mural-chic, bohemian kinda coffee spot – it's just executing that genre very well.

 Entertainment

Hippodrome THEATER
(📋 352-375-4477; www.thehipp.org; 25 SE 2nd Pl) In an imposing historic edifice (1911), the Hippodrome is the city's main cultural center, with a diverse theater and independent-cinema program.

 Shopping

University of Florida Bookstore CLOTHING
(📋 352-392-0194; www.bkstr.com/floridastore/home; 1900 Museum Rd; ⏱ 8am-6pm Mon-Fri, 10am-5pm Sat, noon-5pm Sun) This is the place to come if you're looking for merchandise for the Florida Gators, the University of Florida teams in basketball, baseball and other sports. It makes a terrific Florida souvenir, and it's easily the widest range of choice in the city. They also have books, but they're mostly textbooks. There's parking ($4 for two hours) downstairs, off Reitz Union Drive.

ℹ **Information**

Alachua County Visitors & Convention Bureau (📋 352-374-5260; www.visitgainesville.com; 33 N Main St; ⏱ 8:30am-5pm Mon-Fri) Friendly staff are happy to welcome you to town and advise on the latest happenings.
Pride Community Center (📋 352-377-8915; www.gainesvillepride.org; 3131 NW 13th St; ⏱ 3-7pm Mon-Fri, noon-4pm Sat) For LGBT info.

❶ Getting There & Away

Gainesville Regional Airport (☏ 352-373-0249; www.gra-gnv.com; 3880 NE 39th Ave) is located 10 miles northeast of downtown and is served by a handful of domestic carriers, including Delta and American Airlines. Destinations include Miami, Atlanta, Charlotte and Dallas-Fort Worth.

The **Greyhound bus station** (☏ 352-376-5252; www.greyhound.com; 101 NE 23rd Ave) is a mile or so north of downtown. For most destinations other than Orlando (from $10, two to three hours, five daily), you'll need to change buses.

High Springs

☏ 386 / POP 6137

Quaint High Springs is a hub for antiquers, bikers and locals seeking a getaway. Main St, dotted with shops, galleries and restaurants, is the major north–south divider, and feels lifted out of a *Leave it to Beaver* episode (albeit, a hot and humid *Leave it to Beaver* episode).

That said, the town itself is a sideshow for its namesake: local crystal-clear springs, one of Florida's quiet treasures.

◉ Sights

Poe Springs   SPRING
(☏ 352-548-1210; 28800 NW 182nd Ave; ⊙ 9am-6pm Thu-Sun; 🅿) **FREE** Shallow Poe Springs, which has steps leading all the way down to the bright blue water, is perfect for small children. It's one of the least crowded springs in the area – depending on the time of year, you could find yourself in blissful isolation. From High Springs, follow CR-340 west for 2 miles to reach the park.

Ginnie Springs   SPRING
(☏ 386-454-7188; www.ginniespringsoutdoors.com; 7300 Ginnie Springs Rd; adult/child $14/3.70; ⊙ 8am-7pm Mon-Thu, to 9pm Fri & Sat, to 8pm Sun May-Sep, 8am-4pm Mon-Thu, to 6pm Fri, Sat & Sun Oct-Apr) Of the two springs in High Springs, Ginnie Springs is a little older and more developed than Poe Springs, with a handful of campsites ($22.50) on hand and scuba divers plying its clear waters. Closes a couple of hours earlier in winter.

🛏 Sleeping & Eating

There are some doily-heavy B&Bs in town, as well as chain hotels on the outskirts. Keep in mind Gainesville is only about 30 minutes away if you want more accommodation options.

Great Outdoors Restaurant   AMERICAN **$$**
(☏ 386-454-1288; www.greatoutdoorsdining.com; 18587 High Springs Main St; mains $10-32; ⊙ 11am-9pm Tue-Thu & Sun, to 10pm Fri & Sat; 🍴) This woodsy, lantern-lit steakhouse and saloon, located in the former downtown Opera House, has an inviting patio area for alfresco dining. The menu is old-school Florida, if a little elevated: low country boils, ribs, big burgers and deep-fried seafood.

❶ Getting There & Away

Located about 22 miles north of Gainesville, you'll find High Springs off of US 441 and US 41. There is no bus service here.

WORTH A TRIP

ICHETUCKNEE SPRINGS STATE PARK

Relax in a giant inner tube and float through gin-clear waters at the popular **Ichetucknee Springs State Park** (☏ 386-497-4690; www.floridastateparks.org/parks-and-trails/ichetucknee-springs-state-park; 12087 SW US 27, Fort White; car/bicycle $6/2; ⊙ 8am-sunset; 🅿), plopped on the lazy, spring-fed Ichetucknee River.

Various water sports are available here, but tubing is certainly the most popular. Floats last from 45 minutes to 3½ hours, with scattered launch points along the river. The park runs regular trams (per person $5.50) bringing tubers to the river and also a shuttle service (per person $7.50, May to September) between the north and south entrances.

To minimize the environmental impact, the number of tubers is limited to 750 a day; arrive early as capacity is often reached by mid-morning. Use the south entrance: the shuttle service takes you to the launch points, allowing you to float back down to your car.

You'll see farmers advertising tube rental as you approach the park along Hwy 238 and 47 (the park itself does not rent tubes). Tubes are $5 and one- or two-person rafts cost $10 to $15. At the end of the day, leave your gear at the tube drop at the southern end of the park; it'll be returned.

PAYNES PRAIRIE PRESERVE STATE PARK

Wild horses and bison roam the 20 biological zones that constitute 21,000-acre **Paynes Prairie Preserve State Park** (☑ 352-466-3397; www.floridastateparks.org/parks-and-trails/paynes-prairie-preserve-state-park; 100 Savannah Blvd; per vehicle/bicycle $6/2; ☺8am-sunset; P). This slightly eerie preserve's wet prairie, swamp, hammock and pine flatwoods are crisscrossed by multiple trails that can easily eat up a day of wandering. The 3-mile La Chua Trail takes in the Alachua Sink and Alachua Lake, offering opportunities to spot alligators and sandhill cranes.

Just north of the visitor center, climb the 50ft observation tower for panoramas. Campsites cost $18, and include water and electricity.

The park is about 11 miles south of downtown Gainesville, off of US 441-S.

Barberville

☑ 386

Blink and you'll miss the tiny crossroads town of Barberville, but you'd also miss one of the best re-creations of north-central Florida's frontier past. Amid the palm- and oak-shaded country lanes, you'll find a re-created pioneer settlement that celebrates the people who hacked a place to live out of the nearby vine-clad woods and backwater swamps. Most visitors come here on a day trip from DeLand or elsewhere.

◉ Sights

Barberville Pioneer Settlement　HISTORIC SITE
(☑ 386-749-2959; www.pioneersettlement.org; 1776 Lightfoot Lane, Pierson; adult/child $8/4; ☺9am-4pm Tue-Sat May-Oct, 9am-4pm Mon-Sat & 11am-3pm Sun Nov-Apr; P ♿) ✒ Try to set aside at least an hour to fully explore old Barberville, a re-created pioneer settlement carved from the central Florida woods. Costumed interpreters give child-friendly lessons on Old Florida life in front of blacksmith forges and in rebuilt schoolhouses. Check the website to take advantage of a regular calendar of events, from monthly music workshops to harvest festivals.

☆ Festivals & Events

Fall Country Jamboree　MUSIC
(☑386-749-2959; www.pioneersettlement.org/fall-country-jamboree; Barberville; ☺Nov; ♿) On the first weekend of November, the Pioneer Settlement for the Creative Arts hosts Florida's best pioneer-heritage festival, with folk music and demonstrations of Cracker (rural Floridian) life.

🛍 Shopping

Barberville Roadside Yard Emporium　MARKET
(☑ 386-749-3562; www.barbervilleroadside.com; 140 W SR 40; ☺9am-6pm) Nestled beneath a Spanish-moss canopy, this king of roadside stands fills 3 acres with wrought-iron furniture, gazing balls, pottery and ceramic drop-in sinks. It's along SR 40, plunked halfway between Ocala and Daytona and roughly one-third of the way between DeLand and Palatka. There's even an 8ft-tall aluminum rooster. Who doesn't need one of those?

❶ Getting There & Away

Little Barberville sits at the intersection of US 17 and SR 40. DeLand is about 15 miles south on US 17.

AT A GLANCE

POPULATION
3.5 million

NUMBER OF CRAFT BREWERIES
82

BEST BEACH
Caladesi Island State Park (p422)

BEST FLAMENCO
Columbia Restaurant (p405)

BEST SUNSET BAR
Hurricane (p419)

WHEN TO GO
Mid-Feb–mid-Apr
Peak season, with ideal weather but high prices. Best time for camping, hiking, manatees.

Jun–Sep Hot and rainy (with hurricane threats). Low season means beach bargains; some places close.

Nov–Dec Snowbirds arrive from colder climes. Weather cools and dries; decent off-season prices.

Naples (p444)
SEAN PAVONE / GETTY IMAGES ©

Tampa Bay & Southwest Florida

Florida's Gulf Coast is like an impressionistic watercolor painting, from the dazzling quartz sand and turquoise waters to the manatee-rich mangroves of the coast's north. And the spring-break party crowd rarely get in the way of the sophisticates, as there's enough of it all to go around.

The Gulf Coast's beauty is its main attraction, but variety is a close second: Tampa, St Petersburg, Sarasota and Naples: all offer urban class and exquisite cuisine. There's also family-friendly resorts and theme parks, plus secluded islands and wildlife escapes with rare panthers.

TAMPA BAY

Surrounding the gorgeous deep-water Tampa Bay are two major cities and a seemingly endless expanse of urban-suburban sprawl, forming the state's second-largest metropolitan area. But fear not: the Gulf Coast is edged by some 35 miles of barrier-island beaches. Not many places in the country offer as much big-city sophistication mere minutes from so much dazzling sand. Both Tampa and St Petersburg burble with cultural and culinary excitement as they spruce up their historic districts and polish their arts institutions. The range of adventures on offer – from fine arts to world-class aquariums to hot nightclubs and dolphin cruises – make this compelling region worth a few days of your time.

Tampa

813 / POP 392,890

Often forgotten by tourists in the rush to Miami and Orlando, Tampa has always flown a little below the radar, but this is one city that's really on the upswing. In the heart of downtown, the revitalized Riverwalk along the Hillsborough River glitters with contemporary architecture. For families, there are world-class museums, a fine aquarium, and exciting theme parks. Tampa's sporting teams are among the best in the US and catching a game should be high on the list for sports fans. Within Tampa, Ybor City is both the epicentre of what may just be Florida's most diverse eating scene and southwest Florida's hottest bar and nightclub scene.

Sights

Downtown & the Port

★ Florida Aquarium   AQUARIUM
(813-273-4000; www.flaquarium.org; 701 Channelside Dr; adult/child from $26/22; 9:30am-5pm;) Tampa's excellent aquarium is among the state's best. Cleverly designed, the re-created swamp lets you walk among herons and ibis as they prowl the mangroves. Programs let you swim with the fish (and the sharks) or take a catamaran ecotour in Tampa Bay – check the website carefully before visiting and consider buying one of the the combo tickets that take in additional activities. For better crowd control, tickets are priced by entry time. Parking costs $6.

Tampa Bay History Center   MUSEUM
(813-228-0097; www.tampabayhistorycenter. org; 801 Water St; adult/child $15/11; 10am-5pm) This first-rate history museum presents the region's Seminole and Miccosukee peoples, Cracker pioneers and cattle breeders, and Tampa's Cuban community and cigar industry – it's a fascinating story. The cartography collection, spanning six centuries, dazzles. At the time of research, the museum had just announced an $11-million expansion involving pirate history and a 60ft replica of a pirate ship.

Florida Museum of
Photographic Arts   MUSEUM
(FMoPA; 813-221-2222; www.fmopa.org; the Cube, 400 N Ashley Dr; adult/student $10/8; 11am-6pm Mon-Thu, to 7pm Fri, noon-5pm Sat & Sun) This small, intimate photography museum is housed on the 2nd and 3rd stories of the Cube, a five-story atrium in downtown Tampa. In addition to a permanent collection from Harold Edgerton and Len Prince, temporary exhibits have included the work of Ansel Adams, Andy Warhol and contemporary photographers such as Jerry Uelsmann. Photography courses are also offered.

Tampa Riverwalk   WATERFRONT
(www.thetampariverwalk.com) Downtown, the attractive Tampa Riverwalk connects most sights. Located along the Hillsborough River, this undulating green space, with playgrounds and restrooms, makes a pretty walk from the museums edging Curtis Hixon Park, past the Convention Center, to the aquarium at the far end.

Tampa Museum of Art   MUSEUM
(813-274-8130; www.tampamuseum.org; 120 W Gasparilla Plaza; adult/student $15/5; 10am-5pm Mon-Wed & Fri-Sun, to 8pm Thu) Architect Stanley Saitowitz's dramatically cantilevered museum building appears to float above Curtis Hixon Park overlooking the Hillsborough River. Inside its sculptural shell, six galleries house a permanent collection of Greek and Roman antiquities beside contemporary exhibitions of photography and new media.

Glazer Children's Museum   MUSEUM
(813-443-3861; www.glazermuseum.org; 110 W Gasparilla Plaza; adult/child $15/13; 10am-5pm Mon-Fri, 10am-6pm Sat, 1-6pm Sun;) This crayon-bright, interactive museum provides a creative play space for kids under 10. The staff are delightful and the

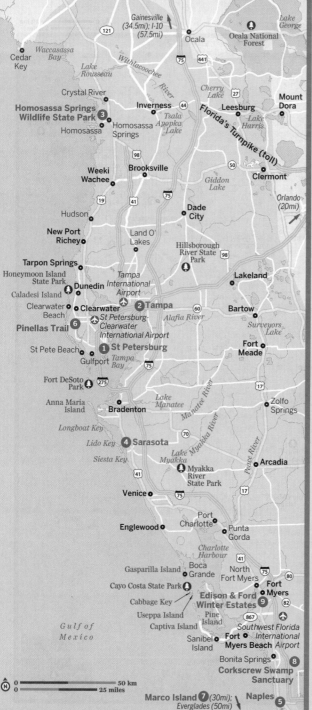

Tampa Bay & Southwest Florida Highlights

1 **St Petersburg** (p409) Sampling craft beer and wandering through Salvador Dalí's dreams in virtual reality.

2 **Tampa** (p396) Spending a few days at roller-coaster-rich Busch Gardens then enjoying a night out in Ybor City.

3 **Homosassa Springs Wildlife State Park** (p423) Paddling the waterways beside manatees.

4 **Sarasota** (p427) Lazing around the marina, visiting the circus museum then learning how to join the circus.

5 **Naples** (p444) Soaking up Southwest Florida's most sophisticated urban center with a glorious beach.

6 **Pinellas Trail** (p412) Freewheeling from St Pete to Tarpon Springs, and rewarding yourself with baklava cheesecake.

7 **Marco Island** (p447) Cruising by mangrove islands and dolphin-spotting.

8 **Corkscrew Swamp Sanctuary** (p445) Admiring bald cypress and wood storks, and watching for panthers.

9 **Edison & Ford Winter Estates** (p436) Studying bright ideas from the region's most famous residents.

Greater Tampa Bay

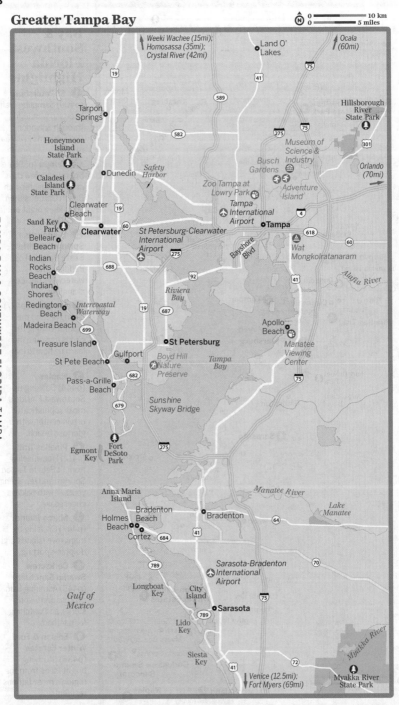

YBOR CITY CIGARS

Tampa's revitalized historic cigar district has a rich heritage. But let's start further south. Due to its proximity to Cuba and its excellent tobacco, Key West had long been the cigar-making capital of the US. When workers started organizing in Key West, the cigar barons figured that the only way to break the union's grip on their factories was to relocate them. In 1886, when Vicénte Martínez Ybor and Ignacio Haya moved their considerable cigar factories – the Principe de Gales (Prince of Wales) and La Flor de la Sanchez y Haya, respectively – to present-day Ybor City, it marked a turning point. Over the next 50 years, Ybor City turned into the cigar capital of the USA, synonymous with quality and epitomized by brands such as Tampa Sweethearts and Hav-a-Tampa. Anyone who loves cigars shouldn't miss Ybor City's annual cigar festival (p401).

Today, the old Tampa Sweethearts factory still stands (at 1301 N 22nd St), and you can learn more about it on an Ybor City historic walking tour (p401).

The most knowledgeable (and legitimate) places to buy cigars in Ybor City:

Metropolitan Cigars (☏813-248-2304; 2014 E 7th Ave; ⊗10am-8pm Mon-Sat, to 4pm Sun) The store itself is actually a humidor; perhaps the best cigar shop in Tampa Bay.

King Corona Cigar Factory (www.kingcoronacigars.com; 1523 E 7th Ave; ⊗9am-midnight Mon-Thu, 9am-2am Fri, 10am-2am Sat, 11am-11pm Sun) The city's largest cigar emporium, complete with an old-fashioned cigar bar.

adjacent Curtis Hixon Park is picnic- and playground-friendly.

⊙ Ybor City

Ybor (ee-bore) City is a short car or trolley ride northeast of downtown. Like the illicit love child of Key West and Miami's Little Havana, this 19th-century district is a multiethnic neighborhood that hosts the Tampa Bay area's hippest party scene. It also preserves a strong Cuban, Spanish and Italian heritage from its days as the epicenter of Tampa's cigar industry. You'll quickly find out why the rooster is Ybor's symbol: the birds are wild and proudly strutting everywhere.

Ybor City Museum State Park   MUSEUM
(☏813-247-6323; www.ybormuseum.org; 1818 E 9th Ave; adult/child under 5 $4/free; ⊗9am-5pm Wed-Sun) This dusty, old-school history museum preserves a bygone era, with cigar-worker houses (open 10am to 3pm) and wonderful photos. The museum has information on a free, self-guided, multimedia tour of Ybor City, accessible with any internet-connected device. The tour includes 21 stops and narration from prominent characters within the community.

⊙ Hyde Park

With Henry B Plant's grand hotel invigorating Tampa's late 19th-century economy, expansion over the river was inevitable. **Old Hyde Park Village** (www.hydeparkvillage.com),

once given over to citrus groves, provided the perfect spot for the city's first suburb. Streetcar services along Swann St and Rome Ave existed as early as 1892. By 1909 the trolley trundled down the 5-mile **Bayshore Boulevard**, which is now lined with some of Tampa's fanciest homes and provides the city's most scenic walking and jogging routes. The Neighborhood Association provides a useful map of the district online.

Henry B Plant Museum   MUSEUM
(☏813-254-1891; www.plantmuseum.com; 401 W Kennedy Blvd; adult/child $10/5; ⊗10am-5pm Tue-Sat, from noon Sun) The silver minarets of Henry B Plant's 1891 Tampa Bay Hotel glint majestically, testimony to the vaunting ambitions of its creator who first brought the railroad to the city – and then extended it so guests could disembark straight into the lobby of his 511-room hotel. Never-before-seen luxuries, such as private baths, telephones and electricity, became the talk of the town, as did the hotel's European decor of Venetian mirrors, French porcelain and exotic furnishings.

Now part of the University of Tampa, one section re-creates the original hotel's gilded late-Victorian world.

⊙ Greater Tampa

Wat Mongkolratanaram   BUDDHIST TEMPLE
(☏813-621-1669; https://wattampainenglish.com; 5306 Palm River Rd; ⊗8:30am-2pm Sun) On

Downtown Tampa

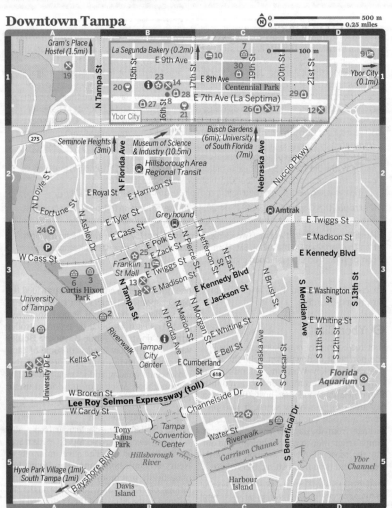

Sundays hundreds of people show up at this striking Buddhist temple for the food and flower markets, lining up for a much-loved beef soup with fish balls. Visitors can also enter the temple barefoot and enjoy traditional music. Orchids and bonsai trees are for sale, as are Thai iced teas, egg rolls and a variety of strange and wonderful desserts (go for the pumpkin cake).

Zoo Tampa at Lowry Park ZOO
(☏ 813-935-8552; https://zootampa.org; 1101 W Sligh Ave; adult/child from $37/27; ⊗ 9:30am-5pm; ⓟ 👶) North of downtown, Tampa's zoo gets you as close to the animals as

possible, with several Florida specialties in the Native Florida Wildlife Habitat, including the critically endangered Florida panther, alligators, black bears and manatees. Other highlights include free-flight aviaries, giraffe feeding, a wallaby enclosure and a rhino 'encounter.'

Manatee Viewing Center WILDLIFE RESERVE
(☏ 813-228-4289; www.tampaelectric.com/manatee; 6990 Dickman Rd, Apollo Beach; ⊗ 10am-5pm Nov–mid-Apr) FREE One of Florida's more surreal wildlife encounters is spotting manatees in the warm-water discharge canals of coal-fired power plants. These placid mammals

Downtown Tampa

show up here so reliably from November through April that this is now a protected sanctuary. Tarpon and sharks can be spotted as well, and a new interactive stingray exhibit in a 10,000-gallon tank allows up-close interaction. The latter can be touched (two fingers only!).

A snack bar, bathrooms and picnic tables round out the sight. It's half an hour from downtown Tampa; take I-75 south to exit 246 and follow the signs.

Museum of Science & Industry   MUSEUM
(MOSI; 📞 813-987-6000; www.mosi.org; 4801 E Fowler Ave; adult/child $13/8, parking $5; ⊙ 10am-5pm; 🅿 ♿) There's something intriguing for all ages at this interactive science museum. Younger kids go straight to Kids in Charge, where a wealth of hands-on activities hides science beneath unadorned play. The frank human body exhibit – with 3D printed fetuses and cautionary looks at pregnancy and health – is best for older kids. Don't miss the IMAX movie; it's included with admission.

🚶 Tours

Ybor City Historic Walking Tours   WALKING
(📞 813-505-6779; www.yborwalkingtours.com; adult/child $20/10) For a guided, 90-minute walking tour of Ybor City, reserve ahead with Ybor City Historic Walking Tours; they typically run twice daily, at 11am and 2pm.

Tours meet at the Vicente Martinez Ybor statue at 7th Ave and 16th St.

🎉 Festivals & Events

Gasparilla Pirate Festival   CULTURAL
(www.gasparillapiratefest.com; ⊙ Jan) On the last Saturday in January, pirates invade and parade in Tampa's version of Mardi Gras.

Florida State Fair   CULTURAL
(www.floridastatefair.com; 4800 US Hwy 301; weekday/weekend $12/14, weekday/weekend rides armband $30/40; ⊙ Feb) Classic Americana for more than 100 years; enjoy rides, food and livestock for two weeks in February.

Gasparilla Music Festival   MUSIC
(📞 813-708-8423; https://gasparillamusic.com; Curtis Hixon Park; ⊙ Mar) Multi-genre music festival on the first or second weekend in March.

Ybor City Cigar Heritage Festival   CULTURAL
(📞 813-358-3455; www.yborcitycigarfestival.com; 1800 E 8th Ave, Centennial Park; ⊙ early Dec) Music and cigars in Centennial Park in early December.

🛏 Sleeping

Gram's Place Hostel   HOSTEL $
(📞 813-221-0596; www.grams-inn-tampa.com; 3109 N Ola Ave, Seminole Heights; dm $28, r $55-65; ❄ @ 🛜) As charismatic as an aging rock

ℹ️ BUSCH GARDENS HOTELS

Near Busch Gardens, at the corner of Busch Blvd and 30th St, you'll find several midrange chain hotels. While they may advertise being 'walkable' to the theme park, it is an extremely long walk that isn't recommended (especially with young kids). Just north of Busch Gardens and across from the University of South Florida, Fowler Ave is also home to a string of dependable midrange chains.

star, Gram's is a small, welcoming hostel for international travelers who prefer personality over perfect linens. Dig the in-ground hot tub. Simple breakfast is included, but there are two fully serviced kitchens. Gram's Place is in Seminole Heights, 2 miles north of the Museum of Art.

Tahitian Inn HOTEL **$$**
(☎813-877-6721; www.tahitianinn.com; 601 S Dale Mabry Hwy, South Tampa; r/ste from $139/199; P❄@🛜🏊🐕) The name is reminiscent of a tiki-themed motel, but this family-owned, full-service hotel offers fresh, boutique stylings on the cheap. There's a nice pool, and the quaint cafe offers outdoor seating by a waterfall and pond. Also, pets are welcome and airport/cruise terminal transportation is included (guests only).

Hilton Garden Inn Ybor City HOTEL **$$**
(☎813-769-9267; www.hiltongardeninn.com; 1700 E 9th Ave, Ybor City; r from $185; P❄🛜🏊) This attractive, efficient and friendly branch of the Hilton Garden chain is just a few blocks from 7th Ave. Rooms are vast and comfortable; there's a nice, private pool area; and the breakfast is generous and cooked to order. An on-call free shuttle is also available for those who want to head downtown.

Hampton Inn &
Suites Ybor City HOTEL **$$**
(☎813-247-6700; www.hilton.com/en/hampton; 1301 E 7th Ave, Ybor City; r from $185; P❄🛜🏊) The red-brick Hampton Inn offers a good level of comfort, a free shuttle downtown and a tiny pool. Its 7th Ave location is perfect for Ybor City's bars and restaurants.

★**Epicurean Hotel** BOUTIQUE HOTEL **$$$**
(☎813-999-8700; www.epicureanhotel.com; 1207 S Howard Ave, South Tampa; r/ste from $314/449;

P❄@🛜🏊) Foodies rejoice! Tampa's coolest hotel, which opened in 2014, is a food-and-drink-themed boutique Eden steeped in detailed design: a zinc bar, reclaimed woods from an 1820s railway station, oversize kitchen tools as door handles, supremely comfortable rooms. The bathrooms even have rugs – it's opulent to the extreme. Warm-toned rooms and one of Tampa's only rooftop bars round out the craft-curated experience.

Le Meridien Tampa HISTORIC HOTEL **$$$**
(☎813-221-9555; www.lemeridientampa.com; 601 North Florida Ave; r from $275; P❄🛜🏊) If you've longed to see the bowels of a federal courthouse but are hesitant to commit crimes, here's your chance. Le Meridien painstakingly restored this century-old courthouse, where judges' chambers and courtrooms now serve as guest rooms and a witness stand has become the front desk for the restaurant, Bizou Brasserie. Also preserved are the crown molding, terrazzo marble and judges' benches.

🍴 Eating

Tampa has an excellent restaurant scene, though precious little is downtown. Ybor City is jam-packed with restaurants, particularly Spanish and Italian, while the Seminole Heights neighborhood (along Florida Ave) is a hipster hangout. Other good spots include gentrified Hyde Park Village, south of downtown, and design-savvy Palma Ceia. SoHo (South Howard Ave) in South Tampa has been dubbed 'restaurant row'; the stretch between Kennedy and Bayshore Blvds is prime.

🍴 Downtown

Taco Bus MEXICAN **$**
(☎813-397-2800; https://taco-bus.com; 505 Franklin St; mains $6.50-12; ⏱11am-midnight Sun-Thu, to 2am Fri & Sat) Taco Bus serves up Mexican comfort food for everyone from cool kids to suits in an informal downtown setting. It's a simple place and the food is damned good.

Oxford Exchange AMERICAN **$$**
(☎813-253-0222; www.oxfordexchange.com; 420 W Kennedy Blvd; mains $12-33; ⏱7:30am-5pm Mon-Wed & Fri, to 9pm Thu, 9am-5pm Sat, 9am-8pm Sun) Built in 1891 as a stable for the Harry B Plant hotel, the reimagined Oxford Exchange takes its inspiration from the

THEME PARKS OF TAMPA

Orlando doesn't hold a monopoly on Florida theme parks. Tampa presents two enormous thrill-seeker destinations: the Africa-themed Busch Gardens, which has some of the country's best roller coasters, and the adjacent Adventure Island water park. If you'll be visiting both, get combo tickets.

Both parks are about 7 miles north of downtown Tampa; take I-275 north to exit 50/Busch Blvd and follow signs. Expect to pay around $20 for parking.

Adventure Island (☑888-800-5447; www.adventureisland.com; 10001 McKinley Dr; admission from $51, parking $15; ☉hours vary) This 30-acre water park has everything a modern, top-flight water park requires: a long lazy river, a huge wave pool, bucket-dumping splash zones, a swimming pool, sandy lounge areas, and enough twisting, plunging, adrenaline-fueled waterslides to keep teens lining up till closing. Adventure Island also features outdoor cafes, picnic and sunbathing areas, a gift shop and a championship sand volleyball complex.

Busch Gardens (☑813-884-4386; www.buschgardenstampa.com; 10165 McKinley Dr; admission from $85, parking $25; ☉10am-6pm, hours vary) This theme park has 10 loosely named African zones, which flow together without much fuss. The entire park is walkable. Admission includes three types of fun: epic roller coasters and rides, animal encounters, and various shows, performances and entertainment. All are spread throughout the park, so successful days require some planning: check show schedules before arriving and plan what rides and animals to visit around the shows. For more on how to interact with manatees responsibly, see the boxed text on p425. Busch Gardens highlights:

Egypt Home to a unique spin coaster called Cobra's Curse featuring a 70ft vertical lift and an encounter with an 80ft snake. There's also Montu, one of the tallest and longest inverted roller coasters in the world.

Pantopia The re-imagined Pantopia drips with elaborate jewels and features animal- and travel-themed restaurants, entertainment, shopping, an indoor theater and rides, of course. At its center is Falcon's Fury, a 335ft-high freestanding drop tower (America's tallest) that plunges riders earthward at 60mph.

Serengeti Plain This 65-acre habitat mimics the African plains, with free-roaming animals including reticulated giraffe, rhino and wildebeest. You can view it from the Serengeti Railway train ride, a Skyride gondola, various walkways or the Serengeti Safari Tour (from $29 to $44 per person), which lets you feed giraffes.

Edge of Africa A walking safari with sightings of hippopotamuses, lions, lemurs, meerkats and crocodiles in an African fishing village. Also here is the ride Cheetah Hunt, a low-to-the-ground scream-fest meant to mimic a cheetah's acceleration.

Morocco You'll find Gwazi, a huge but traditional wooden coaster, along with monkey and ape encounters and the Moroccan Palace Theater, which puts on *Iceploration,* the park's most impressive ice show, combining world-class skaters, larger-than-life puppets, original music and animal stars.

Nairobi Devoted mostly to animals, Nairobi features an elephant interaction area and a flamingo petting station at Animal Connections. The Animal Care Center offers educational behind-the-scenes tours of vets at work with some of the park's 12,000 animals.

Congo The Kumba roller coaster is a long-standing favorite. It features three gulp-inducing loops and a 360-degree spiral. Recover on the Congo River Rapids water ride.

Jungala Designed for younger kids, Jungala has a fantastic climbing structure, a splash area and a zipline ride, as well as encounters with tigers and orangutans.

Stanleyville Another all-star coaster, SheiKra is North America's first dive coaster, which plunges straight down and even goes underground.

Sesame Street Safari of Fun & Bird Gardens The *Sesame Street*–themed Safari of Fun has awesome fenced-in play and climbing structures and splash zones. Don't miss the Elmo and Friends show; reserve ahead to dine with costumed characters. Adjacent Bird Gardens has the quintessential flock of flamingos and a walk-in aviary.

TAMPA BAY SPORTS

Tampa Bay is home to a number of major league sports teams and is certainly the epicenter of Florida's sporting success.

The **Tampa Bay Buccaneers** (www.buccaneers.com) football team won Super Bowl XXXVII in 2002 and consistently reached the NFL play-offs. Their signing of legendary quarterback Tom Brady from the New England Patriots in 2020 raised hopes among Buccaneers fans to fever pitch. The Buccaneers are owned by the Glazer family, who also own Manchester United FC in the UK. The Tampa Bay Buccaneers play their home games at the **Raymond James Stadium** (813-350-6500; http://raymondjamesstadium.com; 4201 N Dale Mabry Hwy) from August (preseason) to December. Single-game tickets can be hard to come by, but try www.buccaneers.com/tickets. Otherwise, Tampa's biggest college-football event is the **Outback Bowl** (813-874-2695; www.outbackbowl.com; Cnr West Tampa Bay Blvd & Dale Mabry Hwy, Raymond James Stadium; tickets from $80; 1 Jan), an NCAA (National Collegiate Athletic Association) football game held on New Year's Day.

The **Tampa Bay Lightning** NHL ice hockey team (www.nhl.com/lightning) is another hugely successful franchise; they won the Stanley Cup in 2003-2004. The Lightning play at **Amalie Arena** (813-301-6500; www.amaliearena.com; 401 Channelside Dr) from October to April. The arena also hosts basketball games, wrestling, football, concerts and ice shows. For tickets, try www.nhl.com/lightning/tickets/single-game-tickets.

Based in St Petersburg, the **Tampa Bay Rays** (www.mlb.com/rays/) play Major League Baseball from April to September and they consistently reach the play-offs; they came runners-up in the 2008 World Series. They play at St Petersburg's **Tropicana Field** (www.mlb.com/rays; cnr 1st Ave S & 16th St S; tickets $9-85) where there's a 360-degree walkway around the ballpark from which fans can observe the action. Huge parking lots line 10th St S near 1st Ave S. For single-game tickets, try https://www.mlb.com/rays/tickets. Baseball fans also won't want to miss the New York Yankees playing spring-training baseball games in March at Tampa's **George M Steinbrenner Field** (813-875-7753; www.gmsfield.com; 1 Steinbrenner Dr), the 10,000-seat stadium modeled after the 'House that Ruth Built' (ie Yankee Stadium in New York).

College sports are also followed avidly in Tampa: the USF Bulls (https://gousfbulls.com) field competitive football, baseball, basketball and other teams. Basketball teams play in the **Yuengling Center** (813-974-3111; www.yuenglingcenter.com; 12499 USF Bull Run Dr) and football games are held at Raymond James Stadium.

venerable Wolseley in London. The American menu is served beneath sculptural palm fronds in a greenhouse atrium, and there's also a wood-paneled bookstore, a Buddy Brew coffee stand and TeBella bar. Beer, wine, craft cocktails and cold-pressed juices are all on offer.

Dio   MEDITERRANEAN $$
(813-341-2525; www.diotampa.com; 519 N Franklin St; mains $12-29; 11am-midnight Mon-Thu, 11am-2am Fri, 8am-2am Sat, 8am-midnight Sun) A beacon of quiet sophistication in the downtown area where good choices are few, Dio is part cafe, part bistro, serving up Lebanese mezze, Greek souvlaki, Italian paninis and all sorts of sandwiches, wraps and salads; the veggie bowls are excellent. It's also good for a lazy coffee at any time.

★ **Ulele**   AMERICAN $$$
(813-999-4952; www.ulele.com; 1810 N Highland Ave; lunch mains $6-15, dinner mains $19-42; 11am-10pm Sun-Thu, to 9pm Fri & Sat;) In a pleasant Riverwalk setting, this former water-pumping station has been transformed into an enchanting restaurant and brewery whose menu harkens back to native Floridian staples made over for modern times. That means liberal use of datil peppers, sides like alligator beans and okra fries (amazing!), mains like local pompano fish and desserts such as guava pie.

Mise en Place   MODERN AMERICAN $$$
(813-254-5373; www.miseonline.com; 442 W Kennedy Blvd; lunch mains $11-16, dinner mains $20-35; 11:30am-2:30pm & 5:30-10pm Tue-Fri, 5:30-11pm Sat) This landmark Tampa restaurant has been a destination for romantic, sophisticated dining for more than 30 years.

The menu emphasizes contemporary American cuisine with Floribbean accents, and constantly evolves with nods to culinary fashions without ever feeling pretentious or 'trendy'. Go all out with the great-value 'Get Blitzed' tasting menu ($60) with wine pairings (an additional $40).

✗ Ybor City

La Segunda Bakery
BAKERY $

(☑813-248-1531; www.lasegundabakery.com; 2512 N 15th St; mains $5-14; ☺6:30am-3pm) At 15th Ave and 15th St, just north of Ybor's main drag, this authentic Spanish bakery cranks out delicious breads and pastries, rich Cuban coffee and maybe Tampa's best Cuban sandwich. Here since 1915, it bustles every morning with a cross section of Tampa society.

Hyppo
ICE CREAM $

(☑813-644-4289; www.thehyppo.com; 1600 E 8th Ave; popsicles from $5; ☺11am-10pm Sun-Wed, to 11pm Thu, to midnight Fri & Sat) On a balmy Tampa evening, there's nothing better than one of Hyppo's weird-and-wonderful popsicle flavours. Try blood-orange cheesecake, peanut butter pie or champagne mango.

★ Columbia Restaurant
SPANISH $$

(☑813-248-4961; www.columbiarestaurant.com; 2117 E 7th Ave; tapas from $5, mains $15-32; ☺11am-10pm Mon-Thu, to 11pm Fri & Sat, noon-9pm Sun) Celebrating its centennial in 2015, this Spanish Cuban restaurant is the oldest in Florida. Occupying an entire block, it consists of 15 elegant dining rooms and romantic, fountain-centered courtyards. Many of the gloved waiters have been here a lifetime, and owner Richard Gonzmart is zealous about authentic Spanish and Cuban cuisine.

Reserve ahead for twice-nightly flamenco Monday to Saturday and look out for one helluva good birthday party. Even if you can't dine here, it's worth a visit just to take a selfie at the exquisite Don Quixote-themed tiled wall outside.

The Stone Soup Company
AMERICAN $$

(☑813-247-7687; www.xsoup4u.com; 1919 E 7th Ave; mains $8-19; ☺10:30am-9pm Sun-Thu, to 11pm Fri & Sat) The soups here have a devoted following, from the lobster bisque or borscht to Mamma's chicken soup, but they also do dumplings, bowl food and the best Cuban sandwich we tasted. The kitchen gets a little overwhelmed when things are busy, so don't come if you're in a hurry. Otherwise, the food's worth the wait.

✗ South Tampa

Wright's Gourmet House
SANDWICHES $

(☑813-253-3838; www.wrightsgourmet.com; 1200 S Dale Mabry Hwy; sandwiches & salads $6-12; ☺7am-6pm Mon-Fri, 8am-4pm Sat) From the outside this place looks like it could be a paint store. The inside isn't much better; green vinyl tablecloths and bare white walls. But the red velvet cake, pecan pie and monster sandwiches (try the beef martini with roast beef, wine-marinated mushrooms and bacon), well, these explain what all the fuss is about.

★ Restaurant BT
FUSION $$$

(☑813-258-1916; www.restaurantbt.com; 2507 S MacDill Ave; mains $29-45; ☺5-10pm Tue-Thu, to 11pm Fri & Sat) ✐ Chef Trina Nguyan-Batley has combined her high-fashion background and Vietnamese upbringing to create this ultra-chic temple to sustainable, locavore gastronomy. She also has the equally delicious BT To Go down the street, serving lunch and takeout meals from 11am to 7:30pm Monday to Saturday.

Haven
MEDITERRANEAN $$$

(☑813-258-2233; http://haventampa.com; 2208 W Morrison Ave; tapas $8-14, butcher's plates $42, cheese monger plates $47; ☺5-10pm Mon-Thu, to 11pm Fri & Sat, 11am-3pm Sun) In 2015 this ambitious Mediterranean venture opened under the same ownership as its famous neighbor, Bern's Steak House, with a new small-plates and charcuterie-centric concept. It feels refined but casual, and excels in house-aged cocktails, wines preserved with the Coravin system and more than 300 different types of whiskey. The cheese monger plate comes with 18 delicious samples and is worth every penny.

Bern's Steak House
STEAK $$$

(☑813-251-2421; www.bernssteakhouse.com; 1208 S Howard Ave,; steaks for 1-2 people $39-95; ☺5-10pm Sun-Thu, to 11pm Fri & Sat) This legendary, nationally renowned steakhouse is an event as much as a meal. Dress up, order caviar and on-premises dry-aged beef, ask to tour the wine cellar and kitchens, and *don't* skip dessert in the specially designed Harry Waugh Dessert Room. Parking $5 plus valet's tip.

✕ Seminole Heights

Ella's Americana Folk Art Cafe AMERICAN **$$**
(✉ 813-234-1000; www.ellasfolkartcafe.com; 5119
N Nebraska Ave; mains $13-18; ☺ 5-11pm Tue & Wed,
11am-midnight Thu-Sat, 11am-8pm Sun) After one
too many Boozy Suzys the visionary outsider
art on Ella's walls starts to make sense. But
it's not just the eccentric art and cocktails
that keep locals loyal; it's also the cozy vibe,
the heartwarming soul food and the weekly
roster of events from live music to craft beer
and cocktail tastings.

Rooster & the Till FUSION **$$**
(✉ 813-374-8940; www.roosterandthetill.com;
6500 N Florida Ave; plates $8-19, 3-course set
menu $20; ☺ 4-10pm Wed & Thu, to 11pm Fri & Sat)
With an impressive culinary pedigree – and
a recent Best Chef South nomination from
the James Beard Foundation – Ferrell Alva-
rez and Ty Rodriguez are behind Seminole
Heights' most ambitious farm-to-table restaurant. Recently expanded, it specializes in
shared and small plates bursting with flavor, most notably a gnocchi with short ribs,
smoked ricotta and pickled peperonata.

🍸 Drinking & Nightlife

Restaurants with great bars include Mise
en Place (p404) and Ella's Americana Folk
Art Cafe in the Museum of Art. For nightlife, Ybor City is party central; SoHo and
Seminole Heights have a more grown-up
atmosphere. Most clubs are open from 10pm
to 3am Thursday to Saturday and charge a
cover of between $10 and $30. Tampa Bay's
alternative weekly is Creative Loafing (www.
cltampa.com), with event and bar listings.

★ Cigar City Brewing BREWERY
(✉ 813-348-6363; www.cigarcitybrewing.com;
3924 W Spruce St; ☺ 11am-11pm Sun-Thu, to 1am Fri
& Sat) This is Tampa's premier craft brewery,
although the original owners were bought
out in 2016. It has dozens of crafted brews
on tap, some exclusive to the brewery. There
are food trucks in the parking lot in the evenings and all day Saturday, and you can take
tours of the brewery for $8 (with tastings of
beer included). You'll find it west of downtown, north off I-275.

Independent Bar BAR
(✉ 813-341-4883; www.independentbartampa.com;
5016 N Florida Ave, Seminole Heights; ☺ 11am-
midnight Sun-Wed, to 1am Thu-Sat) If you appreciate craft brews, roll into this converted gas
station, now a low-key, hip bar in Seminole
Heights. You can count on one or more local
Cigar City brews and it serves some good
pub grub.

Brew Bus Terminal & Brewery CRAFT BEER
(✉ 813-990-7310; www.brewbususa.com; 4101 N
Florida Ave, Seminole Heights; tours $11-62; ☺ 4-
10pm Mon-Thu, noon-midnight Fri, 11am-midnight
Sat, 11am-8pm Sun) Tampa Bay's craft-beer
scene is booming, so it was only a matter of
time before somebody thought to put people on a bus with the beer and drive them
around. Brew Bus also has its own 'terminal'
(a brewery), and offers public and private
tours a few times a week, getting people
drunk all over the Tampa Bay area.

The most popular option, dubbed 'the full
pour,' departs from the terminal on Saturdays
at noon, bringing craft-beer enthusiasts to
three rotating breweries. They get a pint at
each stop, a tour at one place, and two Brew
Bus beers while in transit. It's $62 per person.

Angry Chair Brewing MICROBREWERY
(✉ 813-238-1122; http://angrychairbrewing.com;
6401 N Florida Ave, Seminole Heights; ☺ 4pm-late
Tue-Wed, 3-11pm Thu, noon-midnight Fri & Sat, noon-
9pm Sun) It's how many craft breweries begin: a bunch of people trying to escape 'the
monotony, the rat race and the white-collar
world' got together and made some beer. In
the convivial tasting room, they serve up
hoppy, fruity pale ales and creamy porters
like Two Pump Chump Porter with Hazelnut, among other tasty brews.

Cigar City Cider & Mead MICROBREWERY
(✉ 813-242-6600; www.cigarcitycider.com; 1812 N
15th St, Ybor City; tours $10; ☺ 3-9pm Wed, 3-11pm
Thu, noon-midnight Fri & Sat, noon-8pm Sun) In
historic Ybor City, this tasting room offers
a good selection of honey and apple-based
booze, all brewed with local, natural ingredients. On Saturdays, tours begin at 5pm and
come with a 12oz pour of hard cider, along
with samples of other ciders and mead.

Club Prana CLUB
(www.clubprana.com; 1619 E 7th Ave, Ybor City;
☺ 9pm-3am Thu-Sat) Many nightclubs come
and go, but Club Prana, rising five floors
from its lounge to the rooftop Sky Bar, has
stood the test of time. There's Flirty Thursdays, Foreplay Fridays...you get the idea.

⭐ Entertainment

Arts Tampa Bay (www.artstampabay.com)
maintains a regional cultural calendar.

WHAT'S COOKING IN SOUTHWEST FLORIDA?

The further south you go in Florida, the more Southern culinary influences wane and Latin inflections take over. Wherever you go, you're rarely far from the coast and seafood is an obsession. These are some of the region's signature dishes and some of the places where you can enjoy them:

Oysters Oysters are served every which way, whether raw or fried: Monk's Steamer Bar (p430); Gramma Dot's (p442)

Smoked fish They'll smoke anything down here, including mackerel, mahimahi, mullet and salmon. Eat it whole or in a sandwich: Ted Peter's Famous Smoked Fish (p419)

Cuban sandwich Ham (and sometimes salami and/or turkey) with Swiss cheese, pickles and mustard: The Stone Soup Company (p405); Main Bar Sandwich Shop (p430); Cider Press Cafe (p414)

Blackened grouper Tasty Gulf white fish with crispy blackened skin: Walt'z Fish Shak (p419); Dry Dock (p434); The Dock at Crayton Cove (p446)

Grouper sandwich Grilled grouper, usually served with salad on your choice of bread: Frenchy's Original Cafe (p421); Dry Dock (p434); Sharky's on the Pier (p436); Snook Inn (p448)

Stone-crab claws Floridians wait anxiously every year for the stone-crab season to begin – it runs from mid-October through to mid-May: Charlie's Fish House (p425); Dixie Fish Company (p440)

Lobster mac-n-cheese American comfort food with a Florida twist: Fresh Catch Bistro (p440)

★ **Skipper's Smokehouse** LIVE MUSIC
(☑813-971-0666; www.skipperssmokehouse.com; 910 Skipper Rd, Village of Tampa; cover $5-25; ☺11am-11pm Tue, 11am-midnight Wed-Fri, noon-midnight Sat, 1-9pm Sun) Like it blew in from the Keys, Skipper's is a beloved, unpretentious open-air venue for blues, folk, reggae and gator-swamp rockabilly, beneath beautiful live oaks. It's 9 miles directly north of downtown, on a side street off N Nebraska Ave.

★ **Tampa Theatre** CINEMA
(☑813-274-8981, box office 813-274-8286; www.tampatheatre.org; 711 N Franklin St; tickets adult/child 2-12yr $12/10) This historic 1926 theater in downtown is a gorgeous venue in which to see an independent film. The mighty Wurlitzer organ plays before most movies. Too bad showtimes are so limited, with only one or two films playing on any given day. Look for special events.

Straz Center for the Performing Arts PERFORMING ARTS
(☑813-229-7827; www.strazcenter.org; 1010 MacInnes Pl) This enormous, multivenue complex draws the gamut of fine-arts performances: touring Broadway shows, pop concerts, opera, ballet, drama and more.

Improv Comedy Theater COMEDY
(☑813-864-4000; www.improvtampa.com; 1600 E 8th Ave, Ybor City; tickets $10-30; ☺8pm Thu, 8pm & 10:30pm Fri, 7:30pm & 10pm Sat, 7pm Sun) This comedy club inside the Centro Ybor complex in Ybor City brings the funny five nights a week with local and national acts. You have to be 21 or over to enter.

🔒 Shopping

The most interesting street shopping is in Ybor City. The Columbia Restaurant (p405) gift shop has a notable selection of hand-painted Spanish ceramics. On 8th Ave between 15th and 17th Sts, **Centro Ybor** (www.centroybor.com) is an attractive shopping, dining and entertainment complex.

SoHo (South Howard St) south of Platt is another trendy stretch with cool finds and boutiques.

Dysfunctional Grace Art Co ART
(☑813-842-0830; www.facebook.com/dysfunctionalgrace; 1903 E 7th Ave, Ybor City; ☺11am-6pm Mon, 10am-6pm Tue-Thu, 10am-8pm Fri & Sat) This creepy but awesome art shop contains curios such as a taxidermic giraffe wearing a monocle and a diaphonized zebra moray eel suspended in glycerine. Everything's pricey, but probably worth it. Looking is free.

WORTH A TRIP

HILLSBOROUGH RIVER STATE PARK

When Tampa residents need a woodsy escape, they head to the fantastic 3400-acre Hillsborough River State Park (☏813-987-6771; www.floridastateparks.org/parks-and-trails/hillsborough-river-state-park; 15402 US 301 N; cyclist/car $2/6; ⊙8am-sunset; ♿), just 20 miles (30 minutes) northeast of Tampa. For visiting families, it provides easy, kid-friendly encounters with Florida's wilderness, and you'll find the region's best (non-beach) camping. The best thing to do is get out on the water (canoes two hours/full day $25/50; kayaks per hour $15), gliding beneath Spanish moss on the look out for raptors, deer, foxes and alligators. Morning is best for spotting wildlife.

The flat, winding park roads also make for scenic cycling (bike rental per hour/day $10/25) and there are more than 10 miles of equally easy hiking trails through pine flatwoods and cypress swamps. In summer the biggest draw is the giant half-acre swimming pool (per person $4). On weekends arrive by 8:30am or it might already be full (then you can't enter till someone leaves).

The pretty 114-site campground (sites $24) has good facilities and solar-heated hot water, but not a lot of privacy. Spots along the river are prime and camping is best (and busiest) during the October to March dry season (book up to a year in advance). Midweek is always less busy.

Ybor City Saturday Market MARKET
(www.ybormarket.com; Centennial Park, 8th Ave & 18th St, Ybor City; ⊙9am-3pm Sat) An outdoor market emphasizing arts, crafts and local food products.

La France VINTAGE
(☏813-248-1381; 1612 E 7th Ave, Ybor City; ⊙11am-8pm Mon-Thu, to 10pm Fri & Sat, noon-7pm Sun) Thanks to an influx of wealthy snowbirds, Tampa has a thriving vintage scene. With four street-front windows rotating displays of flapper dresses, ornamental umbrellas, feathered hats and men's leisure suits, La France is like a living museum without a cover charge. Inside you can browse racks of 1930s maxi-dresses, sparkling 1940s swing dresses and mod suits from the '60s.

Some items are newly made from period designs, while others come from estate sales and private sellers.

ⓘ Information

DANGERS & ANNOYANCES

Tampa has big-city problems with homelessness, panhandlers and crime. Both downtown and Ybor City are safe in themselves, but they are bordered by tough neighborhoods; don't wander aimlessly. Panhandlers tend to gather on the median at traffic lights and approach drivers; to end a solicitation, simply shake your head and don't engage.

MEDIA

For local and Florida-wide news and Tampa happenings, try the **Tampa Bay Times** (www.tampabay.com).

MEDICAL SERVICES

Tampa General Hospital (☏813-844-7000; www.tgh.org; 1 Tampa General Circle, Davis Island; ⊙24hr) South of downtown on Davis Island.

TOURIST INFORMATION

Unlock Tampa Bay Visitors Center (☏813-223-2752; www.visittampabay.com; 201 N Franklin St, Ste 102; ⊙10am-5:30pm Mon-Sat, noon-5pm Sun) Good free maps and lots of information.

Ybor City Visitor Center (☏813-241-8838; www.ybor.org; 1600 E 8th Ave; ⊙10am-5pm Mon-Sat, from noon Sun) Provides an excellent introduction with walking-tour maps and info.

ⓘ Getting There & Away

AIR

Tampa International Airport (p527) is the region's third-busiest hub, connecting Tampa with dozens of cities across the US. It's six miles northwest of downtown, off Hwy 589.

HART bus 30 ($3, 25 minutes, every 30 minutes) picks up and drops off at the Red Arrival Desk on the lower level of the airport; exact change is required. Downtown, it runs along Kennedy Blvd and Whiting St.

All major car agencies have desks at the airport. By car, take I-275 to N Ashley Dr, turn right and you're in downtown.

BOAT

Cruise passengers often start or end Caribbean explorations at **Port Tampa Bay** (☏813-905-7678; www.tampaport.com).

BUS

Greyhound (☑ 813-229-2174; www.greyhound. com; 610 E Polk St) serves the region and connects Tampa with Miami (from $21, eight hours, three daily), Orlando (from $12, 1¾ to 2¼ hours, four daily), Sarasota (from $16, 1½ hours, two daily) and Gainesville (from $25, 5¼ hours, one daily). There's free wi-fi on all buses.

CAR & MOTORCYCLE

➤ Between Tampa and Orlando, take the I-4.

➤ The fastest route to Miami is via I-75 south, which turns east at Naples and meets I-95 south at Fort Lauderdale. Another option, with Everglades detours, is to pick up US 41 (Tamiami Trail) at Naples and follow this directly to Miami.

TRAIN

Amtrak (www.amtrak.com) operates at least one daily shuttle between Tampa and Orlando (from $14, two hours) from **Tampa Union Station** (☑ 800-872-7245; www.amtrak.com; 601 N Nebraska Ave).

❶ Getting Around

Getting around Tampa and between Ybor City and Downtown couldn't be easier, with free tram services.

HART In-Towner (⊙ 6am-8:30am & 3:30-6pm Mon-Fri, 11am-7pm Sat) Within downtown, HART's free trolley runs up and down Florida Ave, Tampa St and Franklin St every 15 minutes.

Hillsborough Area Regional Transit (HART; ☑ 813-254-4278; www.gohart.org; 1211 N Marion St; fares/day passes $2/4) HART buses converge at the Marion Transit Center. Routes service the zoo, Busch Gardens, the Henry B Plant Museum and Ybor City.

TECO Line Streetcars (☑ 813-254-4278; www. tecolinestreetcar.org; ⊙ 7am-10pm Mon-Thu, 7am-2am Fri, 8:30am-2am Sat, 8:30am-11pm Sun) HART's free old-fashioned electric streetcars connect downtown's Marion Transit Center with a number of attractions downtown, along with Ybor City, running every 20 to 30 minutes.

St Petersburg

☑ 727 / POP 265,098

Long known as little more than a bawdy spring-break party town and a retirement capital, St Petersburg is now forging a new name for itself as a culturally savvy Southern city. Spurred on by awe-inspiring downtown murals, a revitalized historic district and the stunning Dalí Museum, the downtown energy is creeping up Central Ave, spawning sophisticated restaurants, craft breweries, farmers markets and artsy galleries. All of which is attracting a younger professional

crowd and a new wave of culturally curious travelers. Get here before it becomes a scene.

◎ Sights

When taking in the sights, visitors can confine themselves to a walkable, T-shaped route: along Central Ave, mainly from 8th St to Bayshore Dr, and along Bayshore Dr from the Dalí Museum to the bayfront parks in the Old Northeast neighborhood. From here the pier juts out to sea. While the pier itself is open to walkers, the iconic, inverted pyramid amusement complex at its end remains closed for redevelopment.

★**Salvador Dalí Museum**　　　MUSEUM
(☑ 727-823-3767; www.thedali.org; 1 Dali Blvd; adult/child 13-17yr/child 6-12yr $28/18/10, after 5pm Thu $12/10/10; ⊙ 11am-6pm Wed, Sat & Sun, 11am-8pm Thu & Fri) The theatrical exterior of the extraordinary Salvador Dalí Museum speaks of great things: out of a wound in the towering white shoe box oozes a 75ft geodesic glass atrium. Even better, what unfolds inside is everything a modern art museum devoted to the life, art and impact of Salvador Dalí should be. Even those with no time for his dripping clocks and curlicue mustache will be awed by the museum and its grand works, such as the *Hallucinogenic Toreador*.

The Dalí Museum's 20,000 sq ft of gallery space was designed to display all 96 oil paintings in the collection, along with key works of each era and medium: drawings, prints, sculptures, photos, manuscripts, movies and even a virtual reality exhibit in which guests enter Dalí's dreams. Everything is arranged chronologically and explained in context. The garden out back is also a delight, with a wish tree, a melting clock bench and a giant steel mustache sculpture.

Excellent, free docent tours occur hourly (on the half hour); these are highly recommended to help crack open the rich symbolism in Dalí's monumental works. Audioguides are also free and contain secret, deeply hilarious narration from a voice claiming to be Dalí's mustache. To top everything off, there's a Catalan-inspired cafe and a first-rate gift store. Up to 5000 people have been known to visit in a day, so get here early or wait for everything.

★**Weedon Island Preserve**　　NATURE RESERVE
(☑ 727-453-6500; www.weedonislandpreserve. org; 1800 Weedon Dr NE; ⊙ 7am-sunset) Like a patchwork quilt of variegated greens tossed

St Petersburg

out over Tampa Bay, this 3190-acre preserve protects a diverse aquatic and wetland ecosystem. At the preserve's heart is the excellent Cultural and Natural History Center (open 9am to 4pm Thursday to Saturday and 11am to 4pm Sunday) with exhibits about the natural environment and the early Weedon Island people. Sign up for interpretive boardwalk hikes, or go alone with the online map. The preserve is on Riviera Bay, south off I-92.

St Pete Pier   WATERFRONT
(www.stpetepier.org; off 2nd Ave NE; ☺sunrise-11pm; ⊞) New in 2020, this 26-acre park extending into Tampa Bay has green spaces, public artwork, picnic areas, waterfront restaurants and a marketplace where local vendors sell their wares. Kids will enjoy the splash pad, a sprawling playground area, a new beach area, and a hands-on aquatic themed Discovery Center (adult/child $5/3). The Pier hosts a range of events, including

free outdoor concerts, film screenings and sunset yoga classes.

Don't miss the *Bending Arc*, a tall billowing net sculpture that moves in mesmerizing waves against the breeze, and is also lit up at night.

Chihuly Collection   GALLERY
(☏727-896-4527; www.moreanartscenter.org/chihuly; 720 Central Ave; adult/student $20/13; ☺10am-5pm Mon-Sat, from noon Sun) Dale Chihuly's glass works are displayed at the Metropolitan Museum of Art in New York, the Victoria and Albert Museum (V&A) in London and the Louvre in Paris. But his permanent collection resides here in St Petersburg, at a new location on Central Ave housing his principal works, *Ruby Red Icicle Chandelier* and the multicolored *Persians* ceiling.

The space also contains a meditation garden and a theater that screens a rotation of documentary films. Tickets for the gal-

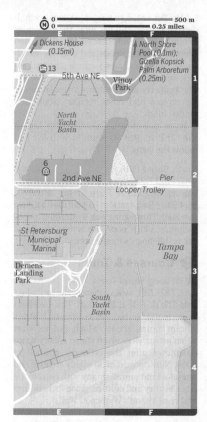

Ⓝ 0 ——————— 500 m
0 ——————— 0.25 miles

Dickens House (0.15mi)

North Shore Pool (0.1mi); Gizella Kopsick Palm Arboretum (0.25mi)

⬛13
5th Ave NE
Vinoy Park

North Yacht Basin

6 🏛
2nd Ave NE
Pier
Looper Trolley

St Petersburg Municipal Marina

Tampa Bay

Demens Landing Park

South Yacht Basin

TAMPA BAY & SOUTHWEST FLORIDA ST PETERSBURG

lery include a glass-blowing demonstration across the street at the affiliated Morean Arts Center.

Morean Arts Center   ARTS CENTER
(☏ 727-822-7872; www.moreanartscenter.org; 719 Central Ave; ⊘10am-5pm Mon-Sat, from noon Sun) FREE This lively community arts center hosts interesting rotating exhibits in all media. If you love glass, don't miss Morean's attached **Morean Glass Studio** where full-blast glassmaking demonstrations occur every hour from 11am to 4pm Monday to Saturday and 1pm to 4pm Sunday. Reserve ahead for a one-on-one 'hot glass experience' ($75) and take home your own creation.

Ask also about its pottery workshops.

Florida Holocaust Museum   MUSEUM
(☏ 727-820-0100; www.flholocaustmuseum.org; 55 5th St S; adult/student $16/8; ⊘10am-5pm) The understated exhibits of this Holocaust museum, one of the country's largest, present mid-20th-century events with moving directness. Temporary, contemporary art exhibits loosely related to the Holocaust and other human rights issues are also displayed. Note: if your car is left in the parking lot a minute past 5pm, it will likely be towed.

St Petersburg
Museum of Fine Arts MUSEUM
(☑727-896-2667; www.mfastpete.org; 255 Beach Dr NE; adult/child 7-18yr $20/10; ☺10am-5pm Tue, Wed & Sat, noon-8pm Thu & Fri, noon-5pm Sun) The Museum of Fine Arts' collection is broad, traversing the world's antiquities and following art's progression through nearly every era.

St Petersburg Museum of History MUSEUM
(☑727-894-1052; www.spmoh.org; 335 2nd Ave NE; adult/child 6-17yr $15/9; ☺10am-5pm Mon-Sat, from noon Sun) As city history museums go, St Pete's is intriguingly oddball: a real 3000-year-old mummy, a two-headed calf and a life-size replica of a Benoist plane, plus exhibits on the bay's ecology and the Tampa Bay Rays baseball team, along with the world's largest collection of autographed baseballs.

Gizella Kopsick Palm Arboretum PARK
(www.stpeteparksrec.org/gizellakopsick; North Shore Dr; ☺sunrise-sunset) FREE This is an open 2-acre garden of more than 800 palms, all signed and lovingly landscaped. There are also large parking lots here and a long, white-sand swimming beach. Keep going along the paved trail, past pretty homes and private docks, all the way to small Coffee Pot Park, where manatees can occasionally be spotted.

Activities
★Pinellas Trail CYCLING
(☑727-582-2100; www.pinellascounty.org/trailgd) This 47-mile county-maintained trail along an abandoned railroad corridor calls to dedicated urban cyclists and runners. The paved path starts along 1st Ave S and Bayshore Dr in St Petersburg and continues, through town, country and suburb, north to Tarpon Springs. Download trail maps and route details online.

Sweetwater Kayak KAYAKING
(☑727-570-4844; www.sweetwaterkayaks.com; 1800 Weedon Dr NE; kayaks per 2/4hr $34/40, SUP per 2/4hr $40/50; ☺rentals 9am-5pm) This local outfitter has the largest selection of seawater kayaks in the area. Knowledgeable staff also lead lessons in foundation skills, sea kayaking and paddleboard yoga, and guide tours (call for prices/scheduling) off Weedon Island Preserve and other nearby St Pete waterways.

Boyd Hill Nature Preserve HIKING
(☑727-893-7326; 1101 Country Club Way S; adult/child $3/1.50; ☺9am-7pm Sun & Tue-Fri, 7am-7pm Sat Mar-Oct, until 6pm Nov-Feb) A low-key hidden oasis, Boyd Hill has more than 6.5 miles of nature trails and boardwalks amid its 390 acres of pine flatwoods and swampy woodlands. Alligators, snowy egrets and bald eagles are among the wildlife you might see. The property also contains a rescue center for raptors and hosts regular events and guided hikes.

From downtown, follow Martin Luther King Jr Blvd (9th St) south to 50th Ave and follow the signs.

North Shore Pool SWIMMING
(☑727-893-7727; www.stpeteparksrec.org/north-shoreaquatic; 901 N Shore Dr NE; adult/child $5/4.50; ☺9am-4pm Mon-Fri, from 10am Sat, from 1pm Sun) Three gorgeous swimming pools, including a kids' pool with waterslide. Rents out paddleboards by the hour.

Courses & Tours
★Walking Mural Tours CULTURAL
(☑727-821-7391; www.stpetemuraltour.com; adult/child $19/11; ☺10-11:30am Sat) This excellent walking tour introduces visitors to St Pete's vibrant mural scene, which got its start when artists were given cheap gallery space downtown after the economy crashed in 2008. Now upward of 30 highly creative and one-of-a-kind murals, many with nods to the city's history and culture, grace its buildings and rival Miami's Wynwood Walls.

The tour begins at the Florida CraftArt (p416), which partnered with St Pete Mural Tour to begin offering the walks. Proceeds go toward commissioning more murals.

St Pete Preservation Walking Tours WALKING
(☑727-824-7802; www.stpetepreservation.org; walking/bicycle tours $10/25; ☺10am Sat Oct-Apr) Join these two-hour tours run by knowledgeable docents from the Preservation Society. Tours take in historic downtown architecture and well-preserved suburbs such as Old Northeast, Bahama Shores and Kenwood. Check the website for meeting points.

Festivals & Events
Art Walk ART
(https://stpeteartsalliance.org/artwalk; ☺5-9pm 2nd Sat of the month) This monthly art event takes place on the second Saturday of each month and involves all the major downtown galleries. You can easily walk the route or you can hop aboard the free trolley service.

Mainsail Arts Festival CULTURAL
(www.mainsailart.org; Vinoy Park; ☺Apr) Live music, food and kids' activities sit alongside 200 art-and-craft exhibitors at this two-day art extravaganza.

Tampa Bay Blues Festival MUSIC
(www.tampabaybluesfest.com; Vinoy Park; three-day pass $110; ☺Apr) Three days of first-rate blues in early April.

International Folk Fair CULTURAL
(www.spiffs.org; Vinoy Park; ☺Oct) A four-day fair in late October showcasing different cultures through traditional foods, crafts and folk dancing.

🛏 Sleeping

With its impressive stock of period homes and newly minted waterfront hotels, St Petersburg has an excellent selection of accommodations. That said, many of the old, locally owned favorites are struggling and even going out of business because they can't compete with the rise of home-sharing services.

Avalon St Petersburg BOUTIQUE HOTEL $
(☑727-317-5508; www.avalonstpetersburg.com; 443 4th Ave N; r/apt from $105/129; 🅿️✳@🛜🏊) Behind the pretty art deco facade, the rooms at this boutique belle have contrasting dark-and-silver colour schemes with splashes of colour. The rooms are classy, the service is professional and the downtown location excellent. It shares a pool with its sister property, Hollander Hotel (☑727-873-7900; www.hollanderhotel.com; 421 4th Ave N; r $115-198; 🅿️⚅✳🛜🏊), a few doors up.

The Cordova Inn BOUTIQUE HOTEL $
(☑727-822-7500; www.cordovainnstpete.com; 253 2nd Ave N; r $89-149; 🅿️✳@🛜) Built in 1921, this stately inn has a gorgeous porch overlooking the street and understated period rooms with claw-foot bathtubs. Some are asplash with modern murals. Service is friendly and helpful and a light breakfast is included in the price. Parking right next door costs $10 per night.

★Dickens House B&B $$
(☑727-822-8622; www.dickenshouse.com; 335 8th Ave NE; r $155-275; 🅿️⚅✳🛜) Five lushly designed rooms await in this passionately restored 1912 Arts and Crafts–style home. The gay-friendly owners whip up a gourmet breakfast often involving egg-white frittata. There's a lovely fern and bamboo garden as well.

Watergarden Inn at the Bay INN $$
(☑727-822-1700; www.innatthebay.com; 126 4th Ave N; r $135-195, ste $200-295; 🅿️✳🛜🏊) This fabulous 1910 inn carved from two old neighborhood houses offers 14 rooms and suites in a mature, half-acre garden. Outside a bright tropical palette and palm-fringed pool give the complex a beachy Key West vibe, while inside four-poster beds, two-person Jacuzzis and fluffy robes conjure romance. The owners are sociable and kind.

Ponce de Leon BOUTIQUE HOTEL $$
(☑727-550-9300; www.poncedeleonhotel.com; 95 Central Ave; r from $118; ✳@🛜) Styling itself as a boutique hotel in the heart of downtown, this place tries hard with bold colours, splashy murals and almost-designer-cool decor; off-site parking is a bummer.

Birchwood Inn BOUTIQUE HOTEL $$$
(☑727-896-1080; www.thebirchwood.com; 340 Beach Dr NE; r incl breakfast from $270; 🅿️✳✳) Rooms are simply gorgeous at this boutique gem: spacious, with claw-foot baths and king canopy beds, and oozing vintage bordello elegance sexed up with a little South Beach sauciness. Canopy (p415), the rooftop bar, is the hottest spot in town for cocktails.

Renaissance Vinoy Resort HOTEL $$$
(☑727-894-1000; www.vinoyrenaissanceresort.com; 501 5th Ave NE; r $185-479; 🅿️✳@🛜🏊) St Pete's coral-pink grande dame, the lavishly renovated 1925 Vinoy, is a sumptuous concoction of period style and 21st-century comforts, including an 18-hole golf course, a private marina, tennis courts, five restaurants and a 5000-sq-ft fitness center. Take note of off-season and online deals. It's worth it just for the gorgeous pool.

🍴 Eating

St Pete's restaurant scene has exploded in recent years, rivaling Tampa just across the bay for its innovative new concepts and exciting openings. Beach Dr remains a well-heeled scene lined with attractive waterfront restaurants, but Central Ave is particularly great for its more experimental and ambitious culinary projects.

Nitally's Thai-Mex Cuisine FUSION $
(☑727-321-8424; www.thaimex.co; 2462 Central Ave N; mains $8-20; ☺11am-1:30pm & 5:30-9:30pm Tue-Fri, 11am-2pm & 5:30-9pm Sat) Owned by a Thai-Mexican couple, this delicious fusion concept worked its way up from a food

truck to a brick-and-mortar establishment. Items like Thai peanut chicken tortillas and Penang mole burritos are winners, but it's the inferno soup challenge, which dares guests to consume a hospital-trip spicy pepper broth, that put this place on the map.

It costs $50 to attempt the challenge and contestants must also sign a waiver. There are 25 different types of hot peppers in the soup, including one of the world's hottest, the ghost pepper.

Cider Press Cafe
CAFE $

(☏727-914-7222; http://ciderpresscafe.com; 601 Central Ave; mains $12-16; ⊙11am-9pm Mon-Thu, 11am-10pm Fri, 10am-10pm Sat, 10am-8pm Sun; ☞) Cool and contemporary decor, great coffee and a vegan-heavy menu with fresh tastes (try the funky feta burger) and a fine Cuban sandwich. There's also a cool beer list and nice brunch. A place to linger.

The Lure
CAFE $

(☏727-914-8000; https://thelurestpete.com/; 661 Central Ave; mains $9-15; ⊙noon-9pm Mon-Fri, 11am-9pm Sat & Sun) They had us with the sashimi lunch, but there's so much that's good – sushi, tapas, poke, cocktails and a mean meatball sandwich. What's not to like at this friendly sidewalk cafe?

Red Mesa Cantina & Lucha Bar
MEXICAN $

(☏727-896-8226; www.redmesacantina.com; 128 3rd St S; tacos from $4.50, mains $10-17; ⊙11am-10pm Sun-Thu, to 11pm Fri & Sat) Rounding out St Pete's plethora of contemporary ethnic cuisine, Red Mesa dishes up tasty, updated Mexican mains, plus a range of interesting ceviches and tacos. The Oaxacan chef also manages an older, sister restaurant to the north, Red Mesa, and a newer fast-food restaurant and market, Red Mesa Mercado. All are worthwhile.

★ Annata Wine Bar
ITALIAN $$

(☏727-851-9582; www.annatawine.com; 300 Beach Dr NE; charcuterie 3/5 selections $14/20, mains $23-28; ⊙4-10pm Sun-Thu, to 11pm Fri & Sat) This swanky wine bar is an anchor of the Beach Dr restaurant scene and also of St Pete's charcuterie obsession, with a range of meats and cheeses and fine Italian wine pairings that will astonish and delight. Service is friendly and the atmosphere is surprisingly chilled – outside, dogs can be served a board of special treats cleverly dubbed 'paw-cuterie.'

Alésia
FRENCH, VIETNAMESE $$

(☏727-345-9701; http://alesiarestaurant.com; 7204 Central Ave, Pasadena; mains $8-19; ⊙11:30am-2:30pm & 5:30-9pm Tue-Fri, 10am-2:30pm & 5:30-9pm Sat) Lovely Alésia, with its big windows, laid-back soundtrack and umbrella-clad courtyard, is the brainchild of Sandra Ly-Flores, Erika Ly and Paul Hsu, who wanted to re-create the French Vietnamese cafes of their Parisian youth. Here you'll agonize over the tiered pastry selection, breakfast on crepes or *croque monsieur,* and linger over bowls of spicy pho and crunchy summer rolls.

Bella Brava
ITALIAN $$

(☏727-895-5515; www.bellabrava.com; 204 Beach Dr NE; mains $9-27; ⊙11:30am-10pm Mon-Thu, to 11pm Fri & Sat, noon-9:30pm Sun; ☞) Anchoring the prime waterfront intersection, trattoria Bella Brava is exactly the kind of place you'd expect to find along Beach Drive, drawing a noisy crowd of young professionals with its contemporary Italian cooking, pizza menu and cocktail bar. There's also sidewalk seating on Beach Dr.

Chattaway
AMERICAN $$

(☏727-823-1594; https://thechattaway.com; 358 22nd Ave S; mains $9-20; ⊙11am-9:30pm Sun-Thu, to 10pm Fri & Sat) A true slice of Old St Pete, this quirky establishment draws regulars back time and again with high tea, tasty burgers and oversized chicken wings. The relaxed outdoor seating area hosts live music regularly and the service couldn't be friendlier. Dogs welcome. Cash only. It's a 10-minute drive south of the centre, along 4th St S.

Mill
MODERN AMERICAN $$

(☏727-317-3930; www.themillrestaurants.com; 200 Central Ave; charcuterie 3 for $18, mains $15-29; ⊙11am-10pm Tue-Thu, 11am-11pm Fri, 10am-11pm Sat, 10am-10pm Sun) The Mill, with its barnyard-chic interior design, is one of St Pete's *it* restaurants, particularly at brunch. Farm equipment is repurposed as abstract art, with rusty gears, a pitchfork and a saddle all polished and arranged to seem devastatingly hip. Menu items are no less of a production, as has always been the case when serial restaurateur and chef Ted Dorsey gets involved.

★ Brick & Mortar
AMERICAN $$$

(☏727-822-6540; www.facebook.com/brickandmortarkitchen; 539 Central Ave; mains $16-41; ⊙5-9pm Tue, 5-10pm Wed & Thu, 4:30-11pm Fri & Sat) A husband-and-wife catering team launched

ST PETE'S CRAFT BEER CRAZE

Since the opening of Dunedin Brewery across the bay in 1996, there's been a growing enthusiasm for locally produced craft beers in the Tampa Bay area. Tourism officials even started marketing a craft-beer trail from Tarpon Springs to Gulfport. Here are six of St Pete's best downtown breweries:

Brewers Tasting Room (☑727-873-3900; www.brewerstastingroom.com; 11270 4th St N; ⊙11am-11pm Sun-Thu, to midnight Fri & Sat) Experimental brewpub with a rotating lineup of beers made by home brewers, accompanied by Cajun food and live music. Located 10 miles north of the Museum of Art.

3 Daughters Brewing (☑727-495-6002; www.3dbrewing.com; 222 22nd St S; ⊙tasting room 10am-6pm) A 30-barrel brewhouse with a range of styles, from light session beers to barrel-aged stouts.

Green Bench Brewing (☑727-800-9836; http://greenbenchbrewing.com; 1133 Baum Ave N; ⊙noon-10pm Tue-Thu & Sun, to midnight Fri & Sat) A red-brick garage now does duty as a 15-barrel brewhouse with a family-friendly beer garden.

Cycle Brewing (www.facebook.com/cyclebrewing; 534 Central Ave; ⊙noon-9pm) Hipster brewhouse with sidewalk seating serving 24 rotating taps of world-class beer. No website but it's on social media.

Ale & the Witch (☑727-821-2533; www.thealeandthewitch.com; 111 2nd Ave NE; ⊙4-11pm Mon-Thu, 4pm-midnight Fri, 3pm-midnight Sat, 3-9pm Sun) The 'Burg's favorite tap house, serving more than 30 craft beers and an $8 'witch flight,' consisting of four 4oz sample servings.

Overflow Brewing Company (☑727-914-0665; www.facebook.com/overflowbrewingco; 770 1st Ave N; ⊙3-10pm Mon-Thu, noon-midnight Fri & Sat, noon-9pm Sun) With names like Possible Iconoclast (a hoppy pilsner), Starlight and Sunbeams (with banana and passionfruit) and all manner of enigmatic monikers, Overflow does serious beers with a playful backstory.

this, well, brick-and-mortar establishment in 2015, and despite the fact that St Pete has been overrun with great restaurants, this New American experiment dominates. Best thing on the menu? A divine house carpaccio with leek, goat's cheese mousse, a touch of truffle oil and a single ravioli stuffed with deliciously runny egg yolk.

🍷 Drinking & Nightlife

The center of the action is Central Ave between 2nd and 3rd Sts, and within a block on all sides. Many Beach Dr restaurants also have lively bar scenes later in the evenings. Kicking off each month, 'First Friday' is an evening block party and giant pub crawl with live music that takes place on Central Ave.

★**St Petersburg**
Shuffleboard Club SPORTS BAR
(☑727-822-2083; http://stpeteshuffle.com; 559 Mirror Lake Dr N; ⊙6-9pm Tue & Thu, 7-11pm Fri) **FREE** Previously a sport reserved for retirees, shuffleboard first transitioned into an all-ages affair on these very courts, which also happen to be the world's oldest and most numerous. Friday nights come alive

when families, hipsters, young people, old people and everybody else show up (toting their own alcohol in many cases) to slide discs back and forth until someone wins.

The shuffleboard nightlife concept has been replicated in many places across the country, including hip Williamsburg in New York City.

Mandarin Hide COCKTAIL BAR
(www.mandarinhide.com; 231 Central Ave N; ⊙4:30pm-3am Tue-Thu, noon-3am Fri & Sat) This dimly lit cocktail bar is totally hipstered out, with craft libations, retro chandeliers and a giant, fake, mounted buffalo head. The pours are heavy and the ingredients fresh, with offerings like Port of Envy, which contains Angel's Envy bourbon, St Germain elderflower liqueur, tawny port and black walnut bitters, along with a splash of ginger beer for effervescence.

Canopy COCKTAIL BAR
(☑727-896-1080; www.thebirchwood.com/the canopy; 340 Beach Dr NE, Birchwood Inn; ⊙4pm-2am) The 5th-floor rooftop bar of the Birchwood Inn (p413) is the hottest ticket in town for late-night drinking thanks to its sexy

ambience and panoramic views of Beach Dr. Couples loiter in the hope of snagging one of the private cabanas, while party-lovers lounge on long sofas warmed by the glow of fire pits.

Mad Hatters Ethnobotanical Tea Bar GAY
(☑727-800-5030; www.madhattersteabar.com; 4685 28th St N, Lealman; ☺24hr) Headed up by two of St Pete's best-known bartenders gone sober, Judah and Levi Love, this trippy tea bar now serves up exotic nonalcoholic concoctions like kava, made from the dried root of a South Pacific plant, and kratom, from the leaves of a Southeast Asian tree containing opioid compounds. Bar games and spooky *Alice in Wonderland* murals abound; service is super-friendly.

☆ Entertainment

For St Pete and some Tampa concert listings, check out *State Media* (www.statemedia.com). Many St Petersburg bars offer live music, but the town has few DJ-fueled nightclubs.

★ Jannus Live CONCERT VENUE
(☑727-565-0550; www.jannuslive.com; 200 1st Ave St N) Well-loved outdoor concert venue inside an intimate courtyard; national and local bands reverberate downtown.

American Stage THEATER
(☑727-823-7529; www.americanstage.org; 163 3rd St N; tickets $29-65) One of the Tampa Bay area's most highly regarded regional theater companies presents American classics and recent Tony winners, along with improv comedy.

Mahaffey Theater PERFORMING ARTS
(☑727-300-2000; www.mahaffeytheater.com; 400 1st St S; tickets $15-70) The gorgeous, 2031-seat Mahaffey Theater hosts a wide range of performing arts, from touring comedy acts to Broadway, dance, the **Florida Orchestra** (☑727-892-3331; www.floridaorchestra.org; 244 2nd Ave N, suite 420; tickets $15-75) and more.

Coliseum Ballroom DANCE
(☑727-892-5202; www.stpete.org/coliseum; 535 4th Ave N; tea dances $7-10) This old-fashioned 1924 ballroom hosts occasional events and has regular tea dances on the first and third Wednesday of each month from October through May.

🛍 Shopping

The main shopping corridor is along Central Ave between 5th and 8th Sts and between 10th and 13th Sts. This ever-expanding hip stretch doesn't lack for funky boutiques, art galleries and antique stores, which are best viewed during the monthly Art Walk (p412).

Saturday Morning Market MARKET
(www.saturdaymorningmarket.com; Al Lang Field, cnr 1st St & 1st Ave S; ☺9am-2pm Sat Oct-May, to 1pm Jun-Sep) For a slice of local life, head down to the Al Lang Field parking lot on Saturday mornings when more than 200 vendors gather for the local farmers market. In summer (from June to September) it moves to the shadier location of Williams Park.

Florida CraftArt ARTS & CRAFTS
(☑727-821-7391; www.floridacraftart.org; 501 Central Ave; ☺10am-5:30pm Mon-Sat, noon-5pm Sun) A nonprofit association runs this gallery store dedicated to Florida craftspeople. Find unusual, unique, high-quality ceramics, jewelry, glass, clothing and art.

Haslam's Book Store BOOKS
(☑727-822-8616; www.haslams.com; 2025 Central Ave; ☺10am-6:30pm Mon-Sat, noon-5pm Sun) A half-block long, with a tremendous selection of new and used books and an excellent Florida section, Haslam's claims to be the largest independent bookstore in the US southeast.

ℹ Information

MEDICAL SERVICES

Bayfront Medical Center (☑727-823-1234; www.bayfrontstpete.com; 701 6th St S; ☺24hr) A convenient option downtown.

John's Hopkins All Children's Hospital (☑727-898-7451; www.allkids.org; 501 6th St S; ☺24hr) The area's largest hospital.

TOURIST INFORMATION

The *Tampa Bay Times* website (www.tampabay. com) is a useful resource. For the wider Clearwater area, check out www.visitstpeteclearwater.com.

St Petersburg Area Chamber of Commerce (☑727-821-4069; www.stpete.com; 100 2nd Ave N; ☺10am-5pm Mon-Sat) This helpful, staffed chamber office has good maps and a driving guide.

ℹ Getting There & Away

AIR

St Petersburg-Clearwater International Airport (☑727-453-7800; www.fly2pie.com; Roosevelt Blvd & Hwy 686, Clearwater) Mainly regional flights; international services to Toronto, Ottawa, and Halifax, Nova Scotia.

BUS

Greyhound (☏727-898-1496; www.greyhound.com; 180 Dr Martin Luther King Jr St N) Buses connect twice daily to Miami (from $20, seven to eight hours), Orlando (from $15, 3½ hours) and Tampa (from $13, 30 minutes).

Pinellas Suncoast Transit Authority (PSTA; ☏727-540-1900; www.psta.net; adult/child $2.25/1.10) St Petersburg buses serve the barrier-island beaches and Clearwater; unlimited-ride Go Cards cost $5 per day.

CAR

➡ From Tampa, take I-275 southwest over the Howard Frankland Bridge. Reach downtown via either I-375 or I-175.

➡ To Sarasota, continue on I-275 south over the Sunshine Skyway Bridge, which connects with I-75 and US 41 (Tamiami Trail).

➡ To St Pete Beach, take I-275 to exit 17, and follow US 682/Pinellas Bayway. Or take Central Ave due west to Treasure Island Causeway; or turn south on 66th St to the Corey Causeway.

➡ To Clearwater Beach, go north on US 19 (34th St in St Petersburg) to Gulf to Bay Blvd; turn west and follow signs.

ℹ Getting Around

Downtown Looper (www.loopertrolley.com; FREE ; ◷7am-10pm Mon-Thu, 7am-midnight Fri, 8am-midnight Sat, 8am-10pm Sun) Old-fashioned trolley cars run a downtown circuit every 15 to 20 minutes; great for sightseeing.

St Pete Beach & Barrier Island Beaches

Just 20 minutes from downtown St Petersburg, Southwest Florida's legendary barrier-island beaches are the sandy soul of the peninsula. This 30-mile-long stretch of languid sun-faded towns and seemingly endless Gulf waters is the perfect antidote to city life and the primary destination of most vacationers from elsewhere in Florida and from further afield. Winter and spring are the high seasons, particularly January through March. During these months, readiness is all: book rooms far in advance, and get up early to beat the traffic and to snag sometimes-elusive beachside parking spaces.

While St Pete Beach is the biggest town, the string of beach communities each has something unique to offer.

◉ Sights

Barrier-island beaches vary greatly, less in terms of their quality than by how amenable they are to day-trippers: some have much more public parking and better access, commerce and hotels, while others are largely residential. From south to north this stretch of beach passes through the sun-faded towns of Pass-a-Grille, St Pete Beach, Treasure Island, Madeira, Redington, Indian Shores, Indian Rocks and Belleair. Limited public parking at Belleair keeps out the day-trippers, who are better served just north at Sand Key and Clearwater.

Parking meters cost $1.50 per hour; some lots have pay-and-display kiosks.

⭐ **Fort DeSoto Park** BEACH
(☏727-582-2100; www.pinellascounty.org/park; 3500 Pinellas Bayway S; ◷sunrise-sunset) FREE
With 1136 acres of unspoiled wilderness, Fort DeSoto is one of Florida's premier beach parks. It includes 7 miles of beaches (including a dog beach), two fishing piers and an extensive nature trail hopping over five interconnected islands. Of its two swimming areas, the long, silky stretch of North Beach is the best, with grassy picnic areas, a cafe and a gift store (open 10am to 4pm Monday to Friday, to 5pm Saturday and Sunday). The cafe organizes hourly bike ($10) and kayak ($23) rentals.

East Beach, meanwhile, is smaller and coarser, and consequently less crowded. The fort after which the park is named, and which dates from the 1898 Spanish-American War, is in the southwest corner of Mullet Key, which was once inhabited by Tocobaga Native Americans. Union troops were later stationed here and on uninhabited **Egmont Key** (www.floridastateparks.org/parks-and-trails/egmont-key-state-park; 4905 34th St S; ◷8am-sunset) during the Civil War. You can visit Egmont's ruined Fort Dade by **ferry** (☏727-393-1947; www.hubbardsmarina.com/egmont; Boardwalk Pl E, Hubbards Marina, Madeira Beach; adult/child 11 & under $25/12.50) from the park. Once there you can explore the fort and abandoned houses, say hello to the protected gopher tortoises and go shelling and snorkeling (equipment hire $5) off the beach.

Fort DeSoto Park is signed off US 682/Pinellas Bayway (exit 17 off I-275). Parking costs $5.

⭐ **Pass-a-Grille Beach** BEACH
(www.pass-a-grillebeach.com; Gulf Way) The epic sliver of sand that is Pass-a-Grille Beach is the most idyllic barrier-island beach, backed only by beach houses and a long stretch of metered public parking. Here you can

watch boats coming through Pass-a-Grille Channel, hop aboard the **Shell Key Shuttle** (🖰 727-360-1348; www.shellkeyshuttle.com; Merry Pier; adult/child $25/12.50; ⊘ shuttles 10am, noon & 2pm) to unspoiled **Shell Key**, and retire for food and ice cream in the laid-back village center.

Seaside Seabird Sanctuary   WILDLIFE RESERVE
(🖰 727-391-6211; www.seasideseabirdsanctuary. org; 18328 Gulf Blvd, Indian Shores; admission by donation; ⊘ 8am-4pm) The largest wild-bird hospital in North America, this sanctuary has more than 100 sea and land birds for public viewing, including a resident population of permanently injured pelicans, owls, gulls and falcons. A couple thousand birds are treated and released back to the wild annually. Unsurprisingly, the place smells a little fishy.

St Pete Beach   BEACH
(🖰 727-367-2735; www.stpetebeach.org; Gulf Blvd) Anchored by the huge, historic Moorish Mediterranean Don CeSar Hotel, St Pete Beach is a long, double-wide strand with parasail booths and chair rentals seemingly every 50ft. It gets crowded with families and spring breakers, who appreciate the big public parking lots, restaurants, bars and motels just steps away.

Treasure Island   BEACH
(Gulf Blvd) Even wider than St Pete Beach and more jam-packed with fun-seekers and motels. Very built up, with lots of public access, volleyball courts and beachside tiki bars, many of which are connected by the Treasure Island Beach Trail – a mile-long, concrete walkway that was revamped in 2013.

Indian Rocks Beach   BEACH
(www.indian-rocks-beach.com; Gulf Blvd) This quieter, family-oriented beach appeals to day-trippers looking for their own stretch of sand. Most of the action is clustered around 17th Ave, where there are public restrooms and several popular seafood restaurants and bars. Headed south there's a nature preserve, and folks can park boats (from 7am to 9pm) at the only free public dock on the Intracoastal Waterway.

🛏 Sleeping

If you don't want a beach-based vacation, Fort DeSoto, Pass-a-Grille and St Pete Beach are an easy day trip from St Petersburg. If, against all advice, you show up without a reservation, cruise Gulf Blvd in St Pete Beach and Treasure Island: the main drag is packed shoulder-to-shoulder with motels, hotels and condos. Low season means deep discounts.

Fort DeSoto
Park Campground   CAMPGROUND $
(🖰 727-582-2100; www.pinellascounty.org/park/ camping.htm; 3500 Pinellas Bayway S; tent sites $34-36, RV sites $40-42; ⊘ office 9am-6pm Sat-Thu, to 9pm Fri; 🅿🏊) The Gulf Coast hardly offers better camping than the 200-plus sites here. Well shaded by thick-growing palms, many face the water and there are good facilities, hot showers, a grassy field and small camp store, in addition to other park concessions. Online reservations can be made three months in advance, but a few first-come, first-served sites are available every Friday.

Bon-Aire Resort Motel   RESORT $$
(🖰 727-360-5596; www.bonaireresort.com; 4350 Gulf Blvd, St Pete Beach; r $119-227; 🅿❄🛜🏊) Family-owned and operated for more than 60 years, the Bon-Aire is one of St Pete's best-kept secrets. Looking pretty much as it did when it was built in 1953, it sits on a wide beach with a variety of rooms and apartments dotted around mature, blooming gardens. Two pools, shuffleboard courts and the locally popular tiki bar, **Sandbar Bill's** (mains $5-10; ⊘ 11am-8pm), keep loyal customers returning. Book ahead.

★ **Postcard Inn**   MOTEL $$$
(🖰 727-367-2711; www.postcardinn.com; 6300 Gulf Blvd, St Pete Beach; r from $245; 🅿❄@🏊) For its vintage 1950s hang-ten style alone, the Postcard Inn leads the pack in St Pete Beach. The long, double-armed shell of a 1957 Colonial Gateway has been transformed into a designer-chic surf shack with rooms sporting murals of wave riders in the curl. Some have hammocks; all surround the sizable pool. Plus there's ping-pong, a tiki bar and beach access.

The recently renamed and revamped hotel restaurant next door, Boathouse, has a smoker and knows how to use it (say yes to the smoked brisket melt).

Don CeSar Hotel   RESORT $$$
(🖰 844-338-1501; www.doncesar.com; 3400 Gulf Blvd, St Pete Beach; r $250-415; 🅿❄@🛜🏊) The magnificent, coral-pink Don CeSar shimmers like a mirage as you approach St Pete Beach from the causeway. Built in 1928, it's the sort of elegant seaside palace you imagine F Scott Fitzgerald spilling cocktails

in, with chandelier-dominated hallways and white cabanas by the glittering pool. You'd never guess that in the '40s it served as a military hospital.

Rooms are more relaxed, light-filled roosts and the full-service, four-diamond property has all you need: fine dining, a European-style spa, kids programs and, most of all, its own sultry beach. The latest addition is an open-air, beachfront sports bar with fire pits.

Inn on the Beach MOTEL $$$
(☑727-360-8844; www.innonbeach.com; 1401 Gulf Way, Pass-a-Grille; r $195-475; P✳☎) For a quiet, relaxing seaside getaway, these 12 rooms and four cottages are unqualified gems. With bright coral and teal accents, functional kitchenettes and lovely tiled bathrooms, these quarters are a pleasure to return to in the evening; a couple of 2nd-floor rooms have stunning Gulf views and the top-floor Ibis honeymoon suite is swoonworthy.

✖ Eating

★**Walt'z Fish Shak** SEAFOOD $
(☑727-395-0732; www.facebook.com/WaltzFish Shak; 224 Boardwalk Pl E, Madeira Beach; mains $5-14; ⊙5-8:30pm Tue-Fri, noon-3pm & 5pm-8:30pm Sat, noon-3pm Sun) At Walter Gerbase's fish shack the idea is simple: the day's domestic-only catch (often featuring grouper, cobia and amberjack) is chalked on the board and you choose one grilled, fried or blackened and served with coleslaw, salad or raw veg. When they run out, that's it for the night. Get there early to grab a table and the best of the day's selection.

Paradise Grille SEAFOOD $
(☑727-954-8957; https://paradisegrille.com; 900 Gulf Way, Passe-a-Grille; mains $6-13; ⊙8am-sunset) With a deck right over the beach, cold beer and the best pound of shrimp on the beach, this is indeed a little slice of paradise. It also does a mean breakfast, and there's a craft market and live music on Fridays, Saturdays and Sundays.

★**Ted Peter's**
Famous Smoked Fish SEAFOOD $$
(☑727-381-7931; www.tedpetersfish.com; 1350 Pasadena Ave, St Pete Beach; mains $8-23; ⊙11:30am-7:30pm Wed-Mon) Since the 1950s, Ted Peter's has been smoking fresh salmon, mackerel, mahimahi and mullet in the little smokehouse here, then dishing it up whole or in sandwich spreads. You eat at outdoor picnic tables; nothing fancy. Cash only. And

if you bring your own catch, they'll smoke it for you for $2 a pound.

Guppy's SEAFOOD $$
(☑727-593-2032; www.3bestchefs.com; 1701 Gulf Blvd, Indian Rocks Beach; lunch mains $12-15, mains $17-40; ⊙noon-10pm, to 10:30pm Fri & Sat) For variety, quality and price, it's hard to beat Guppy's, which packs diners in nightly. Preparations are diverse, skillfully spanning styles (and budgets), from ocean-raised, garlicky cobia to Kona-coffee-dusted deep-sea scallops. Guppy's doesn't take reservations for parties of five or fewer, but its 'call-ahead seating' option gets your name on the wait list an hour before arrival.

🍷 Drinking & Nightlife

Hurricane BAR
(☑727-360-9558; www.thehurricane.com; 807 Gulf Way, Pass-a-Grille; ⊙7am-10pm Mon-Thu & Sun, 8am-11pm Fri & Sat) Skip the mediocre restaurants down below and head straight to the rooftop bar for 360-degree views and the best sundowner spot on the beach. The Bloody Marys are famous here and well paired with the fresh grouper sandwich.

ℹ Information

St Petersburg/Clearwater Area Convention & Visitors Bureau (☑727-464-7200; www.visitstpeteclearwater.com; 8200 Bryan Dairy Rd, Largo; ⊙9am-5pm Mon-Fri) Inconveniently located in Largo, but a good resource.

Tampa Bay Beaches Chamber of Commerce (☑727-360-6957; www.tampabaybeaches.com; 6990 Gulf Blvd, at 70th Ave, St Pete Beach; ⊙9am-5pm Mon-Fri) Extremely helpful; excellent maps and advice.

ℹ Getting There & Away

These islands can be reached from the mainland via the following roads (starting from the southernmost): the Pinellas Bayway, Pasadena Ave S, the Treasure Island Causeway, 150th Av, Park Blvd N, Walsingham Rd and W Bay Dr. Gulf Blvd also connects the northernmost barrier island to Clearwater Beach.

ℹ Getting Around

Suncoast Beach Trolleys (☑727-540-1900; www.psta.net; adult/child $2.25/1.10; ⊙5:15am-10:50pm Sun-Thu, to 12:20am Fri & Sat) ply the entirety of Gulf Blvd, every 20 to 30 minutes, from St Pete Beach north to Clearwater, and connect with other peninsula trolley and bus services.

Tampa Bay Taxi (☑727-398-6577; www.
tampabayferry.com; one way/passes $10/20;
◷10am-7:45pm) transports passengers,
running to Egmont Key and Shell Key from the
Fort De Soto Boat Ramp.

Clearwater & Clearwater Beach

☑727 / POP 116,478

Clearwater Beach is an upscale if somewhat
bland wisp of a barrier island, while its
neighbor to the east is one decidedly low-
class municipality. Clearwater Beach might
make for a better vacation, but Clearwater
makes for more lively dinner conversation,
as the indefatigable Hooters restaurant
chain was invented here in 1983, and its
burgers-and-babes dining concept encap-
sulates the spring-break party scene. While
Clearwater Beach offers idyllic beaches and
parks, Clearwater has a stuck-in-amber,
gray-suited, 1950s-era downtown area.

◉ Sights

Clearwater Marine Aquarium AQUARIUM
(☑727-447-1790; www.seewinter.com; 249 Wind-
ward Passage, Clearwater; adult/child 3-12yr
$25/20; ◷10am-6pm, hours vary) The home of
Winter the dolphin, this nonprofit aquarium rescues and rehabilitates injured sea animals, such as dolphins, sea otters, fish, rays,
loggerhead turtles and Kemp's ridley sea
turtles. It also allows visitors to interact with
the animals, many of which are resident due

CLEARWATER & SCIENTOLOGY

Central Clearwater is dominated by the
international spiritual headquarters of
the Church of Scientology. The Clearwater Church, known as Flag Land Base,
has occupied the historic Fort Harrison
Hotel since the late 1970s.

According to an article in the *Tampa
Bay Times* in 2019, the Church of Scientology has had a presence in the city
since 1975 and the church's footprint
has grown rapidly, especially since 2017
– the church now has direct ties to or
owns 185 properties covering more than
100 acres in the city centre. It all follows
a 1990s article in a Scientology magazine in which the church expressed
the goal of making Clearwater 'the first
Scientology city in the world'.

---

to injuries that prevent their return to the
wild. Regardless, interaction with humans
can be stressful for dolphins and sharks,
and animal welfare experts recommend that
they be kept in sea pens rather than put on
display for paying visitors.

Sand Key Park & Beach BEACH
(1060 Gulf Blvd, Sand Key; ◷7am-sunset) If you
want a less-crowded beach day, free of commercial palaver, head to this 65-acre beach
park. It's at the northern tip of the barrier
island to the south, just over the Clearwater
Pass Bridge. The sand isn't nearly as fine as
at Clearwater Beach, but it's a wide strand
with decent shelling that's popular with local families. It has restrooms and outdoor
showers, but bring lunch. Clearwater's Jolley
Trolley stops here. Daily parking costs $5.

Pier 60 BEACH
(☑727-449-1036; www.sunsetsatpier60.com; 1
Causeway Blvd, Clearwater Beach) In high season,
Clearwater's long stretch of smooth, white
sand becomes a scrum of sun-baked coeds
and extended families. Hotels, resorts and
raucous beach bars line the sand, particularly near Pier 60, where sunset is 'celebrated'
each night with a festive menagerie of musicians, magicians, performers and trinket
stands hawking their wares. On Coronado
Dr across from the pier, activity booths offer
parasailing, fishing, cruises and so on.

🛏 Sleeping & Eating

Parker Manor Resort MOTEL $$
(☑727-446-6562; www.parkermanor.com; 115
Brightwater Dr, Clearwater Beach; r $100-140, 2-bed
apt $170-200; P❋☎❇) On the harbor, but a
walkable distance to the beach, this small,
well-kept complex attracts an older crowd
who enjoy playing billiards in the covered
courtyard and lounging by the small pool.
The motel-style suites are fully loaded for
cooking and extended stays.

Opal Sands Resort RESORT $$$
(☑727-450-0380; www.opalsands.com; 430 S
Gulfview Blvd, Clearwater Beach; from $375; P❋☎)
The latest addition to the luxurious Opal Collection has a glistening-white, semicircular
facade that's the talk of Clearwater Beach.
Rooms are comfy and spacious, featuring
balconies and expansive Gulf views, while the
pool mimics the experience of walking into
the ocean. The oddly named Italian restaurant Sea-Guini is hip and delicious.

SandPearl Resort
RESORT $$$

(☑ 727-441-2425; www.sandpearl.com; 500 Mandalay Ave, Clearwater Beach; r $500-600; ▣✻🅿🛜🌊) Clearwater's Sandpearl is an LEED Silver-certified beach resort within walking distance of Pier 60 and Clearwater's restaurant row. Following all the most fashionable trends, it touts an eco-conscious spa, boat slips, 253 sandy-hued rooms and suites with dark-wood furniture and Gulf-gazing balconies.

Frenchy's Original Cafe
SEAFOOD $

(☑ 727-446-3607; www.frenchysonline.com; 41 Baymont St, Clearwater; mains $8-17; ◷ 11am-11pm) This beach-bum-casual hole-in-the-wall serves grouper sandwiches you'll dream about months later. These crusty beauties on an onion roll go perfectly with its light-and-sweet pineapple coleslaw. Well-loved Frenchy's has four Clearwater locations.

🍸 Drinking & Nightlife

Shephard's Beach Resort
CLUB

(☑ 727-442-5107; www.shephards.com; 619 S Gulfview Blvd, Clearwater Beach) Nine times out of 10 the biggest party in Clearwater Beach is at Shephard's, where three bars and a raucous nightclub brim with revelers. The Tiki Beach Bar often showcases local bands on its stage and (all too frequently) line dancing on its dance floor, while the two-level Wave nightclub and its state-of-the-art light and sound systems feature well-known DJs.

ℹ Information

There is a Clearwater Beach **information booth** (☑ 727-447-7600; www.beachchamber.com; 429 Poinsettia Ave; ◷ 9am-5pm) within walking distance of Pier 60.

ℹ Getting There & Away

Driving from the peninsula, take Hwy 19 to Hwy 60/Gulf to Bay Blvd, and follow it west to Memorial Causeway and the beach. Be warned: beach traffic is a nightmare. If you're coming for sun and fun, ditch the car as soon as you can and walk.

PSTA's Suncoast Beach Trolley (p419) connects downtown Clearwater, Clearwater Beach and the barrier-island beaches south to Pass-a-Grille.

ℹ Getting Around

Jolley Trolley (☑ 727-445-1200; www.clearwaterjolleytrolley.com; adult/child day pass $5/2.50; ◷ 10am-10pm Sun-Thu, to 11:30pm Fri & Sat) Tootles around Clearwater Beach and south to Sand Key.

Gulfport
☑ 727 / POP 12,401

Don't tell anyone, but Gulfport is the cutest, quirkiest little beach town that's not on the barrier island beaches. Nestled at peninsula's end within Boca Ciega Bay, this LGBT-friendly artist community exudes that elusive, easygoing, fun-loving attitude that Florida made famous. The hard-to-resist spell is in full effect on sultry evenings when the trees along Beach Blvd glow with lights and the outdoor restaurants burble with laughter.

It doesn't compare to the barrier islands, of course, but Gulfport does have a beach with a playground and a shady picnic area.

✨ Festivals & Events

Gulfport Art Walk
ART

(3007 Beach Blvd; ◷ 6-10pm 1st Fri & 3rd Sat of month) Get the full dose of Gulfport's wry local sensibilities during the twice-monthly art walk, essentially a low-key street party.

Gulfport Fresh Market
FOOD & DRINK

(https://gulfporttuesdayfreshmarket.com; 3101 Beach Blvd; ◷ 9am-2pm Tue May-Sep, 9am-3pm Oct-Apr) The Tuesday fresh morning market lines Bayshore Dr and is a fun local shindig.

🛏 Sleeping & Eating

Peninsula Inn
INN $$

(☑ 727-346-9800; www.historicpeninsulainn.com; 2937 Beach Blvd; r $155-255; ✻@🛜) If you're tempted to spend the night in Gulfport, the historic Peninsula Inn has been renovated into a pretty, romantic choice. It also has a recommended restaurant, Isabelle's, which serves classic Southern cuisine and live music performances, often involving piano and a Sinatra singer.

ℹ Getting There & Away

➡ To get there from St Petersburg, take I-275 exit 19 onto 22nd Ave S/Gulfport Blvd and turn left onto Beach Blvd into town.

➡ From St Pete Beach, the Corey Causeway connects to Gulfport Blvd.

Honeymoon Island & Caladesi Island

Two of the best beaches in the US are just north of Clearwater: Honeymoon Island, which you can drive to (west on Curlew Rd/Hwy 586 from Dunedin), and the ferry-only Caladesi Island. In fact, the two islands were once part of a single barrier island, split in half during the hurricane of 1921, a reminder of the forces of nature that sometimes batter the state. Together, they offer nearly a thousand acres of coastal wilderness not much changed since Spanish explorers first surveyed this coast in the mid-1500s.

Sights & Activities

★ **Caladesi Island State Park**   STATE PARK
(☏ 727-469-5918; www.floridastateparks.org/parks-and-trails/caladesi-island-state-park; entry per boater/kayaker $6/2; ⏱ 8am-sunset) Directly to the south of Honeymoon, this park is accessible only by boat and is virtually as nature made it: unspoiled and pristine. Consequently, it often tops national beach polls and its 3 palm-lined miles of sugar-sand beaches should make the top of your list, too. Secluded and uncrowded it nevertheless boasts a 110-slip marina, kayak rentals, a tiny cafe, restrooms and showers.

Honeymoon Island State Park   STATE PARK
(☏ 727-241-6106; www.floridastateparks.org/honeymoonisland; 1 Dunedin Causeway; car/cyclist $8/2; ⏱ 8am-sunset; 🐾) This park, so named in the 1940s when marketeers pitched the island as the perfect getaway for newlyweds, is graced with the Gulf Coast's legendary white sand, a dog-friendly beach and warm aquamarine water.

Sail Honeymoon Inc.   KAYAKING
(☏ 727-734-0392; http://sailhoneymoon.com; 61 Causeway Blvd, Dunedin; single/double kayak 2hr $35/45; ⏱ 8am-7pm) Rents kayaks, stand-up paddleboards and trimaran sailboats, which can be used to travel to Caladesi Island.

Eating

South Beach Pavilion Cafe   CAFE $
(www.romantichoneymoonisland.com; Honeymoon Island; mains $6-13; ⏱ 10am-5pm Mon-Fri, from 8am Sat & Sun) Next to the pet beach, this cafe, in addition to sandwiches and snacks, does a special fish fry at 4pm on Fridays, and pancake breakfasts on Saturday and Sunday from 8am to 11am.

Island Cafe   CAFE $
(☏ 727-260-5503; Honeymoon Island; mains $5-11; ⏱ 9am-5pm) On the beach, the Island Cafe serves sandwiches, snacks and beer, and offers bicycle ($22 per hour), kayak ($12 or $25 per hour) and umbrella ($25 per day) rentals.

Getting There & Away

Caladesi Connection Ferry (☏ 727-734-5263; www.caladesiferry.org; adult/child round-trip $16/8; ⏱ 10am-4pm) runs half-hourly ferries to Honeymoon Island beginning at 10am and ending around 4pm. Ferries often fill up, and depart from a pier off Causeway Blvd, just after the end of the Dunedin Causeway. Officially, you must catch a return ferry within four hours. If you're late, passengers with the correct return times board first.

You can also get to Caladesi Island via kayak, stand-up paddleboard or trimaran sailboat from Sail Honeymoon Inc. on Causeway Blvd. It's an easy 15-minute journey to the island.

NATURE COAST

Florida's Nature Coast tracks south from the Panhandle through a largely rural landscape of parkland, preserves and estuaries. As such, it retains more of that oft-promised but hard-to-find Old Florida atmosphere, with its moss-draped rivers, warm-water springs and quiet creeks and bays filled with scallops and tarpon. It's highly recommended to travel here with a boat or kayak, as it's one thing to see these amazing rivers and creeks, but quite another to get out on their crystal-clear waters.

Weeki Wachee Springs

☑ 352 / POP 13
Welcome to where the state's love of a good show meets old-world, small-town Florida: a real-life underwater mermaid show has been running here since 1947 and, were it ever to cease, an essential slice of Florida's soul would be lost forever. Known as the 'City of Mermaids' there's not a city in sight and Weeki Wachee is almost entirely constituted by Weeki Wachee Springs State Park.

Sights & Activities

Weeki Wachee Springs State Park   STATE PARK
(☏ 352-592-5656; www.weekiwachee.com; 6131 Commercial Way, Spring Hill; adult/child 6-12yr $13/8; ⏱ 9am-5:30pm, mermaid shows 11am, 1:30pm & 3pm) Travelers have been lured by the siren song of Weeki Wachee Springs for over seven decades and it remains one of Florida's original roadside attractions. Esther Williams, Danny Thomas and Elvis Presley have all sat in the glass-paneled un-

TAMPA BAY & SOUTHWEST FLORIDA WEEKI WACHEE SPRINGS

derwater theater and watched as pink-tailed mermaids perform pirouettes while turtles and fish swim past. The three daily half-hour shows remain gleeful celebrations of nostalgic kitsch, particularly the mainstay, *The Little Mermaid*. It's a charmingly innocent relic of simpler times.

While there's no mystery to the trick – the mermaids hold air hoses as they swim and gulp air as needed – there's an undeniable theatrical magic to their effortless performances. The park also offers a sedate riverboat cruise and a modest, weekend-only water park, plus picnic areas. Perfect for an afternoon's entertainment.

Prices are reduced in the off-season when the water park is closed, but the show runs 365 days a year.

★ **Boating in Florida**   KAYAKING
(☑ 352-597-8484; 7240 Shoal Line Blvd; single/double kayaks $40/50, stand-up paddleboard $40; ☺ 8am-noon) Kayaking and stand-up paddleboarding on the Weeki Wachee River are perhaps the region's best adventures. Weeki Wachee's spring – a 100ft hole that pumps about 170 million gallons of water daily – is actually the headwater of the river. The 5.5-mile route includes beaches with good swimming and rope swings, plus you'll see fish and even manatees in winter and spring.

ⓘ Getting There & Away

➡ The springs are about 45 miles north of Clearwater via US 19.

➡ It's about an hour from Tampa; take I-75 north to Hwy 50 then head west.

Homosassa Springs

☑ 352 / POP 13,791

As any fly-fisher will tell you, the Homosassa River is a popular feeding ground for the Silver King of the sea world, Atlantic tarpon. Every summer, the river is dotted with flat boats as anglers sit in hushed concentration hoping to see one roll. The tarpon begin to run in May and fade out in July. Then the scallop season takes over, when, for three months, hundreds of people descend on Homosassa to comb the sea-grass beds and fill their 2-gallon-per-day scallop quota. Outlets offer half- and full-day trips for fishing and scalloping.

The warm waters of the river are also a favorite hangout for slow-moving West Indian manatees between October and March.

THE SPRINGS OF CRYSTAL RIVER

Florida has some 700 freshwater springs, 33 of which are categorized as first magnitude, meaning they discharge at least 100 cubic feet of water per second. The Nature Coast boasts several of these high-volume springs, the largest of which are the 30-odd springs that feed Kings Bay, near Crystal River. Maintaining an average temperature of 72°F (22.5°C), the water attracts upwards of 800 manatees (and many more tourists) during the winter months between October and March.

To view them, visit the Homosassa Springs Wildlife State Park, which is quieter than Crystal River (p424).

◉ Sights & Activities

Ellie Schiller Homosassa Springs Wildlife State Park   STATE PARK
(☑ 352-628-5343; www.floridastateparks.org/parks-and-trails/ellie-schiller-homosassa-springs-wildlife-state-park; 4150 S Suncoast Blvd; adult/child 6-12yr $13/5; ☺ 9am-5:30pm) This state park is essentially an old-school outdoor Florida animal encounter that features Florida's wealth of headliner species: American alligators, black bears, whooping cranes, Florida panthers, tiny Key deer and – especially – manatees. Homosassa's highlight is an underwater observatory directly over the springs, where through glass windows you can eyeball enormous schools of some 10,000 fish and ponderous manatees nibbling lettuce.

Various animal presentations happen daily, but time your visit for the manatee program (11:30am, 1:30pm and 3:30pm). The park itself is a short, narrated boat ride from the visitor center.

Homosassa Inshore Fishing   FISHING
(☑ 352-422-4141; www.homosassainshorefishing.com; half-/full-day $350/450) Captain William Toney is a fourth-generation Homosassa fisherman specializing in red fish, trout fishing and scalloping, along with cooking up inshore lunches. You can't get a better guide.

⌇ Sleeping & Eating

MacRae's   MOTEL $$
(☑ 352-628-2602; www.macraesofhomosassa.com; 5300 S Cherokee Way; r from $110; ❈ ☎)

MacRae's is a good, simple sleeping option 3 miles from the Homosassa Springs Wildlife State Park, off W Yulee Rd. It's a fisher's paradise of pseudo log cabins and has 22 rooms (some with kitchens) complete with front-porch rockers. MacRae's also operates the riverfront tiki bar called The Shed, which is perfectly perched for afternoon drinks.

Wallace's at the Greenhouse   BISTRO $$
(☑ 352-503-7276; https://wallacesgreenhouse.com; 2420 S Suncoast Blvd; mains $11-26; ☺ 11am-9pm Wed-Sat) This cute, shamrock-green bistro, with its gluten-free attitude and from-scratch ethos, is a welcome addition to the otherwise unsophisticated dining scene of Homosassa. The menu isn't particularly adventurous, but does feature an excellent cheese platter, some healthy salads, and plenty of local favorites, like fennel-crusted salmon, free-range chicken and grass-fed beef.

❶ Getting There & Away

To reach the center of Homosassa, leave US 19 along Hwy 490/W Yulee Rd (just south of the park) and enter an Old Florida time warp, where live oaks dripping in Spanish moss curtain a roadway dotted with local places to eat and funky galleries.

Crystal River

☑ 352 / POP 3162

Crystal River may be small, but it promises one of Florida's most rewarding (and easily accessible) wildlife encounters. Hundreds of manatees inhabit Kings Bay and the opportunity to see these gentle sea creatures is reason enough to come. But what draws the manatees adds another attraction to the region: Crystal River also has some of the largest freshwater springs anywhere along Florida's Nature Coast. Throw in the chance to go fishing and you'll quickly understand why many travelers enjoy hanging out in this small fishing town for a few days.

◉ Sights

**Crystal River National
Wildlife Refuge**   WILDLIFE RESERVE
(☑ 352-563-2088; www.fws.gov/crystalriver; 1502 SE Kings Bay Dr; ☺ 8am-5:30pm Mon-Fri) The winter home of nearly 20% of Florida's West Indian manatee population, this wildlife refuge protects almost the whole of Kings

Bay. Up to 800 of these gentle, endangered sea creatures have been counted in a single January day and, like any wildlife spectacle, this draws crowds of onlookers, as well as swimmers and snorkelers.

One place to begin is Three Sisters Trail, which leads to **Three Sisters Springs** (☑ 352-586-1170; www.threesistersspringsvisitor.org; 123 NW US 19; adult/child mid-Nov–Mar $20/7.50, Apr–mid-Nov $12.50/7.50; ☺ 8:30am-4:30pm) with a boardwalk for strolling through it all. The area features underwater vents, sand boils and manatee-filled spring waters that feed Kings Bay, the headwaters of the Crystal River. There's no on-site parking, but you can take the trolley to the boardwalk.

🏃 Activities

**Scalloping with
Captain Nick Warhurst**   FISHING
(☑ 352-812-2528; $75) Captain Nick Warhurst, aka Scallop Man, has been taking guests on mollusk hunts in Crystal River and Homosassa for more than three decades. From July to September, he picks guests up at their hotels and boats them through scenic backwaters and out into the Gulf, where scallopers float over grass flats in 4ft to 6ft of water, trying to spot blue scallop 'eyes.'

Upon discovering them, guests dive down, grab the scallops before they can escape, and put 'em in a mesh bag. Once the legal limit is reached (2 gallons per day), the boat heads back to the marina to get the scallops cleaned and cooked. Reserve in advance – these trips get booked up fast.

Crystal River Kayak Co   BOATING
(☑ 352-795-2255; www.crystalriverkayakcompany.com; 1422 SE US 19; 2hr kayak single/double $25/35, canoe double/triple $35/45, SUP from $25, 3hr tour per person $55; ☺ 8am-5pm) Rent your paddling stuff here for manatee excursions. Would-be kayakers must watch a mandatory video about safe interactions with the mammals before the equipment is handed over. This company also runs excellent guided tours of Kings Bay (including a sunset tour) and Chassahowitzka River.

**Bird's Underwater
Dive Center**   WILDLIFE, SNORKELLING
(☑ 352-563-2763; www.birdsunderwater.com; 320 NW US19; manatee tours $60-65, scalloping tours $85; ☺ 9am-5pm) This recommended outdoors company offers snorkeling with manatees, scalloping trips, kayak rentals and

scuba courses. Guidelines regulating the manatee snorkeling are important for the safety of the animals and should be followed at all times: essentially, it's look, but don't touch. The manatee trips leave at 6am and 11am daily.

🛏️ Sleeping & Eating

Plantation on Crystal River HOTEL $

(🖉 352-795-4211; www.plantationoncrystalriver. com; 9301 W Fort Island Trail; r from $107; 🅿 ❄ @ 🛜 🐾) Elegant rooms and a handful of villas make this a fine choice – it's a place you'll love returning to at the end of the day when the day-tripping crowds have moved on. Professional service and a full range of tours round out a good package,

King's Bay Lodge LODGE $$

(🖉 352-795-2850; www.kingsbaylodgefla.com; 506 NW 1st Av; r weekday/weekend $135/150; 🅿 ❄ 🛜) Built in 1957 and redone in 2016 after the floods that accompanied Hurricane Hermine, Kings Bay Lodge is one of a few independently owned hotels in Crystal River. Its 18 rooms surround a large oak tree and are quaint, a touch old-fashioned and well kept. The property also features a spring-fed, natural pool.

Charlie's Fish House SEAFOOD $$

(🖉 352-795-3940; www.charliesfishhouse.com; 224 US 19; sandwiches from $8, mains $12-22; ⊙ 11am-9pm) A long-time local favorite, this waterfront establishment offers fantastic views of Kings Bay, along with reliably good seafood dishes like stone crab claws and crab-meat-stuffed flounder. Charlie's also doubles as a fish market from Monday to Saturday, 8am to 5:30pm, offering oysters and stone crab seasonally, along with grouper, mullet and red snapper. Try the oyster sandwich.

ℹ️ Getting There & Away

Crystal River is 73 miles north of Clearwater via US 19. It's about an hour and a half from Tampa; take I-75 north to Hwy 50 then head west.

Tarpon Springs

🖉 727 / POP 25,571

Tarpon Springs has two unusual claims to fame: sea sponges and that it's billed as America's 'Greek-est' city. How this came to pass is simple: in the 1800s, Greek divers arrived en masse to exploit the Gulf's abundant population of sea sponges. Tarpon Springs soon became known as the 'Sponge

Capital of the World,' remains a leader in the natural sponge market, and loves to show off everything from its sponge docks to its sponge factory. Add to this a strong, vibrant and enduring Greek American identity with fine restaurants and lively festivals, and it's one of Florida's more original town atmospheres.

⊙ Sights

St Nicholas Greek Orthodox Cathedral CATHEDRAL

(🖉 727-937-3540; www.stnicholastarpon.org; 36 N Pinellas Ave; ⊙ 9am-3pm Mon-Fri) Erected in 1907, this historic cathedral doubles as a Greek American community center and host for the yearly Epiphany (p426) celebration. With a stately dome, ornate relics and stained-glass windows, the Neo-Byzantine structure was modeled after the Hagia Sophia in Istanbul, and its 60-ton marble altar, a gift from Greece, was exhibited at the first New York World's Fair.

There are Sunday services in Greek (8:15am) and English (11am).

Historic Sponge Docks HISTORIC SITE

(www.spongedocks.net; Dodecanese Blvd) A 10- to 15-minute walk west along Tarpon Springs' docks from N Pinellas Ave takes visitors past

---

WATCHING MANATEES

Nearly 50 commercial operators offer rentals and guided tours, via every type of nautical conveyance, and the chance to swim with wild manatees. In season, the corralled manatees and crowded bay are a far cry from any natural wildlife interaction, which is better gained by taking one of the area's top-notch paddle tours.

Note that conservationists advise against swimming with or touching manatees, arguing that this causes the animals undue stress – please resist the temptation to swim too close and encourage boat operators and others to give the manatees space.

The best time to go for manatees is November to March, when hundreds come from the ocean into the relatively warm water in the springs to feed on sea grass. Note that although manatees live in Kings Bay year-round, the population dwindles to a few dozen between April and September or October.

working sponging boats loaded up with giant specimens, along with numerous (and fairly tacky) souvenir shops, Greek restaurants and advertisements for local boating excursions. Signage tells the history of the sponge business, which got its start in the late 1800s. There are even sponge smiley faces for sale.

✯✯ Festivals & Events

Epiphany CULTURAL
Each January 6 for the last hundred years or more, the masses have gathered in Tarpon Springs to watch men dive into the water and compete to find a submerged wooden cross. There is also a celebration with Greek food, traditional dancing and a ceremony to honor the cross retriever.

🛏 Sleeping & Eating

★ 1910 Inn B&B $$
(☑ 727-424-4091; www.the1910inn.com; 32 W Tarpon Ave; r $150-200) Distinguished for its Queen Anne architecture and listing in the Historic Registry of Tarpon Springs, this c 1910 home now serves as a charming B&B. Guests adore the light blue-green facade, expansive wraparound porch and rounded tower, and the six units inside feature sky-high ceilings and glistening wood floors. Great location downtown, near St Nicholas Greek Orthodox Cathedral.

SARASOTA HISTORY

Sarasota has seen some things in its time. After marauding Spanish explorers expelled the Calusa people in the 15th century, this land lay virtually empty until the Seminole Wars inspired the Armed Occupation Act (1842), which deeded 160 acres and six months' provisions to anyone who would settle here and protect their farms. Sailing boats and steamships were the only connection to the outside world, until the Tampa railroad came in 1902. Sarasota then grew popular as a winter resort for the affluent, and a number of arts institutions followed. Finally, circus magnate John Ringling decided to relocate his circus here, building a winter residence, art museum and college, and setting the struggling town on course to become the welcoming, well-to-do bastion of the arts it is today.

★ Dimitri's on the Water GREEK $$
(☑ 727-945-9400; www.facebook.com/dimitris onthewatertarponsprings; 690 Dodecanese Blvd; mains $17-38; ☺ 11am-10pm) Tarpon Springs' most ambitious Greek restaurant is set on the Anclote River, with a pleasant outdoor deck and idyllic sunset views. The food is the real draw, though, particularly the oversize lamb wraps, fresh Greek salads and mouthwatering moussaka (a baked, layered eggplant dish with seasoned ground beef and a creamy béchamel).

Hellas Restaurant and Bakery GREEK $$
(☑ 727-943-2400; www.hellasbakery.com; 785 Dodecanese Blvd; mains $8-30; ☺ 11am-10pm Sun-Thu, to 11pm Fri & Sat, bakery from 8:30am) A long-standing favorite for its baklava cheesecake and fall-off-the-bone lamb shank, this Greek restaurant has been killing it since 1970. The place is decked out in a blue-and-white color scheme and showcases plenty of Greek paraphernalia. The service is prompt and upbeat. The bakery opens at 8:30am daily if you're packing for a picnic.

🛍 Shopping

Spongeorama Sponge Factory GIFTS & SOUVENIRS
(☑ 727-943-2164; www.spongeorama.com; 510 Dodecanese Blvd; ☺ 10:30am-5pm) Here you'll find the world's largest collection of natural sea sponges, along with souvenirs of all kinds – art, jewelry, loofahs, paintings, Greek stuff, Florida stuff – you get the point. In back is the Spongeorama Museum, which tells the story of Tarpon Springs' sponge industry through exhibits and a short film.

Tarpon Springs House of Jerky FOOD
(☑ 727-940-8432; www.tarponspringsjerky.com; 840 Dodecanese Blvd; python/alligator jerky $20/22; ☺ 12:30-6pm) A wildly expensive but fun shop selling exotic jerkies, from alligator to python to wild boar.

❶ Getting There & Away

➡ Arriving by car is best, and the city is best accessed from the north or south via N Pinellas Ave, which bisects it.

➡ Intrepid travelers may choose to arrive or depart via bicycle on the Pinellas Trail (p412), a 47-mile bike path that stretches all the way from Tarpon Springs to St Pete.

➡ The closest airport is the St Petersburg-Clearwater International Airport (p416), 17 miles away.

SOUTHWEST GULF COAST

People who prefer Florida's Gulf side over its Atlantic one generally fall in love with this stretch of sun-kissed coastline from Sarasota to Naples. These two affluent, cultured towns set the tone for the whole region, where visits sway between soporific beach days and art-museum meanders, fine dining and designer cocktails. With their rowdy bars and casual fun, Siesta Key and Fort Myers Beach are slight exceptions, but even they don't reach the same pitch of spring-break hysteria that's found to the north.

Sarasota

☑ 941 / POP 57,738

It's easy to fall for Sarasota. An upscale seaside town with some fine places to eat, Sarasota has a touch of class you just don't find in many of Florida's coastal towns. And there are plenty of attractions to turn your head, including a fabulous circus museum, one of Florida's best botanical gardens, a lovely marina, and museums that range from the whimsical to high art. In short, this is coastal Florida at its most agreeable and sophisticated.

◉ Sights

★ **Ringling Museum Complex**   MUSEUM
(☑941-359-5700; www.ringling.org; 5401 Bay Shore Rd; adult/child 6-17yr $25/5; ⊙10am-5pm Fri-Wed, to 8pm Thu; ⊕) The 66-acre winter estate of railroad, real-estate and circus baron John Ringling and his wife, Mable, is one of the Gulf Coast's premier attractions and incorporates their personal collection of artworks in what is now Florida's state art museum. Nearby, Ringling's Circus Museum documents his theatrical successes, while his lavish Venetian Gothic home, Cà d'Zan, reveals the impresario's extravagant tastes. Don't miss the PBS-produced film on Ringling's life, which is screened in the Circus Museum.

➡ **John & Mable Ringling Museum of Art**
The Ringlings aspired to become serious art connoisseurs and they amassed an impressive collection of 14th- to 18th-century European tapestries and paintings. Housed in a grand Mediterranean-style palazzo, the museum covers 21 galleries showcasing many Spanish and baroque works, and includes a world-renowned collection of Rubens canvases, including the *Triumph of the Eucharist* cycle. One wing presents some rotating exhibits and one permanent collection of contemporary art, and the Searing Wing offers *Joseph's Coat*, a stunning 3000-sq-ft James Turrell–designed 'Sky Space.' Opened in 2016, the newest wing contains historical and contemporary Asian art. Free on Mondays (which works only if you don't visit the other museums covered by the main admission price).

➡ **Cà d'Zan**
Ringling's winter home, Cà d'Zan (House of John; 1924–26), displays an unmistakable theatrical flair evocative of his two favorite Venetian hotels, the Danieli and the Bauer Grunwald. Ceilings are painted masterpieces, especially Willy Pogany's *Dancers of Nations* in the ballroom, and even the patio's zigzag marble fronting Sarasota Bay dazzles. Self-guided tours ($10) include the 1st floor's kitchens, taproom and opulent public spaces, while guided tours ($20) add the 2nd floor's stupendous bedrooms and bathrooms.

➡ **Circus Museum**
This is actually several museums in one and they are as delightful as the circus itself. One building preserves the hand-carved animal wagons, calliopes and artifacts from Ringling Bros' original traveling show. Other exhibits trace the evolution of the circus from sideshow to Cirque du Soleil. Yet in the center ring, so to speak, is the miniature Howard Bros Circus: a truly epic re-creation at 1:12 scale of the entire Ringling Bros and Barnum & Bailey Circus in action. This intricately detailed work occupies its own building and is the 60-year labor of love of one man, Howard Tibbels.

Island Park   PARK
Sarasota's marina is notable for Island Park, an attractive green space poking into the harbor. It has a great playground and play fountain, restrooms, tree-shaded benches, a restaurant and tiki bar, plus kayak, jet-ski and boat rentals.

Marietta Museum of Art & Whimsy   MUSEUM
(☑941-364-3399; www.whimsymuseum.org; 2121 N Tamiami Trail; suggested donation $5; ⊙1-4pm Thu-Sat Oct-May) Dedicated to all things whimsical, this bright pink museum and its adjacent outdoor sculpture garden do not fail to inspire. Although exhibits rotate regularly, expect an abundance of hidden surprises, animal sculptures, trippy

Sarasota

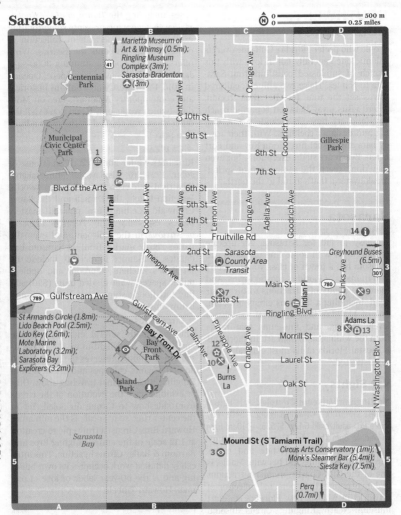

paintings, eclectic textiles and swing chairs to relax in.

Marie Selby Botanical Gardens GARDENS
(☑ 941-366-5731; www.selby.org; 811 S Palm Ave; adult/child 4-11yr $25/15; ☉ 10am-5pm) If you visit just one botanical garden in Florida, choose Selby, which has the world's largest scientific collection of orchids and bromeliads – more than 20,000 species. Selby's genteel outdoor gardens are exceptionally well landscaped and relaxing, with 80-year-old banyan trees, koi ponds and splendid bay views. Art exhibits, a cafe and an enticing plant shop complete the experience.

Marina Jack MARINA
(☑ 941-955-9488; www.marinajacks.com; 2 Marina Plaza) Sarasota's plush deep-water marina is within walking distance of downtown and is well served with alfresco and fine-dining restaurants, numerous sightseeing cruises and private charters. Head here for boat rentals, water sports, sailing and fishing charters.

St Armands Circle SQUARE
(www.starmandscircleassoc.com) Conceived by John Ringling in the 1920s, St Armands Circle is an upscale outdoor mall surrounded by posh residences on St Armands Key. More so

Sarasota

even than the downtown, this traffic circle is Sarasota's social center, where everyone strolls in the early evening, window shopping while enjoying a Kilwin's waffle cone. Numerous restaurants, from diners to fine dining, serve all day.

Art Center Sarasota GALLERY
(☏941-365-2032; www.artsarasota.org; 707 N Tamiami Trail; ☉10am-4pm Mon-Sat) FREE This community-oriented nonprofit gallery has four exhibition spaces that mix local and out-of-town artists. It hosts frequent events, including a lecture series featuring local artists talking about what informs their artistic practice. Donations are appreciated.

🏃 Activities

The pleasant, flat Legacy Trail is a 15-mile paved bike path that connects Sarasota to Venice via the old railroad line that once transported the tents and animals of the Ringling Bros and Barnum & Bailey Circus.

Prepare to run away to the circus with classes at the Circus Arts Conservatory (p431) – a fabulous way to pass the time.

Myakka Outpost KAYAKING
(☏941-923-1120; www.myakkaoutpost.com; 13208 SR 72; canoes/bikes per hour $25/20; ☉9am-5pm) A camp store and cafe inside Myakka River State Park, from where you can also organize tours and kayak, canoe and bike rentals.

☞ Tours

★Siesta Key Rum DISTILLERY
(Drum Circle Distilling; ☏941-702-8143; www.drumcircledistilling.com; 2212 Industrial Blvd; ☉10am-5pm Mon-Thu, to 6pm Fri & Sat, 11am-5pm Sun) FREE The oldest rum distillery in Florida offers an educational and intoxicating

tour in its facility within an industrial park a bit outside of town. You'll learn the entire process of rum-making from the company founder Troy, who is a gifted and hilarious public speaker. Delicious free samples at the end will likely result in purchases.

The beer-barrel rum, with real spices and honey, is a crowd favorite. Tours can be booked by appointment on any day except Thursday, when you can still visit the tasting room.

🎊 Festivals & Events

★Sailor Circus PERFORMING ARTS
(☏941-355-9805; http://circusarts.org; 2075 Bahia Vista St; adult/child $25/20; ☉Apr; ⊕) One of the living circuses in Sarasota is performed by kids and it's incredible. The Sailor Circus, founded in 1949, is a unique extracurricular activity for Sarasota County students, who gear up for one big show over six days in April. They call it 'The Greatest Little Show on Earth,' but don't be fooled: there's nothing little about it.

It includes high wire and trapeze, hand balancing and unicycles, and innumerable midair ballets while dangling from tissues, rings and bars. If you miss the show, consider arranging a tour; customized individually, they include the big tent, costume shop, museum and – hopefully – attending practice. Bring your own kids; just know they will forever after nurture dreams of running away to the circus.

★Forks & Corks FOOD & DRINK
(☏941-365-2800; www.eatlikealocal.com/forks andcorks; ☉Jan-Feb) A multiday epicurean event held in venues throughout Sarasota, including the courtyard of the Ringling Museum of Art (p427). Includes food and wine

tastings, vintner events, seminars, samples from local restaurants and entertainment.

Art & Craft Festivals
ART
(www.artfestival.com; ⊙ Mar or Apr) For two days in late March, an explosion of art and craft stalls dominates downtown Sarasota. The same happens in Siesta Village in late April.

Sarasota Film Festival
FILM
(www.sarasotafilmfestival.com; ⊙ Mar-Apr) If you enjoy seeing serious independent films and wearing your flip-flops to free outdoor screenings at the beach, then head to Sarasota's 10-day film festival.

🛏 Sleeping

Staying downtown in Sarasota is cheaper than staying at the beach, and it's only 3 miles to St Armands Circle and 6 miles to Siesta Key.

Regency Inn & Suites
MOTEL $
(☑ 941-355-7616; www.regencyinnsarasota.com; 4200 N Tamiami Trail; d/ste from $59/74; P ⊝ ❄ 🛜 ⛱) This roadside motel north of the centre has motel rooms that are a cut above average, with contemporary decor and plenty of space. Reception service takes a little time to warm up, but the rooms are outstanding value.

Hotel Ranola
HOTEL $$
(☑ 941-951-0111; www.hotelranola.com; 118 Indian Pl, No 6; r $125-210, ste $215-278; P ⊝ ❄ 🛜) This small hotel has been under new management since January 2019, so previous guests can expect changes, but it's clean, rates are a decent value and it is convenient to the downtown area.

Hotel Indigo
HOTEL $$$
(☑ 941-487-3800; https://hotelindigosarasota. com/; 1223 Blvd of the Arts; r $279-430; P ❄ @ 🛜 ⛱ 🐾) Boutique-style chain that's reliable and attractive, as well as being close to downtown. Rooms are modern and comfortable, with murals depicting wildlife from Marie Selby Botanical Gardens. Good off-season discounts.

🍴 Eating

From Indian comfort curries to Korean BBQ to French bistros, Sarasota has an exciting, multiethnic eating scene and a strong locavore tradition. Log on to www.eatlikealocal.com for details of independent, locally owned restaurants.

Farmers Market
MARKET $
(☑ 941-225-9256; www.sarasotafarmersmarket. org; 1 N Lemon Ave; ⊙ 7am-1pm Sat) This farmers market is one of the best in the state.

Main Bar Sandwich Shop
SANDWICHES $
(☑ 941-955-8733; www.themainbar.com; 1944 Main St; sandwiches from $8; ⊙ 10am-4pm Mon-Sat; 🖐) The Main Bar is a Sarasota classic: an old-school, booth-filled, diner-style deli founded by retired circus performers whose photos blanket the walls. It offers a ton of sandwiches, but – no kidding – order the 'famous' Italian, which instantly transports you to 1958 Brooklyn.

⭐ Indigenous
MODERN AMERICAN $$
(☑ 941-706-4740; www.indigenoussarasota.com; 239 S Links Ave; mains $10-28; ⊙ 5:30-9pm Tue-Sat) Focusing on the popular farm-to-table and hook-to-fork movements, chef Steve Phelps whips up innovative American creations such as Parmesan beignets with honey, pears and thyme, and an ever-popular wild mushroom bisque. Indigenous is housed in a funky, Old Florida bungalow with a broad deck and an intimate 'wine cottage' serving biodynamic and small-production wine labels.

⭐ Owen's Fish Camp
SOUTHERN US $$
(☑ 941-951-6936; www.owensfishcamp.com; 516 Burns Ct; mains $11-28; ⊙ 4-9:30pm Sun-Thu, to 10:30pm Fri & Sat) The wait rarely dips below an hour at this hip, Old Florida swamp shack downtown. The menu consists of upscale Southern cuisine with an emphasis on seafood, including whatever's fresh, and solid regular dishes like scallops with braised pork, succotash and grits, or pecan-crusted trout with crawfish butter.

Monk's Steamer Bar
SEAFOOD $$
(☑ 941-927-3388; www.monkssteamerbar.com; 6690 Superior Ave; mains $8-36; ⊙ 3pm-midnight Mon-Thu, noon-1am Fri & Sat, noon-midnight Sun) Order a spicy oyster shooter (a Bloody Mary with an oyster in it) or oyster 'Monkafellas' (baked with signature toppings) and watch bar staff expertly shuck the gnarly shells in front of you. Or guzzle 2lb of sweet, steamed mussels or Cajun crawdads (crayfish) before lining up for a game of pool at this ever-popular local sports bar.

Antoine's Restaurant
EUROPEAN $$$
(☑ 941-331-1400; www.antoinessarasota.com; 1100 N Tuttle Ave; mains $23-43; ⊙ 5-9pm Thu-Tue) Newly relocated to an otherwise unexciting strip mall northeast of central Sarasota, An-

MYAKKA RIVER STATE PARK

Florida's oldest resident – the 200-million-year-old American alligator – is the star of this 39,000-acre **wildlife preserve** (☑941-361-6511; www.floridastateparks.org/parks-and-trails/myakka-river-state-park; 13208 State Rd 72; car/bike $6/2; ☺8am-sunset). Between 500 and 1000 alligators make their home in Myakka's slow-moving river and its shallow, lily-filled lakes. You can get up close and personal via canoe, kayak and pontoon-style airboat. During mating season in April and May, the guttural love songs of the males ring out across the waters.

The extensive park offers much more besides: its hammocks, marshes, pine flatwoods and prairies are home to a great variety of birds and wildlife, and 38 miles of trails criss-cross the terrain. In winter, airboat trips (adult/child $20/12) depart at 10am, 11:30am, 1pm and 2:30pm; call for summer times. Winter-only wildlife trams run at 11:30am, 1pm and 2:30pm and cost the same. Canoes, kayaks and bicycles can all be rented.

Camping (sites $26) is prime during dry season, from January to April; avoid rainy, buggy summer. The five cabins (per night $70) have kitchens, air-con and linens. Book through www.reserveamerica.com.

To reach the park from Sarasota, take US 41 south to Hwy 72/Clark Rd and head east for about 14 miles; the park is about 9 miles east of I-75.

toine's is a bistro serving perfectly cooked mussels and dishes such as scallop risotto with a candied tangerine sauce or cauliflower blue cheese bisque. But this isn't faddish fusion food: the owners hail from Belgium and the restaurant reflects a classic European style. Save room for the Belgian chocolate desserts; you won't regret it.

Marina Jack's Restaurant SEAFOOD $$$
(☑941-365-4232; www.marinajacks.com; 2 Marina Plaza; sandwiches $12-19, mains $25-37; ☺11:30am-10pm) Anchoring the marina is this well-loved multilevel, multivenue eatery with that quintessential harbor-at-sunset ambience. Be serenaded by steel drums in the relaxed downstairs cafe and lounge, with expansive outdoor seating, tropical cocktails and an easy-on-the-wallet menu. The Bayfront dining room upstairs positions formal tables before curving, two-story windows and serves surf 'n' turf; make reservations.

Drinking & Nightlife

Downtown Sarasota is relatively quiet, perhaps because everyone is busy strolling around St Armands Circle (p428) or Island Park (p427), or is over on Siesta Key.

Perq COFFEE
(☑941-955-8101; www.facebook.com/perqcoffee bar; 1821 Hillview St; ☺8am-4pm Mon-Fri, to noon Sat & Sun) Sophisticated brewing methods and sourcing of single-origin beans make Perq the best third-wave coffee bar in Sarasota.

Jack Dusty BAR
(Ritz-Carlton; ☑941-309-2266; www.ritzcarlton.com/en/hotels/florida/sarasota/dining/jack-dusty; 1111 Ritz-Carlton Dr; ☺7am-11pm) The Ritz-Carlton's gold-trimmed restaurant features one of the sexiest drinking dens in town, with a marble bar, delicious Mote Marina oysters and terrace seating with Gulf views. The bar serves sought-after cocktails such as the Smoking Jacket, with Four Roses single-barrel bourbon, Angostura bitters, burnt sugar syrup and a smoked glass.

☆ Entertainment

★**Circus Arts Conservatory** CIRCUS
(☑941-355-9335, box office 941-355-9805; http://circusarts.org; 2075 Bahia Vista St; ☺9am-5pm Mon-Fri) In addition to putting on the ever-popular Sailor Circus (p429) each year, this circus center offers professional performances along with circus training and summer camp. The performances are usually held in a one-ring European-style big top, and feature Circus Sarasota, a traditional troupe, and Cirque des Voix, which combines singing and orchestral performance with circus arts.

Tickets for performances run between $15 and $55, and most of the revenue goes toward community outreach efforts; for example, a humor therapy program.

Burns Court Cinema CINEMA
(☑941-955-3456; https://filmsociety.org; 506 Burns Lane) This wee theater in an alleyway

off Pineapple Ave presents independent and foreign films. It's run by the Sarasota Film Society (SFS), which screens more than 40 of the year's best international films in November during the annual 10-day Cine-World Film Festival.

 Shopping

Towles Court Artist Colony ARTS & CRAFTS (www.towlescourt.com; 1938 Adams Lane; ⊙11am-4pm Tue-Sat) A dozen or so hip galleries occupy quirky, parrot-colored bungalows in this artists colony. The most lively time to be here is during the art walk on the third Friday of each month (6pm to 9pm). Outside of this, individual gallery hours can be whimsical.

 Information

Arts & Cultural Alliance (www.sarasotaarts.org) All-encompassing event info.

Sarasota Herald-Tribune (www.heraldtribune.com) The main daily newspaper.

Sarasota Visitor Information Center (⊘941-706-1253; www.visitsarasota.org; 1945 Fruitville Rd; ⊙10am-5pm Mon-Fri, to 2pm Sat; 🛜) Very friendly office with tons of info; sells good maps.

❶ **Getting There & Away**

Sarasota is roughly 60 miles south of Tampa and about 75 miles north of Fort Myers. The main roads into town are Tamiami Trail/Hwy 41 and I-75.
Greyhound (⊘941-342-1720; www.greyhound.com; 5951 Porter Way; ⊙8:30-10am & 1:30-6pm) Connects Sarasota twice daily with Miami

(from $18, six to eight hours), Fort Myers (from $15, 2¼ hours) and Tampa (from $15, 1½ hours).

Sarasota-Bradenton International Airport (SRQ; ⊘941-359-2770; www.srq-airport.com; 6000 Airport Circle) Served by many major airlines. Go north on Hwy 41, and right on University Ave.

❶ **Getting Around**

Sarasota isn't that big, but sights are spread out and not well served by public transportation. You'll also want your own car to explore Sarasota's Keys; while Lido and St Armands are really just extensions of downtown, Anna Maria Island is 16 miles north.

Sarasota County Area Transit (SCAT; ⊘941-861-5000; www.scgov.net/SCAT; cnr 1st St & Lemon Ave; fares $1.25; ⊙6am-6:30pm Mon-Sat) Buses have no transfers or Sunday service. Bus 4 connects Ringling Blvd with St Armands Circle and Lido Key Beach; bus 11 heads to Siesta Key.

Sarasota Keys

For sun-worshippers and salty sea dogs alike, Sarasota's Keys offer an irresistible combination of fabulous beaches, laid-back living and endless watery pursuits. Each of the keys, a series of barrier islands that stretch 35 miles from south of Sarasota north to Anna Maria Island, has its own distinct identity, but miles of glorious beach is a common thread.

HISTORIC SPANISH POINT

Explore layers of history at this environmental and archaeological site (⊘941-966-5214; www.historicspanishpoint.org; 337 N Tamiami Trail, Osprey; adult/child 5-12yr $15/7; ⊙9am-5pm Mon-Sat, from noon Sun), which covers a 30-acre peninsula jutting out into Little Sarasota Bay. Covered in shell middens, small pioneer cottages, a chapel and a citrus packing house, the peninsula was bought in 1910 by wealthy widow Bertha Potter Palmer, one of Sarasota's most dynamic entrepreneurs. A museum on the property tells her story beside a unique excavated shell midden and several pioneer homesteads and outbuildings.

Oddly, there were never any Spaniards at Historic Spanish Point. Instead the name derives from a friendly Spanish trader who tipped off early settlers John and Eliza Webb about the idyllic location when they were searching for land to farm in 1867. Eventually the Webbs accumulated the entire peninsula, which they planted with citrus they shipped to market in Cedar Key and Key West. Wander the 1-mile trail (tours via electric cart are also available) around the site and you can see the wooden packing house, Mary's Chapel, the Webb-family cemetery and Frank Guptill's beautiful wooden homestead, which he built for their daughter Lizzie.

Between 1959 and 1962 the Smithsonian Institution partially excavated one of the shell middens. You can enter the mound and see what the layers of shell deposits and prehistoric paraphernalia look like from the inside. It's the only such site in Florida and is quite fascinating.

⊙ Sights

★ Anna Maria Island ISLAND
The perfect antidote to party-loving Siesta Key, Anna Maria Island lies marooned in a 1950s time warp, with sun-faded clapboard houses, teenagers hanging outside ice-cream stores and a clutch of good seafood restaurants. The island has three beach towns: at the southern end is Bradenton Beach, mid-island is Holmes Beach, considered the hub, and at the northern tip is Anna Maria village.

The best beaches are to the south and north. Southern Coquina Beach has plenty of pavilions, lifeguards and restrooms, and is backed by a stand of Australian pines through which the Coquina Bay Walk meanders. To the north, Anna Maria Bayfront Park sits on Tampa Bay, offering views of the Sunshine Skyway Bridge, plus a playground and restrooms. The latter is within walking distance of the City Pier and the center of Anna Maria. The northernmost, lesser-visited and thoroughly gorgeous beach is Bean Point.

The restoration of Anna Maria's 'historic boutique business district' known as Pine Avenue (http://pineavenueinfo.com; Pine Ave; ⊙24hr) FREE has the island abuzz. The renovated, brightly colored homes, boutiques, restaurants and galleries are delightful enough, but tourists will flip for the edible teaching garden out front, with 30 planter boxes filled with stuff like Ethiopian kale and Chinese spinach. Delicious.

Siesta Key BEACH
At 8 miles long, Siesta Key is the area's most popular beach hangout, with a family-friendly village and a public beach of pure quartz sand so fine it's like confectioners' sugar. The enormous parking lot (at the corner of Beach Rd and Beach Way) has an information booth dispensing info on all types of activities and water sports (parasailing, Jet Ski rental, kayaks, bikes and more), plus nice facilities, a snack bar and covered eating areas.

Mote Marine Laboratory AQUARIUM
(☑941-388-4441; www.mote.org; 1600 Ken Thompson Pkwy, City Island; adult/child $20/15; ⊙10am-5pm) The Mote bills itself as a research facility and aquarium, and has a large department dedicated to the study of sharks. Exhibits include a preserved giant squid (37ft long when caught) and a shark tank. In a separate building the aquarium organizes encounters with sea turtles, manatees, otters and alligators, but beware studies show that interaction with sea creatures held in captivity creates stress for them. To get here, head to St Armands Circle, then take John Ringling Blvd north to Ken Thompson Pkwy; follow to end.

Lido Key ISLAND
Lido Key is barely 15-minutes' drive from downtown Sarasota and Lido Beach is an excellent, wide stretch of white sand backed by a number of nature trails. Street and lot parking is free, so expect crowds. A pavilion at the parking lot has food, restrooms and even a small lap swimming pool (☑941-954-4182; 400 Benjamin Franklin Dr; adult/child 4-11yr $4/2; ⊙10am-4:45pm Tue-Sun). About a mile south is South Lido Beach, which has grills and grassy lawns that are extremely popular with picnicking families. Strong currents here discourage swimming.

⊙ Tours

Sarasota Bay Explorers BOATING
(☑941-388-4200; www.sarasotabayexplorers.com; 1600 Ken Thompson Pkwy, Mote Marine Laboratory) Under the supervision of marine biologists, boat cruises trawl a net and then examine the sponges, sea horses and various fish caught. The marine safari (adult/child $48/41) heads out to Lido Key and nearby sandbars where participants get out into the grass flats to commune with crabs, sea horses and sea stars. It also offers guided kayak tours (adult/child $50/40).

⊨ Sleeping

Turtle Beach Campground CAMPGROUND $
(☑941-861-2267; 8862 Midnight Pass Rd, Siesta Key; campsites $32-65; P☎) This county-operated campground is small, caters to RVs, has little privacy and doesn't allow campfires. But it's well worth camping here to be mere steps from Turtle Beach and a quick drive from Sarasota. Max vehicle length is 38ft.

Hayley's Motel MOTEL $$
(☑941-778-5405; www.haleysmotel.com; 8102 Gulf Dr, Anna Maria Island; r from $179; P❋☎🐾) Owner-operated Hayley's offers adults-only motel rooms, one-bedroom suites and buckets of 1950s charm. Super-quaint and competitively priced for Anna Maria Island. You'll find it about a block back from Holmes Beach. There's a $50 fee for pets, though they aren't allowed in high season (February to April) and the beaches on Anna Maria don't allow dogs.

TAMPA BAY & SOUTHWEST FLORIDA SARASOTA KEYS

★ **Harrington House** B&B $$$

(☑941-778-5444; www.harringtonhouse.com; 5626 Gulf Dr, Anna Maria Island; ste/bungalows from $215/240; P❄️🐕🛥️) Sneak away to this beachside B&B and fantasize about your own little seaside paradise. Made up of three former beach houses, the B&B's guest suites and bungalows have sun porches overlooking an idyllic beach. Common rooms ooze Old Florida charm with their wing-back armchairs, mahogany sideboards and candelabra lights. Children under 12 are discouraged.

✖ Eating

Ginny's & Jane E's CAFE $

(☑941-778-3170; www.ginnysandjanees.com; 9807 Gulf Dr, Anna Maria Island; mains $3.50-11; ⏰7:30am-4pm; 🛜) Housed in an old village grocery in the north of Anna Maria Island is this unique cafe, coffee and ice-cream bar, and vintage shop selling furniture, flip-flops, and outsider art and trinkets. The sandwiches are divine, as is the giant hunk of Connie Wolgast's pecan pie. Plop down on the sofa next to other beachcombers; this place is made for socializing.

Sandbar SEAFOOD $$

(☑941-778-0444; http://sandbar.groupersandwich. com; 100 Spring Ave, Anna Maria Island; mains $12-19; ⏰11am-9pm) 🍴 A long-standing favorite haunt in northerly Anna Maria, the Sandbar offers casual dining with toes in the sand, local food on the plate, and a heaping side of innovation. For instance, the caramelized pork slider contains 'local wild hog,' which is part of an effort to control feral pig populations. Although some of the seafood is a bit mediocre, the setting is unbeatable.

Dry Dock SEAFOOD $$

(☑941-383-0102; www.drydockwaterfrontgrill. com; 412 Gulf of Mexico Dr, Longboat Key; mains $16-37; ⏰11am-9pm Sun-Thu, to 10pm Fri & Sat) With a deck overhanging the water and panoramic views from its upstairs dining room impeded only by shady palm fronds, it's hard to beat Dry Dock for waterside dining. Match that with excellent blackened or grilled grouper sandwiches, a half-pound chargrilled burger and Caribbean shrimp tacos and you'll see why the wait time is usually around 40 minutes.

★ **Beach Bistro** MODERN AMERICAN $$$

(☑941-778-6444; www.beachbistro.com; 6600 Gulf Dr, Holmes Beach, Anna Maria Island; mains $16-96; ⏰5-10pm) Sean Murphy's Beach Bistro is Anna Maria's best date night. Perfectly executed Floridian dishes showcase the best locally and nationally sourced farm products, including fresh line-caught seafood, Hudson Valley foie gras and prime USA beef tenderloin. The Bistro Bouillabaisse is legendary, stacked with lobster tail, jumbo shrimp, shellfish and calamari, and stewed in a fresh tomato, saffron and anise flavored broth.

Cottage FUSION $$$

(☑941-312-9300; www.cottagesiestakey.com; 153 Avenida Messina, Siesta Key; tapas $11-15, mains $23-27; ⏰11am-10pm Sun-Thu, to 11pm Fri & Sat) Siesta Key's hottest restaurant serves innovative items like guava slaw, slow-braised Korean short ribs and Hawaiian escolar, which comes with corn and edamame succotash, bathed in a lobster and crab velouté sauce. Pair with a frozen mojito. Perfection.

🍷 Drinking & Nightlife

Doctor's Office COCKTAIL BAR

(☑941-213-9926; https://doctorsofficeami.com; 5312 Holmes Blvd, Holmes Beach, Anna Maria Island; ⏰5-11:45pm) With an eye chart, old filing cabinets and a 'doctor's in' sign on the door, this new craft cocktail establishment makes certain customers aware that, yes, this was once an actual doctor's office. There's no need for such um, cleverness, as the cocktails are fresh and delicious, and the atmosphere lively and elegant.

Gilligan's Island Bar & Grill BAR

(☑941-346-8122; www.gilligansislandbar.com; 5253 Ocean Blvd, Siesta Village; ⏰11am-2am) Classic Florida thatched-roof tiki-bar vibe, with VW bus, outdoor courtyard and strong cocktails. Live music.

ℹ Information

Anna Maria Island Chamber of Commerce (☑941-778-1541; www.annamariaisland chamber.org; 5313 Gulf Dr N, Holmes Beach; ⏰9am-5pm Mon-Fri) Provides info on accommodations, activity providers and island events.

Siesta Key Chamber of Commerce (☑941-349-3800; www.siestakeychamber.com; 5118 Ocean Blvd, Siesta Key; ⏰9am-5pm Mon-Fri, to noon Sat) Tracks daily hotel availability and will help you find a room.

Simply Siesta Key (www.simplysiestakey.com) A comprehensive, online resource.

ℹ Getting There & Away

➡ Anna Maria Island can be accessed via Manatee Ave and Cortes Rd, and it's possible to drive south from there to Longboat Key (which is also accessible from Lido Key to the south).

➡ John Ringling Blvd will take you to Lido Key from the mainland.

➡ Siesta Key can be reached via Siesta Dr and Stickney Point Rd.

➡ A car keeps things simple, but there are also **MCAT** (☑ 941-749-7116; www.ridemcat.org/bus-routes; ◷ 5:30am-8pm Mon-Sat) trolleys and buses between Anna Maria Island and Longboat Key, and **SCAT** (☑ 941-861-5000; ride/7-day pass $1.50/22; ◷ 5:20am-8:40pm Mon-Sat) buses that run between Sarasota and Lido and Siesta Keys.

Venice

☑ 941 / POP 23,376

About the only resemblance Venice has to its Italian namesake is that it's an island in the sea. Venice has scenic, tan-sand beaches but is otherwise a quiet seaside town that's most popular with retirees and families with young kids, who enjoy hunting for sharks' teeth. It also appeals to budget-minded travelers looking for a low-key getaway far from the condos and hard-drinking beach bars elsewhere. Here, entertainment pretty much begins and ends with saluting the tangerine sun's nightly descent into the shimmering ocean.

◉ Sights

★ Venice Beach
BEACH

Where W Venice Ave dead-ends you'll find a covered beach pavilion with restrooms and a snack bar. There's free yoga on the sand daily at 8am and 9am (and also at 5pm on Monday, Thursday and Saturday), and free acoustic music from Saturday to Wednesday from around 5pm to 8pm. Further south is Caspersen Beach.

This area is a top spot for fossil hunters, who often bring specialized sifting gear to search for valuable finds. Sharks' teeth wash up by the millions; all one needs is some patience and a keen eye. An hour or two of looking can net dozens of little teeth, some in excellent condition, others eroded by the waves. Sea turtles also nest here and shorebird watching is excellent.

Nokomis Beach
BEACH

(100 Casey Key Rd, Nokomis) North of Venice on Casey Key, Nokomis is an attractive, low-key beach. Its minimalist-style beach pavilion is an intriguing architectural bauble; it has nice facilities but no kiosks (so bring lunch).

An hour before sundown on Wednesday and Saturday nights things get groovy: the **Nokomis Beach Drum Circle** gathers and its rhythm draws upward of several hundred folks. To get to Nokomis Beach, take US 41 north and then head west on Albee Rd.

Caspersen Beach
BEACH

One-and-a-half miles south of Venice Pier along Harbor Dr, Caspersen is famous for the fossilized prehistoric sharks' teeth that wash up. Most teeth are the size of a fingernail, but occasionally finger-long specimens are found. Its attractive, palmetto-backed sand, playground and paved bike path also make Caspersen popular; there are facilities but no kiosks.

⚡ Activities

Warm Mineral Springs
SPA

(☑ 941-426-1692; 12200 San Servando Ave; ◷ 9am-5pm) Was this warm mineral spring the actual fountain of youth that Spanish explorer Ponce de León was hunting for? So they say. The spring's 84–87°F (28.8–30.5°C) waters have the highest mineral content of any in the US. From US 41 east of North Port, head north 1 mile on Ortiz Blvd.

🛏 Sleeping

Banyan House
RENTAL HOUSE $

(☑ 941-484-1385; www.banyanhouse.com; 519 S Harbor Dr; weekly $550-825;) Suites and apartments within one of Venice's grand old homes are available for weekly rental. They all share a heated pool, a lemon-yellow sunroom, a billiards room and a hammock beneath the namesake banyan tree.

★ Inn at the Beach
RESORT $$$

(☑ 941-484-8471; www.innatthebeach.com; 725 W Venice Ave; r $230-370, ste $352-525; ❄@🛜🏊) Right across from the beach and a perfect choice for an extended stay, this well-managed hotel-style resort worries about the details so you don't have to. Each room's attractive palette of cream yellow, burnt umber and sage avoids seaside cliches, and the kitchenettes are a pleasure to cook in.

🍴 Eating & Drinking

★ Crow's Nest
Marina Restaurant
SEAFOOD $$

(☑ 941-484-9551; www.crowsnest-venice.com; 1968 Tarpon Center Dr; mains $13-36; ◷ 11:30am-9pm Sun-Wed, to 10pm Thu-Sat) With Venice Inlet and marina views from an elegant

2nd-floor dining room within a restored Victorian landmark, this is a longtime surf 'n' turf favorite. Popular dishes include the filet mignon and the Gulf grouper, and do save space for the key lime pie. Downstairs offers a more tavern-y vibe. A charming gazebo and stained-glass windows throughout add style points.

Outside, kayaks and electric boats are available for rent.

★ **Sharky's on the Pier**   BAR

(☑941-488-1456; www.sharkysonthepier.com; 1600 Harbor Dr S; ⊘11:30am-10pm Sun-Thu, to midnight Fri & Sat) With the prime sunset spot at Venice Pier, Sharky's doesn't have to try too hard. It's a typical, middle-of-the-road seafood restaurant (mains $13 to $36) featuring good grouper sandwiches, frozen drinks and a tiki bar perfectly positioned for evening's magic moment.

ℹ Information

Venice Chamber of Commerce (☑941-488-2236; www.venicechamber.com; 597 S Tamiami Trail; ⊘8:30am-5pm Mon-Fri) This helpful office provides good, free maps.

ℹ Getting There & Away

From US 41/Tamiami Trail, Venice Ave heads west directly to Venice Beach. About five blocks east of the beach, the main downtown commercial district lies along W Venice Ave between US 41 and Harbor Dr.

Fort Myers

☑239 / POP 82,254

Fort Myers' brick-lined main street, nestled inland along the Caloosahatchee River, has a certain charm. The city has a handful of excellent natural attractions and some fine museums, including Thomas Edison's fascinating winter home and laboratory. Fort Myers city is separated from Fort Myers Beach by several miles of urban sprawl.

◉ Sights & Activities

The historic district is a six-block grid of streets along 1st St between Broadway and Lee St, extending to the riverfront. It's easily tackled on foot and the area's top attraction, Edison & Ford Winter Estates, is just a five-minute drive southwest.

★ **Edison & Ford Winter Estates**   MUSEUM

(☑239-334-7419; www.edisonfordwinterestates. org; 2350 McGregor Blvd; adult/child $30/18, guided tours adult/child $25/15; ⊘9am-5:30pm) Thomas Edison built his winter home in 1885 and lived in Florida seasonally until his death in 1931. Edison's friend Henry Ford built his adjacent bungalow in 1916. Together, and sometimes side by side in Edison's lab, these two inventors, businessmen and neighbors changed our world. The museum does an excellent job of presenting the overwhelming scope of their achievements. Don't forgo the self-guided audio tour of the estates. Guided tours are also available from 10am to 4pm on the hour.

IMAG History and Science Center   SCIENCE CENTER

(☑239-243-0043; https://theimag.org; 2000 Cranford Ave; adult/student $15/12; ⊘10am-5pm Tue-Sat, from noon Sun) This fascinating science center combines interactive exhibits and even virtual reality, with exhibits like the IMAG's 'Tanked,' which displays fish and their natural habitats, or an exploration of the USS Mohawk, a World War II warship deliberately sunk and turned into an artificial reef in 2012. Kids and grown-ups alike will dig it.

Six Mile Cypress Slough Preserve   NATURE RESERVE

(☑239-533-7550; www.sloughpreserve.org; 7791 Penzance Blvd; parking per hour/day $1/5; ⊘dawn-dusk, nature center 10am-4pm Tue-Sun) FREE With more than 3500 acres of wetlands, this park is a great place to experience southwest Florida's flora and fauna. A 1.2-mile boardwalk trail is staffed by volunteers who help explain the epiphytes, cypress knees, migrating birds and nesting alligators you'll find. Wildlife-watchers should target the winter dry season.

Lee County Manatee Park   WILDLIFE RESERVE

(☑239-533-7275; www.leegov.com/parks; 10901 State Rd 80; parking per hour/day $2/5; ⊘sunrise-sunset daily) FREE December through March, manatees flock up the Orange River to this warm-water discharge canal from the nearby power plant. The waterway is now a protected sanctuary, with a landscaped park and playground in addition to viewing platforms at water's edge, where manatees swim almost at arm's reach.

Fort Myers

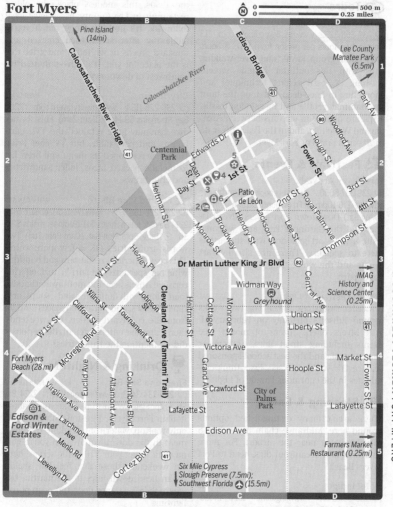

Fort Myers

◎ Top Sights
1 Edison & Ford Winter Estates A5

🛏 Sleeping
2 Hotel Indigo C2

✕ Eating
3 City Tavern C2
   Twisted Vine Bistro .... (see 3)

🍸 Drinking & Nightlife
4 Firestone Sky Bar C2

✦ Entertainment
5 Arcade Theatre C2

🛍 Shopping
6 Franklin Shops C2

ℹ Information
7 Greater Fort Myers Chamber of
   Commerce C2

Tours

Fossil Expeditions BOATING
(☑ 239-368-3252; www.fossilexpeditions.com; 213
Lincoln Ave; tours per person from $50; ⊘ hours
vary) Small-group kayak and river-walking
trips with this outfitter include screen-
washing (a fossil-seeking technique) and
snorkeling in knee-deep water, on the hunt
for mammal, reptile and megalodon fossils.
Trips are usually in streams between Arca-
dia and Wauchula, and in the Peace River, 45
to 70 miles north of Fort Myers.

Festivals & Events

Fort Myers Art Walk ART
(☑ 239-337-5050; www.facebook.com/fortmyers
artwalk; ⊘ 6-10pm 1st Fri of month & 11am-4pm following Sat) Downtown Fort Myers River District and the Gardner's Park area welcome
visitors to 14 art galleries, with the artists
there to socialize. There are also live art
events and the whole thing feels like a big
street party.

Edison Festival of Light CULTURAL
(www.edisonfestival.org; ⊘ Feb) For two weeks
around Edison's birthday on February 11,
Fort Myers offers dozens of mostly free
events including street fairs, antique-car
shows, music and the best school-sponsored
science fair you'll ever see. Everything culminates in the enormous Parade of Light.

Sleeping & Eating

There aren't many distinguished options
around here. Midrange chain hotels line S
Cleveland Ave near the airport. For more
charming and oceanfront digs, head to Fort
Myers Beach.

Hotel Indigo HOTEL $$
(☑ 239-337-3446; www.ihg.com; 1520 Broad-
way; r $115-420; ❀@🛜🏊) Now anchoring
the downtown historic district, this beauty
makes an attractive, reliable stay. The 67
rooms have powder-blue comforters, wall
murals, a mix of wood floors and carpets,
and snazzy glass-door showers. The kicker
is the small rooftop pool and bar, with pan-
oramic views of the scenic riverfront. Valet
parking costs $20.

**Farmers Market
Restaurant** SOUTHERN US $
(☑ 239-334-1687; http://farmersmarketrestaurant.
com; 2736 Edison Ave; mains $5-12; ⊘ 6am-3pm
Mon-Thu, to 7pm Fri & Sat) Pleasing diners with
its simple Southern comfort food since

the 1950s, this modest place, the oldest
restaurant in Lee County, has a loyal local
following. It's nothing fancy, but if you're
hankering after some fried chicken and
mustard greens or whitefish and grits, this
is the place for you. It's a five-minute drive
southwest of downtown.

City Tavern AMERICAN $
(☑ 239-226-1133; www.mycitytavern.com; 2206
Bay St; mains $9-14; ⊘ 11am-2am) This former
dive bar may have retained the TVs, dart-
boards and pool table, but TV chef Brian
Duffy has revamped its menu and brew list
to include packed tacos, killer sandwiches
and craft brews.

★ **Twisted Vine Bistro** AMERICAN $$$
(☑ 239-226-1687; www.twistedvinebistro.com;
2214 Bay St; lunch mains $11-19, dinner mains $22-
36; ⊘ 11am-10pm Mon-Sat, 10am-9pm Sun) Two
words: truffle fries. OK, a few more words.
This cozy American restaurant and boutique
wine bar specializes in surf 'n' turf, offering
certified Angus beef and mouthwatering seafood, along with fantastic salads, soups, artisanal cheeses, and herbs and spices straight
from the courtyard garden. On weekends,
there's also live entertainment. But seriously,
did we mention the truffle fries?

Drinking & Nightlife

Firestone Sky Bar ROOFTOP BAR
(☑ 239-334-3473; www.firestonefl.com; 2224 Bay
St; ⊘ 4pm-late) Want to feel like you're above
it all in Fort Myers? Firestone Sky Bar is the
only rooftop, waterfront drinking establishment in the downtown area, so you're gon-
na want to get your VIP bottle service here.
On weekends, those that feel like shakin'
it can head downstairs to the martini bar,
where there's a dance floor and neon purple
lighting.

Entertainment

★ **Arcade Theatre** THEATER
(☑ 239-332-4488; www.floridarep.org; 2267 1st St;
tickets $25-55; ⊘ Oct-May) The 1908 Arcade
Theatre is home to the **Florida Repertory
Theatre**, one of the best regional theaters
in the state. It produces popular comedies,
musicals and recent Tony winners, such as
The Seafarer.

JetBlue Park STADIUM
(☑ 239-334-4700; https://www.mlb.com/redsox/
spring-training/ballpark; 11500 Fenway S Dr)
March in Fort Myers means major-league

baseball's spring training. **Boston Red Sox** (www.redsox.com) fans literally camp out for tickets to JetBlue Park on Hwy 876.

Shopping

Franklin Shops ARTS & CRAFTS
(☑239-333-3130; 2200 1st St; ⊘10am-8pm Mon-Sat, 11am-6pm Sun) Riding Fort Myers' upsurge in artsy cool, this gift store and gallery represents more than 60 local artists and businesses, which rotate often. Great for only-in-southwest-Florida gifts.

Information

Greater Fort Myers Chamber of Commerce
(☑239-332-3624; www.fortmyers.org; 2310 Edwards Dr; ⊘9am-5pm Mon-Fri) Lots of info and can help you find a room.
Lee Memorial Hospital (☑239-343-2000; www.leememorial.org; 2776 Cleveland Ave; ⊘24hr) The area's largest hospital.

Getting There & Away

A car is essential. US 41/S Cleveland Ave is the main north–south artery. From downtown, both Summerlin Rd/Hwy 869 and McGregor Blvd/Hwy 867 eventually merge and lead to Sanibel Island; they also connect with San Carlos Blvd/Hwy 865 to Fort Myers Beach.

Greyhound (☑239-334-1011; www.greyhound.com; 2250 Widman Way) Connects Fort Myers to Miami (from $20, four hours, two daily), Orlando (from $19, six hours, one daily) and Tampa (from $16, 3¾ hours, two daily).
LeeTran (☑239-533-8726; www.leegov.com/leetran; 3401 Metro Pkwy; adult/child $1.50/0.75) Bus routes run to Fort Myers Beach and Pine Island, but not to Sanibel or Captiva Islands.
Southwest Florida International Airport (RSW; ☑239-590-4800; www.flylcpa.com; 11000 Terminal Access Rd) Take I-75 from Fort Myers and exit 131/Daniels Pkwy.

Fort Myers Beach

☑239 / POP 7077
Like Clearwater Beach and St Pete Beach, Fort Myers Beach foments a party atmosphere year-round, and spring unfolds like one long-running street festival-slash-fraternity bash. And yet, situated on the 7-mile-long Estero Island, Fort Myers Beach has sand and space enough to accommodate all needs and ages. In the north, the so-called Times Sq area is a walkable concentration that verily epitomizes 'sun-bleached seaside party town.' Head south and the beachfront becomes more residential, less crowded and much quieter.

Sights

Bowditch Point Park PARK
(☑239-765-6794; www.leegov.com/parks/beaches/bowditchpoint; 50 Estero Blvd; ⊘7am-sunset) At the island's northernmost tip, Bowditch is a favorite with families and picnickers. The small parking lot (per hour $2) fills up fast, so come early. There's a good snack bar, free boat dockage, and kayak and paddleboard rentals. You'll also find a butterfly garden, picnic areas and a replenished beach that narrows around the tip. It's a good place to view dolphins fishing in the Matanzas Pass and there's a paddle launch onto the Great Calusa Blueway paddling trail.

Lovers Key State Park STATE PARK
(☑239-463-4588; www.floridastateparks.org/parks-and-trails/lovers-key-state-park; 8700 Estero Blvd; car/bike $8/2; ⊘8am-sunset) In the mood for a good hike, bike or kayak, with a chance to spot manatees in spring and summer? Come to Lovers Key, just south (and over a bridge) from Estero Island. Canals and 2.6 miles of trails around inner islands provide head-clearing quietude and bird-watching. The long, narrow beach is excellent for shelling, but erosion can make it too slim to lay a towel at high tide.

Festivals & Events

Fort Myers Beach
Shrimp Festival FOOD & DRINK
(https://fortmyersbeachshrimpfestival.com; ⊘Mar) For two weekends in early to mid-March, Fort Myers celebrates the glorious Gulf pink shrimp with parades, beauty queens, craft fairs and lots of cooking.

American Sandsculpting
Championship CULTURAL
(www.fmbsandsculpting.com; ⊘Nov) Four-day national sand-sculpting event, with amateur and pro divisions, usually held in early November.

Sleeping

Dolphin Inn MOTEL $
(☑239-463-6049; www.dolphininn.net; 6555 Estero Blvd; r $76-148; ❄@🛜🏊) This vintage Old Florida motel is best if you get one of the newly renovated rooms. However, all rooms sport no-fuss furniture and have full kitchens; the best are bayside, overlooking a scenic residential harbor where manatees

WORTH A TRIP

CAYO COSTA STATE PARK

Beautiful Cayo Costa Island is almost entirely a protected 2500-acre state park (☏941-964-0375; www.floridastateparks.org/cayocosta; $2; ☺8am-sunset). While its pale, ash-colored sand may not be as fine as that of other beaches, its idyllic solitude and bathtub-warm waters are without peer. Bring snorkeling gear to help scour sandbars for shells and conchs – delightfully, many still house colorful occupants (who, by law, must be left there). Cycle dirt roads to more distant beaches, hike interior island trails and kayak mangroves.

The ranger station near the dock sells water and firewood, and rents bikes and kayaks, but otherwise bring everything you need. The 30-site campground (from $16 per tent) is exposed and hot, with fire-pit grills, restrooms and showers, but sleeping on this beach is its own reward. Twelve plain cabins (from $30 per night) have bunk beds with vinyl-covered mattresses. January to April is best; by May, the heat and no-see-ums (biting midges) become unpleasant.

The only access is by boat, which doubles as a scenic nature-and-dolphin cruise. Captiva Cruises (p443) offers ferry service to the park from locations in Punta Gorda, Pine Island, Fort Myers, Sanibel Island and Captiva Island.

play. Amenities include a sizable L-shaped pool, communal grills, loaner kayaks, a DVD library and cheap bike rental.

★ **Mango Street Inn** B&B $$
(☏239-233-8542; www.mangostreetinn.com; 126 Mango St; r $120-195; ☀☎☺) Mango Street's affable husband-and-wife owners Dan and Tree have created a winning seaside B&B: its idiosyncratic decor is funky and memorable but relaxed enough to feel homey. The six rooms with full kitchens hug an interior courtyard that has a wood deck and pretty pergola. It's a short walk to the beach, and the B&B offers bikes and beach gear.

Edison Beach House HOTEL $$$
(☏239-463-1530; www.edisonbeachhouse.com; 830 Estero Blvd; ste $150-430; ☀☎☺) This 24-suite hotel was designed smartly from the ground up and proudly maintains impeccable standards. Attractive decor and rattan furniture are pleasing and all suites frame perfect ocean views from nice balconies. The more sizable rooms are comfortable for longer stays. Fully equipped kitchens feature good-quality appliances; each room has a washer-dryer and newly renovated bathroom.

✕ Eating

Heavenly Biscuit BREAKFAST $
(☏239-463-7600; 110 Mango St; items $3-8; ☺7am-1pm Tue-Sun) This unassuming shack offers two genuine delights: sumptuous fresh-baked buttermilk biscuits – overflowing with eggs, cheese and bacon – and tasty

cinnamon rolls. Eat directly off the waxed paper on the tiny porch or get it to go; you can build a bigger breakfast with grits and home fries. It's nothing fancy or highbrow, just a simple thing done right.

★ **Dixie Fish Company** SEAFOOD $$
(☏239-233-8837; www.dixiefishfmb.com; 714 Fishermans Wharf; mains $10-24; ☺11am-10pm) This fish house recently opened in a 1937 wooden structure that originally contained a fish market. The catch comes straight off the local crab and shrimping boats, which can be viewed from the open-air seating area. Dressings are made in house, and the whole fried fish with garlic butter kills it.

Doc Ford's SEAFOOD $$
(☏239-765-9660; www.docfords.com; 708 Fishermans Wharf; mains $10-24; ☺11am-10pm) Part-owner and crime fiction novelist Randy Wayne White once lived on the marina here and he named this scenic wharf eatery, which has two sister restaurants in Sanibel and Capitva, after his beloved mystery-novel protagonist, marine biologist Doc Ford. The wood-sided building with spacious decks, big windows and multiple bars (open till late) emphasizes Floribbean flavors and a Latin American spice rack.

Fresh Catch Bistro SEAFOOD $$$
(☏239-463-2600; www.freshcatchbistro.com; 3040 Estero Blvd; mains $23-30; ☺5-9pm) This nautically themed bistro is a cut above other seafood restaurants on the beach. Inside, a wall of windows frames stunning sunsets or lightning streaks across the waves, and a

vaulted wooden roof arcs over linen-dressed tables. Here diners tuck in to Pine Island clams on ice, Point Judith calamari fried with mild cherry peppers and delicious lobster mac 'n' cheese.

Drinking & Nightlife

Smokin' Oyster Brewery   BAR
(☑ 239-463-3474; https://sob4fun.com; 340 Old San Carlos Blvd; ☺ 11am-11pm Sun-Thu, to 11:30pm Fri & Sat) You can rock up in your bathing suit and flip-flops at this open-air beach bar just steps from Fort Myers Beach. Order a platter of oysters or a bucket of steamed shrimp, corn and red potatoes (mains $8 to $14). Caught your own? Bring it along and they'll cook it up. Every evening there's live music, and happy hour runs from 3pm to 6pm.

❶ Information

Greater Fort Myers Beach Chamber of Commerce (☑ 239-454-7500; www.fortmyers beachchamber.org; 1611 Estero Blvd; ☺ 8am-4pm) Maintains a list of hotel vacancies.

❶ Getting There & Around

The main drag, Estero Blvd, runs the island's length, from Bowditch Point Park in the north to Lover's Key State Park.

Arriving by car, the low-key middle has a large number of end-of-road access points with metered lots. The northern Times Sq area, right where the causeway dumps visitors, has large paid lots (per day $5 to $10).

Key West Express (☑ 239-463-5733; www. seakeywestexpress.com; 1200 Main St; round-trip fare adult/child $155/62) Offers daily sailings to the Keys, departing at 8:30am from a dock on the mainland (take a left just before the causeway). The trip takes 3½ hours one way, so you may want to consider an overnight stay.

LeeTran (p439) Plies the island's length daily, and connects to Fort Myers buses at Summerlin Sq on the mainland.

Sanibel Island

 ☑ 239 / POP 7402

Sanibel is not like other Florida beach communities. It prides itself on its informal and egalitarian spirit, a place where riches are rarely flaunted. More than that, development on Sanibel has been carefully managed: the northern half is almost entirely protected within the JN 'Ding' Darling National Wildlife Refuge. While there are hotels aplenty, the beachfront is free of commercial-and-condo blight. Plus, public beach access is limited to a handful of spread-out parking lots, so there is no crush of day-trippers in one place.

◉ Sights

The quality of shelling on Sanibel is so high that dedicated hunters are identified by their hunchbacked 'Sanibel stoop.' If you're serious, buy a scoop net, get a shell guide from the visitor center and peruse the blog www.iloveshelling.com.

Fourteen miles of largely public-access beaches give you lots of room to choose from. Most beaches except Blind Pass have restrooms; none of the beaches have concessions or snack bars. Parking is $2.50 per hour.

JN 'Ding' Darling
National Wildlife Refuge   WILDLIFE RESERVE
(☑ 239-472-1100; www.fws.gov/dingdarling; 1 Wildlife Dr; car/cyclist/pedestrian $5/1/1; ☺ 7am-sunset) Named for cartoonist Jay Norwood 'Ding' Darling, an environmentalist who helped establish more than 300 sanctuaries across the USA, this 6300-acre refuge is home to an abundance of seabirds and wildlife, including alligators, night herons, red-shouldered hawks, spotted sandpipers, roseate spoonbills, pelicans and anhingas. The refuge's 5-mile **Wildlife Drive** provides easy access, but bring binoculars; flocks sometimes sit at expansive distances. Only a few very short walks lead into the mangroves.

Don't miss the free **visitor center** (open 9am to 4pm), which has excellent exhibits on refuge life and Darling himself. Naturalist-narrated Wildlife Drive tram tours depart from the visitor-center parking lot, usually on the hour from 10am to 4pm. For the best, most intimate experience, canoe or kayak Tarpon Bay (p442).

Bowman's Beach   BEACH
(1700 Bowman's Beach Rd) Bowman's Beach is the quintessential Sanibel beach, a bright dollop of coast and soft white sand, with a playground and excellent facilities. It's remote in the sense that it rarely feels crowded, except perhaps at the height of tourist season. Alphabet cones, angel wings, lightning whelks and horse conch shells all glitter on the powder. Excellent views to the west make for magical sunsets.

Sanibel Historical Village HISTORIC SITE
([☑]239-472-4648; www.sanibelmuseum.org; 950 Dunlop Rd; adult/child $10/free; ⊙10am-4pm Tue-Sat, tours 10:30am & 1:30pm) Well polished by the enthusiasm of local volunteers, this museum and collection of nine historic buildings preserves Sanibel's pioneer past. It gives a piquant taste of settler life, with a general store, post office, cottage and more.

Bailey-Matthews
National Shell Museum MUSEUM
([☑]239-395-2233; www.shellmuseum.org; 3075 Sanibel-Captiva Rd; adult/child 12-17yr/child 5-12yr $24/15/9; ⊙10am-5pm) Like a mermaid's jewelry box, this museum is dedicated to shells, yet it's much more than a covetous display of treasures. It's a crisply presented natural history of the sea, detailing the life and times of the bivalves, mollusks and other creatures who reside inside their calcium homes. It also shows the role of these animals and shells in human culture, medicine and cuisine. Fascinating videos show living creatures. It's nearly a must after a day spent combing the beaches.

Lighthouse Beach BEACH
(112 Periwinkle Way) The most photogenic of the beaches, Lighthouse Beach sports Sanibel's historic metal lighthouse (1884) on the eastern tip of the island. There's also a T-dock, off which pelicans dive-bomb, and a short boardwalk around the point. Park in the lot and walk over a bridge to the narrow beach.

🏃 Activities

Tarpon Bay Explorers KAYAKING
([☑]239-472-8900; www.tarponbayexplorers.com; 900 Tarpon Bay Rd; 2hr canoe & kayak rental from $30; ⊙8am-6pm) Within the Darling refuge, this outfitter rents canoes and kayaks for easy, self-guided paddles in Tarpon Bay, a perfect place for young paddlers. Guided kayak trips (adult $35 to $45, child $25 to $30) are also excellent, and there's a range of other trips and deck talks. Reserve ahead or come early, as trips book up.

Billy's Rentals CYCLING
([☑]239-472-5248; www.billysrentals.com; 1470 Periwinkle Way; bikes per 2hr/day from $5/15; ⊙8:30am-5pm) Billy's rents every type of wheeled contrivance, including joggers, tandems, surreys and scooters. From Monday to Saturday, by reservation, it also offers three Segway tours (per person $65) at 9am, 11:30am and 2pm.

🎭 Festivals & Events

Sanibel Music Festival MUSIC
(www.sanibelmusicfestival.org; 2050 Periwinkle Way, Sanibel Congregational Church; ⊙Mar) A classical- and chamber-music festival that draws international musicians for a month-long concert series every Tuesday and Saturday in March.

'Ding' Darling Days CULTURAL
(www.dingdarlingsociety.org/articles/ding-darling-days; 1 Wildlife Dr; ⊙Oct) A week-long celebration of the wildlife refuge (p441), with birding tours, workshops and guest speakers.

Sanibel Luminary Fest CULTURAL
(⊙Dec) Sanibel's signature street fair occurs the first weekend of December, when paper luminaries line the island's bike paths.

🛏 Sleeping

Sandpiper Inn INN $$
([☑]239-472-1606; www.palmviewsanibel.com; 720 Donax St; r $135-229; [P][❄][🐾][🛜]) Set a block back from the water and in close proximity to the shops and restaurants on Periwinkle Way, this cheery, yellow-and-teal Old Florida inn offers good value for Sanibel. Each of the one-bedroom units has a functional (if dated) kitchen and a spacious sitting area decked out in tropical colors.

Tarpon Tale Inn COTTAGE $$$
([☑]239-472-0939; www.tarpontale.com; 367 Periwinkle Way; r $230-310; [❄][@][🛜]) The charming, tile-floored rooms evoke a bright, seaside mood and are well located for Sanibel's Old Town; each has a shady porch, tree-strung hammock and super-comfy bed (or two), and some offer full kitchens. With the outdoor lounge, library and loaner bikes, this feels like a B&B without the breakfast, although there is a coffee bar with homemade treats.

🍴 Eating

Gramma Dot's SEAFOOD $$
([☑]239-472-8138; www.sanibelmarina.com; N Yachtsman Dr, Sanibel Marina; lunch $11-19, dinner $23-40; ⊙11:15am-8pm) Pull up a bar stool next to the charter-boat captains at this longtime Sanibel Marina favorite. Enjoy a no-fuss fried-oyster sandwich, mesquite-

FLORIDA'S PIRATE COAST

Of all the rum-smuggling, treasure-plundering pirates to have set foot in southwest Florida, José Gaspar, better known as Gasparilla, is the most notorious. He set up his headquarters at Boca Grande on Gasparilla Island, so the story goes, where he built a palmetto palace and furnished it with the treasures he swiped from his high-seas adventures. These days, and despite its popularity as a blue-blooded bolt-hole, Boca Grande has a quaint fishing-village feel and is a great destination for families. It has miles of undeveloped white-sand beaches encompassed within the Gasparilla Island State Park (☑941-964-0375; www.floridastateparks.org/parks-and-trails/gasparilla-island-state-park; 880 Belcher Rd; car/pedestrian $3/2; ☺8am-sunset) where the restored, historic Boca Grande lighthouse has been a beacon to mariners since 1890. If you decide to stay overnight, Anchor Inn (☑941-964-5600; www.anchorinnbocagrande.com; 450 4th St E; r $170-255; P❋☎☀) occupies a 1925 home with four lovely suites, while stately 1913 Gasparilla Inn (☑941-964-4500; www.gasparillainn.com; 500 Palm Ave; r $260-525; P❋☎☀) has a pillared Georgian entrance, bellhops, butlers and rooms with splendidly unpretentious coral-and-pistachio-accented comfort.

On his plundering voyages, Gasparilla was known to seize beautiful women, whom he held captive on the aptly named Captiva Island, according to legend. Captiva Beach (14790 Captiva Dr) has lovely sand and sunsets, and Captiva Cruises (☑239-472-5300; www.captivacruises.com; 11401 Andy Rosse Lane; adult/child from $30/20) offers everything from dolphin and sunset cruises to various island excursions. 'Tween Waters Inn (☑239-472-5161; www.tween-waters.com; 15951 Captiva Dr; r/ste from $270/355, cottages from $295; P❋❋@☎☀❋) combines intimacy with bright rooms and resort-standard facilities and is the island's best option, while South Seas Island Resort (☑239-472-5111; www.southseas.com; 5400 Plantation Rd; r from $469) is like a wonderfully equipped small town just for guests. Mucky Duck (☑239-472-3434; www.muckyduck.com; 11546 Andy Rosse Lane; lunch mains $9-20, dinner $21-53; ☺11:30am-3pm & 5-9:30pm) offers pub meals with brilliant sunsets thrown in; head to Bubble Room (☑239-472-5558; www.bubbleroomrestaurant.com; 15001 Captiva Dr; cakes $8-10, mains $12-28; ☺11:30am-3pm & 4:30-9pm) for its buttercrunch ice-cream pie. Driving is the only way to come and go. The Sanibel Causeway (Hwy 867) charges an entrance toll (cars/motorcycles $6/2).

grilled grouper or the coconut shrimp. A great lunch stop.

★ **Mad Hatter Restaurant**   AMERICAN $$$
(☑239-472-0033; www.madhatterrestaurant.com; 6467 Sanibel-Captiva Rd; mains $29-45; ☺5:30-9pm Tue-Sun) ✐ Vacationing Manhattan urbanites flock to what is widely regarded as Sanibel's best locavore restaurant. Contemporary seafood is the focus, with tempting appetizers such as oysters and a seafood martini, while mains include black-truffle sea scallops, bigeye tuna and a rack of lamb. As the name suggests, it's not stuffy – but it's for culinary mavens seeking quality regardless of price.

★ **Sweet Melissa's Cafe**   AMERICAN $$$
(☑239-472-1956; www.sweetmelissascafe.com; 1625 Periwinkle Way; tapas $9-18, mains $21-46; ☺11:30am-2:30pm & 5-8pm Mon-Fri, 5-8pm Sat) From menu to mood, Sweet Melissa's offers well-balanced, relaxed refinement. Dishes are ever-changing, but may include things like farro fettuccine, escargot with marrow and whole crispy fish. It's creative without trying too hard. Lots of small-plate options encourage experimentation. Service is attentive and the atmosphere upbeat.

❶ Information

Sanibel & Captiva Islands Chamber of Commerce (☑239-472-1080; www.sanibel-captiva. org; 1159 Causeway Rd; ☺9am-5pm; ☎) One of the more helpful visitor centers around; keeps an updated hotel-vacancy list with dedicated hotel hotline, and they even put out buckets of brochures to help after-hours visitors.

❶ Getting There & Away

Driving is the only way to come and go. The Sanibel Causeway (Hwy 867) charges an entrance toll (cars/motorcycles $6/2). Sanibel is 12 miles long, but low speed limits and traffic makes it seem longer. The main drag is Periwinkle Way, which becomes Sanibel-Captiva Rd.

Naples

📞 239 / POP 22,039

For upscale romance and the prettiest, most serene city beach in southwest Florida, come to Naples. This is the Gulf Coast's answer to Palm Beach. Development along the shoreline has been kept residential and the soft white sand is backed only by narrow dunes and half-hidden mansions. More than that, though, Naples is a cultured, sophisticated town, unabashedly stylish and privileged but also welcoming and fun loving with a large population of snowbirds from the Great Lakes. Families, teens, couture-wearing matrons, middle-aged executives and smartly dressed young couples all mix and mingle as they stroll downtown's 5th Ave on a balmy evening. Travelers sometimes complain that Naples is expensive, but you can spend just as much elsewhere on a less impressive vacation.

◉ Sights

Downtown Naples is laid out on a grid. There are two primary retail corridors: the main one is 5th Ave between 9th St S/US 41 and W Lake Dr. The other retail district runs along 3rd St S between Broad Ave S and 14th St S; this area, called Third St South, forms the heart of Old Naples. Throughout the area there's a mix of Mediterranean Revival and board-and-batten Cracker cottages. From spring to fall the Old Naples district hosts a range of events: music, art and a Saturday-morning farmers market. See the online calendar at www.thirdstreetsouth.com.

Naples also features 9 miles of idyllic white-sand beaches, and all downtown parking (off-beach) is free.

★ **Baker Museum**   MUSEUM
(📞239-597-1900; www.artisnaples.org; 5833 Pelican Bay Blvd; adult/child $10/free; ⊙10am-5pm Mon-Fri) The pride of Naples, this engaging, sophisticated art museum is part of the Artis–Naples campus, which includes the fabulous Philharmonic Center next door. Devoted to 20th-century modern art, the museum's 15 galleries and glass-dome conservatory host exciting temporary and permanent shows, ranging from postmodern works to photography, and paper craft to glass sculpture.

★ **Naples Botanical Garden**   GARDENS
(📞239-643-7275; www.naplesgarden.org; 4820 Bayshore Dr; adult/child 4-14yr $20/10; ⊙8am-5pm) This outstanding botanical garden styles itself as 'a place of bliss, a region of supreme delight.' And after spending some time wandering its 2½-mile trail through nine cultivated gardens you'll rapidly find your inner Zen. Children will dig the thatched-roof tree house, butterfly house and interactive fountain, while adults get dreamy-eyed contemplating landscape architect Raymond Jungles' Scott Florida garden, filled with cascades, 12ft-tall oolite rocks and legacy tree species like date palms, sycamore leaf figs and lemon ficus.

Rookery Bay National Estuarine Research Reserve   NATURE RESERVE
(📞239-530-5940; https://rookerybay.org; $5; ⊙learning center 9am-4pm Mon-Fri, plus Sat Jun-Sep) This reserve protects 110,000 acres of coastal lands and marine estuaries at the northern end of the Ten Thousand Islands, just south of Naples and north of Marco Island. A two-story learning center features an auditorium where guests watch an excellent video, along with a marine touch tank and 2300-gallon aquarium with a climb-in bubble. From there, popular activities include kayak and boating tours, a nature walk and birding excursions.

Golisano Children's Museum of Naples   MUSEUM
(C'mon; 📞239-514-0084; www.cmon.org; 15080 Livingston Rd; adult/child $10/12; ⊙10am-5pm Mon, Tue & Thu-Sat, 11am-4pm Sun; 🖈) Designed by kids (and child psychologists) for kids, this interactive children's museum is devoted to learning through play. A trolley takes kids to various exhibits, including a virtual pond, where they can observe fish and growing water plants, and a produce market, where fruit and veggies are sorted and sold to other kid 'customers.' Best of all is the Journey Through the Everglades with its boardwalk winding up into a two-story banyan tree overlooking a mangrove maze.

★ **Naples Municipal Beach**   BEACH
(12th Ave S & Gulf Shore Blvd) Naples' city beach is a long, dreamy white strand that succeeds in feeling lively but rarely overcrowded. At the end of 12th Ave S, the 1000ft pier is a symbol of civic pride, having been constructed in 1888, destroyed a few times by fire and hurricane, and reconstructed each time.

WORTH A TRIP

CORKSCREW SWAMP SANCTUARY

The crown jewel in the National Audubon Society's sanctuary collection, the **Corkscrew Swamp Sanctuary** (☑239-348-9151; www.corkscrew.audubon.org; 375 Sanctuary Rd W; adult/child 6-18yr $14/4; ☺7am-5:30pm, 4:30pm last entry) provides an intimate exploration of six pristine native habitats, including saw grass, slash pine and marsh, along a shady and stunning 2.25-mile boardwalk trail. The centerpiece is North America's oldest virgin bald-cypress forest, with majestic specimens more than 600 years old and 130ft tall. Put simply, Corkscrew is almost as good as the Everglades.

Abundant wildlife includes nesting alligators, night herons, endangered wood storks and trees full of ibis. However, two rare species, when spotted, make the news: the famed ghost orchid and the elusive Florida panther – search for the video of the time a Florida panther shared a boardwalk with a visitor. Volunteers help point out wildlife and signage is excellent; the visitor center rents out binoculars ($3).

The preserve is southeast of Fort Myers and northeast of Naples; take I-75 exit 111 and head east on Hwy 846/Imokalee Rd to Sanctuary Rd; follow the signs. Bring repellent for deer flies in late spring.

Parking is spread out in small lots between 7th Ave N and 17th Ave S, each with 10 to 15 spots of mixed resident and metered parking ($1.50 per hour).

Naples Nature Center   NATURE RESERVE
(☑239-262-0304; www.conservancy.org/nature-center; 1450 Merrihue Dr; adult/child 3-12yr $15/10; ☺9:30am-4pm Mon-Sat year round, plus noon-4pm Sun Jan-Mar) One of Florida's premier nature-conservancy and advocacy nonprofits, the Conservancy of Southwest Florida is a must-visit destination for anyone interested in Florida's environment and its preservation. While the new Discovery Center immerses visitors in southwest Florida environments, with informative films, displays and a rare peek into an avian, reptile and mammal nursery, the 21-acre preserve offers a half-mile trail and naturalist boat rides.

Palm Cottage   HISTORIC BUILDING
(☑239-261-8164; www.napleshistoricalsociety.org/palm-cottage; 137 12th Ave S; adult/child under 10yr $13/free; ☺1-4pm Tue-Sat) The oldest home in Naples and last remaining tabby-mortar cottage in Collier County, this quaint abode was built in 1895 for Henry Watterson, the editor of the *Louisville Courier Journal*. It then offered overflow accommodations for the Old Naples Hotel, hosting movie stars such as Hedy Lamarr. After more recent renovations it now houses the Naples Historical Society, which offers engaging guided tours of the house, in addition to talks by local authors and artists in the adjacent Norris Gardens.

Naples Zoo at Caribbean Gardens   ZOO
(☑239-262-5409; www.napleszoo.com; 1590 Goodlette-Frank Rd; adult/child 3-12yr $23/15; ☺9am-5pm) Caribbean Gardens is an Old Florida attraction that's been updated into an excellent small zoo. It has narrated boat rides in a lake to visit free-roaming, island-bound monkeys, giraffe, lions and a Malayan tiger, but the main reason to come here is the chance to see Athena, a rescued Florida panther, a species that is devilishly difficult to see in the wild. Black bears, alligators, coyotes and the Burmese python are among the Florida residents; last tickets sold at 4pm.

Take the time to learn about the conservation programs the zoo supports across the globe – this is one area where Naples Zoo really punches above its weight.

Delnor-Wiggins Pass State Park   STATE PARK
(☑239-597-6196; www.floridastateparks.org/parks-and-trails/delnor-wiggins-pass-state-park; 11135 Gulf Shore Dr; car/bike $6/2; ☺8am-sunset) This lovely state park and beach extends for a mile from the mouth of the Cocohatchee River. It boasts gorgeous white sands, which are protected during turtle-nesting season (May to October). There's an **observation tower** at the north end, but swimming is best south of the pass' fast-moving waters. The beach has food concessions (at parking lot four) and showers, and every item you might need to hire for a day in the sun. From US 41, take 111th Ave/Hwy 846.

Clam Pass County Park BEACH

(📞 239-252-4000; ☺8am–sunset) This county park covers 35 acres of coastal habitat, including a 0.75-mile boardwalk through a mangrove forest that leads out to a powdery white-sand beach. It's next to Naples Grand Beach Resort, which runs both the water-sports rentals and the free tram that travels between the large parking lot and the well-groomed beach. It's a favorite with families and young adults. The snack bar serves beer and cocktails.

🛌 Sleeping

Gondolier INN $$

(📞 239-262-4858; www.gondolierinnnaples.com; 407 8th Ave S; r $140-225; 🅿❄🤖) This classic 1950s Googie-style bungalow on a quiet street in Old Naples was given a design overhaul in 2018, and the pristine white rooms are some of the loveliest you'll find in town. Warm service and the fact that it's just a few blocks' walk to the beach add to the overall package.

Lemon Tree Inn MOTEL $$

(📞 239-262-1414; www.lemontreeinn.com; 250 9th St S; r $118-224; 🅿❄@🤖🏊) Value for money is high at the Lemon Tree, where 34 clean and brightly decorated rooms (some with passable kitchenettes) form a U around pretty, private gardens. Screened porches, free lemonade and continental breakfasts are nice, but most of all you'll treasure being walking distance to the 5th Ave corridor.

★Escalante BOUTIQUE HOTEL $$$

(📞 239-659-3466; www.hotelescalante.com; 290 5th Ave S; r from $266; 🅿❄@🤖🏊) Hidden in plain sight at 5th Ave and 3rd St, the wonderful Escalante is a boutique hotel crafted in the fashion of a Tuscan villa. Rooms and suites are nestled behind luxuriant foliage and flowering pergolas, and feature plantation-style furniture, European linens and designer bath products.

Inn on 5th HOTEL $$$

(📞 239-403-8777; www.innonfifth.com; 699 5th Ave S; r from $270, ste $550-800; 🅿❄@🤖🏊) This well-polished, Mediterranean-style luxury hotel provides an unbeatable location on either side of 5th Ave. Giant red vases grace the entryway. Stylish rooms are more corporate than romantic, but who complains about pillow-top mattresses and glass-walled showers? Full-service amenities include a 2nd-floor heated pool, business and fitness centers, and an indulgent spa. Free valet parking.

🍴 Eating

The Café CAFE $$

(📞 239-430-6555; www.thecafeon5th.com; 821 5th Ave S; mains breakfast $8-15, lunch $10-16; ☺7:30am-3pm; 🌿) You could easily walk past this unassuming cafe, but then you'd be missing out on a superlative breakfast of fluffy organic eggs, grilled Canadian bacon and perfectly toasted artisan bread. And that's just the standard; Ironman oatmeal topped with flax seeds, almonds, raisins and apples, açaí bowls, crepes and lox bagels topped with pale-pink salmon satisfy healthier cravings.

The Local AMERICAN $$

(📞 239-596-3276; www.thelocalnaples.com; 5323 Airport Pulling Rd N; mains $14-32; ☺11am-9pm; 🤖) 🌿 Aside from the irony of driving 6 miles north of downtown to eat local, this strip-mall farm-to-table bistro is worth the carbon footprint for fab sustainable fare, from the Mediterranean watermelon salad to the grass-fed beef. Try the 'Not Too Effin Hot Sauce,' if you're feeling feisty. Escape tourists. Eat local.

The Dock at Crayton Cove SEAFOOD $$

(📞 239-263-9940.; www.dockcraytoncove.com; 845 12th Ave S; mains $14-38; ☺11am-9pm) Away from the tourist scrum, this casual but classy quayside place is lovely on a balmy South Florida evening. There are so many seafood dishes to turn the head, but consider the key lime black grouper with blue crab cake, the blackened grouper, or the jumbo Gulf shrimp.

★Bha! Bha! Persian Bistro IRANIAN $$$

(📞 239-594-5557; www.bhabhabistro.com; 865 5th Ave S; mains $28-52; ☺5-9pm Sun-Thu, to 10pm Fri & Sat) This experimental, high-end establishment takes its name from the Farsi phrase for 'yum, yum,' and that turns out to be a serious understatement. Wash down the pistachio lamb meatballs with a saffron lemongrass martini, then continue on to a kebab marinated in exotic spices or the duck *fesenjune* ($38), slow braised with pomegranate and walnut sauce.

★USS Nemo SEAFOOD $$$

(📞 239-261-6366; www.ussnemorestaurant.com; 3745 Tamiami Trail N; lunch mains $11-20, dinner mains $27-42; ☺11:30am-2pm Mon-Fri, plus 4-9:30pm Sun-Thu, 4-10pm Fri & Sat) In a nondescript strip mall in north Naples, this popular seafood establishment is festooned in porthole art and known for insanely delicious miso-glazed sea bass and other delicacies. The wine list is extensive and the cocktails are impressive; try the mango bravo with tequila, triple sec, mango and jalapeño. It fills up very quickly; make reservations.

 Drinking & Nightlife

HobNob Kitchen + Bar   COCKTAIL BAR
(☑ 239-580-0070; www.hobnobnaples.com; 720 5th Ave S; ☺ 3:30-9:30pm Mon-Wed, 3:30-10pm Thu-Sat, 4-9pm Sun) This place is about as hipster-chic as Naples gets, with opulent modern decor and craft cocktails. Don't miss the innovative, New American appetizers, particularly the stuffed sweet peppers with chorizo, Italian sausage and crab. The crowd is lively and the bartenders have big personalities.

Happy hour is 3:30pm to 6pm, with 50% off house drinks.

☆ **Entertainment**

★ **Naples Philharmonic**   CLASSICAL MUSIC
(☑ 239-597-1900; www.artisnaples.org; 5833 Pelican Bay Blvd; tickets $22-150) Naples' 85-piece Philharmonic Orchestra is increasingly recognized as one of the country's best young orchestras. Andrey Boreyko became music director in 2014. The season runs from September to June, but the Artis complex within which it lives runs a year-round schedule of concerts and performances, including events for children.

Sugden Community Theatre   THEATER
(☑ 239-263-7990; www.naplesplayers.org; 701 5th Ave; tickets $30-40; ☺ box office 10am-4pm Mon-Fri, 10am-1pm Sat, noon-2pm Sun) Home of the Naples Players, the Sugden boasts two state-of-the-art stages, on the boards of which are enacted seven main-stage performances and four studio productions each year, including four KidzAct performances. It's well attended so book ahead.

ℹ **Information**

Third St Concierge Kiosk (☑ 239-434-6533; www.thirdstreetsouth.com; Camargo Park, 3rd St S; ☺ 10am-6pm Mon-Wed, 10am-9pm Thu & Fri, 9am-9pm Sat, noon-5pm Sun) What's in Old Naples? This friendly outdoor kiosk attendant is glad you asked.

> **DETOUR: THE EVERGLADES**
>
> If you've traveled as far south as Naples, you really owe it to yourself to visit the Everglades (p145). Heading west on the Tamiami Trail/Hwy 41, you can be in Everglades City in half an hour, Big Cypress in 45 minutes and Shark Valley in 75 minutes.

Visitor Information Center (☑ 239-262-6376; www.napleschamber.org; 2390 Tamiami Trail N; ☺ 9am-5pm Mon-Fri) Will help with accommodations; good maps, internet access and acres of brochures.

ℹ **Getting There & Away**

A car is essential; ample and free downtown parking makes things easy. Naples is about 40 miles southwest of Fort Myers via I-75.

Greyhound (☑ 239-774-5660; www.greyhound.com; 3825 Tollgate Blvd) connects Naples daily to Miami (from $19, 3½ hours), Orlando (from $32, 7¼ hours) and Tampa (from $27, 4¾ hours).

Southwest Florida International Airport (p439) is the main airport for Naples. It's about a 45-minute drive north, along I-75, in Fort Myers.

Marco Island

☑ 239 / POP 17,930

The largest and northernmost of the Ten Thousand Islands, Marco Island also offers the highest point of elevation – 58ft above sea level – in all of southwestern Florida. It was the Calusa people who long ago made this vantage point possible with the construction of an enormous shell mound over hundreds of years, which now stands in a residential neighborhood dubbed Indian Hill.

Modern development of the island only began in the 1960s. Draws today include miles upon miles of white-sand beach, boating and fishing among the mangrove islands, and a more relaxed, natural vibe than many of the coastal communities to the north. Shelling is also a big thing, with the best specimens often turning up at Tigertail Beach or on the nearby shores of Keewaydin Island, which remains largely pristine and inaccessible by car.

◉ Sights & Activities

Tigertail Beach BEACH
(400 Hernando Dr; nonresident parking $8) This white-sand, family-friendly beach is ideal for shelling, tide-pool exploration and hanging out at the playground. It also happens to be a fantastic birding site, with abundant shorebirds, gulls and raptors, and plenty of other species flitting among the nearby mangroves and lagoon. Facilities include restrooms, a boardwalk, a picnic area and a concession stand that rents out water toys.

**Hemingway
Water Shuttle** BOATING
(✆ 239-315-1136; www.hemingwaywatershuttle.com; 951 Bald Eagle Dr; adult/child return $44/24; ⊙ departures for Keewaydin at 8:30am, 10:30am, 12:30pm & 2:30pm) A family-owned boating company that departs from **Rose Marina** (✆ 239-394-2502; http://rosemarina.com; 951 Bald Eagle Dr; ⊙ 7am-6pm) out to Keewaydin Island and for an occasional sunset cruise in Marco Island's bay. Kids and adults will love spotting dolphins, manatees and birds (baby ospreys are common) on the way.

☞ Tours

Dolphin Study ECOTOUR
(✆ 239-642-6899; www.dolphin-study.com; 951 Bald Eagle Dr, Rose Marina; adult/child $64/46) One of the best ways to explore the marine ecosystem around Marco Island is with the Dolphin Study, a long-term scientific study of the behavior and movements of southwestern Florida's bottlenose dolphins. Using photo ID of dorsal fins, tour participants have the opportunity to get involved in sighting, counting and confirming individual sightings, data which is then shared with the Mote Marine Laboratory (p433) in Sarasota.

⊟ Sleeping & Eating

Boat House Motel MOTEL $
(✆ 239-642-2400; www.theboathousemotel.com; 1180 Edington Pl; r $115-165; ⓟ ❋ ☎ ☜) The most reasonable accommodations on the island, this 'boatel' in historic Old San Marco is family-owned and quaint, with just 20 rooms adorned in turquoise trim and in some cases featuring views of the Marco River. Those who arrive by boat can tie up at the private dock; there's a charcoal grill to cook your catch.

**Marco Beach
Ocean Resort** CONDO $$$
(✆ 239-393-1400; www.marcoresort.com; 480 S Collier Blvd; r $432-666; ⓟ ❋ ☎ ☜) This condo resort perches on a 5-mile stretch of white-sand beach and is consistently ranked among the top luxury stays in Marco Island. The 98 suites offer full kitchens and private balconies or patios, many with excellent sunset views. There's also a sumptuous spa, a beachfront southern Italian restaurant and nearby golf and tennis facilities.

★ **Doreen's Cup of Joe** CAFE $
(✆ 239-394-2600; www.doreenscupofjoe.com; 257 N Collier Blvd; breakfast $8-17; ⊙ 7:30am-2pm) This charming breakfast-until-midafternoon spot is the perfect place to grab coffee, some freshly squeezed orange juice and a stack of famous key lime pancakes before a morning boat excursion.

Snook Inn SEAFOOD $$
(✆ 239-394-3313; www.snookinn.com; 1215 Bald Eagle Dr; mains $12-29; ⊙ 11am-midnight) Right by the docks and with stunning views of Marco Bay, this long-standing restaurant and bar is the social hub of the island. The kitchen serves up excellent grouper sandwiches and will also fry up your catch. The Chickee Bar offers tasty frozen cocktails and live music every day.

❶ Getting There & Away

➤ Marco Island is directly south of Naples. Semi-regular buses connect Naples with Marco Island ($4.30).

➤ To reach Marco Island by car, go south on Collier Blvd from the junction of Collier Blvd and the Tamiami Trail (US 41).

Pine Island

✆ 239 / POP 7806

The 17-mile-long Pine Island, the region's largest, is a mangrove island with no sandy beaches to call its own, but it offers relaxing, quiet lodgings for anglers, kayakers and romantics fleeing the tourist hordes. It encompasses several communities: Matlacha is the island's center, with a small amount of commerce and funky Old Florida art galleries; you can find boat and fishing charters in the northern communities of Pineland and Bokeelia; and then there's the largely residential St James City at the southern tip. Pine Island is a great jumping-off point for all-day adventures among the region's tarpon-rich waterways and gorgeous barrier islands.

◉ Sights

The tiny fishing village of Matlacha (pronounced mat-la-shay) straddles the drawbridge to Pine Island and provides a quirky window into local life. In addition to its unpretentious fresh-seafood markets and restaurants, a collection of old fishing huts have been transformed into gift shops that sit like a clutch of chattering Day-Glo-painted tropical birds.

☆ Activities

Tropic Star   BOATING
(☎ 239-283-0015; www.cayocostaferry.com; Jug Creek Marina, Bokeelia; ⊙ daily ferry at 9:30am) Cruises and ferries to Cayo Costa depart from Jug Creek Marina. Ferries (adult/child $35/25) take an hour; other options include stops at Cabbage Key for lunch (adult/child $35/25). It also offers private water taxis (per hour $150), which are much faster and offer island-hopping to Useppa and Gasparilla Islands. Parking per half-day/full day/ overnight is $6/8/10.

Gulf Coast Kayak   KAYAKING
(☎ 239-283-1125; www.gulfcoastkayak.com; 4120 Pine Island Rd NW; ⊙ 9am-5pm Nov-May) In Matlacha, just past the drawbridge, Gulf Coast offers several kayak tours (adult/child $55/35) in the wildlife-rich Matlacha Pass Aquatic Preserve. You can also rent a canoe or kayak (half-/full day from $35/50) on a self-guided excursion. Want to kayak the 8 miles *to* Cayo Costa? Talk to them.

Matlacha Bridge   FISHING
They call this causeway between Cape Coral and Matlacha the 'fishingest bridge in the US,' sitting as it does at the center of several dynamic tidal flows. Anglers are here literally 24/7, especially during tarpon season.

🛏 Sleeping & Eating

Tarpon Lodge   INN $$
(☎ 239-283-3999; www.tarponlodge.com; 13771 Waterfront Dr, Pineland; r $125-210; P ❋ 🛜) The atmosphere at this genteel 1926 fishing inn seems barely to have changed since the doors opened. Rooms have a comfortable, stately feel while the dining room has a clubby vibe thanks to its gleaming wooden interior and black-and-white portraits of previous angling patrons. The family also manages the rental cottages on Cabbage Key Island.

Cabbage Key Inn   INN $$
(☎ 239-283-2278; www.cabbagekey.com; Cabbage Key; r $100-175, cottages $180-550) Stay in one of six rooms or eight cottages, all of which are Old Florida atmospheric with pretty touches (Rinehart and Dollhouse are favorites). They're not luxurious: no TVs, no pool and wi-fi only in the restaurant. But you're hardly marooned: the inn serves powerful cocktails and full dinner nightly (and they'll cook your catch), but make reservations (mains $9 to $16).

★ Perfect Cup   BREAKFAST $
(☎ 239-283-4447; www.facebook.com/theperfect cuproastery; 4548 Pine Island Rd, Matlacha; mains $5.50-12; ⊙ 6am-4pm Mon-Sat, to 3pm Sun) A genuine local gathering place, Perfect Cup offers just that: a bottomless mug of flavorful house-roasted coffee ($2.50) to go with its top-quality diner-style fare – creative omelets, French toast and pancakes.

🛍 Shopping

★ Lovegrove Gallery   ARTS & CRAFTS
(☎ 238-938-5655; www.leomalovegrove.com; 4637 Pine Island Rd, Matlacha; ⊙ 10am-5pm daily Nov-Jul, 11am-5pm Fri-Mon Aug-Oct) If Matlacha is unexpectedly groovy for such a sun-faded fishing village, you can thank artist Leoma Lovegrove. Her gallery has transformed a fishing shack into a whimsical vision of tile mosaics and paintings, with a loopy 'Tropical Waterways Garden' in back. Now the whole block is a bona fide slice of roadside Americana, with unusual gift and craft shops.

ℹ Information

For more information, visit www.pineisland chamber.org.

ℹ Getting There & Away

➡ Pine Island is due west of North Fort Myers and is not accessible by public transportation.

➡ By car, take US 41 to Pine Island Rd (Hwy 78) and head west.

➡ Boat charters and water taxis are available at Pineland and Matlacha Marinas.

AT A GLANCE

★

POPULATION
1.3 million

LONGEST RIVER
Suwannee

**BEST SUBTERRAN-
EAN ADVENTURES**
Florida Caverns State
Park (p483)

BEST OYSTERS
Up the Creek Raw
Bar (p486)

BEST LIVE MUSIC
Bradfordville Blues
Club (p481)

📅

WHEN TO GO

Mar Destin, Pensa-
cola and Panama City
Beach get flooded
with partying-hard
spring breakers.

May & Oct Enjoy
the most temperate
weather through
most of the region.

Nov–Feb The tem-
perature and lodging
rates dip; locals turn
out for November's
Florida Seafood
Festival.

Apalachicola (p484)
DATE_98 / SHUTTERSTOCK ©

The Panhandle

The most geographically northern portion of Florida is by far its most culturally Southern side. The Panhandle – that spit of land embedded in the left shoulder of the Florida peninsula – is bordered by Alabama and Georgia, and in many ways the region's beaches are effectively coastal extensions of those states.This is a coast of primal, wind-blown beauty in many places, particularly the undeveloped stretches of salt marsh and slash pine that spill east and west of Apalachee Bay. In other areas, the seashore is given to rental houses and high-rise condos.

Inland, you'll find a tangle of palmetto fans and thin pine woods interspersed with crystal springs, lazy rivers and military testing ranges – this area has one of the highest concentrations of defense facilities in the country.

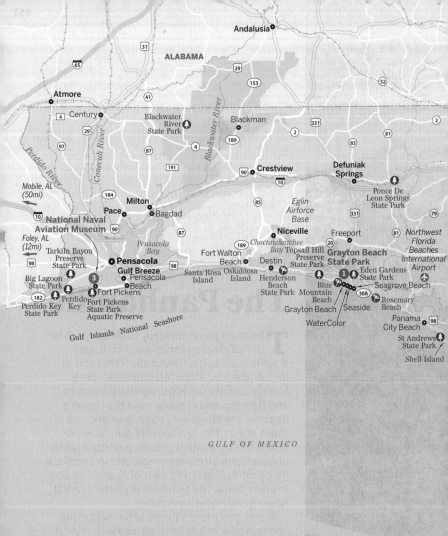

The Panhandle Highlights

1 **Grayton Beach State Park** (p468) Feasting your eyes on the luminous Gulf waters as they lap against one of the country's most beautiful beaches.

2 **Apalachicola** (p484) Embracing your inner romantic in the Gulf's most charming town.

3 **National Naval Aviation Museum** (p454) Marveling at the Blue Angels' death-defying maneuvers and getting hands-on with amazing exhibits.

4 **St George Island State Park** (p482) Walking

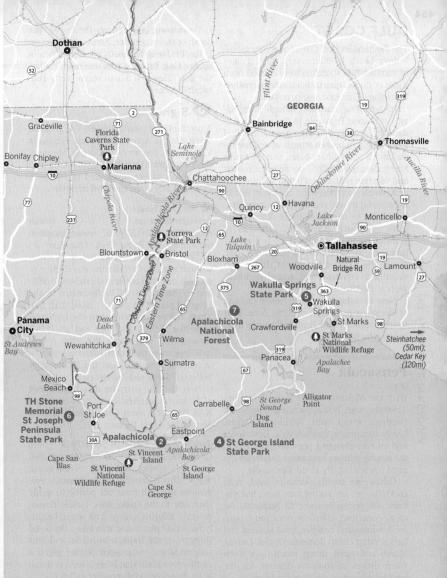

windswept dunes, salt-marsh trails and pristine beaches.

⑤ Wakulla Springs State Park (p488) Boating through a tangle of mossy cypress and mangroves teeming with

manatees, alligators and bird life.

⑥ TH Stone Memorial St Joseph Peninsula State Park (p475) Marveling at the dune, forest and salt marsh

quilt of the best Panhandle wilderness.

⑦ Apalachicola National Forest (p487) Biking, hiking, kayaking or spotting wildlife in Florida's largest forest.

GULF COAST

The Panhandle's Gulf Coast has a very specific draw: beach. Its shimmering, curving miles of vanilla-white shoreline were formed from a glut of silicate quartz that has been crushed by geologic eons into sugary powder.

It's not all sun and sand, though. From Naval Air Station Pensacola in the west to Tyndall Air Force Base in the east, one can find a seemingly unbroken stretch of defense installations and military bases, and the towns here reflect that reality – between the resorts and vacation rentals, you'll find a glut of federal contracting offices and cigar bars servicing active duty and retired service members.

Thanks to clouds of green forest, long acres of coastal marsh and stretches of stunning sand-dune hills, there is a gentle, breeze-blown prettiness to the Gulf Coast. Be on the lookout for decent dining and nightlife in Pensacola and larger base towns such as Destin.

Note that the Gulf Coast, unlike the rest of Florida, is in the Central Time Zone. That means this half of the Panhandle is one hour behind the Big Bend.

Pensacola

📞 850 / POP 52,700

With the Alabama border just a few miles down the road, Pensacola mingles laid-back Southern syrup with Florida brashness. Lively beaches, a Spanish-style Downtown and an ever-changing population thanks to the nearby military base make this by far the most interesting city in the Panhandle.

Urban-chic trends (locavore food, craft cocktails etc) are taking root here, but visitors still primarily come to Pensacola for an all-American, affordable vacation experience: white-sand beaches, fried seafood and bars serving cheap domestic drinks. During March and April, things reach fever pitch when droves of students descend for the weeklong bacchanalia of spring break.

ℹ️ HURRICANE MICHAEL

In October 2018, the Panhandle received a direct hit by devastating Category 5 Hurricane Michael. Tourist hotspots rebounded quickly, but smaller communities like Mexico Beach and natural areas like St George State Park are still rebuilding some two years later.

Downtown, centered on Palafox St, lies north of the waterfront. Across the Pensacola Bay Bridge is the mostly residential peninsula of Gulf Breeze. Cross one more bridge, the Bob Sikes (toll $1), to reach pretty Pensacola Beach.

◉ Sights

A combo ticket (adult/child $8/$4) gets you seven days of access to Historic Pensacola Village, the Pensacola Children's Museum, the TT Wentworth Jr Florida State Museum and Voices of Pensacola, and can be purchased at any of the included museums.

★ **National Naval Aviation Museum**   MUSEUM
(Map p456; 📞 800-327-5002; www.navalaviation museum.org; 1750 Radford Blvd; ⊙ 9am-5pm; 🚼)
FREE A visit to Pensacola is not complete without a trip to this enormous collection of military aircraft muscle and artifacts. Adults and children alike will be fascinated by the range of planes on display: more than 150! That's before we even get to the high-tech stuff like flight simulators and an IMAX theater. You can watch the Blue Angels (p457) practice their death-defying air show at 8:30am most Tuesdays and Wednesdays between March and November.

Note that the entry for non–Department of Defense identification holders is via the NAS Pensacola West Gate located at 1878 South Blue Angel Parkway.

Tarkiln Bayou Preserve State Park   PARK
(📞 850-492-1595; www.floridastateparks.org; 2401 Bauer Rd; vehicle/cyclist $3/2; ⊙ 8am-sunset; 🅿️) 🐾 This fascinating park preserves ecosystems that run from wet prairie to sandy shoreline to the eponymous Tarkiln Bayou, an eerie, alluring spill of dark water, brightly flowering plants and thin trees. Peppered throughout are trails, boardwalks and four species of the endangered pitcher plant, a carnivorous plant that lures insects to death in its digestive, petal-crowned gullet.

The park is located about 15 miles west of Pensacola, and 8 miles north of Perdido Key.

Fort Barrancas & Advanced Redoubt   FORT
(Map p456; 📞 850-934-2600; www.nps.gov/guis/learn/historyculture/advanced-redoubt.htm; 3182 Taylor Rd; $7; ⊙ 8:30am-4:30pm; 🅿️) 🐾 On a dramatic bluff overlooking Pensacola Bay, 19th-century Fort Barrancas was built by enslaved laborers atop an abandoned 18th-cen-

tury Spanish fort. Now part of the National Park Service, the fort has endless dark passageways to explore but not much in the way of displays. A half-mile away via a walking trail lie the ruins of Advanced Redoubt, a Civil War–era fort. Call ahead to ask about scheduled tours.

Historic Pensacola Village   MUSEUM
(Map p460; ☑850-595-5985; www.historic pensacola.org; Tarragona & Church St; adult/child $8/4; ⊙10am-4pm Tue-Sat; P 🖝) 🖉 Pensacola's post-colonial history spans more than 450 years. This fascinating self-contained enclave of photogenic historic homes turned into museums is the perfect starting point for familiarizing yourself with the city. Most can be toured on your own, but a few are accessible only with a guide – tours depart Tivoli House at 11am and 1pm.

Admission is good for one week.

Voices of Pensacola   MUSEUM
(Map p460; ☑850-595-5985; www.historic pensacola.org; 117 E Government St; adult/child $8/4; ⊙10am-4pm Tue-Sat) 🖉 Part oral history archive, part interpretive center, this museum highlights – via videos and audio recordings – the different cultural groups that have contributed to the demographic soup that is Pensacola.

Pensacola Museum of Art   MUSEUM
(Map p460; ☑850-432-6247; www.pensacola museum.org; 407 S Jefferson St; adult/student $7/4; ⊙10am-5pm Tue-Fri, 11am-4pm Sat; P) In the city's former jail (built in 1908), this lovely art museum features an impressive, growing collection of major 20th- and 21st-century artists, spanning cubism, realism, pop art and folk art.

Visitors to Historic Pensacola Village can pick up a ticket to the museum of art there for $5.

Bay Bluffs Park   PARK
(Map p456; www.pensacolascenicbluffs.org; 3400 Scenic Hwy; ⊙sunrise-sunset; P) 🖉 FREE Off Pensacola Scenic Bluffs Hwy, this 32-acre park has wooden boardwalks that lead you along the side of the steep bluffs, through clutches of live oaks, pines, Florida rosemary and holly down to the empty beach below. With all of that said, persistent litter can be an issue.

TT Wentworth Jr Florida State Museum   MUSEUM
(Map p460; www.historicpensacola.org/plan-your-visit/museums-properties/tt-wentworth-museum;

PENSACOLA SCENIC BLUFFS HIGHWAY

This 11-mile stretch of road, which winds around the precipice of the highest point along the Gulf Coast, makes for a peaceful drive or slightly challenging bike ride. You'll see stunning views of Escambia Bay and pass a notable crumbling brick chimney – part of the steam-power plant for the Hyer-Knowles lumber mill in the 1850s – the only remnant of what was the first major industrial belt in the area.

330 S Jefferson St; adult/child $8/4; ⊙10am-4pm Tue & Wed, to 7pm Thu-Sat, noon-4pm Sun; P) Housed in an enormous historic mansion, this state museum showcases two floors of Florida and Pensacola history, and one floor of oddities belonging to its namesake TT Wentworth – a historic-minded 20th-century Pensacola politician – including his famous (and disgusting!) petrified cat.

Pensacola Children's Museum   MUSEUM
(Map p460; ☑850-595-1559; 115 E Zaragoza St; adult/child $8/4; ⊙10am-4pm Tue-Sat; P 🖝) Learn about more than 450 years of local history and have some fun along the way in this compact museum occupying two floors of the historic (and allegedly haunted) Arbona building. Most exhibits are hands-on, and geared toward children 10 and under. The 2nd floor has more to offer kids on the higher side of that age bracket, including a dress-up area.

Pensacola Lighthouse   LIGHTHOUSE
(Map p456; ☑850-393-1561; www.pensacola lighthouse.org; 2081 Radford Blvd; adult/child $7/4; ⊙10am-5:30pm Mon-Sat, from noon Sun; P) Be on the lookout for ghosts of past lighthouse keepers as you climb the 177 steps of this 160ft, 1859 lighthouse, rumored to be haunted. The views are quite stunning, as you might expect. If you're afraid of heights, you can hang back and take a look at the adjacent museum.

🏃 Activities

Garcon Point Trail   HIKING
(FL 281; 🎫) 🖉 FREE The Panhandle's interior hides large swaths of Florida wilderness. One example: the long fields of wiregrass, longleaf pine and oak hammocks that

Pensacola Area

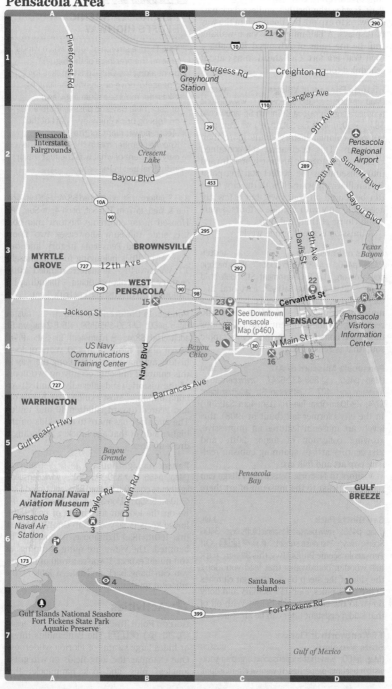

See Downtown Pensacola Map (p460)

290
21

10

Burgess Rd

Greyhound Station

Creighton Rd

110

Langley Ave

29

Pensacola Interstate Fairgrounds

Crescent Lake

9th Ave

Pensacola Regional Airport

289

12th Ave

Summit Blvd

Bayou Blvd

Bayou Blvd

453

10A

90

295

BROWNSVILLE

292

Davis St

9th Ave

Texar Bayou

MYRTLE GROVE

727

12th Ave

WEST PENSACOLA

298

90

98

15

22

Cervantes St

17

23

20

PENSACOLA

Pensacola Visitors Information Center

Jackson St

98

9

W Main St

US Navy Communications Training Center

Bayou Chico

30

16

8

727

Barrancas Ave

WARRINGTON

Gulf Beach Hwy

Bayou Grande

Taylor Rd

Duncan Rd

Pensacola Bay

GULF BREEZE

National Naval Aviation Museum

1

Pensacola Naval Air Station

3

6

173

4

Santa Rosa Island

10

399

Fort Pickens Rd

Gulf Islands National Seashore Fort Pickens State Park Aquatic Preserve

Gulf of Mexico

N 0 ——————— 4 km
0 ——————— 2 miles

Pensacola Area

THE PANHANDLE PENSACOLA

blanket the land cut through by the Garcon Point Trail, about 16 miles east of Pensacola. An easy 1.7-mile loop circles through a flat, vibrantly green plain where the sky touches down to the palmettos.

Look for the trailhead just north of the toll plaza that precedes the bridge to Gulf Breeze.

⭐ Festivals & Events

Blue Angels   AIR SHOW
(☑850-452-3806; www.naspensacolaairshow. com; NAS Pensacola; ⏰8:30am Tue & Wed Mar-Nov) **FREE** To maintain its profile after WWII, and to reinforce its recruitment drive, the US Navy gathered some of its elite pilots to form the Blue Angels, a flight-demonstration squadron traveling to air shows around the country. The squadron's practice sessions can be observed here at their home base twice a week (weather permitting) from spring through autumn.

These days, performing for about 15 million people a year, 'the Blues' (never 'the Angels'), their C130 Hercules support aircraft named Fat Albert and their all-Marine support crew visit about 35 show sites a year. Six jets execute precision maneuvers, including death-defying rolls and loops, and two F/A-18s undertake solo flights; the show culminates in all six planes flying in trademark delta formation.

Bleachers are available for the first 1000 spectators, so arrive early; BYO coffee and lawn chairs. There is also a big performance around Veteran's Day (mid-November).

The viewing area is behind the National Naval Aviation Museum (p454) parking lot.

The name 'Blue Angels' caught on during the original team's trip to New York in 1946, when one of the pilots saw the name of the city's Blue Angel nightclub in the *New Yorker*.

Each of the Blues does a two-year tour of duty. In addition to the six pilots (which always include one marine) is a narrator, who'll then move up through the ranks, and an events coordinator.

Gay Memorial Day   LGBT
(www.johnnychisholm.com; ⊘ late May) A three-day fiesta (across the Memorial Day weekend) of DJ soirees, all-night beach parties, drag shows and general fun and frivolity: crowds reach as many as 50,000, so book ahead!

🛏 Sleeping

Solé Inn   MOTEL $
(Map p460; 🖉 850-470-9298; www.soleinnand suites.com; 200 N Palafox St; r $79-199; P 🌊 ❄ @ 🗢 🗏) Just north of the historic center, this motel is at the quieter end of Palafox St and bursts with mid-century flair. Rooms aren't huge, but price, location and originality make up for the lack of space. And who can complain about the self-serve happy hour between 5pm and 7pm?

The dandelion fountain on the patio is a unique touch.

Lee House   BOUTIQUE HOTEL $$
(Map p460; 🖉 850-912-8770; www.leehouse pensacola.com; 400 Bayfront Pkwy; ste $165-255; 🗢) Waterfront location and historical architectural charm come together at the Lee House, which boasts nine individually appointed suites that were remodeled in 2020. The wrap-around porch dotted with rocking chairs feels plucked from old-time, Gulf South central casting.

Pensacola Victorian B&B   B&B $$
(Map p460; 🖉 850-434-2818; www.pensacola victorian.com; 203 W Gregory St; r $95-150; P 🗢) This stately 1892 Queen Anne building offers four lovingly maintained guest rooms. The standout is Suzanne's Room, with its massive bathroom and vintage claw-foot tub.

The B&B is about a mile north of downtown Pensacola.

New World Inn   BOUTIQUE HOTEL $$
(Map p460; 🖉 850-432-4111; www.newworld landing.com; 600 S Palafox St; r from $170; P 🗢) Peek under the lid of this former box factory and you'll find surprisingly lovely rooms furnished with antiques and luxe bedding. They've got the location game down pat – the attractions of Historic Pensacola Village are just a few blocks away.

There's a fine-dining restaurant, Skopelos, attached.

🍴 Eating

Taqueria El Asador   MEXICAN $
(Map p456; 🖉 850-696-3232; www.facebook.com/ elasadorpcola; 7955 N Davis Hwy; tacos $2, burritos $8; ⊘ 10am-8:30pm Mon-Sat) Florida may not be on the border, but few Mexican restaurants can top El Asador. Its simple setting consists of a smattering of plastic chairs, a smoking grill and a menu of staples (tacos, burritos, tostadas) that are executed to near perfection. The only downside is it's tricky to find: set back from the street, behind a Shell station, about 7 miles north of downtown.

Blue Dot   BURGERS $
(Map p460; 🖉 850-432-0644; www.facebook.com/ bluedotpensacola; 310 N De Villiers St; burgers $6; ⊘ 10:30am-4pm Tue-Fri) The line swells with locals in the know by opening time for these burgers – a simple, greasy and perfectly seasoned affair – and nobody is here to dance. Chips and soda are the only side items, and the lone concession to vegetarians is offering burger toppings on a bun for $2. Cash only.

Get here early – they always run out before closing.

Saigon Oriental Market & Deli   VIETNAMESE $
(Map p456; www.facebook.com/saigonoriental marketanddeli; 604 N Pace Blvd; mains from $3.70; ⊘ 8am-7pm; P ❄ 🍴) This buzzing grocery store and eatery attracts locals of all ages, races and creeds to scarf down pho, bun, bahn mi and other traditional Vietnamese dishes. Most dishes are under $10 and many are under $5, making this a top-notch

budget option. Vegetarians will love the tofu bahn mi and spring rolls.

Don't miss the drink selection, which ranges from Boba teas to lychee juice to Japanese energy drinks.

End of the Line Cafe VEGAN $
(Map p460; ☑850-429-0336; www.eotlcafe.com; 610 E Wright St; items $7-11; ☺10am-10pm Tue-Sat, 11am-2pm Sun; ☏🅿) A funky, fair-trade cafe with velour and vinyl lounges, Pensacola's original vegan cafe serves up casual fare like tempeh reubens and tofu BLTs, as well as cooking classes and cultural events, including open-mic nights.

There's also free wi-fi.

Joe Patti SEAFOOD $
(Map p456; ☑850-432-3315; www.joepattis. com; 534 South B St, at Main St; items from $2.50; ☺7:30am-6pm) At this beloved seafood emporium (established in 1931), get dock-fresh fish and seafood, prepared picnic food and sushi.

Henny Penny's Patisserie DESSERTS $
(Map p456; ☑301-979-0380; www.facebook. com/pg/hennypennyspatisserie; 4412 W Jackson St; cupcakes $2.80; ☺10am-4pm Sun-Fri, to 2pm Sat; 🖪) Take a detour for something sweet at this friendly local bakery. Giant red velvet brownies, key lime cupcakes and elegant fruit tarts fill the pastry cases, and there's plenty of space – and comfy chairs – to enjoy your selection. Snap a photo in front of the colorful mural on the side of the building.

Check the website for occasional evening events like poetry readings and Galentine's Day date nights.

Dharma Blue INTERNATIONAL $$
(Map p460; ☑850-433-1275; www.dharmablue. com; 300 S Alcaniz St; mains $15-30; ☺5-9:30pm Mon-Fri;,10am-2pm&5-9:30pm Sat&Sun; 🖪) The eclectic menu of this compact local favorite ranges from semolina-dusted calamari and blackened catch of the day to mouthwatering sushi. A casual, welcoming vibe extends from the cozy, chandelier-adorned interior to the sunny patio out front.

Five Sisters Blues Cafe CAFE $$
(Map p460; ☑850-912-4856; www.fivesistersblues cafe.com; 421 W Belmont St; mains $7-18; ☺11am-9pm Tue-Thu, to 10pm Fri & Sat, 10am-4pm Sun) Get your weekly dose of blues (Thursday to Sunday) and soul food with a Creole flair (crab cakes, fried green tomatoes, seafood gumbo) at this classic diner just north of Pensacola's historic district. Even more fun – if you can

get a table – are the Sunday jazz brunches: try the chicken and Belgian waffles.

My Favorite Things CAFE $$
(Map p456; ☑850-346-1707; www.facebook.com/ MyFavoriteThingsPensacola; 2183 E Cervantes St; mains $8-23; ☺10am-3pm Tue & Wed, to 9pm Thu & Fri, 9am-9pm Sat, to 3pm Sun) This rustic cafe on the eastern edge of town serves delightful soups, sandwiches and salads, plus a small selection of simple seafood mains including grilled shrimp and pan-seared scallops. Best, however, are the breakfasts: fluffy omelets, decadent French toast and eggs Benedict with Canadian bacon.

The quirky connected shop is worth a browse, if you like novelty items or anything emblazoned with a sassy slogan.

★Iron AMERICAN $$$
(Map p460; ☑850-476-7776; www.restaurant iron.com; 22 N Palafox St; mains $26-46; ☺4:30-10pm Sun-Thu, to 1am Fri & Sat; ☏) Armed with New Orleans experience, chef Alex McPhail works his ever-changing menu magic at Downtown's Iron, which remains a standout of Pensacola's locally sourced, high-end culinary scene. Extremely friendly mixologists know their craft, and McPhail's food – from beer-braised pork belly to Creole-seasoned catch of the day – punches above the Emerald Coast's weight class.

🍷 Drinking & Nightlife

In season, the beachside bars have more of a spring-break vibe (tequila and sozzled new drinkers); Downtown offerings tend to be slightly more sophisticated. Many restaurants have their own bars. Check out www. pnj.com/entertainment for music listings.

Azalea Cocktail Lounge BAR
(Map p456; ☑850-433-9186; www.facebook.com/ azaleacocktaillounge; 810 N Davis St; ☺10:30am-2:30am) So-called 'dives' in trendier cities would kill for a tenth of the vintage cred of Azalea, known as 'the Z.' Friendly bartenders know most patrons by name but new faces are made welcome. Aside from a couple of flat screens, the interior hasn't changed much since the place opened in 1947. Here's hoping it never will.

Cash only (there's an ATM on site). Smoking allowed.

Odd Colony Brewing Co BREWERY
(Map p460; ☑850-285-0743; www.facebook.com/ oddcolony; 260 N Palafox St; ☺4-10pm Mon-Thu, 2-11pm Fri, 11am-11pm Sat, to 10pm Sun; ☏) Hop

Downtown Pensacola

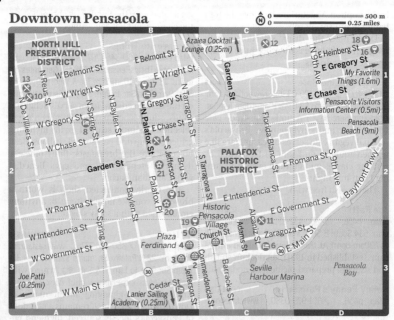

Downtown Pensacola

heads will find much to appreciate at this laid-back craft brewery, which features a creative and ever-rotating beer list. On a recent visit, choices ranged from a kettle sour with sour cherries and plums to a stout with espresso and cinnamon.

There's no food served but food trucks occasionally pull up out back.

Cabaret　　　　　　　　　　　　　GAY
(Map p460; ☑850-607-2020; 101 S Jefferson St; ☉3pm-2:30am) A funky interior and a vibe that ranges from trivia nights to drag shows

is the defining experience at this friendly 'gayborhood' bar, a Pensacola gem that's open to all sexualities.

Elbow Room　　　　　　　　　　　　PUB
(Map p456; ☑850-434-0300; www.facebook.com/ElbowRoomPensacola; 2213 W Cervantes St; ☉4pm-2am Tue-Sat) Although it doesn't have much external visual appeal, this funky, dark, retro dive bar in suburban Pensacola houses a whole world of fun and a mellow vibe.

McGuire's Irish Pub   PUB
(Map p460;   ☑850-433-6789;   www.mcguire
sirishpub.com; 600 E Gregory St; ⊙11am-2am)
This ginormous Irish theme park of a pub
gets rowdy around 9pm and is super popular at dinner time: the pub grub is top-notch.
Try the dry-aged steaks.

Don't try to pay for your drinks with one
of the million dollar bills hanging from the
ceiling – a local once found himself in the
slammer that way!

Roundup   GAY
(Map p460; ☑850-433-8482; www.facebook.com/
theroundupbar; 560 E Heinberg St; ⊙2pm-3am)
For those who like their men manly, check
out this niche-y, neighborhood hangout with
a killer furry-friendly patio. Ladies are welcome, but cowboys, tradies and bikers are
always flavor of the month.

Seville Quarter   CLUB
(Map p460; ☑850-434-6211; www.sevillequarter.
com; 130 E Government St; cover $3-10; ⊙8am-
3am Mon-Sat, from 11am Sun) This monster of
an entertainment complex takes up an entire city block and contains seven separate
eating, drinking and music venues, with an
HG Wells-ian 1890s decor. There's a business
lunch and family tourist crowd on weekdays, and weekend brunches are fairly civilized, but most evenings, enter only if you're
in the mood to party: the crowd here on Pensacola's Bourbon Street is ready to have fun.

☆ Entertainment

Saenger Theatre   THEATER
(Map p460; ☑850-595-3880; www.pensacola-
saenger.com; 118 S Palafox Pl; ⊙box office 10am-
4:30pm Mon-Fri) This Spanish baroque beauty
was reconstructed in 1925 using bricks from
the Pensacola Opera House, which was destroyed in a 1916 hurricane. It now hosts
popular musicals and top-billing music acts
and is home to the Pensacola Symphony Orchestra and the Pensacola Opera.

Vinyl Music Hall   LIVE MUSIC
(Map p460; ☑850-607-6758; www.vinylmusichall.
com; 2 S Palafox Pl; box office noon-5pm Mon-Fri)
This is a solid venue for live music, booking
acts that run from mainstream headliners to
indie. Check the website for listings.

❶ Information

Pensacola Visitors Information Center (Map
p456; ☑800-874-1234; www.visitpensacola.
com; 1401 E Gregory St; ⊙8am-5pm Mon-Fri,

9am-4pm Sat, 10am-4pm Sun) Come to the
foot of the Pensacola Bay Bridge for a bounty
of tourist information, knowledgeable staff and
a free internet kiosk.

❶ Getting There & Away

Pensacola Regional Airport (Map p456;
☑850-436-5000; www.flypensacola.com;
2430 Airport Blvd) is served by most major US
airlines. Primary direct connections outside
Florida include Atlanta, Charlotte, Dallas and
Houston. The airport is 5 miles northeast of
Downtown, off 9th Ave on Airport Blvd. A taxi
costs about $20 to Downtown and around $35
to the beach. Try **zTrip** (☑850-433-3333;
www.ztrip.com/pensacola), previously known
as Yellow Cab, a convenient hybrid of the
rideshare and traditional cab experiences.

The **Greyhound station** (Map p456; ☑850-
476-4800; www.greyhound.com; 505 W
Burgess Rd) is located north of the downtown
area. **Escambia County Transit** (ECAT; ☑850-
595-3228; www.goecat.com; rides $1.75) has a
free trolley service (ECAT) connecting downtown
Pensacola and the beach between Memorial Day
weekend and the end of September.

I-10 is the major east–west thoroughfare used
by buses, and many pass down Palafox St.

Pensacola Beach
☑850 / POP 9310
Distinctly separate from Pensacola itself,
Pensacola Beach is a pretty stretch of powdery white sand; gentle, warm waters;
and a string of mellow beachfront hotels.
The beach occupies nearly 8 miles of the
40-mile-long Santa Rosa barrier island, surrounded by the Santa Rosa Sound and the
Gulf of Mexico to the north and south, and
by the federally protected Gulf Islands National Seashore on either side. Though determined residents have protected much of
the barrier island from development, several
high-rise condos have created a bit of a Gulf
Coast skyline.

The area is a major hub for local entertainment and special events, including Mardi
Gras celebrations, a triathlon, wine tastings,
a summer music series and parades.

◉ Sights & Activities

★**Gulf Islands National Seashore**   PARK
(☑850-934-2600; www.nps.gov/guis; vehicle $20;
⊙sunrise-sunset; 🅿) 𝒫 The highlight of the
Florida Panhandle, this 150-mile stretch
of mostly undeveloped white-sand beach
is a prime example of what the Gulf Coast

looked like before human settlement (which, to be fair, can often be seen from here in the form of high-rises in the distance). The National Seashore is not contiguous, but you'll find portions all along the coast: long swaths of sugar-white dunes crowned with sea oats, a perfect example of pristine flatland beach.

Beach wheelchairs are available at Perdido Key, Santa Rosa Beach and Fort Pickens.

Naval Live Oaks Reservation PARK
(Map p456; ☑ 850-934-2600; www.nps.gov/guis/planyourvisit/naval-live-oaks-area.htm; 1801 Gulf Breeze Pkwy, Gulf Breeze; ☺ 8:30am-4:30pm Mon-Fri; P) ⚑ FREE This section of Gulf Islands National Seashore doesn't actually contain (much) seashore – instead, it consists of groves of local maritime hammock (forest) cut through by 7.5 miles of hiking trails. Local live oaks, prized for their toughness and durability, were used as timber for early American warships.

Fort Pickens HISTORIC SITE
(Map p456; ☑ 850-934-2600; www.nps.gov/guis/learn/historyculture/fort-pickens.htm; 1400 Fort Pickens Rd; 7-day pass pedestrian & cyclist/car $7/15; ☺ sunrise-sunset; P🚻) ⚑ Part of the Gulf Islands National Seashore (p461), this 1834 historic fort perched at the western extent of the Santa Rosa barrier island has survived wars and scores of hurricanes to remain a fascinating and scenic excursion. Pick up a self-guided-tour map from the visitor center.

Shoreline Park UFO Spotting PARK
(Map p456; 800 Shoreline Dr, Gulf Breeze; P) Maybe it's activity from the nearby Pensacola Naval Air Station, but this stretch of the Gulf has apparently had hundreds of UFO sightings in the past few decades, with reports right along the coast. Local skywatchers (including members of the Mutual UFO Network) gather at this park with binoculars and lawn chairs in the hope of a close encounter: as good a reason as any to spread out a beach blanket and gaze at the stars.

MBT Divers DIVING
(Map p456; ☑ 850-455-7702; www.mbtdivers.com; 3920 Barrancas Ave; courses from $289; ☺ 8am-6pm Mon-Sat, to 3pm Sun) The *Oriskany* CV/CVA-34 aircraft carrier, at approximately 900ft long and 150ft tall, was the largest vessel ever sunk as an artificial reef when it was submerged in 2007 off Pensacola Beach. This professional outfitter will gear up and help experienced divers plan their dive. A variety of dive courses are also available, including an exclusive *Oriskany* class.

Courses

Lanier Sailing Academy BOATING
(Map p456; ☑ 850-432-3199; www.laniersail.com/al/pensacola-3; 997 S Palafox St; sailboat rental from $245; ☺ 9am-5pm Tue-Sun) Conditions at Pensacola Bay are perfect for sailing, and this award-winning school offers a variety of courses, including a basic three-day introduction to sailing ($595). Those in the know can rent a Capri 22 from $250 daily.

🛏 Sleeping

Fort Pickens Campground CAMPGROUND $
(Map p456; ☑ 850-934-2622; www.recreation.gov/camping/campgrounds/234704; 1400 Fort Pickens Rd, Gulf Islands National Seashore; tent & RV sites $26; P) ⚑ Amid the windblown trees across from the beach, these two pleasant campgrounds are popular with RV-ers, though you'll see the odd tent or two. There are fire pits, a bathhouse and a small camp store. Park entrance fees to Gulf Islands National Seashore (p461) must be paid separately.

Campsites can be reserved up to six months in advance.

Paradise Inn MOTEL $$
(Map p456; ☑ 850-932-2319; www.paradiseinn-pb.com; 21 Via de Luna Dr; r $99-140; P❄🐾🕐🛜) Across from the beach, this sherbet-colored motel is a lively, cheery place thanks to its popular bar and grill (ask for a quiet room near the parking lot). Compact quarters are spick and span with tiled floors and brightly painted walls.

Holiday Inn Resort HOTEL $$$
(Map p456; ☑ 850-932-5331; www.holidayinnresortpensacolabeach.com; 14 Via de Luna Dr; r from $210; P❄🐾@🛜) This beachfront hotel has inviting rooms with ultra-comfy beds and great showers. Oceanfront rooms have spacious balconies overhanging the soft, white sands and the cool turquoise waters below. Suites and kids suites are available, and the 'Lazy River' pool is killer. Friendly, obliging staff help seal the deal. Excellent value.

🍴 Eating

★Native Café BREAKFAST $
(Map p456; ☑ 850-934-4848; www.thenativecafe.com; 45a Via de Luna Dr; mains $7-15; ☺ 7:30am-3pm Mar-Oct, to 2pm Nov-Feb; 🛜🍴) This funky breakfast and lunch spot, 'owned and oper-

ated by friendly natives,' is a welcome addition to the fried-fish stretch. Try a shrimp po' boy, grilled chicken sandwich, fish tacos, rice and beans or seafood gumbo – or, for a cheap morning jump-start, eggs Benedict or pancakes.

Dog House Deli DINER **$**
(Map p456; ☑850-916-4993; www.doghousedeli. com; 35 Via de Luna Dr; items from $3; ☺8:30am-3:30pm; ⊞) For cheap and easy beachfront eats, try this local favorite, in business for more than 40 years, serving a range of signature or build-your-own dogs as well as a tasty breakfast menu.

Peg Leg Pete's SEAFOOD **$$**
(Map p456; ☑850-932-4139; www.peglegpetes. com; 1010 Fort Pickens Rd; mains $11-30; ☺11am-8pm Sun-Thu, to 9pm Fri & Sat; ⊞) Ah-har, me hearties, walk ye olde plank...you get the idea, this place has a theme going. Pop into Pete's for almost-beachfront oysters, fat grouper sandwiches, crab legs and jumbo sea scallops. There's nothing fancy about the woodsy, somewhat grungy sea-shanty decor with license plates covering the walls, but the service is swift, despite how busy it gets.

Grand Marlin SEAFOOD **$$$**
(Map p456; ☑850-677-9153; www.thegrandmarlin.com; 400 Pensacola Beach Blvd; mains $14-37; ☺11am-10pm Mon-Thu, to 11pm Fri & Sat, 10am-10pm Sun) This versatile seafood restaurant and oyster bar gives you the best of both worlds: enjoy a casual alfresco atmosphere on the best-for-sunset patio, or treat yourself to formal fine dining indoors. Either way, expect excellent service and oceanic delights such as blue crab, lobster mac 'n' cheese (yum!) and fresh-from-the-boat seafood cooked any way you like.

❶ Information

Pensacola Beach Visitors Information Center (Map p456; ☑850-932-1500; www.visit pensacolabeach.com; 7 Casino Beach Boardwalk; ☺9am-5pm Mon-Sat, 10am-3pm Sun) On the right as soon as you enter Pensacola Beach; this is a small place with some useful maps and brochures about goings-on, road closures (due to storms) and anything else beach-oriented.

Perdido Key

☑850 / POP 32,000
The easternmost Florida section of the Gulf Islands National Seashore spans Perdido Key's crystalline waters. These powdery dunes are home to the endangered Perdido Key beach mouse, which blends in well with the white-quartz sands here. There are two coastal state parks in the area: Perdido Key State Park and, on the northern side of the lagoon, between Perdido Key and the mainland, Big Lagoon State Park, with great crabbing in the lagoon's shallows. You'll find several free beach areas along the stretch of Perdido Key town – an otherwise unseemly blot of high-rise condos and share houses.

◉ Sights

Perdido Key State Park STATE PARK
(☑850-492-1595; www.floridastateparks.org; 15301 Perdido Key Dr; vehicle $3; ☺8am-sunset; ℗) ⊘ This alluring coastal state park protects the 247-acre barrier island of the same name, a windblown, sand-strewn landscape of rolling dunes, tufts of beach grass and the soft bending sea oats that give the region such an unmistakable allure.

Big Lagoon State Park STATE PARK
(☑850-492-1595; www.floridastateparks.org; 12301 Gulf Beach Hwy; vehicle $6; ☺8am-sunset; ℗) ⊘ Get a taste of the wilds on the Panhandle at Big Lagoon, a quilt of salt marshes, pine forest, bays, ponds and beaches, all interconnected by boardwalks and easy walking trails. Bird-watchers will be in heaven, as will anyone who wants a little peace and quiet.

Big Lagoon State Park is about 3 miles northeast of Perdido Key.

✷ Festivals & Events

Interstate Mullet Toss CULTURAL
(www.florabama.com/mullet-toss; ☺Apr) Every year, on the last full weekend in April, locals gather on both sides of the Florida–Alabama state line for a time-honored tradition: the mullet toss. The idea – apart from a very fine excuse for a party – is to see who can throw their (dead) mullet (an abundant local fish) the furthest across the border from Florida into Alabama.

People have developed their own techniques: tail first, head first, or breaking its spine and bending it in half for better aerodynamics. The mullet toss is organized by Perdido Key's Flora-Bama Lounge, Package and Oyster Bar (p464), a legendary bar and roadhouse just east of the state line.

Frank Brown International Songwriters' Festival
MUSIC

(☑850-492-7664; www.frankbrownsongwriters.com; ⊘Nov) This 10-day concert series features hundreds of singer-songwriters performing around the Gulf Coast region, including in Perdido Key and Pensacola.

🛏 Sleeping

Big Lagoon State Park Camping
CAMPGROUND $

(☑800-326-3521; www.reserveamerica.com; 12301 Gulf Beach Hwy; campsite $20; ℗) ⬭ There are 68 bucolic campsites in this state park peppered among the pine woods. Electric hookups and drinkable water available.

🍷 Drinking & Nightlife

Flora-Bama Lounge, Package & Oyster Bar
BAR

(☑850-492-0611; www.florabama.com; 17401 Perdido Key Dr; ⊘11am-3am) This legendary bar and roadhouse just east of the state line has live music 365 days a year. It also hosts the annual mullet toss (p463) and Polar Bear Dip (a New Year's dip in the cold sea – comes with a free drink).

Flora-Bama has tried to get mullet tossing into the *Guinness World Records*, but its time hasn't come, yet.

❶ Getting There & Away

Hwy 292 (Gulf Beach Hwy) runs east–west across Perdido Key, and becomes Hwy 182 at the Alabama state line. Gulf Shores, AL, is about 20 miles west on Hwy 292/182 and Pensacola (and I-110) is about 18 miles east on Hwy 292.

Fort Walton Beach

☑850 / POP 22,300

Stretching along US 98 – maybe a little euphemistically relabeled the Miracle Strip – Fort Walton Beach is a jumble of strip malls, beachfront mansions, seaside restaurants and neon. The only exception is a pretty downtown-ish part that rambles from Perry Ave to Florida Place. 'FWB' isn't as tourism-minded as towns like nearby Destin, and the place pretty much feels like a military base town that happens to be perched near the Gulf Coast.

Between Fort Walton Beach and Destin, which bend around Choctawhatchee Bay like two crab claws, lies pristine beachfront owned by the US Air Force, whose largest base, Eglin, is here.

◉ Sights

The most attractive element of Fort Walton Beach lies just outside of its borders: the Okaloosa Day Use Area section of Gulf Islands National Seashore (p461), located just east of town. This long stretch of quiet, windblown dunes and sea oats is jarringly wild when contrasted to the neon strips of beachside development that bracket it. The parking area leads to a beach access point and picnic tables.

Indian Temple Mound & Museum
ARCHAEOLOGICAL SITE

(☑850-833-9595; www.fwb.org/parksrec/page/indian-temple-mound-museum; 139 Miracle Strip Pkwy SE; adult/child $5/3; ⊘noon-4:30pm Mon-Fri, from 10am Sat; ℗) ⬭ One of the most sacred sites for local Native American culture to this day, the 17ft-tall, 223ft-wide ceremonial and political temple mound, built with 500,000 basket-loads of earth and representing what is probably the largest prehistoric earthwork on the Gulf Coast, dates back to somewhere between 800 and 1500 CE. On top of the mound you'll find a re-created temple, which houses a small exhibition center.

The museum offers an extensive overview of 12,000 years of Native American history, and houses flutes, ceramics and artifacts fashioned from stone, bone and shells, as well as a comprehensive research library.

US Air Force Armament Museum
MUSEUM

(☑850-882-4062; www.afarmamentmuseum.com; 100 Museum Dr, Eglin Air Force Base; ⊘9:30am-4:30pm Mon-Sat; ℗) FREE One for military buffs. The exterior of this hangar-style museum, flanked by fighter planes, appears small, but inside are extensive weapons displays – including an F-105 Thunderchief missile and a Warthog simulator – as well as a detailed history of Eglin base, the largest in the US.

Expect an unapologetically pro-American spin on US military history. The museum is about 7 miles northeast of Fort Walton Beach.

Okaloosa Island Pier & Boardwalk
PIER

(1030 Miracle Strip Pkwy E; access $2, fishing adult/child $7.50/4.50; ⊘24hr Apr-Oct, 5am-9pm Nov-Mar; ℗) Stretching out almost a quarter of a mile into the Atlantic, this popular recreational-fishing pier is open 24 hours in the summer and is illuminated for night fishing. Rental gear is available (from $7) and there are no fishing-license requirements.

The pier and adjacent boardwalk are also good for a leisurely stroll, and the neighboring beach is simply a damn fine stretch of sand.

🛏 Sleeping

★ **Aunt Martha's Bed & Breakfast** B&B $
(☎850-243-6702; www.auntmarthasbedandbreak fast.com; 315 Shell Ave SE; r $105-115; 🖩🖵) A short walk from Downtown, this charming inn overlooks the Intracoastal Waterway. Elegant, unfussy rooms with big brass beds look out into the leafy branches of live oak trees. The common area has a baby grand piano, a well-stocked library and French doors that open onto a breezy veranda.

Martha's Southern breakfasts – crawfish quiche, ham and cheese grits, stuffed French toast, you name it – are a veritable feast.

Henderson Park Inn INN $$$
(☎888-836-1105; www.hendersonparkinn.com; 2700 Hwy 98; r from $229; 🖩🖵🖵🖵) This classy shingled inn has 35 tastefully decorated rooms with high-end Egyptian cotton linens, and thoughtful touches such as chocolates on your pillow. Breakfast, lunch, drinks and snacks are all included, making this a popular spot with honeymooners.

🍴 Eating

Stewby's Seafood Shanty SEAFOOD $
(☎850-586-7001; www.stewbys.com; 427 Racetrack Rd NW; items $5-18; ⏰10:30am-9pm; 🅿🖵) Off the main drag, en route to Eglin base, this unpretentious, predominantly takeout restaurant is famed for its signature sandwiches, fried seafood platters and excellent value for money. Go for the soft-shell crab if it's in season.

Bay Café FRENCH $$
(☎850-344-7822; 233 Alconese Ave; mains $18-28; ⏰11am-3pm & 5-10pm; 🅿) Amberjack meunière, pan-seared scallops and filet mignon all feature on the menu of this *très jolie* French cafe on the waterfront beneath the shadow of the Brooks Bridge. Loved by locals for more than 30 years, the cafe has an indoor-outdoor patio with wonderful views of the bay, and an extensive wine list.

🍸 Drinking & Nightlife

Props Brewery & Grill BREWERY
(☎850-586-7117; www.propsbrewery.com; 255 Miracle Strip Pkwy SE; ⏰11am-11pm) A friendly, unassuming spot to down a cold, locally brewed craft beer, check out sports on the big screen or hang in the beer garden to mingle with locals.

❶ Getting There & Away

Fort Walton Beach is about 55 miles west of Panama City Beach and about 41 miles east of Pensacola, along Hwy 98.

Destin–Fort Walton Beach Airport (Northwest Florida Regional Airport; VPS; ☎850-651-7160; www.flyvps.com; 1701 State Road 85 N) serves the Destin–Fort Walton area. In addition, the **Emerald Coast Rider** (☎850-833-9168; www.ecrider.org; $1.50; ⏰8am-7pm Mon-Fri) runs a shuttle service between Fort Walton Beach and Destin.

Destin

☎850 / POP 14,000

Destin has the odd claim of appealing to retirees, families and spring breakers. From the road, the town looks like an endless chain of strip malls, high-rise condos and mini amusement parks. But local beaches are a veritable balm for the soul, and are quite beautiful besides.

Deep-sea fishing is an entrenched part of the area's tradition, with an offshore shelf dropping to depths of 100ft about 10 miles off Destin's east pass. Locals call their town the 'world's luckiest fishing village' – not that it looks much like a village anymore.

◉ Sights

Destin boasts more than 24 miles of beach, which are by far the main draw for visitors. On sunny days, the sand truly is almost uncannily white – ironically, these sea-level beaches derive their pale hue from crushed quartz that washed down from the ancient Appalachian mountains. There are 13 public access points to local beaches. Check www.cityofdestin.com for a full breakdown. Parking around access points is often limited.

Henderson Beach State Park BEACH
(☎850-837-7550; www.floridastateparks.org; 17000 Emerald Coast Pkwy; vehicle $6; ⏰8am-sunset; 🅿🖵) 🏖 Our favorite beach area in Destin is this state park, which includes a 0.8-mile nature trail. There are also some excellent beachside campsites ($30), which include running water and electric hookups.

Arrive early or late in peak season and on weekends – this park is deservedly popular and there's often a wait to get in.

THE PANHANDLE DESTIN

PONCE DE LEON SPRINGS STATE PARK

This park (☎850-836-4281; www.florida
stateparks.org; 2860 Ponce de Leon
Springs Rd, Ponce de Leon Springs; vehicle
$4; ☺8am-sunset; P) features one of
Florida's loveliest and least touristed
springs. The spring has clear, almost
luminescent waters, like something
from a fairy tale, and is studded with
knobby trees and surrounded by lad-
ders for easy swimming access. Two
short, self-guided nature trails skirt the
bank of nearby Blackwater Creek, and
rangers conduct seasonal walking tours.
Bring a picnic – there are plenty of tables and even charcoal grills for a cook-
out. The water temperature remains a
constant 68°F (20°C).

Ponce de Leon Springs State Park
is just off of I-10, about 40 miles north
of the 30A Beaches, around 100 miles
west of Tallahassee and about 90 miles
east of Pensacola.

Shores at Crystal Beach Park   BEACH
(www.cityofdestin.com; 2964 Scenic Hwy 98;
☺sunrise-sunset; P⛵) FREE Although all of
Destin's gleaming, white-sand beaches are
family-friendly, the presence of restrooms, a
picnic area and shaded pavilions makes this
one especially so.

**Destin Boardwalk &
HarborWalk Village**   WATERFRONT
(☎850-687-1237; www.destinboardwalk.com;
102 Harbor Blvd; P⛵) This tourist mecca of
timeshare condos, boutiques, restaurants,
nightclubs and a marina is worth a stroll,
especially if you have kids. Most of the area's tour operators (including private fishing
charters) have kiosks here and there are
plenty of activities to enjoy, albeit at tourist
prices.

🏃 Activities

Just Chute Me   WATER SPORTS
(☎850-398-4827; www.parasaildestin.com; 500
Harbor Blvd; per person from $50; ☺8am-sunset
Mar-Oct) Calm waters and stunning vistas
make the Gulf a great place for parasailing.
This professional operator takes beginners
into the great blue yonder above to gaze at
the great blue wonder below.

It also offers snorkeling excursions and a
dolphin cruise.

ScubaTech   DIVING
(☎850-837-2822; www.scubatechnwfl.com; 301
Harbor Blvd, cnr Marler St; snorkeling from $40,
scuba diving from $110; ☺9am-5pm Mon-Sat, to
4pm Sun) Take advantage of the region's great
diving with this competent outfitter, which
also offers beginner scuba classes. Boat trips
take snorkelers or scuba divers to the many
shipwrecks and reefs in the Gulf – you're
likely to spot fish like grouper and flounder
in addition to sharks and stingray.

👉 Tours

Southern Star Dolphin Cruises   CRUISE
(☎850-837-7741; www.southernstardolphincruise.
com; 100 Harbor Blvd, Suite A; adult/child $29/16)
🚣 This environmentally conscious operator
has been sailing for more than 20 years,
observing the bottlenose dolphins that live
in these temperate waters. Two-hour cruises operate year-round from an 80ft glass-
bottom boat. Check the website for
schedules.

It's right next to the Margaritaville
restaurant.

🛏 Sleeping

You'll find a good spread of accommodations here, ranging from rustic camping to
chain hotels to resorts, though not much
that's distinctive or unique. Most visitors
opt to stay in vacation rentals, which are
listed on a variety of websites, including
www.destinvacation.com and www.destinfl
rentals.com.

**Henderson Beach
State Park**   CAMPGROUND $
(☎850-837-7550; https://floridastateparks.
reserveamerica.com; 17000 Emerald Coast Pkwy;
tent & RV sites $30, day use $6; P) This coastal
paradise has 54 very private sites and good
restrooms amid twisted scrub pines, with a
0.75-mile nature walk through the dune system. It's better suited to RVs than tents.

🍴 Eating

Donut Hole Café & Bakery   BAKERY $
(☎850-837-8824; 635 Harbor Blvd; items from $4;
☺6am-10pm; ⛵) This simple bakery-diner is
a local favorite, serving sit-down breakfasts,
fluffy takeout buttermilk doughnuts and
bakery items, including generous wedges of
decadent key lime pie, all day long.

Boathouse Oyster Bar SEAFOOD $

(☑ 850-837-3645; www.boathouseoysterbardestin.
com; 288 Harbor Blvd; dozen oysters $15; ⊙ 11am-
11pm; P) What looks like a waterfront shed
is...well, a waterfront shed, but a shed where
live music, raw oysters, boiled crawfish, fried
seafood, buckets of cold beer and waterfront
vibes are the reason to come. Closing times
vary, depending on which band is playing. (Hint: bring a dollar bill to add to the
wallpaper.)

McGuire's Irish Pub STEAK $$

(☑ 850-650-0000; www.mcguiresirishpub.com; 33
E Hwy 98; mains $19-40; ⊙ 11am-2am; P ♿) This
enormous Irish-pub-microbrewery-steak-
house is a Panhandle institution. There's
a reason for that; this may be a mall-sized
complex with kitschy stuff on the walls
(which would usually raise our warning
lights), but the steaks and burgers are solid.
Local beers (brewed on site in beautiful copper vats) round out the experience.

McGuire's is extremely popular with local
military families; a good chunk of the US
Navy and Air Force has had a steak or two
(and a beer or four) at this spot. Closing time
varies, but it's usually around 2am.

Craft Bar AMERICAN $$

(☑ 850-460-7907; www.thecraftbarfl.com/destin;
4424 Commons Dr E; mains $15-27; ⊙ 11am-11pm
Mon-Thu, to midnight Fri & Sat, to 10pm Sun; P)
As much restaurant as bar, Craft Bar brings
a bit of 21st-century foodie fanaticism and
craft-beer obsession to Destin (and a few
other spots in North Florida; this is a local
chain). Billing itself as 'a Florida gastropub,'
the airy, modern interior is attached to a
kitchen that serves blackened grouper, ahi
tuna BLTs and bison burgers.

The attached liquor and beer store has a
fantastic selection of booze, and the week-
night happy hour (2pm to 6pm) offers
drinks and bites for just $5 each.

Dewey Destin's SEAFOOD $$

(Dewey Destin's Harborside; ☑ 850-837-7525; www.
destinseafood.com; 202 Harbor Blvd; mains $12-30;
⊙ 11am-9pm; P ♿) Refreshingly human-scale
compared to some of the corporate-
behemoth restaurants on Destin's main strip,
this longtime local favorite serves up simple
fried and steamed seafood platters and cool
rum drinks in a crowded old beach shack
decorated with vintage Florida photos.

The restaurant, owned by descendants of
Destin's founder, has a second location in
Navarre.

Louisiana Lagniappe SEAFOOD $$$

(☑ 850-837-0881; www.thelouisianalagniappe.
com; 775 Gulf Shore Dr; mains $27-42; ⊙ 4:30-9pm
Mon-Fri, to 10pm Sat & Sun; P ♿) Decent New
Orleans-style cooking can be found right
here in Destin, and there's a gorgeous view
overlooking the water to boot. Ocean-fresh
seafood includes grouper topped with soft-
shell crab, redfish topped with – hey, why
not? – more crab plus lobster, and blackened shrimp with smoked tasso ham cream
sauce. Did we mention the views?

⚱ Drinking & Nightlife

HarborWalk Village (just off US 98, on the
very western edge of Destin, before the
bridge to Okaloosa Island) and the boardwalk on Okaloosa Island (p464), about 6
miles west of Destin proper, have plenty
of nightlife – mainly busy, tourist-oriented
pubs and restaurants overlooking the water.
The bars here tend to attract a mix of older
tourists and military folks. While the atmosphere can feel a little casual earlier in the
evening, the party can get raucous later in
the night.

🛍 Shopping

Destin Commons MALL

(☑ 850-337-8700; www.destincommons.com;
4100 Legendary Dr; ⊙ 10am-9pm Mon-Sat, 11am-
7pm Sun) Yes, this is an enormous mall complex, but as outdoor mall complexes go, it's
quite attractive, and an easy place to take
the family, especially on a rainy day. Lose
yourself amid dozens of shops and a gigantic
movie theater.

ⓘ Getting There & Away

Destin is about 45 miles west of Panama City
Beach and about 47 miles east of Pensacola,
along Hwy 98. Destin–Fort Walton Beach Airport
(p465), sometimes still referred to as Northwest
Florida Regional Airport, serves the Destin–Fort
Walton area, with direct services to many US
cities, including Chicago and Tampa.

South Walton & 30A Beaches

☑ 850

Sandwiched between Destin and Panama City
along Scenic Hwy 30A are 16 unincorporat-
ed communities collectively known as South
Walton (or The Beaches of South Walton, if
you love chamber of commerce branding,
but we draw the line at 'SoWal'). Each town

has its own identity, and most are master-planned resort towns with architecture following set themes. If you're wondering what happens when you bake New Urbanism in the Florida sun, here's the answer.

If you only make two stops, we recommend delightful Grayton Beach, which feels as though it was settled by old-school hippies who came into money (stay a night here if you can) and the meticulously manicured village of Seaside, which is so well planned they filmed *The Truman Show* here. Other points of interest include the whimsically named community of WaterColor, Moroccan-themed Alys Beach and the Dutch-inspired hamlet of Rosemary Beach. For more information, check out www.discover30a.com.

◉ Sights

There are more than 50 public access points to the South Walton beaches with varying degrees of accessibility; a complete list can be found at www.visitsouthwalton.com. Find accessibility info at www.destinwheels.com/handicapped-beach-access. Parking lots can fill fast, especially on the weekends, so it's best to arrive early.

★ **Grayton Beach State Park**   STATE PARK
(☑850-267-8300;   www.floridastateparks.org; 357 Main Park Rd, Grayton Beach; vehicle $5; ☺8am-sunset; P) ✎ With nearly 2000 acres of marble-colored dunes rolling down to the water's edge, this state park's beauty is genuinely mind-blowing. The park sits nestled against the wealthy but down-to-earth community of Grayton Beach, home to the famed Red Bar and to the quirky Dog Wall – a mural on which residents paint portraits of their dogs.

Locals flock here for nightly sunsets and to wakeboard on the unique coastal dune lakes that shimmer across the sand from the Gulf. The park also contains the Grayton Beach Nature Trail (start your self-guided tour at the gate), which runs from the eastern side of the parking lot through the dunes, magnolias and pine flatwoods and onto a boardwalk to a return trail along the beach.

Topsail Hill Preserve State Park STATE PARK
(www.floridastateparks.org; 7525 W Scenic Hwy 30A, Santa Rosa Beach; vehicle/pedestrian $6/2; ☺8am-sunset; P) ✎ There's some 1640 acres of natural beauty to discover at Topsail, including quiet white-sand beaches, sun-battered wetlands, sand pine scrub forest, a 2.5-mile nature trail, and three rare coastal

dune lakes – inland bodies of water located less than 2 miles from the coast, connected to the Gulf via outfall channels that run through the dunes.

Accommodation options are available.

Deer Lake State Park   STATE PARK
(☑850-267-8300; www.floridastateparks.org; 6350 E County Rd 30A; car/bicycle/pedestrian $3/2/2; ☺8am-sunset; P) ✎ Named for its eponymous coastal dune lake – a body of water that sits inland from the Gulf, but is connected to it – this park is rich in scrub oaks, magnolia trees, palmetto copses and wildflowers. A boardwalk path makes for a delightful means of observing all of the above.

Blue Mountain Beach   BEACH
(2365 S Scenic Highway 83; ☺sunrise-sunset; P 👫) FREE Towering a cloud-kissing (if by cloud-kissing we mean fog) 64ft-high, 'Blue Mountain' is supposedly the highest point on the pancake-flat Gulf Coast. Be on the lookout for blue lupine flowers, which supposedly gave this alpine peak its name. Relax on the exquisite beach in the shadow of this mighty massif. (Note: the 'mountain' does not actually provide a ton of shade.)

Eden Gardens State Park   STATE PARK
(☑850-267-8320; www.floridastateparks.org; 181 Eden Gardens Rd, Santa Rosa Beach; $4, tours adult/child $4/2; ☺8am-sunset, tours 10am-3pm Thu-Mon; P) ✎ Inland from 30A on a peninsula jutting into Choctawhatchee Bay, manicured gardens and lawns front the 1800s estate home of the Wesleys, a wealthy Florida timber family. The white-columned house was purchased and renovated in 1963 by Lois Maxon, who turned it into a showcase for Louis XVI furniture and many other heirlooms and antiques. Visitors can relax in the oak-lined grounds or the lovely picnic area by the water.

Tours are at the top of each hour, and last approximately 45 minutes.

Inlet Beach   BEACH
(S Orange St & W Park Place Ave; ☺sunrise-sunset; P 👫) FREE This is one of the larger beach access points in South Walton. Inlet Beach itself is hugged by high dunes and old-school A-frame houses, both of which you will walk by as you stroll from the parking lot to a wide sweep of sand.

Dune Allen Beach   BEACH
(Hwy 30A & Fort Panic Rd; ☺sunrise-sunset; P) FREE Simply one of the more pleasant

beaches along South Walton, Dune Allen is a family-friendly slice of sand that's great for the kids, or adults who just want a view of the water and sand between their toes.

Underwater Museum of Art MARINE RESERVE
(http://umafl.org; off Grayton Beach State Park) Roughly 1 mile off Grayton Beach, America's first permanent underwater museum consists of around two dozen sculptures spread around a 1-acre space, with more installations planned in the years ahead. The project, launched in 2018, marries art with conservation, as the works will eventually create an artificial reef and marine habitat in the barren sand flats of the Gulf.

The artwork sits in 58ft (18m) of water, and divers must be certified Open Water Diver to visit. Several dive operators run trips, including **Emerald Coast Scuba** (☑850-837-0955; http://divedestin.net; 503-B Harbor Blvd).

Activities

The area is ideally suited for cyclists. You can follow the 19-mile paved Timpoochee trail, which parallels Scenic Hwy 30A; the 8-mile Longleaf Pine Greenway hiking and cycling trail, paralleling Hwy 30A inland from just east of SR 395 to just before SR 393; and the Eastern Lake trail, which starts in Deer Lake State Park and links up with the western end of the Longleaf Pine Greenway.

If you prefer four wheels to two, allow at least two hours to drive the short stretch of the 30A between Destin and Panama City Beach, even if you're not planning to stop: speed limits are low, kids and cars are plentiful and the beaches are mesmerizing. Find more information at www.waltonoutdoors.com.

30A Bike Rentals CYCLING
(☑850-865-7433; www.30Abikerentals.net; 5399 E County Hwy 30A, Seagrove Beach; ☺rental per day from $20) The flat Florida coast is perfect for casual two-wheeled exploration, and this is a good spot for a bicycle rental, including free delivery and pickup to most locations on 30A. Also rents regular ($20) and beach ($50) wheelchairs by the day or week.

Big Daddy's Bike Shop CYCLING
(☑850-622-1165; www.bigdaddysbikes.com; 2217 W County Hwy 30A, Blue Mountain Beach; rentals from $40; ☺9am-5pm Mon-Sat) 'Dangerously Optimistic since 1998,' Big Daddy will get you wheelin' down picturesque 30A, or on

the beach itself, in no time at all. A plethora of two-wheeled rentals include helmet, lock and free delivery and pickup to most locations on Hwy 30A.

Sleeping

Accommodations on this section of the 30A vary from beachside camping to intimate guesthouses, a luxury resort and a wide selection of private-home and condo rentals. For the latter, try www.graytoncoastrentals.com, www.30avacationrentals.com or www.cottagerentalagency.com. Book your rooms ahead of time, or consider staying in Destin or Panama City Beach if you're on a budget.

Grayton Beach State Park CAMPGROUND $
(☑850-267-8300; https://floridastateparks.reserveamerica.com; 357 Main Park Rd, Grayton Beach; tent & RV sites from $30, cabins $110-130; ℗) ☀ It might be tricky to make spending the rest of your life here in paradise a reality, but it doesn't mean you can't afford to stay here for a short time. Cheap-as-chips camping and compact, cozy cabins make a taste of Grayton Beach living – albeit in the rough – a possibility for everybody. Newer tent sites have electric hookups.

Topsail Hill Preserve State Park CAMPGROUND $
(https://floridastateparks.reserveamerica.com; 7525 W Scenic Hwy 30A, Santa Rosa Beach; tent/RV sites $24/42, cabins $100; ℗☀) ☀ Topsail Hill includes tent sites, RV hookups and quite dapper cabins that come with kitchens and living rooms, and can sleep up to six guests. Rates for cabins drop by around $15 from August to January. Cabins require a two-night minimum stay on weekends.

★Hibiscus Coffee & Guesthouse GUESTHOUSE $$
(☑850-231-2733; www.hibiscusflorida.com; 85 Defuniak St, Santa Rosa Beach; r $135-175, apt $245-285; ℗☎) This delightfully chilled-out garden guesthouse is tucked into a tree-studded corner of the area's oldest township. A variety of self-contained rooms and apartments are done up with tropical prints and funky folk paintings, like an arty friend's beach house.

Free breakfast in the attached cafe.

Pearl HOTEL $$$
(☑877-935-6114; www.thepearlrb.com; 63 Main St, Rosemary Beach; r/ste from $300/430) It's hard to miss the Pearl – this Victorian-style building dominates the architectural landscape,

which is saying something in New Urbanist Rosemary Beach. Inside, you'll find rooms that mush pseudo-historical vibe with integrated guest-service apps that will book your dinner reservations, as well as intelligent lighting and temperature control.

Rosemary Beach Inn BOUTIQUE HOTEL **$$$**
(☑866-348-8952; www.rosemarybeach.com/the-rosemary-beach-inn; 78 Main St, Rosemary Beach; r from $199; P ⟨?⟩) This sunset-red, delightfully renovated hotel in downtown Rosemary Beach is styled like a European inn. There's no lobby, and the 11 guest rooms are quiet and individually decorated, with flat-screen TVs and Keurig coffeemakers. Guests receive complimentary access to the local racquet club and fitness center.

WaterColor Inn & Resort RESORT **$$$**
(☑888-991-8878; www.watercolorresort.com; 34 Goldenrod Cir, WaterColor; r from $350; P @ ⟨?⟩ ⟨≋⟩) This lauded, full-service luxury resort designed by architect David Rockwell occupies almost 500 acres of beachfront land. Contemporary rooms feature soft linens in seaside tones, large windows and balconies. Many have ocean views or are steps from the beach. Free kayak and canoe rentals, and six gorgeous pools to distract you from the stunning waters of the Gulf.

✕ Eating

Meltdown on 30A FAST FOOD **$**
(☑850-231-0952; 2235 E County Hwy 30A, Seaside; items from $5; ⊙10am-9pm, to 10pm Fri & Sat; P) Unless you're gluten- and dairy-intolerant, we dare you to go past this excellent food truck, a vendor of oozy grilled-cheese deliciousness (we couldn't resist the brie, bacon and fig jam creation). It also serves cheese-tastic breakfast biscuits and grits till 11am. Eat in the shade or on the beach – cheap, cheery and... did we mention the cheese?

Cafe Hibiscus BREAKFAST **$**
(☑850-231-1734; www.hibiscusflorida.com/cafe; 85 Defuniak St, Santa Rosa Beach; mains $4-9; ⊙8am-11am; P ☑) Located on the grounds of the Hibiscus Guesthouse (p469), this cafe serves great coffee, tasty granola, fluffy waffles and biscuits smothered in a vegan-sausage gravy. A gorgeous spot for breakfast and caffeine.

Red Bar PUB FOOD **$$**
(☑850-231-1008; www.theredbar.com; 70 Hotz Ave, Grayton Beach; dinner mains $14-25; ⊙11am-3pm & 5-10pm, bar to 11pm Sun-Thu, to midnight Fri

& Sat; P) There's live music most nights at this homey, funky local fave, housed in an old general store stuffed with knick-knacks and oddities. Friendly mobs hunker down for beers, goss and good tunes, and tuck into a small selection of well-prepared dishes, such as crab cakes, shrimp-stuffed eggplant and manicotti.

★ Cafe Thirty-A AMERICAN **$$$**
(☑850-231-2166; www.cafethirtya.com; 3899 E Scenic Hwy 30A, Seagrove Beach; mains $14-39; ⊙5-9pm; P) Set in a sprawling townhouse that echos the beach style of nearby Seaside, this smart-casual fine-dining establishment feels good from the moment you walk through the door. Seafood delights include Maine lobster in paradise and tandoori salmon, but you can enjoy a filet mignon cooked to perfection if you just gotta have some turf with your surf.

Main courses are two-for-one until 6pm.

Roux 30A INTERNATIONAL **$$$**
(☑850-213-0899; www.roux30a.com; 114 Logan La, Ste 1A, Grayton Beach; themed prix-fixe dinner $65; ⊙6-9:30pm Tue & Thu-Sat; P) This odd-duck gem works closely with local farmers and fishers to produce an eclectic, prix fixe menu that jukes from New American to Indian to other world cuisines. Dine at the chef's table and make new friends.

George's at Alys Beach AMERICAN **$$$**
(☑850-641-0017; www.georgesatalysbeach.net; 30 Castle Harbour Dr, Alys Beach; mains $20-45; ⊙11am-3pm & 5-9pm; P ⟨♠⟩) ✎ We give this playful Southern-style coastal seafood spot credit for its menu divisions: 'behave,' which includes locally sourced, organic fare like jerk-crusted snapper, and 'misbehave,' which features fried oyster plates, steaks and the like.

Fish Out of Water SEAFOOD **$$$**
(☑850-641-0017; www.foow30a.com; 34 Goldenrod Cir, WaterColor; mains $23-44; ⊙11:30am-9pm; P) With a menu focusing on local bounty – blackened grouper, Gulf Coast shrimp – a dining room oozing understated good taste and alfresco dining on the breathtaking sunset deck, this is a destination restaurant.

Located inside the WaterColor resort. The shop downstairs sells restaurant-branded merch and other 30A souvenirs.

Bud & Alley's AMERICAN **$$$**
(☑850-231-5900; www.budandalleys.com; 2236 E County Rd 30A, Seaside; mains $30-39; ⊙8am-

9:30pm; P) This landmark seafood restaurant, with dining room and rooftop tables overlooking the Gulf, is worth a visit for the view and the vibe. It's a happening place, especially at sunset, when locals and visitors gather to cheer on the sky while enjoying cold beers and dishes such as seared halibut and grilled shrimp and grits.

☆ Entertainment

Bayou Arts Center   ARTS CENTER
(☑850-622-5970; www.culturalartsalliance.com; 105 Hogtown Bayou Lane, Santa Rosa Beach; ☺8am-4pm) 🖉 Home of the South Walton Cultural Arts Alliance, the Bayou Arts Center serves as a multipurpose space, frequently playing the part of art gallery, performance venue and lecture space, among other roles. Check the website for details on upcoming shows and exhibitions.

🔒 Shopping

★Sundog Books   BOOKS
(☑850-231-5669; www.sundogbooks.com; 89 Central Sq, Seaside; ☺9am-9pm) Need a beach read? Head to this indie bookshop where the shelves are crammed with great literature, book-friendly gifts and the latest bestsellers. Knowledgable booksellers are happy to offer advice.

There's an equally cool record store, Central Square Records, right upstairs.

Modica Market   FOOD & DRINKS
(www.modicamarket.com; 109 Central Sq, Seaside; ☺7am-7pm) This friendly little gourmet grocery is packed with delicious local food and drink to bring a taste of Florida home with you. Or pick from the mouthwatering sandwiches, salads, soups and baked goods – all more than reasonably priced – for a beachside treat.

Blue Giraffe   ART
(☑850-231-5112; www.bluegiraffe30a.com; 13123 E Emerald Coast Pkwy, Inlet Beach; ☺10am-5:30pm) Part gift shop of quirky handmade goods, part gallery of local artists, part showcase of Gulf Coast authors, the Blue Giraffe is a good spot for a South Walton souvenir. The shop supports plenty of local charitable causes and creative initiatives, and the owners are connected to the local arts scene.

Justin Gaffrey Gallery   ART
(☑850-267-2022; https://justingaffrey.com; 21 Blue Gulf Dr, Blue Mountain Beach; ☺9am-5pm Mon-Sat) Self-taught artist Justin Gaffrey is

a Walton County treasure. His work mixes media and textures, and constantly challenges expectations. Catch his gallery of paintings and sculpture.

ℹ Information

Beaches of South Walton Tourist Center
(☑850-267-1216; www.visitsouthwalton.com; 25777 Hwy 331 S; ☺8am-4:30pm) The tourist center is inland, between SR 283 and SR 83. There's also a bulletin board with tourist brochures on the eastern end of Seaside Town Sq.

ℹ Getting There & Away

The South Walton beaches stretch in a thin line along the 30A coast road, starting with Dune Allen (about 15 miles east of Destin) to Carillon Beach (about 13 miles west of Panama City Beach). Bike paths make pedaling through this often congested area easier than driving, though travel by car is still the most common mode of transport.

Panama City Beach
☑850 / POP 13,000

The sandy shores of Panama City Beach are objectively lovely, with dozens of natural, historic and artificial reefs attracting spectacular marine life. But don't expect mellow Old Florida vibes in 'PCB,' an overdeveloped Gulf-front pocket about 10 miles west of unremarkable Panama City. Families come here for cheap vacays, retirees move here to live out their days, and spring breakers flock to party in the sunshine.

Architecturally dire high-rises spring up from the beachfront and block both sunlight and vistas for those on the streets below, which are lined with more strip malls, chain hotels, amusement arcades, uninspiring restaurants and dive bars than good taste allows.

⊙ Sights

★Shell Island   PARK
(☑850-233-0504; www.shellislandshuttle.com; 4607 State Park Lane; round trip adult/child $20/11) 🖉 Offshore from St Andrews State Park (p472), this sandy 'desert' island is fantastic for sunbathing, swimming and snorkeling. There are neither facilities nor shade: wear a hat and plenty of sunscreen. To get here, buy tickets for the Shell Island Shuttle (p474) at Pier Marketplace in the park; there's a trolley service to the boat. Snorkeling packages ($28) and kayak rental (single/tandem $65/75 per

THE PANHANDLE PANAMA CITY BEACH

day) are available – the price includes your shuttle trip. Check website for details and schedules.

St Andrews State Park
STATE PARK

(☏ 850-708-6100; www.floridastateparks.org; 4607 State Park Lane; vehicle/pedestrian $8/2; ☺ 8am-sunset; P) ✈ This peaceful 1260-acre park, a barrier island, is graced with nature trails, swimming beaches and wildlife, including foxes, coyotes, snakes, seabirds and alligators (fear not: gators live in freshwater, and the swimming areas – including the kiddie pool's 4ft-deep water – are in the ocean). On the beach near the jetties, you can still see the circular cannon platforms from when this area was used as a military reservation during WWII.

Excellent waterfront campsites are available year-round for $28, although sites will be limited through 2021 due to damage from 2018's Hurricane Michael.

Man in the Sea Museum
MUSEUM

(☏ 850-235-4101; www.maninthesea.org; 17314 Panama City Beach Pkwy; adult/child $7/5; ☺ 10am-4pm Thu-Sun; P ♿) This museum takes a close look at the history of underwater exploration. Interactive exhibits let you crank up a Siebe pump, climb into a Beaver Mark IV submersible, check out models of underwater laboratory SEALAB III and find out how diving bells really work. There's also a cool collection of old diving suits and undersea treasures.

WonderWorks
MUSEUM

(☏ 850-249-7000; www.wonderworksonline.com/panama-city-beach; 9910 Front Beach Rd; adult/child $29/24; ☺ 10am-7pm Sun-Fri, to 9pm Sat; ♿) Designed to look like an upside-down building, this wacky interactive museum and fun center stands out even on the attraction-studded Miracle Strip. While hands-on exhibits like a hurricane shack, an obstacle climbing course and virtual-reality soccer may give some grown-ups a migraine, kids will have a blast: literally, in the case of the laser-tag maze.

🏃 Activities

Divers are in luck: more than a dozen boats are rusting underwater offshore, including a 441ft WWII Liberty ship and numerous tugs, earning Panama City Beach its nickname Wreck Capital of the South. There are more than 50 artificial reefs made from bridge spans, barges and a host of other sunken structures, as well as natural coral reefs. Visibility varies from 10ft to 80ft, averaging around 40ft. In winter, the average water temperature is 60°F (15.5°C), rising to 87°F (30.5°C) in summer.

Dive Locker
DIVING

(☏ 850-230-8006; www.divelocker.net; 1010 Thomas Dr; discover dive/open-water course $95/345; ☺ 9am-5pm Mon-Sat, to 4pm Sun) This well-respected outfitter and dive school knows all the local dive sites, including artificial reefs based around sunken naval ships and oil supply ships, as well as local inland springs – a unique, only-in-Florida diving experience.

🛏 Sleeping

A plentiful supply of beds means there's usually something for everyone in Panama City Beach – or for everyone's budget, anyway. In terms of taste, there's nothing particularly noteworthy. The code words 'family-friendly' or 'families only' mean you'll avoid spring-breakers, in season. Rates vary dramatically between quieter winter months and heaving summers, and they spike during spring break (March to May).

Wisteria Inn
MOTEL $$

(☏ 850-234-0557; www.wisteria-inn.com; 20404 Front Beach Rd; d from $119; P ♨ 🐾) This sweet little 14-room motel has a variety of tastefully themed rooms from South Beach to Moroccan, as well as poolside mimosa hours and an 'adults only' policy that discourages spring-breakers. It's also very pet-friendly, so feel free to bring Fido. Rates drop like a rock in winter.

Sheraton Bay Point Resort
HOTEL $$$

(☏ 850-236-6000; www.sheratonbaypoint.com; 4114 Jan Cooley Dr; r from $250; ❄ 🛜 🐾 ♨) One of the more comfortable bases in PCB, this pleasantly appointed resort features views of St Andrews Bay, two golf courses, watersports rentals, a lovely pool, three on-site restaurants and a full-service spa. Rooms are cozy, modern and airy.

Holiday Inn Resort
HOTEL $$$

(☏ 850-230-4080; www.hipcbeach.com; 11127 Front Beach Rd; r from $225; P 🛜 ♨) This half-moon-shaped beachfront mega-hotel has large, Gulf-view rooms, as well as family rooms with bunk beds, although it's impossible to fully shake its '70s *Boogie Nights* vibe.

SEACREST WOLF PRESERVE

This **wolf preserve** (☑850-773-2897; www.seacrestwolfpreserve.org; 3449 Bonnett Pond Rd, Chipley; $25; ☺tours 1-4:30pm Sat; ℗) and rescue sanctuary, the only one of its kind in Florida, should fascinate wildlife lovers. Visitors will see and have (limited) interaction with four on-site wolf packs, as well as a slate of wolf puppies, but only after extensive educational lectures. Fair warning: Saturday tours can get crowded, and you may find yourself waiting for long periods with limited views of the animals. That said, if you love wolves, it's worth it. No children under 10. Reservations essential.

There's a decent-sized checklist of clothing you can and can't wear, and other rules to follow; check the website for more information. More expensive VIP tours for one to 10 people are also available at other times ($400 for two people, $75 for each additional participant).

✖ Eating

Andy's Flour Power Bakery
BAKERY **$**

(☑850-230-0014; www.andysflourpower.com; 2629 Thomas Dr; mains from $4; ☺7am-2pm Mon-Sat, from 8am Sun; ♿) Come for hands-down the best breakfasts in town: fluffy rolled omelets cooked to perfection, cheesy grits, breakfast frittata, Belgian waffles and, of course, bacon and eggs, any way you like 'em. Locals are known to start the day with breakfast here and come back for lunch: tasty New York deli–style sandwiches galore on freshly baked breads. Highly recommended.

Hunt's Oyster Bar
SEAFOOD **$**

(☑850-763-9645; www.huntsoysterbar.com; 1150 Beck Ave, Panama City; mains from $10, dozen oysters $15; ☺11am-9:30pm Mon-Sat; ℗) Catch an original Gulf Coast vibe at Hunt's, where oysters have been served up raw, steamed, baked or cheese-topped for more than 50 years. Steaks, gator and grouper are also on the menu.

Near St Andrew's Marina in Panama City, about 7 miles from Panama City Beach.

Dee's Hangout
CREOLE **$$**

(www.deeshangout.com; 529 Richard Jackson Blvd; mains $10-28; ☺11am-8pm Mon-Thu, to 9pm Fri-Sun; ♿) This popular eatery gets points for classic American favorites (burgers and steaks), family-friendly atmosphere and tasty Louisiana-inspired goodness, including barbecue shrimp cooked in a rich butter sauce, po' boys (New Orleans–style sandwiches) served on Leidenheimer Brothers bread straight outta the Crescent City, and red beans and rice.

★ Firefly
AMERICAN **$$$**

(☑850-249-3359; www.fireflypcb.com; 535 Richard Jackson Blvd; mains $25-43, sushi $6-16; ☺5-10pm) This uber-atmospheric, casual fine-dining establishment glistens with hundreds of fairy lights and beckons with seafood dishes including prosciutto-wrapped swordfish, broiled lobster tails and a wide variety of sushi and sashimi.

It was good enough for a former US president: Obama dined here, and the regulars won't let you forget it.

🍸 Drinking & Nightlife

During spring break, most PCB bars are basically filling stations for getting as much alcohol down your throat as quickly as possible. Outside of spring break...well, imagine those bars in slow season. They're kind of sad. Still, a few worthwhile options are available.

Craft Bar
BAR

(☑850-588-7309; www.thecraftbarfl.com; 15600 Panama City Beach Pkwy, Pier Park North; ☺11am-11pm Mon-Thu, to midnight Fri & Sat, to 10pm Sun) Head to this anti-PCB choice to trade pirate-themed camp and beach blanket anarchy for dozens of thoughtfully sourced microbrews on tap, plus craft cocktails and excellent, elevated pub grub (mains $12 to $35) – it shares a menu with its sister location in Destin (p467). Live music on Fridays.

Tootsie's Orchid Lounge
LOUNGE

(☑850-236-3459; www.tootsies.net; 700 S Pier Park Dr; ☺11am-3am) It lacks the dusty character of the Nashville original, but the nonstop live country music is still plenty boot-stompin' for y'all. Closes about a half-hour earlier during the winter.

❶ Getting There & Away

The **Northwest Florida Beaches International Airport** (PFN; ☑850-763-6751; www.iflybeaches.com; 6300 W Bay Pkwy) is served by Delta and

UPON THE SUWANNEE RIVER

Flowing 207 miles, the Suwannee River was immortalized by Stephen Foster in Florida's state song, 'Old Folks at Home.' Foster himself never set eyes on the river, which winds through wild Spanish moss-draped countryside from Georgia, through the Panhandle and to the Gulf of Mexico in the curve of the Big Bend. See it for yourself along the **Suwannee River Wilderness Trail** (www.floridastateparks.org), which covers 169 miles of the river to the Gulf, with nine 'hubs' – cabins – spaced one day's paddle apart. They book up fast, so reserve as early as possible. River camps along the banks of the trail are also in the pipeline. Canoe rentals are available from **American Canoe Adventures** (✆386-397-1309; www.aca1.com; 10610 Bridge St, White Springs; ⊙9am-6pm Wed-Mon), which also offers day trips ($35 to $60) where you're transported upstream and then paddle down, or longer, multi-day excursions covering any portion of the river.

Cultural stops include the **Stephen Foster Folk Cultural Center State Park** (✆386-397-4331; www.floridastateparks.org; 11016 Lillian Saunders Dr, White Springs; vehicle $5; ⊙park 8am-sunset, museum 9am-5pm; P) ✒ north of White Springs (about 100 miles east of Tallahassee). With lush green hills and monolithic live oak trees, the park centers on a museum celebrating the songwriter. Foster's songs were the 1850s version of Norman Rockwell's work for the *Saturday Evening Post:* idealized depictions of an America that perhaps never was. Which of course made them insanely popular. Here you can see eight of his 200-plus tunes depicted in detailed dioramas. The three-day **Florida Folk Festival**, a celebration of traditional Floridian music, crafts, food and culture, takes place in the park every Memorial Day weekend.

At the confluence of the Withlacoochee and Suwannee Rivers, **Suwannee River State Park** (✆386-362-2746; www.floridastateparks.org/parks-and-trails/suwannee-river-state-park; 3631 201st Path, Live Oak; vehicle $5; ⊙8am-sunset; P) ✒ is the site of the biggest Civil War battle in Florida and still contains fortifications. Camping is available, as well as basic cabins that sleep up to six people. The park is 13 miles west of Live Oak, just off US 90 – follow the signs.

Southwest, with daily nonstop flights to Atlanta, Baltimore, Houston, Nashville and St Louis.

For bus services connecting throughout continental USA, head to the **Greyhound** (✆850-785-6111; www.greyhound.com; 917 Harrison Ave, Panama City) bus station, although it's not the most inviting of places for visitors to arrive or depart.

Panama City Beach is almost halfway between Tallahassee (about 130 miles) and Pensacola (95 miles). By car, coming along the coast, Hwy 98 takes you into town; from I-10 take either Hwy 231 or Hwy 79 south.

ⓘ Getting Around

The Bay Town Trolley (www.baytowntrolley.org) runs in Panama City Beach. The service allows flag stops in addition to the official stops, but the schedule is limited to Monday to Saturday between 6am and 8pm. The fare is $1.50 for one ride, or $4 for the day.

Classic Rentals (✆850-235-1519; www.classicrntlsinc.com; 13226 Front Beach Rd; ⊙8am-7pm Mar-May & Sep, to 10pm Jun-Aug, to 5pm Oct-Mar) rents scooters (half-/full day $25/45) and old-school Harleys (half-/full day $85/135).

Shell Island Shuttle (✆850-233-0504; www.shellislandshuttle.com; 4607 State Park Lane; adult/child $20/11; ⊙9am-5pm) takes visitors between Shell Island and St Andrews State Park.

Cape San Blas & Port St Joe

✆850 / POP 3450

Delicate Cape San Blas curls around St Joseph Bay at the southwestern end of the bulge in the Panhandle, starting on the mainland at Port St Joe and ending at its undeveloped, 10-mile-long tip with gorgeous St Joseph Peninsula State Park.

Across the bay, which has gentle rip- and current-free swimming, the town of **Port St Joe** was once known as 'sin city' for the casinos and bordellos that greeted seafarers. Note the switch in time zones from Central to Eastern here: even though Port St Joe is west of some Central Time communities, it goes by Eastern Time.

The Florida Constitution was originally drafted in Port St Joe in 1838, but scarlet fever and hurricanes combined to stymie its progression as one of Florida's boom towns. These days it's anchored by a small historic district that can occupy a visitor for an hour or so.

This region was heavily damaged during Hurricane Michael, but has slowly built its way back.

◉ Sights

★TH Stone Memorial St
Joseph Peninsula State Park   STATE PARK
(St Joseph Peninsula State Park; ✆850-227-1327; www.floridastateparks.org; 8899 Cape San Blas Rd; vehicle $6; ⊙8am-sunset) This lovely park, a quilt of beach and pine forest, brackish bays and fuzzy salt marsh, is a fine slice of increasingly rare Gulf Coast wilderness. Visitors can wander amid sugar-sand beaches that stretch for 1800 acres along grassy, undulating dunes, edging wilderness trails. Cyclists, walkers and bladers can set out on the Loggerhead Run Bike Path, named for the turtles that inhabit the island, which runs about 9 miles to **Salinas Park** (280 Cape San Blas Rd; ⊙sunrise-sunset; P 🐾) 🏊 FREE.

The park has a small concession stand and restrooms. There's accessible beach access via a boardwalk. Unfortunately the park was heavily impacted by Hurricane Michael, which reshaped the delicate peninsula. As of late 2020, campsites and some trails (mainly on the north side of the park) remain closed. Check the website for the latest info.

▤ Sleeping

Port Inn & Cottages   INN $$
(✆850-229-7678; www.facebook.com/pg/port-innfl; 501 Monument Ave/Hwy 98, Port St Joe; r $160-200, cottages from $250; ❄🛜🐾) Recently remodeled after Hurricane Michael and now part of the Ascend Hotel Collection, the Port Inn makes for a pleasant Panhandle overnight stop. A timber porch with rocking chairs runs the full length of this lovely 25-room inn, with front-row seats for the sunsets over the bay. Ten cottages with kitchens are also available.

✗ Eating

★ Sand Dollar Cafe   AMERICAN $
(✆850-227-4865; www.sanddollarcafepsj.com; 301 Monument Ave, Port St Joe; breakfast & lunch plates $10-12; ⊙7am-3pm Thu-Mon; 🖉🏠) This meat-and-three spot is a perfect storm of playful kitsch, warm hospitality, reasonable pricing and innovative Southern home cooking served cafeteria-style. Choices in-

clude juicy meatloaf and tomato chutney and plump crab cakes with an in-house remoulade.

Indian Pass Raw Bar   SEAFOOD $$
(✆850-227-1670; www.indianpassrawbar.com; 8391 Indian Pass Rd, Port St Joe; mains $10-17; ⊙noon-9pm Tue-Sun, Wed-Sat only Jan; P) On a rural stretch of 30A outside Port St Joe, this longtime outpost of old Gulf Coast culture suffered damage in Hurricane Michael but came back brighter and better. The menu, posted above the bar, is simple: oysters three ways (raw, steamed or baked with Parmesan cheese), crab legs and a handful of shrimp dishes.

Of course, you should get the oysters – even if you think you don't like the salty bivalves, you'll be surprised at the sweetness of these guys, drawn fresh from the Gulf. Stay for a slice of key lime pie and impromptu line dancing on the porch.

❶ Getting There & Away

Port St Joe is about 24 miles west of Apalachicola and 70 miles east of Panama City Beach. The fastest route from either town is US 98. If you have the time, we recommend taking State Road 30A, a scenic route that partly hugs the water and extends south of Port St Joe to the state park.

BIG BEND

The crook of Florida's upside down 'L' is home to its state capital, Tallahassee, and an otherwise little-visited region known as Big Bend. The area is characterized by ragged pine woods and freshwater springs of the greater Panhandle mixed with long stretches of salt marsh and thin beachfront. Fishing villages and biker bars perforate the small towns scattered around the region, offset by low-lying Gulf islands and the edges of the Apalachicola National Forest.

Tallahassee

✆850 / POP 196,000

Florida's capital, cradled between gently rising hills and nestled beneath tree-canopied roadways, is geographically closer to Atlanta than it is to Miami. Culturally, it's far closer to the Southern USA than the majority of the state it governs.

Despite its status as a government center, and the presence of two major universities (Florida State and Florida Agricultural &

Mechanical University), the pace here is slower than syrup. That said, there are interesting museums and outlying attractions that will appeal to history and nature buffs and could easily detain a visitor for a day or two.

◎ Sights

★ Tallahassee Museum   MUSEUM
(Map p478; ☑850-575-8684; www.tallahasseemuseum.org; 3945 Museum Rd; adult/child $12/9; ◎9am-5pm Mon-Sat, from 11am Sun; ℙ◢) ◢ Occupying 52 acres of pristine manicured gardens and wilderness on the outskirts of Tallahassee, near the airport, this wonderful natural-history museum features living exhibits of Floridian flora and fauna – including the incredibly rare Floridan panther and red wolf – and has delighted visitors for more than 60 years. Be sure to check out the otters, or try ziplining above the canopy in the Tree to Tree Adventures – a variety of scenarios are available, costing $17 to $45 depending on the options.

Museum of Fine Arts   MUSEUM
(Map p480; ☑850-644-6836; http://mofa.fsu.edu; 530 W Call St; ◎9am-4pm Mon-Fri year-round, 1-4pm Sat & Sun Sep-Apr; ℙ) FREE Florida State University boasts its own Museum of Fine Arts, a newly renovated space that features temporary exhibitions that range from internationally renowned artists to graduating FSU arts students.

Mission San Luis   HISTORIC SITE
(Map p478; ☑850-245-6406; www.missionsanluis.org; 2100 W Tennessee St; adult/child $5/2; ◎10am-4pm Tue-Sun; ℙ◢) ◢ This 60-acre site is home to a 17th-century mission that housed Spanish colonists and Apalachee tribespeople. The compound has been nicely reconstructed, especially the soaring Council House. Tours (included with admission) provide a fascinating taste of life nearly 400 years ago. Costumed interpreters are on-site, and kids who are into history will have a blast.

Meek-Eaton Black Archives   MUSEUM
(Map p478; Southeastern Regional Black Archives Research Center & Museum; ☑850-599-3020; www.famu.edu/BlackArchives; 445 Gamble St; ◎10am-5pm Mon-Fri, noon-4pm Sat; ℙ) ◢ FREE The Meek-Eaton Black Archives holds one of the country's largest collections of African American and African artifacts, as well as thousands of papers, photographs, paintings and documents pertaining to African American life. The 13 museum galleries feature exhibits on African American contributions to medicine and important collateral artifacts like manumission papers and the letters of Zora Neale Hurston.

The complex is located within **Florida A&M University** (FAMU; www.famu.edu; 2400 Wahnish Way), known as FAMU (fam-you). FAMU was founded in 1887; today it's home to about 10,000 students and the only public historically Black college or university (HBCU) in the state.

Tallahassee Automobile
& Collectibles Museum   MUSEUM
(☑850-942-0137; www.tacm.com; 6800 Mahan Dr; adult/student/child under 10yr $18/12/8; ◎8am-5pm Mon-Fri, from 10am Sat, from noon Sun; ℙ) If you like motor vehicles, welcome to heaven! This museum houses a pristine collection of more than 165 unique and historical automobiles from around the world, including an Elvismobile. Top that with collections of boats, motorcycles, books, pianos and sports memorabilia and you've got a full day on your hands. There's even a Tie-Fighter. It is about 8 miles northeast of Downtown, off I-10.

Florida State University   UNIVERSITY
(Map p478; FSU; ☑850-644-2882; www.fsu.edu; Hendry St; ℙ) A liberal-arts school of more than 35,000 undergraduate and graduate students, Florida State University specializes in sciences, computing and performing arts (and football). From September to April, free campus tours depart from **Visitor Services** (850-644-3246; 100 S Woodward Ave) Monday to Friday. Call for a schedule.

Museum of Florida History   MUSEUM
(Map p480; ☑850-245-6400; www.museumofloridahistory.com; 500 S Bronough St; ◎9am-4:30pm Mon-Fri, from 10am Sat, from noon Sun; ◢) FREE Florida's history is splayed out in fun, crisp exhibits, from mastodon skeletons to relics of Florida's Paleo-Indians and Spanish shipwrecks, the Civil War to 'tin-can tourism.'

Florida Historic Capitol Museum   MUSEUM
(Map p480; ☑850-487-1902; www.flhistoriccapitol.gov; 400 S Monroe St; ◎9am-4:30pm Mon-Fri, from 10am Sat, from noon Sun) FREE Adorned with candy-striped awnings and topped with a reproduction of its original glass dome, the 1902 Florida capitol building now houses an interesting political museum, including a restored House of Representatives chamber

ST MARKS NATIONAL WILDLIFE REFUGE

About 25 miles southeast of Tallahassee you'll find the **St Marks National Wildlife Refuge** (☑850-925-6121; www.fws.gov/refuge/St_Marks; 1255 Lighthouse Rd, St Marks; ☻8am-sunset; P), established in 1931 to provide a winter habitat for migratory birds. It spans a whopping 70,000 acres and has approximately 43 miles of Gulf shoreline along its coastal boundary. Within the park's protected marshes, rivers, estuaries and islands, a diverse range of flora and fauna thrives. It's a wildlife photographer's dream, with beautiful contrasts between land, sea and sky.

Be sure to start your visit with a trip to the **visitor center** for information on the park's numerous walking and hiking trails and the lowdown on just how many species of critter live here. If you only have time for a short visit, follow Lighthouse Rd all the way to the coast to enjoy Florida's most photographed **lighthouse**, completed in 1842 and still a functioning beacon today. It's possible to stop along the drive and dip into any of the many trails. Fingers crossed you'll spot a flamingo!

and governor's reception area, numerous portraits, and exhibits on immigration, state development and the infamous 2000 US presidential election.

Florida State Capitol NOTABLE BUILDING
(Map p478; www.floridacapitol.myflorida.com; 400 S Monroe St; ☻8am-5pm Mon-Fri) FREE The stark and imposing 22-story Florida State Capitol's top-floor observation deck affords 360-degree views of the city. In session the capitol is a hive of activity, with politicians, staffers and lobby groups buzzing in and around its honeycombed corridors. There are few states that have as diverse a legislature as Florida's – in one hall, you may hear Cuban Americans from Miami brokering deals with good old boys from the Panhandle. America!

Locals and tourists alike have noted that the new building, a lone shaft with rounded domes on either side, bears striking resemblance to a, um, er...well, go look for yourself.

Knott House Museum HISTORIC BUILDING
(Map p478; ☑850-922-2459; www.museumoffloridahistory.com; 301 E Park Ave; ☻1-3pm Wed-Fri, 10am-3pm Sat; P) FREE This stately, columned 1843 house, affiliated with the history museum, is a quirky attraction. Constructed by George Proctor, a free African-American builder, it was occupied during the Civil War by Confederate and then Union troops before the Emancipation Proclamation was read here in 1865. It's otherwise known as 'the house that rhymes': in 1928 it was bought by politico William V Knott, whose poet wife, Luella, attached verses on the evils of drink to many of the furnishings. Free tours on the hour.

🏃 Activities

Tallahassee's famed oak- and moss-shrouded canopy roads make for lovely afternoon drives and rides. Roads to visit include Old St Augustine Rd, Centerville Rd, Meridian Rd, Miccosukee Rd and Old Bainbridge Rd. Check the Leon County Canopy Roads website (www.leoncountyfl.gov/pubworks/oper/canopy) for info and a map.

Some of the best mountain biking in Florida – some 700 miles of trails – is also found in and around Tallahassee. The Tallahassee Mountain Bike Association (https://tmba.bike) has tons of relevant info on trails and group rides, including the Urban Gorilla, an annual mountain bike ride through the city itself.

Tallahassee-St Marks Historic Railroad State Trail CYCLING
(☑850-487-7989; www.floridastateparks.org; 1358 Old Woodville Rd, Crawfordville; ☻8am-sunset) 🚲 FREE The ultimate treat for runners, skaters and cyclists, this trail has 16 miles of smooth pavement shooting due south, parallel to Route 363, to the Gulf-port town of St Marks. It's easy and flat for all riders, sitting on a coastal plain and shaded at many points by canopies of gracious live oaks.

More experienced riders may opt for forest trails, such as the rugged 7.5-mile Munson Hills Loop trail (p487), which navigates sand dunes and a towering pine forest.

Great Bicycle Shop CYCLING
(Map p478; ☑850-224-7461; www.greatbicycle.com; 1909 Thomasville Rd; ☻10am-6pm Mon-Fri, to 5pm Sat, noon-4pm Sun) Whether you want to mountain bike or just get from A to B,

Tallahassee

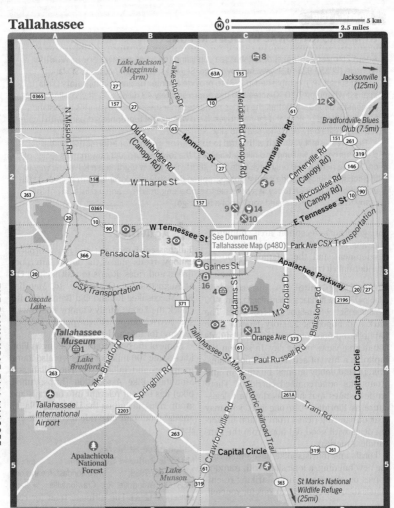

See Downtown
Tallahassee Map (p480)

THE PANHANDLE TALLAHASSEE

this professional outfitter will rent you a bike to cruise around Tallahassee's many excellent bike paths. Rentals start at $35 per day.

🛏 Sleeping

With just a couple of charming exceptions, you'll find that Tallahassee's hotels are mostly midrange chains, clumped at exits along I-10 and along Monroe St between I-10 and Downtown. Be sure to book well ahead during the legislative session and football games, when prices peak.

Little English Guesthouse   B&B $$
(Map p478; ☏850-907-9777; www.littleenglishguesthouse.com; 737 Timberlane Rd; r from $109; ❋ 🕏) In a peaceful residential neighborhood 20 minutes from downtown Tallahassee, London-bred Tracey has turned her suburban house into a homey little English-themed B&B.

Hotel Duval   HOTEL $$$
(Map p480; ☏850-224-6000; www.hotelduval.com; 415 N Monroe St; r $185-309; 🅿 🕏) Slick, sleek and ultra modern, this centrally located 117-room hotel has all the mod cons, and a hip interior that is actually more stylish than pretentious – rare with spots that are

Tallahassee

so overtly design-conscious. The rooftop bar and lounge is open until 2am most nights.

Governor's Inn HOTEL $$$
(Map p480; ☑850-681-6855; www.thegovinn.com; 209 S Adams St; r $240-309; P❋☎) In a stellar Downtown location, this inviting inn has everything from single rooms to two-level loft suites, plus a daily cocktail hour. The interior lobby and common area is attractive but slightly dated (think historical chic). All rooms have refrigerators and flat-screens.

✖ Eating

Mr B's Real Grill BBQ BARBECUE $
(Map p478; ☑850-541-4474; 312 E Orange Ave; ⊙11am-8pm Thu-Sat; P) This ramshackle orange shack in South Tallahassee serves up delicious smoked barbecue – ribs, chopped pork, and all the fixin's – to customers who either take their 'cue to go, or eat at a picnic table.

Dog Et Al HOT DOGS $
(Map p480; www.facebook.com/dogetal; 1456 S Monroe St; hot dogs from $2.10; ⊙11am-8pm Mon-Fri, to 3pm Sat; P♿) There is absolutely nothing fancy about this tiny hot-dog restaurant near Florida A&M – and that's the way its devoted clientele likes it. Jumbo corndogs served with ribbons of mustard and ketchup to chili dogs heaped with cheese: all the classics are here. We love the napkin holders with cheeky sayings ('I used to be decisive. Now I'm not sure.').

Kool Beanz Café FUSION $$
(Map p478; ☑850-224-2466; www.koolbeanz-cafe.com; 921 Thomasville Rd; dinner mains $19-27; ⊙11am-2:30pm & 5:30-10pm Mon-Fri, 5:30-10pm Sat, 10:30am-2pm Sun; P✎) It's got a corny name but a wonderfully eclectic and homey vibe – plus great, creative fare. The menu changes

daily, but you can count on finding something tasty, from hummus plates to monkfish or jerk-spiced scallops to roasted octopus with carrot purée and shoestring potatoes.

Reangthai THAI $$
(Map p478; ☑850-386-7898; www.reangthai.com; 2740 Capital Circle NE; mains $15-25; ⊙11am-2pm & 5-10pm Mon-Fri, 5-10pm Sat, 4-8pm Sun; P✎) Elegant despite its strip-mall setting, Reangthai is the real deal, serving up the kind of spicy, fish saucy, explode-in-your-mouth cuisine so many American Thai restaurants shy away from. Worth the drive.

Andrew's AMERICAN $$
(Map p480; ☑850-222-3444; www.andrewsdowntown.com; 228 S Adams St; mains downstairs $12-25, upstairs $18-44; ⊙downstairs 11:30am-10pm, upstairs 6-10pm Mon-Sat) Downtown's see-and-be-seen political hotspot. At this split-level place, the downstairs (Andrew's Capital Grill and Bar) serves casual burgers and beer. It's somewhere between a family-friendly joint and a bro-kegger, but fun for what it is. Upstairs is Andrew's 228, which offers a more upscale atmosphere and serves Tuscan-Southern fusion cuisine such as pecan-pesto pasta.

Bella Bella ITALIAN $$
(Map p478; ☑850-412-1114; www.thebellabella.com; 123 E 5th Ave; mains $14-19; ⊙11am-10pm Mon-Fri, 4-10pm Sat; P) Come for authentic Italian cuisine in a modern setting. Try the bruschetta and stuffed mushrooms, then move on to creamy pastas or shrimp scampi or chicken Parmesan.

Cypress AMERICAN $$$
(Map p478; ☑850-513-1100; www.cypressrestaurant.com; 320 E Tennessee St; mains $20-44; ⊙5-10pm Mon-Sat; P✎) This unassuming

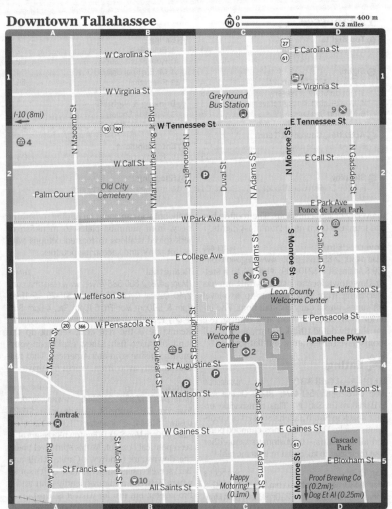

Downtown Tallahassee

spot is the domain of local chef David Gwynn, whose regional Southern food outshines expectations. Start with the grilled veggie salad with poached egg and move on to duck smoked with pecans or basil and ginger shrimp and grits. Don't pull out your phone unless you're at the bar, please.

Drinking & Nightlife

FSU and Florida A&M students can dominate the nightlife scene, though most of the college bars (and there are many) are in and around Tennessee St between Copeland St and Dewey St.

★**Happy Motoring!**   BAR
(Map p480; www.happymotoringtlh.com; 1215 S Adams St; ⊘4:30-10pm Wed, 11:30am-10pm Thu, to midnight Fri & Sat; ⊕) Chill out in this laid-back bar in a former gas station. Local beer and wine is on tap, as well as coffee and creative takes on shandies – think pear cider mixed with ginger ale and elderflower. Food trucks can often be found lined up in front of the astroturf patio (the perfect place for kids to roam).

Tallahassee food truck favorite Tally Mac Shack (www.pickuptallymacshack.com) dishes out inventive mac & cheese combos inside the bar Wednesday to Friday.

Proof Brewing Co   MICROBREWERY
(Map p480; ☑850-577-0517; www.proofbrewingco. com; 1320 S Monroe St; ⊘4-10pm Mon, to midnight Tue-Thu, 11am-1am Fri & Sat, to 10pm Sun) This brewery takes up an entire city block, but the taproom somehow feels cozy. Sofas mix with high-tops and foosball tables to create a convivial atmosphere that spills out onto the back patio on warm nights (ie almost every night in Florida).

Waterworks   BAR
(Map p478; ☑850-224-1887; www.facebook. com/waterworkstallahassee; 1133 Thomasville Rd; ⊘5pm-2am Tue-Thu, 2pm-2am Fri & Sat) This popular, gay-friendly place in midtown has a midcentury Polynesian theme, and packs 'em in with nights of live jazz and Latin salsa as well as rotating DJs.

Behind the main building, sister restaurant the Hideaway serves up breakfast and lunch from 8am to 2pm.

Madison Social   PUB
(Map p478; ☑850-894-6276; www.madison social.com; 705 S Woodward Ave; mains $9-20; ⊘11:30am-2am Mon-Fri, from 10am Sat & Sun; ⊛) This trendy hotspot swarms with a bold and beautiful mix of locals and FSU students, downing drinks at the stellar bar or aluminum picnic tables as the sun sets over Doak Campbell football stadium, the largest continuous brick structure in the USA.

Fermentation Lounge   BAR
(Map p480; ☑850-727-4033; www.fermentation lounge.com; 113 All Saints St, Unit 113; ⊘4pm-midnight Sun-Thu, to 2am Fri & Sat) Sandwiched between the universities, this cool little bar packs a punch: with a chilled vibe attracting an unusual mix of punters from all walks of life and, more importantly, an ever-changing selection of most excellent craft beers and tasty bar snacks.

☆ **Entertainment**

For a comprehensive guide to cultural events in town, such as lectures and art exhibits, visit the handy online calendar at www.tallahasseearts.org.

Junction at Monroe   LIVE MUSIC
(Map p478; ☑800-272-3151; www.junctionat monroe.com; 2011 S Monroe St; ⊘5pm-midnight Wed-Sun) This 1936 warehouse-turned-music-venue is said to have the best acoustics in town. In addition to a well-stocked bar, there's a full casual dining menu with punny names (a Kenny Cheese-ney sandwich or a Brie B King appetizer) that includes vegan options.

Check the website for the performance schedule – events are occasionally booked for days outside of normal business hours.

Bradfordville Blues Club   LIVE MUSIC
(Map p478; ☑850-906-0766; www.bradfordville blues.com; 7152 Moses Lane, off Bradfordville Rd; tickets $15-35; ⊘shows start 8-10pm) Down the end of a dirt road lit by tiki torches, you'll find a bonfire raging under the live oaks at this hidden-away juke joint that hosts excellent national blues acts. Event times and days vary; check online.

🛍 **Shopping**

Railroad Square Art Park   ARTS & CRAFTS
(Map p478; ☑850-224-1308; www.railroadsquare. com; 567 Industrial Dr; ⊘hours vary) This collection of studios, shops, cafes and independent art galleries hosts a festive First Fridays gallery hop monthly. Hours vary by business.

ℹ **Information**

Florida Welcome Center (☑850-488-6167; www.visitflorida.com; 400 S Monroe St, Capitol Building, West Entrance; ⊘8am-5pm Mon-Fri) In the Florida State Capitol, this is a fantastic resource with friendly staff and lots of maps and brochures.

Leon County Welcome Center (☑850-606-2305; www.visittallahassee.com; 106 E Jefferson St; ⊘8am-5pm Mon-Fri) Runs the excellent visitor information center, with brochures on walking and driving tours.

THE PANHANDLE TALLAHASSEE

ⓘ Getting There & Away

Tallahassee is 98 miles from Panama City Beach, 135 miles from Jacksonville, 192 miles from Pensacola, 120 miles from Gainesville and 470 miles from Miami. The main access road is I-10; to reach the Gulf Coast, follow Hwy 319 south to Hwy 98.

Tiny **Tallahassee International Airport** (☑ 850-891-7800; www.talgov.com/airport; 3300 Capital Circle SW) is served by American and Delta for US domestic and international connections, and Silver Airways for direct flights to Tampa and Orlando. It's about 5 miles southwest of Downtown, off Hwy 263. There's no public transportation. Some hotels have shuttles, but otherwise a taxi to Downtown costs around $25: try **Yellow Cab** (☑ 850-999-9999; www.tallahasseeyellowcab.com).

The **Greyhound bus station** (☑ 850-222-4249; www.greyhound.com; 112 W Tennessee St; ⊗ 24hr) is at the corner of Duval, opposite the downtown StarMetro transfer center.

ⓘ Getting Around

Tallahassee is a spread-out city, and it helps to have wheels to get around. For public transport, **StarMetro** (☑ 850-891-5200; www.talgov.com/starmetro; per trip/day $1.25/3), the local bus service for the greater Tallahassee area, has its main transfer point downtown on Tennessee St at Adams St.

Quincy

POP 7540 / ☑ 850

The bucolic village of Quincy makes a nice day trip from Tallahassee. Once nicknamed 'Cola-Cola Town,' Quincy struck it rich in the early 20th century by investing, en masse, in Coke stock – it soon became the wealthiest town per capita in the state. There's an original 1905 Coca-Cola mural on E Jefferson St, and 36 blocks of pretty historic buildings built on the dividends of America's favorite soft drink. The enduring effects of that prosperity make Quincy feel significantly more alive and energetic than many Panhandle towns of a similar size.

Quincy was also a flash point during the Civil Rights movement. The African American population of surrounding Gadsden County was well organized and unafraid of armed resistance against the violent militias that sought to suppress civil rights in other parts of the South.

◉ Sights

Quincy Historic District HISTORIC SITE
FREE It may be small, but Quincy boasts one of the densest concentrations of historic buildings in the state. The area bounded by Sharon, Clark, Stewart and Corry Sts contains 145 historic buildings, including a few wedding-cake mansions. Most historic homes remain private residences, so they're not open to the public, but they make for a scenic stroll. You'll probably be the only one on the sidewalk.

Gadsden Arts Center & Museum ARTS CENTER
(☑ 850-875-4866; www.gadsdenarts.org; 13 N Madison St; suggested donation $5; ⊗ 10am-5pm Tue-Sat; ☷) The Gadsden is a treasure of a museum for a small town like Quincy. It hosts a small collection of local 'vernacular' (folk or self-taught) art, as well as six galleries with rotating exhibitions of regional artwork.

⌐ Sleeping

There isn't much reason to spend the night in Quincy, but if the spirit moves you, there are a handful of B&Bs in historic homes near the town square.

☆ Entertainment

Quincy Music Theatre THEATER
(☑ 850-875-9444; www.quincymusictheatre.com; 118 E Washington St; ☷) Located in the historic Leaf Theater building, this energetic local performing arts center puts on a busy schedule of live theater.

ⓘ Getting There & Away

Quincy isn't served by public transport. The town is 25 miles northwest of Tallahassee, along US 90W.

St George Island

☑ 850 / POP 740

This 28-mile-long barrier island is home to white-sand beaches, bay forests, salt marshes and an inoffensive mix of summer homes and condos. It's a fine spot for shelling, kayaking, sailing, swimming, or just generally zoning out in waterfront bliss. At the end of every street on the island you'll find public beach access and, generally, plentiful parking.

For all that, the highlight of the island is St George Island State Park, which preserves a breathtaking slice of coastal wilderness. The primal, yet gentle, beauty of the dunes and marshes is a world removed from the rental houses mere miles away.

◉ Sights & Activities

★ **St George Island State Park** STATE PARK
(☑ 850-927-2111; www.floridastateparks.org; 1900 E Gulf Beach Dr; vehicle $6; ⊗ 8am-dusk; ℗ ☷)

FLORIDA CAVERNS STATE PARK

Just over an hour from Tallahassee or Panama City, the 1300-acre **Florida Caverns State Park** (☎850-482-1228; www.floridastateparks.org; 3345 Caverns Rd, Marianna; vehicle $5; ⊗8am-sunset; 🖭) on the Chipola River is one of Florida's oldest state parks. Eerie stalactites, stalagmites and flowstone (formed by water flowing over rock) fill the many caves below your feet. You can take a 45-minute guided tour (adult/child $10.75/5; 9am to 4pm) through one of the caves with a volunteer.

They've come up with some quirky names to describe the various rock formations in the cave, from 'wedding cake' to 'bacon.' If you're lucky, you'll spot a tricolored bat (Florida's smallest!) or a salamander. The tour covers a distance of about a mile and is an easy to moderate walk that involves about 50 steps. You'll also have to crouch periodically to scoot under low-hanging rock formations.

Outside, the Blue Hole swimming area makes for a fun – if freezing – dip. Unfortunately, Hurricane Michael destroyed 90% of the park's trees, and aside from the main cave, most areas (including the campsites) remained closed as of late 2020.

As with all parks, plan to have cash (exact change preferred) for the entry fee.

🏝 St George Island at its undeveloped best is found here, in the 9 miles of glorious beach and sand dunes that make up this pristine park. A 2.5-mile nature trail offers exceptional birding opportunities, and throughout the park boardwalks lead to shell-sprinkled beaches, with shallow waters perfect for canoeing, kayaking, and fishing for flounder and whiting. See loggerhead sea turtles from May, when they come ashore to dig nests and lay their eggs, yielding hatchlings that race into the Gulf.

Camping ($24) is permitted at one of the 60 campsites with hookups, or at the Gap Point primitive campsites, accessible by boat or a 2.5-mile hike. As of late 2020, some areas and trails remained closed due to damage from Hurricane Michael – check the website for the latest updates. Note that as with most state parks, it's best to have cash for entry fees (and exact change is preferred).

Apalachicola National Estuarine Research Reserve
WILDLIFE RESERVE

(☎850-670-7700; www.apalachicolareserve.com; 108 Island Dr, Eastpoint; ⊗9am-4pm Tue-Sat) 🏝 Just over the bridge from Apalachicola, in Eastpoint, this reserve provides a great overview of its research site, which encompasses more than 246,000 acres in Apalachicola Bay, with giant aquariums simulating different habitats. A half-mile boardwalk leads down to the river, where you'll find a free telescope on a turret.

St George Lighthouse
LIGHTHOUSE

(☎850-927-7745; www.stgeorgelight.org; 2b E Gulf Beach Dr; adult/child $5/3; ⊗10am-5pm Mon-Wed,

Fri & Sat, noon-5pm Sun; 🅿) Originally built in 1858, this little lighthouse was painstakingly reconstructed in 2008 after collapsing into the sea in 2005 due to erosion. Today you can climb the 92 steps to the top for good water views.

Island Adventures
CYCLING

(☎850-927-3655; www.sgislandadventures.com; 105 E Gulf Beach Dr; bicycle per day from $15; ⊗10am-5pm) This convenient emporium rents out bicycles, beach wheelchairs, fold-out chairs and other types of beach gear.

🚌 Tours

Journeys
BOATING

(☎850-927-3259; www.sgislandjourneys.com; 240 E 3rd St; kayak/boat tour from $40/250; ⊗9am-5pm Mon-Sat) This outfitter leads boat and kayak tours, and rents kayaks (from $50 per day), pontoon boats and catamarans (both $300 per day). All are ideal ways to make the voyage to Cape St George.

🛏 Sleeping

Hotel and motel options are limited, since most visitors to the island rent cottages, which can be anything from a humble beach shack to a multistory mansion. Try homesharing sites or www.resortvacation properties.com.

Buccaneer Inn
MOTEL $

(☎800-847-2091; www.buccinn.com; 160 W Gorrie Dr; r $60-140; 🅿🖭🕸) Right on the Gulf, rooms here are like those of a basic, design-challenged motel – dated green carpet, painted cinder-block walls. But all are clean, bright and surprisingly spacious, and some have kitchenettes.

St George Inn INN $$
(☑850-927-2903; www.stgeorgeinn.com; 135 Franklin Blvd; r $135-275; 🕙🖥️) One of the few historic structures on an island lined with new condo developments, this rambling clapboard inn has comfy, if creaky, rooms and numerous cozy sitting areas filled with dog-eared books. Lots of varied room configurations – twin bunk beds, king/queen suites – though you're paying for the St George Island location.

✖ Eating

Blue Parrot Oceanfront Café SEAFOOD $$
(☑850-927-2987; www.blueparrotsgi.com; 68 W Gorrie Dr; mains $10-32; ⊙11am-9pm; 🖼️🖥️) Out the back of this relaxed and breezy Gulf-front cafe and bar, locals sip rum runners and down oversized po' boys, fish sandwiches and burgers.

ℹ Getting There & Away

A 4-mile-long causeway leads you onto the island, becoming Gulf Beach Dr, also known as Front Beach Dr, at the end. Once you see the lighthouse, turning left brings you to the state park; a right turn takes you toward Government Cut, which separates Little St George Island.

Apalachicola

☑850 / POP 2230

Slow, mellow, shaded by live oaks and flush with historically preserved buildings sweating in the soft Gulf Coast sun, Apalachicola is one of the Gulf's most appealing towns. It's the kind of place that has been discovered by exiles who have fixed up homes and built nice restaurants, bars and bookstores, all threaded together by an attractive grid of walkable streets. 'Apalach' is hugely popular as a romantic weekend getaway – stroll through the historic district at sunset and you'll understand why.

While best known for its increasingly hard-to-find oysters, the fact is this town caters more to tourists and retirees than the fisherfolk who attract said tourist and retirees. That doesn't mean the local seafood isn't still fresh and delicious – just take the idea that this is a fishing town with a grain of (sea!) salt.

◉ Sights

The main sights are well marked on a historic walking-tour guide and map, available free from the Chamber of Commerce (p487) and most B&Bs. Apalachicola's main drag is Ave E, and the entire historic district is easily walked and lined with interesting shops and restaurants.

St Vincent Island WILDLIFE RESERVE
(☑850-653-8808; www.fws.gov/saintvincent) 🏞️ Just a few minutes from Apalachicola, but accessible only by boat, lies this pristine island. Its pearly dunes reveal 5000-year-old geological records, while its pine forests and wetlands teem with endangered species such as red wolves, sea turtles, bald eagles and peregrine falcons. Fishing is permitted on lakes except when bald eagles are nesting (generally in winter). For those sick of the high-rises and bikini-clad crowds of the Gulf beaches, it's the perfect getaway for a day of hiking and solitude.

The island is home to a family of red wolves, one of the last wild populations in the world. These rust-colored wolves once populated the forests and marshes of eastern North America, but were driven to the point of extinction by human expansion and hunting. You probably won't see them – the wolves are notoriously elusive, and reserve managers do what they can to keep them from becoming too comfortable around people – but you may well spot their tracks on the beach.

To get here, hop aboard the **St Vincent Island Shuttle** (☑850-229-1065; www.stvincentisland.com; 690 Indian Pass Rd, Port St Joe; adult/child $10/7), which can also take your bike ($20), or rent you one ($25, including boat trip). Phone for schedules and reservations; they require a certain number of passengers to depart. There is no potable water or food on the island, so carry what you need with you.

The St Vincent National Wildlife Refuge Visitors Center (p487) is located a few minutes walk from downtown Apalachicola, in the historic Fry-Conter house.

Apalachicola Maritime Museum MUSEUM
(☑850-653-2500; www.ammfl.org; 103 Water St; ⊙10am-5pm Mon-Sat; 🅿️) 🏛️ **FREE** This small museum on the banks of the Apalachicola River breaks down the history of oystering, fishing and boat building in Apalachicola – a workshop where traditional boat-building skills are taught and practiced is attached.

The museum also conducts tours of the river and estuary.

Trinity Episcopal Church   CHURCH

([850-653-9550; www.trinityapalachicola.org; 79 6th St) This handsome wooden church was built in New York state and cut into sections, which were shipped down the Atlantic Coast and around the Keys before making their way to this spot where the church was reassembled in 1836.

The public is welcome at Sunday services, which take place at 8am and 10:30am.

John Gorrie State Museum   MUSEUM

([850-653-9347; www.floridastateparks.org; 46 6th St; $2; ⊙ 9am-5pm Thu-Mon; P) Fans of novelty museums will appreciate this tribute to Dr John Gorrie (1803–55), an Apalachicola hero. Gorrie developed a method for cooling the rooms of yellow-fever patients and patented the first ice machine, though he died poor and unaware of how his invention would spur modern refrigeration. Kitchy merch features the slogan 'Keeping it cool since 1851.'

One half of the small museum is devoted to the Florida State Parks system, complete with ranger uniforms and historic photographs.

Activities

Maritime Museum Tours   ECOTOUR

(www.ammfl.org/tours-trips-classes; 103 Water St; tours $15-50) The Apalachicola Maritime Museum runs a series of lovely tours, including eco-tours of the estuary ($40) and cruises around Apalachicola's historic waterfront ($15). Call the museum in advance, as tour times (and availability) can change throughout the year.

Backwater Guide Service   BOATING

([850-899-0063; www.backwaterguideservice. com; tours $200-350; ⊙ by appointment) Offers private wildlife-spotting boat tours, where alligators, wading birds and willowy trees are the main attractions, and fishing charters with the promise of snagging your own red fish or speckled trout for grilling.

Scipio Creek Boardwalk   HIKING

(⊙ sunrise-sunset) Walk off those oysters (and get a capsule view of Gulf Coast flora) on this short and easy trail (0.6 mile round trip). A gravel path through palms, sparkleberries and scrub palmettos eventually transitions to a boardwalk overlooking the sawgrass-strewn shores of Scipio Creek.

Festivals & Events

Apalachicola Farmers Market   FOOD & DRINK

(www.facebook.com/pg/ApalachicolaFarmers Market; 479 Market St, Mill Pond Pavilion; ⊙ 9am-1pm) Local farmers gather rain or shine to sell their wares at Mill Pond Pavilion, on the 2nd and 4th Saturdays of each month.

Florida Seafood Festival   FOOD & DRINK

([850-653-4720; www.floridaseafoodfestival.com; ⊙ early Nov) Stand way, way back at the signature two-day oyster-shucking and -eating contests.

Sleeping

★ Gibson Inn   INN $$

([850-653-2191; www.gibsoninn.com; 51 Ave C; r $109-229; ⚏) This grand 1907 cracker-style inn features recently renovated rooms (no two alike), and a well-appointed lobby that echoes the exterior's period charm. Ask for a 2nd-floor room that opens onto the sprawling veranda.

Whether you're staying here or not, consider dropping in to the attached Franklin bar for the excellent happy hour (5pm to 7pm daily, $3.50 well drinks).

Riverwood Suites   INN $$

([850-653-3848;   www.riverwoodsuites.com; 29 Ave F; r $139-169; P⚏) The four spacious rooms inside this formerly abandoned tin warehouse – the 'Baltimore Building' – have hardwood floors, artsy headboards, modern fixin's and tuck-yourself-away romance. As local hotels go, this one strikes a good balance between historic skin and an interior stuffed with contemporary amenities.

Eating

Hole in the Wall   SEAFOOD $

([850-653-3222; 23 Ave D; half-dozen oysters from $10; ⊙ 11:30am-6pm Tue-Sat) The best place for oysters in Apalachicola is hotly contested, but many locals will send you to this unassuming, no-frills establishment. Service is slow (hey, you're on vacation) but friendly. Sit at the bar to see your oysters shucked before your eyes.

Chowder House   SEAFOOD $

([850-653-1205;   https://the-chowder-house. business.site; 149 Commerce St; mains from $11; ⊙ 8am-4pm Wed-Sat, 9:30am-1:30pm Sun;) Yes you'll love the namesake fish and crab soups – but the delicious breakfasts served up at this family-owned establishment are equally appealing, from chicken and waffles to chorizo frittatas. There's a full vegan menu.

★ Up the Creek Raw Bar   SEAFOOD $$

(☑850-653-2525; www.upthecreekrawbar.com; 313 Water St; mains $7-20; ☺noon-9pm; ▣) You came to Apalachicola to eat oysters; you'd best have a few here. There's a variety of toppers, but we loved the 'classic': lightly cooked with Colby-Jack cheese, chopped jalapeños and bacon – a great way to introduce oyster virgins to the bivalve. The incredible views of the estuary and salt marsh are what makes this place a standout.

Order at the counter and pull up a pew in the shade house or on the deck. A bunch of tasty burgers and salads is available, as well as Pacific-influenced options like poke bowls.

Owl Cafe & Tap Room   MODERN AMERICAN $$

(☑850-653-9888; www.owlcafeflorida.com; 15 Ave D; mains $10-28; ☺11am-3pm & 5:30-10pm Mon-Sat, 10:30am-3pm Sun; ☎) Everyone is catered to in this local favorite, with casual fine dining in the upstairs cafe, and wine room and craft beers and tap-room-only offerings below. The eclectic menu both includes and deviates from the seafood theme: vegetarian pastas, pork tenderloin, chicken marsala and jumbo Gulf shrimp all make appearances. Brunches are wonderful.

Tamara's Café   SOUTH AMERICAN $$$

(☑850-653-4111; www.tamarascafe.com; 71 Market St; dinner mains $16-35; ☺8:00am-10pm Tue-Sun) In the heart of town, Tamara serves up cuisine influenced by the spices of her native Venezuela: grilled, herbed pork chop with shrimp and scallops in a creamy tomato-tarragon sauce, and margarita chicken sautéed in honey, tequila and lime glaze with scallops.

Tamara's Tapas Bar is right next door, with a less formal atmosphere (read: sports bar) and menu with a slightly lower price point.

🍷 Drinking & Nightlife

Oyster City Brewing Company   MICROBREWERY

(☑850-653-2739; www.oystercity.beer; 17 Ave D; ☺tasting room noon-7pm Sun-Thu, to 8pm Fri & Sat) Join the buzzing crowd spilling off the small patio, sipping on a wide roster of beers (the Dirty Blonde ale is a favorite) served in plastic 'go-cups.' Admire the clutter of golf carts parked on the curb. Life is good.

Apalachicola Ice Company   BAR

(www.facebook.com/apalachiceco; 252 Water St; ☺noon-10pm Sat-Mon, 11am-10pm Tue-Fri) You're guaranteed live music almost anytime this casual joint is open. Pull up a barstool or challenge a friend to a game of pool.

High Five Dive Bar   BAR

(131 Commerce St; ☺2-10pm Wed-Sun) A classic Florida dive, this bar in a former warehouse is festooned with twinkle lights and has music memorabilia hanging on the walls. There's live music nightly, with an open mic on Wednesdays; on weekends, expect a crowd on the dance floor.

🛍 Shopping

Richard Bickel Photography   ART

(☑850-653-2828; www.richardbickelphotography. com; 81 Market St; ☺11am-4pm Tue-Sat; ▣) Bickel is a renowned photographer with credits in the *The New York Times*, *Newsweek*, *Die Zeit* and *The Times* (London) among others. He is particularly attracted to water and waterscapes – hence his settling in Apalachicola, where he maintains a gallery of his excellent work.

Bee Inspired Too   ARTS & CRAFTS

(56 Commerce St; ☺10am-5pm Mon-Sat) Everything in this tiny shop is handmade, though not all the artisans are from Florida (or even the USA). Most items are a good value, though prices vary ($18 for hand-printed cotton slippers or $92 for a hand-knit silk poncho). Don't miss the candles and diffuser blends, which are made in Apalachicola.

Downtown Books & Purl   BOOKS

(☑850-653-1290; www.downtownbooksandpurl. com; 67 Commerce St; ☺10am-5:30pm Mon-Sat, 11am-4pm Sun) Need books? How about yarn? How about *both*? Well, you've found the right shop: an adorable, independent bookstore that happens to also include an entire knitting accessory shop. The bookstore contains some excellent small trade books written by local authors, including compilations of Panhandle folklore and quirky guidebooks (not that you need another guidebook).

Tin Shed   ANTIQUES

(☑850-653-3635; www.thetinshednautical.com; 170 Water St; ☺10am-5pm) The Tin Shed really is that: a big shack with a corrugated tin roof, decorated with brightly painted nautical buoys and flags. Inside, you will find – seriously – every damn maritime souvenir under the sun, or the sea, as the case may be.

ℹ Information

Apalachicola Bay Chamber of Commerce
(☑850-653-9419; www.apalachicolabay.org;
17 Ave E; ⊙9am-5pm Mon-Fri) Offers loads of
tourist information, oyster facts, Downtown
walking maps, helpful advice and oyster facts.

**St Vincent National Wildlife Refuge Visitors
Center** (☑850-653-8808; www.fws.gov/
saintvincent; 96 5th St; ⊙10am-3:30pm Mon-
Thu) The information center for visitors headed
to St Vincent National Wildlife Refuge is located
in the historic Fry-Conter house.

ℹ Getting There & Away

Hwy 98 (which becomes Market St) brings you
into town from the east or west – note that it can
be congested with RVs in peak season. It's easy
(and delightful) to wander around downtown
Apalachicola, but you'll need a car to explore the
greater area.

To get to St Vincent Island, hop aboard the St
Vincent Island Shuttle (p484) in Port St Joe.

Apalachicola National Forest

The largest of Florida's three national forests, the **Apalachicola National Forest**
(☑850-643-2282, 850-523-8500; www.fs.usda.
gov/main/apalachicola; entrance off FL 13, FL 67
& other locations; day-use fee $3; ⊙8am-sunset;
🐾) 🐾 occupies almost 938 sq miles – more
than half a million acres – of the Panhandle
from just west of Tallahassee to the Apalachicola River. It's made up of lowlands, pines,
cypress hammocks and oaks, and dozens of
species call the area home, including mink,
gray and red foxes, coyotes, six bat species,
beavers, woodpeckers, alligators, Florida
black bears and the elusive Florida panther.
Numerous lakes and miles of trails make
this one of the most diverse outdoor recreation areas in the state. Over two years after
Hurricane Michael, some loblolly pines still
have a decided lean, and some campsites
and portions of natural areas remain closed,
but the natural beauty still shines through.

◉ Sights

Leon Sinks Geological Area   PARK
(off US 319; vehicle $5; ⊙8am-sunset; 🅿) 🐾
Three trails and boardwalks marked with interpretive signs wind past sinks and swamps
in this fascinating place. Be sure to stay on
the trails, as the karst is still evolving, and
new sinkholes could appear any time. At **Big
Dismal Sink** you'll see ferns, dogwoods and
dozens of other lush plants descending its
steep walls.

The sinks are at the eastern end of Apalachicola National Forest, just west of US 319,
about 10 miles south of Tallahassee.

🏃 Activities

There are plentiful opportunities for paddling along the forest's rivers and waterways. Information on canoeing in the area
and canoe rental is available from the ranger stations and on the excellent website for
Florida Greenways & Trails (www.dep.state.
fl.us/gwt), which have updated lists of outfitters in the surrounding towns. Canoe rentals
cost around $25 to $35 per day.

Powerboats are allowed on the rivers but
not on the glassy lakes.

The **Florida National Scenic Trail** (www.
fs.usda.gov/fnst) cuts a northwest–southeast
swath through the Apalachicola National Forest. Prepare to get soaked if you opt
for the **Bradwell Bay Wilderness** section,
which involves some waist-deep swamp
tramping. You can pick up the trail at the
southeastern gateway, just east of Forest Rd
356 on Hwy 319, or at the northwestern corner on Hwy 12.

Munson Hills Loop   CYCLING
🐾 On the eastern side of the Apalachicola
National Forest is the 7.5-mile Munson Hills
Loop bicycle trail, which starts at the trailhead of the Tallahassee-St Marks Historic
Railroad State Trail. Experienced off-road
cyclists can tackle this area made up of hammock, dunes, hills and brush, though the
soft sand makes it a challenging route.

If you run out of steam halfway through,
take the Tall Pine Shortcut out of the trail,
roughly at the halfway point, for a total distance of 4.5 miles. Alternately, the adjacent
Twilight Trail is a loop trail that adds more
than 9 miles.

🛌 Sleeping

Hickory Landing   CAMPGROUND $
(☑850-643-2282; www.fs.usda.gov; off Hickory
Landing Rd; campsite $10; 🅿) There's drinking
water and 10 campsites here, but not much
else, other than a bucolic forest setting. It's
a designated hunt camp during hunting season (approximately December to January).

🍴 Eating

There are small towns with convenience
stores dotted around the national forest,

WAKULLA SPRINGS STATE PARK

Glowing an otherworldly aqua and overhung with Spanish moss, the natural spring at the center of this 6000-acre **state park** (☑850-561-7276; www.floridastateparks.org; 465 Wakulla Park Dr, Wakulla Springs; vehicle/pedestrian $6/2; ☺8am-sunset; ℗🐾) feels like something from the set of an exotic adventure movie, and indeed parts of *Tarzan's Secret Treasure* and *The Creature from the Black Lagoon* were filmed here. Gushing 1.2 billion gallons of water daily, the spring is deep and ancient: the remains of at least 10 ice-age mammals have been found. Fair warning – this spot can get crowded.

You can swim in the deep, gin-clear waters or dive off the elevated platform. Don't miss the chance to take a 40-minute guided **boat tour** (adult/child $8/5), which glides under moss-draped bald cypress trees and past an array of creatures, including precious manatees (in season), alligators, tribes of red-bellied turtles and graceful wading birds. Tours depart at 11am and 4pm.

You can also crash here: the **Lodge at Wakulla Springs** (☑850-421-2000; www.wakulla springslodge.com; 550 Wakulla Park Dr; r from $130; ℗) is an early 20th-century classic.

but it's a good idea to bring your own food-stuffs. Always dispose of your food responsibly – the forest is home to a population of black bears.

ⓘ Information

Apalachicola Ranger Station (☑850-643-2282; www.fs.usda.gov/apalachicola; 11152 NW SR 20, Bristol) The western half of the forest is controlled by the Apalachicola Ranger Station, northwest of the forest near the intersection of Hwys 12 and 20, just south of Bristol.

Wakulla Ranger Station (☑850-926-3561; www.fs.usda.gov/apalachicola; 57 Taff Dr, Crawfordville) The eastern half of the forest is managed by the Wakulla Ranger Station, just off Hwy 319 behind the Winn-Dixie in Crawfordville.

ⓘ Getting There & Away

You'll need wheels to explore the forest, either a bicycle for the exceedingly fit, or a car for the rest of us. Given that the woods cover such an enormous area, there are multiple entry points, including along SR 65 (easier if you're coming from Apalachicola) and SR 20 (good for those coming from Tallahassee).

Steinhatchee

☑352 / POP 1045

Steinhatchee's (that's *steen*-hatch-ee) claim to fame is its scallop season, which runs from July to early September and brings up to 1000 boats on its opening day to the otherwise peaceful waters of Dead Man's Bay. The season is kind of like a twisted Easter egg hunt, with locals and visitors taking a mesh bag, donning a snorkel and mask, and

and snatching up their own seafood as they swim.

There's not much to the town itself, which consists of a smattering of restaurants and marinas. But it's an inexpensive, off-the-beaten-path choice for those who want to spend time on the Suwannee.

🏃 Activities

Fishing and scalloping is where it's at: depending on the season, cobia, sea trout, mackerel, tarpon and the famous scallops are plentiful.

River Haven Marina BOATING
(☑352-498-0709; www.riverhavenmarinaandmotel. com; 1110 Riverside Dr; ☺9am-5pm) Rent a variety of fishing boats (from $60 per half-day) and kayaks including pick-up and drop-off (per half-day single/tandem $30/40) – great for exploring the local maze of waterways.

🛏️ Sleeping & Eating

Steinhatchee Landing RESORT $$
(☑352-498-0696; www.steinhatcheelanding. com; 315 Hwy 51 NE; cottages $175-350; ❄🐾🏊) This riverside resort community has one-through four-bedroom self-catering cottages clustered around a loop road, with a pool, country store, spa and lusciously manicured grounds bursting with hibiscus and palms. A two-night minimum stay is often required.

Steinhatchee River Inn Motel MOTEL $$
(☑352-498-4049; www.steinhatcheeinn.com; 1111 Riverside Dr; r from $129; ❄🛜🏊) This classic motel-style inn has all-suite rooms, a pool and is close to the marina.

Roy's
SEAFOOD **$$**

(📞352-498-5000; www.roys-restaurant.com; 100 1st Ave S; mains $15-25; ⊘11am-9pm; P🐾) Since 1969, Roy's, which sits overlooking the gulf, has been a favorite for seafood – fresh, locally caught and cooked to order. Platters come with fries, baked potatoes or hush puppies and access to the sprawling salad bar.

❶ Getting There & Away

Coming from either the north or south, take Hwy 19 (also called Hwy 19/27 and Hwy 19/98), then drive west on Hwy 51 to the end, about 12 miles.

Cedar Key

📞 352 / POP 700

Jutting 3 miles into the Gulf of Mexico, this windswept, isolated island will appeal to lovers of history and nature, although at high season the crowds tend to be more of the motorcycle-driving variety. The otherworldly landscape sings with marshes that reflect candy-colored sunsets, and tiny hills offering sweeping island views. Cedar Key is just one of 100 islands (13 of which are part of the Cedar Keys National Wildlife Refuge) that make up this coastal community, which is gloriously abundant with wildlife.

As the western terminus of the trans-Florida railroad in the late 1800s, Cedar Key was one of Florida's largest towns, second only to St Augustine. Its primary industry was wood (for Faber pencils), which eventually deforested the islands; an 1896 hurricane destroyed what was left. Consequently, the trees here are less than 100 years old.

◉ Sights & Activities

Cedar Keys National Wildlife Refuge
WILDLIFE RESERVE

(📞352-493-0238; www.fws.gov/cedarkeys; ⊘8am-sunset; P) 🐾 Home to 250 species of bird (including ibises, pelicans, egrets, herons and double-crested cormorants), 10 species of reptile and one romantic lighthouse, the 13 islands in this refuge can only be reached by boat. The islands' interiors are generally closed to the public, but during daylight hours you can access most of the white-sand beaches, which provide great opportunities for both fishing and manatee viewing.

Cedar Key Museum State Park
MUSEUM

(📞352-543-5350; www.floridastateparks.org; 12231 SW 166th St; $2; ⊘10am-5pm Thu-Mon) 🐾 This eclectic museum features the historic home of St Clair Whitman, a main player in both Cedar Key's pencil factory and fiber mill, who arrived in the area in 1882. At the time of writing, the home was closed for an extended period of renovation (check the website for updates), but Whitman's vast collection of insects, butterflies, glass, sea grass, bottles and infinite varieties of seashells can still be seen in the small exhibit area in the adjacent museum.

Shell Mound
ARCHAEOLOGICAL SITE

(📞352-493-0238; Hwy 326; ⊘sunrise-sunset) Archaeologists from the University of Florida created the informative self-guided walk around this awe-inspiring Native American site. More than one billion oyster shells were amassed to build the mound, which drew a regional crowd for solstice rituals between 400 and 650 CE. Though the mound has been worn down by time (and humans, who harvested the shells for road construction in the 20th century), you can still see the same view (and sunrises/sunsets) from the top that Native Americans once did.

Shell Mound is about 7 miles from central Cedar Key, at the western end of Hwy 326. Follow signs from Hwy 347.

Cedar Key Historical Society Museum
MUSEUM

(📞352-543-5549; www.cedarkeyhistoricalmuseum.org; 609 2nd St; adult/child $1/0.50; ⊘1-4pm Sun-Fri, 11am-5pm Sat) 🐾 This small, well-kept local museum features an extensive collection of Cedar Key historic photographs alongside exhibits on the town's rich industrial history, as well as collections of Native American, Civil War and seafood-industry artifacts.

Kayak Cedar Keys
KAYAKING

(📞352-543-9447; www.kayakcedarkeys.com; 6027 A St; kayaks per 3hr from $35; ⊘10am-4pm) 🐾 The waterways and estuaries in and around Cedar Key make for superb kayaking, which you can access via map-guided tours. This outfitter also will rent you gear and can arrange to take you to offshore clam beds.

☞ Tours

Tidewater Tours
BOATING

(📞352-543-9523; www.tidewatertours.com; 4 Dock St) 🐾 Tidewater Tours runs two-hour nature tours of the islands of the national wildlife refuge ($29), trips along the Suwannee River ($58) and bird-watching treks into the wild marshy coastline ($47).

WORTH A TRIP

MANATEE SPRINGS STATE PARK

Dip into the 72°F (22°C) crystalline waters of this beautiful eponymous **spring** (☑352-493-6072; www.floridastateparks.org; 11650 NW 115th St, Chiefland; vehicle $6; ☺8am-sundown; P⚿). You can scuba dive (bring your gear and register at the office) at the springhead, which gushes 117 million gallons of water per day, or canoe or kayak into the Suwannee (half/full day $20/$40) to spot birds or (in winter) the spring's namesake manatees. On dry land – a spongy combo of sand and limestone shaded by tupelo, cypress and pine – there's the 8.5-mile-long **North End hiking/cycling trail**.

The wheelchair-accessible raised timber boardwalk that traces the narrow spring down to the Suwannee River as it flows to the Gulf and out to sea is a highlight (and a good place from which to spot manatees). Ranger programs include guided canoe journeys, moonlight hikes, nature walks and occasional covered-wagon rides. Contact the park office for details. Snacks and food are served from a walk-up bar-and-grill until 4pm. RV and tent campsites are available at $20 per night.

Manatees are not present in the swimming area of Manatee Springs State Park, though it's worth noting that conservationists advise against touching or crowding them, arguing that this causes the animals undue stress.

🛌 Sleeping

★ Island Hotel
HOTEL **$$**

(☑352-543-5111; www.islandhotel-cedarkey.com; 224 2nd St, at B St; r $100-155; ✳🖧) Listed on the National Register of Historic Places, this 1859 hotel has 10 simple and romantic rooms with original hand-cut wooden walls, a wraparound balcony with rocking chairs, a history of notable guests – including John Muir and President Grover Cleveland – and, by all reports, as many as 13 resident ghosts.

Faraway Inn
MOTEL **$$**

(☑352-543-5330; www.farawayinn.com; 847 3rd St; r/cottages from $100/160; ✳🖧🅿🐾) Overlooking a silent, glassy stretch of bay, this funky little motel complex has rooms and cottages decorated in driftwood art and brightly colored prints. Guests chill on waterfront porch swings to watch mind-blowing sunsets.

🍴 Eating & Drinking

Steamers
SEAFOOD **$**

(www.steamerscedarkey.com; 420 Dock St; dozen oysters $15; ☺11am-9pm Mon-Sat, to 8pm Sun) Perched above Cedar Key's bustling marina, this seafood restaurant has a view of the water, friendly service, a full bar and extremely fresh, plump oysters and clams, thanks to the thriving seafood farms in the area.

Tony's
SEAFOOD **$$**

(☑352-543-0022; www.tonyschowder.com; 597 2nd St; mains $8-28; ☺11am-8pm Mon-Thu, to 9pm Fri-Sun) Creamy, whole-clam-studded clam chowder – Tony's claim to fame – is truly superlative, and a reason to visit this otherwise mediocre seafood restaurant in a Downtown storefront.

Tiki Bar
BAR

(www.lowkeyhideaway.info//tiki-bar; ☺2-9pm Mon-Fri, noon-9pm Sat, 9am-9pm Sun) Tucked behind a motel, this mainly outdoor bar and lounge serves up drinks, like spicy rum runners and margaritas spiked with fresh citrus, in a laid-back atmosphere. Wander down the private dock, or settle in at a picnic table and make new friends.

ℹ Information

Cedar Keys Welcome Center (☑352-543-5600; www.cedarkey.org; 450 2nd St; ☺10am-4pm) The source in town for all things local.

ℹ Getting There & Away

There's no public transportation to Cedar Key, but driving is easy: take Hwy 19/98 or I-75 to Hwy 24 and follow it southwest to the end.

ℹ Getting Around

You'll see locals zipping around in golf ('gulf') carts, which are perfect for traversing the little island; try **Cedar Key Gulf Kart Company** (☑352-543-5090; www.gulfkartcompany.com; 8030 A St; carts per 2hr/day from $25/55).

Understand Florida

History

Florida has the oldest recorded history of any US state, and it sometimes qualifies as the most bizarre too. Something about this swampy peninsula invites exaggeration and inflames desire, then gleefully bedevils those who pursue their visions. Be it Spanish explorers seeking fortunes of gold, Native Americans surviving the colonial onslaught, the great convergence on the state by settlers from both North and Latin America – the constant is epic struggles over land, resilient peoples, great tides of immigration, and inevitably, a crash. It makes for great storytelling.

First Inhabitants & Seminoles

Seminole & Indian Resources

Ah-Tah-Thi-Ki Museum (www. ahtahthiki.com)

Seminole Tribe of Florida (www. semtribe.com)

Miccosukee Tribe (www.tribe. miccosukee.com)

Prior to the arrival of Spanish explorers and settlers, numerous indigenous tribes inhabited the Florida peninsula: the Apalachee in Florida's Panhandle developed the most complex agriculture-based society; other tribes included the Timucua in northern Florida, the Tequesta along the central Atlantic Coast and the fierce Calusa in southern Florida. Legends say it was a poison-tipped Calusa arrow that killed Spanish explorer Ponce de León.

The most striking evidence of these early cultures is shell mounds (middens). Florida's ancestral peoples ate well, and their discarded shells reached 30ft high and themselves became the foundations of villages, as at Mound Key.

When the Spanish arrived in the 1500s, the indigenous population numbered perhaps 250,000. Over the next 200 years, European diseases killed 80% of them. The rest were killed by war or sold into slavery, so that by the mid-1700s, virtually none of Florida's original inhabitants were left.

However, as the 18th century unfolded, Creeks and other tribes from the north migrated into Florida, driven by the European greed for New World territory. These tribes intermingled and intermarried, and in the late 1700s they were joined by numerous runaway black slaves, whom they welcomed into their society.

At some point, these fugitive peoples occupying Florida's interior were dubbed 'Seminoles,' a corruption of the Spanish word *cimarrones,* meaning 'free people' or 'wild ones.' Defying European rule and ethnic catego-

TIMELINE	10,000 BC	AD 500	1513
	After crossing the Bering Strait from Siberia some 50,000 years earlier, humans arrive in Florida, hunting mastodon and saber-toothed tigers, at the end of the last ice age.	Indigenous peoples settle in year-round villages and begin farming, cultivating the 'three sisters' of corn, beans and squash, plus pumpkins, lemons and sunflowers.	Ponce de León lands in Florida, south of Cape Canaveral, believing it an island. Since it's around Easter, he names it La Florida, 'The Flowery Land' or 'Feast of Flowers.'

ry, they were soon considered too free for the newly independent United States, who declared war upon them.

Five Flags: Florida Gets Passed Around

All Floridian schoolchildren are taught that Florida has been ruled by five flags: those of Spain, France, Britain, the US and the Confederacy.

Spain claimed Florida in 1513 – when explorer Ponce de León arrived. Five more Spanish expeditions followed (and one French, raising its flag on the St Johns River), but nothing bore fruit until 1565, when St Augustine was settled. A malarial, easily pillaged outpost that produced

THE UNCONQUERED SEMINOLES

The US waged war on Florida's Seminoles three times. The First Seminole War, from 1817 to 1818, was instigated by Andrew Jackson, who ruthlessly attacked the Seminoles as punishment for sheltering runaway slaves and attacking US settlers.

Trouble was, Florida was controlled by Spain. After Jackson took over Pensacola, Spain protested this foreign military incursion, forcing Jackson to halt.

In 1830, 'Old Hickory,' now President Andrew Jackson, passed the Indian Removal Act, which aimed to move all Native Americans to reservations west of the Mississippi River. Some Seminoles agreed to give up their lands and move to reservations, but not all. In 1835 US troops arrived to enforce agreements, and Osceola, a Seminole leader, attacked an army detachment, triggering the Second Seminole War.

The war was fought guerrilla style by 2000 or so Seminoles in swamps and hammocks, and it's considered one of the most deadly and costly Indian wars in US history. In October 1837 Osceola was captured under a flag of truce and later died in captivity, but the Seminoles kept fighting. In 1842 the US finally called off its army, having spent $20 million and seen the deaths of 1500 US soldiers.

Thousands of Seminoles were killed or marched to reservations, but hundreds survived and took refuge in the Everglades. In 1855 a US army survey team went looking for them, but the Seminoles killed them first. The resulting backlash turned into the Third Seminole War, which ended after Chief Billy Bowlegs was paid to go west in 1858.

But 200 to 300 Seminoles refused to sign a peace treaty and slipped away again into the Everglades. Technically, these Seminoles never surrendered and remain the only 'unconquered' Native American tribe.

In the 1910s, brutally impoverished, the Seminoles discovered that tourists would pay to watch them in their temporary camps, and soon 'Seminole villages' were a mainstay of Florida tourist attractions, often featuring alligator wrestling and Seminole 'weddings.'

In 1957 the US officially recognized the Seminole Tribe (www.semtribe.com), and in 1962 the Miccosukee Tribe (www.miccosukee.com). Both tribes have strong governing structures that ensure indigenous voices are heard in a broader Florida context, as well as numerous cultural and recreational institutions (including casinos that bring in much-needed revenue).

1539	1565	1702	1776
Hernando de Soto arrives in Florida with 800 men, seeking rumored cities of gold. He fights Native Americans, camps near Tallahassee, but, finding no precious metals, keeps marching west.	Pedro Menéndez de Avilés founds St Augustine, which becomes the first permanent European settlement in the New World and is the oldest city in the continental US.	In their ongoing struggle with Spain and France over New World colonies, the British burn St Augustine to the ground; two years later they destroy 13 Spanish missions in Florida.	The American Revolution begins, but Florida's two colonies don't rebel. They remain loyal to the British crown, and soon English Tories flood south into Florida to escape the fighting.

little income, St Augustine truly succeeded at only one thing: spreading the Catholic religion. Spanish missionaries founded 31 missions across Florida, converting and educating Native Americans. They often did so with notable civility, but just as often with far-reaching consequences for indigenous culture.

In 1698 Spain established a permanent military fort at Pensacola, which was thence variously captured and recaptured by the Spanish, French, English and North Americans for a century.

Spain found itself on the losing side of the 1754–63 French and Indian War, having backed France in its fight with England. Afterward, Spain bartered with the English, giving them Florida in return for the captured Havana. Almost immediately, the 3000 or so Spaniards in Florida gratefully boarded boats for Cuba.

The British held Florida for 20 years and did marginally well, producing indigo, rice, oranges and timber. But in 1783, as Britain and the US were tidying up accounts after the close of the American Revolution, Britain handed Florida back to Spain – which this time had supported the winning side, the US.

The second Spanish period, from 1783 to 1819, was marked by one colossal misjudgment. Spain needed settlers, and quickly, so it vigorously promoted immigration to Florida, but this backfired when, by 1810, those immigrants (mainly North American settlers) started demanding 'independence' from Spain. Within a decade, Spain threw up its hands. It gave Florida back to the US for cash in a treaty formalized in 1822. In 1845 Florida became the 27th state of the US, but in 16 short years, it would reconsider that relationship and raise its fifth flag.

El Norte: The Epic and Forgotten Story of Hispanic North America (Carrie Gibson, 2019) traces America's Hispanic history, from the arrival of the Spanish in the 16th century to modern times.

From Civil War to Civil Rights

In 1838 the Florida territory was home to about 48,000 people, of whom 21,000 were black slaves. By 1860, 15 years after statehood, Florida's population was 140,000, of whom 40% were slaves, most of them working on highly profitable cotton plantations.

Thus, unsurprisingly, when Abraham Lincoln was elected president on an antislavery platform, Florida joined the Confederacy of southern states that seceded from the Union in 1861. During the ensuing Civil War, which lasted until 1865, only moderate fighting occurred in Florida.

Afterward, from 1865 to 1877, the US government imposed 'Reconstruction' on all ex-Confederate states. Reconstruction protected the rights of freed African Americans, and led to 19 African Americans becoming elected to Florida's state congress. This radical social and political upheaval led to a furious backlash.

When federal troops finally left, Florida 'unreconstructed' in a hurry, adopting a series of Jim Crow laws that segregated and disenfranchised

1816–58	1823	1835	1845
The three Seminole Wars pit the United States against the Seminole nation and allies, including escaped slaves. Although most Seminoles are exiled, small bands remain in the Everglades.	Tallahassee is established as Florida's territorial capital because it's halfway between Pensacola and St Augustine. Later attempts to move the state capital fail.	In attacks coordinated by Seminole leader Osceola, Seminoles destroy five sugar plantations on Christmas Day and soon after kill 100 US soldiers marching near Tampa, launching the Second Seminole War.	Florida is admitted to the Union as the 27th state. Since it is a slave state, its admission is balanced by that of Iowa, a free state.

African Americans in every sphere of life – in restaurants and parks, on beaches and buses – while a poll tax kept African Americans and the poor from voting. From then until the 1950s, African American field hands in turpentine camps and cane fields worked under a forced-labor 'peonage' system, in which they couldn't leave until their wages paid off their debts, which of course never happened.

The Ku Klux Klan thrived, its popularity peaking in the 1920s, when Florida led the country in lynchings. Racial hysteria and violence were commonplace; most infamously, a white mob razed the entire town of Rosewood in 1923.

In 1954 the US Supreme Court ended legal segregation in the US with *Brown v Board of Education,* but in 1957 Florida's Supreme Court rejected this decision, declaring it 'null and void.' This sparked protests but little change until 1964, when a series of demonstrations, some led by Martin Luther King, Jr, and race riots rocked St Augustine and helped spur passage of the national Civil Rights Act of 1964.

More race riots blazed across Florida cities in 1967 and 1968, after which racial conflict eased as Florida belatedly and begrudgingly desegregated itself. Florida's racial wounds healed equally slowly – as evidenced by more race riots in the early 1980s. Today, despite much progress and the fact that Florida is one of the nation's most ethnically diverse states, these wounds still haven't completely healed. In the weeks following the killing of George Floyd on May 25, 2020, protests associated with the Black Lives Matter movement broke out in cities across Florida, with the largest gatherings in Gainesville and Jacksonville.

Bubble in the Sun: The Florida Boom of the 1920s and How it Brought on the Great Depression (Christopher Knowlton, 2020) and *The Unwinding: Thirty Years of American Decline* (George Packer, 2013) tell the story of the enduring consequences of Florida's boom-bust cycle.

Draining Swamps & Laying Rail

By the middle of the 19th century, the top half of Florida was reasonably well settled, but South Florida was still an oozing, mosquito-plagued swamp. So, in the 1870s, Florida inaugurated its first building boom by adopting laissez-faire economic policies centered on three things: unrestricted private development, minimal taxes and land grants for railroads.

In 10 years, from 1881 to 1891, Florida's railroad miles quintupled, from 550 to 2566. Most of this track crisscrossed northern and central Florida, where the people were, but one rail line went south to nowhere. In 1886 railroad magnate Henry Flagler started building a railroad down the coast on the spectacular gamble that once he built it, people would come.

In 1896 Flagler's line stopped at the squalid village of Fort Dallas, which incorporated as the city of Miami that same year. Then, people came, and kept coming, and Flagler is largely credited with founding every town from West Palm Beach to Miami.

It's hard to do justice to what happened next, but it was madness, pure and simple – far crazier than explorer Ponce de León's Florida-bound

HISTORY DRAINING SWAMPS & LAYING RAIL

1861	1889	1894–95	1912
Voting 62 to seven, Florida secedes from the US, raising its fifth flag, that of the Confederacy. Florida's farms and cattle provide vital Confederate supplies during the ensuing Civil War.	Key West becomes the largest, most populous city in Florida largely due to the wrecking industry – salvaging cargo from ships that sink in the treacherous surrounding waters.	The Great Freeze ruins citrus crops across the agricultural belt in Central Florida. Settlers begin moving to South Florida seeking warmer climes and longer growing seasons.	'Flagler's Folly,' Henry Flagler's 128-mile overseas railroad connecting the Florida Keys, reaches Key West. It's hailed as the 'Eighth Wonder of the World' but is destroyed by a 1935 hurricane.

quest for eternal waters. Why, all South Florida needed was to get rid of that pesky *swamp,* and then it really *would* be paradise: a land of eternal sunshine and profit.

In 1900 Governor Napoleon Bonaparte Broward, envisioning an 'Empire of the Everglades,' set in motion a frenzy of canal building. Over the next 70 years, some 1800 miles of canals and levees were etched across Florida's porous limestone. These earthworks drained about half the Everglades (about 1.5 million acres) below Lake Okeechobee, replacing it with farms, cattle ranches, orange groves, sugarcane and suburbs.

From 1920 to 1925 the South Florida land boom swept the nation. In 1915 Miami Beach was a sand bar; by 1925 it had 56 hotels, 178 apartment buildings and three golf courses. In 1920 Miami had one skyscraper; by 1925, 30 were under construction. In 1925 alone, 2.5 million people moved to Florida. Real-estate speculators sold undeveloped land, undredged land, and then just the airy paper promises of land. Everything went like hotcakes.

Then, two hurricanes struck, in 1926 and 1928, and the party ended. The coup de grâce was the October 1929 stock-market crash, which took everyone's money. Like the rest of the nation, Florida plunged into the Great Depression, though the state rode it out better than most due to New Deal public works, tourism and a highly profitable foray into rum-running.

> After WWII the advent of effective bug spray and affordable air-conditioning did more for Florida tourism than anything else. With these two technological advancements, Florida's subtropical climate was finally safe for delicate Yankees.

Tin-Can Tourists, Retirees & a Big-Eared Mouse

Tourism is Florida's number-one industry, and this doesn't count retirees – the tourists who never leave.

Tourism didn't become a force in Florida until the 1890s, when Flagler built his coastal railroad and his exclusive Miami Beach resorts. In the 1920s, middle-class 'tin-can tourists' arrived via the new Dixie Hwy – driving Model Ts, sleeping in campers and cooking their own food.

In the 1930s, to get those tourists spending, savvy promoters created the first 'theme parks': Cypress Gardens and Silver Springs. But it wasn't until after WWII that Florida tourism exploded. During the war, Miami was a major military training ground, and afterward, many of those GIs returned with their families to enjoy Florida's sandy beaches at leisure.

> At the height of the industry in the 1940s, Florida's sugarcane fields produced one of every five teaspoons of sugar consumed in the US.

In addition, after the war, social security kicked in, and the nation's aging middle class migrated south to enjoy their first taste of retirement. As old folks will, they came slowly but steadily, at a rate of a thousand a week, till they numbered in the hundreds of thousands and then millions. Many came from the East Coast, and quite a few were Jewish: by 1960, Miami Beach was 80% Jewish, creating a famous ethnic enclave.

1923	1926	1933–40	1935
The African American town of Rosewood, in Levy County, is wiped off the map by a white lynch mob; former residents are scattered and resettle elsewhere.	A major hurricane flattens and floods South Florida. Nearly 400 people die, most drowning when Lake Okeechobee bursts its dike. Two years later, another hurricane kills 2000 people.	New Deal public-works projects employ 40,000 Floridians and help save Florida from the Great Depression. The most notable construction project is the Overseas Hwy through the Keys, replacing Flagler's railroad.	'Swami of the Swamp' Dick Pope opens Cypress Gardens, the USA's first theme park, with water-ski stunts, topiary and Southern belles. Allegedly, this inspires Walt Disney to create California's Disneyland.

BLACK MARKET FLORIDA

In 1919, when the US passed the 18th Amendment – making liquor illegal and inaugurating Prohibition – bootleggers discovered something that previous generations of black slaves and Seminoles knew well: Florida can be a good place to hide.

Almost immediately Florida became, as the saying went, 'wet as a frog,' and soon fleets of ships and airplanes were bringing in Cuban and Jamaican rum, to be hidden in coves and dispersed nationwide.

Interestingly, Florida rum-running was conducted mostly by local 'mom-and-pop' operations, not the Mob, despite the occasional vacationing mobster like Al Capone. In this way, Prohibition really drove home the benefits of a thriving black market. When times were good, as in the 1920s, all that (illicit) money got launder-...um...pumped into real estate, making the good times unbelievably great. When hard times hit in the 1930s, out-of-work farmers could still make bathtub gin and pay the bills. Because of this often-explicit understanding, Miami bars served drinks with impunity throughout the 1920s, and local police simply kept walking.

In the 1960s and '70s the story was repeated with marijuana. Down-on-their-luck commercial fishers made a mint smuggling plastic-wrapped bales of pot, and suddenly Florida was asking, 'Recession? What recession?' West Florida experienced a condo boom.

In the 1980s cocaine became the drug of choice. But this time the smugglers were Colombian cartels, and they did business with a gun, not a handshake. Bloody shootouts on Miami streets shocked Floridians (and inspired the *Miami Vice* TV show), but they didn't slow the estimated $10-billion drug business – and did you notice Miami's new skyline? In the 1980s so much cash choked Miami banks that smuggling currency itself became an industry – along with smuggling out guns to Latin America and smuggling in rare birds, flowers and Cuban cigars.

But it wasn't until 1971 when Walt Disney, exempt from a host of state laws and building codes, transformed a patch of Orlando-area wetlands into Disney World and took Florida's tourism boom to a whole new level. How big did it become? In 1950 Florida received 4.5 million tourists, not quite twice its population. By the 1980s, Walt Disney World® alone was drawing 40 million visitors a year, or four times the state population.

Disney had the Midas touch. In the shadow of the Magic Kingdom, Florida's old-school attractions – Weeki Wachee, Seminole Village, Busch Gardens; all the places made famous through billboards and postcards – seemed hokey, small-time. The rules of tourism had changed forever.

Viva Cuba Libre!

South Florida has often had a more intimate relationship with Cuba than with the rest of the US. Spain originally ruled Florida from Havana, and in the 20th century so many Cuban exiles sought refuge in Miami, they

1941–45	1942	1946	1947
The US enters WWII. Two million men and women receive basic training in South Florida. At one point, the army commandeers 85% of Miami Beach's hotels to house personnel.	From January to August, German U-boats sink more than two dozen tankers and ships off Florida's coast. By war's end, Florida holds nearly 3000 German POWs in 15 labor camps.	Frozen concentrated orange juice is invented. As the nation's top orange producer, this event leads to Florida's orange boom, giving birth to the orange millionaires of the '50s and '60s.	Everglades National Park is established after a 19-year effort led by Ernest Coe and Marjory Stoneman Douglas to protect the Everglades from the harm done by dredging and draining.

dubbed it the 'Exile Capital.' Later, as immigration expanded, Miami simply became the 'Capital of Latin America.'

From 1868 to 1902, during Cuba's long struggle for independence from Spain, Cuban exiles settled in Key West and Tampa, giving birth to Ybor City and its cigar-rolling industry. After independence, many Cubans returned home, but the economic ties they'd forged remained. Then, in 1959, Fidel Castro's revolution (plotted partly in Miami hotels) overthrew the Batista dictatorship. This triggered a several-year exodus of more than 600,000 Cubans to Miami, most of them white, wealthy, educated professionals.

In April 1961 Castro declared Cuba a communist nation, setting the future course for US–Cuban relations. The next day, President Kennedy approved the ill-fated Bay of Pigs invasion, which failed to overthrow Castro, and in October 1962, Kennedy blockaded Cuba to protest the presence of Russian nuclear missiles. Khrushchev famously 'blinked' and removed the missiles, but not before the US secretly agreed never to invade Cuba again.

None of this sat well with Miami's Cuban exiles, who agitated for the USA to free Cuba (chanting '*Viva Cuba libre*': long live free Cuba). Between 1960 and 1980, a million Cubans emigrated – 10% of the island's population; by 1980, 60% of Miami was Cuban. Meanwhile, the USA and Cuba wielded immigration policies like cudgels to kneecap each other.

Unlike most immigrant groups, Cuban exiles disparaged assimilation (and sometimes the US), because the dream of return animated their lives. Miami became two parallel cities, Cuban and North American, that rarely spoke each other's language.

In the 1980s and 1990s, poorer immigrants flooded Miami from all over the Latin world – particularly El Salvador, Nicaragua, Mexico, Colombia, Venezuela, the Dominican Republic and Haiti. These groups did not always mix easily or embrace each other, but they found success in a city that already conducted business in Spanish. By the mid-1990s, South Florida was exporting $25 billion in goods to Latin America, and Miami's Cubans were more economically powerful than Cuba itself.

Today, Miami's Cubans are firmly entrenched, to the extent that many of the community's younger generation no longer consider themselves exiles.

> One day in 1963, so the story goes, Walt Disney flew over central Florida, spotted the intersection of I-4 and the Florida Turnpike, and said, 'That's it.' In secret, he bought 43 sq miles of Orlando-area wetlands. He later negotiated unprecedented municipal powers to build his tourist mecca.

Hurricanes, Elections & the Everglades

Florida has a habit of selling itself too well. The precarious foundation of its paradise was driven home in 1992, when Hurricane Andrew ripped across South Florida, leaving a wake of destruction that stunned the state and the nation. Plus, mounting evidence of rampant pollution – fish kills, dying mangroves, murky bays – appeared like the bill for a century of unchecked sprawl, population growth and industrial nonchalance.

1961	1969	1971	May 1980
Brigade 2506, a 1300-strong volunteer army, invades Cuba's Bay of Pigs on April 16. President Kennedy withholds air support, leading to Brigade 2506's immediate defeat and capture by Fidel Castro.	*Apollo 11* lifts off from Cape Canaveral, landing on the moon on July 20, winning the space race with the Russians. Five more lunar-bound rockets take off through 1972.	Walt Disney World® opens in Orlando and around 10,000 people arrive on the first day. The park attracts 10 million visitors during its first year.	In the McDuffie trial, white cops are acquitted of wrongdoing in the death of an African American man, igniting racial tensions and Miami's Liberty City riots, killing 18 people.

Newcomers were trampling what they were coming for. From 1930 to 1980, Florida's population growth rate was 564%. Florida had gone from the least-populated to the fourth-most-populated state, and its infrastructure was woefully inadequate, with too few police, overcrowded prisons, traffic jams, ugly strip malls and some of the nation's worst schools.

In particular, saving the Everglades became more than another environmental crusade. It was a moral test: would Florida really squander one of the Earth's wonders over subdivisions and a quick buck? Remarkably, legislation was passed: the Florida Forever Act and the Comprehensive Everglades Restoration Plan were both signed into law in 2000. Meanwhile, the actual implementation of Everglades restoration has been delayed and held up by bureaucracy and politicking at the federal, state and local levels.

Yet 2000 became even more emblematic of Florida's deeply divided self. That year's tight presidential election between Republican George W Bush and Democrat Al Gore hung on Florida's result. However, Florida's breathtakingly narrow vote in favor of Bush unraveled into a fiasco of 'irregularities,' including defective ballots, wrongly purged voter rolls and mysterious election-day roadblocks. After months of legal challenges and partial recounts, Florida's vote was finally approved, but its reputation had been tarnished.

As the 21st century dawned, Florida's historical tensions – between its mantra of growth and development and the unsustainable demands that placed on society and nature – seemed as entrenched and intractable as ever.

Southernmost Schisms

The beginning of this century was a politically polarizing time across much of the United States, and Florida, being in many ways a microcosm of the nation as a whole, was not immune to the trend. If anything, Florida's ideological divisions were exacerbated by deep boundaries that run along its geographic and ethnic lines.

While the governorship has remained securely in Republican hands since 1999, the state itself is a toss-up in every presidential election (it narrowly broke for George W Bush twice and Barack Obama twice). This is partly due to redistricting practices, widely seen as gerrymandering (ie drawing voting districts to bolster a political party's performance), which have driven a deep rift between the state's political camps. With that said, past governors such as Jeb Bush (George W Bush's younger brother; 1999–2007) and Charlie Crist (2007–11) toed the centrist line within the Republican policy universe, generally skewing towards conservative economics and lenient policies regarding immigration.

In February 2020, Miami-Dade County commissioners voted unanimously to rename their sections of the Dixie Highway (which runs 5786 miles from Miami to Michigan) the Harriet Tubman Highway. The word Dixie is often associated with the pre-Civil War Confederacy when slavery was legal. Harriet Tubman was an escaped slave and abolitionist leader.

1980	1984	1992	1999
Castro declares the Cuban port of Mariel 'open.' The USA's ensuing Mariel Boatlift rescues 125,000 Marielitos, who face intense discrimination in Miami.	TV show *Miami Vice* debuts, combining music-video sensibilities, pastel fashions, blighted South Beach locations and cynical undercover cops battling gun-wielding Miami cocaine cartels.	On August 24, Hurricane Andrew devastates Dade County, leaving 41 people dead and more than 200,000 homeless, and causing $15.5 billion in damage.	On Thanksgiving, five-year-old Elián Gonzalez is rescued at sea, his Cuban mother having died en route. Despite wild protests by Miami's Cuban exiles, the US returns Elián to his father in Cuba.

Indeed, Crist, who supported same-sex marriage but was also pro-gun ownership, made the relatively rare American political move of defection, joining the Democratic Party in 2012. That he did so a month after Barack Obama's re-election did not help his reputation as a political opportunist. His ouster and political conversion came amid the 2008 financial crisis, which particularly devastated the Florida housing market.

Rick Scott, a former CEO and venture capitalist with a pre-election net worth of over $200 million, occupied the gubernatorial office in Tallahassee from 2011–19 and set the state's political compass for the decade. As an unabashedly antiregulation businessman, he was also sympathetic to Everglades protection policies, a tension that mirrored the state's many diverse and divisive interests: the white, conservative northern end, the more liberal and Latin American south, and the mishmash of identities and interests in between. Stand Your Ground, Everglades restoration, climate-change denial and climate-change preparation were the policies of this period, in all their Floridian contradictions.

Florida Today

Florida is undergoing seismic shifts in demographics, state identity, and – if the environment doesn't improve – state topography, thanks to immigration, economic boom-bust cycles and climate change. And just because everyone seems to agree that things can't continue as they are doesn't mean that a change is likely any time soon. Development, real-estate speculation and rapid population growth all continue to put unsustainable pressure on Florida's natural resources. The state's population is projected to double in the period from 2006 to 2060. Something surely has got to give.

As unbelievable as it might seem, Florida is running out of fresh water. The peninsula where Florida resides is largely below sea level, and the ocean is rising – Miami and the Florida Keys are especially vulnerable – even as the peninsula is crumbling. The culprits behind the crumble are artificial canals and waterways dredged in the early 20th century. Those public works directed water away from the Everglades and the South Florida aquifer, eroding the wetlands and depleting freshwater reserves.

Florida is also changing politically. In 2018, Ron DeSantis won Florida's gubernatorial elections. Although the victory margin was less than a single percentage point, DeSantis became the fourth consecutive Republican governor – the last time the Democrats held the governor's mansion was in 1999. In an even closer race, previous governor Rick Scott, also a Republican, won a Senate seat previously held by the Democrats by fewer than 10,000 votes out of 8.1 million votes cast – it was the most expensive race in Senate history.

2000	2000–10	2004	2010
Before the presidential election, Florida mistakenly purges thousands of legitimate voters from rolls. George W Bush then narrowly defeats Al Gore by 537 votes in Florida to win the presidency.	High-rise architecture sweeps Miami; during this period, 20 of the city's 25 tallest buildings are erected, a trend some call the 'Manhattanization' of Miami.	Florida records its worst hurricane season ever, when four storms – Charley, Frances, Ivan and Jeanne – strike the state over two months, causing 130 deaths and $22 billion in damage.	In the Gulf, *Deepwater Horizon*'s offshore oil spill becomes the worst in US history. Oil only affects Panhandle beaches, but Florida tourism plummets, with losses estimated at $3 billion.

But the Republicans don't have things entirely their own way. In the 2018 congressional elections, Democrats won two formerly Republican seats, but then lost two seats in the next election, giving Florida's congressional delegation in Washington a 16–11 Republican–Democrat split. The state Senate leans even more to the right. After the hammering Democrats received in 2020, Florida's legislative chamber had a Republican–Democrat split of 78 to 42. This leaves little hope for a progressive agenda – including the efforts to fight climate change – in the years ahead.

Florida voted for Barack Obama in both 2008 and 2012, but turned to Donald Trump in both 2016 and in 2020. The only thing for certain is that Florida's extraordinarily diverse population – from wealthy retirees to Hispanic immigrants and everyone in between – will keep pundits guessing whenever each election cycle comes around.

TRAYVON MARTIN & STAND YOUR GROUND

One of the most divisive racial and political incidents of the early 21st century in the US began in Florida.

On the night of February 26, 2012, 17-year old-old African American Trayvon Martin walked to his temporary home in the Central Florida town of Sanford. Martin, clad in a hoodie, was carrying a pack of Skittles and some Arizona Iced Tea. To get home quickly, he cut across yards in a gated community. Following him was George Zimmerman, a 28-year-old mixed-race Hispanic and neighborhood watch coordinator. Against the advice of police, Zimmerman confronted Martin, leading to an altercation. In the subsequent fight, Zimmerman received head and facial injuries, and shot and killed the unarmed Martin.

Zimmerman was taken into police custody and released; under Florida's recently passed Stand Your Ground law, police did not believe he had committed a crime. Under the Stand Your Ground statute, in a self-defense incident a victim does not have to exercise the traditional Duty to Retreat, common across American legal code, which states someone who kills in self-defense must have exhausted their opportunities to avoid conflict.

Media attention and a subsequent national outcry led to Zimmerman being rearrested on a charge of second-degree (ie nonpremeditated) murder on April 11, 2012. A trial in the summer of 2013 found Zimmerman not guilty. The decision outraged many, who felt Zimmerman had (literally) gotten away with the murder of an unarmed teenager. On the flip side, gun-rights advocates believed Zimmerman had exercised his rights to self-defense during the course of an assault.

Since the Trayvon Martin incident, Florida has become a petri dish for Stand Your Ground legislation. While the *Journal of the American Medical Association* (JAMA) published a 2016 investigation linking the law to increased homicide rates in the state, as of this writing, the state Senate had passed a bill that relaxed the requirements needed by a defendant to invoke the law's protections. In 2018, the Florida Supreme Court ruled that the Stand Your Ground statute applies to police officers as well as civilians.

2014	2017	2017	2018
Ongoing immigration from Latin America and elsewhere in the United States make Florida the third-most populous state in the US, behind California and Texas.	Around 6.5 million Floridians evacuate from the path of Hurricane Irma, which ended up the costliest in Florida's history, killing 84 people and causing $50 billion damage.	Outgoing president Barack Obama ends 'wet foot, dry foot,' a policy that allows Cubans who make it to the USA without a visa to become permanent residents.	Category 5 Hurricane Michael makes landfall in Florida with winds of up to 155mph wreaking destruction across the state's northwest coast.

People & Culture

Florida's people and culture are a hotpot of accents and rhythms, of pastel hues and Caribbean spices, of rebel yells and Latin hip-hop, of Jewish retirees and Miami Beach millionaires. Florida is, in a word, diverse, both fascinatingly complex and near-on impossible to pin down, making for an intriguing place to explore. And at its heart it's this tension that creates one of the most fascinating social dynamics in the country.

Portrait of a Peninsula

With so many, often contradictory parts, Florida can seem like some kind of Tower of Babel, with nothing holding everything together at its core. Florida is almost too popular for its own good, never able to quite decide whether the continual influx of newcomers and immigrants is its saving grace or what will eventually strain society to breaking point. And yet, Florida is the essence of America, a place that sometimes works and sometimes doesn't, but somehow keeps on going. Perhaps Florida is nothing more or less than the sum of its parts; a complicated place that reflects the broader sweeps of American identity concentrated into one small state.

Ultimately, Florida satisfies and defies expectations all at once. From Cuban lawyers to itinerant construction works, from fixed-income retirees to gay South Beach restaurateurs, it's one of the USA's more bizarre dinner parties come to life. And most residents do have something in common: in Florida, nearly everybody is from someplace else. Nearly everyone is a newcomer and, one and all, they wholeheartedly agree on two things: today's newcomers are going to ruin Florida, and wasn't it great to beat them here?

'Crackers' got the name most likely for the cracking of the whips during cattle drives, though some say it was for the cracking of corn to make cornmeal, grits or moonshine. For a witty, affectionate look at what makes a Cracker, pick up *Cracker: The Cracker Culture in Florida History* (1998) by Dana Ste Claire.

The Rural North

In terms of geography, Florida is a Southern state. Yet culturally, only Florida's northern half is truly of the South. The Panhandle and the rural north welcome those who speak with that distinctive Southern drawl, serve sweet tea as a matter of course and still remember the Civil War. Here, the stereotype of the NASCAR-loving redneck with a Confederate-flag bumper sticker on a mud-splattered pickup truck remains the occasional reality.

Rural Florida, meanwhile, whether north or south, can still evoke America's western frontier. In the 19th century, after the West was won, Florida became one of the last places where pioneers could simply plant stakes and make a life. These pioneers became Florida's 'Crackers', the poor rural farmers, cowhands and outlaws who traded life's comforts for independence on their terms. Sometimes any Florida pioneer is called a Cracker, but that's not quite right: the original Crackers scratched out a living in the backwoods (in the Keys, Crackers became Conchs). They were migrant field hands, not plantation owners, and with their lawless squatting, make-do creativity, vagrancy and carousing, they weren't regarded kindly by respectable townsfolk. But today, all native Floridians like to feel they too share that same streak of fierce, undomesticated self-reliance.

The Urban South

Central Florida and the Tampa Bay area have long been favored destinations for Midwesterners, and here you often find a plain-spoken, Protestant worker-bee sobriety. East Coast Yankees, once mocked as willing dupes for any old piece of swamp, have carved a definable presence in South Florida – such as in the Atlantic Coast's Jewish retirement communities, in calloused, urban Miami, and in the sophisticated towns of the southern Gulf Coast.

And yet, stand in parts of Miami and even Tampa, and you won't feel like you're in the US at all, but tropical Latin America. The air is filled with Spanish, the majority of people are Roman Catholic, and the politics of Cuba, Haiti or Colombia animate conversations.

Multicultural Florida

Like Texas and California, modern Florida has been largely redefined by successive waves of Hispanic immigrants from Latin America. What sets Florida apart is the teeming diversity of its Latinos and their self-sufficient, economically powerful, politicized, Spanish-speaking presence. Not for nothing is Miami often called the 'Capital of Latin America.'

It's worth noting that there are a lot of expats in Florida from Spain, which means some of the state's Spanish-speaking population is not technically Latin American.

Florida has also welcomed smaller waves of Asian immigrants from China, Indonesia, Thailand and Vietnam. And, of course, South Florida is famous for its Jewish immigrants, not all of whom are over 65 or even from the US. There is a distinctly Latin flavor to South Florida Judaism, as Cuban and Latin American Jews have joined those from the US East Coast, Europe and Russia. Overall, Florida is home to 850,000 Jews, with two-thirds in the Greater Miami area.

In *Dream State* (2004), bawdy, gimlet-eyed journalist Diane Roberts weaves her family's biography with Florida's history to create a compelling, unique, hilarious masterpiece: Roberts is like the trouble-making cousin at Florida's family reunion, dishing the dirt everyone else is too polite to discuss.

Cuban Florida

Florida's Cuban exile community (concentrated in Little Havana and Hialeah Park) began arriving in Miami in the 1960s following Castro's Cuban revolution. Educated and wealthy, these Cubans ran their own businesses, published their own newspapers and developed a Spanish-speaking city within a city. Their success aggravated some members of Florida's African American population, who, at the moment the Civil Rights movement was opening the doors to economic opportunity, found themselves outmanoeuvred for jobs by Hispanic newcomers.

IMMIGRATION BY THE NUMBERS

For the past 70 years, the story of Florida has been population growth, which has been driven mostly by immigration. Before WWII, Florida was the least populated state (with less than 2 million). Today it is the third most populated, with an estimated 21.5 million in 2019.

Florida's growth rate has been astonishing – it was 44% for the 1970s. While it's been steadily declining since, it was still over 17% for the 21st century's first decade, twice the national average.

Florida ranks fourth in the nation for the largest minority population (over 8 million), as well as for the largest number and percentage of foreign-born residents (four million people, who make up 20%). In Miami, the foreign-born population exceeds 50%, which is easily tops among large US cities. Close to 900,000 Floridians are undocumented immigrants, many of whom are Cubans – who no longer benefit from the now-dropped, wet-foot, dry-foot, policy that granted Cubans automatic lawful residence if they reached American soil – or 'Dreamers,' undocumented immigrants who arrived in the US as children and were granted temporary protection, a program that President Trump sought to overturn.

PEOPLE & CULTURE MULTICULTURAL FLORIDA

The children of Cuban exiles are now called YUCAs, 'young urban Cuban Americans,' while the next generation of Latinos has been dubbed Generation Ñ (pronounced 'en-yey'), embodying a hybrid culture. For instance, the traditional Cuban *quinceañera*, or *quince*, celebrating a girl's coming of age at 15, is still celebrated in Miami, but instead of a community-wide party, kids now plan trips. With each other, young Latinos slip seamlessly between English and Spanish, typically within the same sentence, reverting to English in front of Anglos and to Spanish or old-school Cuban Spanish in front of relatives.

Other Hispanic Communities

Building on the foundation of the Cuban migration of the '60s, many more Latinos kept arriving in Florida, ranging from the very poorest to the wealthiest. In Miami they found a Spanish-speaking infrastructure to help them, while sometimes being shunned by the insular Cuban exiles who preceded them.

Today, every Latin American country is represented in South Florida. Nicaraguans arrived in the 1980s, fleeing war in their country, and now number more than 100,000. Miami's Little Haiti is home to more than 70,000 Haitians, the largest community in the US. There are 80,000 Brazilians, and large communities of Mexicans, Venezuelans, Colombians, Peruvians, Salvadorans, Jamaicans, Bahamians and more. This has led to significant in-migration around South Florida, as groups displace each other and shift to more fertile ground.

So just how pervasive is Spanish? One in four Floridians speak a language other than English at home, and three-quarters of these speak Spanish. Further, nearly half of these Spanish-speakers admit they don't speak English very well – because they don't need to. This is a sore point with some Anglo Floridians.

To understand the human cost of the Florida real-estate market collapse in 2007, read *Exiles in Eden* (2010) by Paul Reyes, a reporter who joined the family business of 'trashing out' foreclosed homes. George Packer's *The Unwinding* (2013) also uses Tampa as an example of America's economic unraveling.

Life in Florida

Let's get this out of the way first: Florida is indeed the nation's oldest state. It has the highest percentage of people over 65 (more than 20% of Florida's population) – that demographic includes more than *half* of the population of Sumter County (near Orlando). In fact, ever since WWII, South Florida has been 'God's waiting room' – the land of the retiree.

But the truth is, most immigrants to the state (whether from within the US or abroad) are aged 20 to 30. They come because of Florida's historically low cost of living and its usually robust job and real-estate markets.

The Florida Problem

When times are good, what these newcomers find is that there are plenty of low- to midwage construction, tourist and service-sector jobs, and if they can buy one of those new-built condos or tract homes, they're money ahead, as Florida home values usually outpace the nation's. But in bad times when real estate falters – and in Florida, no matter how many warnings people get, the real-estate market does eventually falter – home values plummet, construction jobs dry up and service-sector wages can't keep up with the bills. Thus it is that those 20- to 30-year-olds also leave the state in the highest numbers.

In recent years, the growing wealth gap in America has made it increasingly difficult for middle-income earners to afford rent (let alone a mortgage) in Florida's growing urban areas. While businesses have always been able to fall back on cheap migrant labor from Latin America, the Caribbean and Eastern Europe, there has also usually been an accompanying nucleus of lifer service-industry professionals. Said professionals are increasingly finding Florida unaffordable, though, which bears the question: how can a state that is supported by tourism survive if folks can't afford to live on what the tourism industry pays?

Urban-Rural Divide

Florida's urban and rural divides are extreme. Urban sprawl, particularly around Miami, Orlando and Tampa, is universally loathed – because who likes traffic jams and cookie-cutter sameness? Well, some folks like the sameness; Florida wouldn't be famous for its suburbs and shopping malls if people didn't occupy them. In addition, new immigrants tend to gravitate to the suburbs – the green-lawns predictability rejected by so many Americans seeking a new urbanism are seen as signs of a high quality of life for émigrés from Haiti and Cuba. And 80% of Floridians live within 10 miles of the coast because that's why everyone came – the beach.

Along the peninsula's urbanized edges, everyone rubs up against each other: racial, ethnic and class tensions are a constant fact of life, but they have also calmed tremendously in recent decades. In general, tolerance (if not acceptance) of diversity is the norm, while tolerance of visitors is the rule. After all, they pay the bills.

But wilderness and rural life define much of interior and northern Florida: here, small working-class towns can be as white, old-fashioned and conservative as Miami is ethnic, gaudy and permissive. This is one reason why it's so hard to predict Florida elections, and why sometimes they turn on a handful of votes.

A large military presence in the Florida Panhandle makes for an area that is generally quite conservative in its politics, but thanks to overseas rotations, a bit more cosmopolitan than the deep piney villages of the North Florida interior.

Floridians at Play

Floridians are passionate about sports. If you let them, they'll fervently talk baseball, football, basketball and NASCAR through dinner, dessert and drinks on the porch.

Football

For the majority of Floridians, college football is the true religion. Florida has three of the country's best collegiate teams – the University of Miami Hurricanes, the University of Florida Gators (in Gainesville) and the Florida State University Seminoles (in Tallahassee). Between them, these teams have won nine national championships, and if anything, they are even more competitive with each other. It's hardly an exaggeration to say that beating an in-state rival is – at least for fans, who take deep pleasure in hating their rivals – almost more important than winning all the other games. If you want to cause a scene in Florida, tell an FSU student how much you love the Gators, or mention to a UF student how great the 'Noles are.

Every year on January 1, major football games are played in Orlando (Capital One Bowl), Tampa (Outback Bowl) and Jacksonville (Gator Bowl). Two days later is Miami's Orange Bowl (www.ncaa.com).

Florida also boasts three pro football teams: the Miami Dolphins, Tampa Bay Buccaneers and Jacksonville Jaguars. There's a reason college football is so popular in Florida: in recent years all three professional teams have (sorry, it must be said) royally sucked.

Basketball, Baseball & Ice Hockey

Florida has two pro basketball teams, the Orlando Magic and Miami Heat. The Heat, who won back-to-back NBA championships in 2012 and 2013 (and have since kind of cooled their heels) are loved in Miami and pretty much loathed everywhere else.

When former *David Letterman* writer Rodney Rothman burned out, he decided to test-drive 'retirement' in Boca Raton – at age 28. A good Jewish boy, Rothman crafts a very personal anthropological study of the unsentimental world of Florida retirees in *Early Bird: A Memoir of Premature Retirement* (2005).

PEOPLE & CULTURE FLORIDIANS AT PLAY

> ## INTER MIAMI CF
>
> In early 2020, just before the coronavirus pandemic halted all professional sports in the US, Inter Miami CF (also known as Club Internacional de Fútbol Miami) played its first Major League Soccer (MLS) game. Owned by former Manchester United and Real Madrid star David Beckham – who brings a touch of box office that's right at home in Miami – Inter Miami play at the Inter Miami CF Stadium in Fort Lauderdale.

The 2020 Stanley Cup–winning Tampa Bay Lightning is one of several pro and semipro ice-hockey teams in the state, including the Miami-based Florida Panthers.

Major-league baseball's spring training creates a frenzy of excitement from February each year, when 15 pro teams practice across southern Florida. The stadiums then host minor-league teams, while two pro teams are based here: the Miami Marlins and the Tampa Bay Rays (in St Petersburg). The Minnesota Twins and Boston Red Sox both have their training facilities in Fort Myers.

NASCAR

NASCAR originated among liquor bootleggers who needed fast cars to escape the law – and who later raced against each other. Fast outgrowing its Southern redneck roots to become popular across the US, NASCAR is near and dear to Floridians and hosts regular events in Daytona.

The Daytona International Speedway is NASCAR's spiritual home, and the Daytona 500 is like the Super Bowl to NASCAR fans and easily the biggest event on the calendar. Other NASCAR races also happen at Homestead-Miami Speedway, while part of St Petersburg's waterfront shuts down every March for the street-circuit Firestone Grand Prix of St Petersburg.

Other Sports

Imported sports also flourish in South Florida. One is the dangerous Basque game of jai alai, which is popular with Miami's cigar-smoking wagering types. Another is cricket, thanks to the Miami region's large Jamaican and West Indian population.

Florida Stories: Conquistadores & Pioneers

....

St Augustine (p360)

....

Marjorie Kinnan Rawlings Historic State Park (p386)

....

Museum of Florida History, Tallahassee (p476)

....

Tampa Bay History Center (p396)

....

Historic Pensacola Village (p455)

Religion

Florida is not just another notch in the South's evangelical Bible Belt. It's actually considerably more diverse religiously than its neighboring states.

In Florida, religious affiliations split less along urban/rural lines than along northern/southern ones. About 40% of Florida is Protestant, and about 25% of Protestants are Evangelicals, who tend to be supporters of the religious right. These conservative Protestants are generally concentrated in northern Florida, nearer their Southern neighbors.

The majority of the state's Roman Catholics (who make up 21%) and Jews (3%) live in South Florida. In South Florida, Jews make up 12% of the population, the second-highest percentage after the New York metro area. The high Catholic population reflects South Florida's many Latin American immigrants.

South Florida also has a growing Muslim population, and it has a noticeable number of adherents of Santeria, a mix of West African and Catholic beliefs, and *vodou* (voodoo), mainly practiced by Haitians.

Further, about 17% of Floridians say that they have no religious affiliation. That doesn't mean they lack spiritual beliefs; it just means their beliefs don't fit census categories. For instance, one of Florida's most famous religious communities is Cassadaga, a home for spiritualists for more than 100 years.

The Arts

Florida has a well-earned reputation as a welcoming port for all manner of kitsch and low-brow entertainment. It invented the theme park, spring break, *Miami Vice* and its own absurdist, black-comic semitropical crime noir. But there's so much more. Yes, the colors are always sunshine bright. But at their best, Florida's artistic traditions are simultaneously homegrown and cosmopolitan, and vibrate with the surreal, mercurial truths of everyday life in this state that is, in truth, a mirror onto the American soul.

Literature

Old Florida

Beginning in the 1930s, Florida's literary voice first developed, courtesy mainly of three writers. Ernest Hemingway settled in Key West in 1928 to write, fish and drink, not necessarily in that order. 'Papa' wrote *For Whom the Bell Tolls* (1940) and *A Farewell to Arms* (1929) here, but he only set one novel in Florida, *To Have and Have Not* (1937).

Marjorie Kinnan Rawlings lived in Cross Creek between Gainesville and Ocala. She turned her sympathetic, keen eye on Florida's pioneers – the Crackers who populated 'the invisible Florida' – and on the elemental beauty of the Everglades. Her novel *The Yearling* (1938) won the Pulitzer Prize, and *Cross Creek* (1942) is a much-lauded autobiographical novel. Her original homestead, in Ocala in the state's north, is now a museum.

Rounding out the trio is Zora Neale Hurston, an African American writer born in all-Black Eatonville, near Orlando. Hurston became a major figure in New York's Harlem renaissance of the 1930s, and her most famous novel, *Their Eyes Were Watching God* (1937), evokes the suffering of Florida's rural Blacks, particularly women. In *Seraph on the Suwanee* (1948), Hurston portrays the marriage of two white Florida Crackers. Controversial in her time, Hurston died in obscurity and poverty.

Another famous window on Florida's pioneers is Patrick Smith's *A Land Remembered* (1984), a sprawling, multigenerational saga that highlights the Civil War.

Meanwhile Peter Matthiessen's *Shadow Country* (2008) is an epic literary masterpiece. A trilogy revised into a single work, *Shadow Country* fictionalizes the true story of EJ Watson, a turn-of-the-century Everglades plume hunter who murdered his employees, and who in turn was murdered by the townsfolk. The book won the National Book Award for Fiction in 2008.

Naked Came the Manatee (1998) is a collaborative mystery novel by a constellation of famous Florida writers: Carl Hiaasen, Dave Barry, Elmore Leonard, James Hall, Edna Buchanan and more. It's like nibbling a delectable box of cyanide-laced chocolates.

Noir, Gothic & Crime

Florida writing is perhaps most famous for its eccentric take on hardboiled noir crime fiction. Carl Hiaasen almost single-handedly defines the genre; his stories are hilarious bubbling gumbos of misfits and murderers, who collide in plots of thinly disguised environmentalism, in which the bad guys are developers and their true crimes are against nature. Some other popular names are Randy Wayne White, John D MacDonald, James Hall and Tim Dorsey.

FLORIDA PULP

Florida mystery writers love to tickle the swampy underbelly of the Sunshine State. This list focuses on early novels of famous series.

➡ *Rum Punch* (Elmore Leonard, 1992) Leonard is a master of intricate plots, crackling dialogue and terrific bad guys. Set in Miami, *Rum Punch* inspired Tarantino's *Jackie Brown*.

➡ *Double Whammy* (Carl Hiaasen, 1987) Hiaasen perfected his absurdist, black-comic rage in his second novel; you'll laugh till you cry. *Skinny Dip* and *Hoot* are other gems.

➡ *The Girl in the Plain Brown Wrapper* (John D MacDonald, 1968) The godfather of Florida crime fiction introduces us to Travis McGee, who saves a girl from suicide and gets trouble as thanks.

➡ *Sanibel Flats* (Randy Wayne White, 1990) With crisp prose and tight plotting, White introduces his much-beloved 'retired' NSA agent/marine biologist Doc Ford.

➡ *Miami Blues* (Charles Willeford, 1984) Willeford made it big with this addictive novel about a denture-wearing detective's pursuit of a quirky criminal.

➡ *Cold Case Squad* (Edna Buchanan, 2001) Miami police sergeant Craig Burch leads the cold-case squad in this novel, written by a Pulitzer Prize–winning former crime reporter for the *Miami Herald*.

➡ *Torpedo Juice* (Tim Dorsey, 2005) Zany Serge A Storms only kills people who really deserve it – people who disrespect Florida – as he searches for love in the Keys.

Florida's modern novelists tend to favor supernatural, even monstrously absurd Southern Gothic styles, none more so than Harry Crews; try *All We Need of Hell* (1987) and *Celebration* (1999). Two more cult favorites are *Ninety-two in the Shade* (1973) by Thomas McGuane and *Mile Zero* (1990) by Thomas Sanchez, both writerly, dreamlike Key West fantasies. Also don't miss Russell Banks' *Continental Drift* (1985), about the tragic intersection of a burned-out New Hampshire man and a Haitian woman in unforgiving Miami. Karen Russell's *Swamplandia!* (2011), about the travails of a family of alligator wrestlers, marries Hiaasen-style characters with swamp-drenched magical realism.

New Writing

Recent success stories include Jeff VanderMeer, whose novel *Annihilation* (2014), the first in his Southern Reach trilogy, was turned into a successful Hollywood film. The book was inspired by time spent in St Marks Wildlife Refuge in the state's north. He's not from Florida, but Colson Whitehead's 2019 novel, *The Nickel Boys*, emerged from real-life events at the Florida School for Boys. And Kristen Arnett's bestselling *Mostly Dead Things* (2019) was set in a Florida taxidermy shop.

For Cuban-American literature, Jennine Capó Crucet is always worth tracking down, while Richard Blanco is a celebrated poet.

Cinema & Television

It's a little-known fact that Jacksonville almost became Hollywood. In the 1910s Jacksonville had 30 production companies – far more than Hollywood – who used northern Florida's palm-tree-lined beaches as 'exotic' backdrops for 120 silent films. Instead, religiously conservative Jacksonville decided to run those wild movie types out of town.

Even so, Hollywood has returned to Florida time and again to film both TV shows and movies. Some of the more notable films include the Marx Bros farce *Cocoanuts* (1929), *Creature from the Black Lagoon* (1954; filmed at Wakulla Springs), *Miami Blues* (1990), *The Truman Show*

(1998; filmed at Seaside), *Ulee's Gold* (1997), *Donnie Brasco* (1997), *Get Shorty* (1995), and *Hoot* (2006).

Florida, as setting, has been a main character in numerous TV shows, starting with *Flipper* (1964–67), about a boy and his dolphin, and *I Dream of Jeannie* (1965–70). Set in Cocoa Beach, *Jeannie* was Florida all over: an astronaut discovers a pinup-gorgeous female genie in a bottle, only she never quite fulfills his wishes like he wants.

In the 1980s, *Miami Vice* (1984–90) hit the air, a groundbreaking cop drama that made it OK to wear sport coats over T-shirts and which helped inspire the renovation of South Beach's then-dilapidated historic district. The popular *CSI: Miami* (2002–12) took things up a rung.

Later, *Dexter* (2006–13) dipped past Miami's glamor directly into its bucket of weirdness. The Netflix series *Bloodline* (2015) continues Florida's 'sunshine noir' genre, following the dark history and dealings of a family in the Florida Keys. The 2016 film *Moonlight*, which won best picture at the Academy Awards, is set in Miami, and explores themes of homosexuality, racism and crime.

Miami is one of the centers of American Spanish-language media, especially film and television. The first Spanish-language presidential debate in the United States was hosted at the University of Miami on Univision in 2007, while Spanish-language network Telemundo is based in Hialeah, a suburb of Miami.

Two of the best film festivals in the US are the Miami International Film Festival, a showcase for Latin cinema, and the Florida Film Festival in Orlando.

Music

Florida's musical heritage is rich and satisfyingly diverse. Folk and blues are deep-running currents in Florida music; Ray Charles and Cannonball Adderley were both Floridians. Tallahassee has a notable blues scene, while Tampa has the Tampa Bay Blues Festival. For a taste of Florida's folk-music scene, visit Spirit of the Suwannee Music Park, near Suwannee River State Park.

Florida definitely knows how to rock. Bo Diddley, after helping define rock 'n' roll, settled near Gainesville for the second half of his life. North Florida is also one of the heartlands for Southern rock, which is characterized by roots-laden references to old-school honky tonk overlaid with sometimes folksy, sometimes rowdy lyrics. The late Tom Petty, Lynyrd Skynyrd and the Allman Brothers were Florida's original holy Southern rock trio.

In more recent years, Matchbox Twenty, Dashboard Confessional, Radical Face and Iron & Wine have gotten their start in Florida. Indie-rock sounds are strong across the state, from the expected college towns such as Gainesville to the Latin streetscape of Miami.

The popular musician who most often defines Florida is Jimmy Buffett, whose heart lives in Key West, wherever his band may roam. His

THE FLORIDA HIGHWAYMEN

Beginning in the 1950s, about two dozen largely self-taught African American painters made a modest living selling vivid, impressionistic 'Florida-scapes' on wood and Masonite for about $20 a pop. They sold these romantic visions of raw swamps and technicolor sunsets from the trunks of their cars along I-95 and A1A, hence their name. The Highwaymen were mentored and encouraged by AE 'Beanie' Backus, a white artist and teacher in Fort Pierce. Considered the 'dean' of Florida landscape art, Beanie was also largely self-taught, often preferring the rough strokes of a palette knife over a brush.

Today, this outsider art is highly revered and collected. The largest collection is found in the Orlando Museum of Art. To learn more, pick up Gary Monroe's excellent book *The Highwaymen* (2001) and visit the AE Backus Museum & Gallery (www.backusgallery. com) in Fort Pierce.

fans, known as Parrotheads, are a particularly faithful (some might say obsessed) bunch. If you've never heard Buffet's music, it's basically crowd-pleasing beach tunes with a gentle, anti-authoritarian bent – anarchy while wearing sandals and drinking piña coladas, if you will. In a state where musical tastes tend to divide along sharp cultural fault lines, Buffet's easygoing guitar riffs are a bridge between camps. Conservatives appreciate his yacht-club swagger, even as liberals like his gentle environmentalism.

Miami's gallery scene is unmatched outside of LA and Manhattan. Other notable cities are Fort Lauderdale, West Palm Beach, St Petersburg (for the peerless Dalí Museum), Tampa, Sarasota, Naples and even Orlando.

Orlando (by way of Lou Pearlman, who died in 2016) bestowed upon the world a special genre of music: the boy bands of NSYNC and Backstreet Boys. In fact, in many ways Orlando via Disney is responsible for shaping the soundscape of much of the world's teen- and tween-focused pop music; Disney handlers perfected the art of mass marketability, launching artists such as Miley Cyrus and Britney Spears. Florida's native beat also works its way into the most globally marketed albums, including Boca Raton–born Ariana Grande's Latin-spiced dance numbers.

Rap and hip-hop have flourished in Tampa and Miami, from old-school 2 Live Crew to Trick Daddy, Rick Ross, DJ Khaled and Pitbull, the most visible link between North American hip-hop and Latin American reggaeton. The latter has its roots in Panama and Puerto Rico, and blends rap with Jamaican dancehall, Trinidadian soca, salsa and electronica.

Miami is a tasty mélange of Cuban salsa, Jamaican reggae, Dominican merengue and Spanish flamenco, plus mambo, rumba, cha-cha, calypso and more. Gloria Estefan & the Miami Sound Machine launched a revival of Cuban music in the 1970s, when they mixed Latin beats with disco with hit-single 'Conga.' For a taste of hip-hop Miami-style, check out Los Primeros. The best times to see ensemble Cuban bands – with up to 20 musicians and singers – is during Carnaval Miami.

Electric music is ubiquitous across South Florida, especially in Miami, which celebrates the genre with two of its biggest festivals: the Ultra Music Festival and the Winter Music Conference, both of which kick off in March (the two festivals essentially piggyback off one another).

Architecture

Like its literature, Florida's architecture has some distinctive home-grown strains. These run from the old – the Spanish-Colonial and revival styles of St Augustine – to the aggressively modern, as in Miami and particularly South Beach.

At the turn of the century, Henry Flagler was instrumental in promoting a particularly Floridian Spanish-Moorish fantasia, which blended Italian villas with North African courtyards and open spaces. Prime examples are the monumental Hotel Ponce de León in St Augustine (now Flagler College), Whitehall Mansion in Palm Beach (now Flagler Museum) and Miami's awesome, George Merrick–designed Coral Gables.

Miami Beach got swept up in the art-deco movement in the 1920s and '30s (which Florida transformed into 'tropical deco'), and today it has the largest collection of art-deco buildings in the US. These languished until the mid-1980s, when their rounded corners and glass bricks were dusted off and spruced up with new coats of pastel-pink and aquamarine paint.

Florida's vernacular architecture is the 'Cracker house.' These pioneer homesteads were cleverly designed to maximize comfort, before air-conditioning, in a subtropical climate. Raised off the ground, with windows and doors positioned for cross-ventilation, they had extra-wide gables and porches for shade, and metal roofs reflecting the sun. They weren't pretty, but they worked. A great example is Marjorie Kinnan Rawlings' home in Cross Creek.

Florida's Natural World

Florida's natural world is a fascinating story, one in which charismatic wildlife species roam against a backdrop of an extraordinary patchwork of landscapes. The Everglades is a fragile and precious ecosystem, one of the most important wilderness areas in the Lower 48. It's the panthers and black bears, alligators and manatees who are the headline acts when it comes to animals. And this being Florida, questions of over-development threaten to sweep it all away.

The Land

Florida is many things, but elevated it is decidedly not. This state is as flat as a pancake, or as naturalist Marjory Stoneman Douglas once said, like a spoon of freshwater resting delicately in a bowl of saltwater – a spongy brick of limestone hugged by the Atlantic Ocean and the Gulf of Mexico. The highest point, the Panhandle's Britton Hill, has to stretch to reach 350ft, which isn't half as tall as the buildings of downtown Miami. This makes Florida officially the nation's flattest state, despite being 22nd in total area with 58,560 sq miles.

However, more than 4000 of those square miles are water; lakes and springs pepper the map like bullet holes in a road sign. That shotgun-sized hole in the south is Lake Okeechobee, one of the USA's largest freshwater lakes. Sounds impressive, but the bottom of the lake is only a few feet above sea level – it's so shallow you can practically wade across.

Every year, Lake Okeechobee ever so gently floods the southern tip of the peninsula. Or it tries to – canals divert much of the flow to either irrigation fields or Florida's bracketing major bodies of water: the Gulf of Mexico and the Atlantic Ocean. But were the water to follow the natural lay of the land, it would flow down: from its center, the state of Florida inclines about 6in every 6 miles until finally the peninsula can't keep its head above water anymore. What was an unelevated plain peters out into the 10,000 Islands and the Florida Keys, which end with a flourish in the Gulf of Mexico. Key West, the last in the chain, is the southernmost point in the continental United States.

Southern Ecosystems

When the waters of Okeechobee flood the South Florida plain, they interact with the local grasslands and limestone to create a wilderness unlike any other: the Everglades. They also fill up the freshwater aquifers that are required for maintaining human existence in the ever-urbanizing Miami area. Today numerous plans, which seem to fall prey to private interest and bureaucratic roadblocks, are being discussed for restoring the original flow of water from central to South Florida, an act that would revitalize the 'Glades and, to some degree, address the often-perilous water supply needs of Greater Miami.

What really sets Florida apart, though, is that it occupies a subtropical transition zone between northern temperate and southern tropical

> The Florida chapter of the Nature Conservancy (www.nature.org) has been instrumental in the Florida Forever legislation. Check the web for updates and conservation issues.

climates. This is key to the coast's florid coral-reef system, the largest in North America, and the key to Florida's attention-getting collection of surreal swamps, botanical oddities and monstrous critters. The Everglades gets the most press, and as an International Biosphere, World Heritage Site and national park, this 'river of grass' deserves it. The Keys, too, are dollops of intensely beautiful mangrove forest biomes.

The North & West

The peninsula's north and west are also host to some remarkable landscapes. The white-sand beaches of the Gulf Coast have been gently lapped over geological millennia into wide ribbons of sugar studded with prehistoric shells. The Panhandle's Apalachicola River basin has been called a 'Garden of Eden,' in which ice-age plants survive in lost ravines, and where more species of amphibians and reptiles hop and slither than anywhere else in the US. The Indian River Lagoon estuary, stretching 156 miles along the Atlantic Coast, is the most diverse on the continent. And across North Florida, the pockmarked and honeycombed limestone (called karst terrain) holds the Florida Aquifer, which is fed solely by rain and bubbles up like liquid diamonds in more than 700 freshwater springs.

Wildlife

With swamps full of gators, rivers full of snakes, manatees in mangroves, sea turtles on beaches, and giant flocks of seabirds taking wing at once, how is it, again, that a squeaky-voiced mouse became Florida's

Wildlife Field Guides

Field Guide to Florida (National Audubon Society, 1998)

Florida's Birds: A Field Guide and Reference (David S Maehr, 2005)

Mammals of Florida Field Guide (Stan Tekiela, 2010)

WILD ENCOUNTERS

While yesterday's swamp-buggy rides and alligator wrestling have evolved into today's glass-bottom boats and manatee encounters, the question remains: just because you can do something, does that mean you should? Be involved in protecting nature by considering the best ways to experience it without harming it in the process.

For most activities, there isn't a single right answer; impacts are hotly debated. However, here are a few guidelines:

Airboats and swamp buggies Airboats have a much lighter 'footprint' than big-wheeled buggies, but both are motorized (and loud) and have larger impacts than kayaks or canoes. As a rule, nonmotorized activities are least damaging to wetlands.

Dolphin encounters Dolphins should not be kept in captivity, and Lonely Planet does not recommend places that do so. When encountering wild dolphins in the ocean, it is illegal by federal law to feed, pursue or touch them. Habituating any wild animal to humans can lead to the animal's death, since approaching humans often results in conflict and accidents (as with boats).

Manatee swims When swimming near manatees, a federally protected endangered species, look but don't touch and don't crowd them. 'Passive observation' is the standard. Harassment is a rampant problem that may lead to stricter legislation.

Feeding wild animals In a word, don't. Friendly animals such as deer and manatees may come to rely on human food (to their detriment), while feeding bears and alligators just encourages them to hunt you, your pets or children.

Sea-turtle nesting sites It's a federal crime to approach nesting sea turtles or hatchling runs. Most nesting beaches have warning signs and a nighttime 'lights out' policy. If you do encounter turtles on the beach, keep your distance and don't take flash photos.

Coral-reef etiquette Coral polyps are living organisms and touching or breaking coral creates openings for infection and disease. To prevent reef damage, never touch the coral. It's that simple.

headliner? Florida has wonderful wildlife, both in terms of numbers and sheer variety. You just need to know where to look.

Animals

Birds

Nearly 500 avian species have been documented in the state, including some of the world's most magnificent migratory waterbirds: ibis, egrets, great blue herons, white pelicans and whooping cranes. This makes Florida the ultimate bird-watcher's paradise.

Nearly 350 species spend time in the Everglades, Florida's prime bird-watching spot. But you don't have to brave the swamp. Completed in 2006, the Great Florida Birding Trail (www.floridabirdingtrail.com) runs 2000 miles and includes nearly 500 bird-watching sites. Nine of these are 'gateway' sites, with visitor centers and free 'loan' binoculars; see the website for guides and look for brown road signs when driving.

Among the largest birds, white pelicans arrive in winter (October to April), while brown pelicans, the only pelican to dive for its food, live here year-round. To see the striking pale-pink roseate spoonbill, a member of the ibis family, visit JN 'Ding' Darling National Wildlife Refuge, the wintering site for a third of the US roseate spoonbill population.

About 5000 nonmigratory sandhill cranes are joined by 25,000 migratory cousins each winter. White whooping cranes, at up to 5ft the tallest bird in North America, are nearly extinct; about 100 winter on Florida's Gulf Coast near Homosassa; see www.bringbackthecranes.org for more information.

Songbirds and raptors fill Florida skies, too. The state has more than 1000 mated pairs of bald eagles, the most in the southern US, and peregrine falcons, which can dive up to 150mph, migrate through in spring and fall.

Land Mammals

Easy to find, white-tailed deer is a common species. Endemic to the Keys are Key deer, a Honey-I-Shrunk-the-Ungulate subspecies: less than 3ft tall and lighter than a 10-year-old, they live mostly on Big Pine Key.

Although they are ostensibly native to the American West, the adaptable coyote has been spotted across Florida, appearing as far south as the Florida Keys. Hopefully they won't swim too much further or else they'll end up on Big Pine Key, home of the aforementioned Key deer. The bobcat is a charismatic wild cat species found across the US, including in the Everglades.

The critically endangered red wolf once roamed the bottomlands, marshes and flooded forests of the American eastern seaboard, particularly the southeast. Due to hunting and habitat loss, the red wolf was almost wiped out, but a breeding population has been established at the St Vincent National Wildlife Refuge, located off the coast of the Panhandle.

Other species include marsh rabbits, raccoons and gray foxes.

Florida Panther

Florida's most endangered mammal is the Florida panther. Before European contact, perhaps 1500 roamed the state. The first panther bounty ($5 a scalp) was passed in 1832, and over the next 130 years they were hunted relentlessly. Though hunting was stopped in 1958, it was too late for panthers to survive on their own. Without a captive breeding program, begun in 1991, and a translocation of mountain lions from Texas in the mid-1990s, the Florida panther would now be extinct, and with as few as 130 known to exist, they're not out of the swamp yet. The biggest killers of panthers are motor vehicles. They're devilishly difficult to see,

FLORIDA'S NATURAL WORLD WILDLIFE

Wildlife Resources

Florida Fish & Wildlife Conservation Commission (www.myfwc.com)

Audubon of Florida (https://fl.audubon.org)

Great Florida Birding Trail (www.floridabirding trail.com)

Florida Wildlife Viewing (www.floridawildlife viewing.com)

FLORIDA'S MANATEES

It's hard to believe Florida's West Indian manatees were ever mistaken for mermaids, but it's easy to see their attraction: these gentle, curious, colossal mammals are as sweetly lovable as 10ft, 1500lb teddy bears. Solitary and playful, they have been known to 'surf' waves, and every winter, from November to March, they migrate into the warmer waters of Florida's freshwater estuaries, rivers and springs. Like humans, manatees will die if trapped in 62°F (17°C) water for 24 hours, and in winter Florida's eternally 72°F (22°C) springs are balmy spas.

Florida residents for more than 45 million years, these shy herbivores have absolutely no defenses except their size, and they don't do much, spending most of each day resting and eating 10% of their body weight. Rarely moving faster than a languid saunter, manatees even reproduce slowly; females birth one calf every two to five years. The exception to their docility? Mating. Males are notorious for their aggressive sex drive.

Florida's manatees have been under some form of protection since 1893, and they were included in the first federal endangered species list in 1967. Manatees were once hunted for their meat, and today collisions with boats are a leading cause of manatee death – propeller scars are so ubiquitous among the living that they are the chief identifying tool of scientists.

Population counts are notoriously difficult and unreliable. In 2013 a bloom of red tide algae in southwest Florida and illness caused the death of 16% of the total population of these gentle giants. Another bloom in 2018 killed at least 200 manatees. At the time of writing there were roughly 6000 manatees left in the state.

but they inhabit the Northern Everglades, as well as places like Big Cypress National Preserve (p154), Florida Panther National Wildlife Refuge (p160) and Corkscrew Swamp Sanctuary (p169). To see one in captivity, visit Naples Zoo (p445), Zoo Tampa at Lowry Park (p400), or Palm Beach Zoo & Conservation Society (p239) in West Palm Beach.

Black Bear

Whilst you're highly unlikely to see a panther, Florida black bears have recovered to a population of around 3000 to 4000; as their forests diminish, bears are occasionally seen traipsing through suburbs in northern Florida. There are seven known populations in Florida, including Ocala National Forest (p386), Big Cypress National Preserve (p154) and Apalachicola National Forest (p487), although they also occur across the border in Georgia, Alabama and Mississippi. Naples Zoo (p445) has captive black bears.

Marine Mammals

Florida's coastal waters are home to 21 species of dolphins and whales. By far the most common is the bottlenose dolphin, which is highly social, extremely intelligent and frequently encountered around the entire peninsula. Bottlenose dolphins are the species most often seen in captivity.

The North Atlantic population of about 300 right whales comes to winter calving grounds off the Atlantic Coast near Jacksonville. These giant animals can be more than 50ft long, and are the most endangered species of whale.

River otters are commonly seen in the waterways of the Everglades.

Winter is also the season for manatees, which seek out Florida's warm-water springs and power-plant discharge canals, beginning in November. These lovable, lumbering creatures are another iconic Florida species whose conservation both galvanizes and divides state residents.

Reptiles & Amphibians

Boasting an estimated 184 species, Florida has the nation's largest collection of reptiles and amphibians, and unfortunately, it's growing. No, we're not antireptile, but invasive scaly species are wreaking havoc on Florida's native, delicate ecosystem. Uninvited guests add to the total regularly, many establishing themselves after being released by pet owners. Some of the more dangerous, problematic and invasive species include Burmese pythons, black and green iguanas and Nile monitor lizards.

The American alligator is Florida's poster species, and they are ubiquitous in central and South Florida. They don't pose much of a threat to humans unless you do something irredeemably stupid, like feed or provoke or step on them. With that said, you may want to keep small children and pets away from unfamiliar inland bodies of water. South Florida is also home to the only North American population of American crocodile. Florida's crocs number around 1500; they prefer saltwater, and they're easy to distinguish from gators once you know how.

Turtles, frogs and snakes love Florida, and nothing is cuter than watching bright skinks, lizards and anoles skittering over porches and sidewalks. Cute doesn't always describe the state's 44 species of snakes – though Floridian promoters emphasize that only six species are poisonous, and only four of those are common. Feel better? Of the baddies, three are rattlesnakes (diamondback, pygmy, canebrake), plus copperheads, cottonmouths and coral snakes. The diamondback is the biggest (up to 7ft), most aggressive and most dangerous. But rest assured, while cottonmouths live in and around water, most Florida water snakes are not cottonmouths. And most visitors never even see one.

Naturalist Doug Alderson helped create the Big Bend Paddling Trail, and in his book *Waters Less Traveled* (2005) he describes his adventures: dodging pygmy rattlesnakes, meeting Shitty Bill, discussing Kemp's ridley turtles and pondering manatee farts.

FLORIDA'S NATURAL WORLD WILDLIFE

Sea Turtles

Most sea-turtle nesting in the continental US occurs in Florida. Predominantly three species create more than 80,000 nests annually, mostly on southern Atlantic Coast beaches but extending to all Gulf Coast beaches. Most are loggerhead, then far fewer green and leatherback turtles. Historically hawksbill and Kemp's ridley turtles were also present in numbers as well. All five species are endangered or threatened. The leatherback is the largest, attaining 10ft and 2000lb in size.

GHOST HUNTERS

Florida has more species of orchids than any other state in the US, and orchids are themselves the largest family of flowering plants in the world, with perhaps 25,000 species. On the dial of botanical fascination, orchids rank highly, and the Florida orchid that inspires the most intense devotion is the rare ghost orchid.

This bizarre epiphytic flower has no leaves and usually only one bloom, which is of course deathly white with two long thin drooping petals that curl like a handlebar mustache. The ghost orchid is pollinated in the dead of night by the giant sphinx moth, which is the only insect with a proboscis long enough to reach down the ghost orchid's 5in-long nectar spur.

The exact locations of ghost orchids are kept secret for fear of poachers, who, as Susan Orlean's book *The Orchid Thief* (1998) makes clear, are a real threat to their survival. But the flower's general whereabouts are common knowledge: South Florida's approximately 2000 ghost orchids are almost all in Big Cypress National Preserve and Fakahatchee Strand Preserve State Park. Of course, these parks are home to a great many other wild orchids, as are Everglades National Park, Myakka River State Park and Corkscrew Swamp Sanctuary.

To learn more, see Florida's Native Orchids (www.flnativeorchids.com) and Ghost Orchid Info (www.ghostorchid.info), and visit Sarasota's Marie Selby Botanical Gardens (p428).

During the May-to-October nesting season, sea turtles deposit from 80 to 120 eggs in each nest. The eggs incubate for about two months, and then the hatchlings emerge all at once and make for the ocean. Contrary to myth, hatchlings don't need the moon to find their way to the sea. However, they can become hopelessly confused by artificial lights and noisy human audiences. For the best, least-disruptive experience, join a sanctioned turtle watch; for a list, visit www.myfwc.com/seaturtle, then click on 'Sea Turtle Viewing Opportunities'.

Plants

What Florida lacks in topographical variety, it more than makes up for in plant diversity. The varied nature of the peninsula's flora, including more than 4000 species of plants, is unmatched in the continental US. Florida contains the southern extent of temperate ecosystems and the northern extent of tropical ones, which blend and merge in a bewildering, fluid taxonomy of environments. Interestingly, most of the world at this latitude is a desert, which Florida definitely is not.

Wetlands & Swamps

Visit the website of the Florida Native Plant Society (www.fnps.org), a nonprofit conservation organization, for updates on preservation issues and invasive species and for a nice overview of Florida's native plants and ecosystems.

It takes special kinds of plants to thrive in the humid, waterlogged, sometimes-salty marshes, sloughs, swales, seeps, basins, marl prairies and swamps of Florida, and several hundred specialized native plants evolved to do so. Much of the Everglades is dominated by vast expanses of saw grass, which is actually a sedge with fine toothlike edges that can reach 10ft high. South Florida is a symphony of sedges, grasses and rushes. These hardy, water-tolerant species provide abundant seeds to feed birds and animals, protect fish in shallow water, and pad wetlands for birds and alligators.

The strangest plants are the submerged and immersed species that grow in, under and out of the water. Free-floating species include bladderwort and coontail, a species that lives, flowers and is pollinated entirely underwater. Florida's swamps are abundant with rooted plants with floating leaves, including the pretty American lotus, water lilies and spatterdock. Another common immersed plant, bur marigolds, can paint whole prairies yellow.

Across Florida, whenever land rises just enough to create drier islands, tracts, hills and hillocks, dense tree-filled hammocks occur; ecological zones can shift as dramatically in 1ft in Florida as they do in a 1000ft elsewhere. These hammocks go by many names depending on location and type. Tropical hammocks typically mix tropical hardwoods and palms with semi-deciduous and evergreen trees such as live oak.

Another dramatic, beautiful tree in Florida's swamps is the bald cypress, the most flood-tolerant tree. It can grow 150ft tall, with buttressed, wide trunks and roots with 'knees' that poke above the drenched soil. Cypress domes are a particular type of swamp, which arise when a watery depression occurs in a pine flatwood.

Forests, Scrubs & Flatwoods

Florida's northern forests, particularly in the Panhandle, are an epicenter of plant and animal biodiversity, just as much as its southern swamps. Here, the continent's temperate forests of hickory, elm, ash, maple, magnolia and locust trees combine with the various pine, gum and oak trees that are common throughout Florida, along with the saw grass, cypress and cabbage palms of southern Florida. The wet but temperate Apalachicola forest supports 40 kinds of trees and more insect species than scientists can count.

Central and northern Florida were once covered in longleaf and slash-pine forests, both prized for timber and pine gum. Today, due to logging, only 2% of old-growth longleaf forests remain. Faster-growing slash pine has now largely replaced longleaf pine in Florida's second-growth forests.

Scrubs are found throughout Florida; they are typically old dunes with well-drained sandy soil. In central Florida (along the Lake Wales Ridge), scrubs are the oldest plant communities, with the highest number of endemic and rare species. Sand pines, scrub oak, rosemary and lichens predominate.

Scrubs often blend into sandy pine flatwoods, which typically have a sparse longleaf or slash-pine overstory and an understory of grasses and/or saw palmetto. Saw palmetto is a vital Florida plant: its fruit is an important food for bears and deer (and a herbal medicine that some believe helps prevent cancer), it provides shelter for panthers and snakes, and its flower is an important source of honey. It's named for its sharp saw-toothed leaf stems.

Mangroves & Coastal Dunes

Where not shaved smooth by sand, southern Florida's coastline is often covered with a three-day stubble of mangroves. Mangroves are not a single species; the name refers to all tropical trees and shrubs that have adapted to loose wet soil, saltwater, and periodic root submergence, usually between high and low tides. Mangroves have also developed 'live birth', germinating their seeds while they're still attached to the parent tree. Of more than 50 species of mangroves worldwide, only three predominate in Florida: red, black and white.

Mangroves play a vital role on the peninsula, and their destruction usually sets off a domino effect of ecological damage. Mangroves 'stabilize' coastal land, trapping sand, silt and sediment. As this builds up, new land is created, which ironically strangles the mangroves themselves. Mangroves mitigate the storm surge and damaging winds of hurricanes, and anchor tidal and estuary communities, providing vital wildlife habitats.

Coastal dunes are typically home to grasses and shrubs, saw palmettos and occasionally pines and cabbage palms (or sabal palms, the Florida state tree). Sea oats, with large plumes that trap wind-blown sand, are important for stabilizing dunes.

In Florida, even the plants bite: the Panhandle has the most species of carnivorous plants in the US – a result of its nutrient-poor sandy soil.

National, State & Regional Parks

About 26% of Florida's land lies in public hands, which breaks down to three national forests, 11 national parks, 29 national wildlife refuges (including the first, Pelican Island) and 164 state parks. Attendance is up, with more than 20 million folks visiting state parks annually, and Florida's state parks have three times been voted the nation's best.

Florida's parks are easy to explore. For more information, see the websites of the following organizations:

Florida Fish & Wildlife Commission (www.myfwc.com) Manages Florida's mostly undeveloped Wildlife Management Areas (WMA); the website is an excellent resource for wildlife-viewing, as well as boating, hunting, fishing and permits.

Florida State Parks (www.floridastateparks.org)

National Forests, Florida (www.fs.usda.gov/florida)

National Park Service (www.nps.gov)

National Wildlife Refuges, Florida (www.fws.gov/southeast/florida)

Recreation.gov (www.recreation.gov) National campground reservations.

GLOBAL WARMING & THE KEYS

Call it what you like, but few reputable scientists doubt that global temperatures are increasing, ice caps are melting, and sea levels are rising. Nowhere in the US does this matter more than in the low-lying Florida Keys, a real 'canary in a coalmine' that's being watched worldwide for impacts. In another century, some quip, South Florida's coastline could be a modern-day Atlantis, with its most expensive real estate underwater.

In December 2019, the Florida Keys announced a long-awaited report quantifying the cost of elevating 300 miles of county roads across the Keys. The results were frightening. They took a representative sample of a three-mile road at the southern end of Sugarloaf Key, an island 15 miles from Key West. There are fewer than 30 homes along the stretch of road. To elevate the road 1.3ft to a point where it can be dry and open year round in 2020 would cost $75 million; by 2060, the cost would be $181 million. 'I can't see staff recommending to raise this road,' Rhonda Haag, the county's sustainability director, told the *New York Times*. 'Those are taxpayer dollars, and as much as we love the Keys, there's going to be a time when it's going to be less population.'

Environmental Issues

Florida's environmental problems are the inevitable result of its long love affair with land development, population growth and tourism, and addressing them is especially urgent given Florida's uniquely diverse natural world. These complex, intertwined environmental impacts include erosion of wetlands, depletion of the aquifer, rampant pollution (particularly of waters), invasive and endangered species, and widespread habitat destruction. There is nary an acre of Florida that escapes concern. To its credit, Florida has enacted several significant conservation efforts. In 2000 the state passed the Florida Forever Act, what Florida claims to be the largest public land acquisition program. By 2020, the program had purchased nearly one million acres for public protection and manages 10 times that amount of land for conservation.

Residential development continues almost unabated. The Miami–Fort Lauderdale–West Palm Beach corridor (the USA's fourth-largest urban area) is, as developers say, 'built out,' so developers are targeting the Panhandle and central Florida. Projections for the next 50 years show unrelenting urban sprawl up and down both coasts and painted across central Florida. It is estimated that the state's population will double between 2006 and 2060.

Water Management

In 2000, the US Congress passed the multibillion-dollar Comprehensive Everglades Restoration Plan and the associated Central Everglades Planning Project. Unfortunately, implementation of the latter plan has been problematic due to a lack of approval from federal agencies such as the Army Corps of Engineers.

More than half of Florida's lakes have elevated levels of algae, which leads to frequent toxic blooms that wipe out local wildlife. Though industrial pollution has been curtailed, pollution from residential development (sewage, fertilizer runoff) more than compensates. This is distressing Florida's freshwater springs, which can turn murky and undrinkable, while the pumping of groundwater is causing an increase in sinkholes. Such direct consequences of over-development are worrying signs that the state's waterways may be facing longer-term trouble.

Survival Guide

Directory A–Z

Accessible Travel

The Americans with Disabilities Act (ADA) requires that all public buildings, private buildings built after 1993 (including hotels, restaurants, theaters and museums) and public transit be wheelchair accessible. Some local tourist offices publish detailed accessibility guides but generally it's best to call ahead to confirm what's available. For tips on travel and thoughtful insight on traveling with a disability, download Lonely Planet's free Accessible Travel guide from https://shop.lonely planet.com/categories/accessible-travel.

Telephone companies offer relay operators, available via teletypewriter (TTY) numbers, for the hearing impaired. Most banks provide ATM instructions in braille and via earphone jacks for hearing-impaired customers. All major airlines, Greyhound buses and Amtrak trains will assist travelers with disabilities; just describe your needs when making reservations at least 48 hours in advance. Service animals (guide dogs) are allowed to accompany passengers, but bring documentation.

Some car-rental agencies, such as Budget and Hertz, offer hand-controlled vehicles and vans with wheelchair lifts at no extra charge, but you must reserve them well in advance. **Wheelchair Getaways** (www.accessible vans.com) rents accessible vans. In many cities and towns, public buses are accessible to wheelchair riders and will 'kneel' if you are unable to use the steps; just let the driver know that you need the lift or ramp. Most cities have taxi companies with at least one accessible van; it pays to to call ahead.

Many national and some state parks and recreation areas have wheelchair-accessible paved, graded-dirt or boardwalk trails. US citizens and permanent residents with permanent disabilities are entitled to a free 'America the Beautiful' Access Pass. Go online (www.nps.gov/findapark/passes.htm) for details.

Resources
Disabled Holidays (www.disabledholidays4u.com) Information on disabled travel services and agencies.

Disabled Sports USA (www.disabledsportsusa.org) Offers sport, adventure and recreation programs for those with disabilities. Also publishes Challenge magazine.

Florida State Parks (www.floridastateparks.org/accessibility) Useful statewide accessibility info.

Miami & the Beaches (www.miamiandbeaches.com/plan-your-trip/accessible-travel)

Accessible travel information specific to the Miami area.

Mobility International USA (www.miusa.org) Advises on mobility issues and runs an educational exchange program.

Visit Florida (www.visitflorida.com/en-us/travel-ideas/accessible-travel-in-florida.html) In-depth accessibility guide.

Wheelchair Travel (www.wheelchairtravel.org) An excellent website with many links.

Customs Regulations

For a complete, up-to-date list of customs regulations, visit the website of US Customs & Border Protection (www.cbp.gov). Each visitor is allowed to bring into the US duty-free 1L of liquor (if you're 21 or older), 200 cigarettes (if you're 18 or older) and up to $100 in gifts and purchases.

Discount Cards

There are no Florida-specific discount cards. Being a member of certain groups also gives access to discounts (usually about 10%) at many hotels, museums and sights. Simply carry the appropriate ID.

Seniors Generally refers to those 65 and older, but sometimes those 60 and older. Join the American Association of Retired

Climate

Miami

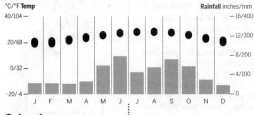

Orlando

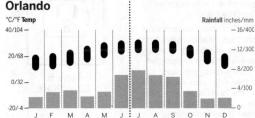

Pensacola

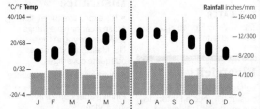

Persons (www.aarp.org) for more travel bargains.

Students Any student ID is typically honored; international students might consider an International Student Identity Card (www.isic.org).

Health

Florida (and the USA generally) has a high level of hygiene, so, Covid-19 pandemic aside, infectious diseases are not a significant concern for most travelers. There are no required vaccines. Despite Florida's plethora of intimidating wildlife, the main concerns for travelers are sunburn and mosquito bites – as well as arriving with adequate health insurance in case of accidents.

Before You Go
HEALTH INSURANCE

The US offers some of the finest health care in the world. The problem is that it can be prohibitively expensive. Citizens from other nations should not even think about travel to the States without adequate travel insurance covering medical care. It's essential to purchase travel health insurance if your policy doesn't cover you when you're abroad. Find out in advance whether your insurance plan will make payments directly to the providers or if they will reimburse you later for any overseas health expenditures.

Accidents and unforeseen illnesses do happen and horror stories of people's vacations turning into

nightmares when they're hit with hefty hospital bills for seemingly innocuous concerns are common. Hospital bills for car accidents, falls or serious medical emergencies can run into the tens of thousands of dollars. Look for an insurance policy that provides at least $1 million of medical coverage. Policies with unlimited medical coverage are also available at a higher premium, but are usually not necessary. You may be surprised at how inexpensive good insurance can be.

USEFUL WEBSITES

MD Travel Health (https://redplanet.travel/mdtravelhealth) Provides complete, updated and free travel-health recommendations for every country.

World Health Organization (www.who.int/ith) The superb book *International Travel and Health* is available free online.

In Florida
AVAILABILITY & COST OF HEALTH CARE

In general, if you have a medical emergency, go to the emergency room of the nearest hospital. If the problem isn't urgent, call a nearby hospital and ask for a referral to a local physician; this is usually cheaper than a trip to the emergency room. Stand-alone, money-making urgent-care centers provide good service, but can be the most expensive option.

Pharmacies (called drugstores) are abundant. However, some medications that are available over the counter in other countries require a prescription in the US. If you don't have insurance to cover the cost of prescriptions, these can be shockingly expensive. Bbring any medications you may need in their original containers, clearly labeled. A signed, dated letter from your physician that describes all of your medical conditions and medications (including generic names) is also a good idea.

ANIMALS & SPIDER BITES

Florida's critters can be cute, but they can also bite and sting. Here are a few to watch out for:

Alligators and snakes Neither attack humans unless startled or threatened. If you encounter them, simply back away calmly. Florida has several venomous snakes, so always seek treatment immediately if bitten.

Bears and wildcats Florida is home to a small population of black bears – if camping, secure all food in sealed containers. If you encounter a bear, stay calm, do not provoke the animal and make a little noise (talking, jiggling keys) to alert the animal of your presence.

Jellyfish and stingrays Florida beaches can see both; avoid swimming when they are present (lifeguards post warnings). Treat stings immediately; they hurt but aren't dangerous.

Spiders Florida is home to two venomous spiders – the black widow and the brown recluse. Seek immediate treatment if bitten by any spider.

INFECTIOUS DISEASES

Giardiasis Also known as traveler's diarrhea. A parasitic infection of the small intestines, typically contracted by drinking feces-contaminated fresh water. Never drink untreated stream, lake or pond water. Easily treated with antibiotics.

HIV/AIDS HIV infection occurs in the US, as do all sexually transmitted infections: incidences of syphilis are on the rise. Use condoms for all sexual encounters.

Lyme Disease Though more common in the US northeast than Florida, Lyme disease occurs here. It is transmitted by infected deer ticks, and is signaled by a bull's-eye rash at the bite and flulike symptoms. Treat promptly with antibiotics. Removing ticks within 36 hours can avoid infection.

Rabies Though rare, the rabies virus can be contracted from the bite of any infected animal; bats are most common, and their bites are not always obvious. If bitten by any animal, consult with a doctor, since rabies is fatal if untreated.

West Nile Virus Extremely rare in Florida, West Nile Virus is transmitted by culex mosquitoes. Most infections are mild or asymptomatic, but serious symptoms and even death can occur. There is no treatment for West Nile Virus.

Zika This mosquito-borne virus has been linked to serious birth defects, including microcephaly, when contracted by expectant mothers during pregnancy. Although the virus was found in Miami-Dade County as recently as 2017, at the time of writing there have been no active, ongoing cases of transmission in the state.

TAP WATER

Tap water in Florida is drinkable and safe.

Electricity

Voltage is 110/120V, 60 cycles. You'll need adaptors to run most non-US devices.

Type A
120V/60Hz

Type B
120V/60Hz

Insurance

➡ It's expensive to get sick, crash a car or have things stolen from you in the US. Make sure you have adequate coverage.

➡ Worldwide travel insurance is available at www.lonelyplanet.com/travel-insurance.

Internet Access

➡ The USA and Florida are wired. Nearly every hotel and many restaurants and businesses offer high-speed internet access. With very few exceptions, most hotels and motels offer in-room wi-fi; it's generally free of charge, but do check for connection rates.

➡ Many cafes and bars (and all McDonald's) offer free wi-fi and most transport hubs are wi-fi hot spots.

➡ For a list of wi-fi hot spots, check Wi-Fi Free Spot (www.wififreespot.com) or Open Wi-Fi spots (www.openwifispots.com).

Legal Matters

In everyday matters, if you are stopped by the police, note that there is no system for paying traffic tickets or other fines on the spot. The patrol officer will explain your options to you; there is usually a 30-day period to pay fines by mail.

If you're arrested, you are allowed to remain silent, though never walk away from an officer; you are entitled to have access to an attorney. The legal system presumes you're innocent until proven guilty. All persons who are arrested have the right to make one phone call. If you don't have a lawyer or family member to help you, call your embassy or consulate. The police will give you the number on request.

Drinking & Driving

To purchase alcohol, you need to present a photo ID to prove your age. Despite what you sometimes see, it is illegal to walk with an open alcoholic drink on the street outside of certain designated zones. More importantly, don't drive with an 'open container'; any liquor in a car must be unopened or else stored in the trunk. If you're stopped while driving with an open container, police will treat you as if you were drinking and driving. A DUI (driving under the influence) conviction is a serious offense, subject to stiff fines and even imprisonment.

LGBT+ Travelers

Florida is not uniformly anything, and it's not uniformly embracing of gay life. The state is largely tolerant, particularly in major tourist destinations, beaches and cities, but this tolerance does not always extend into the more rural and Southern areas of northern Florida. However, where Florida does embrace gay life, it does so with a big

flamboyant bear hug. Miami and South Beach are as 'out' as it's possible to be, with some massive gay festivals. Fort Lauderdale, West Palm Beach and Key West have long supported vibrant gay communities and are now regarded as some of the 'gayest' destinations in the world. Despite the tragedy of the 2016 Pulse nightclub shooting, Orlando retains a vibrant, active and strong gay community. Notable gay scenes and communities also exist in Jacksonville, Pensacola, and, to far lesser degrees, Tampa and Sarasota.

Resources

Damron (www.damron.com) An expert in LGBT+ travel offering a searchable database of LGBT+-friendly and specific travel listings. Publishes popular national guidebooks, including *Women's Traveller, Men's Travel Guide* and *Damron Accommodations*.

Gay Cities (www.gaycities.com) Everything gay about every major city in the US and beyond.

LGBT Visitor Center (www.gogaymiami.com) The best single source for all LGBT+ info on Miami. Check the website for Pink Flamingo–certified hotels (hotels that are most welcoming to the LGBT+ crowd).

Miami Visitors Bureau (www.miamiandbeaches.com/things-to-do/travel-guides/gay-miami) Miami's official tourist bureau

has a useful guide to gay life in the city.

Out Traveler (www.outtraveler.com) Travel magazine specializing in gay travel.

Purple Roofs (www.purpleroofs.com) Lists queer accommodations, travel agencies and tours worldwide.

Money

➡ Major credit cards are widely accepted, and are required for car rentals.

➡ Most ATM withdrawals using out-of-state cards incur surcharges of $3 or so.

➡ Exchange foreign currency at international airports and most large banks in cities.

➡ Personal checks drawn on non-US banks are generally not accepted.

Tipping

Tipping is *not* optional. Only withhold tips in cases of outrageously bad service.

Airport skycaps and hotel bellhops $2 per bag, minimum $5 per cart.

Bartenders 10% to 15% per round or $1 per drink.

Concierges Nothing for simple information, up to $20 for securing last-minute restaurant reservations, show tickets etc.

Housekeeping staff $2 to $4 daily, more if you're messy;

sometimes there's an envelope left in the room for this purpose.

Parking valets At least $2 when handed back your car keys.

Restaurant staff and room service 15% to 25%, unless a gratuity is already charged.

Taxi drivers 10% to 15% of metered fare, rounded up to the next dollar.

Taxes & Refunds

➡ Florida has a state sales tax of 6%. When you add in local (ie city) taxes, the total sales tax rate can go as high as 8%.

➡ Different cities and similar local government entities may also charge hotel and resort taxes.

➡ The USA does not offer reimbursement of sales tax as European nations do with the VAT.

➡ Not all quoted prices include sales tax – always check.

Opening Hours

Standard business hours are as follows:

Banks 8:30am to 4:30pm Monday to Thursday, to 5:30pm Friday; sometimes 9am to 12:30pm Saturday.

Bars Most bars 5pm to midnight; to 2am Friday and Saturday.

Businesses 9am to 5pm Monday to Friday.

Post offices 9am to 5pm Monday to Friday; sometimes 9am to noon Saturday.

Restaurants Breakfast 7am to 10:30am Monday to Friday; brunch 9am to 2pm Saturday and Sunday; lunch 11:30am to 2:30pm Monday to Friday; dinner 5pm to 9:30pm, later Friday and Saturday.

Shops 10am to 6pm Monday to Saturday, noon to 5pm Sunday; shopping malls keep extended hours.

Post

➡ The US Postal Service (www.usps.com) is reliable and inexpensive. For exact rates, refer to http://postcalc.usps.com.

➡ For sending urgent or important letters and packages either domestically or overseas, Federal Express (www.fedex.com) and United Parcel Service (www.ups.com) offer more expensive door-to-door delivery services.

➡ Most hotels will also hold mail for incoming guests.

Public Holidays

New Year's Day January 1

Martin Luther King, Jr Day Third Monday in January

Presidents Day Third Monday in February

Easter March or April

Memorial Day Last Monday in May

Independence Day July 4

Labor Day First Monday in September

Columbus Day Second Monday in October

Veterans Day November 11

Thanksgiving Fourth Thursday in November

Christmas Day December 25

Safe Travel

When it comes to crime, there is Miami, and there's the rest of Florida. As a rule, Miami suffers the same urban problems facing other major US cities such as New York and Los Angeles, but it is no worse than others. The rest of Florida tends to have lower crime rates than the rest of the nation, but any tourist town is a magnet for petty theft and car break-ins.

If you need any kind of emergency assistance, such as police, ambulance or fire-fighters, call ☏911. This is a free call from any phone.

Hurricanes

Florida hurricane season extends from June through November, but the peak is September and October. Relatively speaking, very few Atlantic Ocean and Gulf of Mexico storms become hurricanes, and fewer still are accurate enough to hit Florida, but the devastation they wreak when they do can be enormous. Travelers should take all hurricane alerts, warnings and evacuation orders seriously. For more information, contact the following:

Florida Division of Emergency Management (www.floridadisaster.org) Hurricane preparedness.

Florida Emergency Hotline (☏800-342-3557) Updated storm warning information.

National Weather Service (www.weather.gov)

Telephone

➡ To make international calls from the US, dial ☏011 + country code + area code + number. For international operator assistance, dial 0. To call the US from abroad, the international country code for the USA is 1.

➡ For local directory assistance, dial ☏411.

➡ Always dial 1 before toll-free (☏800, 888 etc) and domestic long-distance numbers. Some toll-free numbers only work within the US.

➡ Pay phones are becoming rarer. Local calls cost 50¢. Private prepaid phonecards are widely available.

Cell Phones

➡ Most of the USA's cell-phone systems are incompatible with the GSM 900/1800 standard used throughout Europe and Asia. Check with your service provider about using your phone in the US.

➡ Cellular coverage is generally excellent, except in the Everglades and parts of rural northern Florida.

➡ In terms of coverage, Verizon has the best network, but AT&T, Sprint and T-Mobile are decent.

Time

Most of Florida is in the US Eastern Time Zone: noon in Miami equals 9am in San Francisco and 5pm in London. West of the Apalachicola River, the Panhandle is in the US Central Time Zone, one hour behind the rest of the state. During daylight saving time, clocks 'spring forward' one hour in March and 'fall back' one hour in November.

Toilets

➡ Sit-down toilets are the norm, with the exception of a few primitive camping facilities.

➡ Public restrooms can be found in some cities and are usually free, and of varying degrees of cleanliness.

Tourist Information

Most Florida towns have some sort of tourist information center that provides local information; be aware that chambers of commerce typically only list chamber members.

Visit Florida (www.visit florida.com) is the state's official tourist website.

Visas

All visitors should reconfirm entry requirements and visa guidelines before arriving. You can get visa information through www.usa.gov, but the US State Department (www.travel.state.gov) maintains the most comprehensive visa information, with lists of consulates and downloadable application forms. US Citizenship & Immigration Services (www. uscis.gov) mainly serves

immigrants, not temporary visitors.

The Visa Waiver Program allows citizens of three dozen countries to enter the USA for stays of 90 days or fewer without first obtaining a US visa. See the ESTA website (https://esta.cbp.dhs.gov) for a current list. Under this program you must have a nonrefundable return ticket and 'e-passport' with digital chip.

Visitors who don't qualify for the Visa Waiver Program need a visa. Basic requirements are a valid passport, recent photo, travel details and often proof of financial stability. Students and adult males must also fill out supplemental travel documents. The validity period for a US visa depends on your home country. The length of time you'll be allowed to stay in the USA is determined by US officials at the port of entry.

To stay longer than the date stamped on your

passport, visit a local USCIS (www.uscis.gov) office.

Volunteering

Volunteer Florida (www.volun teerflorida.org), the primary state-run organization, coordinates volunteer centers across the state. Though it's aimed primarily at Floridians there are short-term volunteering opportunities as well.

Florida's state parks would not function without volunteers. Each park coordinates its own volunteers, and most also have the support of an all-volunteer 'friends' organization (officially called Citizen Support Organizations). Links and contact information are on the website of Florida State Parks (www.floridastateparks.org/volunteers).

Habitat for Humanity (www.miamihabitat.org) does a ton of work building homes and helping the homeless.

Transportation

GETTING THERE & AWAY

Nearly all international travelers to Florida arrive by air, while most US travelers prefer air or car. Florida is bordered by Alabama to the west and north, and Georgia to the north. Major interstates into Florida are I-10 from the west (Alabama), and I-75 and I-95 from the north (Georgia).

Getting to Florida by bus is a distant third option, and by train an even more distant fourth. Major regional hubs in Florida include Miami, Fort Lauderdale, Orlando, Tampa and Jacksonville.

Flights, cars and tours can be booked online at www. lonelyplanet.com/bookings.

Entering the Country

A passport is required for all foreign citizens. Unless eligible under the Visa Waiver Program, foreign travelers must also have a tourist visa.

Travelers entering under the Visa Waiver Program must register with the US government's program, ESTA (https://esta.cbp.dhs.gov), at least three days before arriving; earlier is better, since if denied, travelers must get a visa. Queues at immigration can be very long at busy international airports.

Air

Unless you live in or near Florida and have your own wheels, flying to the region and then renting a car is the most time-efficient option.

Airports & Airlines

Whether you're coming from within the US or from abroad, the entire state is well served by air, with a number of domestic and international airlines operating services into Florida.

Major airports:

Orlando International Airport (MCO; ☑407-825-8463; www.orlandoairports.net; 1 Jeff Fuqua Blvd) Handles more passengers than any other airport in Florida. Serves Walt Disney World®, the Space Coast and the Orlando area.

Miami International Airport (MIA; ☑305-876-7000; www.miami-airport.com; 2100 NW 42nd Ave) One of Florida's busiest international airports. It serves metro Miami, the Everglades and the Keys, and is a hub for American, Delta and US Airways.

Fort Lauderdale-Hollywood International Airport (FLL; ☑866-435-9355; www.broward.org/airport; 100 Terminal Dr) Serves metro Fort Lauderdale and Broward County. It's about 30 miles north of Miami: be sure to check flights into Fort Lauderdale as they are often cheaper or have availability when flights into Miami are full.

CLIMATE CHANGE & TRAVEL

Every form of transport that relies on carbon-based fuel generates CO_2, the main cause of human-induced climate change. Modern travel is dependent on airplanes, which might use less fuel per miles per person than most cars but travel much greater distances. The altitude at which aircraft emit gases (including CO_2) and particles also contributes to their climate change impact. Many websites offer 'carbon calculators' that allow people to estimate the carbon emissions generated by their journey and, for those who wish to do so, to offset the impact of the greenhouse gases emitted with contributions to portfolios of climate-friendly initiatives throughout the world. Lonely Planet offsets the carbon footprint of all staff and author travel.

Tampa International Airport
(TPA; 813-870-8700; www.
tampaairport.com; 4100
George J Bean Pkwy) Florida's
third-busiest airport is located
6 miles southwest of downtown
Tampa and serves the Tampa Bay
and St Petersburg metro area.

Other airports with some
international traffic include
Daytona Beach (386-248-
8030; www.flydaytonafirst.com;
700 Catalina Dr) and **Jacksonville** (JAX; 904-741-
3044; www.flyjax.com; 2400
Yankee Clipper Dr;).

Most cities have airports
and offer services to other
US cities; these airports
include **Palm Beach** (PBI;
561-471-7420; www.pbia.org;
1000 James L Turnage Blvd),
actually in West Palm Beach,
Sarasota (SRQ; 941-359-
2770; www.srq-airport.com;
6000 Airport Circle), **Tallahassee** (Map p478; 850-891-
7800; www.talgov.com/airport;
3300 Capital Circle SW),
Gainesville (352-373-0249;
www.gra-gnv.com; 3880 NE
39th Ave), **Fort Myers** (RSW;
239-590-4800; www.flylcpa.
com; 11000 Terminal Access
Rd), **Pensacola** (Map p456;
850-436-5000; www.fly
pensacola.com; 2430 Airport
Blvd) and **Key West** (EYW;
305-809-5200; www.eyw.
com; 3491 S Roosevelt Blvd).

Tickets

It helps to know that in the
US there are a number of
APEX (Advance Purchase Excursion) fares of seven, 14, 21
and 28 days available, which
can really save you money. It
is prudent to compare flights
into the state between the
handful of significant airline

hubs. The distance between
Orlando, Fort Lauderdale and
Miami, for example, is not
so great, yet each city has
a major airport. Rates can
sometimes fluctuate widely
among these destinations,
depending on season and
demand. If you're lucky, you
could save money by flying
into one airport and out of
the other, or, flying into an
airport a little further from
your destination, and driving.
The combination of Miami
and Fort Lauderdale often
works well in this regard.

Land

Bus

For bus trips, Greyhound
(www.greyhound.com) is the
main long-distance operator
in the US. It serves Florida
from most major cities in
neighboring states and
beyond. It also has the only
scheduled statewide service.

Standard long-distance
fares can be relatively high:
bargain airfares can undercut buses on long-distance
routes; on shorter routes,
renting a car can be cheaper.
Nonetheless, discounted
(even half-price) long-distance bus trips are often
available by purchasing
tickets online seven to 14
days in advance. Then, once
in Florida, you can rent a car
to get around. Inquire about
multiday passes.

Car & Motorcycle

Driving to Florida from
elsewhere in the US is easy.
Incorporating Florida into a
larger USA road trip is very

common, and having a car
while in Florida is often a
necessity: there's lots of
ground to cover and some of
the most interesting places
and state parks are only
accessible by car.

Train

From the East Coast, Amtrak
(www.amtrak.com) makes
a comfortable, affordable
option for getting to Florida.
Amtrak's *Silver Service*
(which includes *Silver Meteor* and *Silver Star* trains)
runs between New York and
Miami, with services that
include Jacksonville, Orlando,
Tampa, West Palm Beach and
Fort Lauderdale, plus smaller
Florida towns in between.

There is no direct service
to Florida from Los Angeles,
New Orleans, Chicago or the
Midwest. Trains from these
destinations connect to the
Silver Service route, but the
transfer adds a day or so to
your travel time.

Amtrak's *Auto Train* takes
you and your car from the
Washington, DC, area to the
Orlando area; this saves you
gas, the drive and having to
pay for a rental car. The fare
for your vehicle isn't cheap,
though, depending on its size
and weight. The *Auto Train*
leaves daily from Lorton, VA,
and goes only to Sanford,
FL. It takes about 18 hours,
leaving in the afternoon and

ROAD DISTANCES

Sample distances and times from various points in the US to Miami:

CITY	DISTANCE (MILES)	DURATION (HR)
Atlanta	660	10½
Chicago	1380	23
Los Angeles	2750	44
New York City	1280	22
Washington, DC	1050	17

arriving the next morning. On the *Auto Train,* you pay for your passage, cabin and car separately. Book tickets in advance. Children, seniors and military personnel receive discounts.

Amtrak lines are subject to federal funding and regulation. Check for the latest fares and routes before you leave for your trip.

Sea

Florida is nearly completely surrounded by the ocean, and it's a major cruise-ship port. Fort Lauderdale is the largest transatlantic harbor in the US. Adventurous types can always sign up as crew members for a chance to travel the high seas. Cruise ships dock at numerous Florida ports, among them Tampa, Miami, Fort Lauderdale (Port Everglades) and Port Canaveral.

GETTING AROUND

Air

The US airline industry is reliable, safe and serves Florida extremely well, both from the rest of the country and within Florida. Air service between Florida's four main airports – Fort Lauderdale, Miami, Orlando International and Tampa – is frequent and direct. Smaller destinations such as Key West, Fort Myers, Pensacola, Jacksonville, Tallahassee and West Palm Beach are served, but less frequently, indirectly and at higher fares.

Airlines in Florida

Domestic airlines operating in Florida:

American (www.aa.com) Has a Miami hub and service to and between major Florida cities.

Delta (www.delta.com) International carrier to main Florida

cities, plus flights from Miami to Orlando and Tampa.

Frontier (www.frontierairlines. com) Serves all major Florida cities.

JetBlue (www.jetblue.com) Major low-cost airline serving key Florida cities.

Southwest (www.southwest. com) One of the US's leading low-cost carriers, offering free baggage and, at times, extremely low fares.

Spirit (www.spirit.com) Florida-based discount carrier serving Florida cities from East Coast US, the Caribbean, and Central and South America.

United (www.united.com) International flights to Orlando and Miami; domestic flights to and between key Florida cities.

Air Passes

International travelers who plan on doing a lot of flying, both in and out of the region, might consider buying an air pass. Air passes are available only to non-US citizens, and must be purchased in conjunction with an international ticket.

Conditions and cost structures can be complicated, but all include a certain number of domestic flights (from three to 10) that must be used within a set time frame, generally between 30 and 60 days. In most cases, you must plan your itinerary in advance, but dates (and even destinations) can sometimes be left open. Talk with a travel agent to determine if an air pass would save you money based on your plans.

The two main airline alliances offering air passes are Star Alliance (www.star alliance.com) and One World (www.oneworld.com).

Bicycle

Regional bicycle touring is very popular. Flat countryside and scenic coastlines make for great itineraries. However, target winter to

spring; summer is unbearably hot and humid for long-distance cycling.

Some Florida cycling organizations run bike tours. Renting a bicycle is easy throughout Florida.

Some other things to keep in mind:

Helmet laws Helmets are required for anyone aged 16 and younger. Adults are not required to wear helmets, but should do so for safety.

Road rules Bikes must obey auto rules; ride on the right-hand side of the road, with traffic, not on sidewalks.

Theft Bring and use a sturdy lock (U-type is best). Theft is common, especially in Miami Beach.

Transporting your bike to Florida Bikes are considered checked luggage on airplanes, but often must be boxed and fees can be high (more than $200).

For more information and assistance, a few organizations can help:

Better World Club (www.better worldclub.com) Offers a bicycle roadside-assistance program.

International Bicycle Fund (www.ibike.org) Comprehensive overview of bike regulations by airline, and lots of advice.

League of American Bicyclists (www.bikeleague.org) General advice, plus lists of local cycle clubs and repair shops.

Boat

Florida is a world center for two major types of boat transport: privately owned yachts and cruise ships.

Each coastal city has sightseeing boats that cruise harbors and coastlines. It really pays (in memories) to get out on the water. Water-taxi services along Intracoastal Waterways are a feature in Fort Lauderdale and around Sanibel and Pine Islands on the Gulf.

Cruises

Florida is a huge destination and departure point for cruises of all kinds. Miami likes to brag that it's the 'cruise capital of the world,' and Walt Disney World® runs its own Disney Cruise Line (https://disneycruise.disney.go.com), which has a number of three- to seven-night cruises throughout the Caribbean, including to Disney's own private island, Castaway Cay.

With the cruise industry having been especially hard hit during the coronavirus pandemic, remember that all of the following information is particularly subject to change.

For specials on other multinight and multiday cruises, see the following:

Cruise.com (www.cruise.com)

CruisesOnly (www.cruisesonly.com)

CruiseWeb (www.cruiseweb.com)

Vacations to Go (www.vacationstogo.com)

Florida's main ports:

Port Canaveral (www.portcanaveral.com) On the Atlantic Coast near the Kennedy Space Center; gives Miami a run for its money.

Port Everglades (www.porteverglades.net; 1850 Eller Drive) Near Fort Lauderdale, and the third-busiest Florida port.

Port of Miami (305-347-4800; www.miamidade.gov/portmiami) At the world's largest cruise-ship port, the most common trips offered are to the Bahamas, the Caribbean, Key West and Mexico.

Port of Tampa (813-905-7678; www.tampaport.com) On the Gulf Coast; rapidly gaining a foothold in the cruise market.

Major cruise companies:

Carnival Cruise Lines (www.carnival.com)

Norwegian Cruise Line (www.ncl.com)

Royal Caribbean (www.royalcaribbean.com)

Bus

The only statewide bus service is by Greyhound (www.greyhound.com), which connects all major and midsize Florida cities, but not always smaller towns (even some popular beach towns). Regional or city-run buses cover Greyhound's more limited areas much better; used together, these bus systems make travel by bus possible, but time-consuming. Megabus (https://us.megabus.com) operates out of five Florida cities – Tallahassee, Jacksonville, Gainesville, Tampa and Miami.

It's always a bit cheaper to take a Greyhound bus during the week than on the weekend. Fares for children are usually about half the adult fare.

Local bus services are available in most cities; along the coasts, service typically connects downtown to at least one or two beach communities. Some cities (such as Tampa and Jacksonville) have high-frequency trolleys circling downtown, while some coastal stretches are linked by seasonal trolleys that ferry beachgoers between towns (such as between St Pete Beach and Clearwater).

Fares generally cost between $1 and $2.50. Exact change upon boarding is usually required, though some buses take $1 bills. Transfers – slips of paper that will allow you to change buses – range from free to 50¢. Hours of operation differ from city to city, but generally buses run from approximately 6am to 11pm.

Car & Motorcycle

Once you reach Florida, traveling by car is the best way of getting around – it allows you to reach areas not served by public transportation.

While it's quite possible to avoid using a car on single-destination trips – to Miami, to Orlando theme parks or to a self-contained beach resort – relying on public transit can be inconvenient for even limited regional touring. Even smaller, tourist-friendly towns such as Naples, Sarasota or St Augustine can be frustrating to negotiate without a car. Motorcycles are also popular in Florida, given the flat roads and warm weather (summer rain excepted).

Automobile Associations

The American Automobile Association (AAA; www.aaa.com) has reciprocal agreements with several international auto clubs (check with AAA and bring your membership card). For members, AAA offers travel insurance, tour books, diagnostic centers for used-car buyers and a greater number of regional offices, and it advocates politically for the auto industry. It also has a handy online route planner that can help you calculate the exact mileage and estimated fuel costs of your intended itinerary.

An ecofriendly alternative is the Better World Club (www.betterworldclub.com), which donates 1% of revenue to assist environmental cleanup; offers ecologically sensitive choices for services; and advocates politically for environmental causes.

In both organizations, the central member benefit is 24-hour emergency roadside assistance anywhere in the USA. Both clubs also offer trip planning and free maps, travel-agency services, car insurance and a range of discounts (car rentals, hotels etc).

Driving Licenses

Foreign visitors can legally drive with their home driver's license. However, getting an International Driving Permit

(IDP) is recommended; this will have more credibility with US traffic police, especially if your home license doesn't have a photo or is in a foreign language. Your automobile association at home can issue an IDP, valid for one year, for a small fee. You must carry your home license together with the IDP at all times. To drive a motorcycle, you need either a valid US state motorcycle license or an IDP specially endorsed for motorcycles.

Insurance

Don't put the key into the ignition if you don't have insurance: it's legally required, and you risk financial ruin without it if there's an accident. If you already have auto insurance (even overseas), or if you buy travel insurance, make sure that the policy has adequate liability coverage for a rental car in Florida; it probably does, but check.

Rental-car companies will provide liability insurance, but most charge extra for the privilege. Always ask. Collision-damage insurance for the vehicle is almost never included in the US. Instead, the provider will offer an optional Collision Damage Waiver (CDW) or Loss Damage Waiver (LDW), usually with an initial deductible of $100 to $500. For an extra premium, you can usually get this deductible covered as well. However, most credit cards now offer collision-damage coverage for rental cars if you rent for 15 days or fewer and charge the total rental to your card. This is a good way to avoid paying extra fees to the rental company, but note that if there's an accident, you sometimes must pay the rental-car company first and then seek reimbursement from the credit-card company. Check your credit-card policy. Paying extra for some or all of this insurance increases the cost of a rental car by around $20 to $40 per day.

Travel insurance, either specific paid policies or free insurance provided by your credit-card company (when your travel arrangements are purchased on their credit cards), often includes cover for rental-car insurances up to the full amount of any deductible. If you plan on renting a vehicle for any significant period of time, the cost of travel insurance, which includes coverage for rental vehicles, is often way cheaper than purchasing the optional insurance from the car-rental company directly. Be prudent and do your research to avoid getting a shock when you go to sign your car-rental contract and discover all the additional charges.

Rental
CAR

Car rental is a very competitive business. Most rental companies require that you have a major credit card; that you be at least 25 years old; and that you have a valid driver's license (your home license will do). Some national companies may rent to drivers between the ages of 21 and 24 for an additional charge. Those under 21 are usually not permitted to rent at all.

Additional drivers are not usually covered under the base rate and an additional daily surcharge will be applied. If someone other than the parties authorized on the rental contract is driving the vehicle and has an accident, all paid insurances will be void: you don't want this to happen. If anyone else is likely to drive the vehicle, they need to be present at the time of collection and are required to submit their driver's license and pay the extra fee. If the additional driver is not able to be present at the time of collection, it is possible to drive into any branch of the rental company and add the additional driver on to your rental agreement at a later date. Charges may

be backdated to the day of collection.

Good independent agencies are listed by Car Rental Express (www.carrental-express.com), which rates and compares independent agencies in US cities; it's particularly useful for searching out cheaper long-term rentals. Auto Europe (www.autoeurope.com) is also good as a clearinghouse for multiple rental agencies.

National car-rental companies:

Alamo (www.alamo.com)

Avis (www.avis.com)

Budget (www.budget.com)

Dollar (www.dollar.com)

Enterprise (www.enterprise.com)

Hertz (www.hertz.com)

National (www.nationalcar.com)

Rent-a-Wreck (www.rentawreck.com)

SixT (www.sixt.com)

Thrifty (www.thrifty.com)

Rental cars are readily available at all airport locations and many downtown city locations. With advance reservations for a small car, the daily rate with unlimited mileage is about $35 to $55, while typical weekly rates are $200 to $400, plus numerous taxes and fees. If you rent from a downtown location, you can save money by avoiding the exorbitant airport fees.

An alternative is Zipcar (www.zipcar.com), a car-sharing service that charges hourly and daily rental fees with gas, insurance and limited mileage included; prepayment is required.

Note that one-way rentals (picking up in one city and dropping off in another) will often incur a prohibitive one-way drop fee. Experimenting with your routing, or returning the vehicle to the city from which you collected it, or one nearby, may help avoid this penalty. Also check if the location that you're collecting the car from is franchised or centrally owned: sometimes the latter will help get any one-way fees waived.

A few major car-rental companies (including Avis, Budget, Enterprise and Hertz) offer 'green' fleets of hybrid, clean diesel or electric rental cars, but they're in short supply. Reserve well in advance.

MOTORCYCLE

To straddle a Harley across Florida, contact EagleRider (www.eaglerider.com), which has offices in Daytona Beach, Fort Lauderdale, Miami, St Augustine, Jacksonville, Pensacola and Orlando. It offers a wide range of models, which start at $150 a day, plus liability insurance.

MOTORHOME (RV)

Forget hotels. Drive your own. Touring Florida by recreational vehicle (RV) can be as low-key or as over-the-top as you wish.

After settling on the vehicle's size, consider the impact of gas prices, gas mileage, additional mileage costs, insurance and refundable deposits; these can add up quickly. Typically, RVs don't come with unlimited mileage, so estimate your mileage up front to calculate the true rental cost.

Inquire about motorhome relocations: sometimes, you can get amazing deals where you're effectively being paid to move the vehicle between cities for its owner – but you'll need to be extremely flexible with your dates and routes.

Adventures On Wheels (www.adventuresonwheels.com) Office in Miami.

CruiseAmerica (www.cruiseamerica.com) The largest national RV-rental firm has offices across South Florida.

Recreational Vehicle Rental Association (www.rvda.org) Good resource for RV information and advice, and helps find rental locations.

Road Rules

If you're new to Florida or US roads, here are some basics:

➡ The maximum speed limit on interstates is 75mph, but that drops to 65mph and 55mph in urban areas. Pay attention to the posted signs. City-street speed limits vary between 15mph and 45mph.

➡ Florida police officers are strict with speed-limit enforcement, and speeding tickets are expensive. If caught going over the speed limit by 10mph, the fine starts at $204. If you're going more than 30mph over the speed limit, that's a mandatory court appearance. Conversely, you may be fined if you're driving too slowly (usually under 40mph) on an interstate.

➡ All passengers in a car must wear seat belts. All children under three must be in a child safety seat.

➡ As in the rest of the US, drive on the right-hand side of the road. On highways, pass in the left-hand lane (but impatient drivers often pass wherever space allows).

➡ Right turns on a red light are permitted after a full stop. At four-way stop signs, the car that reaches the intersection first has right of way. In a tie, the car on the right has right of way.

Hitchhiking

Hitchhiking is never entirely safe in any country, and we don't recommend it. Travelers who decide to hitch

should understand that they are taking a small but potentially serious risk. People who do choose to hitch will be safer if they go in pairs and if they let someone know where they are planning to go. Be sure to ask the driver where they are going first, rather than telling them where you want to go.

Train

Amtrak (www.amtrak.com) trains run between a number of Florida cities. For the purpose of getting around Florida, its service is extremely limited, and yet for certain specific trips its trains can be very easy and inexpensive. In essence, daily trains run between Jacksonville, Orlando and Miami, with one line branching off to Tampa.

The new **MiamiCentral** (Virgin MiamiCentral; https://virginmiamicentral.com; NW 1st Ave, btwn NW 3rd St & NW 8th St; ⊡Government Center) is expected to be the home of Brightline, whose service could run to Orlando, although its launch has been delayed by the coronavirus outbreak.

Walt Disney World® has a monorail and Tampa has a free, old-fashioned, one-line streetcar, but the only real metro systems are in and near Miami. In Miami, a driverless Metromover circles downtown and connects with Metrorail, which connects downtown north to Hialeah and south to Kendall.

Meanwhile, north of Miami, Hollywood, Fort Lauderdale and West Palm Beach (and the towns between them) are well connected by Tri-Rail's double-decker commuter trains. Tri-Rail runs all the way to Miami, but the full trip takes longer than driving.

Behind the Scenes

SEND US YOUR FEEDBACK

We love to hear from travelers – your comments keep us on our toes and help make our books better. Our well-traveled team reads every word on what you loved or loathed about this book. Although we cannot reply individually to your submissions, we always guarantee that your feedback goes straight to the appropriate authors, in time for the next edition. Each person who sends us information is thanked in the next edition – the most useful submissions are rewarded with a selection of digital PDF chapters.

Visit **lonelyplanet.com/contact** to submit your updates and suggestions or to ask for help. Our award-winning website also features inspirational travel stories, news and discussions.

Note: We may edit, reproduce and incorporate your comments in Lonely Planet products such as guidebooks, websites and digital products, so let us know if you don't want your comments reproduced or your name acknowledged. For a copy of our privacy policy visit lonelyplanet.com/privacy.

WRITER THANKS

Fionn Davenport

A huge thanks to Kevin Gibson and Jon Hornbuckle at Universal Orlando; to the Disney gang – Priya, Charlotte, Dave and Nikki; to Diane and Lisa at SeaWorld; to Margaret Henriksson; and to Amy Rodenbrock, Paula Ramirez and Jo Cooke of Visit Orlando. A big thanks to Dyna Stephens for being a terrific landlady, and as always to my wife Laura for being OK with my being away for a whole month!

Anthony Ham

Thanks to Luke Hunter, Tim Tetzlaff, Mark Lotz, Lisa and David Korte and others for their invaluable help. Thanks to the wonderful Vicky Smith and everyone at Lonely Planet for getting this book out there at an extremely difficult time. Thanks to Jan for always being the faithful follower of my journeys. And to Marina, Carlota and Valentina: *os he echado mucho de menos y os quiero.*

Adam Karlin

Thank you: Victoria Smith, Anthony Ham, Regis St Louis, and the rest of the Florida team; Chris Romaguera, for rum, recommendations, and brotherhood; mom and dad for bringing me here; Rachel, Sanda and Isaac for being with me. *Por ti, mami.*

Vesna Maric

Thanks to Vicky Smith for commissioning me. Huge enormous thanks to Atena Sherry for her help and fantastic company, to Kathy in Cocoa for recommendations, Marta Vila for her help. Big love to Angie.

Trisha Ping

Major thanks to everyone who made this research trip so much fun, from family and friends who cheered me on to friendly locals I met along the way. Special shout-out to Vicky Smith and the Melbourne team for hiring me for this gig, and to my travel-writing colleagues, especially MaSovaida Morgan, for being so generous with their time, tips and advice.

Regis St Louis

On the road, I'm grateful to Jeff Kesling in Key Largo, Micah and friends in Islamorada, Jen DeMaria and Bill Keogh in Big Pine Key and Analise Smith and Maura Gannon in Key West. I also thank editor Vicky Smith for inviting me on board and co-authors Adam Karlin and Anthony Ham for their hard work. I'm also indebted to Cassandra and our daughters Magdalena and Genevieve, who make homecoming the best part of travel. On the road, I'm grateful to Jeff Kesling in Key Largo, Micah and friends in Islamorada, Jen DeMaria and Bill Keogh in Big Pine Key and Analise Smith and Maura Gannon in Key West.

ACKNOWLEDGEMENTS

Climate map data adapted from Peel MC, Finlayson BL & McMahon TA (2007) 'Updated World Map of the Köppen-Geiger Climate Classification', Hydrology and Earth System Sciences, 11, 1633–44.

Cover photograph: Tampa Bay, Florida, Aerial Archives / Alamy Stock Photo ©

THIS BOOK

This 9th edition of Lonely Planet's *Florida* guidebook was researched and written by Anthony Ham, Fionn Davenport, Adam Karlin, Vesna Maric, Trisha Ping and Regis St Louis. The 8th edition was written and researched by Adam Karlin, Kate Armstrong, Ashley Harrell and Regis St Louis. The 7th edition was written by Adam Karlin, Jennifer Rasin

Denniston, Paula Hardy and Benedict Walker. This guidebook was produced by the following:

Coordinating editor
Lorna Parkes

Senior product editors
Vicky Smith, Daniel Bolger

Product editors Will Allen, Claire Rourke, Ross Taylor

Regional senior cartographers Hunor Csutoros, Alison Lyall

Assisting editors

Janet Austin, Michelle Bennett, Carolyn Boicos, Kate Connolly, Melanie Dankel, Sasha Drew, Sandie Kestell, Rosie Nicholson, Martine Power, Tamara Sheward, Fionnuala Twomey

Book designer Meri Blazevski, Clara Monitto

Cover researcher
Brendan Dempsey-Spencer

Thanks to Frederik, Coulter, Duncan Ford, Genna Patterson, Lawrence Springall, Angela Tinson

Index

Map Legend

Sights
- Beach
- Bird Sanctuary
- Buddhist
- Castle/Palace
- Christian
- Confucian
- Hindu
- Islamic
- Jain
- Jewish
- Monument
- Museum/Gallery/Historic Building
- Ruin
- Shinto
- Sikh
- Taoist
- Winery/Vineyard
- Zoo/Wildlife Sanctuary
- Other Sight

Activities, Courses & Tours
- Bodysurfing
- Diving
- Canoeing/Kayaking
- Course/Tour
- Sento Hot Baths/Onsen
- Skiing
- Snorkeling
- Surfing
- Swimming/Pool
- Walking
- Windsurfing
- Other Activity

Sleeping
- Sleeping
- Camping
- Hut/Shelter

Eating
- Eating

Drinking & Nightlife
- Drinking & Nightlife
- Cafe

Entertainment
- Entertainment

Shopping
- Shopping

Information
- Bank
- Embassy/Consulate
- Hospital/Medical
- Internet
- Police
- Post Office
- Telephone
- Toilet
- Tourist Information
- Other Information

Geographic
- Beach
- Gate
- Hut/Shelter
- Lighthouse
- Lookout
- Mountain/Volcano
- Oasis
- Park
- Pass
- Picnic Area
- Waterfall

Population
- Capital (National)
- Capital (State/Province)
- City/Large Town
- Town/Village

Transport
- Airport
- BART station
- Border crossing
- Boston T station
- Bus
- Cable car/Funicular
- Cycling
- Ferry
- Metro/Muni station
- Monorail
- Parking
- Petrol station
- Subway/SkyTrain station
- Taxi
- Train station/Railway
- Tram
- Underground station
- Other Transport

Routes
- Tollway
- Freeway
- Primary
- Secondary
- Tertiary
- Lane
- Unsealed road
- Road under construction
- Plaza/Mall
- Steps
- Tunnel
- Pedestrian overpass
- Walking Tour
- Walking Tour detour
- Path/Walking Trail

Boundaries
- International
- State/Province
- Disputed
- Regional/Suburb
- Marine Park
- Cliff
- Wall

Hydrography
- River, Creek
- Intermittent River
- Canal
- Water
- Dry/Salt/Intermittent Lake
- Reef

Areas
- Airport/Runway
- Beach/Desert
- Cemetery (Christian)
- Cemetery (Other)
- Glacier
- Mudflat
- Park/Forest
- Sight (Building)
- Sportsground
- Swamp/Mangrove

Note: Not all symbols displayed above appear on the maps in this book

Trisha Ping

The Panhandle Tricia is a the former Lonely Planet Destination Editor for the Eastern US, and now work as the publisher of BookPage in Nashville. She's a huge fan of train travel, trying new recipes, using a bicycle for transportation and attempting foreign languages. You can follow Tricia on Twitter @editrish and Instagram @ trishaping

Regis St Louis

Florida Keys & Key West Regis grew up in a small town in the American Midwest – the kind of place that fuels big dreams of travel – and he developed an early fascination with foreign dialects and world cultures. He spent his formative years learning Russian and a handful of Romance languages, which served him well on journeys across much of the globe. Regis has contributed to more than 50 Lonely Planet titles, covering destinations across six continents. His travels have taken him from the mountains of Kamchatka to remote island villages in Melanesia, and to many grand urban landscapes. When not on the road, he lives in New Orleans. Follow him on Instagram @regisstlouis.

OUR STORY

A beat-up old car, a few dollars in the pocket and a sense of adventure. In 1972 that's all Tony and Maureen Wheeler needed for the trip of a lifetime – across Europe and Asia overland to Australia. It took several months, and at the end – broke but inspired – they sat at their kitchen table writing and stapling together their first travel guide, *Across Asia on the Cheap*. Within a week they'd sold 1500 copies. Lonely Planet was born.

Today, Lonely Planet has offices in Tennessee, Dublin, Beijing and Delhi, with a network of over 2000 contributors in every corner of the globe. We share Tony's belief that 'a great guidebook should do three things: inform, educate and amuse'.

OUR WRITERS

Anthony Ham

Everglades & Biscayne National Parks, Tampa Bay & Southwest Florida, Northeast Florida Anthony is a freelance writer who travels the world in search of stories. His particular passions are the wildlife, wild places and wide open spaces of the planet, from the Great Plains of the US to the Amazon, East and Southern Africa, and the Arctic. He writes for magazines and newspapers around the world, and his narrative nonfiction book on Africa's lions will be published in 2020. An Australian, he divides his time between Melbourne and Madrid. Anthony also wrote the Plan Your Trip, Understand and Survival Guide sections.

Fionn Davenport

Orlando & Walt Disney World Irish by birth and conviction, Fionn has spent the last two decades focusing on the country of his birth and its nearest neighbor, England. He's written extensively for Lonely Planet and contributed oodles of travel pieces to a host of newspapers and magazines, including the *Irish Times*, *Irish Independent, Irish Daily Mail, Lonely Planet Magazine, Cara, the Independent* and the *Daily Telegraph*.

Adam Karlin

Miami Adam has contributed to dozens of Lonely Planet guidebooks, covering an alphabetical spread that ranges from the Andaman Islands to the Zimbabwe Border. As a journalist, he has written on travel, crime, politics, archeology, and the Sri Lankan Civil War, among other topics. He has sent dispatches from every continent barring Antarctica (one day!) and his essays and articles have featured in the BBC, NPR, and multiple nonfiction anthologies. Adam is based out of New Orleans, which helps explain his love of wetlands, food and good music. Follow his work at http://walkonfine.com/; Instagram @adamwalkonfine.

Vesna Maric

Southeast Florida, Space Coast Vesna lives in London and works as a writer and journalist. As well as having written many guides for Lonely Planet, she is also the author of *Bluebird* (Granta, 2009), a memoir charting her arrival in the United Kingdom as a teenage refugee from Bosnia in 1992.

OVER PAGE | MORE WRITERS

Published by Lonely Planet Global Limited
CRN 554153
9th edition – Jun 2021
ISBN 978 1 78701 569 2
© Lonely Planet 2021   Photographs © as indicated 2021
10 9 8 7 6 5 4 3 2 1
Printed in Singapore

Although the authors and Lonely Planet have taken all reasonable care in preparing this book, we make no warranty about the accuracy or completeness of its content and, to the maximum extent permitted, disclaim all liability arising from its use.